Learning Corel® WordPerfect® Suite 8 Professional

Iris Blanc
Cathy Vento
Marni Ayers Brady

Acknowledgments

To Our Loving Families
Alan, Jaime, Pamela and Mathew – *I.B.*
Jim, Chris, Dirk, Jimmy, Mindi, Anthony, and Tyler – *C.V.*
William and in loving memory of Gerald H. Ayers, Sr. – *M.A.B.*

WITH MANY THANKS to Marni Ayers Brady and Christine Ford for their editorial supervision, support and diligence. It has been our pleasure working with you.

And To Harry Moon: You are a guiding light.

Project Managers	**English Editors**	**Technical Editors**	**Design and Layout**
Christine Ford New York, NY	Byron Nilsson Glen, New York	ali'Zeva Kormendy Tampa, FL	Shu Y. Chen New York, NY
Marni Ayers New York, NY		Christine Ford New York, NY	Midori Nakamura New York, NY
			Maria Kardasheva New York, NY
			Elviro Padro New York, NY

©Copyright 1999 by DDC Publishing

Published by DDC Publishing

All rights reserved, including the right to reproduce this book or portions thereof in any form whatsoever. For information, address DDC Publishing, Inc., 275 Madison Avenue, New York, NY 10016; HTTP://WWW.DDCPUB.COM

ISBN: 1-56243-590-6
Catalog Number: Z28

10 9 8 7 6 5 4 3

Printed in the United States of America.

Corel, WordPerfect, Presentations, and Quattro are either trademarks or registered trademarks of Corel Corporations or Corel Corporations Limited.
Netscape™ Navigator™ is a Trademark of the Netscape™ Communications Corporation.
Microsoft® Internet Explorer and Windows® are registered trademarks of the Microsoft® Corporation.
Yahoo! ™ is a registered trademark of Yahoo! ™
Screen shots reprinted with the permission of Microsoft® Corporation and Corel® Corporations.

All trademarks, registered trademarks, copyrights, and service marks are the property of their respective companies.

Contents

Introduction vii

Log of Exercises ix

Directory of Files xvi

Corel® WordPerfect® Suite 8 Professional Basics 1

Exercise 1 2
    About Corel® WordPerfect® Suite 8 Professional
    Desktop Application Director (DAD)
    Using the Mouse
    Using the Keyboard
    Start Corel WordPerfect Suite 8 Professional
    Close an Application Using the Mouse

Exercise 2 5
    Corel WordPerfect Suite 8 Professional Windows
    Menus, Toolbars, and Commands
    QuickMenus
    Select Menu Items
    The Dialog Box
    Zoom
    Keystrokes Procedures

Exercise 3 11
    Help
    PerfectExpert (While You Work)

WordPerfect 8 15

Lesson 1: Create, Save, and Print Documents

Exercise 1 16
    Start WordPerfect 8
    The WordPerfect 8 Screen
    Document Window Displays
    If You Make an Error…
    View Modes
    Default Settings
    Create a New Document
    Save a New Document
    Close a Document
    Exit WordPerfect 8
    Conventions

Exercise 2 23
    QuickCorrect
    Format-As-You-Go
    Spell-As-You-Go
    Spell Checker
    Prompt-As-You-Go
    Document Properties

Exercise 3 27
    Insertion Point Movements
    Scroll a Document
    Create a Business Letter
    The QuickWords Feature
    The Date/Time Feature

Exercise 4 31
    Address Book
    Preview a Document
    Print

Exercise 5 36
    Summary

Lesson 2: Open and Edit Documents

Exercise 6 37
    Open and Revise a Document
    Open a Recently Saved File
    Open a Document Not Recently Saved
    Insert Text
    Proofreaders' Marks
    Save Changes to a Document

Exercise 7 40
    Open as Copy (Read-Only Document)
    Save As
    Undo
    Redo

Exercise 8 43
    Delete Text
    Select Text
    Undelete
    Undelete vs. Undo

Exercise 9 48
    Preview a Document Before Opening
    Reveal Codes
    Show Symbols
    Delete/Edit Codes

Exercise 10 52
    Change Toolbars
    Hard Space
    Convert Case
    Set Margins
    Set Tabs

Exercise 11 59
    Summary

Lesson 3: Text Alignments and Enhancements

Exercise 12 61
    Center Line
    Flush Right Line
    Vertical Centering (Center Current Page)
    Justification

Exercise 13 65
    Font Faces
    Font Style
    Font Size

Exercise 14 71
    Font Appearance
    Highlight Text

Exercise 15 75
    Ornamental Fonts
    Symbols and Special Characters
    Superscripts and Subscripts
    Remove Font Appearance Attributes

Exercise 16 80
    Bullets and Numbered Lists
    Remove Bullets and Numbers

Exercise 17 85
    Summary

Lesson 4: Format and Edit Documents

Exercise 18 87
    Line Spacing
    Paragraph Spacing

Exercise 19 90
    Format a One-Page Report
    Indent Text
    Hanging Indent
    First-Line Indent

Exercise 20 97
    Move Text
    Cut and Paste
    Drag and Drop
    QuickFormat

Exercise 21 101
    Link Headings

Exercise 22 104
    Copy and Paste
    Drag and Drop
    Append to the Clipboard

Exercise 23 107
    Make It Fit
    Thesaurus

Exercise 24 111
    Grammatik (Grammar Check)
    Grammar-As-You-Go

Exercise 25 115
    Find and Replace Text
    Hyphenate Text

Exercise 26 119
    Outlines

Exercise 27 122
    Summary

Exercise 28 124
    Summary

Lesson 5: Work with Multiple-Page Documents

Exercise 29 126
    Hard vs. Soft Page Breaks
    Second Page Headings
    Headers/Footers
    Edit Headers/Footers
    Insert Page Numbers in Header/Footer
    Turn Off (Suppress) Headers/Footers

Exercise 30 132
    Letters with Special Notations
    Insert Comments
    Bookmarks
    Print Multiple Pages

Exercise 31 139
    Footnotes
    Endnotes
    Edit Footnotes or Endnotes
    Widow and Orphan Lines

Exercise 32 146
    Page Numbering Positions and Formats
    Go To
    File Stamp

Exercise 33 153
    Summary

Lesson 6: Templates; Envelopes and Labels; Macros

Exercise 34 156
    Templates
    PerfectExpert
    Envelopes
    Labels

Exercise 35 164
    Arrange Multiple Documents
    Switch Between Open Documents
    Close Multiple Documents
    Size Windows
    Copy/Move Text from One Open Document to Another

Exercise 36 172
    Repeat Next Action
    Insert a File

Exercise 37 176
    Record a Macro

Exercise 38 179
    Play a Macro

Exercise 39 184
    Summary

Lesson 7: Columns; Tables; Merge

Exercise 40 187
    Columns
    Newspaper Columns
    Parallel Columns

Exercise 41 193
    Create a Table
    Edit a Table in a Graphics box
    Move within a Table
    Enter Text in a Table
    Select Cells, Rows or Columns

Exercise 42 198
    Align Text within a Table
    Insert and Delete Columns and Rows
    Delete a Table
    Resize Columns
    Position a Table Horizontally
    Table Borders
    Cell Lines and Fills
    SpeedFormat

Exercise 43 207
    The Merge Process
    Create a Data File
    Create a Form File

Contents

    Merge the Form and Data Files
    Merge Selected Records
    Merge with Conditions
    Prepare Envelopes While Merging
  Exercise 44..218
    Summary

Lesson 8: Graphics and Text Boxes

  Exercise 45..220
    Graphics Image
    Insert Clipart
    Create a Text Box
  Exercise 46..223
    Select a Graphics Box
    Select a Text Box
    Size a Graphics Box or Text Box
    Position (Move) a Graphics Box
    Delete a Graphics Box or Text Box
    Copy a Graphics Box or Text Box
    Rotate a Text Box
  Exercise 47..228
    Text Wrap Options
    Captions
    TextArt
  Exercise 48..235
    Watermark
    Insert Lines
    Drop Capital
    Reverse Text
  Exercise 49..244
    Summary

Quattro Pro 8..247

Lesson 1: Create, Save, and Edit a Notebook

  Exercise 1..248
    Start Quattro Pro
    The Quattro Pro Window
    Quattro Pro Menu and Toolbars
    Explore the Notebook Using the Mouse and Keyboard
  Exercise 2..252
    Enter Labels
    Make Simple Corrections
    Save and Close a Notebook
    Exit Quattro Pro
  Exercise 3..255
    Numeric Labels and Values
    Label Alignment
    Repeat Labels
  Exercise 4..258
    Summary

Lesson 2: Use Formulas; Format, Copy, and Print

  Exercise 5..259
    Use Formulas
  Exercise 6..261
    Open Files
    Save Files
    Format Data
    Use a Block/Selection

  Exercise 7..264
    Copy Data
    Format Using the Menu
    Print a Notebook Page
    Page View
  Exercise 8..267
    Copy Formulas (Absolute and Relative Reference)
    Format Data (Percents, Fonts, and Font Size)
    QuickFormat
  Exercise 9..271
    Summary

Lesson 3: Use Formulas and Functions; Edit Information; Print Options

  Exercise 10..272
    Use Functions
    Formula Composer
    Quick Sum
    Calc-As-You-Go
  Exercise 11..276
    Change Column Width
    Create a Series
    Comma Format
  Exercise 12..280
    Print Options
    Edit Data
    Documentation Notes
  Exercise 13..284
    Page Setup
    Cell Properties
  Exercise 14..287
    Page Breaks
    Bold
    Headers and Footers
    Cell Reference Checker
  Exercise 15..292
    Print Preview
    Top and Left Headings
  Exercise 16..296
    Summary

Lesson 4: Additional Formatting and Editing; Work with Notebooks

  Exercise 17..297
    Insert Columns and Rows
    Delete Columns and Rows
    Move (Cut/Paste and Drag/Drop)
    Copy (Drag/Drop)
  Exercise 18..301
    Copy and Paste Special
    Transpose Data
  Exercise 19..304
    Lock Titles
    Split Panes
    Copy and Paste Special
  Exercise 20..309
    Notebook Sheets
    Group Sheets
    Print Notebook

Exercise 21 314
    QuickFill
    QuickCell
    Named Blocks
Exercise 22 318
    Templates
    Projects
    PerfectExpert
    Use Projects
    Arrange Notebooks
Exercise 23 322
    3-D Formulas
    Notebook Pages
    Duplicate Notebook Views
Exercise 24 325
    Summary

Lesson 5: Logical and Date Functions; Speed Format; Hide Data

Exercise 25 327
    Insert an IF function
Exercise 26 329
    IF Functions
    Hide Data
Exercise 27 331
    Enter a Date as Numerical Data
    Format Numerical Dates
Exercise 28 333
    SpeedFormat
    Shading and Text Colors
Exercise 29 336
    What-If Tables
    Payment Function
    Protect a Page
Exercise 30 341
    Summary

Lesson 6: Charts

Exercise 31 343
    Create Charts
    Change Chart Types
    Select and Size Inserted Charts
    Enable Graph Editing
Exercise 32 350
    Create Charts with Chart Expert
    Create Charts with Chart Menu
    Chart Subtypes
    Stacked Bar Charts
    Line-Bar Charts
    Change Legend Positions
Exercise 33 355
    Change Chart Font
    Explode Pie Chart Slice
    Print Charts
    Chart Gallery
Exercise 34 359
    Summary

Corel Paradox 8 361

Database Basics 362
    What is Paradox?
    What is a Database?
    What is a Database Management System?
    What are Database Objects?
    How is a Paradox Database Organized?
    What are Paradox Tables?
    How are Paradox Tables Related?
    Paradox 8 Features

Lesson 1: Create a Database

Exercise 1 366
    Database Basics
    Plan the Database
    Startup Expert
    Project Viewer
    Create a Table
    Table Field Types
    Key Field
    Save a Table
Exercise 2 371
    Create Working Directories
    Create and Save a Database Table
Exercise 3 373
    Open a Table
    Enter Records
    Correct Entries
    Change Table Column Width
Exercise 4 376
    Table Guidelines
    Use Project Viewer
    Enter and Edit Data
    Enter Key Field Data
Exercise 5 379
    Forms
    Create a Quick Form
    Enter Records
    Form Design View
    Move Between Views
Exercise 6 384
    Create a Form with Form Expert
Exercise 7 388
    Summary

Lesson 2: Edit and Print a Database

Exercise 8 389
    Modify a Table or Form
    Add, Delete, or Move a Field in a Table
    Add, Delete, or Move a Field in a Form
    Check Box Field
Exercise 9 393
    Validity Checks
    Print
    Print in Landscape
Exercise 10 397
    Edit a Record
    Add a Record
    Delete a Record
    Radio Buttons

Contents

Exercise 11..401
   Enhance Form Design (Background Color, Custom Colors, Frames)
Exercise 12..405
   Summary

Lesson 3: Search and Sort a Database

Exercise 13..408
   Locate Values
   Use Wildcards
   Locate and Replace Data
Exercise 14..412
   Sort Records
   Multiple Sorts
Exercise 15..415
   Filter Fields
   Filter Tables
Exercise 16..418
   Filter Tables
Exercise 17..420
   Summary

Lesson 4: Queries

Exercise 18..423
   Create a Query
   Save a Query
Exercise 19..427
   Open a Query
   Field Checks
   Change Field Names
   Work with Query Files
Exercise 20..430
   Create Queries Using Two Tables
   Summary Operators
Exercise 21..432
   Summary

Lesson 5: Reports

Exercise 22..434
   Reports
   Create Reports with Report Expert
   Modify a Report
   Save a Report
   Print a Report
Exercise 23..438
   Modify a Report
   Change Object Properties
   Header and Footer Settings
Exercise 24..441
   Add Group Band
   Add Summary Field
Exercise 25..445
   Summary

Corel Presentations 8 449

Lesson 1: Create, Save, and Print Slides

Exercise 1..450
   About Corel Presentations 8
   Start Corel Presentations 8
   Create a Presentation
   The Corel Presentations 8 Window
   Slide Layers
   Add Text to Slides
   Add Slides to a Slide Show
   Save a Slide Show
   Close a File/Exit Presentations
Exercise 2..456
   Open a Slide Show
   Slide Views
   Move from Slide to Slide
   Spell Check
   Print a Presentation
Exercise 3..461
   Add Clipart Graphics to Slides
   Use Undo and Redo
   Change Slide Layout
   Change Slide Show Background Master
   Change Background for Individual Slides
Exercise 4..466
   Move, Copy, and Delete Slides
   Slide Sorter View
   Return to Slide Editor View
Exercise 5..470
   Slide Outliner View
   Add Slides in Slide Outliner View
Exercise 6..473
   Insert a Graph
Exercise 7..478
   Create a Table
Exercise 8..481
   Insert an Organization Chart on a Slide
Exercise 9..484
   Summary

Lesson 2: Edit and Enhance Slides

Exercise 10..487
   Select Text
   Align Text
   Change Text Appearance
   Copy and Move Text on a Slide
   Move and Size Placeholders
Exercise 11..493
   Customize the Slide Background
   Customize the Layout
   Customize Bulleted List Slides
Exercise 12..498
   Create Lines, Drawings, and Text Objects
   Change Line, Drawing, and Text Attributes
   Group and Separate Objects
   Combine Objects
   Order Objects
   Contour Text
   Create a Presentations Drawing Outside of a Slide Show
Exercise 13..505
   Use PerfectExpert Projects to Create Presentations
   Insert Date
Exercise 14..510
   Summary

Lesson 3: Work with Slide Shows

   Exercise 15 513
      Show a Presentation
      Slide Transitions
      Add Animation to Bulleted Lists
      Animate Objects
      Slide Show Tools
   Exercise 16 521
      Set Slide Timings and Display Sequences
      Add Sound
      Create Custom Audiences
   Exercise 17 524
      Audience Notes Pages and Handouts
      Speaker Notes
   Exercise 18 528
      QuickKeys
      QuickLinks
      Add Movies
   Exercise 19 532
      Summary

Corel® WordPerfect®
Suite 8 Professional Integration 535

   Exercise 1 536
      Use Several Files in One Application
      Work with Files from Different Applications
   Exercise 2 540
      Copy a Notebook File into a Document File
      Edit a Copied File
   Exercise 3 543
      Integrate a Notebook File and a Document File
      Embed a File
      Edit an Embedded File
      Link a File
      Edit a Linked File
      Integrate a Chart File and a Document File
   Exercise 4 548
      Export a Paradox Database to Quattro Pro
      Insert a Paradox Database into Quattro Pro

   Exercise 5 551
      Merge a Paradox Table with a WordPerfect Document
   Exercise 6 556
      Insert A WordPerfect Outline Into A Presentations Slide Show
      Link A Quattro Pro Chart To A Presentations Slide Show
   Exercise 7 561
      Copy Presentations Text into a WordPerfect Document
      Convert Presentations Slide Shows to .wpg Format
      Insert a Presentations Slide into a WordPerfect Document
   Exercise 8 565
      Internet Basics
      Use Corel WordPerfect to Access the Internet
      Search the Internet
   Exercise 9 571
      Get Help from the Corel Web Site
      Print Web Site Information
      Save a Web Page
      Copy Text from a Web Site into a WordPerfect Document
      Copy Images from the Internet
   Exercise 10 577
      Hyperlinks
      QuickLinks
      Create Hyperlinks in a WordPerfect Document
      Edit Hyperlinks
      Integrate a Presentations Outline into a WordPerfect Document

Index 590

Introduction

ABOUT COREL® WORDPERFECT® SUITE 8 PROFESSIONAL

The Corel® WordPerfect® Suite 8 Professional version includes Corel WordPerfect® 8, Quattro® Pro 8, Corel Paradox® 8, Corel Presentations™ 8, Corel CENTRAL™ 8 and a host of bonus applications such as Corel WEB.sitebuilder, Corel TimeLine, QuickView, Bitstream Font Navigator, Netscape® Communicator, and more. In addition, the suite includes more than 10,000 Clip art images and 150 typographical fonts. The applications and utilities included in the package can be used separately or together to produce professional looking documents.

> ✓ Note: If you are using the standard Corel WordPerfect Suite 8 package, Corel Paradox® and some bonus applications will not be included. Bonus applications are not covered in this book.

The following software applications will be covered in *Learning Corel WordPerfect Suite 8 Professional*.

- **Corel WordPerfect 8**, a word processing program, used for creating and editing documents.
- **Corel Quattro Pro 8**, a spreadsheet program, used for analyses and graphing of numerical data.
- **Corel Paradox 8**, a database program, used for organizing and sorting information.
- **Corel Presentations 8**, a presentation graphics program, used for creating visual presentations.

■ The information created in one application can be easily shared with other applications. For instance, a spreadsheet created in Quattro Pro, or a database created in Paradox, can easily be incorporated into a memo or letter that is created in WordPerfect. Data created in WordPerfect, Quattro Pro or Paradox can be incorporated into Presentations. Such integration of the Corel applications is further detailed in the Integration section of this text.

ABOUT THIS BOOK

Learning Corel® WordPerfect Suite 8 Professional will teach you to use and integrate the four mentioned applications in the Corel WordPerfect Suite 8 Professional package on an IBM PC or compatible computer.

■ Each lesson in this book explains concepts, provides numerous exercises to apply those concepts, and illustrates the necessary keystrokes or mouse actions required to complete the exercises. Lesson summary exercises are provided at the end of each lesson to challenge and reinforce the concepts learned.

■ After completing the exercises in this book, you will be able to use the basic features of each application in the Corel WordPerfect Suite 8 Professional suite with ease.

HOW TO USE THIS BOOK

■ Each exercise contains three parts:

- **NOTES** explain the Corel WordPerfect Suite 8 Professional concept and application being introduced.
- **EXERCISE DIRECTIONS** explain how to complete the exercise and guide you in applying the new concept.
- **KEYSTROKES** outline the keystroke shortcuts and mouse actions required for completing an exercise.

> ✓ Keystrokes and mouse actions are only provided when a new concept is being introduced. However, if you forget the keystroke or mouse action required to perform a task, you can use the Corel WordPerfect Suite 8 Professional Help feature (explained in the Corel Word Perfect Suite 8 Basics section) or the index of this book to find the procedure.

- Before you begin working on the exercises in any Corel WordPerfect Suite 8 Professional application, you should read the section entitled Corel WordPerfect Suite 8 Basics. This section will explain the screens, the Help feature, how to work with application windows, Toolbars, menus, dialog boxes and other necessary preliminary information.

THE DATA AND SOLUTION DISKS

- Data and solutions disks may be purchased separately from DDC Publishing. You may use the data files on the data disk to complete an exercise without typing lengthy text or data. Exercise directions are provided for both data disk and non-data disk users. Exercise directions will include a keyboard icon ⌨ to direct non data disk users to a open document created in a previous exercise and a diskette icon 💾 to direct data disk users to open the document available on disk. For example, a typical direction might read: Open ⌨**TRY** or 💾**03TRY**.

- The data disk contains WordPerfect, Quattro Pro, Paradox, and Presentations files. Each filename begins with the corresponding exercise number and contains an extension that correlates with the program in which the file was created. For example, **03TRY.WPD** would indicate a WordPerfect document, whereas **03TRY.WB3** would indicate a Quattro Pro document.

- In order to maintain the integrity of the data disk, be sure to make a back up copy of the disk, open data files as Read Only, and use the Save As method to save each file under a new name (see explanations of Read Only and Save As in the WordPerfect section of this text).

- The Solution disk may be used for you to compare your work with the final version or solution on disk. Each solution filename begins with the letter "S" and is followed by the exercise number and descriptive filename to which it pertains. For example, **S03TRY** would contain the final solution to the exercise directions in exercise three.

- A directory of data disk and solutions disk filenames are provided in the Log of Exercises section of this book.
  - ✓ *Saving files to some networks may automatically truncate filenames to a maximum of eight characters. Please be aware of the type of network you have as it may affect links between files if filenames are truncated. If your network does truncate filenames, we recommend that you load the data and solution files locally on your hard drive.*

THE INSTRUCTOR'S GUIDE

- While this book can be used as a self-paced learning book, a comprehensive Instructor's Guide is also available. The instructor's guide contains the following:
  - Lesson objectives
  - Exercise objectives
  - Related vocabulary
  - Points to emphasize
  - Exercise settings
  - Exercise illustrations

FEATURES OF THIS TEXT

- Lesson objectives
- Exercise objectives
- Application concepts and vocabulary
- A Log of Exercises, which lists filenames in exercise number order
- A Directory of Files, which lists filenames alphabetically along with the corresponding exercise numbers.
- Exercises to apply each concept
- End of lesson summary exercises to review and test your knowledge of lesson concepts
- Keystrokes and mouse actions necessary to complete each application

Log of Exercises

WordPerfect

Lesson	Exercise	Filename	Data File	Solution File
1	1	WRAP	—	S01WRAP
	2	CORRECT	—	S02CORRECT
	3	SUMMER	—	S03SUMMER
	4	CLELAND	—	S04CLELAND
	5	COMPU	—	S05COMPU
2	6	WRAP	06WRAP	S06WRAP
	7	CORRECT	07CORRECT	S07CORRECT
	8	PEACE	08PEACE	S08PEACE
	9	CLELAND	09CLELAND	S09cleland
		CORRECT	—	—
		WRAP	—	—
	10	CLELAND	10CLELAND	S10CLELAND
		HISTORY	10HISTORY	S10HISTORY
		HISTORY2	—	S10HISTORY2
	11	PILLOW	11PILLOW	S11PILLOW
3	12	PLAY	—	S12PLAY
	13	SCRIPT	13SCRIPT	S13SCRIPT
	14	THEATRE	14THEATRE	S14THEATRE
	15	THEATRE	15THEATRE	S15THEATRE
	16	OFFICE	16OFFICE	S16OFFICE
	17	NETPRO	17NETPRO	S17NETPRO
4	18	YOGA	—	S18YOGA
	19	PEACE	19PEACE	S19PEACE
		PEACE2	—	S19PEACE2
		VITAMIN	19VITAMIN	S19VITAMIN
		VITAMIN2	—	S19VITAMIN2
	20	SAVE	—	S20SAVE
	21	GOLD	21GOLD	S21GOLD
	22	SAVE	22SAVE	S22SAVE
	23	PEACE2	23PEACE2	S22PEACE2
	24	SHOW	24SHOW	S24SHOW
	25	VITAMIN2	25VITAMIN2	S25VITAMIN2
	26	WEDDING	—	S26WEDDING
	27	GYM	27GYM	S27GYM
	28	MAJOR	—	S28MAJOR
5	29	ABROAD	29ABROAD	S29ABROAD
	30	CHILDREN	30CHILDREN	S30CHILDREN
	31	LEARN	31LEARN	S31LEARN
		LEARN2	—	S31LEARN2

Lesson	Exercise	Filename	Data File	Solution File
5 (cont.)	32	JAPAN	32JAPAN	S32JAPAN
		CHILDREN	32CHILDREN	S32CHILDREN
	33	GENERATIONS	33GENERATIONS	S33GENERATIONS
6	34	PICNIC	—	S34PICNIC
		FILES	—	S34FILES
		CUSTOMERS	—	S34CUSTOMERS
		ADDRESSES	—	S34ADDRESSES
	35	ABROAD	35ABROAD	—
		GYM	35GYM	—
		SAVE	35SAVE	—
		STUDENT	35STUDENT	S35STUDENT
		TRAVEL	35TRAVEL	S35TRAVEL
		TRIP	35TRIP	S35TRIP
	36	LEGAL	—	S36LEGAL
		PLAY	36PLAY	S36PLAY
		AD	36AD	S36AD
	38	LEGAL	38LEGAL	S38LEGAL
		SHOW	38SHOW	S38SHOW
	39	LABOUND	—	S39LABOUND
		RANCH	—	S39RANCH
7	40	ACTIVITY	—	S40ACTIVITY
		MINUTES	—	S41MINUTES
	41	EVENTS	—	S41EVENTS
	42	EVENTS	42EVENTS	S42EVENTS
		FUND	—	S42FUND
	43	MTGDATA	—	S43MTGDATA
		MTGFORM	—	S43MTGFORM
		MTGLETTERS	—	S43MTGLETTERS
		PASTDATA	—	S43PASTDATA
		PASTFORM	—	S43PASTFORM
		PASTLETTERS	—	S43PASTLETTERS
	44	DONATEDATA	—	S44DONATEDATA
		DONATEFORM	—	S44DONATEFORM
		DONATELETTERS	—	S44DONATELETTERS
8	45	WORLD	—	S45WORLD
	46	WORLD	46WORLD	S46WORLD
	47	TEXT	47TEXT	
		ACTIVITY	47ACTIVITY	S47ACTIVITY
		PREMIER	—	PREMIER
	48	NETPRO	48NETPRO	S48NETPRO
		THEATRE	48THEATRE	S48THEATRE
	49	ACTIVITY	49ACTIVITY	S49ACTIVITY
		GRADUATE	—	S49GRADUATE

Log of Exercises

Quattro Pro

Lesson	Exercise	Filename	Data File	Solution File
1	2	SALES	—	S02SALES
	3	PAY	—	S03PAY
	4	GRADE	—	S04GRADE
2	5	TRAINS	—	S05TRAINS
	6	TRAINS	06TRAINS	—
		TRAIN2	—	S06TRAIN2
	7	PAY	07PAY	S07PAY
	8	SALES	08SALES	S08SALES
	9	DRINKS	—	S09DRINKS
3	10	TRAINS	10TRAINS	S10TRAINS
	11	APPLI	11APPLI	S11APPLI
	12	PAY	12PAY	S12PAY
	13	APPLI	13APPLI	S13APPLI
	14	EXPENS	14EXPENS	S14EXPENS
	15	INCOME	15INCOME	S15INCOME
	16	GRADE	16GRADE	S16GRADE
4	17	PAY	17PAY	S17PAY
	18	INCOME	18INCOME	S18INCOME
	19	INCOME	19INCOME	S19INCOME
		ISANA	—	S19ISANA
	20	PAY	20PAY	—
		PAYTM	—	S20PAYTM
	21	APPLI	21APPLI	S21APPLI
	22	DPEST	—	S22DPEST
		LEAKEY	—	S22LEAKEY
		WRENCH	—	S22WRENCH
	23	PAYTM	23PAYTM	S23PAYTM
	24	GRADE	24GRADE	S24GRADE
		GRSUM	—	S24GRSUM
5	25	GRSUM	25GRSUM	S25GRSUM
	26	EMP	26EMP	S26EMP
	27	ACCPAY	27ACCPAY	S27ACCPAY
	28	ACCREC	28ACCREC	S28ACCREC
	29	LOAN	29LOAN	S29LOAN
	30	COMM	30COMM	S30COMM
6	31	AIR	31AIR	S31AIR
	32	TICKET	32TICKET	S32TICKET
	33	COMM	33COMM	S33COMM
	34	NCDATA	34NCDATA	S34NCDATA

Paradox

Lesson	Exercise	Filename	Data File	Solution File
1	1	STORES	—	S01STORES
	2	CEQUIP	—	SPORTS\S02CEQUIP
	3	MEMBERS	—	CLUB\S03MEMBERS
	4	STORES	SPORTS\04STORES	SPORTS\S04STORES
		CEQUIP	SPORTS\04CEQUIP	SPORTS\S04CEQUIP
	5	MEMBERS	CLUB\05MEMBERS	CLUB\S05MEMBERS
		MEMFORM	—	CLUB\S05MEMFORM
	6	STAFF	—	SPORTS\S06STAFF
		STAFFRM	—	SPORTS\S06STAFFRM
	7	SFTWARE	—	SPORTS\S07SFTWARE
		SOFORM	—	SPORTS\S07SOFORM
2	8	STORES	SPORTS\08STORES	SPORTS\S08STORES
		STOREFORM	—	SPORTS\S08STOREFORM
		STAFF	SPORTS\S08STAFF	SPORTS\S08STAFF
		STAFFRM	—	SPORTS\S08STAFFRM
	9	CEQUIP	SPORTS\09CEQUIP	SPORTS\S09CEQUIP
		EQUIPFRM	—	SPORTS\S09EQUIPFRM
	10	CHARGES	—	CLUB\S10CHARGES
		CHGFORM	—	CLUB\S10CHGFORM
		MEMBERS	CLUB\10MEMBERS	CLUB\S10MEMBERS
	11	CHGFORM	CLUB\11CHGFORM	CLUB\S11CHGFORM
		CHARGES	CLUB\11CHARGES	CLUB\S11CHARGES
		MEMFORM	CLUB\11MEMFORM	CLUB\S11MEMFORM
	12	CEQUIP	SPORTS\12CEQUIP	SPORTS\S12CEQUIP
		EQUIPFRM	—	SPORTS\S12EQUIPFRM
		STORES	SPORTS\12STORES	SPORTS\S12STORES
3	13	MEMBERS	CLUB\13MEMBERS	CLUB\S13MEMBERS
		MEMFORM	—	CLUB\S13MEMFORM
	14	CEQUIP	SPORTS\14CEQUIP	SPORTS\S14CEQUIP
		EQUIPINV	—	SPORTS\S14EQUIPINV
		EQUIPFRM	SPORTS\14EQUIPFRM	SPORTS\S14EQUIPFRM
		SOFORM	SPORTS\14SOFORM	SPORTS\S14SOFORM
	15	SOFORM	SPORTS\15SOFORM	SPORTS\S15SOFORM
		SFTWARE	SPORTS\15SFTWARE	SPORTS\S15SFTWARE
	16	RECEIPTS	—	CLUB\S16RECEIPTS
		MEMBER	CLUB\16MEMBER	CLUB\S16MEMBER
		CHGFORM	CLUB\16CHGFORM	CLUB\S16CHGFORM
		CHARGES	CLUB\16CHARGES	CLUB\S16CHARGES
	17	INVEN	SPORTS/17INVEN	SPORTS\S17INVEN
		INVFORM	SPORTS/17INVFORM	SPORTS\S17INVFORM
4	18	MEMBERS	CLUB\18MEMBERS	CLUB\S18MEMBERS
		STUDENT	—	CLUB\S18STUDENT

Log of Exercises

Lesson	Exercise	Filename	Data File	Solution File
4 (cont.)	18 (cont.)	ANAHEIM	—	CLUB\S18ANAHEIM
		CHARGES	CLUB\18CHARGES	CLUB\S18CHARGES
		DUES	—	CLUB\S18DUES
	19	STORES	SPORTS\19STORES	SPORTS\S19STORES
		EVENING HOURS	—	SPORTS\S19EVENING HOURS
		CEQUIP	SPORTS\19CEQUIP	SPORTS\S19CEQUIP
		COMPUTER INVENTORY	—	SPORTS\S19COMPUTER INVENTORY
	20	STORES	SPORTS\20STORES	SPORTS\S20STORES
		CEQUIP	SPORTS\20CEQUIP	SPORTS\S20CEQUIP
		COMPUTERS BY STATE	—	SPORTS\S20COMPUTERS BY STATE
		SFTWARE	SPORTS\20SFTWARE	SPORTS\S20SFTWARE
		SOFTWARE TYPES	—	SPORTS\S20SOFTWARE TYPES
	21	VENDORS	—	SPORTS\S21VENDORS
		INVEN	21INVEN	SPORTS\S21INVEN
		JACKET INVENTORY	—	SPORTS\S21JACKET INVENTORY
		REORDER INFORMATION	—	SPORTS\S21REORDER INFORMATION
5	22	STORES	SPORTS\22STORES	SPORTS\S22STORES
		BRANCHES		SPORTS\S22BRANCHES
	23	CEQUIP	SPORTS\23CEQUIP	SPORTS\S23CEQUIP
		COMPUTER EQUIPMENT INVENTORY	—	SPORTS\S23COMPUTER EQUIPMENT INVENTORY
		SFTWARE	SPORTS\23SFTWARE	SPORTS\S23SFTWARE
		SOFTWARE INVENTORY	—	SPORTS\S23SOFTWARE INVENTORY
	24	MEMBERS	CLUB\24MEMBERS	CLUB\S24MEMBERS
		LIST	—	CLUB\S24LIST
		CHARGES	24CHARGES	CLUB\S24CHARGES
		CHG1215	—	CLUB\S24CHG1215
	25	COLLEGE\STAFF	—	COLLEGE\S25STAFF
		COLLEGE\STAFFORM	—	COLLEGE\S25STAFFORM
		COLLEGE\MAIN BUILDING STAFF	—	COLLEGE\S25MAIN BUILDING STAFF
		COLLEGE\ANNEX	—	COLLEGE\S25ANNEX
		COLLEGE\LIST	—	COLLEGE\S25LIST
		COLLEGE\BUDGET	—	COLLEGE\S25BUDGET

Presentations

Lesson	Exercise	Filename	Data File	Solution File
1	1	DIAMOND	—	S01DIAMOND
		CALIBER	—	S02CALIBER
	2	CALIBER	02CALIBER	S02CALIBER
		DIAMOND	02DIAMOND	S02DIAMOND
	3	DIAMOND	03DIAMOND	S03DIAMOND
		CALIBER	03CALIBER	S03CALIBER
	4	CALIBER	04CALIBER	S04CALIBER
	5	SPORTS	—	S05SPORTS
	6	DIAMOND	06DIAMOND	S06DIAMOND
	7	DIAMOND	07DIAMOND	S07DIAMOND
	8	SPORTS	08SPORTS	S08SPORTS
	9	INVEST	—	S09INVEST
2	10	CALIBER	10CALIBER	S10CALIBER
	11	SPORTS	11SPORTS	S11SPORTS
	12	SPORTS	12SPORTS	S12SPORTS
		CALIBER	12CALIBER	S12CALIBER
	13	TIGER	—	—
	14	NEWERA	—	S14NEWERA
3	15	INVEST	15INVEST	S15INVEST
	16	DIAMOND	16DIAMOND	S16DIAMOND
	17	SPORTS	17SPORTS	S17SPORTS
	18	NEWERA	18NEWERA	S18NEWERA
	19	GREEN	—	S19GREEN

Integration

Exercise	Filename	Data File	Solution File
1	TRAINS	—	—
	GRSUM	—	—
	DRINK	—	—
	ACCPAY	—	—
	SUMMER	—	—
2	LOAN	02LOAN	—
	MORTGAGE	02MORTGAGE	—
	LOBUE	—	S02LOBUE
3	MEMO	03MEMO	—
	TICKET	03TICKET	—
	TKTMEMO	—	S03TKTMEMO
4	CEQUIP	04CEQUIP	—
	DEPEQUIP	—	S04DEPEQUIP
5	GRANT	05GRANT	—
	STAFF	05STAFF	—
	DEC10	—	S05DEC10
	DEC10ALL	—	S05DEC10ALL
	NTSTAFF	—	S05NTSTAFF
	NTDEC10.wpd	—	S05NTDEC10.wpd
	NTDEC10.frm	—	S05NTDEC10.frm
6	WEDDING	06WEDDING	—
	WEDPLAN	—	S06WEDPLAN
	WEDBUD	06WEDBUD	S06WEDBUD
7	WEDPLAN	07WEDPLAN	S07WEDPLAN
	LEADS	—	S07LEADS
	CONTACT	07CONTACT	S07CONTACT
9	COREL		S09COREL
	CORHELP	09CORHELP	—
10	INVEST	10INVEST	—
	EXPORT	10EXPORT	S10EXPORT
	NZ	—	S10NZ

Directory of Files

WordPerfect

Filename	Exercise	Page
ABROAD	29, 35	128, 166
ACTIVITY	40, 47, 49	189, 231, 244
AD	36	174
ADDRESSES	34	161
CHILDREN	30, 32	134, 152
CLELAND	4, 9, 10	33, 50, 57
COMPU	5	36
CORRECT	2, 7, 9	25, 41, 50
CUSTOMERS	34	161
DONATEDATA	44	218
DONATEFORM	44	218
DONATELETTERS	44	218
EVENTS	41, 42	196, 203
FILES	34	159
FUND	42	204
GOLD	21	102
GENERATIONS	33	153
GRADUATE	49	244
GYM	27, 35	122, 166
HISTORY	10	55
HISTORY2	10	55
JAPAN	32	148
LABOUND	39	184
LEARN	31	142
LEARN2	31	142
LEGAL	36, 38	173, 180
MAJOR	28	124
MINUTES	40	189
MTGDATA	43	213
MTGFORM	43	213
MTGLETTERS	43	213
NETPRO	17, 48	85, 239
OFFICE	16	82
PASTDATA	43	213
PASTFORM	43	213
PASTLETTERS	43	213
PEACE	8, 19	44, 93
PEACE2	19, 23	93, 108
PICNIC	34	159
PILLOW	11	59
PLAY	12, 36	63, 174
PREMIER	47	231
RANCH	39	185
SAVE	20, 22, 35	99, 105, 166
SCRIPT	13	68
SHOW	24, 38	112, 180
STUDENT	35	167
SUMMER	3	29
TEXT	47	231
THEATRE	14, 15, 48	72, 77, 239
TRAVEL	35	167
TRIP	35	167
VITAMIN	19	93
VITAMIN2	19, 25	93, 117
WEDDING	26	120
WORLD	45, 46	222, 225
WRAP	1, 6, 9	22, 38, 50
YOGA	18	88

Quattro Pro

Filename	Exercise	Page
ACCPAY	27	332
ACCREC	28	335
AIR	31	347
APPLI	11, 13, 21	278, 286, 315
COMM	30, 33	342, 357
DPEST	22	320
DRINKS	9	271
EMP	26	330
EXPENS	14	289
GRADE	4, 16, 24	258, 296, 325
GRSUM	24, 25	325, 328
INCOME	15, 18, 19	294, 302, 306
ISANA	19	306
LEAKEY	22	320
LOAN	29	339
NCDATA	34	359
PAY	3, 7, 12, 17, 20	256, 266, 282, 298, 311
PAYTM	20, 23	311, 323
SALES	2, 8	253, 269
TICKET	32	353
TRAIN2	6	262
TRAINS	5, 6, 10	260, 262, 274
WRENCH	22	320

Paradox

Filename	Exercise	Page
ANAHEIM	18	425
ANNEX	25	448
BRANCHES	22	436
BUDGET	25	448
CEQUIP	2, 4, 9, 12, 14, 19, 20, 23	377, 395, 405, 413, 429, 431, 440
CHARGES	10, 11, 16, 18, 24	399, 403, 419, 425, 443
CHG1215	24	443
CHGFORM	10, 11, 16	399, 403, 419
COMPUTER EQUIPMENT INVENTORY	23	440
COMPUTER INVENTORY	19	429
COMPUTERS BY STATE	20	431
DUES	18	425
EQUIPFRM	9, 12, 14	396, 406, 413
EQUIPINV	14	413
EVENING HOURS	19	429
INVEN	16, 21	420, 432
INVFORM	17	420
JACKET INVENTORY	21	432
LIST	24, 25	443, 448
MAIN BUILDING STAFF	25	448
MEMBERS	3, 5, 10, 13, 16, 18, 24	374, 382, 400, 410, 419, 452, 443
MEMFORM	5, 11, 13	382, 403, 411
RECEIPTS	16	418
REORDER INFORMATION	21	433
SFTWARE	7, 15, 20, 23	388, 416, 431, 440
SOFORM	7, 14, 15	388, 413, 416
SOFTWARE INVENTORY	23	440
SOFTWARE TYPES	20	431
STAFF (SPORTS)	6, 8	386, 391
STAFFRM (SPORTS)	6, 8	386, 391
STAFF (COLLEGE)	25	445
STAFFORM (COLLEGE)	25	445
STORES	1, 4, 8, 12, 19, 20, 22	370, 377, 391, 407, 429, 431, 436
STOREFORM	8	391

Filename	Exercise	Page
STUDENT	18	425
VENDORS	21	433

Presentations

Filename	Exercise	Page
CALIBER	1, 2, 3, 4, 10, 12	454, 459, 463, 467, 489, 502
DIAMOND	1, 2, 3, 6, 7, 16	454, 459, 463, 475, 479, 522
GREEN	19	533
INVEST	9, 15	484, 516
NEWERA	14, 18	510, 530
SPORT	5, 8, 11. 12, 13, 17	471, 483, 495, 502, 526
TIGER	13	507

Integration

Filename	Exercise	Page
CEQUIP	4	549
CONTACT	7	562
COREL	9	573
CORHELP	9	573
DEC10	5	553
DEC10ALL	5	553
DEPEQUIP	4	549
EXPORT	10	580
INVEST	10	580
LEADS	7	562
LOAN	2	541
LOBUE	2	541
NTDEC10	5	553
NTDEC10ALL	5	553
NTSTAFF	5	553
NZ	10	580
STAFF	5	553
TICKET	3	545
TKTMEMO	3	546
WEDBUD	6	557
WEDDING	6	557
WEDPLAN	6, 7	557, 562

Corel® WordPerfect® Suite 8 Professional Basics

Corel WordPerfect 8

Corel Quattro Pro 8

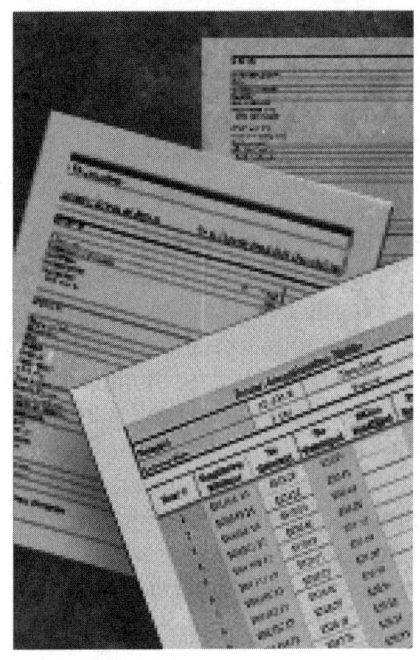

Corel Paradox 8

Corel Presentations 8

COREL WORDPERFECT SUITE OFFICE 8 PROFESSIONAL Basics

Exercise 1

- About Corel® WordPerfect® Suite 8 Professional
- Desktop Application Director (DAD) ■ Using the Mouse
- Using the Keyboard ■ Start Corel WordPerfect Suite 8 Professional
- Close an Application Using the Mouse

NOTES

About Corel® WordPerfect® Suite 8 Professional

- Corel WordPerfect® Suite® 8 Professional provides a full range of powerful tools that may be used independently or in an integrated fashion to perform various office tasks efficiently. Corel WordPerfect Suite 8 Professional includes WordPerfect® (word processing tool), Quattro Pro® (spreadsheet tool), Presentations® (presentation tool), Paradox® (database tool), Envoy (publishing tool), and InfoCentral 8 (a calendar and information management tool). *Envoy and InfoCentral 8 will not be covered in this book.*

- After the software is installed, a program group for Corel WordPerfect Suite 8 Professional appears on the desktop. In addition, the Desktop Application Director, also referred to as DAD, appears on the Taskbar.

Desktop Application Director (DAD)

- The **Desktop Application Director (DAD)** displays icons (symbols) that represent most Corel WordPerfect Suite 8 Professional applications and utilities. DAD is displayed at all times so that you can easily access any Corel WordPerfect Suite 8 Professional application from within windows or easily switch between applications. DAD contains icons for WordPerfect®, Quattro Pro®, Presentations®, Paradox®, and other Corel Office 8 utilities.

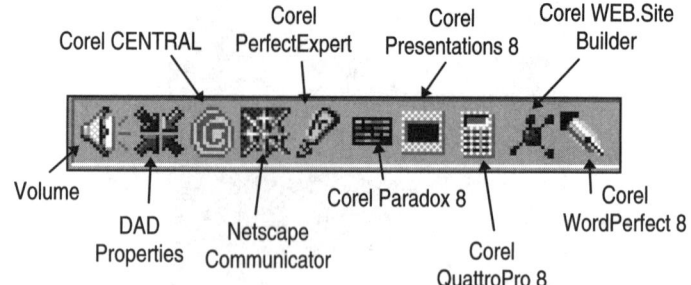

- To identify each DAD icon, place the mouse pointer on the icon. A **QuickTip** will appear with the name or function of the button.

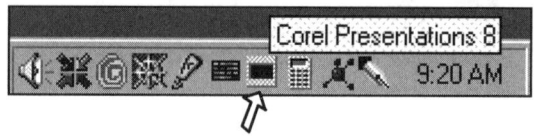

- DAD may be customized to add other applications or utilities you may have installed in your system.

  ✓Note: *The volume icon will only appear if a sound card is installed in your system.*

- All Corel WordPerfect Suite 8 Professional applications and utilities have similar Toolbars, menus, commands, and dialog boxes. The skills learned in one application, such as using the Toolbars, menus, dialog boxes, and Online help features (as well as moving around the screen) are used consistently in all Corel WordPerfect Suite 8 Professional applications.

- You may use the mouse or the keyboard to choose commands and perform tasks.

Using the Mouse

- When the mouse is moved on the tabletop, a corresponding movement of the mouse pointer occurs on the screen. The mouse pointer changes shape depending on the tool being used, the object it is pointing to, and the action it will be performing. The mouse pointer will not move if the mouse is lifted up and placed back on the tabletop.

- The mouse terminology and the corresponding actions described below will be used throughout the book:

Point to	Move the mouse (on the tabletop) so the pointer touches a specific item.
Click	Point to item and quickly press and release the left mouse button.
Right-click	Point to item and press and release the right mouse button.
Double-click	Point to item and press the left mouse button twice in rapid succession.
Drag	Point to item and press and hold down the left mouse button while moving the mouse. When the item is in the desired position, release the mouse button to place the item.
Right-Drag	Point to item and press and hold down the right mouse button while moving the mouse. When the item is in the desired position, release the mouse button to place the item.

- All references to the use of mouse buttons in this book refer to the *left* mouse button unless otherwise specified.

Using the Keyboard

- Computers contain specialized keyboard keys:
  - **Function keys** (F1 through F10 or F12) perform special functions and are located across the top of the keyboard.
  - **Modifier keys** (Shift, Alt, Ctrl) are used in conjunction with other keys to select certain commands or perform actions. To use a modifier key with another key, you must hold down the modifier key while tapping the other key.
  - **Numeric keys**, found on keyboards with a number pad, allow you to enter numbers quickly. When Num Lock is ON, the number keys on the pad are operational, as is the decimal point. When Num Lock is OFF, the cursor control keys (Home, PgUp, End, PgDn) are active. The numbers on the top row of the keyboard are always active.
  - **Escape key** (Esc) is used to cancel some actions, commands, menus, or an entry.
  - **Enter keys** (there are two on most keyboards) are used to complete an entry of data in some applications.
  - **Directional arrow keys** are used to move the active screen insertion point as determined by the tool being used.

Start Corel WordPerfect Suite 8 Professional

- There are two ways to start a Corel WordPerfect Suite 8 Professional application:

- **Using the Windows Taskbar:** The Windows Taskbar appears at the bottom of the screen in all programs running Windows 95. The Taskbar is used to start applications as well as to switch between applications.

Taskbar

Click here to Start Corel WordPerfect
Suite 8 Professional Applications

- After you install Corel WordPerfect Suite 8 Professional software, a **Corel WordPerfect Suite 8** menu item appears when Start is accessed from the Taskbar. Slide the mouse to highlight Corel WordPerfect Suite 8, then slide the mouse to highlight the other applications. Click the left mouse to select the application you wish to access.

COREL WORDPERFECT SUITE OFFICE 8 PROFESSIONAL Basics

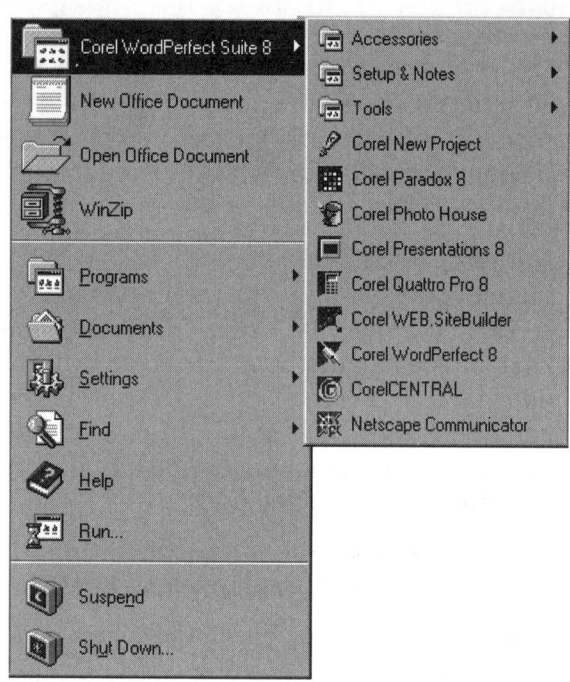

- **Using DAD [Desktop Application Director] on the Taskbar:** Click the desired application icon.

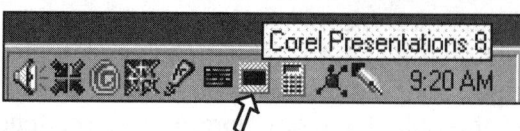

  - To start a second application, hold down the Ctrl key and click on a second application icon.

Close an Application Using the Mouse

- To quickly exit an application using the mouse, click the **Program Close** button ⊠ in the upper right corner of the screen. In the illustration below, you will note two Close buttons. The top Close button closes the program; the bottom Close button closes the document window. Closing a document will be discussed further in each section of this book.

In this exercise, you will use the mouse to start and close Corel WordPerfect Suite 8 Professional applications.

EXERCISE DIRECTIONS

1. Roll the mouse up, down, left, and right on the tabletop or the mouse pad.
2. Place the mouse pointer over each icon on the Desktop Application Director and note the QuickTip notation for each application.
3. Click the DAD icon for Corel WordPerfect 8.
4. Click on the top Close button to exit the WordPerfect program.
5. Click Start on the Windows 95 Taskbar.
6. Highlight Corel WordPerfect Suite 8 Professional, then Corel Quattro Pro 8.
7. Click on the top Close button to exit Quattro Pro.

KEYSTROKES

START A COREL WORDPERFECT SUITE 8 PROFESSIONAL APPLICATION

1. Click **Start** on Taskbar .... [Start]
2. Highlight **Corel WordPerfect 8**.
3. Highlight application.
4. Press **Enter** .... [Enter]

OR

1. Point to application icon on DAD Toolbar.
2. Click to open application.

CLOSE AN APPLICATION

Click **Program Close** Button .... ⊠

OR

1. Click **File** .... [Alt]+[F]
2. Click **Exit** .... [X]

COREL WORDPERFECT SUITE 8 PROFESSIONAL Basics

Exercise 2

- Corel WordPerfect Suite 8 Professional Windows
- Menus, Toolbars, and Commands ■ QuickMenus ■ Select Menu Items
- The Dialog Box ■ Zoom ■ Keystrokes Procedures

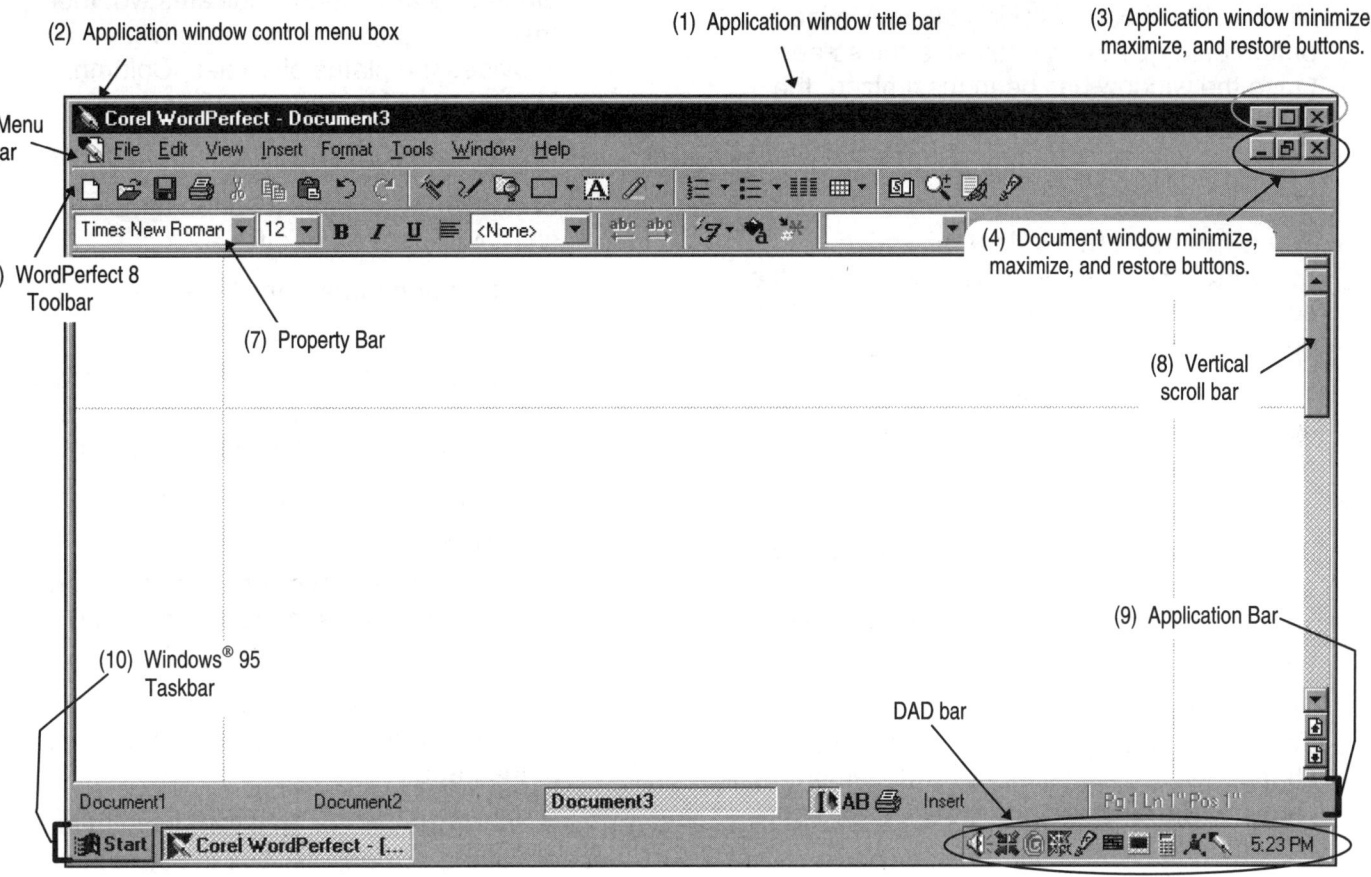

NOTES

Corel WordPerfect Suite 8 Professional Windows

- When you access each Corel WordPerfect Suite 8 Professional application, you will see its opening screen.
- The common parts of all Corel WordPerfect Suite 8 Professional application windows will be discussed using the WordPerfect screen. The specific screen parts for each Corel WordPerfect Suite 8 Professional tool will be detailed in the appropriate sections of this book.

✓ Note: the following universal window parts:

- There are many different bars available in WordPerfect 8 that display when the screen appears. They are: application window title bar, Menu bar, Toolbar, Property Bar, scroll bar(s) and Application Bar.

- The (1) **application window title bar**, located at the top of the application window, displays the program name (WordPerfect, Quattro Pro, etc.) and may also display the name of an opened file if the window is maximized.

COREL WORDPERFECT SUITE 8 PROFESSIONAL Basics

- The (2) **application window control menu box**, located to the left of the application window title bar, can be clicked to access a drop-down menu from which you can choose commands that control the window.

- The (3) **application window minimize, maximize, and restore buttons** are located on the right side of the application window title bar. Clicking the minimize button shrinks the window to an icon. Clicking the maximize button enlarges the window to a full screen. Once the window has been maximized, the maximize button changes to the restore button. Clicking the restore button restores the window to its previous size.

- The (4) **document window minimize, maximize, and restore buttons** function the same as the application window buttons, but only the current document is affected.

- The (5) **Menu bar**, located below the title bar, displays menu names from which drop-down menus may be accessed.

- The (6) **WordPerfect 8 Toolbar**, located below the menu bar, contains buttons that represent some of the most commonly performed WordPerfect tasks. The Toolbar may only be accessed with the mouse.

- The (7) **Property Bar**, located below the Toolbar, provides buttons that let you easily change the appearance of your document. The Property Bar features may be accessed only with the mouse.

- Pointing to and resting the pointer on a Toolbar button or Property Bar drop-down list displays the tool's name and an explanation of its function.

- The (8) **horizontal and vertical scroll bars** are used to move the screen view horizontally or vertically. The scroll box on the vertical scroll bar can be dragged up or down to move more quickly toward the beginning or end of the document.

- The (9) **Application Bar**, located at the bottom of the window, displays the following items:

  - General Status button indicates whether Insert or Typeover mode is active. Provides the status of Tables, Columns, Macros, and Merge features as well.

  - Printer button displays the current printer.

  - Shadow Cursor On/Off button turns shadow cursor on or off.

  - CAPS button turns Caps Lock feature on or off.

  - Combined Position displays page number, vertical line position of insertion point, and horizontal position of the insertion point.

    Pg 1 - The current page number is displayed.

    Ln 1" - The vertical position of the insertion point (in inches) as measured from the top of the page.

    Pos 1" - The horizontal position of the insertion point (in inches) from the left edge of the page.

- The (10) **Windows® 95 Taskbar**, located at the bottom of the screen, displays the start button, all minimized windows, and the Desktop Application Director.

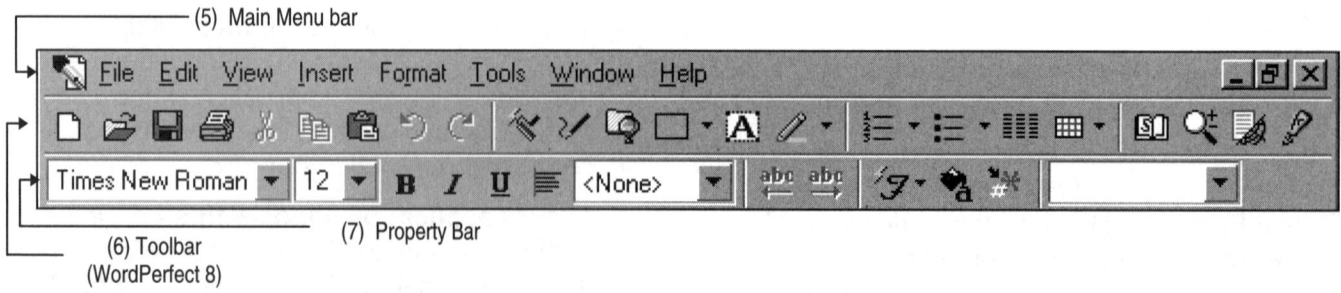

(5) Main Menu bar
(6) Toolbar (WordPerfect 8)
(7) Property Bar

Menus, Toolbars, and Commands

- The Menu bar and Toolbars may be used to access commands. Each application contains a Menu bar and two Toolbars.

- The main Toolbar, located below the Menu bar, contains icons that accomplish many common tasks easily, like saving and printing a file.

- The Property Bar, located below the main Toolbar, contains buttons that access commonly used features. While each application contains both bars and many of the same icons, Property Bar buttons will change based on the task being performed.

- You may display the Toolbars at the top of your screen, or you may hide one or both of them to make room on your screen for text or data. You may also change to one of the other specialized Toolbars available in each application.

- If you are not certain of a Toolbar or Property Bar button's function, position your mouse pointer below the button, and a **QuickTip** will display with the button's name and a description of the task the button can perform.

- Toolbar and Property Bar buttons can only be selected using the mouse. To select a command from a Toolbar or from the Property Bar, use the mouse to point to a button and click once.

QuickMenus

- **QuickMenus** appear when the right mouse button is pressed. The menu items that appear vary depending on where the mouse arrow is pointing or which task is being performed. QuickMenus will be detailed in related exercises.

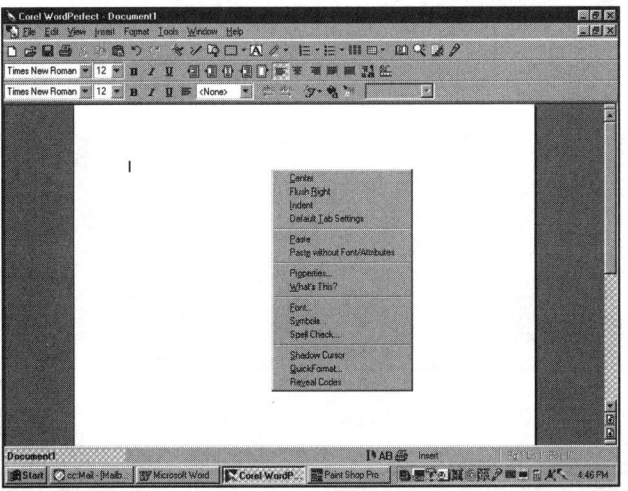

Select Menu Items

- You may use the keyboard, the mouse, or a combination of both to select menu items. Keyboard shortcut keys may also be used to accomplish tasks.

- To access menu bar items:
  - Use the mouse to point to a menu item on the menu bar and click once,

    OR
  - Press Alt + underlined letter in the menu name. A drop-down menu will appear. Note the menu that appears when the WordPerfect 8 Tools menu is accessed:

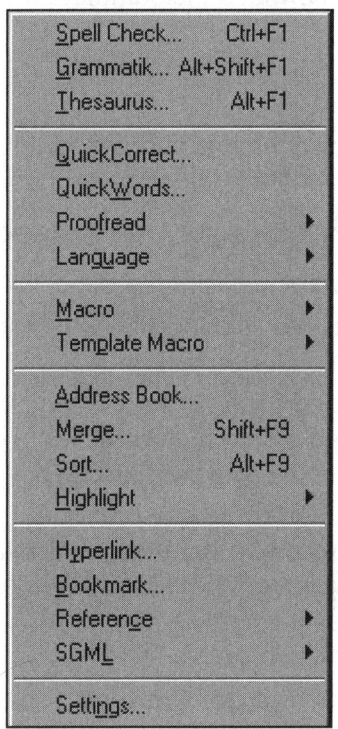

- To select an item from the drop-down menu:
  - Use the mouse to point to the command on the drop-down menu and click once.

    OR
  - Press the underlined letter in the command name.

    OR
  - Use the up or down arrow key to highlight the command, then press Enter.

    OR
  - Press the shortcut keys indicated next to a menu item.

CORAL WORDPERFECT SUITE 8 PROFESSIONAL Basics

✓*Note: Shortcut keys do not automatically display. To make them appear, select Tools, Settings, Environment, Interface, Display shortcut keys.*

- Some menu options are dimmed, while others appear black. Dimmed options are not available for selection while black options are.
- A check mark or dot next to a drop-down menu item indicates that the option is currently selected.
- Some menu items display shortcut keys that may be used to access the feature.
- A menu item followed by an ellipsis (…) indicates that a dialog box (which requires you to provide additional information to complete a task) will be forthcoming.

The Dialog Box

- A dialog box contains different methods to obtain information in order to complete a task.

    The parts of a dialog box are explained below:

    - The **title bar** identifies the title of the dialog box.
    - The **text box** is a location where you type information.
    - **Command buttons** carry out actions described on the button. When a command name has an ellipsis following it, it will access another dialog box.
    - The **drop-down list** is marked with a down arrow. Clicking the drop-down list arrow accesses a short list of options from which a choice should be made.
    - An **increment box** provides a space for typing a value. An up or down arrow (usually to the right of the box) gives you a way to select a value with the mouse.
    - A **named tab** is used to display options related to the tab's name in the same dialog box.
    - **Option buttons** are small circular buttons marking options appearing as a set. You may choose only one option from the set. A selected option button contains a dark circle.
    - A **check box** is a small square box where an option may be selected or deselected. An "X" or "✓" in the box indicates that the option has been selected. If several check boxes are offered, you may select more than one.

- A **list box** displays a list of items from which selections can be made. A list box may have a scroll bar that can be used to show hidden items in the list.
- A **scroll bar** is a horizontal or vertical bar providing scroll arrows and a scroll box that can be dragged up or down to move more quickly through the available options.
- A **preview window** allows you to see the result of your selection.
- A **pop-up list** is marked with an up/down arrow on the right of the button's face.
- **Look-up buttons** contain a graphic on the button's face. Clicking a look-up button displays another dialog box or offers options to assist with entering data. Note the labeled parts in the dialog boxes below:

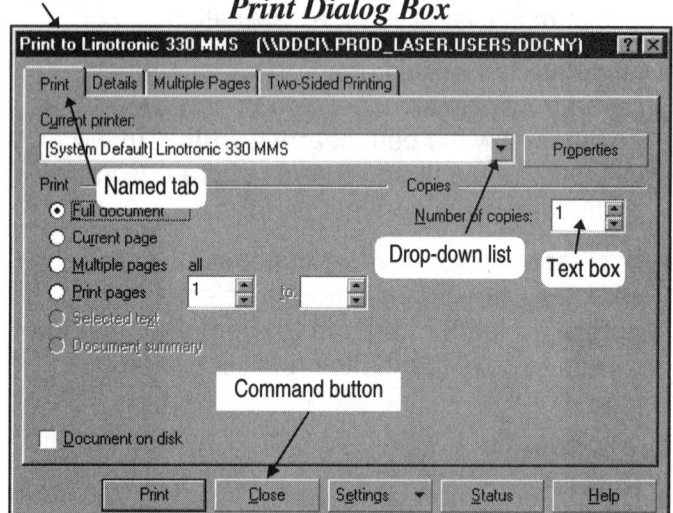

Print Dialog Box

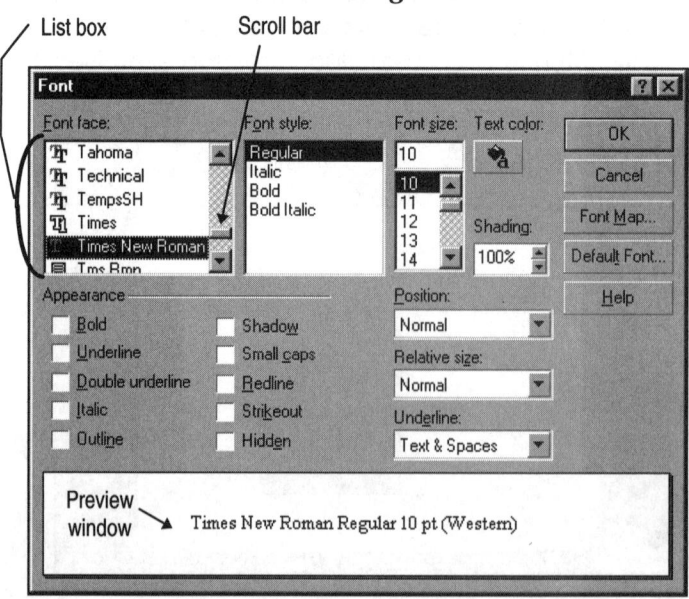

Font Dialog Box

Zoom

- The View menu contains a Zoom option that allows you to set the magnification of the data on the screen. When Zoom is selected, the following dialog box appears:

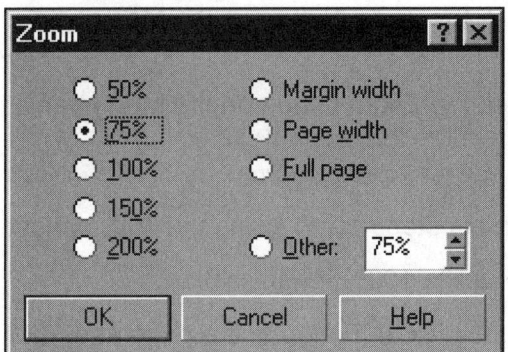

- Clicking a Zoom option button displays document text at 200%, 100%, 75%, etc. You can also access the Zoom feature by clicking the Zoom button on the Menu bar and selecting a magnification amount. This method does not open a dialog box unless you click Other.

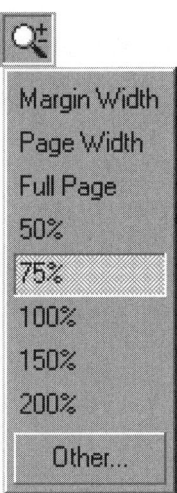

Keystroke Procdures

- Procedures for completing a task will be illustrated as follows throughout this book: Mouse actions are illustrated on the left, keystroke procedures are illustrated on the right, and keyboard shortcut keys are illustrated below the heading. Use whichever method you find most convenient.

    For example:
    SAVE A FILE
    Ctrl + S
    - Click **File**.....Alt + F
    - Click **Save**..........S

COREL WORDPERFECT SUITE 8 PROFESSIONAL   Basics

In this exercise, you will practice using Toolbars, menus, and commands.

EXERCISE DIRECTIONS

1. Open the WordPerfect application.
2. Select View from the Menu bar.
3. Select Toolbars.
4. Deselect Property Bar.
5. Deselect WordPerfect 8 Toolbar and click OK.
   ✓ *Note the change in the screen.*
6. Select View Toolbars and reselect Property Bar and WordPerfect 8 Toolbar to return them to the screen.
7. Select View; select Two Pages.
   ✓ *Note the change in the screen.*
8. Restore the screen to the default view by selecting Page from the View menu.
9. Type your name on the screen.
10. Click the Zoom button on the Menu bar. Select 100%.
11. Click the Zoom button on the Menu bar. Select the 200%.
    ✓ *Note the change in the screen.*
12. Repeat steps 10-11 using the 75% option.
13. Return to 100% magnification.
14. Right-click at the top of the page and note the QuickMenu. Left-click anywhere on the screen to clear menu.
15. Right-click in the middle of the screen and note QuickMenu. Left-click anywhere on the screen to clear the menu.
16. Exit WordPerfect.

KEYSTROKES

MAGNIFICATON/ZOOM

1. Click **Zoom** button on Menu bar .... [Q]
2. Select a zoom option.

   OR

   a. Click **V**iew .... [Alt]+[V]
   b. Click **Z**oom .... [Z]
   c. Select a Zoom option ....
   d. Click **OK** .... [Enter]

HIDE/DISPLAY TOOLBARS (WORDPERFECT)

1. Click **V**iew menu .... [Alt]+[V]
2. Click **T**oolbars............................. [T]
3. Deselect/select desired Toolbar.

   OR

   - Point to the Toolbar.
   - Right-click.
   - Select desired Toolbar.

COREL WORDPERFECT SUITE 8 PROFESSIONAL Basics

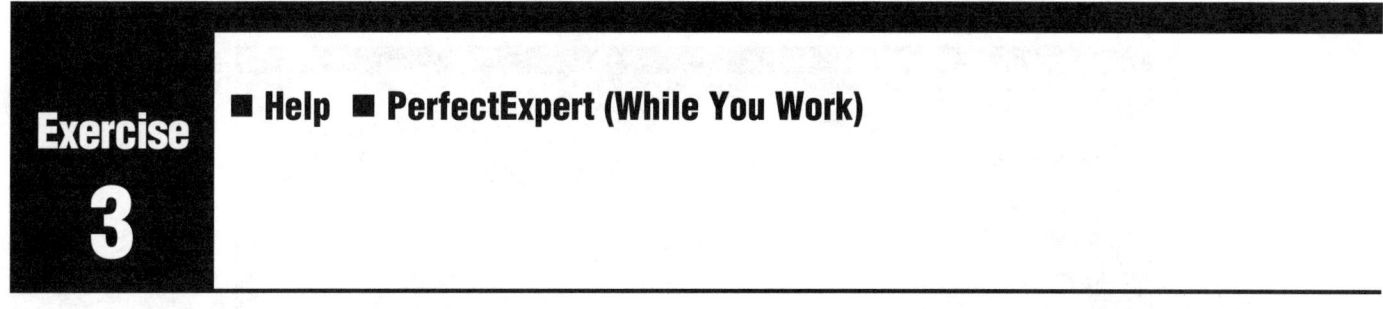

Exercise 3

■ Help ■ PerfectExpert (While You Work)

NOTES:

Get Help

- Help may be accessed by clicking Help on the Menu bar or by pressing F1. Each application's Help menu has some commands in common; in addition, each application has tool-specific help commands. Note the following Help menus from WordPerfect 8 and Paradox 8 and the discussion of the standard commands.

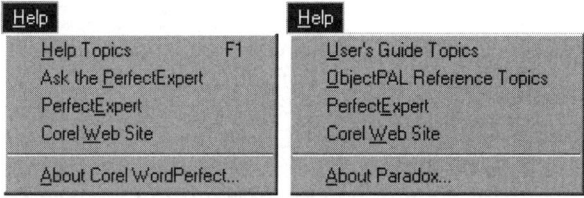

- After you select Help and then Help Topics, the Help Topics dialog box displays with various tabs.

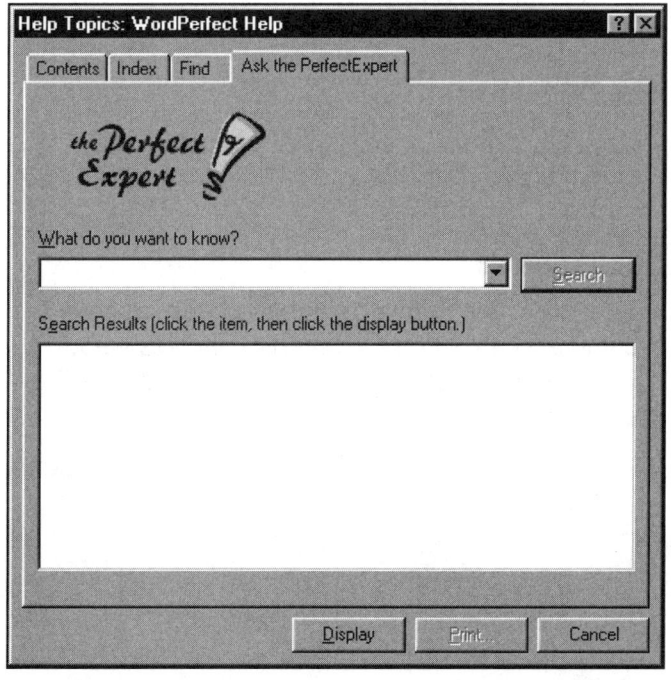

- **Ask the PerfectExpert** searches for answers to your question about a particular topic. In the **What do you want to know?** text box, enter your question and click the Search button. A series of topics in answer to your question displays in the Search Results list box. Double-click any topic in the list box or select the topic and click Display to view the help screen. Note the Ask the PerfectExpert screen:

  ✓Note: Ask the PerfectExpert is not available in Paradox 8.

- **Contents** provides the overall contents of the Help system. Double-clicking the book icon to the left of a topic opens a new set of subtopics. Note the WordPerfect Help Contents page:

- **Index** allows you to enter the first few letters of your topic; the index feature brings you to the index entry. Double-click the entry or select the entry and click Display. The help screen related to your topic is then displayed.

- **Find** accesses the Help database feature. It allows you to search the Help database for the occurrence of any word or phrase in the help topics. The Index and Find features are similar; however, Find offers more options to search for a topic.

  ✓Note: If you are in a Help window, F1 will close the window and open the Help Topics dialog box.

  ✓Note: You may also get help on a particular screen item by pressing Shift + F1, then pointing to any screen icon or location and clicking the left mouse button. A help screen appears explaining the item in question.

- The Corel Web Site help option allows you to access online WordPerfect Help from the Corel Office Web Site if you subscribe to an online service.

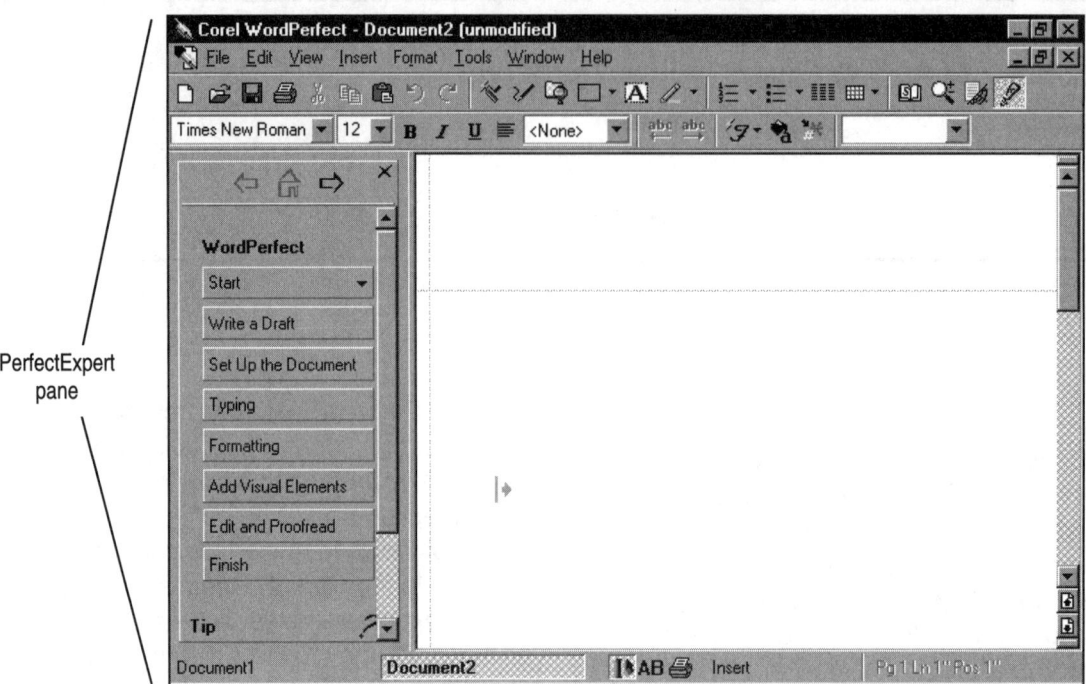

PerfectExpert (While You Work)

- After selecting this help option, a **PerfectExpert** pane displays next to the document window. This pane contains buttons to help you complete tasks. It also displays tips and helpful information during the task completion process.

- The PerfectExpert pane has four icons at the top. Click the back and forward arrows to move backward and forward in the task completion process. Click the home icon to return to the default PerfectExpert pane. To close the PerfectExpert pane, click the Close button on top of the pane.

- To ask a question about a task, click the question mark in the lower right corner of the pane. In the PerfectExpert tab of the Help dialog box that displays, type your question.

✓Note: If you are a new WordPerfect user, it is recommended that you learn the procedures for completing each task before using the PerfectExpert pane. If you used another word processing software package or another version of WordPerfect, using the PerfectExpert pane will make sense to you at this time. **In a later lesson, you will learn to use the PerfectExpert pane to create, enhance, save and send a document.**

Exit Help

- Click Cancel or Close or press Escape, to exit Help.

Conventions

- The exercises in this book have been created using a 12-point font. Because printers vary, your line endings may not appear exactly as the exercises in this text.
  - Changing font style and size will be covered in Lesson 3, Exercise 21.

In this exercise, you will gain practice using the help menus.

EXERCISE DIRECTIONS:

1. Open the Quattro Pro application.
2. Select Help from the Menu bar.
3. Select Help Topics.
4. Select the Contents tab. Do the following:
   - Double-click How Do I.
   - Double-click Learn the Essentials.
   - Double-click Toolbars.
   - Click the Close button.
5. Select Help from the Menu bar.
6. Select Help Topics.
7. Select the Index tab. Do the following:
   - Type **menu** in the text box.
   - Select the topic, **Menu bar**, in the list.
   - Click the Display button.
   - ✓ *Note search results.*
   - Click Cancel, then click Cancel again.
8. Select the Help menu.
9. Select Ask the PerfectExpert.
   - Type, **change column width**.
   - Click Search.
   - ✓ *Note search results.*
10. Click Cancel to exit PerfectExpert.
11. Display the PerfectExpert pane.
    a. Click the Typing button.
    b. Click the Home icon.
    c. Click the Close button on the PerfectExpert pane.
10. Close Quattro Pro.

KEYSTROKES

HELP

F1

1. Click **Help**.................. Alt + H
2. Select desired option.
   OR
   To get help on a particular screen element:
   a. Press **Shift + F1**............... Shift + F1
   b. Click on the desired screen item.

TO DISPLAY/HIDE THE PERFECTEXPERT PANE

1. Click **Help**........................... Alt + H
2. Click **PerfectExpert**........................ E

WordPerfect 8

Lesson 1: Create, Save, and Print Documents

Lesson 2: Open and Edit Documents

Lesson 3: Text Alignments and Enhancements

Lesson 4: Format and Edit Documents

Lesson 5: Work with Multiple-Page Documents

Lesson 6: Templates; Envelopes and Labels; Macros

Lesson 7: Columns; Tables; Merge

Lesson 8: Graphics and Text Boxes

COREL WORDPERFECT 8
Lesson 1: Create, Save, and Print Documents

Exercise 1

- Start WordPerfect 8 ■ The WordPerfect 8 Screen
- Document Window Displays ■ If You Make an Error... ■ View Modes
- Default Settings ■ Create a New Document ■ Save a New Document
- Close a Document ■ Exit WordPerfect 8 ■ Conventions

NOTES

Start WordPerfect 8

- The Windows® 95 taskbar appears at the bottom of the screen on all programs running in Windows 95. WordPerfect may be started using one of the following procedures:

  - **Using the Start button on the Taskbar:** The taskbar allows you to start applications and/or switch between them. Click the Start button on the taskbar; a Corel WordPerfect Suite 8 menu displays (see illustration on the next page). Slide the mouse up to highlight Corel WordPerfect Suite 8. Slide the mouse to the right and down. Then, click the left mouse button to select Corel WordPerfect 8.

  - **Using DAD [Desktop Application Director] on the Taskbar** (if you are using WordPerfect within the Corel WordPerfect 8 Suite, Standard or Professional version. Click the Corel WordPerfect 8 icon .

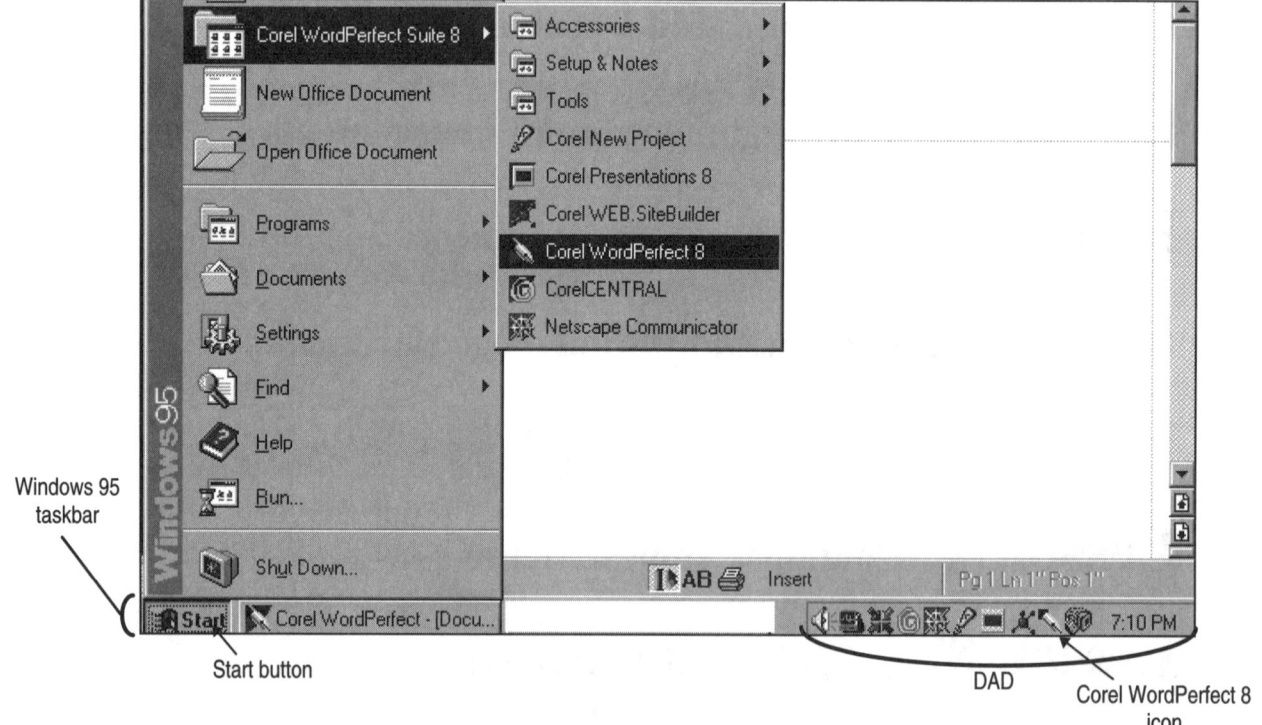

16

The WordPerfect Screen

- After launching the WordPerfect program, the following editing screen appears. Note the name of each screen part in the illustration below and the description provided in the table on pages 4 and 5.

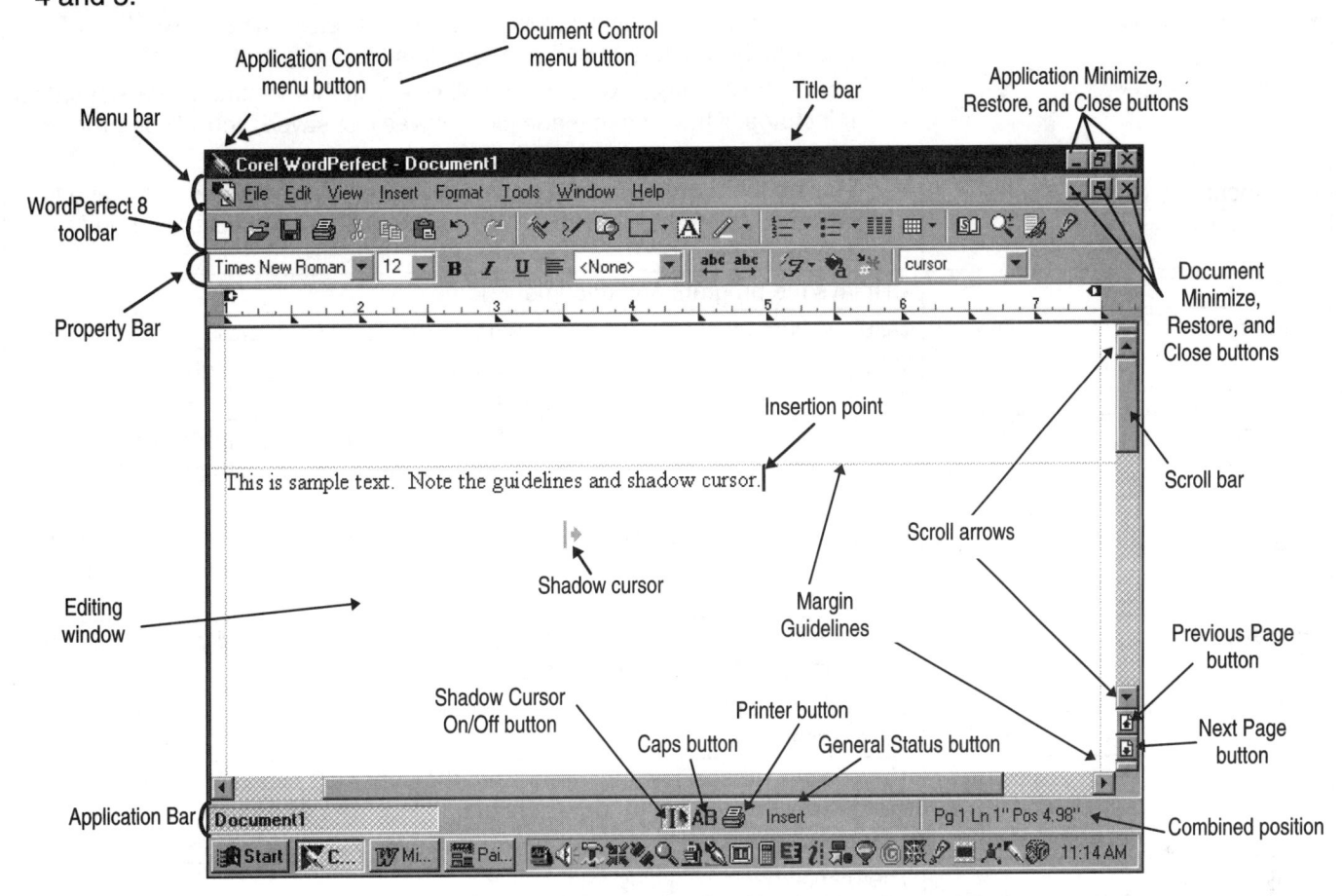

Labels on the illustration: Menu bar, Application Control menu button, Document Control menu button, Title bar, Application Minimize, Restore, and Close buttons, WordPerfect 8 toolbar, Property Bar, Document Minimize, Restore, and Close buttons, Insertion point, Scroll bar, Scroll arrows, Editing window, Shadow cursor, Margin Guidelines, Previous Page button, Shadow Cursor On/Off button, Printer button, Next Page button, Caps button, General Status button, Application Bar, Combined position.

Sample text in editing window: "This is sample text. Note the guidelines and shadow cursor."

Part	Description
Application window	The window within which WordPerfect runs.
Application Control Buttons/Menu:	
• Minimize button	• Shrinks the window to an icon which then appears on the Windows Taskbar.
• Maximize button	• Enlarges the window to a full screen.
• Restore button	• Reduces the application window to its previous size. When a window is reduced, the Restore button changes to a Maximize button.
• Close button	• Closes the window or dialog box. Closing the WordPerfect window will exit WordPerfect.
• Application Control button	• Clicking the WordPerfect 8 Application Control button accesses a menu to Move, Size, Restore, Minimize, Maximize, or Close the WordPerfect 8 window.
Document window (Editing Window)	The window within which a document is contained.

COREL WORDPERFECT 8 Lesson 1: Create, Save, and Print Documents

Part	Description
Document Control buttons/menu:	Appear in the menu bar of a document.
• Minimize button	• Shrinks the document window to an icon at the bottom of the application window.
• Maximize button	• Enlarges the document window to a full screen.
• Restore button	• Reduces the document window to its previous size. When a window is reduced, the Restore button changes to a Maximize button.
• Close button	• Closes the document window or dialog box. If the document was not saved or if changes have been made since it was last saved, you will be prompted to save the document before closing.
• Document Control menu button	• Clicking the WordPerfect 8 Document Control button accesses a menu to Restore, Move, Size, Minimize, Maximize, or Close the document on screen.
Title bar	Displays the program and document name.
Menu bar	Displays items that you can select when executing commands. When an item is selected using the keyboard or the mouse, a group of subitems appears in a drop-down submenu.
Toolbar	A collection of buttons (represented by graphic icons) that enables you to accomplish many common word processing tasks easily, such as saving and printing a file. When you point to the bottom of a toolbar button, a QuickTip displays, and an explanation of that button's function is displayed below the button. You must use the mouse to access toolbar buttons.
Property Bar	Provides buttons that let you easily change the appearance of your document. You must use the mouse to access Property Bar buttons.
Margin guidelines	Dashed lines at the top, bottom, left and right of a page, which display the current margins.
Insertion point	The blinking vertical line that appears in the upper left-hand corner when the WordPerfect document window appears. It indicates where the next typed character will appear and blinks between characters.
Editing window	The blank space for typing text.
Previous and Next Page buttons	The top button moves pages backward through a document; the bottom button moves pages forward through a document.
Scroll bars	Used to move the screen view horizontally or vertically. The scroll box on the vertical scroll bar can be dragged up or down to move the screen view quickly toward the beginning or end of the document. The scroll box on the horizontal scroll bar can be dragged left or right.
Application Bar items:	Appear at the bottom of the screen.
• General Status button	• Indicates whether Insert or Typeover mode is active. Provides the status of Tables, Columns, Macros and Merge features as well.
• Printer button	• Displays the current printer.
• Shadow Cursor On/Off button	• Turns shadow cursor on or off.
• CAPS button	• Turns Caps Lock feature on or off.
• Combined Position	• Displays page number, vertical line position of insertion point, and horizontal position of the insertion point. **Pg 1** - The current page number is displayed. **Ln 1"** - The vertical position of the insertion point (in inches) as measured from the top of the page. **Pos 1"** - The horizontal position of the insertion point (in inches) from the left edge of the page.

Document Window Displays

- The Document Control button, located to the left of the menu bar, can be opened to access a drop-down menu from which you can choose commands to control the document window.

- The document window Minimize, Restore and Close buttons are located on the right of the menu bar. Clicking the Minimize button shrinks the window to an icon which displays at the bottom of the screen. Clicking the Restore button creates a document window (below the Toolbars) including a document Title bar.

- The document Title bar contains the Document Control button as well as the Minimize, Maximize and Control buttons. Clicking the Maximize button on the document Title bar returns the window to the default opening screen. Clicking the Close button closes the document.

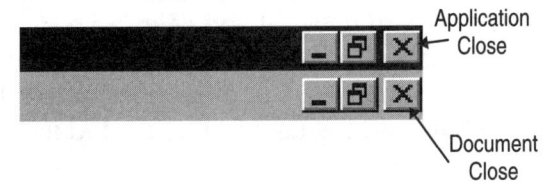

If You Make an Error...

- The following keys will get you out of trouble:
    - **Backspace** — Erases characters to the immediate left of the insertion point.
    - **Escape** — (Or clicking a Cancel button), will back you out of most commands without executing them.
    - **F1** — Accesses Help.

View Modes

- WordPerfect provides various ways to view documents on the screen. You may change view modes by selecting a particular view from the View menu.

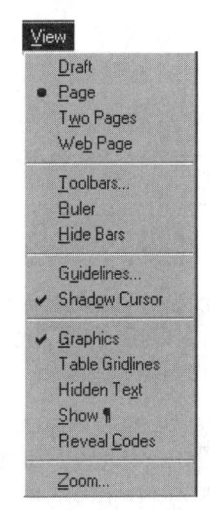

- **Page mode** is the default. It is used to see a document just as it will look when printed. This view allows you to see headers and footers, footnotes and endnotes, columns, etc. The computer may work more slowly in this mode than in draft mode.

- **Draft mode** displays your document without headers, footers, page numbers or other page formatting features. More of the document can be seen on screen in this mode.

- **Two Pages mode** displays two pages side by side.

- **Web Page mode** displays your document as it will appear in HTML format. (See Lesson 13: WordPerfect and the Internet)

Default Settings

- **Default settings** are preset conditions within the program. Settings such as margins, tabs, line spacing, font style, font size and text alignment are automatically set by the WordPerfect program. These settings may be changed as desired. Changing margins, tabs, etc., will be covered in later exercises. WordPerfect 8 default settings include the following:

    - **Margins** are set at 1" on the left, right, top and bottom. Margins are measured from the edges of your page. WordPerfect assumes you are working on a standard 8.5" x 11" page. The line (Ln) and position (Pos) indicators on the Application Bar are displayed in inches. When the insertion point is at the left margin, the Pos indicator displays 1", indicating a 1" left margin; the Ln indicator displays 1", indicating a 1" top margin.

    - **Tab stops** are set every ½ inch.

COREL WORDPERFECT 8 Lesson 1: Create, Save, and Print Documents

Property Bar

Labels on the Property Bar image: Bold, Italics, Underline, QuickFind Previous, QuickFind Next, Insert Symbol, Font Face, Font size, Justification, Select Styles, QuickFonts, Font Color, Prompt-As-You-Go

- The Property Bar displays some default settings. When settings are changed, the new settings will display on the Property Bar.
  - **Font face** (the design of your characters) is defaulted to Times New Roman (or Courier, depending on the printer you are using).
  - **Font size** is set to 12 point. (Font size is measured in points.)
  - **Justification** is set to Left.

Create a New Document

- When you start WordPerfect, a blank screen with guidelines appears, ready for you to begin keyboarding text. WordPerfect assigns "Document1" in the Title bar as the document name (until you provide a name).

- The insertion point will be flashing at the beginning of the document. Text appears at this point when you start typing.

- The **Pos** indicator on the Application Bar shows the insertion point's horizontal position on the page, as measured in inches from the left of the page; the **Ln** indicator shows the insertion point's vertical position, as measured in inches from the top of the page.

- As text is typed, the insertion point automatically advances to the next line. This feature is called **word wrap** or **wraparound**. It is only necessary to use the Enter key at the end of a short line or to begin a new paragraph.

Save a New Document

- Documents must be given a name for identification. A **filename** can contain a maximum of 255 characters, including spaces, and an optional three-character file extension. Filenames and extensions are separated by a period. If you choose not to include a filename extension, WordPerfect automatically assigns the file extension **.wpd**.

- It is recommended that you allow WordPerfect to insert the .wpd file extension for you. Doing so will identify the document as a WordPerfect 8 file to your computer.

- Filenames are displayed in the letter case in which they were originally typed. For instance, If you type a filename in uppercase, it will appear in uppercase. You cannot, however, save one filename in uppercase and save another using the same name in lowercase.

- When saving a file, you must indicate the location where you wish to save it. Documents may be saved on a removable disk or on an internal hard drive. If you save a file to a removable disk, you must indicate that you are saving to the A:, B:, or other designated drive. The hard drive is usually designated as the C: drive.

- If you save to the hard drive, WordPerfect provides folders that you may use to save your work. You also may create your own folders in which to save your work. You will learn to create folders (or directories) in a later exercise. You should use a removable disk to save the exercises in this book.

- When saving a file for the first time, select <u>S</u>ave from the <u>F</u>ile menu, or click the Save button on the toolbar. The following Save File dialog box appears:

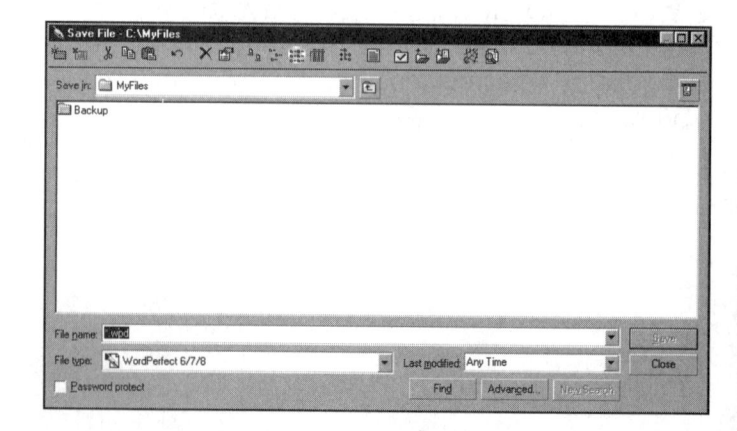

- Note the Save in drop-down list box. WordPerfect displays the current location, or folder, where you can save your file. You can select a different storage location by clicking the drop-down arrow next to the Save in box and selecting the desired drive in which to save the file. The area below the Save in box displays the contents of the current drive. Double-click on the folder in which to save the file. The large area below the Save in drop-down list box displays the contents of the current folder.

- If you wish to save your file to a removable disk, click the list arrow next to the Save in text box and double-click 3½" Floppy (A:) or Removable Disk (which is shown as the F: drive in the illustration below).

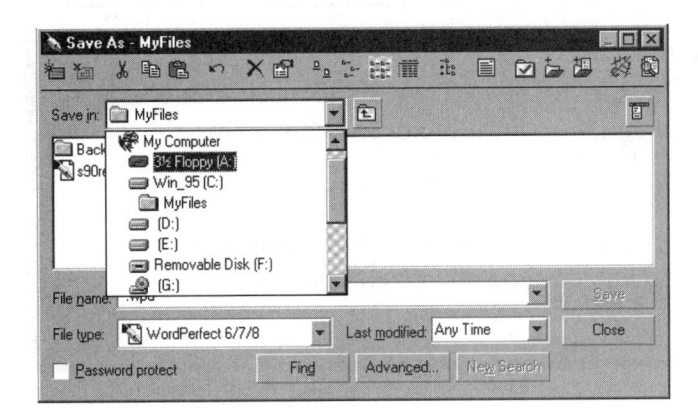

- Once this location is specified, the large area below the Save in text box displays the contents of the disk located in the A: drive.

- Enter a desired filename, or use the one that WordPerfect assigns for you in the File name text box, and click Save to save the document.

- You can save your document in a format other than WordPerfect by clicking the File type drop-down list box and selecting a desired format from the drop-down list. Use this option if you intend to use your file with another software program.

- Once your document is named, the filename appears in the Title bar.

- After saving your document for the first time, you can save the document again and continue working (updating it) by selecting Save from the File menu or by clicking the Save button on the Toolbar. Once the file has been named, the Save File dialog box does not reappear; any changes you have made to your file are simply saved. *Save often to prevent losing data.*

✓Note: By default, the computer automatically saves your open files every 10 minutes.

- Documents may also be saved by selecting Save As from the File menu. Use this command when you want to save your document under a different filename or in a different drive/directory (folder).

Close a Document

- When a document has been saved, it remains on your screen. If you wish to clear the screen, you may close the document window by selecting Close from the File menu, by double-clicking the Document Control button, or by clicking the document Close button.

- If you attempt to close a document before saving it, WordPerfect will prompt you to save it before exiting. You may respond Y for Yes, or N for No.

- If you make a mistake and would like to begin the document again, close the document window without saving it.

- To begin a new document after closing the document window, click the New Blank Document button on the WordPerfect 8 toolbar. This will give you a new document window.

Exit WordPerfect 8

- To exit WordPerfect 8, do one of the following:

  - Click the Program Close button on the Title bar.

  OR

  - Double-click the Application Control menu on the Title bar.

  OR

  - Select Exit from the File menu.

Conventions

- The exercises in this book have been created using a 12-point font. Because printers vary, your line endings may not appear exactly as the exercises in this text.

  - Changing font style and size will be covered in Lesson 3, Exercise 21.

COREL WORDPERFECT 8   Lesson 1: Create, Save, and Print Documents

In this exercise, you will create a two-paragraph document using the word wrap (or wraparound) feature. Use the Backspace key to correct any errors.

EXERCISE DIRECTIONS

1. Start with a clear screen.
2. Begin the exercise at the top of your screen (Ln 1").
3. Type the first paragraph shown below, allowing the text to word wrap to the next line.
4. Correct immediately detected errors using the Backspace key.
   - ✓ *Ignore red slash marks below errors that remain at this time. This feature will be explained in Exercise 5.*
5. Close the file without saving it.
6. Begin the exercise again and complete it. Press the Enter key twice before starting the second paragraph.
7. Save the document; name it **WRAP**.
8. Close the document window.
9. Exit WordPerfect.

When you use WordPerfect 8 to type a document, it is unnecessary to use the "Enter" key at the end of each line. WordPerfect 8 automatically "wraps" text by advancing the insertion point while text is being typed. You will use "Enter" at the end of a short line or to begin a new paragraph.

To save your document, give it a filename and specify the location where you want it to be saved. Once your document has been named, the filename will be displayed in the title bar.

KEYSTROKES

CREATE A NEW DOCUMENT
Ctrl + Shift + N

Click **New Document** button.
OR
1. Click **File** .... Alt + F
2. Click **New** .... N
3. Click **Create** .... Alt + R

SAVE A NEW DOCUMENT
Ctrl + S

Click **Save** button.
OR
1. Click **File** .... Alt + F
2. Click **Save** .... S
3. Click **Save in** text box .... Alt + I
   to select drive or folder.
4. Select desired .... ↓, Enter
   drive or folder.
5. To select subfolder, ... Tab, ↓, Enter
   if necessary, double-click folder.
6. Click in **File name** box .... Alt + N
7. Type filename.
8. Click **Save** .... Alt + S or Enter

CLOSE A DOCUMENT
Ctrl + F4

1. Double-click **Document Control** button.
2. Click **Yes** .... Y
   to save changes.
   OR
   Click **No** .... N
   to abandon changes.
   OR

1. Click **File** .... Alt + F
2. Click **Close** C
3. Click **Yes** .... Y
   to save changes.
   OR
   Click **No** .... N
   to abandon changes.

EXIT WORDPERFECT

Click Program Close button ⊠.
OR
Double-click **Application Control** menu button.
OR
1. Click **File** .... Alt + F
2. Click **Exit** X

COREL WORDPERFECT 8 Lesson 1: Create, Save, and Print Documents

Exercise 2

- QuickCorrect
- Format-As-You-Go
- Spell-As-You-Go
- Spell Checker
- Prompt-As-You-Go
- Document Properties

NOTES

QuickCorrect

- The **QuickCorrect** feature automatically replaces common spelling errors and mistyped words with the correct text as soon as you press the Spacebar.

- There are numerous words already in the word list. However, you can enter additional words that you commonly misspell into the word list by selecting QuickCorrect from the Tools main menu. Select the QuickCorrect Tab in the QuickCorrect dialog box that follows. Enter the misspelled word or abbreviation you want WordPerfect to replace automatically in the Replace text box and type the word you want to use as a replacement in the With text box.

- If you find the QuickCorrect feature annoying, you can deselect the **Replace words as you type** option in the QuickCorrect dialog box.

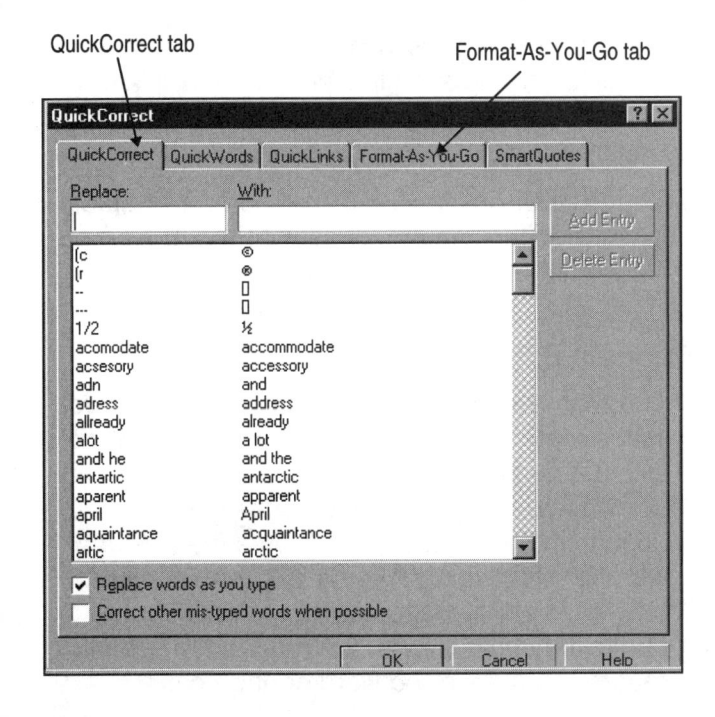

Format-As-You-Go

- **Format-As-You-Go** options found on the Format-As-You-Go tab of the QuickCorrect dialog box allow you to select additional corrections to be included in QuickCorrect. These options include:

  - **Capitalize next letter after end-of-sentence punctuation**, which automatically capitalizes the first letter of a new sentence.

  - **Correct TWo IRregular CApitals**, which automatically converts two initial capital letters of a word to an initial capital letter and a lowercase second letter.

    Note: Click the Exceptions button to specify exceptions to your capitalization settings.

  - **Change two spaces to one space between words**, which automatically converts two spaces to one space between words.

  - **Change one space to two spaces between sentences automatically**, which converts one space to two spaces between sentences.

  - **Change two spaces to one space between sentences**, which converts two spaces to one space between sentences.

Spell-As-You-Go

- The **Spell-As-You-Go** feature underlines spelling errors with red slash marks as you type. To correct a misspelled word, point to the underlined error with your mouse and click the *right* mouse button. A QuickMenu displays with suggested corrections. Click the correctly spelled word in the list and it will replace the incorrectly spelled word in the document. From the QuickMenu option, you can also choose to Add the word to the WordPerfect user word list, Skip in Document, or begin a Spell Check.

COREL WORDPERFECT 8 Lesson 1: Create, Save, and Print Documents

WordPerfect 8 Toolbar

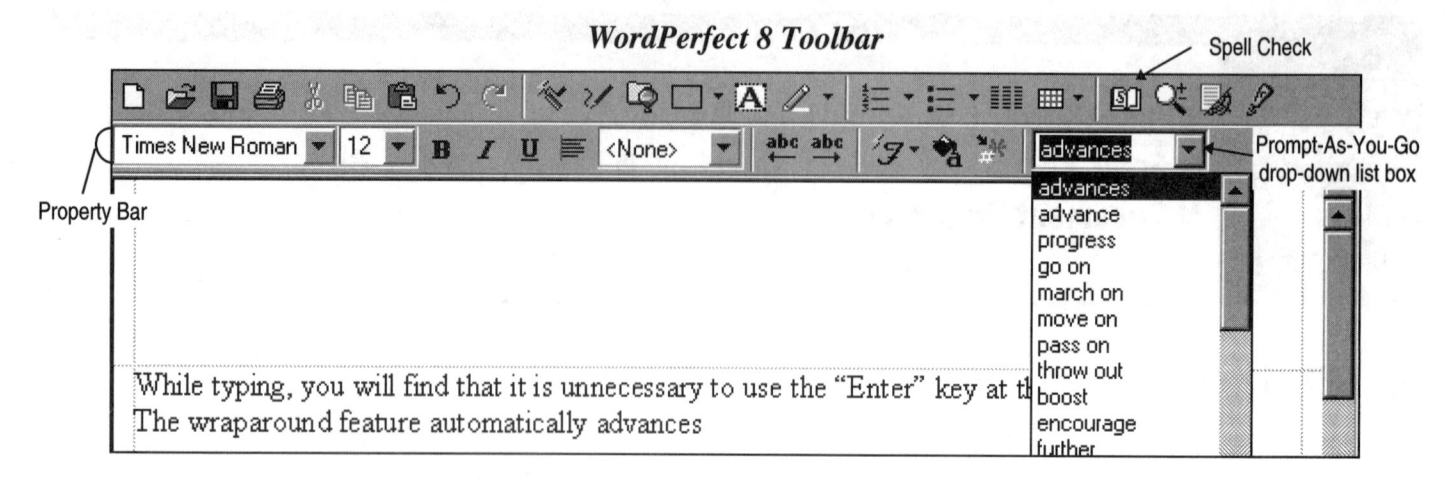

- Spell-As-You-Go is turned on by default. To turn off this feature, click the Off option from the Tools, Proofread menu.

Spell Checker

- WordPerfect's **Spell Check** feature checks your document for general spelling errors, double words, words containing numbers, and irregular capitalization.

- A word, a sentence, a section of a page, an entire page, or an entire document may be checked for spelling errors. When a misspelled or unrecognized word is found, Spell Check offers possible alternatives so you can replace the error.

- Spell Check may be accessed by selecting Spell Check from the Tools menu or by clicking the Spell Check button on the WordPerfect 8 toolbar. You may also click the *right* mouse button in the document window and select Spell Check. The following Writing Tools dialog box will appear:

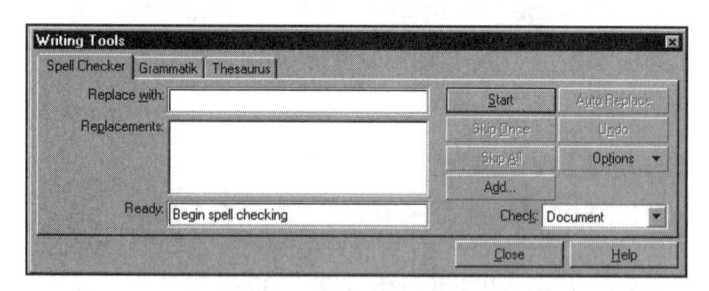

- To avoid having proper names flagged as incorrect spellings during the Spell Check session, add them to the user word list by clicking the Add button in the Writing Tools dialog box.

- Words may be added to the user word list before, after, or during the Spell Check session.

- Spell Check does not find errors in word usage (example: using their instead of there). Finding usage errors will be covered when Grammatik is introduced in Lesson 5, Exercise 36.

Prompt-As-You-Go

- The **Prompt-As-You-Go** feature on the Property Bar provides a list of synonyms as you type. After a word is typed, it displays in the Prompt-As-You-Go drop-down list box. To see a list of words that might substitute for the displayed word, click the list arrow next to the drop-down list box and select a replacement word.

- The Prompt-As-You-Go feature also serves as a spell and grammar checker. If the insertion point is placed on a misspelled word or a possible grammatical error, clicking the list arrow displays a list of corrections.

- If a red word displays in the text box, it indicates a possible spelling error; if a green word displays, it indicates a possible grammatical error. Click the list arrow next to the box to see a list of corrections.

- The Prompt-As-You-Go feature is on by default. To turn off this feature, deselect Prompt-As-You-Go from the Tools, Proofread menu.

Document Properties

- The **Document Properties** feature provides you with a statistical summary of your document. It lists the number of characters, words, lines, sentences, paragraphs and pages in your document. In addition, it indicates the average word length, average words per sentence and maximum words per sentence. This is particularly useful if you are required to submit a report with a specified word or page count.

- Selecting Properties from the File menu will access the document Properties dialog box.
- The Summary tab allows you to save summary information with each document, such as a descriptive name and type, creation and revision date(s), author and typist name(s) and subject. The Information tab includes the document path, character count, word count, sentence, line, paragraph and page count, average word length, average words per sentence, and maximum words per sentence.

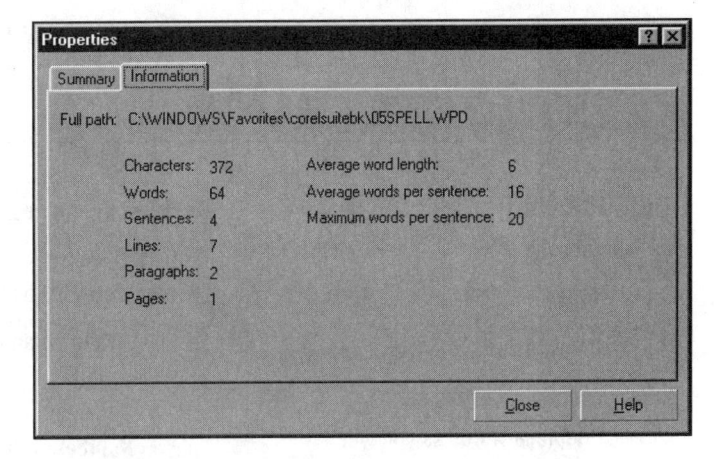

In this exercise, you will type two short paragraphs using word wrap and purposely misspell several words. After typing some of the misspelled words and pressing the Spacebar, you will note that the correct spelling appears. You will then use the Spell Check, Spell-As-You-Go, or Prompt-As-You-Go feature to correct the other misspellings.

EXERCISE DIRECTIONS

1. Start with a clear screen.
2. Access the QuickCorrect feature. Be sure *Replace words as you type* has been selected.
3. Begin the exercise at the top of your screen.
4. Type the paragraphs below exactly as shown, including the circled, misspelled words. Allow the text to word wrap to the next line. After typing the word "QuickCorrect" in the first line, create the following abbreviation for it and add it to QuickWords: qc.
5. Press the Enter key twice to begin a new paragraph.
6. Use the Spell Check, or Spell-As-You-Go feature to correct the misspellings not already corrected by QuickCorrect.
7. Replace the word "avoid" and "mistakes" using the Prompt-As-You-Go list arrow.
8. Using the Document Properties feature, fill out the following summary information about your document:
   Descriptive Name: ... WordPerfect information
   Descriptive Type: .... Report
   Author: .... Your name
   Typist: .... Your name
   Subject: .... Spelling Information
9. Determine the number of words in the document.
10. Save the exercise using the Save button on the toolbar; name it **CORRECT**.
11. Close the document window.

THe WordPerfect QuickCorrect feature automatically corrects spelling errraors and mistyped words when you press teh space bar. The QuickCorrect feature will also correct other mistakes, includeing spacing errors.

General spelling errors, double words, words containing numbers, and irregular capitalizations may all be checkked by the WordPerfect Spell Check feature. You may add words to the user word list to avoid having names erroneously identified as misspellinggs.

Use Prompt-As-You-Go feature to replace "avoid" and "mistakes".

COREL WORDPERFECT 8 Lesson 1: Create, Save, and Print Documents

KEYSTROKES

QUICKCORRECT
Ctrl + Shift + F1

1. Click **T**ools .... `Alt`+`T`
2. Click **Q**uickCorrect .... `Q`
3. Select the **QuickCorrect** tab:
4. Select R**e**place words as you type option .... `Alt`+`E`

   To add words to QuickCorrect dictionary:

   a. Click **R**eplace text box ...... `Alt`+`R`
   b. Type commonly misspelled word to be included.
   c. Click **W**ith text box .... `Alt`+`W`
   d. Type corrected version of word.
5. Click **OK** .... `Enter`

FORMAT-AS-YOU-GO
Ctrl + Shift + F1

1. Click **T**ools .... `Alt`+`T`
2. Click **Q**uickCorrect .... `Q`
3. Click **Format-As-You-Go** tab.
4. Click desired options.
5. Click **OK** .... `Enter`

SPELL CHECK
Ctrl + F1

1. Click **Spell Check** button 📖 on WordPerfect 8 toolbar.

   OR

   a. Click **T**ools .... `Alt`+`T`
   b. Click **Spell Check** .... `S`

   OR

   a. Position mouse on word with error.
   b. Click *right* mouse button.
   c. Click Spe**l**l Check .... `L`

2. Select **Spell Checker** tab ...... `Ctrl`+`Tab`
3. Click **Check** drop-down list box .... `Alt`+`K`
4. Click list arrow and select a Spell Check option:
   - Document
   - Number of Pages
   - Page
   - Paragraph
   - Selected Text
   - Sentence
   - To End of Document
   - Word
5. If an error is found:
   a. Highlight correct spelling from list of Re**p**lacements .... `Alt`+`P`

   OR

   Type correct spelling in the Replace **w**ith box .... `Alt`+`W`

   b. Click **R**eplace .... `Alt`+`R`
   to replace word with correctly spelled word.

   OR

   Click A**u**toReplace .... `Alt`+`U`
   to replace all occurrences.

   OR

   Click Skip **O**nce .... `Alt`+`O`
   to ignore selected word and continue.

   OR

   Click Skip **A**ll .... `Alt`+`A`
   to ignore all occurrences of word in document.

   OR

   Click Ad**d** .... `Alt`+`D`
   to add word to WP dictionary.
6. Click **O**ptions, if desired, to choose spell check options .... `Alt`+`T`
7. Click **U**ndo, if desired, to undo a previous action .... `Alt`+`N`
8. Click **C**lose .... `Alt`+`C`

PROMPT-AS-YOU-GO

1. Position insertion point next to a word.
2. Click Prompt-As-You-Go list arrow and select a word to substitute.

   ✓ *As you type, if a word appears in red in the Prompt-As-You-Go text box, it indicates a spelling error. If the word appears in green, it indicates a grammatical error. Click list arrow to display corrections.*

SPELL-AS-YOU-GO

1. Place mouse on word with red dashed underline.
2. Press right mouse button.
3. Click correct replacement spelling.

DOCUMENT PROPERTIES

1. Click **F**ile .... `Alt`+`F`
2. Click P**r**operties .... `R`
3. Click **Summary** or **Information** tab.
4. Click **OK** or **Close** .... `Enter`

COREL WORDPERFECT 8 Lesson 1: Create, Save, and Print Documents

Exercise 3

- Insertion Point Movements
- Scroll a Document
- Create a Business Letter
- The QuickWords Feature
- The Date/Time Feature

NOTES

Insertion Point Movements

- As noted earlier, the **insertion point** is the blinking vertical bar that shows you where the next typed character will appear. The arrow keys on the numeric keypad, or the separate arrow keys located to the left of the keypad, are used to move the insertion point in the direction of the arrow. You may move the insertion point using the keyboard or the mouse:

  - **Keyboard:** Press the arrow key in the direction you wish the insertion point to move. You may use the arrow keys on the numeric keypad or (depending on your keyboard) the separate arrow keys to the left of the keypad. You can "express" move the insertion point from one point on the document to another using special key combinations. (*See keystrokes at the end of this exercise.*)

  - **Mouse:** Move the mouse pointer to where you want to place the insertion point. Note that when the mouse pointer is moved over white space or a blank line, a light vertical line with an arrow appears. This is called the **shadow cursor**. When the shadow cursor is in the desired position of the white space, you can click to begin typing.

Scroll a Document

- To move the insertion point to a part of the document that does not appear on screen, you can scroll your document vertically by clicking with your mouse on the scroll arrows (up/down arrows) on the right of your document screen.

- To quickly scroll through a document, you may click and drag the scroll box (located on the scroll bar) up or down. Dragging the scroll box down or clicking the scroll-down arrow moves (or scrolls) the page up toward the end of the document; dragging the scroll box up or clicking the scroll-up arrow moves (or scrolls) the page down toward the beginning of the document.

- You can also click in the gray area between the scroll box and the arrows to move a screen up down, right or left. When the part of the document you wish to work with is in view, position your mouse pointer within the document and click where you wish to place the insertion point.

- To scroll one page up or down, click on the Previous or Next Page buttons.

- While the horizontal scroll bar is seldom used, its purpose is to move (or scroll) a document horizontally.

Create a Business Letter

- There are a variety of letter styles used for business and personal use.

- The parts of a **business letter** and the vertical spacing of letter parts are the same regardless of the style used.

Corel WordPerfect 8 ■ Lesson 1 ■ Exercise 3

- A business letter has eight parts:
  - date
  - inside address (to whom and where the letter is going)
  - salutation
  - body
  - closing
  - signature line
  - title line
  - reference initials (the first set of initials belongs to the person who wrote the letter; the second set belongs to the person who typed the letter).

  ✓Note: Whenever you see yo as part of the reference initials in an exercise, substitute your own initials.

- The letter style illustrated in this exercise is a full-block business letter, because the date, closing, signature and title lines begin at the left margin.

- In later exercises, you will learn to use a template to create a business letter.

- A letter generally begins 2.5" from the top of a page. If the letter is long, it may begin 2" from the top of the page. If the letter is short, it may begin 3" or more from the top.

- Margins and font size may also be adjusted to make a letter more balanced on the page.

  ✓Note: Changing margins and font size will be covered in Exercise 15.

QuickWords

- The **QuickWords** feature allows you to save abbreviations in the QuickWords dictionary. When you type the abbreviation, WordPerfect will automatically replace the abbreviation with the expanded text.

- To add abbreviations to the QuickWords dictionary, select the text you want to abbreviate. Then select QuickWords from the Tools menu. In the QuickCorrect dialog box that follows, type the abbreviation for the selected text (abbreviations are not case sensitive) and click Add Entry. The next time you type the abbreviation, the full text will appear after you press the Spacebar.

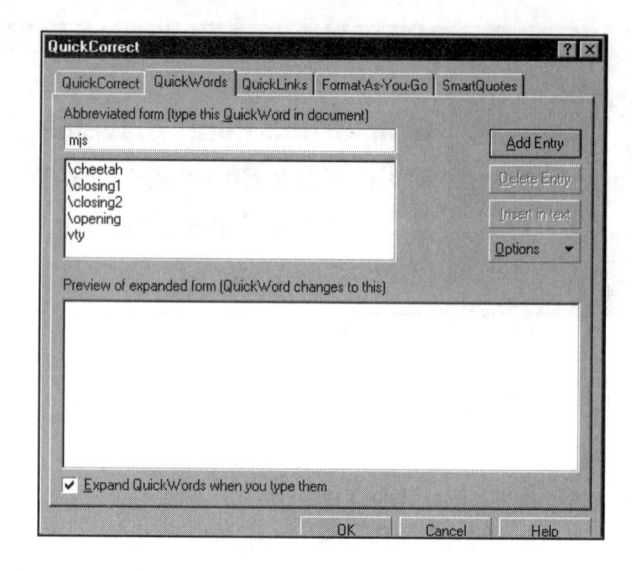

- To turn off this feature, deselect Expand QuickWords When You Type Them at the bottom of the QuickWords tab in the QuickCorrect dialog box.

The Date/Time Feature

- The **Date/Time** feature enables you to insert the current date and time into your document automatically.

- The Date feature gives you two options for inserting the date: **Date Text** or **Date Code**. The date text will insert the current date (which never changes) into your document. The Date Code places a code into your document where the date should appear. The date automatically updates whenever the document is opened or printed.

- To insert date text, press Ctrl + D. Or select Date/Time from the Insert menu and click Insert to insert the date in the default format. To change the date format, click any desired format from the Date/Time formats list.

- To insert a date code, select the Keep the Inserted Date current check box at the bottom of the Date/Time dialog box.

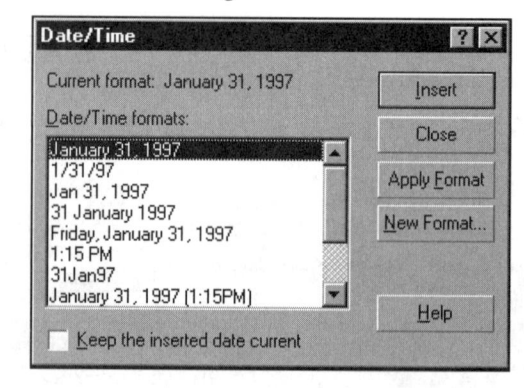

In this exercise, you will create a full-block letter and practice moving the insertion point through the document.

EXERCISE DIRECTIONS

1. Start with a clear screen.
2. Access the QuickCorrect feature. Be sure the Replace words as you type option has been selected.
3. Use the default margins and tabs.
4. Begin the date at approximately Ln 2.5". Use the Date Text feature to insert today's date.
5. Type the letter on the following page exactly as shown. Press the Enter key between parts of the letter as directed in the exercise.
6. After typing the first sentence of body text, create the following abbreviation for the words Wendt, Taylor and Wilkerson and add it to QuickWords: WTW.
7. Use either the Spell Check, Spell-As-You-Go or Prompt-As-You-Go feature to correct any misspellings in the document.
8. Move the mouse pointer above the first paragraph. Note the shadow cursor. Move the insertion point to the top of the screen (Ctrl + Home) and then back to the end of the document (Ctrl + End).
9. Use the scroll box to scroll to the top of the document.
10. Save the file; name it **SUMMER**.
11. Close the document window.

KEYSTROKES

INSERT CURRENT DATE

Ctrl + D

1. Click **Insert** .... Alt + I
2. Click **Date/Time** .... D
3. Click desired format .... ↑ ↓
4. Click **Insert** .... Alt + I

To insert date code:
- Click **K**eep the inserted date current check box .... K

To change date format:
- Click desired format from list of formats .... Alt + D, ↓ ↑
- Select **N**ew Format .... Alt + N
- Click **I**nsert .... Alt + I

SCROLL

Click up/down or left/right arrows on scroll bar until desired text is in view, or click and drag the scroll box up/down to express move the window.

EXPRESS INSERTION POINT MOVEMENT KEYSTROKES

TO MOVE:	PRESS:
One character left	←
One character right	→
One line up	↑
One line down	↓
Previous word	Ctrl + ←
Next word	Ctrl + →
Top of screen	Page Up
Bottom of screen	Page Down
Beginning of document	Ctrl + Home
End of document	Ctrl + End
Beginning of line	Home
End of line	End
First line on previous page	Alt + Page Up
First line on next page	Alt + Page Down

QUICKWORDS

1. Highlight text to be abbreviated.
2. Click **T**ools .... Alt + T
3. Click Quick**W**ords .... W
4. Type an abbreviation for the highlighted text (abbreviations are not case sensitive).
5. Click **A**dd Entry .... A

✓ *QuickWords will automatically replace the abbreviation with the expanded text the next time the word is typed.*

Corel WordPerfect 8 ■ Lesson 1 ■ Exercise 3   29

Ln 2.5"

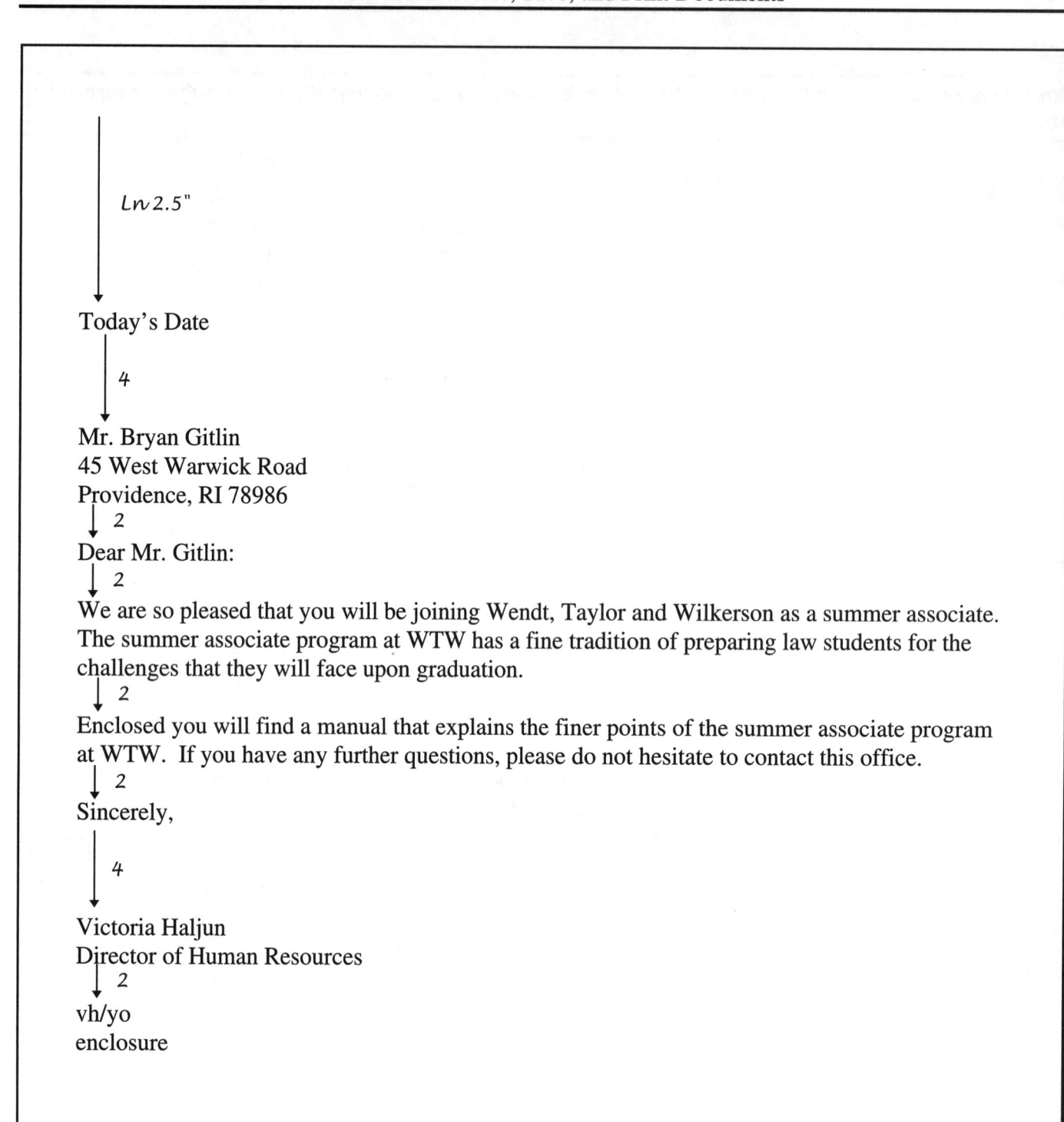

Today's Date

↓ 4

Mr. Bryan Gitlin
45 West Warwick Road
Providence, RI 78986

↓ 2

Dear Mr. Gitlin:

↓ 2

We are so pleased that you will be joining Wendt, Taylor and Wilkerson as a summer associate. The summer associate program at WTW has a fine tradition of preparing law students for the challenges that they will face upon graduation.

↓ 2

Enclosed you will find a manual that explains the finer points of the summer associate program at WTW. If you have any further questions, please do not hesitate to contact this office.

↓ 2

Sincerely,

↓ 4

Victoria Haljun
Director of Human Resources

↓ 2

vh/yo
enclosure

COREL WORDPERFECT 8 Lesson 1: Create, Save, and Print Documents

Exercise 4

- Address Book
- Preview a Document
- Print

WordPerfect 8 Toolbar

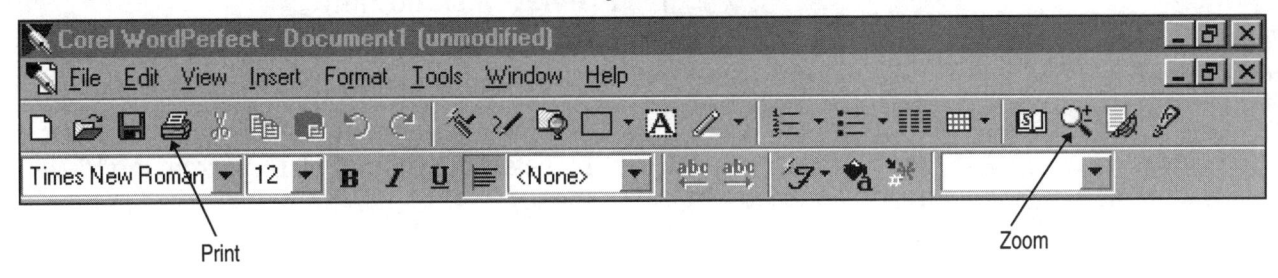

NOTES

Address Book

- The **Address Book** feature allows you to keep the names, addresses, phone numbers, and e-mail addresses of people to whom you send letters frequently. After entering names and addresses into WordPerfect's address book, you can retrieve them into a document when you desire.

- To enter a name and address into the Address Book, select Address Book from the Tools menu.

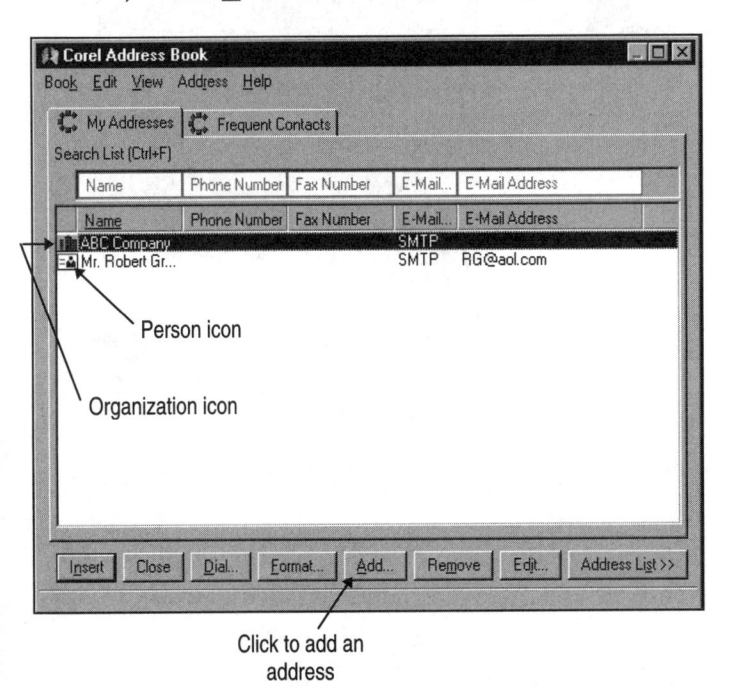

- In the Address Book dialog box, two tabs display: My Addresses and Frequent Contacts. Each tab is considered an individual address book. You can create other address books to allow you to group individuals' phone and address information. For example, you could create an address book (tab) called Computer Club. You would then enter the names and addresses of contacts within that organization or club.

- To add a new address book/tab, select New from the Book menu, type the name for the new address book, and click OK.

Adding an Address

- To add an address, click the tab where you wish to save your information, then click the Add button. You will be prompted to indicate whether the entry is a person, an organization, or a resource. Depending on your selection, a different dialog box displays. If you select person, for example, the New Person Properties dialog box, illustrated on the following page, appears. Fill out the entry form as desired and click OK.

    ✓*Note: Precede each first name entry with a title: Mr., Ms., Dr., etc., so that the title is included when the address is inserted into a document.*

COREL WORDPERFECT 8 Lesson 1: Create, Save, and Print Documents

- In the Address Book list, a small building icon displays next to each organization entry to distinguish it from a personal address entry.

Inserting an Address into a Document

- To insert a name and address into a document, select Address Book from the Tools menu. Then, double-click the desired address to be inserted, or select the address and click Insert.

Preview a Document

- To see how your document will format, or appear on a page, you may preview your work by clicking the Zoom button on the toolbar or by selecting Zoom, Full page from the View menu.

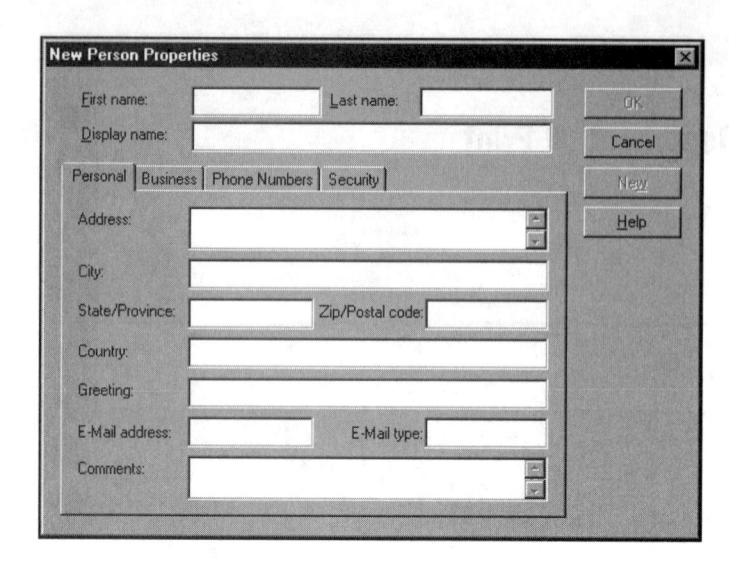

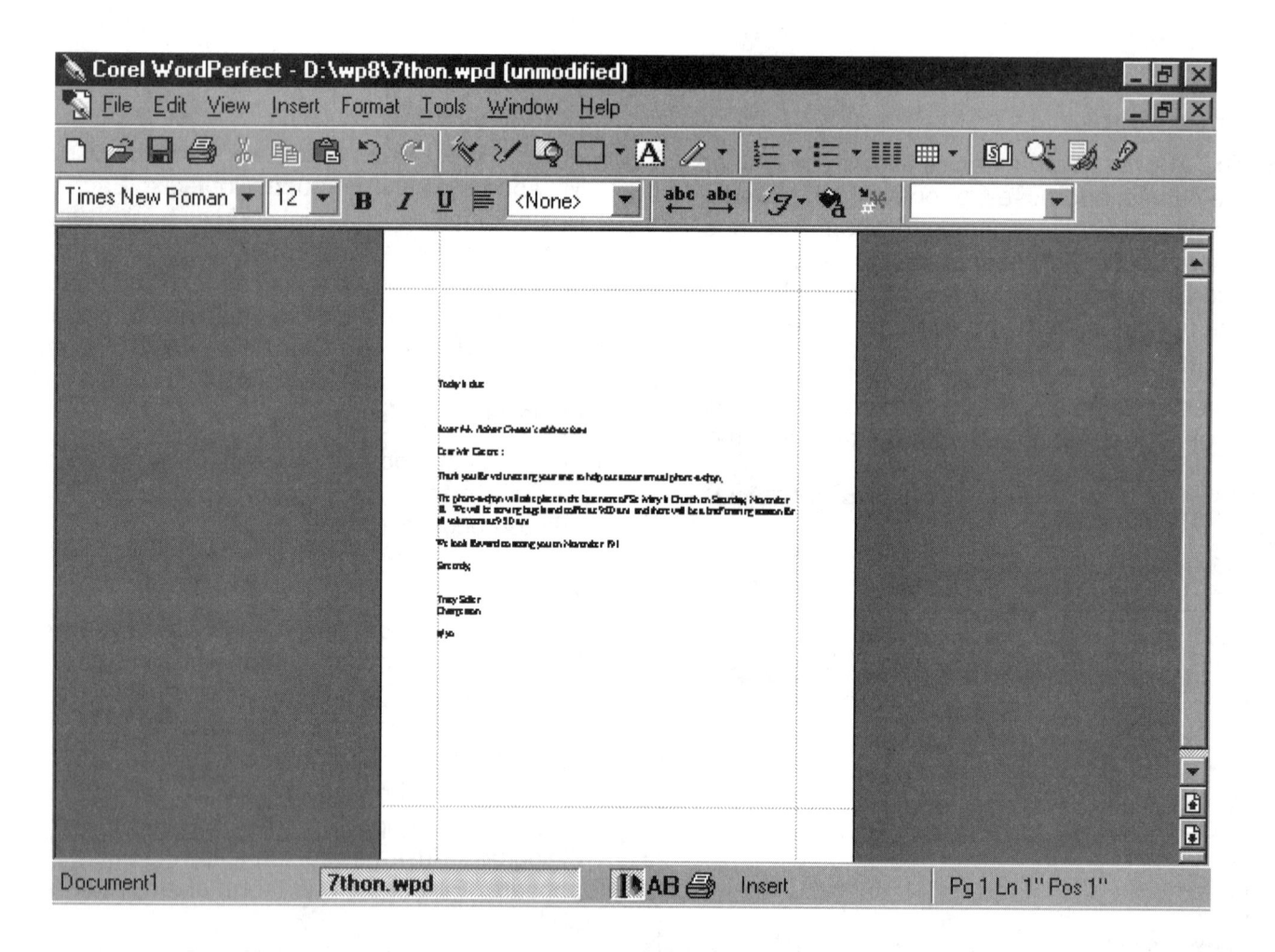

- If you wish to add another entry, click the New button instead of OK when one entry is completed.

Print

- By default, WordPerfect prints the full, on-screen document. However, you can also print a page of the document, selected pages of the document, or selected text within the document. You may also print a single document or multiple documents from a disk without retrieving them to the screen. In this exercise, you will print a full document from a window on your screen.

- Before you print a document, always check to see that your printer is turned on and that paper is loaded.

- There are three ways to print an entire document:
  - Click the Print button on the toolbar.
  - Select File, Print from the menu bar.
  - Press Ctrl + P.

- In the Print dialog box that displays, click Print.

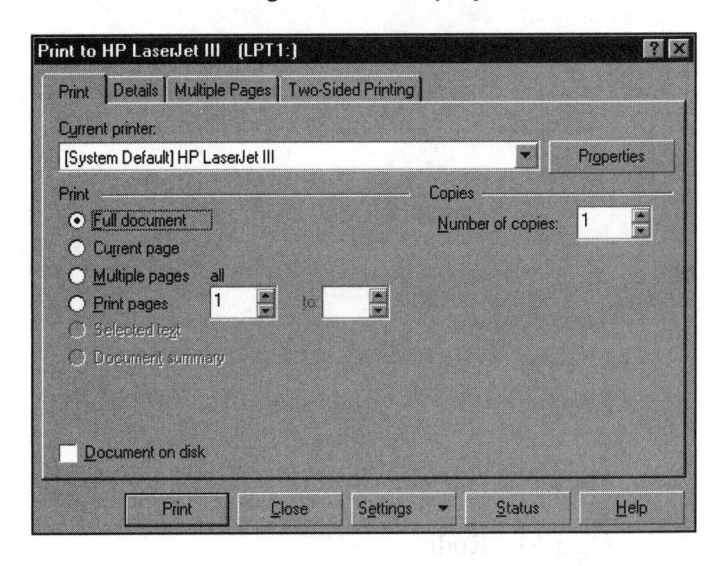

- To cancel a print job, click the Status button. Select the print job to cancel, click Document, Cancel Printing from the menu.

In this exercise, you will enter name and address information using the address book that was created by WordPerfect. You will then create a full-block letter using the Date feature and print one copy of the document.

EXERCISE DIRECTIONS

1. Access the Address Book. Enter the following names and addresses of persons within the My Addresses tab.

   - Ms. Lisa Rodi, University of Texas
     45 Worth Road, Austin, TX 89098
     e-mail: lr@quicknet.com
   - Ms. Julie Garrison, 75 Lincoln Park, No. Miami Beach, FL 33179
     e-mail: Jgarrison@upen.edu
   - Ms. Cheryl Greenwood, 60 Lake Shore Drive, Chicago, IL 60555
     e-mail: gree@ppmail.com
   - Mr. Todd O'Brien, Manager, ACE Company, 550 Broadway, New York, NY 10020
   - Dr. Ellen Sczycpanic, 25 Martins Creek, Winston Salem, NC 27103-4464
   - Ms. Louisa Ruiz, One Hanson Place, Fort Pierce, FL 34982-4448

2. Use the default margins and tabs.

3. Access the QuickCorrect feature. Be sure the Replace words as you type option has been selected.

4. Type the letter on the following page as shown:
   - Use the Date Text feature to insert today's date approximately 2.5" from the top of the page.
   - Press the Enter key between parts of the letter as directed in the exercise.
   - Use the Address Book to insert the inside address shown.

5. Spell check.

6. Preview the document.

7. Print one copy using any of the three methods outlined above.

8. Save the document; name it **CLELAND**.

9. Close the document window.

Today's Date

Use the Address Book to insert Ms. Lisa Rodi's address here.

Dear Ms. Rodi:

CONGRATULATIONS! We are pleased to inform you that you have been selected to join CLELAND HOUSE, a social living group for women at the University of Texas.

Your outstanding academic record and extra-curricular involvement prove your passionate commitment to the University of Texas, and we feel confident that you will be an asset to our dedicated community.

CLELAND HOUSE will be welcoming its new members at a faculty/student reception on March 8.

We look forward to seeing you then.

Sincerely,

Suzanne Silverstein
Membership Director

ss/yo

KEYSTROKES

CREATE A NEW ADDRESS BOOK
1. Click **T**ools .... `Alt`+`T`
2. Click **A**ddress Book .... `A`
3. Click Boo**k** .... `Alt`+`K`
4. Click **N**ew .... `N`
5. Type name of your address book. (e.g., Friends).
6. Click OK .... `Enter`

ADD NAMES TO ADDRESS BOOK
1. Click **T**ools .... `Alt`+`T`
2. Click **A**ddress Book .... `A`
3. Click the tab where you want to add names and address (e.g. Frequent Contacts or Friends).
4. Click **A**dd .... `Alt`+`A`
5. Choose Person or Organization in **S**elect entry type list box.
6. Click OK .... `Enter`
7. Enter the appropriate information.
8. Click OK .... `Enter`

INSERT ADDRESS FROM ADDRESS BOOK INTO A DOCUMENT
1. Position insertion point where address is to be inserted.
   a. Click **T**ools .... `Alt`+`T`
   b. Click **A**ddress Book .... `A`
2. Click the desired tab.
3. Double click name you wish to insert into your document.
   OR
   a. Click the name you wish to insert into your document.
   b. Click I**n**sert .... `Alt`+`N`

PREVIEW A DOCUMENT
Click **Z**oom button on toolbar.
OR
1. Click **V**iew .... `Alt`+`V`
2. Click **Z**oom .... `Z`
3. Click **F**ull Page .... `F`
4. Click OK .... `Enter`

EXIT PREVIEW
Click **Z**oom button on toolbar.
OR
1. Click **V**iew .... `Alt`+`V`
2. Click **Z**oom .... `Z`
3. Click **1**00% .... `1`
4. Click OK .... `Enter`

PRINT
F5 or Ctrl + P
1. Click **P**rint button on toolbar.
   OR
   a. Click **F**ile .... `Alt`+`F`
   b. Click **P**rint .... `P`
2. Click **P**rint tab.
3. Click a print option
   - **F**ull Document .... `Alt`+`F`
   - Cu**r**rent Page .... `Alt`+`R`
   - **M**ultiple Pages .... `Alt`+`M`
   - **P**rint Pages .... `P`, *page numbers*
   - Selected Te**x**t .... `X`
   - Documen**t** Summary .... `T`
   - **D**ocument on Disk .... `D`
4. Click Print .... `Enter`

CANCEL PRINT JOB
1. Click **P**rint button on toolbar.
   OR
   a. Click **F**ile .... `Alt`+`F`
   b. Click **P**rint .... `P`
2. Click **S**tatus .... `Alt`+`S`
3. Click document to cancel.
4. Click **D**ocument .... `Alt`+`D`
5. Click **R**emove .... `R`
6. Click Di**s**play .... `Alt`+`S`
7. Click **C**lose .... `C`

COREL WORDPERFECT 8 Lesson 1: Create, Save, and Print Documents

Exercise 5

■ Summary

In this exercise, you will create a full-block letter using the Date, Address Book and Spell Checker features. You will then preview and print one copy of the completed document.
✓ *The proofreaders' mark for a new paragraph is: ⁋*

EXERCISE DIRECTIONS

1. Type the letter below in full-block style.
2. Use the default margins and tabs.
3. Use the Date Text feature to insert today's date.
4. Send this letter to Ms. Julie Garrison. Use the Address Book to insert the inside address.
5. Spell check.
6. Preview the document.
7. Print one copy.
8. Save the document; name it **COMPU**.
9. Close the document window.

Today's date Dear Ms. Garrison: Thank you for your recent purchase at CompuCenter USA. We hope that you are pleased with your new computer. ⁋ If you should decide you want to grow or update your system, please stop by one of our many convenient locations. Our knowledgeable staff can help you design a system that best meets your needs. ⁋ CompuCenter USA offers the most up-to-date hardware and software for your home and/or office. ⁋ You can also contact our customer service center, available 24 hours a day, at 1-800-555-7654. ⁋ Thank you again for shopping CompuCenter USA. Sincerely, Steven Loga Consumer Services sl/yo

COREL WORDPERFECT 8

Lesson 2: Open and Edit Documents

Exercise 6

- **Open and Revise a Document**
- **Open a Recently Saved File** ■ **Open a Document Not Recently Saved**
- **Insert Text** ■ **Proofreaders' Marks** ■ **Save Changes to a Document**

NOTES

Open and Revise a Document

- A document is revised when corrections or adjustments need to be made. **Proofreaders' marks** are symbols on a printed copy of a document that indicate changes to be made. As each proofreaders' mark is introduced in an exercise in this text, it will be explained and illustrated.

- Before a document can be revised or edited, it must be opened from the disk to the screen.

Open a Recently Saved File

- WordPerfect lists the nine most recently opened files at the bottom of the File menu. To open a recently opened file, select the desired filename from the list.

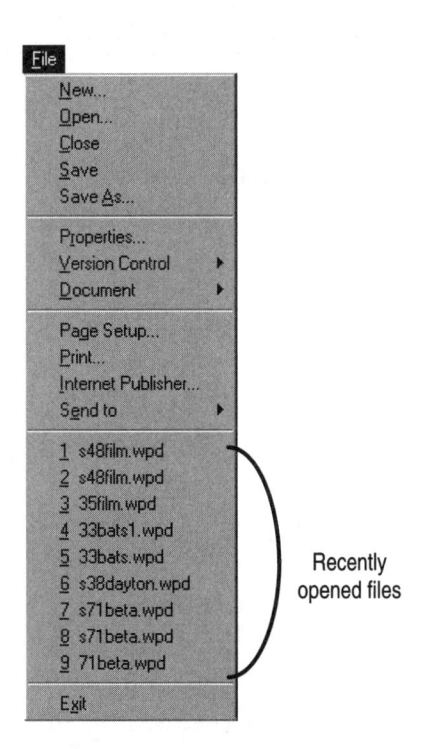

Open a Document Not Recently Saved

- Select Open from the File menu or click the Open button on the toolbar. In the Open File dialog box that appears, double-click the desired file from the list displayed. WordPerfect documents are indicated by the WordPerfect Pen icon. Other document types are noted by different icons.

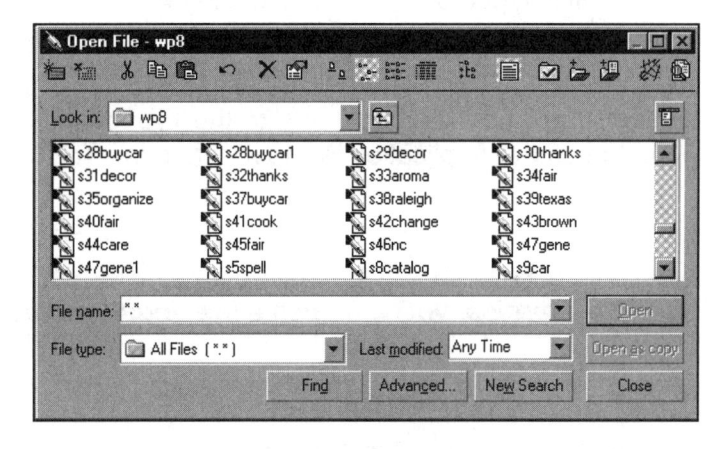

- If the desired file is not listed in the current folder shown in the Look in drop-down list box, click the list arrow next to the Look in box and select a desired drive and/or folder.

- You may also select a file from the history list. Clicking the list box arrow next to the File name box displays the last ten recently saved files.

COREL WORDPERFECT 8   Lesson 2: Open and Edit Documents

Insert Text

- To make corrections, use the insertion point movement keys to move to the point of correction, or use the mouse to click at the point of correction.

- Text is inserted immediately before the insertion point when Insert mode is on. (Insert is the default keyboarding mode indicated on the bottom of the Application Bar.) When typing inserted text, the existing text moves to the right. When inserting a word, the space following the word must also be inserted.

- To create a new paragraph in existing text, place the insertion point immediately to the left of the first character in the new paragraph and press the Enter key twice.

- Another way to edit text is to type over existing text with new text. To put WordPerfect in Typeover mode, press the Insert (Ins) key once or click the Insert button on the Application Bar. In this mode, existing text does not move to the right—it is typed over. (After changing to Typeover mode, note the bottom of the Application Bar—Typeover mode is displayed.)

- Press the Insert key again or click the Typeover button on the Application Bar to return to Insert mode.

Proofreaders' Marks

- Proofreaders' marks are symbols on a printed copy of a document that indicate changes to be made. As each proofreaders' mark is introduced in this text, it is explained and illustrated.

- The proofreaders' mark for insertion is: ∧

- The proofreaders' mark for a new paragraph is: ¶

Save Changes to a Document

- When a document is opened and revisions are made, the revised or updated version must be resaved or replaced. When a document is resaved, the old version is replaced with the new version.

- You may save your changes as you are working or you may save your changes after all corrections have been made. Click the Save button 💾 on the toolbar or select Save from the File menu. Your file will be updated, and the document will remain on the screen for you to continue working.

- It is recommended that you save often to prevent loss of data.

In this exercise, you will open a previously saved document and insert new text.

EXERCISE DIRECTIONS

1. Open **WRAP** or **06WRAP**.
2. Make the insertions indicated below.
3. Use Typeover mode to insert the word "want" in the second paragraph. Return to Insert mode immediately following this step.
4. Save your work.
5. Spell check.
6. Print one copy.
7. Close the file.
8. Close the document window.

When you use WordPerfect 8 to type a document, *you will find that* it is unnecessary to use the "Enter" key at the end of each line. WordPerfect 8 automatically "wraps" text by advancing the insertion point *to the next line* while text is being typed. You will *only need to* use *the* "Enter" *key* at the end of a short line or to begin a new paragraph.

To save your document, *you should* give it a filename *that is relevant to its contents* and *then* specify the location where you want it to be saved. Once your document has been named, the filename will be displayed in the title bar *when the document is in use*.

KEYSTROKES

OPEN A DOCUMENT

CTRL + O

1. Click **Open File** button.

   OR

   a. Click **F**ile .... Alt + F
   b. Click **O**pen .... O

2. Click **L**ook in box .... Alt + L
3. Double-click drive and/or folder containing file to open .... ↓, Enter
4. Select or type desired filename.
5. Click **OK** .... Enter

OPEN A RECENTLY SAVED FILE

1. Click **F**ile .... Alt + F
2. a. Select desired filename .... ↓
      from list of recently opened files.

   OR

   b. Type the number to the left of the filename.

RESAVE A DOCUMENT

Ctrl + S

Click **Save** button on toolbar.

OR

1. Click **F**ile .... Alt + F
2. Click **S**ave .... S

OR

1. Click **F**ile .... Alt + F
2. Click **C**lose C
3. Click **Y**es .... Y
   when prompted to save changes.

INSERT TEXT

1. Place insertion point to left of character that will immediately follow inserted text.
2. Type text.

TYPEOVER

1. Place insertion point where text is to be overwritten.
2. Press **Insert** .... Ins

   OR

   Click **Insert** on the Application Bar.

3. Type text.
4. Press **Insert** .... Ins
   to exit Typeover mode.

   OR

   Click **Typeover** on the Application Bar.

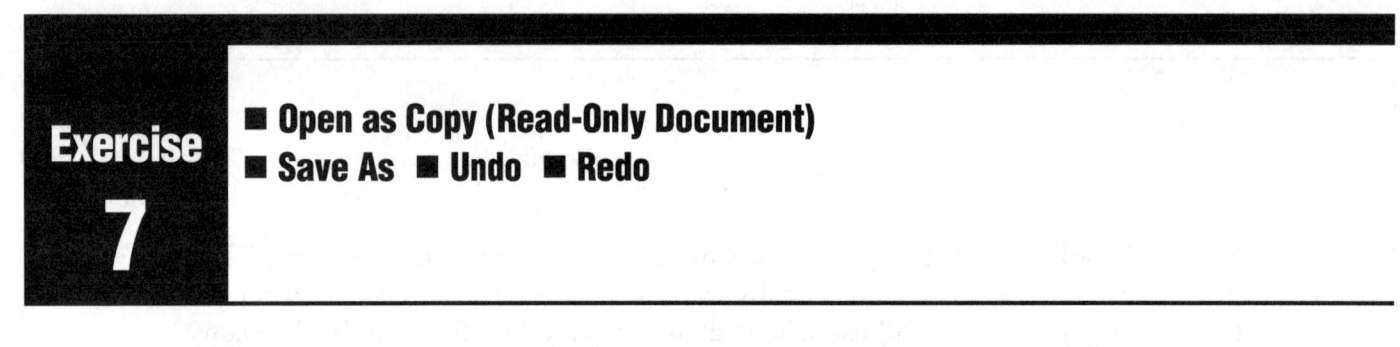

CORELWORDPERFECT 8 Lesson 2: Open and Edit Documents

Exercise 7

- **Open as Copy (Read-Only Document)**
- **Save As** ■ **Undo** ■ **Redo**

Undo   Redo

NOTES

Open as Copy (Read Only-Document)

- If you wish to open a document but not make changes to it, you can click the **Open as copy** option in the Open File dialog box. This will make the document a read-only copy and will require you to save it with a different filename, preventing you from accidentally changing the file.

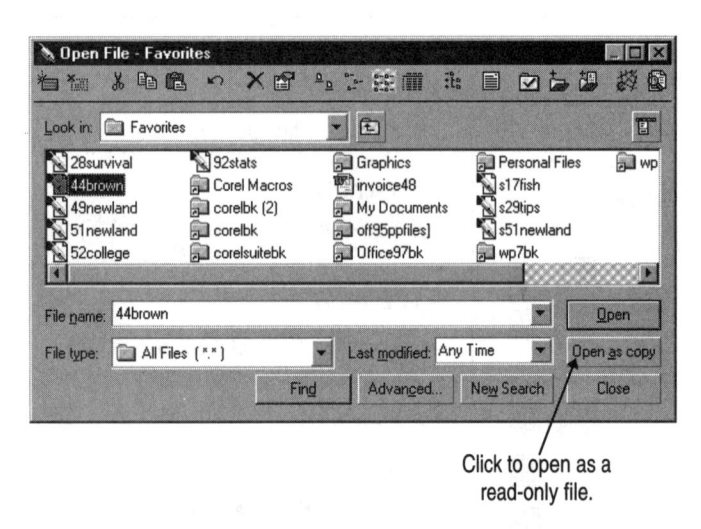

Click to open as a read-only file.

- If you save, close, or exit a document that you opened using the Open as Copy option, WordPerfect automatically displays the Save File dialog box for you to give the file another name, thus leaving the original document intact.

Save As

- If you wish to save any document under a different filename or in a different location, you may select **Save As** from the File menu. When any document is saved under a new filename, the original document remains intact.

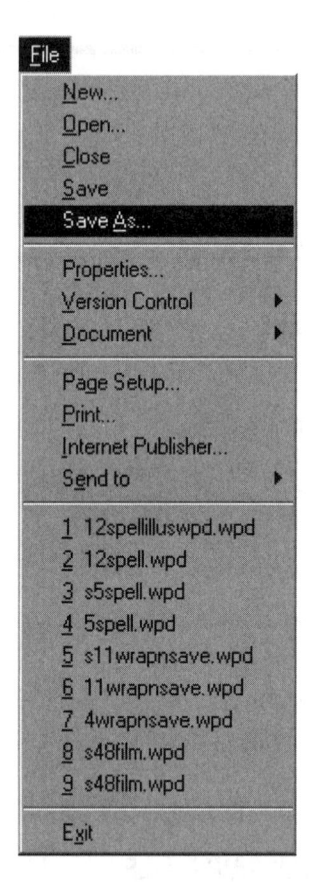

Undo

- The **Undo** feature lets you undo the last change you made to the document.
- WordPerfect remembers up to 300 actions in a document and allows you to undo any or all of them. You can undo all your recent actions by

repeatedly clicking the Undo button on the WordPerfect 8 toolbar, or you can select Undo/Redo History from the Edit menu and choose the action you wish to undo from the list presented. When you choose an action from the list, all actions prior to that action will also be undone.

Redo

- The **Redo** feature allows you to reverse the last undo.
- Like Undo, Redo allows you to reverse up to 300 actions in a document. You can redo an action by repeatedly clicking the Redo button on the WordPerfect 8 toolbar, or you can redo a selected action by selecting Undo/Redo History from the Edit menu and choosing the action to redo.

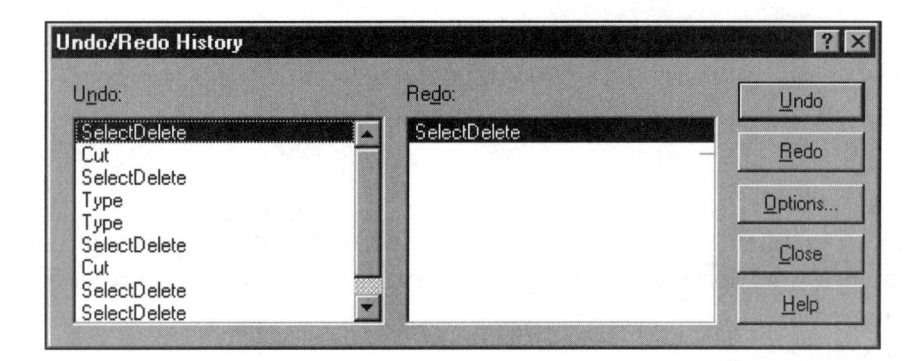

In this exercise, you will insert text at the top of the page and create a full-block letter. To insert the date, press the Enter key eight times to bring the Ln indicator to 2.57". Remember to use the automatic Date feature to insert today's date. After inserting the date, you will use the Address Book to insert the inside address. Text will adjust as you continue creating the letter.

Note: The highlighted words in the illustration may differ from your copy due to substituted words in Exercise 2.

EXERCISE DIRECTIONS

1. Open ⌨**CORRECT** as an Open as copy file, or open 💾**07CORRECT** as an Open as copy file.

2. Make the indicated insertions. (Follow the spacing rules for a full-block letter that were illustrated in Exercise 6.)

3. Use the Date Text feature to insert today's date.

4. Use Typeover mode to replace the word "may" with the word "can" in the last paragraph; return to Insert mode immediately.

5. After typing the initials (mw/yo) in lowercase, undo the action to remove the initials.

6. Retype the initials in uppercase.

7. Preview your work.

8. Modify the document summary information (Properties) as follows:
   Descriptive Name: ... Software Inquiry Response
   Descriptive Type: .... Letter
   Author: .... Your name
   Typist: .... Your name
   Subject: .... Response to Inquiry

9. Access the Information tab in the Properties dialog box and note the number of words in this document.

10. Use Undo to remove the uppercase initials; retype them in lowercase.

11. Print one copy.

12. Close the file; save the changes.

COREL WORDPERFECT 8 Lesson 2: Open and Edit Documents

Today's Date

Insert

*(Use the address book to insert
Todd O'Brien's name and address here)*

Dear Mr. O'Brien:

Thank you for your interest in our how-to computer books. We have a new book on the market that should address all of your WordPerfect needs, including those you mentioned in your letter.

The WordPerfect QuickCorrect feature automatically corrects ^common spelling errors and mistyped words when you press the space bar. The QuickCorrect feature will also correct other errors, including ^capitalization and spacing errors. ^types of

^can General spelling errors, double words, words containing numbers, and irregular capitalizations ~~may~~ all be checked by the WordPerfect Spell Check feature. You may add words to the user word list to keep from having names erroneously identified as misspellings.

Sincerely,

Insert

*Michele Walters
Customer Service Manager*

mw/yo

KEYSTROKES

SAVE AS
F3
1. Click **F**ile .... Alt + F
2. Click **S**ave **A**s .... A
3. Type new filename.
4. Click **O**K .... Enter

OPEN AS COPY
1. Click **F**ile .... Alt + F
2. Click **O**pen .... O
3. Click on the file to open.
4. Click **O**pen **a**s Copy button ..... Alt + A

UNDO
Ctrl + Z
This procedure is to be used immediately after executing the command you wish to undo.

Click **U**ndo button [↺].
OR
1. Click **E**dit .... Alt + E

2. Click **U**ndo .... U

REDO
Ctrl + Shift + R
This procedure is to be used immediately after undoing a command.

Click **R**edo button [↻].
OR
1. Click **E**dit .... Alt + E
2. Click **R**edo .... R

COREL WORDPERFECT 8 Lesson 2: Open and Edit Documents

Exercise 8

- Delete Text
- Select Text
- Undelete
- Undelete vs. Undo

WordPerfect 8 Toolbar

Cut   Paste

NOTES

Delete Text

- The **Delete** feature allows you to remove text, graphics, or codes from a document.

- Procedures for deleting text vary depending upon what is being deleted: a character, previous character, word, line, paragraph, page, remainder of page, or a blank line.

- Use the Backspace key to delete characters and close up spaces to the *left* of the insertion point.

- Use the Delete (Del) key to delete a character or space to the *right* of the insertion point.

- To delete a block of text (words, sentences, or paragraphs), you must first select (highlight) it. (See Select Text methods, right.) Once the block is selected, you may use one of the following deletion methods:
  - Press the Delete key.
  - Click the Cut button on the WordPerfect 8 toolbar.
  - Right-click the mouse button and select Cut.

- When text is deleted using the Cut button, it disappears from the screen and is placed on the Clipboard. The Clipboard is a temporary storage area in the computer's memory. Clicking the Paste button on the WordPerfect 8 toolbar will retrieve the text most recently sent to the Clipboard.

Select Text

- Text may be selected or highlighted in several ways:
  - **Using the keyboard**, by holding down the Shift key while pressing the directional arrow keys.
  - **Using the keyboard in combination with the mouse**, by clicking where the selection should begin, holding down the Shift key, and clicking where the selection will end.
  - **Using the mouse alone,** by dragging the mouse pointer over the desired text.
  - **Using the mouse**, by clicking in the left margin opposite the desired sentence. When the mouse pointer changes to the shape of an arrow pointing upward, click and hold the left mouse button and drag the mouse up or down to highlight as many lines of text as desired.
  - **Using Mouse selection shortcuts**. There are numerous ways to quickly select a word, sentence, paragraph or entire document. See Keystrokes section on page 47 for procedure.

COREL WORDPERFECT 8 Lesson 2: Open and Edit Documents

- **Using the F8 key**, which anchors the insertion point and allows you to use the directional arrow keys to highlight or select text in any direction from the insertion point position. Press F8 to cancel the selection.

■ To abandon any selection process, release the mouse button and click once anywhere on the WordPerfect screen.

Undelete

■ The undelete feature allows you to restore text after it has been deleted. Your insertion point should be in the location where you wish the text to be restored when accessing this task. WordPerfect remembers your last three deletions and allows you to restore them.

■ Undelete may be accessed by pressing Ctrl + Shift + Z. In the undelete dialog box that follows, click Restore to restore highlighted text or click Next or Previous if highlighted text is not what you want to restore.

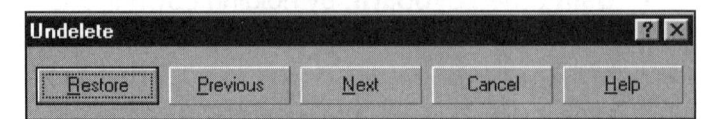

Undelete vs. Undo

■ Undelete lets you restore the most recent deletion or up to three previous deletions at the insertion point. Undo lets you restore deleted information in its original location or reverse the last change or action made to the document.

■ When using Undo to restore deleted text, you must use the command immediately after the deletion is made.

■ Common proofreaders' marks for deleting or moving text are:

delete:

close up space:

move text to the left:

In this exercise, you will use various deletion methods to edit a document. Use block highlighting procedures to delete sentences, words, or blocks of text.

EXERCISE DIRECTIONS

1. Start with a clear screen.
2. Create the exercise as shown in Illustration A, or open 08PEACE.
3. Use the default margins.
4. Begin the exercise on Ln 1".
5. Make the revisions shown in Illustration B of the exercise on page 46. Use the selection and deletion procedures indicated.
6. After deleting the last paragraph, undelete it.
7. Using another deletion method, delete the last paragraph again.
8. Spell check.
9. Print one copy.
10. Save the file; name it **PEACE**.
11. Close the document window.

ILLUSTRATION A

HEALTH AND RELAXATION
HEALTH AND RELAXATION AT THE HUMAN PEACE CENTER

Have you had a bad day, week, month or year? Do you desire the strength that comes from inner peace?

The Human Peace Center was founded in 1985 by William and Kathy Kellman as a healing center for the stressed and over-worked. At the Human Peace Center, relaxation, meditation, and overall health and fitness are promoted through group classes, private meditations, and one-on-one treatments. We tailor each client's program to meet her or his individual needs and concerns.

Because it is sometimes tough to "get away from it all," The Human Peace Center offers you the opportunity to get away while staying close to home.

Are you ready to unwind?

For more information, please write or call our offices:

Human Peace Center, P.O. Box 67543, New York City, NY 90786 / (800) 456-9876

Wellness Center, 45 Oak Park, Chicago, IL 90876 / (987) 876-1234

The benefits of the Human Peace Center will stay with the client long after her or his visit. We emphasize skills and techniques that can be incorporated into a hectic schedule and practiced in the comforts of one's home or private office.

COREL WORDPERFECT 8 Lesson 2: Open and Edit Documents

ILLUSTRATION B

Triple click; press Delete

~~HEALTH AND RELAXATION~~
HEALTH AND RELAXATION AT THE HUMAN PEACE CENTER

Double click; press Delete

Have you had a bad day, week, month or year? Do you desire the strength that comes from ~~inner~~ peace?

Drag to select with mouse; press Delete

Double click; right click, select Cut

The Human Peace Center was founded in 1985 by William and Kathy Kellman as a ~~healing~~ center for the stressed and over-worked. At the Human Peace Center, relaxation, meditation, ~~and overall~~ health and fitness are promoted through group classes, ~~private~~ meditations, and one-on-one treatments. ~~We tailor each client's program to meet her or his individual needs and concerns.~~

Quadruple click to select paragraph; press Delete

~~Because it is sometimes tough to "get away from it all," The Human Peace Center offers you the opportunity to get away while staying close to home.~~

Are you ready to unwind?

For more information, please write or call ~~our offices~~:

Drag to select with mouse; right click, select Cut

Human Peace Center, P.O. Box 67543, New York ~~City~~, NY 90786 / (800) 456-9876

Wellness Center, 45 Oak Park, Chicago, IL 90876 / (987) 876-1234

~~The benefits of the Human Peace Center will stay with the client long after her or his visit. We emphasize skills and techniques that can be incorporated into a hectic schedule and practiced in the comforts of one's home or private office.~~

Position mouse pointer in left margin, click to select; right click, select Cut

Place insertion point immediately to left of the character(s) indicated; press Delete

KEYSTROKES

SELECT (HIGHLIGHT) BLOCKS OF TEXT

USING THE KEYBOARD

Place insertion point where highlight is to begin.

Highlight:	Press:
One character to the left	Shift + ←
One character to the right	Shift + →
One line up	Shift + ↑
One line down	Shift + ↓
To the end of a line	Shift + End
To the beginning of a line	Shift + Home
To the end of a word	Shift + Ctrl + →
To the beginning of a word	Shift + Ctrl + ←
Top of page	Shift + Page Up
Bottom of page	Shift + Page Down
To the end of a paragraph	Shift + Ctrl + ↓
To the beginning of a paragraph	Shift + Ctrl + ↑
To the end of the document	Shift + Ctrl + End
To the beginning of the document	Shift + Ctrl + Home
Entire document	Ctrl + A

USING F8

1. Place insertion point where block highlighting is to begin.
2. Press **F8**............................F8
3. Press any of the directional arrow keys to extend the highlighting.

   OR

   Press any character, punctuation, or symbol (except apostrophe) to highlight to the next occurrence of that key.
4. Press **F8**............................F8
   to cancel mode.

USING THE MOUSE

1. Place insertion point where block highlighting is to begin.
2. Hold down the left mouse button and drag the insertion point to desired location.
3. Release the mouse button.

   OR

1. Place insertion point where block highlighting is to begin.
2. Point to where selection should end.
3. Press **Shift**............................Shift
   and click left mouse button.

MOUSE SELECTION SHORTCUTS

Word:
1. Place insertion point anywhere in word.
2. Double-click left mouse button.

Sentence:
1. Place insertion point anywhere in sentence.
2. Triple-click left mouse button.

   OR

1. Place mouse pointer in left margin, opposite desired paragraph.

   Mouse pointer will point toward the right when you're in the left margin area.

2. Click left mouse button once.

Paragraph:
1. Place insertion point anywhere in paragraph.
2. Quadruple-click left mouse button.

   OR

1. Place mouse pointer in left margin, opposite desired paragraph.

   Mouse pointer will point toward the right when you're in the left margin area.

2. Double-click left mouse button.

Entire Document:

Ctrl + A

1. Click **Edit**............................Alt + E
2. Click **Select**............................L
3. Click **All**............................L

To cancel a selection:

Click anywhere outside the selection.

DELETE

Ctrl + X

Character:
1. Place insertion point to the left of character to delete.
2. Press **Delete**............................Del

   OR

1. Place insertion point to the right of character to delete.
2. Press **Backspace**............................Backspace

Word:
1. Double-click desired word.
2. Press **Delete**............................Del

   OR

1. Place insertion point to the right of word to delete.
2. Press **Ctrl+Backspace**............................Ctrl + Backspace

Block of Text:
1. Select (highlight) block to delete using procedures described above.
2. Click **Cut** button ✂ to place text on the Clipboard.

   OR

   Press **Delete**............................Del

   ✓ *The **Clipboard** is a temporary storage area in computer memory. The text most recently sent to the Clipboard may be retrieved by clicking the Paste button on the WordPerfect 8 toolbar or by pressing Ctrl + V.*

REPLACE DELETED TEXT WITH TYPED TEXT

1. Select (highlight) text to replace using procedures described above.
2. Type new text.

UNDELETE

1. Press **Ctrl + Shift + Z** ... Ctrl + Shift + Z
2. Select desired option:
   - **Restore** to restore............Alt + R
     last deletion.
   - **Next** or **Previous**....Alt + N or P
     to cycle through last three deletions.
3. Click **Restore**............................R

Exercise 9

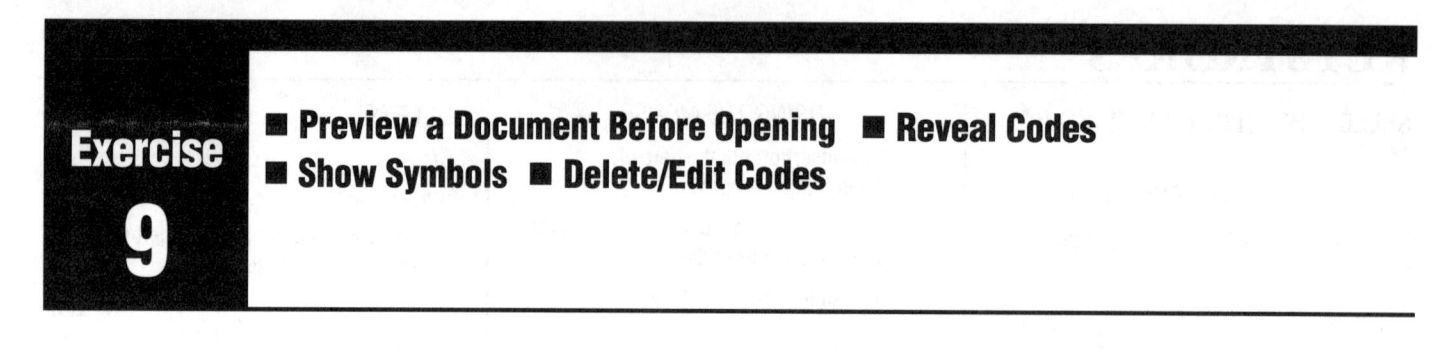

- **Preview a Document Before Opening**
- **Show Symbols**
- **Reveal Codes**
- **Delete/Edit Codes**

NOTES

Preview a Document Before Opening

- In previous exercises, you opened a document to the screen that you knew you wanted to check and print. However, sometimes you might forget the contents of a document and would like to view it before opening or printing it. Or you might want to print a document without opening it first.

- To preview a document before opening it, select Open from the File menu, or click the Open button on the WordPerfect 8 toolbar. In the Open File dialog box which follows, click the file you wish to preview and click the **Preview** button on the dialog box toolbar. A preview screen displays a small portion of the document.

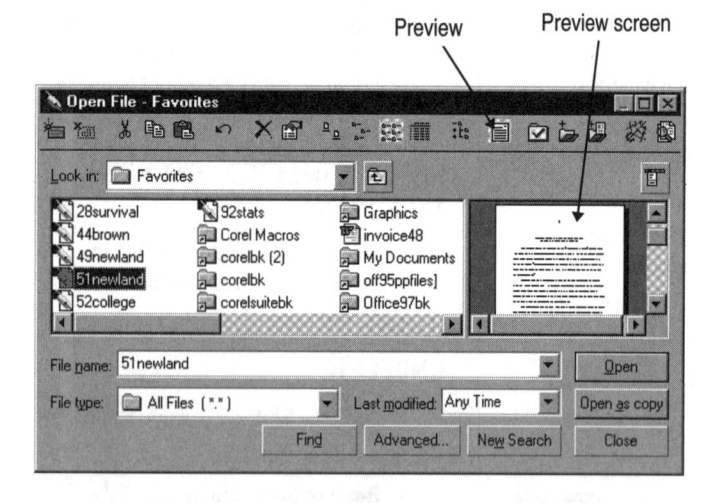

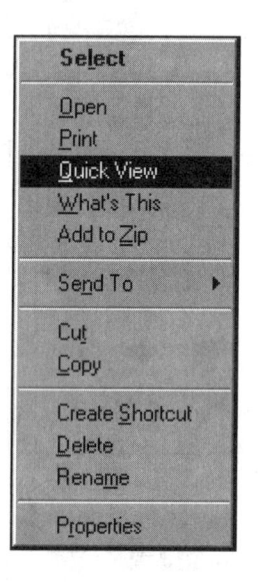

- The Quick View window displays. If this is the document you wish to open, click the Open File for Editing button on the dialog box toolbar.

- To view a larger part of the document, right-click the file you wish to preview and select Quick View from the QuickMenu.

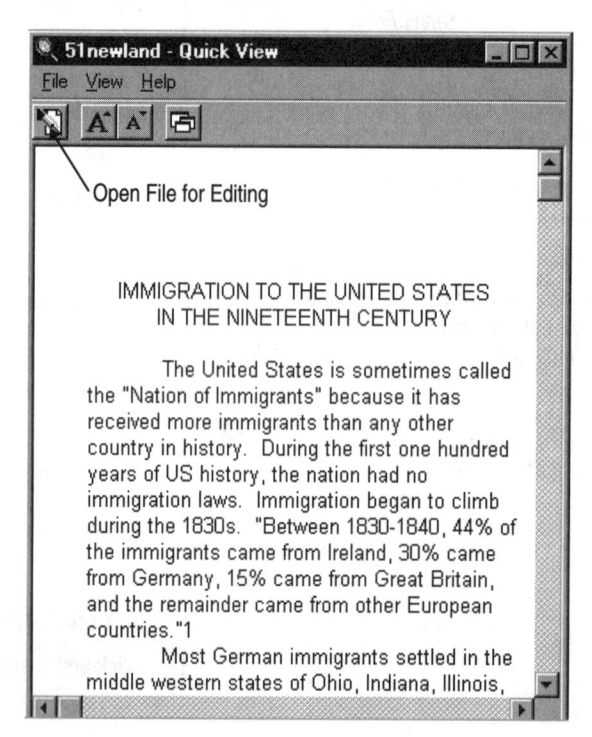

- To print a document without opening it to the screen, right-click the document in the Open File dialog box and select Print from the QuickMenu.

Reveal Codes

- As a document is created in WordPerfect, codes are inserted that determine the document's appearance. These codes are not displayed on the screen but can be revealed when necessary either through the **Reveal Codes** or **Show Symbols** features.

- When Reveal Codes is selected, the document window is divided into two parts. The top part is the normal editing area; the bottom part displays the same text with the codes displayed. A divider line splits the two parts of the window.

- Reveal Codes may be accessed by pressing Alt + F3, by selecting Reveal Codes from the View menu, or by right-clicking the mouse and selecting Reveal Codes.

- As you point to a code with your mouse, a QuickTip explains the code. An example of this screen and its codes appears below.

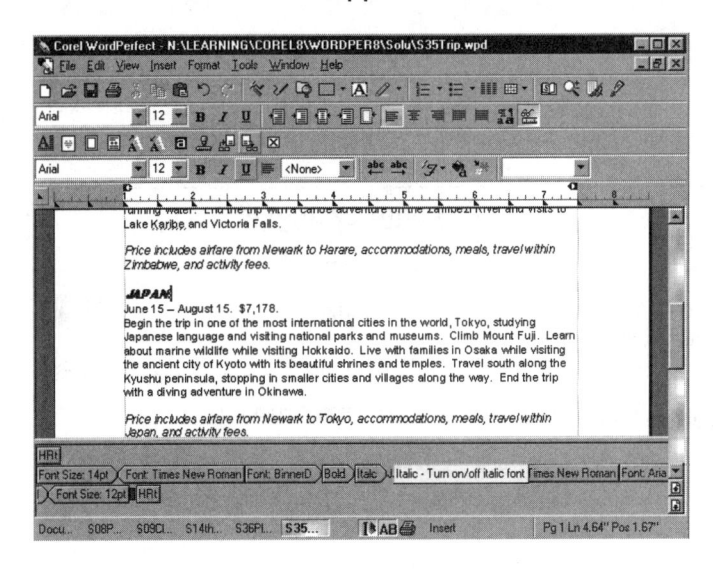

- Reveal Codes may be deselected by pressing Alt + F3 again, or by deselecting the Reveal Codes option under the View menu.

Show Symbols

- When the Show Symbols feature is selected, all the codes that were inserted when the document was created are displayed on screen as various symbols.

- A hard return code is represented by a paragraph symbol (¶); a tab code is represented by an arrow (→); a space is represented by a small solid circle (•). An example of a document with symbols displayed is shown below.

- Show Symbols may be accessed by selecting Show ¶ from the View menu or by pressing Ctrl + Shift + F3.

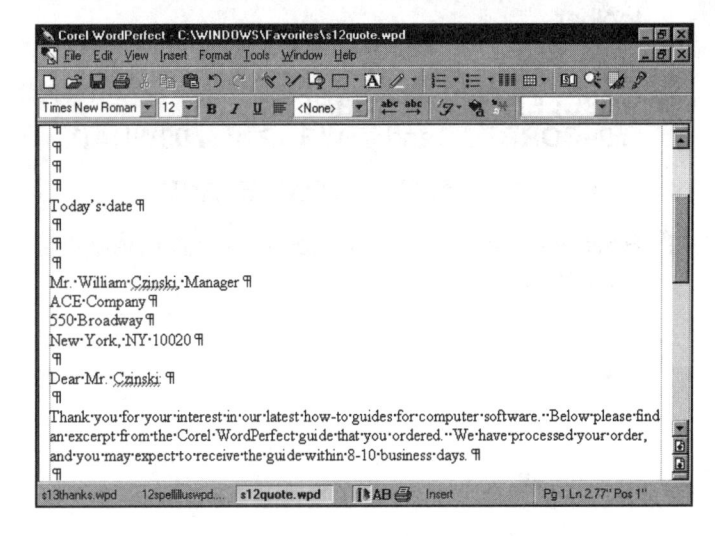

- Show Symbols may be deselected by pressing Ctrl + Shift + F3 or by deselecting the Show ¶ option from the View menu.

Delete/Edit Codes

- **To delete a code in Reveal Codes mode**, use the mouse pointer to click on the code (the insertion point, represented by a red indicator, appears before the code), and press the Delete key. Or, use the mouse pointer to drag the code out of the Reveal Codes window.

- To edit a code in Reveal Codes mode, double-click the code, and a dialog box relating to the feature displays.

- **To delete a code in Show Symbols mode,** move the insertion point to the left of the code and press the Delete key.

- To combine two paragraphs into one, the hard returns that separate the paragraphs must be deleted. Therefore, deleting the paragraph symbols will delete the code. This may be done in either Reveal Codes or Show Symbols mode.

- The proofreaders' mark for "let the orginal stand" is: **stet** or a dotted line below the word(s).

COREL WORDPERFECT 8   Lesson 2: Open and Edit Documents

> *In this exercise, you will edit an exercise you created earlier and use the Reveal Codes feature to assist you.*

EXERCISE DIRECTIONS

1. Start with a clear screen.
2. Click the Open button on the WordPerfect 8 toolbar.
3. Using Quick View, preview **CLELAND** or **09CLELAND**, **CORRECT** or **09CORRECT** and **WRAP** or **09WRAP**.
4. Open **CLELAND** or **09CLELAND**.
5. Reveal codes. Point to each code and view the QuickTip.
6. Make the revisions illustrated on the next page.
7. To combine the two paragraphs (as indicated on the next page), delete the hard return codes in the Reveal Codes screen. Insert spaces where necessary.
8. Preview your work.
9. Print one copy.
10. Close the file; save the changes.

KEYSTROKES

PREVIEW DOCUMENT BEFORE OPENING

1. Click **File** .... Alt + F
2. Click **Open** .... O
3. Click **Toggle Preview On/Off** button ....
4. Click on desired file to preview.

REVEAL CODES

Alt + F3

1. Click **View** .... Alt + V
2. Click **Reveal Codes** C
   ✓ To exit Reveal Codes, repeat this procedure.

DELETE CODES

1. Reveal codes.
2. Use the mouse pointer to drag the code out of the Reveal Codes window.
   OR
   a. Place insertion point to the left of code to delete.
   b. Press **Delete** .... Del

SHOW SYMBOLS

Ctrl + Shift + F3

1. Click **View** .... Alt + V
2. Click **Show ¶** .... S

To exit Show Symbols:

1. Click **View** .... Alt + V
2. Click **Show ¶** .... S

Today's Date

Ms. Lisa Rodi
University of Texas
45 Worth Road
Austin, TX 89098

Dear ~~Ms. Rodi~~ Lisa:

CONGRATULATIONS, Lisa! We are pleased to inform you that you have been selected to join CLELAND HOUSE, a social ~~living~~ group for women at the University of Texas. We were very impressed with your credentials. Your outstanding academic record and extra-curricular involvement prove your ~~passionate~~ in worthy causes commitment to the University of Texas, and we feel confident that ~~you~~ your interests and skills will be an asset to our ~~dedicated~~ community.

CLELAND HOUSE will be welcoming its new members at a faculty/student reception on March 8. We look forward to seeing you then.

Sincerely,

Suzanne Silverstein
Membership Director

ss/yo

COREL WORDPERFECT 8 Lesson 2: Open and Edit Documents

Exercise 10

- Change Toolbars
- Hard Space
- Convert Case
- Set Margins
- Set Tabs

Format Toolbar

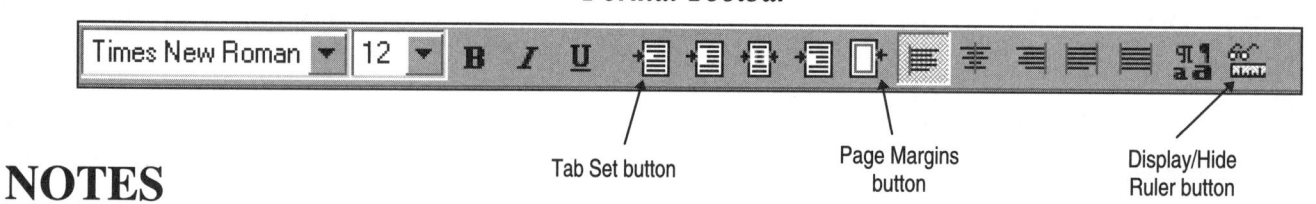

Tab Set button — Page Margins button — Display/Hide Ruler button

NOTES

Change Toolbars

- WordPerfect 8 provides 19 specialized toolbars to make accessing features easier.

- To add another toolbar, point to the current toolbar, right-click and select a toolbar from the list provided or click More… for additional toolbar options. The WordPerfect 8 toolbar is the default.

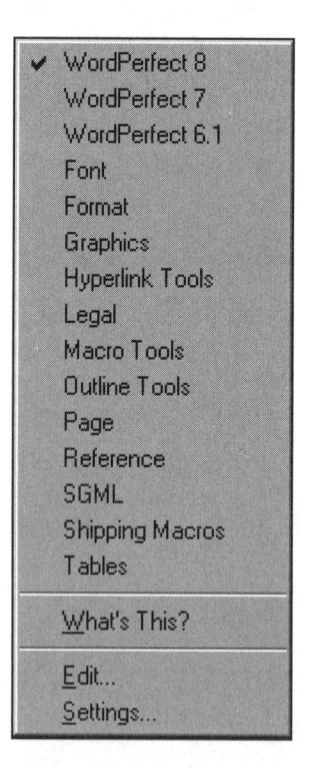

  - ✓ WordPerfect 8
  - WordPerfect 7
  - WordPerfect 6.1
  - Font
  - Format
  - Graphics
  - Hyperlink Tools
  - Legal
  - Macro Tools
  - Outline Tools
  - Page
  - Reference
  - SGML
  - Shipping Macros
  - Tables
  - What's This?
  - Edit…
  - Settings…

- On some toolbars, the left buttons remain constant. Only the buttons on the right change to reflect the new selection.

- The selected toolbar will remain on screen until it is deselected, even if a new document is created.

Hard Space

- To prevent two or more words from splitting during word wrap, a hard space code can be inserted between words. This feature is particularly useful when keyboarding first and last names, dates, equations, and times.

- The procedure for inserting a hard space is to delete the existing space and then hold down the Control key as you press the Spacebar. Or, select Line from the Format menu, select Other Codes, select Hard Space, and click Insert.

Convert Case

- The **Convert Case** feature lets you change selected block of text to Lowercase, Uppercase or Initial Capitals. When you choose Initial Capitals, the first word in each sentence remains capitalized. To change case, select the text to affect, select Convert Case from the Edit menu and select a convert option.

- The proofreaders' mark for changing uppercase letters to lowercase is: / or /
- The proofreaders' mark for changing lowercase letters to uppercase is: ≡

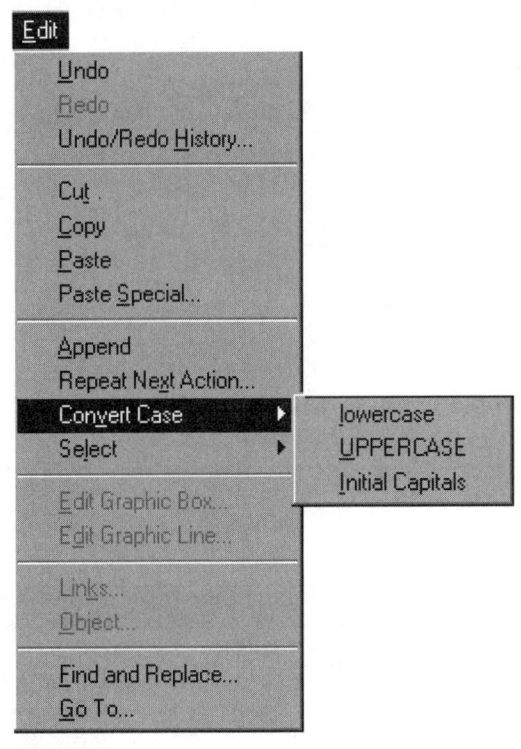

Set Margins

- WordPerfect measures margins in inches. The default margins are 1" on the left and right, and 1" on the top and bottom of the page.
- You can change the margins for an entire document or for selected paragraphs in a document as desired.
- By default, margin changes affect all text from the paragraph containing the insertion point forward. To change the margins for a single block of text, select the paragraphs to change before resetting the margins.
- There are three ways to change left and right margins:

    1. **Drag margin guidelines.** This method is the most convenient way to adjust the margins and immediately see the effect on the document text.
        - To change margins using the guidelines, position the mouse pointer on the left or right, top or bottom margin guideline. When the pointer changes to a left/right or up/down pointing arrow, drag the margin guideline to the desired position. As you drag the guideline, the margin measurement will display onscreen. To change margins for a single block of text, select the text before you drag the margin guidelines.

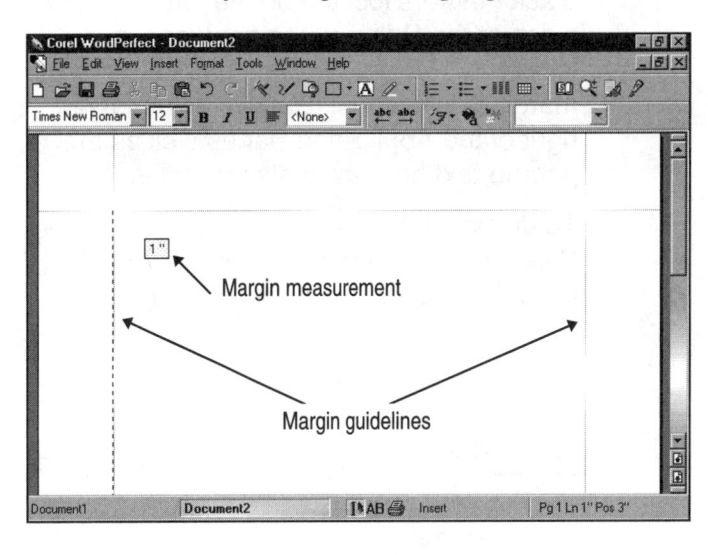

    OR

    2. **Use the Page Margins dialog box.** This method allows for greater precision.
        - To set margins in the dialog box, select Page Setup from the File menu and click on the Page Margins tab, or click the Page Margins button on the Format toolbar. In the Page Setup dialog box that follows, enter the left and right margin amounts. If you want all the margins to be same, check the Make all margins equal check box.

    OR

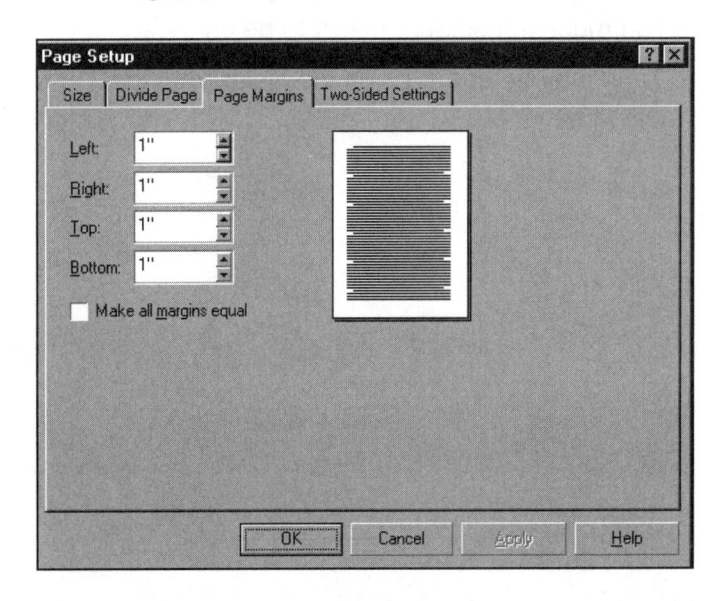

3. **Use the Ruler** This method lets you see the effect of margin changes as you make them.

- To adjust margins using the Ruler, drag the left and/or right margin markers (the solid black markers located on the left and right sides of the Ruler) to the new margin locations. As you drag the marker, note the margin position that displays in the lower right of the Application Bar as well as in the pop-up text box which also displays.

- To display the Ruler, select Ruler from the View menu or click on the Display/Hide Ruler button on the Format toolbar.

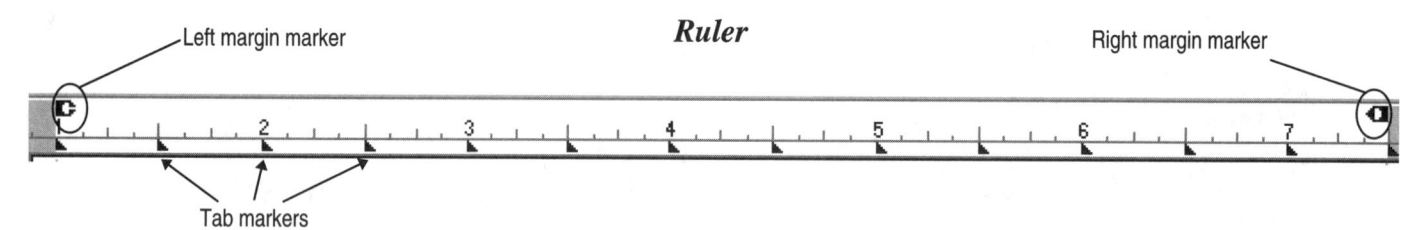

Left margin marker   *Ruler*   *Right margin marker*

Tab markers

Set Tabs

- The Tab key indents a single line of text. Default tabs are set .5" apart. When the Tab key is pressed once, text will advance ½ inch; when the Tab key is pressed twice, text will advance 1 inch, etc.

- If you wish to advance text .8"—or some other distance each time the Tab key is pressed—you can do so by changing the tab settings.

- When you change tab settings in a document, changes take effect from that point forward. If you wish to change tab settings in existing text, you must first select the text to be changed.

- Tabs may be changed on the Ruler or in the Tab Set dialog box.

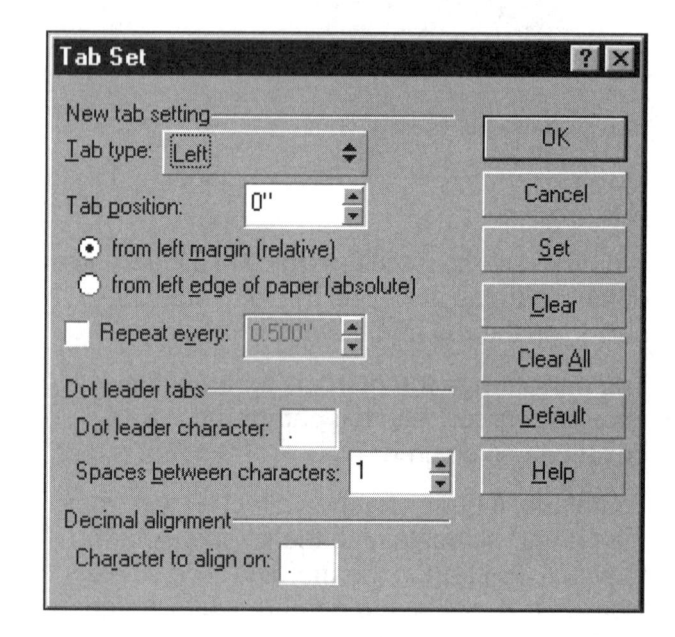

In Part I of this exercise, you will create a full-block letter. You will then edit the letter using the features learned in this lesson and change the format to modified block style. In a modified-block business letter, the date, closing, signature and title lines begin at 4.5". In Part II of this exercise, you will open a letter you created previously, and edit it using the features learned in this lesson. The proofreaders' mark for "let the original stand" is .... or (stet) *.*

EXERCISE DIRECTIONS

PART I

1. Start with a clear screen.
2. Display the Ruler (if necessary).
3. Display the Format toolbar.
4. Type the text as shown in Illustration A or open **10HISTORY**.
   ✓ *If you are using the data disk file (10HISTORY), be sure to place the insertion point at the top of the page before changing the margins and tabs.*
   a. Set 1.5" left and right margins.
   b. Begin the exercise approximately 2.5" from top of page.
   c. Format the letter in full-block style.
5. Spell check.
6. Print one copy.
7. Save the file; name it **HISTORY**.
8. Do not close the document window.
9. Make the indicated revisions as shown in Illustration B on page 56.
   a. Clear all tabs. Set a left-aligned tab stop at 4.5" from left edge of paper.
   b. Use the Convert Case feature to turn NEW BEDFORD HISTORICAL AND PRESERVATION SOCIETY into initial caps.
   c. Use the Convert Case feature to turn Moby Dick (second paragraph) into all caps.
   d. Insert a hard space between names (including the city name New Bedford), dates, and times where ever you see the ◆ symbol.
10. Print one copy.
11. Save the file as **HISTORY2**.
12. Close the document window.

ILLUSTRATION A

Today's date Mr. David Mareira 456 Apple Court New Bedford, MA 08987 Dear Mr. Mareira: Thank you so much for your interest in the NEW BEDFORD HISTORICAL AND PRESERVATION SOCIETY. We are always pleased to welcome new members. ¶ New Bedford is a city that is rich in historical tradition, including both its role in the whaling trade and as a critical stop along the Underground Railroad. In its past, New Bedford has welcomed such noted figures as Frederick Douglass and Herman Melville. ¶ Please feel free to contact our membership office if you have any questions. Otherwise, I look forward to meeting you on November 11. Sincerely, Beth Braun Membership Director bb/yo

ILLUSTRATION B

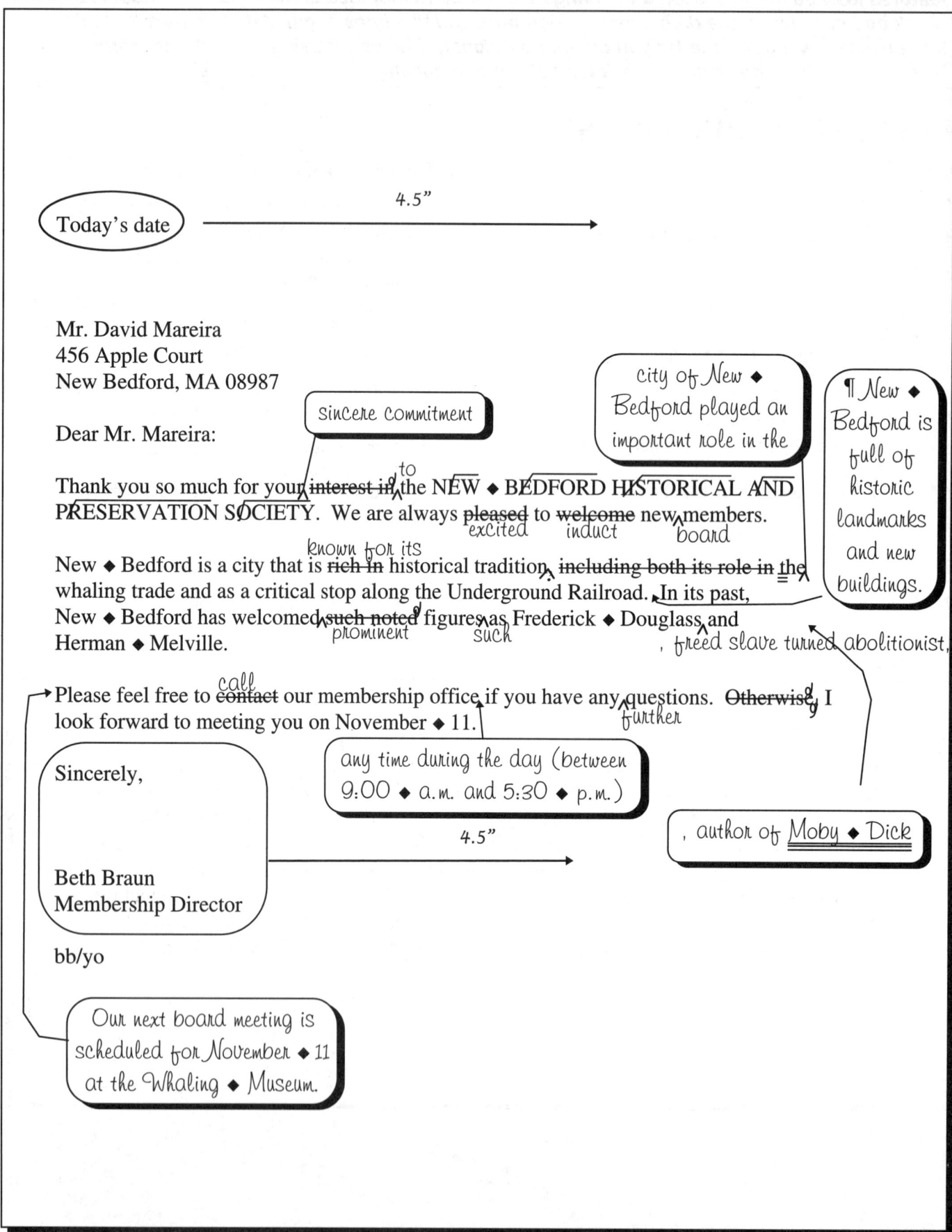

Today's date

Mr. David Mareira
456 Apple Court
New Bedford, MA 08987

Dear Mr. Mareira:

Thank you so much for your ~~interest in~~ [sincere commitment] to the NEW ◆ BEDFORD HISTORICAL AND PRESERVATION SOCIETY. We are always ~~pleased~~ [excited] to ~~welcome~~ [induct] new [board] members.

New ◆ Bedford is a city that is ~~rich in~~ [known for its] historical tradition. ~~including both its role in~~ [The city of New ◆ Bedford played an important role in the] whaling trade and as a critical stop along the Underground Railroad. In its past, New ◆ Bedford has welcomed ~~such noted~~ [such prominent] figures as Frederick ◆ Douglass[, freed slave turned abolitionist,] and Herman ◆ Melville[, author of Moby ◆ Dick].

→ Please feel free to ~~contact~~ [call] our membership office if you have any [further] questions. ~~Otherwise,~~ [And] I look forward to meeting you on November ◆ 11 [any time during the day (between 9:00 ◆ a.m. and 5:30 ◆ p.m.)].

Sincerely,

Beth Braun
Membership Director

bb/yo

[¶ New ◆ Bedford is full of historic landmarks and new buildings.]

[Our next board meeting is scheduled for November ◆ 11 at the Whaling ◆ Museum.]

PART II
1. Open ⌨CLELAND or 💾10CLELAND.
2. Set 1.5" left and right margins.
   ✓ Be sure to place the insertion point at the top of the page before changing the margins, so that change affects entire document.
3. Clear all tabs. Set a left-aligned tab stop at 4.5".
   ✓ Be sure to place insertion point at the top of the page before changing the tabs, so that changes affect the entire document.
4. Make the revisions indicated in Illustration C on page 57.
   ✓ Moving the date and closing to 4.5" makes this a modified-block letter.
5. Insert a hard space between March and 8 (in the third paragraph of the letter.
6. Spell check.
7. Print one copy.
8. Close the file; save the changes.
9. Close the document window.

ILLUSTRATION C

Today's Date ⸺⸺⸺⸺ 4.5" ⸺⸺⸺⸺→

Ms. Lisa Rodi
University of Texas
45 Worth Road
Austin, TX 89098

Dear Lisa:

CONGRATULATIONS, Lisa! We are pleased to inform you that you have been selected to join CLELAND HOUSE, a social group for women at the University of Texas.

We were very impressed with your credentials. ∧as well as ∧Your outstanding academic record and extra-curricular involvement in worthy causes prove your commitment to the University of Texas, and we feel confident that your interests and skills will be an asset to our community.

Your dedication to
CLELAND HOUSE will be welcoming its new members ∧who are joining our organization during the spring semester at a faculty/student reception on March 8. We look forward to seeing you then.
⸺ Insert a hard space.

Sincerely,
⸺⸺⸺⸺ 4.5" ⸺⸺⸺⸺→

Suzanne Silverstein
Membership Director

ss/yo

KEYSTROKES

HARD SPACE

Ctrl + Space

1. Type first word.
2. Click **Format** menu .... `Alt`+`R`
3. Click **Line** .... `L`
4. Click **Other Codes** .... `O`
5. Click **Hard space** .... `P`
6. Click **Insert** .... `Enter`
7. Type next word.

CONVERT CASE

1. Select/highlight text to be converted.
2. Click **Edit** menu .... `Alt`+`E`
3. Click **Convert Case** .... `V`
4. Click a convert option:
   - **Lowercase** .... `L`
   - **Uppercase** .... `U`
   - **Initial Capitals** .... `I`

SET MARGINS (LEFT/RIGHT, TOP/BOTTOM)

Ctrl + F8

1. Place insertion point in paragraph where margin change will begin.

   OR

   Select paragraphs to affect.
2. Click **Page Margins** button on Format toolbar.

   OR

   Drag guideline to desired margin position.

   OR

   a. Click **File** .... `Alt`+`F`
   b. Click **Page Setup** .... `G`
   c. Click appropriate increment box to change desired margin:

   Left .... `Alt`+`L`

   Right .... `Alt`+`R`

   Top .... `Alt`+`T`

   Bottom .... `Alt`+`B`

   d. Type margin amount.

   OR

   Click increment arrows to select margin amount.

   ✓ To make all the margins the same, enter one margin amount and click Make all **m**argins equal check box.

   e. Click **OK** .... `Enter`

SET, CLEAR, OR DELETE TABS

To delete a tab:

Drag the tab marker (triangle) off the Ruler.

To set a tab:

1. Click **Format** .... `Alt`+`R`
2. Click **Line** .... `L`
3. Click **Tab Type** .... `T`
4. Select a type .... `↑↓`
5. Click **Tab position** .... `Alt`+`P`
6. Select a position .... `↑↓`
7. Click **from left margin** .... `Alt`+`M`

   OR

   from left edge .... `Alt`+`E`
8. When tabs are set as desired, click **OK** .... `Enter`

To clear selected tab setting:

1. Follow steps 1-2 above (To set a tab).
2. Click **Clear** .... `Alt`+`C`

   OR

   Click **Clear All** to clear all tabs .... `Alt`+`A`
3. Click **OK** .... `Enter`

Exercise 11

■ Summary

In this exercise, you will create a modified-block letter and edit it using the insert and delete procedures learned.

EXERCISE DIRECTIONS

1. Start with a clear screen.
2. Type and format a modified-block letter from the text shown in Illustration A below, or open **11PILLOW** and format it as a modified-block letter.
3. Place insertion point at the top of the page and clear all tabs; set a tab stop at 4.5" from the left edge of paper; set 1.5" left and right margins.
4. Send this letter to Dr. Ellen Sczyepanic. Use the Address Book to insert the inside address.
5. Make the revisions shown in Illustration B on the next page.
6. Use Reveal Codes to combine the last two paragraphs. Remember to add two spaces at the end of the first sentence.
7. Spell check.
8. Using the Document Properties feature, note the number of words in this document.
9. Preview your work.
10. Using the Convert Case feature, change VP Promotions to uppercase.
11. Print one copy.
12. Save the file; name it **PILLOW**.
13. Close the document window.

ILLUSTRATION A

Today's Date, Dear Dr. Sczycpanic: I am excited to introduce you to Pillow People, the spunkiest girl band to hit the music scene in years. I know you will really enjoy the enclosed CD entitled Rock On. ¶Pillow People's hip music blends the best of folk, rock, country, and soul with creative lyrics. Pillow People's important message is that young women are strong, independent, feisty, and have the ability to do and be anything. We believe that this is a very important message in today's society, and I know you will want to join us in helping to spread the word. ¶If you would like more information about Pillow People, please feel free to contact my assistant, Jane Kramer or myself. Sincerely, Elaine Miller, VP Promotions em/yo enclosure

COREL WORDPERFECT 8 Lesson 2: Open and Edit Documents

ILLUSTRATION B

Today's Date, Dear Dr. Sczycpanic: I am excited to introduce you to Pillow People, the spunkiest girl band to hit the music scene in years. I know you will really enjoy ~~the enclosed~~ *previewing their new* CD, *, which I have enclosed* entitled Rock On. ¶Pillow People's hip music blends the best of folk, rock, country, and soul with creative lyrics. Pillow People's important message is that young women are strong, independent, feisty, and have the ability to do and be anything. We believe that this is a very important message in today's society, ~~and~~ I know you will want to join us in helping to spread the word. ¶If you would like more information about Pillow People, *and their upcoming tour* please feel free to contact my assistant, Jane Kramer, or myself. Sincerely, Elaine Miller, VP Promotions em/yo enclosure

¶ The members of Pillow People are excited about hitting the road and spreading their message in a series of urban and suburban high schools.

COREL WORDPERFECT 8
Lesson 3: Text Alignments and Enhancements

Exercise 12

- Center Line
- Flush Right Line
- Vertical Centering (Center Current Page)
- Justification

NOTES

Center Line

- WordPerfect lets you center a single line or part of a line of text between the left and right margins. Position the insertion point immediately to the left of where you want the centering to begin, and choose one of the following:

    - Select Line, Center from the Format menu.

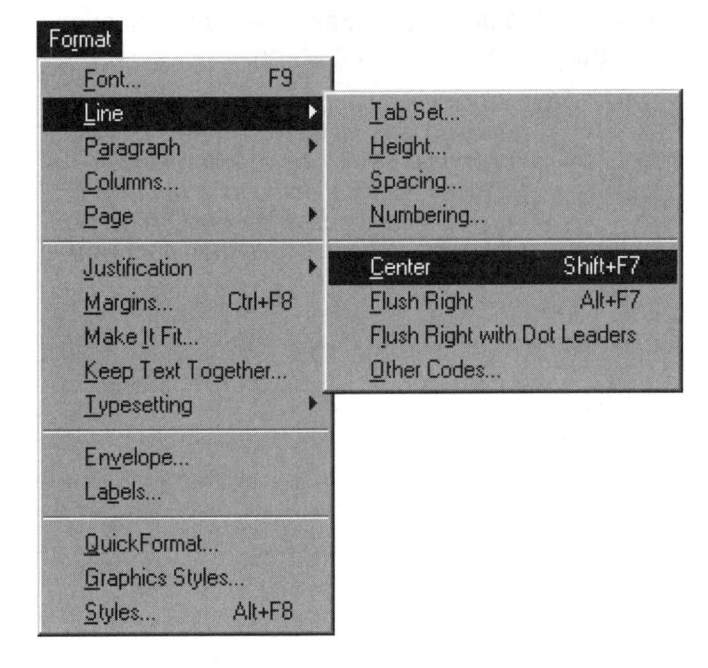

    - Click the *right* mouse button in the document window and select Center.

    - Press Shift + F7.

- Text may be centered before or after typing. If you center a line after it has been typed, press the End key (to bring your insertion point to the end of the line), then press Enter to bring your insertion point back to the left margin.

Flush Right Line

- The Flush Right feature aligns a single line or part of a line of text at the right margin. To flush right text, position the insertion point immediately to the left of where you want the change to begin, and choose one of the following:

    - Select Line, Flush Right from the Format menu.

    - Click the *right* mouse button in the document window and select Flush Right.

    - Press Alt + F7.

- Text may be right aligned before or after typing.

- To align a partial or full line of existing text at the right margin, be sure the line ends with a hard return.

Vertical Centering (Center Current Page)

- Text can also be centered vertically on a page (from top to bottom). If there are hard returns before or after the centered text, WordPerfect will include them in the vertical centering. Therefore, to vertically center text without additional blank lines, start the text at the top of the screen.

- Vertical centering may be accessed by selecting Page, Center from the Format menu.

- In the Center Page dialog box that follows, select whether to center the Current page or the Current and subsequent pages in the document.

Justification

- Justification should be used to affect blocks of text, not individual lines.
- WordPerfect applies left justification to your text by default.
- Justification aligns all text that follows the justification code until another justification code is entered. WordPerfect provides five alignment options:
  - **Left**—All lines are even at the left margin but are ragged at the right margin (the default).

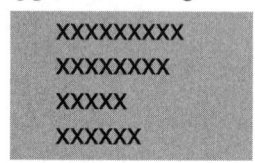

        xxxxxxxxx
        xxxxxxxx
        xxxxx
        xxxxxx

  - **Center**—All lines are centered between the margins.

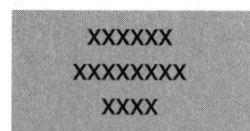

        xxxxxx
        xxxxxxxx
        xxxx

  - **Right**—All lines are ragged at the left margin and are even at the right margin.

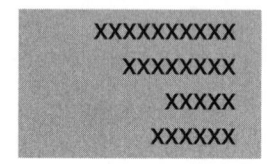

        xxxxxxxxxx
        xxxxxxxx
        xxxxx
        xxxxxx

  - **Full**—All lines are even at the left and right margins, except for the last line of the paragraph.

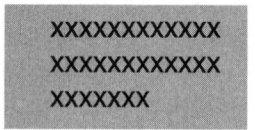

        xxxxxxxxxxx
        xxxxxxxxxxx
        xxxxxxx

  - **All**—All lines are even at the left and right margins, including the last line of the paragraph.

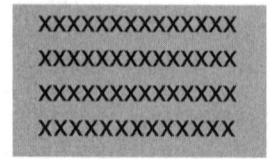

        xxxxxxxxxxxx
        xxxxxxxxxxxx
        xxxxxxxxxxxx
        xxxxxxxxxxxx

- Justification may be changed before or after typing. To change justification before typing, place the insertion point where you want the new justification to begin and select a justification option. To change existing text, select the text to be affected and then select a justification option.
- A justification option may be selected by:
  - Clicking the Justification button on the Property Bar and selecting a justification option.

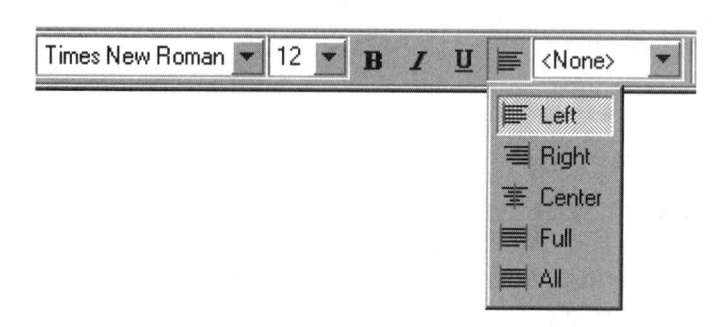

  - Clicking the desired justification button on the Format Toolbar.
  - Selecting <u>J</u>ustification and then a justification option from the Fo<u>r</u>mat Menu.

  CAUTION: *When you change justification of existing text, all text following the code changes. Do not be alarmed. Insert another justification code to return your text to the alignment desired. To avoid this, select the text first, then apply an alignment choice.*

In this exercise, you will create an announcement using various alignment options.

EXERCISE DIRECTIONS

1. Begin the exercise at the top of a clear screen.
2. Display the Format toolbar if it is not currently on screen.
3. Use the default margins.
4. Center the page vertically.
5. Create the announcement below as shown, applying the appropriate alignments and justification.
6. Preview your work.
7. Print one copy.
8. Save the exercise; name it **PLAY**.
9. Close the document window.

FAIR PLAY SPORTS CLUB

Child-like fun
in the company of adults.

Are you tired of the corporate gym mentality? Do you remember the fun you had as a child playing team sports at school or among neighborhood friends? Fair Play Sports Club offers a new and fun way to work out while still gaining the health benefits of a serious gym routine. Fair Play Sports Club now offers team sports for adults at all fitness and experience levels.

Fair Play Sports Club
234 Porter Road
Boston, MA 90786
(890) 890-8909

More information is available at all of our neighborhood locations.

KEYSTROKES

CENTER LINE
Shift + F7

New Text

1. Place insertion point at the beginning of the text to center.
2. Click **Format** .... `Alt` + `R`
3. Click **Line** .... `L`
4. Click **Center** .... `C`
5. Type text.
6. Press **Enter** .... `Enter` to return to left margin.

Existing Text

1. Position insertion point immediately left of where you want the centering to begin.
2. Click *right* mouse button anywhere in document window.
3. Click **Center** .... `C`
4. Press the **End** key.
5. Press **Enter** .... `Enter` to return to left margin.

FLUSH RIGHT
Alt + F7

New Text

1. Place insertion point at beginning of text to set flush right.
2. Click **Format** .... `Alt` + `R`
3. Click **Line** .... `L`
4. Click **Flush Right** .... `F`
5. Type text.
6. Press **Enter** .... `Enter` to return to left margin.

Existing Text

1. Position insertion point at beginning of text to set flush right.
2. Click *right* mouse button anywhere in document window.
3. Click **Flush Right** .... `R`
4. Press the **End** key.
5. Press **Enter** .... `Enter` to return to left margin.

CENTER PAGE
(VERTICALLY CENTER)

1. Place insertion point anywhere on page.
2. Click **Format** .... `Alt` + `R`
3. Click **Page** .... `P`
4. Click **Center** .... `C`
5. Select a page option:
   - **Current page** .... `P`
   - **Current and subsequent pages** .... `S`
   - **No Centering** .... `N`
6. Click **OK** .... `Enter`

ALIGN OR JUSTIFY

1. Place the insertion point where you want new justification to begin.

   OR

   Select text to affect.

2. Click the **Justification** button on the Property Bar and select a justification option from the drop-down menu.

   OR

   Click **Justification** button on Format toolbar.

   OR

   a. Click **Format** .... `Alt` + `R`
   b. Click **Justification** .... `J`
   c. Select a justification option:
      - **Left** .... `L`
      - **Right** .... `R`
      - **Center** .... `E`
      - **Full** .... `F`
      - **All** .... `A`

COREL WORDPERFECT 8 Lesson 3: Text Alignments and Enhancements

Exercise 13

■ Font Faces ■ Font Style ■ Font Size

NOTES

Font Faces

- A **font** is a complete set of characters in a specific face, style and size. Each set includes upper- and lowercase letters, numerals, and punctuation. A font that might be available to you in WordPerfect is **Arial**.

- A font face (often called **typeface** or just **font**) is the design of a character. Each design has a name and is intended to convey a specific feeling.

- You should select typefaces that will make your document attractive and communicate its particular message. As a rule, use no more than two or three font faces in any one document.

- There are basically three types of font faces: serif, sans serif, and script. A **serif** face has lines, curves, or edges extending from the ends of the letter (**T**), while a **sans serif** face is straight-edged (**T**), and **script** looks like handwriting (*T*).

Serif Font Face:
Times New Roman

Sans Serif Font Face:
Arial

Script Font Face:
Brush Script MT

- A serif font face is typically used for document text because it is more readable. Sans serif is often used for headlines or technical material. Script typefaces are used for formal invitations and announcements.

- To change the font before typing text, place the insertion point where you want the change to begin and then select the new font face.

- To change the font for existing text, you must first select the text you want to change and then select the new font face.

- You can select a new font face from the font face list in the Font dialog box.

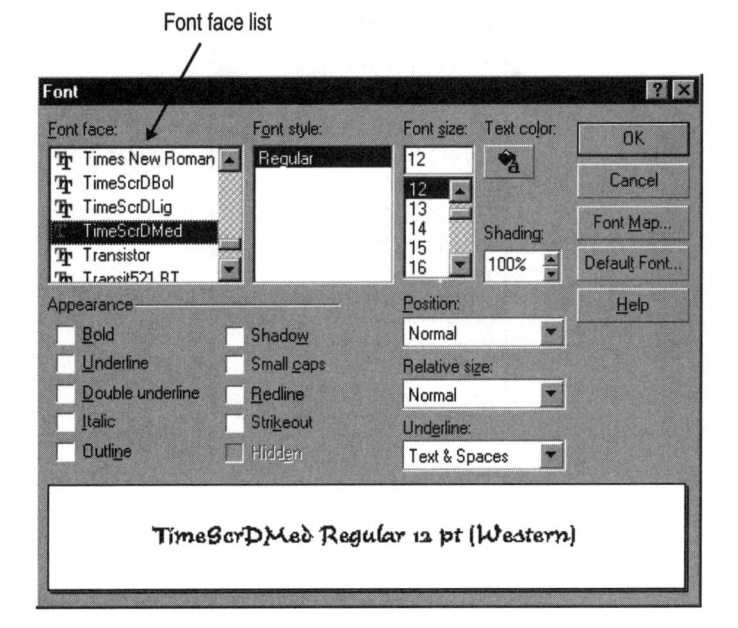

COREL WORDPERFECT 8 Lesson 3: Text Alignments and Enhancements

- The Font dialog box may be accessed by either:
  - Selecting F̲ont from the Fo̲rmat menu.
  - Clicking the *right* mouse button anywhere in the document window and selecting F̲ont.

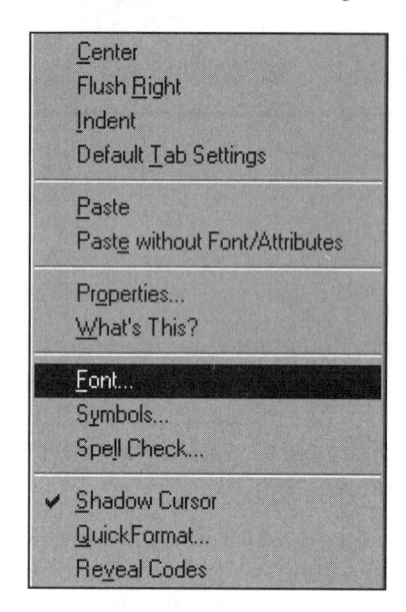

- Font faces can also be changed by clicking the Font Face button on the Property Bar (which drops down a list of font choices as well as a preview window).

- Clicking the QuickFonts button on the Property Bar displays a list of the last ten fonts you used in a document.

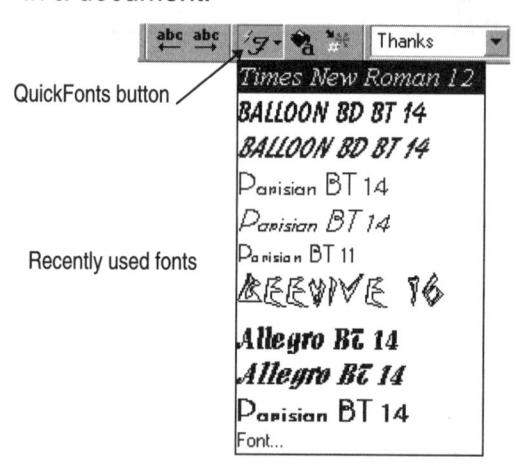

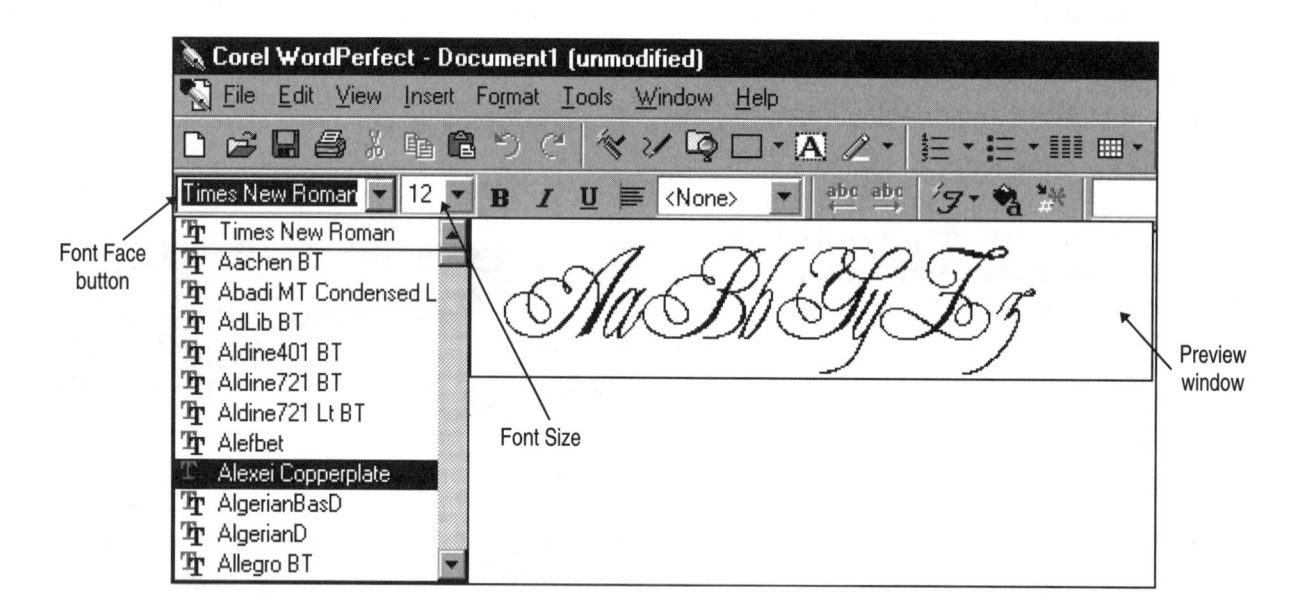

Font Style

- **Font style** refers to the slant and weight of letters, such as bold and italic.

    Font Styles

Times New Roman Regular
Times New Roman Italic
Times New Roman Bold
Times New Roman Bold Italic

- Note the Font dialog box illustrated below. The Font style box lists the styles or weights specially designed and available for the selected font face. You may also apply attributes, such as bold and italic, outline and small caps from the Appearance panel of the Font dialog box. (This will be covered in the next exercise.)

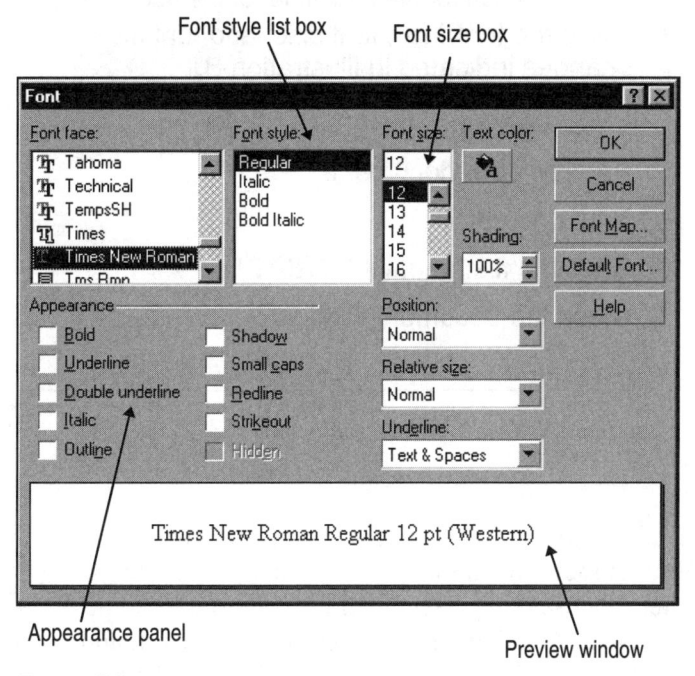

Font Size

- **Font size** generally refers to the height of the font, usually measured in points. There are 72 points to an inch.

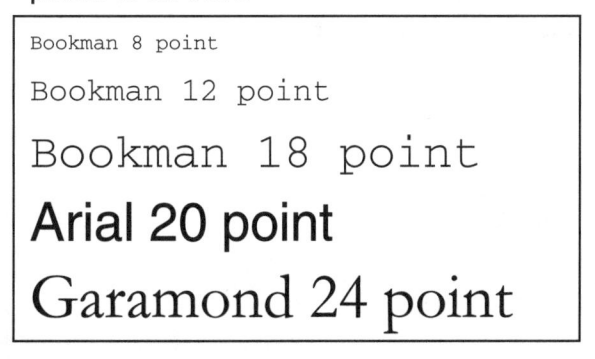

```
Bookman 8 point
Bookman 12 point
```
Bookman 18 point

Arial 20 point

Garamond 24 point

- Font size may be changed in the Font dialog box or by clicking the Font Size button on the Property Bar, which drops down a list of font sizes.

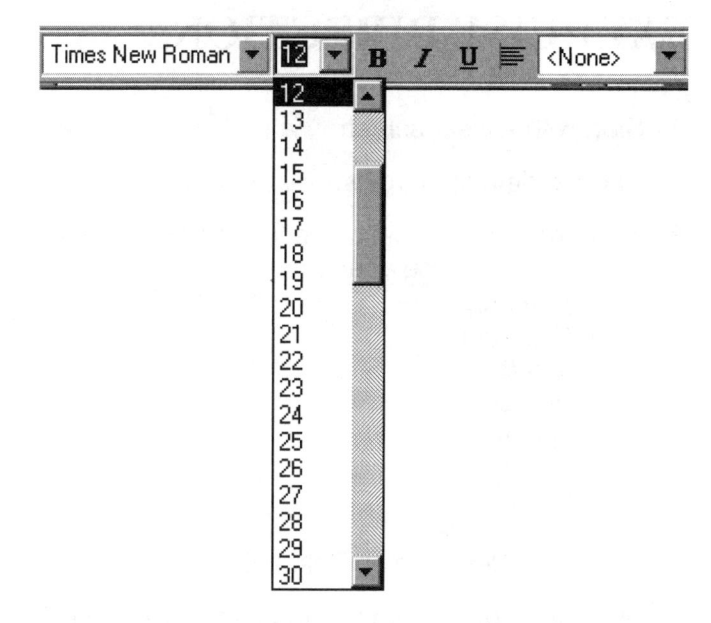

- In the Font dialog box, you can choose a font size from the Font size list. Selected font sizes are displayed in the Preview window. (See illustration, left.)

- To change the font size before typing text, place the insertion point where you want the new size to begin and then select the new font size.

- To change the font size for existing text, you must first select the text you want to change and then select the new font size.

- The fonts that are available to you depend on what you have installed in your system and on your printer's capabilities.

COREL WORDPERFECT 8   Lesson 3:   Text Alignments and Enhancements

> *In Part I of this exercise, you will practice applying font faces, font styles and font sizes to text.*
> *In Part II of this exercise, you will change the font faces, styles and sizes of an announcement.*

EXERCISE DIRECTIONS

PART I

1. Start with a clear screen.
2. Use the default margins.
3. Type the following list at the left margin. Press the Enter key twice after each word.
   - Kaufmann
   - PTBarnum
   - Technical
   - BinnerD
   - 14 point
   - 24 point
   - 48 point
   - Technical Italic
   - Times New Roman Bold Italic
4. Apply the appropriate font face, font size, and font style to each word to match that word.
5. Print one copy.
6. Close the file; do not save the changes.

PART II

1. Start with a clear screen.
2. Type the text shown in Illustration A or open 💾**13SCRIPT**.
   a. Use the default margins.
   b. Center the page vertically.
3. To create Illustration B on page 69:
   a. Use All justification for the two title lines.
   b. Use Full justification for the first paragraph.
   c. Apply the justification as indicated in the illustration for the remainder of the document.
4. Make the font face, font size, and font style changes indicated in Illustration B.
   ✓ *If the exercise runs onto 2 pages, reduce the font size where necessary.*
5. Preview your document.
6. Print one copy.
7. Save the file; name it **SCRIPT**.
8. Close the document window.

ILLUSTRATION A

THE DOWNTOWN SCRIPT-WRITING FESTIVAL
AT THE JONES STREET THEATRE

The West Village Writer's Group, in conjunction with several downtown theatres and writing organizations, is proud to announce its Second Annual Script-writing Festival focusing on today's youth in society. This year's series will focus on the way that today's young writers choose to represent their peers on stage and in film. From the hip and funny to the tragic and prophetic, the staged reading of these fresh new scripts should not be missed by viewers of any and all ages. ¶ The 1998 Program of Staged Readings: ¶ Friday, September 11, 1998 ¶ The Dog Walker ¶ a full-length screenplay by Naisha Cambel ¶ Saturday, September 12, 1998 ¶ Raising Yourself in Manhattan ¶ a full-length play by Dan Waters ¶ Friday, October 29, 1998 ¶ Candle Light ¶ a one-act play by Todd P. Rainer ¶ Saturday, October 30, 1998 ¶ Just Humus, Please ¶ a short film by William Pachello ¶ Friday, November 24, 1998 ¶ Liquid Streets ¶ a full-length play by Megan Culigan ¶ Saturday, November 25, 1998 ¶ Still Thinking ¶ a full-length screenplay by Jules Chen

Second Annual Downtown Script-Writing Festival
Brought to you by the West Village Writer's Group

Special Thanks to:
The Abrams Theatre
and The Jones Street Theatre
for additional support

ILLUSTRATION B

All   *Serif 16 pt*

THE DOWNTOWN SCRIPT-WRITING FESTIVAL
AT THE JONES STREET THEATRE

Full   *Sans serif 11 pt*

The West Village Writer's Group, in conjunction with several downtown theatres and writing organizations, is proud to announce its Second Annual Script-writing Festival focusing on today's youth in society. This year's series will focus on the way that today's young writers choose to represent their peers on stage and in film. From the hip and funny to the tragic and prophetic, the staged reading of these fresh new scripts should not be missed by viewers of any and all ages.

↓2

The 1998 Program of Staged Readings: ← *Serif 14 pt*

↓2

Friday, September 11, 1998 ← *Sans serif, 14 pt*

The Dog Walker ← *Script, 14 pt*

a full-length screenplay by Naisha Cambel ← *Sans serif, 11 pt*

↓2

Saturday, September 12, 1998

Raising Yourself in Manhattan

a full length play by Dan Waters

↓2

Friday, October 29, 1998

Candle light

a one-act play by Todd P. Rainer

↓2

Saturday, October 30, 1998

Just Humus, Please

a short film by William Pachello

↓2

Friday, November 24, 1998

Liquid Streets

a full length play by Megan Culigan

↓2

Saturday, November 25, 1998

Still Thinking

a full-length screenplay by Jules Chen

↓3

Left Justify

Second Annual Downtown Script-Writing Festival
Brought to you by the West Village Writer's Group

↓2

Flush right   *Sans serif 11 pt*

Special Thanks to:
The Abrams Theatre
and The Jones Street Theatre
for additional support

COREL WORDPERFECT 8 Lesson 3: Text Alignments and Enhancements

KEYSTROKES

CHANGE FONT FACE, FONT SIZE, AND FONT STYLE

F9

USING FONT DIALOG BOX

1. Place insertion point where font change will begin (*before* typing).

   OR

   Select text to receive font change (*after* typing).

2. Follow one of the listed procedures to access the Font dialog box.

   a. Click F**o**rmat .... `Alt`+`R`

   b. Click **F**ont .... `F`

   OR

   a. Click *right* mouse button anywhere in the document window.

   b. Select **F**ont.

   ✓ *In the Font dialog box, the currently selected font is displayed in the preview window.*

3. Click in **Font face** list .... `Alt`+`F`

4. Click desired font .... `↓`

5. Click in F**o**nt style box .... `Alt`+`O`

6. Click desired style .... `↓`

7. Click in Font **s**ize box .... `Alt`+`S`

8. Click desired size .... `↓`

USING PROPERTY BAR (FONT FACE AND FONT SIZE ONLY)

Place insertion point where font change will begin (*before* typing).

OR

Select text to receive font change (*after* typing).

To change font face:

1. Click **Font Face** button `Arial ▼`.

2. Select desired font from list.

To change font size:

1. Click **Font Size** button `12 ▼`.

2. Select desired size from list.

USING QUICKFONTS

1. Place insertion point where font change will begin (*before* typing).

   OR

   Select text to receive font change (*after* typing).

2. Click QuickFonts `ᵍ▼` button on Property Bar and select a recently used font (and font attributes) from the drop-down list.

COREL WORDPERFECT 8 Lesson 3: Text Alignments and Enhancements

Exercise 14

- Font Appearance
- Highlight Text

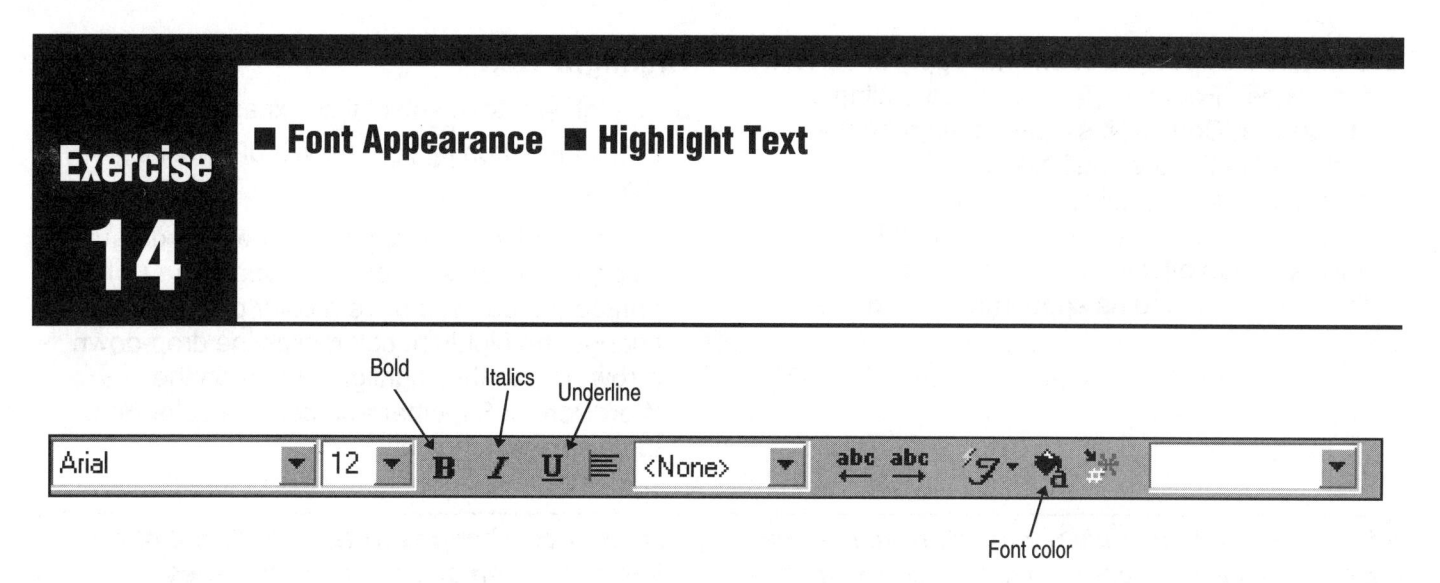

NOTES

Font Appearance

- **Bold**, underline, double underline, *italic*, and highlight are features used to emphasize or enhance text and are referred to as **appearance attributes**. (While highlight is technically not an appearance attribute, it is used to emphasize text.) These features work as on/off toggle switches. You must choose the command to turn on the feature; then choose the command again to turn off the feature.

- In addition to bold, underline, double underline, italics, and highlight, WordPerfect provides other effects. These include outline, shadow, small caps, redline, and strikeout.

- **Redline** and **strikeout** emphasis styles are usually used to indicate that text has been added, deleted, or moved, and are useful when comparing the current document with a different version of a document. Redline displays on screen in red but usually appears shaded, underlined, or with a series of vertical bars (depending on your printer) when printed. Note examples below:

Text may be emphasized before or after typing. To emphasize text before typing, place the insertion point where you want the emphasis to begin and then select the desired appearance attributes. To emphasize text after typing, you must select the text to be affected before selecting the appearance attributes.

- You can apply bold, italic, or underline by clicking on the **B**, *I* or U buttons on the Property Bar.

- You may also use the Font dialog box to access the other appearance attributes. To access the Font dialog box, select Font from the Format menu.

  ✓*Note: There is no highlight option in the Font dialog box. This option must be accessed from the Highlight button on the Toolbar. See Highlight Text on the following page.*

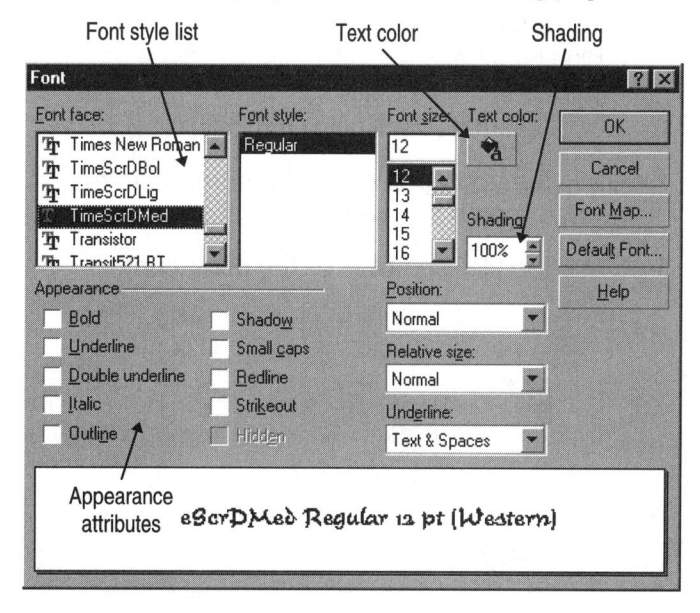

COREL WORDPERFECT 8 Lesson 3: Text Alignments and Enhancements

- Some font appearances will not apply to certain font faces. For example, if you use outline or shadow on Courier, it simply appears bolded. As indicated in the previous exercise, font styles also add bold and italics to a font face, but not all font faces have these styles added. If bold and italic are unavailable in the Font Style list box, they can be added as appearance attributes.

Highlight Text

- To highlight text, select the text and click the Highlight button on the WordPerfect 8 toolbar.
- Highlighted text will appear yellow (the default color) on the screen, but will appear gray when printed (unless you have a color printer). To change the highlight color, click the drop-down arrow next to the Highlight button on the WordPerfect 8 toolbar and select a color from the displayed choices.

In Part I of this exercise, you will practice applying appearance changes to text. In Part II of this exercise, you will create a menu using various text alignments and appearance attributes.

EXERCISE DIRECTIONS

PART I

1. Start with a clear screen.
2. Use the default margins.
3. Type the following list at the left margin of your page. Press the Enter key twice after each word.
   Bold
   Underline
   Double Underline
   Italic
   Highlight
   Outline
   Shadow
   Small Caps
   Redline
   Strikeout
   Blue Font Color
   Dark Green Font Color
   50% Shaded Dark Green Font Color
4. Apply the appropriate font appearance to each word to match that word.
5. Close the file; do not save the document.

PART II

1. Start with a clear screen.
2. Create the menu as shown on the following page or open 🖫**14THEATRE**.
   a. Use the default margins.
   ✓ *The accent mark will be automatically inserted when you type the word café.*
   b. Apply the appropriate text alignments and font changes shown in Illustration B.
3. Center the page vertically.
4. Preview your work.
5. Print one copy.
6. Save the file; name it **THEATRE**.
7. Close the document window.

The Theatre Café

Decorative 30 pt; set font color to red, with a shadow effect

Sans serif 12 pt
45 Maple Road
Cary, NC 91002
(919) 555-5555

Sans serif 17 pt italic
TODAY'S PRESENTATION:

Preview

Cream of Vegetable
Fall Vegetable Terrine with Roasted Pine Nuts
Organic Greens with Peanut Vinaigrette
Endive Salad with Crumbled Blue Cheese and Cranberries

Main Act

Whole Roasted Chicken or Turkey
Smoked Virginia Ham
Grilled Leg of Lamb
Baked Salmon Fillets

decorative 17 pt bold, underlined

Sans serif 10 pt

Supporting Players

Grilled Seasonal Vegetables
Garlic Mashed Potatoes
Butternut Squash with Fresh Ground Cinnamon
Sesame Sauteed Snap Peas with Green Onion

Grand Finale

A wide selection of delicacies baked fresh daily
We include coffee and a variety of herbal teas

Sans serif 14 pt italic

Please call for more information and remember to place your holiday orders early.

KEYSTROKES

FONT APPEARANCE
F9

1. Place insertion point before text to receive appearance change (*before* typing).

   OR

   Select/highlight text to receive appearance change (*after* typing).

2. Click the desired font appearance button on the Property Bar.

   OR

   a. Click **Fo**r**mat** .... `Alt`+`R`

   b. Click **F**ont .... `F`

   c. Click the desired font appearance options.

   d. Click **OK** .... `Enter`

   OR

   a. Click *right* mouse button anywhere in document window.

   b. Click **F**ont .... `F`

   c. Click the desired font appearance options.

   ✓ Double Underline, Outline, Shadow, Small Caps, Redline and Strikeout can only be selected in the Font dialog box. Highlight can only be selected from the Toolbar.

RETURN TO NORMAL OR TURN FEATURE OFF

1. Place insertion point where appearance change will end (*before* typing).

   OR

   Select/highlight text to return to normal (*after* typing).

2. Click the desired font appearance button on the Property Bar to deselect.

   OR

   a. Click **Fo**r**mat** .... `Alt`+`R`

   b. Click **F**ont .... `F`

   c. Click the desired appearance options to deselect.

   d. Click **OK** .... `Enter`

   OR

   a. Click *right* mouse button anywhere in document window.

   b. Click **F**ont .... `F`

   c. Click the desired font appearance options to deselect.

   d. Click **OK** .... `Enter`

COREL WORDPERFECT 8 Lesson 3: Text Alignments and Enhancements

Exercise 15

- Ornamental Fonts
- Symbols and Special Characters
- Superscripts and Subscripts
- Remove Font Appearance Attributes

NOTES

Ornamental Fonts

- **Wingdings, Monotype Sorts**, and **ZapfDingbats** are ornamental or symbol font face collections that are used to enhance a document. Below and to the right are samples from Wingdings and Monotype Sort font collections.

Wingdings Font Collection

Monotype Sorts Font Collection

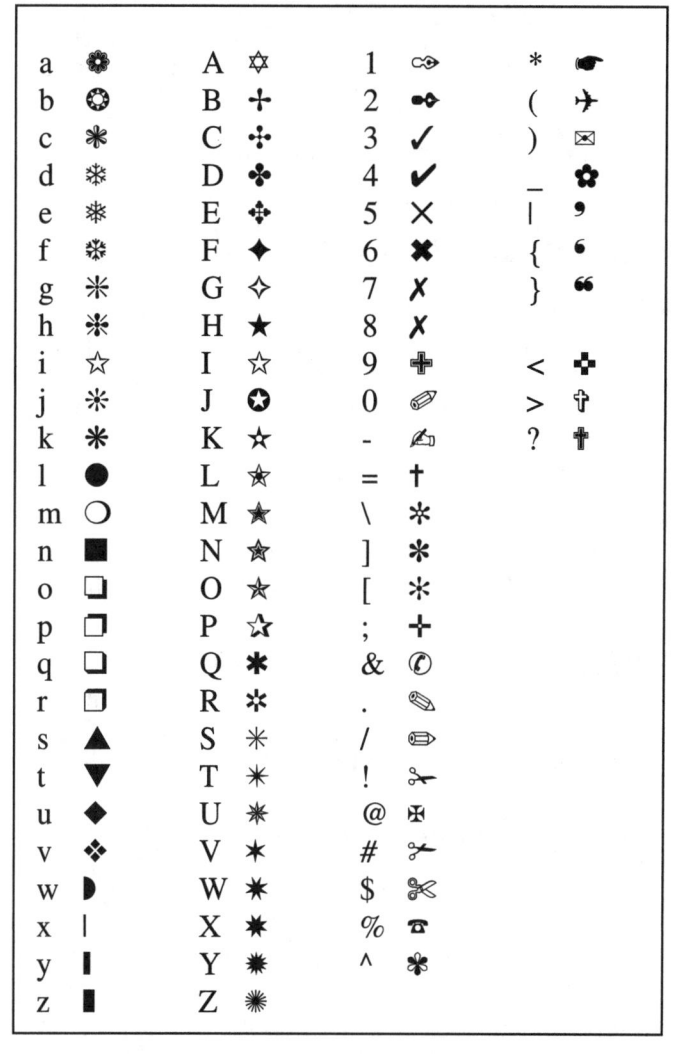

- The upper- and lowercase of each letter and character key provides different Wingdings and/or Monotype Sorts. To choose a Wingdings or a Monotype Sort face, select the font face from the Font Face drop-down list box on the Property Bar and then press the corresponding keyboard letter or character shown in the chart.

Corel WordPerfect 8 ■ Lesson 3 ■ Exercise 15   75

Symbols

- Another source of ornamental fonts is the symbol set called **Iconic Symbols**.

- Symbols may be accessed by selecting Symbol from the Insert menu, or by pressing Ctrl + W. The following dialog box appears, with the most recently used symbol set selected.

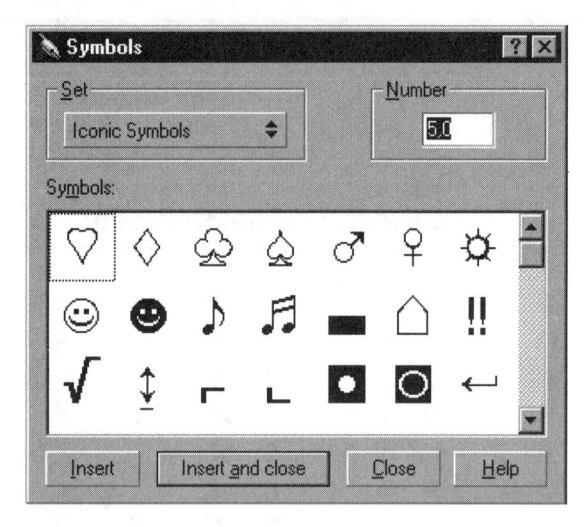

- To select another character set, click on the Iconic Symbols button and select a new symbol set from the list. Each symbol has a number assigned to it. That number is displayed in the Number text box. These numbers can be used to select a specific symbol.

- To insert a symbol from the Symbols dialog box, double-click on the desired symbol or click once on the symbol and then click Insert or click Insert and Close.

- Symbol sets are also found as fonts. They can be accessed through the Font dialog box or from the Font Face drop-down menu on the Property Bar. Each WordPerfect symbol set begins with WP.

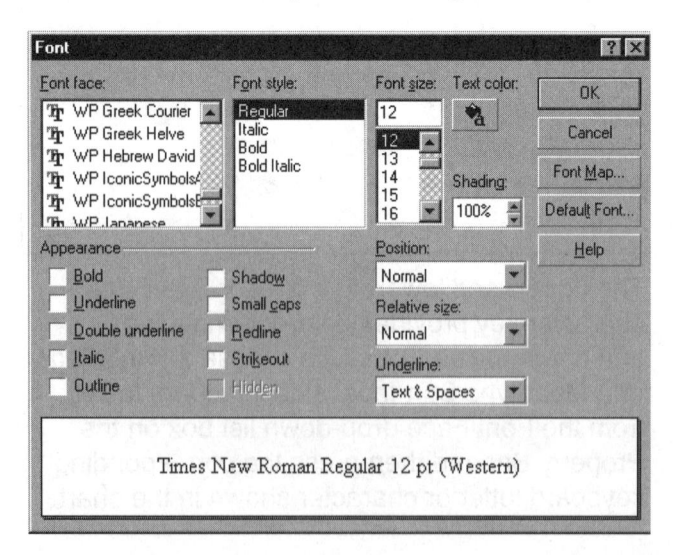

- You may change the size of a symbol font face as you would any other character, by changing the point size.

- Ornamental characters can be used to:

  Separate items on a page:

  > Wingdings
  > ❖❖♦❖❖
  > Graphics

  Emphasize items on a list:

  > ✎dresses
  > ✎coats
  > ✎suits

  Enhance a page:

  > 📖📖📖📖📖
  > BOOK SALE
  > 📖📖📖📖📖

  Add an in-line graphic:

  > Save your document on 💾.

Superscripts and Subscripts

- Superscripts are characters that print slightly higher than the normal typing line; subscripts are characters that print slightly lower than the normal typing line. Note the examples below:

Superscript: A^3
Subscript: H_2O

- Superscript and subscript options may be accessed by clicking the Position list arrow in the Font dialog box, then selecting Superscript or Subscript.

Remove Font Appearance Attributes

- If you decide you would like to remove the font appearance attribute you applied to text, select the text where the style is to be removed and repeat the procedures used to apply the appearance change. You can also remove font appearances by activating the Reveal Codes screen and deleting the codes that were inserted when the styles were applied.

To delete a code in Reveal Codes mode:

- Use the mouse pointer to click on the code and press the Delete key.

- Use the mouse pointer to drag the code out of the Reveal Codes window.

WordPerfect 8 Screen in Reveal Codes Mode

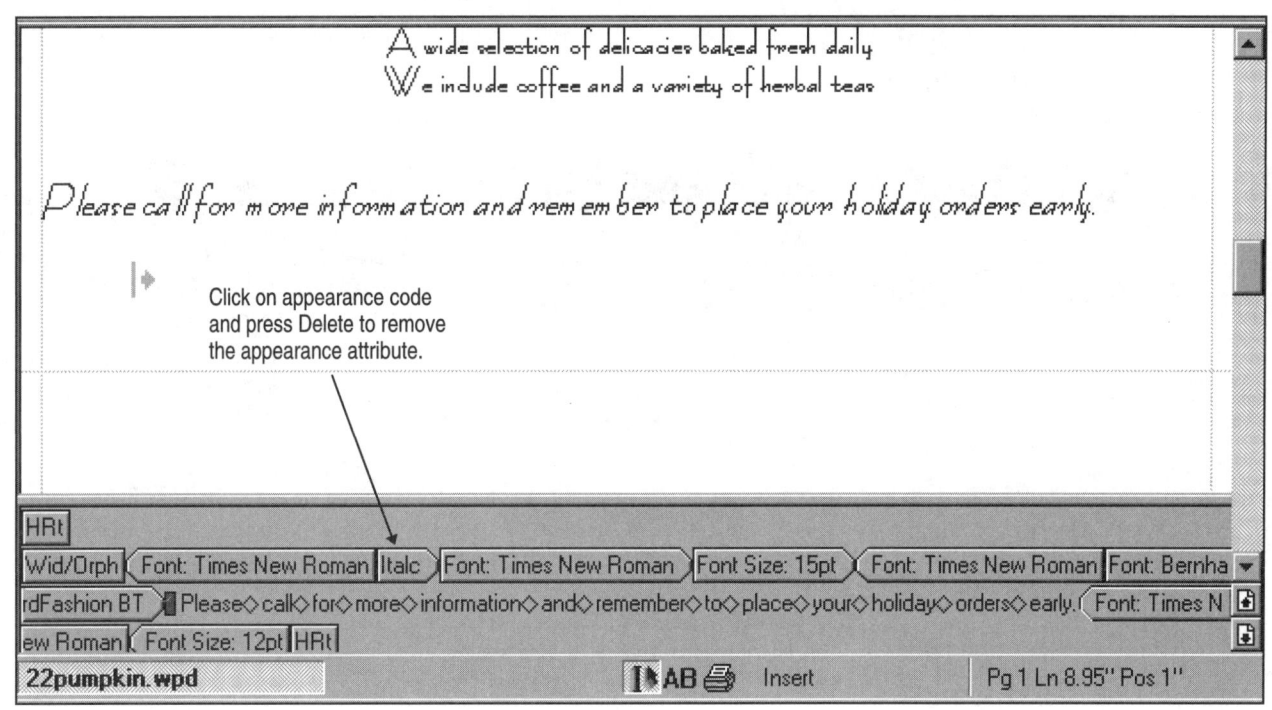

A wide selection of delicacies baked fresh daily
We include coffee and a variety of herbal teas

Please call for more information and remember to place your holiday orders early.

Click on appearance code and press Delete to remove the appearance attribute.

In Part I of this exercise, you will practice applying ornamental fonts and symbols to text. In Part II of this exercise, you will add symbols to a menu you created in a previous exercise and insert superscript characters.

EXERCISE DIRECTIONS

PART I

1. Start with a clear screen.
2. Use the default margins.
3. Type the following paragraph at the left margin exactly as shown:

   Please send us your favorite ⊛ and a ✲ explaining why you like it. Please ◉ me at your earliest convenience. **Do not** ⊘; it takes *too* long. I hope your : is working now. The ◁ drive needed repair. Place the ① next to my ⓢ, *please*. A Ⓢ of H₂0 can comfort a thirsty person.

4. Apply a Wingdings font face to the circled characters.
5. Remove all occurrences of bold and italic.
6. Close the file; do not save the document.

PART II

1. Start with a clear screen.
2. Open ⌨**THEATRE** or 🖥**15THEATRE**.
3. Enhance the document with ornamental fonts from the Wingdings font collection and symbols as indicated:
   a. Use any desired Wingding or symbol.
   b. Type and center the following new paragraph at the bottom of the page, in a sans serif 8-point font:
      Menu items subject to change based on availability of freshest ingredients.
   c. Use a symbol as the superscript after "Today's Presentations" and preceding the last sentence on the page.
4. Preview your document.
5. Print one copy.
6. Print one copy.
7. Close the file; save the changes.

COREL WORDPERFECT 8 Lesson 3: Text Alignments and Enhancements

Remove shadow

❦ The Theatre Café ❦

Insert symbol or Wingding in 30 pt

45 Maple Road
Cary, NC 91002
(919) 555-5555

Remove italics → TODAY'S PRESENTATION: ☆

Insert symbol, 5,80. Format as 12-point superscript

❖ **Preview** ❖

Cream of Vegetable
Fall Vegetable Terrine with Roasted Pine Nuts
Organic Greens with Peanut Vinaigrette
Endive Salad with Crumbled Blue Cheese and Cranberries

❖ **Main Act** ❖

Whole Roasted Chicken or Turkey
Smoked Virginia Ham
Grilled Leg of Lamb
Baked Salmon Fillets

Insert Wingding 12 pt

❖ **Supporting Players** ❖

Grilled Seasonal Vegetables
Garlic Mashed Potatoes
Butternut Squash with Fresh Ground Cinnamon
Sesame Sauteed Snap Peas with Green Onion

❖ **Grand Finale** ❖

A wide selection of delicacies baked fresh daily
We include coffee and a variety of herbal teas

Remove italics

Please call for more information and remember to place your holiday orders early.

☆ Menu items are subject to change due to availability of fresh ingredients.   *Insert text*

Insert symbol, 5,80. Format 8.4 point as superscript

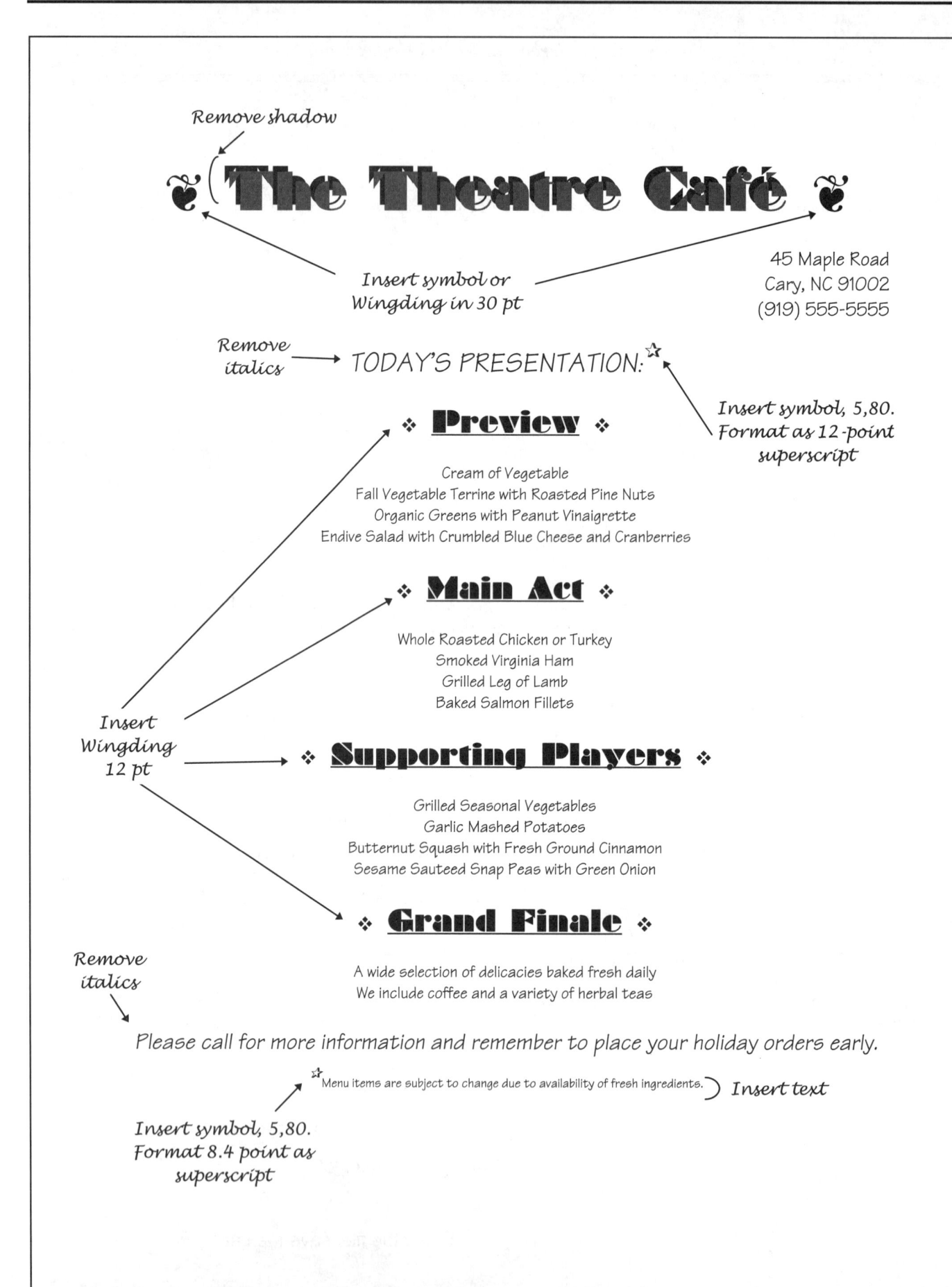

KEYSTROKES

ADD AN ORNAMENTAL FONT
F9

1. Position insertion point where symbol font will begin.
2. a. Click *right* mouse button anywhere in document window.
   b. Click **F**ont .... `Alt`+`F`
   c. Click in **F**ont Face list box..... `Alt`+`F`
   d. Click Wingdings or Monotype ..... `↓`
   e. Click **OK** .... `Enter`

   OR

   a. Click **Font Face** button on Property Bar `Times New Roman ▼`.
   b. Select Wingdings or Monotype Sorts symbol.

   OR

   a. Click Fo**r**mat..................... `Alt`+`R`
   b. Click **F**ont .... `F`
   c. Click in **F**ont Face list box..... `Alt`+`F`
   d. Click Wingdings or Monotype Sorts .... `↓`
   e. Click **OK** .... `Enter`

3. Press the keyboard letter or character for the desired symbol. *(See charts provided on previous pages.)*
4. To turn off symbol font, repeat step 2 and choose a different font.

INSERT SYMBOLS
Ctrl + W

1. Position insertion point to the left of where you wish to insert character.
   a. Click **I**nsert .... `Alt`+`I`
   b. Click S**y**mbol .... `Y`
2. Click **S**et button .... `Alt`+`S` to display character set list.
3. Click desired character set .... `↑` `↓` `Enter`
4. a. Click in Sy**m**bols box......... `Alt`+`M`
   b. Click desired symbol .... `↑↓←→`

   OR

   Type number assigned to symbol in the **N**umber text box......................... `Alt`+`N`, *number*
5. a. Click **I**nsert .... `Alt`+`I`
   b. Click **C**lose .... `Alt`+`C`

   OR

6. Click Insert **a**nd Close............ `Alt`+`A`

FORMAT FONT OR SYMBOL AS SUPERSCRIPT/SUBSCRIPT

1. Select a font or symbol.
2. Click Fo**r**mat .... `Alt`+`R`
3. Click **F**ont .... `F`
4. Click **P**osition drop-down list .... `Alt`+`P`
5. Click **S**uperscript .... `↑` `↓` or **S**ubscript.
6. Click **OK** .... `Enter`

REMOVE FONT APPEARANCE ATTRIBUTE
F9

1. Select/highlight text to change appearance or return to normal.
2. Click appearance change to remove using same procedure used to apply it.

   OR

1. Reveal codes........................ `Alt`+`F3`
2. Drag code off screen.

Corel WordPerfect 8 ■ Lesson 3 ■ Exercise 15   79

COREL WORDPERFECT 8 Lesson 3: Text Alignments and Enhancements

Exercise 16

- **Bullets and Numbered Lists**   ■ **Remove Bullets and Numbers**

WordPerfect 8 Toolbar

Numbering   Bullets

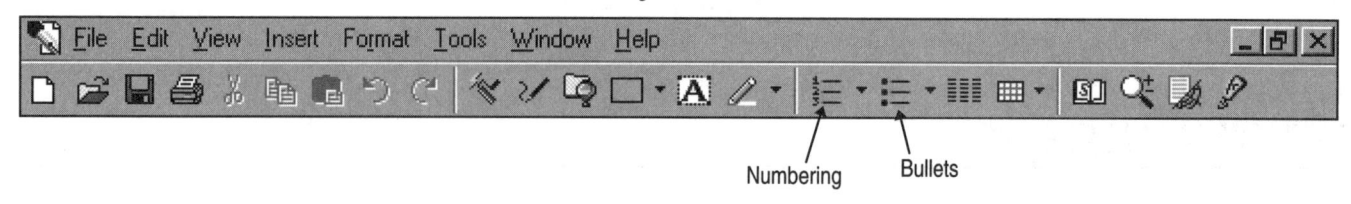

NOTES

Bullets and Numbered Lists

- A **bullet** is a dot or symbol used to highlight points of information or to itemize a list that does not need to be in any particular order.
    - red
    - blue
    - green

- Using the **Bullet and Numbered List** features, you can insert bullets or numbers automatically to create a bulleted or numbered list for each paragraph or item you type. Numbers will increment automatically.
    1. first
    2. second
    3. third

- To create a bulleted or numbered list quickly, click the Bullets or Numbering button on the WordPerfect 8 Toolbar and type your text. Press Enter after each line of text to create a new bullet or number.

    ✓*Note: The Numbering button on the WordPerfect 8 toolbar is also used to create an outline. Outlines will be covered in Lesson 5.*

- To change the bullet style, click the list arrow next to the Bullet button on the toolbar and select another style.

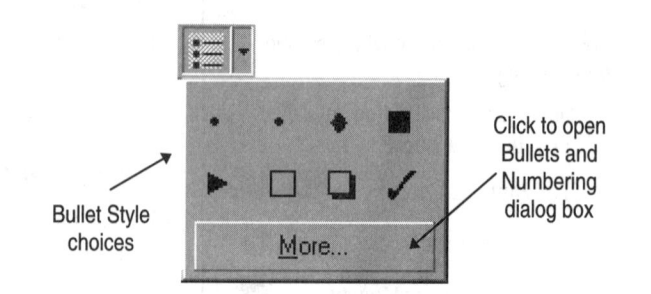

Bullet Style choices

Click to open Bullets and Numbering dialog box

- For additional styles other than those displayed, click the More… option. The Bullets and Numbering dialog box displays (see illustration on the following page). Click the More bullets button and the Symbols dialog box will open. You can select any symbol to serve as a bullet style.

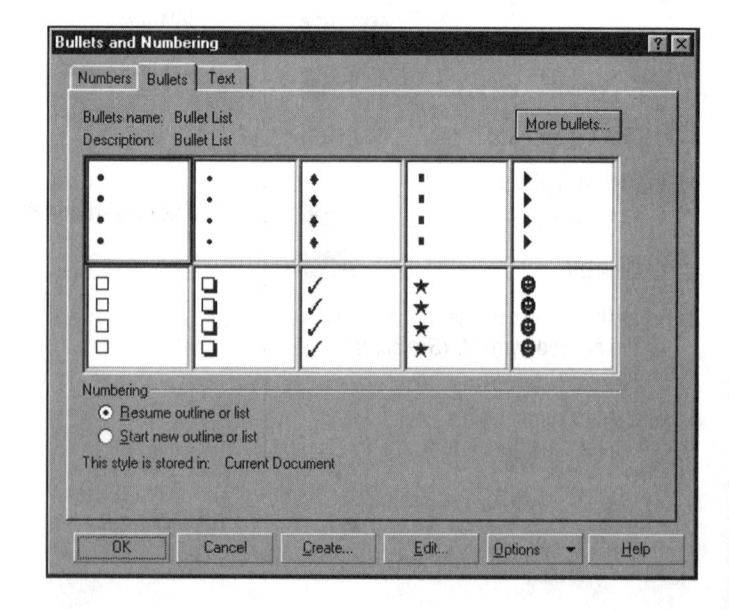

- You can also create a QuickBullet by typing a character (other than a letter or number), followed by a tab. A bulleted list is started. When you press Enter, the bulleted list continues. Type one of the following characters to produce the corresponding bullet:

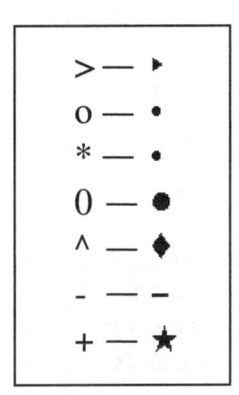

```
> — ▶
o — •
* — •
0 — ●
^ — ◆
- — -
+ — ★
```

- To create numbers quickly, type the number one, followed by a period, followed by a tab (1. →). A numbered list is started. When you press Enter, the numbered list continues.

- You may also access the Bullets and Numbering feature by selecting Outline/Bullets & Numbering from the Insert menu. In the Bullets & Numbering dialog box that follows, click the appropriate tab and select the bullet or number style you desire.

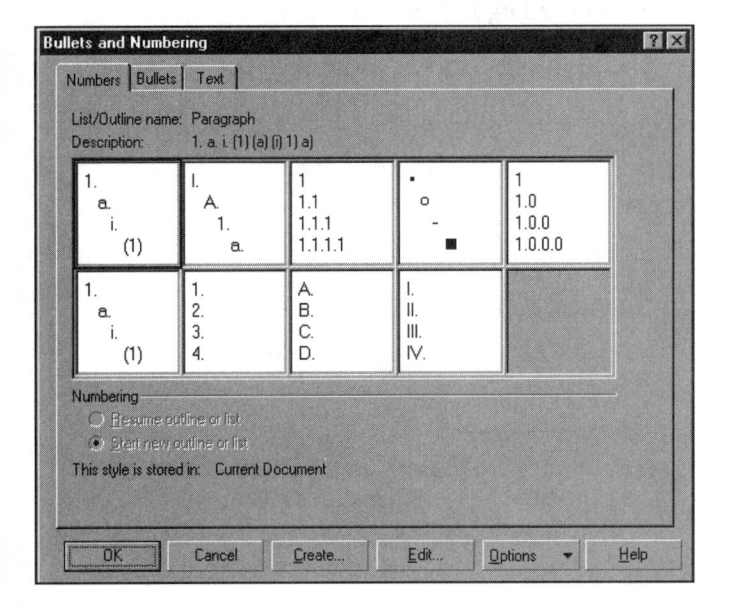

- Once the bullet or number style is chosen, type your text.

- To stop the bullets or numbering, click the appropriate button on the WordPerfect 8 toolbar to deselect the feature or press the Backspace key. The Bullets and Numbering feature will stop at this point.

- If you wish to insert bullets or numbers at a later point in the document, you can select the Bullet button or Number button on the WordPerfect 8 toolbar; the bullet or number style you previously selected in the dialog box displays.

- To begin a new bullet or numbered list, select Outline/Bullets & Numbering from the Insert menu and select the Start new outline or list button at the bottom of the dialog box.

- You can add bullets or numbers to existing text by placing the insertion point in the paragraph to receive a bullet or number (or selecting multiple paragraphs and then applying the desired bullet or number style).

COREL WORDPERFECT 8 Lesson 3: Text Alignments and Enhancements

> *In Part I of this exercise, you will practice applying bullets and numbers. In Part II of this exercise, you will create a flyer using text alignments, enhancements, bullets, and numbers.*

EXERCISE DIRECTIONS

PART I
1. Start with a clear screen.
2. Use the default margins.
3. Type the following at the left margin of your page.
    - Point 1
    - Point 2
    - Point 3
    - Point 4
    - Point 5
4. Select (highlight) all the words and click the Bullets button on the WordPerfect 8 toolbar (select any desired bullet style).
5. Select Outline/Bullets and Numbering from the Insert menu. Select the Numbers tab. Select the "Start new outline or list button." Type the following list:
    - first
    - second
    - third
    - fourth
    - fifth
6. Close the file; do not save the document.

PART II
1. Start with a clear screen.
2. Use the default margins.
3. Type the exercise as shown on the next page or open 🖫**16OFFICE**.
    a. Apply the appropriate alignments and enhancements as shown.
       ✓ Use any desired bullet style for the bulleted items.
       Caution: Apply the bullets to the list of office services <u>before</u> changing the list's alignment. Otherwise, stray bullets, numbers or extra blank lines may be inserted above the list.
    b. Enhance the document with any desired symbols from the Wingdings font collection.
4. Spell check.
5. Preview your document.
6. Vertically center the exercise.
7. Print one copy.
8. Save the file; name it **OFFICE**.
9. Close the document window.

serif 26 pt bold **Big Office Resources**

Sans serif 18 pt For Small and/or Home Offices

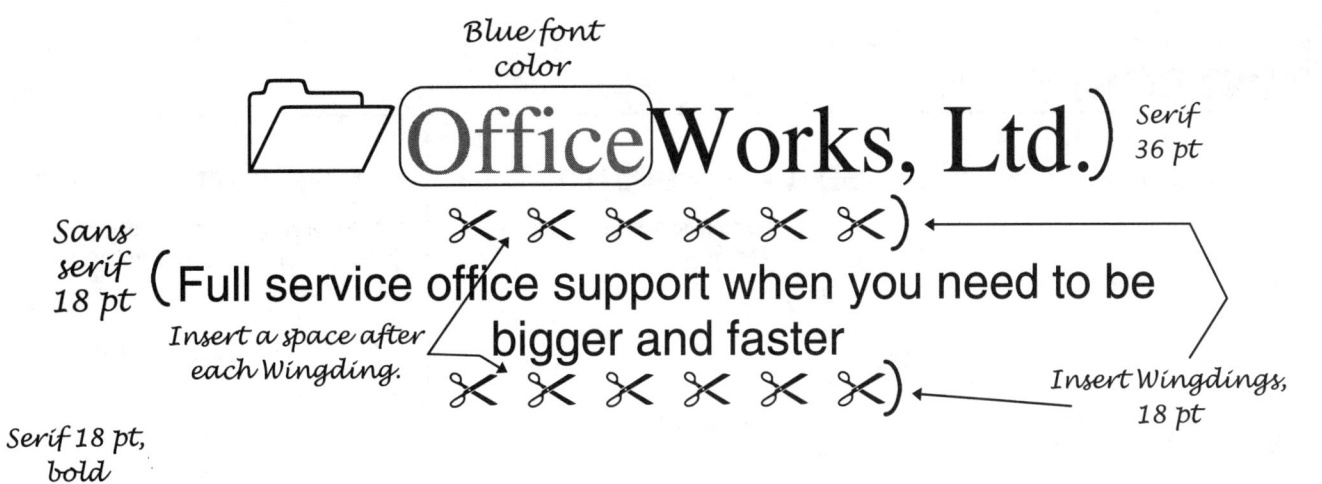

Blue font color Office**Works, Ltd.** *Serif 36 pt*

✂ ✂ ✂ ✂ ✂ ✂

Sans serif 18 pt Full service office support when you need to be bigger and faster

Insert a space after each Wingding.

✂ ✂ ✂ ✂ ✂ ✂

Insert Wingdings, 18 pt

Serif 18 pt, bold

Five Important Reasons to Use Our Service:

Serif 12 pt

1. We work with the client to insure that jobs are done efficiently and correctly.
2. All of our office equipment is the most current and is designed for both large and small work orders.
3. We offer a full range of computer services, including access to the Internet and web site construction.
4. Each client is assigned an account manager to provide individual attention.
5. We guarantee our work.

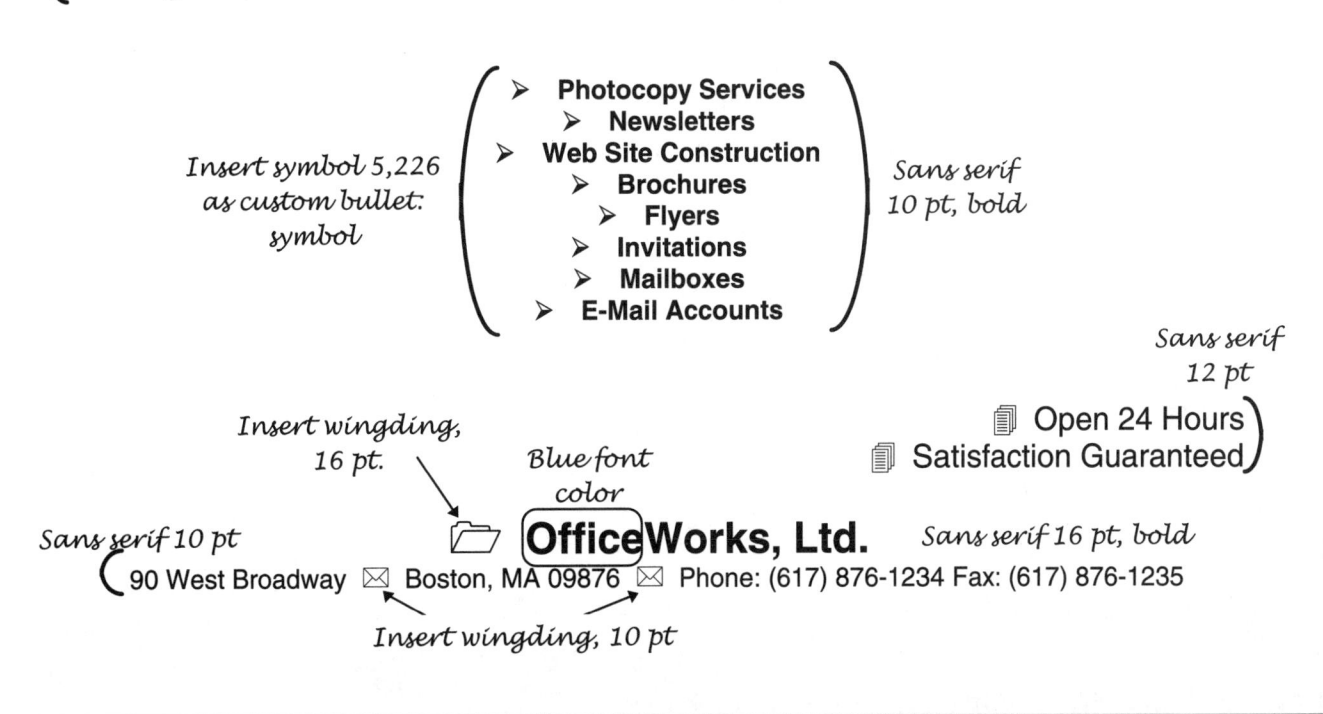

Insert symbol 5,226 as custom bullet: symbol

➢ **Photocopy Services**
➢ **Newsletters**
➢ **Web Site Construction**
➢ **Brochures**
➢ **Flyers**
➢ **Invitations**
➢ **Mailboxes**
➢ **E-Mail Accounts**

Sans serif 10 pt, bold

Sans serif 12 pt

📄 Open 24 Hours
📄 Satisfaction Guaranteed

Insert wingding, 16 pt.

Blue font color 📁 **Office**Works, Ltd. *Sans serif 16 pt, bold*

Sans serif 10 pt 90 West Broadway ✉ Boston, MA 09876 ✉ Phone: (617) 876-1234 Fax: (617) 876-1235

Insert wingding, 10 pt

COREL WORDPERFECT 8 Lesson 3: Text Alignments and Enhancements

KEYSTROKES

CREATE A BULLETED LIST

Ctrl + Shift + B

1. Place insertion point where bulleted list is to begin.

   OR

   Select paragraphs to bullet.

2. Click **Bullets** button on WordPerfect 8 toolbar.

   OR

   Type one of the following characters followed by a tab to display the corresponding bullet.

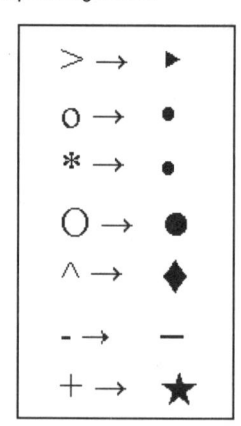

Character	Bullet
> →	▶
o →	•
* →	•
O →	●
^ →	◆
- →	—
+ →	★

   OR

   a. Click **Insert** .... Alt + I
   b. Click **Outline/Bullets & Numbering** .... N
   c. Click **Bullets** tab .... Ctrl + Tab
   d. Click on a bullet choice.
   e. Click **OK** .... Enter

3. Type text.
4. Press **Enter** .... Enter
   to continue list.

CREATE A NUMBERED LIST

1. Place insertion point where numbered list is to begin.

   OR

   Select paragraphs to number.

2. Click **Numbering** button on WordPerfect 8 toolbar.

   OR

   a. Click **Insert** .... Alt + I
   b. Click **Outline/Bullets and Numbering** .... N
   c. Click on Numbers tab.
   d. Click on a numbering style.
   e. Click **OK** .... Enter

3. Type text.
4. Press **Enter** .... Enter
   to continue list.

CHANGE BULLET OR NUMBER STYLE

1. Highlight bulleted or numbered list to be changed.
2. Click **Insert** .... Alt + I
3. Click **Ouline/Bullets Numbering** ..... N
4. Click either the Bullets or the Numbers tab.
5. Click new desired bullet or number style.
6. Click **OK** .... Enter

REMOVE BULLETS OR NUMBERS

1. Place insertion point in paragraph from which bullet or number is to be removed.
2. Click **Bullets** or **Numbers** button.

   OR

   a. Place insertion point at beginning of line from which to remove bullets or numbers.
   b. Press the Backspace key.

Exercise 17

■ Summary

In this exercise, you will create an advertisement using the fonts, appearance changes, and text alignments learned in this lesson.

EXERCISE DIRECTIONS

1. Start with a clear screen.
2. Type the text as shown in Illustration A, or open **17NETPRO**.
3. Use the default margins.
4. To create Illustration B on the next page:
   a. Change the alignments, font faces, colors, styles and sizes as indicated.
   b. Use any desired ornamental font and/or symbol to enhance the document as shown on the next page.
   c. Apply bulleting as shown; use any desired bullet style.
   ✓ Delete any extra returns that may appear when you apply bullets to the two lists.
   ✓ Apply the bullets to the list _before_ right-justifying it.
5. Center the page vertically.
6. Preview your document.
7. Print one copy.
8. Save the file; name it **NETPRO**.
9. Close the document window.

ILLUSTRATION A

Surf the Net
with Netpro

Reasons Why
The Internet is a vast place.
Why not navigate it with the most
efficient Internet service provider?

Netpro offers quick and easy access to the Internet. Are you tired of slow services that force you to wade through several layers of junk before getting down to business? ¶ Netpro can accommodate all of its users simultaneously. Some of the older, better known Internet service providers can no longer handle their current volume of users, resulting in busy signals and long waits. ¶ Netpro is inexpensive. Netpro offers the lowest monthly rate of any other Internet service provider. ¶ Netpro offers a user-friendly customer service line. Customer service representatives are available 24 hours a day to answer calls and provide information. ¶ Netpro is designed to meet all of your Internet needs whether you use the Internet in your home or your office or both. For more information, call 1-800-555-5643 or visit our Web site http://home@netpro.net.

NETPRO
a division of
COMPUTER SERVICE LTD.

ILLUSTRATION B

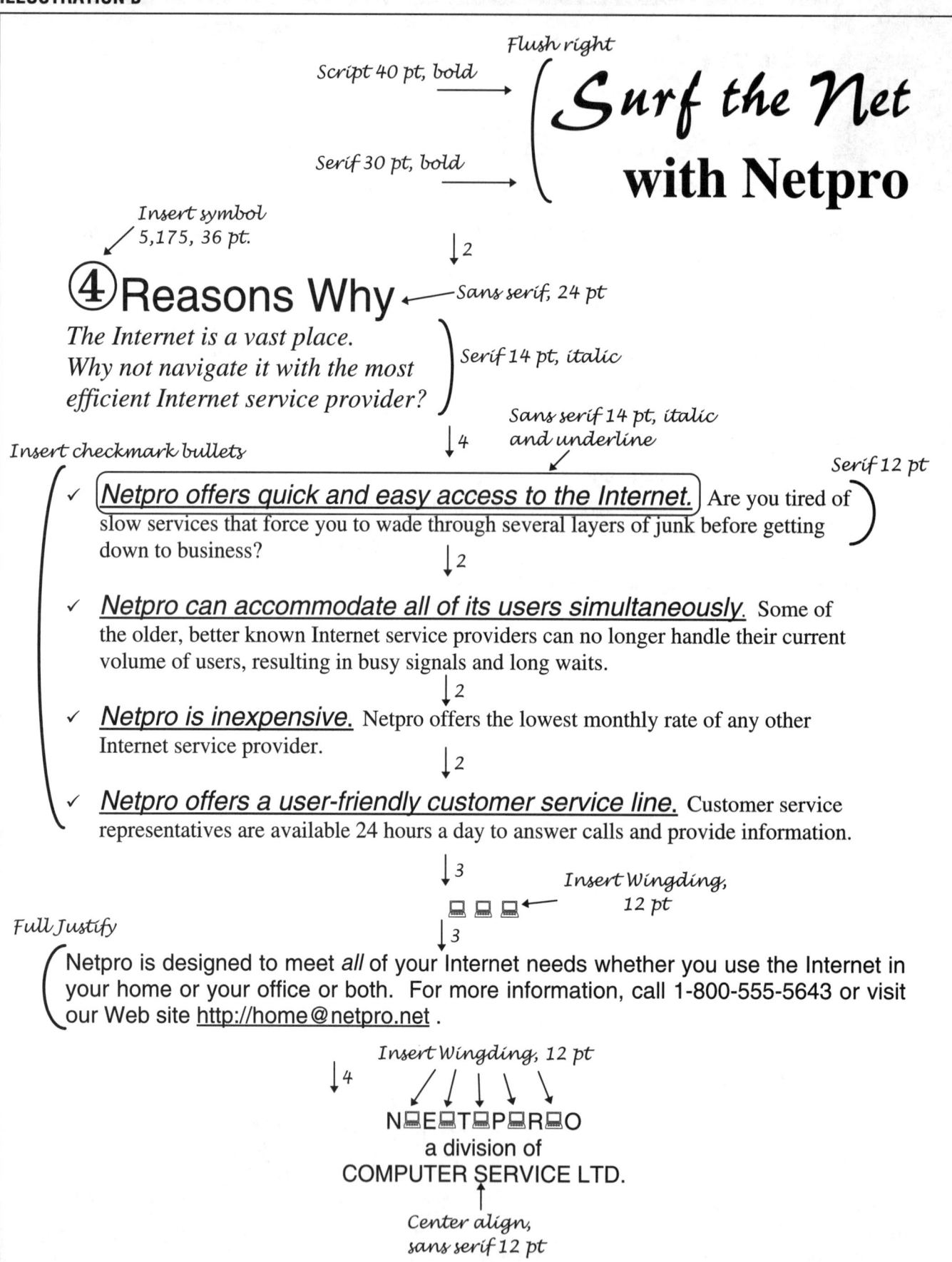

Script 40 pt, bold → *Flush right*

Surf the Net
with Netpro

Serif 30 pt, bold →

Insert symbol 5,175, 36 pt.

↓2

④Reasons Why ← *Sans serif, 24 pt*

The Internet is a vast place. Why not navigate it with the most efficient Internet service provider?) *Serif 14 pt, italic*

↓4

Sans serif 14 pt, italic and underline

Insert checkmark bullets

Serif 12 pt

✓ <u>Netpro offers quick and easy access to the Internet.</u> Are you tired of slow services that force you to wade through several layers of junk before getting down to business?

↓2

✓ <u>Netpro can accommodate all of its users simultaneously</u>. Some of the older, better known Internet service providers can no longer handle their current volume of users, resulting in busy signals and long waits.

↓2

✓ <u>Netpro is inexpensive.</u> Netpro offers the lowest monthly rate of any other Internet service provider.

↓2

✓ <u>Netpro offers a user-friendly customer service line.</u> Customer service representatives are available 24 hours a day to answer calls and provide information.

↓3

💻💻💻 ← *Insert Wingding, 12 pt*

↓3

Full Justify

Netpro is designed to meet *all* of your Internet needs whether you use the Internet in your home or your office or both. For more information, call 1-800-555-5643 or visit our Web site http://home@netpro.net .

↓4

Insert Wingding, 12 pt
↙ ↙ ↓ ↓ ↘ ↘

N💻E💻T💻P💻R💻O

a division of

COMPUTER SERVICE LTD.

↑ *Center align, sans serif 12 pt*

COREL WORDPERFECT 8

Lesson 4: Format and Edit Documents

Exercise 18

- Line Spacing
- Paragraph Spacing

NOTES

Line Spacing

- Use line spacing to specify the spacing between lines of text. A line spacing change affects the paragraph in which the insertion point is located and all text from that point forward. Line spacing may also be applied to selected text.

- If your line spacing is set for double, *two hard returns will result in four blank lines.*

- Line spacing can be changed by selecting Line, Spacing from the Format menu. In the Line Spacing dialog box that follows, enter the desired line spacing amount; the preview window will display the effect of your change.

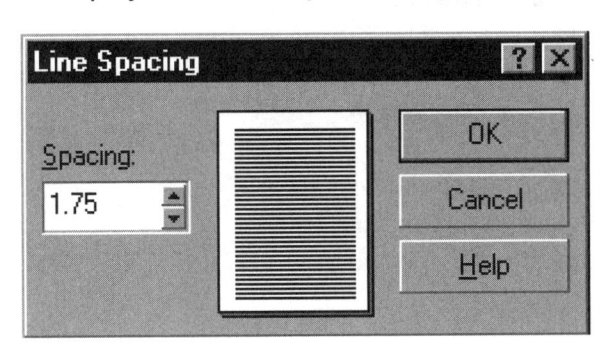

Paragraph Spacing

- You can change the amount of space between paragraphs in the Paragraph Format dialog box. To do so, place the insertion point in the paragraph where you want the change to begin (the new spacing affects all text or selected paragraph(s) from that point forward). Then, select Format, Paragraph, Format. The Paragraph Format dialog box will display.

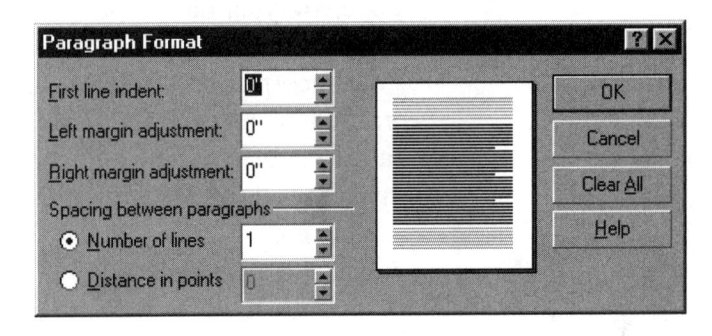

- Enter the amount of space to place between paragraphs in the Number of lines box. Spacing amounts can also be measure in points. To do so, click the Distance in points option and enter the distance amount.

- You can also remove any previously set line and paragraph formatting from the Paragraph Format dialog box. To do so, place the insertion point in the paragraph you want to reset (or press Ctrl + A to select the entire document), access the Format Paragraph dialog box (Format, Paragraph, Format) and press the Clear All button.

COREL WORDPERFECT 8 Lesson 4: Format and Edit Documents

In this exercise, you will create a new document and practice setting margins, as well as line and paragraph spacing.

EXERCISE DIRECTIONS

1. Start with a clear screen.
2. Display the Format toolbar.
3. Click the Page Margins button on the Format toolbar. Set 2" left and right margins.
4. Set the font size to 16 point.
5. Type the three paragraphs shown below.
6. Set line spacing to 1.5" for the second paragraph.
7. Set the spacing between the first and second paragraphs to 2 lines.
8. Set the distance in points between the second and third paragraphs to 10.
9. Change all paragraph spacing to 2 lines between paragraphs.
10. Set all line spacing at 1.25".
11. Save the file; name it **YOGA**.
12. Close the document window.

Yoga strengthens both mind and body! If you're tired of lifting weights and running nowhere on a treadmill, yoga may be the perfect workout for you. If you're experiencing stress or anxiety in your day-to-day life, yoga is definitely the answer.

Yoga incorporates stretching, non-impact aerobic movement, breathing exercises, and relation techniques to help create balance between mind and body. The result? A leaner, stronger body and a calmer, clearer mind. The best part is, once you learn the basics, you can do it anywhere: alone or with a group; at a gym, on your living room floor, or on a beach.

Because you use only your own body weight as resistance, yoga provides a good workout for anyone–regardless of current fitness level. If you want to change your life and your body forever, give yoga a try today!

KEYSTROKES

LINE SPACING

1. Place insertion point in **paragraph** where line spacing change will begin.

    OR

    Select paragraph(s) to receive line spacing change.

2. Click **Format** .... `Alt`+`R`
3. Click **Line** .... `L`
4. Click **Spacing** .... `S`
5. Type desired amount in **Spacing** text box.

    EXAMPLES:

    1.5 = one and one-half space
    2 = double space
    3 = triple space

    OR

    Click increment arrows to select a line spacing amount .... `↓` `↑`

6. Click **OK** .... `Enter`

PARAGRAPH SPACING

1. Place the insertion point in paragraph where new spacing should begin.

    OR

    Select paragraph(s) to affect.

2. Click **Format** .... `Alt`+`R`
3. Click **Paragraph** .... `A`
4. Click **Format** .... `F`
5. Type number of lines to place between .... `Alt`+`N`, *number* paragraphs in the Number of lines box.

    OR

    Type the number of points to place between .... `Alt`+`D`, *number* paragraphs in the Distance in points box.

6. Click **OK** .... `Enter`

RETURN TO PREVIOUS SETTINGS

1. Place insertion point where reset adjustments should begin.

    OR

    Select paragraph(s) to reset.

2. Click **Format** .... `Alt`+`R`
3. Click **Paragraph** .... `A`
4. Click **Format** .... `F`
5. Click **Clear All** .... `Alt`+`A`
6. Click **OK** .... `Enter`

COREL WORDPERFECT 8 Lesson 4: Format and Edit Documents

Exercise 19

- **Format a One-Page Report**
- **Indent Text**
- **Hanging Indent**
- **First-Line Indent**

Format Toolbar

(Hanging Indent, Page Margins)

NOTES

Format a One-Page Report

- A report or manuscript generally begins 2" from the top of the page and is prepared in double space. Each new paragraph begins .5" or 1" from the left margin (tab once). The title of a report is centered and keyed in all caps. A quadruple space follows the title.
- Margins vary depending on how the report is bound. For an unbound report, use margins of 1" on the left and right (the default).

Indent Text

- The **Indent** feature moves a complete paragraph one tab stop to the right and sets a temporary left margin for the paragraph.

> This is an example of text that has an indented paragraph.
>
> > The Indent feature moves a complete paragraph one tab stop to the right and sets a temporary left margin for the paragraph.
>
> Note this example. Text is indented on the left side only.

- The **Double Indent** feature indents paragraph text one tab stop from both margins.

> This is an example of text that has a double-indented paragraph.
>
> > The Double Indent feature moves a complete paragraph one tab stop from the right and left margins.
>
> Note this example. Text is indented on the left and on the right.

- Paragraphs may be indented *before* or *after* text is typed.
- Text is indented to tab settings. Accessing the Indent feature once will indent text .5" to the right; accessing it twice will indent text 1", etc.
- The Indent mode is ended by pressing the Enter key.
- Before accessing the Indent feature, position the insertion point to the left of the first word in the paragraph to be indented.
- The Indent feature may be accessed by doing any of the following:

    1. Place the insertion point to the immediate left of the paragraph to be affected and click the Indent or Double Indent button on the Format toolbar. (This is a quick way to accomplish this task.)

    OR

90

2. Use the Format-As-You-Go QuickIndent feature. When QuickIndent is on, you can left indent a paragraph that begins with a tab by positioning the insertion point at the beginning of the second or subsequent line of the paragraph and pressing Tab. QuickIndent is on by default. To turn it on/off, select QuickCorrect from the Tools menu, click on the Format-As-You-Go tab, and click on the QuickIndent check box.

   OR

3. Selecte Paragraph from the Format menu and select Indent or Double Indent from the resulting submenu.

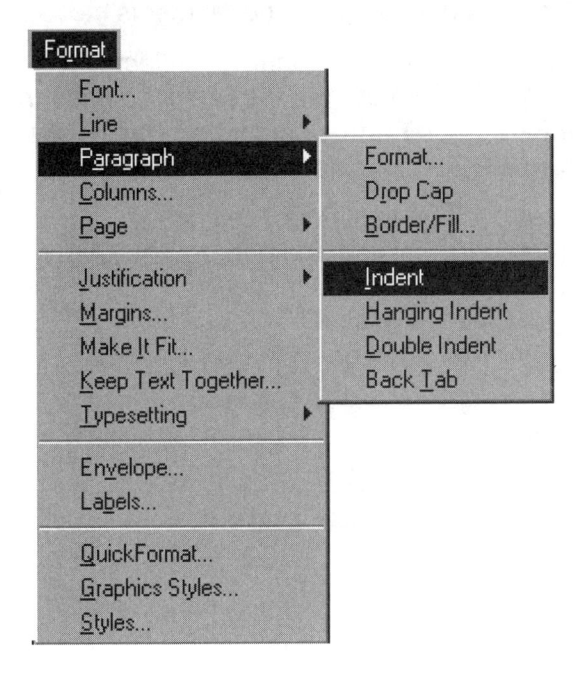

OR

4. Click the *right* mouse button and select Indent. This process is used to indent text *from the left margin only*.

   OR

5. Press the F7 key to indent, or Ctrl + Shift + F7 to double indent.

- To remove an indent, reveal codes and drag the indent code out of the Reveal Codes window. Or, position the insertion point at the beginning of the indented paragraph and press the Backspace key.

- The proofreaders' mark for indenting is:] [

Hanging Indent

- A **hanging indent** is created when all the lines in a paragraph are indented *except* the first line.

- Note the effect of a hanging-indented paragraph. The second and succeeding lines of the paragraph indent to the first tab stop.

> This paragraph is an example of a hanging indent. Note that all the lines in the paragraph are indented except the first line. This can be an effective way to emphasize paragraph text. *This paragraph style is commonly used for bibliographies.*

- A hanging indent may be created in four ways:

  1. by placing the insertion point to the left of the paragraph to be affected and clicking the Hanging Indent button on the Format toolbar. This is a quick way to accomplish this task.

  2. by using the Format-As-You-Go QuickIndent feature. When QuickIndent is on, position the insertion point at the beginning of the second or subsequent line of a paragraph that does *not* start with a tab. Press Tab to create a hanging indent.

  3. by placing the insertion point at the beginning of the paragraph to be affected, or by selecting paragraphs to affect, and selecting Paragraph, Hanging Indent from the Format menu.

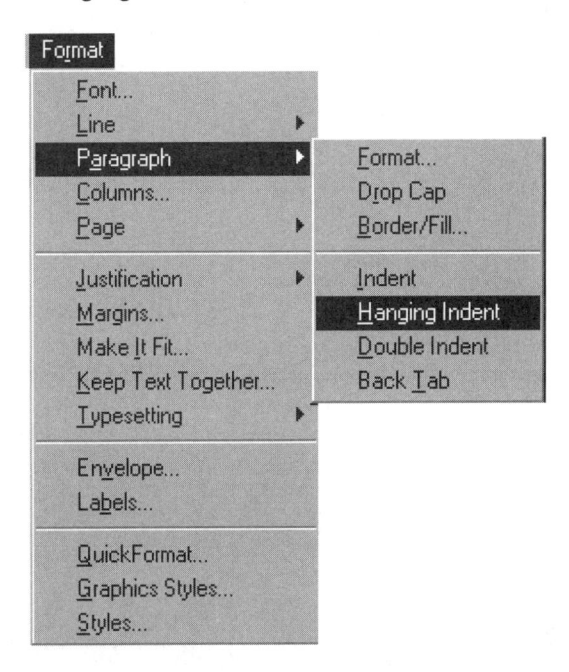

COREL WORDPERFECT 8 Lesson 4: Format and Edit Documents

4. by placing the insertion point at the beginning of the paragraph to be affected, and pressing the Ctrl + F7.

First-Line Indent

- A **first-line indent** lets you set the amount of space the first line of each paragraph indents. Each time you press Enter, the insertion point automatically begins the first line of a paragraph at the indented setting. This feature eliminates the need to use the Tab key to indent each new paragraph.

- First-line indents may be set by selecting Paragraph from the Format menu, then selecting Format from the submenu. In the Paragraph Format dialog box which follows, enter the amount you wish each paragraph to indent in the First line indent increment box.

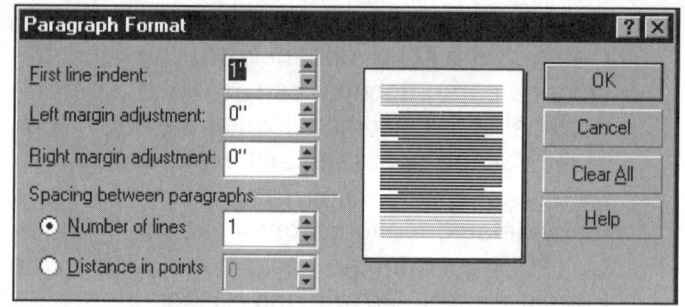

- First-line indents may also be set by dragging the **first-line indent marker** (the top left triangle) *right* on the Ruler to the desired first-line indent position. As the marker is being moved, the Application Bar displays the exact position of the marker. This method allows you to see the effect of your change as the marker is moved.

- To end first-line indent settings, select Paragraph, Format from the Format menu. In the Paragraph Format dialog box that follows, return the First line indent setting to 0".

- To remove first-line indent settings from paragraphs, highlight the paragraphs, then return the First line indent setting to 0".

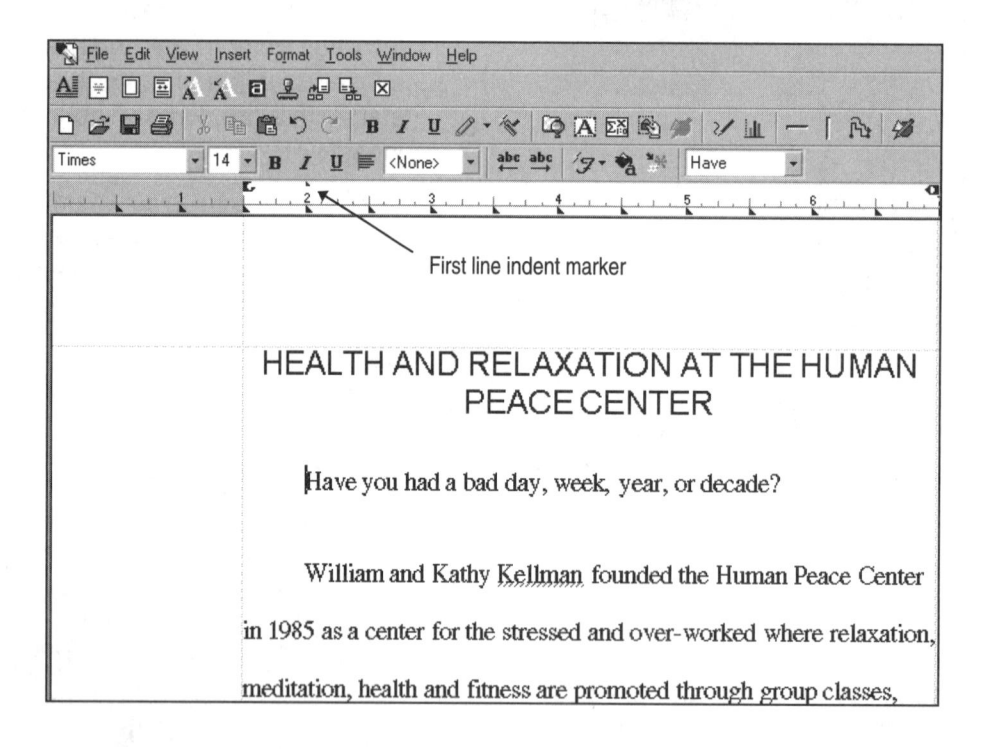

In Part I of this exercise, you will make margin, indentation, line spacing, and alignment adjustments to a document you created earlier. In Part II of this exercise, you will create a one-page report, setting first-line indents for some paragraphs and hanging indents for others. You will also gain more practice using the line spacing, paragraph spacing, margins, and font features.

EXERCISE DIRECTIONS

PART I

1. Open **PEACE** or **19PEACE**.
2. Display the Format toolbar.
3. Center the title and set the font to 18-point sans serif.
4. Set paragraph text to a 14-point serif font.
5. Insert text and make revisions as indicated in Illustration A.
6. Set 1.5" left and right margins.
7. Using first-line indent, indent the first two paragraphs .5" from the left margin.
8. Set the line spacing to 2.0 for the first three paragraphs and the distance between paragraph spacing to 9 points.
9. Set the third paragraph to a 14-point sans serif font.
10. Make the following adjustment to the last five paragraphs:
    a. Set the font to 12-point serif.
    b. Set line spacing to single (1.0).
    c. Set spacing between paragraphs to 1.5.
    d. Double indent .5" from the left and right margins.
    e. Set each center's name, address, and phone number text to Full justification.
    f. Italicize each center's name.
11. Delete any blank lines between all paragraphs.
12. Spell check.
13. Preview your document.
14. Print one copy.
15. Save the file; name it **PEACE**.
16. Set the last five paragraphs (containing the information for each center) to a hanging indent.
17. Print one copy.
18. Save the file as **PEACE2**.
19. Close the file.

PART II

1. Start with a clear screen.
2. Display the Format toolbar.
3. Display the Ruler.
4. Change bottom margin to .5".
5. Type the report shown on page 95 or open **19VITAMIN** and format the title as follows:
    a. Begin title at approximately 2".
    b. Insert any desired symbol before and after the title as shown.
    c. Center the title and set it to a sans serif 14-point bold font.
    d. Set line spacing for paragraph text to 1.25".
    e. Set paragraph spacing to 1.50".
6. Make the following changes to the first four paragraphs.
    a. Set the text to a 12-point serif font.
    b. Set a 1" first-line indent.
    ✓ *Remember, there is no need to tab each new paragraph. The first-line indent automatically advances text 1" when a new paragraph is created.*
    c. Full-justify paragraphs.
7. Center and underline the ESSENTIAL VITAMINS AND MINERALS heading. Set the font to a sans serif 12-point bold.
8. Make the following adjustments to the last four paragraphs:
    a. Set each vitamin name to a 10-point bold sans serif font.
    b. Double-indent the paragraphs .5" from the left and right margins.
9. Spell check.
10. Preview your document.
11. Print one copy.
12. Save the file; name it **VITAMIN**.
13. Create 1" hanging indents on the double-indented paragraphs.
14. Print one copy.
15. Save the file as **VITAMIN2**.
16. Close the file.

COREL WORDPERFECT 8   Lesson 4:   Format and Edit Documents

PART I

Center title in 18-point sans serif

HEALTH AND RELAXATION AT THE HUMAN PEACE CENTER

Press Tab → Have you had a bad day, week, month, or year, or decade? ~~Do you desire the strength that comes from peace?~~

Press Tab → The Human Peace Center ~~was~~ founded in 1985 by William and Kathy Kellman as a center for the stressed and over-worked. ~~At the Human Peace Center,~~ relaxation, meditation, health, and fitness are promoted through group classes, meditations, and one-on-one treatments. ~~Are you ready to unwind?~~

Sans serif 14 point   *where*

For more information, please write or call:

Set location names to italic. Double indent .5"

Human Peace Center, P. O. Box 675, New York ~~City~~, NY 90786 / (800) 456-9876

Wellness Center, 4 Oak Park, Chicago, IL 90876 / (987) 876-1234

Energy Space, 18 Park Street, Portland, OR 90876 / (900) 876-0987

Meditation Zone, 876 West 4 Street, Seattle, WA 12345 / (876) 987-1234   *insert*

The Golden Door, 6 Parker Grove, Clear Lake, CA 78654 / (543) 765-1234

DESIRED RESULT I (PEACE)

HEALTH AND RELAXATION AT THE HUMAN PEACE CENTER

Have you had a bad day, week, year, or decade?

William and Kathy Kellman founded the Human Peace Center in 1985 as a center for the stressed and over-worked where relaxation, meditation, health, and fitness are promoted through group classes, private meditations, and one-on-one treatments.

For more information, please write or call:

Human Peace Center, P. O. Box 675, New York, NY 90786 / (800) 456-9876

Wellness Center, 4 Oak Park, Chicago, IL 90876 / (987) 876-1234

Energy Space, 18 Park Street, Portland, OR 90876 / (900) 876-0987

Meditation Zone, 876 West 4 Street, Seattle, WA 12345 / (876) 987-1234

The Golden Door, 6 Parker Grove, Clear Lake, CA 78654 / (543) 765-1234

DESIRED RESULT II (PEACE2)

HEALTH AND RELAXATION AT THE HUMAN PEACE CENTER

Have you had a bad day, week, year, or decade?

William and Kathy Kellman founded the Human Peace Center in 1985 as a center for the stressed and over-worked where relaxation, meditation, health, and fitness are promoted through group classes, private meditations, and one-on-one treatments.

For more information, please write or call:

Human Peace Center, P. O. Box 675, New York, NY 90786 / (800) 456-9876

Wellness Center, 4 Oak Park, Chicago, IL 90876 / (987) 876-1234

Energy Space, 18 Park Street, Portland, OR 90876 / (900) 876-0987

Meditation Zone, 876 West 4 Street, Seattle, WA 12345 / (876) 987-1234

The Golden Door, 6 Parker Grove, Clear Lake, CA 78654 / (543) 765-1234

PART II

Apply a 1" first line indent and full justification

VITAMINS & MINERALS
Sans serif 14-pt bold

Vitamins and minerals are an essential part of the human body. Both vitamins and minerals are necessary for the body to function properly. They aid in digestion, mental alertness, and resistance to bacterial infection. However, the human body does not manufacture vitamins and minerals on its own, so it is necessary for people to get these important nutrients through other sources. Most vitamins and minerals can be found in foods eaten as part of a regular diet. If a person does not receive all of the necessary vitamins and minerals in her or his daily food intake, she or he must consider taking vitamin and mineral supplements because a deficiency can lead to diseases that can only be cured by a particular vitamin or mineral.

Vitamins are organic substances, which means that they contain carbon and come from materials that are living or have once been alive, such as plants and animals. Minerals are inorganic, meaning they do not contain carbon.

The amount of vitamins and minerals that are required on a daily basis is based upon a person's age, diet, and physical health.

Vitamins and minerals are also known to have some therapeutic benefits and can have a reversing effect on some degenerative diseases.

Double indent .5"

ESSENTIAL VITAMINS AND MINERALS
Sans serif 12-pt bold with underline

VITAMIN C – One of the most popular vitamins found in citrus fruits, carrots, and many other fruits and vegetables. Guards against sickness and may be essential in preventing various forms of cancer.

VITAMIN A – This is essential in the maintenance of healthy skin and internal membranes. It is found in many rose-colored fruits and vegetables.

CALCIUM – Calcium is responsible for strengthening bones and teeth and is essential for women as they mature in preventing osteoporosis. It is found in many dairy products, vegetables, and nuts.

IRON – Iron helps the body produce rich, pure blood, which enables oxygen to be transported around the body, and helps the body maintain a sufficient energy level.

KEYSTROKES

HANGING INDENT
Ctrl + F7

1. Place insertion point at beginning of paragraph to be affected.

   OR

   Select multiple paragraphs to affect.

2. Click **Hanging Indent** button on Format toolbar.

   OR

1. Place insertion point at beginning of paragraph to be affected.

   OR

   Select multiple paragraphs to affect.

2. Click **Format**.................... `Alt`+`R`
3. Click **P**aragraph .... `A`
4. Click **H**anging Indent .... `H`

To end Hanging Indent mode:

Press **Enter** .... `Enter`

FIRST-LINE INDENT

1. Place insertion point where you want the indent to begin (before typing).

   OR

   Place insertion point anywhere within the existing paragraph to be affected.

   OR

   Select multiple existing paragraphs to affect.

2. Click **Format**.................... `Alt`+`R`
3. Click **P**aragraph .... `A`
4. Click **F**ormat .... `F`
5. Click **F**irst Line Indent ...... `Alt`+`F` box.

6. Enter first-line indent amount.

   OR

   Click increment arrows to select a first-line indent amount.

7. Click **OK** .... `Enter`

USING RULER

1. Place insertion point where you want the indent to begin (before typing).

   OR

   Place insertion point anywhere within the paragraph to be affected.

   OR

   Select multiple existing paragraphs to affect.

2. Drag first-line indent marker *right* to desired first-line indent position.

INDENT/DOUBLE INDENT

F7/Ctrl + Shift +F7

1. Place insertion point where indentation should begin.

2. Click **Indent** or **Double Indent** button on Format toolbar.

FOR LEFT INDENT ONLY

1. Place insertion point where indentation should begin.
2. Click right mouse button.
3. Click **I**ndent .... `I`

   OR

1. Place insertion point at the beginning of the second or subsequent lines of a paragraph that starts with a tab.
2. Press the **Tab** key .... `Tab`

   ✓ Repeat steps 1-2 until desired indentation is a achieved.

FOR LEFT AND RIGHT INDENT

1. Place insertion point where indentation should begin.
2. Click **Fo**rmat .... `Alt`+`R`
3. Click **P**aragraph .... `A`
4. Click **I**ndent .... `I`

   OR

   Click **D**ouble Indent .... `D`

   ✓ Repeat steps 1-3 until desired indentation is achieved.

END INDENT MODE

Press **Enter** .... `Enter`

REMOVE INDENT

1. Reveal Codes .... `Alt`+`F3`
2. Drag Indent Code out of window.

   OR

1. Position insertion point at beginning of paragraph.
2. Press **Backspace** .... `Backspace`

RETURN TO PREVIOUS PARAGRAPH SETTINGS

1. Place insertion point where reset adjustments should begin.

   OR

   Select paragraph(s) to reset.

2. Click **Fo**rmat .... `Alt`+`R`
3. Click **P**aragraph .... `A`
4. Click **F**ormat .... `F`
5. Click Clear **A**ll .... `Alt`+`A`
6. Click **OK** .... `Enter`

Exercise 20

- Move Text
- Cut and Paste
- Drag and Drop
- QuickFormat

WordPerfect 8 Toolbar

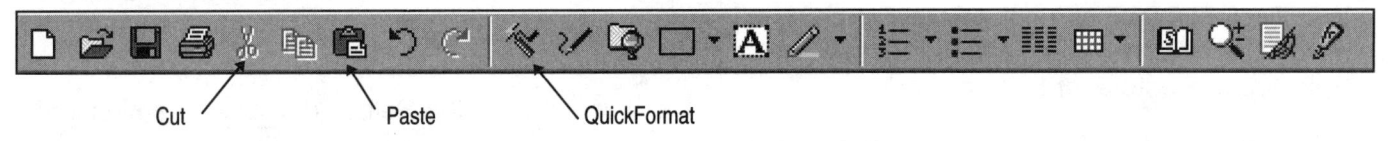

Cut / Paste / QuickFormat

NOTES

Move Text

- WordPerfect provides two methods to move text to another location in the same document or to another document. These methods are called **cut and paste** and **drag and drop**.

Cut and Paste

- The **cut** procedure allows you to "cut," or delete, selected text from the screen and temporarily place it on the Clipboard (temporary storage buffer in your computer). The **paste** procedure allows you to retrieve text from the clipboard and place it in a desired location in the document.

- There are several ways to cut and paste text. Note the keystrokes at the end of this exercise.

- Information remains on the Clipboard until you cut another selection (or until you exit Windows). Therefore, you can paste the same selection into many different locations, if desired.

Drag and Drop

- The **drag and drop** method of moving text allows you to move selected text using your mouse. This method is convenient for moving a word or several words from one location to another.

- Once text to be moved is selected, place the mouse pointer anywhere on the selected text, and click and hold the *left* mouse button as you drag the highlighted text to the new location. The mouse pointer changes to a box with a dotted shadow to indicate that you are dragging text. When you reach the new location, release the mouse button to drop the text into place. Be sure to remove the selection highlight before pressing any key so that you do not delete your newly moved text.

- If you move an indented or tabbed paragraph with formatting codes (double spacing, font changes, etc.), be sure the indent, tab and/or formatting code to the left of the text is moved along with the paragraph. To ensure this, reveal codes and check that the insertion point is to the left of the code to move before selecting text.

- If text was not reinserted at the correct point, you can undo the action by selecting Edit, Undo. It is sometimes necessary to insert or delete spaces, returns, or tabs after completing a move.

- The proofreaders' marks for moving text are: }→ or ◯→ .

QuickFormat

- The **QuickFormat** feature allows you to copy formatting, such as font face, style, size, paragraph spacing, and indents from one part of a document to another.

- QuickFormat can be accessed by highlighting the text that contains the formatting you wish to copy, then selecting QuickFormat from the Format menu. It can also be accessed by clicking the QuickFormat button on the WordPerfect 8 toolbar. In the QuickFormat dialog box which follows, select either the Selected characters, or Headings option.

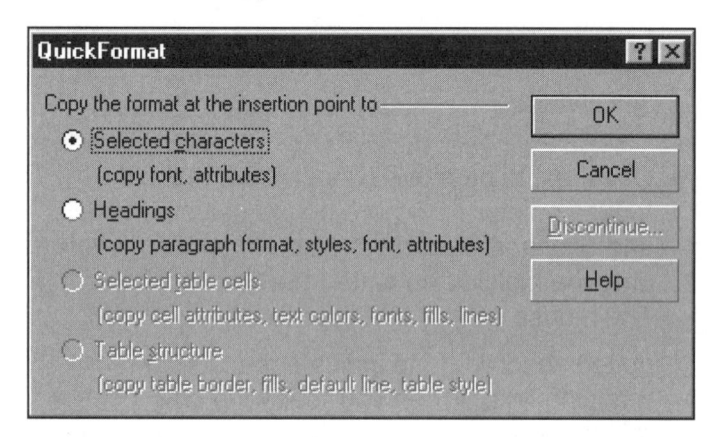

- The **Selected characters** option copies fonts and attributes (italics, bold, underline, size, color, etc.) from selected text containing those attributes to other selected text.

- The **Headings** option copies character attributes as well as paragraph formatting (tabs, centering, indents, styles, etc.) from text within a paragraph to other selected paragraph text. Once the Headings option has been applied to paragraph text, any subsequent format change to one paragraph will cause all previously formatted paragraphs to change and take on the same format, thus creating a link.

- If you choose the Selected character option and click OK, a small paintbrush will appear. If you choose the Headings option, a paint roller will appear. Use the paintbrush or paint roller to "paint" the formatting of the highlighted selection over an unformatted selection. Click the QuickFormat button again to turn the feature off. If you make an error while using QuickFormat, return to the QuickFormat dialog box and click the Discontinue button.

    ✓*Note: If your version of Corel does not perform the Quickformat feature as described above, report the problem to Corel technical support.*

In this exercise, you will move paragraphs, then format them using the QuickFormat feature.

EXERCISE DIRECTIONS

To create Illustration A:

1. Start with a clear screen.
2. Type the exercise exactly as shown below; format the exercise as follows:
   a. Start on Ln 1".
   b. Set right and left margins to 1.5".
   c. Right-align the title text.
   d. Insert a symbol before the title; set it to 72 points.
   e. Set the number "5" character to a 72-point bold font.
   f. Set the remaining title text to a 28-point script font.
3. Move the paragraphs into alphabetical order by doing the following:
   a. Use the drag and drop procedure for the first move.
   b. Use the cut and paste procedure for the second move.
   c. Use any desired procedure for the remaining moves.
5. Press the Enter key once after each capitalized tip. Double indent text twice (1") below each tip.
6. Set the first tip title (Be Realistic) to a sans serif 14-point bold font. Set the color to green.
7. Using the QuickFormat feature, copy the Character formatting to the remaining tip titles.
8. Format the text below the first tip to 10-point sans serif and italic.
9. Using the QuickFormat feature, copy the Character formatting to the remaining text below each tip.
10. Apply full justification to each tip description.
11. Center the current page.
12. Preview your document.
    ✓ Note the Desired Result on page 100.
13. Print one copy.
14. Save the file; name it **SAVE**.
15. Close the document window.

ILLUSTRATION A

5 Ways to Save Money

DO IT YOURSELF. Household tasks, such as laundry, cleaning, and cooking are cheaper if you do them yourself, instead of eating at restaurants or hiring household help. Set time aside every week to prepare for the week ahead.

WAIT FOR SALES AND USE COUPONS. Quality merchandise is available more cheaply if you are conscious of sales and coupons.

BUY IN BULK. Some commonly used household items, such as bathroom products, cleaning supplies, and frozen foods are available from wholesale outlets in large quantities. Think of the long-range needs of your family.

CREATE A BUDGET. Sit down with all members of your family and create a budget. Once a budget is created, it is just as important to stick to it!

BE REALISTIC. Saving money can become difficult if there is a family emergency or unexpected expense. Re-examine the family budget to see where there is some flexibility.

COREL WORDPERFECT 8 Lesson 4: Format and Edit Documents

DESIRED RESULT

> ☞ **5** *Ways to Save Money*
>
> **BE REALISTIC.**
> *Saving money can become difficult if there is a family emergency or unexpected expense. Re-examine the family budget to see where there is some flexibility.*
>
> **BUY IN BULK.**
> *Some commonly used household items, such as bathroom products, cleaning supplies, and frozen foods are available from wholesale outlets in large quantities. Think of the long-range needs of your family.*
>
> **CREATE A BUDGET.**
> *Sit down with all members of your family and create a budget. Once a budget is created, it is just as important to stick to it!*
>
> **DO IT YOURSELF.**
> *Household tasks, such as laundry, cleaning, and cooking are cheaper if you do them yourself, instead of eating at restaurants or hiring household help. Set time aside every week to prepare for the week ahead.*
>
> **WAIT FOR SALES AND USE COUPONS.**
> *Quality merchandise is available more cheaply if you are conscious of sales and coupons.*

KEYSTROKES

MOVE

Ctrl + X, Ctrl + V

Cut and Paste

1. Select text to be moved (cut).
2. a. Click *right* mouse button.
   b. Click **C**ut .... [C]
   OR
   a. Click **E**dit .... [Alt]+[E]
   b. Click Cu**t** .... [T]
   OR
   Click **Cut** button 🗲 on WordPerfect 8 toolbar.
3. Position insertion point where text is to be reinserted.
4. a. Click *right* mouse button.
   b. Click **P**aste .... [P]
   OR
   a. Click **E**dit .... [Alt]+[E]
   b. Click **P**aste .... [P]
   OR
   Click **Paste** button 📋 on WordPerfect 8 toolbar.

Drag and Drop

1. Select text to be moved.
2. Position mouse pointer on selected text.
3. Click and hold left mouse button.
   ✓ *A shadowed box appears.*
4. Drag text to new location.
5. Release mouse button.

QUICKFORMAT

1. Format a character, word, phrase, or paragraph with font face, style, size, color, etc.
2. Select the text that has formatting to be copied.
3. Click **QuickFormat** button on Toolbar.
   OR
   a. Click **For**mat .... [Alt]+[R]
   b. Click **Q**uickFormat .... [Q]
   OR
   a. Click *right* mouse button.
   b. Click **Q**uickFormat .... [Q]
4. Choose Selected **c**haracters .... [C]
   to format a character, word, or phrase.
   ✓ *The mouse pointer changes to a paintbrush.*
   OR
   Choose H**e**adings .... [E]
   to format paragraph.
   ✓ *The mouse pointer changes to a paint roller.*
5. Drag the paintbrush or paint roller over the text to format.
   To turn off QuickFormat:
   Repeat the procedure used in step 3.

COREL WORDPERFECT 8   Lesson 5: Format and Edit Documents

Exercise 21

■ Link Headings

NOTES

Link Headings

- As noted in the previous exercise, the **QuickFormat** feature may be used to link paragraph text together so that when you make a format change to one paragraph, all previously formatted paragraphs change and take on the same format.

- To **link paragraph text**, you must identify the paragraph text that contains the formatting you wish to copy. To do so, place the insertion point within the desired paragraph. Then, click the QuickFormat button on the toolbar. In the dialog box which follows, select Headings.

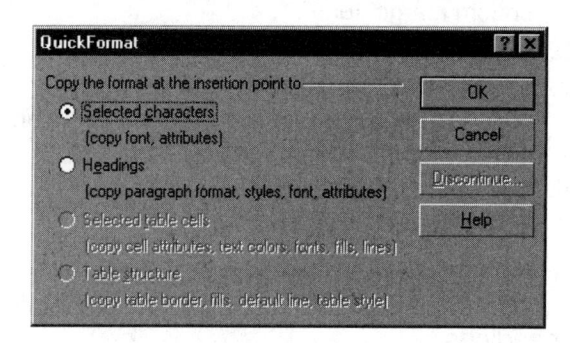

- When the mouse pointer becomes a paint roller, drag it over each paragraph you wish to link. Each paragraph you "paint" receives a heading code. When you make a formatting change to paragraph text you identified as a heading, all linked paragraphs will take on the same format.

    ✓Note: If your version of Corel does not perform the Quickformat feature as described above, report the problem to Corel technical support.

KEYSTROKES

USE QUICKFORMAT TO LINK HEADINGS

1. Format a paragraph with desired alignment, font face, style, size, color, etc.
2. Select the paragraph that has formatting to be copied.
3. Click **QuickFormat** button on Toolbar.
   OR
   a. Click **Format**..................... `Alt`+`R`
   b. Click **QuickFormat** .... `Q`
   OR
   a. Click *right* mouse button.
   b. Click **QuickFormat**..................... `Q`
4. Click **Headings**................................ `E`
   to format an entire heading/paragraph.
   ✓ *The mouse pointer changes to a paint roller.*
5. Drag the paint roller over the paragraph you wish to format.
   To turn off QuickFormat:
   Repeat the procedure used in step 3.

UNLINK HEADINGS

1. Select a linked heading you wish to unlink.
2. Access the QuickFormat feature using any desired method.
3. Click **Discontinue**............................ `D`
4. Choose one of the following options:
   - **Current** heading .... `C`
     to unlink the selected heading only.
   - **All Associated** headings .... `A`
     to unlink all headings.
5. Click **OK** .... `Enter`

Corel WordPerfect 8 ■ Lesson 4 ■ Exercise 21   101

COREL WORDPERFECT 8   Lesson 4: Format and Edit Documents

In this exercise, you will create a flyer and use the Quickformat feature to format selected characters and to link paragraph headings.

EXERCISE DIRECTIONS

PART II

1. Type the text as shown on the next page or open 21GOLD.
   a. Set left and right margins to 1.5"; set top and bottom margin to .5".
   b. Right-align the company name and slogan.
   c. Set the company name to a red 24-point decorative font; set the company slogan to an italic 14-point sans serif font.
   d. Center the first heading (Repairs). Set it to a bold and underlined red, 12-point serif font.

2. Use the Quickformat feature to copy the attributes of the first heading to the remaining headings.

3. Set the description paragraph below the first heading to a 12-point sans serif font.

4. Copy the character and paragraph attributes to the remaining description paragraphs.

5. Set the first contact information paragraph text to italics.

6. Copy the italics to the remaining contact information paragraph text.

7. Right-align any italicized contact information paragraph.
   ✓ *All linked paragraphs will right-align.*

8. Change the color of the contact name, Fleur Johnson, to green.

9. Copy the green font color to each first and last name mentioned in the contact information paragraphs.

10. Center the company name and address information shown at the bottom of the page.

11. Copy the formatting used in the company name at the top of the page to the company name at the bottom of the page.

12. Copy the formatting used in the company slogan a the top of the page to the company name at the bottom of the page.

13. Set the address and phone number to a 14-point sans serif font.

14. Preview the document.

15. Print one copy.

16. Close the file; name it **GOLD**.

Gold Coast Technology
Providing Computer Services to the Chicago Area Since 1987

Repairs
Our in-house technicians offer 24-hour turn around on all warranty and non-warranty repairs. We repair hard drives, cd-rom drives, zip drives, scanners, printers, monitors, and more.

See Fleur Johnston or Greg Owens in the Repairs Department

Data Recovery
Do you have a crashed hard drive or an unreadable disk? No problem! Our staff has the tools to recover your missing or corrupt data.

See Fleur Johnston in the Repairs Department

Memory Upgrades
We sell and install computer memory while you wait. We do installations for both notebooks and desktop computers.

See Tanisha Jones in the Installation Department

Training
Four-hour training sessions available for the following topics: Internet Basics, Creating Web Pages, Word Processing, Windows Environment, Creating Slide Shows, and Working With Images. One-on-one training also available.

See Jo Stein in the Training Department

Sales
We offer a wide variety of both new and used computer equipment and peripherals, including printers, scanners, back-up drives, external drives, cables, batteries and more. All new equipment comes with a two year warranty. All used equipment comes with a six month warranty.

See Wally Zimmerman or Juanita Muniz in the Sales Department

Gold Coast Technology
We're Here to Serve All Your Computer Needs

222 Institute, Suite 7
Chicago, IL 60610
312-555-TECH

Exercise 22

- **Copy and Paste**
- **Drag and Drop**
- **Append to the Clipboard**

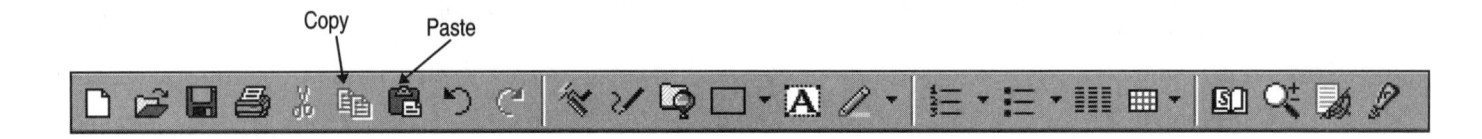

NOTES

- **Copy and paste** and **drag and drop** are features that let you copy text from one location to another.

- **Copying** leaves text in its original location while placing a duplicate in a different location in the same document or another document. (Copying text to another document will be covered in a later lesson.) In contrast, moving removes text from its original location and places it elsewhere.

Copy and Paste

- The procedure for copying text is similar to the procedure for moving text. See keystrokes at the end of this exercise.

- When text is copied, it remains on the screen while a copy of it is placed on the Clipboard.

- Text remains on the Clipboard until you cut or copy another selection (or until you exit Windows). Therefore, you can paste the same selection into many different locations, if desired.

- Text is reinserted or retrieved from the clipboard at the insertion point. Therefore, you should place the insertion point to the *immediate left* of where the text is to be reinserted before following the paste procedures outlined in the keystrokes at the end of this exercise.

Drag and Drop

- Use the drag-and-drop copy method to copy selected text using your mouse.

- Once text to be copied is selected, place the mouse pointer anywhere on the selected text, and press the **Ctrl** key while dragging text to the new location. The mouse pointer changes to a black shadowed box with a plus sign. Drop a copy of the text into its new location by releasing the mouse button. Be sure to release the mouse button *before* releasing the Ctrl key.

- As with the move feature, if text was not copied properly, you can undo the procedure by selecting Undo from the Edit menu.

Append to the Clipboard

- When new text is copied to the Clipboard, the old text is replaced. The **Append to Clipboard** feature allows you to add more text to the Clipboard without deleting text that is already there. To append text to the Clipboard, select the text you want to add, then select Append from the Edit menu.

  ✓*Note: When you paste the Clipboard contents, everything that was appended will be copied to the new location.*

In this exercise, you will use the copy and paste procedures as well as the Append to Clipboard feature to edit a flyer you created earlier. In addition, you will gain practice using the QuickFormat feature.

EXERCISE DIRECTIONS

1. Open **SAVE** or **22SAVE**.
2. Change the top and bottom margins to .5".
3. Center the title.
4. Center the first tip and apply bold and italic formatting.
   - ✓ All remaining tips should change.
5. Using the letter "s" and the Wingdings font, create a line of six diamonds to the right of the first tip.
   - ✓ After the first tip, type the letter "s" six times; select it and change to Wingdings.
6. Use the drag and drop procedure to copy the Wingdings and paste them next to the remaining tips.
7. Change font size of the paragraph below the first tip to 11 points.
   - ✓ All remaining paragraph text should change.
   - ✓ All linked paragraphs should change.
8. Type and center "To Summarize:" three lines below the fifth tip in a serif 14-point bold font, as shown.
9. Append each tip (excluding the Wingdings) to the Clipboard.
   a. Paste the tips two lines below "To Summarize," and press Enter between each tip.
   b. Center-align all summary tips.
   c. Set font to serif 12 points.
   d. Remove italic and bold formatting.
   e. Insert a check mark symbol in front of each tip.
10. Preview your document. Reduce the font size of your document, if necessary, to fit the exercise on one page.
11. Print one copy.
12. Close the file; save the changes.

KEYSTROKES

COPY AND PASTE

Ctrl + C, Ctrl + V

1. Select text to be copied.
2. Click **Copy** button on WordPerfect 8 toolbar.
   OR
   a. Click **Edit** .... Alt + E
   b. Click **Copy** C
   OR
   a. Click *right* mouse button.
   b. Click **Copy** .... O
3. Position insertion point where text is to be reinserted.
4. Click **Paste** button on WordPerfect 8 toolbar.
   OR
   a. Click **Edit** .... Alt + E
   b. Click **Paste** .... P
   OR
   a. Click *right* mouse button.
   b. Click **Paste** .... P

DRAG AND DROP

1. Select text to be copied.
2. Position mouse pointer on selected text.
3. Press and hold **Ctrl** while clicking and holding left mouse button.
   - ✓ A black shadowed box with a plus sign will appear.
4. Drag text to new location.
5. Release mouse button.

APPEND TO CLIPBOARD

1. Select text to append.
2. Click **Edit** .... Alt + E
3. Click **Append** .... A

☞ **5** *Ways to Save Money*

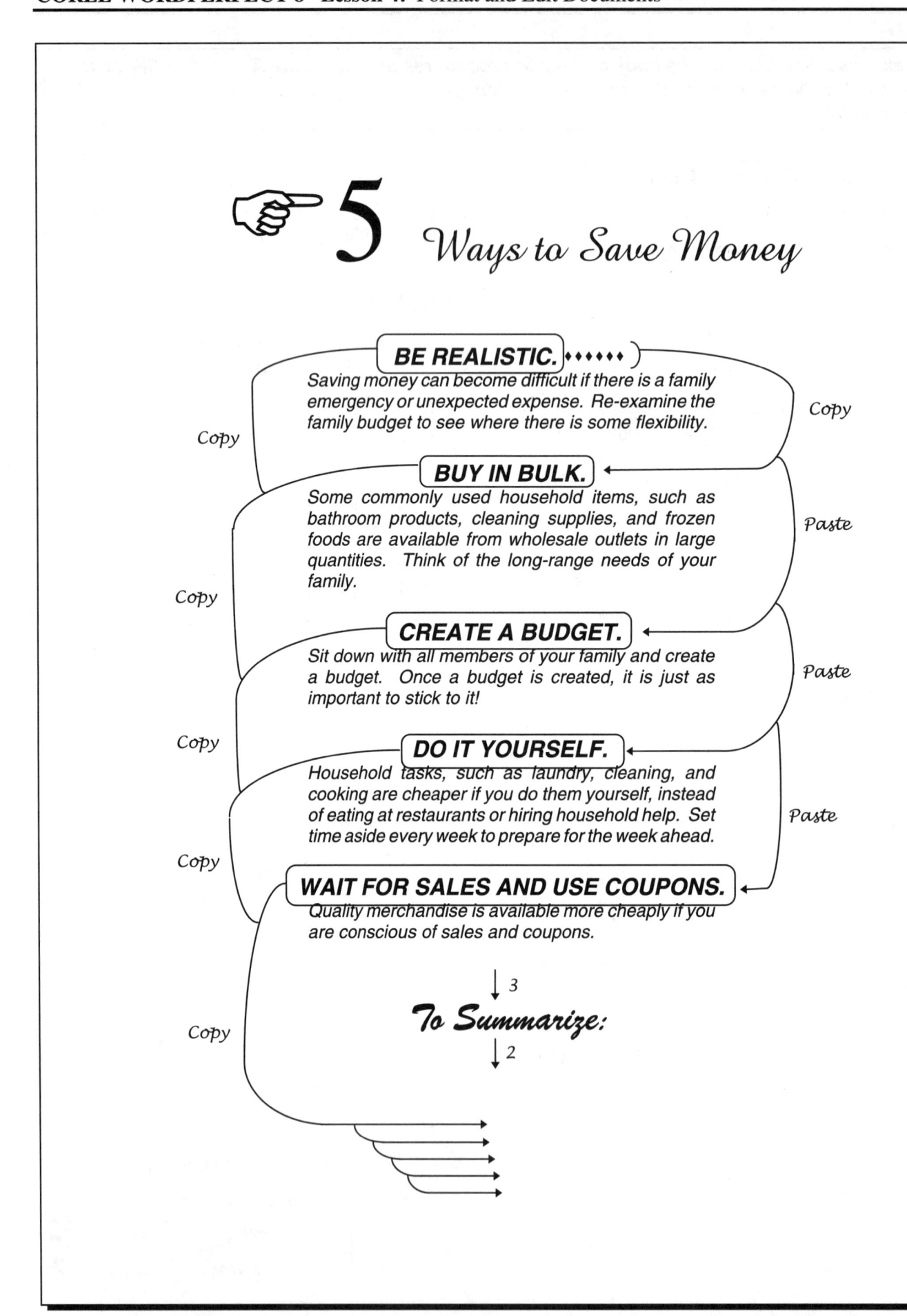

BE REALISTIC. ••••••
Saving money can become difficult if there is a family emergency or unexpected expense. Re-examine the family budget to see where there is some flexibility.

BUY IN BULK.
Some commonly used household items, such as bathroom products, cleaning supplies, and frozen foods are available from wholesale outlets in large quantities. Think of the long-range needs of your family.

CREATE A BUDGET.
Sit down with all members of your family and create a budget. Once a budget is created, it is just as important to stick to it!

DO IT YOURSELF.
Household tasks, such as laundry, cleaning, and cooking are cheaper if you do them yourself, instead of eating at restaurants or hiring household help. Set time aside every week to prepare for the week ahead.

WAIT FOR SALES AND USE COUPONS.
Quality merchandise is available more cheaply if you are conscious of sales and coupons.

↓ 3

To Summarize:

↓ 2

Copy (×5)   *Copy*   *Paste* (×3)

COREL WORDPERFECT 8 Lesson 4: Format and Edit Documents

Exercise 23

- **Make It Fit**
- **Thesaurus**

NOTES

Make It Fit

- The **Make It Fit** feature lets you shrink or expand a document to fill a desired number of pages.

- If, for example, your document fills 1¼ pages, but you would like it to fit on one page, the Make It Fit Expert automatically adjusts margins, font size, and/or line spacing so that the text will shrink to one page.

- You may return your document to the original number of pages by selecting Undo from the Edit menu.

- Make It Fit may be selected from the Format menu. In the dialog box that follows, you must indicate how many pages you wish your document to fill. In addition, you must indicate which items you would like Make It Fit to adjust. If you do not want the margins affected, do not click the margin check boxes.

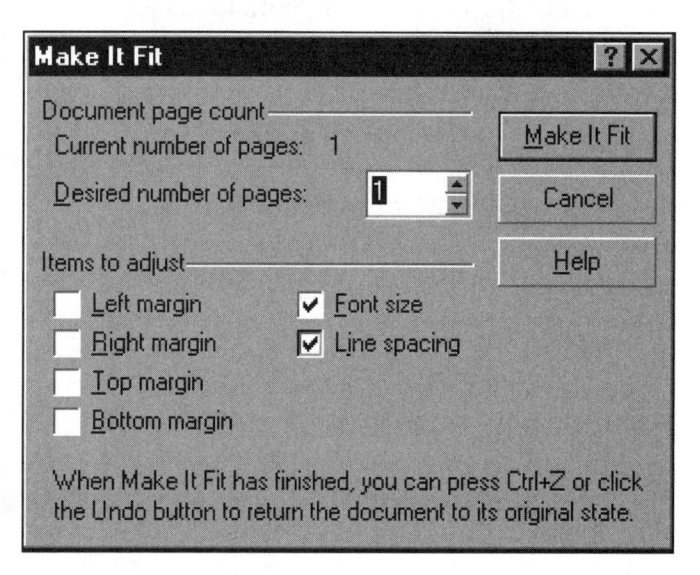

Thesaurus

- The **Thesaurus** feature enables you to select the right word when writing a document.

- The Thesaurus feature lists synonyms (words that have the same meaning) and antonyms (words that have the opposite meaning) for a selected word.

- To access the Thesaurus feature, place the insertion point on the word to be looked up and select Thesaurus from the Tools menu (or press Alt + F1). In the dialog box that follows, a list of related synonyms and antonyms for the selected word displays in the first list box.

- To look up synonyms or antonyms for any of the words listed in the first list box, click on a word in the first list box and click Look Up. A list of synonyms and antonyms for that word will display in the second list box.

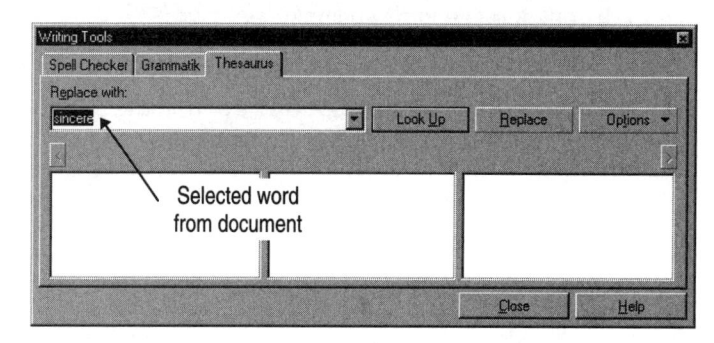

- To look up a word in the second list box, click on the word and click Look Up. A list of synonyms and antonyms will display in the third list box.

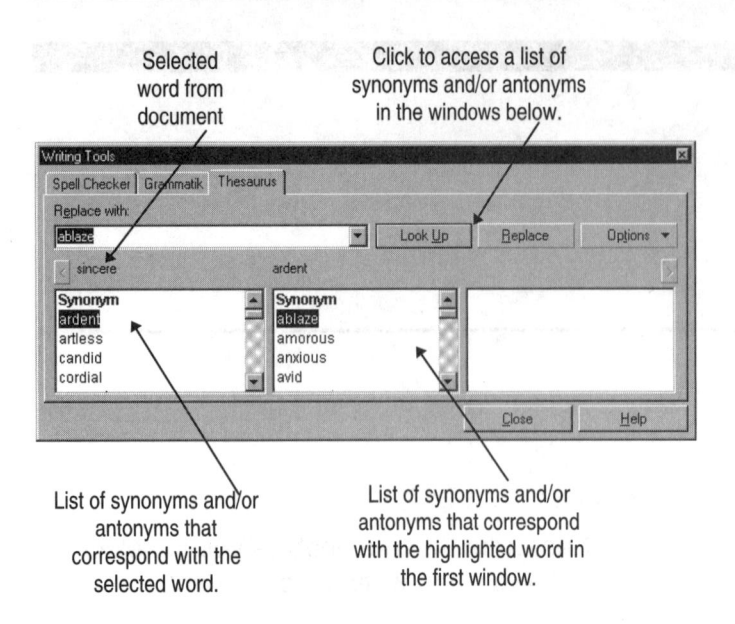

COREL WORDPERFECT 8   Lesson 4: Format and Edit Documents

Writing Tools dialog box (Thesaurus tab):
- Selected word from document
- Click to access a list of synonyms and/or antonyms in the windows below.
- List of synonyms and/or antonyms that correspond with the selected word.
- List of synonyms and/or antonyms that correspond with the highlighted word in the first window.

- To replace a word in your document with a word in the Thesaurus, click on a listed replacement word. Note that it now appears in the Replace with text box. Click the Replace button to replace the original word in your document.

- The Thesaurus feature replaces verbs with the same tense. For example, if you look up the word *inquiring*, the replacement word would include *ing*.

- Remember, the Prompt-As-You-Go feature displays synonyms on the property bar as you type. This is a quick way to find a replacement word.

In this exercise, you will gain more practice copying text. In addition, you will use the Make It Fit feature to keep all text on one page.

EXERCISE DIRECTIONS

1. Start with a clear screen.
2. Open 🖬**PEACE2** or 🖬**23PEACE2**.
3. Insert new paragraphs as indicated in the illustration.
   a. Set line spacing to 2.0.
   b. In the paragraph Format dialog box, set Distance in points to 9.
4. Make the indicated revisions.
   a. Break the title into two lines as shown.
   b. Bold the title.
5. Insert the new center locations as indicated and format them the same way as previous locations.
6. Move the center names into alphabetical order.
7. Preview your document.
8. Use the Make It Fit feature to make the document fit on one page.
   ✓ *Do not make changes to left and right margins. You may, however, include changes to top and bottom margins and font and line spacing.*
9. Place insertion point on each highlighted word and use the Thesaurus feature to select a replacement word.
10. Preview your document.
11. Print one copy.
12. Close the file; save the changes.

HEALTH AND RELAXATION
AT THE HUMAN PEACE CENTER

Have you had a bad day, week, year, or decade?

William and Kathy Kellman founded the Human Peace Center in 1985 as a center for the stressed and over-worked where relaxation, meditation, health, and fitness are promoted through group classes, private meditations, and one-on-one treatments.

Stress can lead to serious medical problems, including high blood pressure, migraine headaches, blurry vision, and sleep disorders. In order to work more efficiently, it is essential for you to learn how to maintain control and channel excess stress in a productive manner. Are you ready to relax?

Human Peace Centers are now available in several locations.

For more information, please write or call:

Human Peace Center, P. O. Box 675, New York, NY 90786 / (800) 456-9876.

Wellness Center, 4 Oak Park, Chicago, IL 90876 / (987) 876-1234

Energy Space, 18 Park Street, Portland, OR 90876 / (900) 876-0987

Meditation Zone, 876 West 4 Street, Seattle, WA 12345/(876) 987-1234

The Golden Door, 6 Parker Grove, Clear Lake, CA 78654 / (543) 765-1234

Clarity Horizon, 1272 Bear Avenue, Claremont, CA 91711 / (909) 333-2727

Spirit Center, 67 Sunshine Street, Winter Haven, FL, 33881 / (941) 555-2289

Vendanta, 7734 Ocean Way, Hilton Head, SC 29926 / (803) 499-9999

KEYSTROKES

MAKE IT FIT

1. Click **Fo_r_mat**.......................... `Alt`+`R`
2. Click **Make _I_t Fit**..................... `I`
3. Click **_D_esired Number**............. `D`
   of Pages text box.
4. Type number of pages you wish document to be.
   OR
   Click number of pages............ `↓` `↑`
   you wish document to be.
5. Click desired items to automatically adjust:
   - **_L_eft Margin**...................... `Alt`+`L`
   - **_R_ight Margin**.................... `Alt`+`R`
   - **_T_op Margin**...................... `Alt`+`T`
   - **_B_ottom Margin**................. `Alt`+`B`
   - **_F_ont Size**......................... `Alt`+`F`
   - **L_i_ne Spacing**................... `Alt`+`I`

6. Click **_M_ake It Fit**...................... `Enter`
   To return document to its original state:
   Ctrl + Z

   Click **Undo** button 🔄 on WordPerfect 8 toolbar.
   OR
   a. Click **_E_dit**........................... `Alt`+`E`
   b. Click **_U_ndo**....................... `U`

THESAURUS

Alt + F1

1. Place insertion point on word to look up.
2. Click **_T_ools**............................ `Alt`+`T`
3. Click **_T_hesaurus**...................... `T`
4. Click **Look _U_p** button............. `Alt`+`U`
5. Click on a Replacement word option in the first dialog box window......... `↑↓`
6. Click **_R_eplace** button............. `Alt`+`R`
   OR
   a. Click **Look _U_p** button
      again................................ `Alt`+`U`
   b. Click on a replacement word option in the 2nd dialog box window.... `↑↓`
   c. Follow steps a and b again, if desired, to view additional choices.
   d. Click **_R_eplace** button......... `Alt`+`R`
   e. If necessary, click **_C_lose** to close dialog box .... `Alt`+`C`

Exercise 24

■ **Grammatik (Grammar Check)** ■ **Grammar-As-You-Go**

NOTES

Grammatik (Grammar Check)

■ **Grammatik** is WordPerfect's grammar check feature that scans your document for errors in spelling, grammar usage, and punctuation. Style errors, including clichés, jargon, and wordiness, are not generally detected.

■ Grammatik checks for errors based on the default writing style, Quick Check. Other writing-style options are available:
- Very Strict
- Formal Memo or Letter
- Documentation or Speech
- Student Composition
- Advertising
- Fiction

■ When a writing style is selected, WordPerfect applies different grammar rules to detect different kinds of writing errors. See the Keystrokes section at the end of this exercise for procedures for selecting a writing style.

■ Grammatik is accessed by selecting Grammatik from the Tools menu, or by pressing Alt + Shift + F1, and selecting the Grammatik tab (if it is not already selected). The following dialog box appears:

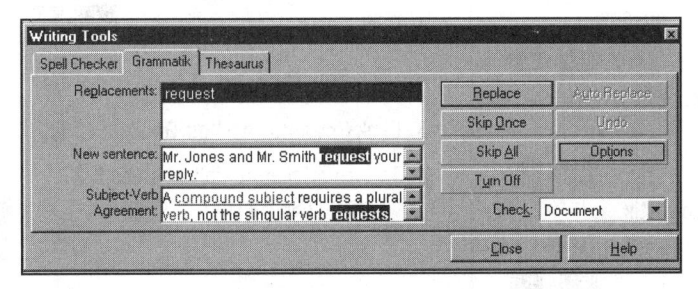

■ When Grammatik detects an error, the window displays the following:

Replacements Displays how to correct the error.

New Sentence Displays the sentence correctly rewritten.

Rule Name Displays the grammar rule that was violated by the error.

■ Grammatik also flags spelling errors.

Grammar-As-You-Go

■ The Grammar-As-You-Go feature checks grammar while you type your document. When a grammatical error is detected, WordPerfect underlines it in blue slash marks. (Spell-As-You-Go underlines spelling errors in red slash marks). To correct an error that is underlined, right click the error and select the correction from the shortcut menu, or select Skip to skip the error, or select Grammatik to open the Writing Tools dialog box. To turn on this feature, select Proofread, Grammar-As-You-Go from the Tools menu.

■ To respond to grammar and spelling errors, click the appropriate button:

Replace	Replaces the highlighted error with a new word.
Skip Once	Ignores the highlighted error for this occurrence only and advances to the next detected error.
Skip All	Ignores the highlighted error for the entire document.
Add	Adds a word to the Grammatik spelling dictionary.
Turn Off	Disables checking for a particular rule.
Auto Replace	Replaces the highlighted error with WordPerfect's suggestion.
Undo	Reverses the last action.
Options	Offers various options to analyze your document.
Close	Closes Grammatik.

COREL WORDPERFECT 8 Lesson 4: Format and Edit Documents

In this exercise, you will create a report and use the Grammatik and Thesaurus features to edit it.

EXERCISE DIRECTIONS

1. Start with a clear screen.
2. Set top and bottom margins to .5".
3. Begin the exercise at the top of the page.
4. Type the exercise exactly as shown (including circled usage errors) in Illustration A or open 💾**24SHOW**.

To create Illustration B:
1. Edit the letterhead as follows:
   a. Set the company name to a sans serif 14-point italic font. Set the font color to red.
   b. Set the first letter of each word to 20 points and underline.
   c. Right-align address information.
   d. Set the address information to the same sans serif font, in 12 points.
   e. Insert a Wingding symbol between Boston and Massachusetts and between Massachusetts and Zip Code.
2. Begin the date at approximately Ln 2.5".
3. Set letter text to a serif 11-point font.
4. Insert a custom bullet in front of each listed show.
5. Move the shows into alphabetical order.
6. Make the indicated revisions as shown.
7. Spell and grammar check your document (correct noun and verb agreement errors only).
8. Use the Thesaurus feature to replace the highlighted words.
   ✓ *Make any necessary corrections to accommodate the new words.*
9. Preview your document.
10. Analyze the document to determine the number of words.
11. Print one copy.
12. Save the file; name it **SHOW**.

KEYSTROKES

GRAMMAR CHECK

Alt + Shift + F1

1. Position insertion point at the beginning of document.
2. Click **T**ools .... Alt+T
3. Click **G**rammatik .... G

   To change writing style:
   a. Click **O**ptions .... Alt+I
   b. Click Check**i**ng Styles I
   c. Select a style from the list box.
   d. Click **S**elect .... Alt+S

4. When an error is detected, click appropriate option:

   • **R**eplace .... Alt+R
     to replace highlighted error with suggested word or phrase in Re**p**lacements box.
   • Skip **O**nce .... Alt+O
     to ignore only this occurrence of highlighted error and advance.
   • Skip **A**ll .... Alt+A
     to skip all occurrences of highlighted error.
   • A**d**d .... Alt+D
     to add word to Grammatik spelling dictionary.
   • U**n**do .... Alt+N

   • Opt**i**ons, Anal**y**sis .... Alt+I, Y
     to apply an analysis option.
5. Click **C**lose .... Alt+C
   to close Grammatik.

GRAMMAR-AS-YOU-GO

1. Click **T**ools .... Alt+T
2. Click Proo**f**read .... F
3. Click **G**rammar-As-You-Go .... G
4. To turn off feature, follow steps 1-2 above and select Off.

ILLUSTRATION A

SHOW-OF-THE-MONTH CLUB
45 Beacon Street
Boston Massachusetts 10657
617-555-5555

Today's date Ms. Tammy Kaufman 678 Winthrop Avenue Brookline, MA 10654
Dear Ms. Kaufman:
We are pleases that you have decided to spend a second season as a member of Boston's *SHOW-OF-THE-MONTH* CLUB. Your participation in *SHOW-OF-THE-MONTH* CLUB gives you the chance to receive less expensive, but good quality, tickets to many of the new shows coming to Boston this season as well as some of the Boston classics, such as *Shear Madness* and the Wang Center's *The Nutcracker*. The following are a list of shows available to you as a member.
Miss Saigon
Smokey Joe's Café
The Capeman
Rent
Shear Madness
Nunsense
The Nutcracker
When you send for tickets, please be sure to indicate the first and second choice of dates, as a limited number of tickets are available for each show. We will try to accommodate you to the best of our ability. All shows listed in bold offer special rate for seniors, children, and large groups. ¶If you have any questions, please do not hesitate to contact our customer service office.
Sincerely, Lisa Krakow Customer Service Representative lk/yo

ILLUSTRATION B

S̲HOW-O̲F-T̲HE-M̲ONTH C̲LUB

45 Beacon Street
Boston❄Massachusetts❄10657
617-555-5555

Today's date

Ms. Tammy Kaufman
678 Winthrop Avenue
Brookline, MA 10654

Dear Ms. Kaufman:

We are pleased that you have decided to spend a second season as a member of Boston's *SHOW-OF-THE-MONTH* CLUB. Your participation in *SHOW-OF-THE-MONTH* CLUB gives you the chance to receive less expensive, but good quality, tickets to many of the shows coming to Boston this season as well as some of the Boston classics, such as *Shear Madness* and the Wang Center's *The Nutcracker*. The following is a list of shows available to you as a member.

Copy and paste below

★ *The Capeman*
★ **Miss Saigon**
★ *Nunsense*
★ **The Nutcracker**
★ **Shear Madness**
★ *Rent*
★ *Smokey Joe's Café*

Place in alphabetical order

The shows listed below will run throughout the entire season:

★ *Nunsense*
★ *Shear Madness*

When you send for tickets through the mail, please be sure to note the first and second choice of dates, as a limited number of tickets are available for each show. We will try to accommodate you to the best of our ability. All shows listed below in bold offer special rates for seniors, children, and large groups.

If you have any questions concerning the above, please do not hesitate to call our customer service office.

Sincerely,

Lisa Krakow
Customer Service Representative

lk/yo

COREL WORDPERFECT 8 Lesson 4: Format and Edit Documents

Exercise 25

■ Find and Replace Text ■ Hyphenate Text

NOTES

Find and Replace Text

- The **Find and Replace** feature scans your document and searches for occurrences of specified words, phrases, or codes. Once the desired text or code is found, it can be edited or replaced.

- Find and Replace may be accessed from the Edit menu. In the Find and Replace Text dialog box which displays, enter the word or phrase to be searched in the Find text box; enter the replacement text or code in the Replace with text box.

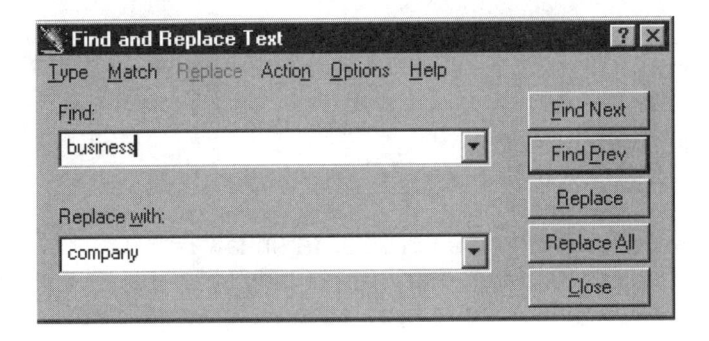

- Then, click the appropriate button to continue your search:

Find Next	To stop at the next occurrence.
Find Prev	To search in a backward direction.
Replace	To confirm each replacement.
Replace All	To replace all occurrences without confirmation.

- WordPerfect searches in a forward direction from the insertion point. To search from the insertion point backward, click the Find Prev button.

- To search for text exactly in the case it was typed (uppercase, lowercase, or initial caps) or in a specific font, choose Case or Font from the Match menu. If, for example, you wanted to find the word HELP and you did not select the Case option, both upper- and lowercase occurrences of the word would be found.

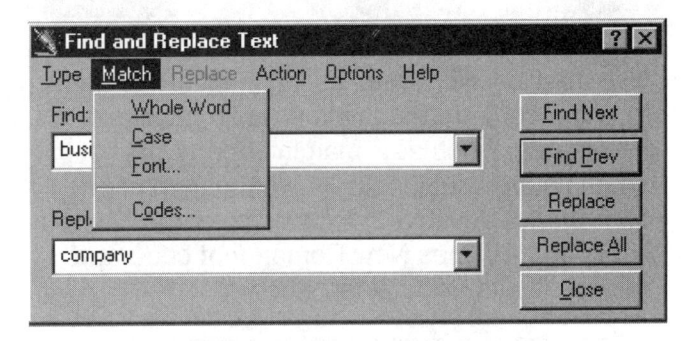

- Use the Whole Word option to select whole words only. For example, if you were searching for the word *the*, and you did not select the Whole Word option, WordPerfect would flag words in which *the* was a part of the word, like *the*se, *the*saurus, *the*sis, etc.

- Use the Codes option to find a code such as Bold On, Bold Off, Left Tab, etc.

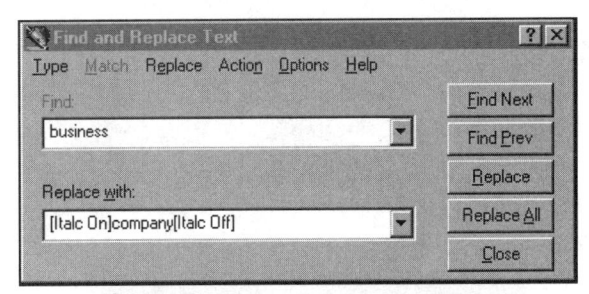

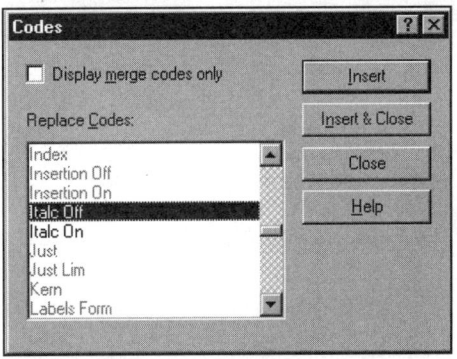

COREL WORDPERFECT 8 Lesson 4: Format and Edit Documents

- The Word Forms option in the Type menu allows you to find and replace words based on the root form of the word. For example, if you select the Word Forms option and you search for the word *call*, WordPerfect would find the words *calls*, *called*, *caller*, and *calling* as well.

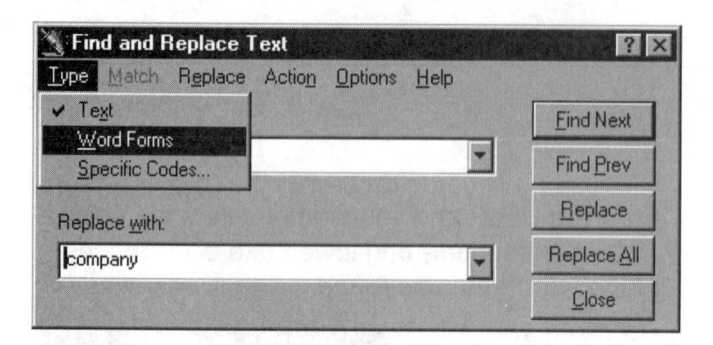

- Use the Specific Codes option in the Type menu to find a code that requires specific numbers or information, such as a margin code. For example, you could find a 1" left margin code and replace it with a 2" left margin code. Or you could find a Times New Roman font code and replace it with an Arial font code.

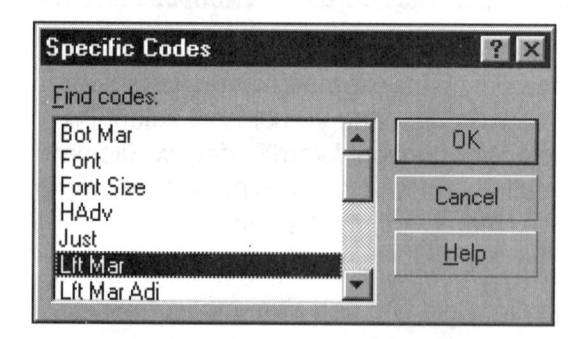

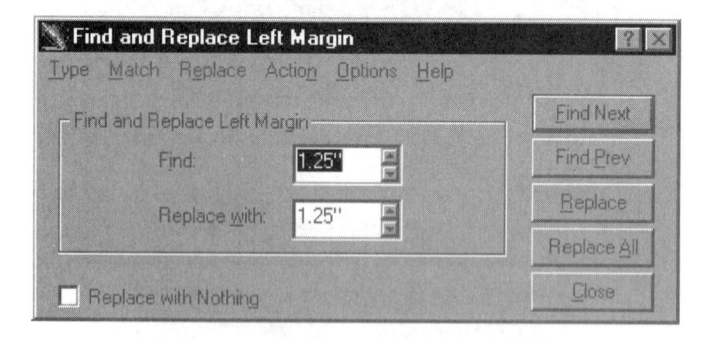

Hyphenate Text

- Hyphenation produces a tighter right margin by dividing words that extend beyond the right margin rather than wrapping them to the next line. If text is full justified and hyphenated, the sentences have smaller gaps between words.

- By default, WordPerfect's hyphenation feature is set to off. In the *off* position, WordPerfect wraps any word extending beyond the right margin. When hyphenation is *on*, a word that starts before the left edge of the hyphenation zone and extends beyond the right edge of the zone will be hyphenated.

- Hyphenation may be accessed by selecting Language, Hyphenation from the Tools menu. In the Line Hyphenation dialog box which follows, you may change the width of the space a word must span before hyphenation divides it by changing the hyphenation zone. *Increase* the percentage of the zone to hyphenate *fewer* words; *decrease* to hyphenate *more* words.

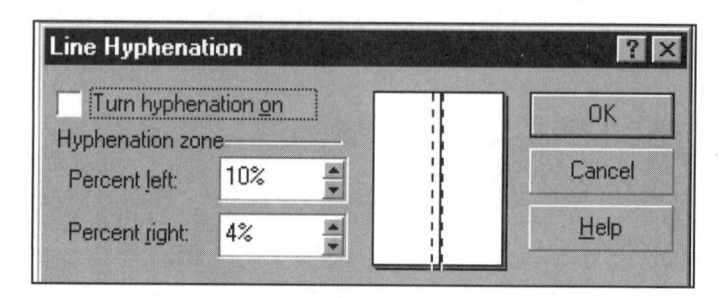

- To keep words such as sister-in-law or self-control together, even if they span the hyphenation zone, type each word with a hard hyphen (Ctrl + -).

> In Part I of this exercise, you will practice using the Find and Replace feature. In Part II of this exercise, you will use the Find and Replace feature to quickly place the insertion point on certain words, then use the Thesaurus feature to replace those words.

EXERCISE DIRECTIONS

1. Start with a clear screen.
2. Type the paragraph below at the top of your screen:

    A PC is a PC is a PC. Not true. Not all PCs are the same. SUMIT PCs outperform all others on the market today. Call your SUMIT dealer today.

3. Use the Find and Replace feature to find each occurrence of PC and replace it with Personal Computer.
4. Use the Find and Replace feature to find each occurrence of SUMIT and replace it with SUMMIT.
5. Close the file; do not save the exercise.

1. Open **VITAMIN2** or **25VITAMIN2**.
2. Use the Find and Replace feature to place your insertion point on each of the following words in the document. Then use the Thesaurus feature to replace each word:
    - therapeutic
    - deficiency
3. Use the Find and Replace feature to locate the word "essential" and replace it with "fundamental."
4. Set the left hyphenation zone to 4% and hyphenate the document.
5. Print one copy.
6. Close the file; save the changes.

KEYSTROKES

FIND AND REPLACE TEXT/CODES

F2 then step 4

1. Place insertion point at top of document.
2. Click **Edit** .... Alt+E
3. Click **Find and Replace** .... F
4. Type text to be searched .... Alt+I
   in **Find** text box.
5. Type replacement text .... Alt+W
   in **Replace with** text box.
   To find specific text:
   a. Click **Match** .... Alt+M
   b. Click **Whole Word** .... W
      OR
      Click **Case** C
      OR
      Click **Font** .... F

To find/replace codes:
a. Click **Match** .... Alt+M
b. Click **Codes** .... O
c. Click code .... ↓↑
   to be searched/replaced.
d. Click **Insert** .... Alt+I
   to insert each selected code.
e. Click **Insert & Close** .... Alt+N
   to return to **Find and Replace** dialog box.

To find/replace specific codes:
a. Click **Type** .... Alt+T
b. Click **Specific Codes** .... S
c. Click specific code .... ↓↑
   to be searched.
d. Click **OK** .... Enter

6. Click **Find Next** .... Alt+F
   to search for each occurrence.
7. Click one of the following options:
   - **Replace** .... Alt+R
   - **Replace All** .... Alt+A
8. Click **Close** .... Alt+C

HYPHENATION

1. Position insertion point where hyphenation is to begin.
2. Click **Tools** .... Alt+T
3. Click **Language** .... U
4. Click **Hyphenation** .... H
5. Click **Turn Hyphenation on** .... Alt+O
   check box.
   To change hyphenation zone:
   a. Click **Percent left** .... Alt+L
      text box.
   b. Type a new left percentage.
   c. Click **Percent right** .... Alt+R
      text box.
   d. Type a new right percentage.
6. Click **OK** .... Enter

ⵖVITAMINS & MINERALSⵖ

Vitamins and minerals are an essential part of the human body. Both vitamins and minerals are necessary for the body to function properly. They aid in digestion, mental alertness, and resistance to bacterial infection. However, the human body does not manufacture vitamins and minerals on its own, so it is necessary for people to get these important nutrients through other sources. Most vitamins and minerals can be found in foods eaten as part of a regular diet. If a person does not receive all of the necessary vitamins and minerals in her or his daily food intake, she or he must consider taking vitamin and mineral supplements because a deficiency can lead to diseases that can only be cured by a particular vitamin or mineral.

Vitamins are organic substances, which means that they contain carbon and come from materials that are living or have once been alive, such as plants and animals. Minerals are inorganic, meaning they do not contain carbon.

The amount of vitamins and minerals that are required on a daily basis is based upon a person's age, diet, and physical health.

Vitamins and minerals are also known to have some therapeutic benefits and can have a reversing effect on some degenerative diseases.

ESSENTIAL VITAMINS AND MINERALS

VITAMIN C – One of the most popular vitamins found in citrus fruits, carrots, and many other fruits and vegetables. Guards against sickness and may be essential in preventing various forms of cancer.

VITAMIN A – This is essential in the maintenance of healthy skin and internal membranes. It is found in many rose-colored fruits and vegetables.

CALCIUM – Calcium is responsible for strengthening bones and teeth and is essential for women as they mature in preventing osteoporosis. It is found in many dairy products, vegetables, and nuts.

IRON – Iron helps the body produce rich, pure blood, which enables oxygen to be transported around the body, and helps the body maintain a sufficient energy level.

COREL WORDPERFECT Lesson 4: Format and Edit Documents

Exercise 26

■ Outlines

NOTES

Outlines

- An **outline** is used to organize information about a subject for the purpose of making a speech or writing a report.

- An outline contains many topics and subtopics, or levels. WordPerfect's Outline feature automatically formats each level of topic and subtopic differently.

- The Outline feature is accessed by selecting Outline/Bullets & Numbering from the Insert menu. In the Bullets and Numbering dialog that displays, click on the Numbers tab and select a numbering style.

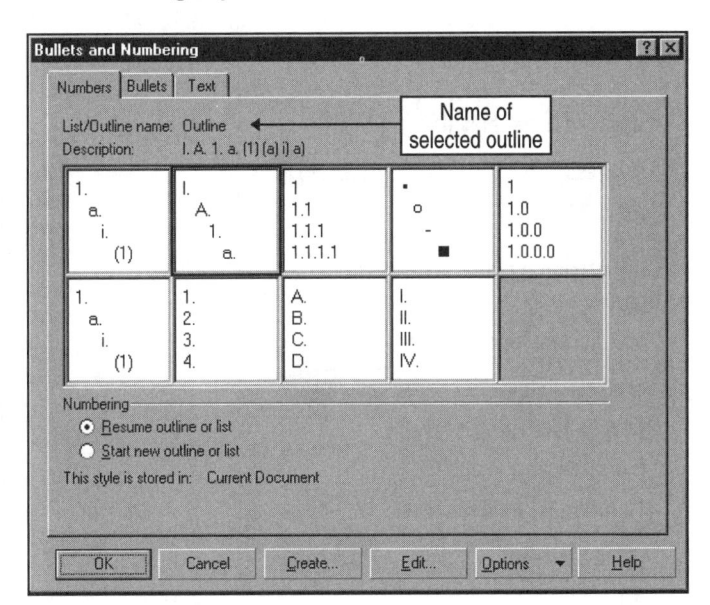

- Outlines include several levels of information. A traditional outline, like the one illustrated below, uses Roman numerals to indicate the first outline levels (I, II, III, etc.), capital letters to indicate the second outline levels (A, B, C, etc.), and Arabic numerals to indicate the third outline levels (1, 2, 3, etc.). When you select an outline style, its name displays at the top of the dialog box.

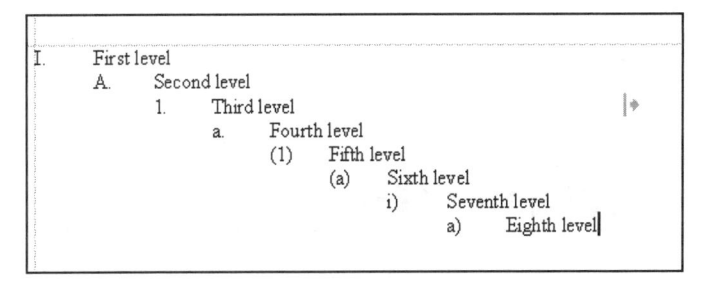

```
I.    First level
      A.   Second level
           1.   Third level
                a.   Fourth level
                     (1)   Fifth level
                           (a)   Sixth level
                                 i)   Seventh level
                                      a)   Eighth level
```

- A document using a traditional outline may contain a title. If a title is desired, type the title, press Enter three times, then access the Outline feature and begin typing. The Application Bar will display the outline level where your insertion point is located.

- **To advance from one level to the next**, press the Tab key or click the Demote button on the Property Bar.

- **If you make an error by advancing too far to the next level**, press Shift + Tab or click the Promote button on the Property Bar.

- **To turn off outline numbering, click in text outside the outline.** If an undesired number remains, press the Backspace key to remove it.

- After selecting a numbering style and clicking OK, the first level of the outline displays along with an Outline Property Bar which provides buttons to make outlining easy.

- Creating a new outline will end a previous one.

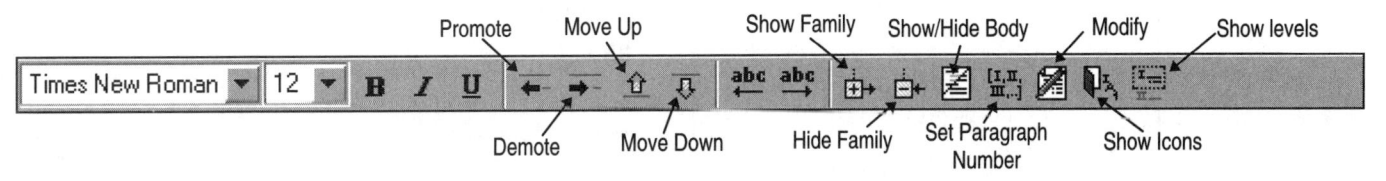

Corel WordPerfect ■ Lesson 4 ■ Exercise 26   119

COREL WORDPERFECT Lesson 4: Format and Edit Documents

In this exercise, you will use the Outline feature to create a traditional outline.

EXERCISE DIRECTIONS

1. Start with a clear screen.
2. Set left margin to 1.5".
3. Begin the exercise at the top of the page (Ln 1").
4. Center the title; set the font to 14-point bold sans serif. Press Enter three times after the title. Return to left alignment and to a 12-point sans serif font without bold.
5. Create the outline shown on the following page using the Outline feature and the Paragraph numbering style.
6. Spell check.
7. Center the document vertically on the page.
8. Preview your file.
9. Print one copy.
10. Save the exercise; name it **WEDDING**.
11. Close the document window.

KEYSTROKES

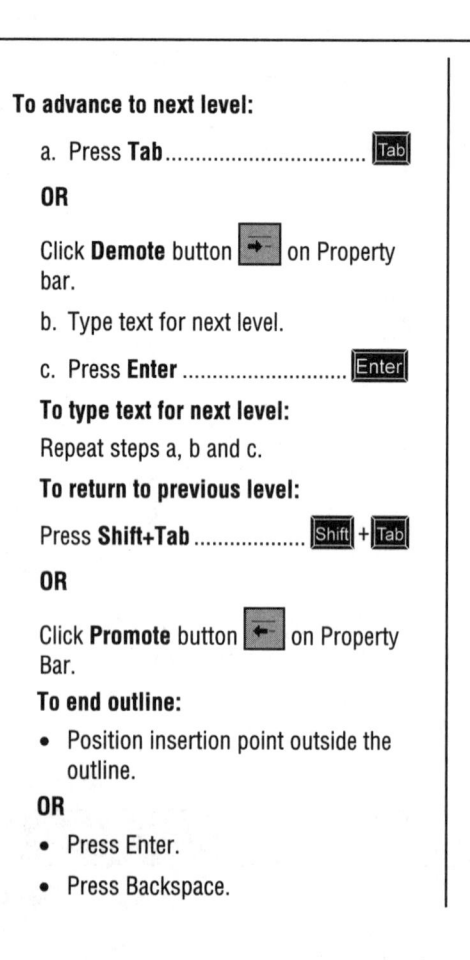

OUTLINE

1. Place insertion point where outline is to begin.
2. Click **Insert** .... Alt + I
3. Click **Outline/Bullets & Numbering** .... N
   a. Select desired outline style.
   b. Click **OK** .... Enter

   ✓ *As you highlight a choice, a description of the style appears at the top of the dialog box.*

To create the outline:
a. Type text for first level.
b. Press **Enter** .... Enter

To advance to next level:
a. Press **Tab** .... Tab

OR

Click **Demote** button on Property bar.

b. Type text for next level.
c. Press **Enter** .... Enter

To type text for next level:
Repeat steps a, b and c.

To return to previous level:
Press **Shift+Tab** .... Shift + Tab

OR

Click **Promote** button on Property Bar.

To end outline:
- Position insertion point outside the outline.

OR

- Press Enter.
- Press Backspace.

THE WEDDING

1. Overview
   a. Date
   b. Location
   c. Band/DJ
   d. Florist
   e. Caterer
   f. Budget
2. Date
   a. Length of time from engagement
   b. Bride's and Groom's work and/or school schedule
   c. Indoor or outdoor wedding
3. Locations
   a. Bride's and Groom's hometowns or current place of residence
   b. House of worship
   c. Type of party: catering hall, country club, private home, hotel
   d. Availability
4. Band/DJ
   a. Hear or see band or DJ before hiring
   b. Location of party
5. Florist
6. Caterer
7. Budget
   a. Who is paying for wedding?
      i. Bride's family
      ii. Groom's family
      iii. Bride and Groom
         (1) Fixed budget
         (2) Flexible
      iv. Combination
         (1) Decide on budget before planning begins
            (a) Who will contribute what amount and for what?
         (2) Develop a list of priorities
         (3) Allow for unexpected expenses

COREL WORDPERFECT 8 Lesson 4: Format and Edit Documents

Exercise 27

■ Summary

In this exercise, you will create a letter using the features learned in this lesson.

EXERCISE DIRECTIONS

1. Start with a clear screen.
2. Use the default margins.
3. Type the text as shown in Illustration A (including circled usage errors) or open 27GYM.

To Create Illustration B on Page 123

4. Make the following adjustments:
   a. Begin the letterhead at the top of the screen.
   b. Center and Set the letterhead to a 24-point sans serif font.
   c. Set the paragraph text to a 13-point serif font.
   d. Begin the date line at approximately Line 2.
   e. Create a full-block letter from the text.
5. Add the text as indicated and do the following:
   a. Insert a smile face bullet preceding each class.
   b. Move the classes into alphabetical order.
   c. Indent each bullet item .5" from the left margin.
6. Search for all occurrences of "play" and replace with "fitness."
7. Search for all occurrences of "FPSC" and replace with "FFSC."
8. Place the insertion point on each highlighted word in Illustration B and use the Thesaurus feature to substitute the word.
9. Use Grammatik to correct the circled usage errors.
10. Spell check.
11. Use Make It Fit to fit the letter on one page.
12. Hyphenate the document and set the left and right hyphenation zone to 4%.
13. Print one copy.
14. Save the exercise, name it **GYM**.
15. Close the document window.

ILLUSTRATION A

Fair Play Sports Club

Today's Date Ms. Eva Brown 78 West 87 Street, Apartment 34 New York, NY 10023 Dear Ms. Brown: Subject: Fair Play Sports Club Membership¶ We are so glad that you have decided to join Fair Play Sports Club (FPSC). FPSC offers the most inclusive membership program at the lowest rates in the city. Your dues offer you access to all of our gyms that are conveniently located in all New York City neighborhoods. Furthermore, we (is) constantly expanding!¶ In addition, we offer new members three free sessions with a personal trainer. This trainer will meet with you to assess your Play level and work with you to plan a workout schedule that will help you reach your personal health goals. All of our trainers are board certified and have come to FPSC with years of experience and abundant enthusiasm. We believe that our Play team is the best in the city.¶ FPSC is constantly working to improve the level of service that we provide to our members. If at any time you feel that there is something lacking or you have a suggestion, please do not hesitate to contact a member of our management team.¶ Welcome to FPSC! We look forward to seeing (your) at the gym. Sincerely, Your Name Membership Director eb/yo

Fair Play Sports Club

Today's Date

Ms. Eva Brown
78 West 87 Street, Apartment 34
New York, NY 10023

Dear Ms. Brown:

Subject: Fair Play Sports Club Membership

We are so glad that you have decided to join Fair Play Sports Club (FPSC). FPSC offers the most inclusive membership program at the lowest rates in the city. Your dues offer you access to all of our gyms that are conveniently located in all New York City neighborhoods. Furthermore, we is constantly expanding!

You will find that we offer more variety than most local health clubs. Our daily class schedule include the following:

- Aerobic Aqua Motion
- Kick Boxing
- Power Boxing
- Power Cycling
- Step Aerobics
- Urban Dance
- Yoga

(Indent bullets .5") *(Insert text)*

In addition, we offer new members three free sessions with a personal trainer. This trainer will meet with you to assess your Play level and work with you to plan a workout schedule that will help you reach your personal health goals. All of our trainers are board certified and have come to FPSC with years of experience and abundant enthusiasm. We believe that our Play team is the best in the city.

FPSC is constantly working to improve the level of service that we provide to our members. If at any time you feel that there is something lacking or you have a suggestion, please do not hesitate to contact a member of our management team.

Welcome to FPSC! We look forward to seeing your at the gym.

Sincerely,

Your Name
Membership Director

eb/yo

COREL WORDPERFECT 8 Lesson 4: Format and Edit Documents

Exercise 28

■ Summary

In this exercise, you will create an outline and apply some of the features learned in this lesson.

EXERCISE DIRECTIONS

1. Start with a clear screen.
2. Use the default margins.
3. Create the outline shown in Illustration A on the following page.
   a. Set 2" left and right margins.
   b. Select the Paragraph outline option.
   c. Use a sans serif 12-point font.
4. Select the first heading (Reasons for Majoring in Public Policy) and change the font to bold, 14 points.
5. Use QuickFormat to set same attributes for the second heading (Reasons for Majoring in Cultural Anthropology).
6. Select the first second level heading (Pre-vocational) and set the font attributes to bold and italic.
7. Use QuickFormat to copy the character formatting to the remaining second level headings.
8. Use the Thesaurus feature to substitute the highlighted words.
9. Set the distance in points between paragraphs to 9.
10. Use Make It Fit, if necessary, to keep text on one page. Adjust top and bottom margins only.
11. Spell check.
12. Preview your work.
13. Print one copy.
14. Save the file; name it **MAJOR**.
15. Close the document window.

ILLUSTRATION A

1. **Reasons for Majoring in Public Policy**
   a. *Pre-Vocational*
   b. *Practical*   ← *Use Prompt-As-You-Go feature to replace highlighted words.*

2. **Reasons for Majoring in Cultural Anthropology**
   a. *Scope*
      i. Global
      ii. Inter-disciplinary
   b. *Small Major*
      i. Small Classes
         (1) Most classes taught in seminar format
         (2) Better student/student interaction
   c. *Academics*
      i. Grading based on more than just subjective testing
         (1) Class Participation
         (2) Papers
         (3) Presentations
         (4) Journals
      ii. Study abroad opportunities
         (1) Asia
            (a) Japan
            (b) China
         (2) Africa
            (a) Zimbabwe
            (b) Botswana
   d. *Requirements*
      i. Foundations in Cultural Anthropology
      ii. Skeletal structure left to student and advisor discretion
      iii. Optional honors thesis

COREL WORDPERFECT 8
Lesson 5: Work with Multiple-Page Documents

Exercise 29

- Hard vs. Soft Page Breaks
- Second Page Headings
- Headers/Footers
- Edit Headers/Footers
- Insert Page Numbers in Header/Footer
- Turn Off (Suppress) Headers/Footers

NOTES

Hard vs. Soft Page Breaks

- WordPerfect assumes you are working on an 8½" x 11" page. Since WordPerfect uses default 1" top and bottom margins, there are exactly 9" of vertical space on a standard page for entering text.

- Therefore, when text is entered beyond the bottom margin (the last line of the 9 inches), it continues at the top margin of the next page. A solid horizontal line marks the page break.

- Once the insertion point is below the page break line, the Pg indicator on the Application Bar displays Pg 2 and the Ln indicator displays 1".

- When WordPerfect automatically ends the page, it is referred to as a **soft page break**.

- To end the page before the last line above the bottom margin, you can enter a **hard page break** by selecting New Page from the Insert menu or by pressing Ctrl + Enter. Text can still be added above the page break, but the hard page break will always begin a new page.

  ✓Note: In Draft view, a soft page break is represented by a single line and a hard page break is represented by a double line.

- A hard page break may be deleted by moving the insertion point to the end of the page before the hard page break, and pressing Delete or revealing your codes and deleting the [HPg] code.

Second-Page Headings

- A multiple-page letter requires a heading on the second and succeeding pages. The heading should begin at 1" and include the name of the addressee (to whom the letter is going), the page number, and the date. To include a heading on the second and succeeding pages, a header may be created.

Headers/Footers

- A **header** is the same text appearing at the top of every page or every other page, while a **footer** is the same text appearing at the *bottom* of every page or every other page.

- After the desired header or footer text is typed once, the header/footer feature will automatically insert it on every page or on specific pages of your document.

- You can create two different headers (specified as either A or B) and two different footers (specified as either A or B) anywhere in the document. You can have up to two headers and two footers active on any given page.

- Headers and footers can be created by placing the insertion point on the first page on which you want the header or footer to display and selecting Header/Footer from the Insert menu.

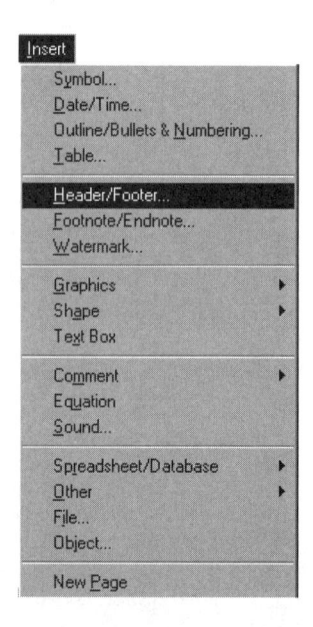

```
Insert
  Symbol...
  Date/Time...
  Outline/Bullets & Numbering...
  Table...
  Header/Footer...
  Footnote/Endnote...
  Watermark...
  Graphics      ▶
  Shape         ▶
  Text Box
  Comment       ▶
  Equation
  Sound...
  Spreadsheet/Database  ▶
  Other         ▶
  File...
  Object...
  New Page
```

126

Header/Footer Property Bar

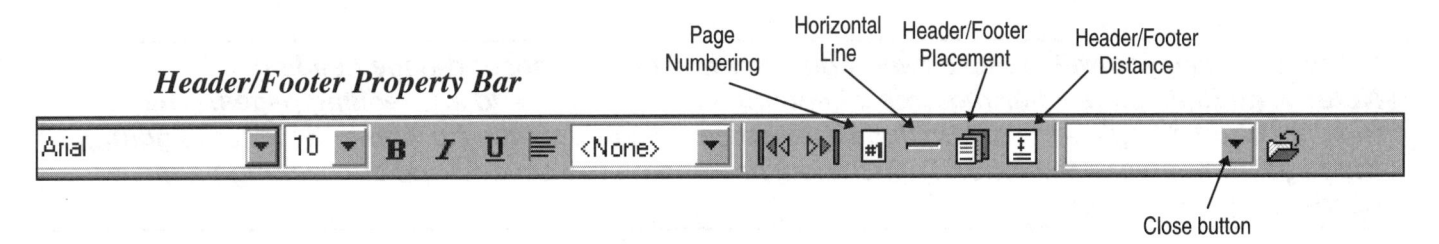

Labels on property bar: Page Numbering, Horizontal Line, Header/Footer Placement, Header/Footer Distance, Close button

- In the Headers/Footers dialog box that follows, select the header or footer to create and click <u>C</u>reate. Then, type the header/footer text.

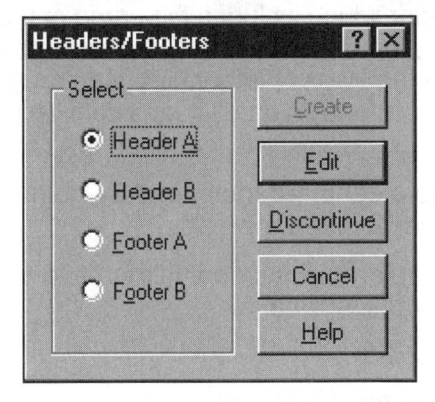

- Because headers and footers display by default in <u>P</u>age and/or T<u>w</u>o Page views, it is easiest to create and/or edit them in these views.

- When you create a header or footer, the Property Bar displays new buttons to make it easy to use Header/Footer features.

- When you click outside the header or footer area, the Property Bar buttons become deactivated.

- The header prints just below the top margin; the footer prints just above the bottom margin.

- The distance between the text and header or footer may be changed. To do so, click the Header/Footer <u>D</u>istance button on the Property Bar and make the desired adjustments in the dialog box that follows.

- Headers, footers and page numbers may be inserted before or after the document is typed.

- If you want headers and footers to align with the body text, you must drag the header/footer boundaries to align with your margins. Or, you can set margins for the header or footer by positioning your insertion point inside the header or footer boundary and selecting <u>M</u>argins from the Fo<u>r</u>mat menu. You can also set your margins for the document. (See Ex. 47 for setting document margins.)

Edit Headers/Footers

- To edit a header or footer, click inside the header or footer boundary or select <u>H</u>eader/Footer from the <u>I</u>nsert menu and click <u>E</u>dit.

Insert Page Numbers in Header/Footer

- Page numbers may be included as part of the header or footer text by clicking the Page Numbering button on the Property Bar. Position the insertion point where you want the page number before clicking the Page Numbering button. (Inserting page numbers independently of the header or footer will be covered in Exercise 50.)

Turn Off (Suppress) Headers/Footers

Page Toolbar

- You can turn off (suppress) headers or footers and page numbers on the current page (of your insertion point) by clicking outside of the header/footer area and selecting <u>P</u>age, <u>S</u>uppress from the Fo<u>r</u>mat menu or by clicking the Suppress button on the Page toolbar and selecting the item to suppress. Since headers or footers and page numbers should *not* appear on the first page of a multiple-page document, they must be suppressed.

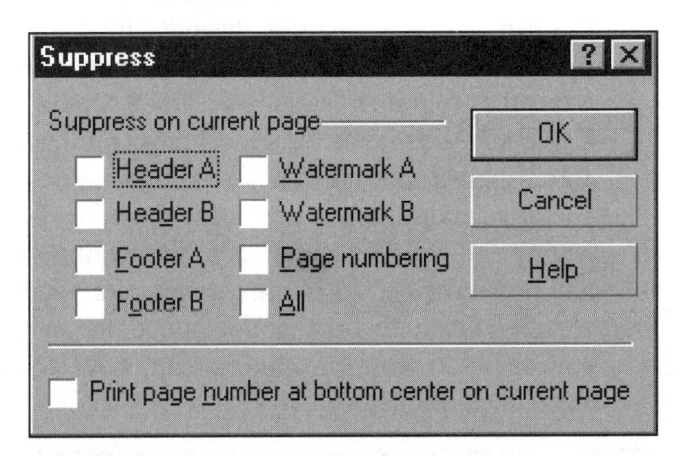

Corel WordPerfect 8 ■ **Lesson 5** ■ **Exercise 29**

COREL WORDPERFECT 8 Lesson 5: Work with Multiple-Page Documents

In this exercise, you will create a two-page letter and insert a second-page heading.
Note: A multiple-page letter requires a heading on the second and succeeding pages. The heading should begin at 1" and include the name of the addressee (to whom the letter is going), the page number, and the date. To include a heading on the second and succeeding pages, a header may be created.

EXERCISE DIRECTIONS

1. Start with a clear screen.
2. Type and format a modified-block letter from the text shown in Illustration A below or open 29ABROAD and format it as a modified-block letter.
   a. Set 1" left and right margins.
   b. Type the date line at approximately Ln 1.5".
   c. Indent the date 4.5" from the left margin.
   d. Use a 12-point serif font for all document text except side heading (Job titles).

Create Illustration B on pages 129 and 130 as follows:

3. Use QuickFormat to set all side job title headings to an italic, 14-point sans serif font.
4. Double indent each job description twice from the left and right margins 1".
5. Insert new text (shown in script) using same font size and style as used for other paragraph text.
6. Position your insertion point on page one. Create a header which includes the name of the addressee (Ms. Claire Ways), the page number (using the Page Numbering button on the Property Bar), and today's date in sans serif 10 point as shown; suppress the header on the first page.
7. Create a centered footer in a 24-point script font that reads: Work Abroad
8. Make any necessary adjustments to prevent awkward line breaks.
9. Spell check.
10. Preview the document.
11. Edit the footer to read:
    Student Life Incorporated
12. Print one copy.
13. Save the file; name it **ABROAD**.
14. Close the document window.

ILLUSTRATION A

Today's Date Ms. Claire Ways 507 Bay Road, Apartment #3-C San Francisco, CA 94102 Dear Ms. Ways: I am writing to inform you that you have been accepted to our Work Abroad program for the summer of 1999. We at Student's Life have been successfully placing qualified college students in various areas of overseas employment since 1979. ¶ We have carefully reviewed your resume and application and, based on your experience and language skills, would like to place you in Paris, France. ¶ The following is a list of possible job opportunities that meet your qualifications: ¶ Assistant English Teacher ¶ Work with a principal instructor to create English lesson plans for grades 6-8. Job responsibilities include: assistant facilitator in the classroom, after-school one-on-one student tutor, accompanying students on field trips, creating a mentor program to assist students. ¶ Media Translator ¶ Help translate American, English, and Canadian news items for a local news radio station that broadcasts daily programs in English. Job responsibilities include: reading American, English, and Canadian news clips, working with a team of translators to transcribe the information into French, and working with advertisers. ¶ Living and working abroad is a very exciting opportunity that is sure to add to your future job and life experiences. In order to prepare yourself for the challenges and excitement that lie ahead, it is mandatory that you attend one of prescheduled orientations. Please contact one of counselors to set up an appointment. ¶ Welcome aboard! Sincerely, Rianna Howard Work Abroad Coordinator rh/yo

ILLUSTRATION B - PAGE 1 OF 2

Today's Date

Ms. Claire Ways
507 Bay Road, Apartment #3-C
San Francisco, CA 94102

Dear Ms. Ways:

I am writing to inform you that you have been accepted to our Work Abroad program for the summer of 1999. We at Student's Life have been successfully placing qualified college students in various areas of overseas employment since 1979.

We have carefully reviewed your resume and application and, based on your experience and language skills, would like to place you in Paris, France.

The following is a list of possible job opportunities that meet your qualifications:

Assistant English Teacher
Work with a principal instructor to create English lesson plans for grades 6-8. Job responsibilities include: assistant facilitator in the classroom, after-school one-on-one student tutor, accompanying students on field trips, creating a mentor program to assist students.

Insert text:
Junior Journalist
Assist senior editors and journalists at a small bi-monthly publication that targets Americans living in France. Job responsibilities include: desktop publishing, proofreading and copy editing.

Media Translator
Help translate American, English, and Canadian news items for a local news radio station that broadcasts daily programs in English. Job responsibilities include: reading American, English, and Canadian news clips, working with a team of translators to transcribe the information into French, and working with advertisers.

Edit footer to read "Student Life Incorporated" → *Work Abroad*

Ms. Claire Ways
Page 2
Today's Date

Create header then suppress on page one.

Insert text

If you know which opportunity you would be interested in pursuing, please contact a counselor at our main office to set up an interview. If the listed employment opportunities do not suit you, please contact a counselor immediately. She or he will gladly provide you with additional opportunities from our large database of employment clientele.

Living and working abroad is a very exciting opportunity that is sure to add to your future job and life experiences. In order to prepare yourself for the challenges and excitement that lie ahead, it is mandatory that you attend one of prescheduled orientations. Please contact one of counselors to set up an appointment.

Welcome aboard!

                                                Sincerely,

                                                Rianna Howard
                                                Work Abroad Coordinator

rh/yo

Work Abroad

KEYSTROKES

INSERT HARD PAGE BREAK

1. Place insertion point where new page is to begin.
2. Press **Ctrl + Enter** .... [Ctrl]+[Enter]

   OR

   a. Click **Insert** .... [Alt]+[I]
   b. Click **New Page** .... [P]

DELETE HARD PAGE BREAK

1. Place insertion point immediately after hard page break line.
2. Press **Backspace** .... [Backspace]

   OR

1. Reveal Codes .... [Alt]+[F3]
2. Place insertion point on hard page break code (HPg).
3. Press Delete .... [Del]

CREATE HEADERS/FOOTERS

1. Place insertion point on first page where you want new header/footer to appear.
2. Click **Insert** .... [Alt]+[I]
3. Click **Header/Footer** .... [H]
4. Select **Header A** or **Header B** .... [A] or [B]
5. Click **Create** .... [C]
6. Type header/footer text.

To add a page number:

1. Position insertion point where number will appear.
2. Click **Page Numbering** button on Property Bar.

To adjust distance between header/footer and document text:

1. Click

   Header/Footer Distance button on Property Bar.
2. Type amount of space in text box.

   OR

   Click increment arrows.
3. Click **OK** .... [Enter]

SUPPRESS HEADER/FOOTER/PAGE NUMBER ON CURRENT PAGE

1. Place insertion point on page where text is to be suppressed.

   a. Click **Format** .... [Alt]+[R]
   b. Click **Page** .... [P]
   c. Click **Suppress** .... [U]

   OR

   Click **Suppress** button on Page toolbar.
2. Click appropriate check box to suppress desired item.
3. Click **OK** ....

EDIT HEADER/FOOTER

1. Place the insertion point on first page of header or footer you want to change.
2. Click **Insert** .... [Alt]+[I]
3. Click **Header/Footer** .... [H]
4. Choose which header or footer you wish to edit.
5. Click **Edit** .... [E]
6. Edit header/footer text.

Exercise 30

- Letters with Special Notations
- Insert Comments
- Bookmarks
- Print Multiple Pages

NOTES

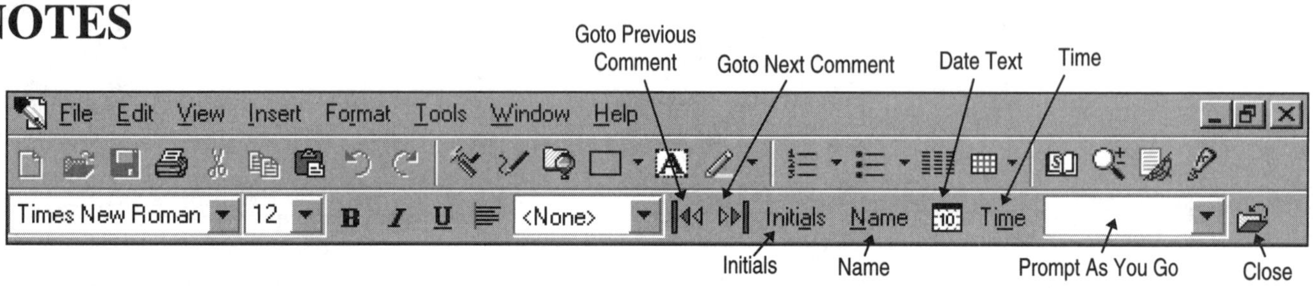

Toolbar labels: Goto Previous Comment, Goto Next Comment, Date Text, Time, Initials, Name, Prompt As You Go, Close

Letters with Special Notations

- Letters may include special parts in addition to those learned thus far. The letter in this exercise contains a mailing notation, a subject line, and enclosure and copy notations.

- When a letter is sent by a special mail service such as Express Mail, Registered Mail, Federal Express, Certified Mail or by hand (via a messenger service), it is customary to include an appropriate mailing **notation** on the letter. When a letter is faxed, a fax notation may also be included on the letter. This notation is placed a double space below the date and typed in all caps.

- The **subject** line identifies or summarizes the body of the letter. It is typed a double space below the salutation. A double space follows it. It may be typed at the left margin or centered in modified-block style. "Subject" may be typed in all caps or in upper- and lowercase. "Re" (in reference to) is often used instead of "Subject."

- An **enclosure** or **attachment notation** is used to indicate that something else besides the letter is included in the envelope. The enclosure or attachment notation is typed a double space below the reference initials and may be typed in several ways (the number indicates how many items are enclosed in the envelope):

    ENC.   Enclosure   Enclosures (2)
    Enc.   Encls.   Attachment
    Encl. Encls (2)   Attachments (2)

- If copies of the document are sent to others, a **copy notation** is typed a double space below the enclosure/attachment notation (or the reference initials if there is no enclosure/attachment). A copy notation may be typed in several ways:

    Copy to: cc: (courtesy copy)
    Copy to   pc: (photocopy)
    c: copy

Insert Comments

- Comments are hidden notes or annotations that you or a reviewer can add to a document. Comments do not print with the document. They can, however, be converted to text in the document and then printed. Each comment can be set to include the initials of the person making the comment.

- To insert a comment, position your insertion point where you wish to insert the comment. Then, select Comment, Create from the Insert menu. A comment window displays for you to type your comment. Comment buttons will display on the Property Bar so you can easily add your initials, name, date, or time to the comment. You may change the font face, size, color and justification and add emphasis features (bold, highlight, etc.) to your comment. Click the Close button when you finish typing your comment.

- The comment appears in the left margin as either an icon or your initials within a small box if you are in Page or Two-Page view. In Draft view, the comment appears as a shaded box.

  ✓Note: *Initials will only display if you have specified them in Environmental preferences.*

- To delete a comment, right-click on the comment or comment icon and select Delete from the QuickMenu.

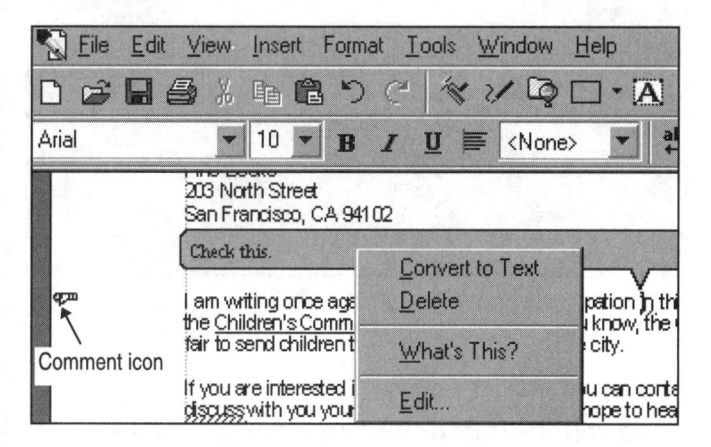

- To read your comment in Page or Two-Page view, click on the icon or initial box in the left margin. To convert the comment to regular document text, display the comment, right-click the comment, then select Convert to Text from the QuickMenu.

- To edit a comment, double-click on the comment icon or initial box or on the shaded comment box in Draft view. This brings you back to the Comment window.

Bookmarks

- The **Bookmark** feature allows you to mark a location in a document so you can return quickly to that location. This is a convenient feature if, for example, you are editing a large document and have to leave your work for a time. When you return to work, you can open your file, find the bookmark in your document and quickly return to the place you had marked. Or, you might not have all the information needed to complete your document when you begin. Setting a bookmark will enable you to return to the section of the document which needs development or information inserted.

- There are two types of bookmarks: a QuickMark and a named bookmark. You can have only one QuickMark in a document, but you can have as many named bookmarks in a document as you desire. The bookmark name can be the first line of a paragraph, one word or one character.

- To insert a bookmark, position your insertion point at the bookmark location, then select Bookmark from the Tools menu. In the Bookmark dialog box that follows, click Create, type a bookmark name and click OK. The name of your bookmark will be added to the Bookmarks window. To set a QuickMark, click the Set QuickMark button.

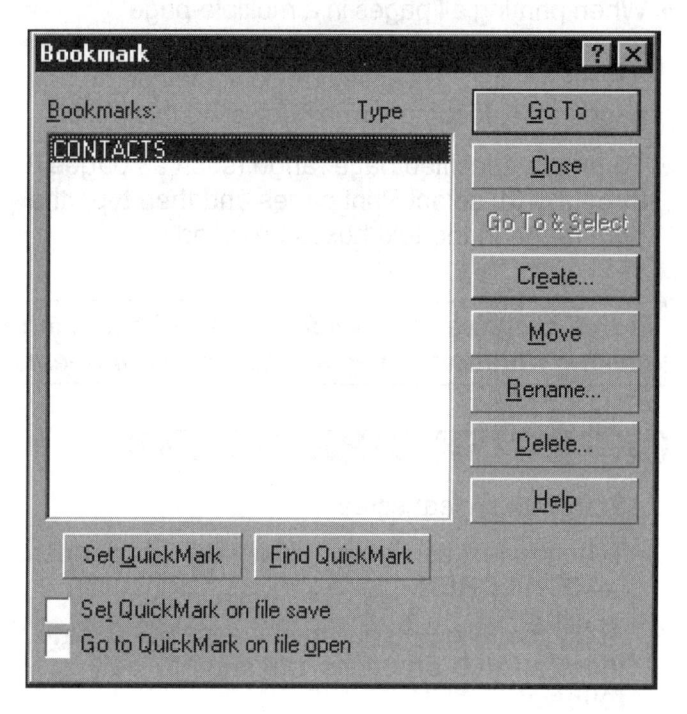

- To return to a bookmark, select Bookmark from the Tools menu. In the Bookmark dialog box that follows, click the bookmark name to which you wish to return, and click Go To. To return to a QuickMark, click the Find QuickMark button. You can also use the Go To feature to return to a bookmark location (see right).

- Your insertion point may be anywhere in the document when finding a bookmark.

Print Multiple Pages

- WordPerfect prints the full document by default. However, you can specify how much of the document you wish to print: current page, multiple pages, selected text, document summary, or document on disk.

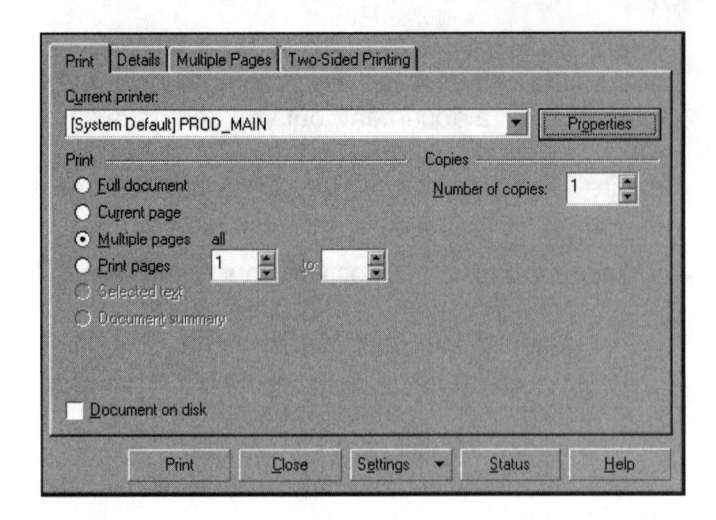

COREL WORDPERFECT 8 Lesson 5: Work with Multiple-Page Documents

- To print various pages within a document (such as pages 2, 4, 7 and pages 12-20, etc.), select the Multiple Pages option, then click the Multiple Pages tab of the Print to dialog box and enter the page numbers and range you wish to print.

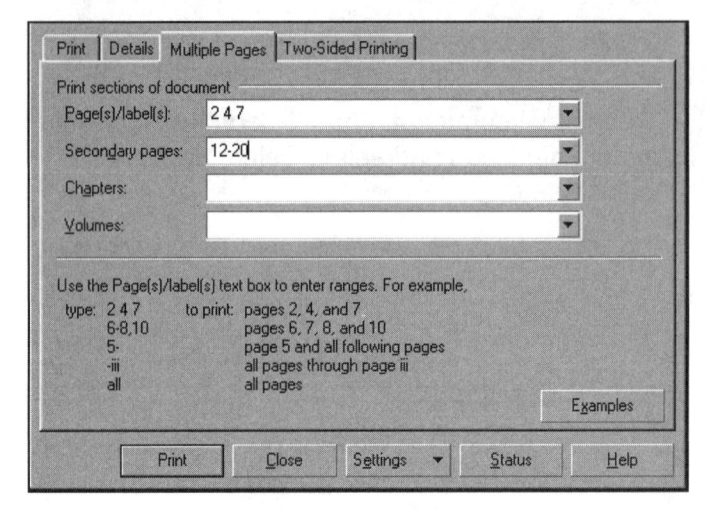

- When printing all pages in a multiple-page document, select the Full Document from the Print drop-down list. The insertion point may be on any page in the document when selecting this option.

- To print a specified page range (such as pages 3 through 10), select Print pages and then type the print range in the text boxes provided.

In this exercise, you will format a full-block letter from a rough-draft copy and insert special mailing notations. You will also add comments to the document.

EXERCISE DIRECTIONS

1. Start with a clear screen.
2. Type the text as shown in Illustration A, or open 🖫**30CHILDREN**.
3. Apply the following document settings. **Create Illustration B on pages 136 and 137 as follows**:
    a. Set left and right margins to 1.25".
    b. Create a centered letterhead in a 16-point sans serif font that reads: CHILDREN FIRST
    c. Insert a 16-point wingding on each side of the heading.
    d. Begin the letter at approximately 2.5" from the top of the page.
    e. Italicize the words "The New York Times" in the first paragraph.
4. Type the new text as shown.
5. Insert the following special notations in the letter (refer to Illustration B for proper placement):
    - REGISTERED MAIL
    - Re: CHILDREN FIRST CAPITAL CAMPAIGN
    - mv/yo
    - Enclosure
    - Copy to: Beth Billingham
6. Create a header that includes the name of the addressee, the page number code preceded by the word "Page", and today's date in sans serif 10 point; suppress the header on the first page.
    ✓ *Be sure to also set left and right header margins to 1.25".*
7. Add the following comments where shown.
    - Include Packet B with Mailing.
    - Journalists' names available upon request.
8. Add the following bookmarks where shown.
   Name the first one:
       Ms. Furman-Burke Quote

   Name the first one:
       Senator Deacon Quote
9. Use Make-It-Fit feature, if necessary, to make letter fit on two pages.
10. Preview the document.
11. Print one copy.
12. Save the file; name it **CHILDREN**.
13. Close the file; save the changes.

ILLUSTRATION A

Today's Date
Ms. Abigail Porter
30 United Nations Plaza
New York, NY 10018
Dear Ms. Porter:
Thank you for your sincere interest in Children First's capital campaign. I am pleased to enclose an information packet that includes summaries of our programs, our annual report, copies of our most recent newsletter and news articles in local papers that highlight the work that we are doing. As I am sure you know, we have recently been the focus of several articles in the City section of The New York Times.¶
Here are some of the great things that people are saying about Children First: ¶
Ms. Mary Furman-Burke, President of the National Foundation for Children and Senior Consultant to the Vice-President of the United States on family policy, said: ¶
"I am proud that Children First was founded in my home state." ¶
As a prominent member of the National Committee on Children and Families, Ms. Martha Manning also praised Children First and said: ¶
"Children First has paved the way for improved services for children and families. Their hard work has resulted in significant changes in New York City." ¶
These are just some of the positive reactions that we have had to our programs. I know that you will enjoy reading through our literature and learning more about us. We will be sure to include you on our mailing list, so that you receive all press updates and information concerning special events and meetings. ¶
I would also like to arrange an appointment for you to meet with our Executive Director, Beth Billingham. I will contact you later this week, so that we can find a time that is convenient for you. ¶Cordially, Marta Villarta Director of Development

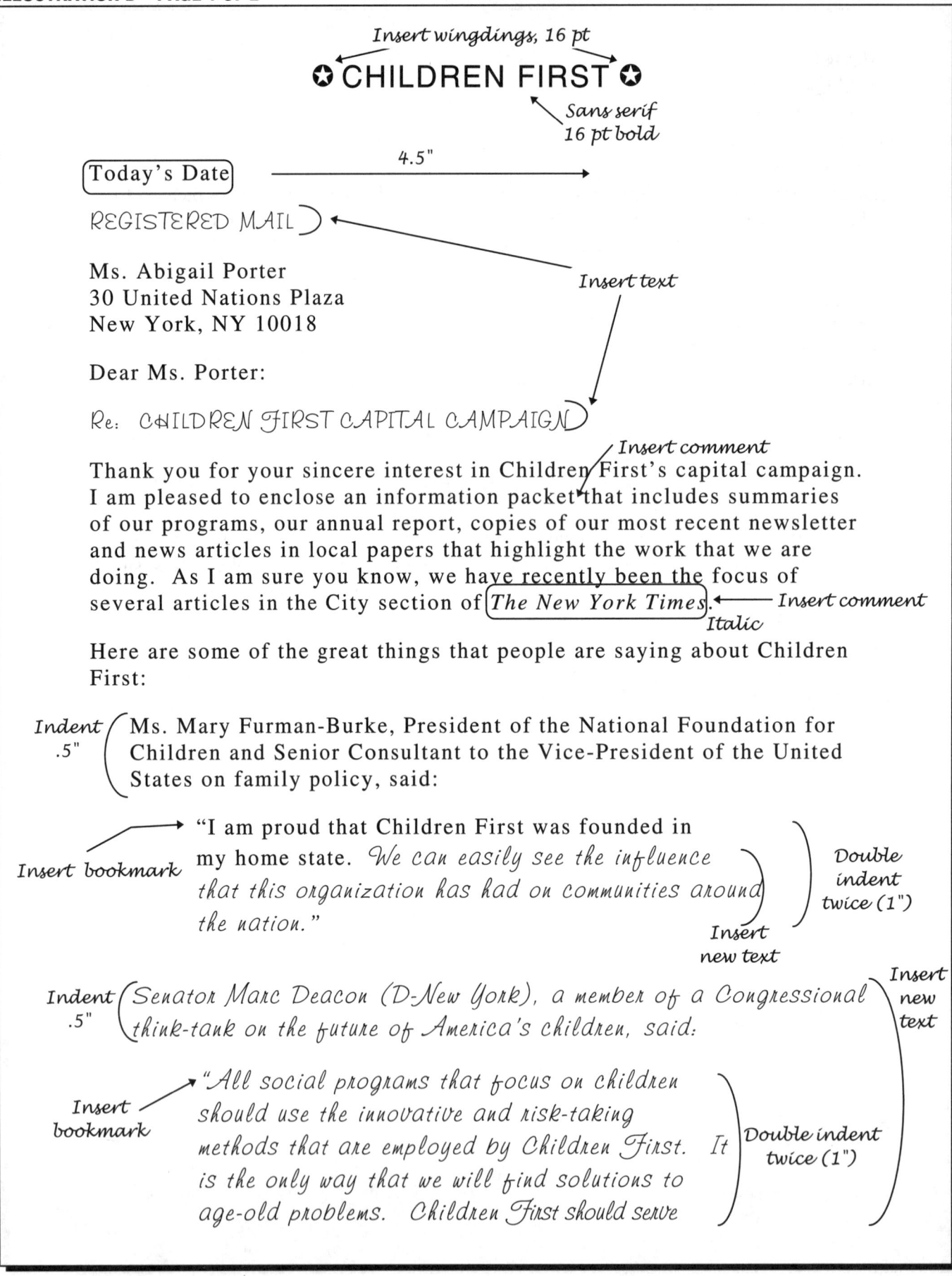

ILLUSTRATION B – PAGE 1 OF 2

Insert wingdings, 16 pt

✪ CHILDREN FIRST ✪

Sans serif 16 pt bold

Today's Date ←—— 4.5" ——→

REGISTERED MAIL *(Insert text)*

Ms. Abigail Porter
30 United Nations Plaza
New York, NY 10018

Dear Ms. Porter:

Re: CHILDREN FIRST CAPITAL CAMPAIGN

Insert comment

Thank you for your sincere interest in Children First's capital campaign. I am pleased to enclose an information packet that includes summaries of our programs, our annual report, copies of our most recent newsletter and news articles in local papers that highlight the work that we are doing. As I am sure you know, we have recently been the focus of several articles in the City section of *The New York Times*. ←—— *Insert comment* / *Italic*

Here are some of the great things that people are saying about Children First:

Indent .5" — Ms. Mary Furman-Burke, President of the National Foundation for Children and Senior Consultant to the Vice-President of the United States on family policy, said:

Insert bookmark → "I am proud that Children First was founded in my home state. *We can easily see the influence that this organization has had on communities around the nation.*" *Double indent twice (1")* / *Insert new text*

Indent .5" — *Senator Marc Deacon (D-New York), a member of a Congressional think-tank on the future of America's children, said:* *Insert new text*

Insert bookmark → "*All social programs that focus on children should use the innovative and risk-taking methods that are employed by Children First. It is the only way that we will find solutions to age-old problems. Children First should serve* *Double indent twice (1")*

Ms. Abigail Porter
Page 2
Today's Date

as a national model when thinking about creating policy for the twenty-first century.") **Insert new text**

Indent .5" (As a prominent member of the National Committee on Children and Families, Ms. Martha Manning also praised Children First and said:

"Children First has paved the way for improved services for children and families. Their hard work has resulted in significant changes in New York City.") *Double indent twice (1")*

These are just some of the positive reactions that we have had to our programs. I know that you will enjoy reading through our literature and learning more about us.

We will be sure to include you on our mailing list, so that you receive all press updates and information concerning special events and meetings.

I would also like to arrange an appointment for you to meet with our Executive Director, Beth Billingham. I will contact you later this week, so that we can find a time that is convenient for you.

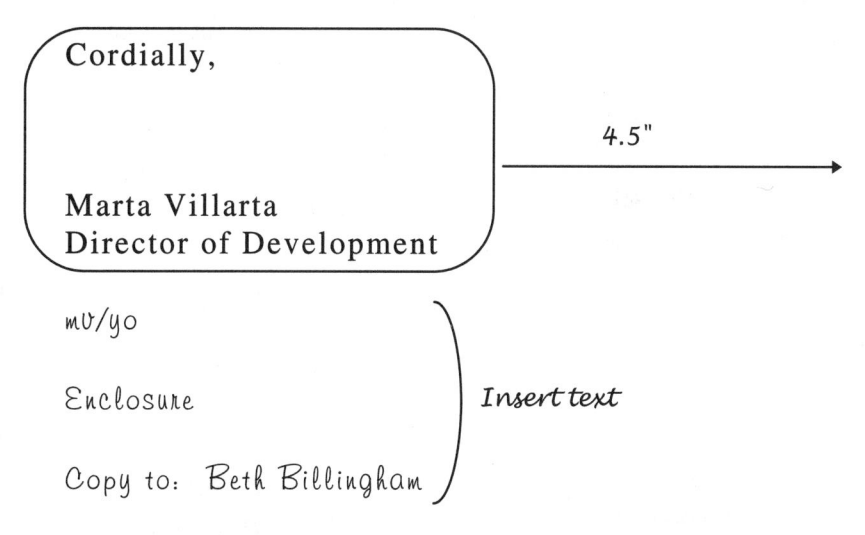

Cordially,

⟶ 4.5"

Marta Villarta
Director of Development

mv/yo

Enclosure   ) *Insert text*

Copy to: Beth Billingham

KEYSTROKES

INSERT COMMENTS

1. Place insertion point where you want to insert comment.
2. Click **I**nsert .... Alt + I
3. Click Co**m**ment .... M
4. Click **C**reate .... Alt + C
5. Type comment in window.
   - Click buttons on Comment Feature Bar to add desired items:

     | Initials | Initials |
     | Name | Name |
     | Date | :10: |
     | Time | Time |

6. Click the **Close** button.

Convert comment to text:

1. Click comment to convert to text.
2. Click **I**nsert .... Alt + I
3. Click Co**m**ment .... M
4. Click Convert to **T**ext .... T

   OR

   In Page or Two Page View:
   - Click the comment icon.
   - Right click the comment.
   - Click **C**onvert to Text C

DELETE A COMMENT

1. Right click the comment or comment icon.
2. Click **D**elete .... D

EDIT A COMMENT

1. Double-click comment icon or initial box.

   ✓ *The comment window opens.*

2. Retype the comment as desired.
3. Click the **Close** button.

SET A BOOKMARK

1. Place insertion point where you want to set bookmark.
2. Click **T**ools .... Alt + T
3. Click **B**ookmark .... B
4. Click Cr**e**ate .... E
5. Click in **Bookmark name** text box.

   ✓ *The **Bookmark Name** text box automatically displays text following the insertion point.*

6. Click **OK** .... Enter

   to accept text as bookmark name.

   OR

   Type new bookmark name.

7. Click **OK** .... Enter

FIND BOOKMARK

1. Click **T**ools .... Alt + T
2. Click **B**ookmark .... B
3. Highlight name of bookmark to find.
4. Click **G**o To .... G

Exercise 31

- Footnotes
- Endnotes
- Edit Footnotes or Endnotes
- Widow and Orphan Lines

NOTES

Footnotes

- A **footnote** gives information about the source of quoted material. The information includes the author's name, the publication, the publication date, and the page number from which the quote was taken.

- There are several footnoting styles. Traditional footnotes are printed at the bottom of a page. A separator line separates footnote text from the text on the page.

- A reference number appears immediately after the quote in the text, and a corresponding footnote number or symbol appears at the bottom of the page.

- The Footnote feature automatically inserts the reference number after the quote, inserts the separator line, numbers the footnote, and formats your page so that the footnote appears on the same page as the reference number. If you desire endnotes instead of footnotes, WordPerfect will change footnote information into endnotes and, if desired, back again to footnotes. (See **Endnotes** on the following pages.)

- The actual note may be viewed in Page view if you scroll to the bottom of the page. To see how the page will format, select Two Page from the View menu, or click the Zoom button on the WordPerfect 8 toolbar and select Full Page.

- Footnotes are inserted by placing the insertion point at the end of the text you want to footnote and selecting Footnote/Endnote from the Insert menu. In the Footnote/Endnote dialog box that follows, select Footnote Number, enter the note number, and click Create.

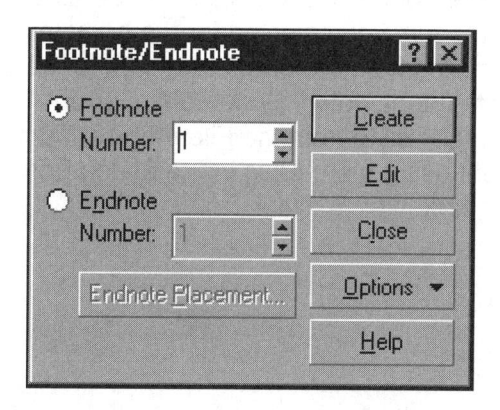

IMMIGRATION TO THE UNITED STATES
IN THE NINETEENTH CENTURY

The United States is sometimes called the "Nation of Immigrants" because it has received more immigrants than any other country in history. During the first one hundred years of US history, the nation had no immigration laws. Immigration began to climb during the 1830s. "Between 1830-1840, 44% of the immigrants came from Ireland, 30% came from Germany, 15% came from Great Britain, and the remainder came from other European countries."[1]

Most German immigrants settled in the middle western states of Ohio, Indiana, Illinois, Wisconsin and Missouri. With encouragement to move west from the Homestead Act of 1862, which offered public land free to immigrants who intended to become citizens, German immigrants comprised a large portion of the pioneers moving west. They were masterful farmers and they built prosperous farms.

The movement to America of millions of immigrants in the century after the 1820s was not simply a flight of impoverished peasants abandoning underdeveloped, backward regions for the riches and unlimited opportunities offered by the American economy. People did not move randomly to America but emanated from very specific regions at specific times in the nineteenth and twentieth centuries. "It is impossible to

[Footnote number]
[Separator line]

[1]Lewis Paul Todd and Merle Curti, *Rise of the American Nation* (New York: Harcourt Brace Jovanovich, Inc., 1972), 297.

COREL WORDPERFECT 8 Lesson 5: Work with Multiple-Page Documents

- In the screen that follows, the first footnote number appears, ready for you to type the first footnote. After entering the footnote text, click the Close button to return to body text.

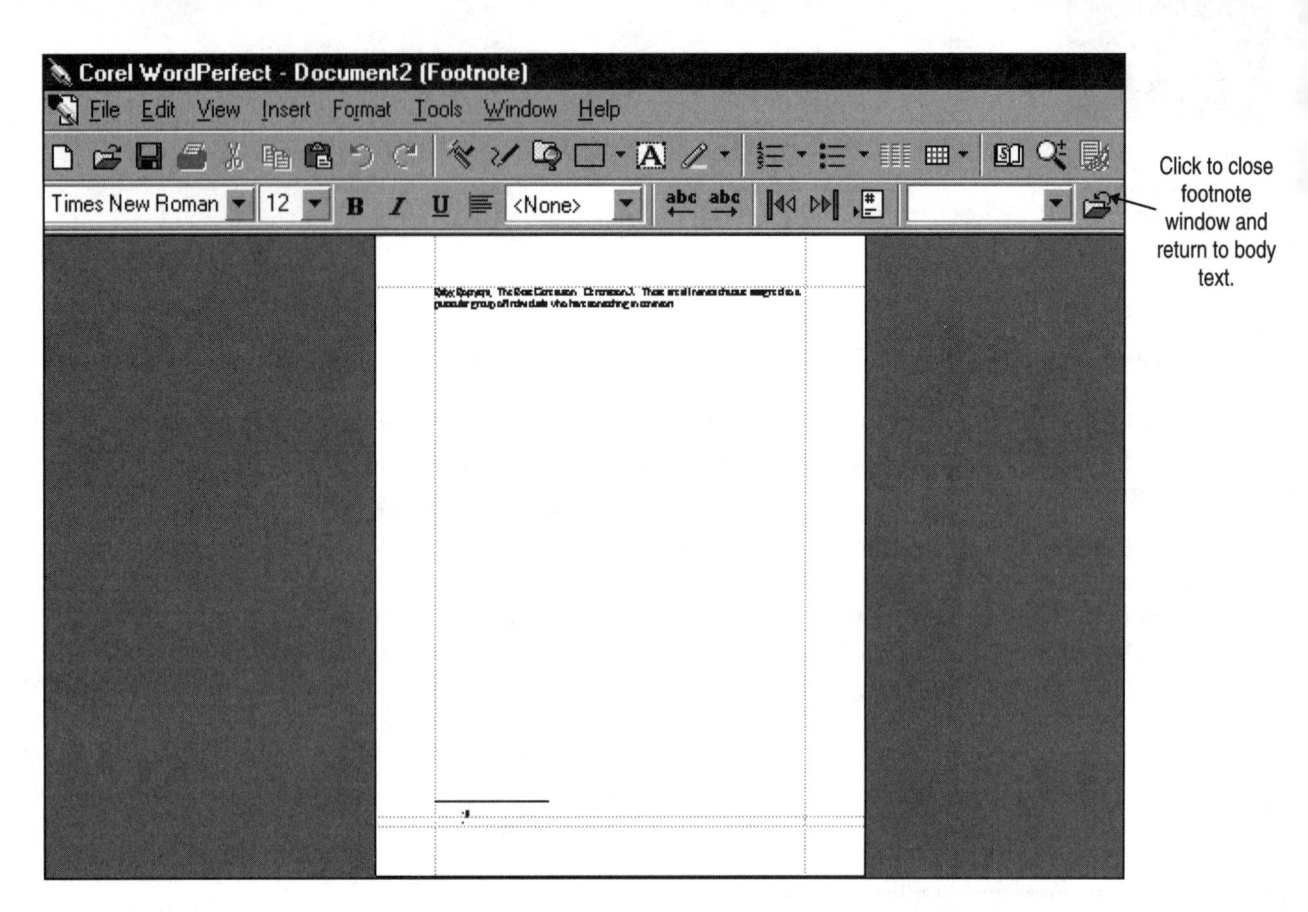

Click to close footnote window and return to body text.

- Footnote/Endnote buttons display on the Property Bar to make it easier to work with this feature.

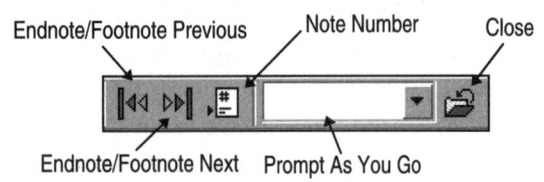

  Endnote/Footnote Previous — Note Number — Close
  Endnote/Footnote Next — Prompt As You Go

- Footnotes and endnotes are printed using the document default font, which may be different from the font you selected for the body text. To change the footnote or endnote font to match the body text font, select Document, Current Document Style from the File menu. Change the font using the menus in the Styles Editor dialog box.

- Similarly, a margin change does not affect footnote text margins. To change margins for the entire document including the footnote text, you must change document margins. To do so, select Document, Current Document Style from the File menu. In the Styles Editor dialog box that follows, select Margins from the Format menu. Make the desired margins changes and click OK.

Endnotes

- An **endnote** contains the same information as a footnote, but is printed at the end of a document or on a separate page and differs in format. Compare the endnote illustrations below with the footnotes shown in the exercise illustrated on page 139.

Endnotes at the End of a Document

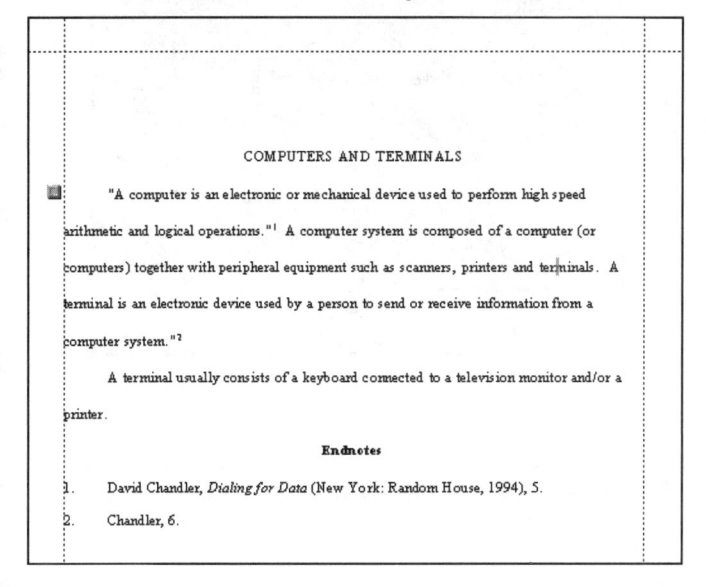

Endnotes on a Separate Page

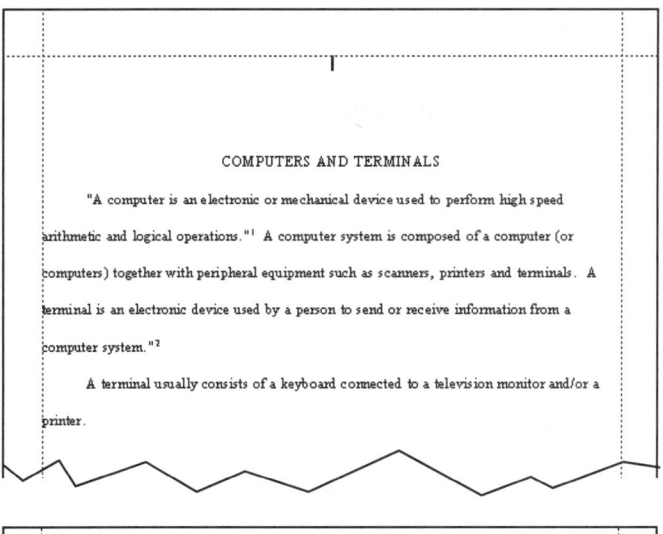

- When endnotes are created, they appear at the end of the document text. Each note number is indicated by an Arabic number and a period. You may space twice after the period or use the Indent button on the Format toolbar before typing endnote text.

- To force endnotes onto a separate page, place the insertion point below the last line of document text and press Ctrl + Enter or click Insert, New Page.

- Like footnotes, endnotes may be viewed in Page or Two Page view if you scroll to the bottom of the page. To see how the page will format, select Two Page from the View menu, or click the Zoom button on the WordPerfect 8 toolbar and select Full Page.

- To create an endnote, place the insertion point at the end of the text you want to note. Then, select Footnote/Endnote from the Insert menu. In the Footnote/Endnote dialog box that follows, select Endnote Number. Type the endnote number, and click Create. After entering the endnote, click the Close button to return to the document text.

- To convert footnotes into endnotes or endnotes into footnotes, click the appropriate button on the Shipping Macros toolbar.

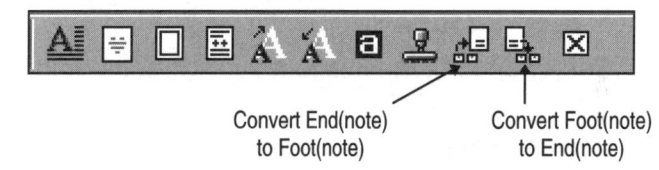

Convert End(note) to Foot(note)
Convert Foot(note) to End(note)

Edit Footnotes or Endnotes

- If you need to make a correction to a footnote or endnote, you may return to the footnote window and edit the note. When you edit, add, or delete footnotes or endnotes, WordPerfect renumbers and reformats them as necessary.

- To edit a footnote or endnote, select Footnote/Endnote from the Insert menu. In the dialog box that follows, type the footnote or endnote number you want to edit and click Edit. This will display the footnote or endnote screen and place your insertion point in the footnote or endnote to be edited. You can also edit a footnote or endnote by clicking in the footnote or endnote area of the document and making the desired changes.

COREL WORDPERFECT 8   Lesson 5:   Work with Multiple-Page Documents

- To move to the previous or next note, click the Next or Previous button on the Property Bar. Click the Close button to return to your document when you have completed your edits.

- To delete, copy or move a footnote or endnote, edit the reference mark, not the footnote or endnote text. If you delete, copy or move the footnote or endnote text, the reference number will remain where it was inserted. When you delete, copy or move reference numbers, WordPerfect renumbers and reformats all footnote and endnote references and text.

Widow and Orphan Lines

- A **widow** occurs when the last line of a paragraph is printed by itself at the top of a page. An **orphan** occurs when the first line of a paragraph appears by itself at the bottom of a page. Widow and orphan lines should be avoided.

- The Keep Text Together feature eliminates widows and orphans in a document. It may be accessed by selecting Keep Text Together from the Format menu. In the Keep Text Together dialog box which follows, click the Widow/Orphan check box to turn on the feature.

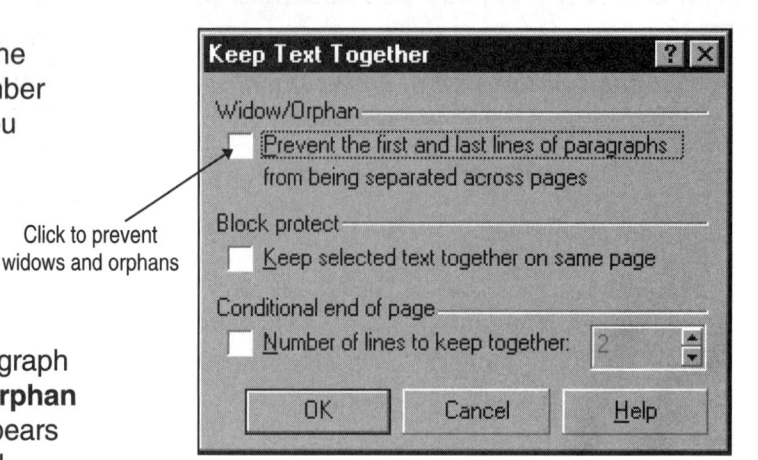

Click to prevent widows and orphans

Keep Text Together dialog box:
- Widow/Orphan: Prevent the first and last lines of paragraphs from being separated across pages
- Block protect: Keep selected text together on same page
- Conditional end of page: Number of lines to keep together: 2
- OK / Cancel / Help

In this exercise, you will create a report with footnotes, then convert the footnotes into endnotes appearing on a separate page.

EXERCISE DIRECTIONS

1. Start with a clear screen.
2. Create the report shown on the following page, or open **31LEARN**.
3. Center and set the title to a serif 16-point bold font.
4. Begin the exercise on approximately Ln 2".
5. Use a serif 13-point font for the document.
6. Set 1.25" left and right margins for the entire document.
   - ✓ *If you want the header, footer, and/or footnotes to align with the body text, you must set margins for the document, not for the page. If you want the document font face, size, and style to apply to header or footer text, you must change the default document font settings. See the keystrokes on page 145 to do so.*
7. Set line spacing to double after typing the title.
8. Set paragraph indentation as indicated in the illustration.
9. Create the following header using a serif 10 point italic font: LEARNING ABOUT THE INTERNET. Include a page number as part of the header. Suppress the header and page number on the first page.
10. Create each footnote as it appears in the illustration.
11. Use widow and orphan protection.
12. Spell check.
13. Preview your document.
14. Edit the header to read, INTERNET.
15. Print one copy.
16. Save the file; name it **LEARN**.
17. Display the Shipping Macros toolbar.
18. Convert all footnotes to endnotes and force them onto a separate page. Insert an indent, two spaces, or a tab between the endnote numbers and text.
19. Print one copy.
20. Save the file as **LEARN2**.
21. Close the document window.

LEARNING ABOUT THE INTERNET

The Internet, or "information superhighway" to which it is often referred, is a communications system that can be accessed by the public. It is used to access information about anything, from the weather in Africa, to the latest presidential address, to current movie reviews.

The Internet is a huge computer network. Actually, it is the world's largest computer network. This network allows the computers that are connected to share information with each other. The information flows from one computer to another over electronic wires. This information can be letters, (called e-mail on the Internet), reports, magazine articles, books, pictures, etc. Computers are even able to exchange music and videos over these electronic wires!

The Internet provides services. The two most frequently used services are e-mail and the World Wide Web.

E-mail is a system that allows messages to be sent from one computer to another. These messages might include sounds, pictures, spreadsheets, as well as software files. Before using e-mail, it is necessary that both correspondents have e-mail "addresses." An e-mail address has the same function as a home address—it allows mail to be appropriately delivered to the correct mailbox, and thus, the correct recipient. E-mail addresses usually contain three parts. The first part is the account name; the second part is the domain name and the third part contains an extension which classifies the computer user's address as belonging to a company, government agency or a school. The domain name is "the address, or name, of the company, Internet service provider or school that is giving the Internet access."[1] The account name and the domain name are separated by an "@" symbol. A common e-mail address for Peter Clark at Tennessee State University who gets his Internet service from the university might be: pclark@tsu.edu. "Edu." represents an educational address.

The World Wide Web, or the WWW, is the "fastest growing service on the Internet."[2] It is also the most visual and interesting service on the Internet. The WWW is made up of pages which are created by companies, individuals, schools and government agencies around the world. Each page has an address and can be accessed by typing the exact address in an appropriate textbox on the screen. Pages are also accessed by conducting a search of the pages on the WWW. This is done by using search engines, such as Lycos, Excite, Yahoo and Infoseek. After entering the subject to be searched, the search engine provides topics relating to your inquiry. These topics are underlined and highlighted and can be accessed by clicking them. These underlined, highlighted words are known as *hypertext*—links to other pages relating to the search topic.

---

[1] Samantha Blane, *Using E-mail* (New York: University Press, 1996), 25.

[2] Ned Peterson, *The Internet and Beyond* (New York City: Halpern Publishers 1997), 3.

"Hypertext is text that is highlighted and/or underlined, which when clicked on with the left mouse button, will provide access to additional information that it describes."[3] "The World Wide Web is a system without boundaries. It has no capacity limit, either. Web pages are being added every minute of the day, all over the world."[4]

You might hear the term, "URL." This stands for "Uniform Resource Locator," a formal name for "web address." A typical URL might be **http://www.vicinity.com.** This address provides a direct link to a particular Web page. So, instead of clicking hypertext links to get to a particular page, you can enter the URL the quick way to go to the source.

The Internet is an amazing information and communication source that has made the world a much smaller place. International communication has become as simple as the touch of a button, and visits to other countries have been made possible by viewing the vast photographs and videos that can be accessed on the Internet.

---

[3] Natasha Banks, *Understanding the Internet* (Los Angeles: CompuBooks, Inc. 1996), 104.

[4] Banks, 106.

KEYSTROKES

CHANGE DOCUMENT MARGINS

1. Click **F**ile .... `Alt`+`F`
2. Click **D**ocument .... `D`
3. Click Current **D**ocument Style .... `D`
4. Click Fo**r**mat .... `Alt`+`R`
   in **Styles Editor** dialog box.
5. Click **M**argins .... `M`
6. Change left and right margins.
7. Click **OK** .... `Enter`
8. Click **OK**. .... `Enter`

CHANGE CURRENT DOCUMENT FONT STYLE OR SIZE

1. Click **F**ile .... `Alt`+`F`
2. Click **D**ocument .... `D`
3. Click Default **F**ont .... `F`
4. Select desired option(s):
   - **F**ont face .... `Alt`+`F`, `↕`
   - Font **s**ize .... `Alt`+`S`, `↕`
   - F**o**nt style .... `Alt`+`O`, `↕`
5. Click **OK** .... `Enter`

FOOTNOTE

1. Type up to the first reference number.
   OR
   Place insertion point at the location where first reference number will appear.
2. Click **I**nsert .... `Alt`+`I`
3. Click **F**ootnote/Endnote .... `F`
4. Select **F**ootnote .... `Alt`+`F`
5. Type footnote number to create.
6. Click **C**reate .... `Alt`+`C`
   ✓ *A blank window appears displaying the separation line and the assigned footnote number.*

7. Type footnote text.
8. Click **C**lose button 📁 to return to body text.
   ✓ *The reference number is automatically inserted in the document.*
9. Repeat steps 1-8 for each footnote.

ENDNOTE

1. Type up to the first reference number.
   OR
   Place insertion point where reference number will appear.
2. Click **I**nsert .... `Alt`+`I`
3. Click **F**ootnote/Endnote .... `F`
4. Select E**n**dnote .... `Alt`+`N`
5. Type endnote number to create.
6. Click **C**reate .... `Alt`+`C`
   ✓ *A blank window appears with an automatically assigned reference number.*
7. Type endnote text.
8. Click **C**lose button 📁 to return to body text.
9. Repeat steps 1-8 for each endnote.

PLACE ENDNOTES ON SEPARATE PAGE

1. Place insertion point at the end of the last line of text.
2. Press **Ctrl + Enter** .... `Ctrl`+`Enter`
   OR
   a. Click **I**nsert .... `Alt`+`I`
   b. Click New **P**age .... `P`

EDIT FOOTNOTE OR ENDNOTE

1. Click **I**nsert .... `Alt`+`I`
2. Click **F**ootnote/Endnote .... `F`
3. Select **F**ootnote Number .... `Alt`+`F`
   OR
   Select E**n**dnote Number .... `Alt`+`N`
4. Type footnote or endnote number to edit.
5. Click **E**dit .... `Alt`+`E`
6. Make desired correction.
7. To move from note to note,
   click **Endnote/Footnote Previous** button ⏮.
   OR
   click **Endnote/Footnote Next** button ⏭.
8. Click **C**lose button 📁 to return to body text.

CONVERT FOOTNOTES TO ENDNOTES OR ENDNOTES TO FOOTNOTES

1. Display Shipping Macros toolbar (Right click on current toolbar and select Shipping Macros).
2. Click **Convert End to Foot** button or Click **Convert Foot to End** button.

SET WIDOW/ORPHAN PROTECTION

1. Place insertion point on page where you want protection to begin.
2. Click Fo**r**mat .... `Alt`+`R`
3. Click **K**eep Text Together .... `K`
4. Click **P**revent the First and Last ..... `P`
   Lines of Paragraphs from Being Separated Across Pages check box.
5. Click **OK** .... `Enter`

Exercise 32

- **Page Numbering Positions and Formats**
- **Go To**
- **File Stamp**

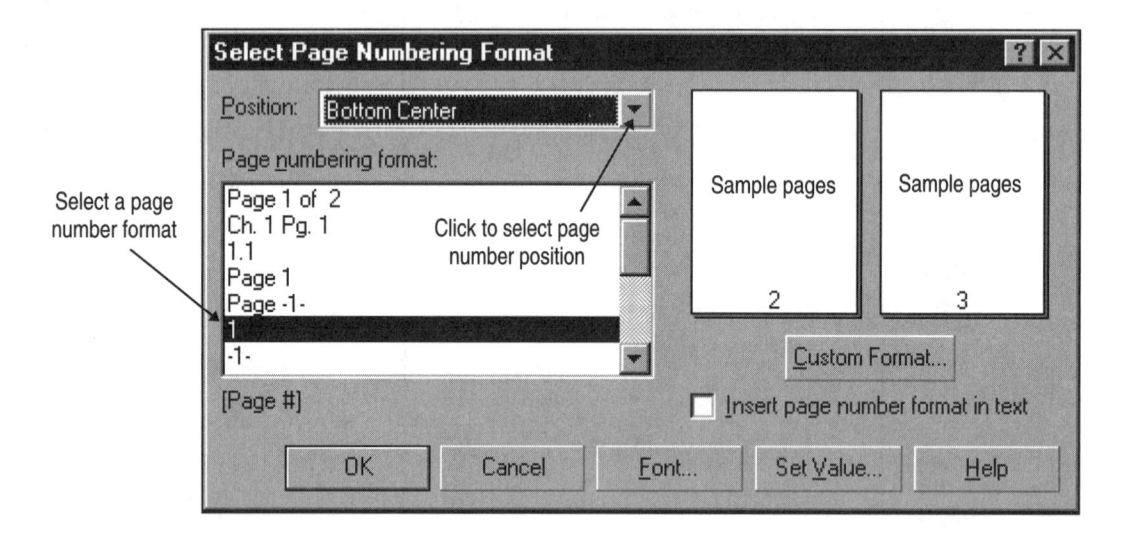

NOTES

Page Numbering

- WordPerfect 8 numbers pages automatically. In exercise 29, you used the Insert page Number button on the Header/Footer Property Bar to insert a page number into a header. You can also use the **Page Numbering** feature to insert page numbers in various positions within a document.

- To display page numbers, you must turn on the **Page Numbering** feature. Once the feature is turned on, you can choose a page numbering style and position.

- To turn on page numbering, select Page, Numbering from the Format menu. In the Select Page Numbering Format dialog box that follows, select a page number Position from the drop-down menu and a Page numbering format from the list box. The preview window displays your selection.

- Page numbers appear in the default font. To change the page number font, click the Font button in the select Page Numbering Format dialog box, and select a new font style, size, or color.

- To create a page number style other than those preformatted by WordPerfect, click the Custom Format button, and choose a desired option.

- Like headers and footers, page numbers should not appear on the first page of a multiple-page document. See Ex 45, Keystrokes section for instructions to suppress page numbers.

Go To

- The **Go To** feature may be used to advance quickly to a specific place in your document. You can advance to a specific position in the document, a specific page, a bookmark or a specific table and cell.

- To access the Go To feature, select Go To from the Edit menu or press Ctrl + G. In the Go To dialog box that follows, click the desired go to option and the place you wish to go to within that option. After clicking OK, your insertion point will jump to the go to location you specified.

- To insert the filename in a header or footer, use the File Stamp button on the Shipping Macros toolbar. This method opens the File Stamp Options dialog box in which you can change the font size and style, indicate a justification option for the filename, and select a header or footer in which to place it.

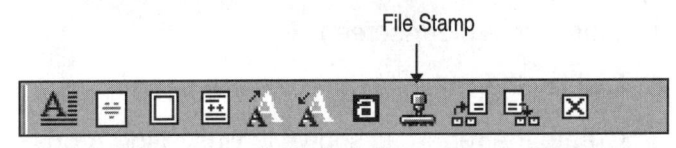

File Stamp

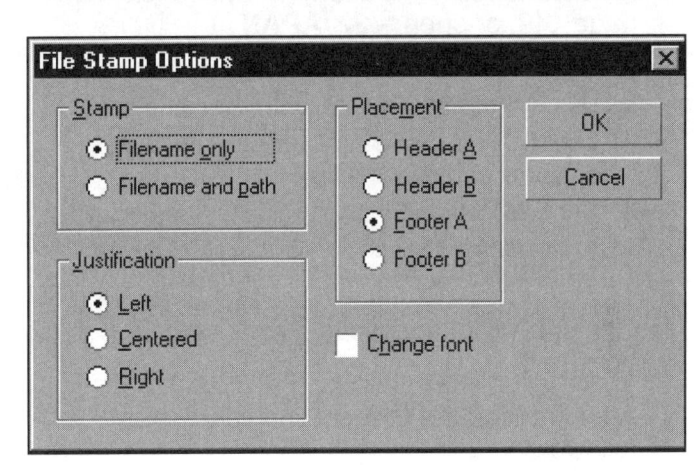

✓ *Note: If the Filestamp feature does not work, check to see that the Filestmp macro is included in the Macros folder (C:\Corel\Suite8\Macros). If it is not, you can run a custom install to install it.*

- The **File Stamp** feature allows you to insert the current filename in a document or within a header and/or footer.

- Including a filename and path on a document is a convenient way to later locate that file in the computer. In a letter, filenames are generally indicated below the typist's initials and should appear on the file copy only. In a report, filenames may be indicated as footer text at the bottom left or right of the document. It is recommended that the filenames that appear in a letter or a report use a font size that is smaller than the body text.

- To insert a filename, select Other, Filename (or Path and Filename) from the Insert menu. This method will insert the document filename at the insertion point position.

COREL WORDPERFECT 8 Lesson 5: Work with Multiple-Page Documents

> In Part I of this exercise, you will create a report with endnotes, a header, and a bottom right-aligned page number. You will also insert the filename and path into your document. Remember to suppress the header and page number on the first page. In Part II of this exercise, you will open a document you created earlier and use the GoTo feature to access bookmarks.

EXERCISE DIRECTIONS

PART I

1. Start with a clear screen.
2. Display the Shipping Macros toolbar.
3. Create the report as shown in Illustration A on page 149, or open **32JAPAN**.
   a. Begin the exercise on approximately Ln 2".
   b. Use a serif 12-point font for the document.
   c. Use the Endnote feature to insert reference numbers and endnote text.
   d. Set 1.25" left and right margins for the document.
   ✓ *Change the font size and the margins using the Current Style feature (select File, Document, Current Style).*
4. Center and set the title to a sans serif 16-point bold font.
5. After creating the title, set line spacing as follows:
   - First paragraph   1.0
   - Remaining paragraphs   2.0

   ✓ *The report shown is single spaced. Be sure to double space your report as indicated. It should come to three pages total.*
6. Double indent the first paragraph of quotation text 1".
7. Create a 1" first line indent for each body text paragraph.
   ✓ *Do not indent headings.*
8. Format the first heading (An Introduction) to a 12-point sans serif bold font. Use QuickFormat to format the remaining headings.
9. Create the following right-aligned header using a script 14-point font: Dreaming Japan
10. Insert page numbering.
    a. Use Page 1 of 1 number format.
    b. Position it at the bottom right of the page.
11. Suppress the header and page numbering on the first page.
12. Turn hyphenation on.
13. Use widow/orphan protection.
14. Spell check.
15. Edit the header to read: Japan
16. Insert the filename and path using the File Stamp button on the Shipping Macros toolbar.
    a. Position the filename and path at the bottom left of the document as Footer A.
    b. Size the filename and path to an 8-point font.
    ✓ *The page number will now appear inside the footer along with the filename and path.*
    c. Suppress the Footer on the first page.
17. Double space all body text.
18. Preview your document.
19. Adjust any awkward page breaks, if necessary.
20. Print one copy.
21. Save the file; name it **JAPAN**.
22. Close the document window.

JAPAN

I dreamt of Japan long before I went there. Moss gardens, straw-mat rooms, wooden bridges arching in the moonlight, paper lanterns with the fire glowing inside. Whenever I paged through photography books of traditional Japan, I found myself gasping with appreciation. Three rocks, a gnarled pine tree, raked white sand: awe.[1]

AN INTRODUCTION

The country of Japan is an archipelago consisting of four main islands – Kyushu, Shikoku, Honshu, and Hokkaido – and about 3,900 smaller islands. Since Japan is so large with so many different landscapes, ranging from small fishing communities to large urban centers, from flat plains to towering mountain ranges, the climate varies from region to region and from season to season. The Japanese people have a "sense of uniqueness" that theirs is a culture and race distinct from any other, but "Theories regarding the racial origins of the Japanese cite both the north and the south – Manchuria and Siberia, and the South China or Indochina regions – as likely possibilities."[2] And most Japanese, while identifying themselves as either Shinto or Buddhist, do not have the same strict religious boundaries as one finds in the West.

ART AND TRADITION

The Japanese have several artistic forms of expression that are well-known and considered to embody the tradition and spirit of Japan. At a most basic level, most Americans are familiar with the simplicity of origami, a method of folding paper into beautiful formations, such as birds. In addition, the Japanese practice a form of traditional calligraphy, scripting the ancient *kanji*, characters where "each single character contains a concept… Each character has many layers of meaning, giving *kanji* especially rich connotative powers."[3] In addition, the Japanese have strong traditions in textiles, ceramics, painting, and bamboo work.

There are five forms of traditional Japanese theater—the two most significant are *noh* and *kabuki*. *Noh* drama is considered classical and dates back to the early fifteenth century. "As an art form, its high degree of stylization, lack of overt action, and monotonous-sounding vocal declamation makes it a distinctly acquired taste."[4] In contrast, *kabuki* is much more modern. "*Kabuki* is the equivalent of cabaret spectacular, soap opera, morality play, religious pageant, and tear-jerker. It is music and dance and story and color and pathos and farce and everything a theater-goer could want."[5]

PART I (Page 2 of 2)

Japan

LANGUAGE

The Japanese language is complex and often seems impenetrable to the outsider. The language is based on three alphabets: *kanji*, *katakana* and *hiragana*. *Kanji* is a hieroglyphic, character-based script that was inherited from the Chinese. There are over eighteen hundred *kanji*, and the Japanese use them all. *Katakana* and *hiragana* are supportive alphabets that are often used to incorporate foreign terminology or contemporary meanings into the Japanese language.

THE CHANGING ENVIRONMENT

Industrialization and modernization have brought about many changes to the culture and natural environment that one often thinks of when thinking of Japan. "Forget rocks and raked sand! Neon everywhere, billboards as far as the eye could see, concrete apartment blocks dingy with pollution. Even the details radiated a sense of urbanization run amok."[6] This transformation is often dismissed as the necessary price to pay for economic prosperity and an increased role in the global culture and marketplace. However, Japan is still a place like no other. "The changes taking place in the cultural world, the rumblings of economic revolution in the bureaucracy and in business – all of this is exciting in a way in which Japan has not been exciting for decades."

1. APA Publications, *Insight Guides: Japan* (Boston: Houghton Mifflin, 1997), 63.

2. Davidson, Cathy N., *36 Views of Mount Fuji* (New York: Plume, 1993), 5.

3. Kerr, Alex, *Lost Japan* (Australia: Lonely Planet Publications, 1996), 123.

4. APA Publications, 99.

5. APA Publications, 100.

6. Davidson, 5.

Use Filestamp feature to insert file name and path.

Page 2 of 2

PART II

✪ CHILDREN FIRST ✪

Today's Date

REGISTERED MAIL

Ms. Abigail Porter
30 United Nations Plaza
New York, NY 10018

Dear Ms. Porter:

Re: CHILDREN FIRST CAPITAL CAMPAIGN

Thank you for your sincere interest in Children First's capital campaign. I am pleased to enclose an information packet that includes summaries of our programs, our annual report, copies of our most recent newsletter and news articles in local papers that highlight the work that we are doing. As I am sure you know, we have recently been the focus of several articles in the City section of *The New York Times*. *[Insert new bookmark; name it Articles.]*

Here are some of the great things that people are saying about Children First:

> Ms. Mary Furman-Burke, President of the National Foundation for Children and Senior Consultant to the Vice-President of the United States on family policy, said:

> > "I am proud that Children First was founded in my home state. We can easily see the influence that this organization has had on communities around the nation." *[Move Senator Deacon quote here.]*

> Senator Marc Deacon (D-New York), a member of a Congressional think-take on the future of America's children, said:

> > "All social programs that focus on children should use the innovative and risk-taking methods that are employed by Children First. It is the only way that we will find solutions to age-old problems. Children First should serve

[Use File Stamp feature to insert filename and path.]

Ms. Abigail Porter
Page 2
Today's Date

[Move Ms. Furman-Burke quote here] as a national model when thinking about creating policy for the twenty-first century."

As a prominent member of the National Committee on Children and Families, Ms. Martha Manning also praised Children First and said:

> "Children First has paved the way for improved services for children and families. Their hard work has resulted in significant changes in New York City."

These are just some of the positive reactions that we have had to our programs. I know that you will enjoy reading through our literature and learning more about us.

We will be sure to include you on our mailing list, so that you receive all press updates and information concerning special events and meetings.

I would also like to arrange an appointment for you to meet with our Executive Director, Beth Billingham. *[Insert new Bookmark; name it Beth Billingham.]* I will contact you later this week, so that we can find a time that is convenient for you. *[Use GoTo feature to jump to Beth Billingham bookmark and insert new text.]*

Cordially,

Marta Villarta
Director of Development

mv/yo

Enclosure

Copy to: Beth Billingham

COREL WORDPERFECT 8 Lesson 5: Work with Multiple-Page Documents

PART II

1. Start with a clear screen.
2. Open **CHILDREN** or **32CHILDREN**.
3. Insert a new bookmark in the first and last paragraphs as shown. Name the first bookmark "Articles"; name the second bookmark "Beth Billingham."
4. Use the Go To feature to jump to the Articles bookmark. Insert the following new text (as shown in the illustration):

    There have been many positive reactions to these articles. For example, these articles have attracted new volunteers and donors and, as a result, we will be able to re-open one of our pre-school programs in Brooklyn that was closed due to changes in the city's budget.

5. Use the Go To feature to jump to the Beth Billingham bookmark. Insert the following new text (as shown in the illustration):

    Beth has been our fearless leader for more than ten years, and she will be able to give you a sense of our organization's past, as well as a glimpse into the directions that we will be heading towards in the twenty-first century.

6. Switch the Ms. Mary Furman-Burke quote with the Senator Marc Deacon quote as shown.
   Hint: Use mouse to drag and drop each quote.
7. Insert a bottom-centered page number; suppress it on the first page.
8. Insert the filename using the File Stamp.
    a. Position the filename and path at the bottom left of the document as footer A.
    b. Size the filename and path to an 8-point font.
    ✓ *The page number will now appear inside the footer along with the filename and path.*
    c. Suppress the Footer on the first page.
9. Use Widow/Orphan protection.
10. Turn Hyphenation on.
11. Use Make-it-fit feature, if necessary, to make the letter fit on two pages.
12. Spell check.
13. Print one copy.
14. Close the file; save the changes.

KEYSTROKES

PAGE NUMBERING

1. Place insertion point at beginning of document or page.
2. Click **Format** .... Alt+R
3. Click **Page** .... P
4. Click **Numbering** .... N
5. Click **Position list box** .... Alt+P, ↕
6. Click page number position option:
   - No page numbering
   - Top Left
   - Top Center
   - Top Right
   - Top Outside Alternating
   - Top Inside Alternating
   - Bottom Left
   - Bottom Right
   - Bottom Outside Alternating
   - Bottom Inside Alternating

To change numbering format:

Select a numbering format option from the **Page numbering format** list box .... Alt+N

To change numbering font:

a. Click **Font** button .... Alt+F
b. Make desired selections.
c. Click **OK** twice .... Enter, Enter

USE GO TO FEATURE

1. Click **Edit** .... Alt+E
2. Click **Go To** .... G
3. a. Click **Position** .... Alt+P
    a. Click desired page position from drop-down list.
    OR
    a. Click **Page Number** .... Alt+N
    b. Type desired page number .... ↕
    OR
    a. Click **Bookmark** .... Alt+B
    b. Click desired bookmark from drop-down list .... ↕
4. Click **OK** .... Enter

FILE STAMP

1. Click **File Stamp** button 🖋 on Shipping Macros toolbar.
2. Select desired option in File Stamp Options dialog box.
    OR
1. Position insertion point where filename is to be inserted.
2. Click **Insert** .... Alt+I
3. Click **Other** .... O
4. Click **Filename** .... F
    OR
    Path and Filename .... P

Exercise 33 ■ Summary

In this exercise, you will create a report with footnotes. The report will be bound on the left; therefore, you will need to place the footer and page numbers accordingly.

EXERCISE DIRECTIONS

1. Type the exercise on the following pages or open 💾**33GENERATIONS**.
2. Set the Current Document Style for a 2" left margin, a 1.5" right margin, and a 13-point font.
3. Format the document as a left-bound report. Begin the document on the appropriate line.
4. Center and set the title to a sans serif 16-point bold font.
5. Single space then double indent quoted paragraphs 1" from the left and right margins.
6. Set line spacing for the remaining paragraphs to double.

   ✓ *The report shown is single-spaced. Be sure to double space your report as indicated. It should result in four pages.*

7. Set a .5" first line indent for all remaining paragraphs.
8. Use the Footnote feature to insert reference numbers and footnote text as indicated in the illustration.
9. Create a right-aligned footer in a sans serif 12-point bold font that reads:
   GENERATIONS: A SOCIAL REVIEW
10. Include a page number in any style at the top right corner of the page.
11. Suppress the footer and page number on the first page.
12. Edit the footer to read GENERATIONS.
13. Full justify the document.
14. Use widow/orphan protection.
15. Display the Shipping Macros toolbar.
16. Use the File Stamp feature to insert the filename. Position it at the top left of the document. Change the font size to 8 point.
17. Spell check.
18. Print pages 2 and 4.
19. Print the full document.
20. Save the file; name it **GENERATIONS**.
21. Close the document window.

GENERATIONS (Page 1 of 2)

GENERATIONS

Double space all body text

Students of American culture feel that invoking "generations" may help explain a great variety of other phenomena, such as historical change, social conflict, progress or declensions, immigrant adaption, certain aesthetic movements, as well as scholars' own interests; yet more often than not, the concept of the "generation" itself remains unexplained and unquestioned.[1] *Single space quotation paragraphs*

Baby Boomers. The Beat Generation. Generation X. These are all names that are assigned to a particular group of individuals who have something in common whether it is a particular form of artistic expression or a set of circumstances that surrounds the years of their births. While these names are often used in the popular media and invoke a variety of meanings, the concept of a generation is an important tool for social scientists who study American history and culture. Werner Sollers, an American History scholar, explains it this way, "Though it defies measurability, the generation is first and foremost a mental concept which has been experienced as well as used to interpret experience throughout American History."[2]

One reason that social scientists have chosen to focus on generations is that individuals define themselves as part of a group, and oftentimes one clear and concrete social sub-group is a generation. For example, Japanese immigrants to the United States refer to themselves and their American born children as *Issei*, *Nisei*, or *Sansei*, to separate the generations by time and place of birth. In studying Japanese immigration and settlement, social scientists have found it helpful to understand the characteristics that are attributed to each of these generations and to determine why these terms are useful for the Japanese people who have created them.

A second example is that of Generation X, a term used to describe individuals born between the years 1961-1981. Though this terminology was originally used by "generational outsiders" and has many negative connotations (including laziness and lack of focus), people who are in their twenties have now begun using this name to describe themselves and to identify themselves as a potentially powerful group. Lauren Zinn

---

[1] Sollers, Werner. *Beyond Ethnicity: Consent and Descent in American Culture*, (New York and Oxford: Oxford University Press, 1986)

[2] Sollers, 210.

explains in *Business Week*, "…this current crop of 18-to-29 year olds is the second largest group of young adults in U.S. history. They're already starting to set tastes in fashion and popular culture."[3]

There are several criticisms that are launched against those who study generations. One such criticism is that it is impossible to determine who is and who is not part of a particular generation. David Reisman has said, "It is not easy to say when one generation ends and another begins, for people are not produced in batches, as are pancakes, but are born continuously."[4] A second critique is that many times the characteristics that describe a particular generation are inconsistent or contradictory. Alexander Star wrote in *The New Republic* about Generation X:

> "How can one generalize about a group that is said to be politically disengaged and politically correct, obsessed with surfaces and addicted to irony, scarred by Watergate and Vietnam and unaware of them, technologically savvy, and unconditionally ignorant, busy saving the planet and creating electricity and noise, prematurely careerist and proud to be lazy, and unwilling to grow up and too grown up already?"[5]

Finally, critics argue that studying generations as bound social sub-groups ignores the impact that one generation has on the generation that follows it.

Who gets to have the final say about the creation and study of generations? As long as people continue to define themselves or allow themselves to be defined as part of a generation, generations will continue to exist as a social concept. And as long as scholars study American history and culture, there will be those who will study generations. In their book *Generations: The History of American's Future, 1854 to 2069*, William Strausse and Neil Howe predict the characteristics of "generations" straight into the next century. What generation do you belong to in this century? What generation will you belong to in the next?

---

[3]Zinn, Lauren, "Move Over Boomers: the busters are here - and they're angry." *Business Week*. 14 December 1992: 74 - 82.

[4]Sollers, 209.

[5]Star, Alexander. "The Twentysomething Myth," *The New Republic*. 4, 11 January 1993: 22-25.

COREL WORDPERFECT 8
Lesson 6: Templates; Envelopes and Labels; Macros

Exercise 34
- Templates
- PerfectExpert
- Envelopes
- Labels

NOTES

Templates

- A **template** is a skeleton document that may contain formatting, graphics, and/or text. It can be used over and over again to create new documents.

- Using WordPerfect's predesigned templates and projects, you can create documents such as newsletters, menus, faxes, letters, and resumes (as well as other documents).

- To use a template or project to create a document, select New from the File menu. The New dialog box displays with the Create New tab selected.

New Dialog Box

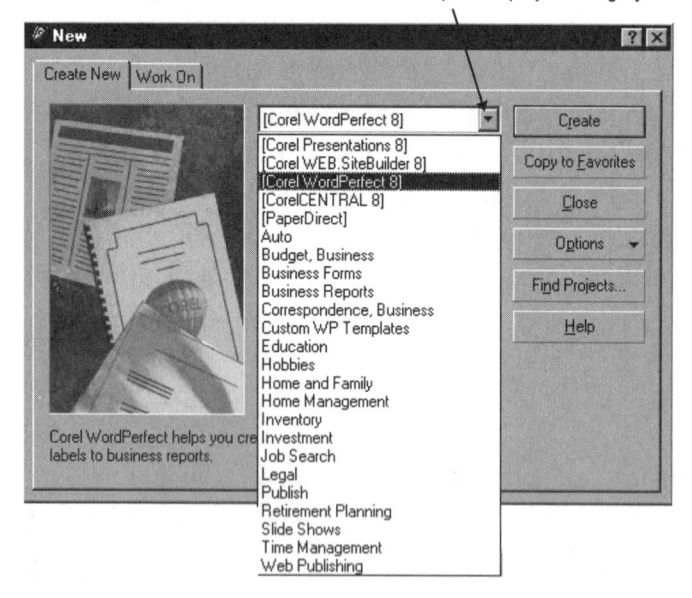

- Templates and other projects are arranged into categories. Click the down arrow to select the desired category from the drop-down list.

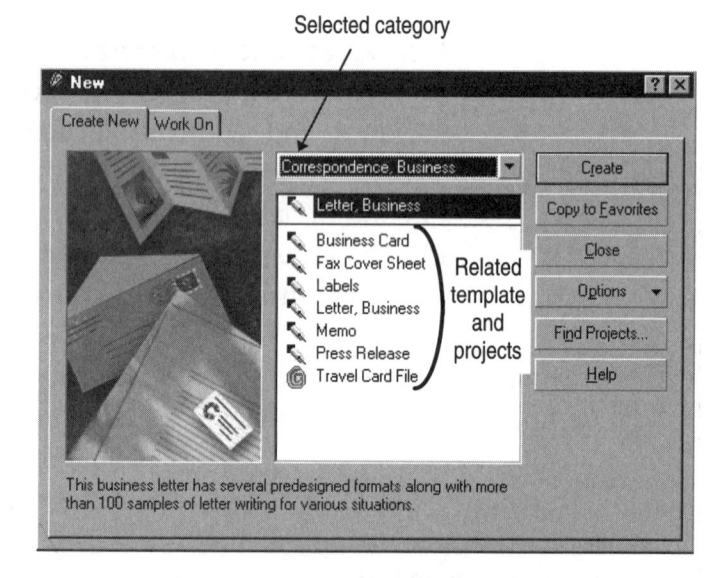

- Note the related templates and projects that display in the selection list box. Double-click a template or project to open it.

  ✓*Note: While templates are included with your software CD-ROM, they do not automatically install to your hard disk with a typical installation of WordPerfect.*

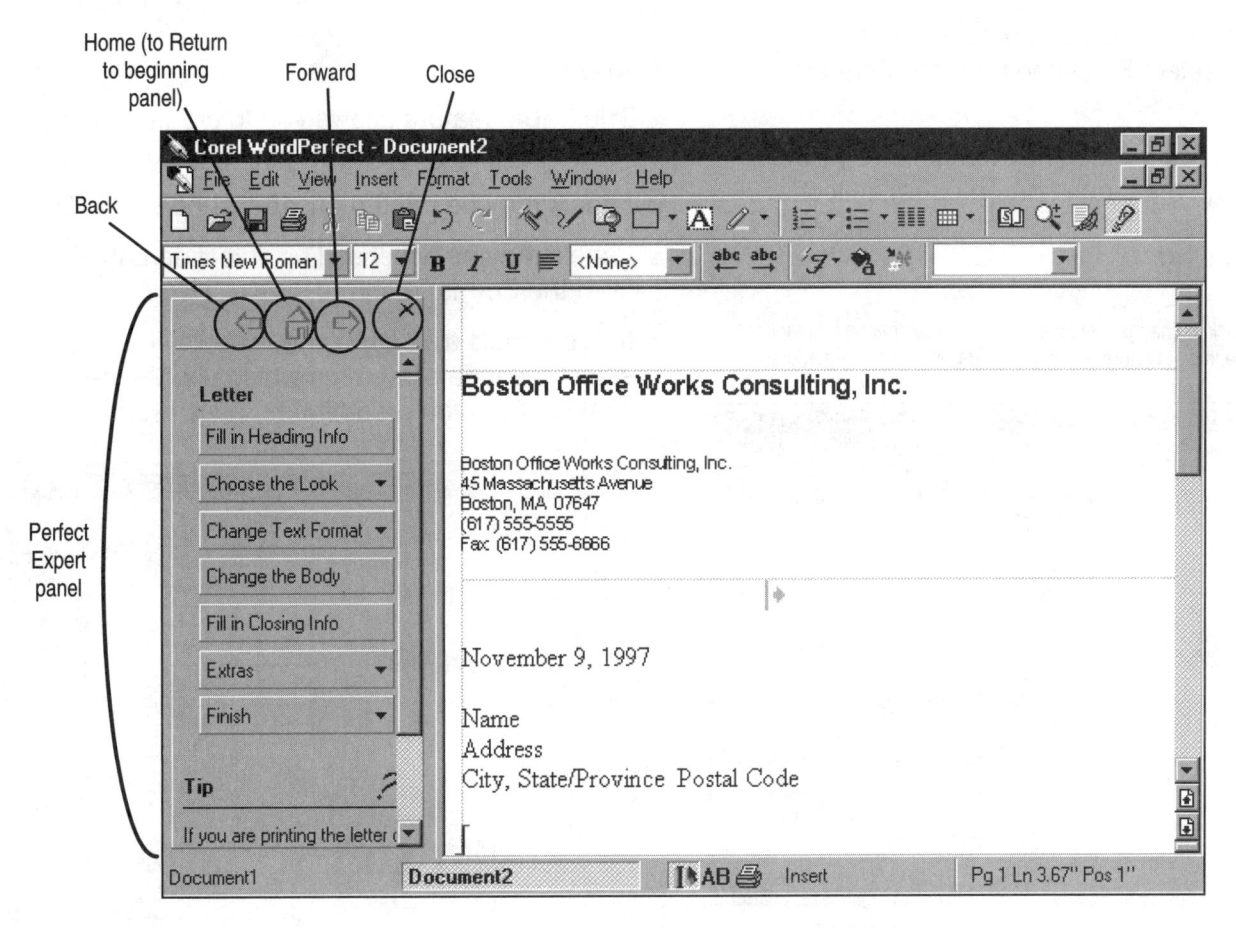

PerfectExpert

- Once you open a template or project, a **PerfectExpert** panel appears on the left side of the document window. PerfectExpert is a feature that provides options for creating and completing the document.

- If you select Letter, Business in the selection list box from the Correspondence, Business category, the following PerfectExpert panel appears. The first time you use the PerfectExpert, you will be prompted to provide your personal information. This information will be used in the return address and signature portions of any templates you access through the PerfectExpert. To step through the letter-creation process, click each button and make the desired selections. To replace sample text, select the text, then retype it. Click the back and forward icons to cycle through the options. Click the house icon to return to the template's beginning panel. To close the panel, click the Close icon ☒ in the top right corner of the panel. To redisplay the panel, select PerfectExpert from the Help menu.

Envelopes

- **Envelopes** can be created while using the PerfectExpert to create a letter or they can be created independently. Envelopes can also be created during the merge process (see The Merge Process, Exercise 43).

- To create envelopes to accompany the letters you create using the PerfectExpert, click the Finish button in the PerfectExpert panel and select Create an Envelope.

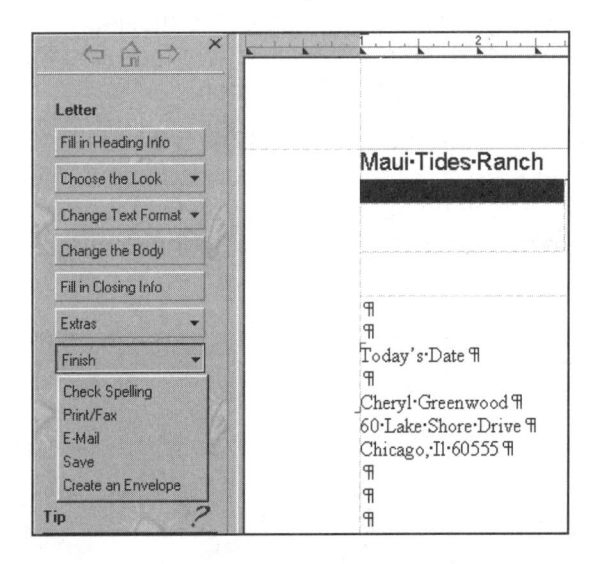

COREL WORDPERFECT 8   Lesson 6:   Templates; Envelopes and Labels; Macros

- To create an envelope independent of a template, select En_v_elope from the Fo_r_mat menu.

- In the Envelope dialog box that follows (using either of the mentioned procedures), select an envelope size from the En_v_elope definitions drop-down list.

Click to change font face, size, etc., of return address.

Click to change font face, size, etc., of mailing address.

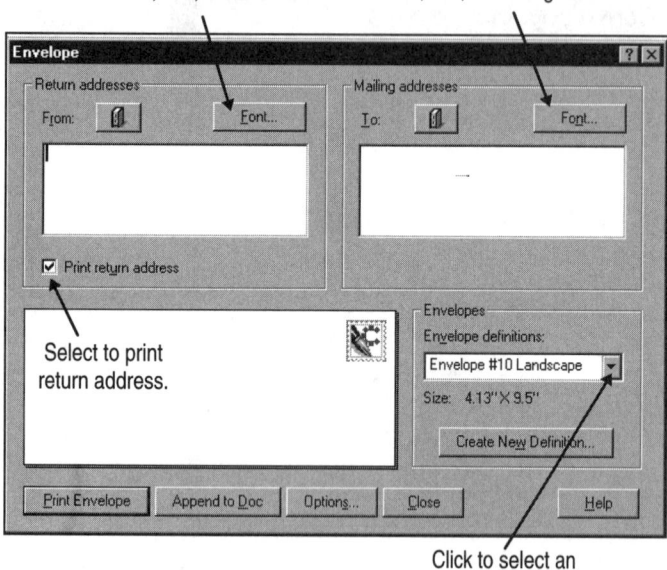

Select to print return address.

Click to select an envelope size.

- If a document containing an address is onscreen (in the current document window), WordPerfect automatically brings the mailing address into the mailing addresses window.

- You may also type an address in the Return addresses window. To ensure that the return address is printed, select the Print ret_u_rn address check box.

- To change the appearance of the mailing address text, select a desired font face and font size by selecting the Fo_n_t button.

- Clicking the Append to _D_oc button inserts the envelope file at the end of your document; the _P_rint Envelope button allows you to print your envelope without appending it to the document.

Labels

- The **Label** feature allows you to create mailing labels, file folder labels, or diskette labels.

- Labels may be printed on label sheets or rolls.

- Labels may be accessed by selecting La_b_els from the Fo_r_mat menu.

- In the Labels dialog box that follows, you may select the type of label on which you will be working from the predefined _L_abels list.

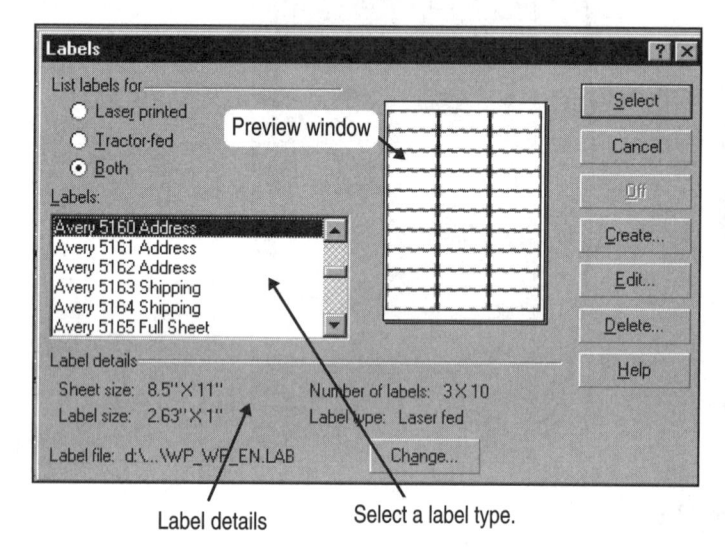

Preview window

Label details   *Select a label type.*

- For each label type you highlight, information about the label and sheet size displays in the Label details area of the dialog box, and an illustration of the label arrangement displays in the preview window.

- Once the label format has been specified, the first blank label displays ready for you to start keyboarding text. Once the label is filled, a new label appears.

- If you do not enter enough text to fill a label, press Ctrl + Enter to end the text you are keyboarding and display a new label.

- The Application Bar reports each new label as a new page. WordPerfect calls these **logical pages**, as opposed to the **physical page**, or sheet, to which the labels are physically attached.

- To see labels as they will be arranged when you print, select T_w_o Pages from the _V_iew menu.

- When you print a single page, the entire physical page is printed.

158

In Part I of this exercise, you will use PerfectExpert to create a memorandum and a set of file labels. A memorandum is a communication sent within a company. In Part II of this exercise, you will use PerfectExpert to create a letter and an envelope. In Part III of this exercise, you will create address labels.

EXERCISE DIRECTIONS

PART I

1. Start with a clear screen.
2. Click File, New.
3. Select Memo from the Correspondence, Business category, and click Create.
   - ✓ *If you have not used this feature previously, a pop-up menu will appear, "Personalize Your Templates." Click OK and select Person. Click OK in the "New Person Properties" dialog box that appears, fill in your personal information, and then click OK again.*
4. Use the following PerfectExpert options to complete the document:
   a. Click the Choose a Look button and select Cosmopolitan.
   b. Click the Fill in Heading Info button and enter the following in the Memo Heading dialog box:
      - To: Rachel Stein
      - From: Your name
      - Date: Today's
      - Subject: Company Volleyball Team
   c. Delete the sample body text and type the body text shown in Illustration A on the following page.
   d. Click the Home icon on the PerfectExpert panel.
   e. Click the Finish button and select Check Spelling. Then, click the Finish button again and select Save, and name the file **PICNIC**.
5. Close the PerfectExpert panel.
6. Preview the full page of the document.
7. Print one copy.
8. Start a new document.
9. Create the following four file labels. Use Avery 5066.

   Interoffice Memorandums
   January-March 1999

   Corporate Events
   January-March 1999

   Current Projects
   January-March 1999

   Business Related Articles
   January-March 1999

10. Print one copy of the label sheet.
11. Save the file; name it **FILES**.
12. Close both document windows.

COREL WORDPERFECT 8   Lesson 6: Templates; Envelopes and Labels; Macros

ILLUSTRATION A

MEMORANDUM

To: Rachel Stein
From: Your Name
Date: Today's Date
Subject: Company Volleyball Team

Congratulations! Our company volleyball team has once again won the Annual Corporate Olympics pennant. This award represents a sincere level of commitment to our corporation, and I am truly grateful to you for your sense of commitment and team work.

To celebrate, I would like to invite you and your family to a picnic in Forest Edge Park on Sunday, August 24 at 1:00 p.m. The corporate management team will be sponsoring the picnic. Lunch and soft drinks will be provided.

I look forward to seeing you, your family, and all of your teammates at this victorious event.

PART II

1. Start with a clear screen.
2. Click File, New.
3. Select Letter, Business from the Correspondence, Business category, and click Create.
4. Use the following PerfectExpert options to complete the document:
   ✓ *The last selected Address Book entry will automatically display as the letterhead. This can be changed using the Fill-in Heading option.*
   a. Click the *Fill-in Heading Info* button and enter the following in the Heading Information dialog box:
   To: Click Address Book button and select Ms. Julie Garrison. (If her information has not been entered, do so now. See Exercise 4 for her address information).

   From: Click Address Book button and enter the following organization:
   Boston Computer Consulting, Inc.,
   45 Massachusetts Avenue
   Boston, MA 07647
   phone: (617) 555-5555, fax: (617) 555-6666.

   Date: Today's

   Greeting: Dear Ms. Garrison:

   b. Click the Choose a Look button and select Elegant.
   c. Click the Change Text Format button and select Full Block.
   d. Click the Change the Body button, delete the sample body text and enter the body text shown in Illustration B.
   ✓ *After completing the body text you will have to press the End button once to move your insertion point outside of the "body text" region.*
   e. Click the Fill-in Closing Info button and select the following:
   Complimentary Closing: Sincerely
   Sender's Title: Manager
   Writer's Initials: je
   Typist's Initials: yo
   Enclosures: 1
   ✓ *The writer's name is not included in the closing info fill-in options, and the spacing for a full-block letter does not conform to the standard format. Therefore, you will need to add the writer's name (in addition to making spacing adjustments) after the letter is completed.*
   f. Click the Extras button and select Center Page Vertically.
   g. Click the Finish button and select Check Spelling.
   h. Click the Finish button and select Create an Envelope. The envelope return address should read:
   James Elton
   Boston Computer Consulting, Inc.
   45 Massachusetts Avenue
   Boston, MA 07647
   i. Append the Envelope to the document.
   j. Click the Finish button and select Save; name the file **CUSTOMERS**.

5. Insert the writer's name (James Elton) as shown in Illustration B on the following page.
6. Create a hard space between the words "nine" and "years" in the first sentence of the second paragraph. Make any additional spacing adjustments to match the spacing shown in Illustration B.
7. Print one copy of both the letter and the envelope.
8. Close the file; save the changes.

PART III

1. Start with a clear screen.
2. Create the following six address labels. Use Avery 5260.

   Samantha Purdy
   12 Maple Drive
   Woodlands, TX 77381

   Libby McGuire
   5796 Broadway
   New York, NY 10028

   Brian Howard
   376 River Road
   Colorado Springs, CO 80935

   Kiandra Coleman
   333 West 25 Street
   Tacoma, WA 98402

   Tyler Stevenson
   3259 Bay Avenue
   San Francisco, CA 94103

   Kristi Morgan
   500 West Main Street
   Louisville, KY 40202

3. Print one copy of the label sheet.
4. Save the file; name it **ADDRESSES**.
5. Close the document window.

ILLUSTRATION B

Boston Computer Consulting, Inc.

Today's Date

Ms. Julie Garrison
555 Madison Avenue
New York, NY 10016

Dear Ms. Garrison:

Thank you for your interest in Boston Computer Consulting, Inc. We understand you will be opening an office in Medford, Massachusetts sometime next year.

Our company has been analyzing the technological needs of Boston area businesses for the past nine years. Our purpose is to assist businesses in becoming fully technologically automated and integrated. Our service consists of determining software and hardware needs, facilitating Internet access, designing and hosting a company Web page, and employee training. In addition, we will also analyze your business processes–such as bookkeeping, accounts receivable, invoice processing, mailing lists, etc., –and then suggest automated alternatives. Our goal is to create an office environment that will save you time and money by automating tasks that in the past were time consuming and cumbersome.

I have enclosed a brochure that explains all of our services in further detail. If you have any questions or would like to arrange a meeting, please do not hesitate to contact me directly at (617) 555-5555.

Sincerely,

James Elton
Manager

je/yo

Enclosures: 1

Boston Computer Consulting, Inc.
45 Massachusetts Avenue
Boston, MA 07647
(617) 555-5555
Fax: (617) 555-6666

KEYSTROKES

OPEN A TEMPLATE

1. Click **File**............................. Alt+F
2. Click **New**............................. N
   To fill in Personal Information:
   a. Click **Options** button .... Alt+P
   b. Click **Personal Information** .... E
   c. Choose an address book entry.
3. Click the down arrow and select a category..................................... ↓↑
4. Double-click on desired template or project.
5. Click button(s) on PerfectExpert panel to step through and select options.
   To close PerfectExpert panel:
   - Click Close button X
   To display PerfectExpert panel:
   - Click **Help**.......................... Alt+H
   - Click **PerfectExpert** .... E

CREATE AN ENVELOPE

FROM MAIN MENU

1. Click **Format**......................... Alt+R
2. Click **Envelope**...................... V
3. Click **Envelope definitions**..... Alt+V
4. Select envelope size drop-down list .... ↓↑
5. Click **To** text box .... Alt+T
6. Type address in **Mailing addresses** window.
   ✓ If a document containing an inside address is on screen, the mailing address will automatically be inserted into the Mailing addresses window.
7. Click **From** text box .... Alt+R
8. Type return address in **Return addresses** window.
   To print return address:
   Click **Print return address** check box.............................. Alt+U
9. Select printing option:
   Click **Append to Doc** .... Alt+D
   to insert the envelope at the end of the current document.
   OR
   Click **Print Envelope** .... Alt+P
   to print envelope immediately without appending it to the current document.

CREATE LABELS

1. Click **Format** .... Alt+R
2. Click **Labels** .... B
3. Select a label type:
   - **Laser printed** .... Alt+R
   - **Tractor-fed** .... Alt+T
   - **Both** .... Alt+B
4. Click in **Labels** list box .... Alt+L
5. Highlight label type .... ↓↑
6. Click **Select**........................... Alt+S
7. Type address for first label.
8. Press **Ctrl + Enter** to advance to the next label .... Ctrl+Enter
9. Load labels into printer.
10. Print as a normal document.

COREL WORDPERFECT 8 Lesson 6: Templates; Envelopes and Labels; Macros

Exercise 35

- **Arrange Multiple Documents**
- **Switch Between Open Documents**
- **Close Multiple Documents**
- **Size Windows**
- **Copy/Move Text from One Open Document to Another**

NOTES

- WordPerfect lets you open and work with up to nine documents at one time. This is a convenient feature for moving and/or copying text from one document to another. As each document is opened, the document name appears as a button on the Application Bar.

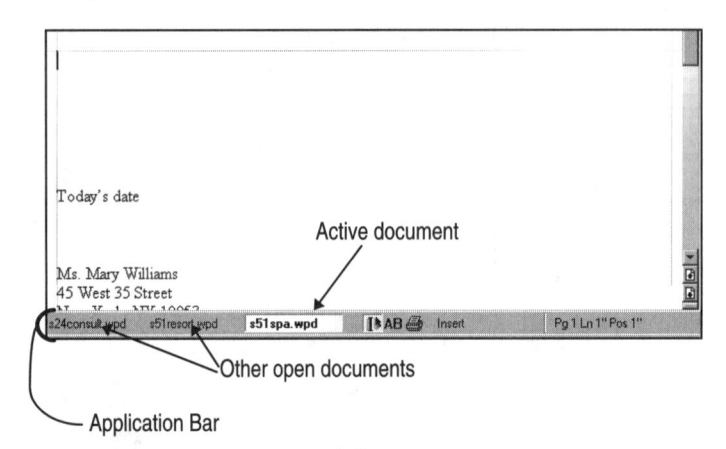

- The area where you type your document is called the **document window**.

- You may open multiple files individually or all at once in the same operation. To open multiple files at one time from the Open dialog box, hold down the Ctrl key as you select each of the desired files, then click Open.

- **Windowing** lets you view those documents as you work with them.

Arrange Multiple Documents

- When you open more than one document window, you can decide how you want them arranged. To choose a document arrangement option, select the desired option from the Window menu. Each option is described below.

Cascade Documents

- One option is to **cascade** document windows. Cascaded windows overlap so that the title bar of each window is displayed. Note the illustration (below) of three cascaded documents.

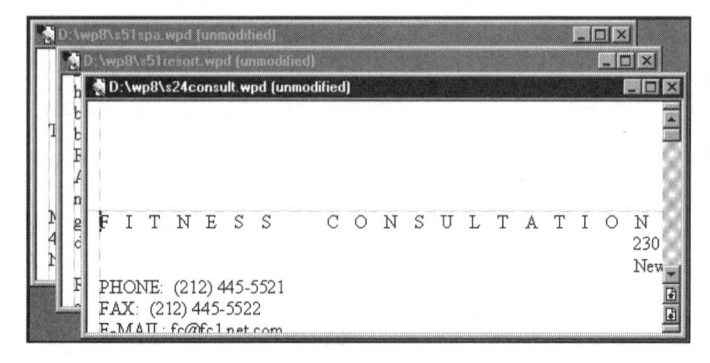

- The colored title bar indicates the **active window**. To change the active window, click the title bar of the desired window. The active window will display on top of the other windows.

Tile Documents

- Another arrangement option is to **tile** document windows. This allows you to view several documents at one time. Tiled windows are arranged on the screen with no overlapping.

- You may choose to tile your documents horizontally or vertically. Horizontally tiled documents are arranged side by side (Tile Side by Side) while vertically tiled documents are tiled one below the other (Tile Top to Bottom). The active window is indicated by the colored title bar. The title bars of the inactive windows are shaded gray. Note the illustrations on the next page which shows documents tiled top to bottom and side by side.

Documents Tiled Top to Bottom

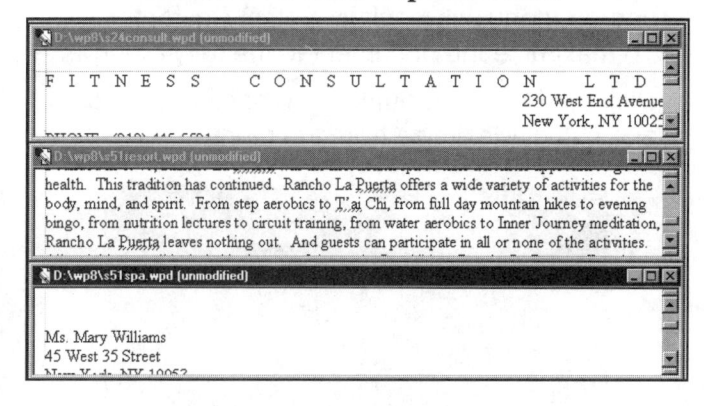

Documents Tiled Side by Side

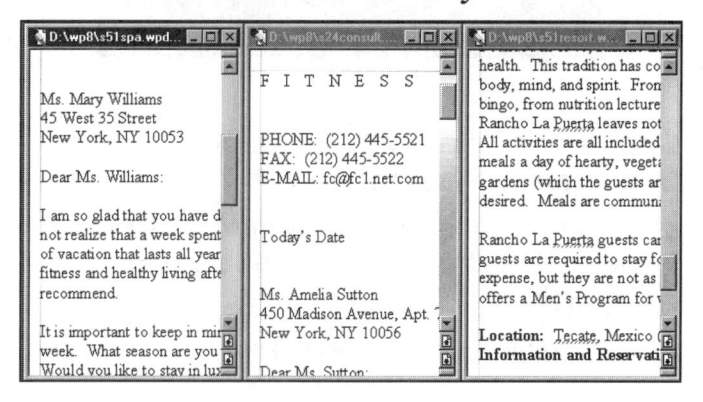

Switch Between Open Documents

- You can switch between open documents (whether they are currently displayed or not) by clicking their names on the Application Bar or by selecting the document you want to display from the Window menu. You can also press Ctrl+F6 to cycle through all open documents.

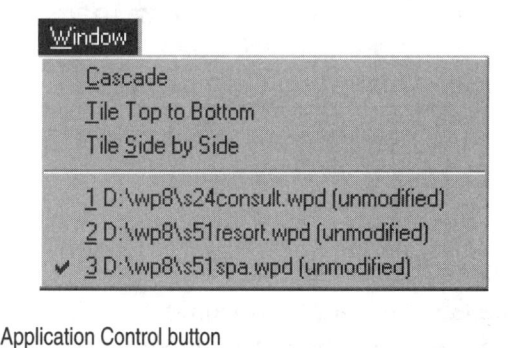

Close Multiple Documents

- As you close each document, you can save its contents. To close an active document, double-click the Document Control button to the left of the title bar, or click the Close button to the right of the title bar, or select Close from the File menu, or press Ctrl+F4.

Size Windows

Maximizing a Window

- When you begin a new document, WordPerfect provides a full-screen or **maximized** window ready for you to begin typing. The buttons (application controls) on the WordPerfect title bar let you size and arrange the WordPerfect application window in the Windows screen. The buttons to the left and right of the menu bar are document controls that allow you to size and arrange the current document window.

    ✓Note: If you have a document open that is not maximized and open a new one, the new one opens in reduced size.

- To maximize a window, click the Maximize button.

- When a document is maximized, the Restore button becomes active on the menu bar.

Separating the Document Window from the Application Window

- When you click the Restore button in a maximized document window, your document separates from the application window. This allows you to view several documents at once.

Application Control button

Application Control buttons

Minimize button (Click to reduce document to a desktop icon.)

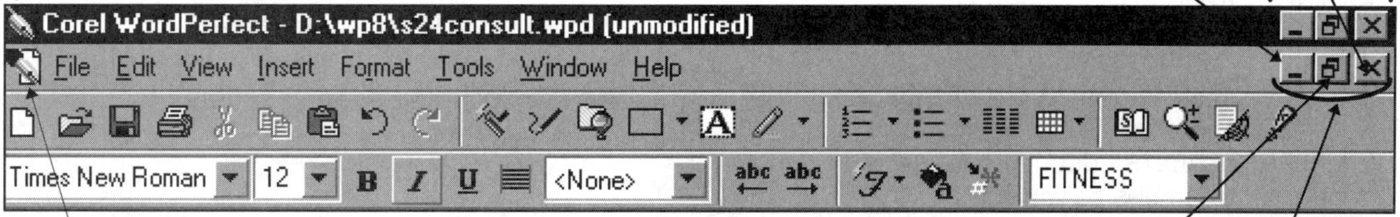

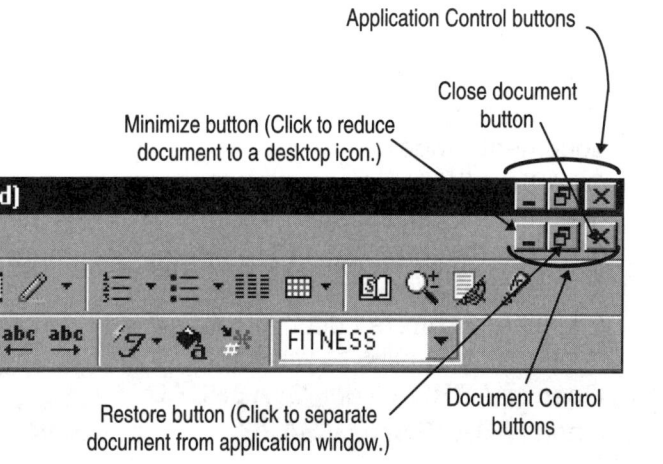

Close document button

Document Control button

Restore button (Click to separate document from application window.)

Document Control buttons

COREL WORDPERFECT 8 Lesson 6: Templates; Envelopes and Labels; Macros

Minimizing a Window

- To minimize a document to an icon, click the Minimize document button [—] to the right of the document title bar. The document is reduced to a small rectangular icon at the bottom of the screen, which displays the document name along with control buttons (Restore, Maximize, and Close).

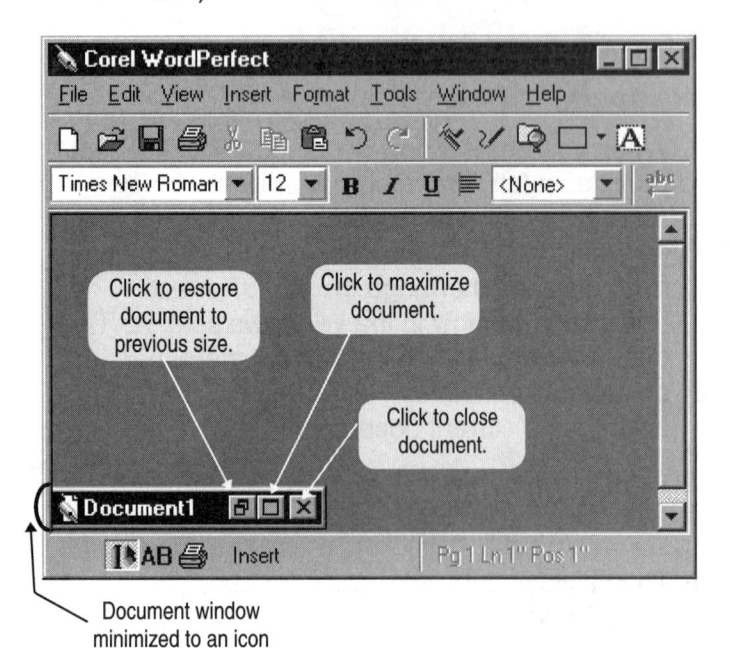

Document window minimized to an icon

- To return the document to a separate document window, click the Restore button [🗗] (the Restore button then changes to a Maximize button), or click anywhere on the icon and a pop-up menu will display. Select Restore. To maximize the document to the full screen, click the Maximize button [□] or click the icon and select Maximize from the menu.

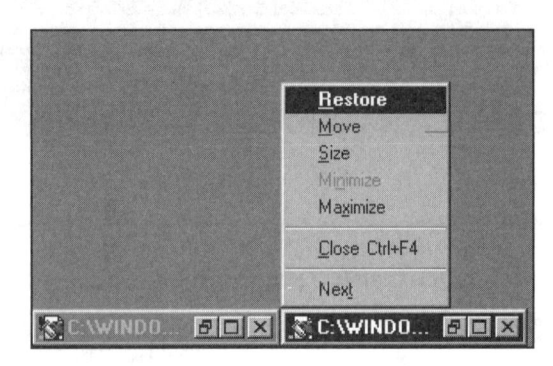

Copy/Move Text from One Open Document to Another

- The procedure for copying or moving text from one document to another is the same as copying/moving text within the same document.

- Opening multiple documents allows you to copy or move text easily from one document to another since you can actually see where the text is coming from and where it is going.

- When you finish working in a document, close the file. Then tile or cascade the windows again to provide larger windows for the remaining documents.

In Part I of this exercise, you will open several documents, minimize and/or maximize them, and practice different document arrangements. In Part II of this exercise, you will open multiple documents and copy text from one document to another. (See Illustration C on page 169.)

EXERCISE DIRECTIONS

PART I

1. Open **GYM** or **35GYM**.
2. Click the Restore button to create a separate document window.
3. Click the Minimize button to reduce the document to an icon.
4. Click the Restore button to return the document to a separate document window.
5. Click the Maximize button to return the document to a full-size window.
6. Open **ABROAD** or **35ABROAD**.
7. Open **SAVE** or **35SAVE**.
8. Cascade the documents.
9. Make GYM the active document.
10. Make ABROAD the active document.
11. Tile the documents side by side.
12. Maximize GYM (they will all maximize).
13. Tile the documents top to bottom.
14. Close each document window.

PART II

1. Start with a clear screen.
2. Open 📁**35TRAVEL** or type the letter as shown in Illustration A. Format it as follows:
   a. Use the default margins. Begin the exercise on approximately Ln 2.5".
   b. Use the full-block letter style.
   c. Use the default font size and style.
   d. Save the file; name it **TRAVEL**.
3. Open 📁**35STUDENT** or type the letter as shown in Illustration B.
   a. Use the default margins.
   b. Use a decorative 24-point font to create the following letterhead text at Ln 1".
      Summer Student Adventures
   c. Type the dateline on approximately Ln 2.5".
   d. Use the modified-full block letter style.
   e. Save the file; name it STUDENT.
4. Open 📁**35TRIP**, or type the flyer as shown in Illustration C on page 169. Format it as follows:
   a. Use the default margins.
   b. Begin the document at Ln 1".
   c. Center the title. Set the title to a decorative 14-point font. Set "Four" to 30 points, bold.
   d. Set the document to a sans serif 12-point font.
   e. Set each program name to a bold decorative font as shown.
   f. Italicize the inclusive price information for the first two programs, as shown.
   g. Save the file; name it **TRIP**.
5. Open ⌨**ABROAD** or 📁**35ABROAD**.
6. Tile all documents, top to bottom.
7. Copy the footer from ABROAD to both STUDENT and TRAVEL.
6. Make TRIP the active document.
7. Copy all text for the first two programs (ZIMBABWE and JAPAN) and paste it into TRAVEL as shown in Illustration D. (Leave a double space between programs.)
8. Paste the same text (Zimbabwe and Japan) into STUDENT as shown in Illustration D. (Leave a double space between programs.)
9. Return to the TRIP document and copy all text for the third and fourth programs (ENGLISH ADVANCE and THE LIVING ENVIRONMENT) and paste into STUDENT as shown in Illustration D.
10. Close **ABROAD** and **TRIP**.
11. Maximize STUDENT.
12. Double indent all pasted program information in STUDENT.
13. Create a 10-point, left-aligned header in STUDENT, which includes the addressee's name, today's date, and the appropriate page number.
14. Suppress the header on the first page.
15. Make any necessary adjustments to the text in both STUDENT and TRAVEL. Avoid awkward page breaks.
16. Spell check each document.
17. Print one copy of each document.
18. Close **STUDENT** and **TRAVEL**; save all changes.

COREL WORDPERFECT 8   Lesson 6: Templates; Envelopes and Labels; Macros

ILLUSTRATION A

Today's Date Ms. Margaret Sanger Travel Time 5247 Maple Drive Studio City, CA 91607 Dear Ms. Sanger: Subject: New Summer Abroad Programs ¶ As a travel agency representative for Student Life Inc., we would like to take this opportunity to inform you of our upcoming summer programs. The descriptions listed below are for the new travel abroad programs that we are currently offering to students.¶ We anticipate that these summer programs will fill up quickly; therefore, we have set an earlier response deadline because of the extensive planning that will be required. You can expect that students may be contacting you as early as December 1 to make their travel arrangements for the following two programs: ¶ As always, we look forward to doing business with you. Cordially, William Reid President Copy to: Annie Huff, Tour Coordinator wr/yo

ILLUSTRATION B

Today's Date Ms. Anne Richardson 89 Park Avenue New York, NY 90876 Dear Ms. Richardson: Thank you for your inquiry about our summer programs for 1999. Our summer programs for high school students are designed to provide both fun and excitement that is educationally enhanced. Enclosed is our brochure outlining the many summer programs that we offer. However, we are adding four new programs this summer, and I am sure that you will want to know about them. ¶ The first two programs are travel programs.¶
In addition to our travel programs, we also offer a wide variety of language and study programs at several American universities and universities abroad. These programs often require pre-testing. You can contact our office if you have specific questions about our requirements. ¶ We expect that our new programs will fill up quickly. Therefore, if you are interested in one of these programs, we recommend that you contact us as soon as possible. ¶ We hope that you will choose to join us this summer. If you have any questions or concerns, please do not hesitate to contact this office. Sincerely, William Reid President wr/yo Enclosure

ILLUSTRATION C

Student Life Inc. Announces
Four New Travel Abroad Programs

ZIMBABWE:
June 6 – August 9. $5,456.
Travel to one of the most beautiful and rapidly developing countries in Africa. Begin the trip in Harare, the capital city, learning about urban development and social geography. Visit Hwange National Park and Mana Pools, two of the country's game parks, studying wildlife management. Hike in the western Motopos Hills. Live with families in Chiweshe, a small, rural community, and see how life exists without electricity or running water. End the trip with a canoe adventure on the Zambezi River and visits to Lake Karibe and Victoria Falls.
Price includes airfare from Newark to Harare, accommodations, meals, travel within Zimbabwe, and activity fees.

JAPAN:
June 15 – August 15. $7,178.
Begin the trip in one of the most international cities in the world, Tokyo, studying Japanese language and visiting national parks and museums. Climb Mount Fuji. Learn about marine wildlife while visiting Hokkaido. Live with families in Osaka while visiting the ancient city of Kyoto with its beautiful shrines and temples. Travel south along the Kyushu peninsula, stopping in smaller cities and villages along the way. End the trip with a diving adventure in Okinawa.
Price includes airfare from Newark to Tokyo, accommodations, meals, travel within Japan, and activity fees.

ENGLISH ADVANCE (located on the campus of Dartmouth College):
June 21 – August 10. $2,155.
A course that teaches critical thinking and writing skills while studying both classic literature and contemporary authors. The program also includes a reflexive in-depth seminar about the way that English is taught in high schools and universities and explores the future of the canon.

THE LIVING ENVIRONMENT (located on the campus of the University of Vermont):
June 21 – August 10. $2,155.
Begin to study environmental science and the way that day to day living is affected by changes in the environment. This program is divided between in-class seminars and multiple day excursions to the working farms, mountain ranges, and lake communities in Vermont.

COREL WORDPERFECT 8 Lesson 6: Templates; Envelopes and Labels; Macros

ILLUSTRATION D

TRAVEL

Today's Date

Ms. Margaret Sanger
Travel Time
5247 Maple Drive
Studio City, CA 91607

Dear Ms. Sanger:

Subject: New Summer Abroad Programs

As a travel agency representative for Student Life Inc., we would like to take this opportunity to inform you of our upcoming summer programs. The descriptions listed below are for the new travel abroad programs that we are currently offering to students.

We anticipate that these summer programs will fill up quickly; therefore, we have set an earlier response deadline because of the extensive planning that will be required. You can expect that students may be contacting you as early as December 1 to make their travel arrangements for the following two programs:

As always, we look forward to doing business with you.

Cordially,

William Reid
President

Copy to: Annie Huff, Tour Coordinator

wr/yo

STUDENT

Summer Student Adventures

Today's Date

Ms. Anne Richardson
89 Park Avenue
New York, NY 90876

Dear Ms. Richardson:

Thank you for your inquiry about our summer programs for 1999. Our summer programs for high school students are designed to provide both fun and excitement that is educationally enhanced. Enclosed is our brochure outlining the many summer programs that we offer. However, we are adding four new programs this summer, and I am sure that you will want to know about them.

The first two programs are travel programs.

In addition to our travel programs, we also offer a wide variety of language and study programs at several American universities and universities abroad. These programs often require pre-testing. You can contact our office if you have specific questions about our requirements.

We expect that our new programs will fill up quickly. Therefore, if you are interested in one of these programs, we recommend that you contact us as soon as possible.

We hope that you will choose to join us this summer. If you have any questions or concerns, please do not hesitate to contact this office.

Sincerely,

William Reid
President

wr/yo

Enclosure

TRIP

Student Life Inc. Announces
Four New Travel Abroad Programs

ZIMBABWE:
June 6 – August 9. $5, 456.
Travel to one of the most beautiful and rapidly developing countries in Africa. Begin the trip in Harare, the capital city, learning about urban development and social geography. Visit Hwange National Park and Mana Pools, two of the country's game parks, studying wildlife management. Hike in the western Motopos Hills. Live with families in Chiweshe, a small, rural community, and see how life exists without electricity or running water. End the trip with a canoe adventure on the Zambezi River and visits to Lake Karibe and Victoria Falls.

Price includes airfare from Newark to Harare, accommodations, meals, travel within Zimbabwe, and activity fees.

JAPAN:
June 15 – August 15. $7,178.
Begin the trip in one of the most international cities in the world, Tokyo, studying Japanese language and visiting national parks and museums. Climb Mount Fuji. Learn about marine wildlife while visiting Hokkaido. Live with families in Osaka while visiting the ancient city of Kyoto with its beautiful shrines and temples. Travel south along the Kyushu peninsula, stopping in smaller cities and villages along the way. End the trip with a diving adventure in Okinawa.

Price includes airfare from Newark to Tokyo, accommodations, meals, travel within Japan, and activity fees.

ENGLISH ADVANCE (located on the campus of Dartmouth College):
June 21 – August 10. $2,155.
A course that teaches critical thinking and writing skills while studying both classic literature and contemporary authors. The program also includes a reflexive in-depth seminar about the way that English is taught in high schools and universities and explores the future of the canon.

THE LIVING ENVIRONMENT (located on the campus of the University of Vermont):
June 21 – August 10. $2,155.
Begin to study environmental science and the way that day to day living is affected by changes in the environment. This program is divided between in-class seminars and multiple day excursions to the working farms, mountain ranges, and lake communities in Vermont.

ABROAD

Today's Date

Ms. Claire Ways
507 Bay Road, Apartment #3-C
San Francisco, CA 94102

Dear Ms. Ways:

I am writing to inform you that you have been accepted to our Work Abroad program for the summer of 1999. We at Student's Life have been successfully placing qualified college students in various areas of overseas employment since 1979.

We have carefully reviewed your resume and application and, based on your experience and language skills, would like to place you in Paris, France.

The following is a list of possible job opportunities that meet your qualifications:

Assistant English Teacher
Work with a principal instructor to create English lesson plans for grades 6-8. Job responsibilities include: assistant facilitator in the classroom, after-school one-on-one student tutor, accompanying students on field trips, creating a mentor program to assist students.

Junior Journalist
Assist senior editors and journalists at a small bi-monthly publication that targets Americans living in France. Job Responsibilities include: desktop publishing, proofreading and copy editing.

Media Translator
Help translate American, English, and Canadian news items for a local news radio station that broadcasts daily programs in English. Job responsibilities include: reading American, English, and Canadian news clips, working with a team of translators to transcribe the information into French, and working with advertisers.

Student Life Incorporated

KEYSTROKES

OPEN MULTIPLE DOCUMENTS

Ctrl + O

1. Click **File** .... `Alt` + `F`
2. Click **Open** .... `O`

   OR

   Click **Open** button 📂 on toolbar.

3. Press the **Ctrl** key and click each file to be opened.

   OR

   To select consecutive files, click the name of first file in group, use the scroll bar/box as needed to bring last file of desired group into view, then **Shift + click** (press Shift while you click) on the name of that file.

4. Click **Open** .... `Enter`

CASCADE DOCUMENTS

1. Click **Window** .... `Alt` + `W`
2. Click **Cascade** .... `C`

TILE DOCUMENTS

1. Click **Window** .... `Alt` + `W`
2. Click **Tile Top to Button** .... `T`

   OR

   Click **Tile Side by Side** .... `S`

SWITCH BETWEEN OPEN DOCUMENTS

- Click any visible portion of desired document.

  OR

- Click the document name on the Application Bar.

  OR

1. Click **Window** .... `Alt` + `W`
2. Click desired document .... `↑/↓`

   OR

- Press **Ctrl + F6** .... `Ctrl` + `F6` to view the next document.

  OR

- Press **Ctrl + Shift + F6** ...... `Ctrl` + `Shift` + `F6` to view previous document.

MOVE/COPY TEXT FROM ONE OPEN DOCUMENT TO ANOTHER

1. Open each file from which text is to be copied or moved. (See OPEN MULTIPLE DOCUMENTS above.)
2. Open a new file to receive the moved/copied text.

   ✓ *To make the Copy/Move procedure easier, tile the open documents.*

3. Click in the window where text is to be moved/copied from.
4. Highlight text to copy/move.

To copy text:

Ctrl + C

   a. Click **Edit** .... `Alt` + `E`
   b. Click **Copy** .... `C`

   OR

   Click **Copy** button 📋 on toolbar.

To cut (move text):

Ctrl + X

   a. Click **Edit** .... `Alt` + `E`
   b. Click **Cut** .... `T`

   OR

   Click **Cut** button ✂ on toolbar.

5. Click in window where text is to be moved/copied to.

   OR

   - Click the document name in the Application Bar to where text is to be moved/copied

6. Position insertion point where text is to be inserted.

To Paste text:

Ctrl + V

   a. Click **Edit** .... `Alt` + `E`
   b. Click **Paste** .... `P`

   OR

   Click **Paste** button 📋 on toolbar.

Exercise 36

- **Repeat Next Action**
- **Insert a File**

NOTES

Repeat Next Action

- The Repeat Next Action feature lets you repeat an action a specific number of times. For example, suppose you want to insert a row of 22 asterisks or hyphens, or paste an item from the Clipboard 15 times. The Repeat Next Action feature lets you set the desired number of repeats by selecting Repeat Next Action from the Edit menu. In the Repeat dialog box that follows, enter the number of times to repeat the next action in the increment box and click OK. The next action you perform will repeat the number of times you specified.

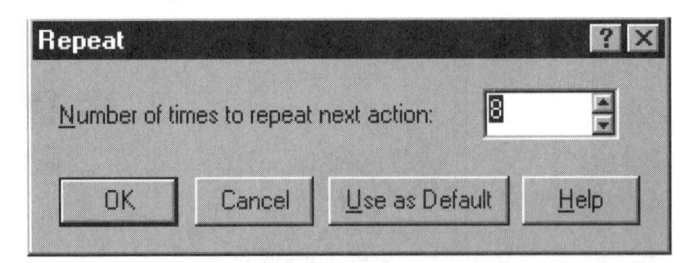

Insert a File

- When you insert a file into a document, the inserted file is made part of the current document. The original file remains intact and can be inserted into another document if desired. This is different than opening a document. When you open a document, each opened document is layered over the previous one.

- A file may be inserted by selecting File from the Insert menu.

- In the Insert File dialog box that follows, you must select the drive and folder containing the file you wish to insert, click the desired filename and click Insert.

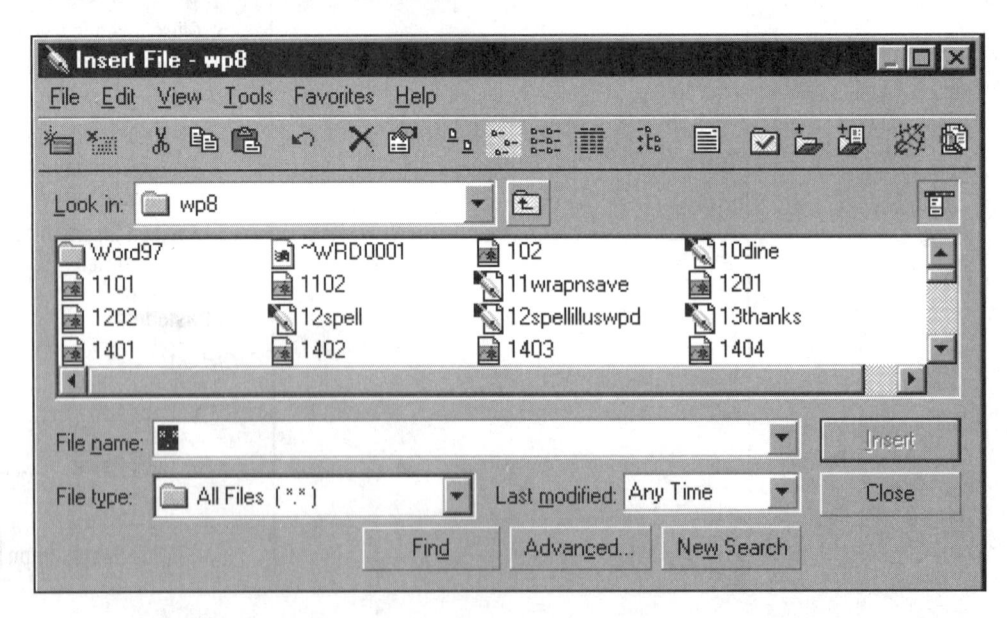

In Part I of this exercise, you will practice using the Repeat Next Action feature. In Part II of this exercise, you will use the Repeat Next Action feature to create a legal "caption" for an Order to Show Cause. Captions are headings used in court-filed legal documents. An Order to Show Cause will be explained in a later exercise when it is created. In Part III of this exercise, you will create a letter and insert a previously created file into it.

EXERCISE DIRECTIONS

PART I
1. Start with a clear screen.
2. Set the Repeat action to 10 and click OK. Type an asterisk.
3. Close the document window.

PART II
1. Create the legal caption shown in Illustration A below:
   a. Begin the caption on approximately Ln 2".
   b. Type the first two lines as shown in all caps and bold. Press Enter once.
   c. Set the Repeat action to 64, then type the hyphen once. Insert an "x" at the end of the hyphens.
   d. Press Enter twice. Set a bookmark; name it Plaintiff. Press Enter once.
   e. Display the Ruler. Clear all tab stops. Set left-aligned tab stops at 1.5", 2", and 4" from left margin.
   f. Tab to 3".
      - Type "Plaintiff,".
   g. Tab to 5".
      - Type ORDER TO SHOW CAUSE in all caps.
      - Underline and bold Order to Show Cause.
      - Press Enter twice.
   h. Tab to 2.5".
      - Type "–against–".
   i. Tab to 5".
      - Type "Index No."
      - Press the Spacebar twice after "Index No. " and create a bookmark; name it **Index No**.
      - Press Enter twice.
   j. Create a bookmark; name it **Defendant**. Press Enter once.
   k. Tab to 3".
      - Type "Defendant,".
      - Press Enter twice.
   l. Set Repeat action to 64, then type the hyphen once. Insert an "x" at the end of the hyphens.
2. Print one copy.
3. Save the file; name it **LEGAL**.
4. Close the document window.

ILLUSTRATION A

```
        SUPREME COURT OF THE STATE OF NEW YORK
        COUNTY OF NEW YORK
        ------------------------------------------------------------x
        Set a bookmark.
                                Plaintiff,              ORDER TO SHOW CAUSE

                        -against-                       Index No.   Set a bookmark.
        Set a bookmark.
                                Defendant,

        ------------------------------------------------------------x
```

COREL WORDPERFECT 8 Lesson 6: Templates; Envelopes and Labels; Macros

PART III

1. Open ⌨**PLAY** or 💾**36PLAY**. Format it as shown on Illustration B.
   a. Center the title and set it to a 24-point decorative font.
   b. Center the next two lines and set the font to a 20-point script font.
   c. Set the body and address information to a 12-point sans serif font.
   d. Right align the address information.
   e. Set the last line to a 10-point sans serif font.

2. Close the file; save as **PLAY**.

3. Open 💾**36AD**, or type the letter shown in Illustration C on page 175. Format it as follows:
   a. Use the default left and right margins. Set .5" top and bottom margins.
   b. Begin the letterhead at Ln .5". Set the letterhead title to a decorative font in 18-point bold. Set the address and phone number information to a sans serif font in 10-point bold.
   c. Right-align the letterhead name and address; left-align the phone and fax information.
   d. Use a serif 12-point font for the document.
   e. Begin the date at approximately Ln 2.5".

4. Insert ⌨**PLAY** or 💾**36PLAY** where indicated. Leave a double space before and after the insert.
   ✓ *After you insert the file, it may be necessary to return the left and right margins to 1" for the last paragraph.*

5. Spell check.

6. Use the Make-It-Fit feature to fit all text on one page. (Adjust font sizes and line spacing only.)

7. Print one copy.

8. Save the file as **AD**.

9. Close all files.

ILLUSTRATION B

> FAIR PLAY SPORTS CLUB
>
> *Child-like fun*
> *in the company of adults.*
>
> Are you tired of the corporate gym mentality? Do you remember the fun you had as a child playing team sports at school or among neighborhood friends? Fair Play Sports Club offers a new and fun way to work out while still gaining the health benefits of a serious gym routine. Fair Play Sports Club now offers team sports for adults at all fitness and experience levels.
>
> Fair Play Sports Club
234 Porter Road
Boston, MA 90786
(890) 890-8909
>
> More information is available at all of our neighborhood locations.

ILLUSTRATION C

Fair Play Sports Club
234 Porter Road
Boston, MA 90786
Phone: (900) 555-9989
Fax: (900) 555-8888

Today's Date

Ms. Carrie Weaver
MICA Advertising, Inc.
32 Farwell
Chicago, IL 66766

Dear Ms. Weaver:

The following is the advertising copy that we would like to run in several local business journals as well as in the business section of *The Boston Sun*. This copy incorporates many of the ideas that were discussed in last week's planning meeting, which you and your partner, James Newburg, attended. When you have had a chance to look it over, please give me a call.

We have several graphics that we are proposing to go with the copy. The art department will route the various options to you once the copy has been approved.

Sincerely,

Insert PLAY file.

Susan Porter
Marketing Manager

sp/yo

DESIRED RESULT

KEYSTROKES

REPEAT NEXT ACTION

1. Click **E**dit .... Alt+E
2. Click Repeat Ne**x**t Action X
3. Enter **N**umber of ...... Alt+N, *number times to repeat next action.*

4. Click **OK** .... Enter

INSERT FILE

1. Place the insertion point where you want file inserted.
2. Click **I**nsert .... Alt+I

3. Click **F**ile I
4. Type filename in the Filename text box or select name of document to insert.
5. Click **I**nsert .... Enter

COREL WORDPERFECT 8 Lesson 6: Templates; Envelopes and Labels; Macros

Exercise 37

■ Record a Macro

Macro Edit Feature bar

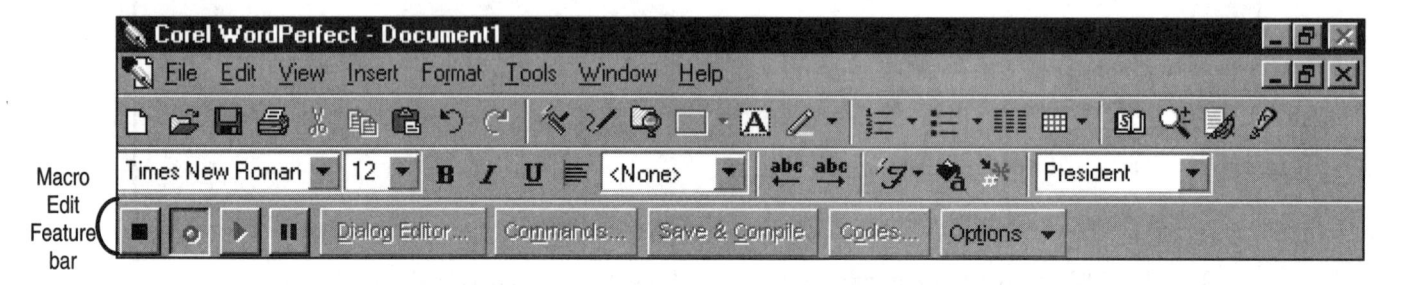

NOTES

- A **macro** is a saved series of commands and keystrokes which may be *played back* at a later time.

- Macros may be used to record often-used phrases, like the complimentary closing of a letter. When the phrase is needed, it is played back.

- A macro also may be used to automate a particular task, such as changing margins and/or line spacing.

- Rather than press many keys to access a feature, it is possible to record the process and play it back with fewer keystrokes.

- Macro features can be easily accessed from the Macro Tools toolbar or the Macro Edit Feature bar. Before recording your macro, display the Macro Tools toolbar (right-click the WordPerfect 8 Toolbar, select Macro Tools) and/or the Macro Edit feature bar (Tools, Macro, Macro Toolbar).

    ✓Note: The Macro Edit Feature bar will automatically display when you record a macro.

- To record a macro, select Macro, Record from the Tools menu, press Ctrl+F10, or click the Record button on the Macro Tools toolbar.

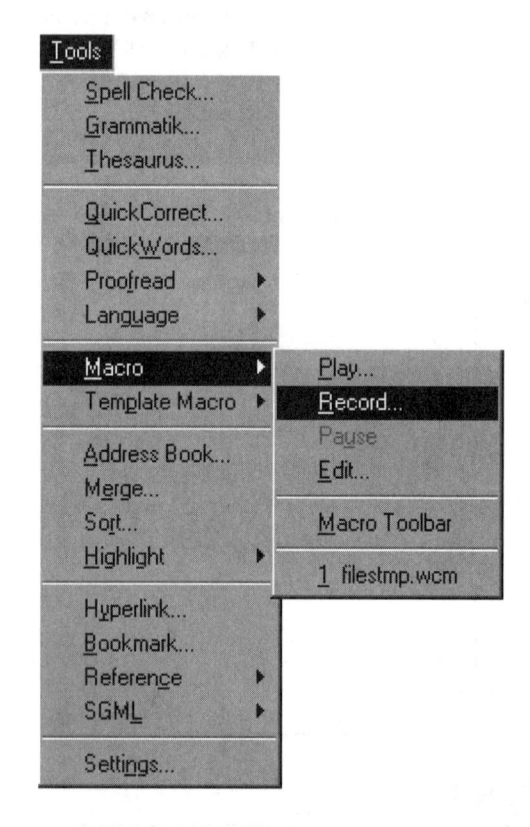

- In the Record Macro dialog box that follows, type the name of your macro in the File name text box. Then, click the Record button.

    ✓Note: Unless you specify another location, WordPerfect automatically saves macros in the C:\COREL\OFFICE\MACROS\WPWIN directory and assigns a **.wcm** extension.

176

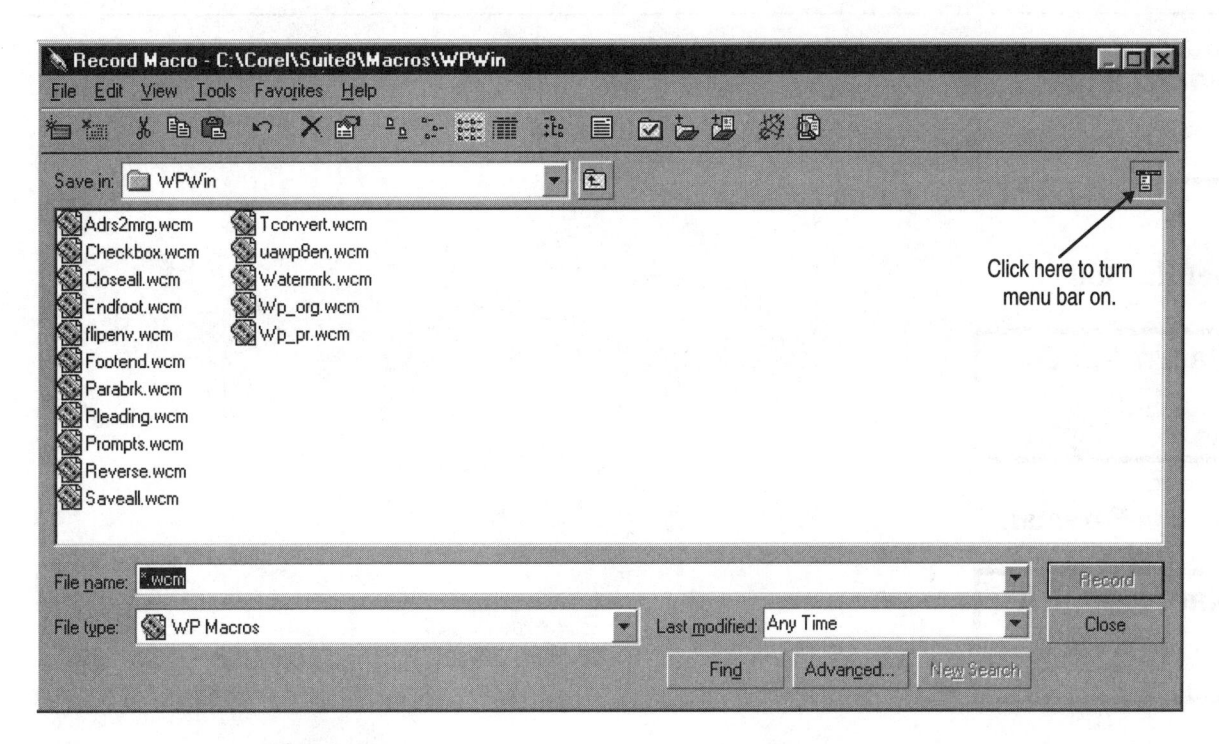

- The Macro Edit toolbar displays to provide a quick way to access macro-related tasks.

- If you wish to create a macro to change margins, for example, you will need to access the Margins dialog box during the recording session. To record selections from the dialog box, change the settings and proceed as usual.

- Record a macro carefully. When recording begins, the mouse pointer changes to a warning circle and Macro Record displays on the Application Bar.

- Any keyboard or mouse actions will be recorded into the macro. Before ending a macro, always return to the default document font. Otherwise, any new text will take on the appearance of the font used during Macro recording.

- To stop recording, click the Stop Macro Play or Record button on the Macro Edit toolbar.

  ✓ Note: The macro exercises in this text will not cover programming commands. (See your Corel WordPerfect Suite 8 documentation for macro programming command information.)

In this exercise, you will create several macros. You will play them back in subsequent exercises.

EXERCISE DIRECTIONS

1. Start with a clear screen.
2. Access the Macro Tools toolbar.
3. Create macro #1 as shown in the illustration on the following page; name it **P**. Use a serif 12-point bold font. Insert a hard space (Ctrl + spacebar) between first and last names.
   ✓ *If you are recording a macro with a font change, you must return the font back to the default before you stop recording.*
4. Close the document window without saving the changes.
5. Create macro #2; name it **D**. Use a serif 12-point bold font. Insert a hard space between first and last names.
6. Close the document window without saving the changes.
7. Create macro #3; name it **LA**. Use a bold sans serif 14-point font as shown.
8. Close the document window without saving the changes.
9. Create macro #4 (change margins); name it **M**.
10. Close the document window without saving the changes.

Corel WordPerfect 8 ■ Lesson 6 ■ Exercise 37

COREL WORDPERFECT 8   Lesson 6:   Templates; Envelopes and Labels; Macros

| Macro #1: P |

Gerald Holt

| Macro #2: D |

Gladys Foreman

| Macro #3: LA |

LA BOUND

| Macro #4: M |

1. Press Ctrl + F8.
2. Click Left margin up increment arrow and select 1.5".
3. Click Right margin up increment arrow and select 1.5".
4. Click OK.

KEYSTROKES

DISPLAY MACRO TOOLS TOOLBAR
1. Right-click WordPerfect 8 toolbar.
2. Select Macro Tools.

DISPLAY MACRO EDIT TOOLBAR
1. Click **Tools** .... Alt + T
2. Click **Macro** .... M
3. Click **Macro** toolbar .... M

RECORD MACRO
Ctrl + F10, name macro, record it, Ctrl + F10

1. Click **Record** button 🖭 on Macro Tools toolbar.
   OR
   Click **Tools** .... Alt + T
2. Click **Macro** .... M
3. Click **Record** .... R
4. Type macro name.
5. Click **Record** .... Enter

6. Provide keystrokes and mouse actions to be recorded.
   ✓ *If your macro contains any font appearance changes, be sure to return the font to the document default before ending the macro.*

7. To stop recording macro:

8. Click **Stop Record** button ■ on Macro Edit toolbar.
   OR
   a. Click **Tools** .... Alt + T
   b. Click **Macro** .... M
   c. Click **Record** .... R

Exercise 38

■ Play a Macro

Play Macro (toolbar button indicated)

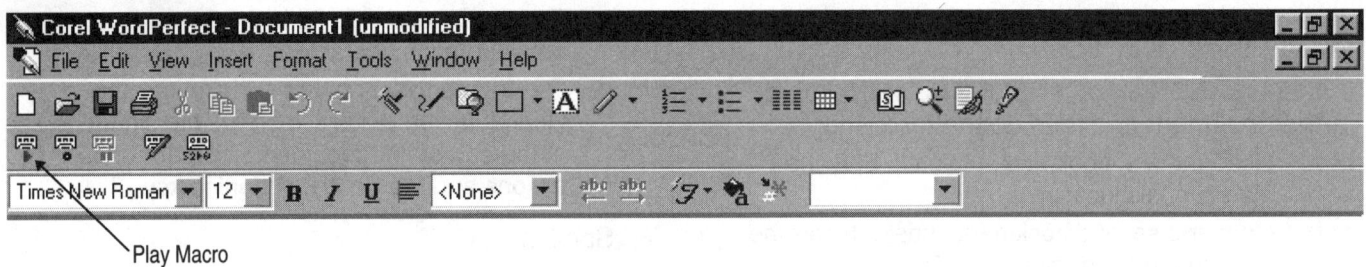

NOTES

Play a Macro

- Once a macro has been recorded and saved, it can be *played* into your document whenever desired.

- To play a macro, select Macro, Play from the Tools menu, press Alt + F10, or click the play button on the Macro Tools Toolbar.

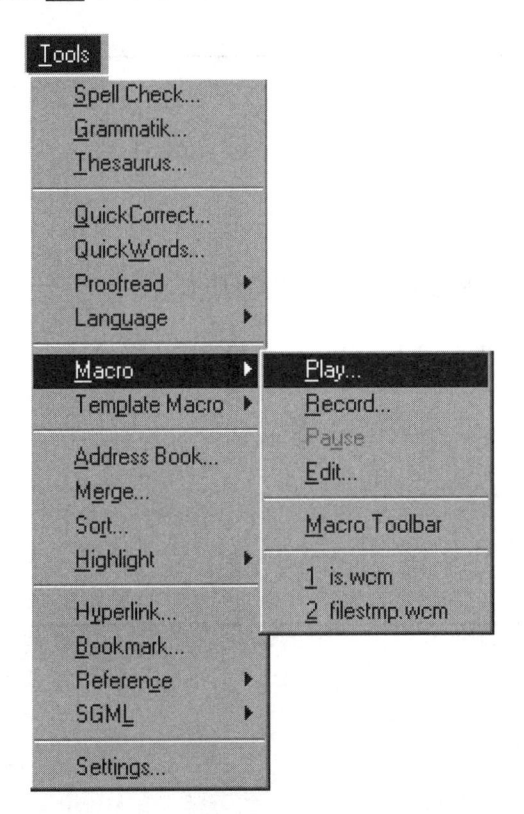

- In the Play Macro dialog box that follows, type the macro name to play in the File name text box. Or, select a macro from the filenames listed in the window. You will notice that there are macros listed that you did not create. WordPerfect has provided you with numerous macros to automate a variety of tasks. To determine what each macro does, right-click the macro and select QuickView from the QuickMenu.

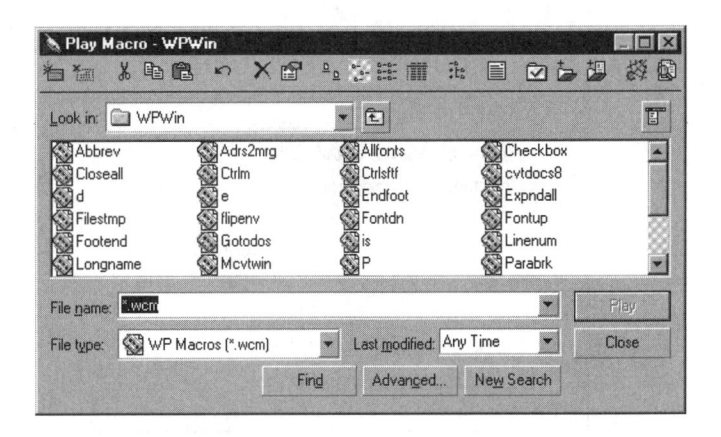

- When you select Tools, Macro, a list of the most recently played and/or recorded macros displays. You can select a macro to play back from the macros listed. (*see Illustration of drop-down menu on the left.*)

COREL WORDPERFECT 8 Lesson 6: Templates; Envelopes and Labels; Macros

> *In this exercise, you will create an Order to Show Cause and, where indicated, play the macros you created earlier. You will then insert the caption created earlier to complete the Order to Show Cause. An Order to Show Cause is an emergency application to the court for remedy to imminent harm. (See Desired Result, pages 182 and 183.)*

EXERCISE DIRECTIONS

1. Start with a clear screen.
2. Turn widow/orphan on.
3. Insert **LEGAL** or **38LEGAL** at the top of the document and then do the following:
   a. Go to the first bookmark, Plaintiff. Play the P macro in this location.
   b. Go to the second bookmark, Index. Insert the following Index number: 500000/98
   c. Go to the third bookmark, Defendant. Play the D macro in this location.
4. Clear all tab stops. Set left aligned tabs at .5", .75", 1", 3.5" from the left margin.
5. Insert **38SHOW**, or create the Order to Show Cause as shown in Illustration B.
   a. Begin the document two lines below the caption.
   b. Set the line spacing to double for the text.
   c. Play the P and D macros wherever they appear in the text.
   d. At the end of the document, press enter twice. Tab to 4.5" and type "E N T E R," spacing between each character.
   e. Press enter twice, tab to 4.5" and use the Repeat action feature to create the signature line at the end of the document. Use 30 repeat actions and the Shift + Underline key.
6. Spell check.
7. Insert page numbers. Position them at the bottom right of second and subsequent pages. Choose any desired format.
8. Preview your document.
9. Print one copy.
10. Save the file; name it **SHOW**.
11. Close the document window.

ILLUSTRATION A

```
    SUPREME COURT OF THE STATE OF NEW YORK
    COUNTY OF NEW YORK
    ----------------------------------------------------------------X

 Play D Macro at the
  Plantiff bookmark        Plaintiff,           ORDER TO SHOW CAUSE

                            -against-           Index No.


 Play D Macro at the
  Defendant bookmark       Defendant,
    ----------------------------------------------------------------X
```

ILLUSTRATION B

Upon reading and filing the annexed Affidavit of the Plaintiff, **P**, sworn to on the 15th day of March, 1999, the Affirmation of Thomas Quinn, Esquire, of the law firm of Quinn, Davis and Marino, dated the 15th day of March, 1999, the Summons and Verified Complaint heretofore served herein, and upon all the prior papers and proceedings in this action,

LET THE DEFENDANT, **D**, SHOW CAUSE before a Justice of this Court, to be assigned herein, to be held at the Supreme Court, New York County, at the Courthouse thereof located at 60 Centre Street, Room 555, New York, New York, on the 19th day of March, 1999, at 9:30 o'clock in the forenoon or as soon thereafter as counsel can be heard, why an order should not be made and entered herein directing the following relief:

1. Granting to the Plaintiff, **P**, leave to amend the Complaint, pursuant to CPLR 3025;

2. Directing the Defendant, **D**, to produce and allow discovery of documents and things, pursuant to CPLR Section 3120(a) and related sections; and

3. For such other and further relief as the Court may deem just and proper.

Sufficient cause appearing therefore, let personal service of a copy of this Order, the Summons and Verified Complaint, and the papers upon which it is based upon **D** on or before the day of March 16, 1999, be deemed good and sufficient service.

SUPREME COURT OF THE STATE OF NEW YORK
COUNTY OF NEW YORK
---x

Gerald Holt

        Plaintiff,   **<u>ORDER TO SHOW CAUSE</u>**

    -against-   Index No. 500000/98

Gladys Foreman

        Defendant,

---x

   Upon reading and filing the annexed Affidavit of the Plaintiff, **Gerald Holt**, sworn to on the 15th day of March, 1999, the Affirmation of Thomas Quinn, Esquire, of the law firm of Quinn, Davis and Marino, dated the 15th day of March, 1999, the Summons and Verified Complaint heretofore served herein, and upon all the prior papers and proceedings in this action,

   LET THE DEFENDANT, **Gladys Foreman**, SHOW CAUSE before a Justice of this Court, to be assigned herein, to be held at the Supreme Court, New York County, at the Courthouse thereof located at 60 Centre Street, Room 555, New York, New York, on the 19th day of March, 1999, at 9:30 o'clock in the forenoon or as soon thereafter as counsel can be heard, why an order should not be made and entered herein directing the following relief:

1. Granting to the Plaintiff, **Gerald Holt**, leave to amend the Complaint, pursuant to CPLR 3025;

2. Directing the Defendant, **Gladys Foreman**, to produce and allow discovery of documents and things, pursuant to CPLR Section 3120(a) and related sections; and

3. For such other and further relief as the Court may deem just and proper.

DESIRED RESULTS - Page 2 of 2

> Sufficient cause appearing therefore, let personal service of a copy of this Order, the Summons and Verified Complaint, and the papers upon which it is based upon **Gladys Foreman** on or before the day of March 16, 1999, be deemed good and sufficient service.
>
> ENTER
> _____
>
> -2-

KEYSTROKES

PLAY A MACRO

Alt + F10

1. Position insertion point where macro is to play.
2. Click **Play** button on Macro Tools toolbar.

   OR

   a. Click **Tools** .... Alt + T
   b. Click **Macro** .... M
   c. Click **Play** .... P

3. Double-click desired macro to play.

   OR

   Type the macro name to play.

4. Click **Play** .... Enter

COREL WORDPERFECT 8 Lesson 6: Templates; Envelopes and Labels; Macros

Exercise 39

■ **Summary**

In Part I of this exercise, you will create a press release for a new film using a PerfectExpert template and other features learned in this lesson. A press release is a document that is prepared and sent to various newspapers and magazines announcing a new product, production, publication, etc. In part II of this exercise, you will use a PerfectExpert template to create a letter and print an envelope.

EXERCISE DIRECTIONS

1. Start with a clear screen.
2. Click File, New.
3. Select Press Release from the Correspondence, Business category, and click Create.
4. Use the following PerfectExpert options and Macro feature to complete the document as shown in Illustration A.
   ✓ *The last selected Address Book entry will automatically display in the press release. This can be changed using the Edit Sections option.*
   - Click the Edit Sections button. Select each section and edit it as follows:
     - Company Name: Change as shown in Illustration A. Bold the name and address text.
     - Contact Info: Change as shown in Illustration A.
     - Subtitle: Bold the text.
     - Headline: Change as shown in Illustration A. Center and bold headline text. Play the **LA** macro (created in Exercise 37) wherever LA BOUND appears in the document.
     - Body: enter the text as shown in the illustration. Change line spacing to 1.5". Play the macro wherever LA BOUND appears in the document.
5. Play the Filestamp macro. Insert the filename (not the path) as a footer on the bottom left of the page.
   ✓ *If this feature is unavailable, skip this step.*
6. Spell check.
7. Use Make-It-Fit, if necessary, to keep text on one page.
8. Preview your document.
9. Print one copy.
10. Save the file; name it **LABOUND**.
11. Close the document window.

PART II
1. Start with a clear screen.
2. Click File, New.
3. Select Letter, Business from the Correspondence, Business category, and click Create.
4. Use the PerfectExpert options to complete the document shown in Illustration B on page 186.
   a. Click the *Fill in Heading Info* button and enter the following in the Heading Information dialog box:
      To: Click Address Book button and select Ms. Cheryl Greenwood. (If his information has not been entered, do so now. See Exercise 4 for address information).
      From: Click Address Book button and enter the following organization:
      Maui Tides Ranch
      39 Keoki Drive
      Kihei, HI 96753-544
      Phone: 425-555-4545
      Fax: 425-555-7777
      Date: Today's
      Greeting: Dear Ms. Greenwood:
   b. Choose any desired look for the letter.
   c. Type the body text as shown in Illustration B.
   d. Click the Fill in Closing Info button and select the following:
      Complimentary Closing: Sincerely
      Sender's Title: Manager
      Writer's Initials: cf
      Typist's Initials: yo
      Enclosures: 1
      ✓ *The writer's name is not included in the closing info fill-in options, and the spacing for a full-block letter does not conform to the standard format. Therefore, you will need to add the writer's name (in addition to making spacing adjustments) after the letter is completed.*

a. Spell check the letter.
b. Click the Finish button and select Save; name the file **RANCH**.
c. Create an Envelope
   – Do not include a return address.
   – Use a number 10 Landscape envelope, if available.
   – Append it to the document.
5. Insert the writer's name (Carla French) as shown in Illustration B on page 186.
6. Print one copy of the letter and the envelope.
7. Close the file; save the changes.

ILLUSTRATION A

PRESS RELEASE

First Degree Cinema ⎫
555 Fifth Avenue   ⎬ *Company Name*
New York, NY 10022   ⎭

For more information contact: ⎫
First Degree Cinema   ⎬ *Contact Information*
(800)555-4444   ⎭

FOR IMMEDIATE RELEASE ⎤ *Subtitle*

Headline — **First Degree Cinema introduces LA BOUND written and directed by Sherry Lynn Greco to be previewed at the New York Film House on December 1, 1998.**

Body, 1.5 line spacing

First Degree Cinema is proud to introduce to the romantic-comedy film audience Sherry Lynn Greco's hilarious new film, **LA BOUND**.

Something is amiss in the extremely successful life of Dallas advertising executive Lisa Everett. On the eve of her own wedding, Lisa Everett decides to flee her wealthy fiancé, Rupert, in search of a long-lost love in Los Angeles. After she steals her fiancé's car and flees for LA, she meets a host of unusual characters, including a new best friend, Rosetta, who introduces her to a world of excitement that Lisa has never experienced. When Lisa does eventually make it to Los Angeles–minus Rupert's car and all savings that she previously had–she is faced with a difficult decision: Should she return to her secure life in Dallas or risk everything to start again with nothing in a town where she knows only one person, whom she hasn't even found yet.

LA BOUND is a romantic adventure that is sure to keep audiences at the edge of their seats. Told to the audience from the narrative of Lisa–who is just as brilliant and beautiful as she is confused and angry–**LA BOUND** will appeal to anyone who's ever been at a cross road in life and dared to explore other options.

LA BOUND is writer/director Sherry Lynn Greco's first feature film. She is a graduate of the University of Miami Film School, where her thesis film, TAKE YESTERDAY AWAY, took first place in the annual Florida Student Film Festival. She lives in Chicago with her husband and five dogs.

ILLUSTRATION B

Maui Tides Ranch

Maui Tides Ranch
39 Keoki Drive
Kihei, HI 96753-5544
425-555-RIDE
Fax: 425-555-7777

Today's Date

Cheryl Greenwood
60 Lake Shore Drive
Chicago, Il 60555

Dear Ms. Greenwood:

We are delighted that you will be joining us for one week, beginning June 7, 1999.

Your vacation package includes: all meals, a four-hour horseback ride daily, access to our health spa, and a lovely one-room ocean view suite. I have enclosed a brochure that further details your accommodations.

At Maui Tides Ranch, we believe that the best of Maui can only be explored by horseback. Automobiles limit your access to the true beauty of the island. We are certain you too will find this to be true.

Sincerely,

Carla French
Manager

cf:yo

Enclosures/1/

COREL WORDPERFECT 8

Lesson 7: Columns; Tables; Merge

Exercise 40

- Columns
- Newspaper Columns
- Parallel Columns

NOTES

Columns

- The **Columns** feature allows text to flow from one column to another.

  WordPerfect provides four column types:

  - *newspaper columns,* in which text flows down one column to the bottom of a page then starts again at the top of the next column.
  - *balanced newspaper columns*, in which text flows down one column to the bottom of a page then starts again at the top of the next column and is adjusted on the page so that the columns are equal in length.
  - *parallel columns*, in which text moves across the columns.
  - *parallel columns with block protect*, similar to parallel columns, except that if a column extends beyond a page break, the entire column is moved to the next page.

Regular Newspaper Columns

Newspaper columns allow text to flow from one column to another. This is an example of a regular newspaper column. When text reaches the bottom of one column, it automatically wraps to	the top of the next column. The gutter space is set by WordPerfect, but may be changed, as desired.

Balanced Newspaper Columns

This is an example of a balanced newspaper column. Each column is adjusted on the page so that it is equal in length. No matter how much text is typed, the columns will always balance so that they are equal in length. As with	regular newspaper columns, the gutter space is set by WordPerfect, but may be changed as desired. Use this where you want as much text as possible to stay together in the section, like the top and bottom of a page.

Parallel Columns

Monday	Meeting with John Smith at 9:00 a.m.
Tuesday	Lunch appointment with Randy Grafco to discuss merge.
Wednesday	Meeting with Sasha Mann at 10:30 a.m.

- The Column feature is accessed by selecting Columns from the Format menu.

- You can also create columns quickly by clicking the columns button on the WordPerfect 8 toolbar and selecting the number of columns you want to create.

- In the Columns dialog box that follows, select a column type and define the number of columns. You can also adjust the space between columns and the width of each column. To change the amount of space between columns, enter the amount of space in the Space between text box. To change column widths, enter the desired widths in the Column width boxes. If you choose not to make any adjustments, the default settings will apply.

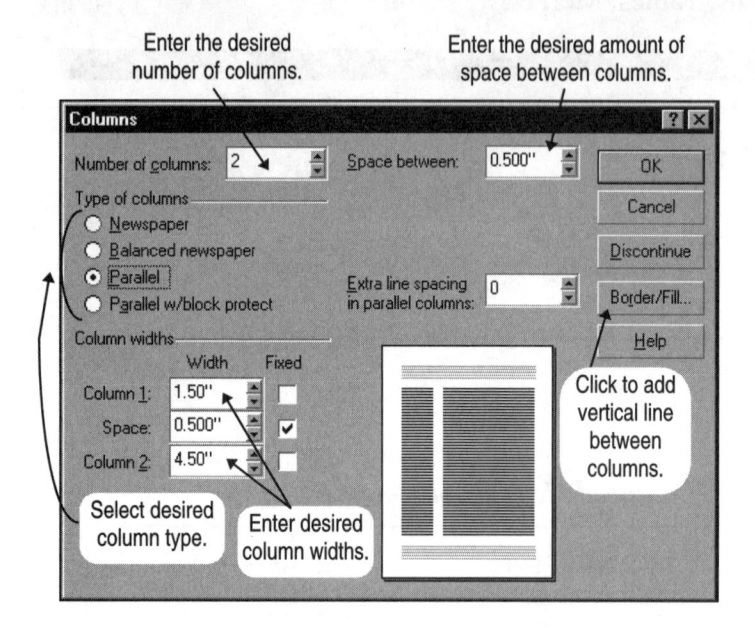

Columns dialog box callouts

- Enter the desired number of columns.
- Enter the desired amount of space between columns.
- Click to add vertical line between columns.
- Select desired column type.
- Enter desired column widths.

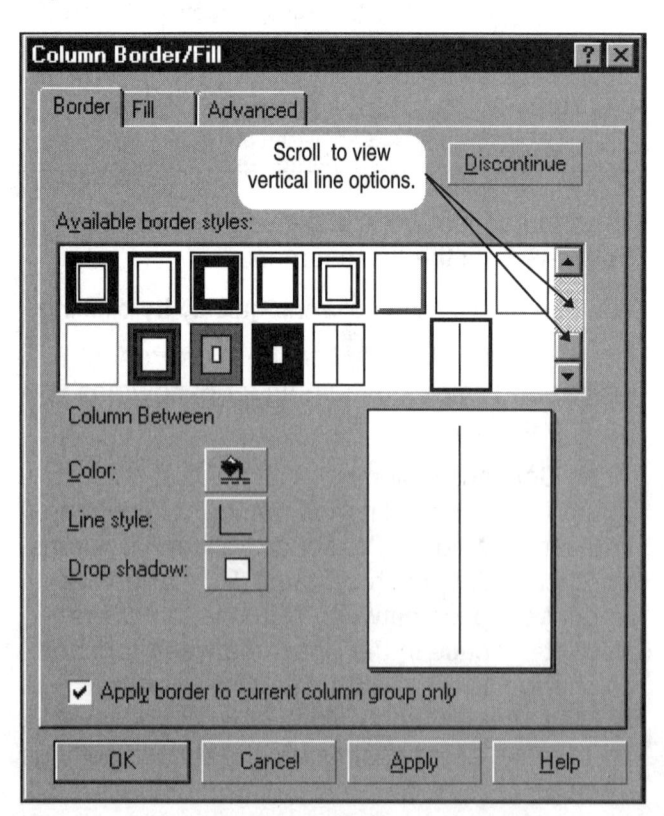

- Click the mouse in the desired column to move the insertion point quickly from column to column.
- Columns may be created *before* or *after* typing text. To create them after typing text, select the text to format in columns and then apply the desired column settings.

Newspaper Columns

- Newspaper and balanced newspaper columns are particularly useful when creating newsletters, pamphlets, brochures, lists, or articles.
- You can retrieve text from a file into newspaper-style columns. When retrieving text from a file into columns, be sure your insertion point is within the column mode.
- After text is entered in one column, enter a hard column break (Ctrl + Enter) to force the insertion point to move to the next column.

Parallel Columns

- Parallel columns are particularly useful when creating a list, script, itinerary, minutes of a meeting, or any document in which columns are read horizontally.
- After text is entered in one column, enter a hard column break (Ctrl + Enter) to force the insertion point to move to the next column.

- The column feature is turned *on* when you click OK. You must turn *off* the Column feature when you complete the columnar part of your document.
- To include a vertical line between columns, click the Border/Fill button in the Columns dialog box. In the Column Border/Fill dialog box that follows, click the Border tab, then click the vertical line between columns option in the list of Available border styles. You must scroll down to see this option.

Column Border/Fill dialog box callout

- Scroll to view vertical line options.

In Part I of this exercise, you will create a three-column newsletter using newspaper-style columns. In Part II of this exercise, you will create minutes of a meeting using parallel columns.

EXERCISE DIRECTIONS

PART I

1. Start with a clear screen.
2. Use the default margins.
3. Begin the exercise on Ln 1".
4. Type the title, shown in Illustration A on page 190 in a sans serif 18-point bold font. Return to serif 12 point and press Enter three times.
5. Set line spacing to 1.3.
6. Create the remainder of the newsletter shown in Illustration A using a three-column, *regular* newspaper-style format. Use the default gutter space between columns.
7. Center (within the column) and set the headlines to a sans serif 14-point bold font. Press Enter twice after each headline.
8. Set column paragraph text to a serif 12-point font.
9. Insert a vertical line (border) between columns.
10. Full justify document text.
11. Spell check.
12. If necessary, adjust the bottom margin (drag the guide) to keep all text on one page.
13. View your document as a full page and compare with Illustration A.
14. Print one copy.
15. Save the file; name it **ACTIVITY**.
16. Close the document window.

PART II

1. Start with a clear screen.
2. Use the default margins.
3. Begin the exercise on approximately Ln 2".
4. Type the text shown in Illustration B on page 191.
5. Center the main heading in a sans serif 16-point bold font.
    a. Use any desired special character before and after the heading as shown.
    b. Center the minor headings in a sans serif 12-point italic font.
    c. Center five symbols to separate the date from the body text. Return to serif 12 point and press the Enter key three times after the special characters.
6. Create a two-column, parallel style format.
7. Change the width of column one to 1.5". Change the width of column two to 4.5". Use the default distance between columns.
8. Set the side headings to a sans serif 12-point italic font. Set the body text to a serif 12-point font.
9. Set the "New Business" heading to uppercase, bold, italic, and underline.
10. Spell check.
11. View your document as a full page and compare with Illustration B.
12. Print one copy.
13. Save the file; name it **MINUTES**.
14. Close the document window.

COREL WORDPERFECT 8 Lesson 7: Columns; Tables; Merge

ILLUSTRATION A

Student Activity Monthly Newsletter

NEW STUDENT WELCOME FAIR

The Administration department will sponsor a Welcome Fair for all new students on August 28. Packets will be available to inform students of all on-campus activities and clubs, nearby restaurants and shops, dormitory information, etc. Several clubs and organizations will be represented by information booths. If you would like to add a flyer or brochure to the packet, or if you wish to register a booth for your club or organization, please see Dean Stella Samuels in the Administration Department. A barbecue lunch will be served on the Main Lawn from noon to 2:00 p.m., followed by a get-acquainted session in which new students will have the opportunity to ask a panel of peers any university-related questions. Dean Samuels will wrap up the event with a talk at the Union Podium.

CAMPUS EMPLOYMENT

With the arrival of the fall semester, several campus employment opportunities have opened up. The French and Italian Languages department is seeking tutors for French 1 and Italian 1. Applicants must be fluent in either French or Italian and have completed a minimum of 3 years of college-level French or Italian. If interested, please see Dr. Vincineau Monday through Wednesday in Room 760 of the French and Italian Building. The Math and Science department is also seeking tutors as well as lab workers. Many positions and levels of employment are available. If interested, see Dr. Martin on Tuesdays and Thursdays in Room 317 of the John Hall Math and Science Building.

ESSAY CONTEST

The University's 32nd Annual Personal Heritage Essay Contest is underway. All students are encouraged to write a 5,000-word essay that details their history and family background. Scholarship money will be awarded to the top ten winners.

❀❀❀ NATIONAL CHILDREN'S GROUP ❀❀❀
BOARD OF DIRECTORS

Board Committees

❀❀❀❀❀

Present	Will Smith, Lisa Krakow, Byron Wendall, Sarah Porter, Elaine Miller, Wendy Cohen, Suzanne Feldstein
Announcements	The meeting for next month is going to be rescheduled. Please see Elaine if you have any conflict with April 12th. We will be welcoming two new members to the development committee at that meeting.

NEW BUSINESS

Newsletter	There have been delays in the current issue of the newsletter because of a change in office staff. We need volunteers to work on the next edition, so that we can get it out in time for the benefit.
AIDS Walk	Children First will be sending a team to participate in this year's AIDS walk. We will be considered a sponsor team and, as such, will receive the money that we raise.
Benefit	Please see the attached memo that Lisa has prepared on the progress of this year's benefit.
Endowment	We are close to our goal on the endowment campaign. Please speak with Wendy if you have specific questions.
Adjournment	The meeting was adjourned at 12:00 p.m.

COREL WORDPERFECT 8 Lesson 7: Columns; Tables; Merge

KEYSTROKES

CREATE COLUMNS

1. Place insertion point where column is to begin.
   OR
   Select existing text to include in columns.
   a. Click **Format** .... `Alt`+`R`
   b. Click **Columns** .... `C`
2. Click a column type:
   - **Newspaper** .... `Alt`+`N`
   - **Balanced newspaper** .... `Alt`+`B`
   - **Parallel** .... `Alt`+`P`
   - **Parallel w/block protect** ... `Alt`+`A`
3. Change the following options as desired:
   Number of columns:
   a. Click **Number of columns** text box .... `Alt`+`C`
   b. Type desired number of columns OR use increment arrows .. `↓`/`↑` to choose desired number of columns.

Space between text boxes:
   a. Click **Space between** text box .... `Alt`+`S`
   b. Type desired distance.
Insert a vertical line between columns:
   a. Click the **Border/Fill** button .... `Alt`+`R`
   b. Select an **Available border** style .... `Alt`+`V`, `↕`
      - Scroll down .... `↓`/`↑` to vertical line option.
   c. Click **OK** .... `Enter`
4. Click **OK** .... `Enter`

FORCE TEXT TO A NEW COLUMN

1. Position insertion point where new column is to begin.
2. Press **Ctrl + Enter** .... `Ctrl`+`Enter`

TURN OFF COLUMNS

Place insertion point outside column area.
OR
1. Place insertion point where column is to be turned off.
2. Click **Format** .... `Alt`+`R`
3. Click **Columns** .... `R`
4. Click **Off** .... `O`

MOVE INSERTION POINT FROM COLUMN TO COLUMN

Click in desired column.

CREATE COLUMNS WITH CUSTOM WIDTHS

1. Place insertion point where column is to begin.
2. Click **Format** .... `Alt`+`R`
3. Click **Columns** .... `C`
4. Click **Column 1** text box .... `Alt`+`1`
5. Type desired width.
6. Click **Column 2** text box .... `Alt`+`2`
7. Type desired width.
8. Repeat procedure .... `Tab`, *number* for each additional column.
9. Click **OK** .... `Enter`

COREL WORDPERFECT 8 Lesson 7: Columns; Tables; Merge

Exercise 41

- Create a Table ■ Edit a Table in a Graphics box ■ Move within a Table
- Enter Text in a Table ■ Select Cells, Rows or Columns

NOTES

	Column A	Column B	Column C	Column D
Row 1				
Row 2				
Row 3				

- The **Table** feature allows you to organize information into columns and rows without using tabs or tab settings.

- A table consists of **rows**, which run horizontally and are identified by number (1, 2, 3, etc.), and **columns**, which run vertically and are identified by letter (A, B, C, etc.). The rows and columns intersect to form empty boxes, called **cells**. Note the example above of a table with three rows and four columns.

- Text, graphics, numbers, or formulas are entered into cells after you have defined the structure of your table—that is, how many columns and rows you require for your table.

Create a Table

- Select Table from the Insert menu. In the Create Table dialog box that follows, indicate the desired number of columns and rows in the Columns and/or Rows increment boxes. Then click the Create button.

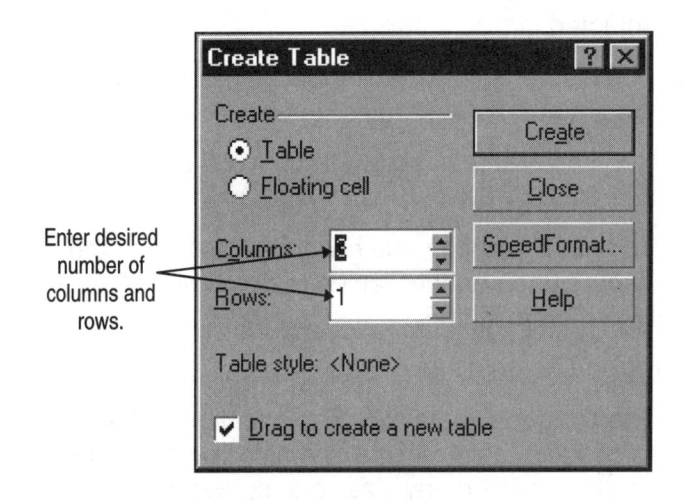

Enter desired number of columns and rows.

- You can also create tables quickly by clicking the Tables QuickCreate button on the WordPerfect 8 toolbar and dragging the mouse pointer to select the desired number of rows and columns. Double-clicking this button will bring you to the Create Table dialog box.

Drag down and to the right to select the desired number of columns and rows

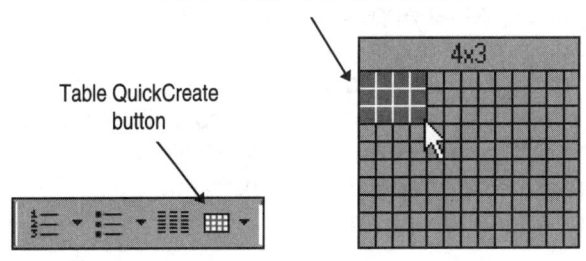

Table QuickCreate button

Corel WordPerfect 8 ■ Lesson 7 ■ Exercise 41

COREL WORDPERFECT 8 Lesson 7: Columns; Tables; Merge

Tables Toolbar

Table Menu — Vertical Alignment — Rotate Cell — Tables Toolbar

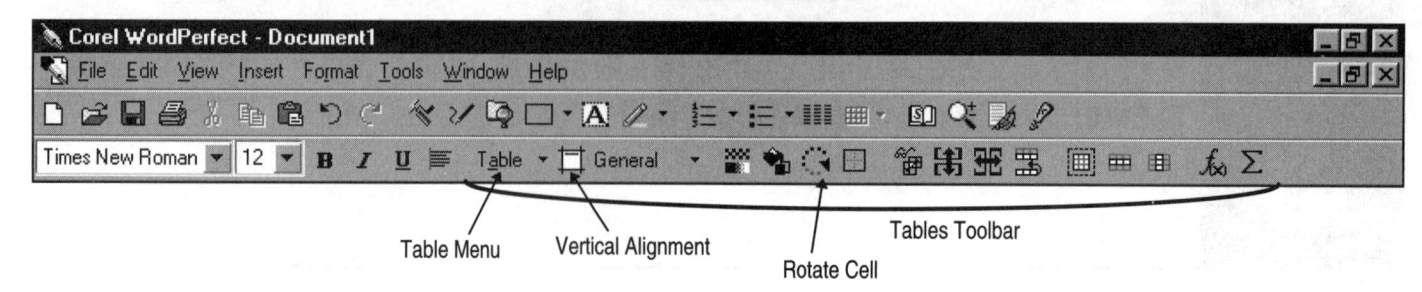

- When you select a table (or a cell, column, or row within a table), table related toolbar buttons automatically appear on the Property Bar. The Table Property Bar buttons are convenient for accessing table-related tasks.

- You may want to display the Tables toolbar by right-clicking the current toolbar and selecting Tables. This toolbar will remain onscreen until it is deselected, even if a table (or table cell) is not selected.

- The columns adjust automatically to fit between the left and right margins.

- You can create a table with up to 64 columns and 32,767 rows.

- To display column and row indicators, click the T<u>a</u>ble button on the Tables toolbar and select Ro<u>w</u>/Col Indicators.

Drag-to-Create a New Table

- The Drag-to-Create New Table feature allows you to create a table within a graphics box. The box can be drawn to any size, and placed in any position within your document. You can also flow text around it. (Flowing text around a graphics box will be covered in Lesson 12). Table columns and rows will span the box frame.

- To activate the Drag-to-Create feature, select the Drag-to-Create a New Table check box on the Create Table dialog box. After entering the desired number of columns and rows and clicking Cre<u>a</u>te, a special pointer appears. Position the pointer where you want the upper left corner of the box to begin and drag down diagonally to the desired position for the lower right corner of the box. Then, release the mouse button. Your table will display within a graphics box. To hide the box frame, click anywhere outside the table.

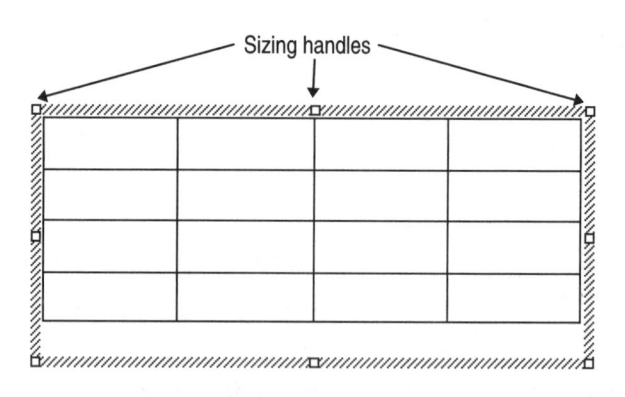

Sizing handles

- Once activated, the Drag-to-Create option remains selected until you deselect it.

Edit a Table in a Graphics Box

- You can reduce, enlarge, stretch, move or delete the graphics box containing a table when the sizing handles are displayed.

- *To size a table graphics box*, click the table to display the box frame and its sizing handles. Position the mouse pointer on a handle until it becomes a double-headed arrow. Drag any one of the four *corner* handles to size the box (and table) proportionally. Drag any one of the four *middle* handles to change the box height or width.

- *To position a table graphics box*, click the table to display the box frame and position your mouse on the frame (not on a handle). When the pointer becomes a four headed arrow, drag the box to the desired location.

- *To delete a table graphics box* and it contents, click the table to display the box frame, click on the frame again to display only the sizing handles and press the Delete key.

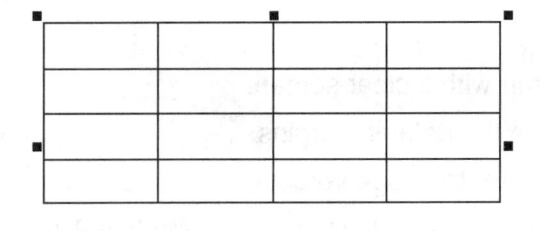

Move within a Table

- The insertion point moves in a table the same way it moves in a document. You may use the mouse to click in the desired cell, press the Tab key to move from cell to cell, or use keystrokes to move around the cells. (See Keystrokes section on page 197.)

- If there is no text in a cell, the directional arrow keys move the insertion point from cell to cell; otherwise, they move the insertion point through text in the cell.

- When the insertion point is in a table cell, the Application Bar indicates the cell location by displaying the cell's column letter and row number.

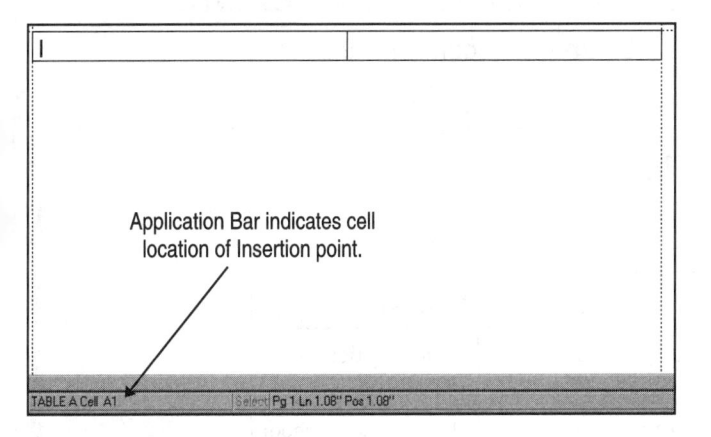

Enter Text in a Table

- As you enter text in a table cell, the cell expands downward to accommodate the text. Pressing Enter in a cell also expands the cell vertically.

- Use the Tab key to advance the insertion point from one cell to the next, even at the end of the row. When the insertion point is in the last cell of a table, pressing the Tab key creates a new row.

- You can advance text to a tab setting within a cell by pressing Ctrl + Tab.

Selecting Cells, Rows or Columns

- When working with tables, it is often necessary to select a cell, a row, a column or a group of cells, rows or columns before performing an action (like aligning, deleting, or sizing text). The following selection shortcuts will make this task easier:

  - To select a cell or row, position the mouse to the right of a vertical line until the pointer changes to a single-headed, horizontal arrow. Click once to select the cell, or double-click to select the entire row. Or, you can click the row indicator to select the row.

  - To select a cell or a column, position the mouse pointer below a horizontal line until it becomes a single-headed, vertical arrow. Click to select the cell, or double-click to select the entire column. Or, you can click the column indicator to select the column.

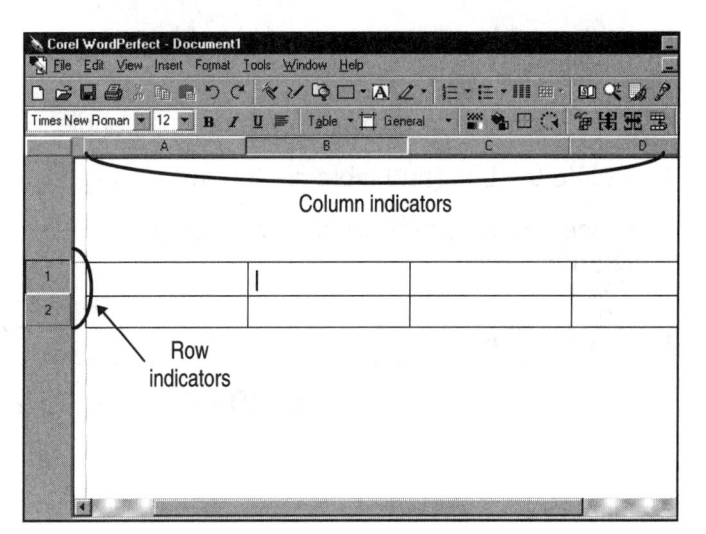

  - To select all the cells in the table, position the mouse pointer on any line in the table until it becomes a vertical or horizontal arrow and triple-click the mouse button. You can also select the entire table by clicking the Select Table button on the Table Property Bar.

  ✓*Note: The Table Property Bar will display different buttons for accessing table-related tasks depending on whether you select a cell, column or row.*

Corel WordPerfect 8 ■ Lesson 7 ■ Exercise 41

COREL WORDPERFECT 8 Lesson 7: Columns; Tables; Merge

In Part I of this exercise, you will use the Drag-to-Create feature to create a table.
In Part II of this exercise, you will create a table using 4 columns and 5 rows.

EXERCISE DIRECTIONS

PART I
1. Start with a clear screen.
2. Use the default margins.
3. Using the Drag-to-Create table feature, create a table with 3 columns and 2 rows in any desired size. Click outside the table to hide the frame.
4. Display the column and row indicators.
5. Enter the following text.

1st Term	2nd Term	3rd Term
Pass	Pass	Pass

6. Click inside the table to display the frame and sizing handles.
7. Enlarge the box proportionally (drag a corner handle)
8. Widen the box to any desired size (drag a middle right or left handle).
9. Click the frame to display only the sizing handles.
10. Delete the box (and table contents).
11. Close the document window without saving changes.

PART II
1. Start with a clear screen.
2. Use the default margins.
3. Center the page vertically.
4. Create the table shown in Illustration A on the next page using four columns and six rows. (Do not use the Drag-to-Create feature.)
5. Enter the table text as shown. Bold the column headings.
6. Preview your document.
7. Print one copy.
8. Display column and row indicators.
9. Change table font sizes and faces as follows:
   - Row 1 titles to 16-point bold.
   - Column A text to a sans serif bold font.
10. Center the title above the table as shown.
    - Set font to 18 points, sans serif.
    - Return font to 12 points and press the Enter key three times.
11. Print one copy.
12. Save the exercise; name it **EVENTS**.
13. Close the document window.

ILLUSTRATION A

1999 UNIVERSITY SPECIAL EVENTS

Event	Date	Location	Sponsor
New Student Welcome Picnic	September 2	Campus Main Library Lawn	Administration Department
Fall Fest Carnival	October 17	Huff Pavilion	Huff Business School
Pilgrim Celebration Dinner	November 19	Wyndham Hall	Theatre Department
Winter Dance	December 12	Railley Hall	Advanced Technology Club
Summer Celebration Dinner and Dance	May 28	Wyndham Hall	Science Department

KEYSTROKES

CREATE A TABLE
F12

1. Position insertion point at left margin where you want table to begin.
2. Follow one of listed procedures below:
   a. Click **Table** button [icon] on the WordPerfect 8 toolbar.
   b. Drag to select desired number of columns and rows.
   c. Release mouse.

   OR

   a. Click **Insert**.................. Alt + I
   b. Click **Table**.................. T
   c. Click **Columns** box......... O
   d. Type desired number or click increment buttons to select number of columns............. ↑ ↓
   e. Click **Rows** box .... Alt + R
   f. Type desired number or click increment buttons to select number of rows................ ↑ ↓

   To Drag-to-Create Table:
   - Click **Drag-to-Create Table** check box.................. Alt + D

   g. Click **Create** .... Alt + A

   If Drag-to-Create Table was Selected:
   - Drag mouse pointer diagonally to desired size.
   - Release mouse.
   - Click outside frame to hide box.
   - Click inside table to display frame and sizing handles.

ENTER TEXT IN TABLES

1. Click cell to receive text.
2. Type text.
3. Press **Tab**........................ Tab
   to advance to next cell.

   OR

   Use the following insertion point movements:

TO MOVE:	PRESS:
One cell right	Tab
One cell left	Shift + Tab
One cell down	↓
One cell up	↑
First cell in row	Home, Home
Last cell in row	End, End
Top line of multi-line cell	Alt + Home
Bottom line of multi-line cell	Alt + End

DISPLAY COLUMN LETTERS AND ROW NUMBERS

- Click Tables button [Table ▼] on Tables toolbar.
- Select **Row/Col Indicator** .... W

SELECT CELLS, COLUMNS, ROWS OR TABLES

1. Click inside the table.
2. Display row and column indicators:
   - Click **Table**.................. Alt + A
   - Click **Row/col indicator**........... W

To select a cell:
- Click inside the cell

To select a row:
- Click the row indicator.

   OR
- Highlight the row.

To select a column:
- Click the column indicator.

   OR
- Highlight the column.

To select the entire table:
- Click the rectangle in the top left corner of the row and column indicators to select the table.

   OR
- Click **Edit**.................. Alt + E
- Click **Select**.................. L
- Click **Table**.................. T

COREL WORDPERFECT 8 Lesson 7: Columns; Tables; Merge

Exercise 42

- Align Text within a Table
- Insert and Delete Columns and Rows
- Delete a Table
- Resize Columns
- Position a Table Horizontally
- Table Borders
- Cell Lines and Fills
- SpeedFormat

NOTES

Align Text within a Table

- WordPerfect allows you to change the alignment of text for a cell, column, or the entire table.
- You can horizontally align text left, center, right, full, all, or at the decimal. You can vertically align text at the top, bottom or center of a cell. In addition, text can be rotated within a table cell in 90-degree increments.
- You can align text either during the table creation process or afterward.

Alignment Examples

Left	Decimal Align: .1
	10.0
	1000.00
Center	**Full** justify needs more than one line to show its effect.
Right	**All** justify also needs more than one line to show its effect.
Top	Text at the top
Bottom	Text at the bottom
Center	Text in the center
Text Rotated 90 degrees	Text rotated 90 degrees

- To align text in a table cell, place the insertion point in any cell, or select (highlight) several cells, rows, or columns, in which you wish to align text. Then, click Table on the Table Property Bar and select Format from the drop-down menu. Or, you can right-click within a table and select Format from the QuickMenu.

- In the Properties for Table Format dialog box that follows, click the Cell tab and choose an alignment option from the Horizontal, Vertical or Rotate drop-down list boxes. Vertical alignment can also be changed by selecting the Vertical Alignment button [icon] on the Table Property Bar and selecting an alignment option.

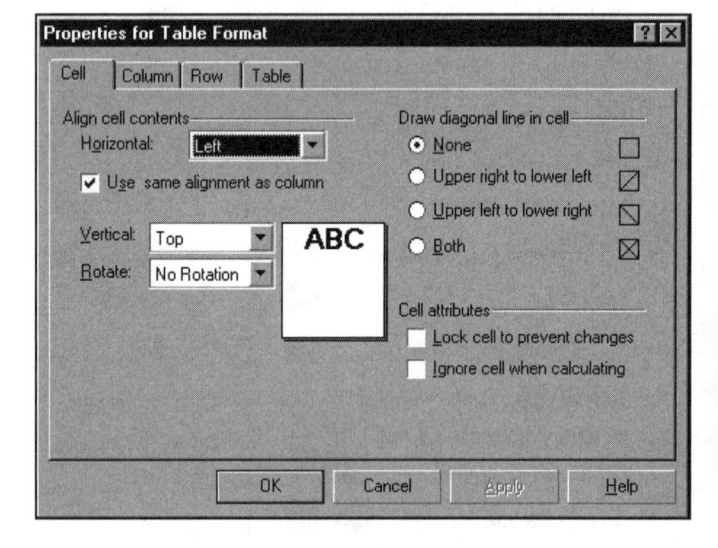

- To align text in a column or table, click the Column, or Table tab and make the desired selections. Text rotation and vertical alignment selection can only be made within the Cell tab.

- To set the distance from the margin for a decimal-aligned column, click the column tab, select From right margin, and enter the distance.

Insert Columns and Rows

- One or more rows and/or columns may be inserted in a table before or after the insertion point position.

- To insert a column or row, position the insertion point in the column or row where the insertion will occur. Click the T<u>a</u>ble button on the Table Property Bar and select <u>I</u>nsert, or right-click and select <u>I</u>nsert from the drop-down menu.

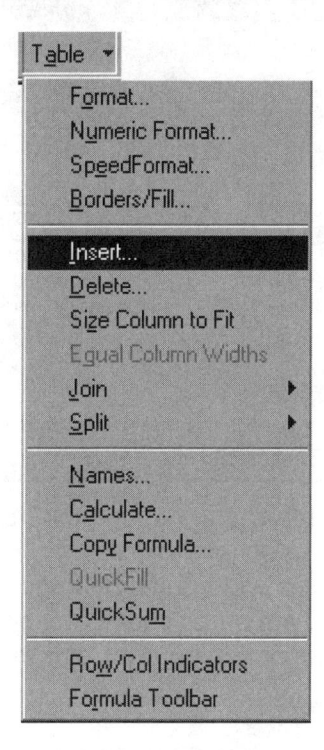

- In the Insert Columns/Rows dialog box that follows, click either the <u>C</u>olumns or <u>R</u>ows option, and enter the number of columns and/or rows you wish to insert in the increment box(es). Then, click either the <u>B</u>efore or <u>A</u>fter option to indicate if you wish the column or row to be inserted before or after the insertion point.

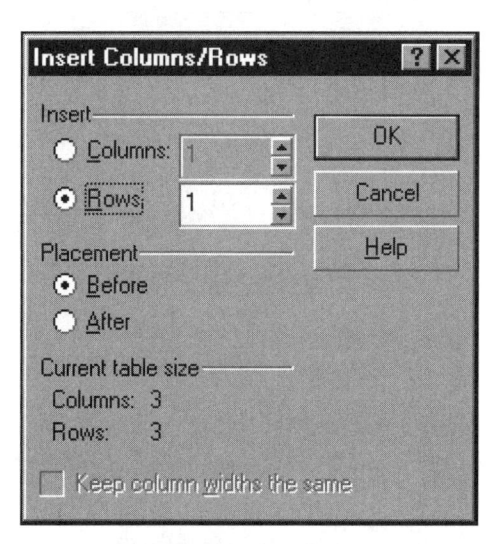

- The text in the inserted column or row takes on the same formatting as the row or column of the insertion point.

- To insert rows at the end of the table, position the insertion point in the last cell and press the Tab key.

Delete Columns and Rows

- To delete a column or row, position the insertion point in the column or row to be deleted or select the column(s) and/or row(s) to be deleted. Then, click T<u>a</u>ble on the Table Property Bar (or right-click) and select <u>D</u>elete from the drop-down menu. In the Delete dialog box that follows, click either the <u>C</u>olumns or <u>R</u>ows option to indicate whether you wish to delete a column or row and the number of columns or rows to delete (if you did not select (highlight) them first).

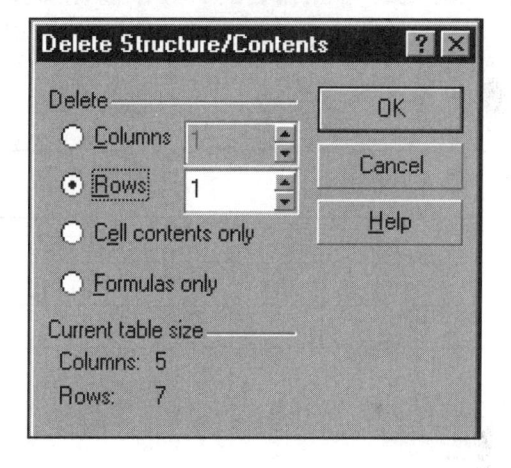

Delete a Table

- To delete the entire table, select the table, then click the T<u>a</u>ble button on the Table Property Bar (or right-click) and select <u>D</u>elete from the drop-down menu. In the Delete Table dialog box that follows, click the <u>E</u>ntire table option.

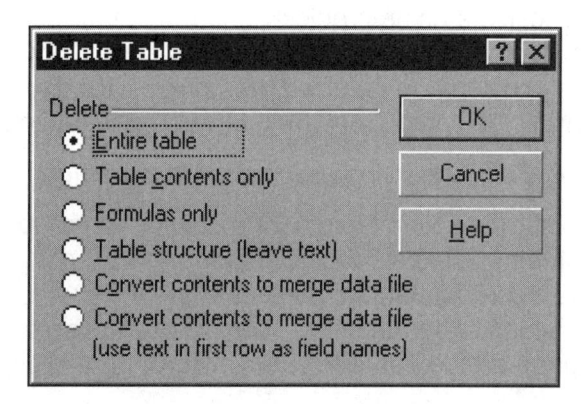

Sizing Columns

- Columns may be resized using a specific measurement or by dragging the vertical lines between columns to the desired width.

- Dragging the vertical lines between the columns allows you to see the immediate effect of the change on the table as it is being made. To do this, place the mouse pointer on a vertical line between the columns to be sized. (To adjust table size, place the mouse pointer on the far left or right vertical line.) The pointer's shape changes to a table sizing arrow. Press and hold the mouse as you drag the dotted line left or right to the desired column width or table size. As you drag the vertical line between columns, the column widths to the left and right of the vertical line display.

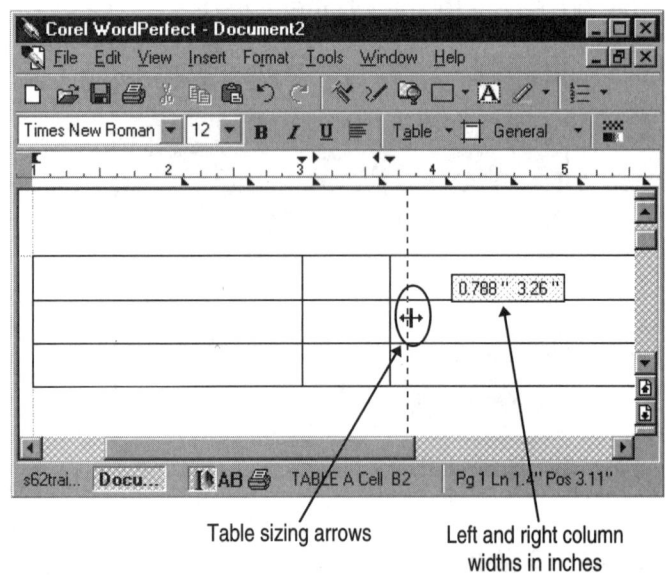

Table sizing arrows   Left and right column widths in inches

- When you resize a column by dragging, the column next to the one you are resizing will be reduced or widened. If you hold down the Ctrl key while dragging, the remaining columns will retain their original size.

- To resize a column quickly and retain the widths of all other columns, position the insertion point in the column to be sized, and press Ctrl+< to shrink the column or Ctrl+> to widen the column.

Sizing Columns Using a Specific Measurement

- To set the column width for a column or group of columns using a specific measurement, position the insertion point in the column or highlight the columns to be affected. Then, click the Table button on the Table Property Bar (or right-click) and select Format. In the Properties for Table Format dialog box that follows, click the Column tab and enter the desired column width amount in the Width increment box.

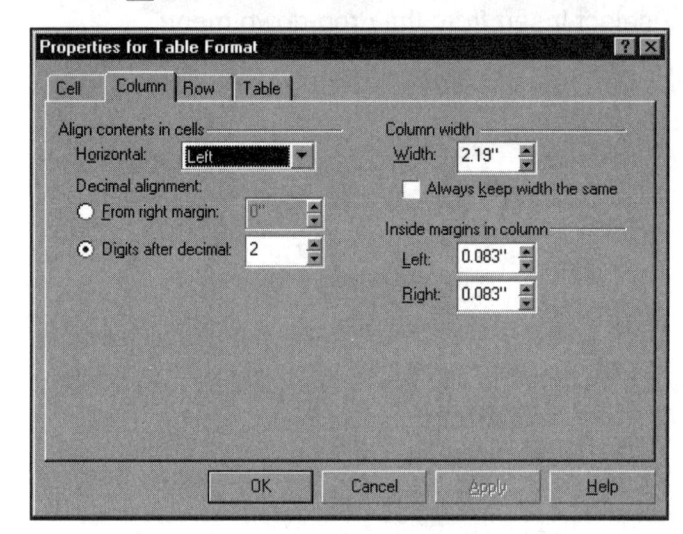

- Sometimes making an adjustment to one column may slightly affect another column. To insure that a column's width remains intact, click the *Always keep the same* check box below the Column width option on the Column tab.

Size Column to Fit

- The Size-Column-to-Fit feature automatically adjusts the column width to fit the longest text entry. Highlight the column(s) you wish to adjust. Then, select the Table button on the Table Property Bar (or right-click), and choose the Size Column to Fit option from the drop-down menu.

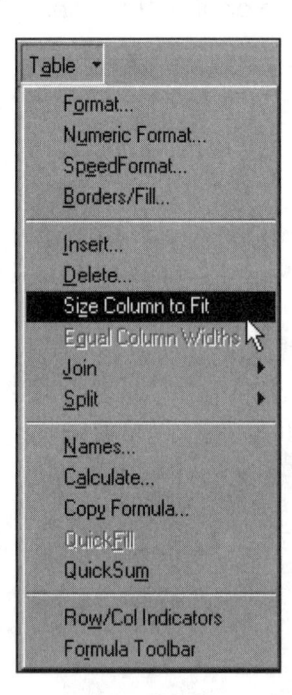

Position a Table Horizontally

- WordPerfect sets column widths in a table to spread out evenly between the margins whether your table contains two or ten columns. When you change column widths, WordPerfect keeps the same left margin. This means the table is no longer centered across the page.

- To center the table horizontally, click the Table button on the Tables toolbar (or right-click) and select Format. In the Properties for Table Format dialog box that follows, click the Table tab and choose Center from the Table position on page drop-down list.

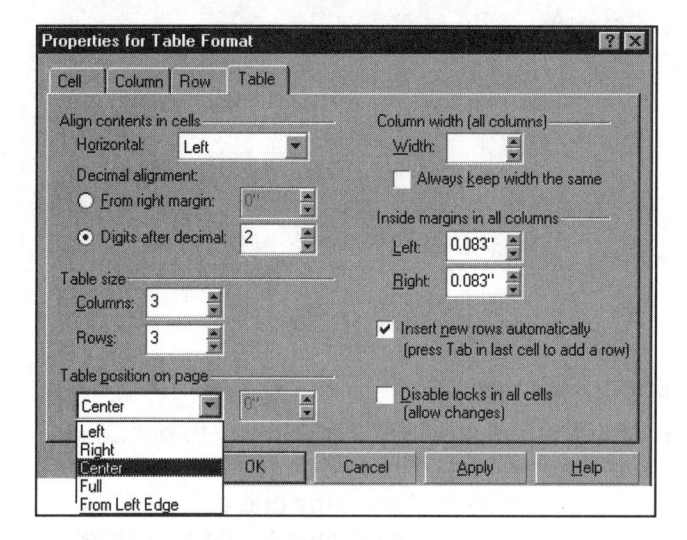

- You may also choose to position the table to the left or right of the page, or a specific distance from the left edge of the page.

Table Borders

- Tables may be enhanced by changing the line styles of the entire table or of selected cells. The fill feature lets you emphasize a cell, row or column by adding a pattern or shade.

- A **table border** is a line (or lines) that surrounds a table. **Cell lines** divide the columns and rows to form the cells. By default, tables print with a single line around the outer edge (table border) and single lines that divide columns and rows (cell lines). Note the example below:

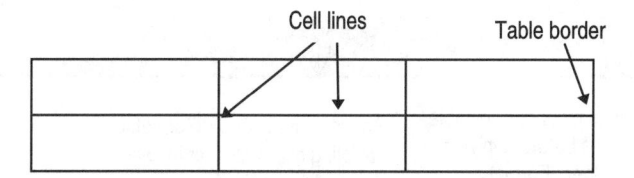

- WordPerfect lets you change the table border and cell line style, and provides you with numerous line types.

Thick Table Border and Dashed Cell Lines

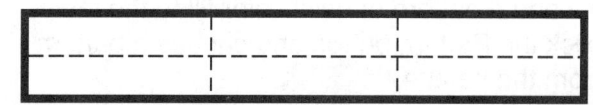

- To change table borders and cell lines, select the table. Then, click the Table button on the Tables toolbar (or right-click) and select Borders/Fill from the drop-down menu. In the Properties for Table Borders/Fill dialog box that follows, click the Table tab (it should already be selected) and select a table border from the Border drop-down palette and/or a line style from the Line drop-down palette. For each cell line style and table border type you select, you will see a sample in the Preview window.

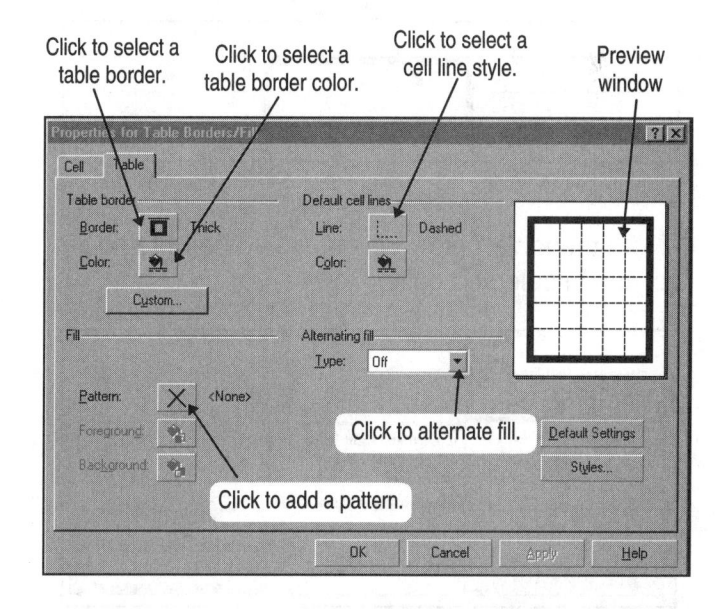

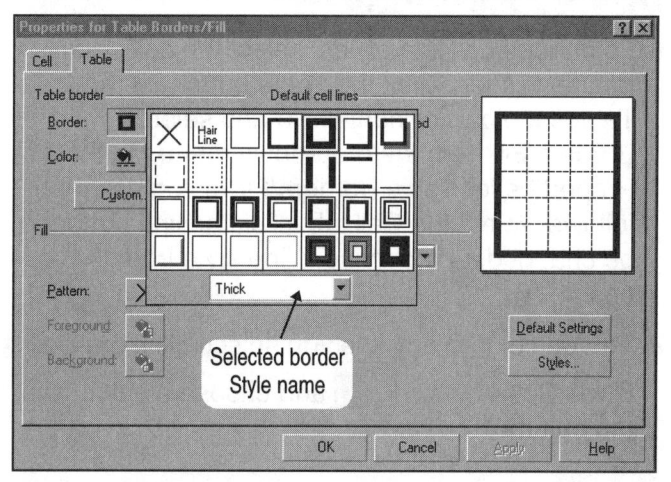

- To change the table border color, click the Color button below the Border button, and choose a color from the palette. To change a cell line color, click the Color button below the Line button, and choose a color from the palette.

- To add a pattern or solid color fill to the table, click the Pattern button and choose a pattern from the palette.

- You can add patterns to alternating rows and/or columns by selecting the Alternating fill Type button.

Cell Lines and Fills

- You can change the line and fill styles for a single cell, for selected cells or for parts of a cell.

- Lines that surround the selection *are outside lines*; lines within the selection are *inside lines*.

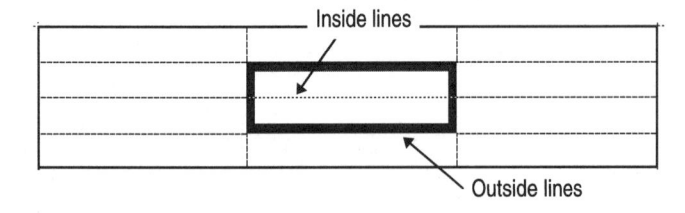

- Note the table below which uses different line styles in selected cells.

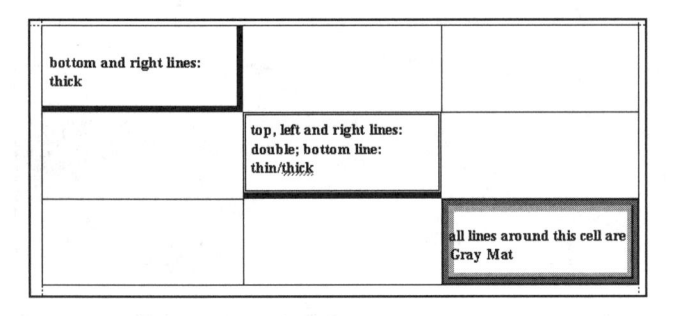

- To change cell line styles, select the cell or cells to affect. Then, click the Table button on the Tables toolbar (or right-click) and select Borders/Fill from the drop-down menu. In the Properties for Table Borders/Fill dialog box that follows, select the Cell tab, click the line button to be changed, and choose a line style from the palette.

- To add color to any line you select, click the Cell Lines Color button and choose a color from the palette.

- To add a pattern or solid color fill to a selected cell, click the Fill button. If you have a color monitor and/or printer, click the Foreground button and select a color. If you chose a pattern that allows for two colors, click the Background button and select a background color.

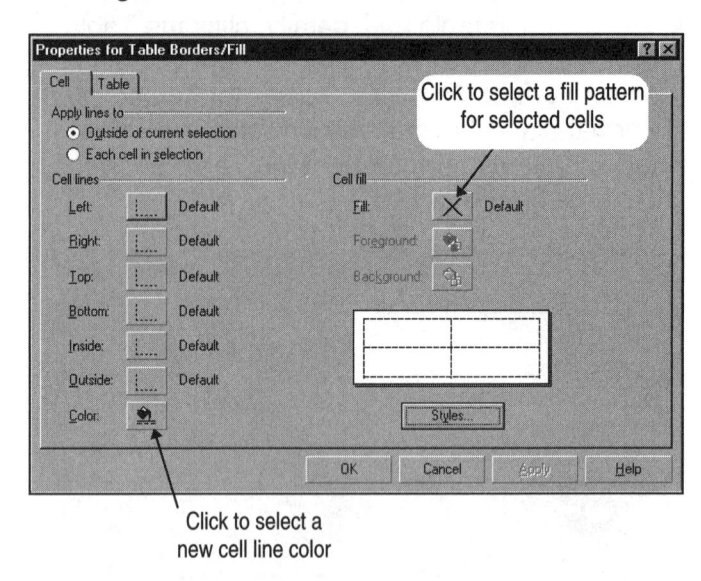

SpeedFormat

- WordPerfect provides a quick way to enhance the appearance of tables through its **SpeedFormat** feature. Any one of WordPerfect's 40 predefined formatting styles can be applied to your table.

- To access SpeedFormat, click the Table button on the Tables toolbar (or right-click) and select SpeedFormat from the drop-down menu. In the Table SpeedFormat dialog box that follows, select a style from the available styles listed on the left and note its effect in the preview window.

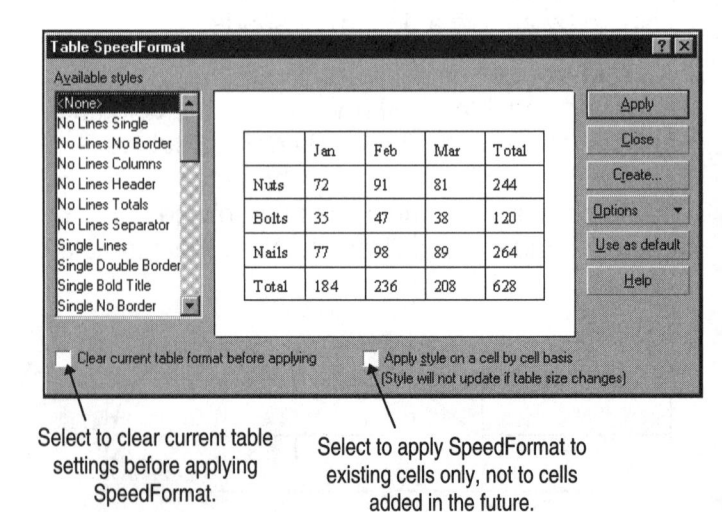

In Parts I and II of this exercise, you will insert columns and rows, as well as adjust column widths in a table you created previously. In Part II, you will create and then edit a new table.

EXERCISE DIRECTIONS

PART I

1. Start with a clear screen.
2. Open **EVENTS** or **42EVENTS**.
3. Display the column and row indicators.
4. Insert one row and one column, and enter text as shown in Illustration A on the following page.
   a. Set column A width to 1.25". Choose Always keep width the same option from the Column tab in the Properties for Table Format dialog box.
   b. Set column D width to 1.2"; choose Always keep width the same.
   c. Set column E widths to 1.2"; choose Always keep width the same.
5. Use the Size-Column-to-Fit feature to adjust the width of column B.
6. Center align text in Row 1 and Column 1.
7. Vertically center the cell contents of rows 2-7.
8. Horizontally center the table on the page.
9. Add a Heavy Double Style border around the table.
10. Apply a light gray fill to row 1.
11. View the full document.
12. Print one copy.
13. Close the file; save the changes.

PART II - ILLUSTRATION A

1999 UNIVERSITY SPECIAL EVENTS

Insert column

Event	Date	Time	Location	Sponsor
New Student Welcome Picnic	Sept. 2	Noon to 3:00 p.m.	Campus Main Library Lawn	Administration Department
Fall Fest Carnival	Oct. 17	5:00 p.m. to Midnight	Huff Pavilion	Huff Business School
Pilgrim Celebration Dinner	Nov. 19	7:00 p.m.	Wyndham Hall	Theatre Department
Winter Dance	Dec. 12	7:00 p.m to Midnight	Railley Hall	Advanced Technology Club
Spring Forward Picnic	Mar. 21	Noon to 3:00 p.m.	Campus Main Library Lawn	Student Government
Summer Celebration Dinner and Dance	May 28	6:00 p.m. to Midnight	Wyndham Hall	Science Department

Insert row

COREL WORDPERFECT 8   Lesson 7:   Columns; Tables; Merge

PART II

1. Start with a clear screen.
2. Create the table as shown in Illustration B.
3. Save the file; name it **FUND**.
4. Set top and bottom margins to .5".
5. Display the column and row indicators.
6. Decimal align all columns containing numeric data.
7. Horizontally center the table on the page.

To create Illustration C:

8. Insert a centered title above the table.
   - Set font to 36-point decorative, bold.
   - Return font size to 12 points and press Enter three times.
9. Insert one column after the ACTIVITY column and enter text as shown.
10. Decimal align the cells in the new column.
11. Delete Row 6 (Antique Auction).
12. Use Size Column to Fit feature to size all columns.
    - Center and set column titles font to sans serif.
    - Center and bold each activity name in Column A.
13. Use any desired SpeedFormat to format the table.
14. Preview the document.
15. Print one copy
16. Close the file: save the changes.

PART II - ILLUSTRATION B

ACTIVITY	FY 98	GOAL 1999	FY 98 10/98-5/99	% GOAL
Annual Appeal	51,332.00	60,000.00	55,555.00	91.6
Direct Mail	21,476.00	25,000.00	15,500.00	62.0
Museum Benefit	90,350.00	100,000.00	107,000.00	107.0
Summer Concert	33,445.18	50,000.00	35,000.00	70.4
Antique Auction	9,232.00	10,000.00	500.00	5.0
Meet the Artist Dinner	27,640.50	30,000.00	8,100.00	27.0
Misc.	7,330.00	9,000.00	4,225.00	84.5

PART II - ILLUSTRATION C

1999 Fund-Raising Analysis

Insert column

ACTIVITY	FY 97	FY 98	GOAL 1999	FY 98 10/98-5/99	% GOAL
Annual Appeal	49,660.00	51,332.00	60,000.00	55,555.00	91.6
Direct Mail	18,596.00	21,476.00	25,000.00	15,500.00	62.0
Museum Benefit	78,211.00	90,350.00	100,000.00	107,000.00	107.0
Summer Concert	25,990.00	33,445.18	50,000.00	35,000.00	70.4
Antique Auction	32,777.00	9,232.00	10,000.00	500.00	5.0
Meet the Artist Dinner	24,722.00	27,640.50	30,000.00	8,100.00	27.0
Misc.	6,019.00	7,330.00	9,000.00	4,225.00	84.5

KEYSTROKES

ALIGN TEXT WITHIN CELLS, COLUMNS, OR TABLE

Ctrl + F12

1. Place insertion point in table.
   OR
   Select a cell, several cells, several columns, or an entire table to receive alignment change.
2. Follow one of the procedures listed below:
   a. Click right mouse button.
   b. Click **F**ormat .... `O`
   OR
   a. Click **Table** button `Table ▼` on Tables toolbar.
   b. Select **F**ormat .... `O`
3. Select desired tab:
   - Cell
   - Column
   - Table
4. Click appropriate **Align Cell Contents** drop-down list boxes and select desired alignment options.
5. Click **OK** .... `Enter`

INSERT ROWS/COLUMNS

1. Place the insertion point in the row or column that will precede or follow the desired insertion.
2. Click **Table** button on Table Property Bar .... `Alt`+`A`
   OR
   Click *right* mouse button.
3. Click **I**nsert .... `I`
4. Click to insert:
   - **C**olumns .... `Alt`+`C`
   - **R**ows .... `Alt`+`R`
5. Type number of columns and/or rows to be inserted.
   OR
   Click increment arrows .... `↓``↑`
6. Click desired **Placement**:
   - **B**efore .... `Alt`+`B`
   - **A**fter .... `Alt`+`A`
7. Click **OK** .... `Enter`

DELETE ROWS/COLUMNS

1. Place insertion point in column or row to delete.
   OR
   Select columns or rows to delete.
2. Click **Table** button on Table Property Bar .... `Alt`+`A`
   OR
   Click *right* mouse button.
3. Click **D**elete .... `D`
4. Click item to be deleted:
   - **C**olumns .... `Alt`+`C`
   - **R**ows .... `Alt`+`R`
5. Type number of columns or rows to delete.
   OR
   Click increment arrows .... `↓``↑`
6. Click **OK** .... `Enter`

COREL WORDPERFECT 8 Lesson 7: Columns; Tables; Merge

DELETE TABLE OR CELL CONTENTS

1. Select entire table.
2. Click **Ta**ble button on Table Property Bar .... `Alt` + `A`
3. Click **D**elete .... `D`
4. Click a delete option:
   - **Entire table** .... `E`
   - **Table contents** .... `C`
   - **Formulas only** .... `F`
   - **Table structure (leave text)** ...... `T`
5. Click **OK** .... `Enter`

SIZE COLUMNS

To see immediate changes:

1. Place mouse pointer on a vertical line separating the column until it changes to a table sizing arrow............ ↔
2. Drag arrow to desired width.

OR

1. Place mouse pointer in column to change.
2. Click Ctrl + > to increase column width or Ctrl + < to decrease column width.

OR

a. Place insertion point in cell or select column(s) containing longest text.
b. Click *right* mouse button.
c. Click **Si**ze Column to Fit .... `Z`

OR

To set specific measurements:

a. Place insertion point in column.

   OR

   Select several columns to format.
b. Click **Ta**ble button on Table Property Bar .... `Alt` + `A`

   OR

   Click *right* mouse button.
c. Click **F**ormat .... `O`
d. Select **C**olumn tab.
e. Click in **W**idth text box .... `Alt` + `W`
f. Type a column width amount.

   OR

   Click increment arrows .... `↓` `↑`

To keep width of current column same:

Click Always **K**eep Width the Same check box .... `Alt` + `K`

g. To retain all adjustments made to column widths:

   Click **OK** .... `Enter`

POSITION TABLE ON PAGE HORIZONTALLY

1. Place insertion point in table.
2. Click **Ta**ble button .... `Alt` + `A` on Table Property Bar.

   OR

   Click *right* mouse button.
3. Click **F**ormat .... `O`
4. Click **T**able tab .... `Ctrl` + `Tab`
5. Click Table **p**osition on page drop-down list box .... `Alt` + `P`
6. Select desired position:
   - **L**eft .... `L`
   - **R**ight .... `R`
   - **C**enter .... `C`
   - **F**ull .... `F`
   - **F**rom Left Edge .... `F`, `F`
     and type amount from left edge.

   OR

   Click increment arrows............ `↓` `↑`
7. Click **OK** .... `Enter`

TABLE BORDERS, LINES, AND FILLS

1. Select table.
   - Click **Change Table Border** button on Table Property Bar.

   and/or
   - Click **Change Default Line Style** button on Table Property Bar.

   OR

2. Click **Ta**ble button on Table Property Bar .... `Alt` + `A`
3. Click **B**orders/Fill .... `B`
4. Click on **T**able tab .... `Ctrl` + `Tab`

   OR

5. Click on **L**ine style button .... `Alt` + `L`
6. Click desired line style from drop-down palette............. `↓` `↑`
7. Click on **B**order style button ... `Alt` + `B`
8. Click desired border style from drop-down palette............. `↓` `↑`
9. Click **P**attern button `X`.
10. Click on desired pattern from drop-down palette.
11. Click **F**oreground button.
12. Select a color ....
13. If applicable, select **B**ackground button.
14. Select a color ....
15. Click **OK** .... `Enter`

CELL LINES AND FILLS

1. Select cells to affect.
2. Click **Ta**ble button on Table Property Bar............... `Alt` + `A`
3. Click **B**orders/Fill .... `B`
4. Click on Cell tab.
5. Click lines to affect:
   - **L**eft .... `L`
   - **R**ight .... `R`
   - **T**op .... `T`
   - **B**ottom .... `B`
   - **I**nside .... `I`
   - **O**utside .... `O`

✓ *When you change all sides of a single cell, the **I**nside option will have no effect.*

6. Click desired line style from drop-down palette.............
7. Click **F**ill button `X`.
8. Click **F**oreground button.
9. Select a color ....
10. If applicable, select **B**ackground button.
11. Select a color ....
12. Click **OK** .... `Enter`

SPEEDFORMAT

1. Click **Ta**ble button on Table Property Bar............. `Alt` + `A`
2. Click **Sp**eedFormat .... `E`
3. Select a desired style.
4. Click **A**pply .... `Enter`

206

COREL WORDPERFECT 8 — Lesson 7: Columns; Tables; Merge

Exercise 43

- The Merge Process
- Create a Data File
- Create a Form File
- Merge the Form and Data Files
- Merge Selected Records
- Merge with Conditions
- Prepare Envelopes While Merging

NOTES

The Merge Process

- The **Merge** feature allows you to mass produce letters, envelopes, mailing labels, and other documents so they appear to be personalized.

- The merge exercises in this lesson illustrate the mail merge feature using typical letters. However, other document types may be merged, such as envelopes, fill-in forms, reports or catalogs.

- The merge process combines a **form document file** with a **data source** file to produce merged documents.

Form Document File

Today's date

FIELD(TITLE) FIELD(FIRST) FIELD(LAST)
FIELD(ADDRESS)
FIELD(CITY), FIELD(ST) FIELD(ZIP)

Dear FIELD(TITLE) FIELD(LAST):

This letter is to confirm your reservation of the FIELD(ROOM) at the FIELD(HOTEL) for the FIELD(EVENT) you are planning on FIELD(MONTH). At the FIELD(HOTEL), we aim to meet all of your needs when you are planning an event of any sort.

I know that you are working closely with FIELD(REP), but if there is anything that I can do to help make your event run more efficiently, please let me know.

Sincerely,

Luis Cueva
Hilton Manager

lc/yo

Placeholders (merge codes) for variable information

\+

Data Source File

TITLE	FIRST	LAST	ADDRESS	CITY	ST	ZIP	ROOM	HOTEL	EVENT	MONTH	REP
Ms.	Barbara	Williams	34 Walker Road	Boston	MA	17896	Fulton	Boston Hilton	Medical Conference	January 12	Bob
Mr.	Gregg	Parker	556 West 34 Street	New York	NY	10021	Eaton	Midtown Hilton	Wedding	May 8	Beth
Ms.	Sarah	Dunham	8970 Oak Court	Rockville	MD	78967	Ballroom	Washington Hilton	Donor Reception	April 12	Bob
Mr.	Wendall	Homer	88 Flowers Drive	Durham	NC	20019	Fulton	Raleigh Hilton	Business Dinner	March 13	Natasha

=

Merged Documents

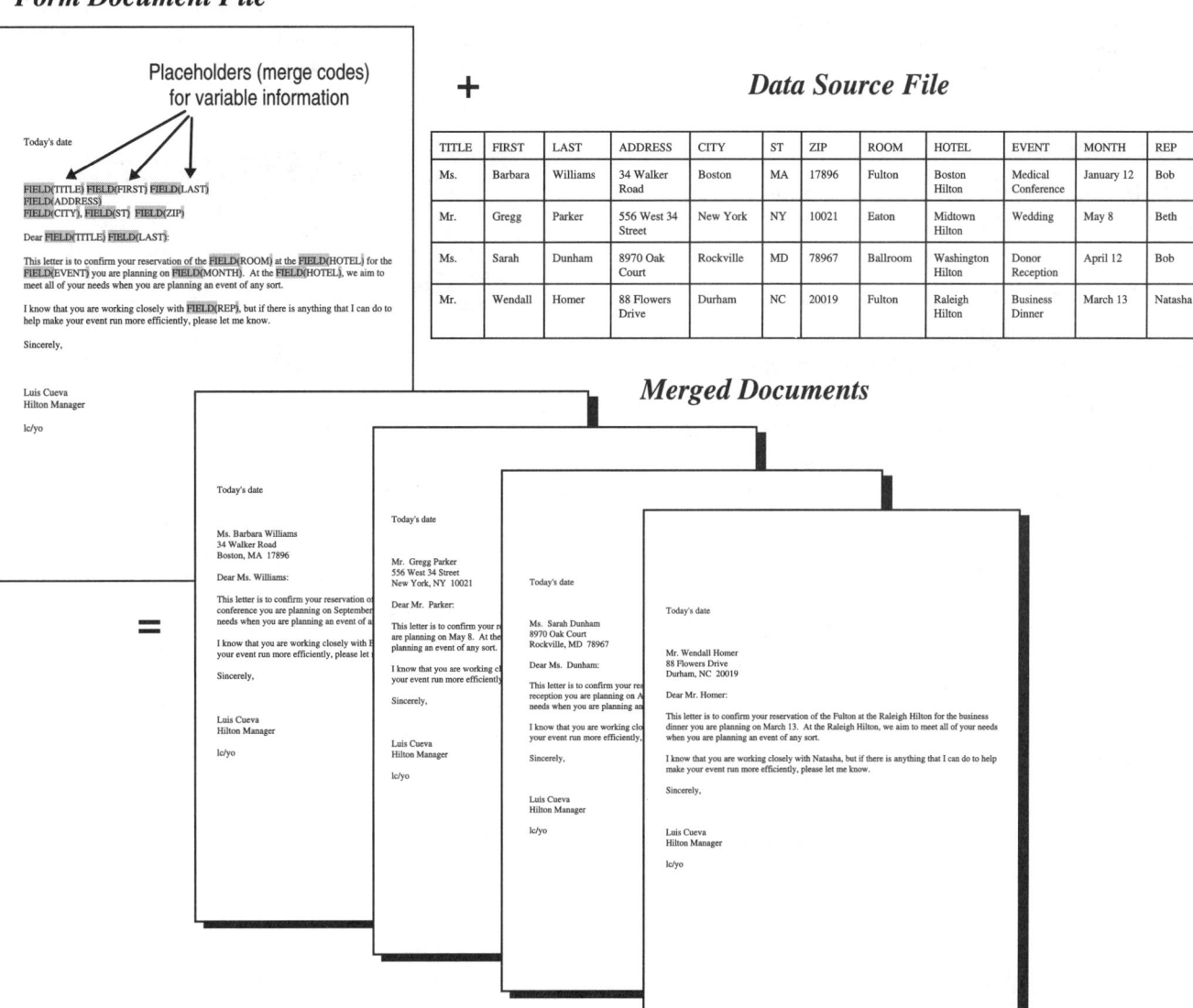

COREL WORDPERFECT 8 Lesson 7: Columns; Tables; Merge

- The same data source file may then be used to produce the envelopes and/or labels, making it unnecessary to type the name and address list a second time.

- There are three steps in the mail merge process:

    1. Create the data source file that contains the variable information (actual names and addresses of those receiving the letter).

    2. Create a form file that contains the text that will not change, and codes indicating where variable information will be inserted (see illustration on previous page).

    3. Merge the form and data source files to create individual personalized letters.

    ✓ *Note: Before creating the data source file, you should create a rough copy of the form file you wish to send. This will help you determine what variables will be included in your letter. Then you can create and insert the proper merge codes in your data source file.*

Create a Data File

- The data source file contains the actual names, addresses, cities, states, and zip codes (as well as other variable information) for each recipient of the form file.

- A data file may contain many records. A **record** is a collection of related information about one person or thing. The information in each record is divided into fields. When data is arranged in a table format, the fields are divided into columns. Each row is a record.

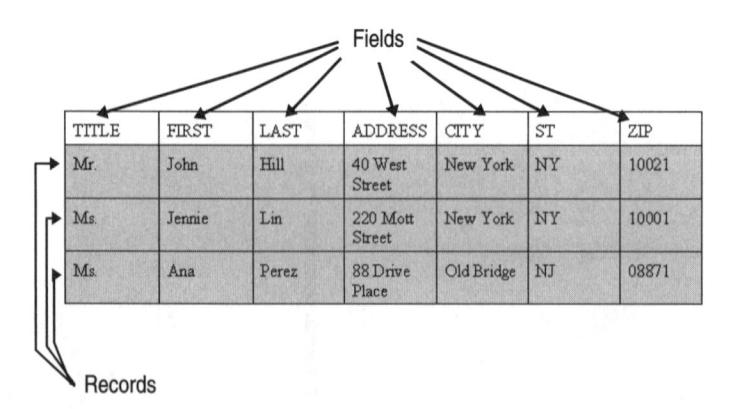

TITLE	FIRST	LAST	ADDRESS	CITY	ST	ZIP
Mr.	John	Hill	40 West Street	New York	NY	10021
Ms.	Jennie	Lin	220 Mott Street	New York	NY	10001
Ms.	Ana	Perez	88 Drive Place	Old Bridge	NJ	08871

- To create a data file, select Merge from the Tools menu. In the Merge dialog box that displays, click Create data.

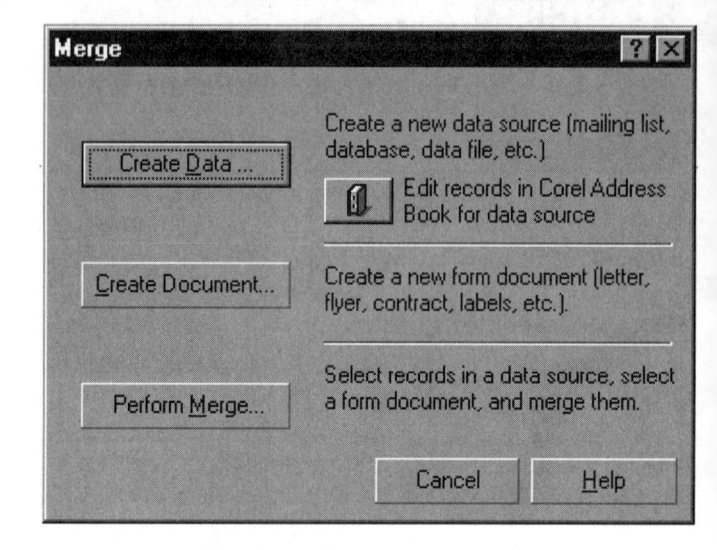

- If you entered any information (even a space) in the current document window, you will be prompted to indicate whether you want to Use the file in the active window or create a New document window.

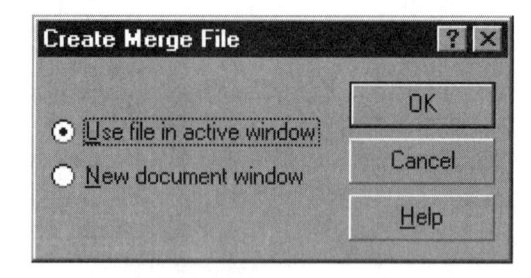

- When the Create Data File dialog box appears, type the name of the field in the Name a field text box, then press Enter or click Add to enter the field name. Each field is named for what information will eventually be inserted into that location. For example, the first field in an inside address is the title, so you would enter the field name "Title" in the Name a field text box. The second field is the first name, so you would enter the field name "First" in the Name a field text box, etc.

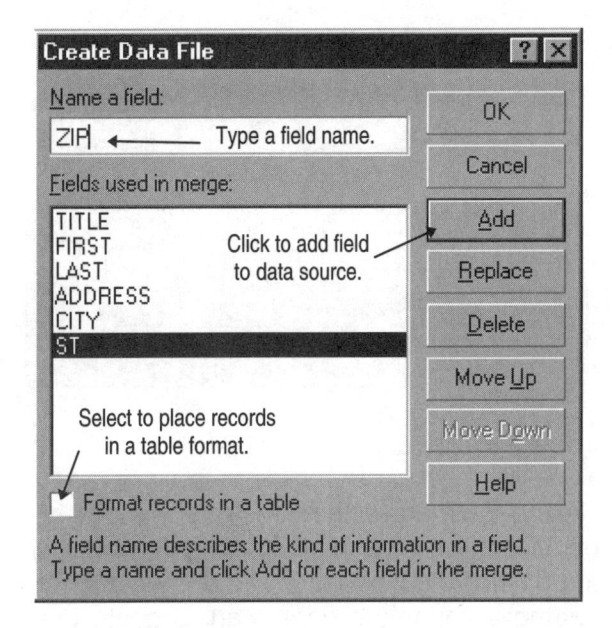

- To format the data file in a table format, select the Format records in a table check box. When all field names have been entered, click OK.

- In the Quick Data Entry dialog box that follows, enter the actual data next to each field name. After entering the necessary information into all the fields for the first record, click the New Record button and repeat the procedure for the next record.

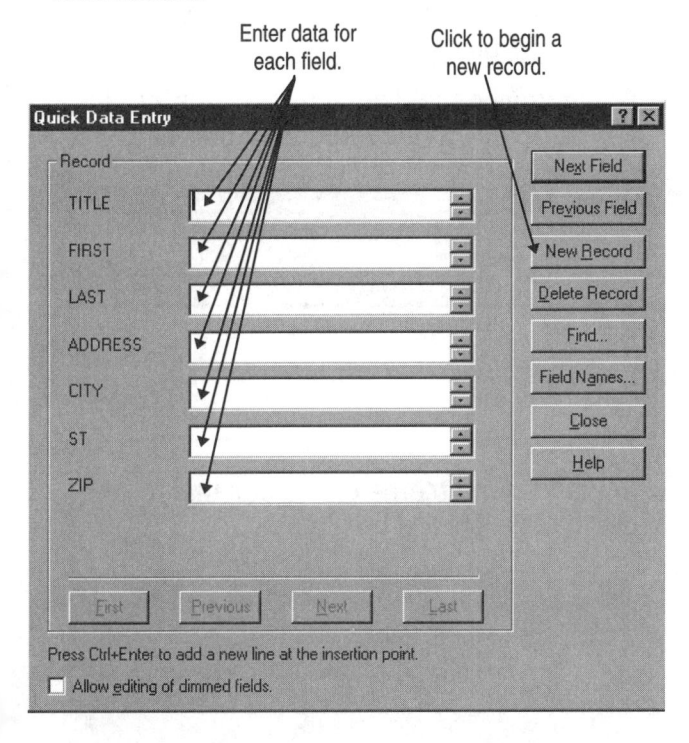

- When all the records have been entered, click the Close button; you will be prompted to save the data file. WordPerfect adds the file extension **.dat** to saved data files.

- Note the following illustration of records entered in a data file table format and the Merge feature bar, which is automatically displayed. The Merge feature bar provides a quick way to access merge-related tasks.

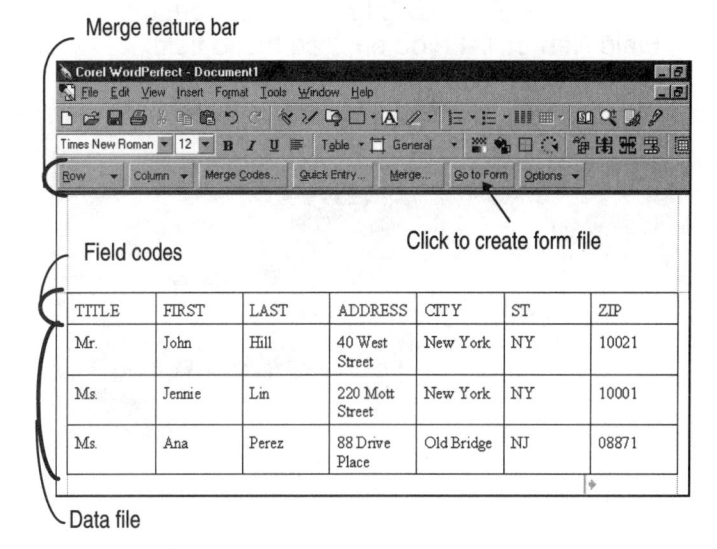

- Most punctuation (such as the comma after a city) should not be inserted in the data file; it should be inserted in the form file. However, a period after a title should always be included in the data file.

Create a Form File

- The form file contains information that does not change. All formatting, punctuation, margins, spacing, etc., as well as graphics and paper size information, should be included in the form file.

- After creating the data file, click the Go To Form button on the Merge feature bar to create the form document. In the Associate dialog box that follows, click the Create button. A new document window appears.

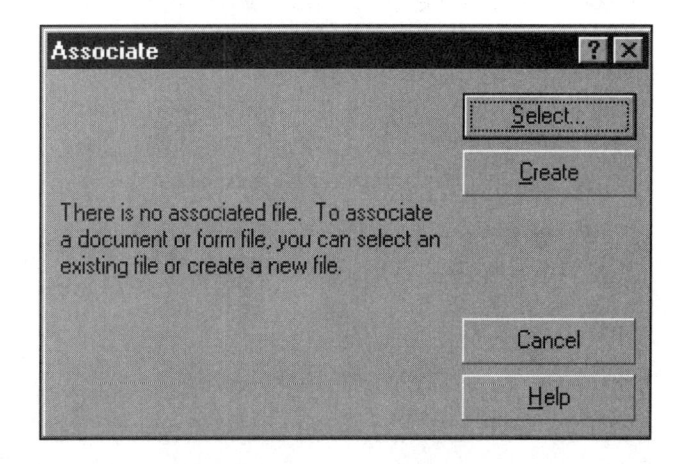

COREL WORDPERFECT 8   Lesson 7: Columns; Tables; Merge

- Type the letter until you reach the first field location (first variable). Then, click the Insert Field button on the Merge feature bar. The Insert Field Name or Number dialog box displays for you to select an appropriate field name, (TITLE, FIRST, LAST, etc.) from the Field Names list (you entered these field names when you created the data source file). The field name will be inserted as a code.

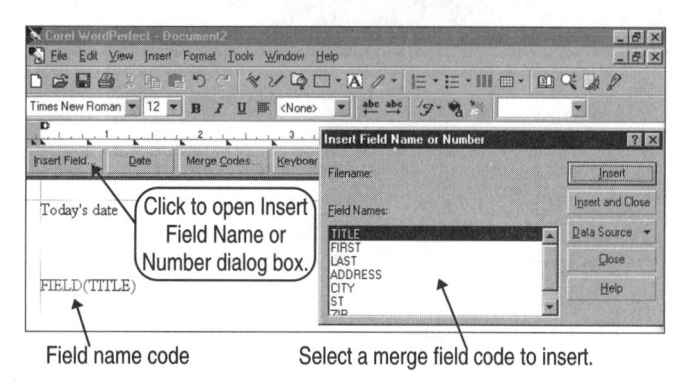

- Repeat this procedure for each variable in the letter. Insert spaces and punctuation before and after field codes as you would if you were typing actual text. When the letter is complete, save it. WordPerfect adds the file extension **.frm** to saved form files.

Merge the Form and Data Files

- To merge the form and data files, click the Merge button on the Merge feature bar.

- In the Perform Merge dialog box that follows, enter the name of the Form file and Data source file you wish to merge.

- The default output merges the files to a new document, showing you the merged files on the screen and allowing you to save it. This new third document appears as separate pages, each one representing a personalized letter. This document may be saved under its own filename. If you wish to change the output destination, click the Output button and make another selection.

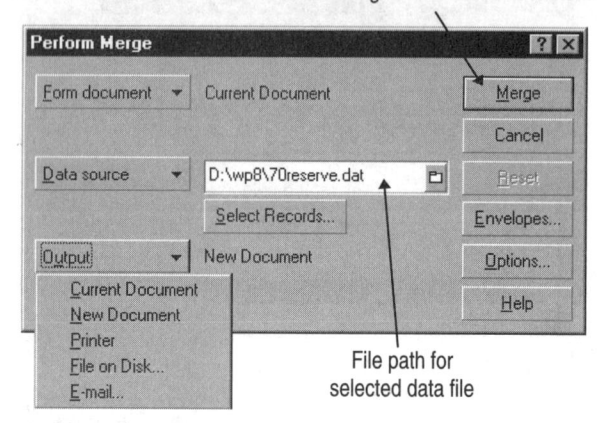

- Saving the merged third document under its own filename is particularly helpful if you wish to edit individual pages of the document. For example, you might want to add a postscript (PS) or special mailing notation to selected letters.

- Click the Merge button to merge the data and form files.

Merge Selected Records

- Rather than merging all the records contained in a data file, it is possible to merge selected records by marking them at the beginning of the merge process.

- After creating the data and form files, click the Merge button on the Merge feature bar.

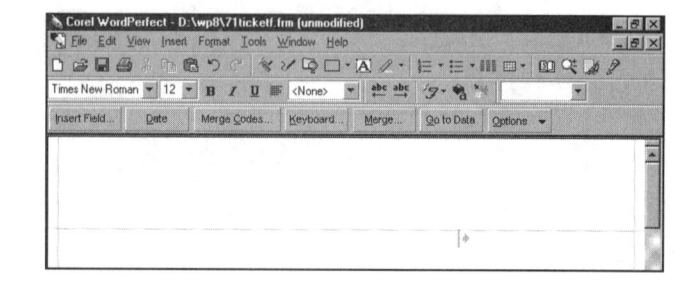

- In the Perform Merge dialog box that follows, click the Select Records button.

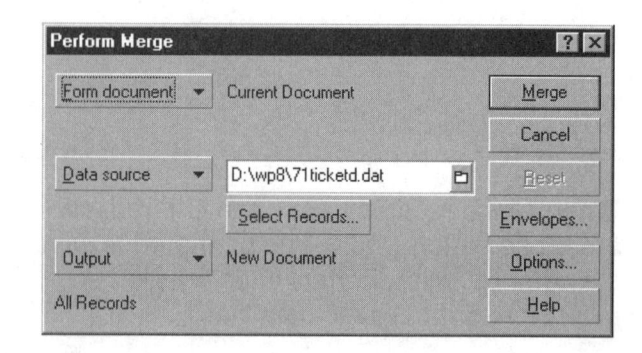

- In the Select Records dialog box that follows, click the Mark records button. This produces a list of records in the Record list window. Click the check box next to the records you wish to merge.

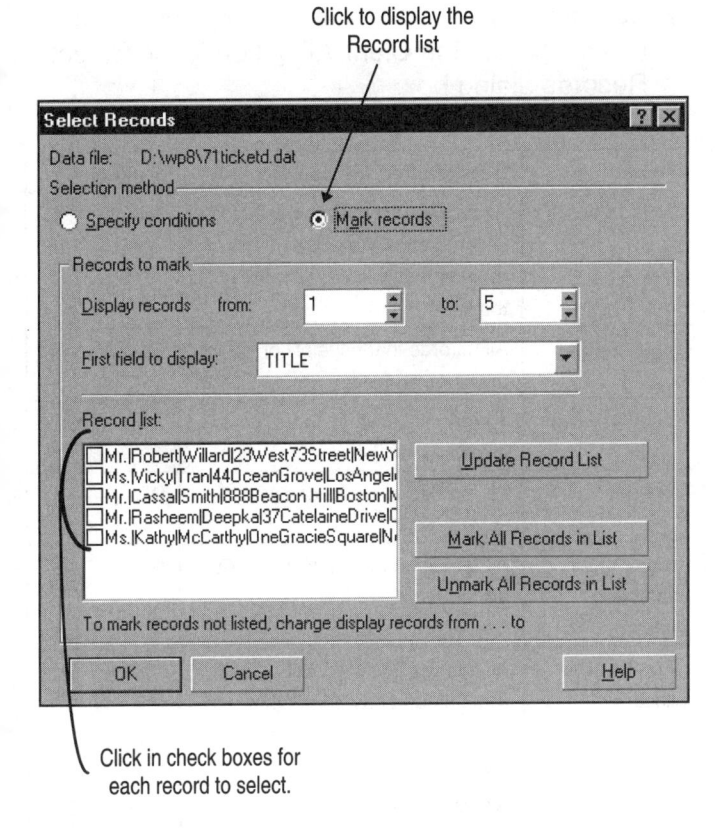

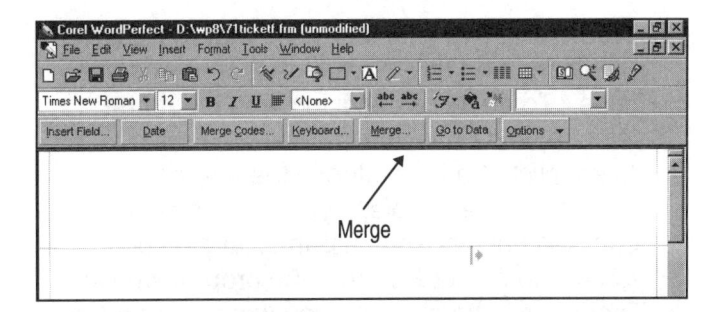

- In the Perform Merge dialog box that follows, click the Select Records button.

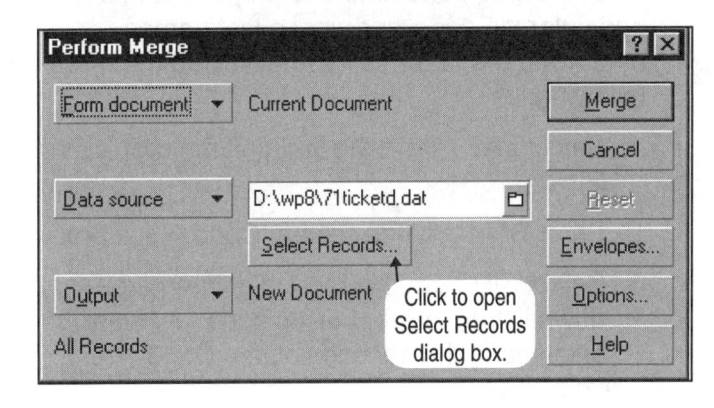

- In the Select Records dialog box that follows, click Specify conditions.

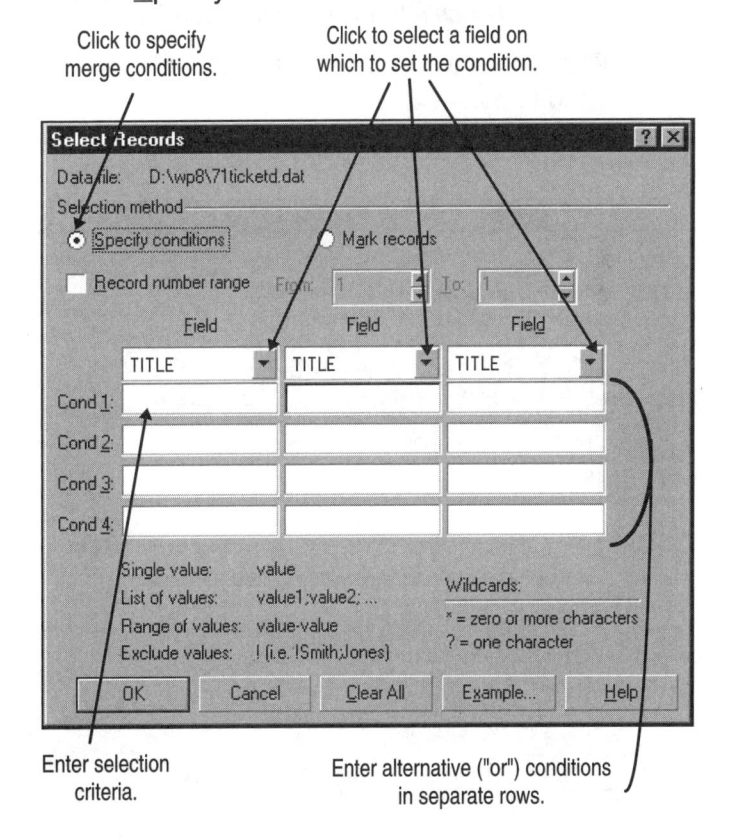

Merge with Conditions

- In addition to merging specific records, you can define **conditions** that data records must meet to be included in the merge. For example, you might want to merge only those letters in a specific zip code or job title. Or, you might want to merge letters only for individuals who owe more than $200 and live in New Jersey.

- To define conditions for a merge, first create the data and form files; then, click the Merge button on the Merge Feature Bar. Or, if the Merge Feature Bar is not on screen, select Tools, Merge and click Perform Merge.

Corel WordPerfect 8 ■ Lesson 7 ■ Exercise 43   211

- A table displays with four rows that represent conditions and three columns that represent fields. To define a condition, you must first select a field on which to enter a condition. To do so, click the list button in the first field column. For example, if you want to send letters to only those in a particular zip code, you would select ZIP from the drop-down list. Then, enter the zip code you want selected in the Cond 1 text box.

- If you want to send letters to only those in a particular zip code *and* whose last names begin with the letter "B," you would do the following:

  1. Select LAST from the first-column drop-down list.

  2. Enter B* in the first column Cond 1 text box.

  3. Select ZIP from the second-column drop-down list and enter the zip code you want selected in the second column Cond 1 text box.

     ✓Note: There is an "and" relationship between criteria **within** a Condition row and an "or" relationship **between** condition rows.

  4. Click OK when you finish specifying conditions.

  5. Click Merge to merge the documents.

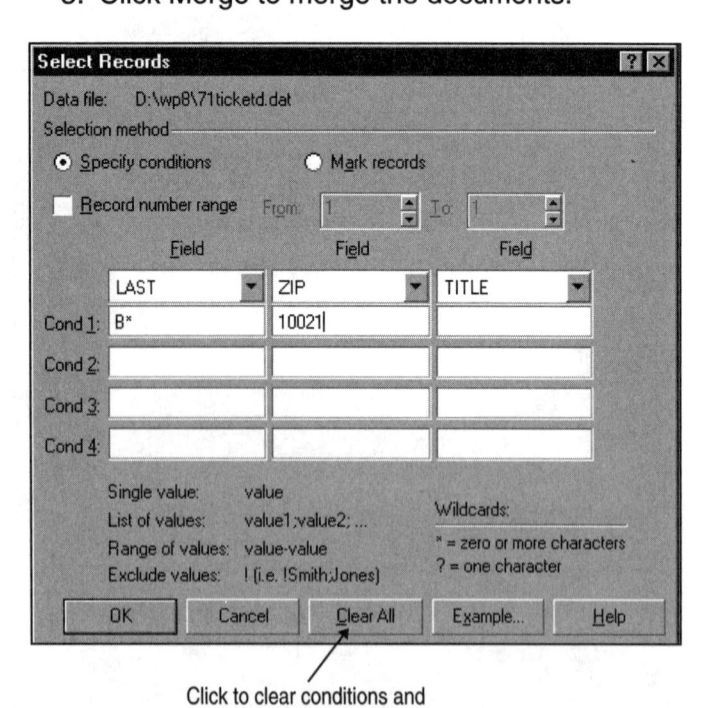

- A record is selected for merge if it meets any one of the conditions you define as selection criteria. See the table to the right for symbols you can use to define criteria for selecting records to be merged.

- Before merging again with different conditions, you must click the Clear All button in the Select Records dialog box.

Criteria	Records that will be Selected	Examples
Single value	All records in which the selected field matches the value (only records that have exactly NJ in the field)	NJ
List of values	All records that have NJ or NY in the selected field.	NJ;NY
Range of values	All records in which the selected field is within the range of values.	5,000-8,000
Excluded values	All records *except* those who live in New York.	!NY
Zero or more characters wildcard	All records that start with *New* in the selected field.	New*
One-character wildcard	All records that start with 1, end with 081 and have one other character in place of the question mark.	1?081
Greater than or less than	All values greater than 300 or less than 300.	>300 or <300

Prepare Envelopes While Merging

- WordPerfect makes it possible for you to create envelopes while merging a letter or other form file. (See Exercise 49 to create envelopes and labels without merging.)

- After specifying the form and data filenames to merge in the Perform Merge dialog box, click the Envelopes button.

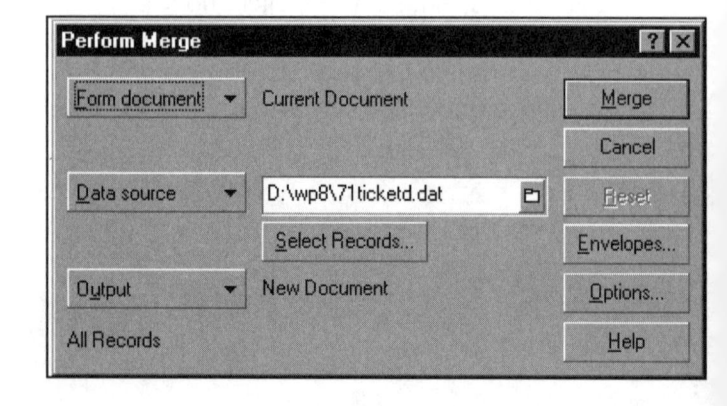

In Part I of this exercise, you will create and merge form and data source files. In Part II of this Exercise, you will create form and data source files, merge selected records, and prepare envelopes for each letter.

EXERCISE DIRECTIONS

PART I

1. Start with a clear screen.
2. Create a data file from the records shown in Illustration A on the following page. Format the data file as a table.
3. Use the default margins.
4. Begin the exercise on Ln 1".
5. Save the file; name it **MTGDATA**.
   ✓ When the data table displays on screen, field information may appear on two lines. Do not be concerned. Text will insert properly during the merge process.
6. Create the form letter file as shown in Illustration B, inserting appropriate merge fields as shown.
7. Use the default margins.
8. Begin the exercise on approximately Ln 2.5".
9. Spell check.
10. Save the file; name it **MTGFORM**.
11. Merge the form file with the data file to a new document.
12. Save the merged letters under a new filename: **MTGLETTERS**.
13. Close the document window.

PART II

1. Create the data file from the records shown in Illustration C on page 215. Format the data file as a table.
2. Use the default margins.
3. Begin the exercise on Ln 1".
4. Save the file; name it **PASTDATA**.
5. Create the form letter file as shown in Illustration D on page 215.
6. Use the default margins.
7. Begin the exercise on approximately Ln 2.5".
8. Spell check.
9. Save the file; name it **PASTFORM**.
10. Merge the form file with the data file to a new document.
11. Define the following criteria for the merge: merge and print letters for only those individuals who live in New Jersey and owe more than $200.
    HINT: In the ST field, enter the single value NJ; in the AMOUNT field, enter single value >200.
12. Print the full document (one copy of each merged letter).
13. Prepare an envelope for each letter in the merge.
14. Save the merged letters under a new filename: **PASTLETTERS**.
15. Close the document window.

COREL WORDPERFECT 8 Lesson 7: Columns; Tables; Merge

ILLUSTRATION A (MTGDATA)

TITLE	FIRST	LAST	ADDRESS	CITY	ST	ZIP
Mr.	Kevin	Burkett	12 Oak Drive	Wellesley	MA	09876
Ms.	Gillian	Leviton	456 Winthrop Street	Brookline	MA	09876
Mr.	Ross	Freedman	7 Willis Square	Brighton	MA	09564
Ms.	Amy	Vernick	89 Willow Road	Acton	MA	06754

ILLUSTRATION B (MTGFORM)

Today's Date

FIELD(TITLE) FIELD(FIRST) FIELD(LAST)
FIELD(ADDRESS)
FIELD(CITY), FIELD(ST) FIELD(ZIP)

Dear FIELD(TITLE) FIELD(LAST):

Children First, Inc. cordially invites you to attend our annual meeting of the Board of Directors on Wednesday, April 2. This year's meeting will be held at the Long Wharf Marriott and will begin at 7:00 p.m.

We like to keep our friends well appraised of our activities. Thus, we will feature speakers from both our Board of Directors as well as some of our program directors. There will be a dessert reception immediately following the meeting.

Please let me know if you would like to attend and if you will be bringing a guest. I do hope that you will be able to join us.

Sincerely,

Susan Wilton
Executive Director

sw/yo

ILLUSTRATION C (PASTDATA)

TITLE	FIRST	LAST	ADDRESS	CITY	ST	ZIP	AMOUNT	DATE
Mr.	James	Platt	One Gracie Terrace	New York	NY	10022	255.55	April 18
Ms.	Shanna	O'Neil	48 Endor Avenue	Brooklyn	NY	11221	256.98	March 1
Mr.	Ray	Todd	3 Windsor Drive	West Long Branch	NJ	07764	450.50	March 15
Ms.	Janie	Babit	187 Beach 147 Street	Queens	NY	11694	128.86	Februrary 28
Ms.	Stephanie	Miller	137 Brighton Avenue	Perth Amboy	NJ	08861	615.75	February 15
Ms.	Jackie	Lee	876 Ocean Parkway	Seaside	NJ	07765	449.08	April 15

ILLUSTRATION D (PASTFORM)

Today's date

FIELD(TITLE) FIELD(FIRST) FIELD(LAST)
FIELD(ADDRESS)
FIELD(CITY), FIELD(ST) FIELD(ZIP)

Dear FIELD(TITLE) FIELD(LAST):

We would like to remind you, FIELD(TITLE) FIELD(LAST), that your account is currently past due. As you can see from the enclosed statement, you have an outstanding balance of FIELD(AMOUNT). This balance was due on FIELD(DATE).

We need your cooperation in resolving this matter so that we can continue to give you the service we have provided you for many years.

Please mail your remittance for FIELD(AMOUNT) today, so that we will not have to forward your account to our Collections Department.

Cordially,

Carol Horowitz
Accounts Receivable Manager

ch/yo
Enclosure

COREL WORDPERFECT 8 Lesson 7: Columns; Tables; Merge

KEYSTROKES

CREATE A DATA FILE
Shift + F9

1. Click **T**ools .... **Alt** + **T**
2. Click M**e**rge .... **E**
3. Click Create **D**ata .... **Alt** + **D**
4. Click **U**se file in active window .... **U**

   OR

   Click **N**ew Document Window .... **N**
5. Click OK .... **Enter**
   - Click OK .... **Enter**

   ✓ *These options will not appear if you have a clear unmodified screen open when the merge command is accessed.*

6. Click **N**ame a field text box .... **Alt** + **N**
7. Type the first field name.
   EXAMPLE: TITLE
8. Click **A**dd .... **Alt** + **A** or **Enter**
9. Repeat steps 7 and 8 to create each field name to be used in the form file.
10. Click F**o**rmat records
    in a table .... **Alt** + **O**
11. Click OK .... **Enter**

    ✓ *The Quick Data Entry dialog box appears.*

12. To enter data:
    a. Type data for first field in **Quick Data Entry** dialog box.
    b. Click
       Ne**x**t Field .... **Alt** + **X** or **Enter**
    c. Repeat steps a-b for each field to receive data.
13. After all fields are entered in first record:
14. Click New **R**ecord ... **Alt** + **R** or **Enter**
15. Repeat steps a-c above for each record.
16. Click **C**lose .... **Alt** + **C**
17. Save the file .... **Enter** or **Y**

    ✓ *Save this file as usual.*

CREATE A FORM FILE

1. a. Click **T**ools .... **Alt** + **T**
   b. Click M**e**rge .... **E**
   c. Click
      Create Document button ...... **Alt** + **C**

   OR

   If document is on screen:

   a. Click Go To Form ..... **Alt** + **Shift** + **G**
      on Merge feature bar.
   b. Click **C**reate .... **Alt** + **C**
2. Type to the first field location.
3. Click **I**nsert Field .... **Alt** + **Shift** + **I**
   on Merge feature bar.
4. Click on **F**ield Name
   to insert .... **Alt** + **F**, ↓ ↑
5. Click **I**nsert .... **Enter**
6. Type to the next field location.
7. Type remainder of document repeating steps 4-8 until done.
8. Click **C**lose .... **Alt** + **C**

   ✓ *Save this file as usual.*

MERGE FORM AND DATA FILES

1. Click **M**erge button
   on Merge feature Bar .... **Alt** + **Shift** + **M**

   OR

   a. Click **T**ools .... **Alt** + **T**
   b. Click M**e**rge .... **E**
   c. Click Perform **M**erge .... **Alt** + **M**
2. To select a form file:
   a. Click **F**orm document
      button .... **Alt** + **F**
   b. Click **C**urrent Document .... **C**
      if desired form file is the active open document.

   OR

   - Click **F**ile on Disk .... **F**
   - Select a form file to merge.
   - Click Select.

3. To select a data file:
   a. Click **D**ata source
      button .... **Alt** + **D**
   b. Click **F**ile on Disk .... **F**
   c. Select a data file to merge.
   d. Click Select.
4. To select output:
   a. Click **O**utput File
      button .... **Alt** + **U**
   b. Select an output source:
      - **C**urrent Document .... **C**
      - **N**ew Document .... **N**
      - **P**rinter .... **P**
      - **F**ile on Disk .... **F**
      - **E**-mail .... **E**
4. Click **M**erge .... **Alt** + **M**

MERGE SELECTED RECORDS

1. Create the data and form document files.
2. Click **M**erge .... **Alt** + **Shift** + **M**
   on Merge feature bar.
3. Click **F**orm document drop-down list
   button .... **Alt** + **F**
4. Click **C**urrent Document .... **C**
   if the desired form document is open.

   OR

   Click **F**ile on Disk .... **F**
   and select a file to merge.
5. Click **D**ata source drop down list
   button .... **Alt** + **D**
6. Click **C**urrent Document .... **C**
   if the desired form document is open.

   OR

   Click **F**ile on Disk .... **F**
   and select a file to merge.

7. To merge only select records:
   a. Click **S**elect Records .... `Alt`+`S`
   b. Click M**a**rk Records .... `Alt`+`A`
   c. Click check box for each record you wish to merge.
   d. Click OK .... `Enter`
8. Click **M**erge .... `Alt`+`M`

MERGE WITH CONDITIONS
Shift + F9

1. Click **T**ools .... `Alt`+`T`
2. Click M**e**rge .... `E`
3. Click Perform **M**erge .... `M`
   OR
   Click **M**erge on the
   Merge feature bar .... `Alt`+`Shift`+`M`
4. Click **F**orm document .... `Alt`+`F`
5. Click **C**urrent Document .... `↓`, `C`
   if form file is the active document.
   OR
   a. Click **F**ile on Disk .... `↓`, `F`
   b. Select form file to merge.
6. Click **D**ata source button .... `Alt`+`D`
7. Click **F**ile on Disk .... `↓`, `F`
   and select data source file.
8. Click O**u**tput button .... `Alt`+`U`
9. Select **N**ew Document .... `↓`, `N`
10. Click **S**elect Records .... `Alt`+`S`
11. Click **S**pecify conditions
    option .... `Alt`+`S`
12. Click **F**ield list arrow in first column
    and select a field on which you will set
    a condition .... `Alt`+`F`, `↓`, `↑`
13. Click Cond **1** text box .... `Alt`+`1`
    and type selection criteria.

14. Click fi**e**ld list arrow in second column
    and select a field ...... `Alt`+`E`, `↓`, `↑`
    on which you will set a condition.
    OR
    Click on the Cond **2** row .... `Alt`+`2`
    to add another condition to the first field.
15. Repeat steps 12-14 to select a third
    fiel**d** on which to set conditions or to
    add conditions to a field which has
    been selected.
16. Click OK .... `Enter`

CREATE ENVELOPES WHILE MERGING

1. Click **T**ools .... `Alt`+`T`
2. Click M**e**rge .... `E`
3. Click Perform **M**erge .... `M`
   OR
   Click **M**erge on the
   Merge feature bar .... `Alt`+`Shift`+`M`
4. Click **F**orm document
   button .... `Alt`+`F`
5. Click **C**urrent Document .... `↓`, `C`
   if form file is the active document.
   OR
   a. Click **F**ile on Disk .... `↓`, `F`
   b. Select **form** file to merge.
6. Click **D**ata source button .... `Alt`+`D`
7. Click **F**ile on Disk .... `↓`, `F`
   and select data source file.
8. Click O**u**tput button .... `Alt`+`U`
9. Select **N**ew Document .... `↓`, `N`
10. Click **E**nvelopes .... `Alt`+`E`
    ✓ *The Envelope dialog box appears.*

11. Select an envelope size from En**v**elope
    Definitions drop-down list (Use your
    printer's default) ...... `Alt`+`V`, `↓`, `↑`
12. Click **Mailing addresses** text box.
13. Click F**i**eld .... `Alt`+`I`
    ✓ *Data file's Field Name list appears.*
14. Select first field name needed for address.
15. Click **I**nsert and Close .... `Alt`+`N`
    • Add/Delete spaces and returns as needed.
16. Repeat steps 11-13 for each field in the mailing address.
17. Set desired **Return Address** criteria:
    • For no Return Address, deselect
      Print ret**u**rn address .... `Alt`+`U`
    • To include Return Address, select
      Print ret**u**rn address .... `Alt`+`U`
18. Type desired address in **Return addresses** text box.
19. Click OK .... `Enter`
    to return to **Perform Merge** box.
20. Click **M**erge .... `Alt`+`M`
    to perform merge.

COREL WORDPERFECT 8   Lesson 7: Columns; Tables; Merge

Exercise 44

■ Summary

In this exercise, you will create a data file. You will then create a full-block letter as a form file, insert letterhead text and a table, and then merge the two documents, setting a condition for the merge.

EXERCISE DIRECTIONS

1. Start with a clear screen.
2. Create a data file from the information shown in Illustration A on the following page. Use a table format for the data.
3. Save the data file; name it **DONATEDATA**.
4. Create a form file from the information shown in Illustration B on the following page.
   a. Set 1.25" left and right margins.
   b. Create the letterhead shown at the top of the page.
      - Center the organization's name using a script font in 36-point bold. Set the font color to red.
   c. Begin the date on approximately Ln 2.5".
   d. Use a serif 12-point font for the document.
5. Save the form file; name it **DONATEFORM**.
6. Merge the form and data files only for those records in which a donation of over $300 was made.
7. Prepare envelopes for the merged letters.
8. Save the merged letters under a new document name, **DONATELETTERS**.
9. Print one copy of the merged file and the envelopes.
10. Close the document window.

ILLUSTRATION A (DONATEDATA)

TITLE	FIRST	LAST	COMPANY	ADDRESS	CITY	STATE	ZIP	1998 CONTRIBUTION
Mr.	Tom	Mason	Web Mania, Inc.	560 Madison Avenue	New York	NY	10022	$500
Mr.	Phelps	Welles		6790 Magnolia Street	Fall City	WA	98024	$1,200
Ms.	Dana	Dowell	Right Stage	675 6 Street	Los Angeles	CA	91606	$1,000
Ms.	Jade	Smith		6798 Belmont	Chicago	IL	60610	$75
Mr.	Henry	Thompson	Sheer Electronics	89 Brown Street	Sea Cliff	NY	11579	$350

ILLUSTRATION B (DONATEFORM)

Children First, Inc.

Today's Date

FIELD(Title) FIELD(First) FIELD(Last)
FIELD(Company)
FIELD(Address)
FIELD(City), FIELD(State) FIELD(Zip)

Dear FIELD(Title) FIELD(Last):

Thanks to regular annual donations such as yours, FIELD(Title) FIELD(Last), Children First, Inc. has been able to help thousands of children in need. We survive on your individual and corporate-sponsored tax deductible contributions.

Please note the Quarterly Contributions table below. Thanks to your donation of FIELD(1998 CONTRIBUTION), we will be able to help even more children in the year to come.

QUARTERLY CONTRIBUTIONS

Year	1st Quarter	2nd Quarter	3rd Quarter	4th Quarter
1998	$6,670	$7,900	$7,880	$13,890
1997	$5,590	$6,380	$8,750	$13,120
1996	$4,420	$5,760	$9,532	$12,740

Should you have any questions about our organization, please feel free to contact our main office.

Sincerely,

Judith George
Vice President

jg/yo

COREL WORDPERFECT 8

Lesson 8: Graphics and Text Boxes

Exercise 45

- Graphics Image
- Insert Clipart
- Create a Text Box

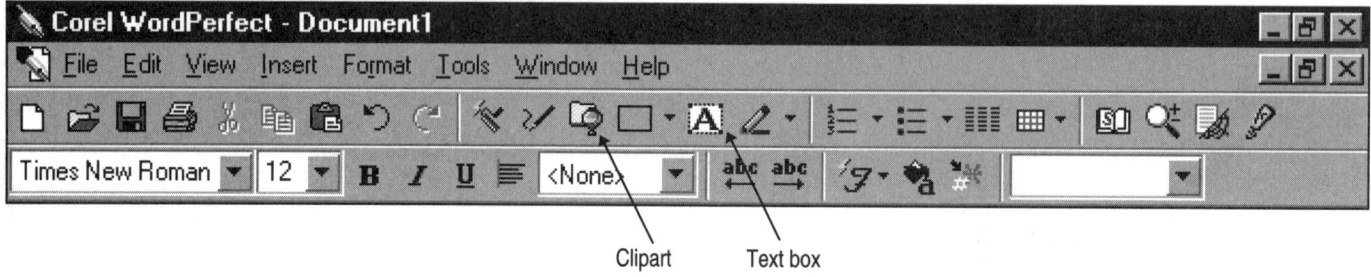

NOTES

- **Graphics** are design elements, such as pictures, charts and lines, used to make a visual statement. The ability to combine graphics and text enables you to create documents such as letterheads, newsletters, brochures and flyers in which these design elements contribute to the effectiveness of the message.

Graphics Boxes

- WordPerfect places graphics into a "box" which is called a **graphics box**. A graphics box can contain an image, text, watermark, table, chart, or equation. (Equations will not be covered in this text.) There are numerous predefined box styles. For example, the "box" around a graphic image (clipart, chart, picture or drawing) is invisible because, by default, there is no box border. A box containing text has, by default, a thin border around all sides of the box. Note the illustrations below.

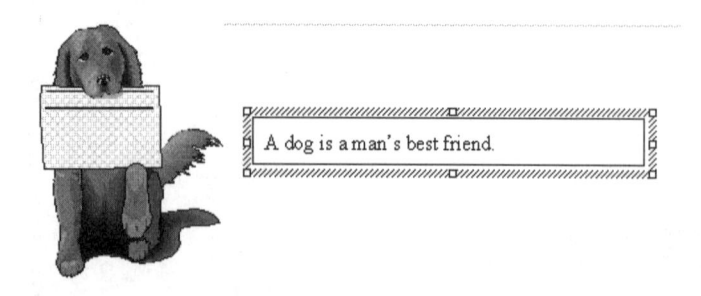

Insert Clipart

- Clipart boxes are the most widely used graphics box types. To insert a clipart graphic, position your insertion point where you want the graphic inserted. Then, select Graphics, Clipart from the Insert menu or click the Clipart button on the WordPerfect 8 Toolbar. The Scrapbook dialog box displays.

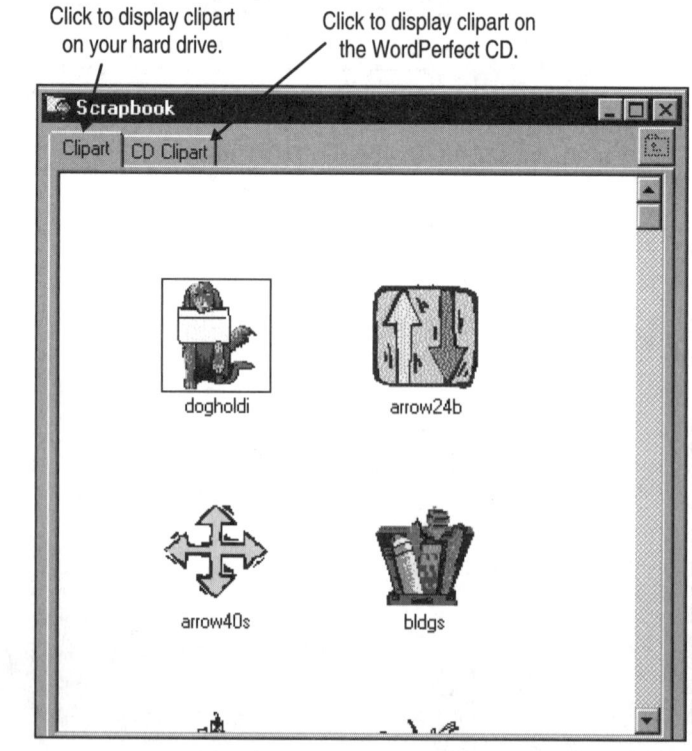

- Corel WordPerfect provides thousands of Clipart images, some of which were copied to your hard drive when you installed WordPerfect. These images display in the Scrapbook. The remaining Clipart images, drawings and photos are located on the WordPerfect CD. To insert one of the images on the CD, insert the CD and click the CD Clipart tab in the Scrapbook dialog box.

- There are two ways to insert clipart from the Scrapbook into your document:

  1. Drag the image you want off the Scrapbook page into your document. When you release the mouse, the image will appear within the dotted box border. Then, close the Scrapbook by clicking the Close button ▣ in the Scrapbook window.

     ✓ Note: It is difficult to place the image using this method since the Scrapbook window blocks the document. To insert the image into a particular place in the document, use the next method. Do not worry if the image is not in the desired position or in the desired size at this time. You will learn to edit it in the next exercise.

  OR

  2. Right-click on the image and select Copy from the QuickMenu. Close the Scrapbook. Then, click the Paste button ▣ on the WordPerfect 8 toolbar. The image will display at the insertion point position.

Create a Text Box

- A **text box** is typically used for setting off special text, such as tables, charts, sidebars, and callouts. As noted earlier, WordPerfect automatically applies a thin border around all sides of a text box.

- To create a text box, select Te**x**t Box from the **I**nsert menu, or select the Text Box button ▣ on the WordPerfect 8 Toolbar. When the text box first appears, it is aligned at the right margin and pre-sized by WordPerfect. Type the text you want to appear in the box. Note that the box contains sizing handles. When sizing handles appear on a box, the box is in edit mode. Click outside the box to remove the handles.

- You can resize and reposition a text box within your document, and you can edit the text within the box (see Exercise 76 to edit a graphics box).

KEYSTROKES

INSERT CLIPART

1. Position the insertion point where you wish to insert the graphic.

2. Click **Clipart** button ▣ on WordPerfect 8 toolbar.
   OR
   a. Click **I**nsert............... [Alt]+[I]
   b. Click **G**raphics............... [G]
   c. Click **C**lipart............... [C]
   ✓ The scrapbook displays.

3. Drag the desired graphic off the Scrapbook page into the document. Close the Scrapbook.
   OR
   a. Right-click the desired graphic.
   b. Click **C**opy .... [C]
   c. Click **Close** button [X].
   d. Click the **Paste** button ▣ on the WordPerfect 8 toolbar.

CREATE A TEXT BOX

1. Click **Text Box** button ▣ on WordPerfect 8 toolbar.
   OR
   a. Place insertion point where you want text box to be inserted (vertically on the page).
   b. Click **I**nsert............... [Alt]+[I]
   c. Click Te**x**t Box .... [X]
   ✓ A text box appears with an active insertion point.

2. Type text into box.

3. Click anywhere outside the text box to deselect it.

COREL WORDPERFECT 8 Lesson 8: Graphics and Text Boxes

In this exercise, you will create three graphics images and a text box. In the next exercise, you will edit them.

EXERCISE DIRECTIONS

1. Start with a clear screen.
2. Position the insertion point at the top left corner of your screen. Use the copy and paste method to insert the LIGHTBUL graphic from the Scrapbook.
3. Press the Enter key 16 times.
4. Use the copy and paste method to insert the OLDKEY graphic from the Scrapbook.
5. Use the copy and paste method to insert the GLOBE01 graphic from the Scrapbook on the right side of the page as shown.
6. Press the Enter key 16 times.
7. Create a text box and enter the following text using the default font:

    Good ideas make the world go round!
8. Print one copy.
9. Save the file; name it **WORLD**.
10. Close the document window.

COREL WORDPERFECT 8   Lesson 8: Graphics and Text Boxes

Exercise 46

- Select a Graphics Box   ■ Select a Text Box
- Size a Graphics Box or Text Box
- Position (Move) a Graphics Box   ■ Delete a Graphics Box or Text Box
- Copy a Graphics Box or Text Box   ■ Rotate a Text Box

Graphics Property Bar

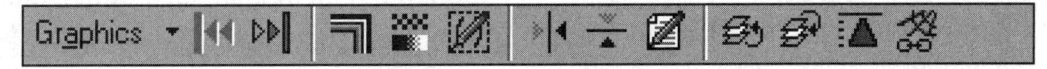

NOTES

Select a Graphics Box

- The sizing handles must be displayed to edit a graphics box; that is, to delete, copy, or change its size or position.
- To select a graphics box and display its sizing handles, click the image. The Graphics Property Bar will also display. The Graphics Property Bar contains buttons that make graphics editing tasks easier.

Selected graphics sizing handles

Select a Text Box

- Click the top, bottom, left, or right edge of the text box to display solid sizing handles along with the Graphics Property Bar. Click inside the box to display hollow sizing handles. When solid sizing handles appear, you can size, position, copy or delete the box. When hollow sizing handles appear, you can edit the box contents as well as size or position the box. You cannot delete a text box when hollow sizing handles are displayed.

  ✓Note: *Once you have displayed hollow sizing handles, you must click outside the text box before you can display the solid handles.*

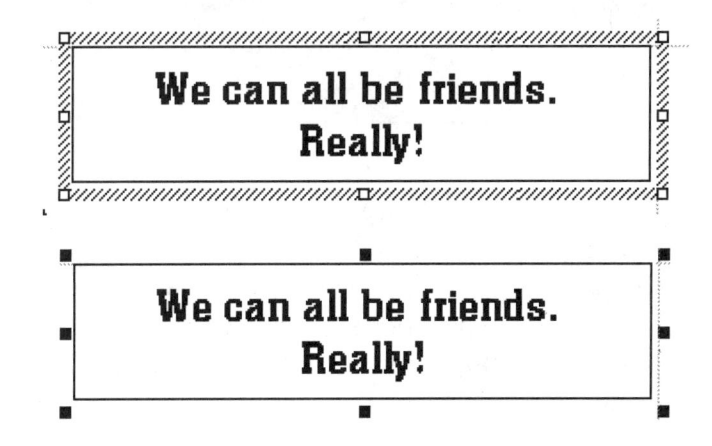

We can all be friends. Really!

We can all be friends. Really!

COREL WORDPERFECT 8   Lesson 8: Graphics and Text Boxes

Size a Graphics Box or Text Box

- To size a graphics or text box using the mouse, point to one of the sizing handles until the pointer becomes a double-headed arrow (↔). Then, drag a corner handle to size the box and retain the box proportions; drag a top or bottom middle handle to change the box height, and/or drag a left or right middle handle to change the box width.

- The size of a graphics or text box may also be adjusted by a specific amount. Select the box so that solid handles appear. Right-click and select Size from the QuickMenu or click Graphics on the Graphics Property Bar and select Size from the drop-down menu.

- In the Box Size dialog box that follows, click the Set option and enter the desired width and height by typing the values in the appropriate text boxes. Choose Full to fill the page with the image, or choose Maintain proportions to create a proportioned image.

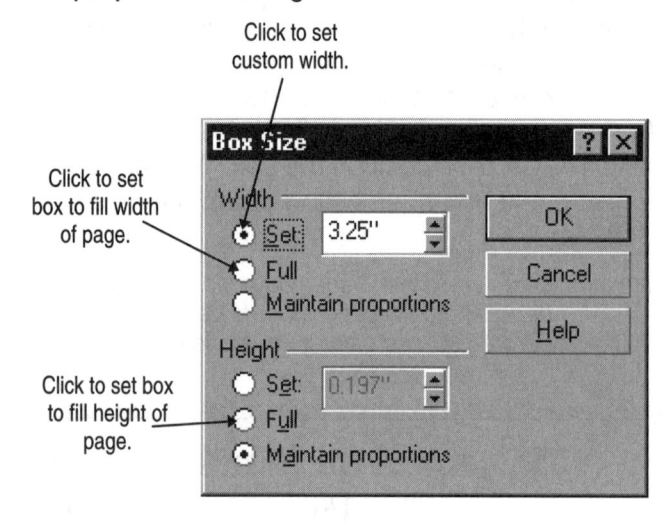

Click to set custom width.

Click to set box to fill width of page.

Click to set box to fill height of page.

Position (Move) a Graphics or Text Box

- To position a graphics box or text box using the mouse, point, click and hold down the mouse button until the pointer becomes a four-headed arrow (✣). Then, drag the box to the desired location.

- You can also position a graphics or text box using specified positions. Select the box, then click Graphics on the Graphics Property Bar and select Position, or right-click the selected box and choose Position from the QuickMenu. In the Box Position dialog box that follows, specify the desired Horizontal or Vertical position in the Horizontal and/or Vertical increment box. Be sure to also specify from what point on the page the distance specified will be calculated (e.g., from the right margin, top margin, etc.)

- To center a box between the margins, attach it to the page, enter zero in the Horizontal and/or Vertical boxes and select Center of Margins from the Horizontal and/or Vertical from drop-down lists.

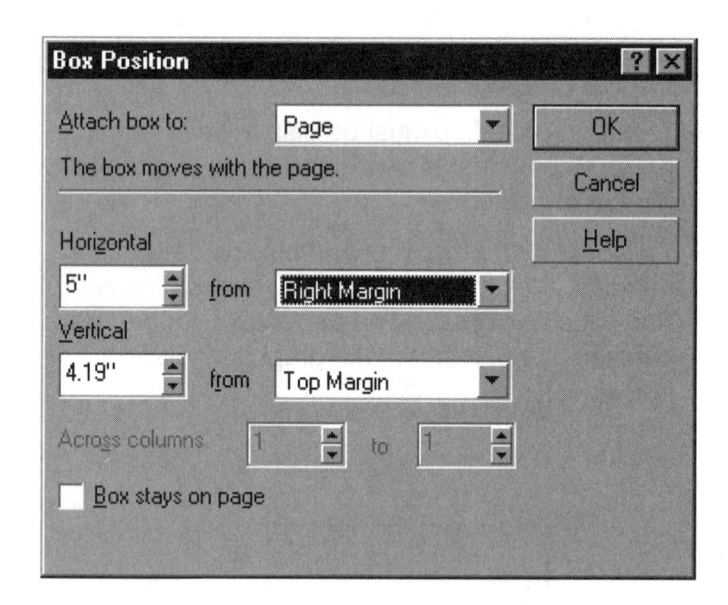

Delete a Graphics or Text Box

- To delete a graphics or text box, select the box to display the solid sizing handles, and press the Delete key or click the Cut button on the WordPerfect 8 toolbar.

Copy a Graphics or Text Box

- To copy a graphics box, select the box, and select Copy from the Edit menu or click the Copy button on the WordPerfect 8 toolbar. Position the insertion point where the copied box should appear. Then, select Paste from the Edit menu or click the Paste button on the WordPerfect 8 toolbar.

Rotate a Text Box

- The text box may be rotated counterclockwise in 90-degree increments. Select the text box so that solid handles display, then click Graphics on the Graphics Property Bar and click Content, or right-click the text box and choose Content from the QuickMenu. In the Box Content dialog box that follows, enter a rotation amount.

- To edit the text within the box, select Edit from the Box Content dialog box. The Text Box Editor window opens. You can then change the alignment, font size, or style of the text using the methods learned previously.

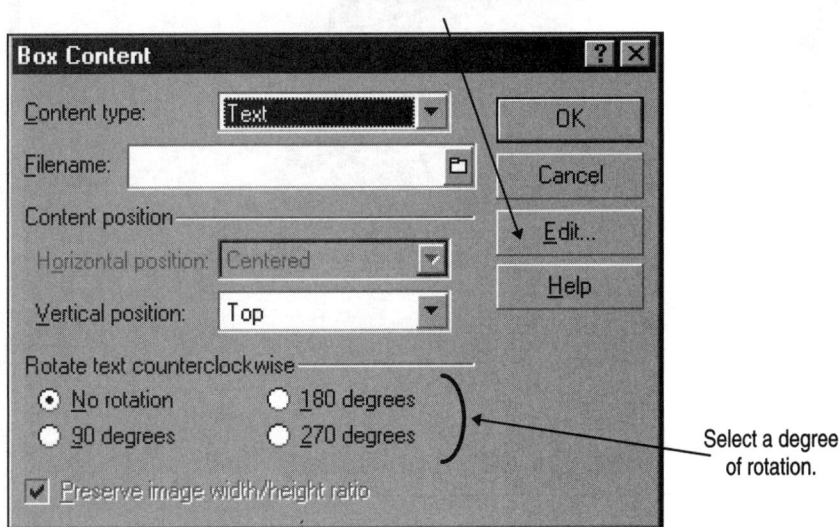

In this exercise, you will edit the graphics inserted in the previous exercise to create a scene.

EXERCISE DIRECTIONS

✓ It will be helpful to view the page in Full Page view while working through the exercise (View, Zoom, Full Page).

1. Open **WORLD** or open **46WORLD**.
2. Select the LIGHTBUL graphic. Size it to 2.50" wide by 2.37" high. Move it to the top right position as shown in the Desired Result.
3. Select the OLDKEY graphic. Size it to 2.5" wide by 2.15" high, and position it at the top left of the page as shown in the Desired Result.
4. Select the GLOBE01 graphic. Size it to 3.50" wide by 3.57" high. Position it at the bottom center of the page as shown.
5. Select the text box.
   a. Edit the text within the box to read:
      Key players and great ideas make the world go round!
   b. Center the text within the box and set the font to a decorative 18-point bold font.
   c. Extend the length of the text box so that the text does not wrap to the second line.
   d. Position the box in the center of the page as shown.
6. Create another text box.
   a. Type and center the following text in a sans serif 16 point bold font:
      PEOPLE AND IDEAS
   b. Rotate the text box 90 degrees and position it to the left of the GLOBE01 graphic, as shown.
   c. Copy the text box and position the copy to the right of the GLOBE01 graphic as shown.
7. Print one copy.
8. Close the file; save the changes.
9. Close the document window.

COREL WORDPERFECT 8 Lesson 8: Graphics and Text Boxes

DESIRED RESULT

Key players and great ideas make the world go round!

PEOPLE AND IDEAS

PEOPLE AND IDEAS

KEYSTROKES

SELECT A GRAPHICS BOX
Point to the image and click.

SELECT A TEXT BOX

To display solid handles:

Point to the top, bottom, left or right edge of the text box and click.

To display hollow handles:

Point inside the box and click.

DELETE A GRAPHICS OR TEXT BOX
Ctrl + X

1. Select box.
2. Press **Delete** key.............................. `Del`

   OR

   Click **Cut** button ✂ on WordPerfect 8 toolbar.

POSITION A GRAPHICS OR TEXT BOX

1. Select the graphics or text box (see above).
2. Hold down mouse until pointer changes to a four-headed arrow.
3. Drag box to desired position.

   OR

1. Select the graphics or text box so that solid handles display.
2. Click **Graphics** button .... `Alt`+`A` on Graphics Property Bar.

   OR

   - Right-click box.

3. Select **P**osition................................ `P`

   To position horizontally:

   a. Click **Hori**z**ontal** .... `Alt`+`Z`
   b. Type desired horizontal measurement.
   c. Click Horizontal **from** list arrow to select where graphic placement should be measured from..... `Alt`+`F`

   d. Select a placement option:
   - **Left Edge of Page**
   - **Left Margin**
   - **Right Margin**
   - **Center of Margins**
   - **Left Column**
   - **Right Column**
   - **Centered in Columns**

   To position vertically:

   a. Click **V**ertical..................... `Alt`+`V`
   b. Type desired vertical measurement.
   c. Click vertical **from** list arrow to select where graphic placement should be measured from.............. `Alt`+`R`

   d. Select a placement option:
   - **Top of Page**
   - **Top Margin**
   - **Bottom Margin**
   - **Center of Margins**

4. Click **OK** .... `Enter`

SIZE A GRAPHICS OR TEXT BOX

1. Select the box (see above).
2. Drag the sizing handles to desired box size.

   OR

   - Select the box.
   - Click **Graphics** button on Graphics Property Bar.

   OR

   - Right-click box.

3. Select **S**ize .... `Z`

   To set height and width:

   a. Click **S**et........................... `Alt`+`S`
   b. Type desired width.
   c. Click **S**et text box .... `Alt`+`E`
   d. Type desired height.

   To have box fill page horizontally:

   Click **F**ull for Width............... `Alt`+`F`

   To have box fill page vertically:

   Click F**u**ll Height..................... `Alt`+`U`

4. Click **OK** .... `Enter`

COPY A GRAPHICS OR TEXT BOX
Ctrl + C, Ctrl + V

1. Select the box.
2. Click **E**dit.............................. `Alt`+`E`
3. Click **C**opy .... `C`
4. Click location on page where copied graphic should appear.
5. Click **E**dit.............................. `Alt`+`E`
6. Click **P**aste .... `P`

ROTATE TEXT BOX

1. Select a text box to rotate so that solid handles display.
2. a. Click **Graphics** button on Graphics Property Bar............. `Ctrl`+`Shift`+`A`

   b. Click C**o**ntent........................... `O`

   OR

   a. Right-click text box.
   b. Click Co**n**tent.......................... `N`

2. Select desired degree of rotation:
   - **N**o Rotation .... `Alt`+`N`
   - **9**0 Degrees .... `Alt`+`9`
   - **1**80 Degrees .... `Alt`+`1`
   - **2**70 Degrees .... `Alt`+`2`

3. Click **OK** .... `Enter`

   To edit text in a rotated box:

   a. Click the **E**dit button.......... `Alt`+`E`
   b. Edit text as desired.
   c. Click **C**lose .... `Shift`+`Alt`+`C`

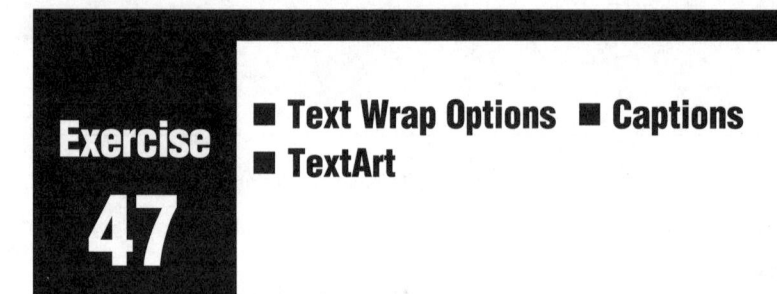

COREL WORDPERFECT 8   Lesson 8: Graphics and Text Boxes

Exercise 47
- Text Wrap Options
- Captions
- TextArt

NOTES

Text Wrap Options

- WordPerfect provides you with numerous options for wrapping text around a graphics or text box. You can control the type and position of the text wrap. Note some of the text wrap options illustrated below:

Behind text

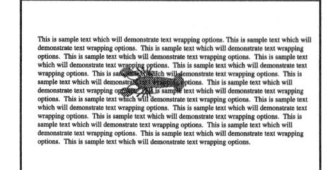

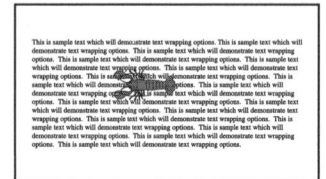

In front of text

Square (left side)

Square (both sides)

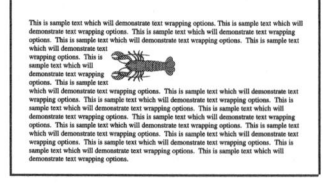

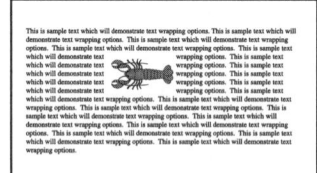

Contour (both sides)

Neither side

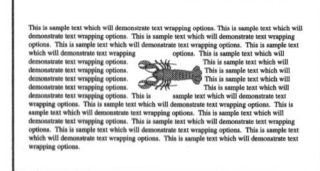

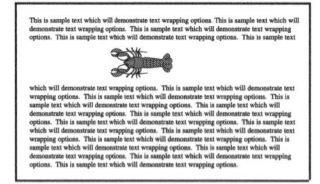

- To **wrap text** around a graphic or text box, you must insert the graphic or text box into the text. Then, click to select the box, click the Wrap button on the Graphics Property bar and select a wrap option from the drop-down menu, or right-click on the box and select Wrap from the QuickMenu. In the Wrap Text dialog box that follows, click to choose a wrap option.

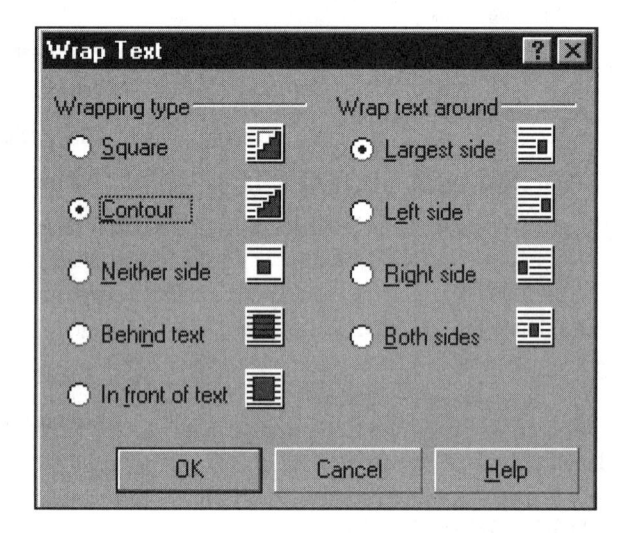

- The *Contour* option flows text in a silhouette pattern up to and around the selected sides of the image.

- The *In front of text* option places the box in front of text, thus affecting the readability of the text where the box is displayed.

- The *Behind text* option places the box behind the text so that both the text and the box are visible.

- When using text wrap, carefully proofread the text that flows around the graphic. You may need to adjust the graphic position to avoid awkward word breaks.

Captions

- A **caption** is explanatory text that appears with a graphic.

- WordPerfect will automatically number captions for you. If you insert or delete a captioned graphic box, WordPerfect will renumber the boxes to reflect the change.

- You can create a caption using one of the following three methods:
    1. Click to select the graphic to receive the caption. Click the caption button on the Graphics Property Bar ▫. Backspace to delete the Figure number (if desired) and type the caption. This method does not give you immediate access to caption formatting options.

       OR

    2. Click to select the graphic to receive the caption. Click the Graphics button on the Graphics Property Bar and select Caption from the drop-down menu. The Box Caption dialog box displays.

       OR

    3. Right-click the graphic to receive the caption. Select Caption from the QuickMenu. The Box Caption dialog box displays.

- In the Box Caption dialog box that follows (methods 2 and 3), click Edit and type your caption. A box or figure number appears below the box, with the insertion point in place for you to type the caption. Normal editing and formatting features apply here. For example, to delete the figure number, press the Backspace key.

- You can position the caption on any side of the box by clicking the Side of box list arrow and choosing an option. You can choose where you want the caption to be positioned in relation to the box border by selecting Inside or Outside Border from the Border drop-down list. You can also choose how you want the caption text aligned by selecting from the Position drop-down list and choosing an alignment option.

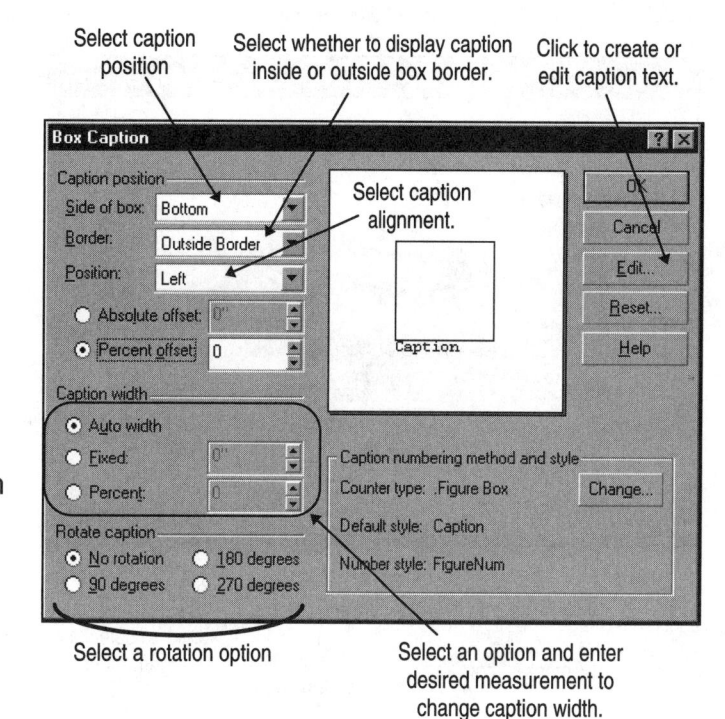

- By default, the caption width matches the graphic width. However, you can set your own Caption width by choosing the Fixed or Percent option and indicating an amount.

- The caption can be rotated to appear along any side of the box by choosing a Rotation option.

TextArt

- WordPerfect's **TextArt** feature allows you to create striking text effects for special uses, such as flyer headlines or logos. Waves, pennants, circles, and crescents are among the included effects.

- To create a TextArt effect, select Graphics, TextArt from the Insert menu. In the Corel TextArt 8.0 dialog box that follows, you can enter up to 58 characters on one, two, or three lines. Or, you can select text to be used for TextArt and then access the TextArt feature.

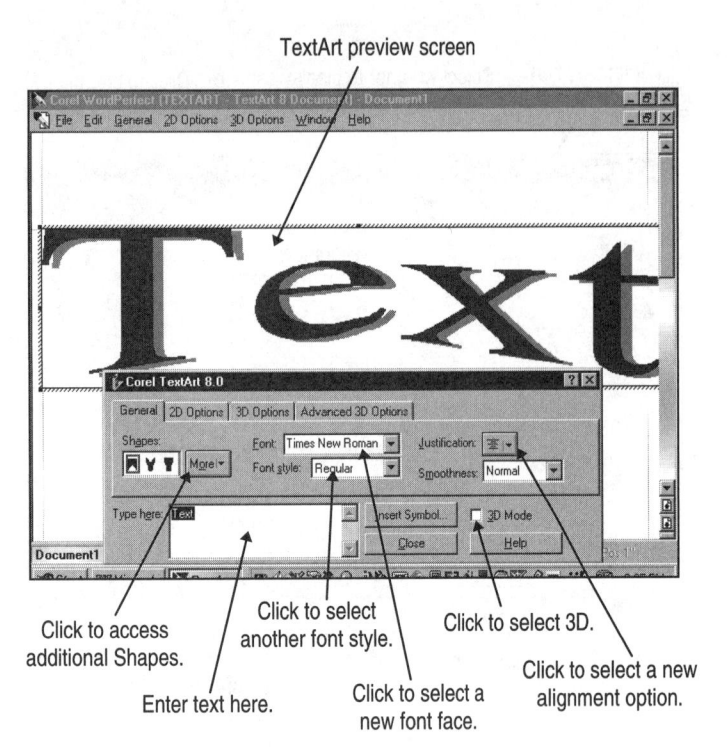

COREL WORDPERFECT 8 Lesson 8: Graphics and Text Boxes

TextArt preview screen

Click to access additional Shapes.

Enter text here.

Click to select another font style.

Click to select a new font face.

Click to select 3D.

Click to select a new alignment option.

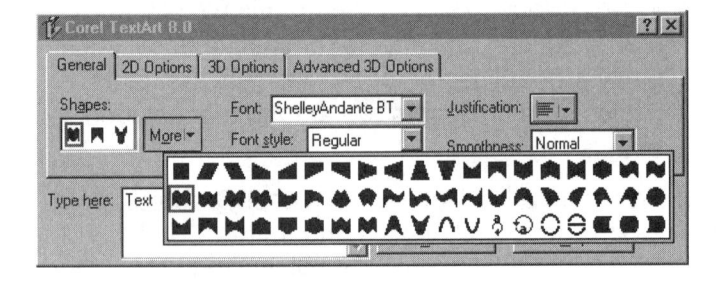

- You can also change the text color and enhance the design with patterns, shadows, and borders by clicking the 2D or 3D tab and choosing the desired options.

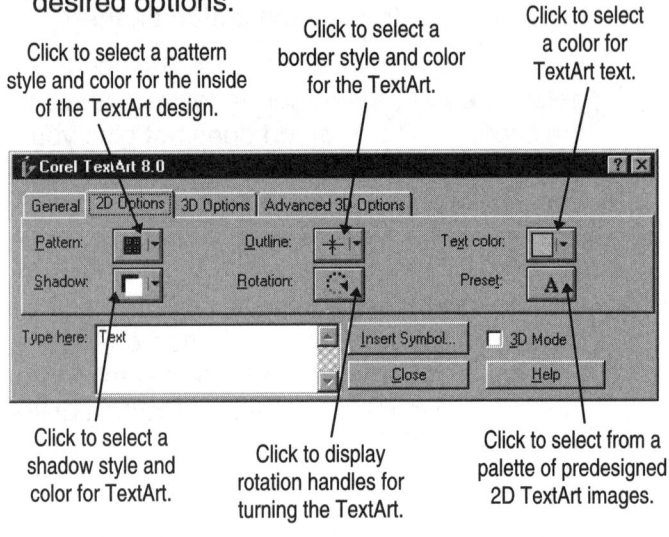

Click to select a pattern style and color for the inside of the TextArt design.

Click to select a border style and color for the TextArt.

Click to select a color for TextArt text.

Click to select a shadow style and color for TextArt.

Click to display rotation handles for turning the TextArt.

Click to select from a palette of predesigned 2D TextArt images.

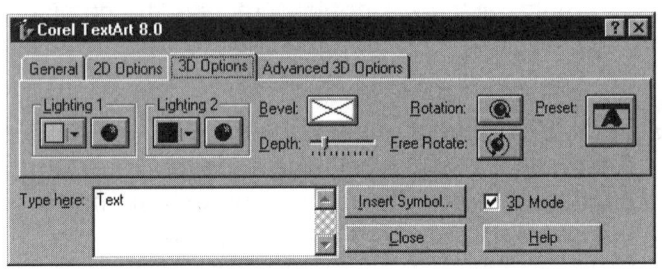

- Once the text to be used for TextArt has been identified, select a TextArt shape to apply from the Shapes palette, or click on the More button to select additional shapes. You can also select a different font, font style, and justification option by clicking the appropriate button in the Corel TextArt 8.0 dialog box and choosing the option.

- The TextArt image is placed in a graphics box that can then be positioned and sized like any other graphics box.

- To edit a TextArt image, double-click on it.

- To return to the main document, click Close or click outside of the dialog box.

In Part I of this exercise, you will practice wrapping text using different wrap options. In Part II of this exercise, you will enhance a newsletter created earlier with TextArt, graphics and captions. In Part III of this exercise, you will create an invitation using TextArt and graphics.

EXERCISE DIRECTIONS

PART I
1. Start with a clear screen.
2. Open **47TEXT** or type the following sentence and then copy and paste it 17 times (within the same paragraph).

    In this exercise, we will wrap text around graphics images and text boxes.

3. Insert any desired graphic in the center of the text.
4. Wrap the graphic using each of the following options:
   - Neither side
   - Behind text
   - In front of text
   - Square (largest side)
   - Square (both sides)
   - Contour (both sides)
   - Contour (left side)
5. Insert any desired caption below the graphic.
6. Change the caption rotation to 90 degrees.
7. Close the file; do not save the changes.

PART II
1. Open **ACTIVITY** or open **47ACTIVITY**.
2. Change the font size of the headline text to 12 point.
3. Insert a relevant graphic in the first column as shown in Illustration A on the following page.
   a. Size it to approximately .93" wide by .65" high.
   ✓ *Make necessary adjustments to graphic size to avoid distortion of graphic.*
   b. Apply a Contour (left side) text wrap.
4. Insert a relevant graphic in the second column as shown.
   a. Size it to approximately .66" wide by .93" high.
   b. Apply a Neither side text wrap.
   c. Insert and center the caption shown in sans serif 9-point bold.
5. Insert a relevant graphic in the third column as shown.
   a. Size it to approximately .867" wide by .52" high.
   b. Apply a Contour both sides text wrap.
6. Make any adjustments necessary so the text does not split awkwardly.
7. Print one copy.
8. Close the file; save the changes.

PART III
1. Start with a clear screen.
2. Use the default margins.

To create the invitation in Illustration B:
3. Type the text as shown.
4. Center the text horizontally and vertically on the page.
5. Change font sizes and styles as indicated.
6. Create a TextArt object for the words, Liquid Streets.
   a. Select any desired shape.
   b. Place the TextArt object as shown.
   c. Size it as desired.
7. Insert the BLDGS Clipart graphic at the bottom of the page.
   a. Size it to approximately 3.48" wide by 1.88 high.
   b. Insert and center the following caption in a 14-point script font:

      A comedy about life in New York City.
8. Print one copy.
9. Save the file; name it **PREMIERE**.
10. Close the document window.

ILLUSTRATION A

Student Activity Monthly Newsletter

NEW STUDENT WELCOME FAIR

The Administration department will sponsor a Welcome Fair for all new students on August 28. Packets will be available to inform students of all on-campus activities and clubs, nearby restaurants and shops, dormitory information, etc. Several clubs and organizations will be represented by information booths. If you would like to add a flyer or brochure to the packet, or if you wish to register a booth for your club or organization, please see Dean Stella Samuels in the Administration Department. A barbecue lunch will be served on the Main Lawn from noon to 2:00 p.m., followed by a get-acquainted session in which new students will have the opportunity to ask a panel of peers any university-related questions. Dean Samuels will wrap up the event with a talk at the Union Podium.

CAMPUS EMPLOYMENT

With the arrival of the fall semester, several campus employment opportunities have opened up. The French and Italian

Earn While You Learn

Languages department is seeking tutors for French 1 and Italian 1. Applicants must be fluent in either French or Italian and have completed a minimum of 3 years of college-level French or Italian. If interested, please see Dr. Vincineau Monday through Wednesday in Room 760 of the French and Italian Building. The Math and Science department is also seeking tutors as well as lab workers. Many positions and levels of employment are available. If interested, see Dr. Martin on Tuesdays and Thursdays in Room 317 of the John Hall Math and Science Building.

ESSAY CONTEST

The University's 32nd Annual Personal Heritage Essay Contest is underway. All students are encouraged to write a 5,000-word essay that details their history and family background. Scholarship money will be awarded to the top ten winners.

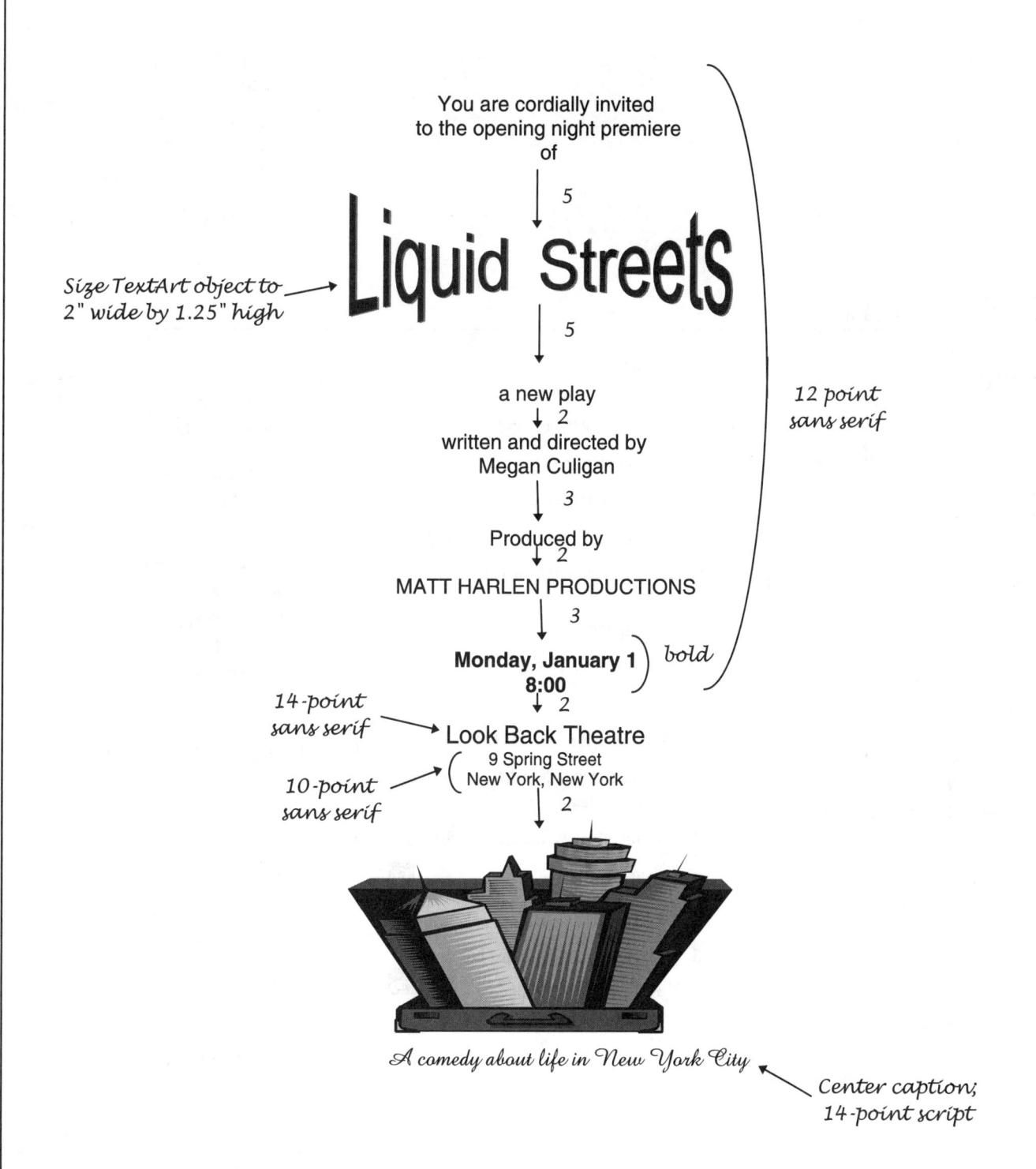

ILLUSTRATION B

You are cordially invited
to the opening night premiere
of

↓ 5

Liquid streets

↓ 5

a new play
↓ 2
written and directed by
Megan Culigan
↓ 3
Produced by
↓ 2
MATT HARLEN PRODUCTIONS
↓ 3
Monday, January 1) *bold*
8:00
↓ 2
Look Back Theatre
9 Spring Street
New York, New York
↓ 2

A comedy about life in New York City

Size TextArt object to 2" wide by 1.25" high → (points to Liquid streets)

12 point sans serif (brace around main text block)

14-point sans serif → Look Back Theatre

10-point sans serif → 9 Spring Street / New York, New York

Center caption; 14-point script → A comedy about life in New York City

KEYSTROKES

WRAP TEXT

1. Select graphic.
2. Click the **Wrap** button [icon] on the Graphics Property Bar.
   OR
   a. Right-click the graphic.
   b. Click **W**r**ap** .... `R`
3. Select a wrapping option.

ADD A CAPTION

1. Select the graphic.
2. Click the **Caption** button [icon] on the Graphics Property Bar.
3. Backspace to delete figure number (if desired) .... `Backspace`
4. Type the caption.
5. Apply formatting options from Format menu, if desired.
   OR
1. Select the graphic.
2. Click the **Graphics** button on the Graphics Property Bar .... `Shift`+`Alt`+`A`
3. Click **C**aption .... `C`
   OR
   a. Right-click the graphic.
   b. Select **C**aption .... `A`
4. Select caption options (if desired).
5. Click **E**dit .... `Alt`+`E`
6. Backspace to delete the Figure number (if desired).
7. Type caption.
8. Apply formatting options from Format menu (if desired).

CREATE A TEXTART IMAGE

1. Place insertion point where you want to insert the image.
2. Click **I**nsert .... `Alt`+`I`
3. Click **G**raphics .... `G`
4. Click Te**x**tArt .... `X`
5. Click in the **Type h**ere text box and enter desired text .... `Alt`+`E`
6. Select a TextArt shape from the **Shapes** box. Click **More** and select desired shape from palette.
   a. Click **F**ont list arrow .... `Alt`+`F` and select desired font.
   b. Click Font **s**tyle list arrow .... `Alt`+`S` and select desired style, if applicable.
   c. Click **J**ustification button and select justification option, if desired.
   d. Click **3D Mode** check box to convert image to 3D, if desired .... `Alt`+`3`

To enhance a TextArt design:

a. Click the 2D option, 3D option or Advanced 3D **Options** tab in the Corel TextArt 8.0 dialog box.
b. Click to select the desired options.

To rotate text box:

a. Click 2D or 3D Options tab.
b. Click **R**otation button and select a desired rotation from the palette.
   OR
• Click **Free Rotate** in 3D TAB and drag on a rotation handle in desired direction.

7. Click **C**lose .... `Alt`+`C`
   to exit the TextArt dialog box.
8. Click anywhere outside the text image.

Exercise 48

- Watermark
- Drop Capital
- Insert Lines
- Reverse Text

NOTES

Watermark

- A **watermark** is a lightened graphics image or text that prints in the background behind the printed text. A watermark can appear on every page of your document or on selected pages. You can also create two watermarks (Watermark A and Watermark B), which can appear on odd pages, even pages, or every page. (See Keystrokes section, CREATE A WATERMARK.)

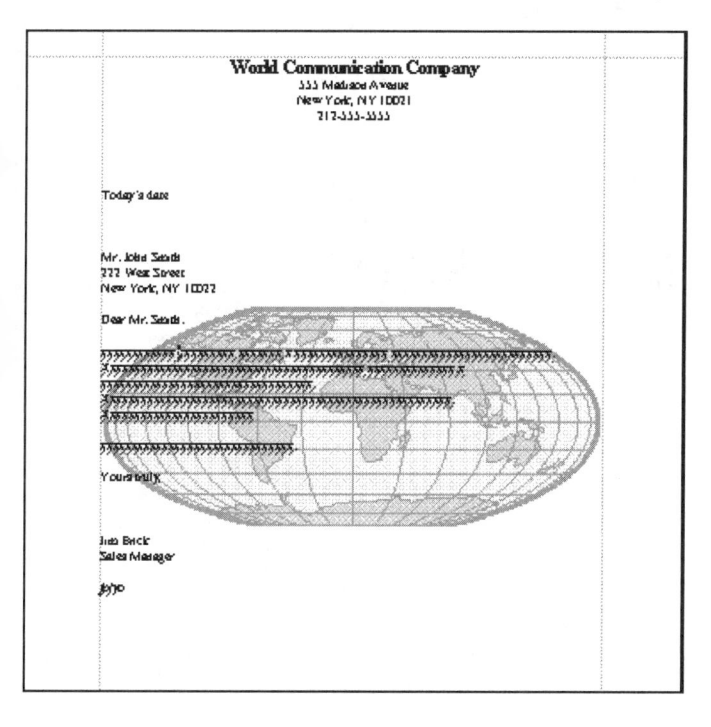

- To create a watermark select Watermark from the Insert menu. In the Watermark dialog box that follows, select Watermark A or B and click Create.

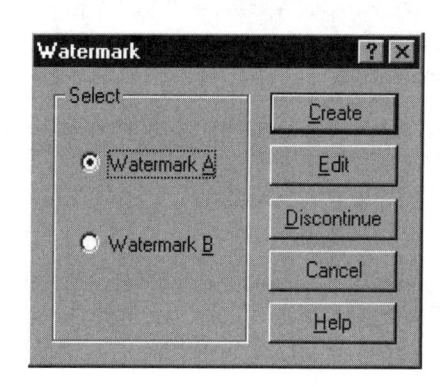

- A blank watermark window displays along with the Watermark Property Bar. You can insert a graphics image, a file, or typed text. You can edit text content, apply font changes and use most editing features within the watermark window.

- To use text as a watermark, type the desired text in the watermark window. Apply any desired font face, size, style and other text formatting.

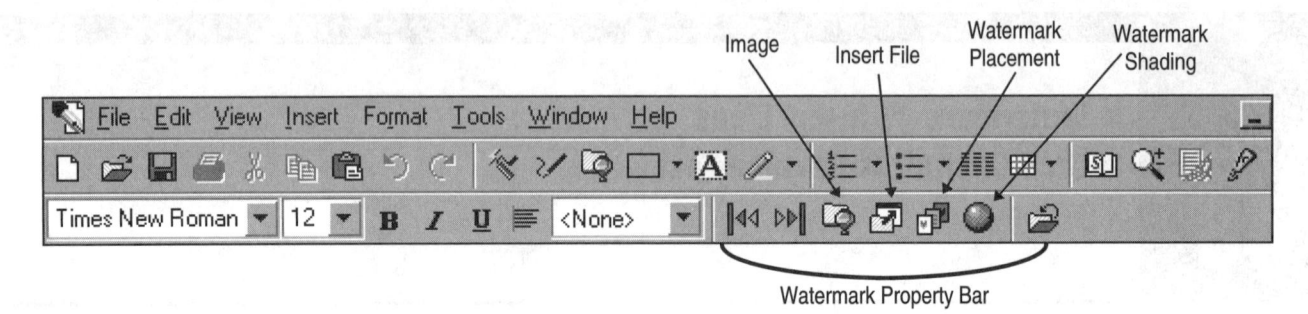

COREL WORDPERFECT 8 Lesson 8: Graphics and Text Boxes

Toolbar callouts: Image, Insert File, Watermark Placement, Watermark Shading — Watermark Property Bar

- If you choose to insert a graphics image as a watermark, select the Image button on the Watermark Property Bar. Locate the image to insert in the Insert Image dialog box that follows and click Insert.

- To insert a file as a watermark, click the Insert File button on the Watermark Property Bar. Locate the file in the Insert File dialog box that follows and click Insert.

- To suppress a watermark on the current page, select Format, Page, Suppress and select Watermark A and/or Watermark B and click OK.

- To edit a watermark, click in the page containing the watermark, select Watermark from the Insert menu and click Edit.

- To adjust the shading of a watermark image or watermark text, select the Shading button on the Watermark Property Bar. In the Watermark Shading dialog box that follows, enter the desired shading percentage for the watermark text and/or image.

Watermark Shading

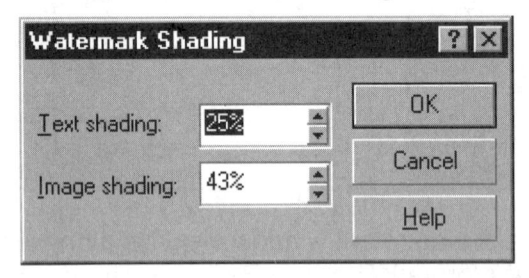

- Page borders, along with any other graphic image, may be used as watermarks.

Insert Lines

- You can insert horizontal, vertical and diagonal lines in your document. **Lines** are used to create designs, separate parts of a document, or draw attention to a particular place.

- You can adjust the position, length, and thickness of lines as well as change line styles.

- Horizontal and vertical lines can be inserted by selecting Horizontal Line or Vertical Line from the Insert, Shape submenu. WordPerfect automatically inserts a full line (a single line that extends from the left to the right margin, or a single line that extends from the top to the bottom margin) at the insertion point position.

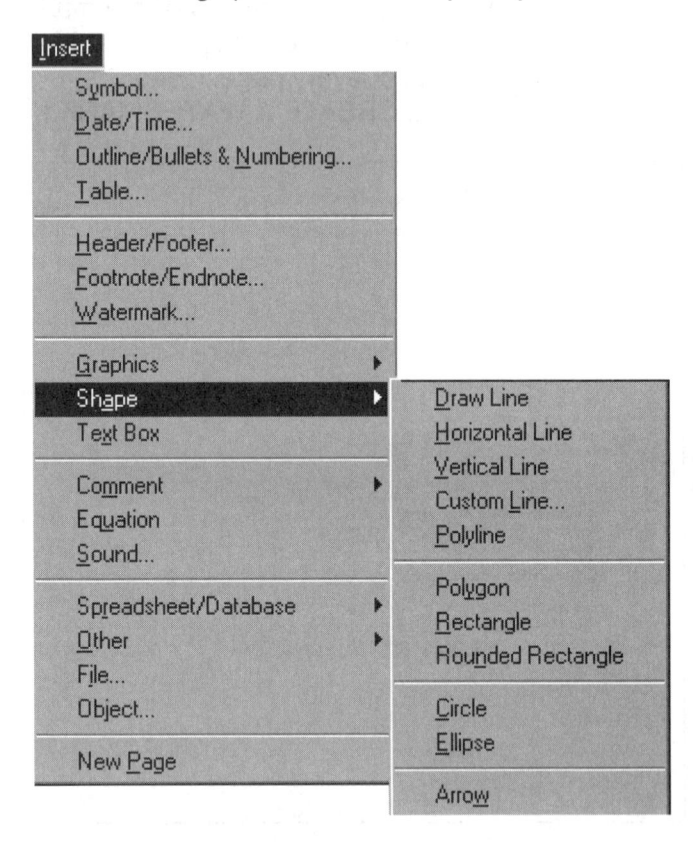

- To create a specified line thickness, color, size, or style, select Custom Line from the Insert, Shape submenu. In the Create Graphics Line dialog box that follows, select Horizontal line or Vertical line. Then, click the appropriate button and choose a desired Line style, Line color, and/or Line thickness from the palette of choices that display. Enter the length in the Length increment box. You can also change the amount of space above and/or below a horizontal line by selecting the Space above/below line buttons and entering a spacing amount.

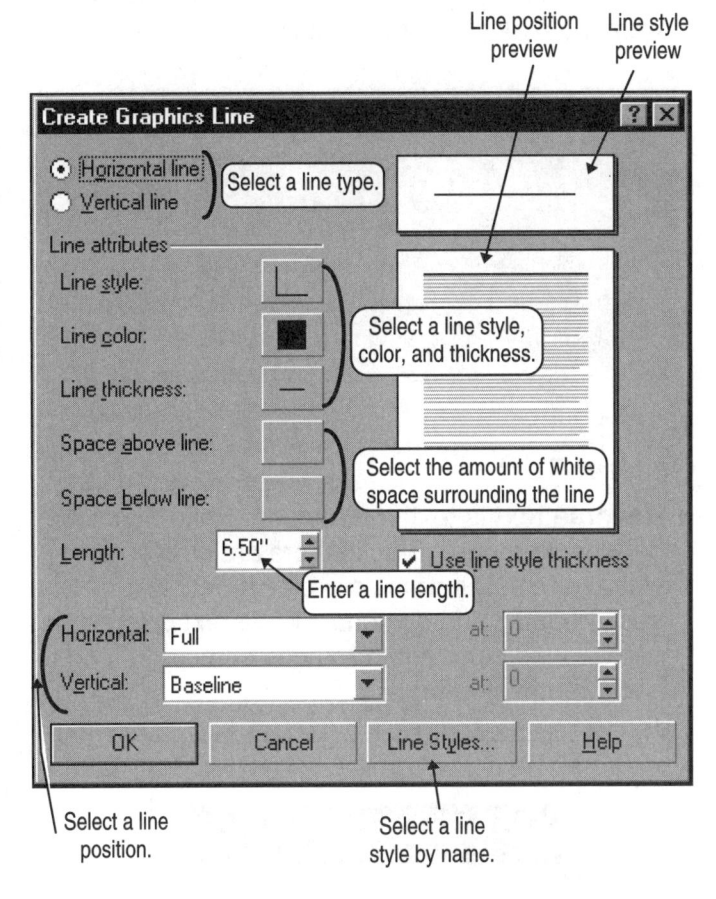

Labels on Create Graphics Line dialog: Line position preview, Line style preview, Select a line type, Select a line style, color, and thickness, Select the amount of white space surrounding the line, Enter a line length, Select a line position, Select a line style by name.

Labels on Line Property Bar: Line Style, Line Thickness, Line Color, Line Graphic Edit, Line Property Bar.

✓ Note: You can select a Line style by sight or by name. When you click the Line style button, a palette of predefined styles displays. Select a desired line style from the palette or click the Line Styles button at the bottom of the dialog box and select one by name.

- The preview window will display your selection. Click OK to select your choices. The line will appear in the document window.

- You can customize or edit an existing line by selecting the line (handles will appear), then clicking the Line Graphic Edit button  on the Line Property Bar, or right-clicking the line and selecting Edit Horizontal (or Vertical) Line. In the Edit Graphics Line dialog box that follows, make the desired changes to your line.

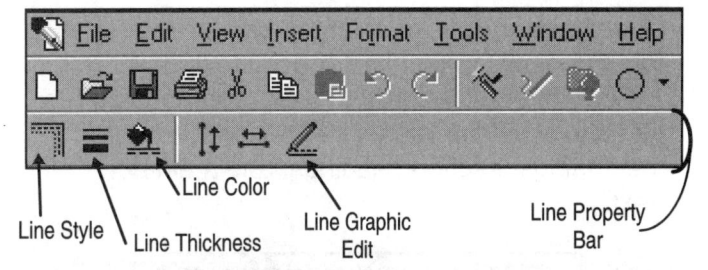

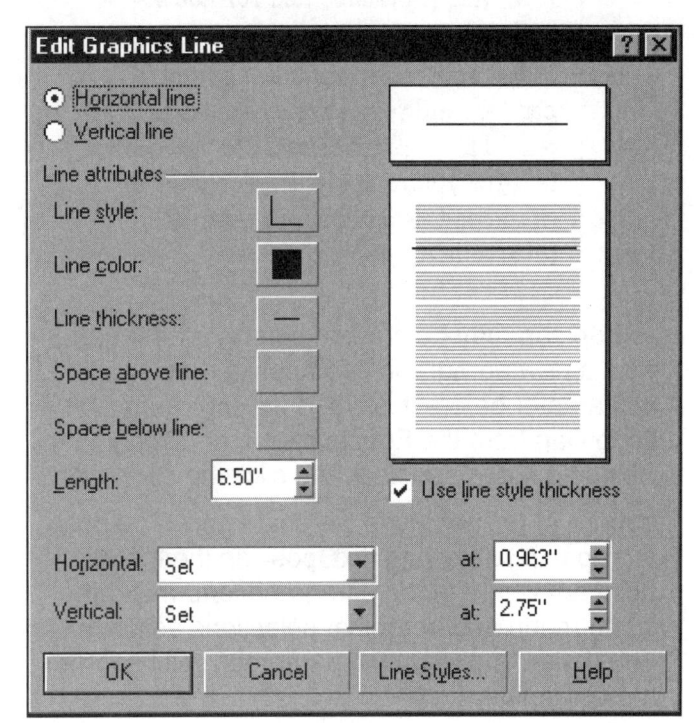

- To move a line with the mouse, click to select it, then drag it to a new position.

- To change the size or thickness of a line, click to select it, then drag one of the sizing handles to enlarge or reduce its width and/or length.

- The line color may be changed by selecting the shape, then clicking the Line Color button  on the Shape Property Bar and selecting a color from the palette.

- Lines, like graphic images and boxes, may be copied and deleted.

- You can quickly copy a line by selecting the line, then holding down the Ctrl key while you drag. You can also use the Copy and Paste procedures learned earlier.

- To delete a line, select it and press Delete.

Drop Capital

- A **drop capital** is an enlarged capital letter that drops below the first line of body text. It is usually the first letter of a paragraph and is often used to draw the reader's attention to chapter beginnings, section headings, and main body text.

> This is practice text for you to text for you to apply drop cap apply drop capitals and revers capitals and reverse text. This is pra text. This is practice text for you to text for you to apply drop capitals a drop capitals and reverse text. This reverse text.

- A drop cap may be created before or after you type a new paragraph. To apply a drop capital to a character before it is typed, select P<u>a</u>ragraph, D<u>r</u>op Cap from the Fo<u>r</u>mat menu, or display the Shipping Macros toolbar and click the Drop Cap button. Then, type the character. To apply a drop cap to existing text, position the insertion point anywhere in the paragraph, and make the same menu and/or toolbar selections as above. The first character in the paragraph will become a drop capital.

- After you access the Drop Cap feature, a Drop Cap Property Bar displays, giving you options for editing the drop capital.

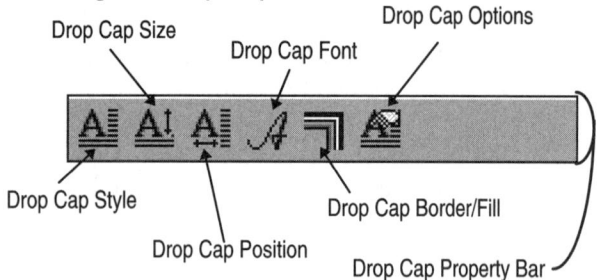

  Drop Cap Size — Drop Cap Options
  Drop Cap Font

  Drop Cap Style — Drop Cap Border/Fill
  Drop Cap Position — Drop Cap Property Bar

- You can select a different predefined drop cap style or you can customize the drop capital by changing the font style, height, position, border or fill style of the capital letter. (See Keystrokes section on page 242 for specific procedures.)

You can also capitalize the first word of the paragraph rather than only the first letter by clicking the Drop Cap Options button on the Drop Cap Property Bar and choosing an option from the dialog box that follows.

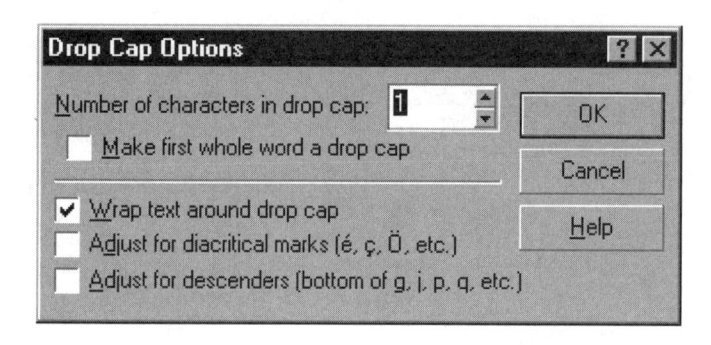

Drop Cap Options
- <u>N</u>umber of characters in drop cap: 1
- <u>M</u>ake first whole word a drop cap
- ✓ <u>W</u>rap text around drop cap
- A<u>d</u>just for diacritical marks (é, ç, Ö, etc.)
- Adjust for descenders (bottom of g, j, p, q, etc.)

OK | Cancel | Help

Reverse Text

- **Reverse text** is text that appears white against a dark background. Black letters are converted to white (or color) letters on a black (or color) background. You can choose the text color, background color and darkness of the background shading.

> **REVERSE TEXT**

- To reverse text, select the text you wish to reverse, then click the Reverse Text button on the Shipping Tools toolbar. You can also reverse text by selecting <u>M</u>acro from the <u>T</u>ools menu and choosing *reverse.wcm*. (The *reverse.wcm* macro automates the process of reversing text). In the Reverse Text Options dialog box that follows, choose a <u>T</u>ext color and Fill style/color option. You can also choose to place the selected text in a text box or apply reverse text to the whole paragraph.

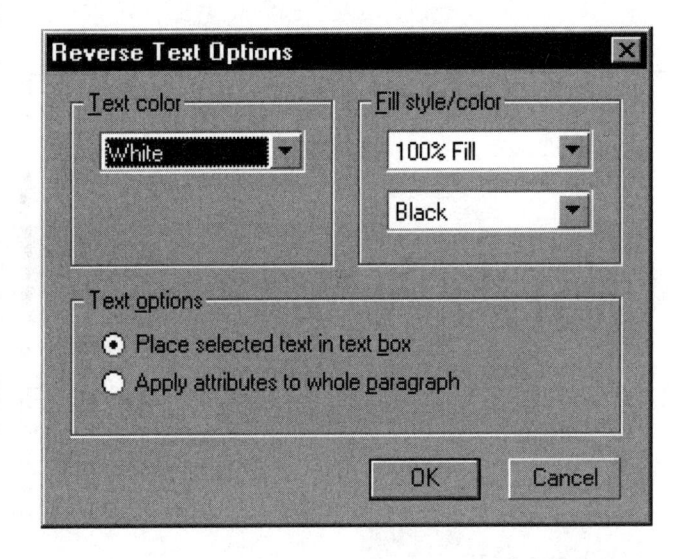

- WordPerfect places text that has been reversed in a graphics box. If you click on the reversed text, handles appear. The text within the graphics box can be edited and formatted like any other text and you can move, size, add a border and change the fill color of the graphics box as you would any other graphics or text box.

- If you chose to apply reverse text to an entire paragraph, click the paragraph, then click Format, Paragraph, Border/Fill to change its fill and/or borders.

In Parts I and II of this exercise, you will enhance two documents you created earlier using drop capitals, watermarks, lines, and reverse text.

EXERCISE DIRECTIONS

PART I
1. Open **NETPRO** or **48NETPRO**.
2. Insert the COMPPL Clipart graphic as a watermark image.
3. Set the second line of the flyer heading (With NetPro) to reverse text. Select white for the font color and black for the background color.
4. Create a drop cap in the first and second paragraph of the body text as shown in Illustration A.
5. Remove italic formatting as indicated in the illustration.
6. Insert a horizontal double line above the last three lines, as shown in Illustration A.
7. Preview the document. Make any adjustments necessary to keep the document on one page.
8. Print one copy.
9. Close the file; save the changes.

PART II
1. Open **THEATRE** or **48THEATRE**.
2. Insert the ACTIV004 Clipart graphic (CD Clipart/Leisure/Activities/Activ004), or a relevant graphic, as a watermark image.
3. Insert the new text as shown in Illustration B.
   a. Use a 12-point sans serif font.
   b. Create a drop cap.
   c. Indent the paragraph .5" from the left margin.
4. Highlight each of the menu categories and set to reverse text. Select white for the font color and light red for the background color.
5. Insert a vertical line at the left margin.
   - Use the Thin/thick 3 line style.
   - Set the line color to red.
6. Preview the document. Make any adjustments necessary to keep the document on one page.
7. Print one copy
8. Close the file; save the changes.

COREL WORDPERFECT 8 Lesson 8: Graphics and Text Boxes

ILLUSTRATION A

Surf the Net
with Netpro

④Reasons Why

*T*he Internet is a vast place. Why not navigate it with the most efficient Internet service provider?

← Remove italics

✓ <u>**Netpro offers quick and easy access to the Internet**</u>. Are you tired of slow services that force you to wade through several layers of junk before getting down to business?

✓ <u>**Netpro can accommodate all of its users simultaneously**</u>. Some of the older, better known Internet service providers can no longer handle their current volume of users, resulting in busy signals and long waits.

✓ <u>**Netpro is inexpensive**</u>. Netpro offers the lowest monthly rate of any other Internet service provider.

✓ <u>**Netpro offers a user-friendly customer service line**</u>. Customer service representatives are available 24 hours a day to answer calls and provide information.

← Create a drop-cap

Netpro is designed to meet *all* of your Internet needs whether you use the Internet in your home or your office or both. For more information, call 1-800-555-5643 or visit our Web site http://home@netpro.net.

← Insert a horizontal double line

N▢E▢T▢P▢R▢O
a division of
COMPUTER SERVICE LTD.

ILLUSTRATION B

🎭 The Theatre Café 🎭

45 Maple Road
Cary, NC 91002
(919) 555-5555

Insert At the Theater Café, we entertain you as well as feed you. Every evening at 7:00 p.m. we provide an array of entertainment in the Becket Room—everything from live music and cabaret acts, to new play readings.

TODAY'S PRESENTATION ✯

❖ Preview ❖

Cream of Vegetable
Fall Vegetable Terrine with Roasted Pine Nuts
Organic Greens with Peanut Vinaigrette
Endive Salad with Crumbled Blue Cheese and Cranberries

❖ Main Act ❖

Whole Roasted Chicken or Turkey
Smoked Virginia Ham
Grilled Leg of Lamb
Baked Salmon Fillets

❖ Supporting Players ❖

Grilled Seasonal Vegetables
Garlic Mashed Potatoes
Butternut Squash with Fresh Ground Cinnamon
Sesame Sauteed Snap Peas with Green Onion

❖ Grand Finale ❖

A wide selection of delicacies baked fresh daily
We include coffee and a variety of herbal teas

Please call for more information and remember to place your holiday orders early.

✯ Menu items are subject to change due to availability of fresh ingredients.

KEYSTROKES

CREATE A WATERMARK

1. Click **I**nsert .... `Alt`+`I`
2. Click **W**atermark .... `W`
3. Click Watermark **A** .... `A`
   OR
   Click Watermark **B** .... `B`
4. Click **C**reate .... `C`
   ✓ *Watermark Property Bar and Watermark window appear.*
5. Click **Watermark Placement** button 🗗 on Watermark Property Bar.
6. Select desired placement option:
   - **O**dd Pages .... `O`
   - **E**ven Pages .... `E`
   - E**v**ery Page .... `V`
7. Click OK .... `Enter`

To insert image as watermark:

a. Click **I**mage button 🖼 on Watermark Property Bar.
b. Select image to be inserted.
c. Click **I**nsert .... `Enter`

To insert text as Watermark:

a. Click in watermark window until cursor appears.
b. Type desired text.
c. Format text as desired.

To insert a file as a Watermark:

a. Click **Insert File** button 📂 on Watermark Property Bar.
b. Select file.
c. Click **I**nsert .... `Enter`

8. Click **C**lose button 📂 on Watermark Property Bar.
9. Type document text as desired.

EDIT A WATERMARK

1. Click on page containing Watermark.
2. Click **I**nsert .... `Alt`+`I`
3. Click **W**atermark .... `W`
4. Click Watermark **A** .... `A`
   OR
   Click Watermark **B** .... `B`
5. Click **E**dit button .... `Alt`+`E`
6. Edit watermark as desired.

To change shading:

a. Click **Shading** button ⚫ on Watermark Property Bar.
b. Click **T**ext shading .... `Alt`+`T`
c. Type desired shade amount or click increment arrows .... `↓` `↑`
d. Click **I**mage shading .... `Alt`+`I`
e. Type desired shade amount ..... `↓` `↑` or click increment arrows.
f. Click OK .... `Enter`

7. Click **C**lose button 📂 on Watermark Property Bar.
8. Type document text as desired.

CREATE VERTICAL OR HORIZONTAL LINE

Ctrl + F11

1. Place insertion point at desired line position.
2. Click **I**nsert .... `Alt`+`I`
3. Click Sh**a**pe .... `A`
4. Click **V**ertical Line .... `V`
   OR
   Click **H**orizontal Line .... `H`

CREATE A CUSTOM VERTICAL OR HORIZONTAL LINE

1. Follow steps 1-3, above.
2. Click Custom **L**ine .... `L`
3. Click **V**ertical .... `Alt`+`V`
   OR
   Click H**o**rizontal .... `Alt`+`O`
4. Select the drop-down arrow next to one or more of the following options:
   - Select Line **s**tyle button .... `Alt`+`S`
   - Select Line **c**olor .... `Alt`+`C`
   - Select Line **t**hickness .... `Alt`+`T` button.
   - Select **B**order offset .... `Alt`+`B`
5. Click **L**ength text box .... `Alt`+`L`

To position line on page:

a. Click **H**orizontal list arrow and select a placement option .... `Alt`+`R`, `↑` `↓`
b. Click **V**ertical list arrow and select a placement option .... `Alt`+`E`, `↑` `↓`

6. Click OK .... `Enter`

DRAW LINES

1. Click **I**nsert .... `Alt`+`I`
2. Click Sh**a**pe .... `A`
3. Click **D**raw Line .... `D`
4. Place mouse pointer where line will begin.
5. Drag mouse pointer to where line will end.
6. Release mouse button.

CHANGE LINE COLOR, WIDTH, AND PATTERN

1. Select the line.

To change line color:

2. Click the **Line Color** button on the Graphics Property Bar.
3. Select a color from the drop-down palette.

To change line width:

4. Click the **Line Width** button on the Graphics Property Bar.

   OR

   Click **Line Style** on the Lines Property Bar.
5. Select a thickness from the drop-down palette.

To change line pattern:

6. Click the **Line Pattern** button on the Graphics Property Bar.
7. Select a pattern from the drop-down palette.

DROP CAPITAL

1. Place insertion point at beginning of paragraph to receive drop cap.

   OR

   Place insertion point where you want to insert drop cap.
2. Click **Drop Cap** button on Shipping Macros toolbar.

   OR

   a. Click **F**o**rmat** .... Alt+R
   b. Click **P**aragraph .... A
   c. Click **D**rop Cap .... R

   ✓ *To edit a drop cap, place insertion point before the Drop Cap and select appropriate buttons on the Drop Cap Property Bar:*

   - Click **Style** button and select desired drop cap style.
   - Click **Size** button and click desired size.
   - Click **Position** button and click desired position.
   - Click **Font** button and select font options.
   - Click **Border/Fill** button and select desired border/fill options.
   - Click **Options** button and select how many characters to include and other options.

REVERSE TEXT

1. Select text to reverse.
2. Click **Reverse Text** button on Shipping Macros toolbar.

   OR

   a. Click **T**ools .... Alt+T
   b. Click **M**acro .... M
   c. Click **P**lay .... P
   d. Select **Reverse.wcm**.
3. Select desired options, within the Reverse Text options dialog box.
4. Click **OK** .... Enter

COREL WORDPERFECT 8 Lesson 8: Graphics and Text Boxes

Exercise 49

■ Summary

In Part I of this exercise, you will use the graphics features learned in this lesson to enhance a newsletter created earlier. In Part II of this exercise, you will use graphics features to create an invitation.

EXERCISE DIRECTIONS

PART I

1. Open **ACTIVITY** or **49ACTIVITY**.
2. Create and then center the dateline information as shown in Illustration A on page 245 using a sans serif 10-point bold font. Use any desired special character between dateline information. Press Enter twice.
3. Create a .020" thick full horizontal line and place it above the dateline.
4. Change the nameplate to any desired TextArt design. (highlight the nameplate, then select TextArt from the Graphics menu.)
   a. Use a sans serif font.
   b. Size it to 2½" wide x 1" high and place it as shown.
5. Insert any desired graphic and place it to the right of the nameplate, as shown.
6. Create drop initial capitals for the paragraphs shown.
7. Set the headlines to reverse text.
   ✓ *Text may align left. Align to center, if necessary.*
8. Create a text box within the first column and enter the text shown in a sans serif 10-point bold italic font.
9. Apply a double border around the text box, and then size the box to approximately 1.78" wide by 2.63" high and position it as shown.
10. Adjust placement and size of the graphics within each column if necessary.
11. Adjust top and bottom margins, if necessary, to make the newsletter fit on one page.
    ✓ *Once all text and graphics are adjusted to the first page, it may appear as though the columns are spilling to the second page. This is due to the column borders. Only the first page will print.*
12. Preview your document.
13. Print one copy of the newsletter.
14. Close the file; save the changes.

PART II

1. Start with a clear screen.
2. Insert the GRAD5 Clipart graphic (CD Clipart/Spec_Occ/Graduan/Grad5), or a relevant graphic, as a watermark image. Press Enter nine times.
3. Type the invitation text as shown in Illustration B on page 246.
   a. Set the font to 14-point script.
   b. Center all text horizontally.
5. Create a TextArt image for the line that reads: KATRINA ANN JONES
   a. Set the font to sans serif.
   b. Set the text color to purple and apply any desired style.
   c. Size the TextArt object to approximately Ln 3.15" wide by .82" high and place as shown.
6. Set RSVP (813) 555-9762 to reverse text.
7. Create a text box as shown in Illustration B.
   a. Type text using a sans serif 14-point font.
   b. Create a drop cap.
   c. Set justification to full.
8. Using the Violet Mat line style, insert a vertical line at the left margin. Copy the vertical line and paste it at the right margin, as shown.
9. Preview the document. Make any adjustments necessary to keep the document on one page.
10. Print one copy.
11. Close the file; name it **GRADUATE**.

Student Activity Monthly Newsletter

Volume 4, Number 8 ✳ A Student Services Publication ✳ August 1998

NEW STUDENT WELCOME FAIR

The Administration department will sponsor a Welcome Fair for all new students on August 28. Packets will be available to inform students of all on campus activities and clubs, nearby restaurants and shops, dormitory

> **Q: What's the best way to make new acquaintances on campus?**
>
> **A: Attend regular study groups, join an established club or organization, and live on campus.**

information, etc. Several clubs and organizations will be represented by information booths. If you would like to add a flyer or brochure to the packet, or if you wish to register a booth for your club or organization, please see Dean Stella Samuels in the Administration Department. A barbecue lunch will be served on the Main Lawn from noon to 2:00 p.m., followed by a get-acquainted session in which new students will have the opportunity to ask a panel of peers any university-related questions. Dean Samuels will wrap up the event with a talk at the Union Podium.

CAMPUS EMPLOYMENT

With the arrival of the fall semester, several campus employment opportunities have opened up. The

Earn While You Learn

French and Italian Languages department is seeking tutors for French 1 and Italian 1. Applicants must be fluent in either French or Italian and have completed a minimum of 3 years of college-level French or Italian. If interested, please see Dr. Vincineau Monday through Wednesday in Room 760 of the French and Italian Building. The Math and Science department is also seeking tutors as well as lab workers. Many positions and levels of employment are available. If interested, see Dr. Martin on Tuesdays and Thursdays in Room 317 of the John Hall Math and Science Building.

ESSAY CONTEST

The University's 32nd Annual Personal Heritage Essay Contest is underway. All students are encouraged to write a 5,000-word essay that details their history and family background. Scholarship money will be awarded to the top ten winners.

COREL WORDPERFECT 8   Lesson 8: Graphics and Text Boxes

ILLUSTRATION B

You are cordially invited to attend a college graduation party in honor of

↓ 4x

KATRINA ANN JONES

↓ 4x

June 1, 1999

↓ 3x

7:00 p.m.

↓ 3x

Lakeview Harbor
32 Palm Pass Road
Winter Haven, FL

↓ 3x

RSVP (813) 555-9762 ← Reverse Text

We are very proud of Katrina and her many accomplishments at the University. Please join us in celebrating this tremendous occasion with a lakeside evening of dinner, dancing and college memories. Please feel free to bring a guest.

Set TextArt object to sans serif, purple. Size it to 3.15" wide x .82" high

14-point sans serif

246

Quattro Pro 8

Lesson 1: Create, Save, and Edit a Notebook

Lesson 2: Use Formulas; Format, Copy, and Print

Lesson 3: Formulas and Functions; Edit Information; Print Options

Lesson 4: Additional Formatting and Editing; Work with Workbooks

Lesson 5: Logical and Date Functions; SpeedFormat; Hide Data

Lesson 6: Charts

QUATTRO PRO 8

Lesson 1: Create, Save, and Edit a Notebook

Exercise 1

- Start Quattro Pro
- The Quattro Pro Window
- Quattro Pro Menu and Toolbars
- Explore the Notebook Using the Mouse and Keyboard

NOTES

Start Quattro Pro

- Quattro Pro, like the other programs in the Corel Office 8 Professional package, may be started from the Windows 95 Taskbar, or by using DAD (See Corel Office Basics, Exercise 1):

  - Click Start on the Windows Taskbar, highlight Programs, select Corel WordPerfect Suite 8, and then select Corel Quattro Pro 8.

  - Click the Corel Quattro Pro icon on the **Desktop Application Director (DAD)** on the Windows 95 Taskbar.

The Quattro Pro Window

- The Corel Quattro Pro 8 screen displays when the program is first started. (*See Illustration A.*)

- The default notebook displays at least fourteen pages, lettered A through M, that contain rows and columns made up of cells. Some screens will display more notebook tabs.

- The active cell is the cell that is ready to receive data or a command. You can change the active cell in a notebook by using the mouse or keyboard.

- When you change the active cell, the cell reference box, located on the left side of the input line, shows the new cell reference. The cell reference identifies the location of the active cell in the notebook page by the column and row headings.

  ✓Note: *Note the location of the cell reference on the Input line displaying the address of the active cell.*

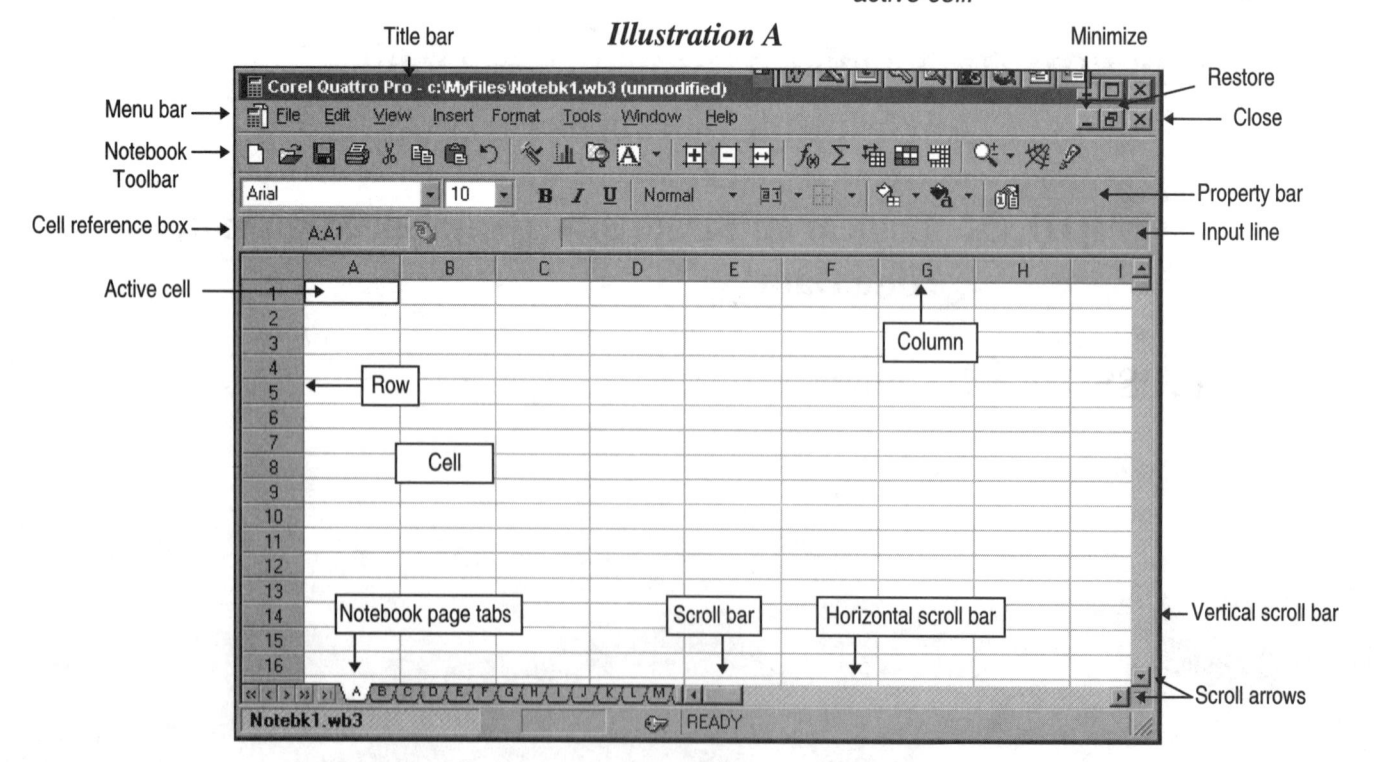

Illustration A

248

Quattro Pro Menu and Toolbars

- As shown in Illustration A, the default Quattro Pro window contains the menu bar, Notebook Toolbar, Property Bar and Input line. The first eight buttons are similar to those discussed in the WordPerfect section of this text, while the other buttons and bars are specific to Quattro Pro. There are eight toolbars available in Quattro Pro that may be displayed as needed.

Explore the Notebook Using the Mouse and Keyboard

- The **notebook** window displays a limited portion of the notebook page. It is possible to view other portions of the page by **scrolling** to the desired location. You can scroll to different areas on a page by using the mouse or keyboard. Scrolling does not change the active cell.

- There are 256 columns and 8192 rows in a notebook page. Although fourteen notebook pages are visible, there are actually 256 pages available in a notebook. The pages are lettered from A through IV, as are the columns.

    ✓Note: Note the illustrations of the outer edges of a notebook page in Illustration B.

Illustration B

Top Left Edge (A1)

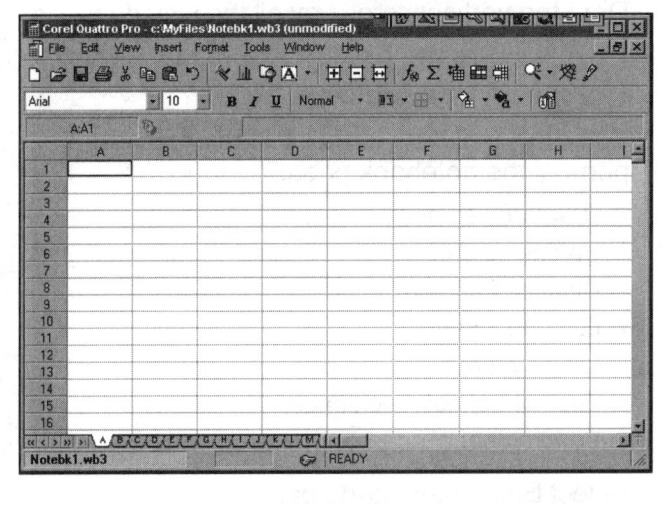

Top Right Edge (IV1)

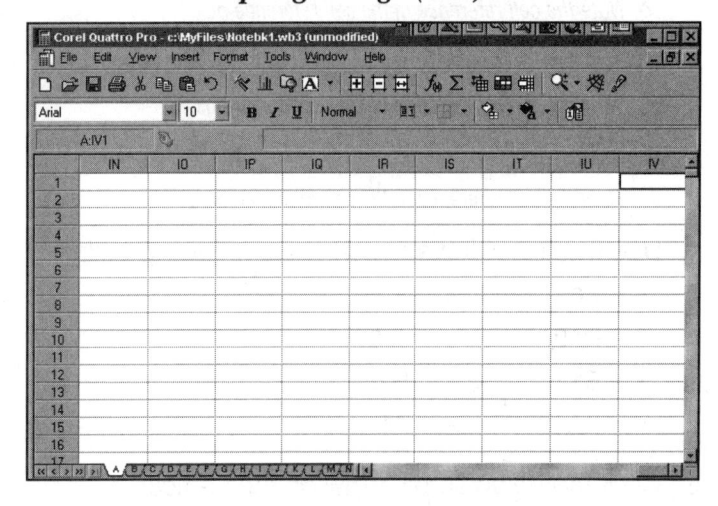

Bottom Left Edge (A8192)

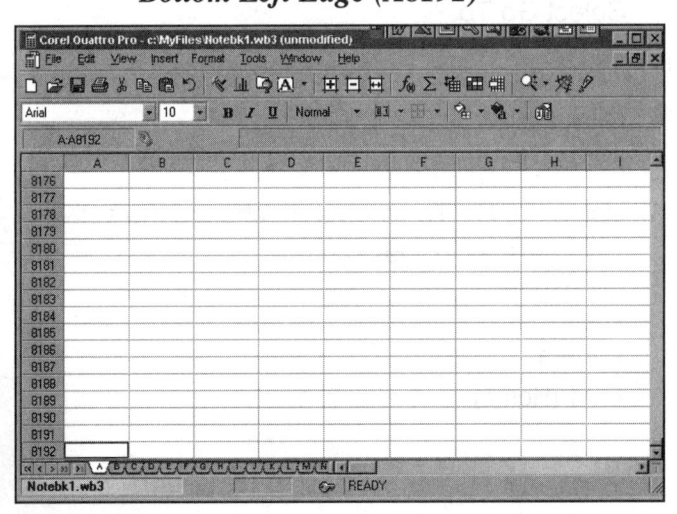

Bottom Right Edge (IV8192)

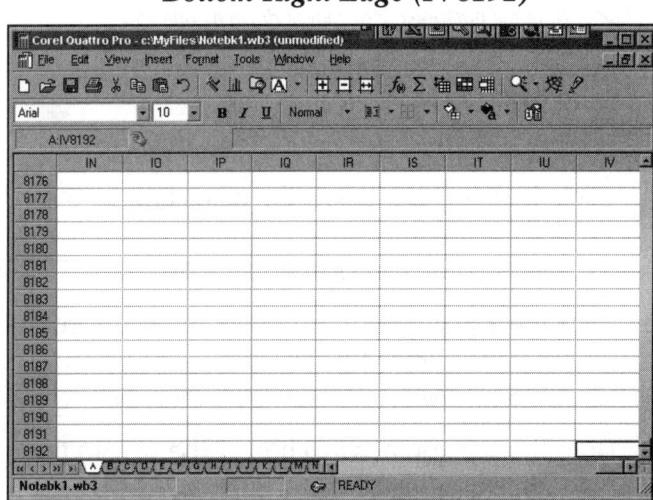

Quattro Pro 8 ■ Lesson 1 ■ Exercise 1

QUATTRO PRO 8 Lesson 1: Create, Save, and Edit a Notebook

- You can also change the active cell in a notebook page by selecting the Go To command on the Edit menu or by pressing F5.

  ✓ *Note: Note the Go To dialog box that appears when Go To is selected or F5 is pressed. The letter before the colon (:) represents the active notebook page, while the letter and number after the colon (:) represent the active cell.*

Go To Dialog Box

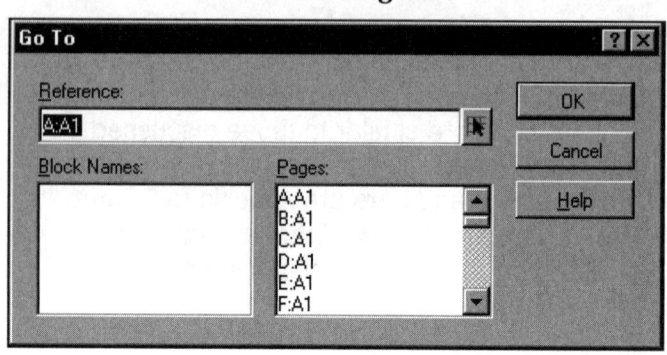

In this exercise, you will use the scroll bars as well as the menu bar and the Go To command to move around the notebook.

EXERCISE DIRECTIONS

1. Click cell E5 to make it active.
   ✓ *Note the cell reference in the cell reference box.*
2. Press the left arrow key until cell C5 is selected.
   ✓ *Note the cell reference in the cell reference box.*
3. Select cell C9.
   ✓ *Note the cell reference in the cell reference box.*
4. Use the arrow keys to select the following cells:
   - A6
   - R19
   - B14
   - AA45
   - G2
   - J33
   - H20
   - A1
5. Click the down scroll arrow on the vertical scroll bar.
   ✓ *Note the notebook page moves down by one row.*
6. Click the right scroll arrow on the horizontal scroll bar.
   ✓ *Note the notebook page moves right by one column.*
7. Click the scroll bar below the scroll box on the vertical scroll bar.
   ✓ *Note the notebook page moves down by one screen.*
8. Click the scroll bar to the right of the scroll box on the horizontal scroll bar.
   ✓ *Note the notebook page moves right by one screen.*
9. Drag the horizontal scroll box all the way to the right on the scroll bar.
   ✓ *Note how the view of the notebook page has changed.*
10. Drag the vertical scroll box all the way down on the scroll bar.
    ✓ *Note how the view of the notebook page has changed.*
11. Use the scroll bars to move to the following parts of the notebook page:
    - Down one screen
    - Up one screen
    - Right one screen
    - Left one screen
    - Lower left of notebook page
    - Top right of notebook page
    - Bottom right of notebook page
12. Select Edit on the menu bar.
13. Select Go To.
14. Type A10 in the Reference text box.
15. Click OK.
    ✓ *Note the active cell is A10.*
16. Using the Go To command, change the active cell to the following:
    - AB105
    - BG200
    - K965
    - A1 (Home)

KEYSTROKES

CHANGE ACTIVE CELL USING THE KEYBOARD

To Move:	Press:
One cell right	→
One cell left	←
One cell down	↓
One cell up	↑
One screen up	Page Up
One screen down	Page Down
One screen right (Ctrl+right arrow)	Ctrl + →
One screen left (Ctrl+left arrow)	Ctrl + ←
First cell in current row (End+left arrow)	End + ←
Last cell in current row (End+right arrow)	End + →
First cell in notebook page (Home)	Home

CHANGE ACTIVE CELL USING THE MOUSE

Click desired cell.

✓ If desired cell is not in view, use the scroll bars to move area of notebook page containing cell into view, then click the cell.

SCROLL USING THE MOUSE

The vertical scroll bar is located on the right side of the notebook window. The horizontal scroll is located on the bottom of the notebook window.

To scroll one column left or right:

Click left or right scroll arrow.

To scroll one row up or down:

Click up or down scroll arrow.

To scroll one screen up or down:

Click vertical scroll bar above or below the scroll box.

To scroll one screen right or left:

Click horizontal scroll bar to right or left of the scroll box.

To scroll to the beginning columns:

Drag horizontal scroll box to the extreme left of the scroll bar.

To scroll to the beginning rows:

Drag vertical scroll box to the top of the scroll bar.

To scroll quickly to an area in a notebook page:

Drag scroll box to desired position on the scroll bar.

✓ The limits of the scrolling area will depend on the location of data in the notebook page.

To scroll quickly to the last row where data was entered:

Press Ctrl and drag vertical scroll box to the bottom of the scroll bar.

CHANGE ACTIVE CELL USING GO TO

F5

1. Click **E**dit .... Alt + E
2. Click **G**o To .... G
3. Type cell reference .... *cell reference* in **R**eference text box.

   ✓ If you are going to a cell within the same notebook page you need only type the column and row reference. Otherwise, type the notebook page, a colon (:) and the column and row number.

4. Click **OK** .... Enter

QUATTRO PRO 8 Lesson 1: Create, Save, and Edit a Notebook

Exercise 2

- Enter Labels
- Make Simple Corrections
- Save and Close a Notebook
- Exit Quattro Pro

NOTES

Enter Labels

- The **status** of a cell is determined by the first character entered.
- When an alphabetical character or a symbol (` ~ ! % ^ & * _ \ | [ ] { } ; : ' " < > , ?) is entered as the first character in a cell, the cell contains a **label**.
- By default, each cell is approximately eight (8) characters wide; however, it is possible to view an entered label that is longer than the cell width if the cell to the right is blank.
- As a label is being entered, it appears on the Input line.

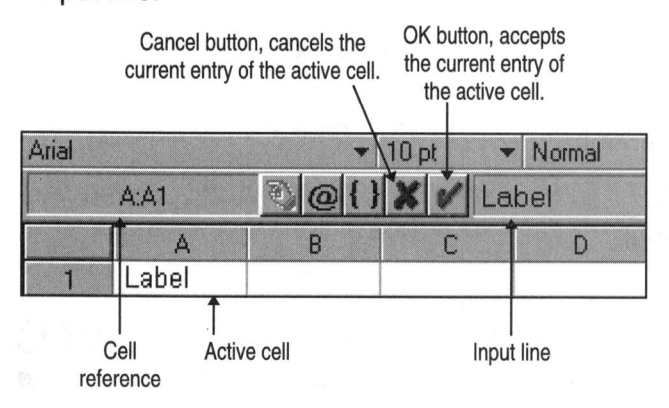

It is entered in the cell after you do one of the following:

- Press an arrow key
- Click another cell
- Click the OK button on the Input line
- Press Enter

- The contents of a label will automatically align to the left of the cell, making it a left-justified entry.

Make Simple Corrections

- Before data is entered, the Backspace key may be used to correct an error. To delete the entire entry, press the Escape key or click the Cancel button on the input line. After text is entered, a correction may be typed directly over the existing text.
- Existing text may also be edited by selecting the cell, then pressing F2 or double-clicking on the cell with the mouse.

Save and Close a Notebook

- As with text files, each notebook should be saved on a removable disk or on a hard drive for future recall and must be given a name for identification. A saved notebook is called a file.
- Prior to Windows 95, filenames were limited to eight characters. Now filenames may be more descriptive, since the limit for the name, drive and path is 255 characters. When you save a file, Quattro Pro automatically adds a period and a filename extension (**.wb3**) to the end of the filename. Because Quattro Pro identifies file types by their extension, you should not type the filename extension.
- A notebook must be saved before closing, or all current or updated entries will be lost. Notebooks should be saved often as you work, so that your most current work is not lost if a problem occurs. If you attempt to close a notebook or exit Quattro Pro before saving, you will be asked if you want to save the changes.

    ✓Note: If you make a mistake and want to begin again, you may choose to close the notebook without saving it.

- A notebook may be saved by clicking the Save button ![] on the Toolbar or by selecting Save from the File menu. The dialog box that appears allows you to name the path, folder, and file.

Exit Quattro Pro

- After all open files have been saved and closed, you can exit the application. Select Exit from the File menu. If prompted, click Yes to save any additional changes. Click No if you do not wish to save the most recent changes.

Save File Dialog Box

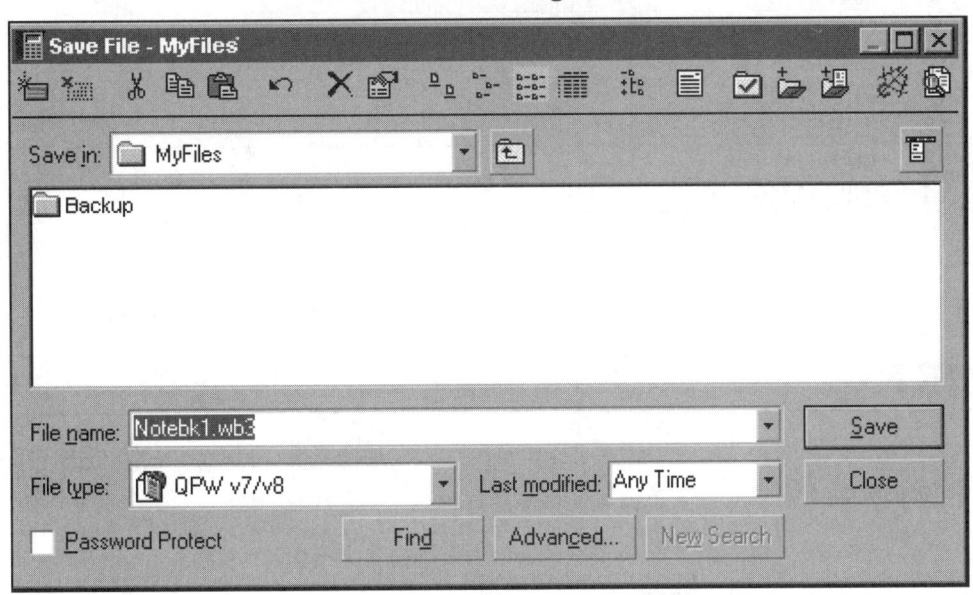

In this exercise, you will begin to create a notebook page for Air Control Systems, Inc. by entering labels. Numeric data will be entered in a later exercise.

EXERCISE DIRECTIONS

1. Go to cell B2.
2. Type your name while looking at the input line.
   ✓ Note the Cancel and Enter buttons to the left of the input area.
3. Cancel the entry by pressing the Escape key or by clicking the Cancel button ![].
4. Create the notebook on the following page.
5. Enter the labels in the exact cell locations shown in the illustration.
6. Correct errors using the Backspace key or strikeover method.
7. Save the notebook; name it **SALES**.
8. Close the notebook.

QUATTRO PRO 8 Lesson 1: Create, Save, and Edit a Notebook

A	A	B	C	D	E	F	G
1		AIR CONTROL SYSTEMS, INC.					
2		YEAR-TO-DATE SALES					
3							
4					DATE:		
5							
6	SALESPERSON		A/COND	HEATING	TOTAL	% OF TOTAL	
7							
8	ARTURO						
9	CHESTERTON						
10	DAVIS						
11	FERNANDEZ						
12	JORGENSON						
13	MARTIN						
14	WILLIAMS						

KEYSTROKES

ENTER A LABEL

✓ Labels are left-aligned and cannot be calculated.

1. Click cell .... *cell*
   to receive label.
2. Type label text .... *label text*
3. Press any **arrow key** .... [↕]
   to enter label and move to next cell.

   OR

   Click **OK** button .... [✓]
   on the Input line.

   OR

   Press Enter.

SAVE A NEW NOTEBOOK

1. Click **F**ile .... [Alt]+[F]
2. Click **S**ave **A**s .... [A]

   To select a drive:

   a. Click **S**ave **i**n .... [Alt]+[I]
   b. Select desired drive letter ... [↓], [↑]

   To select a folder:

   Double-click folder
   name in Save in box ...... [Tab], [Tab], [↓]

3. Double-click **N**ame .... [Alt]+[N]
4. Type filename .... *filename*
5. Click **S**ave .... [Enter]

CLOSE A NOTEBOOK

1. Click **F**ile .... [Alt]+[F]
2. Click **C**lose .... [C]

   If a Save Changes in Notebook message appears:

   Click **Y**es .... [Y]
   to save changes to the notebook.

   ✓ If you have not previously saved the notebook, the Save As dialog box appears. (See SAVE A NEW NOTEBOOK, left.)

   OR

   Click **N**o .... [N]
   to close without saving the changes.

🌐 EXIT QUATTRO PRO

Alt + F4

1. Click **F**ile .... [Alt]+[F]
2. Click **E**xit .... [X]

   If a Save Changes in Notebook message appears:

   Click **Y**es .... [Y]

   ✓ If you have not previously saved the notebook, the Save As dialog box appears. (See SAVE A NEW NOTEBOOK, left.)

   OR

   Click **N**o .... [N]
   to close without saving the changes.

QUATTRO PRO 8 Lesson 1: Create, Save, and Edit a Notebook

Exercise 3

- **Numeric Labels and Values**
- **Label Alignment**
- **Repeat Labels**

NOTES

Numeric Labels and Values

- When a number or a symbol (+-.@#=$) is entered as the first character in a cell, the cell contains a **value**.

- A value is entered after you do one of the following:
  - Press Enter
  - Click another cell
  - Press an arrow key
  - Click the OK button ✔ on the input line

- If a value is longer than the cell, Quattro Pro displays the number in scientific notation, or asterisks (********) appear in the cell. In either case, the column width must be reset. *(Setting column width will be covered in Exercise 11.)*

- A **numeric label** is a number that will not be used in a calculation. Examples of numeric labels are social security numbers or identification numbers. To indicate that such numbers are to be treated as labels and not values, it is necessary to begin the entry with one of the following label prefixes:
  - an apostrophe (') to left-align the numbers
  - double-quotes (") to right-align the numbers
  - a carat (^) to center-align the numbers

- Label prefixes are not displayed on the notebook page but are shown on the Input line, as illustrated below:

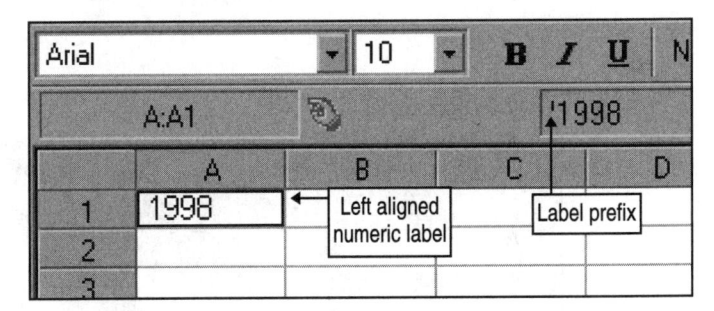

Label Alignment

- A value automatically aligns to the right of the cell, making it a right-justified entry, and a label automatically aligns to the left of the cell. Since labels are left-justified and values are right-justified in a cell, column titles (which are labels) will not appear centered over numeric data. When necessary, alignment may be adjusted. For example, column title labels above numeric data may be centered or right-aligned to improve the appearance of the notebook page. Note the illustration of how data is aligned in cells.

QUATTRO PRO 8 Lesson 1: Create, Save, and Edit a Notebook

- Label alignment may be adjusted by following any of the three methods outlined below:
  - Enter a label prefix in a cell (as mentioned above).
  - Select the cells to be aligned and choose an alignment option on the Property Bar *(see illustration below)*. Note that the default alignment setting is "general" which means that values are right-aligned and labels are left aligned.
  - Select the cells to be aligned and choose Selection from the Format menu. Then click the Alignment tab and choose the desired horizontal and vertical alignment options.

Repeat Labels

- If you wish to repeat data across an entire cell, you can use the repeat label prefix (\) before typing the character. For example, if you wish to repeat a $ across a cell, type \$ and the dollar sign will repeat to fill the cell.

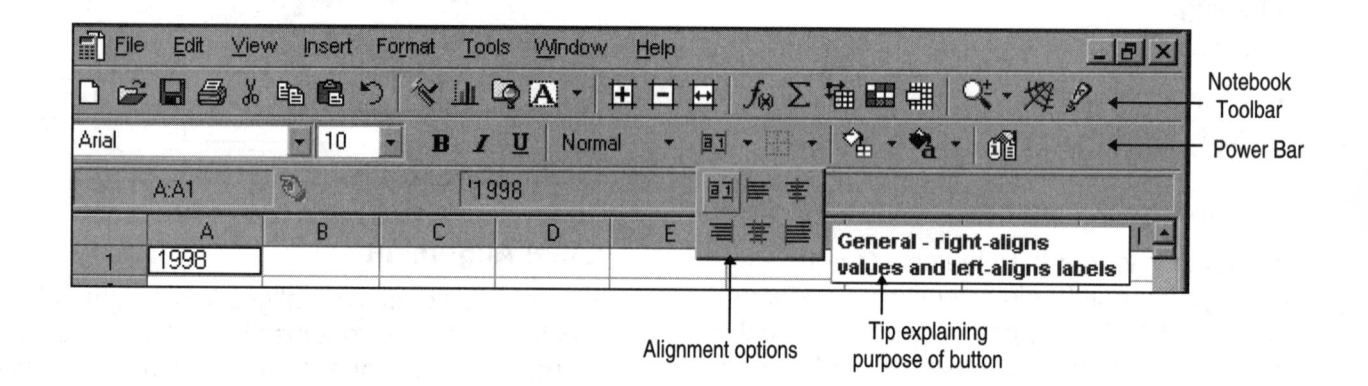

(illustration of Quattro Pro screen showing Notebook Toolbar, Power Bar, Alignment options, and Tip explaining purpose of button: "General - right-aligns values and left-aligns labels")

In this exercise, you will create a payroll for employees of the Medallion Music Stores. Gross Pay refers to total salary earned before taxes; Federal With. Tax refers to the amount withheld for Federal Taxes. Soc. Sec. Tax and Medicare Tax refers to the amount deducted for these benefits. Net Pay refers to salary received after taxes are deducted.

EXERCISE DIRECTIONS

1. Create the notebook page as illustrated on the following page.

2. Enter the labels in the exact cell locations shown in the illustration.
   ✓ *Enter the Employee numbers as numeric labels, not as values.*

3. Correct any errors.

4. Right-align the Hourly Rate and Hours Worked column headings.

5. Enter the company logo MMs as a repeat label in cells A1 and I1.

6. Save the notebook; name it **PAY**.

7. Close the notebook.

	A	B	C	D	E	F	G	H	I
1	MMsMMsM		MEDALLION MUSIC STORES						MMsMMs
2			PAYROLL						
3									
4	Employee	Employee	Hourly	Hours	Gross	Federal	Soc. Sec	Medicare	Net
5	Number	Name	Rate	Worked	Pay	With. Tax	Tax	Tax	Pay
6									
7	272	Engelson	7.25	21					
8	320	Gomez	7.75	19					
9	322	Jordan	8.25	21					
10	330	Kelly	9.95	35					
11	340	Romano	9.75	35					
12	341	Unger	8.45	15					

Title and subtitle (labels) — row 1–2
Column headings (labels) — rows 4–5
Numeric labels — column A
Labels — column B
Values — columns C, D

KEYSTROKES

ENTER A NUMERIC LABEL

✓ *Numbers entered as numeric labels cannot be calculated.*

1. Click cell.. *cell* to receive numeric label.
2. Press:
   a. " to right-align label .... ["]
   b. ^ to center label .... [^]
   c. ' to left-align label .... [']
3. Type number............................. *number*
4. Press arrow key .... [→]

REPEAT LABEL

✓ *Data can be repeated to fill a cell.*

1. Type \... [\ ]
2. Type data to repeat .... *data*
3. Press Enter .... [Enter]

ENTER A VALUE

✓ *Numbers entered as values are right-aligned and can be calculated.*

1. Click cell.. *cell* to receive value.
2. Type number............................. *number*
   ✓ *Begin entry with a number from zero to nine or a decimal point. Precede a negative number with a minus sign (-), or enclose it within parentheses().*
3. Press Enter .... [Enter]
   ✓ *If Quattro Pro displays asterisks (*******) or the number is in scientific notation, the column is not wide enough to display the value. Quattro Pro stores the value in the cell but cannot display it. To see the entry, adjust the column width.*

SELECT (HIGHLIGHT) A RANGE OF CELLS USING THE MOUSE

1. Point to interior of first cell to select.
2. Drag through adjacent cells until desired cells are highlighted.

SELECT (HIGHLIGHT) A RANGE OF CELLS USING THE KEYBOARD

1. Press arrow keys .... [↔]
2. Press Shift + arrow keys..... [Shift]+[↔] until adjacent cells to select are highlighted.

ALIGN LABELS USING THE PROPERTY BAR

1. Select cell(s) containing label(s)............................. [Shift]+[↔]
2. Click the Align button .... [▣] on the Property Bar.
3. Click General, Left, Center, Right, or Center across block .... [↑][↓]

QUATTRO PRO 8 Lesson 1: Create, Save, and Edit a Notebook

Exercise 4

■ Summary

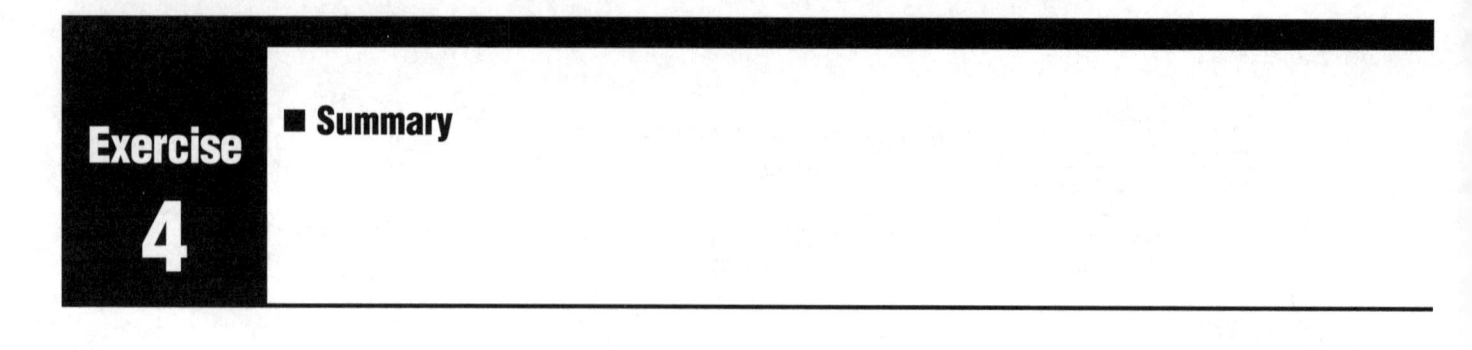

Mr. Foster, the teacher of Science 105, would like you to prepare a notebook for quiz marks for the Spring 199- term.

EXERCISE DIRECTIONS

1. Create a Three-line notebook page title using the labels provided with the information above. Place all CLASS, TERM, and TEACHER data in column A.

2. Leave a blank column (column C) between NAME and LAB 1. Enter IDNO as numeric labels. Right-align column labels for quiz marks.

3. Save and close the notebook; name it **GRADE**.

A	A	B	C	D	E	F
1	CLASS:					
2	TERM:					
3	TEACHER:					
4						
5	IDNO.	NAME		LAB 1	LAB 2	LAB 3
6						
7	1245	Bell, D.		90	88	92
8	4123	Dorchester, T.		55	70	75
9	1255	Garcia, L		75	80	82
10	3331	Levine, M.		78	75	80
11	2121	Livingston, F.		77	85	80
12	1234	Pella, J.		80	75	82
13	2323	Ruiz, G.		82	80	85
14	1332	Trevino, S.		92	85	80
15	2143	West, D.		98	90	95
16	1112	Zdan, M.		82	85	85

QUATTRO PRO 8

Lesson 2: Use Formulas; Format, Copy, and Print

Exercise 5 ■ Use Formulas

NOTES

Use Formulas

- A formula is an instruction to calculate a number and may include actual numbers or cell addresses.

- A formula is entered in the cell where the answer should appear. As you type the formula, it appears in the cell and on the Input line. After a formula is entered, the answer is displayed in the cell, and the formula is displayed on the Input line.

- A formula must begin with a period, plus, minus, open parenthesis, at symbol, dollar sign, or equal sign (.+-(@$=). Generally, the plus sign is used since it is on the numeric keypad. There should be no spaces between mathematical operators and cell references. If you include extraneous spaces, Quattro Pro 8 will delete them when you press the Enter key.

- **Cell references** and **mathematical operators** are used to develop formulas. The cell reference can be typed or inserted into a formula. For example, the formula +C3+C5+C7 results in the addition of the values in these cell locations. Therefore, any change to the values in these cell locations causes the answer to change automatically.

- The standard mathematical operators used in formulas are:

    + Addition   - Subtraction
    * Multiplication   / Division
    ^ Exponentiation

- It is important to consider the order of mathematical operations when preparing formulas. Operations enclosed in parentheses have the highest priority and are executed first; exponential calculations are executed second. Multiplication and division operations have the next priority and are completed before any addition and subtraction operations.

- All operations are executed from left to right in the order of appearance. For example, in the formula +A1*(B1+C1), B1+C1 is calculated before the multiplication is performed. If the parentheses were omitted, A1*B1 would be calculated first and C1 would be added to that answer. Each procedure results in a different outcome.

- Multiplication and division formulas may result in answers with decimal places. These numbers can be rounded off using a formatting feature. *(See Format Data, Exercise 6.)*

- When using a percentage as a numeric factor in a formula, you can enter it either with a decimal or with the percent symbol. For example, you may enter either .45 or 45% to indicate 45 percent in a formula.

Quattro Pro 8 ■ Lesson 2 ■ Exercise 5

QUATTRO PRO 8 Lesson 2: Use Formulas; Format, Copy, and Print

A notebook will be used to calculate markup and sales tax on items in the Hobby Train Store inventory. MARKUP refers to the amount added to the cost of goods to determine the selling price; in this case, it will be calculated at 25%. The SALES TAX percentage for this exercise will be 8% and, as illustrated, the percent has been changed to .08 in the formula.

EXERCISE DIRECTIONS

1. Create the notebook page below.
2. Enter the labels and values in the exact cell locations shown in the illustration. The ITEM numbers should be entered as numeric labels.
3. Enter the formula, as illustrated, in the MARKUP column to calculate a 25% markup. Note that after the formula is entered, the answer appears in the cell and the formula is visible on the Input line.
4. Enter formulas in the MARKUP column for the remaining items using the appropriate cell addresses.
5. Enter the formula to calculate the first SELLING PRICE, which is COST plus MARKUP.
6. Enter the formula to calculate SALES TAX at 8% of the SELLING PRICE.
7. Enter the formula to calculate TOTAL PRICE, which is the total of the sales tax and selling price values.
8. Complete the formulas for the remaining items using the appropriate cell addresses for each formula.
9. Check formula entries for accuracy.
10. Save and close the notebook; name it **TRAINS**.

A	A	B	C	D	E	F
1		HOBBY TOY TRAIN STORE				
2						
3				SELLING	SALES	TOTAL
4	ITEM	COST	MARKUP	PRICE	TAX	PRICE
5	124	84	+B5*.25	+B5+C5	+D5*.08	D5+E5
6	238	35				
7	432	18				

KEYSTROKES

ENTER A FORMULA USING MATHEMATICAL OPERATORS

1. Click cell .... [↕↔]
   to receive formula.
2. Press + ... [+]
3. Type formula .... *formula*
   using cell references and mathematical operators.
   Example: +A1*(B2+B10)/2

   ✓ *You can select cells by clicking on them, instead of typing references, to tell the formula which cells you wish to reference.*

To insert cell references by selecting cells:

a. Click cell where formula will be inserted.
b. Type preceding operator.
c. Select first cell you want formula to reference.
d. Type desired operator or parenthesis.
e. Repeat steps above as needed.
f. Press **Enter** .... [Enter]

QUATTRO PRO 8   Lesson 2: Use Formulas; Format, Copy, and Print

Exercise 6

- Open Files
- Save Files
- Format Data
- Use a Block/Selection

NOTES

Open Files

- Notebooks that have been saved and closed must be opened using the same drive designation and filename used during the saving process. The Open File dialog box contains a drop-down list with the drives or folders and a box containing a list of the files in that directory. In addition to opening a previously saved file, you may preview it, search for the file, or list details or properties about the file. Note the illustration of the Open File dialog box below.

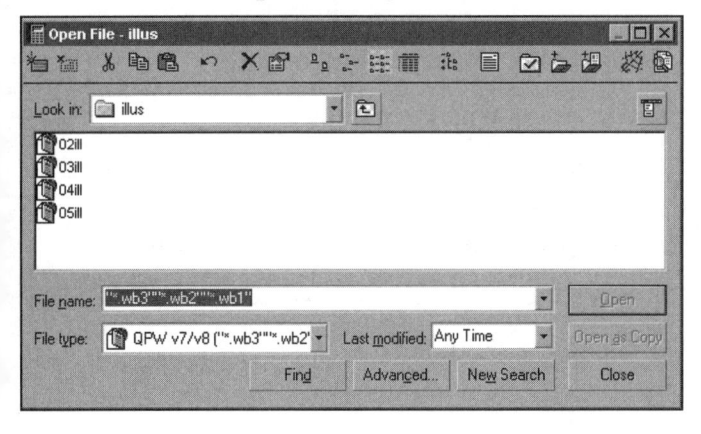

- When the File menu is accessed, a list of the last ten files used is provided at the bottom of the menu. Clicking the filename of one of these recently used files is a quick way to open a file.

- A newly opened notebook becomes the active notebook and hides any other open notebooks. Open notebooks can be made active by selecting the file from the Window menu.

Open Dialog Box

Save Files

- When you resave a workbook using the Save command from the File menu, the new version of the file overwrites the previous version.

- Use the Save As command from the File menu, or press F3, to change the filename. This is the easiest way to save both the original file and the revised one as separate notebooks. Simply give the revised file a new name.

Format Data

- You can change the appearance of data to make it more attractive and readable by formatting it. Some available number formats are normal, currency, percent, date, or comma. Note the illustration of the number format button on the Property Bar.

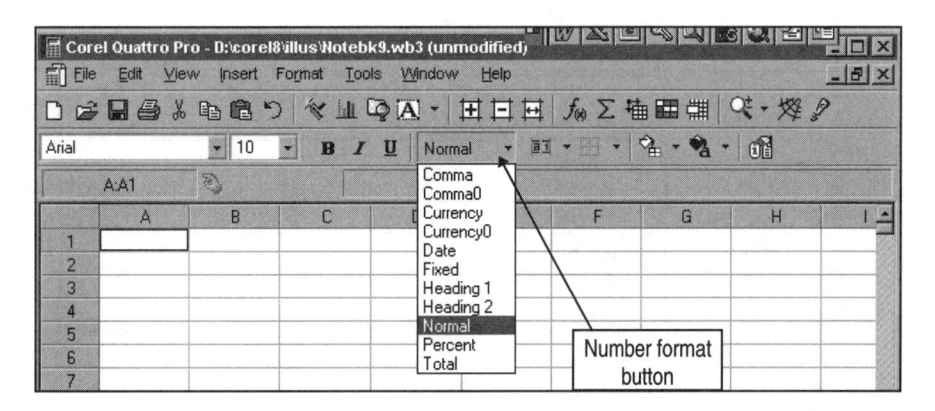

QUATTRO PRO 8 Lesson 2: Use Formulas; Format, Copy, and Print

- The following formats may be used for formatting number values:

Normal	Displays numbers without added decimal places or as entered.
Fixed	Displays numbers with two decimal places.
Currency0	Displays numbers with dollar signs and no decimal places.
Currency	Displays numbers with dollar signs and two decimal places.

  ✓Note: Other formats will be introduced in later exercises.

Use a Block/Selection

- A block or selection is a defined area or range in a notebook. For example, the cells F4, F5, and F6 can be indicated as **F4:F6; A1:G2** indicates all the cells in columns A through G in rows one and two. You can format data in a column or row by selecting the block of cells containing the data to format.

- Cell contents may be formatted before or after data is entered.

- As noted in Exercise 3, label text is left-aligned while values are right-aligned in a cell. The alignment button on the Property Bar may be used to align a column heading in a single cell or all the column titles in a selected range.

In this exercise, you will add data to the TRAINS notebook and format money columns and column titles. In addition, the file will be saved using the Save and Save As options.

EXERCISE DIRECTIONS

1. Open 📂**TRAINS** or 💾**06TRAINS**.
2. Select the block of data in cells B3:F4.
3. Right-align column titles using the alignment button on the Property Bar.
4. Enter the new item data as illustrated below.
5. Enter formulas to complete the information for the new data using a 25% markup and an 8% sales tax.
6. Select the block of data in cells B5:F10.
7. Format the data for Fixed using the number format button on the Property Bar.
8. Select the data in cells F5:F10.
9. Format the data for Currency using the number format button on the Property Bar.
10. Save/overwrite the notebook file.
11. Format cells F5:F10 for Fixed using the number format button on the Property Bar.

    HINT: *The change in step 11 is to be saved in the TRAIN2 file.*

12. Save the notebook as **TRAIN2**.
13. Close the notebook.

	A	B	C	D	E	F	
1		HOBBY TOY TRAIN STORE					
2							
3					SELLING	SALES	TOTAL	← Block B3:F4
4	ITEM	COST	MARKUP	PRICE	TAX	PRICE	
5	124	84	21	105	8.4	113.4	
6	238	35	8.75	43.75	3.5	47.25	
7	432	18	4.5	22.5	1.8	24.3	← Block B5:F10
8	504	22.85					
9	589	31.75					
10	590	29.85					

KEYSTROKES

OPEN A NOTEBOOK FILE

To open a recently used file:
1. Click **File**.................... `Alt`+`F`
2. Select file from list at the bottom of the menu.

To open any file:
1. Click **Open** button ....
   on Toolbar.
   OR
   a. Click **File**.................. `Alt`+`F`
   b. Click **Open**.................. `O`

To select a drive:
a. Click **Look in** .... `Alt`+`L`
b. Select desired drive letter........... `↓`

Files in current directory of selected drive appear in window.

To list files of a different type:
a. Click **File type** .... `Alt`+`Y`
b. Select file type........................ `↓`

Only files of specified type appear in window.

✓ Use this option to change the kinds of files displayed in the Open window. For example, if you wanted to open a Lotus file into notebook page, you would select the 1-2-3 v4/v5("*.wk") item in the drop-down list.

2. Click file to open in Open window.
   OR
   a. Select **File Name** list box.. `Alt`+`N`
   b. Select file to open.................. `↓`
3. Click **Open**. .... `Enter`

RESAVE/OVERWRITE A NOTEBOOK FILE

Click **Save** button ....
on Toolbar.
OR
1. Click **File** menu .... `Alt`+`F`
2. Click **Save** .... `S`

SAVE AS

Saves and names the active notebook.

1. Click **File**.................... `Alt`+`F`
2. Click **Save As** .... `A`

To select a drive:
a. Click **Save in** .... `Alt`+`I`
b. Select desired drive letter........... `↓`

To select a folder:
a. Double-click folder name
   in Save window .... `Tab`, `↓`
b. Select **File name** .... `Alt`+`N`
c. Type filename .... *filename*

SELECT (HIGHLIGHT) A BLOCK OF CELLS USING THE MOUSE

✓ *A block of cells is two or more cells. Cells in a selected block are highlighted and the active cell within the selection is white.*

To select a range of adjacent cells:
1. Point to interior of first cell to select.
2. Drag through adjacent cells until desired cells are highlighted.

To select entire row or column:
Click row heading or column heading to select.

To select adjacent rows or columns:
1. Point to first row heading or column heading to select.
2. Drag through adjacent headings until desired rows or columns are highlighted.

SELECT (HIGHLIGHT) A BLOCK OF CELLS USING THE KEYBOARD

To select a block of adjacent cells:
1. Press arrow keys ....
   until first cell to select is highlighted.
2. Press **Shift** + arrow keys ..... `Shift`+

To select entire row containing active cell:
Press **End** + **Shift** + **Right**
arrow .... `End`+`Shift`+`→`

To select entire column containing active cell:
Press **End** + **Shift** + **Down**
arrow .... `End`+`Shift`+`↓`

To select adjacent rows:
1. Press arrow keys to select first cell in first row.
2. Press and hold **End** + **Shift** . `End`+`Shift`
   then press **Left arrow** .... `←`
   to highlight first row.
3. Still pressing **End** + **Shift**,
   press **Up** or **Down** arrow .... `↑`, `↓`
   to highlight adjacent rows.

FORMAT NUMBERS USING THE PROPERTY BAR

Applies commonly used number formats.

1. Select cells to format (see above).
2. Click **Number format button** on the Property Bar.
3. Select a style .... `↑` `↓`

QUATTRO PRO 8 Lesson 2: Use Formulas; Format, Copy, and Print

Exercise 7

- Copy Data
- Format Using the Menu
- Print a Notebook Page
- Page View

NOTES

Copy Data

- Formulas may be copied:
  - Horizontally or vertically
  - To another cell or range of cells
  - To another notebook page or notebook
- When a formula is copied, the cell references change relative to their new location. To copy data, select the cell to be copied, click the Copy button on the Toolbar, select the block or cell to receive the data, and click the Paste button on the Toolbar. The Edit, Copy and Edit, Paste commands on the menu bar may also be used.

Format Using the Menu

- In the last exercise, we formatted numbers by selecting the data and pressing the appropriate button on the toolbar. Selected data can also be formatted by clicking the **Format**, **Selection** commands. The Active cells dialog box, as illustrated below, contains tabs for formatting various aspects of data. When you select a format on the Numeric Format tab, as illustrated below, a set of additional choices may appear within the setting.

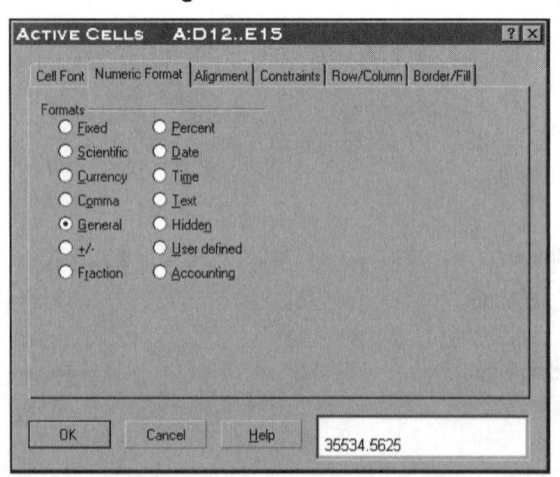

Print a Notebook Page

- The notebook, selected notebook page(s), or a the selected range of data may be printed using the Print command on the File menu. You can also use the Print button on the Toolbar. When you access the Print command, Quattro Pro allows you to select various print options. You can preview the print output by selecting the Print Preview button in the Spreadsheet Print dialog box or by selecting Print Preview from the File menu.

Spreadsheet Print Dialog Box

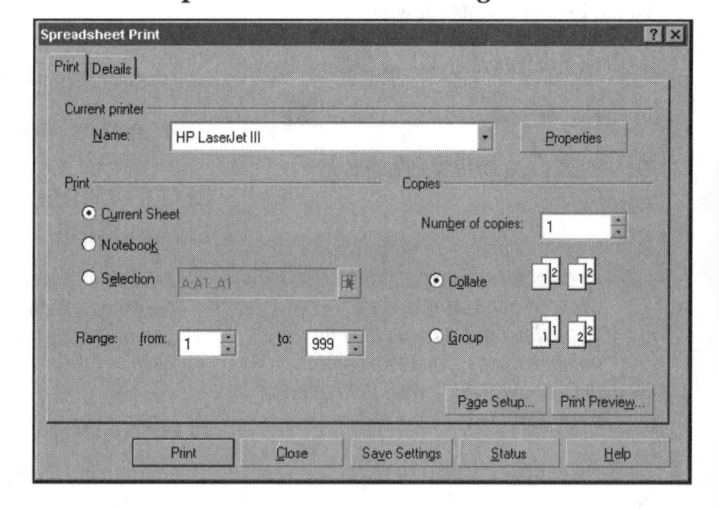

- Quattro Pro uses the default page size (usually 8½" x 11") of the current printer. The page size settings can be accessed by selecting the Page Setup option from the File menu. The top and bottom default page margins are set at .33"; the right and left default page margins are set at 0.40". Click the Print Margins tab from the Spreadsheet Page Setup dialog box to access the margin settings, as illustrated on the next page.

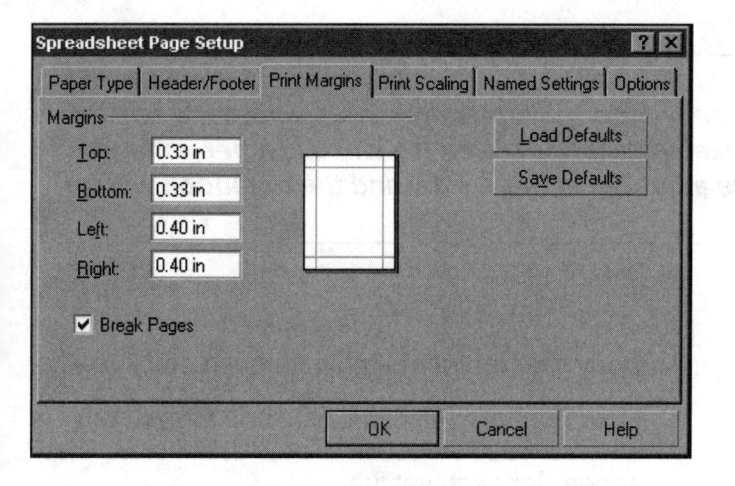

- If you select the Page view, Quattro Pro displays the actual spreadsheet page as it will print on your printer. This is sometimes called the WYSIWYG or "what you see is what you get" view. In page view, margins are indicated with a dotted line and page breaks, fonts, headers and footers will display. While in Page View, you can move margins by dragging the dotted lines and noting the margin settings as you move the line. The mouse cursor turns into a double arrow as you drag the margin line. You can get to the Page Setup dialog by double clicking or right clicking in a margin.

Page View

- As you will note on the View menu illustrated below, Draft is the default view setting for notebooks. Draft view does not display margins, headers, footers and other features that may exist in the notebook, but it is the most efficient view.

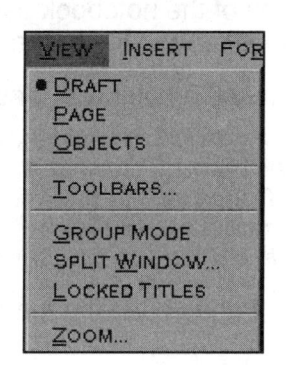

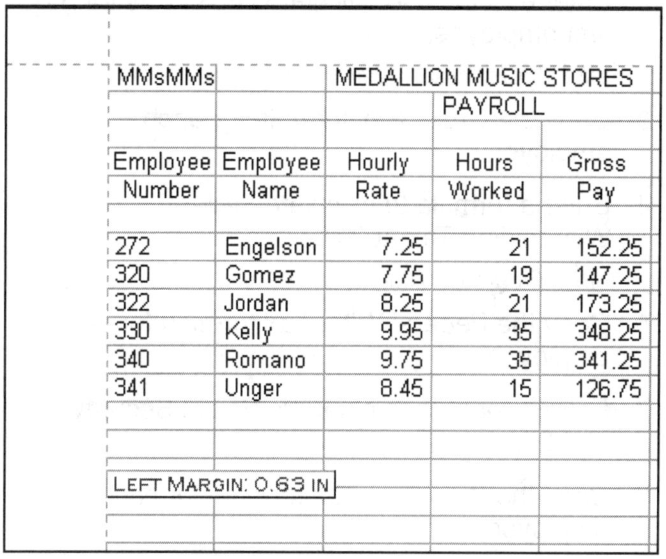

KEYSTROKES

COPY AND PASTE

Ctrl + C, Ctrl + V

Copies the data once and overwrites existing data in the destination cells.

1. Select cell(s) to copy.
2. Click **Copy** button..........................
   OR
   a. Click **Edit**..................... `Alt` + `E`
   b. Click **Copy**..................... `C`
3. Select destination cell(s).
   ✓ *Select an area the same size as the area to copy, or select the upper left cell in the destination cell range. The destination can be in the same notebook page, another sheet, or another notebook.*
4. Click **Paste** button..........................

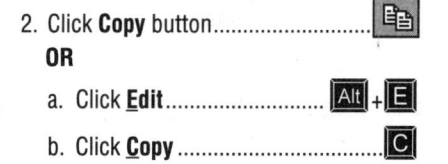

OR

a. Click **Edit**............................ `Alt` + `E`
b. Click **Paste**.............................. `P`

FORMAT SELECTION USING THE MENU (NUMERIC DATA)

1. Select the block of data.
2. Click **Format**..................... `Alt` + `R`
3. Click **Selection**....................... `E`
4. Select Numeric Format tab.
5. Select desired format.
6. Make any additional settings as required.
7. Click **OK**............................. `Enter`

CHANGE TO PAGE VIEW

1. Click **View**............................ `Alt` + `V`
2. Click **Page**............................... `P`

PRINT A NOTEBOOK PAGE

Prints notebook page data using the current page settings.

✓ *When printing a notebook page, Quattro Pro will print only the print area, if you defined it.*

Ctrl + P

Click **Print** button..............................
on Toolbar.
   OR
   a. Click **File**........................ `Alt` + `F`
   b. Click **Print**............................ `P`
   c. Select **Current Sheet**........ `Alt` + `U`
   d. Click **OK**.......................... `Enter`

Quattro Pro 8 ■ Lesson 2 ■ Exercise 7   265

QUATTRO PRO 8 Lesson 2: Use Formulas; Format, Copy, and Print

> You will complete the Medallion Music Stores payroll by entering formulas to calculate the taxes and net pay. Federal Withholding Taxes are normally determined using a table where the tax varies according to your salary and number of exemptions; however, we will use a percentage rate for this problem. The payroll margins will be adjusted in Page view and the notebook will be printed using the Print command.

EXERCISE DIRECTIONS

1. Open **PAY** or **07PAY**.
   - ✓ If you are using the data disk, you should make the disk read-only to preserve the data files. Instructions will be given to save the file as a new file.

2. Enter a formula to calculate Gross Pay for the first employee.
   HINT: Hours Worked * Hourly Rate

3. Copy the Gross Pay formula for each employee.

4. Enter a formula to calculate Federal Withholding Tax at 20%.
   HINT: Gross Pay * 20%

5. Copy the Federal With. Tax formula for each employee.

6. Enter a formula to compute Social Security Tax at 6.2%.

7. Copy the Soc. Sec. Tax formula for each employee.

8. Enter a formula to compute Medicare Tax at 1.45%.

9. Copy the Medicare Tax formula for each employee.

10. Enter a formula to calculate Net Pay.
    HINT: Deduct all taxes from the gross pay.

11. Copy the Net Pay formula for each employee.

12. Click Format, Selection, Numeric Format tab and test each selection to note the choices that appear for each setting.

13. Select values in columns E, F, G, H, and I and use the Format, Selection, Fixed format setting for two decimal places on the Numeric Format tab.

14. Center all column labels.

15. Print one copy of the notebook page using default settings for paper and margins.

16. Close and save the notebook, or save as **PAY**.
    - ✓ If you are using the PAY file you created previously, you are asked to save changes to update the file before closing the notebook. If you are using the data disk, you must use the Save As command to create a new PAY file since the data file should be kept on a read-only disk.

17. Select View, Page to see the margin settings and page view.

18. Drag the right margin and note the double arrow cursor and the margin settings.

19. Close the notebook without saving these settings.

A	A	B	C	D	E	F	G	H	I
1	MMsMMs			MEDALLION MUSIC STORES					MMsMMs
2				PAYROLL					
3									
4	Employee	Employee	Hourly	Hours	Gross	Federal	Soc. Sec	Medicare	Net
5	Number	Name	Rate	Worked	Pay	With. Tax	Tax	Tax	Pay
6									
7	272	Engelson	7.25	21					
8	320	Gomez	7.75	19					
9	322	Jordan	8.25	21					
10	330	Kelly	9.95	35					
11	340	Romano	9.75	35					
12	341	Unger	8.45	15	▼	▼	▼	▼	▼
13									

QUATTRO PRO 8 Lesson 2: Use Formulas; Format, Copy, and Print

Exercise 8

- Copy Formulas (Absolute and Relative Reference)
- Format Data (Percents, Fonts, and Font Size)
- QuickFormat

NOTES

Copy Formulas (Absolute and Relative Reference)

- In some cases, a value in a formula must remain constant when copied to other locations. This is referred to as an **absolute reference**. To identify a cell as an absolute value, a dollar sign ($) must precede the column and row references for that cell. In this exercise, we must divide each salesperson's sales by total sales to find the percentage of total sales. To copy the total sales cell reference and have it stay constant in every formula, we must make it an absolute reference. For example, in the formula +E8/$E$16, in the illustration on page 269, the reference to E16 is an absolute reference. The dollar signs may be typed with the cell reference or you may press F4 to enter the dollar signs after you key in the cell address.

Format Data (Percents, Fonts, and Font Size)

- Formatting may be used to change decimal answers into a percentage format.

- Quattro Pro lets you apply desktop publishing features to create a more attractive screen view and printout. Your monitor and printer, however, must be able to support these features.

- Notebook page enhancements such as changing the font and font size can be accomplished using the Property Bar. Note the above right illustration of the Property Bar with the font button selected:

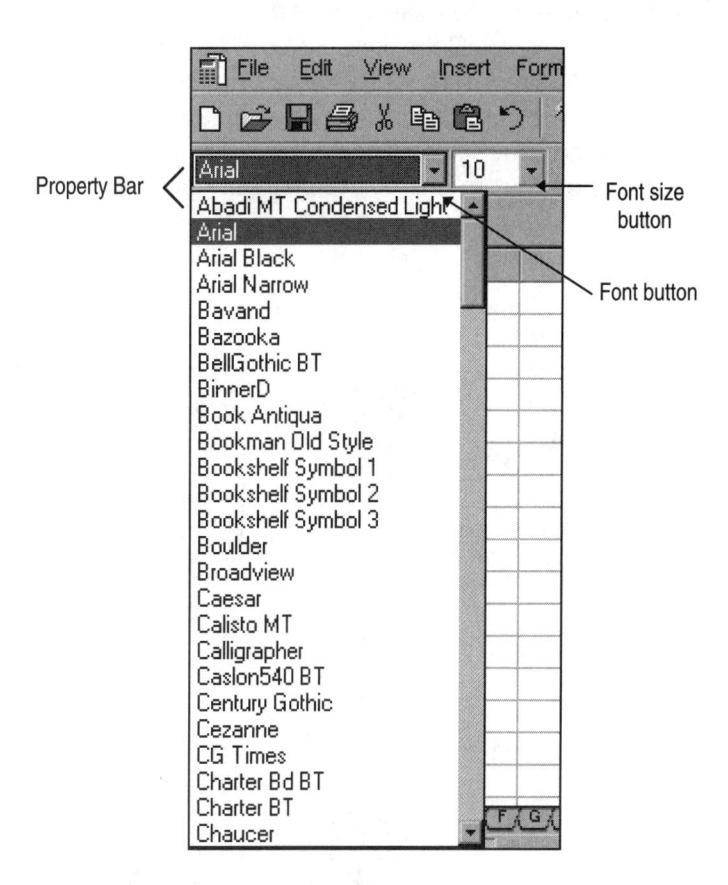

- A **font** is a set of characters that share a design style and name. Since Windows TrueType fonts are scalable, a single TrueType font can be set to a variety of sizes. The current font name is displayed on the Font button Arial, and the current font size is displayed on the Font size button 10 on the Property bar.

QUATTRO PRO 8   Lesson 2: Use Formulas; Format, Copy, and Print

- The **font size** is an attribute that sets the height of characters in a scalable font. This size is measured in points. A point is 1/72 of an inch. When the size of a font is changed, Quattro Pro automatically adjusts the row height but does not adjust the column width.

- As shown in Illustration A, the easiest way to apply a new font or font size is to select the cells to format and then select the font or font size via the Font or Font size buttons on the Property Bar. However, you can also use the Cell Font tab in the Active Cells dialog box. The dialog box, in Illustration B, is opened using the Fo<u>r</u>mat, <u>S</u>election commands. You can copy and paste formatting (background color, font, numeric format, etc.) from one cell to another cell using QuickFormat.

- When a font and font size are selected, Quattro Pro immediately formats the text in the selected cells.

- You can change the font or font size for characters you select while editing a cell.

QuickFormat

- Once you have formatted a cell, you can copy and paste formatting (font, numeric format, etc.) to another cell using the QuickFormat button on the Notebook toolbar. To QuickFormat, select a cell or range with the format you wish to copy. Click the QuickFormat button, then select the range to receive the same format. You can continue to apply the format until you deselect the button.

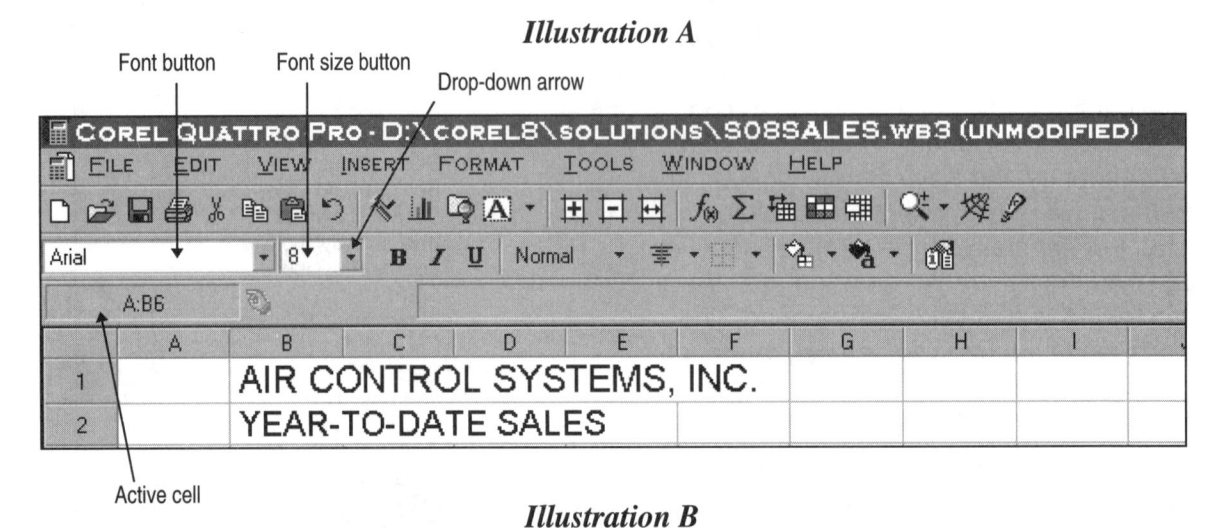

Illustration A

Illustration B

In this exercise, you will complete and format the Year-to-Date Sales report for Air Control Systems, Inc. for July 1, 1998, by calculating total sales and percent of total sales for each salesperson, and formatting.

EXERCISE DIRECTIONS

1. Open ⌨**SALES** or 💾**08SALES**.
2. Enter sales data and the date of the report, as shown.
3. Enter a formula to determine TOTAL for each salesperson.
   HINT: A/COND + HEATING
4. Copy the TOTAL formula for each salesperson.
5. Enter the label TOTALS in cell A16.
6. Enter a formula in cell C16 to calculate TOTALS for the A/COND column.
7. Copy the column TOTALS formula to cells D16 and E16.
8. Enter the formula to find the % OF TOTAL using an absolute reference as illustrated.
9. Copy the % OF TOTAL formula for each salesperson.
10. Copy the TOTALS formula to find the total of the % OF TOTAL column.
11. Use the Format, Selection commands to format the money columns (C, D, and E) for fixed with two decimal places.
12. Use the Format, Selection commands to format the % OF TOTAL column for percents with two decimal places.
13. Center column C, D, and E labels.
14. Make the font changes indicated below using the toolbar:
    - Main title: Arial 16 point
    - Secondary title: Arial 14 point
    - Column titles: Arial 10 point
15. Make the font change indicated below using the menu:
    - Data in rows: MS Sans Serif 10 point
      ✓ *If your system does not have this font, choose a different font.*
16. To use QuickFormat:
    - Select any row of data just formatted.
    - Select the QuickFormat Button.
      (The Mouse cursor turns into a paint roller.)
    - Select the totals line of the notebook.
    - Deselect the QuickFormat button.
17. Print one copy of the notebook page.
18. Close and save the notebook, or save as **SALES**.

A	A	B	C	D	E	F	G
1			AIR CONTROL SYSTEMS, INC.				
2			YEAR-TO-DATE SALES				
3							
4					DATE:	07/01/98	
5							
6	SALESPERSON		A/COND	HEATING	TOTAL	% OF TOTAL	
7							
8	ARTURO		1245.67	2348.92		=E8/$E$16	
9	CHESTERTON		3458.91	4567.89			
10	DAVIS		3543.55	2345.87			
11	FERNANDEZ		4545.85	9587.85			
12	JORGENSON		9875.67	15875.98			
13	MARTIN		8756.89	4587.34			
14	WILLIAMS		7758.85	4587.95	▼	▼	
15							
16	TOTALS						
17							

QUATTRO PRO 8 Lesson 2: Use Formulas; Format, Copy, and Print

KEYSTROKES

ENTER FORMULAS FOR ABSOLUTE CONDITIONS

1. Select cell to receive formula.
2. Press **+** or **=** .... [+] or [=]
3. Type formula .... *formula* using absolute references and mathematical operators.

   Example of a formula using absolute references: +$A$1*($B$2+$B$10)/2

   ✓ You can select cells instead of typing absolute references to tell Quattro Pro which cells you wish the formula to reference.

To insert cell references by selecting cells:

   a. Click formula where cell reference will be inserted.

   ✓ If necessary, type preceding operator or parenthesis.

   b. Select cell(s) you want formula to reference. Reference appears in formula.

   c. Press **F4** .... [F4] until absolute reference appears.

   d. Type desired operator or parenthesis.

   e. Repeat steps a-d as needed.

4. Press **Enter** .... [Enter]

CHANGE FONT USING THE FONT BOX

1. Select cells or characters in cells to format.
2. Click **Font** drop-down arrow on Property Bar.
3. Select desired font .... [↑][↓]

CHANGE FONT SIZE USING THE FONT SIZE BOX

1. Select cells or characters in cells to format.
2. Complete one of the following procedures:

   a. Click **Font size** button . [10 pt ▼] drop-down arrow on Property Bar.

   b. Select a number in list .... [↑][↓]

   OR

   a. Click **Font size** button . [10 pt ▼] on Property bar.

   b. Enter desired number .... *number*

3. Press **Enter** .... [Enter]

270

QUATTRO PRO 8 Lesson 2: Use Formulas; Format, Copy, and Print

Exercise 9

■ Summary

Hillside Academy would like you to prepare a daily report analyzing beverage sales quantities. They would also like to determine each beverage's percent of total sales.

EXERCISE DIRECTIONS

1. Create an appropriate three-line title for your notebook page. *Include a line for the date and use today's date.*

2. Enter a listing of each BEVERAGE and the quantity SOLD as listed below:

   ✓ *Allow columns A and B for BEVERAGE list.*

BEVERAGE	SOLD
Whole Milk	238
Skim Milk	122
Chocolate Milk	45
Orange Juice	75
Soft Drinks	320
Diet Soft Drinks	240

3. Skip one line below the list, enter the label TOTAL, and find the total number of beverages sold.

4. Add a column % OF TOTAL.

5. Find what percent each beverage quantity is of the total.

6. Copy the TOTAL formula from C13 to D13.

7. Format % OF TOTAL column for two-place percents.

8. Use font and font size changes to enhance the spreadsheet as follows:
   - Main title – 14 point Arial
   - Subtitles – 12 point Arial
   - Column headings, data and totals – 10 point Times New Roman

9. Right-align SOLD column heading.

10. Print one copy of the notebook page.

11. Save the notebook; name it **DRINKS**.

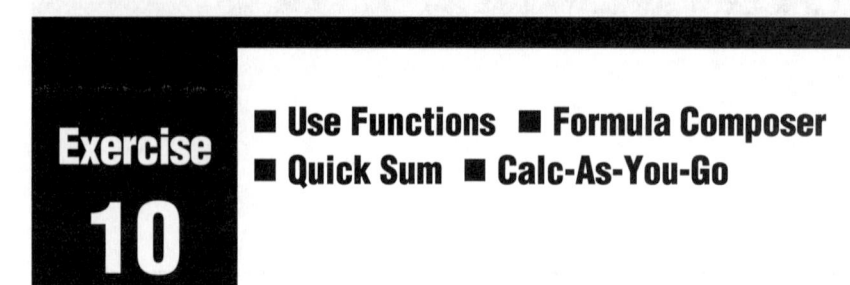

QUATTRO PRO 8

Lesson 3: Formulas and Functions; Edit Information; Print Options

Exercise 10

- Use Functions
- Formula Composer
- Quick Sum
- Calc-As-You-Go

NOTES

Use Functions

- A **function** is a built-in formula that performs a special calculation automatically. For example, the @SUM function can be used with a range of cells to add all values in the specified range. To add the values in A4, A5, and A6, for example, the function would appear in the formula as follows: @SUM(A4..A6)

- Functions appear in formulas in the following order: first the @ sign, then the function name (in either uppercase or lowercase), followed by an open parenthesis; then the number, cell, or range of cells to be affected, followed by a close parenthesis.

- A function may be used by itself, or it may be combined with other functions.

- Quattro Pro provides functions that are used for statistical and financial analysis or for database operations:

    @AVG()   Finds the average value in a range of cells.
    @COUNT()   Counts all the non-blank cells in a range. Cells containing values as well as labels are counted.
    @MAX()   Indicates the highest value in a range of cells.
    @MIN()   Indicates the lowest value in a range of cells.
    @SUM()   Adds all values in a range of cells.

- The data you must supply to complete the functions are called **arguments**. For example, in @MAX(A1..A5) the range of cells A1 to A5 is the argument.

- You can type or insert functions into formulas. If you are typing a function and you wish to start the formula with a function, first type an "at" sign (@). You can also insert a function by clicking Insert, Function, which will display the Functions dialog box. You can also use the Formula Composer as illustrated on the following page. In either case, the @ sign is automatically entered as part of the assistance provided by Quattro Pro.

Insert Function Dialog Box

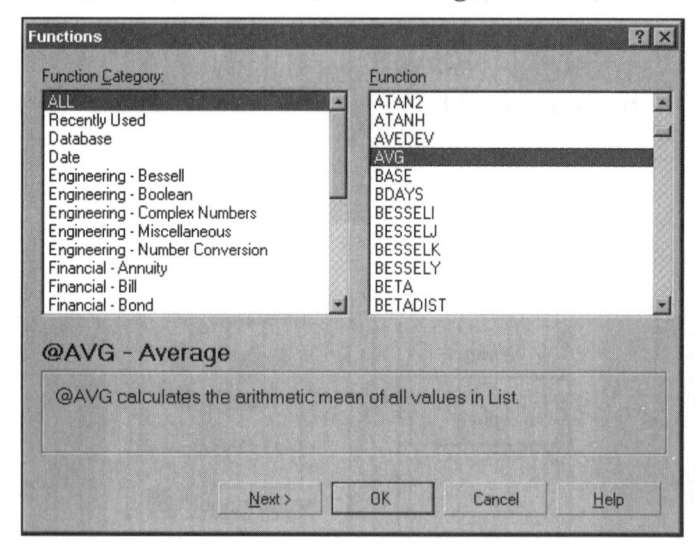

Formula Composer

- The Formula Composer button [fx], located on the Toolbar, lets you insert functions into formulas by selecting the function from a list. It evaluates the formula as you enter it to determine proper syntax. When you press the @ button, on the button bar of the Formula Composer dialog box, the **Functions** dialog box displays, as illustrated on the previous page.

Quick Sum

- Quattro Pro provides a quick method to enter the @SUM function. After entering the data to be added, move to the next cell and click the Sigma button [Σ] on the Toolbar. The formula then automatically displays on the Input line and the answer appears in the cell.

Calc-As-You-Go

- Calc-As-You-Go lets you quickly evaluate a selection of cells. You can select cells, and you can see the sum, average, count, maximum value, and minimum value for those cells at the bottom-right of the screen. Note the illustration below. These numbers are for your information and cannot be copied electronically from this location.

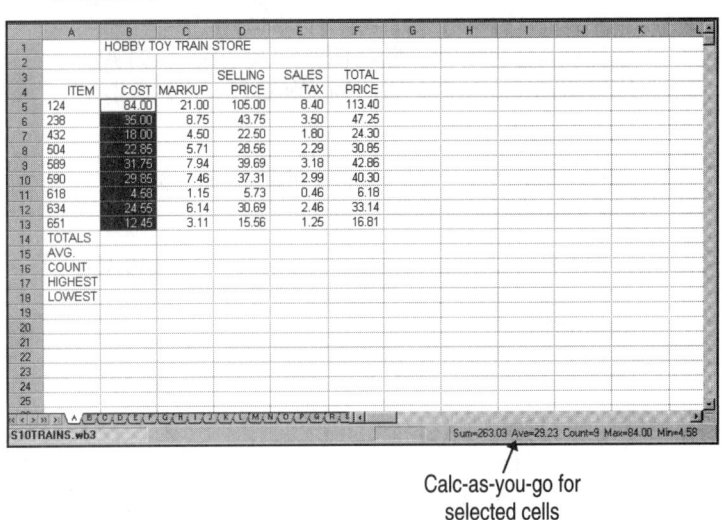

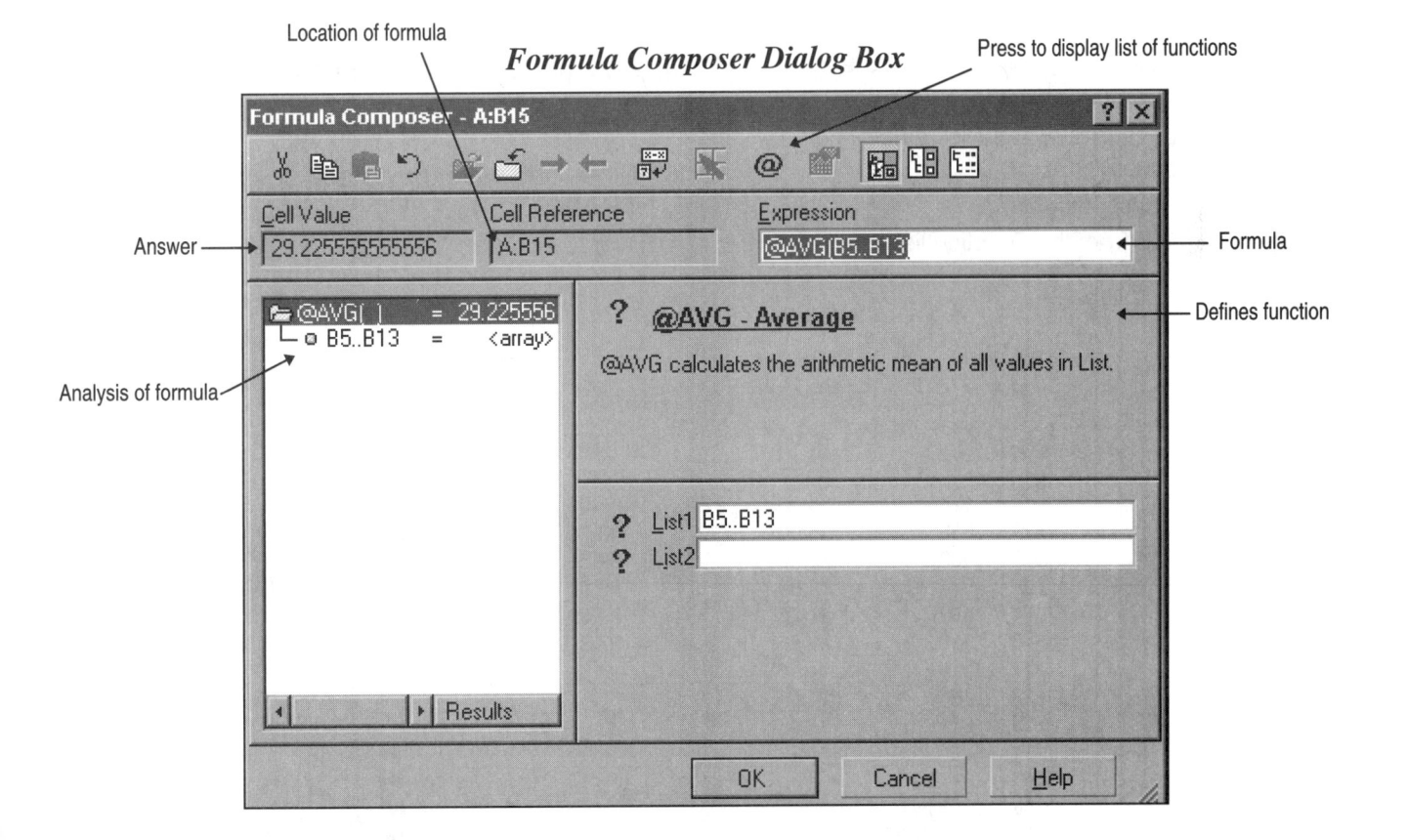

Formula Composer Dialog Box

Quattro Pro 8 ■ Lesson 3 ■ Exercise 10

QUATTRO PRO 8 Lesson 3: Formulas and Functions; Edit Information; Print Options

> You will be adding more items to the TRAINS notebook and summarizing the information using SUM, AVG, MAX, COUNT and MIN functions. Calc-As-You-Go will be viewed and functions will be entered using the keyboard, Formula Composer, and Quick Sum.

EXERCISE DIRECTIONS

1. Open ⌨TRAINS or 💾10TRAINS.

2. Enter new data as shown in the illustration.

3. Copy the formulas from the MARKUP, SELLING PRICE, SALES TAX, and TOTAL PRICE columns in the block C10:F10 to the block C11:F13.

4. Enter summary labels in column A, as indicated.

5. Enter a SUM function formula to total the COST column. Copy the formula to the remaining columns.

6. Use the Sigma button on the Toolbar to total the MARKUP column. Copy the formula across to the remaining columns.

7. Enter an AVG function formula to average the Cost column. Copy the formula to the remaining columns.

8. Use the Formula Composer to enter the COUNT function as follows:
   - Place the cursor in B16 and click the Formula Composer button.
   - Click the @ function button.
   - Select COUNT from the Function list and click OK.
   - Click in the area between the parentheses in the function formula.
   - Click the Point to Cell or Block button and select the COST data in B5:B13.
   - Press Enter twice.
   - Copy the formula to the remaining columns.

9. Enter MAX and MIN functions with the keyboard or using the Formula Composer. Copy formulas to the remaining columns.

10. Select the values in the cost column in B5:B13.

11. View the Calc-As-You-Go data on the status bar at the bottom right of the display. Compare answers to the summary data for that column.

12. Format all money amounts for fixed with two decimal places. Use QuickFormat.

13. Format the TOTAL PRICE summary data for currency.

14. Format COUNT row for normal.

15. Print one copy of the notebook.

16. Close and save the notebook, or save as **TRAINS**.

A	A	B	C	D	E	F
1		HOBBY TOY TRAIN STORE				
2						
3				SELLING	SALES	TOTAL
4	ITEM	COST	MARKUP	PRICE	TAX	PRICE
5	124	84.00	21.00	105.00	8.40	$113.40
6	238	35.00	8.75	43.75	3.50	$47.25
7	432	18.00	4.50	22.50	1.80	$24.30
8	504	22.85	5.71	28.56	2.29	$30.85
9	589	31.75	7.94	39.69	3.18	$42.86
10	590	29.85	7.46	37.31	2.99	$40.30
11	*618*	*4.58*				
12	*634*	*24.55*				
13	*651*	*12.45*				
14	TOTALS					
15	AVG.					
16	COUNT					
17	HIGHEST					
18	LOWEST					

KEYSTROKES

INSERT A FUNCTION USING KEYBOARD

1. Type @.. @
2. Type function name .... *function name*
3. Type open parenthesis .... (
4. Type arguments or block arguments separated by an ellipsis.
   Ex. A1..A5
5. Type close parenthesis ....)

INSERT A FUNCTION USING MENU

1. Click cell.. *cell* to contain formula.
2. Click **Insert**............................. Alt+I
3. Click **Function**............................. U
4. Follow steps 4-9 below.

INSERT A FUNCTION USING FORMULA COMPOSER

1. Click cell.. *cell* to contain formula.
   OR
   Click formula where function will be inserted.
2. Click **Formula Composer** button.... *f(x)* on Toolbar.
   OR
   a. Click **Insert** menu.............. Alt+I
   b. Click **Function** .... U

3. Click @ button.............................. @
4. Select a category in
   Function Category list............ Alt+C
5. Select a function in
   Function list............................ Alt+F
6. Click **OK** .... Enter
7. Type arguments and data. Depending on the function, enter the following kinds of data:
   - Numbers (constants) – type numbers (integers, fractions, mixed numbers, negative numbers) as you would in a cell.
   - References – type or insert cell references.
   - Named references or formulas – type or insert named references or formulas.
   OR
   a. Click **Point** button..................
   b. Highlight range of data.
   c. Press **Enter**............................. Enter
8. Repeat step 7, as needed.
9. Click **OK** .... Enter
   ✓ *Quattro Pro will inform you if you have entered incorrect arguments.*

USE QUICK SUM

1. Enter data to be added.
2. Place cursor in answer location. (The cell below or to the right of the data.)
3. Click **Sigma** button........................ Σ

USE CALC-AS-YOU-GO

1. Select block to be calculated.
2. View sum, average, count, maximum value, and minimum value on status bar.

Quattro Pro 8 ■ Lesson 3 ■ Exercise 10   275

QUATTRO PRO 8   Lesson 3: Formulas and Functions; Edit Information; Print Options

Exercise 11

- Change Column Width
- Create a Series
- Comma Format

NOTES

Change Column Width

- It is sometimes desirable to change (widen or narrow) the column widths so text or values can fit or have a better appearance. Only the width of an entire column or a group of columns may be changed, not the width of a single cell. You can select a column (or range of columns) and then use the QuickFit button on the Toolbar. The column width will adjust automatically to fit the longest current entry, or entries below a selected all.

- You can also use the mouse to manually drag a column to a desired width. Simply place the mouse between the top of two columns. When the cursor changes to a crosshair, drag the column to the desired width.

- All notebook pages in a notebook are set for a **standard column width** (default setting). The default setting represents the number of characters displayed in a cell using the standard font. Change column width by placing your cursor in the column to be changed and then selecting Format, Selection, and the Row/Column tab. Note the default column setting in the illustration to the right. Auto Width sets the column to fit the widest entry. You can quickly set the column to fit the widest entry and bypass this dialog box by using QuickFit from the Format menu.

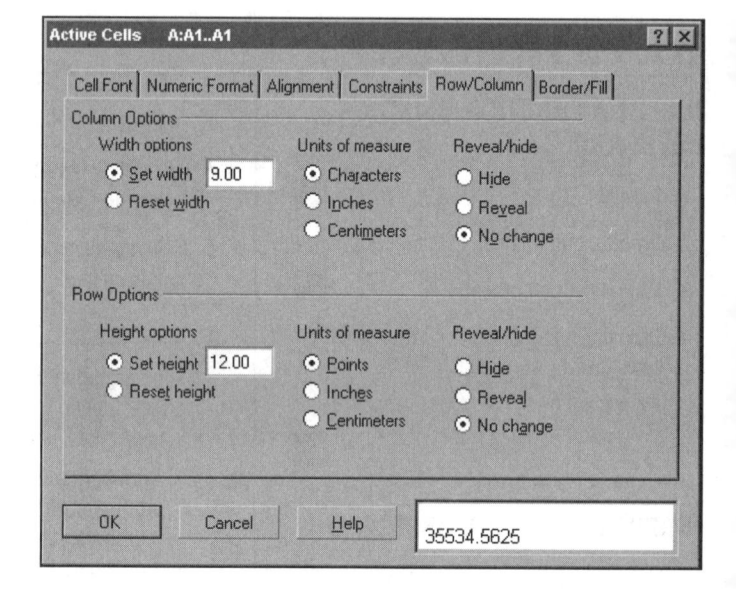

- When you enter long labels, the text flows into the next column if the cell to the right is empty. If the next cell is not empty, text that exceeds the column width is covered by the data in the cell to the right.

- Quattro Pro displays numeric data that exceeds the column width by filling the cell with asterisks (********), by displaying the number in scientific notation, or by hiding the numeric data–depending on which number type has been selected.

Create a Series

- You can use the Fill command on the Edit menu to quickly enter sequential values in a range of cells. You can enter sequential numbers, dates, or times in any increment (e.g., 2, 4, 6, 8 or 5, 10, 15, 20 or January, February, March, April). In addition, you can define a pattern of entries to fill a block by using the Edit, Fill, Define QuickFill selection. Note the illustration of the Fill Series dialog box used to set a sequential range of numbers beginning with 350. The ending value need not be set if you select the cells before opening this dialog box.

- In the illustration below, the cells box contains the block A5..A12 and at the right you will note a Select Arrow. You can use this to collapse the dialog box and select the block. Then you can maximize the dialog box to complete your settings.

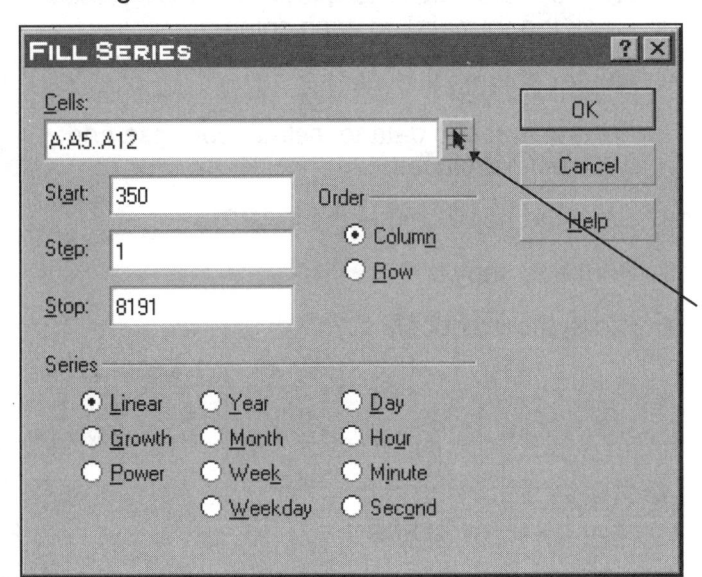

Comma Format

- To make large numbers more readable, formatting may be used to include commas. To do so, highlight the block of cells, columns or rows to receive the comma format and click Format, Selection. Click on the Numeric Format tab, click the Comma option and then Enter the number of decimal places.

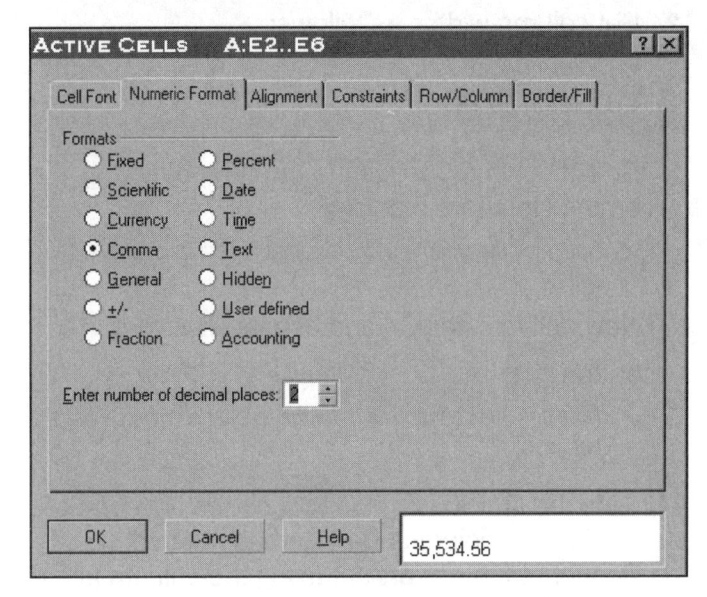

Quattro Pro 8 ■ Lesson 3 ■ Exercise 11

QUATTRO PRO 8 Lesson 3: Formulas and Functions; Edit Information; Print Options

> You will create a notebook page for Best Home Appliances showing employees' quarterly SALES and COMMISSIONS earned. Each employee receives a 15% commission on sales.

EXERCISE DIRECTIONS

1. Create the notebook as shown on the following page or open 11APPLI.

2. Set column widths as follows:
   - Column A: 5
   - Column B: 15

3. Select column C. Use the QuickFit button on the Notebook Toolbar.
   - ✓ Note how the column width expands for the long entry in cell C2.

   Now activate cell C4 and use the QuickFit button.
   - ✓ Note how the column width fits the longest entry in C4 or below.

4. Use the QuickFit button on the Notebook Toolbar for columns B-F, and as needed throughout this exercise, using the column titles as the QuickFit starting point.

5. Select the block for EMP. NO. in cells A6:A10. Use the Fill, QuickFill option on the Edit menu.

6. Copy BASE SALARY to the remaining employees.
   - ✓ All employees have the same base salary.

7. Enter a formula to find COMMISSIONS for the first employee. The commission rate is 15% of sales. Copy the formula to the remaining employees.

8. Enter a formula to find 1ST QTR. EARNINGS for the first employee by adding BASE SALARY and COMMISSIONS for the quarter. Copy the formula to the remaining employees.

9. Enter formulas using functions to find TOTALS, AVERAGES, HIGHEST, and LOWEST values. Copy the formulas to each column.

10. Center column title labels.

11. Format numeric data to include commas and two decimal places.

12. Save the notebook; name it **APPLI**.

13. Print one copy.

14. Close the notebook.

	A	B	C	D	E	F
1			BEST HOME APPLIANCES			
2			QUARTERLY SALES AND SALARY REPORT			
3						
4	SMN.		BASE	1ST QTR.		1ST QTR.
5	NO.	SALESMAN	SALARY	SALES	COMMISSIONS	EARNINGS
6	350	Larry Fridga	3200.00	15,785.96		
7		Jose Micronez		21,895.95		
8		Marie Steerio		20,750.90		
9		Brian Stovely		25,920.85		
10		Patricia Washer		28,875.90		
11						
12		TOTALS				
13		AVERAGES				
14		HIGHEST				
15		LOWEST				

KEYSTROKES

CHANGE COLUMN WIDTHS USING THE MENU

1. Select any cell(s) in column(s) to change.
2. Press **F12**.................................. `F12`

   OR

   a. Click **F**o**rmat**.................. `Alt`+`R`
   b. Click **Se**l**ection**..................... `E`
3. Click **Row/Column** tab .... `Ctrl`+`Tab`
4. Type number (0-299)................*number* in **Se**t **Width** text box.

   ✓ *Number represents number of characters that can be displayed in cell using the standard font. You can change the units of measure by selecting **In**c**hes** or **Centi**m**eters** from the **unit** group.*
5. Click **OK**................................... `Enter`

CHANGE COLUMN WIDTHS USING THE MOUSE

Change One Column Width

1. Point to right border of column heading to size.

   Pointer becomes a ⬄
2. Drag ⬄ left or right.

Change Several Column Widths

1. Select columns to size.
2. Point to right border of any selected column heading. Pointer becomes left and right arrows.
3. Drag ⬄ left or right.

SET COLUMN WIDTH TO FIT LONGEST ENTRY

1. Select column to size.
2. Click................................... ⬄

   OR

   a. Click **F**o**rmat**.................. `Alt`+`R`
   b. Click **Q**uickFit.......................... `Q`

CREATE A SERIES OF NUMBERS, DATES, OR TIMES USING THE MENU

1. Select cell(s) containing cells to fill.
2. Click **E**dit menu .... `Alt`+`E`
3. Click **F**ill .... `I`
4. Click **F**ill Series .... `F`

To enter starting value:

a. Click **S**tart........................ `Alt`+`A`
b. Enter start value .... *start value*

To change proposed step value:

a. Click **St**e**p** .... `Alt`+`E`
b. Type step value .... *number* in **Ste**p text box.

To change proposed direction of series:

Select desired **Order** in option:

- **R**ows................................ `Alt`+`R`
- Colum**n**s........................... `Alt`+`N`

To change proposed series type:

Select desired **Series** option:

- **L**inear .... `Alt`+`L`
  to increase/decrease each value in series by number in **Ste**p value text box.
- **G**rowth .... `Alt`+`G`
  to multiply each value in series by number in **Ste**p value text box.
- **P**roperty .... `Alt`+`P`
  to increase each value in series exponentially.
- You may also choose **Y**ear, **M**onth, **W**eek, **W**eekday, **D**ay, **H**our, **M**inute Sec**o**nd.

To set stop value for series:

✓ *Type a stop value if you want series to end at a specific number.*

a. Click **S**top .... `Alt`+`S`
b. Type stop value .... *number*
5. Click **OK**................................... `Enter`

FORMAT DATA FOR COMMAS

Press **F12**................................... `F12`

OR

1. Click **F**o**rmat**........................ `Alt`+`R`
2. Click **Se**l**ection** .... `E`

OR

1. Right-click.
2. Select **Cell Properties**.
3. Select **Numeric Format** tab ... `Ctrl`+`Tab`
4. Click **C**omma............................. `O`
5. Click **E**nter number of decimal Place .... `Alt`+`E`
6. Use arrows or enter number ..... ⬇⬆
7. Click **OK**................................... `Enter`

Quattro Pro 8 ■ Lesson 3 ■ Exercise 11   279

QUATTRO PRO 8 **Lesson 3:** Formulas and Functions; Edit Information; Print Options

Exercise 12

- Print Options
- Edit Data
- Documentation Notes

NOTES

Print Options

- When the **Print** command is accessed, the Spreadsheet Print dialog box allows you to select various print options. Note the illustrations of the Spreadsheet Print dialog box below showing the Print and Details tabs.

Spreadsheet Print Dialog Box

- The **Page Setup** button, in the Spreadsheet Print dialog box, is used to access page-setting options. Note the illustrations of the Paper Type and Print Scaling tabs of the Spreadsheet Page Setup dialog box. The other setting tabs are for Header/Footer, Print Margins, Named Settings, and Options.

Paper Type Tab on Spreadsheet Page Setup Dialog Box

Print Scaling Tab on Spreadsheet Page Setup Dialog Box

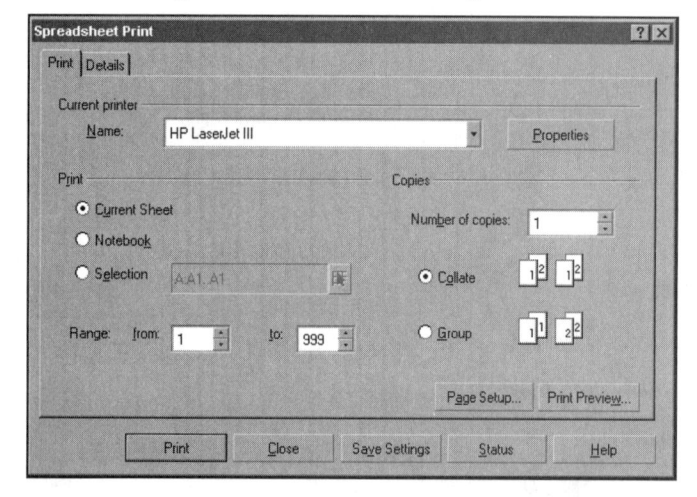

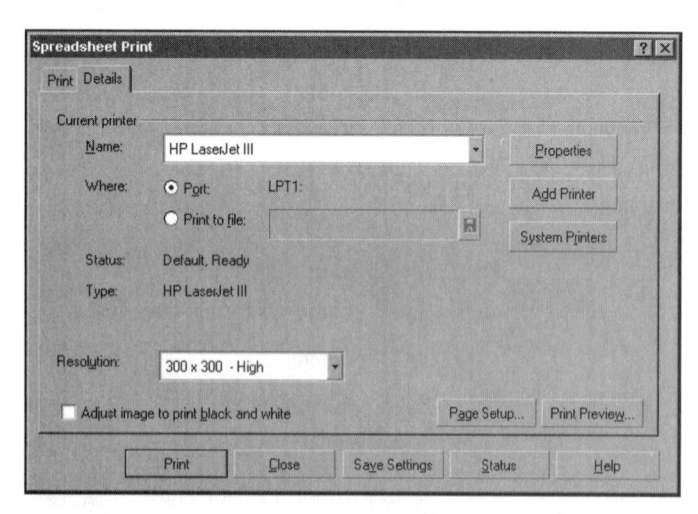

- In the Spreadsheet Print dialog box you can select the **Print Preview** button to review, on screen, the output your settings will yield.

280

- When you select the Options tab from the Page Setup box, you can set various print options for the Notebook sheet, such as gridlines, or row/column headings, as shown in the Spreadsheet Page Setup box below.

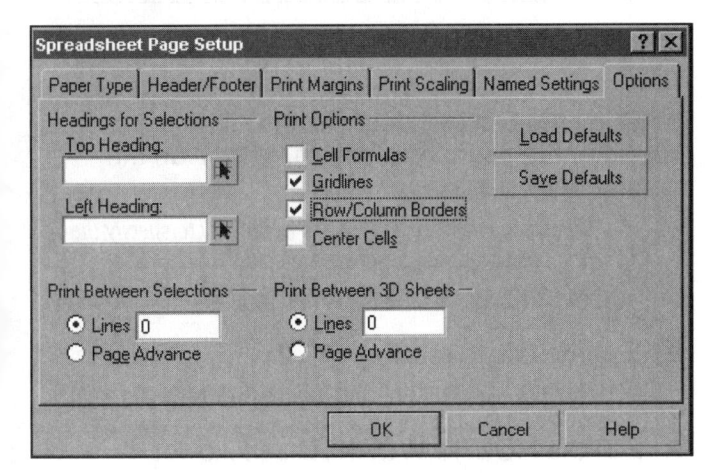

- If you selected Page Setup from the Spreadsheet Print dialog box, you will be returned to that box to activate printing after you make your settings. You can also use file, Page Setup to go into setup directly. In that case, a Print button will appear on the Page Setup dialog box.

Edit Data

- Data may be changed either before or after it has been entered in a cell.

- To clear or edit a cell's content before it is entered, choose one of the following methods:
  - Use the backspace key to correct a keystroke,
  - Press the Escape key, or
  - Click the Cancel button on the Input line.

- To clear or edit a cell's content after it is entered:
  - Replace or overwrite the entire entry with new data,
  - Edit part of the entry by enabling cell editing F2,
  - Erase a single cell entry Del,
  - Select and erase a range of cell entries Del.

- You can enable cell editing by pressing F2 or by double-clicking the cell. The cursor will then appear at the end of the entry and the data will appear on the Input line. You can then use the backspace key or cursor arrows to edit as desired.

- You can erase entries by selecting the cell(s) and then clicking Edit, Clear, or pressing the Delete key.

Documentation Notes

- When a notebook is created by one person and then used by others, formulas used to create the report should be documented or explained. Entering an explanatory note with each formula can do this. The note will display on the Input line when the formula cell is selected.

- To enter a note, type a semi-colon (;) immediately after the formula, then type the note. For example: +C7*D7; Hours times rate per hour. When you select the formula cell the formula and note will display on the input line.

QUATTRO PRO 8 Lesson 3: Formulas and Functions; Edit Information; Print Options

In this exercise, you will complete the payroll for Medallion Music Stores for the week ending February 6, 199-. You will then copy the entire notebook page to a new location and edit entries to create another payroll for the week ending February 13, 199-. Documentation notes will be added to several formulas.

EXERCISE DIRECTIONS

1. Open **PAY** or **12PAY**.
2. Clear the PAYROLL label from the subtitle.
3. Enter a new subtitle in column D: PAYROLL FOR THE WEEK ENDING 2/6/9-
4. Enter the new row labels at the bottom of the notebook, as indicated.
5. Find Totals and Averages for columns from Gross Pay to Net Pay.
6. Format Totals and Averages for two decimal places.
7. Enter documentation notes in the formulas listed by enabling cell editing, adding a semicolon and adding the notes shown below:
   E7: Hours worked times hourly pay.
   F7: Used 20% of Gross Pay.
   G7: Used 6.2% of Gross Pay.
   H7: Used 1.45% of Gross Pay.
8. Copy the block of data (A2:I15) that represents the entire payroll, as shown, to A17 on the notebook page.
   ✓ *When copying a block, it is only necessary to specify the first position as the destination block.*
   – ON THE BOTTOM PAYROLL –
9. Edit the title to read:
   PAYROLL FOR THE WEEK ENDING 2/13/9-
10. Edit the HOURS WORKED as follows:

    | Engelson | 26 |
    | Gomez | 23 |
    | Jordan | 20 |
    | Kelly | 30 |
    | Romano | 32 |
    | Unger | 22 |

11. Adjust format for payroll values if necessary.
12. Preview the printout of this file.
13. Print one copy of the February 13 payroll.
14. Close and save the notebook, or save as **PAY**.

A	A	B	C	D	E	F	G	H	I	J
1	MMsMMs			MEDALLION MUSIC STORES					MMsMMs	
2				PAYROLL FOR THE WEEK ENDING 2/6/98						
3										
4	Employee	Employee	Hourly	Hours	Gross	Federal	Soc. Sec	Medicare	Net	
5	Number	Name	Rate	Worked	Pay	With. Tax	Tax	Tax	Pay	
6										
7	272	Engelson	7.25	21	152.25	30.45	9.44	2.21	110.15	
8	320	Gomez	7.75	19	147.25	29.45	9.13	2.14	106.54	
9	322	Jordan	8.25	21	173.25	34.65	10.74	2.51	125.35	
10	330	Kelly	9.95	35	348.25	69.65	21.59	5.05	251.96	
11	340	Romano	9.75	35	341.25	68.25	21.16	4.95	246.89	
12	341	Unger	8.45	15	126.75	25.35	7.86	1.84	91.70	
13										
14	Totals								▶	
15	Averages								▶	
16										
17										

Copy block A2:I15 to A17.

KEYSTROKES

EDIT CELL CONTENTS AFTER IT IS ENTERED (ENABLE CELL EDITING)

1. Double-click cell to edit.

    OR

    a. Select cell to edit .... `↑↓`
    b. Press F2 .... `F2`

    An insertion point appears in the active cell and these buttons appear on the formula bar:

    ❌ Cancel button – cancels changes made in cell.

    ✓ OK button – accepts changes made in cell.

2. Click desired data position in cell or in formula bar.

3. Type new data .... *data*

    OR

    Press **Backspace** .... `Backspace`
    to delete character left of insertion point.

    OR

    Press **Delete** .... `Del`
    to delete character right of insertion point.

    To accept changes:

    Press **Enter** .... `Enter`

    OR

    Click **OK** button .... ✓
    on the formula bar.

    To cancel changes:

    Press **Escape** .... `Esc`

    OR

    Click **Cancel** button .... ❌
    on the formula bar.

EDIT CELL CONTENTS WHILE TYPING

To delete character to the left of insertion point:

Press **Backspace** .... `Backspace`

To cancel all characters:

Press **Escape** .... `Esc`

ERASE CONTENTS OF CELL OR RANGE

1. Select cell or range containing contents to erase.

2. Press **Delete** .... `Del`

    OR

    a. Click **Edit** .... `Alt`+`E`
    b. Click **Clear** .... `E`

🌐 PRINT PREVIEW

1. Click **Print** button on Standard Toolbar .... 🖨

2. Click **Print Preview** .... `Alt`+`W`

    OR

    a. Click **File** .... `Alt`+`F`
    b. Click **Print Preview** .... `T`

    – FROM PREVIEW WINDOW –

    To view next page:

    Click **Next Page** button .... ▶

    To view previous page:

    Click **Previous Page** button .... ◀

    To view a magnified portion of the page:

    Left-click area of page to magnify.

    OR

    a. Click **Increase Zoom** button ...... 🔍+

    OR

    Click **Reduce Zoom** button .... 🔍−

    b. Right-click any area of page to return to full page view.

3. Click
    Close the Print Preview button ..... 🖨
    to exit Print Preview.

🌐 PRINT RANGE OF CELLS

Prints data in range using the current page settings.

✓ When printing a range, this procedure will override a print area, if you defined one.

1. Select range of cells to print.
2. Click **File** menu .... `Alt`+`F`
3. Click **Print** .... `P`
4. Click **Selection** .... `E`
5. Click **Print** .... `Enter`

🌐 SET PRINT OPTIONS FOR WORKSHEET

1. Click **File** menu .... `Alt`+`F`
2. Click **Print** .... `P`
3. Click **Page Setup** .... `Alt`+`A`
4. Select desired tab .... `Ctrl`+`Tab`
5. Select desired setting .... `Tab`
6. Enter setting or use list box .... `↑↓`
7. Click **OK** .... `Enter`

Exercise 13

■ Page Setup ■ Cell Properties

NOTES

Page Setup

- Quattro Pro uses the default page size (usually 8 ½"x11") of the current printer. To change the page size, select Print from the File menu, click the Page Setup button, and select the Paper Type tab. Use the following Page Setup options to control the print output for the selected page size.

- Paper Type options include:
  - **Type:** The size of paper on which to print the notebook page.
  - **Orientation:** Portrait prints the notebook page vertically on the paper. Landscape prints the notebook page horizontally on the paper.

Page Setup Dialog Box With Paper Type Tab Selected

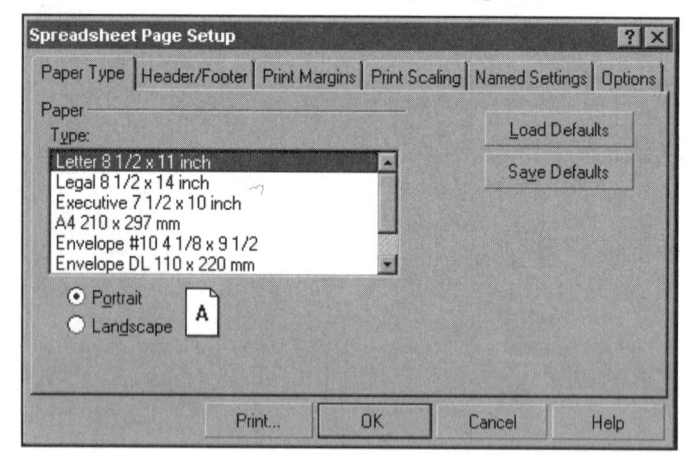

- Header/Footer options include:
  - **Header:** Text to be printed at the top of each notebook page.
  - **Footer:** Text to be printed at the bottom of each notebook page.
  - **Header Font:** Sets the font for the header text.
  - **Footer Font:** Sets the font for the footer text.

- Print Margins options include:
  - **Top, Bottom, Left, Right:** Sets the size for a notebook page's top, bottom, left, and right margins.
  - **Break Pages:** Configures Quattro Pro to break pages when a line count is reached.

Page Setup Dialog Box With Print Margins Tab Selected

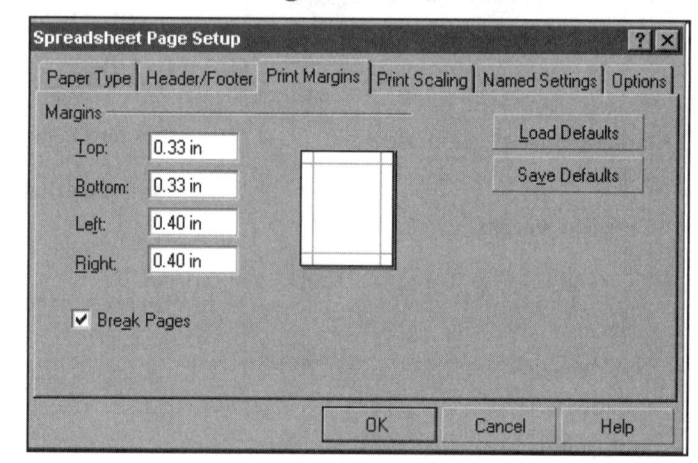

- Print Scaling options include:
  - **Print to % of normal size.** Sets percentage (1-1000) to increase or decrease size of data printed on a page. Margins do not change; thus if data is too large for the page, the output will go to additional pages. The default setting is for 100%.
  - **Print to desired width.** Prints notebook so that it fits on as few pages as possible. If you set a wide notebook to print on one page, it will scale the fonts and margins so that it fits.

- The Named Settings tab options include:
  - **New Set:** Type the name for a new print setting.
  - **Add:** Adds the setting to the list.
  - **Use:** Uses the selected named print setting.
  - **Update:** Replaces the settings stored under the selected name with the current print settings.
  - **Delete:** Deletes the selected named setting.
- And finally the Options tab includes settings to print Top and Left headings to label data on multiple page reports, Cell Formulas, Gridlines, Row/Column borders, Centered Cells Entries, Print Between Selections and Print Between 3-D Sheets.

Cell Properties

- You may apply several formatting options at once when you format text or values by using the **Active Cells** dialog box. To access the Active Cells dialog box, select the block of cells you wish to format, and then choose one of the following methods:
  - Select Selection from the Format menu
  - Right-click (on the block of cells) and choose Cell Properties
  - Press F12

- Note in the illustration below that, although the Cell Font tab is currently displayed, the box also contains five other tabs that contain cell and block formatting options. Settings for column widths, data alignment, font, color, and numeric formats can be set all at once for a block of data using this dialog box.

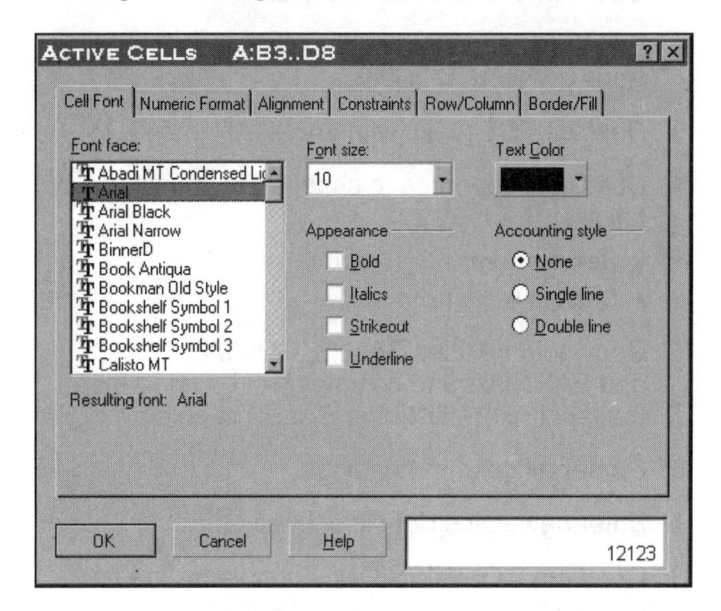

KEYSTROKES

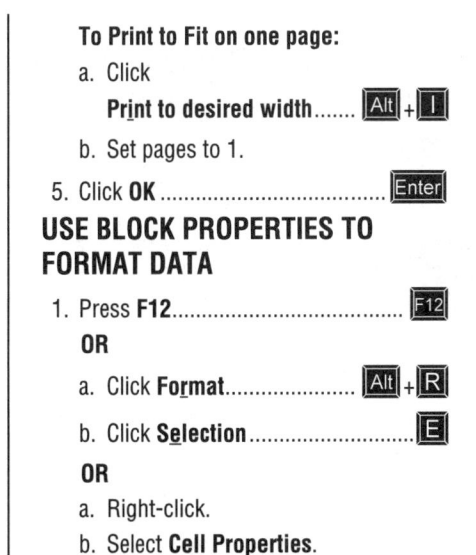

CHANGE SCALE OF PRINTED DATA
1. Click **File** .... Alt+F
2. Click **Print** .... P
3. Click **Page Setup** .... A
4. Select **Print Scaling** tab.

   To reduce or enlarge data on printed sheet:
   a. Click **Print to % of normal size** .... Alt+R
   b. Type percentage (1-100) .... Tab + number

To Print to Fit on one page:
   a. Click **Print to desired width** .... Alt+I
   b. Set pages to 1.
5. Click **OK** .... Enter

USE BLOCK PROPERTIES TO FORMAT DATA
1. Press **F12** F12
   OR
   a. Click **Format** .... Alt+R
   b. Click **Selection** .... E
   OR
   a. Right-click.
   b. Select **Cell Properties**.

2. Select appropriate tab .... Ctrl+Tab from the following:
   - **Cell Font**
   - **Numeric Format**
   - **Alignment**
   - **Constraints**
   - **Row/Column**
   - **Border/Fill**
3. Use list boxes and/or buttons to set options.
4. Click **OK** .... Enter

QUATTRO PRO 8 Lesson 3: Formulas and Functions; Edit Information; Print Options

In this exercise, you will add data to the Best Home Appliances report, set column widths, and use cell properties and page setup commands.

EXERCISE DIRECTIONS

1. Open **APPLI** or **13APPLI**.
2. Edit the second line of the title. Add: JANUARY-JUNE.
3. Replace 1ST QTR. with JAN-MAR in cell D4.
4. Use Cell Properties to change column widths as follows:
   - Select columns G, H, and I.
   - Change width to 14.
5. Copy column titles SALES, COMMISSIONS, and EARNINGS to columns G, H, and I. Insert the label APR-JUN over SALES in column G.
6. Center all column headings.
7. Enter new sales data in column G.
8. Copy the COMMISSIONS formula for the first employee in column E to column H.
9. Copy the COMMISSIONS formula down for each employee.
10. Enter the label 2ND QTR. over EARNINGS in column I.
11. Enter a formula in column I to compute BASE SALARY + COMMISSIONS for the second quarter.
12. Copy the BASE SALARY + COMMISSIONS formula down for each employee.
13. Find TOTALS, AVERAGES, HIGHEST, and LOWEST for the second quarter. (Copy formulas using one copy command.)
14. Use Cell Properties to format numeric data for commas and two decimal places.
15. Use Page Setup to change the scale setting to fit the notebook page on one page.
16. Check your scale setting using Print Preview.
17. Print one copy.
18. Close and save the notebook, or *save as* **APPLI**.

	A	B	C	D	E	F	G	H	I
1			BEST HOME APPLIANCES						
2			QUARTERLY SALES AND SALARY REPORT				JANUARY - JUNE		
3				JAN-MAR					
4	SMN.		BASE	1ST QTR.		1ST QTR.			
5	NO.	SALESMAN	SALARY	SALES	COMMISSIONS	EARNINGS			
6	350	Larry Fridga	3,200.00	15,785.96	2,367.89	5,567.89	22,758.85		
7	351	Jose Micronez	3,200.00	21,895.95	3,284.39	6,484.39	25,675.89		
8	352	Marie Steerio	3,200.00	20,750.90	3,112.64	6,312.64	24,567.81		
9	353	Brian Stovely	3,200.00	25,920.85	3,888.13	7,088.13	25,975.75		
10	354	Patricia Washer	3,200.00	28,875.90	4,331.39	7,531.39	29,656.54		
11									
12		TOTALS	16,000.00	113,229.56	16,984.43	32,984.43			
13		AVERAGES	3,200.00	22,645.91	3,396.89	6,596.89			
14		HIGHEST	3,200.00	28,875.90	4,331.39	7,531.39			
15		LOWEST	3,200.00	15,785.96	2,367.89	5,567.89			

QUATTRO PRO 8 Lesson 3: Use Formulas and Functions; Edit Information; Print Options

Exercise 14

- Page Breaks
- Bold
- Headers and Footers
- Cell Reference Checker

NOTES

Page Breaks

- Before printing, you may set hard page breaks and add headers and footers.

- Quattro Pro inserts soft page breaks based on the current paper size, scaling, and margin settings. You can override the automatic page breaks by inserting hard page breaks in your notebook page. When you click Insert, Page Break, Quattro Pro stops printing on the current page and starts printing on the top of a new page. A line drawn down or across the page denotes hard page breaks.

- You can remove soft page breaks by choosing Page Setup from the File menu, selecting the Print/Margins tab and deselecting the Break Pages check box. Hard page breaks may be removed by placing your cursor on the page break, and clicking Insert, Page Break, Delete.

Bold

- Labels or values may be emphasized by bolding the characters. Select the text and press the Bold button **B** on the Notebook Toolbar.

Headers and Footers

- Headers and footers are used when you want to repeat the same information at the top (header) or bottom (footer) of every page.

- Headers/footers are limited to a single line of text. You can specify different fonts for headers and footers.

- The following table lists special characters you can use to format header and footer text.

Code	Description
|	(vertical bar) Determines the position of the text: left-aligned, right-aligned, or centered.
#d	Enters the current date in the Short Date International format. (02/06)
#D	Enters the current date in the Long Date International format. (02/06/98)
#ds	Enters the current date in Short Date format. (20-Feb)
#Ds	Enters the current date in Long Date format. (20-Feb-98)
#t	Enters the current time in Long Time International format. (18:47)
#ts	Enters the current time in Short Time format. (06:47PM)
#Ts	Enters the current time in Long Time format. (06:48:49PM)
#p	Enters the current page number.
#P	Enters the number of pages in the document.
#f	Enters just the name of the notebook being printed (EXPENSE.WB2).
#F	Enters the name and path of the notebook being printed (C:\DATA\EXPENSE.WB2).
#n	Prints the remainder of the header or footer on a second line.
#	(number sign) Enters the current page number. Use for compatibility with Quattro Pro for DOS.
@	Enters the current date (per your computer's calendar). Use for compatibility with Quattro Pro for DOS.

✓Note: *If you want a # or @ character to appear in your header or footer without being treated as a header or footer code, type a backslash (\\) character before the # or @.*

- Header and Footer information can be added and edited by selecting the Header/Footer tab on the Spreadsheet Page Setup dialog box. Note the illustration of the text settings provided in the Header/Footer tab and compare it with the illustration of the headers and footers that result from those settings. The vertical bar is used to separate or set left-aligned, centered, or right-aligned text. One vertical bar centers the text and two vertical bars right-align the text. For example, to display a centered filename, you would enter |#f, as illustrated in the Footer below, and to display a right-aligned filename, you would enter | |#f.

- Headers and footers are only displayed on the screen in Print Preview mode.

    ✓Note: Top and bottom margins may have to be increased when using headers and footers.

Spreadsheet Page Setup Dialog Box, Header/Footer Tab

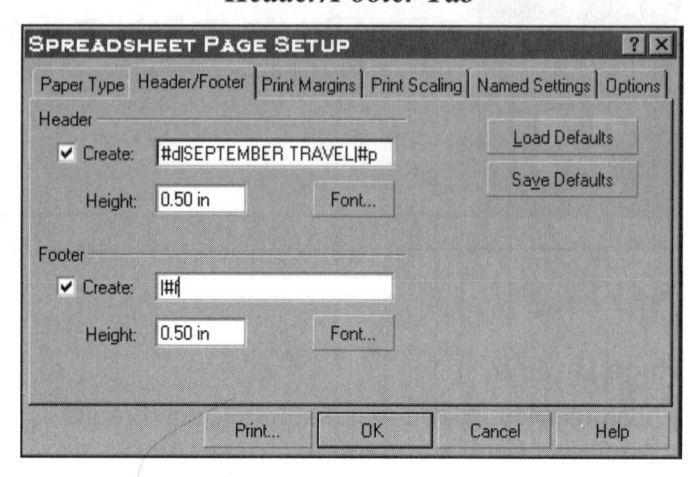

Header

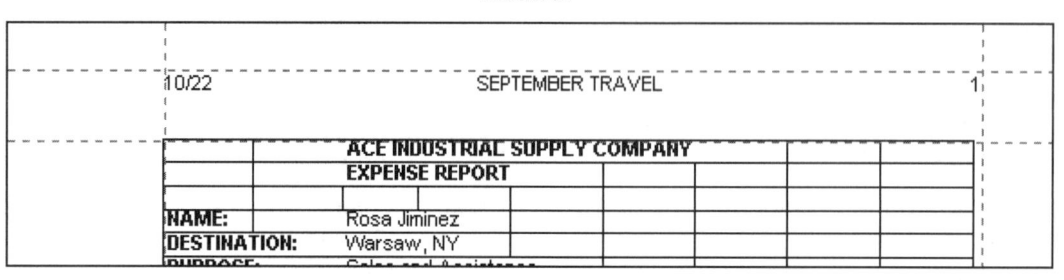

Footer

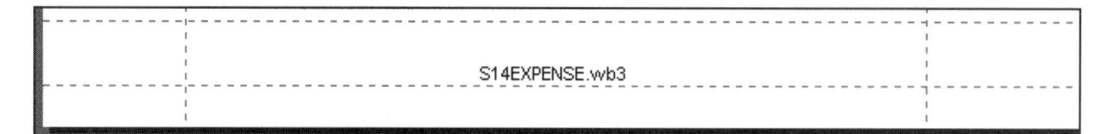

Cell Reference Checker

- To fix errors you might encounter when copying formulas that contain references to cell addresses, Quattro Pro provides the Cell Reference Checker. The Cell Reference Checker shows you how a formula you copy appears in the new location and checks if the formula should adjust to the new location using "relative" cell addresses or change to contain the original formula using "absolute" cell addresses. For example, suppose you copy a formula that references values in the range E12..E20. If you want the formula at the new location to continue referencing the values, then the formula's reference should be to $E$12..$E$20, making the reference "absolute"; otherwise, the formula's reference is "relative" to the new location.

- When a formula at the new location refers to cells that are empty, the Cell Reference Checker indicates that the new formula uses empty cells, as shown in the illustration below. Cell Reference Checker assumes you want the copied formula to reference the same cell addresses as in the original formula. To change the formula to contain the original formula using absolute cell addresses, click Fix It, then click Close. To have the formula adjust to the new location using relative cell addresses, click Close.

- Turn on or turn off the Cell Reference Checker by clicking Tools, Settings, General, Cell Reference Checker.

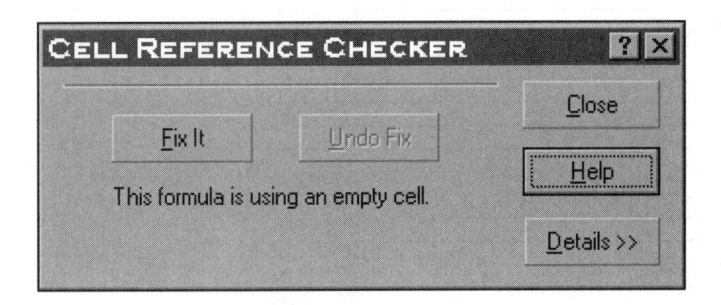

In this exercise, you will create a travel expense report for one of the engineers at the Ace Industrial Supply Company. The September travel report will include two trips, each printed on a separate page with a header and footer.

EXERCISE DIRECTIONS

1. Create the top notebook page shown on the next page, or open 🖫14EXPENS.
   - ✓ Enter the days of the month as numeric labels. Bold headings as illustrated.
2. Set column C width to 7.
3. Use cell properties to format block D12:I36 for fixed number format.
4. Find Mileage reimbursement at $.35 per mile in cell D14.
5. Check setting for Cell Reference Checker: Click Tools, Settings, General Tab, and activate Cell Reference Checker.
6. Find for TRANSPORTATION:
   - TOTALS – Enter formula to find the horizontal total for the Airplane row, columns E-H.
   - Copy the formula down for all Transportation items.
     - ✓ The cell reference checker dialog box will display informing you that cells are empty in the new locations. Click Fix it and note that the correction is to use absolute references. Since we are aware of the empty cells and still wish to use relative cell addresses, click Undo Fix and Close.
   - TOTAL TRANSPORTATION: Enter formula to find the total of column E from row 12 down.
   - Copy the formula across for all columns of data.
     - ✓ Click Close if Cell Reference Checker appears. You would Fix it if you wanted the cell references to be absolute.

7. Find for DAILY EXPENSES:
   - Copy TOTALS formula down for all rows of data.
   - TOTAL DAILY EXPENSES: Enter a formula to total the DAILY EXPENSES items.
8. Copy formula for all columns.
9. Find TOTAL EXPENSES for each day and for the TOTALS column by adding TOTAL TRANSPORTATION and TOTAL DAILY EXPENSES.
10. Copy the formula for all columns.
11. Copy the entire top notebook page to cell A41.
12. Create a page break at cell A39.
13. Edit the DESTINATION, PURPOSE, DATES, and all EXPENSES to display the data for the next trip, as indicated.
14. Print the file to fit columns to the page with the following header/footer specifications:
    - Header: left-justified date, centered title that reads SEPTEMBER TRAVEL, right-justified page number.
    - Footer: centered file name.
    (See dialog box illustration above.)
15. Close and save the notebook file; name it **EXPENS**.

QUATTRO PRO 8 Lesson 3: Formulas and Functions; Edit Information; Print Options

	A	B	C	D	E	F	G	H	I
1			ACE INDUSTRIAL SUPPLY COMPANY						
2			EXPENSE REPORT						
3									
4	NAME:		Rosa Jiminez						
5	DESTINATION:		Warsaw, NY						
6	PURPOSE:		Sales and Assistance						
7	DATES:		9/12-9/15/--						
8									
9			MILES	@.35	1	2	3	4	TOTALS
10		DATES:			09/12	09/13	09/14	09/15	
11	TRANSPORTATION:								
12	Airplane				86.55				
13	Car Expenses:								
14			Miles	297					
15			Tolls		12.85		3.75	12.85	
16			Parking		17.85				
17			Rental						
18	Taxi								
19	Train								
20	Other								
21									
22	TOTAL TRANSPORTATION								
23									
24	DAILY EXPENSES:								
25	Hotel				125.75	126.75	127.75	128.75	
26	Meals				68.56	58.94	72.85	76.89	
27	Telephone, Fax, etc.				14.78	13.89	12.75	8.54	
28	Copy Services					12.75		13.45	
29	Entertainment						85.67		
30	Fees, etc.								
31	Tips				15.00	10.00	25.00	20.00	
32	Other								
33									
34	TOTAL DAILY EXPENSES								
35									
36	TOTAL EXPENSES								
37									
38									
39									
40									
41			ACE INDUSTRIAL SUPPLY COMPANY						
42			EXPENSE REPORT						
43									
44	NAME:		Rosa Jiminez						
45	DESTINATION:		Miami, Fla.						
46	PURPOSE:		Sales and Assistance						
47	DATES:		9/25-9/28/--						
48									
49			MILES	@.35	1	2	3	4	TOTALS
50		DATES:			09/25	09/26	09/27	09/28	
51	TRANSPORTATION:								
52	**Airplane**				385.95				
53	Car Expenses:								
54			Miles						
55			Tolls		7.50	3.50	3.50	7.50	
56			Parking			8.50	8.50		
57			Rental		45.00	45.00	45.00	45.00	
58	Taxi								
59	Train								
60	Other								
61									
62	TOTAL TRANSPORTATION								
63									
64	DAILY EXPENSES:								
65	**Hotel**				98	98	98	98	
66	Meals				82.58	78.85	81.56	35.85	
67	Telephone, Fax, etc.				12.98	23.45	14.56	6.78	
68	Copy Services								
69	Entertainment					245.67			
70	Fees, etc.								
71	Tips				20	50	13	15	
72	Other								
73									
74	TOTAL DAILY EXPENSES								
75									
76	TOTAL EXPENSES								

Page break → row 39

KEYSTROKES

INSERT HARD PAGE BREAKS

✓ *After you insert a hard page break, Quattro Pro adjusts the soft page breaks that follow it.*

1. Select row where new page will start.
2. Click **I**nsert .... `Alt`+`I`
3. Click **P**age Break .... `P`

REMOVE HARD PAGE BREAKS

✓ *After you remove a hard page break, Quattro Pro adjusts the soft page breaks that follow it.*

1. Select the cell containing the page break.
2. Click **I**nsert .... `Alt`+`I`
3. Click **P**age Break .... `P`
4. Click **D**elete .... `D`

DISABLE SOFT PAGE BREAKS

1. Click **F**ile .... `Alt`+`F`
2. Click Pa**g**e Setup .... `G`
3. Select **P**rint Margins tab .... `Ctrl`+`Tab`
4. Disable the Bre**a**k Pages option .... `Alt`+`A`
5. Click OK .... `Enter`

SET HEADER AND FOOTER OPTIONS

Adds text or special codes to top or bottom of each page.

1. Click **F**ile .... `Alt`+`F`
2. Click Pa**g**e Setup .... `G`
3. Select **H**eader/Footer tab ...... `Ctrl`+`Tab`
4. Create header/footer text.
5. Place insertion point where code will appear.
6. Type desired code:
   | Moves text to next alignment position–left, center, or right.
   #p   Inserts current page number.
   #P   Inserts total number of pages in document.
   #d   Inserts current date in short format.
   #t   Inserts current time.
   #f   Inserts the name of the notebook.
   #p of #p   Inserts current page number and total number of pages.

CHANGE HEADER/FOOTER FONT

To change the header/footer font:

1. Follow steps 1-3 (under Set Header and Footer Options).
2. Click He**a**der Font .... `Tab`
   OR
   Click **F**ooter Font .... `Tab`
3. Click **T**ypeface .... `Alt`+`T`
4. Select a typeface .... `↓` `↑`
5. Click **P**oint Size .... `Alt`+`P`, `↓` `↑`
6. Select desired font options.
7. Click OK .... `Enter`

ACTIVATE CELL REFERENCE CHECKER

1. Click **T**ools .... `Alt`+`T`
2. Click S**e**ttings .... `E`
3. Select **G**eneral tab .... `Ctrl`+`Tab`
4. Activate C**e**ll Reference Checker .... `Alt`+`E`
5. Click OK .... `Enter`

USE CELL REFERENCE CHECKER

If Cell Reference checker dialog box appears:

1. Click **F**ix It .... `Alt`+`F`
2. Note suggested correction.
3. If you agree, click **C**lose .... `Alt`+`C`
4. If you disagree, click **U**ndo Fix .... `Alt`+`U`
5. Click **C**lose .... `Alt`+`C`

QUATTRO PRO 8 Lesson 3: Formulas and Functions; Edit Information; Print Options

Exercise 15

■ Print Preview ■ Top and Left Headings

Print Preview Toolbar

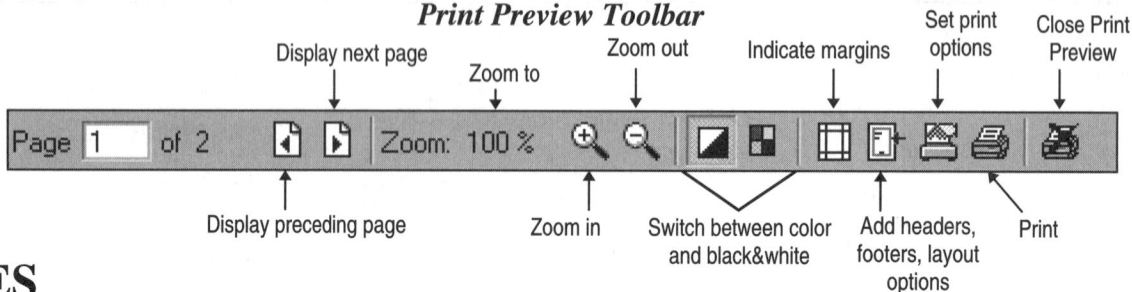

Display next page — Zoom to — Zoom out — Indicate margins — Set print options — Close Print Preview

Page 1 of 2   Zoom: 100 %

Display preceding page — Zoom in — Switch between color and black&white — Add headers, footers, layout options — Print

NOTES

Print Preview

- When working with multiple pages or when establishing print settings, it is advisable to preview your report prior to printing by selecting Print Preview from the File menu. The Print Preview screen has a Toolbar, illustrated above, which allows you to advance through multiple pages in the report, zoom in or out for a better view, switch between color and black and white output views, enter margin grids, change the layout, set print options, print, or simply return to the notebook.

Top and Left Headings

- As a print option, you may print **top and left headings** which come from rows and columns in the notebook. Notebook headings may be useful when:

    - Printing a range that is too wide or too long to fit on one page. Headings will then display on the remaining pages to clarify the data.

    - Printing part of a columnar series of data that does not have column or row headings immediately adjacent to the column of data you wish to print.

- The top or left headings you select from the notebook:

    - Should not be included in the print range.

    - Will appear only on the pages that follow the page containing the heading data.

- Top and left headings are set by selecting Page Setup from the File menu, clicking on the Options tab, and inputting the top or left ranges to indicate which rows or columns you want repeated on every page of the printed notebook. In the illustrated dialog box below, column A is set as the left headings range.

- Note that the Spreadsheet Page Setup Options dialog box below also shows the Gridlines and Row/Column Borders options selected. These settings are used to produce the notebooks illustrated on the following page.

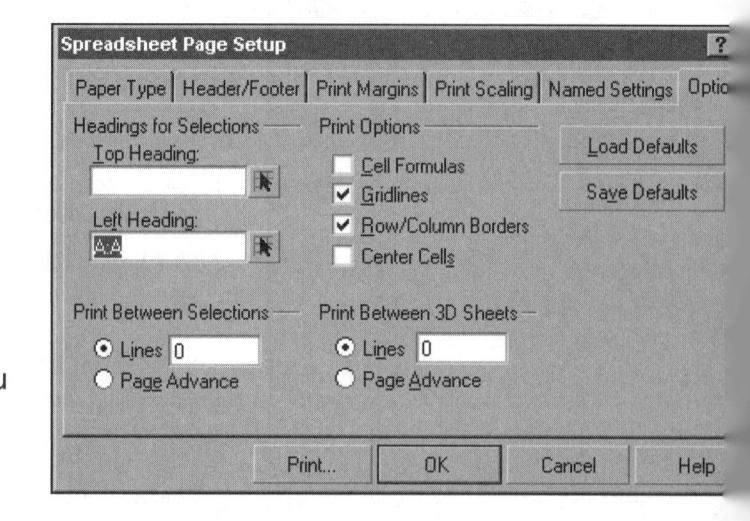

292

✓ *NOTE:* Note the illustrations below. They show the first and second pages of a notebook page that is too wide for one page (using 100% sizing). Since left headings were set for column A, both pages show the labels contained in that column.

Page 1

Left heading →

A	A	B	C	D	E	F	G
1			YANOV COMPUTER STORES				
2			COMPARATIVE INCOME STATEMENT				
3			FOR THE MONTHS ENDED 19–				
4							
5			JANUARY	FEBRUARY	MARCH	APRIL	MAY
6	INCOME:						
7	Commissions		15,689.48	17,865.92	19,876.34	21,781.85	17,656.45
8	Consultations		4,218.47	5,678.98	7,210.56	5,434.49	4,656.23
9	Total Income		19,907.95	23,544.90	27,086.90	27,216.34	22,312.68
10							
11	EXPENSES:						
12	Advertising		145.00	145.00	145.00	165.00	130.00
13	Rent		2,100.00	2,100.00	2,100.00	2,100.00	2,100.00
14	Salaries		10,765.85	10,765.85	10,765.85	10,765.85	10,765.85
15	Payroll Taxes		1,104.55	1,104.55	1,104.55	1,104.55	1,104.55
16	Supplies		143.67	312.85	210.00	215.70	312.65
17	Utilities		287.43	297.81	289.45	278.45	201.16
18	Other		98.76	145.87	24.56	113.45	186.39
19	Total Expenses		14,645.26	14,871.93	14,639.41	14,743.00	14,800.60
20							
21	NET INCOME		5262.69	8672.97	12447.49	12473.34	7512.08

Page 2

Left heading →

A	A	H	I	J
1				
2				
3				
4				
5		JUNE	TOTALS	AVERAGES
6	INCOME:			
7	Commissions	18,234.98	111,105.02	31,744.29
8	Consultations	3,875.98	31,074.71	8,878.49
9	Total Income	22,110.96	142,179.73	40,622.78
10				
11	EXPENSES:			
12	Advertising	170.00	900.00	257.14
13	Rent	2,100.00	12,600.00	3,600.00
14	Salaries	10,765.85	64,595.10	18,455.74
15	Payroll Taxes	1,104.55	6,627.30	1,893.51
16	Supplies	215.98	1,410.85	403.10
17	Utilities	197.40	1,551.70	443.34
18	Other	210.43	779.46	222.70
19	Total Expenses	14,764.21	88,464.41	25,275.55
20				
21	NET INCOME	7346.75	53,715.32	15,347.23

QUATTRO PRO 8 Lesson 3: Formulas and Functions; Edit Information; Print Options

In this exercise, you will create a comparative income statement for Yanov Computer Stores. To print data for only the last three months, it is necessary to set a left heading for the labels in the first column.

EXERCISE DIRECTIONS

1. Create the notebook page as illustrated, or open 15INCOME.

2. Set column widths as follows:
   - Column A: 18
   - Column B: 5
   - Column C-J: 12

3. Format the entire data block for commas with two decimal places.

4. Find for each month:
   - Total Income
   - Total Expenses
   - NET INCOME (Income-Expenses)

5. Find for each item in the income statement:
   - TOTALS
   - AVERAGES

6. Format new data for commas with two decimal places.

7. Center all column headings.

8. Set column A as a left heading as follows: Select Page Setup from the File menu and select the Options tab. Select or enter column A as the left header.
   - ✓ *If you select column A using the selector arrow, the dialog box will collapse. Click the Maximize button to re-display the dialog box, after you have selected the column.*

9. Create a header that includes the page number and total pages centered on the page.
   Hint: 1#p of #p.

10. Select the data to print in B1 to J22 (excluding the heading.) In Page Setup, be sure that scaling is set to 100% of normal size. Preview both pages of the notebook.
    - ✓ *Page one will show column A with JANUARY through JUNE data. Page two will show column A with TOTALS through AVERAGES data, as illustrated.*

11. Print one copy of the two-page report. On the Print dialog box, the Selection option which displays the selected range should be selected.

12. Change width for columns C-J to Quickfit settings.

13. Print one copy of the April-June data with column titles:
    - Highlight the April-June columns. Enter commands to print the selection.
    - Preview the print selection. (The column border was set previously.)
      - ✓ *The April-June data will be shown with the column titles in column A.*
    - Print the selection.

14. Save the notebook file; name it **INCOME**.

15. Close the notebook.

	A	B	C	D	E	F	G	H	I	J	K
1			YANOV COMPUTER STORES								
2			COMPARATIVE INCOME STATEMENT								
3			FOR THE MONTHS ENDED 19–								
4	▶18	▶5	▶12	▶12	▶12	▶12	▶12	▶12	▶12	▶12	
5			JANUARY	FEBRUARY	MARCH	APRIL	MAY	JUNE	TOTALS	AVERAGES	
6	INCOME:										
7	Commissions		15,689.48	17,865.92	19,876.34	21,781.85	17,656.45	18,234.98			
8	Consultations		4,218.47	5,678.98	7,210.56	5,434.49	4,656.23	3,875.98			
9	Total Income							▶	▼	▼	
10											
11	EXPENSES:										
12	Advertising		145.00	145.00	145.00	165.00	130.00	170.00			
13	Rent		2,100.00	2,100.00	2,100.00	2,100.00	2,100.00	2,100.00			
14	Salaries		10,765.85	10,765.85	10,765.85	10,765.85	10,765.85	10,765.85			
15	Payroll Taxes		1,104.55	1,104.55	1,104.55	1,104.55	1,104.55	1,104.55			
16	Supplies		143.67	312.85	210.00	215.70	312.65	215.98			
17	Utilities		287.43	297.81	289.45	278.45	201.16	197.40			
18	Other		98.76	145.87	24.56	113.45	186.39	210.43			
19	Total Expenses							▶			
20											
21	NET INCOME							▶	▼	▼	

KEYSTROKES

SET REPEATING PRINT TITLES FOR NOTEBOOK PAGE

Sets titles to print on current and subsequent pages.

1. Click **File** .... `Alt`+`F`
2. Click **Page Setup** .... `G`
3. Select **Options** tab .... `Ctrl`+`Tab`

To set columns as repeating print headings:

a. Choose **Left heading**. .... `Alt`+`F`

b. Select columns in notebook page.

   OR

   Type column reference.

✓ *Columns must be adjacent. To remove print titles, delete the reference.*

To set rows as repeating print titles:

a. Click **Top heading** .... `Alt`+`T`

b. Select rows in notebook page.

   OR

   Type row reference.

✓ *Rows must be adjacent. To remove print titles, delete the reference.*

4. Click **OK** .... `Enter`

QUATTRO PRO 8 Lesson 3: Formulas and Functions; Edit Information; Print Options

Exercise 16

■ Summary

Mr. Foster would like to continue to add grades to his notebook and average the grades. He has administered three major examinations this term for his English 852 class.

EXERCISE DIRECTIONS

1. Open **GRADE** or **16GRADE**.
2. Add the column headings as indicated in the illustration. Adjust column widths as necessary.
3. Enter the grades for quizzes 1, 2, and 3.
   ✓ *A Blank cell indicates that the student was absent for the quiz.*
4. Find for each student:
   - LAB AVERAGE
   - QUIZ AVERAGE
5. Enter summary labels at the bottom of the notebook as illustrated.
6. Find for each lab and quiz:
   - NO. OF PAPERS
   - CLASS AVERAGE
   - HIGHEST GRADE
   - LOWEST GRADE
7. Format all averages to one decimal place.
8. Center all column titles.
9. Create a series to number students consecutively beginning with 1 in the STUDENT NUMBER column.
10. Print one copy in landscape orientation so that it fits on one page.
11. Close and save the file; name it **GRADE**.

A	A	B	C	D	E	F	G	H	I	J	K	L
1	CLASS:		SCIENCE 105									
2	TERM:		SPRING 199-									
3	TEACHER:		MR. FOSTER									
4							LAB				QUIZ	STUDENT
5	IDNO.	NAME		LAB 1	LAB 2	LAB 3	AVERAGE	QUIZ 1	QUIZ 2	QUIZ 3	AVERAGE	NUMBER
6												
7	1245	Bell, D.		90	88	92		92	90	93		1
8	4123	Dorchester, T.		55	70	75		58	69	78		
9	1255	Garcia, L		75	80	82		70	78	80		
10	3331	Levine, M.		78	75	80		75	80	80		
11	2121	Livingston, F.		77	85	80		75	82	85		
12	1234	Pella, J.		55	45	55		57	45			
13	2323	Ruiz, G.		82	80	85		85	78	88		
14	1332	Trevino, S.		92	85	80		90	82	85		
15	2143	West, D.		45	56	58	▼		46	50	▼	▼
16	1112	Zdan, M.		82	85	85		85	80	83		
17												
18	NO. OF PAPERS										▶	
19	CLASS AVERAGE										▶	
20	HIGHEST GRADE										▶	
21	LOWEST GRADE										▶	

Exercise 17

- Insert Columns and Rows
- Delete Columns and Rows
- Move (Cut/Paste and Drag/Drop)
- Copy (Drag/Drop)

Lesson 4: Additional Formatting and Editing; Work with Workbooks

NOTES

Insert Columns and Rows

- It is recommended that you save the notebook before you insert, delete, move, or copy data so you can retrieve the original notebook page in the event of an error. Inserting, deleting, moving, or copying data can affect formulas and data. Check that formulas are correct after an insert, delete, move, or copy operation.

- Columns and/or rows may be inserted or deleted to change the structure of a notebook page. Inserting a column or row creates a blank area. Existing columns or rows shift to allow for the newly created space. To insert columns or rows, select Row or Column from the Insert menu. New rows appear above the insert point and new columns appear to the left of the insert point. Or you can use the Insert Cells button on the Notebook Toolbar. When you click the button or select Insert, Cells, the dialog box below displays.

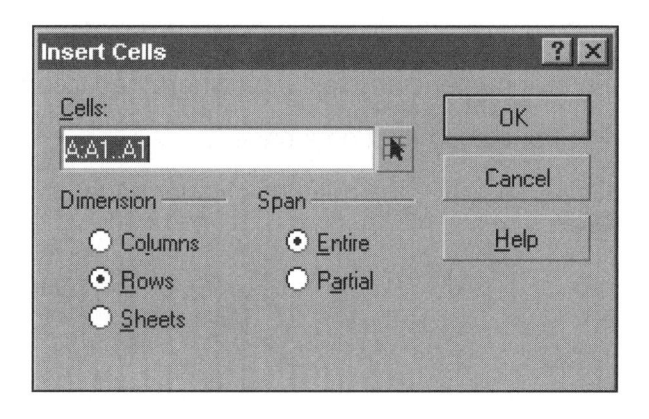

- You can insert rows, columns, or pages from the Insert Cells dialog box. The Span options allow you to set whole or partial columns, rows, or page.

Delete Columns and Rows

- When a column or row is deleted, all data in that column or row is eliminated. Remaining columns or rows shift to fill in the space left by the deletion. To delete a column or row, select the row or column and select Edit, Delete, and then Row or Column. Or, you can use the Delete Block button on the Notebook Toolbar. The button will display a Delete Cells dialog box illustrated below.

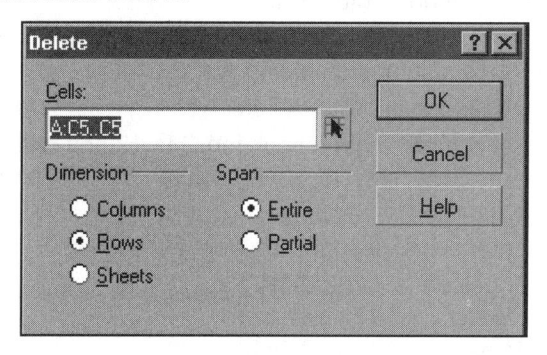

Move (Cut/Paste and Drag/Drop)

- When you move data, the data is removed from one location and inserted into another. You may choose to overwrite existing data or insert the data and shift existing data in the direction that you specify. The Cut (Ctrl+X) and Paste (Ctrl+V) commands are on the Edit menu and may be activated using either the keyboard or Toolbar. These commands may also be activated by right-clicking the active cell. Moving data can also be accomplished by selecting the range and dragging it to the paste location (known as **drag and drop**). The mouse pointer will change to a double crossbar during the drag and drop procedure.

- The format of data will be moved along with the data itself.

QUATTRO PRO 8 Lesson 4: Additional Formatting and Editing; Work with Workbooks

Copy (Drag/Drop)

- Data and its format may also be copied by using the drag and drop method. To copy a cell or a range of cells, select the cell or range, position the mouse so it becomes a hand with a double cross bar and press the Ctrl key. Then click and drag the cell to its new location. Next release the mouse.

In this exercise, you will insert, delete, and move columns and rows to include additional information in the Medallion Music Stores payroll notebook page. In addition, a new payroll notebook page will be created below the existing one for the new pay period.

EXERCISE DIRECTIONS

1. Open **PAY** or **17PAY**.

2. Make the following changes on the top payroll as shown in the illustration below:
   - Insert a new column A.
   - Move all the data and headings in column C (Emp. Name column) to column A.
   - Move logo in cell B1 to cell A1.
   - Set column width for column C to 12 and enter the label Soc. Sec. No. as the column title. Center the column heading.
   - Enter social security numbers as follows:

Engelson	070-12-3821
Gomez	174-16-1234
Jordan	108-12-0810
Kelly	102-12-3111
Romano	108-28-4429
Unger	060-10-3100

   - Copy the Soc. Sec. No. column title and data from the 2/6/9- payroll to the 2/13/9- payroll.
   - Copy the entire 2/13/9- payroll, including the title, to a new location below the existing notebook page.

3. Make the following changes on the bottom payroll only:
   - Edit the subtitle to read:
     FOR THE WEEK ENDING 2/20/9-
   - Delete the row containing data for Jordan.
   - Insert a row where necessary to maintain alphabetical order for a new employee named Polla.
     Enter the following information for Polla:
     Employee Number: 335
     Soc. Sec. No.:   222-30-1010
     Hourly Rate: $8.75
   - Edit the HOURS WORKED as follows:

Engelson	28
Gomez	25
Kelly	22
Polla	18
Romano	30
Unger	26

   - Copy payroll formulas to complete Polla's data.

4. Format numeric and text data where necessary.

5. Print one copy to fit on a page.

6. Close and save the notebook file, or *save as* **PAY**.

Insert new column A.

	A	B	C	D	E	F	G	H	I
1	MMsMMs				MEDALLION MUSIC STORES				MMsMMs
2					PAYROLL FOR THE WEEK ENDING 2/6/98				
3									
4	Employee	Employee	Hourly	Hours	Gross	Federal	Soc. Sec	Medicare	Net
5	Number	Name	Rate	Worked	Pay	With. Tax	Tax	Tax	Pay
6									
7	272	Engelson	7.25	21	152.25	30.45	9.44	2.21	110.15
8	320	Gomez	7.75	19	147.25	29.45	9.13	2.14	106.54
9	322	Jordan	8.25	21	173.25	34.65	10.74	2.51	125.35
10	330	Kelly	9.95	35	348.25	69.65	21.59	5.05	251.96
11	340	Romano	9.75	35	341.25	68.25	21.16	4.95	246.89
12	341	Unger	8.45	15	126.75	25.35	7.86	1.84	91.70
13									
14	Totals				1289.00	257.80	79.92	18.69	932.59
15	Averages				214.83	42.97	13.32	3.12	155.43
16									
17					PAYROLL FOR THE WEEK ENDING 2/13/98				
18									
19	Employee	Employee	Hourly	Hours	Gross	Federal	Soc. Sec	Medicare	Net
20	Number	Name	Rate	Worked	Pay	With. Tax	Tax	Tax	Pay
21									
22	272	Engelson	7.25	26	188.50	37.70	11.69	2.73	136.38
23	320	Gomez	7.75	23	178.25	35.65	11.05	2.58	128.96
24	322	Jordan	8.25	20	165.00	33.00	10.23	2.39	119.38
25	330	Kelly	9.95	30	298.50	59.70	18.51	4.33	215.96
26	340	Romano	9.75	32	312.00	62.40	19.34	4.52	225.73
27	341	Unger	8.45	22	185.90	37.18	11.53	2.70	134.50
28									
29	Totals				1328.15	265.63	82.35	19.26	960.92
30	Averages				221.36	44.27	13.72	3.21	160.15

Move column B data to the new column.

KEYSTROKES

INSERT COLUMNS/ROWS

These commands Insert blank columns or rows and shifts existing columns or rows to make room for the insertion.

1. Select as many adjacent columns or rows as you want to add to notebook page.
   - ✓ *If you select cells, be sure to select the entire column or row option in the dialog box. New columns will be placed to the left of the highlighted columns. New rows will be placed above the highlighted rows.*

2. Click **Insert** .... `Alt` + `I`
3. Click **Co**l**umn** .... `L`

   OR

   Click **R**ow .... `R`

DELETE COLUMNS/ROWS

Deletes columns or rows and the data they contain. Existing columns or rows shift to fill in the space left by the deletion.

1. Select column(s) or row(s) to delete.
   - ✓ *Be sure to select the entire column or row. When deleting more than one row or column, select adjacent columns or rows.*

2. Click **E**dit .... `Alt` + `E`
3. Click **D**elete .... `D`
4. Choose **Co**l**umns** .... `Alt` + `L`

   OR

   Choose **R**ows .... `Alt` + `R`

INSERT CELLS

1. Place cursor at point of insertion.
2. Click **I**nsert .... `Alt` + `I`
3. Click **C**ells .... `C`
4. Click **Co**l**umns** .... `Alt` + `L`

   OR

   Click **R**ows .... `Alt` + `R`

   OR

   Click **S**heets .... `Alt` + `S`

5. Click **OK** .... `Enter`

🌐 MOVE (CUT/PASTE) USING THE MENU

Ctrl + X, Ctrl + V

Moves data in a cell, or a range of cells, to another area.

1. Select cell or range to move.
2. Click **E**dit menu .... `Alt` + `E`
3. Click Cu**t** .... `T`
4. Select cell or range to receive data.
   - ✓ *You only have to specify the top left cell. The destination range can be in another notebook or notebook page.*
5. Click **E**dit .... `Alt` + `E`
6. Click **P**aste .... `P`

🌐 MOVE (DRAG AND DROP)

Moves data in a cell, or range of cells, to another area.

1. Select cell or range to cut.
2. Move mouse pointer to edge of range.
   Pointer becomes a crossbar.
3. Click and move to new location.
4. Release mouse button.

🌐 COPY (DRAG AND DROP)

Copies data in a cell, or range of cells, to another area.

1. Select cell or range to copy.
2. Move mouse pointer to edge of range.
   Pointer becomes a crossbar.

To copy and overwrite existing data in destination cells:

a. Press **Ctrl** .... `Ctrl`
   and click left mouse button.
   Pointer becomes a hand and a crossbar.
b. Drag border outline to new location.
c. Release the key, then mouse button.

QUATTRO PRO 8 Lesson 4: Additional Formatting and Editing; Work with Workbooks

Exercise 18

■ Copy and Paste Special ■ Transpose Data

NOTES

Copy and Paste Special

■ **Paste Special** is a feature that gives you added control during the pasting process once data has been copied. As shown in the illustration of the Paste Special dialog box on the right, you can select which features in a block will be pasted, i.e. Formula Cells, Label Cells, Number Cells, Properties or Cell Comments. The following options are also available: Avoid Pasting Blanks, Transpose Rows and Columns, and Paste Formulas as Values. In this exercise, we will use the Transpose feature in the Paste Special dialog box.

Transpose Data

■ Use the **Transpose** feature to copy and rearrange data so that data in rows can be copied to columns and vice versa. Data can be transposed by copying the data and then choosing Paste Special from the Edit menu and clicking the Transpose Rows and Columns option. Note the illustration of the Paste Special dialog box and the illustration of transposed data. The labels in column B, when transposed are pasted to row 5.

Paste Special Dialog Box

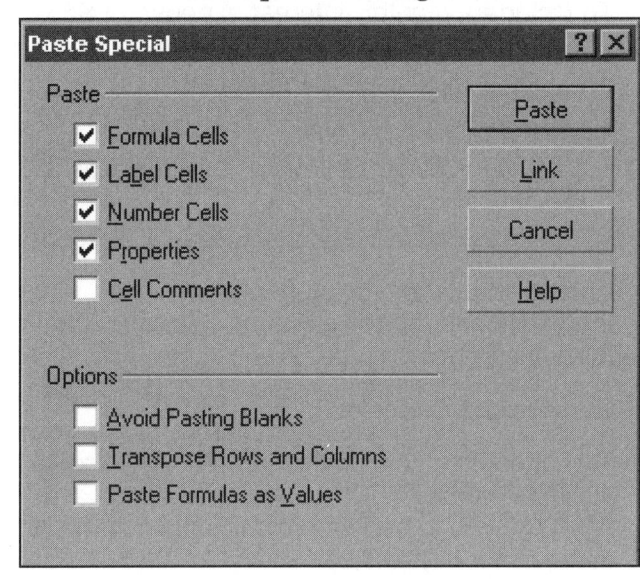

Transposed Data

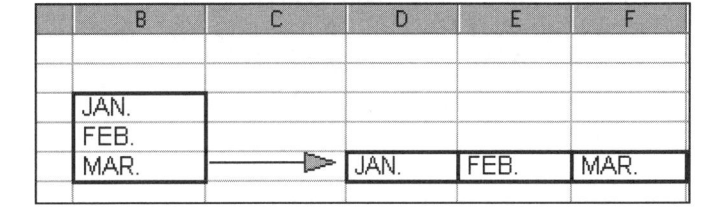

■ Note the following precautions when transposing data:

- Choose an area outside the selected range in which to copy the transposed data; otherwise, the data will become garbled.

- If you are transposing values that are the result of formulas, you must also select the Paste Formulas as Values option in the Paste Special dialog box, since the formulas will not work in their new locations.

QUATTRO PRO 8 Lesson 4: Additional Formatting and Editing; Work with Workbooks

In this exercise, you will insert a new expense item in the Yanov Computer Store notebook. In addition, you will use transposed data from the Income Statement to prepare an income statement analysis.

EXERCISE DIRECTIONS

1. Open **INCOME** or **18INCOME**.

2. Delete column B.

3. Set Column widths for Column B through column H to 12.

4. To include a monthly interest expense of $25:
   - Insert a row between Utilities and Other.
   - Enter the label: Interest.
   - Enter $25 for each month.
   - Copy the TOTALS and AVERAGES formulas for the interest line.
   - Format the interest line for two decimal places.

5. Enter new title and column labels below the existing notebook page, as illustrated on the following page.

6. Center column labels.

7. Transpose the column titles JANUARY through JUNE, including TOTALS and excluding AVERAGES, to become row titles in column A in the range A29:A35.

8. Transpose Total Income data for JANUARY through JUNE, including TOTALS and excluding AVERAGES, to become row data for column B in the range B29:B35.
   - ✓ *Be sure to select the Paste Formulas as Values option when transposing.*

9. Transpose Total Expenses data for JANUARY through JUNE, including TOTALS and excluding AVERAGES, to become row data for column D in the range D29:D35.
   - ✓ *Be sure to select the Paste Formulas as Values option when transposing.*

10. Transpose NET INCOME data for J0ANUARY through JUNE, including TOTALS and excluding AVERAGES, to become row data for column F in the range F29:F35.
    - ✓ *Be sure to select the Paste Formulas as Values option when transposing.*

11. Enter formulas in the % OF TOTAL columns to find what percent each item is of the six month total for each item.
    HINT: Use an absolute reference for the TOTAL in the formulas.

12. Format % OF TOTAL columns for percentage with one decimal place.

13. Print one copy to fit on a page. Change previous print settings as follows.
    - Remove option to print left headings.
    - Change print selection to print the notebook.

14. Close and save the notebook file, or *save as* **INCOME**.

	A	B	C	D	E	F	G	H	I	J
1			YANOV COMPUTER STORES							
2	*Delete column B*		COMPARATIVE INCOME STATEMENT							
3			FOR THE MONTHS ENDED 19–							
4										
5			JANUARY	FEBRUARY	MARCH	APRIL	MAY	JUNE	TOTALS	AVERAGES
6	INCOME:									
7	Commissions		15,689.48	17,865.92	19,876.34	21,781.85	17,656.45	18,234.98	111,105.02	31,744.29
8	Consultations		4,218.47	5,678.98	7,210.56	5,434.49	4,656.23	3,875.98	31,074.71	8,878.49
9	Total Income		19907.95	23544.9	27086.9	27216.34	22312.68	22110.96	142179.73	40622.78
10										
11	EXPENSES:									
12	Advertising		145.00	145.00	145.00	165.00	130.00	170.00	900.00	257.14
13	Rent		2,100.00	2,100.00	2,100.00	2,100.00	2,100.00	2,100.00	12,600.00	3,600.00
14	Salaries		10,765.85	10,765.85	10,765.85	10,765.85	10,765.85	10,765.85	64,595.10	18,455.74
15	Payroll Taxes		1,104.55	1,104.55	1,104.55	1,104.55	1,104.55	1,104.55	6,627.30	1,893.51
16	Supplies		143.67	312.85	210.00	215.70	312.65	215.98	1,410.85	403.10
17	Utilities		287.43	297.81	289.45	278.45	201.16	197.40	1,551.70	443.34
18	Other		98.76	145.87	24.56	113.45	186.39	210.43	779.46	222.70
19	Total Expenses		14645.26	14871.93	14639.41	14743	14800.6	14764.21	88464.41	25275.5457
20										
21	NET INCOME		5262.69	8672.97	12447.49	12473.34	7512.08	7346.75	53715.32	15347.2343
22			*Transpose*							
23										
24			INCOME STATEMENT ANALYSIS							
25			YANOV COMPUTER STORES							
26										
27			TOTAL	%OF	TOTAL	%OF	NET	% OF		
28	MONTH		INCOME	TOTAL	EXPENSES	TOTAL	INCOME	TOTAL		
29										
30										
31										
32										
33										
34										
35										

Insert row (pointing to row 17)

KEYSTROKES

TRANSPOSE DATA

Copies and transposes data from horizontal to vertical arrangement and vice versa.

Ctrl + C

1. Select range to transpose.
2. Click **E**dit .... Alt + E
3. Click **C**opy C
4. Click upper-left cell .... ↑↓←→
   to receive transposed data.
5. Click **E**dit .... Alt + E
6. Click Paste **S**pecial .... S
7. Click **T**ranspose Rows
   and Columns .... Alt + T

   If formulas are to be transposed:
   Click
   Paste Formulas as **V**alues .... Alt + V

8. Click **OK** .... Enter

QUATTRO PRO 8 Lesson 4: Additional Formatting and Editing; Work with Workbooks

Exercise 19

- **Lock Titles**
- **Split Panes**
- **Copy and Paste Special**

NOTES

Lock Titles

- Quattro Pro provides two methods for working with large notebook pages: locking titles to keep them in view and splitting the window into panes that can be scrolled.

- To keep headings or titles in view at the left or top edge of the notebook page when scrolling, it is necessary to hold, or lock, them in place. To lock row or column titles, place your cursor in the row or column after the titles area, then select Locked Titles from the View menu. A blue line will appear to the left of and/or above the cursor. You can scroll the worksheet as illustrated below and the titles will remain locked.

	A	K	L	M	N
2					
3					
4			HALF-YEAR		3RD QTR.
5	INCOME:	JULY	AUGUST	SEPTEMBER	TOTALS
6	Commissions	17,444.84	16,545.83	19,589.45	53,580.12
7	Consultations	3,415.89	2,454.91	3,456.79	9,327.59
8	Total Income	20,860.73	19,000.74	23,046.24	62,907.71
9					
10	EXPENSES:				

Split Panes

- You can view different sections of a large notebook page at one time by splitting the screen into separate panes. Each pane can be used to access information from different parts of the document. For example, you may wish to compare data at the top of your notebook with the data at the bottom. Splitting the window into separate panes allows you to see both sections.

- When you split a window vertically, the panes move together when you scroll up or down, but they move independently when you scroll left and right.

- When you split a window horizontally, the panes move together when you scroll left or right, but they move independently when you scroll up and down.

- A notebook can be divided into panes using the pane splitter button, which is located in the lower right corner of the notebook, or by selecting Split Window from the View menu. The Pane Splitter button and the Split Windows dialog box are illustrated below and at the top of the next column, with an example of a vertically split screen view.

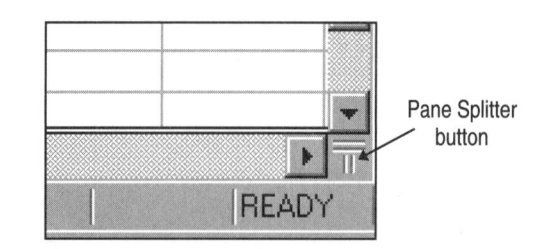

Split Window Dialog Box

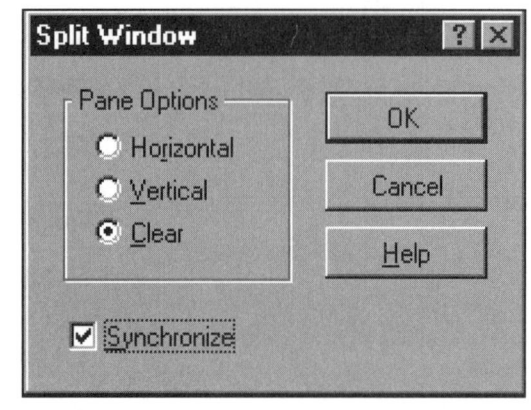

304

Vertically Split Screen

	A	B	C	D		K	L	M	N
1		COMPARATIVE INCOME STATEM			1				
2		FOR THE MONTHS ENDED 19–			2				
3					3				
4		JANUARY	FEBRUARY	MARCH	4	HALF-YEAR			3RD QTR.
5	INCOME:				5	JULY	AUGUST	SEPTEMBER	TOTALS
6	Commissions	15,689.48	17,865.92	19,876.3	6	17,444.84	16,545.83	19,589.45	53,580.12
7	Consultations	4,218.47	5,678.98	7,210.5	7	3,415.89	2,454.91	3,456.79	9,327.59
8	Total Income	19,907.95	23,544.90	27,086.9	8	20,860.73	19,000.74	23,046.24	62,907.71
9					9				

- When you click the Synchronize option for a split notebook page, the top and/or left panes lock when you scroll through the notebook page.

Copy and Paste Special
- New notebooks can be created to store new or extracted data.
- Use the Copy and Paste Special commands to copy part of a notebook page into another notebook. The dialog box that appears depends on the type of data copied to the clipboard.

- If you want to paste the results of formulas, mark the Paste Formulas as Values check box in the Paste Special dialog box. If you want to paste the formulas themselves, leave the check box blank.

- When working with more than one notebook at a time, you can use the Window menu to select the notebook you want to activate.

QUATTRO PRO 8 Lesson 4: Additional Formatting and Editing; Work with Workbooks

> *In this exercise, you will divide the Yanov Computer Stores data into quarterly information by inserting and deleting columns. Because inserting or deleting columns from the top portion of the notebook page will affect the bottom portion, you will first extract the bottom portion of the notebook page, save it to another file, and delete it from the original. The top portion of the notebook page will then be expanded and edited.*

EXERCISE DIRECTIONS

1. Open **INCOME** or **19INCOME**.

2. Use the Copy and Paste Special commands to extract the Income Statement Analysis portion of the notebook page to a new notebook:
   - Copy Income Statement Analysis portion of notebook.
   - Open new notebook.
   - Click cell A1.
   - Paste Special, using Paste Formulas as Values option.
   - Save the new notebook file; name it **ISANA**.

3. Switch to the **INCOME** notebook.

4. Delete the Income Statement Analysis portion from the **INCOME** notebook page.

5. Insert a column between MARCH and APRIL and enter the column titles:
   1ST QTR.
   TOTALS

6. Find 1ST QTR. TOTALS.

7. Format the new column for two decimal places and adjust column width as necessary.

8. Copy the formula to the remaining items.

9. Insert a column between JUNE and TOTALS and enter the column title:
   2ND QTR.
   TOTALS

10. Copy the formulas for 1ST QTR. TOTALS to the column for 2ND QTR. TOTALS.

11. Edit column title TOTALS to read:
    HALF-YEAR
    TOTALS

12. Delete the AVERAGES column.

13. Edit the formula in the HALF-YEAR TOTALS column to add 1ST QTR. TOTALS and 2ND QTR. TOTALS.

14. Lock titles in column A.

15. Enter third quarter data indicated below beginning in the next available column of your notebook page.

	JULY	AUGUST	SEPTEMBER
Commissions	17,444.84	16,545.83	19,589.45
Consultations	3,415.89	2,454.91	3,456.79
Advertising	125.86	225.67	225.68
Rent	2100.00	2100.00	2100.00
Salaries	9856.58	9856.58	10,810.59
Payroll Taxes	985.67	985.67	985.67
Supplies	145.67	135.75	156.89
Utilities	186.86	175.69	145.55
Interest	25.00	25.00	25.00
Other	105.54	98.56	145.95

16. Copy and edit formulas, where necessary, to complete the notebook page.

17. Find 3RD QTR. TOTALS.

18. Copy the formula to the remaining items.

19. Center all column heading labels. Set column width for columns K-N to 12.00.

20. Format numeric data for two decimal places.

21. Print one copy of **INCOME** in landscape orientation to fit on a page.

22. Close and save the notebook; name it **INCOME**.

23. In the **ISANA** notebook: format and align data as needed.

24. Print one copy.

25. Close and save the notebook; name it **ISANA**.

YANOV COMPUTER STORES
COMPARATIVE INCOME STATEMENT
FOR THE MONTHS ENDED 19—

Insert Column: 1st QTR TOTALS
Insert Column: 2nd QTR TOTALS
Delete column

	JANUARY	FEBRUARY	MARCH	APRIL	MAY	JUNE	TOTALS	AVERAGES	JULY	AUGUST	SEPTEMBER
INCOME:											
Commissions	15,689.48	17,865.92	19,876.34	21,781.85	17,656.45	18,234.98	111,105.02	31,744.29			
Consultations	4,218.47	5,678.98	7,210.56	5,434.49	4,656.23	3,875.98	31,074.71	8,878.49			
Total Income	19,907.95	23,544.90	27,086.90	27,216.34	22,312.68	22,110.96	142,179.73	40,622.78			
EXPENSES:											
Advertising	145.00	145.00	145.00	165.00	130.00	170.00	900.00	257.14			
Rent	2,100.00	2,100.00	2,100.00	2,100.00	2,100.00	2,100.00	12,600.00	3,600.00			
Salaries	10,765.85	10,765.85	10,765.85	10,765.85	10,765.85	10,765.85	64,595.10	18,455.74			
Payroll Taxes	1,104.55	1,104.55	1,104.55	1,104.55	1,104.55	1,104.55	6,627.30	1,893.51			
Supplies	143.67	312.85	210.00	215.70	312.65	215.98	1,410.85	403.10			
Utilities	287.43	297.81	289.45	278.45	201.16	197.40	1,551.70	443.34			
Interest	25.00	25.00	25.00	25.00	25.00	25.00	150.00	42.86			
Other	98.76	145.87	24.56	113.45	186.39	210.43	779.46	222.70			
Total Expenses	14,670.26	14,896.93	14,664.41	14,768.00	14,825.60	14,789.21	88,614.41	25,318.40			
NET INCOME	5237.69	8647.97	12422.49	12448.34	7487.08	7321.75	53,565.32	15,304.38			

INCOME STATEMENT ANALYSIS
YANOV COMPUTER STORES

MONTH	TOTAL INCOME	% OF TOTAL	TOTAL EXPENSES	% OF TOTAL	NET INCOME	% OF TOTAL
JANUARY	19,907.95	14.0%	14,670.26	16.6%	5237.69	9.8%
FEBRUARY	23,544.90	16.6%	14,896.93	16.8%	8647.97	16.1%
MARCH	27,086.90	19.1%	14,664.41	16.5%	12422.49	23.2%
APRIL	27,216.34	19.1%	14,768.00	16.7%	12448.34	23.2%
MAY	22,312.68	15.7%	14,825.60	16.7%	7487.08	14.0%
JUNE	22,110.96	15.6%	14,789.21	16.7%	7321.75	13.7%
TOTALS	142,179.73	100.0%	88,614.41	100.0%	53,565.32	100.0%

Extract to new notebook ISANA.

KEYSTROKES

COPY AND PASTE SPECIAL (EXTRACT DATA)

Copies a portion of the current notebook page to a new notebook.

Ctrl + C

1. Copy range to extract to the clipboard:
   a. Select range of notebook page to extract.
   b. Click **E**dit .... Alt + E
   c. Click **C**opy C
2. Open a new notebook:
   a. Click **F**ile .... Alt + F
   b. Click **N**ew .... N
3. Use Paste Special command:
   a. Click **E**dit .... Alt + E
   b. Click Paste **S**pecial .... S
   c. Click Paste Formulas as **V**alues .... Alt + V
      to copy data as it appears in cells (results of formulas).
   d. Click **P**aste .... P
4. Save and name the new notebook.
   a. Click **F**ile .... Alt + F
   b. Click Save **A**s .... A
   c. Type new filename .... *filename*
   d. Click **S**ave .... Alt + S

CREATE NEW NOTEBOOK

Opens a new notebook based on the default template.

Click **New Notebook** button on the Standard toolbar ....

OR

1. Click **F**ile .... Alt + F
2. Click **N**ew .... N

SELECT NOTEBOOK

✓ *When more than one notebook is open, the notebook you want to access may be hidden or reduced to an icon. In order to use a hidden or reduced notebook, follow one of the listed methods.*

Click anywhere on notebook window.

OR

Double click on a Notebook icon.

OR

1. Click **W**indow menu .... Alt + W
2. Select name of notebook .... ↓
   near bottom of the menu.

SPLIT NOTEBOOK PAGE INTO PANES USING SPLIT BOXES

Provides simultaneous scrolling of up to two panes. You can lock panes (see right) to prevent top, left, or both panes from scrolling.

1. Click **V**iew .... Alt + V
2. Click Split **W**indow .... W
3. Select options.

OR

1. Point to the **Split View** button on the scroll bar.
   ✓ *Pointer becomes a* ←|→
2. Drag pointer along scroll bar until split bar is in desired position.

REMOVE SPLIT BARS

Point to **Split View** button on the scroll bar.

Drag split bar to the top, bottom, left, or right.

OR

1. Click **V**iew .... Alt + V
2. Click Split **W**indow .... W
3. Click **C**lear C
4. Click OK .... Enter

ADJUST NOTEBOOK PAGE PANES

1. Point to **Split View** button on the scroll bar.
   Pointer becomes a ←|→
2. Drag pointer along scroll bar until split bar is in desired position.

MOVE BETWEEN NOTEBOOK PAGE PANES

Click desired pane.

OR

Press **F6** F6
until active cell is in desired pane.

LOCK TITLES

Locks top and/or left pane when scrolling. Select column to the right or row below data to be locked.

1. Click **V**iew .... Alt + V
2. Click **L**ocked Titles L

UNLOCK TITLES

1. Click **V**iew .... Alt + V
2. Click **L**ocked Titles L

QUATTROPRO 8 Lesson 4: Additional Formatting and Editing; Work with Workbooks

Exercise 20

- Notebook Sheets
- Group Sheets
- Print Notebook

NOTES

Notebook Sheets

- By default, each new notebook contains 256 notebook sheets labeled A through IV. Sheet tabs show the names of the sheets *(see illustration below)*.

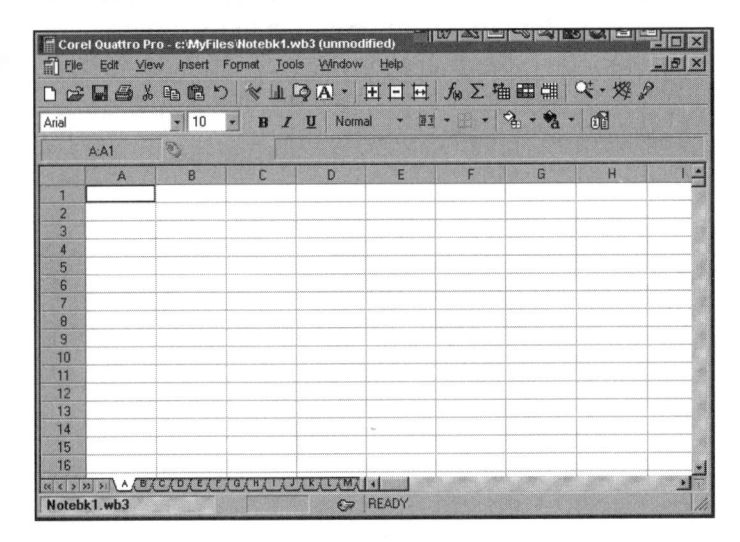

Active Sheet Dialog Box

- Quattro Pro lets you work with sheets by using the Active Sheet dialog box. This dialog box displays when you right-click the sheet tab and select Sheet Properties. You may then set such features as page display, name, colors, protection, default cell widths, and a zoom factor. These features let you modify your notebook sheets to fit your work objectives. Note the illustration of the Active Sheet dialog box at the top right. To rename a sheet tab quickly, you can double-click the tab and enter the new name.

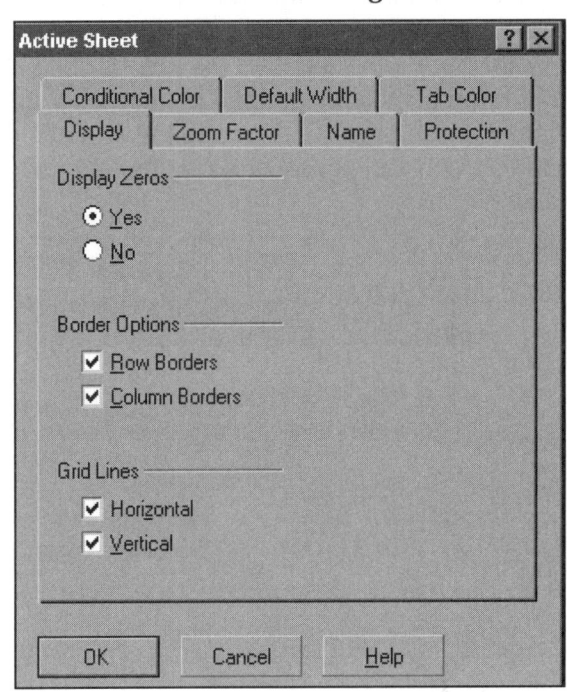

- Quattro Pro provides tab scrolling controls at the lower left of the notebook window. You can click these buttons to move the sheet tab display. Note that the last scroll control moves you to and from the Objects sheet. The Objects sheet is always the last sheet in a notebook and is used to display icons for every chart in the notebook. This sheet will be discussed in Lesson 6, Exercise 31, Charts.

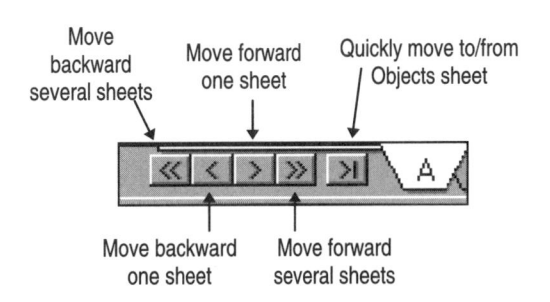

Move backward several sheets
Move forward one sheet
Quickly move to/from Objects sheet

Move backward one sheet
Move forward several sheets

- You can insert new sheets by selecting Shee<u>t</u> from the <u>I</u>nsert menu.

Group Sheets

- You can select multiple sheets, which is called **grouping**, to work on several sheets simultaneously. Select each of the sheets while holding down the Shift key, then select <u>N</u>ame, <u>G</u>roup of Sheets from the <u>I</u>nsert menu to name and define the group.

- Once pages are grouped, Group Mode must be enabled in order to view and make changes to the pages as a group. Select <u>G</u>roup Mode from the <u>V</u>iew menu and a check will appear next to the command indicating that it is active. Selected page tabs will then appear with an underline connecting the grouped pages, as illustrated below.

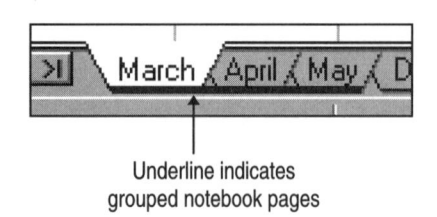

Underline indicates grouped notebook pages

- Formats changed on one page will now affect all grouped pages. To make formatting changes to individual pages in the group, you must first deselect <u>G</u>roup Mode from the <u>V</u>iew menu to disable the command. If you wish to enter data through all pages at once, you must press Ctrl + Enter to enter the text while in group mode.

Print Notebook

- You can tell Quattro Pro to print all the data on all the sheets in your notebook by selecting File, <u>P</u>rint and choosing the <u>N</u>otebook option in the Spreadsheet Print dialog box. When you select the notebook option, Quattro Pro will print all data on as few pages as possible. You can also click the P<u>a</u>ge Setup button (in the Spreadsheet Print dialog box), select the Print Scaling tab and choose Print to desired width to fit the entire notebook on one or more pages. Or, select Print to % of normal size to manually adjust the desired print size.

In this exercise, you will create a payroll template for future use. To do this, you will delete unnecessary sheet tabs, insert and rename sheet tabs, and work with grouped sheets to edit data on more than one notebook page at a time.

EXERCISE DIRECTIONS

1. Open **PAY** or **20PAY**.
2. Resave the notebook file as **PAYTM**.
3. Click page tab labeled B to select it.
   - ✓ *Note that page B is empty.*
4. Select Page A.
5. Use tab scrolling buttons to scroll to last page.
6. Select Page A, double-click and rename the page February.
7. Insert a page using Insert, Sheet, and name it March.
8. Move the March page to the right of the February page. (Click and drag the sheet tab.)
9. Select and double-click page C, rename it April.
10. Select the February page. To make payrolls uniform:
    - Jordan has left our employment; delete the Jordan rows in the top two payrolls.
    - Copy the Polla information from the last payroll to the first two payrolls in the correct order. (Be sure to insert a row first.)
    - Edit the titles in each week's payroll to read: FOR THE WEEK ENDING
        - ✓ *Delete the dates.*
11. Select all the data on the FEBRUARY page and copy it to the clipboard.
    - HINT: *You can click the Select All button (the top left corner of the worksheet) to select the entire notebook page.*
12. Paste the worksheet to cell A1 on the March and April pages.
13. Select the February page.
14. Click cell A1 to deselect the range.
15. Select all the pages in the notebook (February through April):
    - Select the sheets while the Shift key is down.
    - Click Insert, Name, Group of Sheets and name the group FebApr.
    - Check that Group Mode is selected on the View menu.
16. WHILE ALL PAGES ARE GROUPED
    a. Use Edit, Clear, Values to clear the data in the cells containing the hours worked for each employee in each payroll week. (Do not delete the column.) This will result in zeros for payroll data.
    b. Deselect View, Group Mode.
    c. Check that each page contains identical data.
    d. Set page setup print scaling to fit on one page when printed.
       - ✓ *There are no print page options for a group.*
17. Print preview and print the entire notebook.
    - ✓ *All sheets will print on one page. You can print one sheet at a time by using the Current Sheet option on the print dialog box.*
18. Close and save the notebook file.

QUATTRO PRO 8 Lesson 4: Additional Formatting and Editing; Work with Workbooks

△	A	B	C	D	E	F	G	H	I	J
1	MMsMMs				MEDALLION MUSIC STORES					MMsMMs
2					PAYROLL FOR THE WEEK ENDING 2/6/98					
3										
4	Employee	Employee	Soc. Sec.	Hourly	Hours	Gross	Federal	Soc. Sec	Medicare	Net
5	Name	Number	No.	Rate	Worked	Pay	With. Tax	Tax	Tax	Pay
6										
7	Engelson	272	070-12-3821	7.25	21	152.25	30.45	9.44	2.21	110.15
8	Gomez	320	174-16-1234	7.75	19	147.25	29.45	9.13	2.14	106.54
9	Jordan	322	108-12-0810	8.25	21	173.25	34.65	10.74	2.51	125.35
10	Kelly	330	102-12-3111	9.95	35	348.25	69.65	21.59	5.05	251.96
11	Romano	340	108-28-4429	9.75	35	341.25	68.25	21.16	4.95	246.89
12	Unger	341	060-10-3100	8.45	15	126.75	25.35	7.86	1.84	91.70
13										
14		Totals				1289.00	257.80	79.92	18.69	932.59
15		Averages				214.83	42.97	13.32	3.12	155.43
16										
17					PAYROLL FOR THE WEEK ENDING 2/6/98					
18										
19	Employee	Employee	Soc. Sec.	Hourly	Hours	Gross	Federal	Soc. Sec	Medicare	Net
20	Name	Number	No.	Rate	Worked	Pay	With. Tax	Tax	Tax	Pay
21										
22	Engelson	272	070-12-3821	7.25	26	188.5	37.7	11.69	2.73	136.38
23	Gomez	320	174-16-1234	7.75	23	178.25	35.65	11.05	2.58	128.96
24	Jordan	322	108-12-0810	8.25	20	165.00	33.00	10.23	2.39	119.38
25	Kelly	330	102-12-3111	9.95	30	298.50	59.70	18.51	4.33	215.96
26	Romano	340	108-28-4429	9.75	32	312.00	62.40	19.34	4.52	225.73
27	Unger	341	060-10-3100	8.45	22	185.90	37.18	11.53	2.70	134.50
28										
29		Totals				1328.15	265.63	82.35	19.26	960.92
30		Averages				221.36	44.27	13.72	3.21	160.15
31										
32					FOR THE WEEK ENDING 2/20/19					
33										
34	Employee	Employee		Hourly	Hours	Gross	Federal	Soc. Sec	Medicare	Net
35	Name	Number		Rate	Worked	Pay	With. Tax	Tax	Tax	Pay
36										
37	Engelson	272	070-12-3821	7.25	28	203.00	40.60	12.59	2.94	146.87
38	Gomez	320	174-16-1234	7.75	25	193.75	38.75	12.01	2.81	140.18
39	Kelly	330	102-12-3111	9.95	22	218.90	43.78	13.57	3.17	158.37
40	Polla	335	222-30-1010	8.75	18	157.50	31.50	9.77	2.28	113.95
41	Romano	340	108-28-4429	9.75	30	292.50	58.50	18.14	4.24	211.62
42	Unger	341	060-10-3100	8.45	26	219.70	43.94	13.62	3.19	158.95
43										
44		Totals				1285.35	257.07	79.69	18.64	929.95
45		Averages				214.23	42.85	13.28	3.11	154.99

Copy A1:J45 to March and April sheets.

Delete row (row 10)

Delete row (row 25)

KEYSTROKES

SELECT SHEETS

Select One Sheet

1. If necessary, click tab scrolling controls to scroll.. [« < > » >|] [A] a hidden sheet tab into view.
2. Click desired sheet tab.

Select Multiple Sheets

1. Click the first sheet tab in the selection.
2. Press the **Shift** key, then click the last sheet in the selection.

   Black line appears under tabs.

Select (Group) Consecutive Sheets

IMPORTANT: *When you group sheets, formatting applied to one sheet is duplicated on all sheets in the group.*

1. Click first sheet tab to select.
2. If necessary, click tab scrolling controls to scroll... [« < > » >|] [A] a hidden sheet tab into view.
3. Press **Shift** and click .... [Shift] last sheet tab to select.

   Black line appears under tabs.

NAME GROUP OF SHEETS

1. Click **Insert** .... [Alt]+[I]
2. Click **Name** .... [N]
3. Click **Group of sheets** .... [G]
4. Type name of group .... *name*
5. Click **OK** .... [Enter]

ACTIVATE GROUP MODE

Alt + F5

1. Click **View** .... [Alt]+[V]
2. Click **Group Mode** .... [G]

   Blue line appears under group.

To deactivate group mode:

Alt + F5

1. Click **View** .... [Alt]+[V]
2. Click **Group Mode** .... [G]

DELETE SHEETS

Delete One Sheet

1. Click sheet tab to delete.
2. Click **Edit** .... [Alt]+[E]
3. Click **Delete** .... [D]
4. Click **Sheet(s)** .... [Alt]+[S]

Delete Multiple Sheets

1. Click the first sheet tab.
2. Press **Shift** and click. .... [Shift] last sheet tab to select.
3. Follow steps 2-4 above.

RENAME A SHEET

1. Double-click sheet tab to rename.
2. Type new name .... *name*
3. Press **Enter** .... [Enter]

   OR

   a. Right-click sheet tab.
   b. Select **Edit Sheet Name**.
   c. Type new name .... *name*
   d. Click **OK** .... [Enter]

INSERT SHEETS

Insert One Notebook Sheet

1. Click sheet tab of the sheet you want to follow the new sheet.
2. Click **Insert** .... [Alt]+[I]
3. Click **Sheet** .... [T]
4. Click **OK** .... [Enter]

   Quattro Pro inserts sheet and makes the new sheet active.

Insert Multiple Notebook Sheets

1. Select as many sheets as you wish to insert in the desired location using the **Shift** key.
2. Click **Insert** .... [Alt]+[I]
3. Click **Sheet** .... [T]

   Quattro Pro inserts sheets and makes the last new sheet active.

MOVE SHEETS WITHIN A NOTEBOOK

Move One Sheet

Drag sheet tab to desired sheet tab position.

Move Multiple Sheets

1. Select sheets to move.
2. Drag selected sheet tabs to desired sheet tab position.

🌐 PRINT NOTEBOOK

Prints notebook sheet data using the current page settings.

1. Click **File** menu .... [Alt]+[F]
2. Click **Print** .... [P]
3. Click **Notebook** .... [K]
4. Click **Print** .... [Enter]

Quattro Pro 8 ■ Lesson 4 ■ Exercise 20

QUATTRO PRO 8 Lesson 4: Additional Formatting and Editing; Work with Workbooks

Exercise 21

■ QuickFill ■ QuickCell ■ Named Blocks

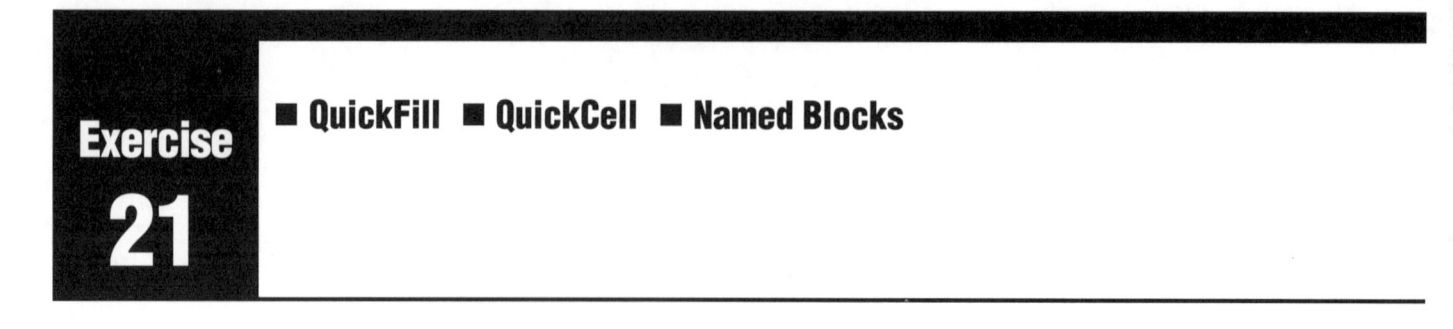

NOTES

QuickFill

- The **QuickFill** feature is used to enter a series of labels or values in columns, rows, or on tabs. The Quick Fill dialog box, illustrated below, will appear when you click the QuickFill button on the Notebook Toolbar. You can select a series name and then use or modify the suggested series elements to be filled into your notebook.

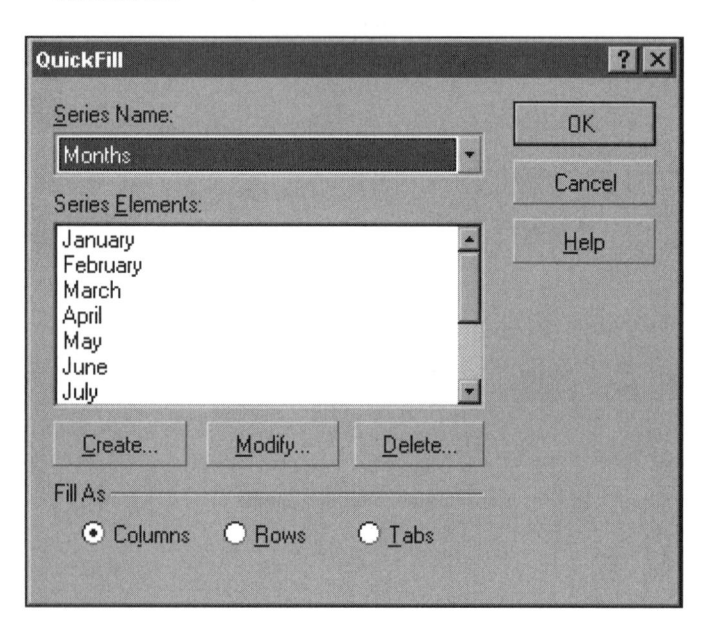

QuickCell

- QuickCell is a feature in QuattroPro 8 that allows you to drag any cell to the Application Bar at the bottom of the window. You can then see its updated value as you change other cells elsewhere in the spreadsheet. To drag a cell, select the cell until the arrowhead crossbar appears and the cell is outlined in yellow. Drag the cell and place it on the QuickCell in the application bar. Note the application bar with 123 in the QuickCell location in the illustration at the top right.

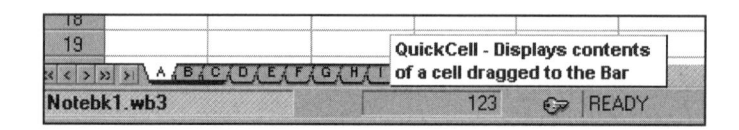

Named Cells

- Quattro Pro allows you to assign a name to a cell or block of cells rather than use the cell reference for identification. To assign a name to a block, click Insert, Name and Cells or press Ctrl+F3. The Cell Names dialog box, illustrated below, is then used to define the name of the range of cells.

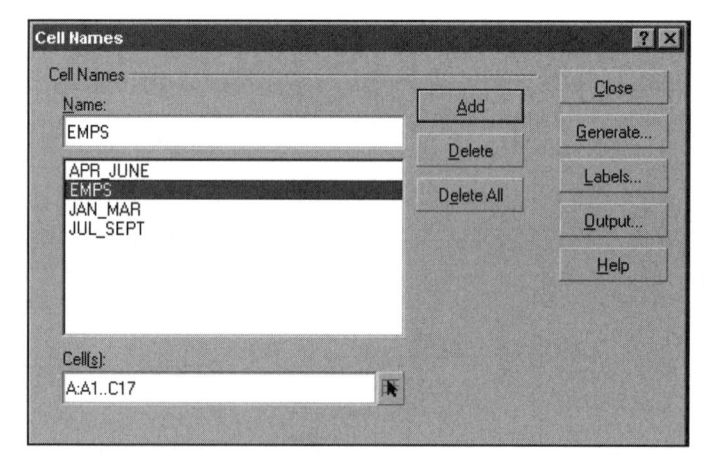

- Named cell ranges make formulas easy to read and understand, and makes printing and combining blocks easier to accomplish. For example, when you define a print selection area you can type the name of the cells (such as EMPS), rather than typing the cell reference (such as A1:C17). In addition, you can move quickly to named cells by pressing F5 and selecting the named cells from the list that appears. Note the illustration on the next page.

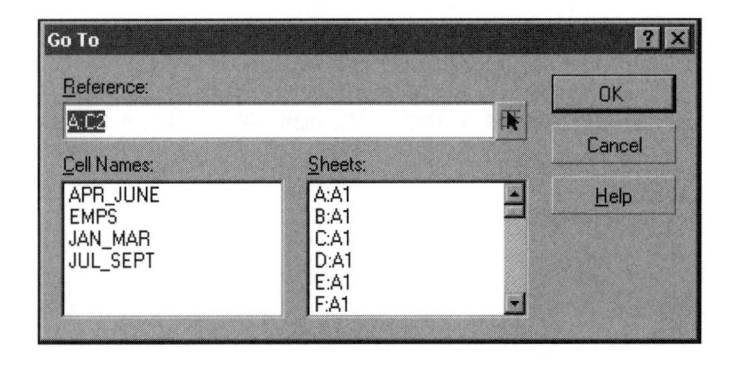

- Cell names may contain up to 64 characters and may consist of letters, numbers, underscores (_), backslashes (\), periods (.), and question marks (?), as well as other special characters. You should keep cell names short and descriptive.
- A list of the named cell ranges you create and their corresponding cell references can be inserted on the notebook page by selecting the Output button in the Cell Names dialog box.
- A named block can be modified by changing the range or the name.

In this exercise, you will include third-quarter sales commission data for Best Home Appliances as well as add named blocks in the report for printing and for later use in combining files.

EXERCISE DIRECTIONS

1. Open APPLI or 21APPLI.
2. Edit the title to read:
   QUARTERLY SALES AND SALARY REPORT – JANUARY– SEPTEMBER
3. Insert a row at the bottom of the list to include a new employee hired on July 1. Employee Number, 321; Name, Dora Wazeter; Base Salary, $3200.
   ✓ *Format base salary to be consistent with other formatting.*
4. Copy column headings from columns G-I to columns J-L. Edit column headings as indicated in the illustration.
5. Lock columns A-C for vertical titles.
6. Change column widths to 14 for columns J and L and to 15 for Column K.
7. Enter July-Sept sales data as indicated in the illustration or as listed below:

Larry Fridga	28,450.78
Jose Micronez	32,456.98
Marie Steerio	31,875.67
Brian Stovely	30,568.90
Patricia Washer	35,689.98
Dora Wazeter	28,456.78

8. Format all data to be consistent with notebook formats.
9. Copy the COMMISSIONS formulas to the new column.
10. Find JULY-SEPT SALARY using BASE SALARY + COMMISSIONS.
11. Copy the formula to the remaining employees.
12. Clear the lock.
13. Edit the formulas for TOTALS, AVERAGES, HIGHEST, and LOWEST in the BASE SALARY column to include the new employee data.
14. Copy the edited formulas to all columns.
15. Test the use of QuickCell as follows:
    a. Select the total July-Sept. sales, in J13, so that the arrowhead crossbar appears and the cell is outlined in yellow.
    b. Drag the cell to the QuickCell in the Application bar.
    c. Cut the last sales value in J11.
    d. Note the change in the QuickCell.
    e. Paste the last sales value back to J11.
16. Create the following named cells:

EMPS	A1:C17
JAN_MAR	F1:F17
APR_JUNE	I1:I17
JUL_SEPT	L1:L17

17. Use F5 to select the EMPS cells. Print one copy of EMPS.
18. Beginning at cell B19, insert list of named cells by using the Insert, Names, Cells, Output commands.
19. Enter the Sales Summary title and column headings as illustrated.

QUATTRO PRO 8 Lesson 4: Additional Formatting and Editing; Work with Workbooks

20. Use QuickFill to enter the Quarter labels. Use the Quarter 5 series name which creates the labels illustrated.

21. Transpose the TOTALS, AVERAGES, HIGHEST, and LOWEST values from the Quarterly Sales and Salary Report for each quarter.

22. Print one copy in landscape orientation with print scaling set to Fit to 1 page.

23. Close and save the notebook file, or *save as* **APPLI**.

A	A	B	C	D	E	F	G	H	I	J	K	L
1			BEST HOME APPLIANCES									
2			QUARTERLY SALES AND SALARY REPORT									
3												
4	SMN.		BASE	JAN-MAR		1ST QTR.	APR-JUN		2ND QTR.	JULY-SEPT.		3RD QTR.
5	NO.	SALESMAN	SALARY	SALES	COMMISSIONS	EARNINGS	SALES	COMMISSIONS	EARNINGS	SALES	COMMISSIONS	EARNINGS
6	350	Larry Fridga	3,200.00	15,785.96	2,367.89	5,567.89	22,758.85	3,413.83	6,613.83	**28,450.78**		
7	351	Jose Micronez	3,200.00	21,895.95	3,284.39	6,484.39	25,675.89	3,851.38	7,051.38	**32,456.98**		
8	352	Marie Steerio	3,200.00	20,750.90	3,112.64	6,312.64	24,567.81	3,685.17	6,885.17	**31,875.67**		
9	353	Brian Stovely	3,200.00	25,920.85	3,888.13	7,088.13	25,975.75	3,896.36	7,096.36	**30,568.90**		
10	354	Patricia Washer	3,200.00	28,875.90	4,331.39	7,531.39	29,656.54	4,448.48	7,648.48	**35,689.98**		
11	355	**Dora Wazeter**	**3,200.00**							**28,456.78**		
12												
13		TOTALS	19,200.00	113,229.56	16,984.43	32,984.43	128,634.84	19,295.23	35,295.23			
14		AVERAGES	3,200.00	22,645.91	3,396.89	6,596.89	25,726.97	3,859.05	7,059.05			
15		HIGHEST	3,200.00	28,875.90	4,331.39	7,531.39	29,656.54	4,448.48	7,648.48			
16		LOWEST	3,200.00	15,785.96	2,367.89	5,567.89	22,758.85	3,413.83	6,613.83			
17												
18			*Edit formulas.*									
19												
20												
21												
22												
23												
24			SALES SUMMARY									
25												
26			TOTALS	AVERAGES	HIGHEST	LOWEST						
27		Quarter1										
28		Quarter2										
29		Quarter3										
30												
31		*Create labels with QuickFill.*		*Transpose data for summary table.*								
32												
33												
34												

KEYSTROKES

NAME/MODIFY CELLS USING THE MENU

1. Select cells to be named.
2. Click **I**nsert .... `Alt`+`I`
3. Click **N**ame .... `N`
4. Click **C**ells .... `C`
5. Type name for block .... *name* in **N**ame text box.
6. Click **A**dd .... `Alt`+`A`

   To delete a name:

   a. Click name to delete .... `Tab`, `↓` in list box.
   b. Click **D**elete .... `Alt`+`D`
   c. Click **C**lose .... `Alt`+`C`

   To change a name:

   a. Click name to change .... `Tab`, `↓` in list box.
   b. Select name in **N**ame edit box.
   c. Type new name for block.
   d. Click **A**dd .... `Alt`+`A`
   e. Click old name to delete in list box.
   f. Click **D**elete .... `Alt`+`D`

   To change reference a name refers to:

   a. Click name .... `Tab`, `↓` to edit in list box.
   b. Drag through existing reference .. `Tab` in cells text box.
   c. Select cells in notebook page to reference.

      OR

      Type new reference .... *reference*

7. Click **A**dd .... `Alt`+`A`
8. Click **C**lose .... `Alt`+`C`

SELECT NAMED CELLS

1. Press **F5** .... `F5`
2. Select name in **C**ell Names list .... `Alt`+`C`, `↓`
3. Click **OK** .... `Enter`

INSERT LIST OF NAMED CELLS

Inserts a list of named cells and their corresponding references in current notebook sheet.

1. Select upper-left cell in block to receive list.
2. Click **I**nsert .... `Alt`+`I`
3. Click **N**ame .... `N`
4. Click **C**ells .... `C`
5. Click **O**utput .... `Alt`+`O`
6. Click **OK** .... `Enter`
7. Click **C**lose .... `Alt`+`C`

   ✓ *Quattro Pro includes page names.*

PRINT NAMED CELLS

1. Select named cells.
2. Click **F**ile menu .... `Alt`+`F`
3. Click **P**rint .... `P`
4. Click S**e**lection .... `Alt`+`E`
5. Click **P**rint .... `Enter`

USE QUICKCELL

1. Select cell to be monitored.
2. When arrowhead crossbar appears and the cell is outlined in yellow, drag the cell to the Application Bar.
3. The cell value will be shown in the QuickCell location.

QUATTRO PRO 8 Lesson 4: Additional Formatting and Editing; Work with Workbooks

Exercise 22

- Templates ■ Projects ■ PerfectExpert
- Use Projects ■ Arrange Notebooks

NOTES

Templates

- When you need to create more than one notebook that will contain similar formatting, data and formulas, you can save a model notebook with the desired formats and formulas as a template. Saving a Quattro Pro document into the **\Corel\Suite8\Template\Custom QP Templates** directory turns it into a template file. Note the illustration of the path below. The Custom QP Templates directory is listed on the New file dialog box. When you open a template file, Quattro Pro opens a copy of it and leaves the original file intact so you can use it again. When data is added to this type of notebook, it is saved under a new name to preserve the original file.

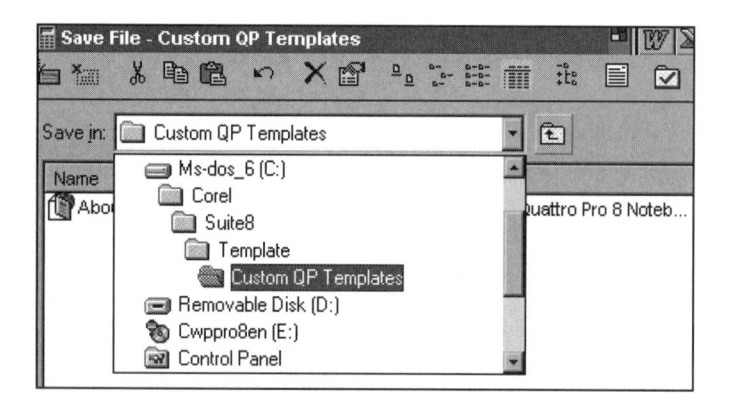

CD to run the project. If projects are not enabled, File, New creates a blank notebook. To enable QuickTemplates click Tools, Settings, File Options, then check Enable QuickTemplates.

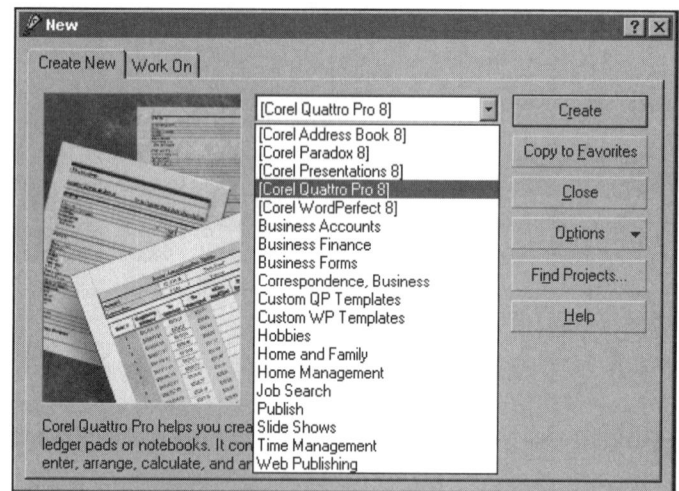

PerfectExpert

- The PerfectExpert is part of the help system in Corel 8 that allows you to search for answers to "natural language" questions. It also provides access to projects or templates. You can open the PerfectExpert to search for a project to complete a task by clicking the Find Projects button on the New dialog box or by clicking **Help, Ask the Perfect Expert** from the menu. When the dialog box appears, as illustrated on the next page, enter the task that needs to be completed and a list of related projects will appear. You can select the desired project and click Create to open the template file.

Projects

- A project is a notebook template provided in the Corel 8 Suite that you can use to serve as the basis for a new notebook. When you click **File, New** you can select a project category from a drop-down list, as illustrated at the right. The projects to be used with Corel Quattro Pro provide the formatting and structural skeleton for common spreadsheets and data entry forms used in business and at home. Although the categories and projects are listed, you must use the Corel WordPerfect Suite program

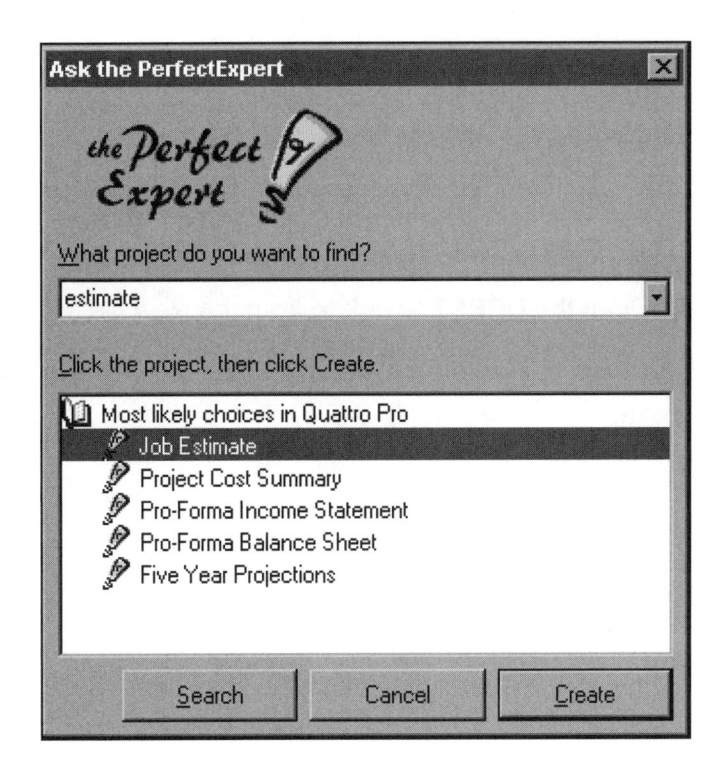

- The PerfectExpert panel appears on the left side of the screen, which is used like a toolbar to complete or customize the project. The option to Insert Sample Data provides an example to view how the project template works. You can customize the template with your information and save and open versions under new filenames. When you save your customized version of the template, use the path to templates discussed in the first paragraph. To close the PerfectExpert panel, click the X or close button in the top right corner.

Arrange Notebooks

- When working with a number of open files, you may want to use the Cascade, Tile Top to Bottom, or Tile Side by Side options available on the Window menu. These options allow you to position the notebook windows so that they are all visible at once, allowing you to quickly move from one notebook to another.

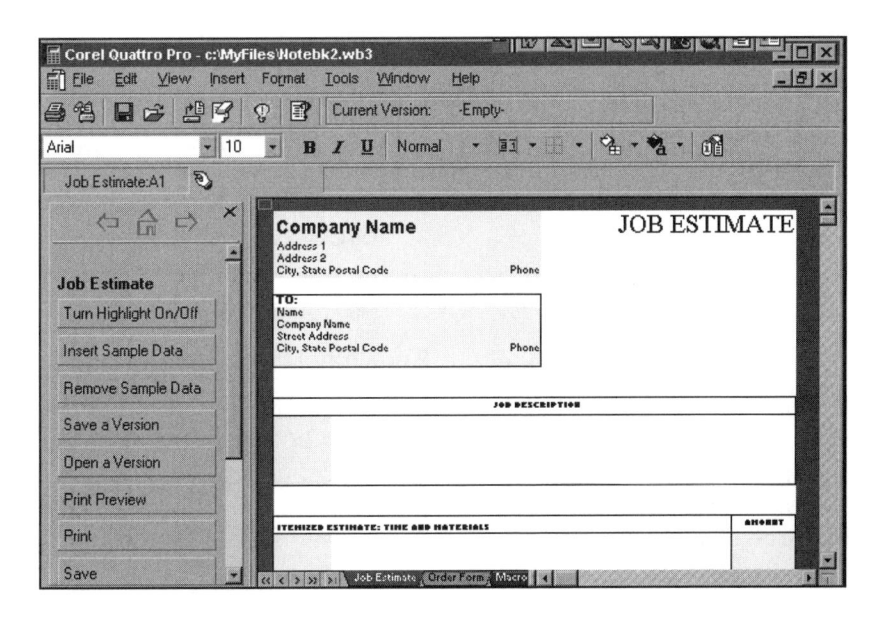

Use Projects

- The Corel 8 CD-ROM provides project formats created with Quattro Pro and other suite applications that can be used or modified for your own purposes. There are also order forms for additional templates included in some projects. When you click Create to open a project, the model notebook displays with preset formats and formulas. Note the illustration of the Job Estimate project below. The notebook has three sheets; the Job Estimate or project sheet, an Order sheet for additional templates, and a Macros sheet.

QUATTRO PRO 8 Lesson 4: Additional Formatting and Editing; Work with Workbooks

> In this exercise you will explore the Quick Templates that are available on the Corel 8 CD-ROM for Quattro Pro. You will customize the Job Estimate template for your firm, Dribbler Plumbing, and prepare two job estimates. The estimates will be arranged on the screen so that both are viewed simultaneously.

EXERCISE DIRECTIONS

1. Insert the Corel WordPerfect 8 Suite CD-Rom.
2. Use the File menu to open the New dialog box.
3. Click Find Projects to locate a template for estimating the price of a job.
4. In the Ask the PerfectExpert dialog box enter "estimate" in the What project do you want to find box. Click Search.
5. Select Five-Year Projections and click Create.
6. Select the Insert Sample Data button on the PerfectExpert panel to insert sample data.
7. Scroll to view the notebook and note the Balance Sheet data.
8. Remove all data with the Remove Sample Data button on the PerfectExpert panel.
9. Close the project and the panel using the Close buttons and answer No to prompts to save the file.
10. Click File, New, Find Projects, Search and select and create the Job Estimate template.

    ✓ *The search word "estimate" was still in the dialog box.*

11. Scroll down the panel display and read the Tip for this project.
12. Enter the company name and address below by selecting the Company Name line, entering the data, and using the down arrow to move to the next line.

    Dribbler Plumbing
    432 Piper Street
    Suite 10
    Bergenfield, NJ 07621   201-555-4320

13. Scroll down and enter your name on the Prepared By line at the bottom of the form.
14. Enter @TODAY on the date line to use the current system date.
15. Turn the highlight off the data areas by clicking the Highlight On/Off button on the PerfectExpert panel.
16. Save this form as a template using the Save As command and the directory path illustrated on page 318. Name it **DPEST**. Close the file.
17. Open the **DPEST** template from the New file dialog box under the Custom QP Templates directory. Enter the data as follows:

    To:
    Mrs. John Leakey
    325 Dogwood Street
    Bergenfield, NJ 07621

    Job Description:
    Install new 1¼" return piping. Flush boiler. Add boiler cleaner.

Itemized Estimate:	AMOUNT
Materials	$110.25
Labor	285.00

    ✓ *The total will automatically calculate.*

18. Save the notebook as **LEAKEY** in your data directory.
19. Print one copy.
20. Open the **DPEST** template again and enter data as follows:

    To:
    Mr. Sam Wrench
    54 Water Street
    Bergenfield, NJ 07621

    Job Description:
    Install kitchen sink and compactor.

Itemized Estimate:	AMOUNT
Sink	$255
Compactor	125
Labor	400

21. Save the notebook as **WRENCH** in your data directory.
22. Use the Window, Cascade command to view the notebooks.
23. Select the **LEAKEY** notebook.
24. Select the Tile option from the Window menu to view both notebooks.
25. Select the **WRENCH** notebook.
26. Close both files.

Dribbler Plumbing
432 Piper Street
Suite 10
Bergenfield, NJ 07621   201-555-4320

JOB ESTIMATE

TO:
Name
Mr. Sam Wrench
54 Water Street
Bergenfield, NJ 07621   201-555-7434

JOB DESCRIPTION
Install kitchen sink and compactor.

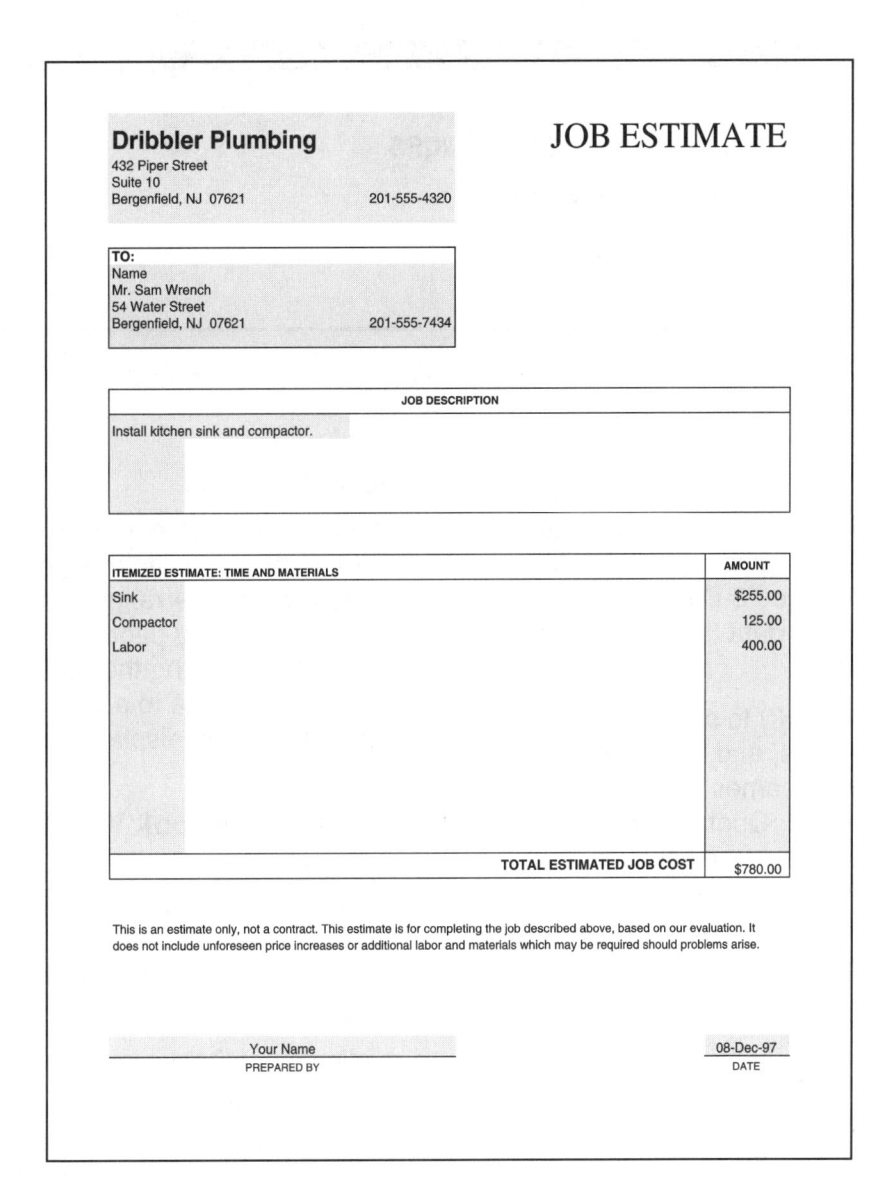

ITEMIZED ESTIMATE: TIME AND MATERIALS	AMOUNT
Sink	$255.00
Compactor	125.00
Labor	400.00
TOTAL ESTIMATED JOB COST	$780.00

This is an estimate only, not a contract. This estimate is for completing the job described above, based on our evaluation. It does not include unforeseen price increases or additional labor and materials which may be required should problems arise.

Your Name   08-Dec-97
PREPARED BY   DATE

KEYSTROKES

FIND AND CREATE PROJECTS

1. Click **F**ile .... Alt + F
2. Click **N**ew .... N
3. Click Fi**n**d Project .... Alt + N
4. Enter search word(s).
5. Click **S**earch .... Alt + S
6. Select project.
7. Click **C**reate .... Alt + C

CREATE A TEMPLATE NOTEBOOK

Saves and names the active notebook as a template file.

1. Customize a project to be saved as a template.
2. Click **F**ile .... Alt + F
3. Click Save **A**s .... A
4. Change directories to **\COREL\SUITE8\TEMPLATE\Custom QP Templates**.
5. Double-click in **N**ame .... Alt + N
6. Type filename .... *filename*
7. Click **S**ave .... Alt + S or Enter

ARRANGE NOTEBOOK WINDOWS

1. Click **W**indow .... Alt + W
2. Click **C**ascade or **T**ile .... C or T

Exercise 23

- 3-D Formulas
- Notebook Pages
- Duplicate Notebook Views

NOTES

3-D Formulas

- You can create references to values that exist in any page or range of pages in a notebook. These references are called 3-D references because they summarize data through the pages rather than on one page.

- Quattro Pro uses a colon (:) to separate a page name from cell references, and two periods (..) between notebook page names to indicate a range of notebook pages. Quotation marks are used if the notebook page name contains a space. In addition, the name of a group can be used in a 3-D formula if you want all the pages in a group to be included in the formula.

- You can type a 3-D reference in a formula, or you can insert it by selecting the desired cells in the notebook page while typing or editing a formula. Note the illustrations showing examples of 3-D references and formulas.

To refer to:	3D reference examples:
Cells in a **different notebook page** (range A1:D1 in Sales 96)	"Sales 96":A1..D1
Cells in **range of notebook pages** (ranges A1..D3, on page C through page E)	C..E:A1..D3 or C:A1..E:D3
Cells in a **group of pages** (cells E7..E9 in the group, FebApr)	FebApr:E7..E9
Add cells E7..E9 in the group, FebApr	=Sum(FebApr:E7..E9)

Notebook Pages

- You should consider copying a page when you need to create multiple pages that contain similar or identical data arrangements. You can use the page tabs to copy pages and the data they contain by selecting the tab, pressing Ctrl and dragging the page to a new location. The page (March) will then display as a copy (March_2).

Duplicate Notebook Views

- You can create duplicate views of the active notebook by selecting New View from the Window menu. This allows you to view different pages of the same notebook simultaneously.

- Consider the following when working with duplicate notebook views:

  - Quattro Pro places the new notebook view in front of the active notebook window. Therefore, if the active notebook is maximized, you will not be able to see the new notebook.

  - Duplicate notebook views are indicated in the title bar that shows the notebook name followed by a colon and a number. For example, NOTEBK1:1

  - Your system memory determines the number of duplicate views you can have open at one time.

  - Closing a duplicate view will not close the notebook.

  - You can add or edit data in the original or duplicate view.

In this exercise, you will add a summary page to the PAYTM file and enter formulas containing 3-D references to the February, March, and April notebook pages. You will also open a duplicate notebook window so you can view the Totals notebook page while you change values in the February notebook page.

EXERCISE DIRECTIONS

1. Open 📖**PAYTM** or 💾**23PAYTM**.

2. Copy the March page to a new page, to the right of the original.

3. Rename March_2 page; name it Totals.

4. Move the Totals tab to the right of April by dragging the tab into place.

5. Select a previously defined group by clicking View, Group mode. *(A dark line should appear below the February, March and April sheets. Check for the group name by clicking Insert, Name, Group of Sheets.)*

6. Select February and, while notebook pages are grouped, enter values in the HOURS WORKED columns for each employee as listed below:

   - On the first payroll, enter 10 hours for Engelson using Ctrl+Enter to input the number.
   - Copy 10 for all employees for the first payroll week.
   - On the second payroll, enter 20 hours for Engelson, again using Ctrl+Enter to input the number.
   - Copy 20 for all employees for the second payroll week.
   - On the third payroll, enter 30 hours for Engelson, using the same method to input the number.
   - Copy 30 for all employees for the third payroll week.

7. Turn View Group mode off, deselect grouped pages and check that test values have been entered on each month's notebook page.

8. Select cell E7 in the Totals notebook page and enter a 3-D formula that adds the values in cell E7 in the February, March, and April notebook page.

   HINT: The completed formula would read: +February:E7+March:E7+April:E7, if the formula cells are selected using the mouse. Or, you can type @SUM(February..April:E7) or @Sum(febapr:E7), and 30 (the sum of the values) should appear in the cell.

9. Copy the formula for each employee in the first week of the payroll.

10. Enter a 3-D formula on the Totals page to add the values in E22 on all sheets.

11. Copy the formula for all employees on the last two payrolls.

12. Open a duplicate notebook window and arrange them in a tiled fashion. Note the names of the windows.

13. Both notebooks should be on the Totals page with A1 in the top left corner. Select one notebook and move to the February page.

14. On the February notebook page, change the HOURS WORKED values in the first payroll week to 50 for each employee.

    ✓ *Note that the Totals notebook page in the duplicate window shows updated values.*

15. Change the HOURS WORKED values for the first payroll back to 10.

16. Close the duplicate notebook window.

17. Select the Totals notebook page and set it to fit on one page when printed.

18. Print the Totals notebook page.

19. Select View, Group Mode to group February, March, and April pages.

20. Select the February notebook page and delete all values in HOURS WORKED.

21. Deselect Group Mode and check that test values have been deleted on each month's notebook page and that Totals page shows zeros in the HOURS WORKED column.

22. Save **PAYTM** as a template file.

23. Close the notebook file.

Quattro Pro 8 ■ Lesson 4 ■ Exercise 23   323

KEYSTROKES

COPY PAGES WITHIN A NOTEBOOK

✓ *Quattro Pro will rename pages that you copy.*

Copy One Page by Dragging

Press **Ctrl** and drag page tab to copy to desired page tab position.

Copy Multiple Pages by Dragging

1. Select pages to copy.
2. Press **Ctrl** and drag selected page tabs to desired page tab position.

INSERT 3-D REFERENCE IN FORMULA

1. If necessary, type or edit formula.
2. Place insertion point in formula where reference will be inserted.
3. Select page containing cell(s) to reference.
   ✓ *When you click a page tab, its name appears in the formula bar.*
4. Select cell(s) to reference.
   ✓ *When you select the cell(s), the complete 3-D reference appears in the formula bar.*

To enter a 3-D reference for a range of notebook pages:

Press **Shift** and click last notebook page tab to reference.

5. Type or insert remaining parts of formula.
6. Press **Enter** .... `Enter`

TYPE A 3-D REFERENCE IN FORMULA

1. If necessary, type or edit formula.
2. Place insertion point in formula where reference will be typed.
3. Type the page name.............. *page name*

To type a 3-D reference for a range of notebook pages:

a. Type two periods .... `.` `.`

b. Type last page name in range.

4. Press colon .... `:`
5. Type cell reference or range.
   EXAMPLES: A..C:A1..C1
              or "Total Sales":A1..A5

OPEN A DUPLICATE NOTEBOOK WINDOW

Creates a new view for active notebook window.

1. Click **Window** .... `Alt` + `W`
2. Click **New View** .... `N`

CLOSE A DUPLICATE NOTEBOOK WINDOW

Click **Close** button .... `X`

QUATTRO PRO 8 Lesson 4: Additional Formatting and Editing; Work with Workbooks

Exercise 24

■ Summary

Mr. Foster administered two additional quizzes plus a final examination to his class. He needs to revise the notebook page he prepared earlier to include the new test data and two new students. In addition, Mr. Foster's supervisor has requested a separate notebook page showing student names and final exam averages.

EXERCISE DIRECTIONS

✓ You may lock row labels when it is helpful to facilitate data entry.

1. Open **GRADE** or **24GRADE**.
2. Insert rows in alphabetical sequence for two students who were admitted late and have been transferred in from another class. Enter the information below, as shown in the illustration on the following page, and extend the quiz and lab average formulas for the new rows.

   3105 Hart, M. labs 82, 90 quizzes 85, 86 Adm. 5/1
   1898 Sanders, J. labs 69, 72 quizzes 75, 70 Adm. 5/1

3. Insert two new columns after QUIZ 3, as shown, for QUIZ 4 and QUIZ 5.
4. Enter QUIZ 4 and QUIZ 5 data. Leaving blanks for absentees, from the list below.

   ✓ The Final Exam data will be entered in step 7 of this exercise.

	QUIZ 4	QUIZ 5	FINAL EXAM
Bell, D.	89	94	92
Dorchester, T.	79	80	74
Garcia, L.	81	78	75
Hart, M.	84	85	82
Levine, M.	78	82	75
Livingston, F.	85	80	82
Pella, J.	65	64	65
Ruiz, G.	78	79	79
Sanders, J.	75	77	75
Trevino, S.	80	84	80
West. D.	60	65	65
Zdan, M.	85	84	86

5. Edit the formulas in the QUIZ AVERAGE column to include the new data and to create averages for the new students.
6. Delete the STUDENT NUMBER column (the last column).
7. Create a new column after QUIZ AVERAGE for FINAL EXAM. Enter the grades shown in the FINAL EXAM column at bottom left in the new column.
8. Create a new column for FINAL AVERAGE after the FINAL EXAM column.
9. Find the FINAL AVERAGE for each student if the Quiz Average and Final Exam are each worth 25% of the final average and the Test Average is worth 50% of the Final Average.

   HINT: @AVG(Quiz Average, Lab Average, Quiz Average, Final Exam) Use commas to separate cell addresses.

10. Format averages to one decimal place and center all new column headings.
11. Check the accuracy of the summary formulas for NUMBER OF PAPERS, CLASS AVERAGE, HIGHEST GRADE, and LOWEST GRADE, and copy them for the new columns of data.
12. Save the notebook file, or save as **GRADE**.
13. Print one copy in landscape orientation to fit on one page.
14. Using the Copy and Paste Special feature, copy columns A:C and the FINAL AVERAGE column to a separate notebook. Use the Paste Formulas as Values option for FINAL AVERAGE data.
15. Save the new file; name it **GRSUM**.
16. Print one copy of **GRSUM**.
17. Close the notebook files.

QUATTRO PRO 8 Lesson 4: Additional Formatting and Editing; Work with Workbooks

	A	B	C	D	E	F	G	H	I	J	K	L
1	CLASS:		SCIENCE 105									
2	TERM:		SPRING 199-									
3	TEACHER:		MR. FOSTER							*Insert two columns*		*Insert two columns*
4												
5	IDNO.	NAME		LAB 1	LAB 2	LAB 3	AVERAGE	QUIZ 1	QUIZ 2	QUIZ 3	QUIZ AVERAGE	STUDENT NUMBER
6												
7	1245	Bell, D.		90	88	92	90.0	92	90	93	91.7	1
8	4123	Dorchester, T.		55	70	75	66.7	58	69	78	68.3	2
9	1255	Garcia, L		75	80	82	79.0	70	78	80	76.0	3
10	**3105**	**Hart, M.**	Enter data		**82**	**90**			**85**	**86**		
11	3331	Levine, M.		78	75	80	77.7	75	80	80	78.3	4
12	2121	Livingston, F.		77	85	80	80.7	75	82	85	80.7	5
13	1234	Pella, J.		55	45	55	51.7	57	45		51.0	6
14	2323	Ruiz, G.		82	80	85	82.3	85	78	88	83.7	7
15	**1898**	**Sanders, J.**	Enter data		**69**	**72**			**75**	**70**		
16	1332	Trevino, S.		92	85	80	85.7	90		85	87.5	8
17	2143	West, D.		45	56	58	53.0		46	50	48.0	9
18	1112	Zdan, M.		82	85	85	84.0	85	80	83	82.7	10
19												
20	NO. OF PAPERS			10	12	12	10	9	11	11		*Delete column*
21	CLASS AVERAGE			73.1	75.0	77.8	75.1	76.3	73.5	79.8		
22	HIGHEST GRADE			92	88	92	90.0	92	90	93		
23	LOWEST GRADE			45	45	55	51.7	57	45	50		

insert two rows

326

QUATTRO PRO 8

Lesson 5: Logical and Date Functions; SpeedFormat; Hide Data

Exercise 25

■ Insert an IF function

NOTES

Insert an IF Function

- An **IF statement** is a logical function which sets up a conditional statement to test data. The truth or falsity of the condition will determine the results of the statement.

- The format for an IF statement is:

  @IF(Condition, True Expression, False Expression)

- Using this formula, if the condition is true, the function results in True Expression; if the condition is false, the function results in False Expression.

- For example, in this exercise, the teacher uses an IF statement to determine the final grade based on the final average and a passing grade of 65. Therefore, an IF statement can be used to test whether the final average is greater than 64.9. If so, then the student passes and the word PASS is entered in the function location. If the condition is false, the word FAIL is entered in the function location.

  ✓Note: Note the breakdown of one of the IF statement formulas used in this problem. Since PASS and FAIL are text, you must enclose them in quotation marks (").

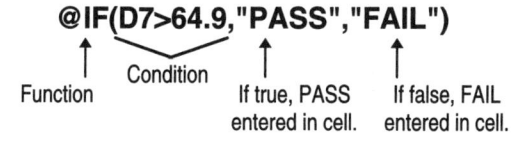

  @IF(D7>64.9,"PASS","FAIL")
  ↑   ↑   ↑   ↑
  Function Condition If true, PASS If false, FAIL
                       entered in cell. entered in cell.

- IF statements may use conditional operators as listed below:

=	Equals	<=	Less than or equal to
>	Greater than	>=	Greater than or equal to
<	Less than	&	Used for connecting text (concatenation)
<>	Not equal to		

  ✓Note: IF statements may be used in combination with OR, AND, and NOT statements to evaluate complex conditions.

QUATTRO PRO 8 Lesson 5: Logical and Data Functions; SpeedFormat; Hide Data

In this exercise, you will use an IF statement to calculate the FINAL GRADE and CREDITS GRANTED for Mr. Foster's class based on a 65% passing grade.

EXERCISE DIRECTIONS

1. Open **GRSUM** or **25GRSUM**.
2. Insert the following columns after FINAL AVERAGES and center the headings:
   FINAL   CREDITS
   GRADE   GRANTED
3. Enter an IF statement for the first student in the FINAL GRADE column that will produce the word PASS if the final average is greater than 64.9, and FAIL if it is not.
4. Copy the formula to the other students.
5. Enter an IF statement for the first student in the CREDITS GRANTED column that will produce the number three if the final average is greater than 64.9, and zero if it is not.
6. Copy the formula to the other students.
7. Center all new entries.
8. Delete the row containing Number of Papers.
9. Print one copy of the notebook page.
10. Close and save the notebook file, or *save as* **GRSUM**.

A	A	B	C	D	E	F	G	H	I
1	CLASS:		SCIENCE 105						
2	TERM:		SPRING 199-						
3	TEACHER:		MR. FOSTER						
4				FINAL	FINAL	CREDITS			
5	IDNO.	NAME		AVERAGE	GRADE	GRANTED			
6									
7	1245	Bell, D.		91.2					
8	4123	Dorchester, T.		71.2					
9	1255	Garcia, L		77.1					
10	3105	Hart, M		84.3					
11	3331	Levine, M.		77.2					
12	2121	Livingston, F.		81.4					
13	1234	Pella, J.		58.1					
14	2323	Ruiz, G.		81.0					
15	1898	Sanders, J		73.3					
16	1332	Trevino, S.		83.5					
17	2143	West, D.		57.8					
18	1112	Zdan, M.		84.5	▼	▼			
19									
20	NO. OF PAPERS			12			Delete row		▶
21	CLASS AVERAGE			76.7					
22	HIGHEST GRADE			91.2					
23	LOWEST GRADE			57.8					

KEYSTROKES

INSERT AN IF FUNCTION USING FORMULA COMPOSER

✓ *You can also type a function to insert it.*
1. Click cell.
2. Click **Formula Composer** button f_∞ on toolbar.
3. Click **@** button in Expression group.
4. Select **Function Category** list . [Alt]+[C]
5. Select **Logical** .... [↓][↑]
6. Select **Function** list............ [Alt]+[F]
7. Select **IF** function .... [↓][↑]
8. Click **OK**................................ [Enter]
9. Click **Condition** box............. [Alt]+[O]
10. Type condition.

✓ *You can click cells in notebook page to insert cell references.*
11. Click **TrueExpr** box .... [Alt]+[T]
12. Type the argument if condition is true.
13. Click **FalseExpr** box .... [Alt]+[F]
14. Type the argument if condition is false.
15. Click **OK** .... [Enter]

Exercise 26

- **IF Functions**
- **Hide Data**

NOTES

IF Functions

- An **IF** statement may be created to perform one calculation if the condition is true and perform another calculation if the condition is false. For example, if sales are over $50,000, multiply the sales by 3% commission, otherwise multiply sales by 2%.

- When creating a condition using the greater than operator (>), make sure to use the correct value. If you are looking for all values of 5 or over, you should use >4.9 or >=5, not >5.

- A condition may test the presence of specific text entries. As discussed in the previous exercise, any text in an IF function should be enclosed in quotation marks.

  For example: @IF(D7="M",4,5) If the data is M, then enter 4, otherwise enter 5.

Hide Data

- Data that should not be viewed by all users of a notebook or data that is not necessary for a report may be **hidden**.

- To hide rows or columns, select a cell in the row or column to be hidden and then select Selection from the Format menu, click the Row/Column tab, and select the Reveal/Hide options from the row or column section.

- You can reverse the hide operation by selecting the columns or rows on both sides of the hidden area, returning to the Row/Column tab and selecting the Reveal option.

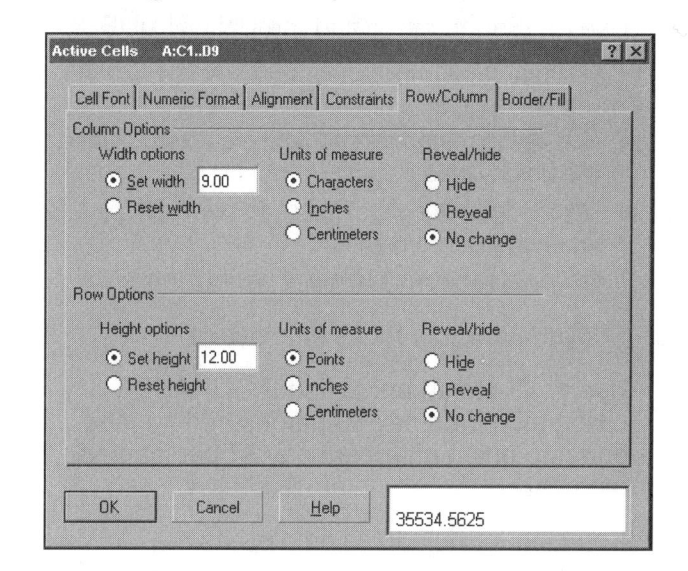

- You can use the mouse to reveal a single row or column by placing the mouse pointer slightly to the right of the hidden column's border and dragging it to the right.

- To view all hidden column and rows at once, click Edit, Select All, then click Format, Selection and select the Reveal options. (This is the easiest way to reveal row 1 or column A when they are hidden.)

KEYSTROKES

REVEAL/HIDE COLUMNS OR ROWS

1. Select a cell in the column or row to be hidden, or select the area around data to be revealed.
2. Click **Format** .... `Alt`+`R`
3. Click **Selection** .... `E`
4. Select **Row/Column** tab .... `Ctrl`+`Tab`

   For column options
5. Click **Hide** .... `I`

   or **Reveal** .... `V`

   OR

   For row options

   Click **Hide** .... `D`

   or **Reveal** .... `L`
6. Click **OK** .... `Enter`

QUATTRO PRO 8   Lesson 5: Logical and Data Functions; SpeedFormat; Hide Data

In this exercise, Strong Equipment Manufacturing Co. is preparing a notebook to calculate miscellaneous payroll deductions for its employees. Union dues, insurance, and locker and uniforms charges will be calculated based on union or non-union membership.

EXERCISE DIRECTIONS

1. Create the worksheet below or open **26EMP.WB3**.

2. Center data and column headings in the NUMBER INSURED, U/N and M/F columns.

3. Center S.S.NO. and NAME column headings.

4. Right-align the remaining column headings and adjust column width as necessary.

5. Use an IF function to find the UNION DUES.
   - Union and non-union members are noted with U or N.
   - Non-union members should have a zero placed in the Union Dues column.
   - Union members pay dues of $5 per week plus $2 for each insured member.

   HINT: IF data equals "U", 5+NUMBER INSURED*2,0.

6. Copy the formula for all employees.

7. Use an IF statement to find INSURANCE. Union members pay $3 per insured member, and non-union members pay $7 per insured member.

8. Copy the formula to all employees.

9. Use an IF statement to find LOCKER + UNIFORMS deduction. Males pay $4 per week and females pay $5 per week due to variations in uniforms and locker facilities.

   HINT: If M/F data is "M", then $4, otherwise $5.

10. Copy the formula to all employees.

11. Find the TOTAL MISC. DEDUCTIONS.

12. Find the TOTALS for the columns indicated in the illustration.

13. Format all money data to two decimal places.

14. Bold titles, column headings, and TOTALS line.

15. Insert a blank column in column A; set width to 2.00.

16. Hide the Social Security Number (S.S.NO.) column.

17. Print one copy of the worksheet.

18. Reveal the S.S.NO. column.

19. Close and save the workbook file; name it **EMP**.

	A	A	B	C	D	E	F	G	H	I
1				FITNESS EQUIPMENT PLUS MFG. CO.						
2				MISCELLANEOUS PAYROLL DEDUCTIONS						
3				TREMONT PLANT						
4										
5				NUMBER			UNION		LOCKER +	TOTAL MISC.
6		S. S. NO.	NAME	INSURED	U/N	M/F	DUES	INSURANCE	UNIFORMS	DEDUCTIONS
7		101-45-5689	Bicycla, Ethel	2	N	F				
8		020-57-3388	Deltoid, Danny	1	U	M				
9		123-45-7890	Kemper. Betty	3	U	F				
10		234-45-5678	Nautilia, Nancy	4	N	F				
11		234-23-4455	Roww, Jose	3	U	M				
12		121-34-5656	Quintana, Jay	2	U	M				
13		124-45-5777	Treadwell, Sam	4	N	M	▼	▼	▼	▼
14										
15			TOTALS							

QUATTRO PRO 8 Lesson 5: Logical and Data Functions; SpeedFormat; Hide Data

Exercise 27

- Enter a Date as Numerical Data
- Format Numerical Dates

NOTES

Enter Date as Numerical Data

- As previously noted, dates can be entered as label data, but when there is a need to add or subtract dates, they must be entered as numerical data.

- Quattro Pro recognizes the appropriate number format based on the way you enter data. For example, if you enter 25%, the entry is recognized as a value with the percent format. This also applies to dates.

Format Numerical Dates

- If you enter a date in one of the standard formats, Quattro Pro automatically recognizes the entry as a numerical date value or serial value.

  ✓ Note: To view a serial value for a date, enter the date in number format.

- Illustrated below are some of the standard date formats that Quattro Pro recognizes as numerical date values. Notice the serial value for the dates listed. When you subtract one date value from another, Quattro Pro subtracts the serial values of the numbers and displays the result.

Formats	Date	Example Entries	Serial values
mm/dd/yy	January 1, 1900	1/1/00	1
dd-mmm-yy	February 23, 1998	23-Feb-98	35484
dd-mmm	July 25, 1998	25-Jul	36001
mmm-yy	July 1, 1998	Jul-98	35612

- In the Quattro Pro date system, the date December 3, 1899 is represented by the serial value 0.

KEYSTROKES

ENTER DATE AS NUMERICAL DATA

✓ Dates entered as numerical data are right-aligned and can be calculated.

1. Select cell to receive date.

   To enter a specific date:

   Type date .... *date in valid format*

   You may use the following formats:
   - **mm/dd/yy** .... (e.g. 6/24/94)
   - **dd-mmm** .... (e.g. 24-Jun)
   - **dd-mmm-yy** .... (e.g. 24-Jun-94)
   - **mmm-yy** .... (e.g. Jun-94)

2. Press **Enter** .... `Enter`

✓ If Quattro Pro displays number signs (######), the column is not wide enough to display the date. To see the entry, double-click the right border of the column heading.

FORMAT NUMERICAL DATES

1. Select cells containing numerical dates to format.

2. Press **F12** .... `F12`

   OR

   a. Click **Format** .... `Alt`+`R`

   b. Click **Selection** .... `E`

   OR

   a. Right-click cells.

   b. Click **Cell Properties**.

3. Click **Numeric Format** tab.

4. Select desired format... `↓`, `Shift`+`Tab`
   in Date Formats list, for example:
   - **DD-MMM-YY**
   - **DD-MMM**
   - **MMM-YY**
   - **Long Date Intl.** (mm/dd/yy)
   - **Short Date Intl.** (mm/dd)

5. Click **OK** .... `Enter`

QUATTRO PRO 8 Lesson 5: Logical and Data Functions; SpeedFormat; Hide Data

In this exercise, Wheeler Auto Supply Co. is creating a workbook to determine the due date of invoices, the due date for cash discounts, the discounts, and the amounts paid as determined by the date paid. The Net Terms refer to the number of days given to pay the invoice in full. The Discount Terms reflect the number of days within which payment must be made to earn the discount.

EXERCISE DIRECTIONS

1. Create the notebook page as shown below, or open 27ACCPAY.

2. Complete the following steps:
   - Center all column headings.
   - Center data in the NET TERMS, DISCOUNT TERMS, and DISCOUNT RATE columns.
   - Format titles and column headings for bold.
   - Enter dates as values with MM/DD/YY (Long Date Intl.) format (no label prefix).
   - Adjust column width as necessary.

3. Find DUE DATE:

   HINT: INVOICE DATE+NET TERMS

   ✓ This formula adds the serial value of a date with a number and the result is a serial value.

4. Format the date serial number for Long Date International format, MM/DD/YY.

5. Find the DISCOUNT DATE.

   HINT: INVOICE DATE+DISCOUNT TERMS

6. Format the date serial number for Long International format.

7. Find the DISCOUNT: Use an IF statement to determine if a discount has been earned.

   HINT: If the date paid is earlier (less than) than the discount date, then multiply the amount of the invoice by the discount rate, otherwise enter a zero.

8. Format DISCOUNT for two decimal places.

9. Find AMOUNT PAID.

   HINT: AMOUNT-DISCOUNT.

10. Format AMOUNT PAID for two decimal places.

11. Find totals for the AMOUNT, DISCOUNT, and AMOUNT PAID columns.

12. Format totals for two decimal places.

13. Create a name for the cells on the entire notebook page. Name it PRINTALL.

14. Print one copy of the block PRINTALL, using landscape orientation to fit on one page.

15. Save and close the file; name it **ACCPAY**.

A	A	B	C	D	E	F	G	H	I	J	K	L
1			WHEELER AUTO SUPPLY CO.									
2			ACCOUNTS PAYABLE									
3												
4		INVOICE		NET	DUE	DISCOUNT	DISCOUNT	DISCOUNT	DATE			AMOUNT
5	INVOICE	DATE	VENDOR	TERMS	DATE	TERMS	RATE	DATE	PAID	AMOUNT	DISCOUNT	PAID
6	A22889	05/02/98	Roto Parts Inc.	45		20	3%		05/18/98	1245.78		
7	1497856	05/06/98	Davis Polish Co.	30		15	3%		06/01/98	235.78		
8	JU-78901	05/08/98	E & E Auto Supplies	90		30	2%		06/20/98	975.78		
9	2234	05/09/98	Geneva Car Mats	45		15	5%		05/21/98	568.89		
10	87A5568	05/10/98	Fraser Batteries Co.	120		30	2%		06/10/98	895.45		
11	245689	05/11/98	Nordino & Sons	60		20	1%		06/30/98	1895.85		
12	A22907	05/11/98	Handy Mirrors Co.	30	▼	10	3%	▼	05/20/98	458.85	▼	▼
13												
14			TOTALS									

QUATTRO PRO 8 Lesson 5: Logical and Data Functions; SpeedFormat; Hide Data

Exercise 28

■ SpeedFormat ■ Shading and Text Colors

NOTES

SpeedFormat

- Quattro Pro provides built-in formats which can be applied to a block of data to give the notebook a professional appearance. These formats are called **SpeedFormats** and include number formats, fonts, borders, patterns, colors, alignments, row heights, and column widths. You can apply SpeedFormats to column and row headings, the body of the report and totals. The heading area is not included in the formats.

- Select the area to be formatted and then select SpeedFormat, from the Format menu or click the SpeedFormat button to display a dialog box with a selection of table formats that may be applied to a range of data. *(See the illustration below.)* You may add a customized format to SpeedFormats by creating your own format and then clicking the Add button to include it on the SpeedFormat list of options.

SpeedFormat Dialog Box

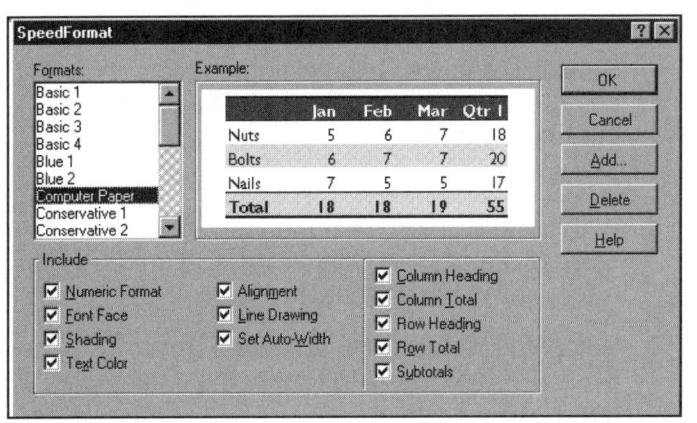

Shading and Text Colors

- Custom formats may be set using the Active Cells dialog box, which is accessed by clicking Selection on the Format menu. As illustrated below, the Border/Fill tab in the dialog box provides a palette of colors that can be used to color the background of a selected cell or block.

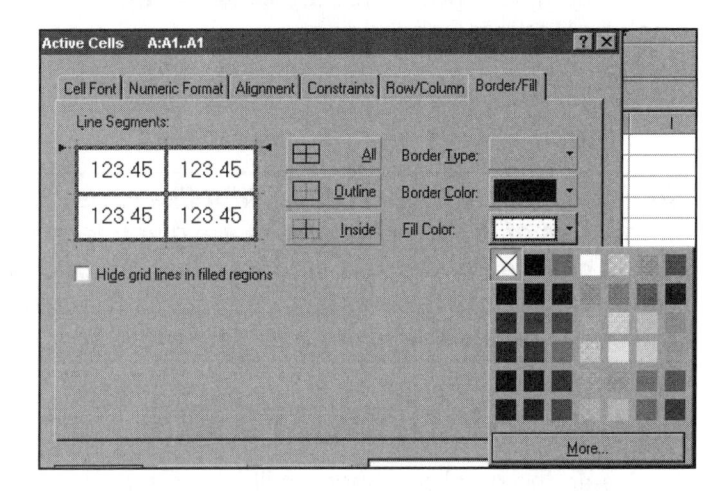

- If you select the "More" button at the bottom of the color palette box, you will be able to blend colors in the Shading dialog box. The Color 1 and Color 2 palettes are used to blend or mix colors. For example, if you select red in Color 1 and yellow in Color 2, those colors will be at either end of the Blend spectrum that appears on the next page. Shades that transition between those colors will appear in the middle. You can then select orange, a blend of red and yellow, from the middle of the spectrum. Note the illustration of the Shading tab on the next page.

QUATTRO PRO 8 Lesson 5: Logical and Data Functions; SpeedFormat; Hide Data

Shading Tab

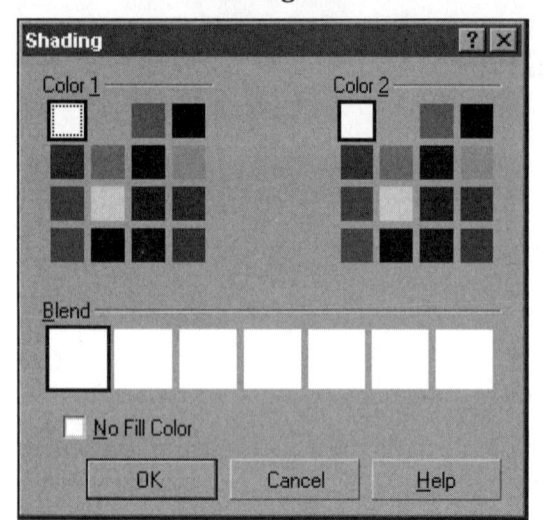

- The Text Color option on the Cell Font tab in the Active Cell dialog box is used to color the text in a selected cell. Text colors are limited to the palette illustrated on the right.

- While a block is selected, you may set all the format options at once using the various tabs in the Active Block dialog box. If you will be reusing a format, it may be saved as a SpeedFormat option using the SpeedFormat dialog box and the ADD button.

Text Color Tab

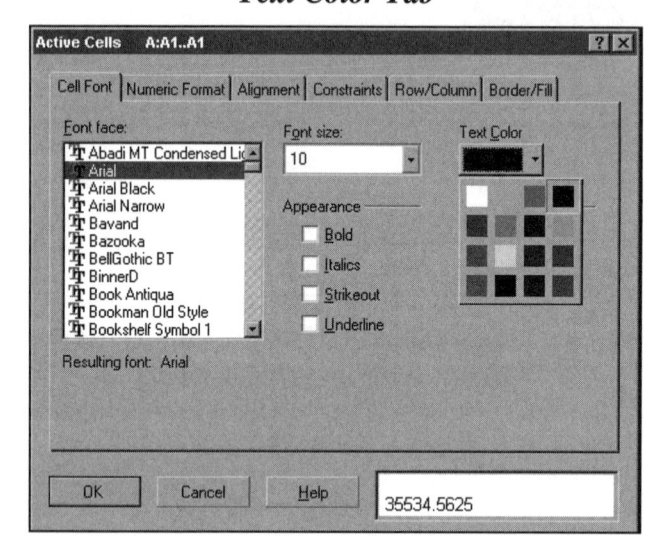

In this exercise, Global Office Supplies is determining the number of days each account has been unpaid as of 9/1/98. Customers are given terms of ten to thirty days to pay the bills. A late fee of 1% is charged on unpaid amounts that are outstanding for more than thirty days past their due date. (Accounts Receivable are records for customers who owe money to a company. Aging of accounts receivable is done to determine how many days the customers' payments are overdue.)

EXERCISE DIRECTIONS

1. Create the notebook page as illustrated, or open 🖫**28ACCREC**.

2. Find the DUE DATE.
   HINT: *INVOICE DATE+TERMS*
   Format the serial value for DD-MMM-YY date format. Adjust column width as necessary.

3. Find the DAYS UNPAID.
   HINT: *DATE-DUE DATE*
   ✓ The reference to the date in C4 should be an absolute reference.

4. Find the LATE FEE. Use an IF statement. If the days unpaid are greater than 30, find 1% of the amount, otherwise enter zero. Format the fee for fixed with two decimal places.

5. Find AMOUNT DUE by adding LATE FEE and AMOUNT. Format for two decimal places.

6. Copy the formulas to the remaining invoices.

7. Total and format all money columns.

8. Select the range A1:I3 and use the Format, Selection (Active Cells) dialog box to set the Fill color to navy, the cell font color to white, and the Font to bold.
   ✓ The colors will appear different while the cells are selected.

9. With the block still selected, add this format to SpeedFormat by clicking Format, SpeedFormat, Add. Name this format Navy. Click OK.

10. Select the range A5:I6 and use Format, SpeedFormat, Navy to format the column headings.

11. Select the Total line, A18:I18 and use Format, SpeedFormat, Navy to format the line.

12. Select the range A7:I17, select Format, SpeedFormat and view all the choices provided in the dialog box.

✓ As you highlight each table format, an example of the style appears in the Sample box.

13. Select Grey 3 and deselect the Numeric Format, the Column Heading, and the Column Total features since the heading, numbers, and Totals have been formatted. Click OK.

14. Adjust column widths as necessary.
15. Print one copy so that it all fits on one page, without gridlines.
16. Save and close the file; name it **ACCREC**.

A	A	B	C	D	E	F	G	H	I
1			GLOBAL OFFICE SUPPLIES						
2			AGING OF ACCOUNTS RECEIVABLE						
3									
4	DATE:		09/01/98						
5	INVOICE	INVOICE			DUE	DAYS			AMOUNT
6	DATE	NO.	CUSTOMER	TERMS	DATE	UNPAID	AMOUNT	LATE FEE	DUE
7	06/02/98	23486	George Hall	10			210.56		
8	06/05/98	23487	Mary Davis	20			334.58		
9	06/08/98	23488	Sandra Marsh	20			98.56		
10	06/11/98	23489	Jean Oliver	30			289.56		
11	06/12/98	23490	Sandra Marsh	30			456.98		
12	06/16/98	23491	Kathy King	20			325.45		
13	06/19/98	23492	George Hall	10			105.56		
14	06/21/98	23493	Mary Davis	20			110.85		
15	06/25/98	23494	Kathy King	30			58.75		
16	06/30/98	23495	Sandra Marsh	30	▼	▼	39.56	▼	▼
17									
18			Totals						

KEYSTROKES

APPLY SPEEDFORMAT

1. Select range of data to be formatted.
2. Click the **SpeedFormat** button ....
   OR
   a. Click **Format** .... `Alt`+`R`
   b. Click **SpeedFormat** .... `F`
3. Select desired format.
4. Click **OK** .... `Enter`

ADD FORMAT TO SPEEDFORMAT

1. Select formatted range of data to be added to list.
2. Click the **SpeedFormat** button ....
   OR
   a. Click **Format** .... `Alt`+`R`
   b. Click **SpeedFormat** .... `F`
3. Click **Add** .... `Alt`+`A`
4. Enter format name.
5. Click **OK** .... `Enter`

APPLY COLOR TO CELL BACKGROUND

1. Select cell or range of cells.
2. Right-click cells.
3. Choose **Cell Properties**.
4. Click **Border/Fill** tab .... `Ctrl`+`Tab`
5. Select or create the color you want.
6. Click **OK** .... `Enter`

APPLY COLOR TO TEXT

1. Select range of cells.
2. Right-click cells.
3. Click **Cell Properties**.
4. Click **Cell Font** tab .... `Ctrl`+`Tab`
5. Click **Text Color** .... `Alt`+`C`
6. Select color.
7. Click **OK** .... `Enter`

QUATTRO PRO 8 Lesson 5: Logical and Data Functions; SpeedFormat; Hide Data

Exercise 29

- What-If Tables
- Payment Function
- Protect a Page

NOTES

What-If Table

- A **What-If table** is used to answer a question based on one or two factors that might influence the outcome. What-if tables are created by selecting Numeric Tools, and then What-If from the Tools menu as illustrated below.

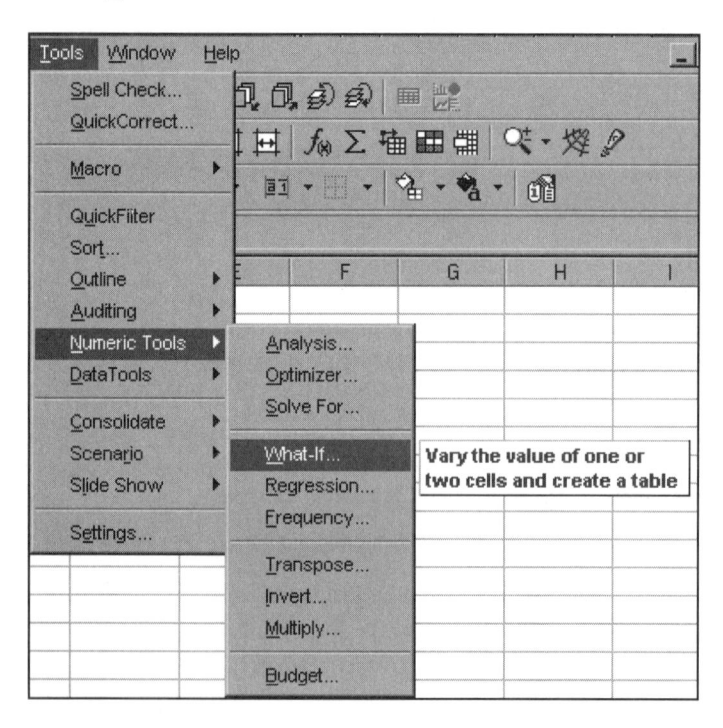

- The table created in a what-if problem enables you to find the best solution to a problem by presenting a range of solutions based on one or two **variables**. A what-if table evaluates a series of answers using input values you supply. The top row and left-most column of the table are call **substitution values**. The first substitution value in both the top row and left-most column are called **input values** and are listed at the bottom of the notebook.

- For example, if you want to purchase a home and can only afford to spend $1,000 per month on your mortgage payment, you might want to determine the maximum mortgage amount you can afford to borrow and the number of years for which you should apply. A what-if table should be created showing the mortgage payments for various loan amounts and loan payment periods. Then you can determine what you can afford.

- When you use the what-if table command, Quattro Pro uses the formula in the upper-left corner of the table to calculate the substitution values. What-if tables that require two sets of substitution values (a row and a column) are called **two-variable what-if tables**. Note the illustration of the What-If dialog box.

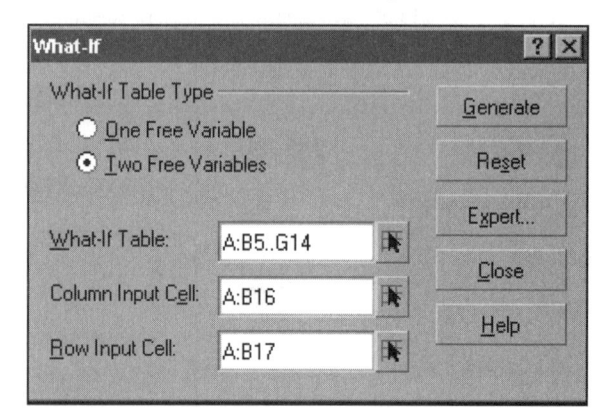

- The format of a two-variable what-if table must meet the following criteria:
  - The column and row input values that the formula will use must be outside of the table.
  - The formula must be in the top-left cell of the table range and must refer to the column and row input values.
  - The substitution values for the table must be arranged in the top row and left-most column of the table, as shown in Illustration A.

Illustration A

	A	B	C	D	E	F	G	H
1		ALISHA AND MARTIN LOBUE						
2		MONTHLY MORTGAGE PAYMENT TABLE AT 8%						
3	Formula cell							
4					TERM IN YEARS			
5		=PMT(B16,.08/12,B17*12)	10	15	20	25	30	
6	PRINCIPAL	$100,000.00						
7		$105,000.00						
8		$110,000.00						
9		$115,000.00						
10		$120,000.00						
11		$125,000.00						
12		$130,000.00						
13		$135,000.00						
14								
15	Input cells							
16	column:	100000						
17	row:	10						
18								
19								

(What-if data table range covers the block C5:G13. Input cells are the first column and row cells.)

- To create the table values, select the what-if table range (which includes the formula), then indicate the row and column input cells (the cells that contain the column and row input values), and then click Generate to create the table.

Payment Function

- The **PMT (payment) function** can be applied to calculate a loan payment amount using principal, interest rate, and number of payment periods. The PMT function uses the following format and contains three parts, as defined below.

  The arguments for the PMT function are:

  @PMT (Pv, Rate, Nper)

  Pv Present value – total amount that a series of future payments is worth now (for example, the principal or amount of the loan).

  Rate Interest rate per period (for example, interest/12 represents the interest per month).

  Nper Number of payment periods (for example, term*12 months).

  ✓Note: The rate and the number of payment periods (nper) must be expressed in the same manner. For example, if you are calculating a monthly payment at a % annual rate of interest for 25 years, you must enter .08/12 as the rate and 25*12 to get the number of monthly payment periods (nper).

Protect a Page

- It is possible to protect, or **lock**, an entire notebook page, individual cells, or a range of cells from accidental changes or unauthorized use. When a notebook page is protected, the message "Protected Cell or Block" will appear when you try to change the contents of a locked cell.

- To protect a document, click Format, Sheet, click the Protection tab and then click Enable Cell Locking.

Format Sheet Protection Dialog Box

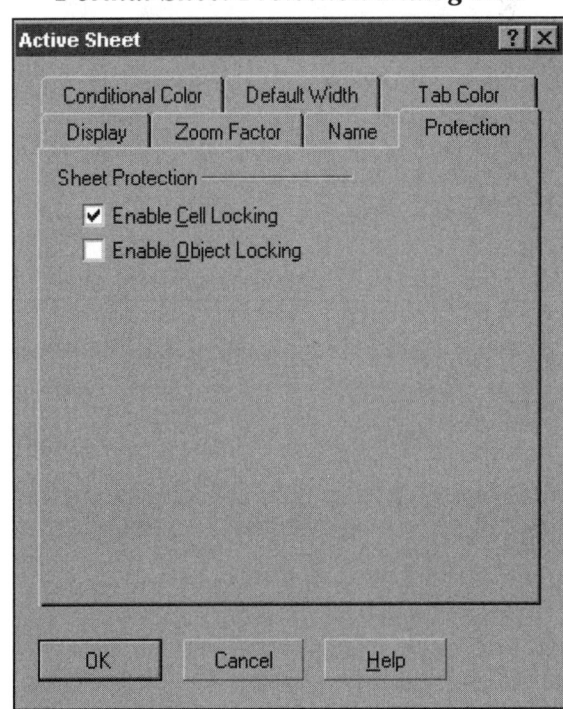

QUATTRO PRO 8   Lesson 5: Logical and Data Functions; SpeedFormat; Hide Data

- When a notebook is protected, by default, all cells are protected and data entry is disabled.

- To enable certain cells to receive data in a protected notebook page, you must unlock those individual cells. To unlock a cell or block of cell, select the block, click Format, Selection, click the Constraints tab and click the Unprotect option.

    important: *If you set a password when protecting a notebook page and you forget the password, you will not be able to make changes to the notebook page.*

Format Cells Constraints Tab

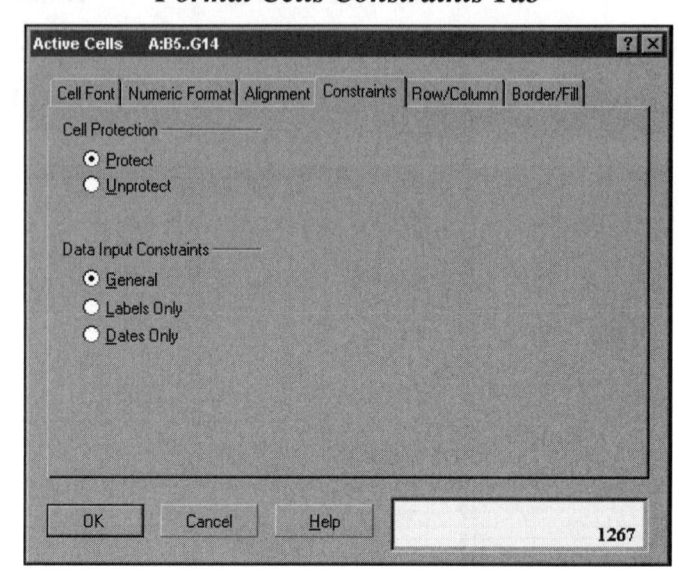

In this exercise, you will create a mortgage payment table for Alisha and Martin Lobue to determine payment amounts at 8% for various principal amounts and numbers of years. The table will be formatted using SpeedFormat, and the notebook page will be protected.

EXERCISE DIRECTIONS

1. Create the notebook page below, or open **29LOAN**.

2. Find in B5 the monthly mortgage payment for $100,000 at 8% for 10 years using the locations of the input cell data for principal and term.

   HINT: @PMT (pv, rate, nper)

   @PMT(B16, .08/12, B17*12)

   ✓ The formula must reference the input values in cells B16 and B17. These input values will not affect the computed values in the table. Note that to determine monthly payments, the rate and nper values have been adjusted by a factor of 12.

3. Create a two-variable what-if table by selecting the table range then completing the What-If dialog box. Click Generate. (See illustrated dialog box on page 336.)

4. Select the table data beginning in row 5 and use the Legal Pad SpeedFormat. Deselect Column Headings and Number Format.

5. Select the top four rows of the notebook and format the block for light yellow to match the table.

6. Adjust column widths as necessary.

7. Save the file; name it **LOAN**.

8. Print one copy.

   ❓ Based on the data in the table, what would be the highest principal you can borrow with a payment of approximately $1,000 a month?

9. Use the Format, Sheet commands and the Protection tab to enable cell locking feature.

10. Use the Format, Selection commands and the Constraints tab to unprotect the top three rows of the notebook.

11. Go to cell C8, F11, and G13 and try to edit the data.

    ✓ A protection message should appear.

12. Go to the third row of the title and enter, March 1998.

    ✓ Since this area was unprotected, you can change these cells.

13. Save and close the file; name it **LOAN**.

A	A	B	C	D	E	F	G
1		ALISHA AND MARTIN LOBUE					
2		MONTHLY MORTGAGE PAYMENT TABLE AT 8%					
3							
4					TERM IN YEARS		
5			10	15	20	25	30
6	PRINCIPAL	$100,000.00					
7		$105,000.00					
8		$110,000.00					
9		$115,000.00					
10		$120,000.00					
11		$125,000.00					
12		$130,000.00					
13		$135,000.00					
14							
15	Input cells						
16	column:	100000					
17	row:	10					

QUATTRO PRO 8 Lesson 5: Logical and Data Functions; SpeedFormat; Hide Data

KEYSTROKES

TWO-VARIABLE WHAT-IF TABLES

What-if tables generate values that change depending on one or two values in a formula. For example, a two-variable input table displays the results of changing two values in a formula.

The row input cell is used to indicate an initial input value to which the formula will refer.

The column input cell is used to indicate an initial input value to which the formula will also refer.

Although instructions listed below are for a two-variable what-if table, you could also create a one-variable what-if table that would find answers for a single row or column of substitution values.

CREATE A TWO-VARIABLE WHAT-IF TABLE

1. Select cells outside the table you will be using to serve as row and column input cells.
2. Enter initial value .... *number* in row input cell.
3. Enter initial value .... *number* in column input cell.
4. Enter series of substitution ...... *numbers* values in left-most column.
5. Enter series of substitution ...... *numbers* values in top row.
   - ✓ *The first cell in row and column will contain the formula.*
6. Click upper-left cell .... [icon] in table.
7. Type formula .... *formula*
   - ✓ *Formula must refer to row and column input cells.*
8. Select all cells in what-if table range.
   - ✓ *Select cells containing formula substitution values and cells where results will be displayed.*
9. Click **Tools** .... `Alt`+`T`
10. Click **Numeric Tools** .... `N`
11. Click **What If** .... `W`
12. Click **Two Free Variables** .... `Alt`+`T`
13. Select What-If table range using the mouse .... `Alt`+`W`, [icon]
14. Select
    Column Input Cell .... `Alt`+`E`, [icon]
15. Select **Row Input Cell** .... `Alt`+`R`, [icon]

    OR

    Type cell references for entire table, column input and row input cells.
16. Click **Generate** .... `Alt`+`G`
17. Click **Close** .... `Alt`+`C`

USE THE PMT FUNCTION

Applies the PMT function to find the monthly payment for a principal for a specific number of years.

1. Click cell where answer should appear.
2. Click [$f_{(x)}$] on toolbar.
3. Click [@].
4. Click **Financial-Annuity** in Function Category list .... `Alt`+`R`, [icon]
5. Click **PMT**
   in Function List .... `Alt`+`F`, [icon]
6. Click **OK** .... `Enter`
7. Click **Monthly Payment** option.
8. Click **Pv** and enter value .... `Alt`+`V`
   - ✓ *The principal is the amount of the loan. You can type the amount or type the cell reference containing the amount.*
9. Click **Rate** and enter value .... `Alt`+`A`
   - ✓ *The rate is a percentage. You can type the percentage or type the cell reference containing the percentage.*
10. Click **Nper** and enter value .... `Alt`+`N`
    - ✓ *Nper is the number of years. You can type the number or type the cell reference containing the number.*
11. Click **OK** .... `Enter`

PROTECT A PAGE (ENABLE CELL LOCK)

Prevents changes to locked cells, graphic objects, embedded charts in a notebook page, or chart items in a chart page.

1. Click **Format** .... `Alt`+`R`
2. Click **Sheet** .... `H`
3. Click **Protection** tab .... `Ctrl`+`Tab`
4. Click **Enable Cell Locking** .... `C`
5. Click **OK** .... `Enter`

   To password protect page:
   a. Right-click notebook title bar when document window is *not* maximized.
   b. Select **Active Notebook Properties**.
   c. Click **Password Level** tab.
   d. Choose a password protection level (**None**, **Low**, **Medium**, or **High**) .... `↓``↑`
   e. Click **OK** .... `Enter`
   f. Type the **Password**.
   g. Click **OK** .... `Enter`
   h. Verify the password by retyping it.
   i. Click **OK** .... `Enter`

UNPROTECT A PAGE

1. Right-click page tab to unprotect.
2. Click **Sheet Properties**.
3. Click the **Protection** tab .... `Ctrl`+`Tab`
4. Clear the **Enable Cell Locking** or **Enable Object Locking** check boxes.

   If page is password protected:
   a. Right-click on notebook title bar.
   b. Select **Active Notebook Properties**.
   c. Click **Password Level**.
   d. Click **None**.
   e. Click **OK**.

LOCK/UNLOCK CELLS IN A NOTEBOOK PAGE

- ✓ *By default, all cells and objects in a notebook page are locked.*

1. Select block to unlock or lock.
2. Click **Format** .... `Alt`+`R`
3. Click **Selection** .... `E`
4. Select **Constraints** tab .... `Ctrl`+`Tab`
5. Click **Unprotect** .... `U`
   or **Protect** .... `P`

QUATTRO PRO 8 Lesson 5: Logical and Data Functions; SpeedFormat; Hide Data

Exercise 30

■ Summary

In this exercise, you will create a notebook for Clearview Window Replacements, Inc., to analyze its sales and commissions for the month and quarter. The staff receives a base salary of $1,200 per month plus a 10% commission on all sales.

There is a bonus incentive plan as follows:
Under $10,000   no bonus
$10,000 - up   3% additional commission on sales of $10,000 or more.

EXERCISE DIRECTIONS

1. Create the worksheet as illustrated or open 📄30COMM.

2. Find COMMISSION. The commission is 10% of sales.

3. Format the commission for commas with two decimal places and copy the formula for all sales staff.

4. Find BONUS. Enter an IF function that does the following:
   IF (SALES are greater than or equal to 10000, (Sales-10000)*.03, otherwise, zero.)

5. Format the bonus for two decimal places and copy the formula for all sales.

6. Enter the salary data as shown on the illustration. Format for commas with two decimal places.

7. Find the MONTHLY EARNINGS by totaling the COMMISSION, BONUS, and SALARY columns.

8. Format the monthly earnings for commas with two decimal places and copy the formula for all sales.

9. Find the summary TOTALS.

10. Enter an IF function to enter a note for those who sold less than $8,500 to "See Mr. Booster" or a "-" for the others.

11. Rename page A to JANUARY.

12. Copy the worksheet onto sheets B, C, and D.

13. Rename the copies FEBRUARY, MARCH, and FIRST QUARTER.

14. Change the third line of the headings to reflect the month on the FEBRUARY and MARCH sheets.

15. Enter the data listed below on the new sheets:

SALES STAFF	FEBRUARY SALES	MARCH SALES
Anderson, Louis	14,895.65	12,656.80
Cusick, Ann	10,454.87	5,222.34
Haebich, Gunther	8,310.00	10,234.56
Mahoney, Daniel	6,458.98	15,434.89
Rothman, Paula	10,568.92	8,333.00
Santoro, Ralph	15,878.45	8,450.40
Unitas, Marie	16,344.54	10,333.89
Williams, Charles	14,456.80	10,650.00

16. On the FIRST QUARTER sheet, change the third line of the heading to state:
    FIRST QUARTER SUMMARY

17. Delete all Notes text and numeric data except for TOTALS formulas.

QUATTRO PRO 8 Lesson 5: Logical and Data Functions; SpeedFormat; Hide Data

18. Enter a three-dimensional formula to summarize the JANUARY, FEBRUARY, and MARCH sheet data in the SALES column for Louis Anderson.

19. Copy the formula down and across for all numeric columns.

20. In the Notes column, enter an IF function that will print "Congratulations on a great quarter." for SALES over $35,000, and no message "-" for sales under that amount. Adjust column width.

21. Print one copy of the notebook.
    - ✓ In Page Setup, enable Print Between Selections on the Options tab, and set lines to 2; on the Print Scaling tab, enable Print to desired width and set to 1 page wide and 1 page high.

22. Save and close the notebook; name it **COMM**.

A	A	B	C	D	E	F	G	H
1			CLEARVIEW WINDOW REPLACEMENTS, INC.					
2			SALES AND COMMISSION REPORT					
3			JANUARY					
4							MONTHLY	
5	SALES STAFF		SALES	COMMISSION	BONUS	SALARY	EARNINGS	NOTE:
6	Anderson, Louis		9,450.85			1200		
7	Cusick, Ann		12,785.90			1200		
8	Haebich, Gunther		14,656.45			1200		
9	Mahoney, Daniel		8,333.92			1200		
10	Rothman, Paula		12,455.95			1200		
11	Santoro, Ralph		9,454.87			1200		
12	Unitas, Marie		8,566.86			1200		
13	Williams, Charles		10,353.82			1200		
14								
15	TOTALS							

QUATTRO PRO 8
Lesson 6: Charts

Exercise 31
- Create Charts
- Change Chart Types
- Select and Size Inserted Charts
- Enable Graph Editing

NOTES

Create Charts

- Charts present and compare data in a graphic format and are always linked to the data that they plot. When you change data in the plotted area of a notebook page, the data and visual graphics in the linked chart also change. A chart may be created by selecting Chart from the Insert menu, or by using the Floating Chart button on the Notebook Toolbar.

- To create a chart using the Notebook Toolbar, first select the data, then click the Floating Chart button, and then click the insertion point location on the notebook page. Here are some guidelines for selecting data to chart:

  - The selection should be rectangular.
  - The selection should not contain blank columns or rows.

- The selection determines the orientation (in columns or rows) of the data series. However, orientation may be changed as desired.

- Typically, a chart or graph will contain the following elements:

  Chart data — Values the chart represents.
  Series labels — Labels identifying the charted values. These labels appear in the chart legend, which identifies each data series.
  Category labels — Labels identifying each data series shown on the x or y-axis.

  ✓Note: Note the illustration of a labeled vertical bar chart showing chart elements.

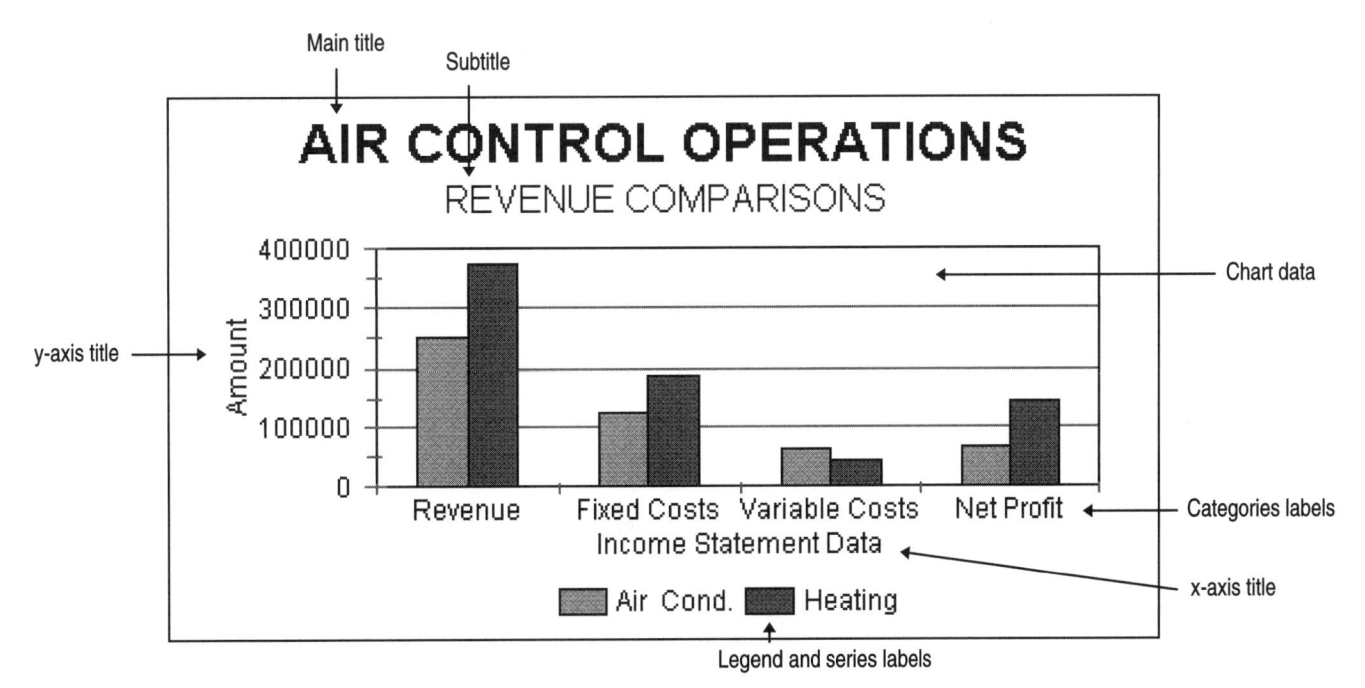

A	A	B	C	D	E	F	G
1	COMPARISON OF AIR CONTROL REVENUES						
2							
3		Air Cond.	Heating				
4	Revenue	250925	374850				
5	Fixed Costs	122850	185678			Fixed Costs	185678
6	Variable Costs	62450	43567			Variable Costs	43567
7	Net Profit	65625	145605			Net Profit	145605
8							
9							
10			This selection results in a column, line or comparison chart since more than one series of data is selected.			This selection (a copy of only the Heating data) results in a Pie chart since only one series is selected.	
11							
12							
13							
14							
15							

- The illustration above shows two selections that would result in different charts. Both selections are rectangular. The second selection is for a pie chart and contains only one value range. If you wish to select the labels and data for Heating revenues for a pie chart, you would hide column B or the Air Conditioning data, or move the data to a new area on the notebook as illustrated.

- Most charts (excluding pie charts) also typically contain the following:

    y-axis Represents the value scale and is usually vertical. Scale values are entered automatically, based on the values being graphed.

    x-axis Represents the data series categories and is usually horizontal.

    x-axis title Describes the x-axis (horizontal) data. *(See Income Statement Data in the illustration on the previous page.)*

    y-axis title Describes the y-axis (vertical) data. *(Amount in the illustration on the previous page.)*

- To create a chart using the Floating Chart button:

    1. Select the notebook page data to plot.

    2. Click the Floating Chart button [icon] on the Notebook Toolbar.

    3. Click once on the desired chart location or click and drag the chart to the desired size.

These steps will create a floating chart on the notebook page. A copy of the chart will also appear as an icon on the **Objects** sheet, the last sheet in the notebook. Charts may be copied, moved, or edited from the Objects sheet or from the notebook sheet. Note the illustration below of the objects sheet and the chart icon.

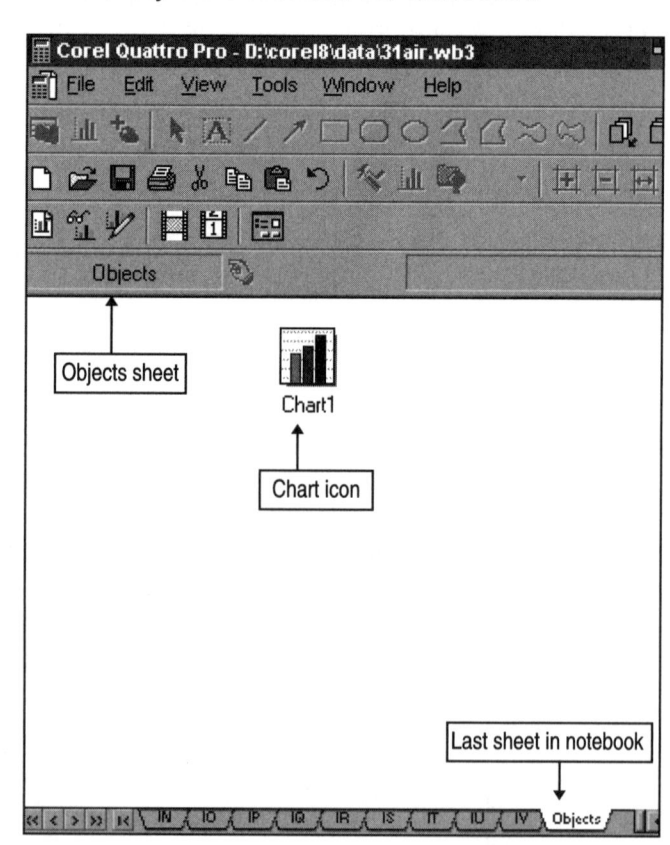

Change Chart Types

- Quattro Pro provides many chart types. In this exercise we will discuss and explore three chart types: Bar, line, and pie *(illustrated on page 348)*.
  - Bar charts compare individual or sets of values. The height or length of each bar is proportional to its corresponding value in the notebook page.
  - Line charts are especially useful when plotting trends, since lines connect points of data and show changes over time effectively.
  - Pie charts are circular charts used to show the relationship of each value in a data range to the entire data range. The size of each wedge represents the percentage each value contributes to the total.

- Only one numerical data range may be used in a pie chart. The data in that range is represented as pie slices. The data range must be adjacent to the data labels when using the Floating Chart button to create a pie chart. Therefore, it may sometimes be necessary to copy the labels and values to another section of the notebook or to hide unwanted data in order to plot the chart.

- Pie charts may be formatted to indicate the percentage each piece of the pie represents of the whole.

- Charts can be copied and then edited to produce a different chart type that uses the same notebook page data.

Select and Size Inserted Charts

- You can click an inserted chart once to format it as an object, or to size, move, and copy it. The selected object will display a border outline with handles, as shown below. Drag the border to size the chart or use the mouse to drag and drop or move the object. A chart may be copied using the Edit menu or Toolbar buttons.

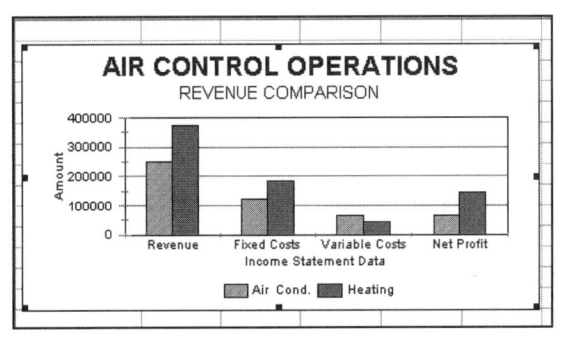

Enable Chart Editing

- To edit a chart, double-click the graph you want to change on the Objects page or on the notebook page. The chart will display in a dotted border, as shown below, and a Chart menu will appear on the menu bar. Use the Chart menu to edit items on the graph.

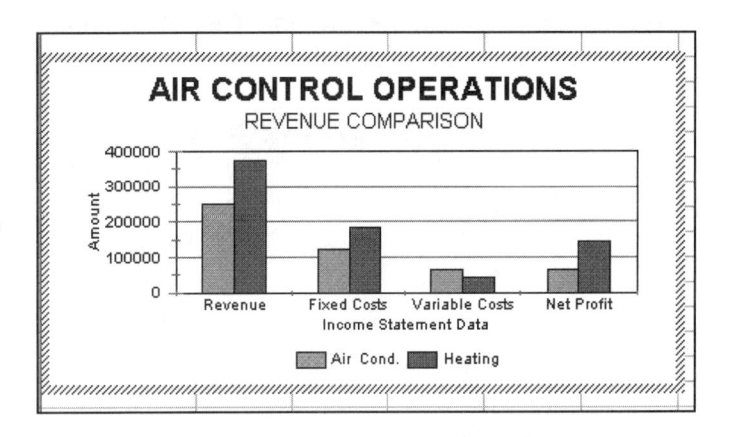

- When charts are created using the Floating Chart button, titles are not included. Double-click the chart and edit to include the titles by selecting Titles from the Charts menu and completing the Chart Titles dialog box as illustrated below.

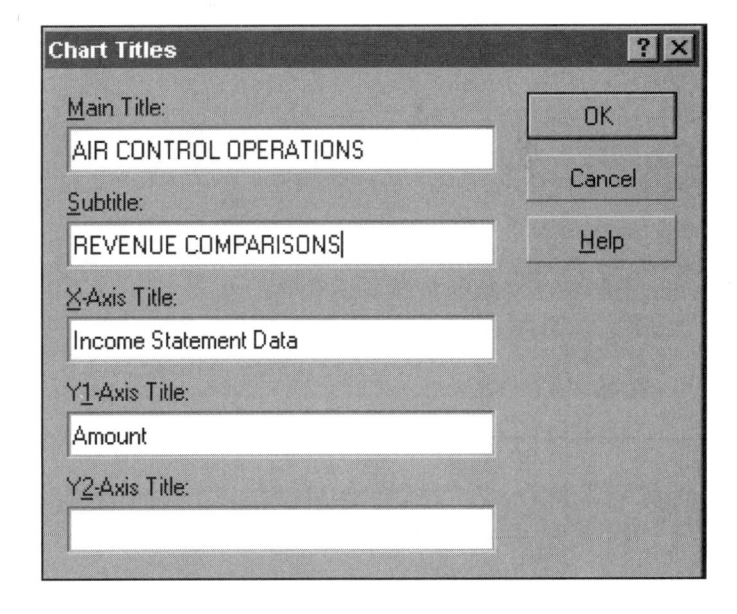

QUATTRO PRO 8 Lesson 6: Charts

- When the floating chart is created, the default chart type is a three-dimensional bar chart. You may change the chart type by double-clicking the chart and selecting Type/Layout from the Chart menu. The Chart Types dialog box appears containing a drop-down list for chart categories. Each chart type selected will display a different variety of subtypes. In the illustration below, the Bar category is selected and the illustrations are the subtypes of bar charts that may be selected.

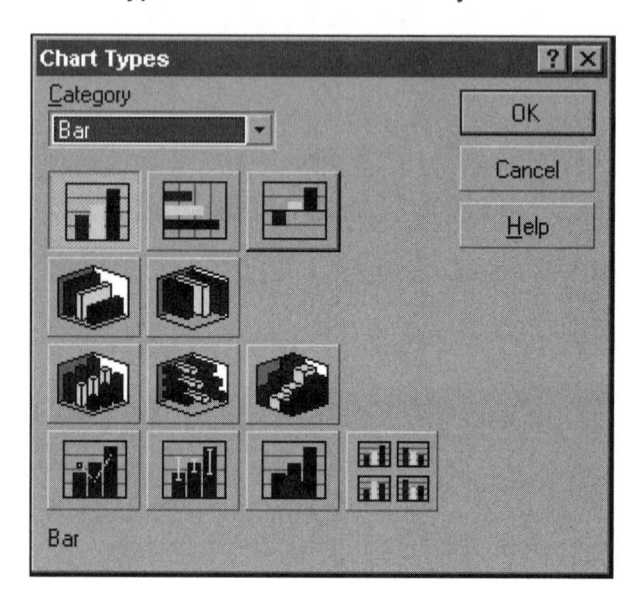

- All chart items, such as legends and titles, can be changed and enhanced by clicking on them and making changes through the Chart menu. When you right-click a chart or chart element, Quattro Pro displays a shortcut menu containing relevant commands, as illustrated below.

    Right-Click Menu for Chart Items

- After editing is complete, return to the notebook by clicking on the Notebook sheet.

In this exercise, you will use an air conditioning and heating comparison worksheet to prepare and modify several charts presenting the data graphically.

EXERCISE DIRECTIONS

1. Create the worksheet as illustrated below or open 🖫31AIR.

	A	B	C	D
1	COMPARISON OF AIR CONTROL REVENUES			
2				
3		Air Cond.	Heating	
4	Revenue	250925	374850	
5	Fixed Costs	122850	185678	
6	Variable Costs	62450	43567	
7	Net Profit	65625	145605	

2. Use the Floating Chart button to create a floating bar chart in the notebook. Select data as highlighted in the illustration, comparing air conditioning and heating revenues, then click the Floating Chart button.

   ✓ *When selecting notebook data to chart, the selection area must be rectangular and a blank cell should be included in the selection. The selection of a blank cell helps Quattro Pro correctly identify the category and data series labels.*

   - Place chart in the range A9:F21. (A 3-D bar chart, with legends but without titles, will appear.)

3. Enable chart editing by double-clicking the chart. Right-click the chart to open the shortcut menu and choose Titles. Insert the following information and click OK.

   Main title: AIR CONTROL OPERATIONS
   Subtitle: REVENUE COMPARISON
   X-axis title: Income Statement Data
   Y-axis title: Amount

4. Return to the notebook by clicking anywhere else on the notebook sheet.

5. Click on the chart once, displaying the handles around the chart, and copy the chart to A22.

6. Double-click the chart in A22 to enable chart editing. Change the chart type to an Area/Line chart by selecting Type/Layout from the Chart menu. Select the first line chart in the category options.

7. To create a pie chart for Air Conditioning:
   - Select labels and values for Air Conditioning for Fixed Costs, Variable Costs, and Net Profit. (Omit Revenues.)
   - Place the chart in the range A35:F47.

8. Edit the pie chart and insert a chart title and subtitle as follows:
   AIR CONDITIONING
   Revenue Dollar

9. In the notebook, change Fixed Costs to Fixed Expenses.

   ✓ *Linked text changes in chart labels.*

10. Change the label back to Fixed Costs.

11. Create a pie chart of Fixed Costs, Variable Costs, and Net Profit labels and data for Heating data.
    - Copy the labels for Fixed Costs, Variable Costs, and Net Profit to E5.
    - Copy the data for Heating to F5.
    - Select the heating labels and data in E5:F7 and click the Floating Chart button.
    - Place the pie chart in the range A48:E61.
    - Add a chart title and subtitle: Heating, Revenue Dollar.

12. If necessary, move and size charts to align them.

13. In Page Setup set notebook to fit on one page.

14. Use Print Preview to view and print the notebook.

15. Move to the last page of the notebook, the Objects page, by using Move to Objects Page button ▶| at the bottom of the window.

16. Double-click on one of the charts.

17. Close chart using ✕ button at the top right of screen.

18. Return to the notebook and to page A by using the Return from Objects Page button |◀. *(The same button changes to a return button.)*

19. Save and close the workbook file; name it **AIR**.

QUATTRO PRO 8 Lesson 6: Charts

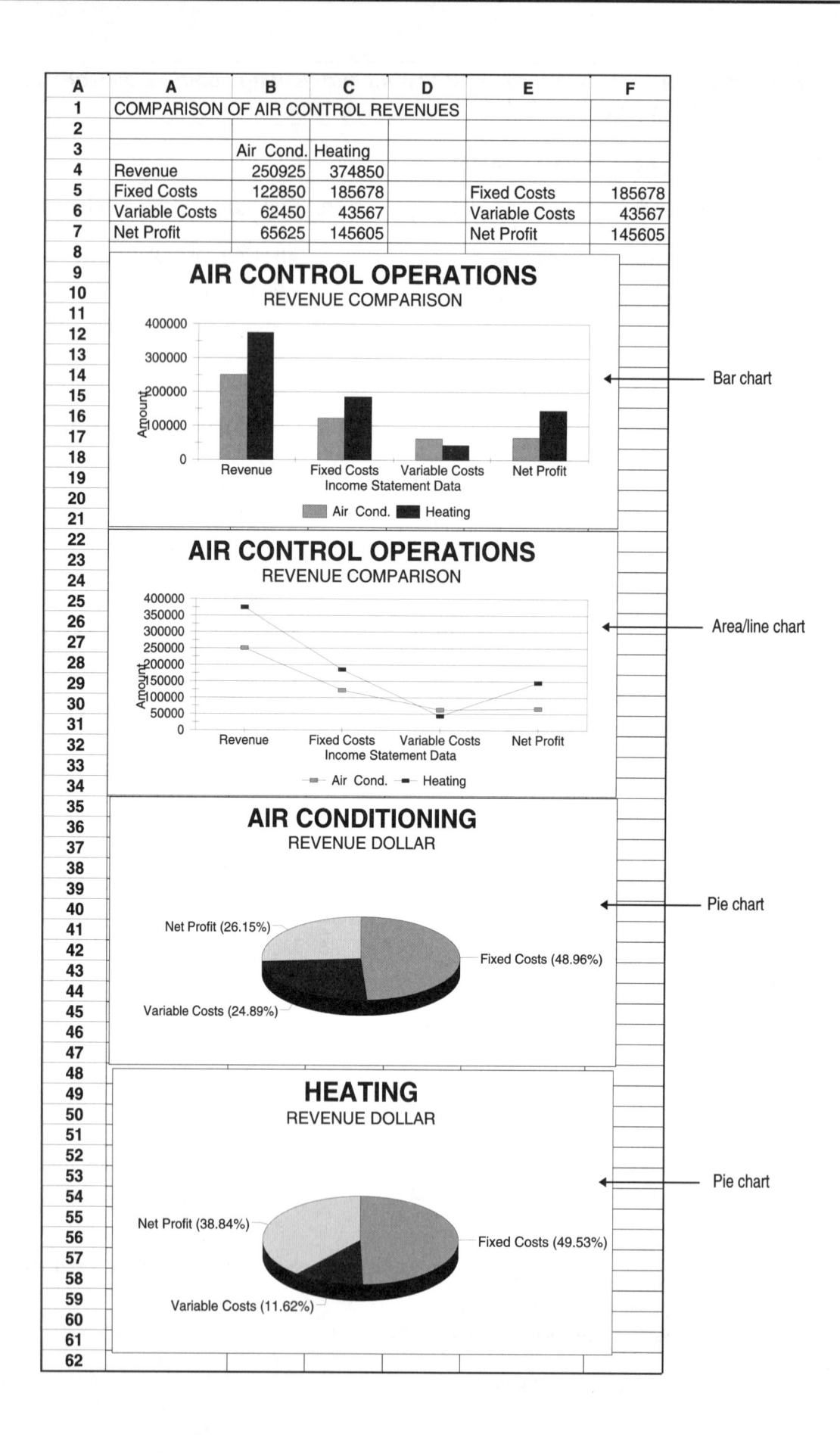

	A	B	C	D	E	F
1	COMPARISON OF AIR CONTROL REVENUES					
2						
3		Air Cond.	Heating			
4	Revenue	250925	374850			
5	Fixed Costs	122850	185678		Fixed Costs	185678
6	Variable Costs	62450	43567		Variable Costs	43567
7	Net Profit	65625	145605		Net Profit	145605

AIR CONTROL OPERATIONS
REVENUE COMPARISON

← Bar chart

AIR CONTROL OPERATIONS
REVENUE COMPARISON

← Area/line chart

AIR CONDITIONING
REVENUE DOLLAR

Net Profit (26.15%)
Fixed Costs (48.96%)
Variable Costs (24.89%)

← Pie chart

HEATING
REVENUE DOLLAR

Net Profit (38.84%)
Fixed Costs (49.53%)
Variable Costs (11.62%)

← Pie chart

KEYSTROKES

USE TOOLBAR TO CREATE A GRAPH

1. Select cells containing data to plot.
2. Click **Chart** button ....
3. Click location on notebook and drag to desired size. (Chart appears on notebook page and also on objects page as an icon.)
4. Edit chart to add titles or to change chart type.

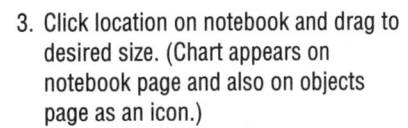

SELECT CHART AS AN OBJECT

Click chart once.

When chart is selected as an object, it can be sized, moved, or copied. Handles (black squares) appear on chart border.

ENABLE CHART EDITING

Double-click chart.

(Chart displays with a wide dotted border.)

CHANGE CHART TYPE

Available types depend upon the selected chart category.

In chart edit mode:

1. Click **Chart** .... Alt + C
2. Click **Type/Layout** .... Y
3. Select **Category** .... ↓ , Enter
4. Select type .... Tab + →
5. Click **OK** .... Enter

ADD TITLES TO CHART

In chart edit mode:

1. Click **Chart** .... Alt + C
2. Click **Titles** .... T
3. Click **Main Title** .... Alt + M
4. Enter title.
5. Click **Subtitle** .... Alt + S
6. Enter title.
7. Click **X-Axis Title** .... Alt + X
8. Enter title.
9. Click **Y1-Axis Title** .... Alt + 1
10. Enter title.
11. Click **Y2-Axis Title** .... Alt + 2
12. Enter title.
13. Click **OK** .... Enter

SIZE INSERTED CHARTS

1. Select chart.
2. Point to handle on side of border to size.
   ✓ *To size object proportionally, point to corner handle.*

To size object without constraints:

Drag border outline until desired size is obtained.

QUATTRO PRO 8 Lesson 6: Charts

Exercise 32

- Create Charts with Chart Expert
- Create Charts with Chart Menu
- Chart Subtypes
- Stacked Bar Charts
- Line-Bar Charts
- Change Legend Positions

NOTES

Create Charts with Chart Expert

- In the last exercise, charts were created using the Floating Chart button on the toolbar. You can also create charts by selecting the area to be charted and then selecting Chart from the Insert menu. The Chart Expert: Step 1 of 5 dialog box will appear with a sample chart, the range selected and plotting options.

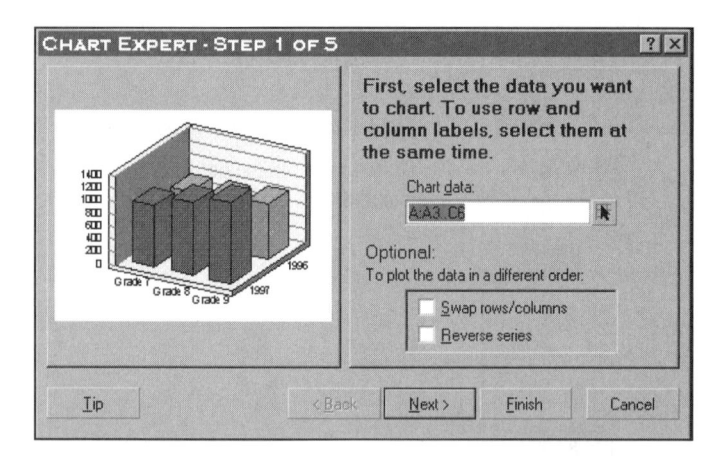

- When you click Next, the Step 2 of 5 dialog box displays providing options as to the general chart type you wish to create. As you select the type, the resulting chart is illustrated in the dialog box.

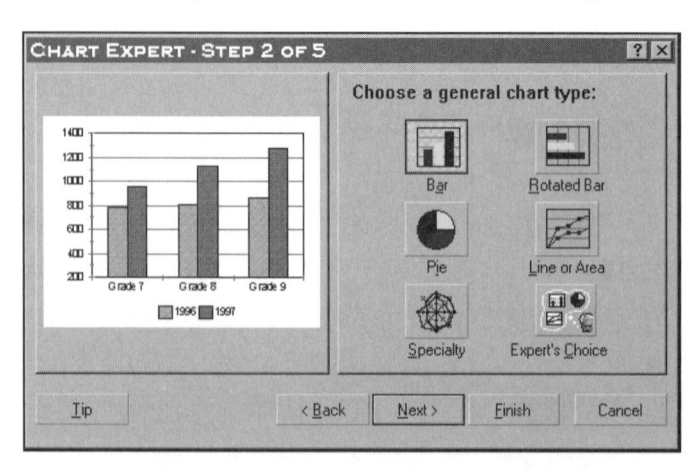

- The third dialog box provides specific chart types or subtypes within the general chart type you chose in Step 2.

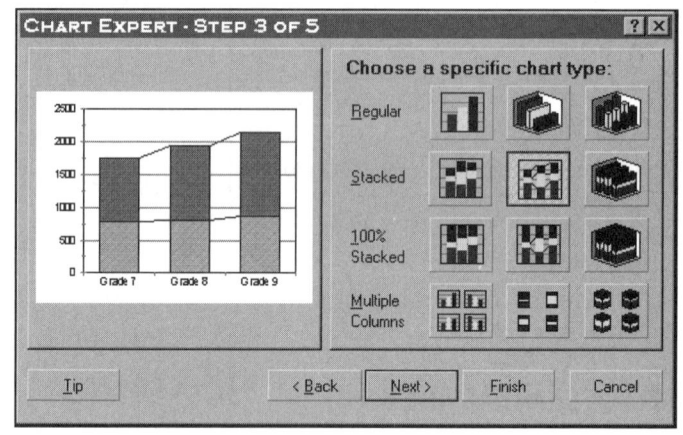

- Step 4 provides color scheme options for the chart. A no change selection will result in the illustrated chart.

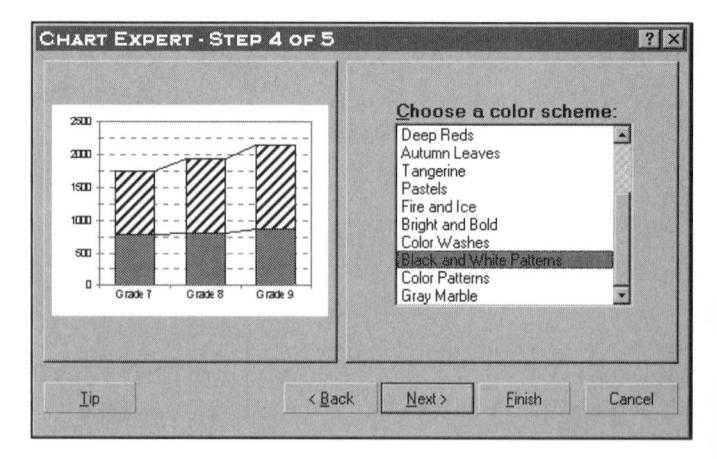

350

- The last dialog box, Step 5, provides settings for titles, subtitles, and axis labels. As you enter the labels, they are placed on the illustration. You must also set the destination of the chart in the current sheet or in a chart window.

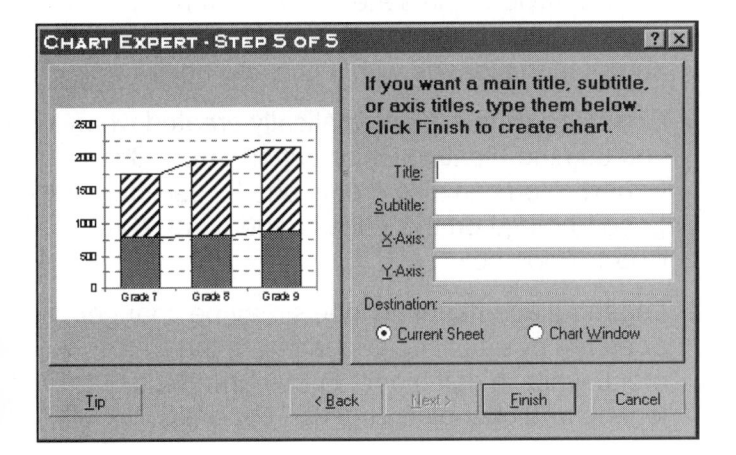

- When you select placement on the current sheet, you will be able to click and drag the completed chart into position. When you select placement on a chart window, the chart will display in a window that is named with the filename and the chart name. A chart window is a separate window within the file that can only be accessed by using the Object sheet in the notebook. Note the illustration of the Window menu, showing objects in the current file and on the object sheet.

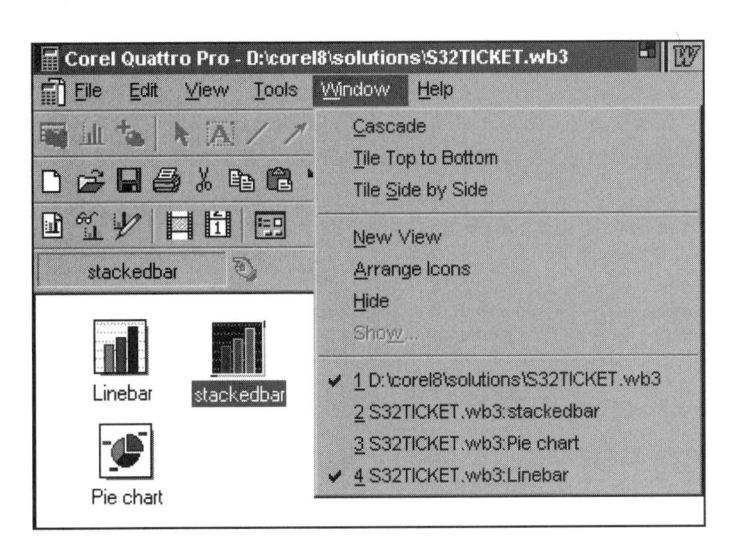

Create Charts with Chart Menu

- When you are in a chart window or in chart edit mode, the Chart menu will display. You can then create a new chart by clicking Chart, New Chart. The New Chart dialog box contains the Series, Type, Titles, and Name tabs which you complete to create the chart. The Name tab allows you to give the chart a name other than Chart1, Chart2, etc. Note the illustration of the Name tab below.

New Chart Dialog Box - Name Tab

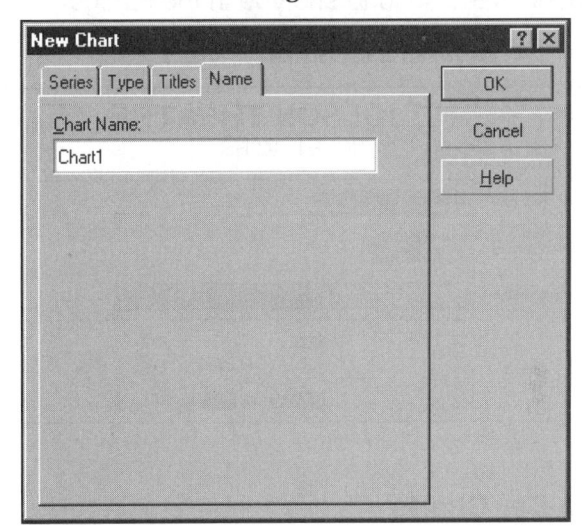

- When you use this method to create a chart, the chart is placed on the Objects sheet, as with a chart window. A chart that appears as an icon on the Objects sheet can be placed on any notebook page by copying and pasting it to the desired location. On the Objects sheet you can double-click a chart icon to edit the chart and name or rename the chart. You can also select the chart icons and print them. To move quickly to the Objects sheet, click the Objects sheet scroll button or click View, Objects.

Chart Subtype

- A goal of charting data is to select a chart type and format that will best present the notebook page data. Chart **subtypes**, such as the three dimensional variation, offer additional options to standard chart types. Once you select a chart type, the subtypes display graphically for selection.

Quattro Pro 8 ■ Lesson 6 ■ Exercise 32

Stacked Bar Charts

- The **stacked bar chart** is an example of one chart type category that offers several subtypes. This chart type is used to show the total effect of several sets of data. For example, in the illustration below, each bar has two sections, which represent ticket sales for March and April. Together, these sections represent the total sales for the seats for the two months. The chart illustrated is called the Rotated 2-D Stacked Bar, which is the second subtype in the category.

Rotated 2-D Stacked Bar Chart

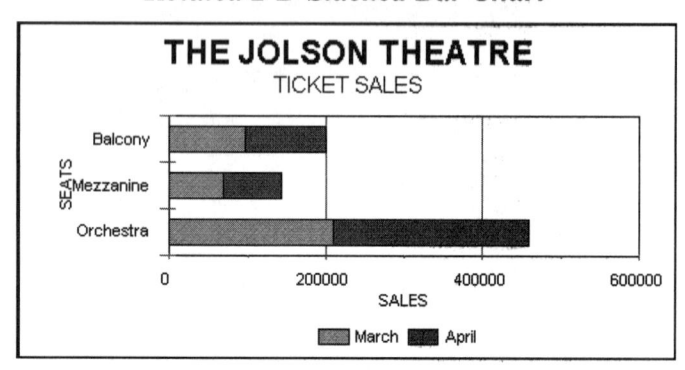

Line-Bar Charts

- The **Line-Bar**, or combination chart, is a subtype in the Bar category that lets you plot the data using lines and bars to present a clear comparison. For example, in the illustration below, a line is used to plot the March data and bar to plot the April data.

Line-Bar Chart

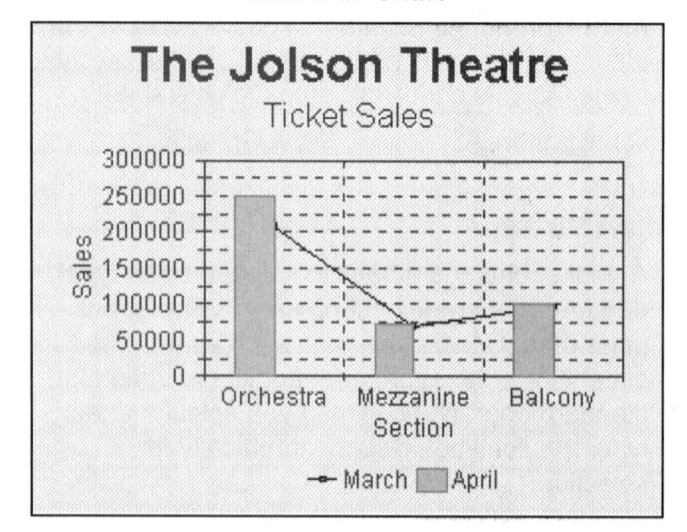

Change Legend Positions

- Any part of a chart may be edited by selecting the part and using the right-click menu.

- A legend is a series label with a sample of the color or style of the series. For example, in the chart at bottom left, March and April data are shown in the legend with a line and bar sample.

- **Chart legends** are automatically created when you use the Floating Chart button or the Chart Expert. You can also create one by selecting the Legend range on the Series page of the New Chart dialog box.

- Legend placement and labels may be changed or edited by selecting Legend from the Chart menu while in edit mode, or by right-clicking the legend and changing Legend Properties.

In this exercise you will create stacked bar, pie, line, and line-bar charts. Charts will be named and edited using the Object sheet and the Chat menu..

EXERCISE DIRECTIONS

1. Create the notebook as illustrated below or open 📁**32TICKET**.

	A	B	C
1	THE JOLSON THEATRE		
2	TICKET SALES		
3		March	April
4	Orchestra	208480	250340
5	Mezzanine	68450	73680
6	Balcony	97450	102343
7			

2. To create a stacked bar graph:
   - Select graph data, A3:C6.
   - Select Chart from the Insert menu.
   Chart Expert displays with the chart data range and a sample chart.
   - Click Next.
   - Click Rotated Bar as the general chart category.
   - Click Next.
   - Click the first Stacked rotated bar subtype.
   - Click Next.
   - Select Pastels as the color scheme.
   - Click Next.
   - Enter titles as follows:
     Main Title: The Jolson Theatre
     Subtitle: Ticket Sales
     X-Axis Title: Section
     Y-Axis Title: Sales
   - Select Chart Window as the destination for the chart.
   - Click Finish.
   The chart will appear in a chart window.

3. Switch back to the notebook using the Window menu.

4. Move to the Objects page and right-click the icon.

5. Use the right-click quick menu to copy the icon.

6. Select Icon properties and name the chart STACKBAR. Click OK.

7. Return to Sheet A and paste the chart in A10:E24.

8. Return to the Object sheet and note that an icon was created for this object called Chart1.

9. Return to Sheet A and double-click to edit the chart. Right-click on the chart legend. Change legend properties so that the legend appears on the right side of the chart.

10. Paste the Stacked Bar chart again to F10.

11. Enable chart editing and change the type to the Bar category, Line-Bar subtype.

12. While still in edit mode, create a new pie chart showing April sales as follows:
    - Select, New Chart from the Chart menu.
    - Type in the X-Axis block A4..A6, or use the 🔲 to select the block.
    - Type in the 1st Series block C4..C6, or use the 🔲 to select the block.
    - Select the Titles tab and enter the following titles:
      The Jolson Theatre
      April Ticket Sales
    - Select the Name tab and name the graph Pie.
    - Click OK.

13. Copy the pie chart from the Object sheet and paste it to A26:J40.

14. Use the Floating Chart button to create a line chart for the March and April data, place it in A41, and size it to match the smaller charts.

15. Select the chart with one click, and delete the chart by pressing the Delete key.

16. Set the notebook to print on one page.

17. Preview and print the notebook sheet.

18. Close and save the notebook file, or *save as* **TICKET**.

Quattro Pro 8 ■ Lesson 6 ■ Exercise 32   353

QUATTRO PRO 8 Lesson 6: Charts

KEYSTROKES

CREATE CHARTS WITH CHART EXPERT

1. Select data to be graphed.
2. Click **I**nsert .... `Alt`+`I`
3. Click C**h**art .... `H`
4. Step 1 of 5:
   If series data is not correct, reselect data for each series using 🔲 button.
5. Click **N**ext .... `Alt`+`N`
6. Step 2 of 5:
   Choose a general chart type:
   - **B**ar .... `Alt`+`A`
   - **R**otated Bar .... `Alt`+`R`
   - P**i**e .... `Alt`+`I`
   - **L**ine or Area .... `Alt`+`L`
   - **S**pecialty .... `Alt`+`S`
   - Expert's **C**hoice .... `Alt`+`C`
7. Click **N**ext .... `Alt`+`N`
8. Step 3 of 5:
   Choose a specific chart type:
   - **R**egular .... `Alt`+`R`, `Tab`
   - **S**tacked .... `Alt`+`S`, `Tab`
   - **1**00% Stacked .... `Alt`+`1`, `Tab`
   - **M**ultiple Columns .... `Alt`+`M`, `Tab`
9. Click **N**ext .... `Alt`+`N`
10. Step 4 of 5:
    Select a color scheme .... `↓`
11. Click **N**ext .... `Alt`+`N`
12. Step 5 of 5:
    Enter title and tab to next title:
    - Titl**e** .... `Alt`+`E`
    - **S**ubtitle .... `Alt`+`S`
    - **X**-Axis .... `Alt`+`X`
    - **Y**-Axis .... `Alt`+`Y`
    Destination:
    Click **C**urrent sheet .... `Alt`+`C`
    OR
    Click Chart **W**indow .... `Alt`+`W`
13. Click **F**inish .... `Alt`+`F`

CREATE CHARTS WITH CHART MENU

1. Select data to be charted.
2. Double-click a chart to enter chart edit mode.
3. Click **C**hart .... `Alt`+`C`
4. Click **N**ew Chart .... `N`
5. On **Series** tab, if series data is not correct or if you have not done step 1, select data for each series using 🔲 button.
6. Click **Type** tab .... `Ctrl`+`Tab`
7. Click **C**ategory .... `↓`, `Enter`
8. Select a subtype .... `Tab`, `→`
9. Select **Titles** tab .... `Ctrl`+`Tab`
10. Click **M**ain Title .... `Alt`+`M`
11. Type main title.
12. Click **S**ubtitle .... `Alt`+`S`
13. Type subtitle.
14. Click **X**-Axis Title .... `Alt`+`X`
15. Type X-Axis title.
16. Click Y**1**-Axis Title .... `Alt`+`1`
17. Type Y1-Axis Title.
18. Select **N**ame page .... `Ctrl`+`Tab`
19. Type chart name.
20. Click **OK** .... `Enter`

SELECT CHART ITEMS

Select chart items (such as the legend or a data series) prior to selecting commands to change the item in some way.

✓ *Quattro Pro marks the currently selected graph item with squares and displays its name in the name box.*

Enable chart editing by double-clicking the chart.

To select next or previous class of graph items:

Press Tab or Shift Tab.

To select a specific item with the mouse:

Click chart item.

To select a data series:

Click any data marker in data series.

To select a data marker:

1. Click any data marker in data series.
2. Click data marker in selected series.

To select the graph area:

Click any blank area outside plot area.

To select the plot area:

Click any blank area inside plot area.

To select the legend:

✓ *Legend items are the legend entry and key.*

Click legend.

To deselect a selected graph item:

Press **Escape** .... `Esc`

DELETE AN INSERTED CHART

1. Select inserted graph as an object.
2. Press **Delete**.

POSITION LEGEND IN CHART

1. Enable chart editing.
2. Right-click legend.
3. Select **Legend Properties**.
4. Select **Legend Position**.
5. Select desired position:
   - None
   - Bottom
   - Right
6. Click **OK**.

GO TO OBJECTS SHEET

Click **Objects scroll** button .... 🔲
OR
1. Click **V**iew .... `Alt`+`V`
2. Click **O**bjects .... `O`

QUATTRO PRO 8 Lesson 6: Charts

Exercise 33

- Change Chart Font
- Explode Pie Chart Slice
- Print Charts
- Chart Gallery

NOTES

Change Chart Font

- Due to size or appearance constraints, you may wish to change the font size of text labels. Remember that any object on a chart may be formatted once you are in chart edit mode. In chart edit mode, select the label to be formatted and choose Selected Object from the Format menu. Or, right click the object and select the Properties item from the menu that appears.

- For example, to change the font size of a chart title, enable chart editing, select the chart title, right-click the object, and then select Chart Title Properties. You can set alignment, text font, text settings, box settings, and fill settings for the chart title. The properties dialog box will provide the settings tabs that are appropriate for the object selected. Note the illustration of the dialog box that appears when Chart Title Properties, or Format, Selected Object is selected.

Chart Title Properties Dialog Box

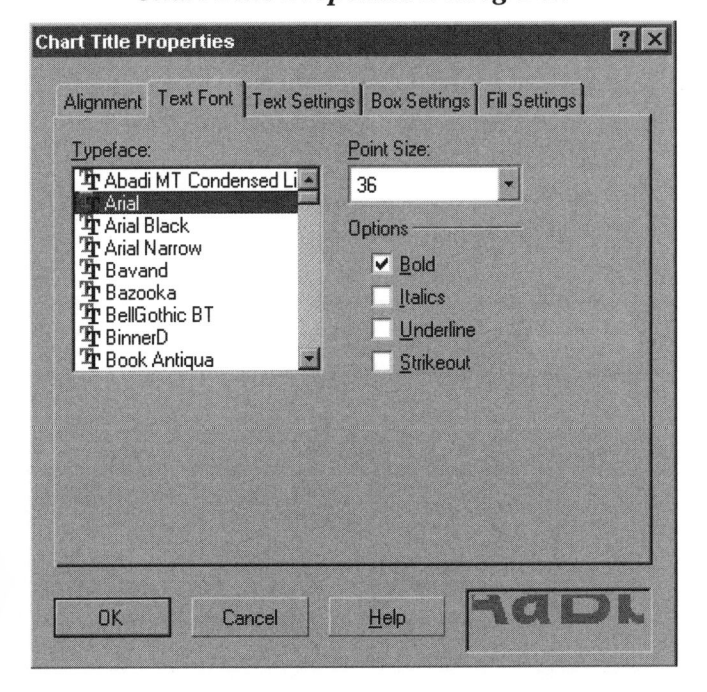

Explode Pie Chart Slice

- To highlight one aspect of pie chart data, you may wish to explode a slice of the pie. To explode a pie chart slice, select the segment in chart edit mode, click Format, Selected Object or right-click and select Pie Chart Properties. The dialog box that appears contains an Explode Slice tab that can be used to enable the setting. Note the illustration of the setting and the resulting pie chart below.

Pie Chart Dialog Box - Explode Slice Tab

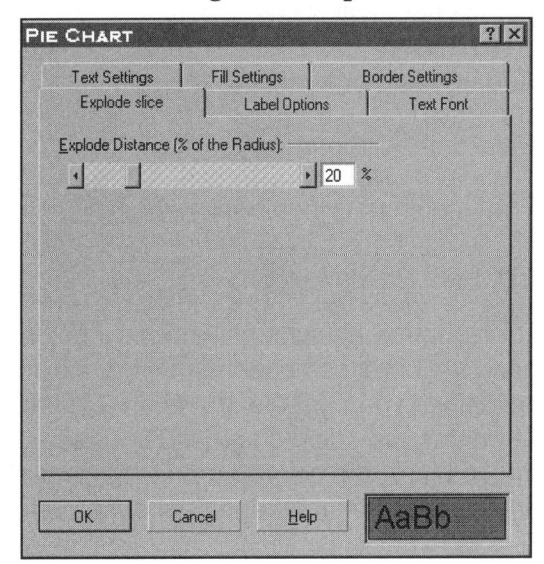

Pie Chart with Exploded Slice

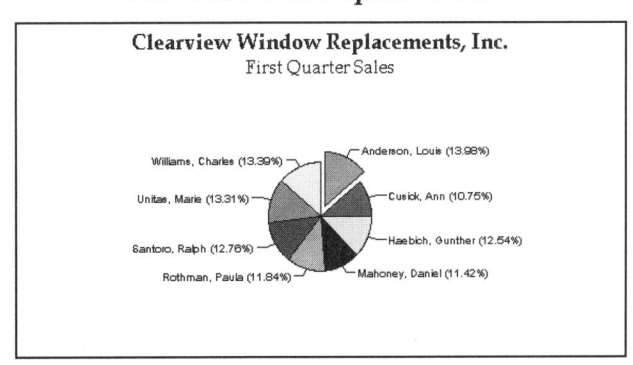

QUATTRO PRO 8 Lesson 6: Charts

Print Charts

- Charts can be printed with the notebook sheet or as separate pages. You can select an inserted chart to print it apart from the notebook sheet. When printing a selected inserted chart or a chart page, you can change the page orientation from the Paper Type tab in the Page Setup dialog box.

- You can use Print Preview to see how a notebook page or chart will print.

    From Print Preview, you can also:

    - View the Previous or Next page when more than one page will be printed.

    - Zoom in or out to view the chart.

    - Change from color to black and white view by using the black and white icon or the color icon.

    - Change the page margins by dragging the guidelines that appear when you select the Margin button.

    - Add headers or footers to the printout.

    - Set Printer Options.

    - Print the chart or notebook page.

    - Exit Print Preview.

- If your computer equipment includes a color monitor, the chart components will be shown in colors. When you print the charts on a black and white printer, the colored text and lines are printed in black; the colored areas are printed in different shades of gray; and the background color is ignored.

Chart Gallery

- When you are in chart edit mode, you can view the chart and data in various other configurations by selecting **Gallery** from the **Chart** menu. The Chart Gallery dialog box, illustrated below, lets you view the data using all the subtypes for the selected chart and using other types and subtypes as well.

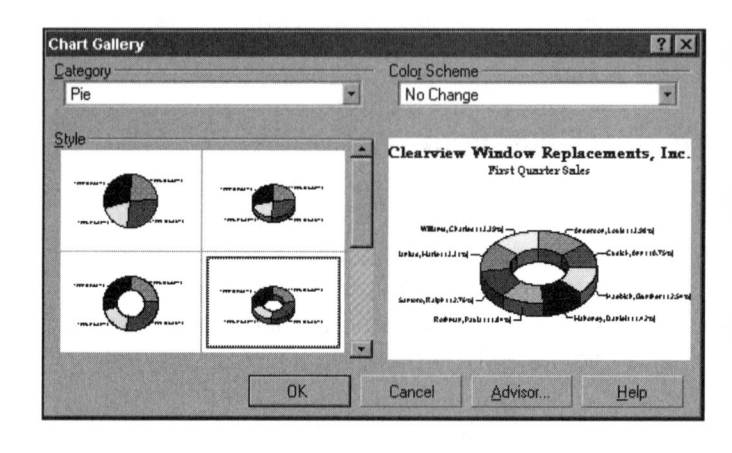

In this exercise, you will create a pie and bar chart for an existing notebook. The pie chart fonts will be changed and one slice will be exploded for emphasis. You will use the Chart Gallery to change the chart subtype. One chart will be printed on a separate page and the notebook will be printed with all the charts.

EXERCISE DIRECTIONS

1. Open **COMM** or **33COMM**.
2. Move to the First Quarter page.
3. Create a pie chart using Chart Expert to display the sales for each employee:
   - Hide column B.
   - Select A6:C13 for data to be charted.
   - Click Insert, Chart.
   - Set type for pie chart.
   - Set titles as follows:
     Main Title: Clearview Replacement Windows, Inc.
     Subtitle: First Quarter Sales
   - Place the chart in the current workbook.
4. Locate the chart in the range A17:I36.
5. Enable chart editing and select the chart title
6. Change the font to Book Antiqua, Bold and the font size to 24 by selecting Chart Title Properties from the right-click shortcut menu.
7. Select the chart subtitle.
8. Change the subtitle font to Book Antiqua 20.
9. Select any series label, right-click and select Pie Chart Properties.
10. Set text font to Book Antiqua, 12 point.
11. Select the Louis Anderson data slice and right-click to set Pie Chart properties to explode the slice 35%.
12. Enable chart editing and select Gallery from the Chart menu.
13. View all options for pie and other chart types. Select the doughnut subtype for pie charts, then explode the Louis Anderson data slice again, as above.
14. Enable chart editing by double-clicking the chart and select New Chart from the Chart menu.
15. Create a stacked rotated bar chart comparing sales from each month using the following series settings by selecting or entering the blocks:
    - X-Axis: January:A6..A13
    - Legend: January:C3, February:C3, March:C3
    - 1st Series: January:C6..C13
    - 2nd Series: February:C6..C13
    - 3rd Series: March:C6..C13

    Set type:
    - Select Stacked Bar type, rotated 2-D subtype.

    Set titles:
    - Main Title: Clearview Window Replacements, Inc.
    - Subtitle: Comparison of First Quarter Sales
    - X-Axis: Staff
    - Y-Axis: Amount

    Name the chart, Comparison.
16. Return to the notebook and copy the chart from the objects page to A37:I57.
17. Enable chart editing and select the appropriate chart elements to make the following changes:
    - Chart main title to Book Antiqua, 24 point, bold
    - Chart subtitle to Book, Antiqua, 20 point.
    - Set legend properties to move legend to bottom of chart and set text to Book Antiqua,16 point.
    - X and Y-axis text to Book Antiqua, 16 point.
    - X and Y-axis titles to Book Antiqua, 18 point.
18. Return to the notebook and set page setup to fit notebook and charts on one page.
19. Print preview.
20. Change orientation to landscape using the Print Options button. Return to portrait mode.
21. Print preview and change margins to center the data on the page.
22. Print one copy of the notebook and charts.
23. Select the Doughnut chart, print preview, and print a copy of the chart in landscape orientation.
24. Close and save the notebook file, or *save as* **COMM**.

QUATTRO PRO 8 Lesson 6: Charts

First Quarter	A	B	C	D	E	F	G	H	I	J	K	L
1			CLEARVIEW WINDOW REPLACEMENTS, INC.									
2			SALES AND COMMISSION REPORT									
3			FIRST QUARTER SUMMARY									
4							MONTHLY		NOTE:			
5		SALES STAFF	SALES	COMMISSION	BONUS	SALARY	EARNINGS					
6		Anderson, Louis	37,006.30	3,700.63	1,133.32	3,600.00	8,433.95		Congratulations on a great quarter			
7		Cusick, Ann	28,463.11	2,846.31	486.12	3,600.00	6,932.43					
8		Haebich, Gunther	33,201.01	3,320.10	733.65	3,600.00	7,653.75					
9		Mahoney, Daniel	30,227.79	3,022.78	815.23	3,600.00	7,438.01					
10		Rothman, Paula	31,357.87	3,135.79	453.73	3,600.00	7,189.52					
11		Santoro, Ralph	33,783.72	3,378.37	881.77	3,600.00	7,860.14					
12		Unitas, Marie	35,245.29	3,524.53	1,001.76	3,600.00	8,126.29		Congratulations on a great quarter			
13		Williams, Charles	35,460.62	3,546.06	819.09	3,600.00	7,965.16		Congratulations on a great quarter			
14												
15		TOTALS		26474.571	6324.674	28800	61599.24					

KEYSTROKES

CHANGE CHART FONTS

1. Enable chart editing. (Double-click chart.)
2. Select text object.
3. Right-click object.
4. Select (Specific) **Properties**.
5. Select **Text Font** tab.
6. Select **T**ypeface...................... `Alt`+`T`
7. Select font .... `↓`
8. Select **P**oint Size .... `Alt`+`P`
9. Select size .... `↓`
10. Select **Options**
    a. **B**old................................ `Alt`+`B`
    b. **I**talics .... `Alt`+`I`
    c. **U**nderline .... `Alt`+`U`
    d. **S**trikeout .... `Alt`+`S`
11. Click **OK** .... `Enter`

EXPLODE PIE SLICE

1. Enable chart editing. (Double-click chart.)
2. Select slice to be exploded.
3. Right-click object.
4. Select **Pie Chart Properties**.
5. Select **Explode Slice** tab.
6. Select **E**xplode .... `Alt`+`E`
7. Enter distance or use mouse slide.
8. Click **OK**.............................. `Enter`

PRINT CHARTS

Print chart page or inserted chart as part of the notebook sheet.

1. Select notebook sheet or chart sheet.
2. Follow steps to **PRINT A NOTEBOOK PAGE**, Lesson 2, Exercise 7.

SET PAGE ORIENTATION OF PRINTED PAGE

FROM PRINT DIALOG BOX

1. Click **F**ile .... `Alt`+`F`
2. Click **P**rint........................... `P`
3. Click P**a**ge Setup button......... `Alt`+`S`
4. Click **Paper Type** tab
5. Click T**y**pe .... `Alt`+`Y`
6. Click P**o**rtrait .... `Alt`+`O`
   OR
   Click Lan**d**scape .... `Alt`+`D`
7. Click **OK** to return to page or Print Preview .... `Enter`

USE CHART GALLERY

1. Enable chart editing.
2. Click **C**hart........................... `Alt`+`C`
3. Click **G**allery .... `G`
4. Click and select
   Category .... `Alt`+`C`, `↓`
5. Select **S**tyle .... `Alt`+`S`, `Tab`
6. Select Color Scheme...... `Alt`+`R`, `↓`
7. Click **OK** .... `Enter`

QUATTRO PRO 8 Lesson 6: Charts

Exercise 34

■ Summary

You have been asked to analyze employment trends in the state of North Carolina using data from the 1980 and 1990 census reports. You will create a notebook page using the data below and create several graphs as directed.

EXERCISE DIRECTIONS

1. Create a notebook page using the data below, or open 34NCDATA.

	A	B	C	D
1	N.C. EMPLOYMENT IN SELECTED INDUSTRIES			
2				
3		1980	1990	Change
4	Agriculture, etc.	64,447	80,161	24.4%
5	Mfg., nondurable	414,416	347,224	-16.2%
6	Mfg., durable	405,728	306,212	-24.5%
7	Finance, real estate	181,953	246,037	35.2%
8				

2. Format labels and values appropriately and set column widths where needed.
3. Create a rotated bar chart comparing 1980 and 1990 trends and place it on the notebook sheet.
4. Include appropriate titles.
5. Change typeface and point size, if necessary.
6. Using the same data and titles above, create line and line-bar charts below the rotated bar chart.
7. Create a pie chart of 1990 data. Hide columns or copy the pie chart data to the right of the original data. Explode the section of the pie representing the largest employment area in the state.
8. Include appropriate titles.
9. Change typeface and point size, if necessary.
10. Use Edit, Cut and then Edit, Paste to move each chart to a separate sheet in the notebook.
    ✓ Do not delete the source charts on the objects page.
11. Rename each sheet containing a chart as follows:
    BAR CHART
    LINE CHART
    LINEBAR CHART
    PIE CHART
12. Enable editing for each chart listed below and use the Chart Gallery to change the charts as follows:
    BAR CHART   The top right, or second, Rotated Bar subtype.
    LINE CHART The bottom right, or fourth, Line or Area chart subtype.
    PIE CHART   The top right, or second, Pie Chart subtype.
13. Rename Page A; name it DATA.
14. Print the pie and line bar charts on separate pages.
15. Close and save the notebook file, name it **NCDATA**.

Corel Paradox 8

DATABASE BASICS

Lesson 1: Create a Database

Lesson 2: Edit and Print a Database

Lesson 3: Search and Sort a Database

Lesson 4: Queries

Lesson 5: Reports

CORAL PARADOX 8 — Database Basics

Database Basics
- What is Paradox? ■ What is a Database?
- What is a Database Management System?
- What are Database Objects?
- How is a Paradox Database Organized? ■ What are Paradox Tables?
- How are Paradox Tables Related? ■ Paradox 8 Features

NOTES

What is Paradox?

- Paradox 8 is the **database management system** in the Corel WordPerfect Suite 8 Professional package. To understand what a database management system is and what it can do, you need to study the database basics information in this section.

What is a Database?

- A **database** is an organized collection of company or personal data. An address book or a library's card catalog is a database; an office filing cabinet can also contain a database.

- Examples of manual databases are illustrated below. To use and maintain them requires manual labor and a lot of time. Suppose you have two hundred people listed in your address book. To update the telephone number and address of a friend who just moved to Tucson, you must page through the book, locate the entry, and make the change.

Examples of Manual Database Records

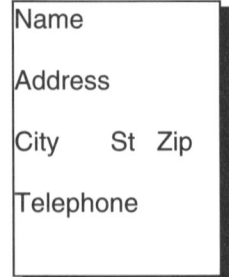

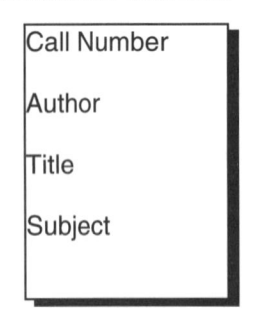

```
Name
Address
City    St   Zip
Telephone
```
Address Book Entry

```
Call Number
Author
Title
Subject
```
Card Catalog Entry

- A **Paradox database** is the electronic equivalent of a manual database. It lets you organize the facts and provides a way to maintain the data electronically. To update the friend's telephone number who moved to Tucson, you simply retrieve the friend's record and make the change.

What is a Database Management System?

- Paradox is a database management system that provides data maintenance features and functions to store, search, filter, query, and report data in the database. For example, suppose you want a list of books about political science. To do this manually, you must read the card catalog entries and write down each political science book. Such a manual search could be quite time-consuming. With an automated database management system like Paradox, however, you can locate all the political science books with its search function and a few simple keystrokes.

What are Database Objects?

- To help you use your database efficiently, modern database management systems, like Paradox, provide **database objects**. Database objects are the tools you need to store, maintain, search, analyze, and report data in your database.

- In the Paradox exercises, you will learn about the four database objects listed below.

Table Data is automatically formatted into a table or spreadsheet format. Each column provides specific information about an aspect of the database (such as branch, item, manufacturer, etc.). Each row in a table represents one record in the database.

	BRANCH	ITEM	MFG	MODEL	COST	PURDATE
1	Big Apple	Computer	GBM	PC220	$1,348.50	6/5/96
2	Sunset	Computer	GBM	Notepad 500C	$2,199.00	6/10/96
3	Pacific	Computer	GBM	Notepad 600	$1,399.00	6/15/96
4	Pacific	Hard Drive	Barton	LPS80 220 MB	$199.00	6/20/96
5	Sunset	Hard Drive	Wilson	CFS4 330 MB	$250.00	7/10/96
6	Pacific	Printer	BP	Laserjet	$1,479.00	7/15/96
7	Bean Town	Computer	Debb	Notebook 586	$1,889.00	1/10/97
8	Lakeview	Computer	Debb	P200	$2,507.52	1/12/97

Form A format that displays one record (one row from a table) at a time. Forms are used to enter or update data. A form can be designed and customized to contain all database fields or only those you wish to display.

BRANCH:	Pacific	MODEL:	Laserjet	WTY:	N
ITEM:	Printer	COST:	$1,479.00	ASSIGNED TO:	Accounting
MFG:	BP	PURDATE:	7/15/96	SERIAL #:	88842

Query A structured way to tell Paradox to retrieve data that meets certain criteria from one or more database tables. For example, a query may request that Paradox retrieve data on hardware assigned to Accounting that is not under warranty. The results of the query would be displayed in a table, as shown below.

	ITEM	MFG	MODEL	COST	PURDATE	WTY	ASSIGNED TO:
1	Hard Drive	Barton	LPS80 220 MB	$199.00	6/20/96	N	Accounting
2	Printer	BP	Laserjet	$1,479.00	7/15/96	N	Accounting

Report A formatted way to display information retrieved from the database. A report formats and analyzes data that you specify. Note the partial view of a report below.

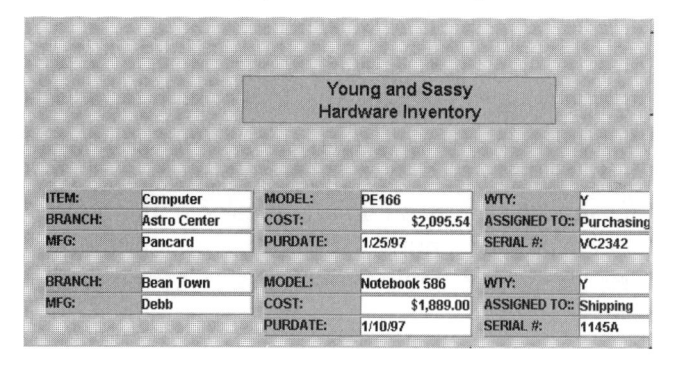

Young and Sassy Hardware Inventory

ITEM:	Computer	MODEL:	PE166	WTY:	Y
BRANCH:	Astro Center	COST:	$2,095.54	ASSIGNED TO:	Purchasing
MFG:	Pancard	PURDATE:	1/25/97	SERIAL #:	VC2342

BRANCH:	Bean Town	MODEL:	Notebook 586	WTY:	Y
MFG:	Debb	COST:	$1,889.00	ASSIGNED TO:	Shipping
		PURDATE:	1/10/97	SERIAL #:	1145A

How is a Paradox Database Organized?

- The Paradox database management system displays database objects in the Project Viewer for the Working Directory. As illustrated below, the Project Viewer for the WORK directory has a list of database objects on the left. As you select each object, the files of that type in the selected directory are displayed. Each Paradox object has a different extension. For example, as shown below, tables have a .db extension. As you select each object, you will display lists of the named objects of that type.

Paradox Project Viewer

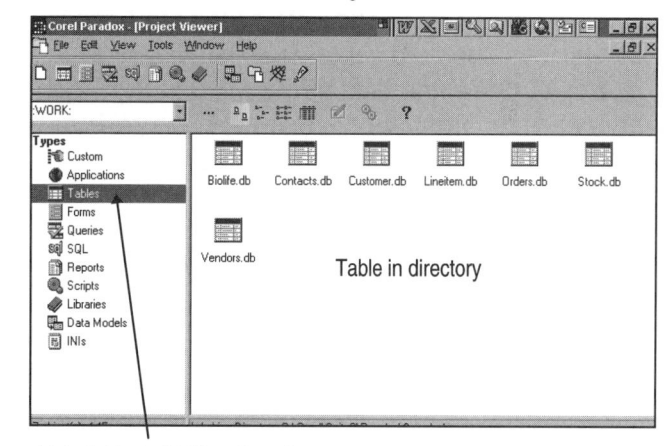

List of objects (Table selected)

Corel Paradox 8 ■ Database Basics

- Using Paradox, you organize the data itself into separate electronic storage containers called **tables**. Each table contains data about a particular part of the entire subject.

  In the illustration on the previous page, there are many tables that represent different aspects of a diving shop's business, i.e. vendors, contacts, customers, orders, etc. These tables, along with others you may create, form the database. By organizing its data into an electronic database consisting of a number of tables, the company replaces filing cabinets with their electronic equivalent.

What are Paradox Tables?

- A Paradox table is a group of rows and columns. Each row contains one **record**. A record is a set of details about a specific item. For example as illustrated below, one record in a company's hardware inventory table will contain details on one of its BP printers, giving a product identifier, the manufacturer, model number, cost, and purchase date. When data processing people ask about the "BP printer record," they want to know the details in the table row where the printer is described.

- Each column in the table represents a **field**, headed by a **field name**. Each row in the column contains specific data called the **field contents**. The field contains a detail. For example, under the field name MFG in the hardware records, the field content entry BP identifies the manufacturer of that piece of equipment. When data processing people ask, "What's in the manufacturer field?", they are asking about the field contents of a particular record.

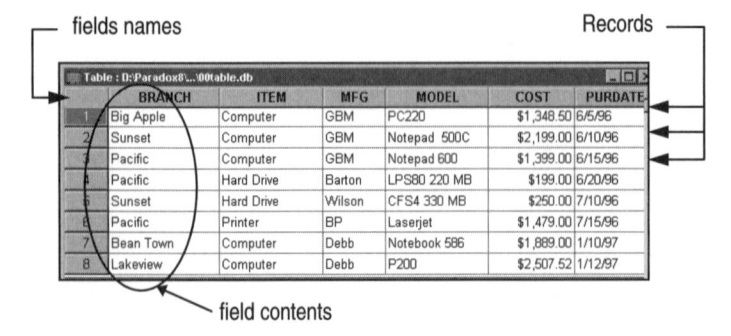

How are Paradox Tables Related?

- If you open several tables of data and do not relate them you have created a **flat-file database.** This type of database examines only one table at a time and cannot use data from all of the tables in a search, query, or report. For example, if you have one table for your address book and another table for holiday cards, and do not relate them, you are working with flat-file databases that cannot be used together. In that case, each table is a separate database.

- In a Corel Paradox **relational database**, you can extract specific information from any table and assemble it in a meaningful way. You could combine addresses from one table with names in the holiday table to get a holiday address list. This would save you time since you would not have to enter the addresses in both tables.

- When designing a database consisting of many tables and database objects, you should provide at least one field in each Paradox table that is the same as that in another table. This **key field** relates the tables to each other so that you can create queries from several or all the tables in the database. Relating tables also prevents data duplication and makes data easier to maintain, because an update in a single field can update information in many tables. The key field used to relate tables should be unique, should identify the record, and should not be duplicated. For example, in a library database, an obvious candidate for a field common to all tables is a book's call number.

fields names — Records

	BRANCH	ITEM	MFG	MODEL	COST	PURDATE
1	Big Apple	Computer	GBM	PC220	$1,348.50	6/5/96
2	Sunset	Computer	GBM	Notepad 500C	$2,199.00	6/10/96
3	Pacific	Computer	GBM	Notepad 600	$1,399.00	6/15/96
4	Pacific	Hard Drive	Barton	LPS80 220 MB	$199.00	6/20/96
5	Sunset	Hard Drive	Wilson	CFS4 330 MB	$250.00	7/10/96
6	Pacific	Printer	BP	Laserjet	$1,479.00	7/15/96
7	Bean Town	Computer	Debb	Notebook 586	$1,889.00	1/10/97
8	Lakeview	Computer	Debb	P200	$2,507.52	1/12/97

field contents

Catalog Table

BOOK	TITLE	AUTHOR	PUBLISHER	SUBJECT
453.34	Harry's Time	Barton	Milton Press	History
646.54	Pearl Cooks	Harding	Janus and	Cookbook
657.54	The Winning Way	Martin	Price Brothers	Politics

Purchases Table

BOOK	PUBLISHER	TELEPHONE	DATE	PRICE	INVOICE
635.43	Kingston Press	201-555-8746	6/2/97	$19.45	452332
646.54	Harding	705-555-2345	6/5/97	$25.95	53443

Book number field used to relate data in separate tables. This field can be a key field because the book number is unique data that identifies the records.

Paradox 8 Features

- PerfectExpert—Corel 8 task oriented applications than allow you to use model files for Paradox applications.
- ProjectViewer—Improved usability makes objects easier to create, find, open, and edit.
- Paradox Experts—Step by step screens are provided to assist you in creating every type of database object.
- Sample Application—A complete Paradox database is included to demonstrate the capabillities of the software.
- Supports Internet and Hyperlink features.

Be sure you know the answers to these questions before moving on to the next exercise.

REVIEW QUESTIONS

1. What is a database?
2. What are some examples of databases?
3. What is the benefit of an electronic database over a manual database?
4. What are some of the functions provided in a database management system?
5. What capability does a relational database provide?
6. What are database objects?
7. What is a table?
8. What is a record?
9. What is a field?
10. What is a form?
11. What is a query?
12. What is a database report?
13. What is the Project Viewer?
14. What are the field contents?
15. How can data in different tables be related?

COREL PARADOX 8 Lesson 1: Create a Database

Exercise 1

- **Database Basics** ■ **Plan the Database** ■ **Startup Expert**
- **Project Viewer** ■ **Create a Table** ■ **Table Field Types**
- **Key Field** ■ **Save a Table**

NOTES

Database Basics

- Paradox is a **relational database management system**. A **database** is a collection of information (**data**) organized into one or more tables. In a **relational database**, two or more tables have data in common which relates, or links, them together. They are usually stored in the same directory or folder, referred to as the **working directory**. Each table stores data pertaining to a specific aspect or category of the information being organized.

- For example, a corporation that has many stores can create one table that contains general information for each store (like the name, location, etc.) and a second table that contains a listing of computer equipment in each store. These tables would both be stored in the same directory (the working directory) and would be related by a key field, such as a branch name or number common to both tables. Each table would contain information about a specific aspect of the company, but when related or connected in a database, the tables would provide a more complete picture of the corporation.

- Each table in a database contains data in rows called **records**. Each record contains information about one item: for example, one item in the computer equipment inventory. A group of records make up a table, and a group of tables make up a database.

- Each record contains categories of information about the record. Each category is referred to as a **field**. There are two parts to a field: the **field name** and the **field contents**. Note the illustration of the STORES table, below, providing information about branch stores.

Stores Table

	BRANCH ID	ADDRESS	TELEPHONE	CITY	ST	ZIP	MANAGER ID
1	01NY	210 Green Street	800-555-3434	New York	NY	10012	FL15
2	02MA	100 Revere Square	800-555-4343	Boston	MA	02101	RO45
3	03IL	42 Lake Road	800-555-6929	Chicago	IL	60601	CR12
4	04RI	14 Ocean Lane	800-555-1010	Providence	RI	02901	WA43

(Field names point to the header row. Records point to the numbered rows. Field contents points to "Providence".)

Plan the database

- Before creating a database, you should plan the fields you want to include in each table—that is, what type of information the database should contain and how you wish to organize it. Plan your database on paper first by writing the field names that would best identify the information entered as field contents. If you want to access information simultaneously from two or more tables, you should have these tables share common field names and contents. The planning and development phase is very important since using key fields to link tables can save data entry. Within a corporation, database consultants generally provide this expertise. You can also develop your database in stages and link tables for optimum results throughout the development process, as we will do throughout this Paradox section.

- It is often advisable to organize data into its smallest units for the greatest flexibility. For example, using field names of FIRST and LAST gives you more options than using NAME for the entire name.

Startup Expert

- To start Paradox, click Start on the Windows Taskbar, click Corel WordPerfect Suite 8, then click Corel Paradox 8. Or, you can click the Paradox button on the Desktop Application Director (DAD). When you first open Paradox, the **Startup Expert** screen appears, as illustrated.

    ✓Note: The Startup Expert screen will not appear if the **Don't Show the Startup Expert again** option has been selected.

From the Startup Expert preliminary screen you can:

- Use the Paradox Database Expert, which contains predefined databases you may use for your data.
- Give a name to a database you wish to create yourself.
- Name a database you have already created.
- Open an existing database.

Successive screens prompt you according to the option you have chosen. In this exercise, we will explore an existing database and name a new database.

Project Viewer

- Behind the Startup Expert, you will see the **Project Viewer**. This window provides a view of all the objects in a database. **Database objects** can be tables, forms, queries, reports, etc. The illustration below shows the Project Viewer screen for the SAMPLE database. The Tables object is selected and a list of tables in the database appears. This screen, showing the tables within the database, shows all the table files in the WORK directory with a **.db** extension, the default extension for all Paradox tables.

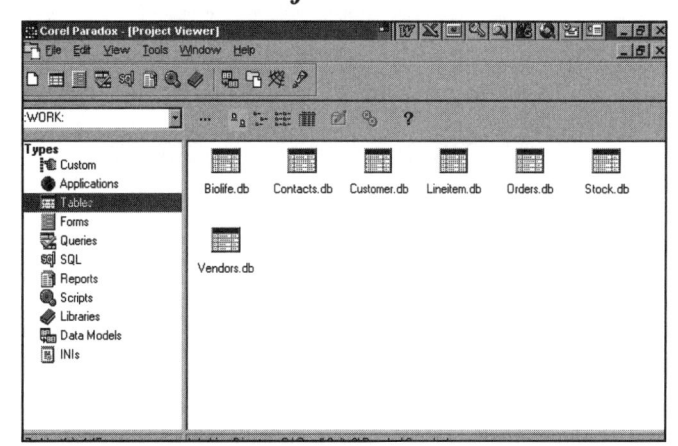

Project Viewer

Create a Table

- A table may be created using the **Table Expert**, which can be launched from the Startup Expert, or by clicking <u>T</u>ools, <u>E</u>xperts, selecting Table and then clicking the <u>R</u>un Expert button [Run Expert]. The Table Expert provides table templates that can be customized for your own purposes.

- You can also create a table by clicking <u>F</u>ile, <u>N</u>ew, or by clicking the New button on the toolbar. When the New dialog box appears, as illustrated below, select Corel Paradox 8 in the top box, select New Table from the list box of objects, and click C<u>r</u>eate. You will then be presented with the New Table dialog box that provides choices for creating the table. Use the <u>B</u>lank table selection.

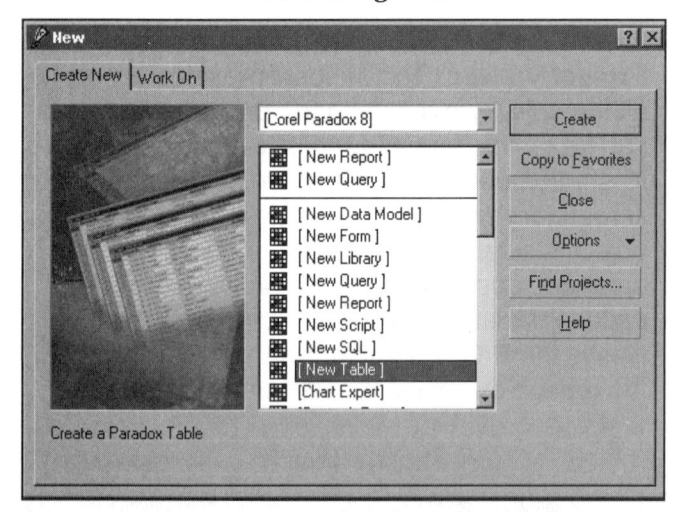

New Dialog Box

New Table Dialog Box

- When you click Blank Table, the Create Paradox 7 & 8 Table dialog box appears. The **Field roster** defines the field names, types, sizes, and whether or not a field is a key field. (Key fields are discussed on the next page.) After the field name is entered, you must enter the field type and size. Note the illustration of the dialog box below with the drop-down list displayed for field type.

Create Paradox 7 & 8 Table

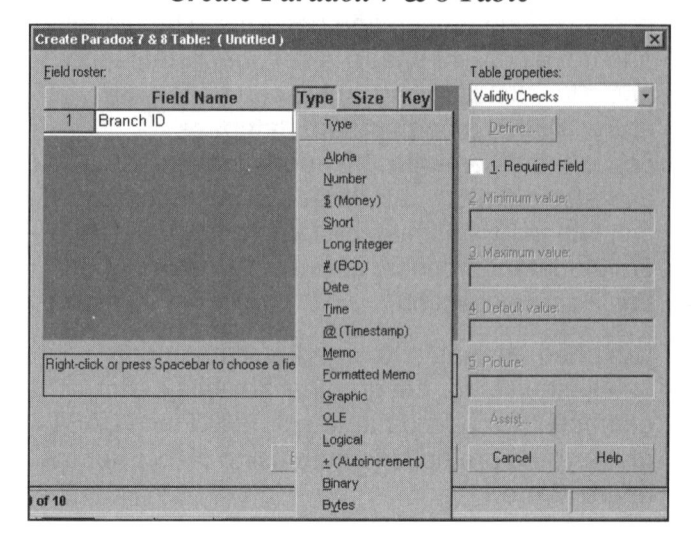

Table Field Types

- The most common field type is **Alpha**, which consists of alphanumeric text. The list of data types is displayed by right-clicking the Type field or by pressing the spacebar while the cursor is in the Type column of the Field Roster.

- When naming a field consider the following naming rules:

  - The maximum length of a field name is 25 characters.

  - A field name cannot start with a blank space (unless it is enclosed in quotation marks), but it can contain blank spaces.

  - Each field name in a table must be unique.

  - A field name should not contain certain characters if you plan to use the table in a query. These characters are the comma (,), pipes (|), and exclamation point (!).

The size allowed for each field type is listed below along with the symbol that you can use to select the field type.

Symbol	Size	Type
A	1-255	Alpha
N	N/A	Number (can contain only numbers)
$	N/A	$(Money)
S	N/A	Short
I	N/A	Long Integer
#	0-32	#(BCD)
D	N/A	Date
T	N/A	Time
@	N/A	@(Timestamp)
M	1-240	Memo (Can be any length. The assigned size tells Paradox how much of the memo will be stored in the table. Anything over the specified size is stored in the .MB file.)
F	0-240	Formatted Memo (Lets you format text including typeface, style, color, and size.)
G	0-240	Graphic (Lets you store a graphic image in the field. Graphics are not saved with the table, but are stored in separate files.)
O	0-240	OLE
L	N/A	Logical
+	N/A	+(AutoIncrement)
B	0-240	Binary
Y	1-255	Bytes

Key Field

- Although it is possible to create tables without it, a **key** should be created for every table in a database because:
    - It ensures that each record will be unique.
    - The table is sorted by the key field.
    - It enables keyed tables to be linked together.
    - It provides a means to ensure the accuracy of linked data.
    - It expedites querying, searching and locating data.

- The key field must be a field with unique values. An EMPLOYEE ID field would be appropriate because each employee would have a unique ID. Since it is not possible to key all tables with one unique field, Paradox allows multiple-field, or composite, keys. Multiple-field keys will not be discussed in this text.

- The key for a table must be at the beginning of the Field roster. If the key consists of only one field, it must be the first field in the Field roster.

Save a Table

- After defining the fields in the Field roster, a table must be named and saved by clicking on the Save As button in the Create Paradox 7 & 8 Table dialog box. The table will be stored in the directory or folder that has been set as the default directory. All related files should be saved in this directory, thereby making them readily available for opening, editing and linking. If you want the database files to be private or separated into groups, you need to create separate working directories in the Save As dialog box or using Windows Explorer. This will be discussed later in the text.

COREL PARADOX 8 Lesson 1: Create a Database

Sports Duds Stores opened branches throughout the United States during the last several months. In order to keep track of the branches and the cities in which the branches are located, you have been asked to create a database to organize information relating to these stores. In this exercise, you will explore the Sample database and Expert screens, view completed tables, and create the first table for Sports Duds Stores.

EXERCISE DIRECTIONS

1. Start Paradox 8 using the Start button on the Taskbar or the DAD Paradox icon.
2. Open a Database should be the default selection. Select Sample in the Database box. Click Next. Click Finish.
3. In the Project Viewer, click Tables, Forms, Queries, and Reports and note the files that have been created in each object category. (No files are stored in the Queries category.)
4. Click on the Tables icon and double-click on the CUSTOMER.DB table.
5. Use the scroll bar to view the records in the CUSTOMER table.
6. Close the table using the Close button and view several other tables. Notice that each table presents information about one aspect of a dive equipment business.
7. Close the Project Viewer.
8. Select File, New, then New Table, under the Corel Paradox 8 category. Click Create.
9. Select Blank Table.
10. Click OK to table type: Paradox 7 and 8.
11. Create a table using the information provided in steps a-i and in the table below:

    | BRANCH ID | A | 5 | * |
    | ADDRESS | A | 20 | |
    | TELEPHONE | A | 12 | |
    | CITY | A | 13 | |
    | ST | A | 2 | |
    | ZIP | A | 5 | |
    | MANAGER ID | A | 4 | |

    a. Type the field name.
    b. Press Tab.
    c. Right-click on Type and select the desired field type. (ALPHA)
    d. Press Tab.
    e. Enter the field size.
    f. Define the Branch field as a key field by double clicking in the Key column or pressing the spacebar.
    g. Press Tab.
    h. Repeat steps a-e and g until the table is complete.
    i. Save the table; name it **STORES**.
    ✓ *By default, the STORES table will be saved in the Corel\Suite 8\Paradox\Samples directory. Select a different drive and/or directory if you wish to save it in another location.*
12. Close the **STORES** Field roster box.

KEYSTROKES

CREATE NEW TABLE

1. Click
   OR
   a. Click **File** .... Alt+F
   b. Click **New** .... N
2. Select Corel Paradox 8 .... ↓
3. Select New Table .... ↓
4. Click **Create** .... Alt+R
5. Click **Blank** .... Alt+B or Enter
6. Click **OK** .... Enter
7. Click on field name then define a field name.
8. Press **Tab** .... Tab
9. Right-click to display Type list.
   OR
   Press **Spacebar** .... Space
10. Select type .... ↓↑
    or press underscored character for type.
11. Press **Tab** .... Tab
12. Define a field size.
13. Press **Tab** .... Tab
14. Repeat steps 5-11 until table is complete.
15. Save the table.

SAVE TABLE
FROM THE CREATE PARADOX 7&8 TABLE DIALOG BOX

1. Click **Save As** .... Alt+A
2. Click **Save in** .... Alt+I
3. Select directory .... ↓
4. Click **File name** .... Alt+N
5. Type table name.
6. Click the **Display Table** option .... Alt+B
7. Click **Save** .... Alt+S
   ✓ *The table will be left open if the Display table option is checked.*

COREL PARADOX 8 Lesson 1: Create a Database

Exercise 2

- **Create Working Directories**
- **Create and Save a Database Table**

NOTES

Create Working Directories

- In Paradox, each table is saved as a file in the default directory WORKING, which is created by Corel. Note the illustration below. A Corel Paradox **working directory** is the directory Corel Paradox uses by default to open and save files. In the illustration, the Working directory is given an alias of WORK. However, if you are creating tables for unrelated data that will not be used together, you would find it useful to organize your work by creating separate working directories for each database. If you were working on one project, however, all tables and database objects would most likely remain in one directory.

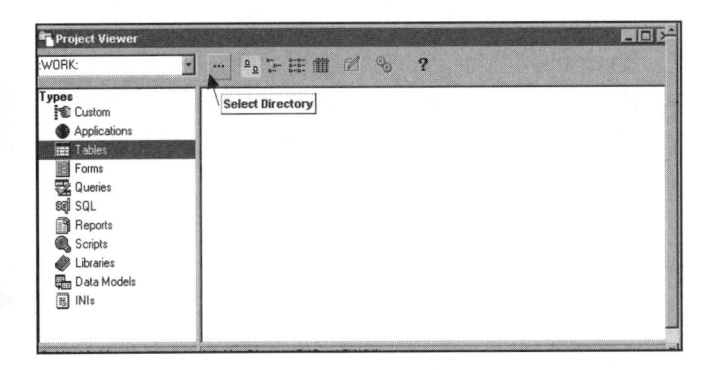

- New directories can be created outside of Paradox using Windows Explorer or during the Save As process. If you then want to use tables from a directory called d:\data\sports, you can change the working directory. Directions for this task will be included in the exercise. For the purposes of this text, it is advisable that you create a directory or a folder for data and subdivide it with subdirectories for each database scenario.

- Change your working directory by selecting Working Directory from the File menu. Select the new working directory by using the Select Directory button, then select it from the Directory Browser dialog box, as illustrated below. Once the directory is selected you can change the directories with the Working Directory or Database drop-down list within the Project Viewer.

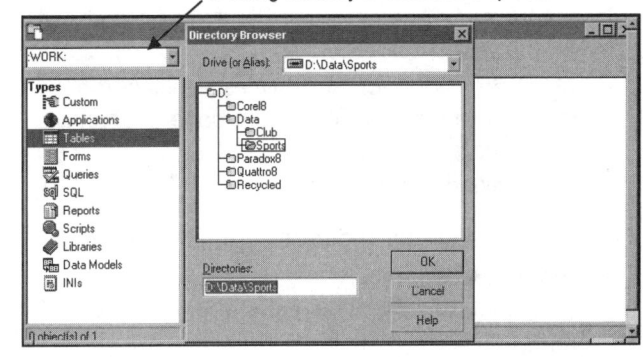

- You can open the Project Viewer by clicking the Project Viewer button on the Toolbar, or by selecting Project Viewer from the Tools menu.

Create and Save a Database Table

- Tables store data about different areas of your business. One database may contain all the related data for a company. In Exercise 1, you created a table for STORES which contained information about each branch. You will now create a table for CEQUIP, listing computer equipment purchased for each store. To correlate information between tables, the tables should have data in common, such as the Branch ID field.

- Field types that do not allow a field size entry are Date, Time, Number, and $.

COREL PARADOX 8 Lesson 1: Create a Database

> You will first set up a separate working directory for the firm called SPORTS and change the working directory. In order to keep track of computer equipment purchased by Sport Duds Stores, your employer has asked you to create an inventory table for your corporation database.

EXERCISE DIRECTIONS

1. Create a directory for the Sports Duds Stores database using Windows Explorer:
   a. Click Start.
   b. Click Programs.
   c. Click Windows Explorer.
   d. Click the drive that contains the STORES data from Exercise 1.
   e. Double click the directory where the STORES data is stored and note the Stores.db and Stores.PX files. (If you selected the default location, the path will be: Corel\Suite 8\Paradox\Working\
   f. In the Paradox folder, click File, New, Folder.
   g. On the New folder type over "New folder" with the name "DATA."
   h. In the Data folder, click File, New, Folder.
   i. On the New Folder, type over "New Folder" with the name "SPORTS."
   j. Move the Stores.db and Stores.PX files from their location into the SPORTS database directory using drag and drop.
   k. Close Windows Explorer.

2. Change the working directory to SPORTS:
   a. Start Paradox.
   b. Click File, Working Directory on the Paradox menu.
   c. Enter the path to the new directory, which should be the old directory with the \SPORTS subdirectory added. For example, c:\Corel\Suite 8\Paradox\DATA\SPORTS or a:\SPORTS.
   d. Click OK.

3. Open Project Viewer using the Project Viewer button on the Toolbar.

4. Select the new working directory

   a. Click the Select Directory button [...] on the Project Viewer.
   b. Select the new directory, SPORTS. (Change the drive if necessary.)
   c. Click OK.

5. Note the new working directory \SPORTS, which includes the STORES table files.

6. Create a new table using the field data listed below. (Do not create a key field.)
   ✓ In this table, Branch ID cannot be a key field since there will be several occurrences of the same branch. Remember that key field data items must be unique.

Field Name	Type	Size
Branch ID	A	5
Item	A	15
Mfg	A	8
Model	A	15
Cost	$	
Purdate	Date	
Wty	A	1

7. Save the table; name it **CEQUIP**.
   ✓ If you added an eighth field by mistake, Paradox will not let you save the table without entering more field data. To eliminate a field that was added in error, click on the previous field number.

8. Close the table.

9. Open the Project Viewer and click on Tables. Note the Stores and Cequip tables.

10. Click on the Working Directory or Database drop-down list arrow and note the available directories.

11. Close the Project Viewer.

KEYSTROKES

DISPLAY PROJECT VIEWER

1. Click **Project Viewer** button .... [icon]
   on the Global Toolbar.
   OR
2. Click **Tools** .... Alt+T
3. Click **Project Viewer** .... P

CHANGE WORKING DIRECTORY

1. Click **File** .... Alt+F
2. Click **Working Directory** .... W
3. Click **Working Directory** .... Alt+W

4. Enter directory
   OR
   Click **Browse** .... Alt+B
   Select directory.
5. Click OK .... Enter

COREL PARADOX 8 Lesson 1: Create a Database

Exercise 3

- Open a Table
- Enter Records
- Correct Entries
- Change Table Column Width

NOTES

Open a Table

- A saved table can be opened, for viewing or editing, by highlighting and double-clicking the desired table name in Project Viewer. Or you can right-click on a table name and choose Open; select Open from the File menu, click Table and select the file; or, click the Open Table button on the Standard toolbar.

- Tables have two modes of operation, View and Edit mode. You can switch to Edit mode by pressing F9, or by clicking the Edit Data button on the Toolbar. If you wish to add or change data, you must be in Edit mode. A row and column format, similar to a spreadsheet, is displayed with the previously entered field names as the column headings. The table view gives you an efficient way to work with more than one record on the same screen. In this view, as illustrated below, each row will contain the data of a single record.

Paradox Table

	MEMBER ID	LAST	FIRST	ADDRESS	CITY	PHONE
1	CE9701	Ceedee	Carol	808 Summer Street	Anaheim	(213)555-4987
2	MO9702	Modem	Miles	154 Newburg Road	Anaheim	(213)555-4837
3	SO9703	Sort	Stuart	1551 Dean Street	Beverly Hills	(213)555-3010
4	MO9704	Monitor	Michael	17 Pine Street	Beverly Hills	(213)555-9275
5	MO9705	Mouse	Trina	3954 Wood Avenue	Anaheim	(213)555-7283
6	IC9708	Icon	Sheila	417 Specific Court	Anaheim	(213)555-7284

records

Enter Records

- To enter records in the table, type the data below each field name as you would in a spreadsheet. Use the Tab key or cursor arrows to advance from field to field. To advance to the next (record) row, click in the new row, or use the Tab key or the direction-arrow keys. When you leave a record, your data will automatically be saved in the table.

- It is recommended that field data be entered in upper- and lowercase so that it may be used in word processed files. Field headings may be entered in uppercase to distinguish them from field data.

- Data entered into a table is automatically saved when you close the table or switch back to View mode by pressing F9 again.

- Once records have been added to a table, you can use the navigation buttons on the Standard Toolbar, as illustrated below, to scroll through the records.

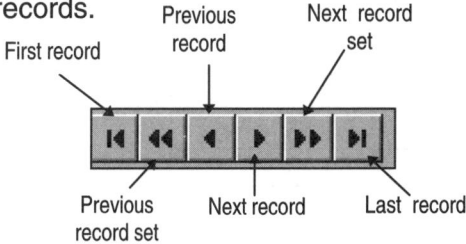

  First record | Previous record | Previous record set | Next record | Next record set | Last record

- You may use Control + D (duplicate) to copy an entry from the record above to the active record. Or, you may use the Copy or Cut and Paste options to quickly enter repetitive data. You can copy either one cell entry or an entire record. To select an entire row or record after it has been entered, double-click the shaded area to the left of the first field in the row record number area.

COREL PARDOX 8 Lesson 1: Create a Database

Correct Entries

- Use the Backspace key to correct an error made while typing an entry. If you have already advanced to another field, you can return to the field that needs correction by clicking in the field, pressing Shift+Tab, or by using the direction arrow keys on the keyboard. Retype the entry, and then move to another field. You can enter edit mode and edit field contents by pressing F2 or Ctrl + F, or by selecting Field View from the View menu.

Change Table Column Width

- You may find that the default column width for a field is not appropriate for your entries, and/or that the table is too wide to fit on one screen. Column size can be changed at any time by clicking and holding the mouse on the right column border and dragging it to size. The stored field size is *not* affected by the column display size.

You are the president of CCU, a computer users' group based in California. One of your responsibilities is to send announcements, catalogs, and newsletters to the members. To make your mailings easier, you have decided to create a table for your computer group's members. In this exercise, you will create a new directory and a table. You will save the table, add members' names, and close the table.

EXERCISE DIRECTIONS

1. Use Windows Explorer to create a subdirectory for the new table and database in your Data folder.
   - Name the directory CLUB and close Windows Explorer.
   - In Paradox, change the working directory to CLUB.
2. Create a table using the field names and sizes indicated below.
   - ✓ *Use the Alpha field type for all fields. Use Member ID as the key field.*

Field Names	Size
Member ID	6
Last	10
First	8
Address	20
City	15
Phone	14

3. Save the table; name it **MEMBERS**.
4. Open the MEMBERS table.
5. Switch to Edit mode by pressing F9.
6. Use the data in the illustration at the top of the next page to enter the information for each member into your table. Use Control+D to repeat field entries, such as Anaheim, to save time.
7. Use the mouse to adjust column widths to accommodate the longest entry in each field.
8. Using the Toolbar navigation buttons, click on the First Record, Next Record and Last Record buttons and observe their functions.
9. Proofread and correct any errors.
10. Close the MEMBERS table.
11. Save view properties, if prompted, by clicking the Yes button.

CCU MEMBERSHIP LIST

MEMBER ID	LAST	FIRST	ADDRESS	CITY	PHONE
CE9701	Ceedee	Carol	808 Summer Street	Anaheim	(213) 555-4987
MO9702	Modem	Miles	154 Newburg Road	Anaheim	(213) 555-4837
SO9703	Sort	Stuart	1551 Dean Street	Beverly Hills	(213) 555-3010
MO9704	Monitor	Michael	17 Pine Street	Beverly Hills	(213) 555-9275
MO9705	Mouse	Trina	3954 Wood Avenue	Anaheim	(213) 555-7283
IC9706	Icon	Sheila	417 Specific Court	Anaheim	(213) 555-7284
WA9707	Wave	Bette	1584 F. Street	North Hollywood	(213) 555-9174
MI9708	Midi	Carl	1956 Park Avenue	North Hollywood	(213) 555-5192
GR9709	Graphic	John	P.O. Box 2333	North Hollywood	(213) 555-8129
DI9710	Disk	Amy	237 Albee Street	North Hollywood	(213) 555-8917
BO9711	Boolean	Bob	19 Wilson Court	Anaheim	(213) 555-5265
FR9712	Franz	Reid	72 Young Avenue	Beverly Hills	(213) 555-0912

KEYSTROKES

OPEN TABLE WITH THE MOUSE

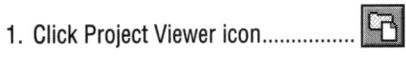

1. Click Project Viewer icon..............
2. Click Tables.
3. Double-click on the desired table.

OPEN TABLE WITH THE MENU

1. Click **File**.......................... Alt + F
2. Click **Open** .... O
3. Click **Table**........................ T
4. Click desired file or enter filename.
5. Click **Open** .... Alt + O

CHANGE TABLE COLUMN WIDTH

Click right border of the field and drag border to desired size.

EDIT FIELD CONTENTS

Before moving to the next/previous field, data may be edited by backspacing and correcting the entry.

After data is entered:

1. Move to the field:
2. Press **Tab**........................ Tab
   OR
   Press **Shift + Tab** .... Shift + Tab
   OR
   Click on the field.
3. Press **F9**........................ F9
   to go into Edit mode.
   OR
   a. Click **View** .... Alt + V
   b. Click **Edit Data** .... E
4. Make corrections.
5. Press **Enter** .... Enter
   to save changes to field.

In table restructure mode:

1. Press **F2**........................ F2
   OR
   Press **Ctrl + F** .... Ctrl + F
   OR
   Click **View** .... Alt + V
2. Click **Field View** .... F

COREL PARADOX 8 Lesson 1: Create a Database

Exercise 4

- Table Guidelines
- Use Project Viewer
- Enter and Edit Data
- Enter Key Field Data

NOTES

Table Guidelines

- To create tables that provide flexibility and optimum data handling keep the following guidelines in mind:
  - Use only one aspect of data for each field. For example, separate a name into Title, Last, and First so that you can query each aspect.
  - Use all necessary data to completely identify the data.
  - Use small tables rather than entering all data in one large table.
  - Do not duplicate information in tables other than data needed for key linking fields.

Use Project Viewer

- If you are working in one table and wish to open a different table or database object, you may use Project Viewer to do so. To open Project Viewer, click Tools, Project Viewer, or click the Project Viewer button, or use the Window menu if Project Viewer is open. If several tables or objects are open and you wish to move among them, you may use the Window menu, as illustrated below, to switch to the object you wish to display.

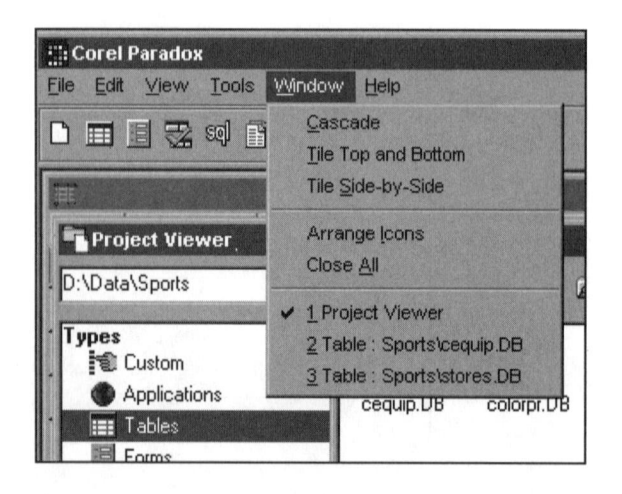

Enter and Edit Data

- You can navigate around a table using the Toolbar buttons, as discussed in Exercise 3, or you can use keyboard shortcuts.

Ctrl + D	Copy an Entry
Home	Move to first field in a record
End	Move to last field in a record
Esc	Undo a field edit (prior to exiting the field)

- As discussed in Exercise 3, you may correct errors during data entry or after the record or table is complete. There is no need to perform a Save command when entering or editing information in Edit mode since records are automatically saved when a table is closed or when you switch back to View mode.

Enter Key Field Data

- When you have a key field and complete entering a record, Paradox will automatically alphabetize key field text data or arrange numeric data in ascending order.

In this exercise, you will enter records into the STORES and CEQUIP tables. You will make several edits, as directed, and save the tables.

EXERCISE DIRECTIONS

1. Open Project Viewer and switch to the \SPORTS working directory.

2. Open **STORES.DB** or **04STORES.DB**.

3. Switch to Edit mode (F9) and enter the data listed in Table A below:

TABLE A

BRANCH ID	ADDRESS	TELEPHONE	CITY	ST	ZIP	MANAGER ID
NY01	210 Green Street	800-555-3434	New York	NY	10012	FL15
MA02	100 Revere Square	800-555-4343	Boston	MA	02101	RO45
IL03	42 Lake Road	800-555-6929	Chicago	IL	60601	CR12
RI04	14 Ocean Lane	800-555-1010	Providence	RI	02901	WA43
CA05	2145 Pacific Drive	800-555-0054	Los Angeles	CA	90002	SE34
GA06	14 Peach Street	800-555-1212	Atlanta	GA	30303	ME14
CA07	32 Hill Drive	800-555-3030	San Francisco	CA	94101	JO12
CT08	1470 River Street	800-555-4040	New London	CT	06320	LE17
NC09	135 Pine Street	800-555-8080	Raleigh	NC	27601	PR15
PA10	321 Bell Lane	800-555-5050	Philadelphia	PA	19019	FR33

4. Move to the Providence branch record and change the MANAGER ID from WA43 to TH12 by re-entering the data.

5. Move to the Chicago branch record and change the telephone number to 800-555-2929.

6. Close the table.

7. Open **CEQUIP.DB** or **04CEQUIP.DB**.

8. Switch to Edit mode and enter the data listed in Table B below. Use Ctrl+D for repetitive entries.

9. Use the Toolbar to move to the previous record until you reach the Wilson Hard Drive for the CA07 branch.

10. Change the purchase date for the Wilson Hard Drive to 7/10/97.

11. Close the table.

TABLE B

BRANCH ID	ITEM	MFG	MODEL	COST	PURDATE	WTY
NY01	Computer	GBM	PC220	$1248.50	6/5/97	Y
NY01	Printer	GBM	ColorJet II	$335.00	6/8/97	Y
CA07	Computer	GBM	Notepad 500C	$2199.00	6/10/97	Y
CA05	Computer	GBM	Notepad 600	$1399.00	6/15/97	Y
CA05	Hard Drive	Barton	LPS80 220MB	$199.00	6/20/97	Y
CA07	Hard Drive	Wilson	CFS4 330MB	$250.00	6/10/97	N
CA05	Printer	BP	Laserjet	$1479.00	7/15/97	N
MA02	Computer	Debb	Notebook 586	$1889.00	1/10/98	Y

KEYSTROKES

DATA ENTRY SHORTCUTS

1. Move to first field in record .... [Home]
2. Move to last field in record .... [End]
3. Move to first field in table .. [Ctrl]+[Home]
4. Move to last field in table ..... [Ctrl]+[End]
5. Duplicate information from field in record above selected field ..... [Ctrl]+[D]
6. Undo a field .... [Esc] or [Alt]+[Backspace]
7. Enter current date in date field .. [Space] (once each for month, day, year)

OPEN PROJECT VIEWER

Project Viewer allows you to view all database objects. It filters the contents of the current working directory into categories, such as tables, forms, etc., and displays only those objects appropriate to the currently selected icon in the left panel.

1. Click **Tools** .... [Alt]+[T]
2. Click **Project Viewer** .... [P]

If Project Viewer is open but not visible:

1. Click **Window** .... [Alt]+[W]
2. Select **Project Viewer** .... [↓], [Enter]

From a Table:

Click **Project Viewer** button................. 🗂

COREL PARADOX 8 Lesson 1: Create a Database

Exercise 5

- Forms
- Create a Quick Form
- Enter Records
- Form Design View
- Move Between Views

NOTES

Forms

- You may view or enter data in a database in either a table or form. A table displays the data in a column and row format, similar to a spreadsheet grid. Each row is a record and each column is a field.

- A **form** is a database object that allows you to design the display of data from one or more tables. Forms are good tools for data entry and can be used to enter and edit the data in the tables. Any change you make to the data in the form is reflected in the table. You can create forms that display one record at a time, multiple records, or only certain fields of a table. A form can contain design features, such as lines, boxes, graphics, shading, or special colors.

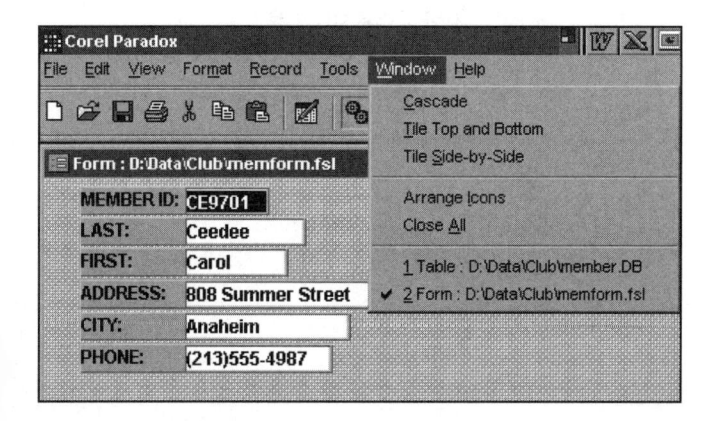

- You can return to the table by pressing F7, by using the Window menu, as illustrated bottom left, or you can click in the Table window to activate it. Note that Paradox uses .fsl as the extension for a saved form file.

- You can create several forms for one table. Forms simply offer you different ways of viewing information that is stored in a table. For example, the sales division of a company may only need viewing access to its customer's Name, Address and Phone number data, whereas accounts receivable may need access to sales information. A separate form may be created for each group's viewing needs and saved as its own .fsl file.

Create a Quick Form

- To quickly create a form from an open table, press F7 or click Tools, Quick Design, Quick Form to view the default form for the table. The Form window will open in front of the open Table window. The navigation buttons on the Toolbar can be used to scroll through the records in a table in either Table view or Form view.

Enter Records

- Data can be entered into a table, but many companies use forms for data entry because each record can be viewed separately. Records may be entered in Form view using the same Toolbar buttons and keyboard shortcuts as used for entering data in a table. You must be in Edit mode (press F9) to enter data and the data you enter in a form is actually stored in the Table. To move to the next record, use the Next Record button ▶ and press Insert or Page Down to insert a new, blank record.

- Note the illustration on the next page of the active Toolbar when in Form view. Note that you can move to Form Design and Edit mode from the Toolbar.

Corel Paradox 8 ■ Lesson 1 ■ Exercise 5   379

COREL PARADOX 8 Lesson 1: Create a Database

Form View Toolbar

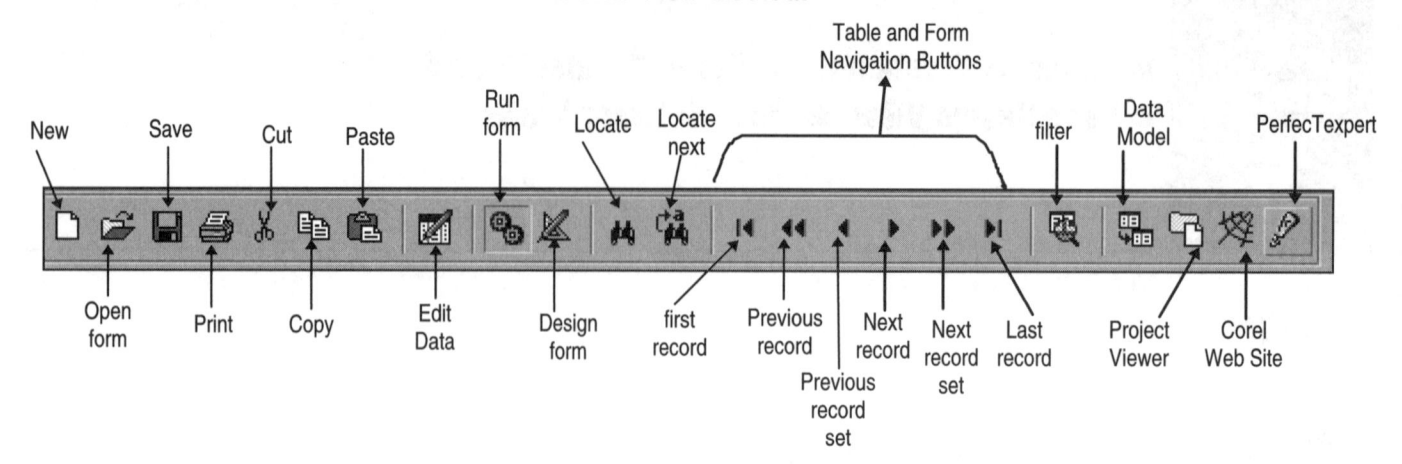

Toolbar buttons (left to right): New, Open form, Save, Print, Cut, Copy, Paste, Edit Data, Run form, Design form, Locate, Locate next, first record, Previous record, Previous record set, Next record, Next record set, Last record (Table and Form Navigation Buttons), filter, Data Model, Project Viewer, Corel Web Site, PerfecTexpert

Design Form View

- You can only make changes to a form or save a form while in **Form Design** mode. You can switch to Form Design mode in Form view by clicking the **Design Form** button  on the Toolbar or by pressing F8. Note the illustration of Form Design mode below.

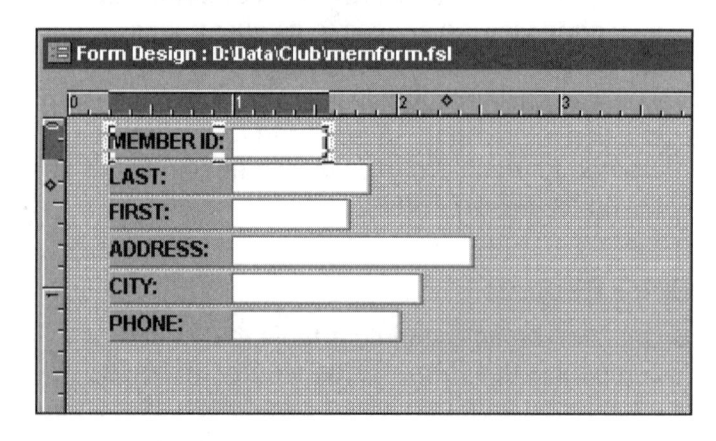

  Form Design : D:\Data\Club\memform.fsl
  - MEMBER ID:
  - LAST:
  - FIRST:
  - ADDRESS:
  - CITY:
  - PHONE:

- In Form Design mode, you can change a selected field's properties, such as font, size, color, styles, or alignment. To change an object on a form, click on the object while in Form Design. Handles will appear around the object, as shown on the Member ID field in the illustration above. Right-click and select Properties to display a dialog box with tabs for every type of property setting. For example, if you want to color the background of a field, you would select the General tab and click the desired color.

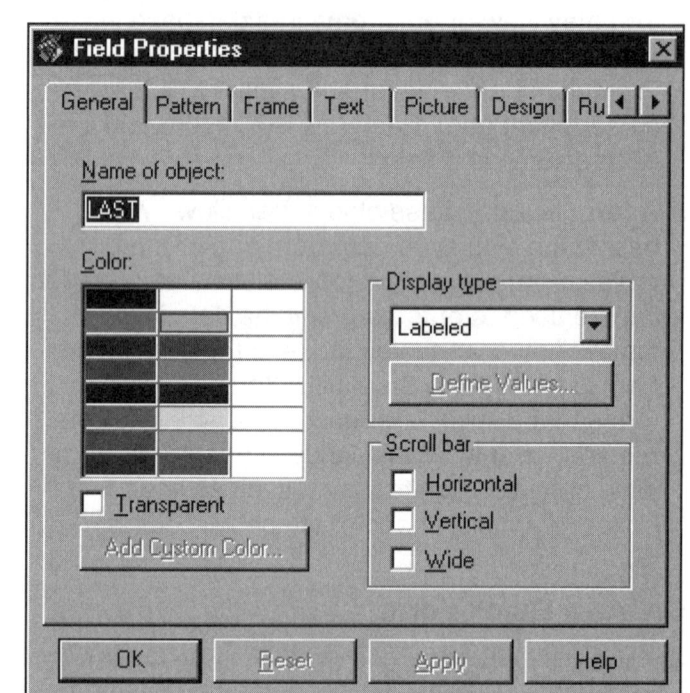

Field Properties dialog box — tabs: General, Pattern, Frame, Text, Picture, Design, Ru...
- Name of object: LAST
- Color:
- Transparent
- Add Custom Color...
- Display type: Labeled
- Define Values...
- Scroll bar: Horizontal, Vertical, Wide
- Buttons: OK, Reset, Apply, Help

- If you wish to format only the data font, color, alignment, etc. (and not the field name), you must double-click on the desired data area. When handles appear, right-click and select Properties to display the EditRegion Properties dialog box, as illustrated on the next page.

  ✓Note: *Making font changes may result in a need to reset the item's size.*

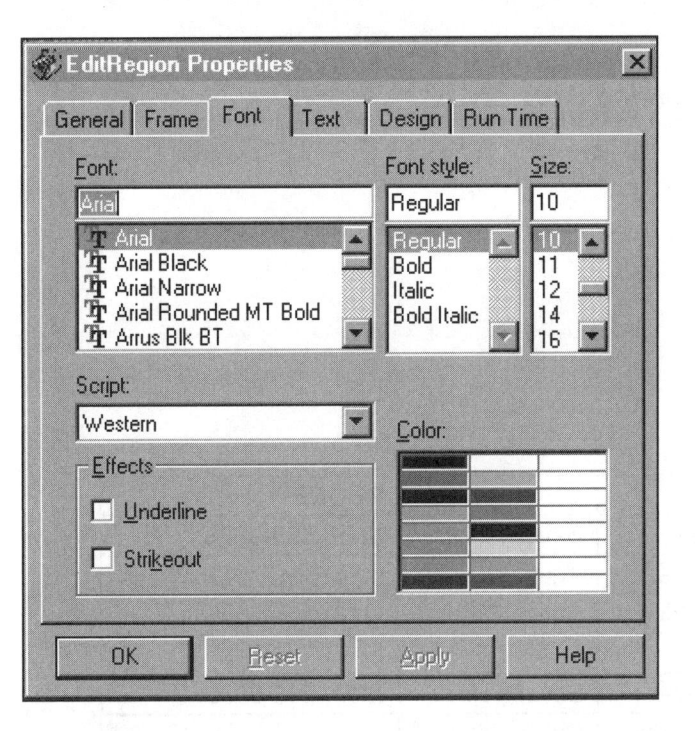

- If you discover that the Form view data areas need adjusting, you must return to Form Design mode to make changes. To resize a field, click on the item, then click and hold down the left mouse button on one of the handles, and drag in the desired direction. You can also move each field on the screen to redesign the layout of the form. Note the illustration of a form with font, color, and placement changes.

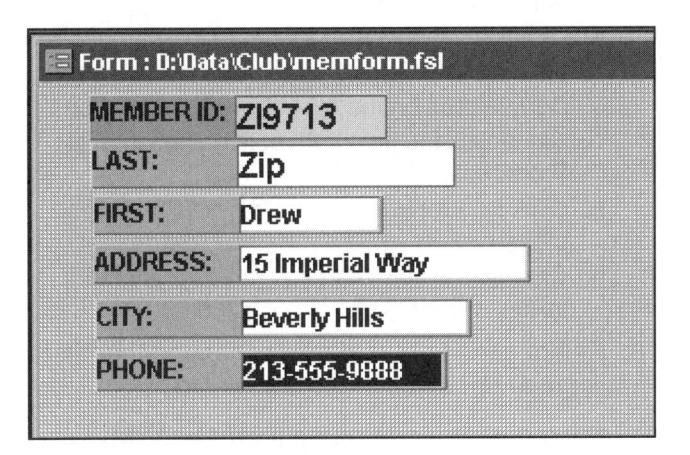

Move Between Views

- You can move between Form view and Design view by pressing F8, clicking the Run Form button, or by using the Window menu. You can return to the Table from the Form view by pressing F7 or by using the Window menu. The Window menu will list all open database objects.

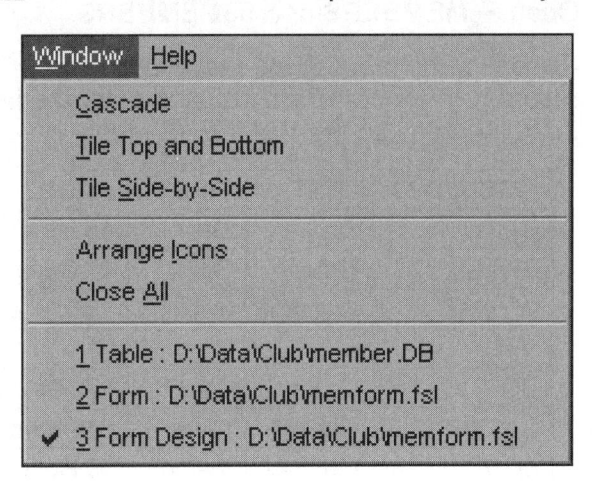

Corel Paradox 8 ■ Lesson 1 ■ Exercise 5

COREL PARADOX 8 Lesson 1: Create a Database

> *CCU has added more members and would like to create a form for data entry. The form will be enhanced in Design view and saved in the Club working directory.*

EXERCISE DIRECTIONS

1. Open Project Viewer, switch your working directory to \CLUB, and select the Tables object.
2. Open **MEMBERS** or **05MEMBERS**.
3. Switch to Edit mode (F9). Move to the last record (Ctrl+End). Press Tab and enter the first three records into the MEMBERS table:

MEMBER ID	LAST	FIRST	ADDRESS	CITY	PHONE
ZI9713	Zip	Drew	15 Imperial Way	Beverly Hills	(213) 555-9888
SI9714	Sistem	Sally	27 Ocean Avenue	Anaheim	(213) 555-7777
WY9715	Wyndow	Walter	188 Riverside Drive	Culver City	(213) 555-7655
CO9716	Coller	Jenny	879 Beverly Drive	Beverly Hills	(213) 555-6676
CA9717	Cable	Cleo	666 Santa Ana Drive	Culver City	(213) 555-9988
MA9718	Matricks	Martin	90 Rodeo Drive	Beverly Hills	(213) 555-2222

4. Press F7 to create a Form view of the table.
5. Press F7 to return to the table.
6. Click Tools, Quick Design, Quick Form to create a Form view of the table again.
7. Scroll through all the records using the Toolbar navigation buttons or by pressing Page Up or Page Down.
8. Move to the last field on the last record. (Use Ctrl+End, End.)
9. Click the Next button to display a blank form.
10. Add the last three records from the list above into the quick form.
11. Move to the next blank record.
12. Click the Design Form button on the Toolbar, or press F8, to go into Form Design mode.
13. Change the font of the MEMBER ID field edit region:
    a. Double-click on the MEMBER ID field in the data area to the right of the field name.
    b. Right-click on the selected edit region, then choose Properties.
    c. Click the Font tab in the EditRegion Properties dialog box.
    d. Change the font size to 12 point, and the font style to bold.
    e. Click OK.
14. Set the LAST field edit region to 12 point bold as well.
15. Color the MEMBER ID field:
    a. Double-click on the MEMBER ID field name.
    b. Right-click the field name, choose Properties.
    c. Click the General tab in the Field Properties dialog box.
    d. Change the field name color background to light blue. Click OK.
    e. Double-click on the MEMBER ID edit region.
    f. Right-click the field edit region, choose Properties.
    g. Click the General tab in the Field Properties dialog box.
    h. Change the field data color background to yellow. Click OK.
16. Select each field and move them so that there is some space between each field.
17. Save the form and name it **MEMFORM**.
18. Press F8 or use the Window menu to return to Form view mode. Check the appearance of the form.
19. Press F7 or use the Window menu to switch to Table view.
20. Check that the three new records have been added to the table.
21. Close all database objects.

KEYSTROKES

CREATE QUICK FORM

1. Open table.
2. Press F7

   OR

   Click **T**ools .... `Alt`+`T`

   Click **Q**uick Design .... `Q`

   Click Quick **F**orm .... `F`

ENTER DATA IN FORM VIEW

✓ *Ensure that both the table and the form are open.*

1. Use F7 to toggle between Form and Table mode.
2. Press **F9** .... `F9`
   for Edit mode.
3. Click **Insert** button on the keyboard to add next record .... `Ins`

   OR

   Click **Next Record** button .... ▶
   on Toolbar.

   OR

   Press **Page Down** .... `Page Down`
4. Type data in first field.
5. Press **Tab** .... `Tab`
6. Repeat steps 3-5 until complete.

SWITCH TO FORM DESIGN

From Form view:

Click **Form Design** button ....
OR

Press **F8** .... `F8`

SWITCH TO FORM VIEW

From Form Design mode:

Press **F8** .... `F8`

CHANGE FORM DESIGN

1. Select item:

To select field name and edit region:
- Click field to be changed.
- Right-click.

OR

To select only the edit region:
- Double-click on edit region of field.
- Right-click.

2. Click **Properties**.
3. Select appropriate tab.
4. Change desired settings.
5. Click **OK** .... `Enter`

COREL PARADOX 8 Lesson 1: Create a Database

Exercise 6

■ **Create a Form with Form Expert**

NOTES

Create a Form with Form Expert

- If you wish to create a form that contains fields from more than one table or set form enhancements, you can use the Form Expert to create the form. When you click Tools, Experts, the Experts dialog box, as illustrated below, appears.

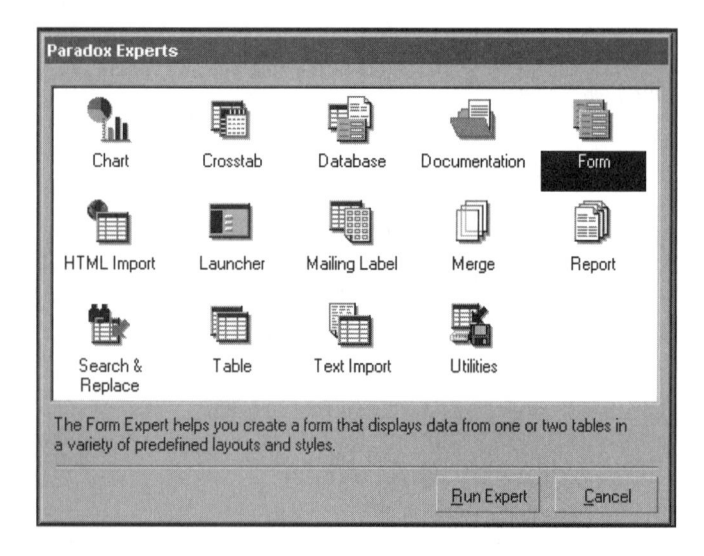

- If you click the Form icon and Run Expert, the Form Expert will launch. The first screen, illustrated top right, determines if you will be using data from one, two, or multiple tables to create the form.

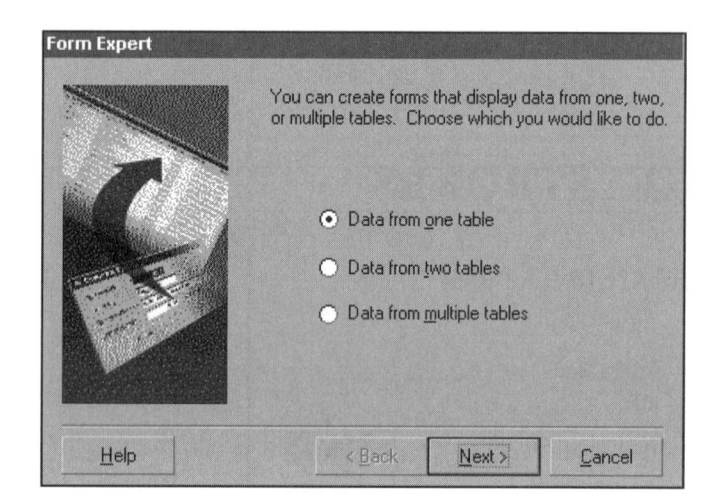

- The second screen provides a drop-down list of tables and a list of the available fields. You can select some or all of the fields.

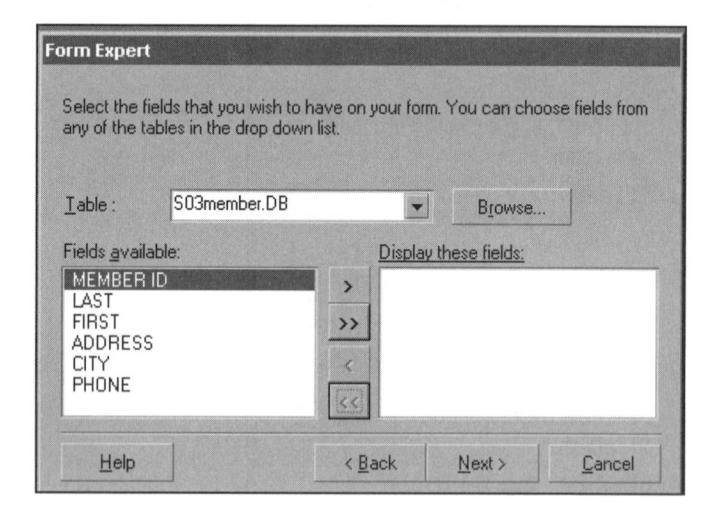

- The third screen, illustrated on the next page, allows you to select the format or type of form you wish to use. The first selection is the default setting and displays the data from one record at a time.

384

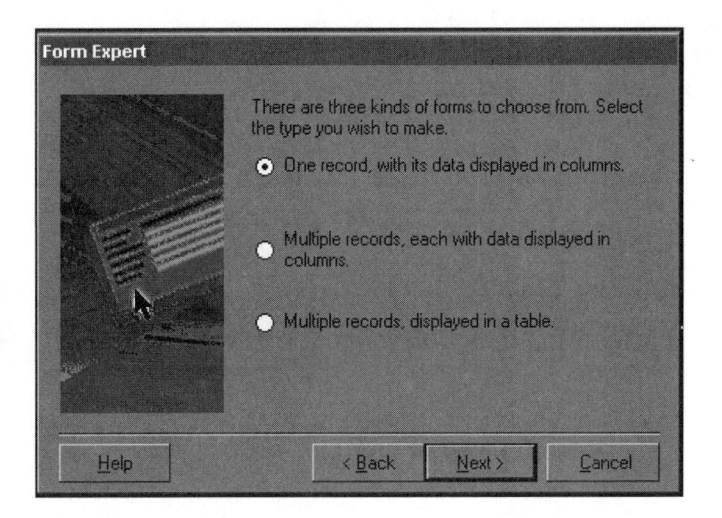

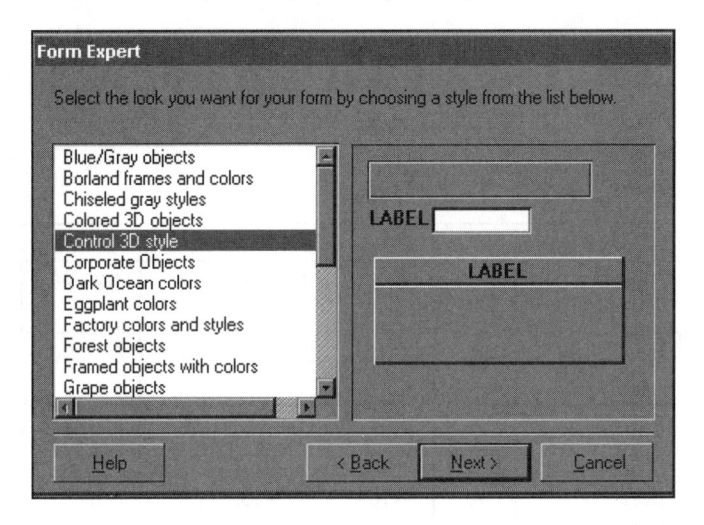

- The last screen allows you to name the form, provide the location in which to save that form, and select either design or run mode for the next view of the form.

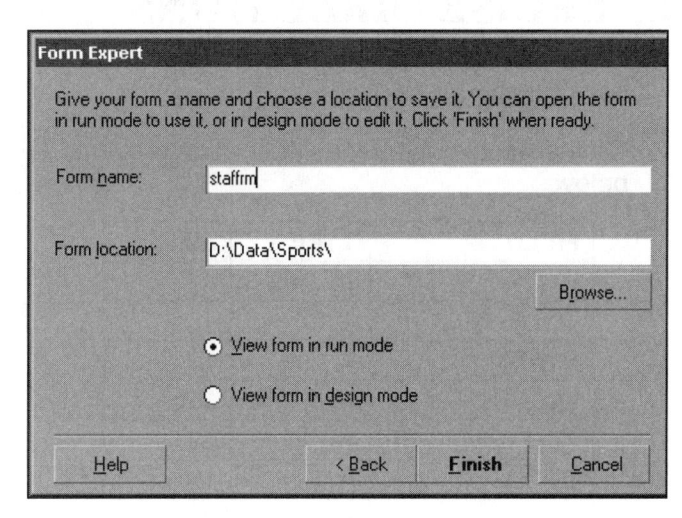

- On the fourth screen you are presented with a list of styles for the form. As you select each style, a sample displays to the right of the list.

COREL PARADOX 8 Lesson 1: Create a Database

In this exercise, you will create and enter data into a new table containing data about the Sports Duds store managers. You will use Form Expert to create a form from the new table.

EXERCISE DIRECTIONS

1. Open Project Viewer and switch to the \SPORTS working directory.
2. Create a table using the information provided below:

FIELD	TYPE	SIZE
ID	A	4
TITLE	A	4
FIRST	A	10
LAST	A	15
ADDRESS	A	22
CITY	A	15
ST	A	2
ZIP	A	5
PHONE	A	12
HIRED	D	

3. Set ID as a Key field.
4. Save the table; name it **STAFF**.
5. Enter the data below into the new table in Edit mode:

ID	TITLE	FIRST	LAST	ADDRESS	CITY	ST	ZIP	PHONE	HIRED
CR12	Mr.	William	Craemer	1205 Windy Road	Chicago	IL	60601	312-555-3621	4/23/96
FL15	Mr.	Michael	Florio	156 East Fifth Street	New York	NY	10014	212-555-3434	2/15/96
FR33	Ms.	Elaine	Franz	3385 Franklin Street	Philadelphia	PA	19019	215-555-6412	2/1/97
JO12	Mr.	Mark	Josephson	1254 Trolley Avenue	San Francisco	CA	94101	415-555-1753	7/15/97
LE17	Mr.	Elliot	Leland	1705 Water Road	New London	CT	06320	203-555-2353	9/15/96
ME14	Ms.	Pamela	Meehan	1409 Bravely Drive	Atlanta	GA	30303	404-555-2411	5/1/96
PR15	Mr.	Daniel	Price	1565 Chapel Road	Raleigh	NC	27601	919-555-6322	2/1/97
RO45	Ms.	Sara	Rodriguez	450 Freedom Lane	Boston	MA	02101	617-555-6424	3/10/96
SE34	Mr.	Lawrence	Seligman	3434 Palm Drive	Los Angeles	CA	90002	213-555-6312	4/15/96
WA43	Ms.	Tess	Walenda	43 Dune Drive	Providence	RI	02901	401-555-3167	3/1/97

6. Create a new form using the Form Expert by clicking Tools, Experts, Form.
7. Click Run Expert and respond to the screens as follows:
   a. Select Data from one table and click Next.
   b. Select STAFF.DB as the table.
   c. Select all the fields from the STAFF.DB table. (Use the >> button to display all the fields.) Click Next.
   d. Select One record with its data displayed in columns. Click Next.
   e. Select Corporate Objects as the look for the form. Click Next.
   f. Save the form and name it **STAFFRM**. Click Finish.
8. Switch to Form Design using the View, Design Form commands.
9. Rearrange the fields so that they are placed as shown in the illustration below:
10. Save the form design.
11. Switch to the Form view in Edit mode and enter the information for two new employees: ID: HE23, Ms. Nilda Hernandez, 2382 Adams Place, Bronx, NY, 10458, 718-555-6453, hired on 11/15/97 and ID: TR54, Mr. Robert Tribunio, 5422 Star Road, Los Angeles, CA 90002, 213-555-7357, hired on 11/20/97.
12. Close the form and table.

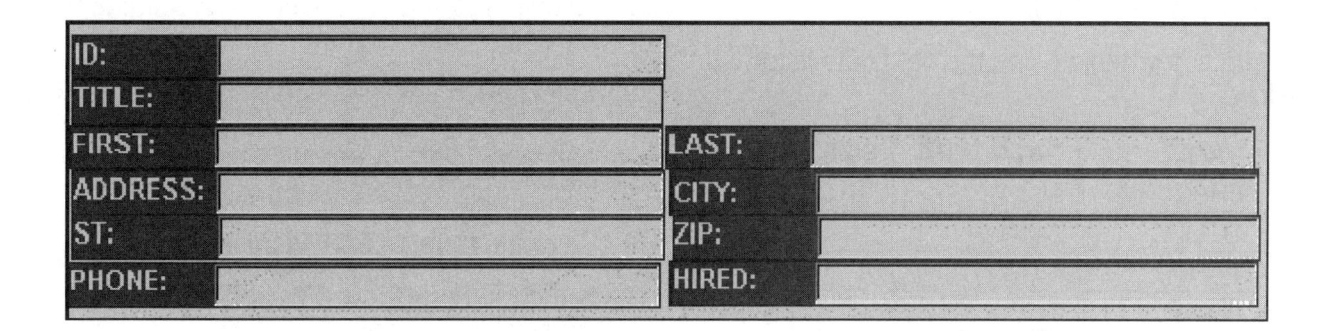

KEYSTROKES

CREATE A FORM WITH FORM EXPERT

1. Click **Tools** .... Alt+T
2. Click **Experts** .... E
3. Click **Form** icon .... Form
4. Click **Run Expert** .... Alt+R
5. Select table choice:
   a. Data from **o**ne table .... Alt+O
   b. Data from **t**wo tables .... Alt+T
   c. Data from **m**ultiple tables .. Alt+M
6. Select **N**ext .... Alt+N
7. Select **T**able .... Alt+T, ↓
8. Select **F**ields **a**vailable Alt+A, ↓, Tab, Enter
9. Repeat until all desired fields are selected.
10. Click **N**ext .... Alt+N
11. Select form type:
    a. One record with its data displayed in columns .... ↓, Enter
    b. Multiple columns, each with data displayed in columns ..... ↓, Enter
    c. Multiple records, displayed in a table. .... ↓, Enter
12. Click **N**ext .... Alt+N
13. Select the look you want .... ↓
14. Click **N**ext .... Alt+N
15. Enter Form **n**ame .... Alt+N, *type name*
16. Click **F**inish .... Alt+F

COREL PARADOX 8 Lesson 1: Create a Database

Exercise 7

■ Summary

At Sports Duds, you are the staff member responsible for ordering and evaluating software products used at company stores. To keep track of the types of software, their prices, and where they are stored, you have been asked to set up a new table and form for the SPORTS database.

EXERCISE DIRECTIONS

1. Open Project Viewer and switch your working directory to \SPORTS.

2. Create a new table using the field data listed below:

NAME	DATA TYPE	SIZE
BRANCH ID	Alpha	16
TITLE	Alpha	11
TYPE	Alpha	17
PRICE	$	
PURDATE	Date	
STORED	Alpha	4

3. Save the table; name it **SFTWARE**.

4. View the **SFTWARE** table.

5. Press F7 to create a Quick Form.

6. Switch to Form Design mode (F8).

7. Select the BRANCH ID field object. Change the color properties to light blue.

8. Select the BRANCH edit region. Make the following changes: font size–12 point; font style–bold; text alignment–center (Text tab).

9. Select each field, starting with the last field, and move each one down to allow more space between fields. Keep the fields aligned on the left.

10. Save the form as **SOFORM** in Form Design.

11. Switch to Form view (F8). Note the results of your enhancements.

12. Check for any design adjustments that must be made and make these adjustments in Form Design mode.

13. In Form view, go into Edit mode by pressing F9.

14. Enter the software data listed below.

15. Switch to the **SFTWARE** table to verify data. Make any corrections.

16. Close the table, form and Project Viewer.

BRANCH ID	TITLE	TYPE	PRICE	PURDATE	STORED
CA07	Word-O	Word Processing	499.85	6/12/97	D230
NY01	Micro Words	Word Processing	459.80	6/14/97	C330
CA05	PerfectWord	Word Processing	499.85	7/18/97	B235
IL03	PerfectWord	Word Processing	499.85	7/20/97	A135
IL03	Calla7	Spreadsheet	594.20	8/21/97	A138
NY01	Trenta8	Spreadsheet	475.50	8/21/97	C338
MA02	BBS	Communications	111.50	9/15/97	D230
GA06	Officemate	Integrated	479.95	9/15/97	B238
CA07	Harwood	Graphics	299.95	1/30/98	D230
IL03	Pagemaker	Desktop	399.40	2/15/98	A114

COREL PARADOX 8
Lesson 2: Edit and Print a Database

Exercise 8
- Modify a Table or Form
- Add, Delete, or Move a Field in a Table
- Add, Delete, or Move a Field in a Form
- Check Box Field

NOTES

Modify a Table or Form

- Fields may be added, moved, or deleted in a table or a form. When you add a field to an existing table or form, it is not automatically added to the other views of this record.

- For tables, all structural changes must be made in the **Restructure Paradox 7 & 8 Table dialog box**. You must be certain that no forms or tables that use this data are running when structural changes are being made. You can open an existing table by double-clicking on it in the Project Viewer. Then open the Restructure Table dialog box by clicking the Format, Restructure Table commands, or click the Restructure button on the Standard toolbar.

- Structural changes in a form must be made in Design view. Enter Design mode by double-clicking the form in the Project Viewer, then clicking the Design Form button on the Toolbar or pressing F8.

Add, Delete, or Move a Field in a Table

- In the Restructure Paradox 7 & 8 Table dialog box, as illustrated above right, you can create space for a new field by clicking where you want to insert the new field, then pressing the Insert key. To delete a field, simply click on the field, and then press Ctrl+Delete. You will be asked to confirm the deletion, and when you agree, the field will be deleted and the remaining data will reposition itself. The best way to move a field is to drag it to its new position.

Restructure Paradox 7 & 8 Table

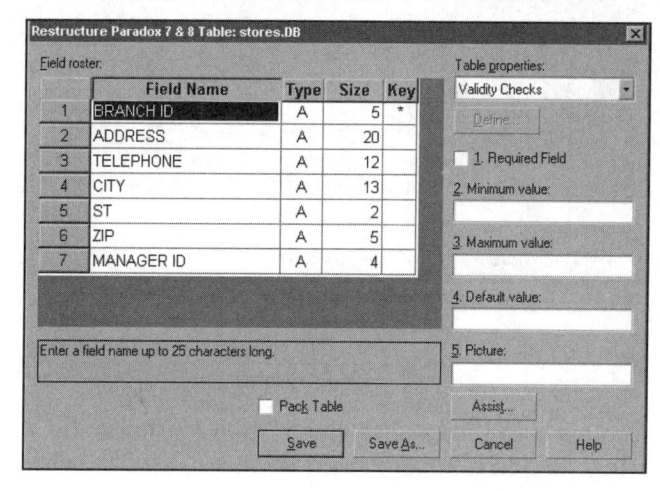

Add, Delete, or Move a Field in a Form

- If a field is added to a table, it is not automatically added to the form. A new field may be added to a form directly by clicking the Field Tool button on the Toolbar in Form Design mode. This will activate the Field Expert which is a set of dialog boxes that will define the field, its contents and its format, as well as establish if the data is independent of a table or connected to a field in a specific table.

- To delete a field in a form, select the field in design view and press Delete. You can also right-click the field and use the quick menu to Cut the field. You can move fields by selecting and dragging the field to its new location.

- If you make changes to a table, and wish to reflect those changes in the form, you can add and delete fields as discussed above. Or, you can click the Quick Form button on the Toolbar, which recreates the form from the updated table. The old form will be overwritten when the new form is saved with the same name.

COREL PARADOX 8 Lesson 2: Edit and Print a Database

Check Box Field

- If you want to add a field that uses a special functionality or a different format, you should add the field to the form using the Field Tool and Field Expert. Once you place the new field, the Field Expert screen displays, as shown below, which allows you to set the type of field. The edit field is the type we have been using. The check box field provides a check box that can be checked to show a true or yes condition.

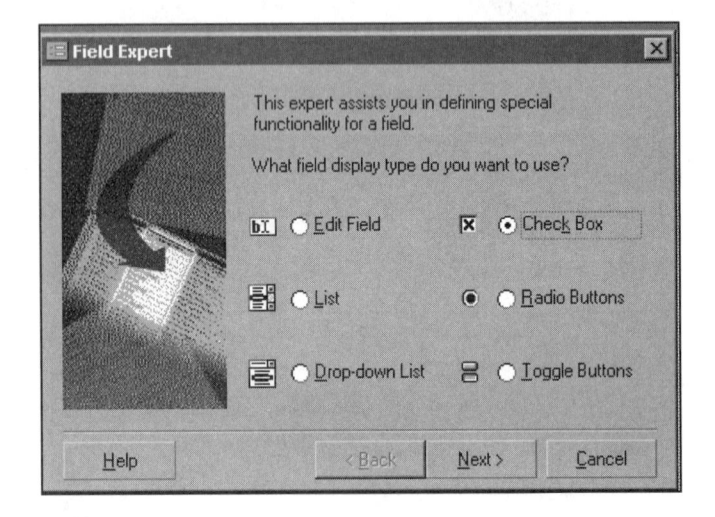

- You will then be asked if you wish to attach the new field to a specific field in a table. If the field is attached, any entry you make in the form will be added to the same field in the table. Note the illustration, above right, attaching the field to the Eve field in the Stores table.

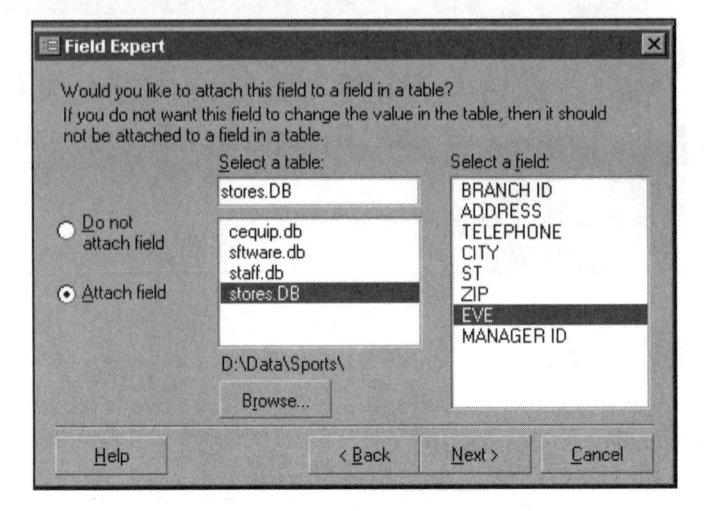

- The next screen allows you to set the meaning of the check box. The default settings are for True and False. You can either accept the default True/False settings, or enter your own text, such as Yes/No as shown in the illustration below. When you check the check box on the form, the entry "Yes" will appear in the table. When you leave the check box empty, a "No" condition will be assumed.

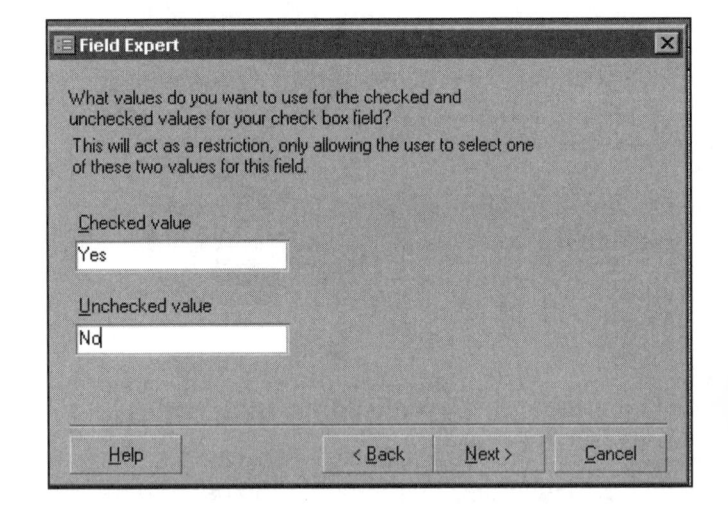

> Your manager at Sports Duds has asked you to add and delete fields on the STORES table and enter new data. You will be adding an EVE field to indicate if the store is opened evenings. In addition, you will add a field to a form and add new data for the field.

EXERCISE DIRECTIONS

1. Open Project Viewer and switch to the \SPORTS database.
2. Open **STORES** or **08STORES**.
3. Click F7 to create a form for this table.
4. Switch to Design view and save the form as **STOREFORM**.
5. Close the form and return to the STORES table.
6. Click Format, Restructure Table to open the dialog box.
7. Add a new field after the ZIP field by pressing Insert while on the Manager ID field name:

   EVE (Type—Alphanumeric; Size—3)
8. Delete the MANAGER ID field.
9. Save the changes you made, confirm the deletion, and return to the table. Note the changes in the table.
10. Open the form STOREFORM. Note that the Members ID data is no longer present since the table data, the source of form data, was deleted. Also, the EVE field is not included.
11. Switch to Form Design and select the blank "Label" field, which is a placeholder for the Member ID data. Delete the field.
12. Add a field for EVE to the form:
    a. Click the Field Tool on the Form Design toolbar.
    b. Place and drag a new field to the right of the Branch ID field. A blank field will appear.
    c. On the Field Expert screen, select Check Box. Click Next.
    d. Select Attach field. Select the STORES.DB table and the EVE field. Click Next.
    e. Set the values that the checks represent by entering Yes into the Checked value box and No into the Unchecked value box. Click Next.
    f. Enter the name of the field, EVE. Click Next.
    g. Accept the default style. Click Finish.
    h. Make any adjustments to the placement of the new field. It should be on the same line as Branch ID.
    i. Save the form design.
13. Switch to Form View (F8) and check the Yes conditions for the following branches that are open in the evenings: New York, Boston, Chicago, Los Angeles, San Francisco, Philadelphia.
14. Switch to the STORES table. Note the entries in the EVE field.
15. Close the form and table.
16. Open the **STAFF** or **08STAFF** table.
17. Use Format, Restructure Table to add a new field for BRANCH ID (Text, Size: 4) after the ID field.
18. Save the new design.
19. Use Quick Form to create a related form for this table.
20. Switch to Design view and save the form as **STAFFRM**, which will overwrite the old form.
21. Add Branch ID data to each staff record in the table or form as follows:

ID	BRANCH ID
CR12	IL03
FL15	NY01
FR33	PA10
HE23	NY01
JO12	CA07
LE17	CT08
ME14	GA06
PR15	NC09
RO45	MA02
SE34	CA05
TR54	CA05
WA43	RI04

22. Close the form and table.

KEYSTROKES

ADD/DELETE FIELD IN A TABLE

1. Click For**m**at .... `Alt`+`M`
2. Click Res**t**ructure Table .... `T`

Add a field:

3. Click the field directly below where you want to add the new field.
4. Press **Insert** .... `Ins`

Delete a field:

3. Select field to delete.
4. Press **Ctrl + Delete** .... `Ctrl`+`Del`
5. Click **S**ave .... `Alt`+`S`

ADD/DELETE FIELD IN A FORM

1. Switch to Form Design .... `F8`

  ✓ *Dialog box may vary depending on the type of field you choose.*

Add a field:

2. Select Field Tool and place, click and drag into position.
3. On the Field Expert screens:

   a. Select type of field:

   Edit**f**ield .... `Alt`+`E`

   List .... `Alt`+`L`

   Drop-down list .... `Alt`+`D`

   Chec**k** box .... `Alt`+`K`

   Radio button .... `Alt`+`R`

   Toggle button .... `Alt`+`T`

   b. Click **N**ext .... `Alt`+`N`

   c. Select **D**o not attach field.. `Alt`+`D`

   Click **N**ext .... `Alt`+`N`

   OR

   Select **A**ttach field .... `Alt`+`A`

   Select a table .... `Alt`+`S`, `↓`

   Select a **f**ield .... `Alt`+`F`, `↓`

   Click **N**ext .... `Alt`+`N`

   d. Enter **L**abel .... *label*

   e. Click **N**ext .... `Alt`+`N`

   f. **S**elect a style .... `Alt`+`S`, `↓`

   g. Click **F**inish .... `Alt`+`F`

Delete a field

2. Select field to be deleted.
3. Press **Delete** .... `Del`
4. Click **F**ile .... `Alt`+`F`
5. Click **S**ave .... `S`

MOVE FIELD IN A TABLE

1. Click For**m**at .... `Alt`+`M`
2. Click Res**t**ructure Table .... `T`
3. Click the field selector (the number to left of field name).
4. Click and drag field selector to new position.

MOVE FIELD IN A FORM

1. Switch to Form Design from Form view .... `F8`
2. Select field to be moved.
3. Drag to new position.

COREL PARADOX 8 Lesson 2: Edit and Print a Database

Exercise 9

- Validity Checks ■ Print ■ Print in Landscape

NOTES

Validity Checks

- Once a table is created, employees will enter new records as necessary. To ensure that data is accurate, it is possible to establish rules or validity checks for fields to verify that data meets certain requirements. The **Validity Checks** feature is available in the Create Paradox Table and the Restructure Paradox 7 & 8 Table dialog boxes. Note that the validity checks option is selected in the Table properties drop-down list in the Restructure Paradox 7 & 8 Table dialog box below.

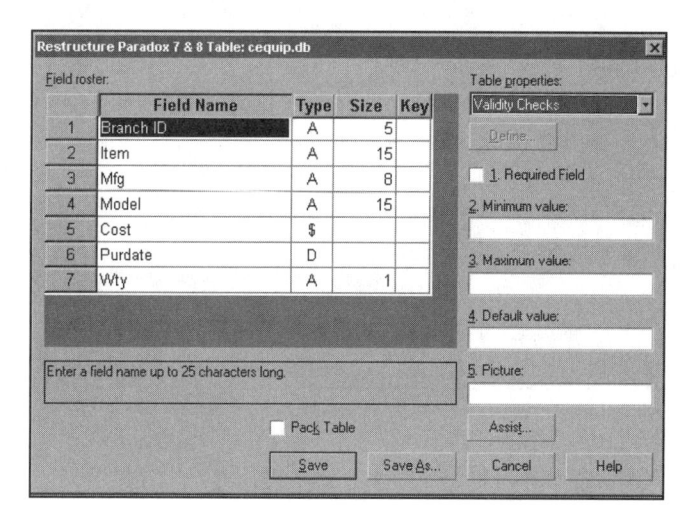

- The Restructure Paradox 7 & 8 Table dialog box has two main sections: the Field roster and the Table properties sections. Use the F4 key to move from the Field roster to the Table properties section and the Shift+Tab or Alt+F to return.

- Paradox provides five types of validity checks:

  1. **Required field**: If this is selected, the field cannot be left blank.

  2. **Minimum value**: You can specify a minimum numeric value for the field, but the entry must be equal to or greater than this amount.

  3. **Maximum value**: You can specify a maximum numeric value for this field, but the entry must be equal to or less than this amount.

  4. **Default value**: You can specify a default value for the field which will be used if data is not entered. This will save data entry time if an entry is generally the same value.

  5. **Picture**: A picture is a pattern of characters defining what a user can type into a field during data entry or editing, or in response to a prompt. Therefore a picture validity check is a string of characters that restricts the type of information that can be entered. For example, a picture of #####{-####} would represent a 12345 or 12345-6789 configuration for a zip code and a {Yes,No} picture would represent either a Yes or No entry.

- If you try to enter data into a form or table (while in Edit mode) that does not meet the requirements of any preset validity checks, you will not be allowed to move to the next field. An error message will appear on the status bar at the bottom of the screen explaining the problem.

- When a table is saved, Validity Checks are saved in a file with the table's name and the .VAL file extension. You will be asked if the validity checks should be enforced on existing data when saving the new structure.

Print

- You can get a printout of current screen data in either Table view or Form view. To print the current screen data, either choose the Print option from the File menu, or click the Print button on the Toolbar. The dialog box that appears gives you the ability to choose the print range, number of copies, and overflow handling options. Note the Print File dialog box below.

Print File Dialog Box

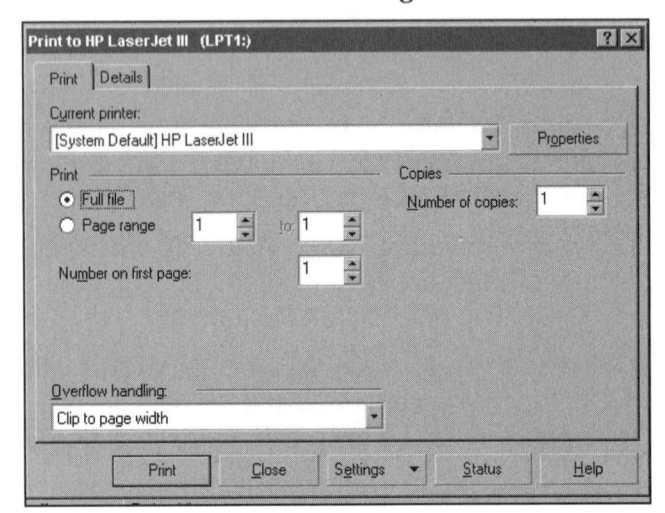

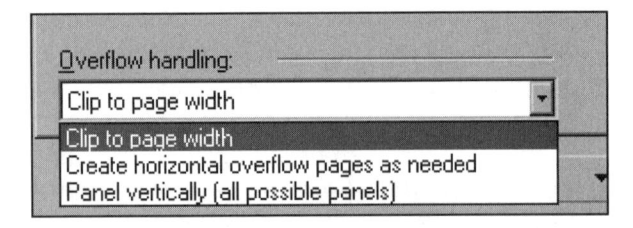

- The Status button on the Print dialog box will display the printer status and the Settings button will allow you to save printer settings. The Overflow handling drop-down list, as illustrated above provides options for handling data that will not fit on one page.

Print in Landscape

- If you are printing a table that is wide, you should use landscape mode for a better view of the data. You can specify landscape mode by clicking Properties on the Print dialog box. On the Properties screen for a HP LaserJet III, illustrated below, you will note the Orientation and Paper size settings along with tabs for other setup features.

    ✓Note: Setup options may vary, depending on your printer type.

Printer Properties Dialog Box

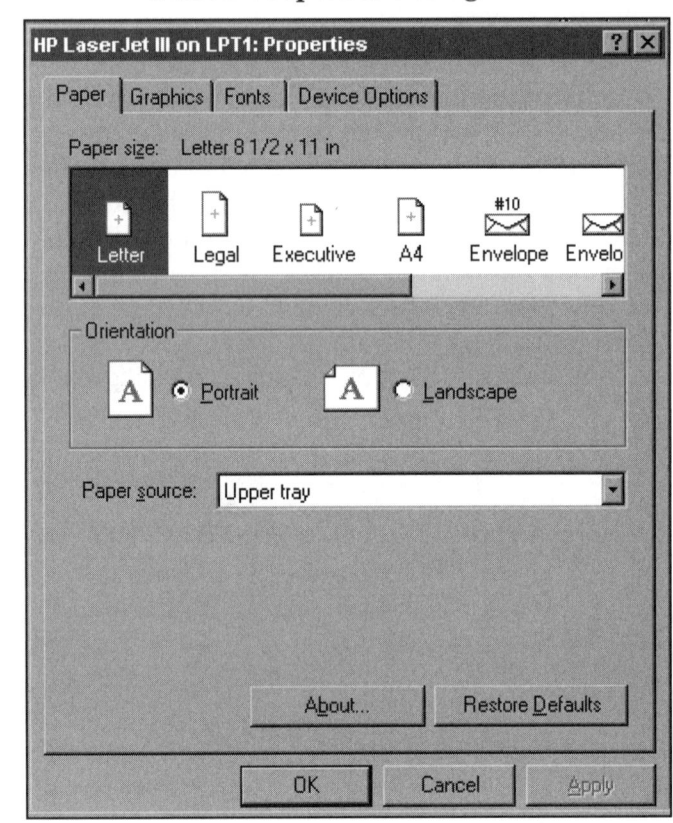

Sports Duds stores will be adding validity checks and additional data to its tables. Tables and forms will be printed.

EXERCISE DIRECTIONS

PART I

1. Open Project Viewer and switch your working directory to \SPORTS.
2. Open ⌨CEQUIP or 💾09CEQUIP.
3. Click Format, Restructure Table to open the Restructure Paradox 7 & 8 Table dialog box.
4. Move to each field, as listed at the right, and set the validity checks indicated. Use F4 to move to the Table properties section and Shift+Tab to return to the Field roster.
5. When finished, click Save to save the settings. You will be asked to confirm the validity checks for each setting, and if you wish to apply the settings to current data. Therefore, you will have seven warning screens, one for each setting. Answer yes to all screens to save the settings and apply them to current data.

✓ *If you make an error, you can open the Structure box, correct the error and save the settings again. If you need to delete the validity checks file to clear an error, you can find the file using Windows Explorer. The file will be named CEQUIP.val.*

FIELD	VALIDITY CHECK
Branch ID	Required Field
Item	Required Field
Mfg.	Required Field
Model	Required Field
Cost	Minimum: 100 (Items less than $100 would be considered supplies.)
Purdate	Required Field
Wty	Default Value: Y Picture: {Y,N} (Yes or No in the indicated format.)

PART II

6. From Table view, switch to Edit mode.
7. Enter the data listed below: (Be sure to enter N in the WTY column for the Zip Drive since the default setting enters Y in this field.)

BRANCH	ITEM	MFG.	MODEL	COST	PURDATE	WTY
IL03	Computer	Debb	P200	2507.52	1/12/98	Y
IL03	Printer	Jokidota	BJ800	355.00	1/12/98	Y
NC09	Computer	Pancard	PE166	2095.54	1/25/98	Y
NC09	Zip Drive	Howell	Z100	169.95	1/25/98	N

PART III

8. Attempt to enter the data on the next page, some of which contains errors or omissions, and note the messages that appear at the bottom of the screen. Use the corrected information listed under the incorrect data to complete the entries.
9. Print a copy of the table in landscape orientation.
10. Use the F7 to create a form for this table.
11. In Form Design mode, select the entire BRANCH ID field and set the following properties: (Right-click and use the Properties command.)
    Color: light blue
12. Select the Branch ID field edit area and make the following property settings:
    Color: light blue
    Font: 12 point, bold
    Text Alignment: center
13. Move the fields so that they are separated from one another.

COREL PARADOX 8 Lesson 2: Edit and Print a Database

14. Save the form as **EQUIPFRM**.
15. Press F8 to View Data in the form.
16. Move through the records and locate the computer purchased on 6/15/97.
17. Print a copy of that record in portrait orientation.
18. Close the form and table.

	BRANCH ID	ITEM	MFG.	MODEL	COST	PURDATE	WTY
Entry	RI04	Computer	Pancard		2095.54	1/29/98	Y
Correction				PE166			
Entry	RI04	Printer	BP	LaserJet	13.03	1/29/98	U
Correction					1303.00		Y

KEYSTROKES

PRINT DATA IN TABLE

1. Open table to print.
2. Click **F**ile .... `Alt`+`F`
3. Click **P**rint .... `P`
4. Click to select:
   - **Full file** .... *(default)*
   - **Page range** .... `↓`
   - **to** .... `Alt`+`T`
5. Click **Number of copies** text box .... `Alt`+`N`
   and type desired number of copies.
6. Click **Print** .... `Enter`

PRINT DATA IN FORM

1. View form to print.
2. Click **F**ile .... `Alt`+`F`
3. Click **P**rint .... `P`
4. Click **N**umber of copies box ... `Alt`+`N`
   and type desired number of copies.
5. Click **OK** .... `Enter`

SETUP LANDSCAPE MODE

1. Click **F**ile .... `Alt`+`F`
2. Click **P**rint .... `P`
3. Click **P**roperties .... `Alt`+`O`
4. Select **Paper size** .... `Alt`+`Z`, `→`
5. Click **L**andscape .... `Alt`+`L`
6. Click **OK** .... `Enter`

SET VALIDITY CHECKS

1. Open table.
2. Click **Format** .... `Alt`+`M`
3. Click **R**estructure table .... `T`
4. Select field to receive setting .... `↓`
5. Press **F4** .... `F4`
6. Select setting and enter requirements:
   1. **R**equired field .... `Alt`+`1`
   2. **M**inimum Value .... `Alt`+`2`
   3. **M**aximum Value .... `Alt`+`3`
   4. **D**efault Value .... `Alt`+`4`
   5. **P**icture .... `Alt`+`5`
7. Click **S**ave .... `Alt`+`S`
   You will be asked to confirm and apply each setting on a separate warning screen.
8. Click **OK** .... `Enter`

COREL PARADOX 8 Lesson 2: Edit and Print a Database

Exercise 10

- Edit a Record
- Add a Record
- Delete a Record
- Radio Buttons

NOTES

Edit a Record

- To change data that has already been entered in a field, highlight the existing data and retype the new data in edit mode. This may be done in either Table or Form view. You may also double-click on the section of the data that needs revising, or press F2 or Ctrl + F, and make the needed changes.

- To delete the contents of a field, select the data then press the Delete key, Backspace, or select the Delete option from the Edit menu.

Add a Record

- Records may be added in either Table or Form view by pressing Enter on the last field of the last record, or by pressing Insert anywhere in the table.

Delete a Record

- Records may be deleted in either Table or Form view by pressing Ctrl + Delete. Paradox will renumber the records when a record is added or deleted.

Radio Buttons

- In some cases, data in a field is a choice from a list of specific entries. For example, you can list specified items that can be charged to club members, (such as dues, newsletters, publications, etc.) and then use **radio buttons** on a form to select the item instead of typing it. Each value for the field is listed with a button beside it to provide a quick way to enter data. Note the illustration of a radio button field below.

Radio Button Field for a Form

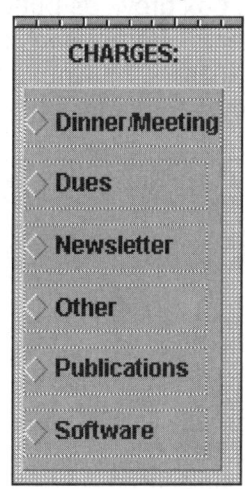

CHARGES:
- Dinner/Meeting
- Dues
- Newsletter
- Other
- Publications
- Software

- Radio buttons are created in Form Design mode by right-clicking the field and opening the Properties dialog box. On the General tab, as illustrated on the next page, select Radio Buttons in the Display type drop-down list and click Define Values to enter the values to be used for this field.

COREL PARADOX 8 Lesson 2: Edit and Print a Database

Field Properties Dialog Box

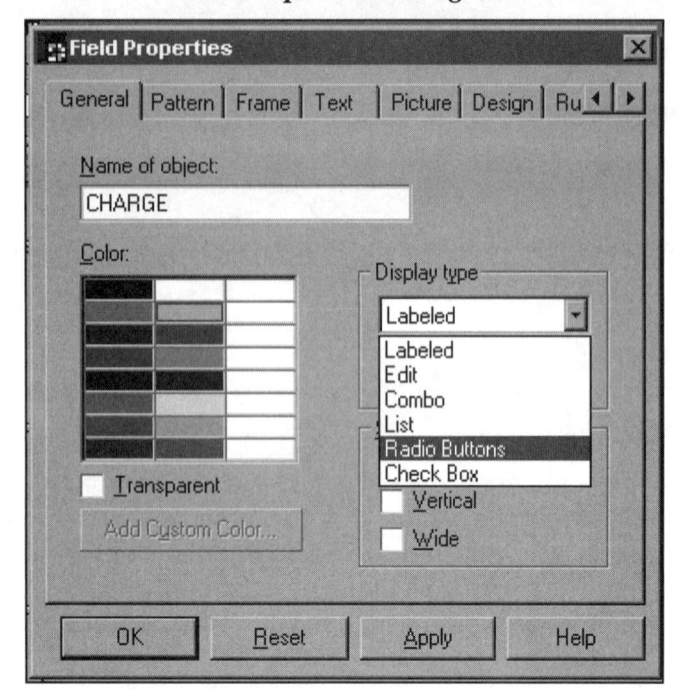

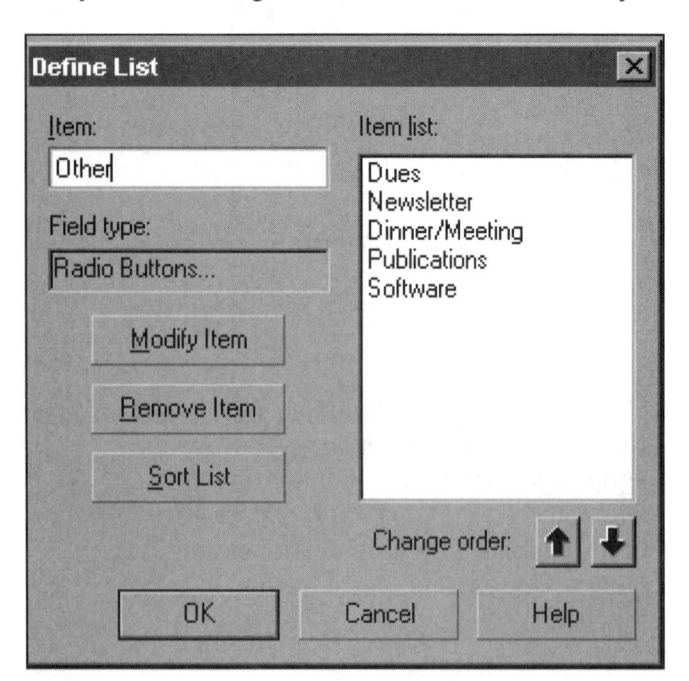

- Once you have created the Radio Buttons field for the form, you may wish to label the radio buttons section with a field name. This can be done in Form Design view by clicking the text tool button [A] on the Toolbar and entering the field label in a position above the radio buttons. Note the illustration of the Form Design with a new label placed above the radio button field.

Form with Radio Button Field

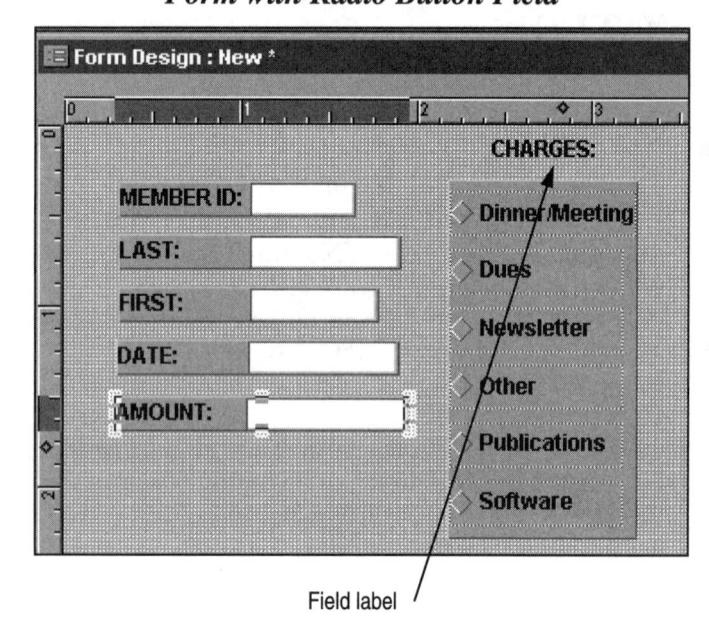

- In the Define List dialog box (illustrated below), you can enter each item in the Item box, press the Enter key and the item will move to the Item list. The dialog box provides buttons to Modify and Remove items. Item names can be sorted into alphabetical order, making data entry easier, or you can change the order of items manually.

398

The CCU group will be adding a new table to its database for the charges that members incur. A form will be created for the data, and a field will be formatted to display radio buttons. The Field will be labeled in Form Design mode using the text tool. Data will be added and deleted from tables or forms.

EXERCISE DIRECTIONS

PART I

1. Open Project Viewer and switch your working directory to \CLUB.

2. Create a new table, using the fields and table properties indicated below:

FIELD	TYPE	SIZE	VALIDITY CHECKS
Member ID	Alpha	6	Required Field
Last	Alpha	10	Required Field
First	Alpha	8	
Date	Date		Required Field
Amount	Number		Required Field
Charge	Alpha	15	Required Field

3. Save the table; name it **CHARGES**.

4. View the table.

PART II

5. Click F7 or the Toolbar Quick Form button to create a form for this table.

6. Switch to Form Design mode.

7. Select the Charge field and right-click to select Properties.

8. Change the Display type to Radio Buttons and click Define Values.

9. Key the following items into the item box and press the Enter key after each item:
   Dues
   Newsletter
   Dinner/Meeting
   Publications
   Software
   Other

10. Click Sort List to sort the list into alphabetical order. Click OK to close the Define List dialog box, then click OK again to close the Field Properties dialog box.

11. In the Form Design window, use the Text Tool button to add the label, CHARGES. Set the label text for bold style.

12. Adjust placement of the radio button field so that it is to the right of the other fields; adjust the label so that it is above the radio buttons. (See the form design illustration on the previous page.)

13. Adjust the placement of the other fields to allow space between the fields.

14. Save the form as **CHGFORM**.

15. Press F8 to return to the form.

16. Enter the following data into the form in Edit mode using the radio buttons for the Charge field data.

MEMBER ID	LAST	FIRST	DATE	AMOUNT	CHARGE
SO9703	Sort	Stuart	11/15/97	$59.95	Software
MO9704	Monitor	Michael	11/16/97	$15.00	Newsletter
GR9711	Graphic	John	11/18/97	$35.00	Publications
WA9709	Wave	Bette	11/19/97	$25.00	Dues
DI9712	Disk	Amy	11/20/97	$10.00	Other

Corel Paradox 8 ■ Lesson 2 ■ Exercise 10

COREL PARADOX 8 Lesson 2: Edit and Print a Database

PART III

17. Switch to Project Viewer.
18. Open **MEMBERS** or **10MEMBERS**.
19. Add the new members listed below to the end of the MEMBERS table in Edit mode.

MEMBER ID	LAST	FIRST	ADDRESS	CITY	PHONE
BO9719	Boot	Barry	6 Terminal Drive	North Hollywood	(213) 555-1122
WE9720	Web	Warren	15 Design Road	Anaheim	(213) 555-5454
BU9721	Bugg	Barbara	345 Systems Street	Culver City	(213) 555-9191
CH9722	Chipp	Charley	231 Board Avenue	Beverly Hills	(213) 555-7171

20. Carl Midi has asked to be removed from our club listings. Check the Charges table to note if he has charged any items. If not, delete his record from the MEMBERS table.

PART IV

21. Use the Window menu to switch to CHGFORM. Add the following data: (Use navigation buttons to add the new data.)

MEMBER ID	LAST	FIRST	DATE	AMOUNT	CHARGE
ZI9713	Zip	Drew	11/22/97	$30.00	Dinner/Meeting
WY9715	Wyndow	Walter	11/22/97	$30.00	Dinner/Meeting

22. Switch to the CHARGES table.
23. Print the table.
24. Close the tables and form.

KEYSTROKES

EDIT DATA

Paradox automatically saves changes to fields when you move to the next record.

If you are entering data into a field that has validity checks, you cannot move from that field until the validity check requirement is met.

1. In Edit mode, place insertion point in field to change.
   OR
   Click and drag to select field contents.
2. Type desired new value.

DELETE RECORD

In Edit mode:

1. Scroll to the record to be deleted.
2. Press **Ctrl + Delete** .... Ctrl + Del

SET FORM RADIO BUTTON FIELD

In Design Form mode:

1. Select the field to be displayed with radio buttons.
2. Right-click and select **Properties** .... R
3. Click **Display type** .... Alt + Y

4. Select **Radio Buttons** .... ↓
   on drop-down list.
5. Click **Define Values** .... Tab , Alt + D
6. Click **Item** .... Alt + I
7. Enter first item/value for field.
8. Press **Enter** .... Enter
9. Repeat steps 7-8 until list is complete.
10. To sort list; click **Sort List** ...... Alt + S
11. Click **OK** .... Enter
12. Click **OK** .... Enter
    to close Field Properties box.

COREL PARADOX 8 Lesson 2: Edit and Print a Database

Exercise 11

Enhance Form Design (Background Color, Custom Colors, Frames)

NOTES

Enhance Form Design

- Many companies use forms as their main method of entering data and viewing records. Forms can be enhanced to make data attractive and easier to read. We have already changed the color and font size of field data in previous exercises. Note the illustration of a form with background color, field frames, field color, and font changes.

Form View

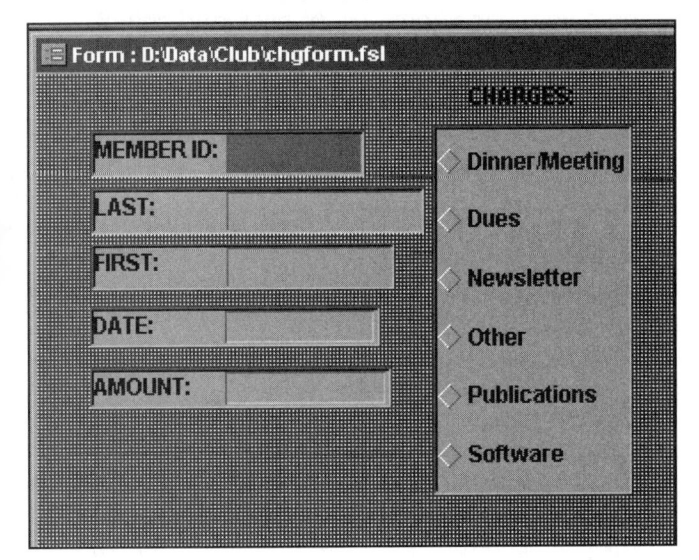

- You can change the background color or pattern of a form by selecting the background while in Form Design mode, right-clicking, then selecting Properties. The Page Properties dialog box will display on the General tab. As you will note in the illustration to the right, several colors are available for selection, along with an Add Custom Color button.

- To create a custom color, click on a blank color box, then click Add Custom Color. Colors may be customized for field areas and form backgrounds using the Custom Color dialog box (illustrated on the next page) by sliding the Red, Green, and Blue bars to create a custom color.

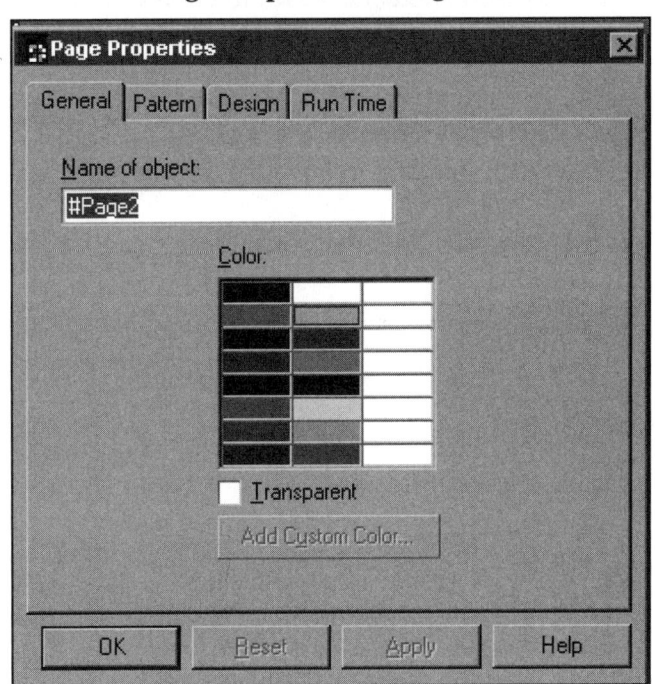

Page Properties Dialog Box

COREL PARADOX 8 Lesson 2: Edit and Print a Database

Custom Color Dialog Box

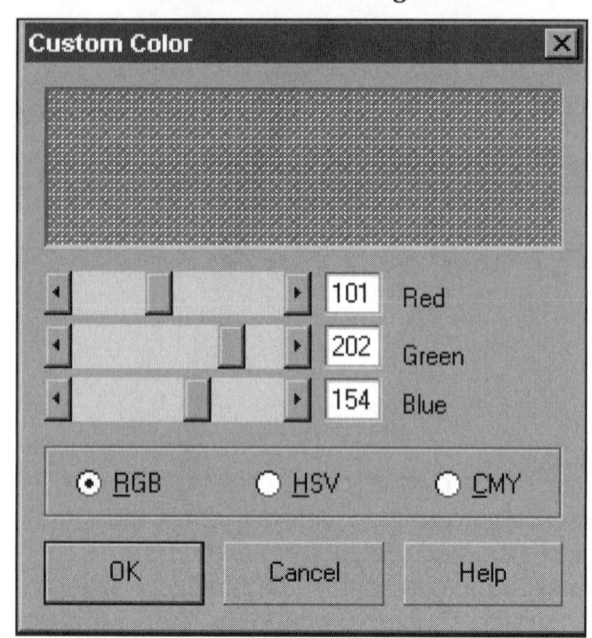

Frame Tab - Field Properties Dialog Box

- **Frames** can be used to highlight fields on a form. You can select the Frame tab from the Field Properties dialog box and choose from various colors, line styles, and line thickness options. Note the illustration of the Frame tab of the Field Properties dialog box at the top right, and an example of a form with a framed field.

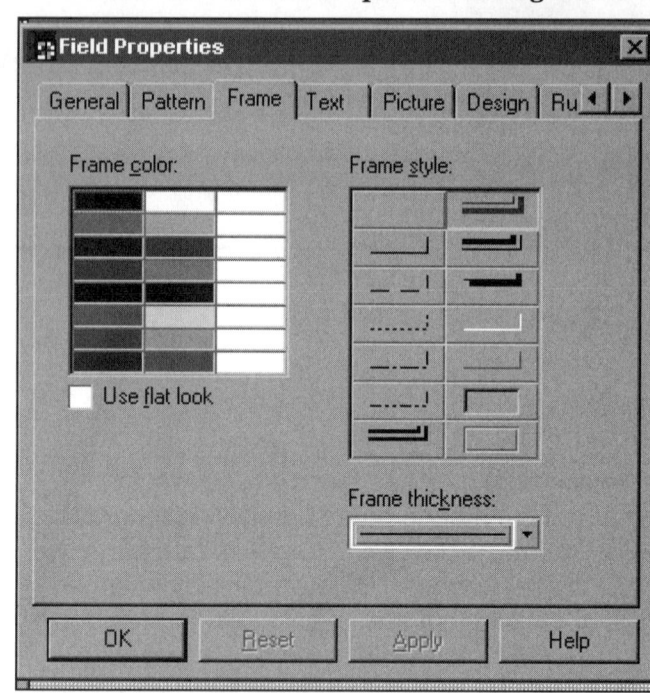

- If you wish to apply the same Properties setting to several items on a form, press the Shift key and select each item. Right-click and select Properties.

    ✓Note: You can also hold the Shift key and drag a box around the items to be selected and enhanced.

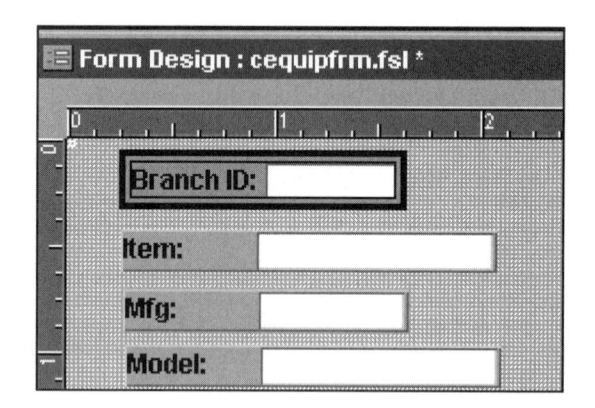

The CCU group has decided to enhance its forms. In addition, data will be added to the MEMBERS and CHARGES tables, and corrections to will be made to existing data.

EXERCISE DIRECTIONS

1. Open Project Viewer and switch your working directory to \CLUB.

2. Open **CHGFORM** or **11CHGFORM**.

3. Switch to Form Design mode.

4. Right-click on the background of the form and select Properties.

5. To set a custom color background:
   a. Click on one of the blank color locations.
   b. Click Add Custom Color.
   c. Click and slide Red bar to 9 (or type 9).
   d. Click and slide Green bar to 157 (or type 157).
   e. Click and slide Blue bar to 47 (or type 47). (Or create any background color you wish.)
   f. Click OK.
   g. Click Apply.
   h. Click OK.

6. Make the following changes to all fields: (Select each field and hold down the Shift key. Right-click and select Properties.)
   a. Select each field's edit region (data area) and change the color to light gray.
   b. Add the indented frame style (right column, frame six).

7. Move the fields so that they are spaced as shown in the Form View illustration on page 401.

8. Select the edit region (data area) for the Member ID, Last, and First name fields and change the font to Book Antiqua, Regular, 12 point.

9. Save the changes in the form design.

10. In Edit mode, enter the new charges as indicated in the table below:

MEMBER ID	LAST	FIRST	DATE	CHARGE	AMOUNT
BO9719	Boot	Barry	12/1/97	Dues	$25.00
WE9720	Web	Warren	12/2/97	Dues	$25.00
WE9720	Web	Warren	12/2/97	Newsletter	$15.00
BU9721	Bugg	Barbara	12/3/97	Dues	$25.00
CO9716	Coller	Jenny	12/3/97	Publications	$50.00
CH9722	Chipp	Charley	12/3/97	Dues	$25.00

11. Close the form and switch to Project Viewer.

12. Open the **CHARGES** or **11CHARGES** table and check your data entry.

13. Close the table and the form.

14. Open **MEMFORM** or **11MEMFORM**.

15. Enhance this form, in Form Design mode, using the same frame and data format, but changing to a different background color.

16. Save the changes.

17. Switch to Form view and scroll through records to make the following changes in Edit mode:

18. Drew Zip has moved to 23 Hillside Street in Beverly Hills and has kept the same telephone number.

19. Martin Matricks has changed his telephone number from 555-2222 to 555-2651.

20. Print a copy of the Drew Zip record.

21. Close all database objects.

KEYSTROKES

CHANGE FORM BACKGROUND COLOR

In Form Design mode:

1. Right-click on the form background.
2. Select **P**roperties .... `R`
3. Select **C**olor
   on the **General** tab .... `Alt`+`C`, `↑↓`

   OR

   Select a custom color:
   - Click one of the blank color locations .... `→`
   - Click Add C**u**stom Color .... `Alt`+`U`
   - Move slides of each color bar until desired color is obtained.
4. Click **OK** .... `Enter`
   to save custom color.
5. Click **A**pply .... `Alt`+`A`
6. Click **OK** .... `Enter`

ADD FRAME TO FIELD

In Form Design mode:

1. Right-click on the field.
2. Select **P**roperties .... `R`
3. Select **Frame** tab.
4. Select Frame **s**tyle ... `Alt`+`S`, `↓``↑`
5. Click **OK** .... `Enter`

SELECT MULTIPLE FORM ITEMS TO ADJUST OR DESIGN

Hold Shift and drag box .... `Shift`+*drag*
around objects to be selected.

OR

1. Select first item.
2. Press and hold **Shift** key .... `Shift`
3. Select next item.
4. Repeat as necessary.

COREL PARADOX 8 Lesson 2: Edit and Print a Database

Exercise 12

■ Summary

In an earlier exercise, you created an inventory table called CEQUIP for Sports Dud's computer inventory and you began to make entries. In this exercise, you will add new fields to the table and enter new information into the database. A form will be created and enhanced, and data will be added using the form. In addition, you will be adding new branches to the STORES table and editing existing records.

EXERCISE DIRECTIONS

PART I

1. Open Project Viewer and switch your working directory to \SPORTS.
2. Open the 🖳CEQUIP or 💾12CEQUIP.
3. Restructure the table to add two alpha fields at the end of the existing table:
   ASSIGNED TO (Alpha - 15)
   SERIAL # (Alpha - 7)
4. Save the new structure.
5. Add the new field data listed below.
   ✓ You should maximize the table window or scroll to view all fields in this table.

BRANCH ID	ITEM	MFG	MODEL	COST	PUR. DATE	WTY	ASSIGNED TO	SERIAL #
CA05	Printer	BP	LaserJet	$1479.00	7/15/97	N	Accounting	88842
CA05	Computer	GBM	Notepad 600	$1399.00	6/15/97	Y	Accounting	671150
CA05	Hard Drive	Barton	LPS80 220 MB	$199.00	6/20/97	Y	Accounting	54219
CA07	Computer	GBM	Notepad 500C	$2199.00	6/10/97	Y	Accounting	AB2059
CA07	Hard Drive	Wilson	CFS4 300MB	$250.00	7/10/97	N	Purchasing	12345
IL03	Computer	Debb	P200	$2507.52	1/12/98	Y	Accounting	765498
IL03	Printer	Jokidota	BJ800	$355.00	1/12/98	Y	Accounting	43567
MA02	Computer	Debb	Notebook 586	$1889.00	1/10/98	Y	Shipping	1145A
NC09	Computer	Pancard	PE166	$2095.54	1/25/98	Y	Purchasing	VC2342
NC09	Zip Drive	Howell	Z100	$169.95	1/25/98	N	Purchasing	324222
NY01	Computer	GBM	PC220	$1248.50	6/5//97	Y	Accounting	651198
NY01	Printer	GBM	ExecJetII	$335.00	6/8/97	Y	Accounting	55211
RI04	Computer	Pancard	PE166	$2095.54	1/29/98	Y	Accounting	BV3452
RI04	Printer	BP	LaserJet	$1303.00	1/29/98	Y	Accounting	1213H

COREL PARADOX 8 Lesson 2: Edit and Print a Database

PART II

6. Create a Quick Form from this table.

7. In Form Design mode, enhance the form by changing font size, field placement, and background color.

8. Add a Radio Button for the Assigned To field. Use the following to define field values:
   - Accounting
   - Purchasing
   - Shipping
   - MIS
   - Sales
   - Administration
   - Other

9. Sort the items.

10. Move the Radio Button field to the right of the other fields.

11. Use the Text Tool to add a label above the radio buttons. Use ASSIGNED TO: as the label and set it for bold. Move the label in place above the radio buttons.

12. Save the form; name it **EQUIPFRM**, replacing the previous form with the same name.

13. In Edit mode, add the records listed below.

PART III

14. Switch to the CEQUIP table. Make the following edits:
    - The correct cost of the GBM PC220 purchased on 6/5/97 was $1348.50; make the correction.
    - The Barton hard drive is not under warranty; make the correction.
    - The GBM ColorJet II Printer purchased on 6/8/97 is no longer in use; delete the record from the table.

15. Print one copy of the table in landscape mode.

16. Close the table and form.

BRANCH	ITEM	MFG	MODEL	COST	PUR.DATE	WTY	ASSIGNED TO	SERIAL #
GA06	Printer	NIC	FGE/3V	$539.00	2/3/98	N	Purchasing	87098
CA05	Printer	BP	Deskjet	$429.00	2/5/98	Y	Accounting	99911
CA07	Printer	BP	Deskjet	$429.00	2/6/98	Y	Purchasing	22230
GA06	Computer	Canton	Notebook	$2436.00	2/10/98	Y	MIS	98763

PART IV

17. Open the ⌨STORES or 💾12STORES table.

18. Add the new branches to the table as listed below:

BRANCH ID	ADDRESS	TELEPHONE	CITY	ST	ZIP	EVE
PA11	196 Patriot Avenue	800-555-1234	Philadelphia	PA	19018	Yes
NJ12	1453 Fashion Drive	800-555-5170	Paramus	NJ	07843	No
CA13	352 Shore Drive	800-555-6431	San Diego	CA	92102	No
DC14	167 Congress Avenue	800-555-0055	Washington	DC	20003	No
AZ15	9087 Cactus Drive	800-555-1133	Phoenix	AZ	85004	Yes
CO16	65 Mountain Road	800-555-9898	Denver	CO	80204	Yes
CT17	45 Fifth Street	800-555-0987	Stamford	CT	06902	No
FL18	124 Atlantic Avenue	800-555-8181	Miami	FL	33107	No
OH19	245 Rock Avenue	800-555-8484	Cleveland	OH	44109	Yes
MD20	432 Ocean Street	800-555-2333	Annapolis	MD	21401	No

19. The Boston, MA branch, MA02, closed; make the following updates to our tables.
    a. Delete the MA02 record from the STORES table.
    b. Switch to the CEQUIP table. The Notebook 586 computer from MA02 has been reassigned to the Accounting department of PA11, the new Philadelphia store. Make the update to the table.
    c. Switch to the STAFF table. Ms. Rodriguez, the manager of the MA02 store, has left our employment. Delete her record from the STAFF table.
    d. Switch to the SFTWARE table. Software for the MA02 store has been transferred to the PA11 store.

20. Print the STORES table in landscape mode.

21. Close all database objects.

COREL PARADOX 8

Lesson 3: Search and Sort a Database

Exercise 13

- Locate Values
- Use Wildcards
- Locate and Replace Data

NOTES

Locate Values

- The **Record** menu in Table and Form views contains commands that assist in locating records. You may wish to find a specific record for editing or informational purposes. After opening a table in either Table or Form view, select Lo_c_ate, _V_alue from the _R_ecord menu, or press Ctrl+Z, or click the Locate button on the Toolbar to display the Locate Values dialog box (illustrated below).

Locate Value Dialog Box

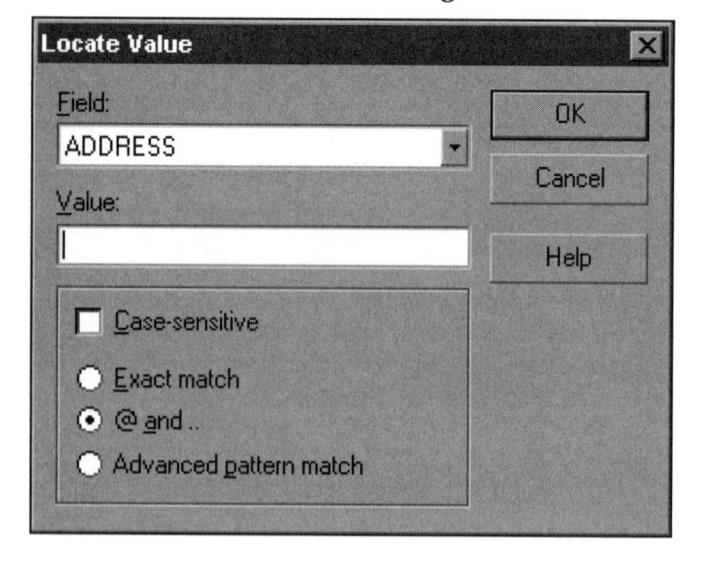

- After entering the value you wish to locate in the _V_alue box, set the Locate Value conditions:
  - **_F_ield** - Indicates the field you want to search. By default, it lists the field that contains the cursor. Click the drop-down arrow to select another field to search.

  - **_C_ase-sensitive** - Select to match capitalization as typed, or if not selected, search will ignore case of entry.

  - **_E_xact match**—Check Exact match if you do not want to treat pattern characters as wildcards.

  - **@ _a_nd ..**—Wildcards. @ stands for any character, and .. stands for any number of characters, including none.

  - **Advanced Pattern match**—Check Advanced pattern match if you want to use an extended list of wildcards in your search. (Click the Help button for the extended list of wildcards.)

- When all the appropriate conditions have been set, click OK to begin the search. The first record containing the search value is presented, with the search value highlighted. You can now view or edit the located record.

- To search for another record that contains the same data, select _R_ecord, Locate Nex_t_, or click the Locate Next button , or press Ctrl+A to move to the next occurrence. Either the next matching record is presented, or a message indicating that the search value was not found is displayed.

Use Wildcards

- A **wildcard operator** is a symbol used in a search value to substitute for unknown characters. There are two wildcard operators that broaden the locate command, the ellipsis (..) and the "at" symbol (@).

- The ellipsis (..) is used to indicate an unknown group of characters. For example; if you were searching for a particular name but were certain of only the first two letters, you would indicate the search value as *Br...* This will find all records in which the last name begins with *Br*.

- The "at" symbol (@) is used to substitute for an unknown single character. If you were searching for a particular name but were uncertain of some characters in the spelling, the search value could be entered as, for example, *Br@wn* or *Br@w@* or *B@@wn*. This would find records with any letter in the @ wildcard operator location.

Locate and Replace Data

- You may determine that you wish to locate all occurrences of a specific value and replace it with another value. In this case, you should use the Locate and Replace feature. This feature is available in Edit mode of a Form or Table. Select Lo_c_ate, and _R_eplace from the _R_ecord menu, or press Shift+Ctrl+Z, to open the dialog box (illustrated below). Enter the _F_ield, _V_alue, and Replace _w_ith value in the dialog box.

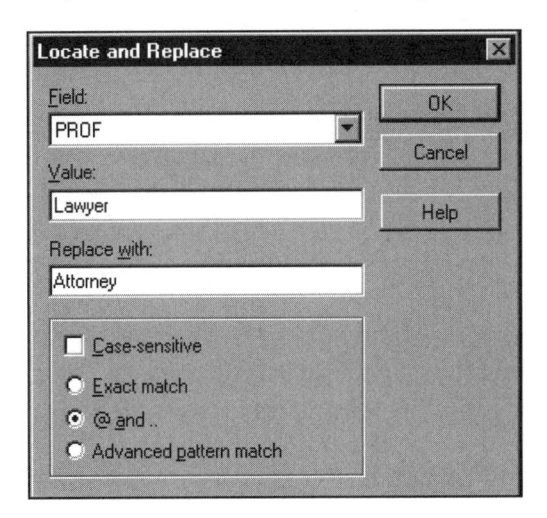

- The settings for the Find and Replace dialog box are the same as those for the Locate Value dialog box. These settings will locate and replace values as specified, stopping at each occurrence of the value and allowing you to determine if it should be replaced. Note the illustration of the Found a Match dialog box that appears for each occurrence of the value. You may elect to change all occurrences without viewing each one.

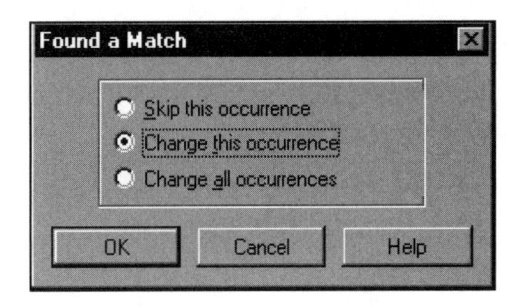

COREL PARADOX 8 Lesson 3: Search and Sort a Database

> CCU, your computer users' group, has decided to add a field to its MEMBERS table. In addition, several new members have joined CCU and you have been notified that several members' records need to be updated. After updating the records, you will be in a better position to generate membership information.

EXERCISE DIRECTIONS

PART I
1. Open Project Viewer and switch your working directory to \CLUB.
2. Open **MEMBERS** or **13MEMBERS**.
3. Use the Restructure feature to add two new fields to the table as follows:
   - Insert after the CITY field: ZIP (Alpha–5)
     Hint: Press Insert while on the PHONE field.
   - Insert after the PHONE field: PROF. (Alpha–15)
   - Save the changes.
4. Add the new information to the records of the present members as listed below:
   ✓ *For easier data entry, you can temporarily move the PROF field next to the ZIP field. Return it after data is entered.*

PART II
5. Use Quick Form to create an updated form for the table.
6. In Form Design Mode, change the background and field colors, and add field frames.
7. Save the form as **MEMFORM**, replacing the original form.
8. Add the new members shown on the next page at the end of the records in Form view:

MEMBER ID	LAST	ZIP	PROF
BO9711	Boolean	92803	Student
BO9719	Boot	91615	Accountant
BU9721	Bugg	90311	Lawyer
CA9717	Cable	90311	Teacher
CE9701	Ceedee	92803	Student
CH9722	Chipp	90210	Chiropractor
CO9716	Coller	90210	Lawyer
DI9710	Disk	91615	Student
FR9712	Franz	90210	Orthopedist
GR9709	Graphic	91615	Teacher
IC9706	Icon	92803	Editor
MA9718	Matricks	90210	Accountant
MO9702	Modem	92803	Banker
MO9704	Monitor	90210	Student
MO9705	Mouse	92803	Lawyer
SI9714	Sistem	92803	Manager
SO9703	Sort	90210	Teacher
WA9707	Wave	91615	Manager
WE9720	Web	92803	Teacher
WY9715	Wyndow	90311	Sales
ZI9713	Zip	90210	Lawyer

MEMBER ID	LAST	FIRST	ADDRESS	CITY	ZIP	PHONE	PROF.
FO9723	Folder	Fred	45 Anita Street	Anaheim	92803	(213) 555-7199	Sales
GR9724	Graphiks	Gene	231 Fifth Street	Culver City	90311	(213) 555-0091	Insurance
IM9725	Image	Iggy	79 Sunny Drive	Beverly Hills	90210	(213) 555-1009	Student

PART III

9. Switch to Table view. Using Record, Locate, Value, search the database for the answers to the following questions. Make note of the answers.
   - Which members live in Anaheim? (CITY field)
   - Which members live in Beverly Hills? (CITY field)
   - Which members are Lawyers? (PROF. field)
   - How many members are Students? (PROF. field)
   - What is Trina Mouse's profession? (LAST field)

10. Switch to **MEMFORM**. In Edit view, locate the record for Michael Monitor. Make the following changes to his record:
    - His new address is 32 Oak Street.
    - His new phone number is (213) 555-8750.

11. Locate the record for Bette Wave. Make the following changes to her record:
    - Her new name is Bette Wave-Sim.
    - Her new address is 1745 River Street, located in North Hollywood, 91615.
    - Her new phone number is (213) 555-8520.

12. Locate the record for Sheila Icon. Change her phone number to (213) 555-7255.

13. Locate and replace all occurrences of the value Lawyer with Attorney in the PROF. field.

14. Close the **MEMBERS** table and the **MEMFORM** form.

KEYSTROKES

LOCATE VALUES

Ctrl+Z

In Form or Table view:

1. Click **Locate Field Value** button .....
   OR
   a. Click **Record** .... Alt+R
   b. Click **Lo**c**ate** C
   c. **V**alue V
2. Select **F**ield .... Alt+F, ↓
3. Enter **V**alue .... Alt+V, value
4. Set options as desired:
   - **C**ase sensitive .... Alt+C
   - **E**xact match .... Alt+E
   - **@** a**nd** .... Alt+A
   - Advanced **p**attern match ..... Alt+P
5. Click **OK** .... Enter

Value will be located, or a status bar message will appear noting that the value was not found.

6. To locate next occurrence of the value:

   Ctrl+A

   a. Click **R**ecord .... Alt+R
   b. Click Locate Nex**t** .... T
   OR
   Click **Locate Next** button ....

LOCATE AND REPLACE DATA

Shift+Ctrl+Z

In Form or Table Edit mode only:

1. Click **R**ecord .... Alt+R
2. Click **Lo**c**ate** C
3. Click **R**eplace .... R
4. Select **F**ield .... Alt+F, ↓
5. Enter **V**alue .... Alt+V, value to be located.

6. Enter Replace **w**ith value .... Alt+W, value
7. Set options as desired:
   - **C**ase sensitive .... Alt+C
   - **E**xact match .... Alt+E
   - **@** a**nd** .... Alt+A
   - Advanced **p**attern match ... Alt+P
   - Click **OK** .... Enter

If a match is found the Found a Match dialog box will appear; if not a status bar message will appear, noting that the value was not found.

In the Found a Match dialog box:

1. Select desired action:
   - **S**kip this occurrence .... Alt+S
   - Change **t**his occurrence .. Alt+T
   - Change **a**ll occurrences .. Alt+A
2. Click OK .... Enter

Corel Paradox 8 ■ Lesson 3 ■ Exercise 13   411

COREL PARADOX 8 Lesson 3: Search and Sort a Database

Exercise 14

■ Sort Records ■ Multiple Sorts

NOTES

Sort Records

- Records may be arranged in an order best suited for locating and updating records. Sorting allows you to rearrange the records so that you can view them according to the task at hand.
- You can sort records to provide:
  - Data arranged in alphabetical or numerical order.
  - Data arranged by size (largest to smallest or smallest to largest).
  - Data arranged into groups (for example; all people who live in Washington).
  - A method to find duplicate entries.
- Records are best sorted in Table view. To sort data in Table view, select Sort from the Format menu, or, when in Table or Form view, you can use Tools, Utilities, Sort. Paradox will not allow you to sort a table if it is also open in Form view. You must close the form first. When you select the Sort command, the Sort Table dialog box will appear. All the fields in the table are listed so that you can add the desired fields to the sort order list.

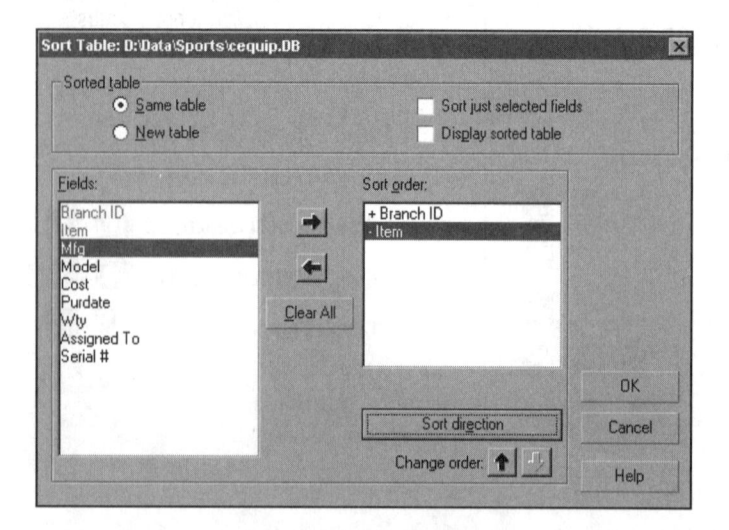

- The dialog box provides choices as to how the table should be sorted, under the Sorted table heading:
  - **Same table:** Overwrites the existing order of the table. (Not available for keyed tables.)
  - **New table:** Creates a new table that you can name, while preserving the original table. If you have a key in the table, you must save the sort to a new table since the key places the table in order.
  - **Sort just selected fields:** Sorts only the selected fields but all the fields are displayed.
  - **Display sorted table:** If you are sorting to a new table, this selection displays the table after it is sorted.
- To add a field to the sort order list on the Sort Table dialog box, select the field from the list and click the right arrow button. A field may be removed from the Sort order list by selecting the field under Sort order and clicking the left arrow button.
- Tables can be sorted in either ascending or descending order. **Ascending order** arranges text in alphabetical order from A to Z, or in numerical order from lowest to highest. Dates and Times are sorted from the oldest to the most recent date and time. **Descending order** is the opposite. The Sort direction button will change the order of the selected field. A plus sign (see BRANCH in the illustration) means ascending sort, and a minus sign (see ITEM in the illustration) means descending sort.

Multiple Sorts

- Several fields (columns) of data may be sorted at one time, and each field's sort order can be set independently to provide a sort on multiple criteria. The order, or priority, of the fields listed in the Sort order box may be changed by selecting the field and clicking one of the Change order arrows to move it either up or down in the list.

Your manager at Sports Duds has requested lists of information from the CEQUIP table that requires sorting records. In this exercise, you will sort records on one or more fields and create new tables with sorted data.

EXERCISE DIRECTIONS

1. Open Project Viewer and switch your working directory to \SPORTS.
2. Open **CEQUIP** or **14CEQUIP**.
3. Use Format, Sort to sort the table in the following way:
   - In ascending order (+) by BRANCH ID.
   - In ascending (+) order by ITEM.
   - In descending (-) order by COST.
4. Select the Same table option in the Sorted Table section of the dialog box.
5. Click OK to sort.
6. Print a copy of this sort in landscape mode.
7. Sort the table in the following way:
   - In ascending order by ITEM.
   - In ascending order by MFG.
   - In ascending order by BRANCH ID.
8. Select the New table and name the table **EQUIPINV**. Also select the Display sorted table option.
9. Print a copy of this sort in landscape mode.
10. Close the table.
11. Switch to Project Viewer and open **EQUIPFRM** or **14EQUIPFRM**.
12. Use Tools, Utilities, Sort. Open the **CEQUIP** table, and sort in ascending order by PURDATE. Select the Same table option.
    - ✓ *You will not be able to complete the sort since the table selected relates to the open form.*
13. Close the form.
14. Switch to Project Viewer and open **SOFORM** or **14SOFORM**.
15. Use Tools, Utilities, Sort. Open the **CEQUIP** table, and sort as listed below:
    - In ascending order by PURDATE.
    - In ascending order by BRANCH ID.
    - In descending order by COST.

    Select the Same table and Display sorted table options.
    - ✓ *Because you were sorting a table that was not in use by an open form, the commands will sort the table.*
16. Print a copy of this sort in landscape mode.
17. Close the form and tables.

COREL PARADOX 8 Lesson 3: Search and Sort a Database

KEYSTROKES

SORT RECORDS IN TABLE VIEW

1. Click **Format**.......................... `Alt`+`M`
2. Click **Sort**............................. `S`
3. Select **Sorted table** options:... `Alt`+`T`
   - **Same table** .... `S`
   - **New table** .... `N`
   - **Sort just selected fields**.................... `Alt`+`J`
   - **Display sorted table** .... `P`
4. Select **Fields** .... `Alt`+`F`
5. Click desired field .... `↑``↓`
6. Click right arrow .... `→`
   to list fields in **Sort order** box.
7. Repeat steps 4-6, as desired.

To change sort direction:

1. Select field in **Sort order** box...... `Alt`+`O`, `↑``↓`
2. Click **Sort direction** .... `Alt`+`E`

To change order of priority of sort:

1. Select field.............. `Alt`+`O`, `↑``↓` in **Sort order** box.
2. Click Change order up or down arrow.................. `↑``↓`
3. Click **OK**.................................. `Enter`

SORT RECORDS IN FORM OR TABLE VIEW

✓ *The form view of the table to be sorted cannot be in use when sorting in Table view.*

1. Click **Tools** .... `Alt`+`T`
2. Click **Utilities** .... `U`
3. Click **Sort**................................... `S`
4. Select table to be sorted.
5. Click **OK**.................................. `Enter`
6. Follow steps in SORT RECORDS IN A TABLE.

414

Exercise 15: Filter Fields ■ Filter Tables

NOTES

Filter fields

- Sometimes the most efficient way to get information from a table is to isolate, or filter out, only those records that satisfy a specific set of conditions.

- Records may be filtered using the Field Filter or Filter Tables dialog boxes. To filter fields, click on the filter button or right-click a field in a table (or a field object on a form) and select Filter. The Field Filter dialog box will appear requesting the value to be filtered from the selected field. The illustrated setting will filter only those records with a value of CA07 in the Branch field. Filters are case-sensitive, therefore enter the value exactly as it should appear in the table. After filtering, a table can be edited, sorted, or printed.

Field Filter Dialog Box

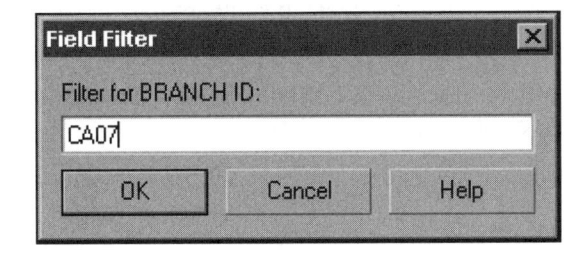

- To reverse the filter and display all records, right-click the field, click Filter, and remove the value setting.

Filter Tables

- If you wish to set filter data based on conditions, you must use the Filter Tables dialog box. When you click on the filter button on the toolbar or when you click Format, Filter in a table, or Record, Filter in a form, the Filter Tables dialog box will appear, as illustrated.

Filter Tables Dialog Box

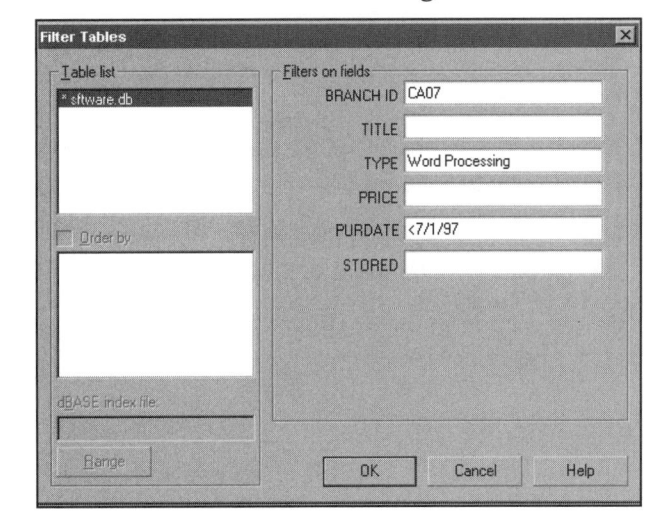

- In the Filter Tables dialog box, the Table list displays the table being filtered. The Filters on fields section lists the fields in the table and conditions for the filter. Notice in the illustration that the less than sign (<) is being used to indicate a date earlier than 7/1/97. The conditions set in the illustration will result in all records that represent Word Processing software from the CA07 branch purchased before 7/1/97.

- To remove a filter and display all the records, you must re-open the Filter Tables dialog box and clear the filter settings.

COREL PARADOX 8 Lesson 3: Search and Sort a Database

> *In this exercise, you will add data to the SOFTWARE table and use field and table filters to answer questions about the data in several tables or forms in the SPORTS database.*

EXERCISE DIRECTIONS

1. Open Project Viewer and switch your working directory to \SPORTS.

2. Open 💾**SOFORM** or 💾**15SOFORM**.

3. In Form Design mode, enhance the form by changing the background color, and setting field color and frame options.

4. Create a Radio Button field for TYPE using the following field values:

   - Communications
   - Spreadsheet
   - Desktop
   - Integrated
   - Graphics
   - Word Processing
   - Database
   - Other

5. Sort the list.

6. Arrange fields to allow spaces between items. Save the form as **SOFORM**, replacing the original layout.

7. Add the new data listed in the table below using Form view in Edit mode.

8. Use Project Viewer to switch to the 💾**SFTWARE** table or open 💾**15SFTWARE**.

9. Check that data was entered correctly.

10. Use the Field Filter method to answer the following questions, removing the filter between questions:

    HINT: Right-click the field, select Filter, enter desired value, click OK.

    a. How many copies of Graphics software do we have? (TYPE field)
    b. Which branches have copies of Trenta? (TITLE field)
    c. Which software packages do we have in all branches for Desktop publishing? (TYPE field)
    d. What was purchased on 9/15/97? (DATE field)
    e. What software is in the NY01 branch? (BRANCH field)

11. Use the Field Filter to find software purchased for the GA06 branch.

12. Edit the PURDATE field and change the date of the 9/15/97 purchase to 9/16/97.

13. Use the Filter Tables dialog box to find the answers to the following questions, clearing conditions between filters:

    HINT: Click Table, Filter and enter conditions for appropriate fields.

    a. Which word processing software titles were purchased before 8/31/97?
    b. Which word processing software titles cost less than $300.00?

14. What spreadsheet software titles do we have that cost less than $500?

15. Clear all filters.

16. Close the form and table.

BRANCH	TITLE	TYPE	PRICE	PURDATE	STORED
GA06	BBS	Communications	99.50	11/2/97	A15
GA06	WordEX	Word Processing	259.42	11/5/97	A15
NJ12	WordEX	Word Processing	259.42	11/15/97	B110
CT08	Trenta	Spreadsheet	202.55	1/30/98	A101
CT08	Harwood	Graphics	287.49	1/30/98	A101
CA07	Trenta	Spreadsheet	202.55	2/10/98	B235
RI04	Word-O	Word Processing	389.95	2/12/98	D230
CA05	PublishDesk	Desktop	289.95	2/15/98	A135
NC09	Tulip7	Spreadsheet	389.95	2/16/98	D230

KEYSTROKES

USE FIELD FILTER

In a table:

1. Right-click on field to be filtered.
2. Select **Filter**.
3. Enter value .... *value*
   to be filtered
4. Click **OK** .... `Enter`

USE TABLE FILTER

From a Form or Table:

1. Click **Tools** .... `Alt`+`T`
2. Click **Utilities** .... `U`
3. Click **Sort** .... `S`
4. Select table to filter.
5. Click **Filters on fields** .... `Alt`+`F`, `↓`
   Select fields to be filtered.
6. Enter filter condition .... *condition*
7. Click **OK** .... `Enter`

From a Table:

1. Click **Format** .... `Alt`+`M`
2. Click **Filter** .... `F`
3. Click **Table list** .... `Alt`+`T`, `↓`
   and select table, if necessary.
4. Click **Filters on fields** .... `Alt`+`F`, `↓`
   Select fields to be filtered.
5. Enter filter condition.
6. Click **OK** .... `Enter`

COREL PARADOX 8 Lesson 3: Search and Sort a Database

Exercise 16

■ **Filter Tables**

NOTES

Filter Tables

- The Filter Tables dialog box discussed in Exercise 15 is used when you have multiple criteria to be defined. You can use comparison operators to narrow, or limit, the resulting record set of a filter. The comparison operators are:

=	Is equal to (The default symbol can be omitted.)
<	Is less than
<=	Is less than or equal to
>	Is greater than
>=	Is greater than or equal to
<>	Is not equal to

- The ellipsis (..), the wildcard operator discussed in Exercise 13, may also be used with filter conditions. For example, if you wanted to filter out the members whose last names begin with C, you would enter C.. in the Last field in the Filters on fields section of the Filter Tables dialog box. To clear a filter, remove the criteria settings.

- If you have a filtered set of records you can filter it again for records that meet additional filter conditions.

In this exercise, you will add a new table for RECEIPTS to the CLUB database. Field filters and table filters with comparison operators will be used to edit and answer questions about the records.

EXERCISE DIRECTIONS

PART I

1. Open Project Viewer and switch your working directory to /CLUB.

2. Create a new table using the following field structure.

FIELD NAME	TYPE	SIZE	VALIDITY CHECKS
Member ID	Alpha	6	Required field
Last	Alpha	10	Required field
First	Alpha	8	Required field
Date	Date		Required field
Check#	Alpha	5	
Amount	Number		Required field

3. Save the table and name it **RECEIPTS**.

PART II

4. Open the **RECEIPTS** table.

5. Enter the data from the list of receipts below.

MEMBER ID	LAST	FIRST	DATE	CHECK#	AMOUNT
MO9704	Monitor	Michael	12/5/97	605	15.00
WA9709	Wave-Sim	Bette	12/10/97	1851	25.00
SO9703	Sort	Stuart	12/11/97	3421	59.95
ZI9713	Zip	Drew	12/18/97	324	30.00
WY9715	Wyndow	Walter	12/29/97	2345	30.00
GR9711	Graphic	John	12/30/97	1689	35.00
WE9720	Web	Warren	1/5/98	8769	25.00
CO9716	Coller	Jenny	1/8/98	6542	50.00

PART III

6. Open Project Viewer and open 🖬**MEMBERS** or 🖬**16MEMBERS**.

7. Use the Filter Tables dialog box to answer the following questions:
   ✓ *Clear the filter between questions.*
   a. Which member, whose last name begins with a C, is a chiropractor?
   b. Which members live in Beverly Hills and are attorneys?

8. Filter on Anaheim in the City field.

9. Edit all area codes from (213) to (818). Clear the filter.

10. Filter on North Hollywood in the City field.

11. Edit all area codes from (213) to (817). Clear the filter.

12. Filter on Culver City in the City field.
    ✓ *Because Culver City contains the name of the field, Paradox will return an empty table. You must enclose "Culver City" in quotes.*

13. Edit all area codes from (213) to (214). Clear the filter.

PART IV

14. Open Project Viewer and open 🖬**CHGFORM** or 🖬**16CHGFORM**.

15. Add the data below:

MEMBER ID	LAST	FIRST	DATE	AMOUNT	CHARGE
FO9723	Folder	Fred	12/8/97	Dues	25.00
GR9709	Graphiks	Gene	12/10/97	Dues	25.00
IM9725	Image	Iggy	12/12/97	Dues	25.00
IM9725	Image	Iggy	12/12/97	Dinner/ Meeting	30.00
BO9719	Boot	Barry	12/15/97	Dinner/ Meeting	30.00

16. Open 🖬**CHARGES** or 🖬**16CHARGES**.

17. Use Table Filter to answer the following questions:
    a. What types of charges were greater than $25.00?
    ✓ *Do not clear the filter before answering the next question.*
    b. Which of these charges were made after 12/1/97?
    ✓ *This is subset of a subset.*

18. Print these records.

19. Clear the filters and close all tables and forms.

COREL PARADOX 8 Lesson 3: Search and Sort a Database

Exercise 17 — Summary

PART I

> The manager of Sports Duds in New York has decided to create an inventory system for his store. The clothing inventory includes style number, type of garment, color, size, and vendor. In this exercise, you will create a table to keep track of the number of garments on hand. You will then search the table when customers or other branches call about availability of stock or when information is needed for reordering merchandise.

EXERCISE DIRECTIONS

1. Switch to the /SPORTS directory.
2. From the information listed on the next page, create a table with a suitable structure:
   - Use the column headings as field names.
   - Determine field properties from the information shown in the fields. (Inventory values are numeric.)
   - Set the Type, Color, and Vendor fields as required fields.
   - Set the Style field as a key field.
3. Save the table as **INVEN**.
4. Open the table.
5. Create a Quick Form from the table.
6. Enhance the form as desired.
7. Set the Type field for radio buttons and define the following items:
   - Jacket
   - Crew Top
   - T-Shirt
   - T-Top
   - Pants
   - Shorts
8. Sort the values and add the label TYPE for the field.
9. Save the form as **INVFORM**.
10. Enter the data provided in the table on the next page in either Form or Table view.
11. Locate the following information on the table:
    a. What color is style number T1327?
    b. What color Jackets do we have in stock?
    c. What are the style numbers for blue items?
12. Use locate and replace to change the color Blue to Navy.
13. Close the table and form.

STYLE	TYPE	COLOR	P	S	M	L	XL	VENDOR
J2354	Jacket	Black	4	4	2	4	2	Winner
C3276	Crew Top	White	5	6	6	4	3	Grand Co.
P4532	Pants	Tan	2	12	12	4	4	Amella
S7823	Shorts	Blue	4	15	16	3	14	Amella
T1327	T-Shirt	Green	12	17	34	12	12	Amella
P4653	Pants	Black	5	7	4	34	12	Winner
C3654	Crew Top	Black	3	6	8	8	8	Winner
J2543	Jacket	White	3	3	5	5	5	Grand Co.
S7932	Shorts	Black	5	4	4	6	8	Winner
T1421	T-Top	White	10	15	15	14	18	Grand Co.
P4821	Pants	Blue	13	32	30	26	30	Amella
C3911	Crew Top	Blue	23	32	26	36	32	Amella
S7214	Shorts	Blue	3	6	33	23	17	Amella
P4276	Pants	White	12	18	20	18	16	Grand Co.
J2399	Jacket	Blue	17	21	26	21	18	Amella

PART II

Sally Jogger, your boss at Sports Duds in NY, has asked you to enter additional data into the clothing inventory you created earlier, (INVEN). In addition, she would like you to add a new field and then provide lists from sorted or filtered data to respond to various questions.

EXERCISE DIRECTIONS

1. Open Project Viewer and switch your working directory to \SPORTS.

2. Open **INVEN** or **17INVEN**.

3. Restructure INVEN to add the PRICE numeric field after the COLOR field. Save the table.

4. Open **INVFORM** or **17INVFORM**.

5. Add the PRICE field to the form design and save the new design.

6. Using the table or form, add the highlighted information to the PRICE field as indicated for existing data, and add the new data listed on the next page.

COREL PARADOX 8 Lesson 3: Search and Sort a Database

STYLE	TYPE	COLOR	PRICE	P	S	M	L	XL	VENDOR
C3276	Crew Top	White	15.75	5	6	6	4	3	Grand Co.
C3654	Crew Top	Black	15.25	3	6	8	8	8	Winner
C3911	Crew Top	Navy	14.75	23	32	26	36	32	Amella
J2354	Jacket	Black	35.50	4	4	2	4	2	Winner
J2399	Jacket	Navy	32.25	17	21	26	21	18	Amella..
J2543	Jacket	White	34.25	3	3	5	5	5	Grand Co.
P4276	Pants	White	22.35	12	18	20	18	16	Grand Co.
P4532	Pants	Tan	21.75	2	12	12	4	4	Amella
P4653	Pants	Black	22.75	5	7	4	34	12	Winner
P4821	Pants	Navy	21.50	13	32	30	26	30	Amella
S7214	Shorts	Navy	13.15	3	6	33	23	17	Amella
S7823	Shorts	Navy	13.65	4	15	16	3	14	Amella
S7932	Shorts	Black	12.75	5	4	4	6	8	Winner
T1327	T-Shirt	Green	10.25	12	17	34	12	12	Amella
T1421	T-Top	White	10.50	10	15	15	14	18	Grand Co.
C3281	Crew Top	Green	15.75	9	10	15	20	25	Amella
T1422	T-Shirt	Red	10.50	8	12	15	22	30	Winner
S7623	Shorts	Red	13.65	8	10	12	18	20	Winner
P4246	Pants	Navy	22.35	10	12	15	18	22	Grand Co.
J2544	Jacket	Black	34.25	8	8	8	8	10	Winner
C3912	Crew Top	Red	14.75	8	8	10	12	16	Winner
T3654	T-Top	Red	10.75	10	10	15	20	25	Winner
T1328	T-Shirt	Navy	10.25	12	15	15	20	23	Amella
S7215	Shorts	Black	13.15	5	8	10	12	10	Winner
P4533	Pants	Green	21.75	10	15	15	20	20	Amella

7. The following item is no longer in stock. Delete the record.
   - P4532 Tan Pants

8. Sort the records in each of the following ways and answer the questions:
   ✓ *Because this table has a key field, you cannot sort within this table. Save the first sort and then use the new table for sorting. Click "display the table" to view it after the sort.*

   a. Sort in ascending order by COLOR and ascending order by PRICE within each color. Name the table COLORPR and set the table to display.
      - What is the lowest priced style for a black jacket?
   b. Use the COLORPR table to sort in ascending order by TYPE and descending order by PRICE:
      - How much is the most expensive crew top?
   c. Use the COLORPR table to sort in ascending order by COLOR, in ascending order by TYPE, and ascending order by STYLE:
      - Which colors do we have stock in at this time? Which color is most prevalent?

9. Print a copy of the COLORPR table in landscape mode.

10. Use table or field filters to answer the following questions:
    a. Which Shorts styles and colors are presently in stock?
    b. What is the style number for a Petite Navy Crew Top of which five or more are in stock?
    c. Which Jacket styles were purchased from Amella?
    d. Which styles and types are White and have more than ten items in Large and Extra Large?

11. Print one copy of the last filtered list in landscape mode.

12. Remove all filters and print one copy of the table in landscape orientation.

13. Close the table and form.

COREL PARADOX 8

Lesson 4: Queries

Exercise 18

- Create a Query
- Save a Query

NOTES

Create a Query

- A **query** can use advanced techniques to isolate a group of records, determine which fields to include and in what order, calculate data, and use data from more than one table. Queries are used to create datasets that answer a question. They can be saved, printed, and used as the basis for a form or report.

- A query is created by selecting New, Query from the File menu or by right-clicking the Queries icon in Project Viewer, listed under Types, and selecting New. The Select File dialog box displays, as illustrated below, and lists the database tables in the current working directory that may be used for the query. You can also open tables from a different directory, if desired. The directory can be changed and the desired database selected. Select the tables to be included in the query and click Open.

Select File Dialog Box

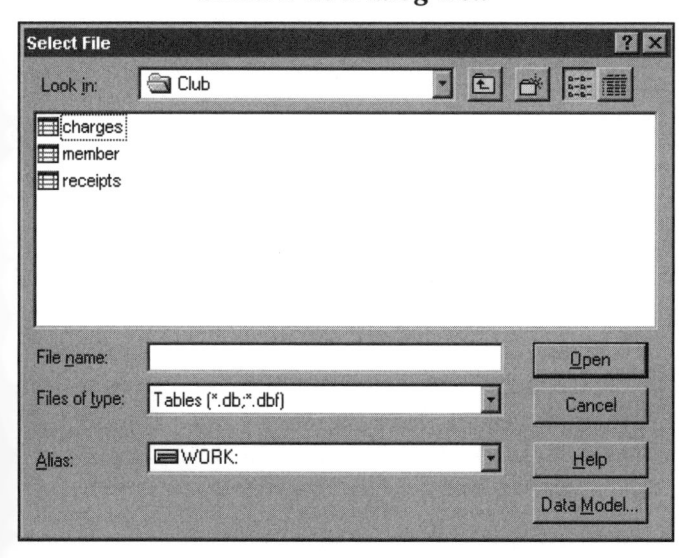

- After the table(s) is selected and the Select File dialog box is closed, the Query form appears in a window.

- Paradox uses a method called **query by example** (QBE) to ask questions about the data. You give Paradox an example of the result you want, and Paradox gives you the result in a temporary table named Answer in your PRIVATE directory.

Query Form

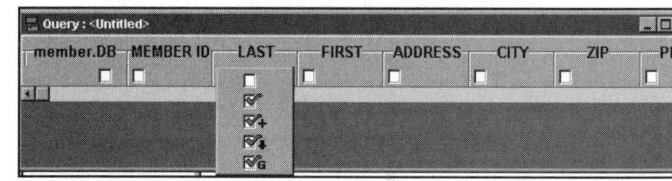

- On the Query form, there is a check box under each field, and also under the table name which can be checked to include all the fields in the query. When you right-click the check box, you see the different types of checks you can use. Check the boxes under the fields to tell Paradox which fields to include in the Answer table by either clicking with the mouse or by pressing F6 for a check or Shift+F6 for other forms of the check.

- The checks are as follows:

    Check: shows all unique values for a field in ascending order.

    CheckPlus: shows all values in a field, including duplicates, without sorting, as they appeared in the table. A Check Plus will override any Check or CheckDescending selections.

COREL PARADOX 8 Lesson 4: Queries

☑↓ **CheckDescending:** shows unique values sorted in descending order.

☑G **GroupBy:** specifies that the query will use the field to group records in a query. This field will not appear in the answer table.
An empty check box clears any check.

- To see the results of your Query Design, use the Run Query option from the Query menu, press F8, or press the Run Query button on the toolbar. In the query design partially shown below we checked the LAST, FIRST, PHONE, and PROF. fields. The sorted table, automatically named ANSWER.DB. appears below.

Query form

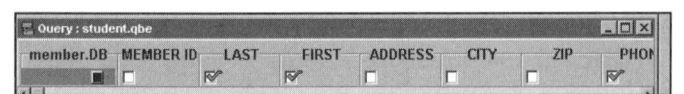

Answer Table

	LAST	FIRST	PHONE	PROF
1	Boolean	Bob	(818)555-5265	Student
2	Boot	Barry	(817)555-1122	Accountant
3	Bugg	Barbara	(214)555-9191	Attorney
4	Cable	Cleo	(214)555-9988	Teacher
5	Ceedee	Carol	(818)555-4987	Student
6	Chipp	Charley	(213)555-7171	Chiropractor
7	Coller	Jenny	213-555-6676	Attorney
8	Disk	Amy	(817)555-8917	Student
9	Folder	Fred	(818)555-7199	Sales
10	Franz	Reid	(213)555-0912	Orthopedist
11	Graphic	John	(817)555-8129	Teacher
12	Graphiks	Gene	(214)555-0091	Insurance
13	Icon	Sheila	(818)555-7255	Editor

- If you wish to select records with a specific item in a field, you can enter the criterion in the space after the check box. The box will expand to fit the criterion. You can use comparison operators (< > >= etc.), or merely enter the item you wish to select from the field. The criterion must be in the same case and exactly like the table data to filter correctly. Notice, in the illustration below, that the Charge field has a criterion of Dues, but it is not checked. This will result in an Answer table with LAST, FIRST, and DATE fields for records with Dues in the CHARGES field.

Query Form

Save a Query

- Save the query by selecting Save, or Save As from the File menu, or Close without saving. Query names can contain a maximum of 64 characters including spaces and thus can be named to identify the contents. The query design will be saved using the name you specify with a **.qbe** extension. Note the file name dues.qbe in the illustration above.

The CCG would like to query its data and develop answer sets to be used for telephoning members or calling segments of the membership list. The query form window will be used with various criteria and checks to query the table.

EXERCISE DIRECTIONS

1. Open Project Viewer and switch your working directory to \CLUB.

2. From Project Viewer, right-click on Queries, then click New.

3. In the Select File dialog box, open **MEMBERS.db** or **18MEMBERS.db**, then choose OK.

4. Check the LAST, FIRST, PHONE, and PROF. fields to tell Paradox to display only those fields in the Answer table.

5. Click the Run Query button on the Toolbar to see the results in the Answer Table. Notice the table is sorted by the data in the LAST field (Last name).

6. Print a copy of the list of members and their telephone numbers.

7. Close the Answer table.

8. Modify the query to tell Paradox to list members who are students in the Answer table. Leave the check in the field and type Student in the PROF. field.

9. Run the query.

10. Examine the Answer table, then close it.

11. Save the query as **STUDENT.qbe**. Close the query.

12. Define a new query for the MEMBER table, which selects the Member ID, Last, First, and Phone fields for members who live in Anaheim. Do not include the City field in the Answer table.
    Hint: Enter Anaheim in the City field but do not check the field.

13. Run the query. Print a copy of the answer table. Close the table.

14. Save the query as **ANAHEIM.qbe**. Close the query.

15. Define a new query on the **CHARGES.db** table or **18CHARGES.db**.

16. Select the fields with appropriate checks to display all records in the DATE, AMOUNT and CHARGE fields, sorted so that the DATE and AMOUNT fields display in descending order.

17. Run the query. Print a copy of the answer table. Close the table.

18. Modify the query as follows:
    - Produce a listing of MEMBER ID, LAST, FIRST, and DATE fields only for Dues charges.
    - The CHARGE and AMOUNT fields should not be displayed.

19. Run the query. View and close the table.

20. Save the query as **DUES.qbe**.

21. Close all tables and queries.

KEYSTROKES

CREATE A QUERY

1. From Project Viewer:
   a. Select and right-click **Queries**.
   b. Click **New** .... [N]
   OR
   From menu:
   a. Click **File** .... [Alt]+[F]
   b. Click **New** .... [N]
   c. Click **Query** .... [Q]
2. In Select File dialog box, Select table(s) to be included. (Hold **Ctrl** key to select more than one table.)
3. In Query Form window, Check fields to be included in the query.
4. To set specific query selections, Right-click check box and make selection (or press **Shift+F6** to cycle through options):

   Check shows all unique values for that field in ascending order.

   CheckPlus shows all values in a field without sorting, as they appeared in the table. A CheckPlus will override any Check or CheckDescending selections.

   CheckDescending shows unique values sorted in descending order.

   GroupBy specifies a group of records to use in a query. This field will not appear in the answer table.

   An empty check box clears any check.
5. To enter field values:
   a. Click in field to right of check box.
   b. Type value.

RUN QUERY

F8

If Query is open:

Click Run Query button ....

OR

1. Click **Query** .... [Alt]+[Q]
2. Click **Run Query** .... [R]

SAVE QUERY

1. Click **File** .... [Alt]+[F]
2. Click **Save** .... [S]
   OR
   Click **Save As** (if new) .... [A]
3. Enter filename.
4. Click **OK** .... [Enter]

OPEN QUERY

1. Click on **Queries** icon in Project Viewer.
2. Right-click on name of query.
3. Select **Run Query** .... [R]
   OR
   Double-click name of query.

COREL PARADOX 8 Lesson 4: Queries

Exercise 19
- Open a Query
- Field Checks
- Change Field Names
- Work with Query Files

NOTES

Open a Query

- To open an existing query, click Queries in Project Viewer and double-click the query you wish to open or click File, Open, Query. Or, click the Open Query button on the Toolbar. A query may be opened, changed and resaved, or saved as a new query.

Field Checks

- You can clear a check in a query by clicking on the check, or by pressing F6. If you wish to select or remove all the checks in a table, click on the check box at the left edge of the query form, underneath the table name. Thus to use all the fields in a query, click on the table name check box.

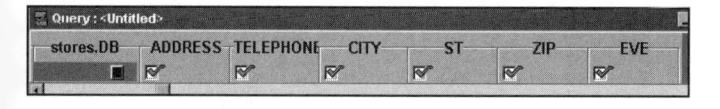

✓Note: All fields are selected because the STORES.DB box was clicked.

Change Field Names

- When you check fields to be part of an answer table, the field names in the answer table are taken from the original table. If you wish to change the name of a field in the answer table (for printing purposes, for example), you can indicate the new name in the query. In the field you wish to change in the answer table, enter AS followed by the new field name. See the illustration top right, where the City field will appear AS Store Location. This setting will not change the field name in the table, however.

Query Form

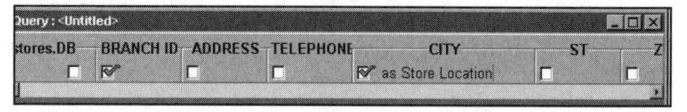

Work with Query Files

- If you wish to rename a query, click the query in the Queries section of Project Viewer until the cursor is at the end of the query name, then edit the name. Note the illustration below of the menu that appears when a query name is right-clicked. You can use this menu to open, run, design, cut, copy, create a shortcut, delete, or set properties for a query.

Query Quick Menu

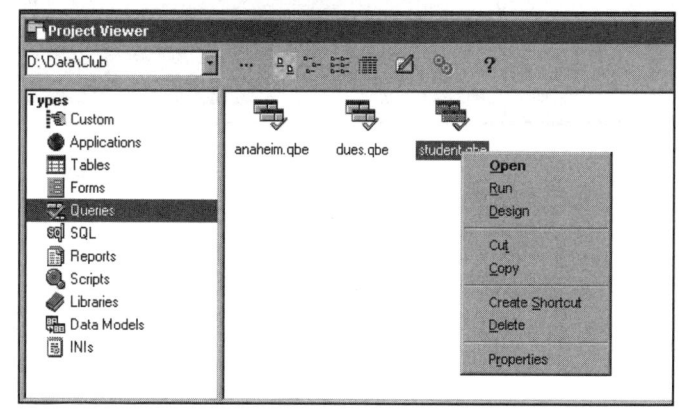

COREL PARADOX 8 Lesson 4: Queries

- If you wish to view the answer table with a different layout, you may move columns to rearrange data. You may also sort fields to present information as desired. With a query open, click Query, Properties, or click on the Query Properties icon on the toolbar to display the Query Properties dialog box. The Structure tab, illustrated below, allows you to rearrange fields in the answer table. The field order determines the emphasis of the sort order in the answer table. For example, you might want to place the ST field first for a listing of stores by state.

Query Properties Structure tab

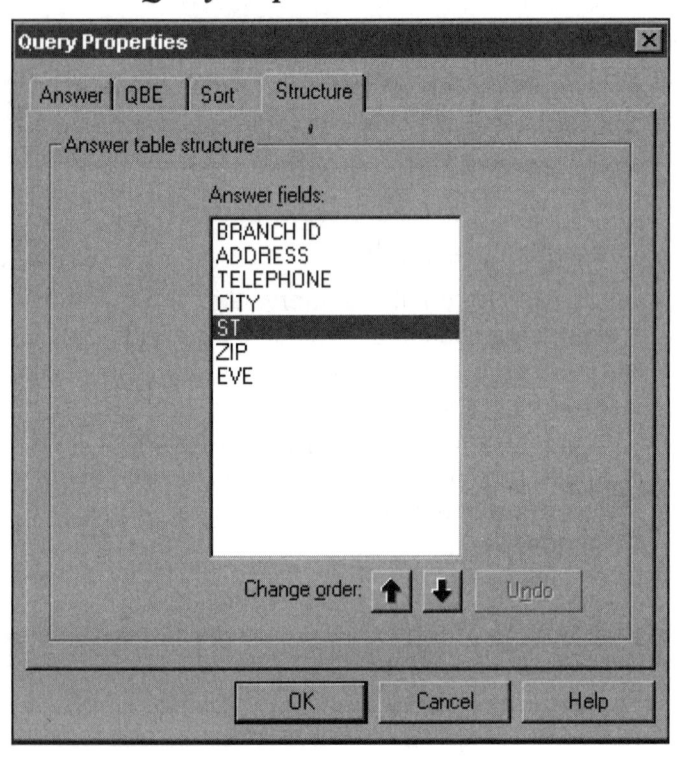

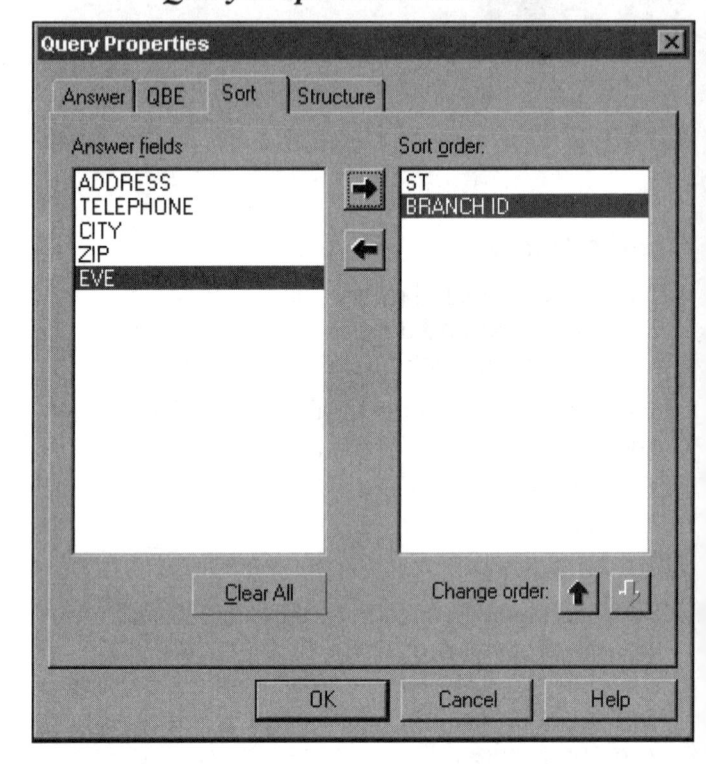

- You can set sort properties, or review settings made with check marks, by selecting the Sort tab of the Query Properties dialog box. Note the illustration of the Sort tab of the Query Properties dialog box below.

Query Properties Structure tab

428

> Your manager at Sports Duds has many questions about the branch stores and their computer hardware. You can provide the answers using queries.

EXERCISE DIRECTIONS

1. Open Project Viewer and switch your working directory to \SPORTS.
2. Create a new query, using the **STORES** or **19STORES** table to develop a listing of stores with evening hours sorted by state:
   a. Select all fields by clicking the table name box.
   b. Enter settings to change field names as follows:
   c. City field   as STORE LOCATION
   d. ST field   as STATE
   e. Enter a criteria to display only stores with evening hours.
   HINT: In Eve field, enter Yes. Deselect the check in the field.
   f. Open the Query Properties dialog box. Select the Sort tab and double-click on the ST field in the Answer Fields list box. Click OK.
   g. Run the query.
3. Print a copy of this table. Close the Answer table.
4. Save the query as **EVENING HOURS**.
5. Create queries to answer each of the following questions.
   ✓ *Do not save the queries you create to answer these questions.*
   a. What are the Branch IDs for stores located in Atlanta?
   b. What cities in CA (California) have branches?
   c. What are the Branch IDs for stores located in Philadelphia?
6. Clear the query design.
7. Query the **CEQUIP** or **19CEQUIP** table to display a list of computers:
   a. Include BRANCH ID, MFG., MODEL, COST, PURDATE, and WTY.
   b. Do not display the ITEM field, but enter a criterion for Computer items.
   c. Change field names as follows:
      - Purdate field name to Date Of Purchase.
      - Mfg. field name to Manufacturer.
      - Wty. field name to Warranty.
   d. Run the query and adjust column width, as necessary.
8. Print the table and then close the answer table.
9. Save the query as **COMPUTER INVENTORY**.
10. Close all database objects.

KEYSTROKES

OPEN QUERY

In Project Viewer:
   a. Click **Queries**.
   b. Right-click name of query.
   c. Select **Open**

OR

Double-click query to open.

From the Toolbar:
- Click **Open Query** button

RENAME QUERY

In Project Viewer:
1. Click **Queries**.
2. Click query to be renamed.
3. Click again.
4. Edit text to enter new query name.

SET SORT AND TABLE STRUCTURE QUERY PROPERTIES

In a Query Form window:
1. Click **Query** .... Alt+Q
2. Click **Properties** .... P
3. Select desired tab .... Ctrl+Tab
4. Sort tab:
   a. Click **Answer fields** .... Alt+F
   b. Select field .... ↓
   c. Click right arrow.
   d. Add fields to **Sort order** as desired.

To Change order of sort:
   a. Select field in **Sort order** list box.
   b. Click **Change order** .... Alt+R
   c. Click up or down arrow.
   d. Click **OK** .... Enter

5. Structure tab:
   a. Click **Answer fields** .... Alt+F
   b. Select field .... ↓
      in **Fields** list box
   c. Click **Change order** .... Alt+R
   d. Click up or down arrow.
   e. Click **OK** .... Enter

COREL PARADOX 8 Lesson 4: Queries

Exercise 20

- **Create Queries Using Two Tables**
- **Summary Operators**

NOTES

Create Queries Using Two Tables

- One of the advantages of a relational database is that you can combine data from two tables into one answer table. When you query more than one table, you must join the tables by a common field. You can then select fields from each table as desired. The joined fields are fields in each table that contain the same information. For example, the BRANCH ID field that appears in the STORES and CEQUIP tables can be used to join these two tables.

- When you create a query, you can add additional tables to the query design by clicking the Add Table button on the toolbar, or by selecting multiple tables in the Select File dialog box. The new table will be added to the design.

- The joined fields do not have to have the same field name, but the field types must be compatible. You can join up to 24 tables in a single query. The joining of fields is called **creating an example element**. To join fields, click the **Join Tables button** and then click in the appropriate field of each table to be joined. Paradox will enter an example element (highlighted with a different color) to join the tables, as illustrated below in the Branch ID field.

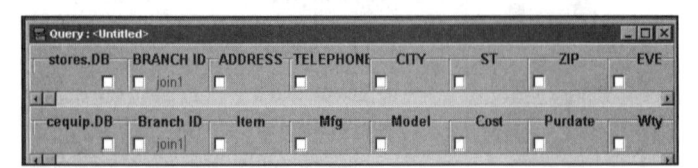

- Once you join the tables, you can select fields and set criteria and properties, as with a single-table query.

Summary Operators

- You can do simple and complex calculations with data by using summary operators. A **summary operator** performs a calculation on a group of records. For example, in the query illustrated below, you are calculating the total price of each type of software. The field you wish to group, TYPE, is checked and CALC SUM is entered in PRICE, the field to be totaled.

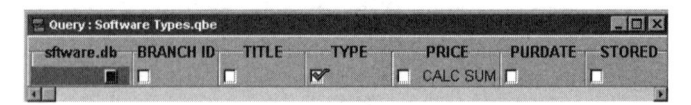

- The answer table illustrated shows each type of software and the total price paid for each group. You can use AVERAGE, MAX, MIN, and COUNT in the same manner; for example CALC MAX will calculate the highest value in the group. Paradox creates a new column for the calculation result and names it Sum of PRICE by default. You can change this name by following the summary operator with "AS (desired new field name)."

- If you do not group data by checking a field, but only enter a summary operator, you will display the AVERAGE, MAX, MIN, SUM, or COUNT for all the records. In the case of the COUNT operator, if you wish to count all records you must enter CALC COUNT ALL in order to count all records including duplicates; otherwise, you will get a count of unique records.

- You may enter summary operators in upper- or lowercase letters.

In this exercise, you will create a query that combines data from two tables and prints the results. In addition, you will use summary operators to develop totals and averages for our software inventory.

EXERCISE DIRECTIONS

1. Open Project Viewer and switch your working directory to \SPORTS.
2. Create a new query using the **STORES** or **20STORES** table.
3. Click the Add Table button and add the **CEQUIP** or **20CEQUIP** table.
4. The query result should be a list of computers owned by branches, which includes the city and state location of the branch:
   a. Click the Join Tables button and then the Branch ID fields to join the tables on the Branch ID field.
   b. Check the CITY, ST, MODEL, COST, PURDATE, ASSIGNED TO, SERIAL # fields.
   c. Change field names as follows:
   d. PURDATE as Date of Purchase
      ST as State
   e. In the Item field, set a criterion for Computer.
   f. Use Query Properties to select State as the field to sort by and to place State in the first position on the Structure tab.
   g. Run the query.
   h. Adjust column width as necessary.
5. Set to print in landscape mode and print one copy of the answer table.
6. Close the answer table and save the query as **COMPUTERS BY STATE**.
7. Close the query.
8. Create a new query using the **SFTWARE** or **20SFTWARE** table.
9. The query result should summarize the types of software and total paid for each type of software.
   a. Check Type field.
   b. Enter summary operator, CALC SUM, in the Price column. (Do not check the column.)
   ✓ *To rename the field in the Answer table, type CALC SUM AS Total Cost.*
   c. Run the query.
   d. Adjust column width as necessary.
10. Print answer table.
11. Close the answer table.
12. Save the query as **SOFTWARE TYPES**.
13. Change the summary operator to either CALC AVERAGE, CALC MAX, CALC MIN, or CALC COUNT, and run the query to answer the following questions:
    a. What is the average cost of Word Processing software?
    b. What is the average cost of Desktop Publishing software?
    c. What is the highest price we paid for Word Processing software?
    d. What is the lowest price we paid for Word Processing software?
    e. How many total spreadsheet software packages do we have?
14. Close the answer table.
15. Modify the query design to find the total value of all software.
    HINT: Do not check the Type field.
16. What is the total value of all our software?
17. Close the answer table and query without saving changes.
18. Close all database objects.

KEYSTROKES

ADD ADDITIIONAL TABLE TO QUERY
In Query Form window:
1. Click **Add Table** button ....
2. Select **Table**.
3. Click **Open**.
   OR
   Double-click table name.

JOIN TABLES FOR QUERY
In Query design:
1. Click **Join Table** button.................
2. Click field in first table.
3. Click similar field in second table.

ENTER SUMMARY OPERATORS
In Query Form window:
1. Check field to group.
2. Enter
   CALC SUM
   CALC AVERAGE
   CALC MIN
   CALC COUNT
   in field to be calculated.

COREL PARADOX 8 Lesson 4: Queries

Exercise 21 ■ Summary

Sports Duds will be adding a VENDOR table to its database. You will use queries to answer questions about the data in several tables, and you will use summary operators to gather information about inventory.

EXERCISE DIRECTIONS

PART I

1. Open Project Viewer and switch your working directory to \SPORTS.

2. Create a new table with the fields and data as listed below. Make the VEN ID field a key field and all other fields required. Save the table as **VENDORS**.

3. Enter the data listed below:

VEN ID	VENDOR	ADDRESS	CITY	ST	ZIP	PHONE
AM12	Amellla	P.O. Box 432	Fargo	ND	58103	800-555-4323
FR43	Franzie	45 Jog Road	Orlando	FL	38802	800-555-4998
GR76	Grand Co.	P.O. Box 324	Raleigh	NC	27605	800-555-2156
JO95	Joggers	36 Runny Ave.	Albany	NY	12205	800-555-7634
SE23	Seeling	542 10th Avenue	St. Louis	MO	63107	800-555-2811
WI90	Winner	76 Park Road	Cleveland	OH	44109	800-555-3098

PART II

4. Create a new query using the ⌨INVEN or 💾21INVEN table.
   a. Use the STYLE, COLOR, P, S, M, L, XL, and PRICE fields.
   b. Enter a criterion in the Type field for Jacket.
   c. Change STYLE heading to print as STYLE NO.
   d. Run the query.
   e. Adjust column widths if necessary.

5. Print one copy of the answer table.

6. Close the answer table and save the query as **JACKET INVENTORY**.

PART III

7. Create queries to answer the questions below. Do not save the queries or the answer tables.
   a. How many Red Crew Tops do we have in XL in all styles?
   b. How many Navy Shorts do we have in XL and L in all styles?
   c. What types of items do we carry in Red that cost less than $14.00?
   d. In which style do we have the highest number of Petite Shorts?
   e. In which style do we have the highest number of XL Crew Tops?
   f. In which style do we have the highest number of M Red items?
   g. What are the styles of Petite T-Shirts that are available?
   h. In which style number do we have the most Green Medium items?
   i. Which style Crew Top has the lowest number of P items on hand?
   j. What is the highest Jacket price?

8. Create a new query for the NY branch to determine reorder information including the style numbers provided by each vendor, using the **INVEN** or **21INVEN** table.
   a. Add the **VENDORS** table to the query.
   b. Join the NAME field in the Vendors table with the VENDOR field in the INVEN table.
   c. Check the Style, Type, Color, Price fields in the INVEN table.
   d. Check the Ven. ID, Name, and Phone fields in the VENDORS table.
   e. Change Phone to print as TELEPHONE.
   f. Use Query Properties to place the Vendor ID and Name fields in the first and second positions for sort and structure properties
   g. Run the query.
   h. Adjust column widths if necessary.

9. Print a copy in landscape.

10. Save the query as **REORDER INFORMATION**.

11. Close all database objects

COREL PARADOX 8
Lesson 5: Reports

Exercise 22

- Reports
- Create Reports with Report Expert
- Modify a Report
- Save a Report
- Print a Report

NOTES

Reports

- **Reports** are design elements that allow you to customize the way you present or print data. You can sort and group records, calculate totals, and lay out your data in many different ways. Reports can be based on tables, forms, or queries.

- Reports can include:
  - Report headers and footers.
  - Page headers and footers.
  - Summary statistics.
  - Objects imported from other sources (such as graphics).

- You can design a report from scratch in the Report Design window (see the illustration below), which looks and behaves very much like the Form Design window, or you can let Paradox design a report for you by using the Report Expert. Once the report is designed, it can be modified in Report Design mode.

Report Design Mode

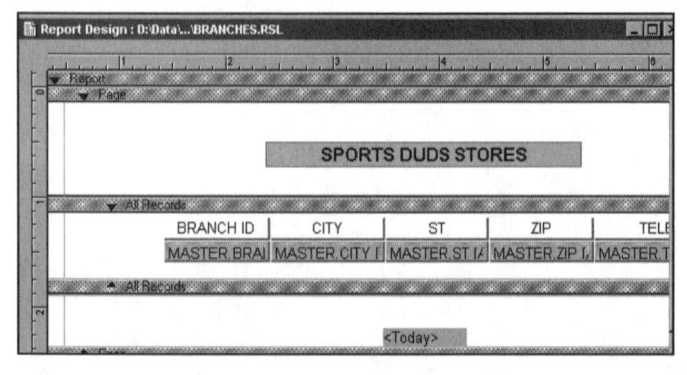

Create Reports with Report Expert

- To begin creating a report with the Report Expert:

  1. Right-click on the Reports icon in the Project Viewer, and select <u>N</u>ew.

  2. Select <u>E</u>xpert.

  3. Respond to a series of questions on six screens to select:

     a. How many tables to include.

     b. Which table(s) to include (tables or queries can be included). Note the illustration of the second screen with a drop-down list of tables and queries that can be used. You also select the fields to display based on the table or query you select.

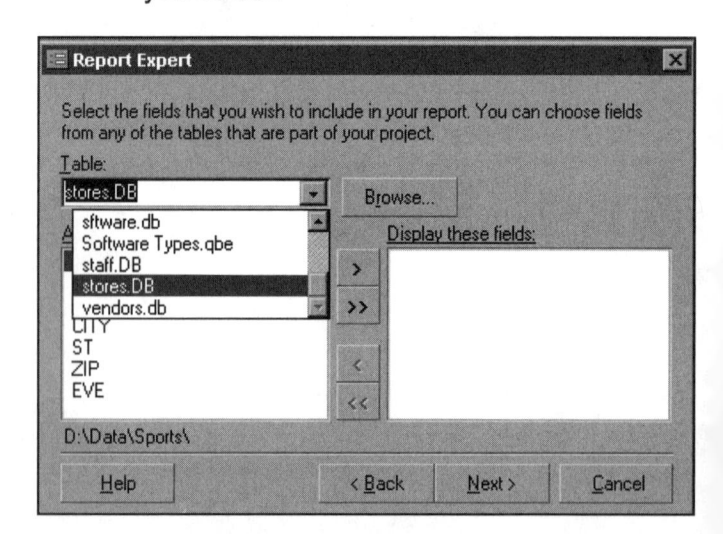

     c. A grouping field (optional) to organize the report. This will be discussed in Exercise 24.

d. Which style sheet is to be used for the report and how records will be displayed (individually or showing multiple records).

e. Whether to include a title, page numbers, headers, footers, etc.

f. The name of the report and the working directory and whether you want to print it. Click Finish on the final Expert screen and a report is generated. Note the illustration of a report below.

Example of a Report

- You can also access the Report Expert by clicking the Perfect Expert button, while in Table or Form view, and then selecting Report from the Perfect Experts window that appears as illustrated below. The Perfect Expert window appears to the left of your screen containing icons for Experts. Scroll down and select the Report icon to move into the Expert screens discussed.

Perfect Expert Window

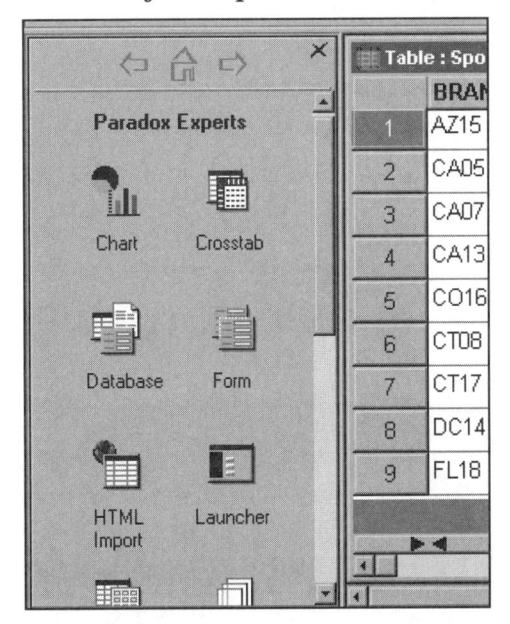

Modify a Report

- You can modify the layout of a report by switching to Report Design mode. Click the Design Report button on the Toolbar while the report is running.

- You may want to move items to adjust alignment of titles and column headings. To move a report detail item, click and hold down the mouse button within the item's boundary, and drag the item to the desired position. The rulers at the top and left side of the screen can be used to help position the item.

- You can view changes to the report at any time by clicking the Run Report button on the Toolbar.

Save a Report

- Reports are named and saved on the last screen of Report Expert. If you create the report from the report design screen or if you make modifications, you can select the Save (if new or updating a report) or Save As option from the File menu. Click the Reports icon in Project Viewer to display a list of saved reports. Your new report will appear here with the **.RSL** extension.

Print a Report

- You can print an open report by selecting Print from the File menu, or by clicking the Print button on the Toolbar. You may set the printer to landscape mode since orientation is determined by the printer setup feature.

COREL PARADOX 8 Lesson 5: Reports

> *Your manager at Sports Duds must submit reports to the president of the company. You have been asked to create these reports from your tables.*

EXERCISE DIRECTIONS

1. Open Project Viewer and switch your working directory to \SPORTS.

2. Right-click Reports and select New.

3. Click on Expert.

4. In step 1 of the Report Expert, choose Data from one table, then click Next.

5. In step 2, select **STORES** or open **22STORES** in the proper directory. *(If you get a message that there are no tables in the directory, use the Browse button to locate the SPORTS directory and the STORES table.)* Select all the fields except EVE by clicking the pointer arrow, then click Next.

6. In step 3, bypass the group screen and click Next.

7. In step 4, select the Control 3D Style and Multiple Records, then click Next.

8. In step 5, click the Title Text box and enter Sports Duds Stores as the title. Click Show date, then click Next.

9. In step 6, name the report **BRANCHES.rsl** and select the correct path and directory using the Browse button. Click Finish.

10. Click the Report Design button to view the report design.

11. Select the title text box and move it so that it begins at the 3 inch mark on the horizontal ruler.

12. Click in the title text box after the word STORES, and press Enter to move to a new line. Type Branch Data as a subtitle.
    ✓ *You may have to click several times on this text box to select it.*

13. Select column title ST and change it to State.

14. Save the report design.

15. Click the Run Report button on the Toolbar.

16. Print the report.

17. Close the report.

KEYSTROKES

OPEN REPORT EXPERT

From Project Viewer:
1. Right-click **Reports**.
2. Click **N**ew .... N
3. Click **E**xpert .... E

From Table or Form view:
1. Click **Experts** Button ....
2. Click **R**eport .... ↓

CREATE REPORT WITH REPORT EXPERT

1. Follow one of the steps above to open Report Expert.
2. Step 1:
   - Click Data from **o**ne table .... Alt+O
   OR
   Click Data from **t**wo tables .... Alt+T
   - Click **N**ext .... Alt+N
3. Step 2:
   - Select table or query .... ↓
     to use for report.
   - Click **B**rowse to locate directory, if necessary .... Alt+R
   - Select **A**vailable fields .. Alt+A, ↓ ↑
   - To display each field, click .... >
   - To select all fields, click .... >>
   - Click **N**ext .... Alt+N

4. Step 3:
   - Select field for grouping.
   - To display each field, click .... >
   - Click **N**ext .... Alt+N
5. Step 4:
   - Select style sheet .... ↓
   - Select **I**ndividual Records .. Alt+I
   Or
   Select **M**ultiple Records .... Alt+M
   - Click **N**ext .... Alt+N
6. Step 5:
   - If desired, click **Title**.
   - Enter title .... ↓, title
   - If desired, click **Page numbering**.
   OR
   Select **Page N** .... ↓
   OR
   Page N of M .... ↓
   - If desired, click **Show date**.
   - If desired, click **Show time**.
   ✓ *These choices also have a drop down list for placement in the header or footer.*
   - Click **N**ext .... Alt+N
7. Step 6:
   - Enter report name ... Alt+N, name
   If necessary, select **L**ocation .... Alt+L
   Click **Browse** to select the directory.
   If desired, click **P**rint Report ..... Alt+P
   - Click **F**inish .... Alt+F

SWITCH TO REPORT DESIGN

While running a report:
Click Design button ....

SWITCH TO RUN REPORT

While designing a report:
Click Run Report button ....

MODIFY REPORT

In Report Design window:
1. Click on design item (eg. text box, table frame, etc.).
2. Drag to desired position.

SAVE REPORT

In Report Design window:
1. Click **F**ile .... Alt+F
2. Click Save **A**s .... A
3. Name report.
4. Click S**a**ve .... Enter

PRINT REPORT

1. Click **F**ile .... Alt+F
2. Click **P**rint .... P
3. Click OK .... Enter

COREL PARADOX 8 Lesson 5: Reports

Exercise 23

- Modify a Report
- Change Object Properties
- Header and Footer Settings

NOTES

Modify A Report

- The Report Expert simplifies the process of creating basic reports. However, the results may sometimes yield unwanted items, exclude desired items, or provide insufficient formatting. To solve these problems, all aspects of a report can be changed in the Report Design window.

- The Report Design window consists of bands that represent the parts of a report. The parts of a report are the Report, Page, and Record bands, as illustrated below. Every band has a top and bottom (header and footer). The Group band, an optional band, will be discussed in Exercise 24. To change the size of a band, click on the boundary line to select the band. You will know it is selected when it changes color. Move the mouse toward the top of the selected band until you see a double-headed arrow, click on the resizing handles, then drag up or down. You may have to repeat this adjustment a number of times.

- The items or objects on a report may be edited by clicking on the object to select it, then making the necessary changes. For example, if you wish to change a field name heading for a report, you can select it, then edit the text to become the column heading you desire. To delete an object, click on it, and when the resizing handles appear, press the Del key. If the column headings of a report are changed, the size of the report frame may have to be adjusted to fit all the fields in the report. Select the last field and use the sizing handles to adjust the size of the report frame.

Report Design Window

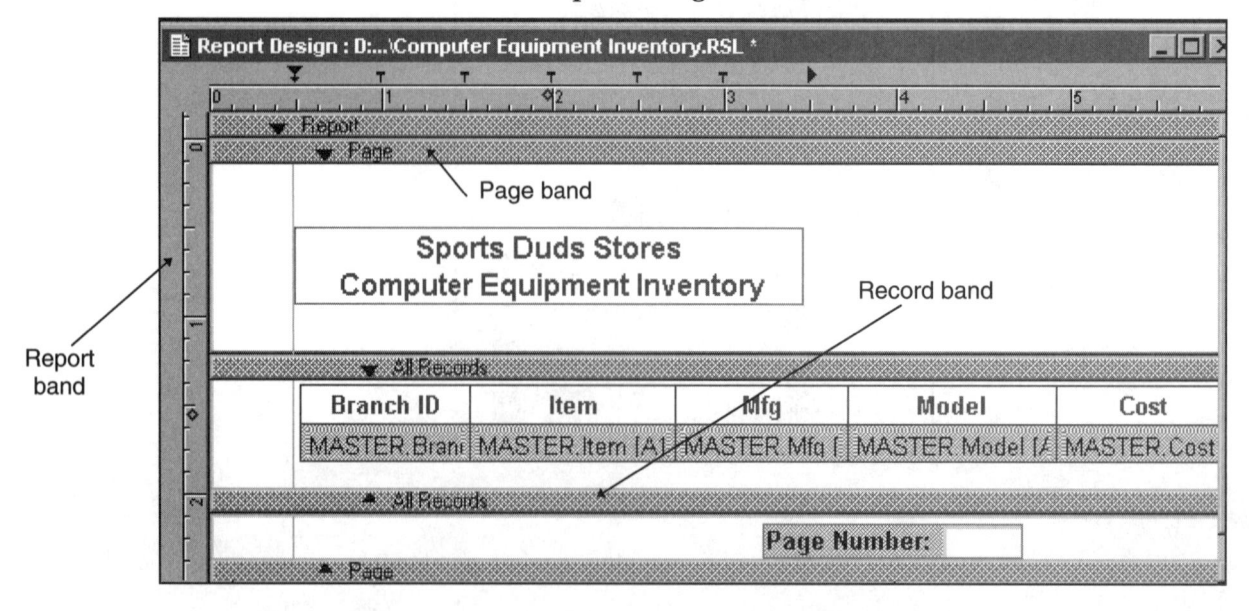

Change Object Properties

- To change an object's font, font size, alignment, color, border, or shading, you must right-click the object and select Properties. The Properties dialog box, with tabs appropriate to the object selected, will appear. Note, for example, the illustration of the Text Properties dialog box that appears when a page header text object is right-clicked.

Text Properties Dialog Box

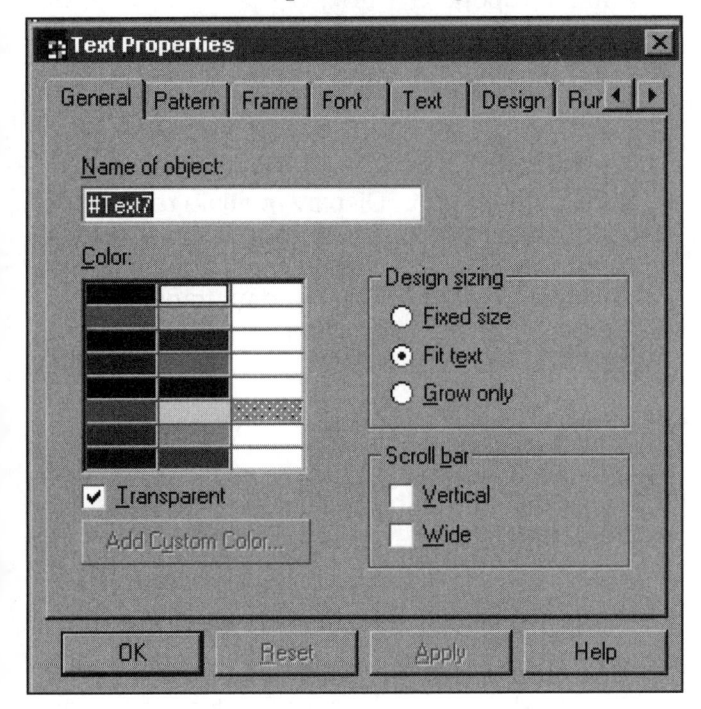

- If you wish to change the properties of a group of objects at once, select the first object and hold down the Shift key while selecting the other items. Right-click and set the desired properties. All selected objects will receive the selected properties.

Header and Footer Settings

- On step 5 of the Report Expert, you may set headers and footers that include the title, page numbers, and date and/or time stamp(s). Use Page numbering, Show date and Show time options to place page numbers, or the date and/or time, in a specific location on the header or footer. Note the illustration below of the Step 5 screen.

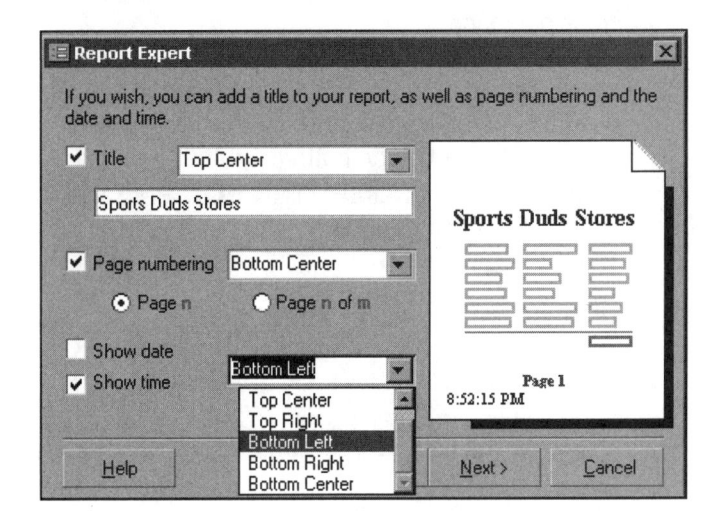

KEYSTROKES

CHANGE OBJECT PROPERTIES

In Report Design:

1. Right-click item to be changed.
2. Select **Properties** .... [R]
3. Select appropriate tab.
4. Make desired changes.
5. Click **OK** .... [Enter]

Corel Paradox 8 ■ Lesson 5 ■ Exercise 23   439

COREL PARADOX 8 Lesson 5: Reports

> To prepare for a computer equipment inventory audit, you have been asked to prepare a report that will list specific information about the computer equipment in all branches of the Sports Duds stores.

EXERCISE DIRECTIONS

1. Open Project Viewer and switch your working directory to \SPORTS.

2. Right-click Reports, and then choose New.

3. Create a new report using the Report Expert as follows:
   a. Select data from one table.
   b. Select **CEQUIP** or **23CEQUIP** as the table for the report. Display all fields except the Wty and Assigned to fields.
   c. Bypass the group Screen and click Next.
   d. Select the Mint Objects style sheet and display multiple records.
   e. Title the report Sports Duds Stores. Set the title to print at the Top Left. Select the page numbering option to print at the bottom left and the date to print at the bottom right.
   f. Name the report **COMPUTER EQUIPMENT INVENTORY**.
   g. Click Finish.

4. Switch to Report Design window.

5. Change Record Headers:

   MFG. to MANUFACTURER
   PURDATE to PURCHASED

6. Add the subtitle, Computer Equipment Inventory, to the title text box. Select the box; place the cursor at the end of the text, press Ente, and type the subtitle.

7. Select the title text box. Change property of the title font size to 16 points.

8. Adjust the title text box so that the title and subtitle fit on two lines. Set the text properties to left align the titles.

9. Select the text for each column heading (except Cost) by pressing the Shift key between selections. Right-click and set Alignment to Left on the Text tab of the Text Properties dialog box.

10. Right-align the text for the Cost column heading.

11. Save the report design.

12. Run the report.

13. Change the printer properties to landscape mode and print the report.

14. Create a new report using the **SFTWARE** or **23SFTWARE** table for the report. Show all fields in the report. Display multiple records per page, select the Sunshine objects style, and center the title of the report, Sports Duds Stores Software Inventory. Set the date to display at the center of the footer, and name the report **SOFTWARE INVENTORY**.

15. Change PURDATE column heading to PURCHASED.

16. Adjust the size of the last field to fit into the table frame.

17. Set the title text box font to 16 points, and adjust it to display as a two-line title.

18. Select the Master:Price item to set format of Price field data for Windows $. Use the Format tab of the Properties dialog box.

19. Select all the shaded areas on the report and change the color property to light gray.

20. Save the report design.

21. Run the report.

22. Print a copy after setting print properties to landscape mode.

23. Close all database objects.

COREL PARADOX 8 Lesson 5: Reports

Exercise 24

■ Add Group Band ■ Add Summary Field

NOTES

Add Group Band

- As illustrated in Exercise 23, a report is divided into bands – the Report, Page, and Record bands. In the previous two exercises, reports were produced that listed the data as it appeared in the table. By grouping records and adding summary data you can make report information more useful. For example, if you were producing a list of members, it might be beneficial to group the members by city to determine the number of members in each location.

- You can add a group band in Report Expert by selecting the field to group on the third screen of Report Expert, as illustrated below.

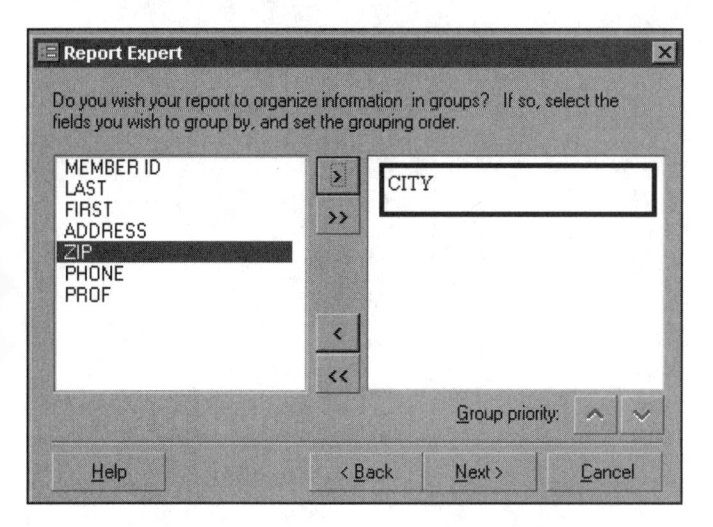

- Once you select a field for grouping, a new screen displays, illustrated at top right, providing summary options. You can select fields to be summarized and a summary feature such as Sum, Count, Max, Min, etc. This feature will summarize the field selected within the group chosen on the previous screen.

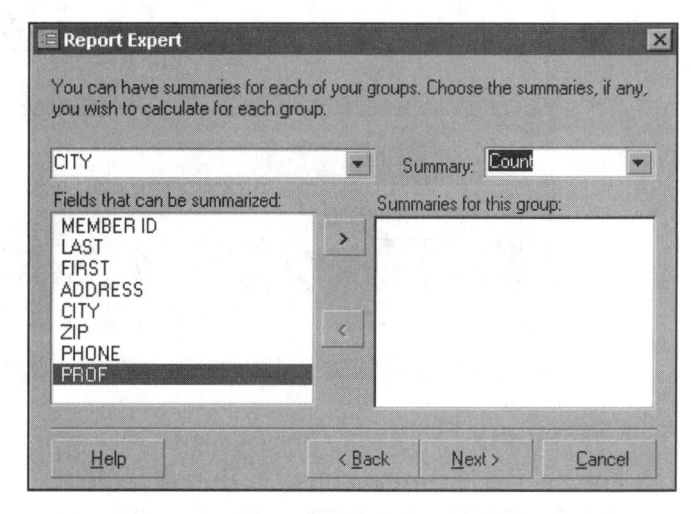

- To add a group band after the report is designed, click Insert, Group Band, or click the Add Group Band button on the Toolbar, in Report Design mode. The Define Group dialog box, illustrated below, appears.

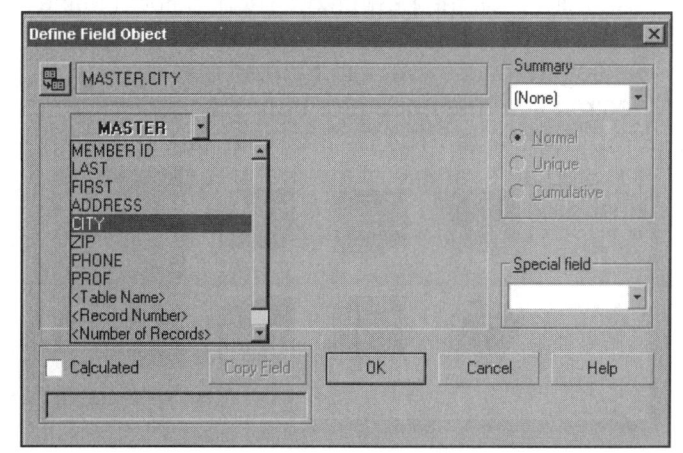

Define Group Dialog Box

- To produce a membership list by city, select CITY as the group field. A new group band will be added to the report design with the City field added to the band, as shown in the illustration below. When a field is added to a group band, it is not automatically removed from the record band. The CITY field must be deleted from the record area to eliminate duplication of data.

Report Design Window

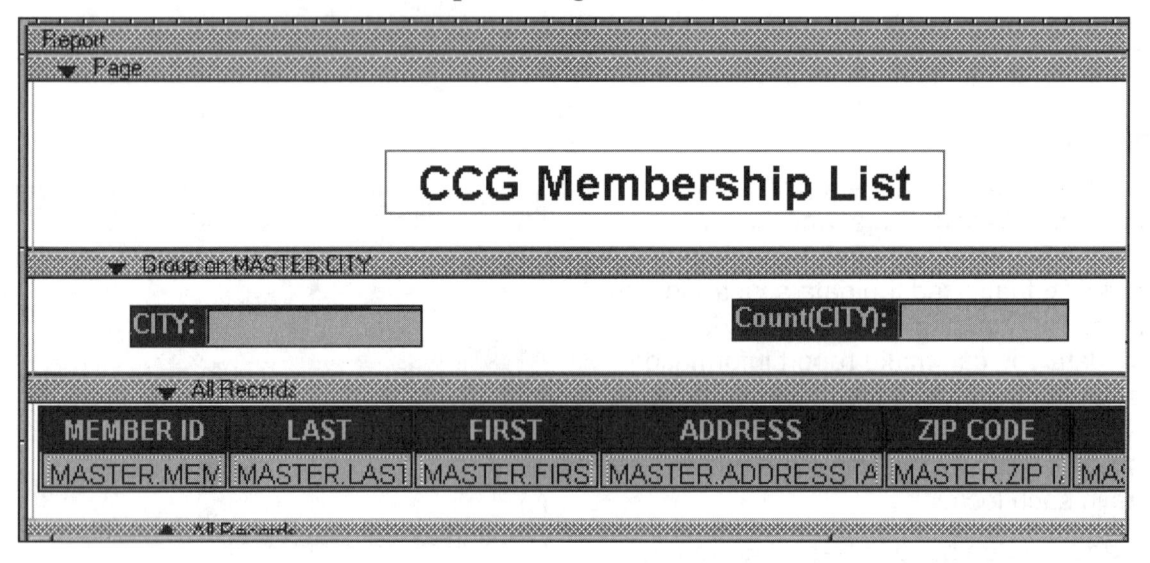

Add Summary Field

- Summary fields can be added in Report Expert or added later to a grouped report. A subtotal or summary field for the group can be added to the design by first clicking the Field Tool button and then clicking in the new group band. When you add a field, the Paradox Field Expert will open to assist you in defining the field. To define the field on your own, cancel the Field Expert and right-click the new field. Then, select Define Field to open the Define Field Object dialog box. Select the field to be summarized and the desired summary operator from the respective drop-down lists. The Define Field Object dialog box and an example of the grouped report is illustrated at right.

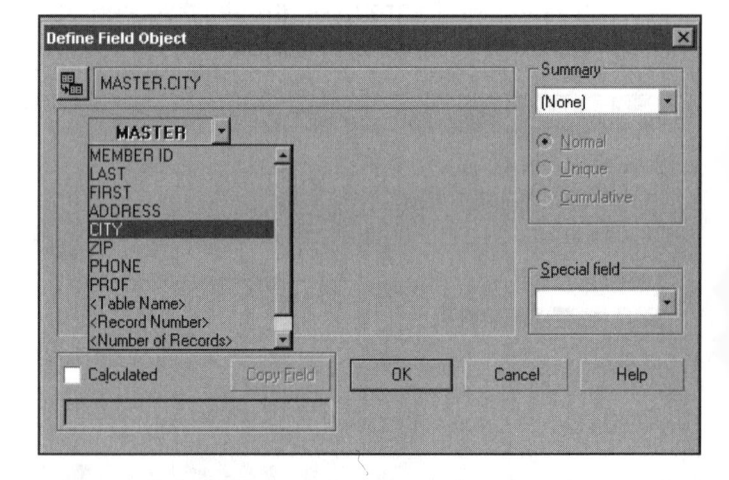

In this exercise, you will create two reports for the CCG club that will require the grouping and summarizing of report data. You will add groups to a report with the menu and with Report Expert.

EXERCISE DIRECTIONS

PART I

1. Open Project Viewer and switch your working directory to \CLUB.
2. Right-click Reports and choose New.
3. Create a new report using the Report Expert as follows:
   a. Select data from one table.
   b. Select **MEMBERS** as the table for the report, or use **24MEMBERS**.
   c. Display all fields except PROF.
   d. Bypass the Group option, click Next.
   e. Select the Corporate objects style sheet and multiple records.
   f. Title the report CCG Membership List, set Page N of M to appear at the bottom right and set the date to appear at the bottom left.
   g. Name the report **LIST**.
   h. Create the report.
4. Switch to Report Design mode.
5. Change column heading for ZIP to ZIP CODE.
6. Select Insert, Group Band from the menu, or click the Add Group Band button and group the members by CITY. *Note the new group band.*
7. Select and delete the CITY field and header. Move fields together to eliminate the blank column. *Select the column divider and move it to the left.*
8. Add a summary field to count the number of members in each city:
   a. Click the Field Tool button, and then click in the right end of the group band above the Zip Code field.
   b. Cancel the Field Expert screen.
   c. Right-click the new field and select Define Field.
   d. Select CITY from the drop-down list for the table.
   e. Select Count from the Summary drop-down list.
   f. Click OK.
9. Format the title text to an 18-point font.
10. Save the report design.
11. Run the report, set print properties to print in landscape mode, and print the report.

PART II

1. Create a new report using the **CHARGES** table for the report, or use **24CHARGES**.
   a. Display all fields
   b. Group on CHARGES.
   c. Summarize the AMOUNT field with a SUM function. *Select AMOUNT, select SUM, and then select the right arrow button. The summaries for the group should appear as Sum(CHARGE AMOUNT).*
   d. Select the Corporate objects style sheet and multiple records.
   e. Title the report, CCG CHARGES Month Ended 12/15/97.
   f. Set Page N to display at the center of the footer. Name the report **CHG1215**.
2. Switch to Report Design mode.
3. Set the title box font to 16 points.
4. If necessary, modify the size of the title box so that the title becomes a two-line title.
5. Set format of the AMOUNT and SUM AMOUNT fields to Windows $ on the Format tab of the Field Properties dialog box.
6. Make any alignment settings as needed.
7. Save the report design.
8. Run and print the report.
9. Close all database objects.

KEYSTROKES

ADD GROUP BAND

In Report Design mode:

1. Click **I**nsert .... `Alt`+`I`
2. Click Group **B**and .... `B`
3. Select **F**ield .... `Alt`+`F`, `↓`
4. Click **OK** .... `Enter`
   OR
   Click **Add Group Band** button on the Toolbar .... `⊕`

ADD FIELD

In Report Design:

1. Click **Field Tool** button .... `bī`
2. Click and drag on report to place new field.

DEFINE FIELD OBJECT

1. Right-click field to be defined.
2. Select **D**efine Field .... `D`
3. Select field from drop-down list.

To summarize a field:

1. Click Summ**a**ry .... `Alt`+`A`
2. Select summary operator .... `↓`
3. Select summary specification:
   - **N**ormal .... `Alt`+`N`
   - **U**nique .... `Alt`+`U`
   - **C**umulative .... `Alt`+`C`
4. Click **OK** .... `Enter`

COREL PARADOX 8 Lesson 5: Reports

Exercise 25 ■ Summary

The Human Resources Department of Barnes College has hired you to work on their database. One of your first jobs is to help organize information about the faculty. Once the information is organized, you will be asked to update and modify it, as well as create several reports requested by the college President.

This summary exercise will review and apply all concepts learned throughout the Paradox 8 sections of this book.

EXERCISE DIRECTIONS

Create and Save a Table:

1. Create a new directory using Window Explorer; name it COLLEGE.

2. Change your working directory to \COLLEGE.

3. Create a table using the field names and properties indicated below STAFID is a key field:

FIELD NAME	TYPE	SIZE	VALIDITY CHECK
STAFID	Alpha	5*	
TITLE	Alpha	3	
LAST	Alpha	10	Required field
FIRST	Alpha	8	
DEPT	Alpha	4	Required field
BUDGET	Number		Max. Value 5000
BLDG	Alpha	1	
NO OF CLASSES	Number		
START	Date		
TENURE	Alpha	1	

4. Save the table; name it **STAFF**.

5. Switch to Table view.

Enter Records:

6. Use Quick Form to create a form for the table.

7. In Form Design mode, change the BLDG field to display as a radio button display for the BLDG field. Enter M or A as the item values to represent the Main or Annex buildings.
   a. Add a text label, BUILDING, above the radio buttons in bold.
   b. Enhance the form design by:
      • Adding a light custom background color.
      • Change the field object color to light gray.
   c. Move the items for better appearance.

8. Save the form as **STAFFORM**.

9. Enter the records listed in the table on the following page.

10. Switch to Table view and print one copy.

11. Close all database objects if you do not have time to complete the next segment. Otherwise, move to next step.

COREL PARADOX 8 Lesson 5: Reports

STAFID	TITLE	LAST	FIRST	DEPT	BUDGET	BLDG	NO OF CLASSES	START	TENURE
MAE88	Dr.	Martinez	Jose	Eng	2000	M	5	9/16/88	Y
ROE88	Ms.	Roberts	Diana	Eng	2500	M	4	9/18/88	Y
HAE95	Dr.	Harris	Sally	Eng	2500	M	5	9/16/95	Y
BEM86	Mr.	Bergen	Paul	Math	1500	A	3	9/14/86	N
PRS88	Mr.	Price	Robert	Sci	2000	A	3	9/14/88	N
CRS90	Mr.	Creighton	Matthew	Math	1200	A	2	1/10/90	N
BRP90	Ms.	Bryson	Jaime	PE	1200	M	3	9/15/90	N
CHS88	Ms.	Chang	Julie	Sci	1600	M	4	9/15/88	Y
BRH91	Ms.	Brewster	Donna	Hist	2000	A	5	2/1/91	Y
ANH89	Mr.	Anderson	Harvey	Hist	2000	A	5	1/10/89	N
BRL89	Dr.	Brown	Donald	Lang	1400	M	3	2/1/89	Y
MAS90	Mr.	Martinelli	William	Sci	1200	A	2	9/16/90	N
ZHS86	Dr.	Zhan	Rafu	Sci	2000	M	5	9/9/86	Y
BRE97	Ms.	Browning	Paula	Eng	1500	A	4	9/10/97	N
NGL97	Dr.	Ng	Tom	Lang	1800	M	3	9/11/97	N
GRM96	Mr.	Greene	Ralph	Math	1400	A	5	2/5/92	N
LIB96	Ms.	Linn	Sarah	Bus	1800	A	4	2/3/96	N
FEB96	Mr.	Fernandez	Ricardo	Bus	1800	A	3	1/20/96	N
KRB94	Dr.	Kramer	Mel	Bus	2000	A	5	2/10/94	Y
GRP95	Mr.	Grosso	Lenny	PE	1400	M	2	9/13/95	Y

Modify the Table/Add Records:

12. Open the **STAFF** table in the COLLEGE directory.

13. To keep track of faculty members' years of teaching experience, restructure the table and add one new field, EXP, with a Number format.

14. From the list on the following page, enter the experience information into the table.

STAFID	TITLE	LAST	FIRST	DEPT	BUDGET	BLDG	NO OF CLASSES	START	TENURE	EXP
ANH89	Mr.	Anderson	Harvey	Hist	2000	A	5	1/10/89	N	12
BEM86	Mr.	Bergen	Paul	Math	1500	A	3	9/14/86	N	14
BRE97	Ms.	Browning	Paula	Eng	1500	A	4	9/10/97	N	8
BRH91	Ms.	Brewster	Donna	Hist	2000	A	5	2/1/91	Y	8
BRL89	Dr.	Brown	Donald	Lang	1400	M	3	2/1/89	Y	10
BRP90	Ms.	Bryson	Jaime	PE	1200	M	3	9/15/90	N	9
CHS88	Ms.	Chang	Julie	Sci	1600	M	4	9/15/88	Y	13
CRS90	Mr.	Creighton	Matthew	Math	1200	A	2	1/10/90	N	10
FEB96	Mr.	Fernandez	Ricardo	Bus	1800	A	3	1/20/96	N	9
GRM96	Mr.	Greene	Ralph	Math	1400	A	5	2/5/92	N	8
GRP95	Mr.	Grosso	Lenny	PE	1400	M	2	9/13/95	Y	11
HAE95	Dr.	Harris	Sally	Eng	2500	M	5	9/16/95	Y	13
KRB94	Dr.	Kramer	Mel	Bus	2000	A	5	2/10/94	Y	7
LIB96	Ms.	Linn	Sarah	Bus	1800	A	4	2/3/96	N	9
MAE88	Dr.	Martinez	Jose	Eng	2000	M	5	9/16/88	Y	15
MAS90	Mr.	Martinelli	William	Sci	1200	A	2	9/16/90	N	16
NGL97	Dr.	Ng	Tom	Lang	1800	M	3	9/11/97	N	10
PRS88	Mr.	Price	Robert	Sci	2000	A	3	9/14/88	N	18
ROE88	Ms.	Roberts	Diana	Eng	2500	M	4	9/18/88	Y	12
ZHS86	Dr.	Zhan	Rafu	Sci	2000	M	5	9/9/86	Y	15

15. Several teachers' records were left out of the table. Add the following records.

STAFID	TITLE	LAST	FIRST	DEPT	BUDGET	BLDG	NO OF CLASSES	START	TENURE	EXP
HOS90	Dr.	Hochman	Pamela	Sci	2000	M	5	9/9/90	Y	17
TRS89	Mr.	Tracey	Charles	Sci	1400	A	3	2/10/89	N	13
GOP92	Ms.	Godiva	Kayli	PE	1600	A	4	2/10/92	Y	16
BEL96	Mr.	Bertinelli	Thomas	Lang	1500	A	3	9/10/96	N	8
HAM97	Dr.	Hawkins	Joyce	Math	2000	A	5	2/10/97	N	5

Sort and Search the Table:

16. Sort the table in ascending order by DEPT and LAST name. Save the sort to a new table titled DEPT and select the display table option.

17. Print a copy of this list.

18. Sort the DEPT table by Dept and Last name in ascending order, and sort Start date in descending order.

19. Print a copy of this list.

20. Save the DEPT table and switch to the STAFF table using the Window menu.

21. Select Locate, Value from the Record menu, or click the Locate button, to search the database for the answers to the following questions:

   a. Which teachers work in the English Department?
   b. In which building does Ralph Greene work?

22. Locate and Replace all Lang Dept entries; change to LA.

23. Use Format, Filter to search the table, find the answers to each of the following questions:

   a. Which professors work in the main building and have more than 10 years experience?
   b. Which English teachers hold a doctoral degree?
   c. Which Math teachers work in the Annex and have a supply budget of at least $1400?

24. Create a query using STAFF to locate professors who work in the M (Main) Building sorted by Dept:

COREL PARADOX 8 Lesson 5: Reports

- Include the fields listed: DEPT, STAFID, TITLE, LAST, FIRST, and TENURE.
- Set Query Properties to structure the query in the field order listed above.
- Set a criterion in the Bldg field for M.
- Save the query in the COLLEGE directory; name it **MAIN BUILDING STAFF**.

25. Run the query.
26. Print the Answer table.
27. Close the Answer table and the query.
28. Create and save a new query using the STAFF table to list those teaching in the Annex who have four or more classes:
    - Include the fields listed: STAFID, TITLE, LAST, FIRST, NO OF CLASSES, and DEPT.
    - Set Query Properties to structure the query in the field order listed above.
    - Set criteria to select Annex teachers who teach four or more classes.
    - Save the query in the COLLEGE directory as **ANNEX**.
29. Run the query.
30. Print the Answer table.

Prepare Reports:

Report I:

31. Create a new report with the Report Expert and respond as follows:
    a. Use one table.
    b. Use the STAFF table.
    c. Display all fields.
    d. Select the Mint objects style sheet and display Multiple records.
    e. Title the report Barnes College Staff, and set Page N of M to appear in the center of the footer.
    f. Name the report **LIST**.
32. Switch to Report Design and add the subtitle By Department.
33. Set title font to 16 points and adjust the size or placement of the title text box, if necessary.
34. Add a group band to group the report by DEPT.
35. Delete the DEPT field from the Record band.
36. Move the column border to eliminate the blank column.
37. Use the Field tool to add a field to the group band.
38. Cancel the Field Expert, right-click and use the Define field dialog box set the field to count the Dept data.
39. Format the Count data to Normal.
40. Make any adjustments necessary to make the report more attractive.
41. Save the report.
42. Print one copy by setting print properties to landscape mode.

Report II:

43. Create a new report with the Report Expert and respond as follows:
    a. Use one table.
    b. Use the STAFF table.
    c. Select fields: STAFID, LAST, DEPT, BUDGET, and BLDG.
    d. Group the report by DEPT.
    e. Summarize the BUDGET field with the Sum summary function.
    f. Select the Mint objects style sheet and display Multiple records.
    g. Title the report Barnes College Department Budgets, set Page N of M as a centered footer, and show the date as a centered footer.
    h. Name the report **BUDGET**.
44. Switch to Report Design and set title to a 16-point font. Adjust the size of the title box so that the title is on one line.
45. Format the Budget and Sum Budget fields to Windows $.
46. Make any adjustments necessary to make the report more attractive.
47. Save the report.
48. Print one copy.
49. Close all open windows.

Corel Presentations 8

Lesson 1: Create, Save, and Print Slides

Lesson 2: Edit and Enhance Slides

Lesson 3: Work with Slide Shows

COREL PRESENTATIONS 8 Lesson 1: Create, Save, and Print Slides

Exercise 1

- About Corel Presentations 8 ■ Start Corel Presentations 8
- Create a Presentation ■ The Corel Presentations 8 Window
- Slide Layers ■ Add Text to Slides ■ Add Slides to a Slide Show
- Save a Slide Show ■ Close a File/Exit Presentations

NOTES

About Corel Presentations 8

- **Corel Presentations 8** is the presentation component of Corel WordPerfect Suite 8 that allows you to create slide shows as well as posters, drawings and charts to be used in other presentations.

- A **presentation**, also known as a slide show, is a collection of slides related to a topic which may be shown while an oral report is given to help summarize data and emphasize report highlights. From the presentation slides, you can prepare handouts for the audience, speaker notes for use during the presentation, and/or outlines to provide an overview of the presentation. In addition, you can use slides to create a table of contents, overhead transparencies, and/or 35 mm slides of your presentation.

- Slides may include text, drawings, charts, outlines, and/or graphics.

- Outlines created in WordPerfect or data created in Paradox or Quattro Pro may be imported into a Presentations slide. (See Integration Section, Exercise 11.)

Start Corel Presentations 8

- To start Presentations, click the Corel Presentations 8 icon on the Desktop Application Director (DAD).

- Or, you may click the Start button on the Windows 95 Taskbar, highlight Corel WordPerfect Suite 8, then click to select Corel Presentations 8.

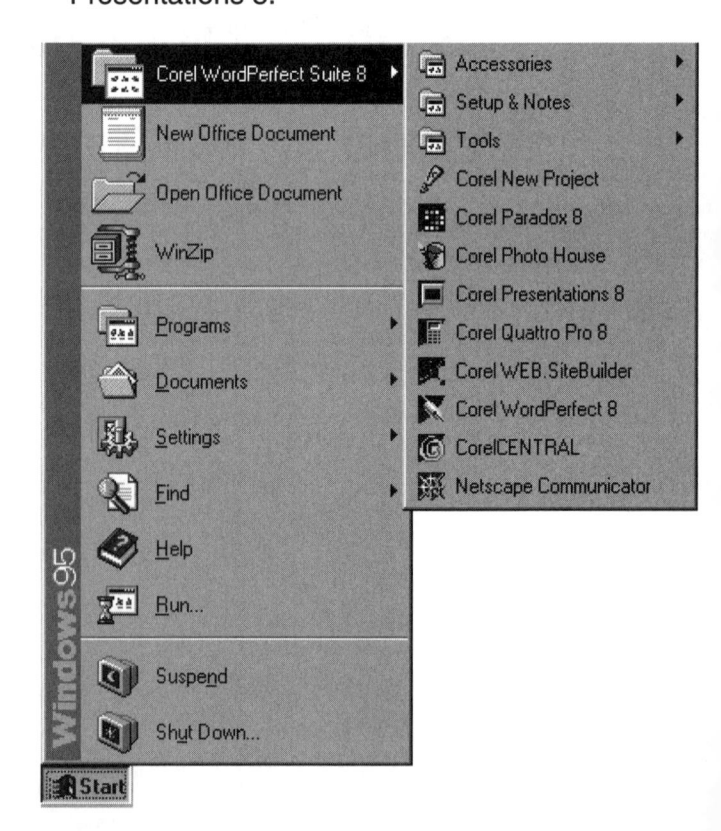

- After launching Corel Presentations 8, the New dialog box appears which displays two tabs: Create New and Work On. The Create New tab provides a list of options for creating a slide show, a drawing, or an original background master (Presentations Master). In addition, it also provides preformatted templates, which guide you through creating an annual report, a budget report, a market research report, a birthday banner, a congratulations banner, and more.

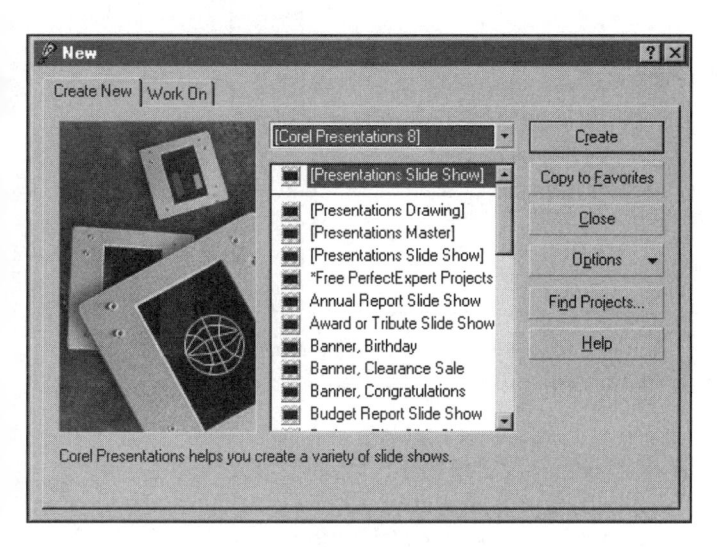

Create a Presentation

- To create a new slide show, select the **[Presentations Slide Show]** option from the Create New list box and click Create. The Startup Master Gallery dialog box appears (unless the *Do not show this dialog when beginning a new slide show* option was previously checked).

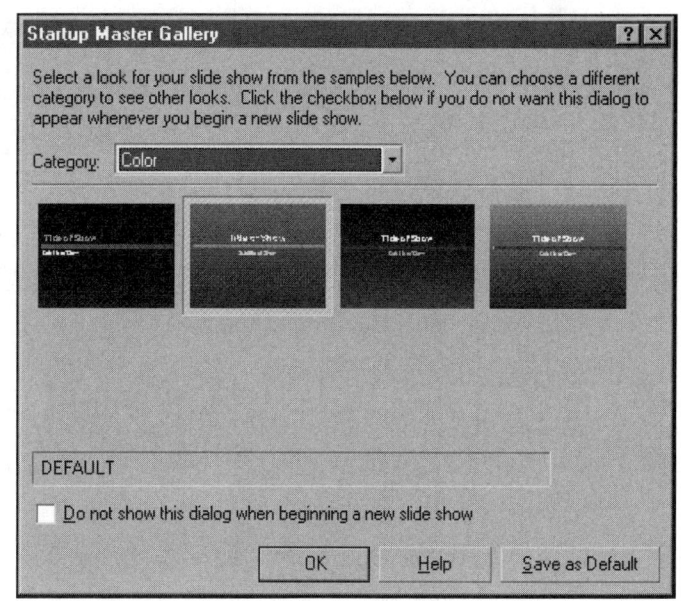

- The **Master Gallery** provides predefined background templates that you can use to help design your slide show. Each template contains Smart Color Matching, so that the text, data charts, organization charts, and bullets that you add to your slides will all coordinate with the selected background color.

- In addition to the default Color category background option, Presentations 8 also provides master templates for the following categories: 35 millimeter, Business, Design, Nature, Printout, and Theme. These may be selected from the Category drop-down list in the Master Gallery dialog box.

- Once you select a Master Gallery background option and click OK, the Corel Presentations 8 window appears.

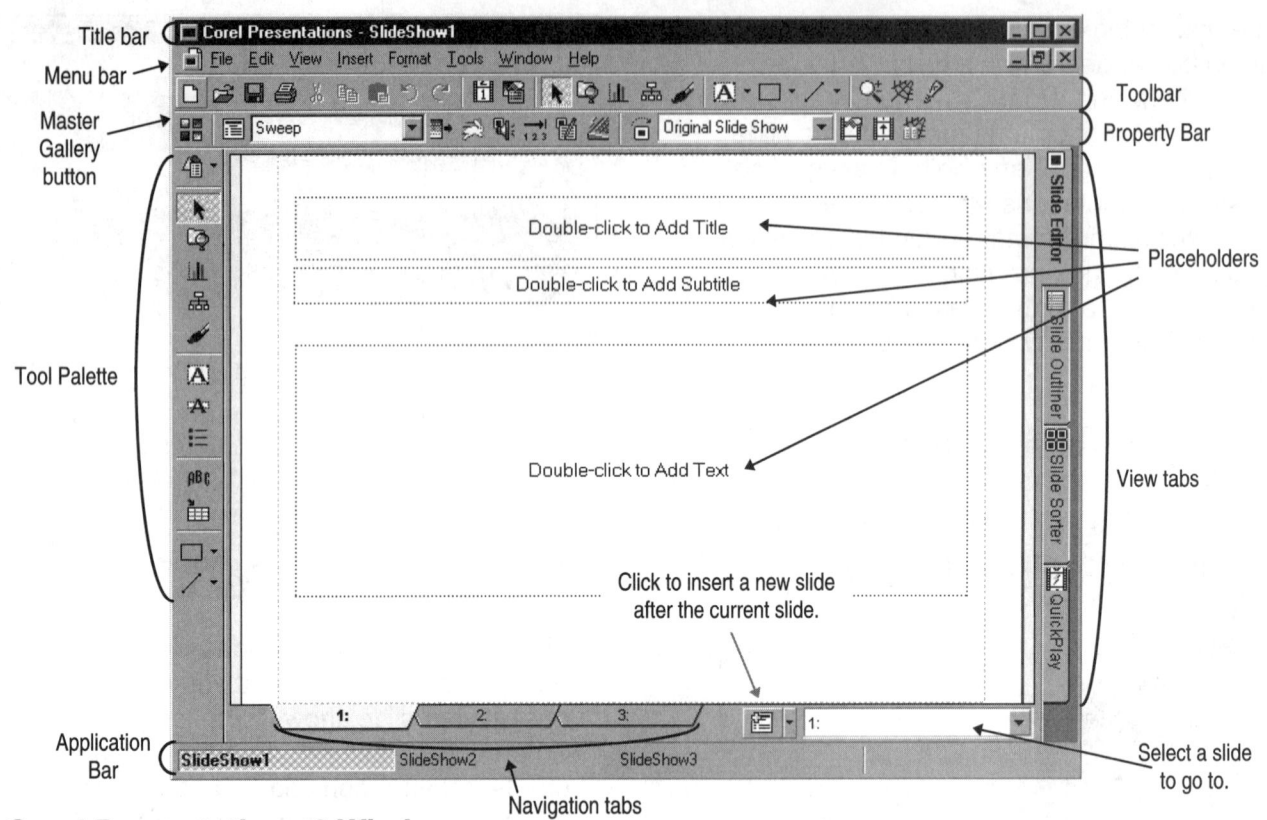

COREL PRESENTATIONS 8 Lesson 1: Create, Save, and Print Slides

The Corel Presentations 8 Window

- Corel Presentations 8 places the title SlideShow1 (unmodified) in the **title bar** of each slide show you create. After the slide show is saved, the filename appears in the title bar.

- The **Toolbar** contains buttons to give you quick access to features you use most often. These buttons work like other Toolbar buttons in the Corel WordPerfect Suite.

- The **Property Bar** located below the Toolbar, contains buttons that change depending on what is selected onscreen: text placeholder, graphic object, text box, etc. In general, it displays buttons that make formatting more efficient.

- The **Tool Palette**, located down the left side of the screen, contains common tools for adding graphics to slides or for drawing images on slides.

- **View tabs**, located down the right side of the screen, allow you to easily switch between slide views: Slide Editor, Slide Outline, Slide Sorter, and QuickPlay. (Slide views will be covered in Exercise 2.).

- The **Application Bar**, located at the bottom of the screen, displays all open slide show documents as well as the cursor location. It allows you to easily move between presentations and drag objects from one presentation to another.

- The **Navigation tabs**, located above the Application Bar, allow you to quickly move to any slide within the current slide show.

Slide Layers

- Every slide consists of the following three layers:

  1. The **Background Master Layer** contains designs and colors that give the slide an appealing look. All slides within a slide show usually contain the same background. The Background Layer can be selected from the Master Gallery when you begin a new slide show.

  2. The **Layout Layer** contains placeholders that determine the position and format of text or objects on the slide. Presentations 8 provides seven preformatted layout options to choose from: Title, Bulleted List, Text, Org Chart, Data Chart, Combination, and None.

  3. The **Slide Layer**, which is the top layer, contains drawings, text, Clipart, and other items.

  ✓Note: The Background and Layout Layer will be discussed further in Exercise 2.

Add Text to Slides

- Most Corel Presentations 8 layout layers contain **placeholders** (an empty box or boxes) which identify the placement and location of text on the slide. Each placeholder contains directions to help you complete the slide.

- **Title and subtitle** placeholders contain the format for title and subtitle text, while **text** placeholders include the format and design for bulleted lists or plain text.

- To type text into a placeholder, double-click inside the placeholder and type the desired text. Presentations 8 uses a preset font style and size, however, you may change these attributes if desired. To insert text into the next placeholder on a slide, press the down arrow key or double-click the next placeholder.

Add Slides to a Slide Show

- To add a new slide to the slide, click the drop-down arrow to the right of the **Add a new slide after the current slide** button (above the Application Bar) and select a new slide layout option.

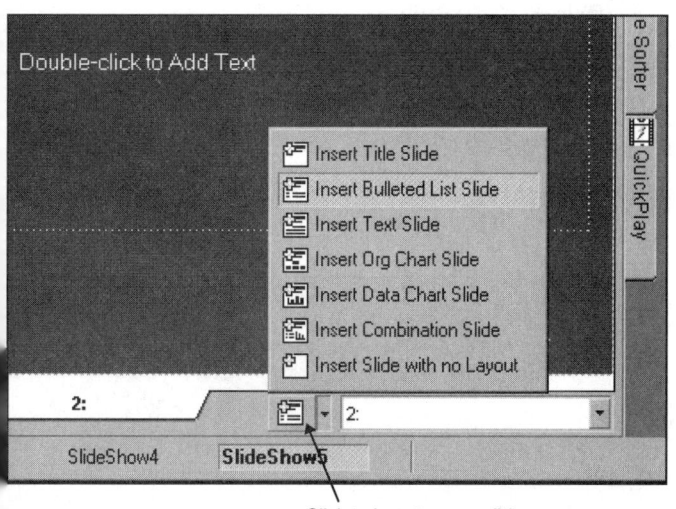

Click to insert a new slide after the current slide.

- Or, select <u>N</u>ew Slide from the <u>I</u>nsert menu. The following New Slide dialog box appears onscreen.

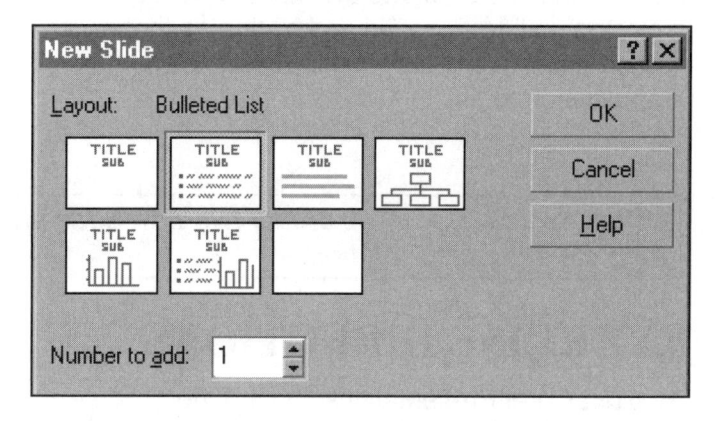

- Click a slide layout option and then type the number of slides you wish to insert in the Number to <u>a</u>dd text box.

- The **Bulleted List** layout lets you format bulleted lists. A bulleted list format typically follows the title slide.

- Six different bullet levels are available. Pressing the Tab key indents text and produces sub-levels of bulleted items. Corel Presentations 8 displays the first three sub-levels with a different bullet as well as reducing the text size for each new level. Press Shift + Tab to return to the previous bullet level.

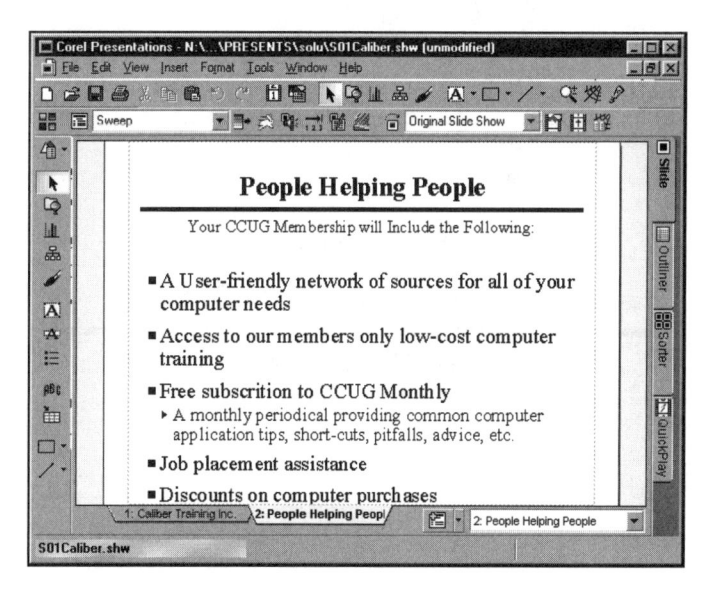

Save a Slide Show

- Slide shows are saved using the same procedures used to save WordPerfect documents and Quattro Pro spreadsheets.

- Corel Presentations 8 automatically adds a .SHW extension to slide shows saved for the first time.

Corel Presentations 8 ■ Lesson 1 ■ Exercise 1

COREL PRESENTATIONS 8 Lesson 1: Create, Save, and Print Slides

Close a File/Exit Presentations

- Presentations 8 follows the same procedures for closing a slide show file and exiting as those used in the WordPerfect and Quattro Pro application tools.

- If the slide show you are working on has been modified or has not yet been saved, you will be prompted to save it.

In this exercise, you will create two new slide shows containing Title and Bulleted List slides and then save the presentation.

EXERCISE DIRECTIONS

1. Start Corel Presentations 8 using the Windows 95 Taskbar.
2. Create a new slide show.
3. Accept the Default master background option (green) and the title layout for the first slide.
4. Create the title slide as shown in the first slide of Illustration A.
5. Insert a new Bulleted List slide after the current slide.
   - Type the bullet items as shown in slide two of Illustration A.
6. Save the presentation; name it **DIAMOND**.
7. Close the slide show.
8. Create a new slide show.
9. Choose ICE (blue) as the master background option and accept the default Title slide for the first slide.
10. Type the title slide information as shown in the first slide of Illustration B on the next page.
11. Insert a Bulleted List slide as the second slide. Type the bullet items as shown in slide 2 of Illustration B on the next page.
12. Save the presentation; name it **CALIBER**.
13. Close the slide show.

ILLUSTRATION A

Diamond Natural Food Stores

1st Quarter Management Meeting
January 20, 1999

Meeting Objective

Review and Plan Ahead

- Review 1998 Accomplishments
- Review 1998 Sales
- Announce New Management Hierarchy
- Review Top Selling Products
- Set Goals for 1999
- Develop Mission Statement

ILLUSTRATION B

Caliber Training Inc.

Lisa Scully, President

People Helping People

Your CCUG Membership Will Include the Following:

- A user-friendly network of sources for all of your computer needs
- Free subscription to CCUG MONTHLY
  ▸ A monthly periodical providing common computer application tips, short-cuts, pitfalls, advice, etc.
- Job placement assistance
- Discounts on computer purchases

KEYSTROKES

START PRESENTATIONS

Click the **DAD Corel Presentations 8** icon.....................

OR

1. Click **Start** .... Ctrl + Esc
2. Highlight **Corel WordPerfect Suite 8** .... ↑
3. Click **Corel Presentations 8** ...... → ↓

CREATE NEW SLIDE SHOW

1. Click **File** .... Alt + F
2. Click **New** .... N
3. Select **[Corel Presentations 8]** template.
4. Click **[Presentations Slide Show]** template .... ↓ ↑
5. Click **Create** .... Alt + R
6. Click a background **Color** from the **Master Gallery**.
   OR
   a. Click **Category** drop-down list.............. Alt + Y
   b. Select new category .... ↓ ↑
   c. Click on a background choice .... Tab, ↑↓
7. Click **OK** .... Enter

ADD NEW SLIDE

Click **Insert a new slide after current slide** on the Application Bar.

OR

1. Click **Insert** .... Alt + I
2. Click **New Slide** .... N
3. Click **Layout** .... Alt + L
4. Click one of the following Layout options:...................... ↓ ↑
   - Title
   - Bulleted List
   - Text
   - Org Chart
   - Data Chart
   - Combination
   - None
5. Click **Number to add** .... Alt + A
6. Type number of slides to add.... ↓ ↑
7. Click **OK** .... Enter

ADD TEXT TO PLACEHOLDERS

1. Double-click desired placeholder.
2. Type text and press **Enter** to move to a new line................ Enter
3. Press **down arrow** to move to next text object .... ↓

SAVE PRESENTATION

Ctrl + S

Click **Save** button on Toolbar ....

OR

1. Click **File** .... Alt + F
2. Click **Save** .... S
3. Type the slide show name in the **Filename** text box.
4. Select alternate drive and directory, if desired.
5. Click **OK** .... Enter

EXIT COREL PRESENTATIONS 8

Alt + F4

Click **Program Close** button X

OR

1. Click **File** .... Alt + F
2. Click **Exit** X

COREL PRESENTATIONS 8 Lesson 1: Create, Save, and Print Slides

Exercise 2

- Open a Slide Show
- Slide Views
- Move from Slide to Slide
- Spell Check
- Print a Presentation

NOTES

Open a Slide Show

- A slide show that has already been created may be opened when you start the Presentations 8 application. Click the **Work On** tab when the New dialog box displays and select the desired file from those displayed in the list box. Presentations 8 displays the most recently opened slide shows in the list.

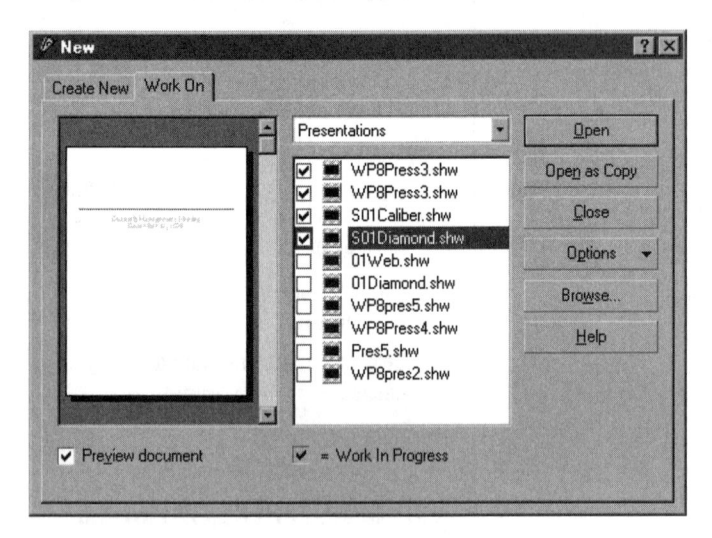

- You can also open a slide show document using the same procedures used to open other Corel WordPerfect Suite 8 applications.

Slide Views

- There are four different ways of viewing your presentation:

  - **Slide Editor view,** the default, allows you to see a single slide on screen. You may edit or modify all text, graphic objects, and placeholders in this view.

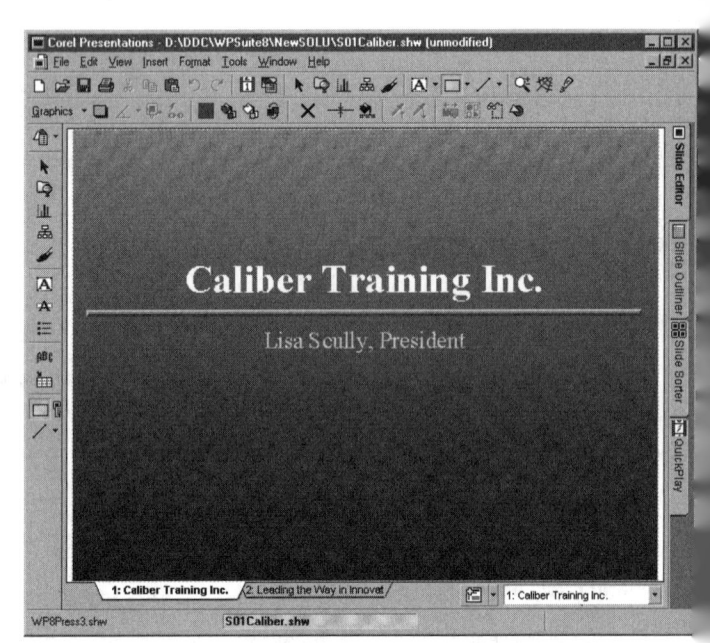

  - **Slide Outliner view** displays slide text in a notebook page layout to give an overview of the content of a presentation. Only text can be edited in this view, not graphic objects or placeholders. Use this view to organize your presentation. *(This view will be detailed in Exercise 5.)*

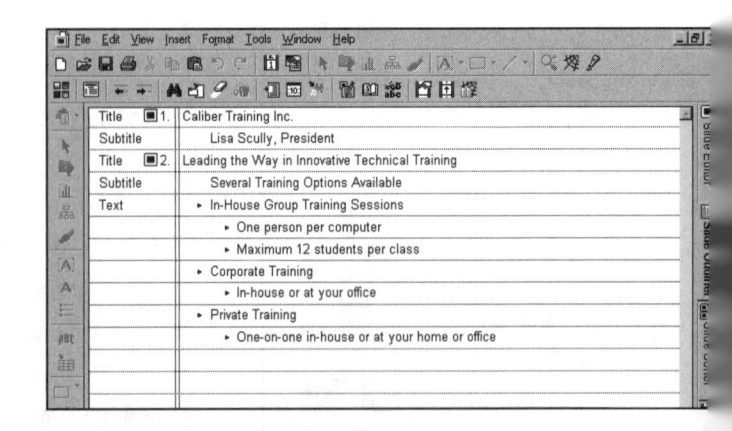

- **Slide Sorter view** allows you to see miniature copies of your slides on screen so that you can see the flow of the presentation. Use this view to move, copy, and delete slides. (Moving, copying, and deleting slides will be detailed in Exercise 4.) Slide Sorter view may also be used to set slide transitions and animation. (Slide transitions and animation will be detailed in exercise 15.)

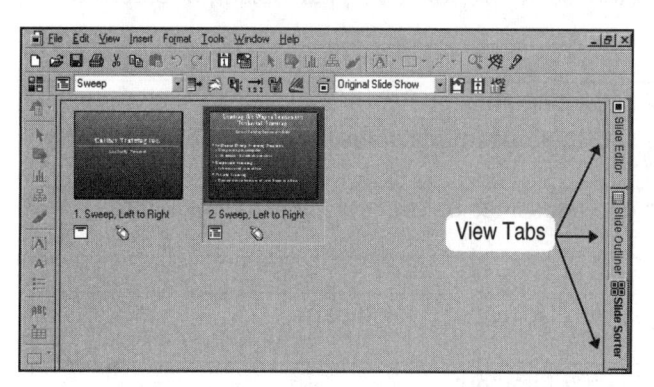

- **QuickPlay view** allows you to play the current slide as it will display in the final slide show—complete with transitions, animation, and other slide enhancements.

■ Views may be changed by clicking the appropriate **View tab** to the right of the screen or by selecting the desired view from the View menu.

Move from Slide to Slide

■ When there are a number of slides included in a slide show, you will find it necessary to move from slide to slide to edit, enhance, or view slide information. Corel Presentations 8 offers a variety of ways to select and display slides in Slide view:

- Press the **PgDn** key to display the next slide or the **PgUp** key to display the previous slide.
- Click the **Navigation tabs** located above the Application Bar. Each tab represents a numbered slide in the presentation.
- Click the **Select a slide to go to** drop-down list, located above the Application Bar, and choose the desired slide.

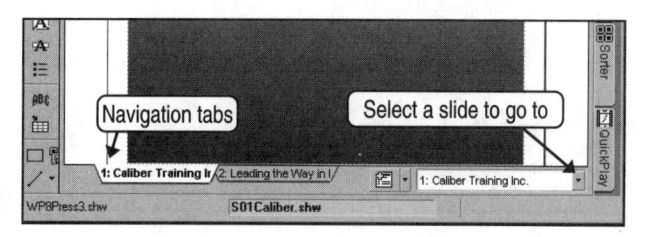

Spell Check

■ To **spell check** all slide placeholder text within a presentation, you must go to the Slide Outliner view. From Slide Outliner view, select Spell Check from the Tools menu or click the right mouse button and select Spell Check. (The spell check procedures are the same as those used in the other Corel WordPerfect 8 Suite applications.)

Print a Presentation

■ Slides in your presentation may be used as an onscreen slide show or to create and **print** transparencies, audience notes, speaker notes, handouts, or an outline. When you select Print from the File menu or click the Print button on the Toolbar, Corel Presentations 8 lets you choose various output options for printing these documents.

Print Tab

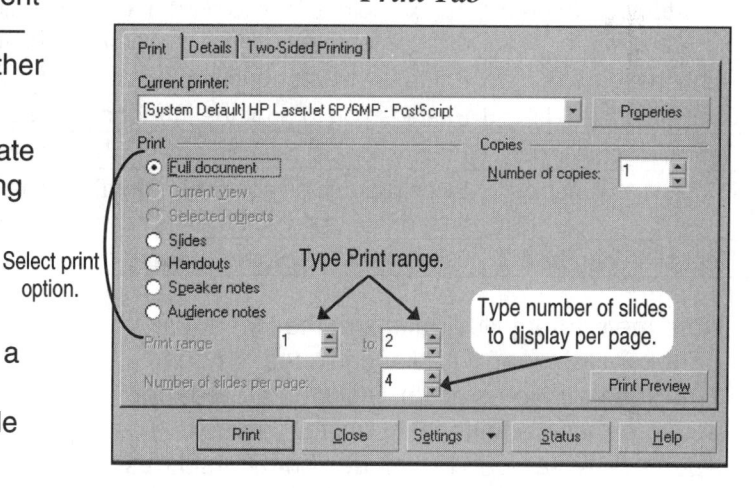

Details Tab

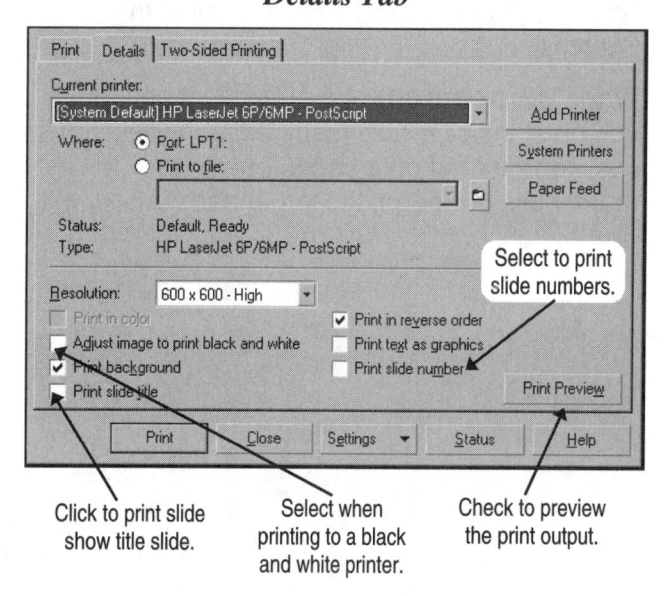

Corel Presentations 8 ■ Lesson 1 ■ Exercise 2 457

COREL PRESENTATIONS 8   Lesson 1: Create, Save, and Print Slides

- The <u>F</u>ull Document option on the Print tab in the Print dialog box prints all slides. This is the default option. Additional options within the Print and Detail tabs of the Print dialog box include:

Print Tab Options	*Description*
Current <u>v</u>iew	Prints only what is shown on your screen. For example, if zoom settings are set to 200%, the Current view option prints only the portion of the slide displayed in the window.
Selected o<u>b</u>jects	Prints only those objects you have selected, such as a text box, placeholder, or graphics object.
S<u>l</u>ides	Prints slides from slide show.
Hando<u>u</u>ts	Prints a thumbnail sketch of each slide in the presentation.
S<u>p</u>eaker notes	Prints a thumbnail sketch of each slide with the presenter's notes displayed below on each slide.
Au<u>d</u>ience notes	Prints a thumbnail sketch of each slide and adds lines below each slide to make note-taking easier.
Print <u>r</u>ange	Allows you to select specific slides to print.
N<u>u</u>mber of slides per page	Lets you identify how many slide images will display per printed page.
Print Previe<u>w</u>	Allows you to preview the printed results prior to output.
A<u>d</u>just Image to print black and white	Adapts color slides to print black and white. Use this option if you plan to use your slides as overhead transparencies or if you have a printer that only prints in black and white.
Print back<u>g</u>round	Prints the master background layer of slides.
Print slide <u>t</u>itle	Enables you to print the introductory title page of your presentation.
Print in re<u>v</u>erse order	Prints slides in reverse order, which makes collating documents easier.
Print te<u>x</u>t as graphics	Skips graphic objects when printing. This is convenient when you wish to save printing time or ink or if you have a printer that does not have strong graphic capabilities.
Print slide n<u>u</u>mber	Prints the slide order numbers on the printed document(s).

- Note the printout illustrations of the Handouts, Speaker Notes, and Audience Notes options. The Speaker Notes option includes an area for you to provide additional notes for yourself. The Audience Notes option includes horizontal lines for notetaking. (The Audience Notes and Speaker Notes options will be detailed in Exercise 17.)

- When you select any one of the print options, you must indicate how many thumbnail sketches you want printed on a page. The fewer thumbnails per page, the larger each image will display.

Handouts

Diamond Natural Food Stores

1rst Quarter Management Meeting
January 20, 1999

Meeting Objective

Review and Plan Ahead

- Review 1998 Accomplishments
- Review 1998 Sales
- Announce New Management Heirarchy
- Review Top Selling Products
- Set Goals for 1999
- Develop Mission Statement

Speaker Notes   *Audience Notes*

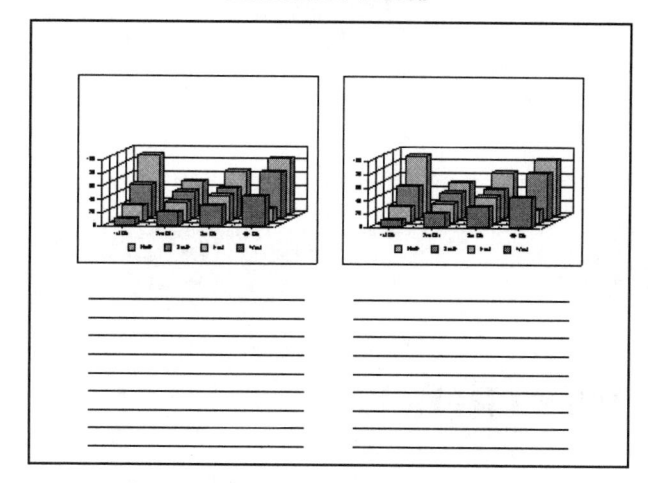

In this exercise, you will add new slides to a previously created presentation. You will then use different slide views to see the flow of your presentation.

EXERCISE DIRECTIONS

1. Start Presentations.
2. Select the Work On tab.
   ✓ If a Corel Presentations 8 slide show is already running, select File, Open to open a slide show.
3. Open 💾**CALIBER** or 💾**02CALIBER**.
4. Display slide 2 by clicking the appropriate Navigation tab.
5. Display slide 1 by clicking the appropriate Navigation tab.
6. Add a new Bulleted List slide and type the following information:
   ✓ The new slide will be inserted after slide 1. You will move it in a later exercise.

> **Classes Available**
> For Macintosh, Windows, and NT Environment
> - Word Processing
> - Database Management
> - Spreadsheet Power
> - Graphic Design
> - Web Page Design

7. Switch to Slide Sorter view.
8. Switch back to Slide Editor view.
9. In the Print dialog box, change Print selection to Handouts, then change the Number of slides per page to three. Print one copy in black and white.
10. Close the file; save the changes.
11. Open 💾**DIAMOND** or 💾**02DIAMOND**.
12. Display slide 2 using the PgDn key.
13. Display slide 1 using the PgUp key.
14. Add a new Bulleted List slide and type the following information:

> **1998 Accomplishments**
> Year in Review
> - Opened 6 new stores
> - Developed 5 new product lines
> - Promoted 2 District Managers to Regions Managers
>   ➢ Julie Garrison
>   – District 11 to Region 3
>   ➢ JR Greenwood
>   – District 14 to Region 2

15. Switch to Slide Sorter view.
16. Switch to Slide Outliner view.
17. Spell check.
18. Print one copy.
19. In the Print dialog box, change Print selection to Handouts Notes, then change Number of slides per page to two. Print one copy in black and white.
20. Close the file; save the changes.

Corel Presentations 8 ■ Lesson 1 ■ Exercise 2   459

KEYSTROKES

OPEN PRESENTATION

1. Click the **DAD Corel Presentations 8 icon**......................................
2. Click **Work On** tab................ `Ctrl`+`Tab`
3. Click slide show name in drop-down list.

   Click **Open**............................ `Alt`+`O`

   OR

   Double-click desired slide show name from those listed.

   OR

   Click **Browse**........................ `Alt`+`W`
   - Browse and select desired file.

   Click **Open**............................ `Alt`+`O`

If a slide show is open and you wish to open another:

1. Click **File**............................. `Alt`+`F`
2. Click **Open**........................... `O`
3. Type slide show name in **Name** text box.

   OR
   - Double-click desired slide shown from those listed.
4. Click **OK**............................... `Enter`

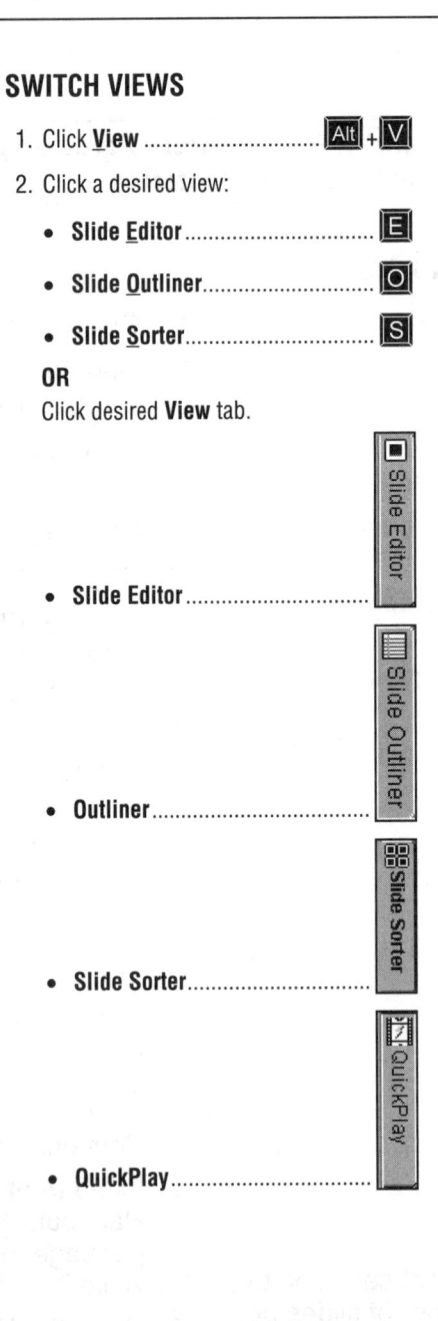

SWITCH VIEWS

1. Click **View**........................... `Alt`+`V`
2. Click a desired view:
   - Slide **E**ditor....................... `E`
   - Slide **O**utliner.................... `O`
   - Slide **S**orter...................... `S`

   OR

   Click desired **View** tab.

   - Slide Editor........................ [Slide Editor]

   - Outliner............................. [Slide Outliner]

   - Slide Sorter....................... [Slide Sorter]

   - QuickPlay.......................... [QuickPlay]

MOVE FROM SLIDE TO SLIDE

Press **PgUp** or **PgDn** ...... `PageUp` or `PageDown` to display previous or next slide.

OR
- Click **Navigation tabs** above Application Bar.

OR
- Click **Select a slide to go to** button above Application Bar.
- Select desired slide.

SPELL CHECK

✓ *The Spell-As-You-Go feature is inactive in this application.*

Ctrl + F1

1. Switch to **Slide Outliner** view.
2. Click **Tools**.......................... `Alt`+`T`
3. Click **Spell Check**................ `S`

PRINT A PRESENTATION

Ctrl + P

Click **Print** button on Toolbar............

OR

1. Click **File**............................. `Alt`+`F`
2. Click **Print**........................... `P`
3. Select desired options from Print and Details tabs.
4. Click **OK**............................... `Enter`

COREL PRESENTATIONS 8 Lesson 1: Create, Save, and Print Slides

Exercise 3

- Add Clipart Graphics to Slides
- Use Undo and Redo
- Change Slide Layout
- Change Slide Show Background Master
- Change Background for Individual Slides

NOTES

Add Clipart Graphics to Slides

- **Graphics** on slides can help capture the audience's attention during a slide show. Graphics can be added to your slides by clicking the Clipart button on the Toolbar or the Tool Palette or by selecting Graphics, Clipart, from the Insert menu. The Scrapbook dialog box appears displaying **Clipart** images that are installed on your system. These are the same images that are available in each of the Corel WordPerfect Suite 8 applications.

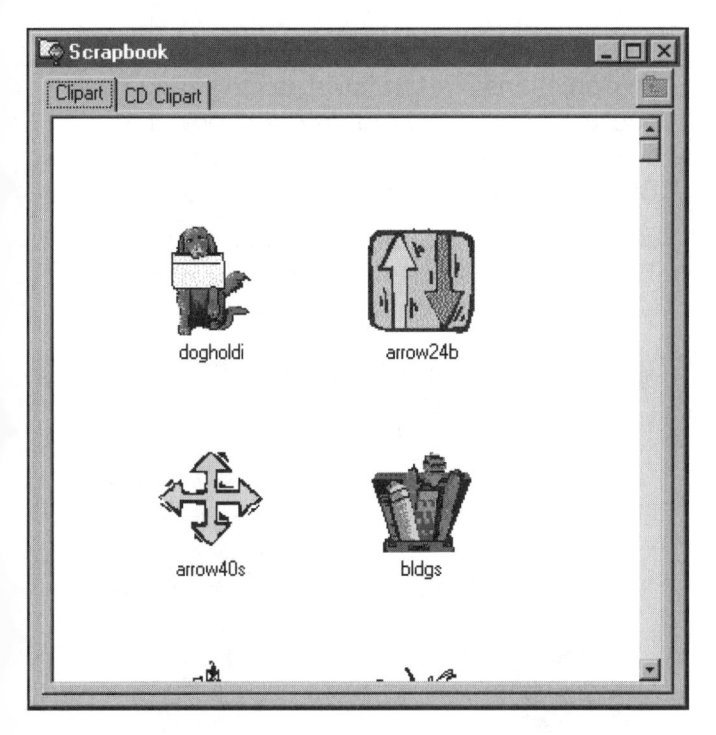

- Click the CD Clipart tab (if you have access to your Corel WordPerfect Suite 8 installation CD-ROM) to preview the categories of graphic images available on the CD-ROM.

- There are two ways to insert a Clipart image from the Scrapbook: click on the image and select Edit, Copy, and then click on your slide and select Edit, Paste. Or, drag and drop the image directly onto the slide. The second method allows you to control the immediate placement of the image.

- Once the graphic is inserted, it appears with handles. When handles appear, you can size the graphic, just as you did with WordPerfect graphics. Simply drag a top or bottom-middle handle to change the height, drag a left or right middle handle to change the width, or drag a corner handle to size the graphic proportionally.

- You can move the graphic by displaying the handles and then placing the pointer within the graphic (not a handle). Next, click and hold the left mouse button while dragging the graphic to a desired location.

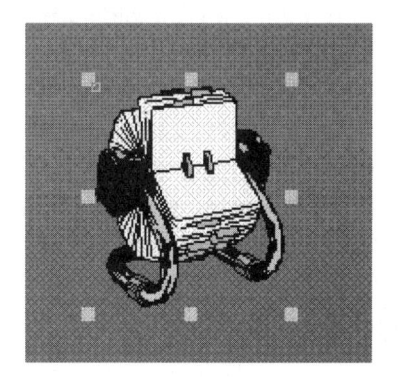

COREL PRESENTATIONS 8 Lesson 1: Create, Save, and Print Slides

Use Undo and Redo

- Like other Corel WordPerfect Suite 8 applications, the Undo feature reverses the most recent action and the Redo feature returns the action. These features are available only in Slide Editor view. They may be accessed from the Edit menu (by clicking Undo or Redo) or by clicking the Undo or Redo buttons.

Change Slide Layout

- The layout (or template) of a slide may be changed at any time. If you have graphics or other objects on the slide when changing the layout, they may be rearranged.

- Use Slide Editor view when changing an individual slide layout. Use Slide Sorter when changing the layout of several slides.

- To change the layout of a slide, select the Layout button on the Property Bar, then choose the desired layout for the current slide.

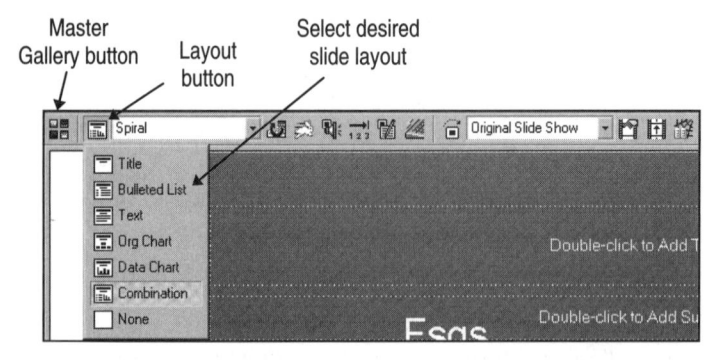

Change Slide Show Background Master

- In Exercise 1, you learned to choose a background master for your slide when you created a new slide show. Corel Presentations 8 also allows you to change that background at any time.

- To change a slide show's master background, you must first access the **Master Gallery** dialog box. To do so, select Master Gallery from the Format menu or click the Master Gallery button on the Property Bar.

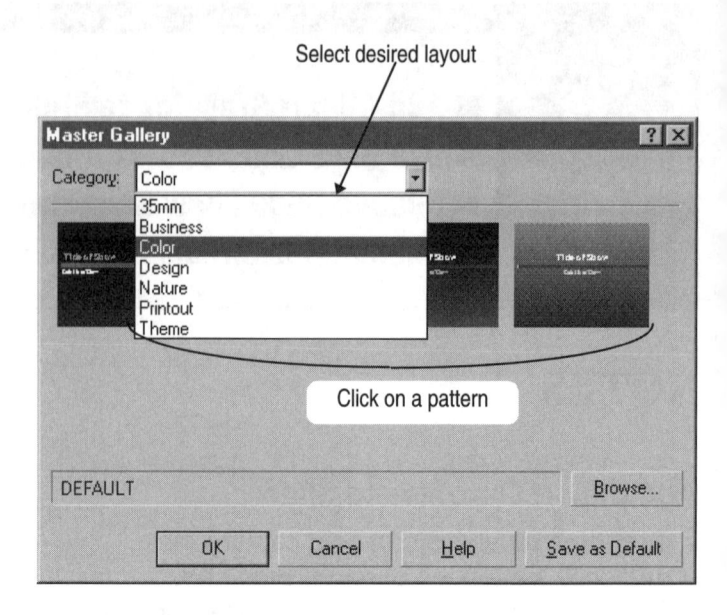

- Choose a category from the Category drop-down list, select one of the available patterns, and click OK to change the background master of all slides in your slide show (with the exception of those that were changed individually—see CHANGE BACKGROUND FOR INDIVIDUAL SLIDES, below).

Change Background for Individual Slides

- Presentations 8 also allows you to change the background layer of **individual slides**. To change an individual slide background, select **Background Gallery** from the Format menu or click the Slide Appearance button on the Toolbar. The Slide Properties dialog box opens with the Appearance tab selected.

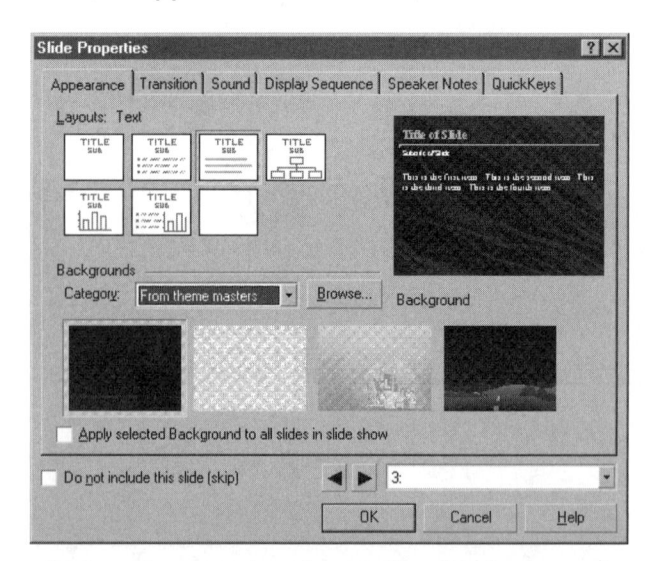

✓Note: You can also change the slide layout option from this dialog box.

- The background options are identical to those available in the Master Gallery. The only difference is that you are applying the new background choice *only* to the slide you selected. The remaining slides in your slide show will still contain the background you chose in the Master Gallery.

- To change the individual slide background, choose a category from the Category drop-down list, click on a desired background pattern, and click OK. A background change made to an individual slide will override changes made to the Background Master.

In this exercise, you will add two new slides to each of the presentations you created in previous exercises. You will also use the Master Gallery and Background Gallery to change the backgrounds.

EXERCISE DIRECTIONS

PART I

1. Open **DIAMOND** or **03DIAMOND**.
2. Add a Bulleted List slide as slide 4.
3. Enter the bulleted list information shown in Illustration A on page 464.
4. Insert a relevant Clipart graphic. Size it appropriately.
5. Add another new Bulleted List slide as slide 5.
6. Enter the bulleted information shown in Illustration B on page 464.
7. Insert two or more relevant Clipart graphic(s). Size them as shown.
8. Undo the last action.
9. Redo the last action.
10. Switch to Slide Sorter view.
11. Change the background master to PARCHMENT (found under the Theme Category of the Master Gallery).
12. Change the background of slide 4 to Background 5 (found in the Theme category).
    ✓ *Text color will be changed in a later exercise to allow it to be read more easily.*
13. Change the layout for slide 4. Select Text as the new layout.
14. Change the layout back to Bulleted List.
15. Switch to Slide Outliner view.
16. Spell check.
17. In the Print dialog box, change Print selection to Handouts and change number of slides per page to 6.
18. Print one copy in black and white.
19. Save the changes and close the file.

PART II

1. Open **CALIBER** or **03CALIBER**.
2. Add a new Bulleted List slide as slide 4.
3. Enter the bulleted list information shown in Illustration C on page 464.
4. Add another new Bulleted List slide as slide 5.
5. Enter the bulleted information shown in Illustration D.
6. Insert a relevant Clipart graphic in the approximate size shown.
7. Click the slide 3 navigation tab.
8. Insert a relevant Clipart graphic in the approximate size shown.
9. Switch to Slide Sorter view.
10. Switch back to Slide Editor view.
11. Spell check.
12. Change the background to CHISEL (found in the Business category of the Master Gallery).
13. Change the background for slide 5 to Purple Design 1 (found in the Purple category).
14. Change the layout for slide 5. Select text as the new layout. (Adjust the graphic size and placement if necessary.)
15. In the Print dialog box, change the Print selection to Handouts and the number of slides per page to 2.
16. Print one copy in black and white.
17. Save the changes and close the file.

COREL PRESENTATIONS 8 Lesson 1: Create, Save, and Print Slides

ILLUSTRATION A

1998 Accomplishments
Year in Review

- Opened 6 New Stores
- Developed 5 New Product Lines
- Promoted 2 District Managers to Regional Managers
  - Julie Garrison
    - District 11 to Region 3
  - J.R. Greenwood
    - District 14 to Region 2

ILLUSTRATION B

Exciting New Product Lines
We're Not Just Granola Anymore!

- Kava Time Organic Coffee
- Smart Sweets Baked Goods
- Jenna's Farm Dairy Products
- Casey's All Natural Cosmetics
- Environment-Right Household Products
  - Laundry Detergent
  - All-Purpose Cleaner
  - Window Cleaner

ILLUSTRATION C

We Aim to Train
Several Training Options Available

- In-House One and Two-Day Training Sessions
  - One person per computer
  - Maximum 12 students per class
- In-House Six-Week Certificate Programs
- Corporate Training
  - In-house or at your office
- Private Training
  - One-on-one in-house or at your home or office

ILLUSTRATION D

New Levels of Classes
Go Beyond the Beginner and Intermediate Levels!

Multimedia 3
Create action-packed interactive CD-ROMS
Word Processing 3
Improve typing skills and speed
Advanced Word Processing, such as mail-merge, macros, graphics, etc.
Web Page Design 2
Learn HTML coding language
Use several editors to create intricate Web pages

KEYSTROKES

INSERT CLIPART

1. Click **I**nsert .... `Alt`+`I`
2. Click **G**raphics .... `G`
3. Click **C**lipart .... `C`
4. Click on **C**lipart tab
   or CD **C**lipart tab .... `Alt`+`Tab`
5. Click desired Clipart image .... `C`
6. Drag image to slide
   OR
   a. Right-click on image.
   b. Click **C**opy .... `C`
   c. Click on slide.
   d. Click **E**dit .... `E`
   e. Click **P**aste .... `P`
7. Click Close to close Scrapbook ... `Enter`

UNDO LAST ACTION

Click **U**ndo button ....
OR
a. Click **E**dit .... `Alt`+`E`
b. Click **U**ndo .... `U`

REDO LAST ACTION

Click **R**edo button ....
OR
a. Click **E**dit .... `Alt`+`E`
b. Click **R**edo .... `R`

CHANGE SLIDE LAYOUT

1. Click **L**ayout button ....
   on the Property Bar.
   OR
   a. Click Fo**r**mat .... `Alt`+`R`
   b. Click Layo**u**t Gallery .... `U`
2. Click **L**ayouts .... `L`
3. Click on a layout option.
4. Click OK .... `Enter`

CHANGE SLIDE SHOW BACKGROUND MASTER

1. Click **M**aster Gallery button ....
   on the Property Bar.
   OR
   a. Click Fo**r**mat .... `Alt`+`R`
   b. Click **M**aster Gallery .... `M`
2. Click Categor**y** .... `Alt`+`Y`
3. Click desired category.
4. Click on desired background option.
5. Click OK .... `Enter`

CHANGE BACKGROUND OF INDIVIDUAL SLIDES

1. Click on desired slide.
2. Click Fo**r**mat .... `Alt`+`R`
3. Click **B**ackground Gallery .... `B`
4. Click
   Background Categor**y** .... `Alt`+`Y`
5. Click desired category.
6. Click on desired background option.
7. Click OK .... `Enter`

Corel Presentations 8 ■ Lesson 1 ■ Exercise 3

COREL PRESENTATIONS 8 Lesson 1: Create, Save, and Print Slides

Exercise 4

- **Move, Copy, and Delete Slides**
- **Slide Sorter View**
- **Return to Slide Editor View**

NOTES

Move, Copy, and Delete Slides

- Each slide in a slide show is part of the entire presentation. Slides may be moved, copied, or deleted within the slide show.
- You should save a slide show before moving, copying, or deleting slides to prevent loss of data.

Slide Sorter View

- You may move, copy, or delete slides from all views using menu commands or cut/copy and paste procedures. However, it is easier and more efficient to perform these tasks in **Slide Sorter view** since all slides are displayed in miniature. In this view, you can easily see the flow of the entire slide show.

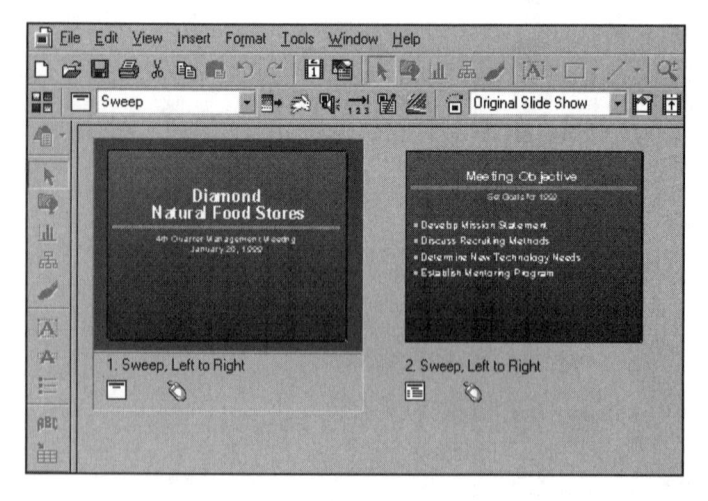

- To move, copy, or delete a slide in Slide Sorter view, click the Slide Sorter tab or select Slide Sorter from the View menu.

- Select the slide to be moved, copied, or deleted. Selected slides appear with a sunken (embossed) and shaded background. You can select slides using one of several techniques:
  - Click the desired slide.
  - Press the insertion point arrow keys until the desired slide is selected.
  - Press and hold down the Shift key as you click to select multiple slides. Selecting multiple slides allows you to move, copy, or delete them as a group. You cannot undo changes made in Slide Sorter view.

- The easiest way to move a slide in Slide Sorter view is to select it and drag it to a new location. When the slide is being moved, the mouse pointer changes to a slide with a diagonal arrow, and a vertical bar identifies the new position of the slide (as indicated in the illustration below). When the vertical bar is in the position where you want to place the slide, release the mouse button.

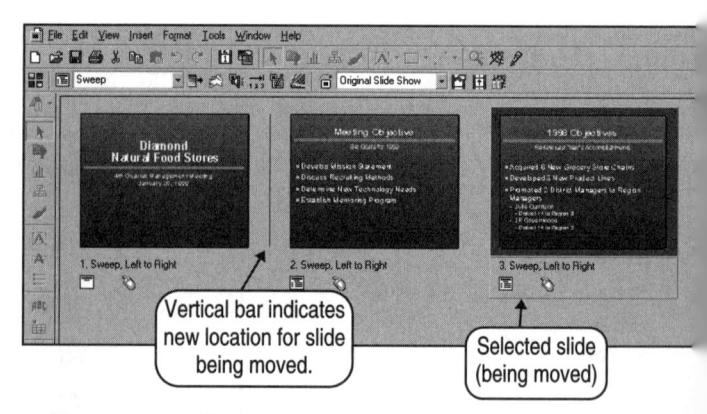

- To copy a slide, press the Ctrl key as you drag the slide to a new location.

- To delete a slide, select the slide and press the Delete key, or select Delete Slide(s) from the Slide menu.

Return to Slide Editor View

- Because you cannot edit slide contents in Slide Sorter view, you will need to return to Slide Editor view to make changes and adjust text. You can return to Slide Editor view using one of the following techniques:

- Double-click a slide in Slide Sorter view.
- Double-click a slide icon in Slide Outliner view.
- Select the desired slide and click the Slide Editor tab.
- Select the desired slide and select Slide Editor from the View menu.

In this exercise, you will insert slides into an existing slide show. You will then move, copy, and delete slides.

EXERCISE DIRECTIONS

1. Open CALIBER or 04CALIBER.
2. Insert a new Bulleted List slide as slide 3.
3. Enter the information shown in Illustration A.
4. Insert a new Bulleted List slide as slide 4.
5. Enter the information shown in Illustration B on page 468.
6. Create a new Bulleted List slide as slide 8.
7. Enter the information shown in Illustration C on page 468 and insert a relevant graphic.
8. Switch to Slide Sorter view.
9. Move slide 5 (Classes Available) so that it becomes slide 4.
10. Delete the slide entitled WE AIM TO TRAIN (slide 6).
11. Copy slide 5 (Fall Schedule) and drag it to the slide 6 position.

  ✓ You will now have two Fall Schedule slides. The second one will be edited in a later exercise.
  ✓ The contents of the duplicate slide will be edited in Exercise 10.

12. Switch to Slide Editor view.
13. Change the background master to ARROWS found in the Business category of the Master Gallery.

  ✓ Slide 7 will not change. It will still contain the individual background set earlier.

14. Print one copy as Handouts with 8 slides per page in black and white.
15. Switch to Slide Outliner view.
16. Spell check.
17. Switch to Slide Sorter view. Compare the order of slides with the Desired Result on page 469.
18. Close the file; save the changes.

ILLUSTRATION A

What is CCUG?

A.K.A. Caliber Computer User Group

- A volunteer-run computer user group, educating the community in computer technology.
  - Annual membership includes:
    - Access to inexpensive classes
    - Free meetings
    - Free access to our extensive computer and multimedia lab

COREL PRESENTATIONS 8 Lesson 1: Create, Save, and Print Slides

ILLUSTRATION B

Fall Schedule
In-House Training Only

- Word Processing 1
  - Monday and Wednesday 6:00 p.m. – 9:00 p.m.
  - Thursday and Friday 1:00 p.m. – 4:00 p.m.
- Desktop Publishing 3
  - Saturday 9:00 a.m. – 4:00 a.m.
- Graphic Design
  - Thursday and Friday 6:00 p.m. – 9:00 p.m.
- Spreadsheet Power
  - Monday and Wednesday 6:00 p.m. – 9:00 p.m.

ILLUSTRATION C

Weekly CCUG Meetings
Valuable Door Prizes Awarded!

- Every Wednesday at 7:00 p.m.
- Topics include:
  - Demos of popular new software or hardware
  - Introduction of new technology
  - Discussions regarding popular software
- Meetings hosted by:
  - Popular vendors
  - Computer and multimedia professionals
  - CCUG President, Lisa Scully

KEYSTROKES

MOVE SLIDES

1. From Slide Sorter view, select slide to move.
2. Drag slide to new location.

OR

- Click **E**dit .... Alt + E
- Click Cu**t** .... T
- Move insertion point to new slide location.
- Click **E**dit .... Alt + E
- Click **P**aste .... P

COPY SLIDES

Ctrl + C, Ctrl + V

1. From Slide Sorter view, select slide to copy.
2. Press **Ctrl** while dragging slide to new location.

OR

a. Click **E**dit .... Alt + E
b. Click **C**opy C
c. Click on slide to the left of desired location.
d. Click **E**dit .... Alt + E
e. Click **P**aste .... P

DELETE SLIDES

From Slide Sorter View:

1. Select slide(s) to delete.
2. Press **Delete** key .... Del

From Any View:

1. Select Slide(s) to delete.
2. Click **E**dit .... Alt + E
3. Click **D**elete .... E

   OR

   Click **D**elete Slide(s) .... D

4. Click **Y**es or **N**o .... Y or N

   OR

1. Select Slide(s) to delete.
2. Click **E**dit .... Alt + E
3. Click Cle**a**r .... A
4. Click S**l**ide # .... Alt + L
   to clear current slide only.

   OR

   Click **E**ntire **s**lide show ...... Alt + S
   to delete all slides in a slide show.

5. Click **C**lear .... Alt + C

DESIRED RESULT

Slide 1

Caliber Computer User Group

Lisa Scully, President

Slide 2

People Helping People

Your CCUG Membership Will Include the Following:

- A user-friendly network of sources for all of your computer needs
- Free subscription to CCUG MONTHLY
  - A monthly periodical providing common computer application tips, short-cuts, pitfalls, purchasing advice, etc.
- Job placement assistance
- Discounts on computer purchases

Slide 3

What is CCUG?

A.K.A. Caliber Computer User Group

- A volunteer-run computer user group, educating the community in computer technology.
  - Annual membership includes:
    - Access to inexpensive classes
    - Free meetings
    - Free access to our extensive computer and multimedia lab

---

Slide 4

Classes Available

For Macintosh, Windows, and NT Environments

- Word Processing
- Database Management
- Spreadsheet Power
- Graphic Design
- Web Page Design

Slide 5

Fall Schedule

In-House Training Only

- Word Processing 1
  - Monday and Wednesday 6:00 p.m. – 9:00 p.m.
  - Thursday and Friday 1:00 p.m. – 4:00 p.m.
- Desktop Publishing 3
  - Saturday 9:00 a.m. – 4:00 a.m.
- Graphic Design
  - Thursday and Friday 6:00 p.m. – 9:00 p.m.
- Spreadsheet Power
  - Monday and Wednesday 6:00 p.m. – 9:00 p.m.

Slide 6

Fall Schedule

In-House Training Only

- Word Processing 1
  - Monday and Wednesday 6:00 p.m. – 9:00 p.m.
  - Thursday and Friday 1:00 p.m. – 4:00 p.m.
- Desktop Publishing 3
  - Saturday 9:00 a.m. – 4:00 a.m.
- Graphic Design
  - Thursday and Friday 6:00 p.m. – 9:00 p.m.
- Spreadsheet Power
  - Monday and Wednesday 6:00 p.m. – 9:00 p.m.

Slide 7

New Levels of Classes

Go Beyond the Beginner and Intermediate Levels!

- Multimedia 3
  - Create action-packed interactive CD-ROMS
- Word Processing 3
  - Improve typing skills and speed
  - Advanced Word Processing, such as mail merge, macros, graphics, etc.
- Web Page Design 2
  - Learn HTML coding language
  - Use several editors to create intricate Web pages

Slide 8

Weekly CCUG Meetings

Valuable Door Prizes Awarded!

- Every Wednesday at 7:00 p.m.
- Topics include:
  - Demos of popular new software or hardware
  - Introduction of new technology
  - Discussions regarding popular software
- Meetings hosted by:
  - Popular vendors
  - Computer and multimedia professionals
  - CCUG President, Lisa Scully

COREL PRESENTATIONS 8 Lesson 1: Create, Save, and Print Slides

Exercise 5

- Slide Outliner View
- Add Slides in Slide Outliner View

NOTES

Slide Outliner View

- **Slide Outliner** view displays slide text as titles and subtitles in an outline format to give an overview of the contents of a slide show. This view is usually used to organize a slide show.

- Slide Outliner view may be used before creating text on slides to organize your thoughts in an outline format. Or, you may create your presentation on slides first, then switch to Slide Outliner view to see the flow of your slide show in an outline format. It can also serve as a Table of Contents which, when exported to WordPerfect 8 can be printed separately and distributed to your audience (see the Integration section for details on exporting to WordPerfect 8).

- Note the illustration below of the DIAMOND slide show displayed in Slide Outliner view. A slide icon, a number, and a text placeholder mark each slide on the left. Slide text is shown on the right.

- Graphics and objects do not appear in Slide Outliner view.

- To display Slide Outliner view, click the Slide Outliner navigation tab or select Slide Outliner from the View menu.

- You can change to Slide Outliner view after creating a slide show, or you can create an entire presentation in Slide Outliner view. Once you change views, the outline will convert to a series of slides.

- In Slide Outliner view, use the Tab key to promote the outline to the next level, and use Shift + Tab to demote the outline to the previous level. As you promote or demote outline levels, Presentations 8 changes the placeholder type for the level from Title to Subtitle to Text (Bullet Chart).

- To view the result of text added in Slide Outliner view, double-click the slide icon displayed on the left.

- When you use the Spell Check feature in Slide Outliner view, your entire presentation will be checked for spelling errors.

Add a New Slide in Slide Outliner View

- A new slide may be added in Slide Outliner View using any one of the following procedures:

  - Place the insertion point at the end of a line and press Ctrl + Enter.

  - Select New Slide from the Insert menu.

  - Click the arrow next to the Insert a *new slide after the current slide* button above the Application Bar, and select the type of slide you want to insert.

In this exercise, you will create a slide show in Slide Outliner view. After creating the slide show, you will move slides, add a new slide, and print the slide show.

EXERCISE DIRECTIONS

1. Create a new slide show.
2. Use the default background master.
3. Select a Title layout as the first slide.
4. Switch to Slide Outliner view.
5. Enter the following titles and subtitles to create your outline.
   ✓ *In the outline below, numbered items represent the title and slide number, indented items represent subtitles, and bulleted items represent bulleted list text.*

   1. Fair Play Sports Club
      Boston, MA
         ✓ *Change layout to Bulleted List.*
   2. FPSC is More Than Just a Gym
      We're a Professional Fitness Complex.
      - Professional Fitness Staff and Personal Trainers
      - Classes on the Hour, Every Hour
      - Spa Facility
      - Swimming Pool
      - Rock Climbing Wall
      - Health and Juice Bar
   3. We're Expanding Every Day
      Clubs Opening Soon In:
      - Dover
      - Brookline
      - Foxwood
      - Watertown
      - Wellesley
      - Natick
   4. FPSC's High Success Rate
      Why more people are working out with us.
      - People want more activity choices.
        - Traditional aerobics can be boring.
        - Doing the same activity daily can cause repetitive injuries.
      - Our workout equipment is top of the line.
        - Updated once a year, or sooner when needed.
        - We have more equipment than any fitness center in the New England area.
        - Our guarantee: you'll never have to wait in line.

6. Spell check.
7. Switch to Slide Sorter view.
8. Move slide 4 to become slide 3.
9. Switch to Slide Editor view and display slide 2.
10. Insert a relevant graphic.
11. Display slide 4.
12. Insert a relevant graphic.
13. Change the background master to SUMMER (found in the Nature Category of the Master Gallery).
14. Switch to Slide Outliner view.
15. Insert a new Bulleted List slide after slide 3 that reads:

> Our Professional Staff Means Business
>   You're Not Alone at FPSC
>   - 20 staff members on the floor at all times
>   - Class limit of 1 instructor per 15 students
>   - Bi-weekly health readings:
>   - Cholesterol readings
>   - Body fat and muscle mass analysis
>   - Nutrition advice
>   - Once a month free private training sessions
>   - Additional sessions available at a nominal fee

16. Switch to Slide Outliner view.
17. Spell check.
18. Switch to Slide Sorter view. Compare the order of slides with the Desired Result illustration on page 472.
19. Print one copy as Handouts with 5 slides per page in black and white.
20. Save the file; name it **SPORTS**.
21. Close the window.

COREL PRESENTATIONS 8   **Lesson 1:** Create, Save, and Print Slides

DESIRED RESULT

Slide 1:
Fair Play Sports Club
Boston, MA

Slide 2: FPSC is More Than Just a Gym
We're a Professional Fitness Complex.
- Professional Fitness Staff and Personal Trainers
- Classes on the Hour, Every Hour
- Spa Facility
- Swimming Pool
- Rock Climbing Wall
- Health and Juice Bar

Slide 3: FPSC's High Success Rate
Why More People are Working Out With Us.
- People want more activity choices.
  - Traditional aerobics can be boring.
  - Doing the same activity daily can cause repetitive injuries.
- Our workout equipment is top of the line.
  - Updated once a year, or sooner when needed.
  - We have more equipment than any fitness center in the New England area.
  - Our guarantee: you'll never have to wait in line.

Slide 4: Our Professional Staff Means Business
You're Not Alone at FPSC
- 20 staff members on the floor at all times
- Class limit of 1 instructor per 15 students
- Bi-monthly health readings:
  - Cholesterol readings
  - Body fat and muscle mass analysis
  - Nutrition advice
- Once a month free private training sessions
  - Additional sessions available at a nominal fee

Slide 5: We're Expanding Every Day
Clubs Opening Soon In:
- Dover
- Brookline
- Foxwood
- Watertown
- Wellesley
- Natick

KEYSTROKES

SWITCH TO SLIDE OUTLINER VIEW

Click **Slide Outliner** View tab............ [Slide Outliner]

OR

1. Click **View** .... Alt + V
2. Click **Slide Outliner** .... O

ADD SLIDES IN SLIDE OUTLINER VIEW

1. Position insertion point at the end of the last line in the outline.
2. Press **Ctrl + Enter**.

ADD TEXT IN SLIDE OUTLINER VIEW

Press **Tab** .... [Tab]
to indent or add subtitles
and text (bullet) items.

   ✓ To add a bulleted item under the Title line, press **Enter** and then press **Tab**.

OR

Press **Shift+Tab** to go back one level.

Exercise 6

■ Insert a Graph

Data Chart Toolbar

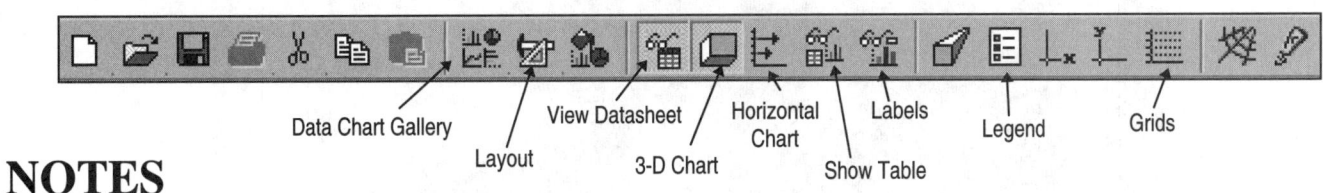

(Toolbar labels: Data Chart Gallery, Layout, View Datasheet, 3-D Chart, Horizontal Chart, Show Table, Labels, Legend, Grids)

NOTES

Insert a Graph

- Thus far, you have been working with Title and Bulleted List slide layouts. Corel Presentations 8 provides other layouts that help to display data. The **Data Chart layout** allows you to create a graph on a slide. You can also import graphs that have been created in Quattro Pro. (See Integration Chapter to import a Quattro Pro chart and workbook data.)

- To insert a slide that contains a graph placeholder, click the arrow next to the *Insert a new slide after the current slide* button above the Application Bar. From the drop-down list that appears, select Insert Data Chart Slide or Insert Combination Slide.

  ✓Note: *A combination layout has four placeholders: title, subtitle, bulleted list (on the left), and data chart (on the right).*

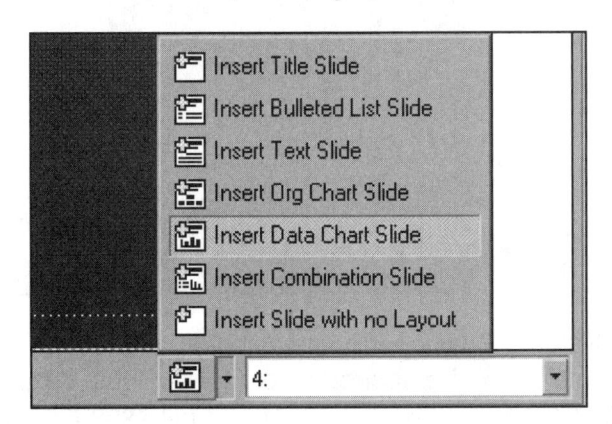

- On the data chart slide that follows, double-click the placeholder as directed to add data chart.

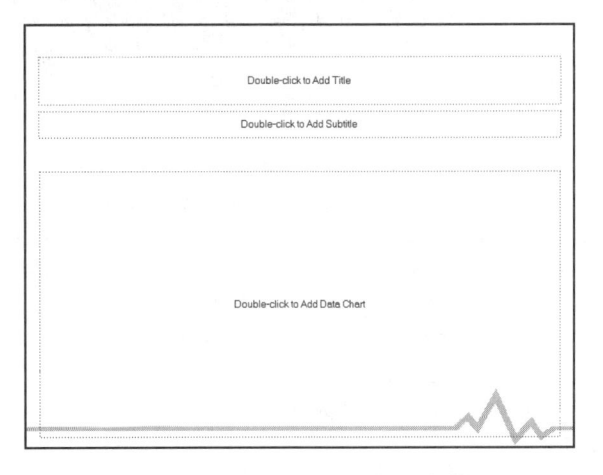

- The Data Chart Gallery dialog box will appear so that you may choose a desired Chart type. The default Chart type is Bar (Vert), a vertical bar chart. Select a desired chart type from the Chart type list, then choose one of the display options, and click OK.

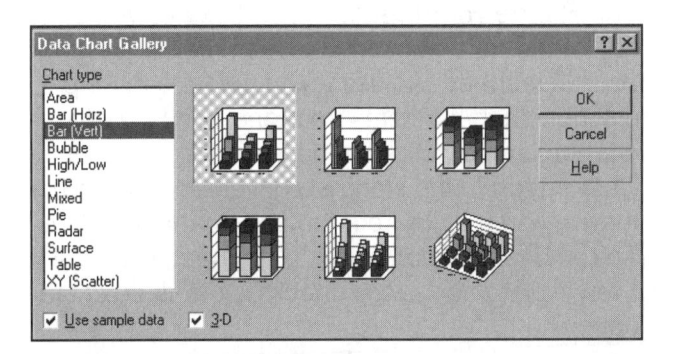

- The Data Chart toolbar will display along with the **Datasheet** and the **Range Highlighter** dialog boxes.

COREL PRESENTATIONS 8 Lesson 1: Create, Save, and Print Slides

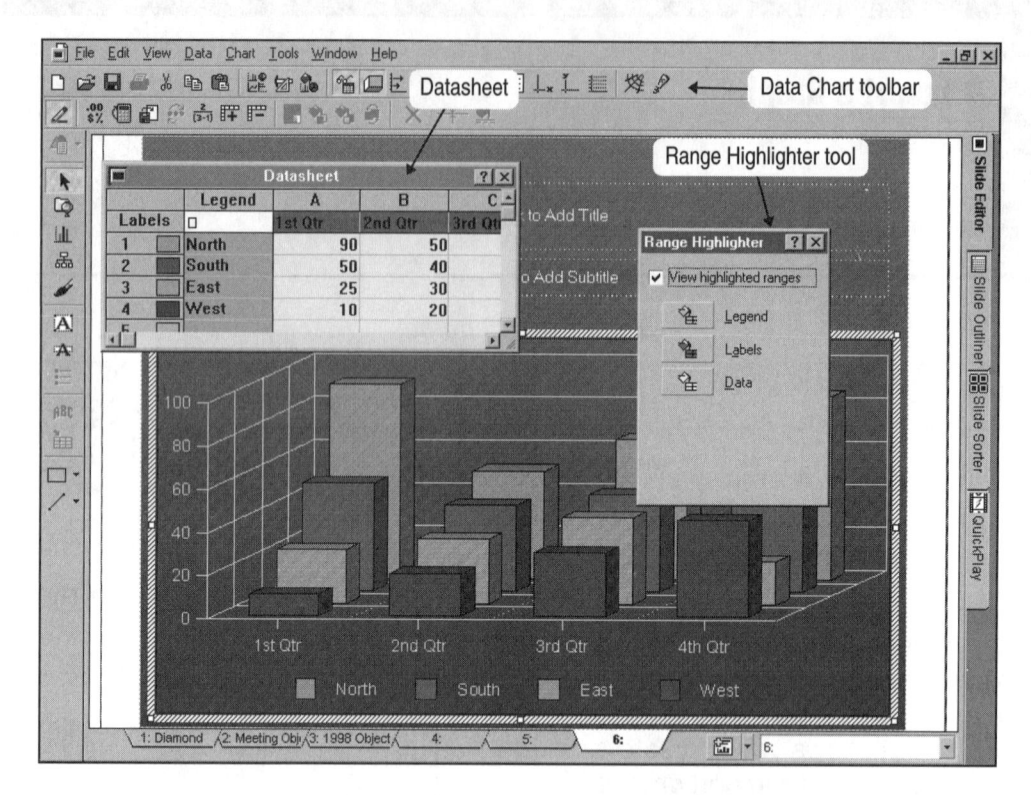

- The datasheet contains sample data to assist you with data placement. You must delete the sample data before you enter your own data. To delete data from the datasheet, click Edit, Clear All and then click Yes to confirm the deletion. Enter the data you wish to chart on the datasheet, just as you did in a Quattro Pro spreadsheet. The graph will reflect the new data.

- To hide the datasheet, click the View Datasheet button on the Data Chart toolbar. To bring the datasheet table back into view, double-click the graph placeholder and then click the View Datasheet button again.

- The **Range Highlighter** dialog box allows you to adjust the data, legend, and label colors within your datasheet. Adjusting the colors can help distinguish these items from one another. To change a color, click on the Legend, Label, or Data button in the Range Highlighter box, and then select a color from the palette that displays. To remove all color from a Datasheet, click the *View highlighted range* check box to deselect the option.

- You may enhance your graph with data labels. **Data labels** let you indicate the exact value of each data point. Click the Labels button on the Data Chart toolbar. To adjust the location or appearance of the data label, select Data Labels from the Chart menu.

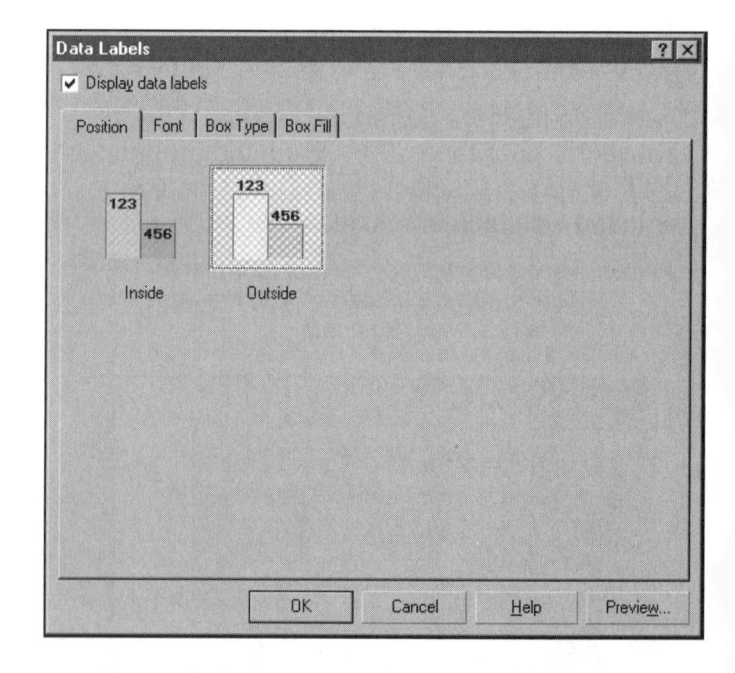

- Click the Position tab and select Inside or Outside for the desired placement of label data. Click the Font, Box Type, and/or Fill Type tabs to make any adjustments to these data label display options.

- To add a **legend**, click the data chart placeholder, then click the Legend button on the Data Chart toolbar, or select Legend from the Chart menu. The Legend Properties dialog box displays.

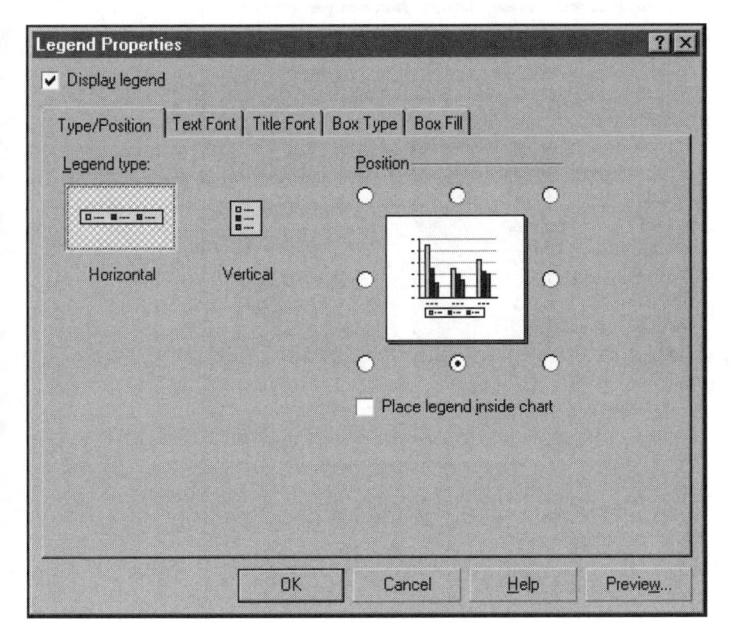

- To place the legend inside the actual chart area, click the Type/Position tab and check the **Place legend inside chart** option. Click the Horizontal or Vertical options to change the Legend type and click any of the Position buttons to adjust the placement on the slide.

- To add a chart to a slide that does not have a chart placeholder, select Chart from the Insert menu. Then, click on the slide and drag to create an area for the chart to be inserted (similar to inserting a graphic). The Data Chart Gallery displays. Follow the same procedures reviewed in this exercise to create the chart.

In this exercise, you will insert a Data Chart slide into a previously created presentation. You will also use the Range Highlighter tool.

EXERCISE DIRECTIONS

1. Open **DIAMOND** or **06DIAMOND**.
2. Add a new Data Chart slide.
3. Enter the slide title and subtitle shown in Illustration A on page 476.
4. Create a vertical bar chart using the format shown in the illustration.
5. Delete the data from the datasheet and enter the new data shown below:

	1996	1997	1998
Produce	4,276	4,852	6,025
Dairy	3,375	3,004	4,537
Grains	5,789	6,521	7,990
Soy	4,756	5,380	7,045
Household Products	2,589	3,042	3,350
Other	1,963	2,245	2,980

6. Use the Range Highlighter tool to shade the legend, label, and data cells on the datasheet.
7. Display all labels.
   ✓ *If data labels appear to be crowded, click on each data point and adjust it slightly.*
8. Move the new Data Chart slide to become slide 4.
9. Switch to Slide Editor view.
10. Display slide 3 (1998 Accomplishments).
    - Insert a relevant graphic, as shown in Illustration B.
11. Insert a new Bulleted List slide.
    - Add the title, subtitle and bulleted text as shown in Illustration C.
    - Move the slide to become slide 7.
12. Print one copy as Handouts with 6 slides per page in Black and White.
13. Close the file; save the changes.

ILLUSTRATION A

Units Sold Nationally

Three-Year Comparison of Product Categories

	1996	1997	1998
Other (Y1)	1,963	2,245	2,980
Household Products (Y1)	4,756	5,380	7,045
Soy (Y2)	2,589	3,042	3,350
Grains (Y1)	5,789	6,521	7,990
Dairy (Y1)	3,375	3,004	4,537
Produce (Y1)	4,276	4,852	6,025

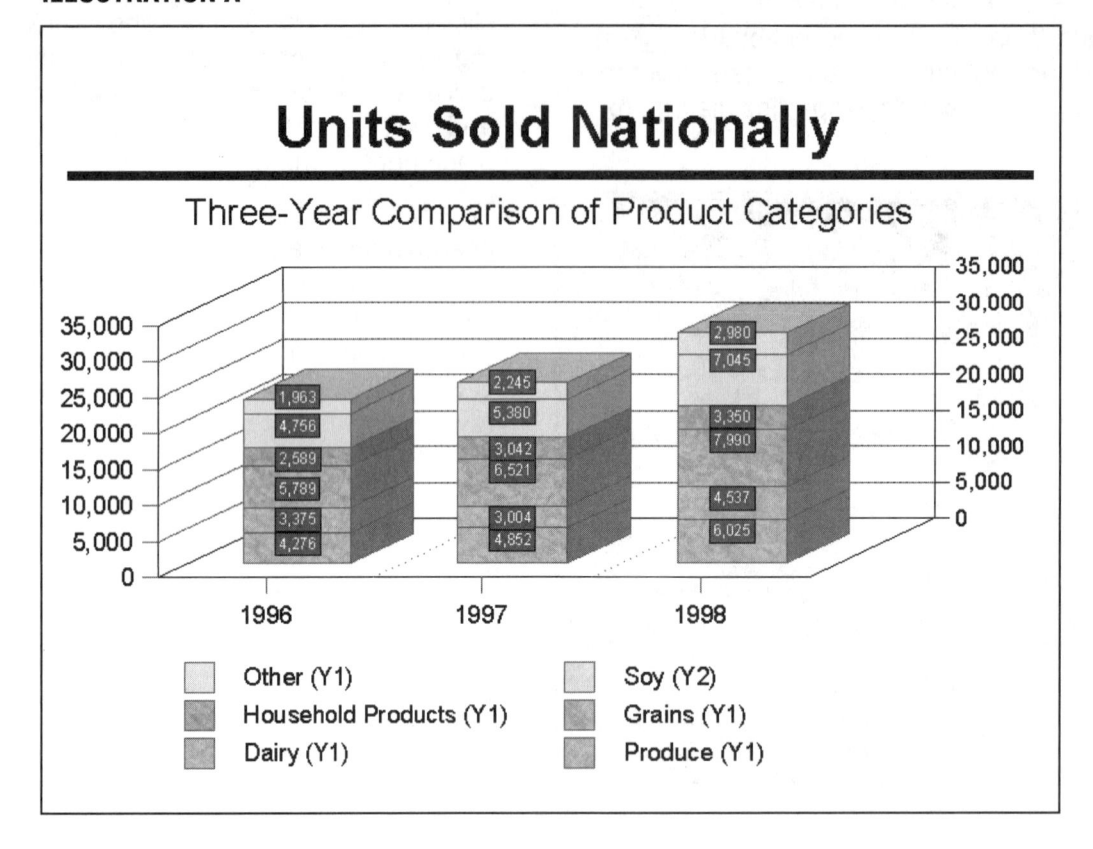

ILLUSTRATION B

1998 Accomplishments

Year in Review

- Opened 6 New Stores
- Developed 5 New Product Lines
- Promoted 2 District Managers to Regional Managers
  - Julie Garrison
    - District 11 to Region 3
  - J.R. Greenwood
    - District 14 to Region 2

ILLUSTRATION C

Goals for 1999

Let's Break New Ground in '99!

- Product Expansion
- New Markets
- Lower Operating Costs
- Increase Revenue

KEYSTROKES

CREATE A GRAPH

1. **On a new slide:**
   a. Click **Insert a new slide after current slide** .... button on Application bar.
   b. Click **Insert Data Chart Slide** or **Insert Combination Slide** ...
   c. Double click placeholder.
   OR
   a. Click **Insert** .... Alt + I
   b. Click **New Slide** .... N
   c. Click **Layout** .... Alt + L
   d. Click **Data Chart** or **Combination**
   e. Click **OK** .... Enter
   f. Double click placeholder.
   OR
   On an existing slide:
   a. Click **Select Layout** button .... on Property Bar.
   b. Click **Data Chart** or **Combination** ....
   OR
   a. Click **Format** .... Alt + R
   b. Click **Layout Gallery** .... U
   c. Click **Layout** on Appearance tab .... Alt + L
   d. Click **Data Chart** or **Combination**
   e. Click **OK** .... Enter
   f. Double click placeholder.
   OR
   a. Click **Insert** .... Alt + I
   b. Click **Chart** .... A
   c. Drag mouse to desired size and release.
2. Click desired **Chart type** .... Alt + C
3. Click **OK** .... Enter
4. Delete the sample data in the datasheet:
   a. Click **Edit** .... Alt + E
   b. Click **Clear All** .... A
   c. Click **Yes** to confirm deletion ...... Y
   d. Click **OK** .... Enter
5. Enter the data you wish to chart in the datasheet.
6. Press **Tab** .... Tab
   to advance to the next datasheet cell.
   OR
   Press **Shift + Tab** .... Shift + Tab
   to move to the previous cell.
7. Click outside the graph to return to Corel Presentations 8 slide.

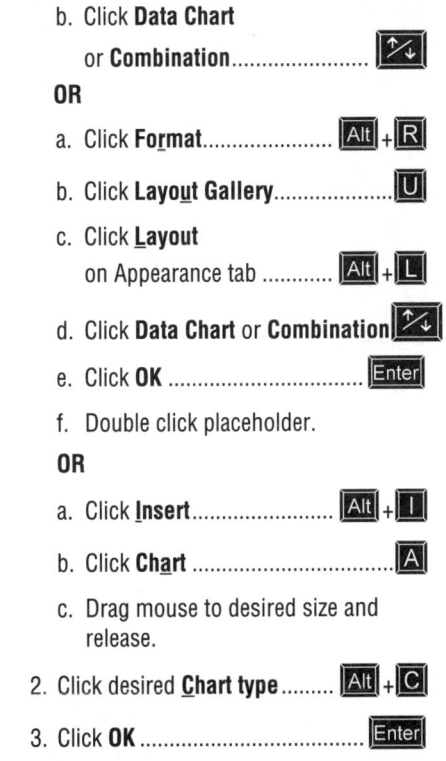

HIDE OR VIEW DATASHEET

1. Double-click on a graph placeholder.
2. Click the **View Datasheet** button on Toolbar to hide the datasheet.........
3. Click the **View Datasheet** button ... again to view.

COREL PRESENTATIONS 8 Lesson 1: Create, Save, and Print Slides

Exercise 7

Create a Table

Data Chart Toolbar

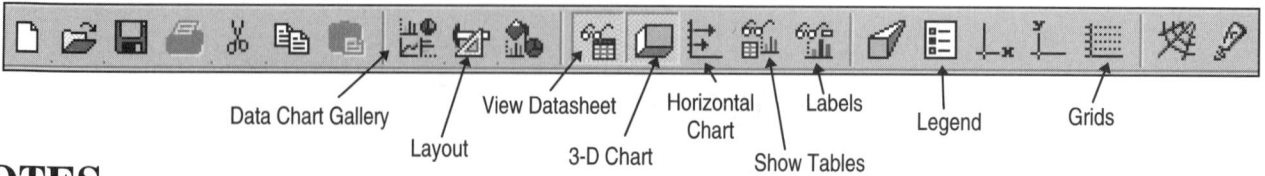

Data Chart Gallery — Layout — View Datasheet — 3-D Chart — Horizontal Chart — Labels — Show Tables — Legend — Grids

NOTES

Create a Table

- A **table** may be added to Corel Presentations 8 using the same procedures used to add a graph. To create a table, select Data Chart as the slide layout and double-click the data chart placeholder. In the Data Chart Gallery dialog box that follows, select Table as the Chart type and choose from the table layouts that display.

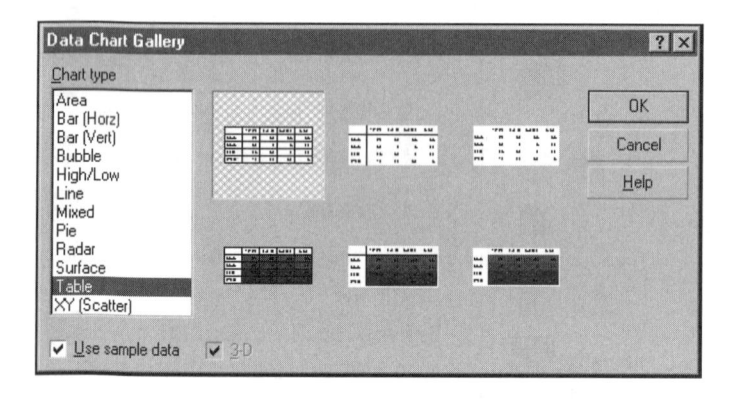

- In the Datasheet dialog box that follows, enter your data in place of the sample data.

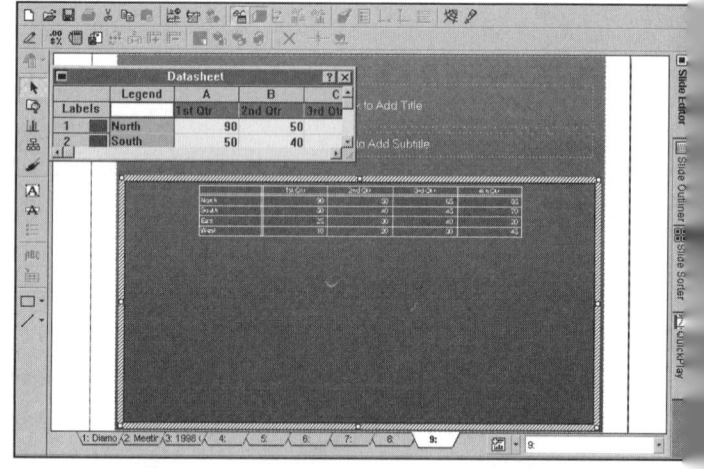

- The font size may appear small. To change font attributes, click the Layout button on the Data Chart toolbar. In the Table Properties dialog box which follows, click the Font tab and make the desired changes.

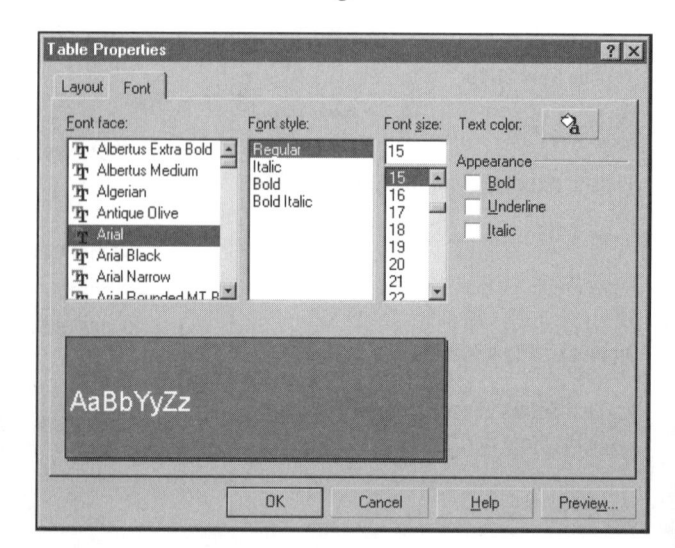

478

- Click the Layout tab on the Table Properties dialog box to make adjustments to the fill color, line color, gradation, etc.

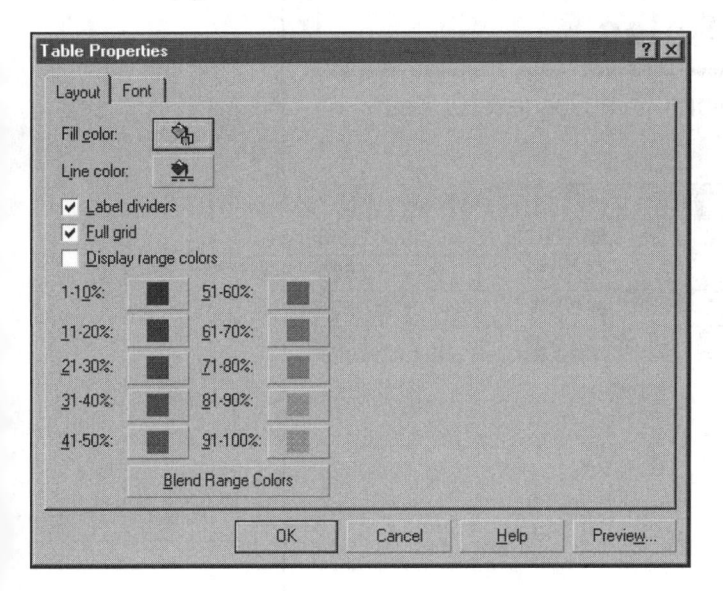

- You may also insert a table within a graph by clicking the Show Table button on the Data Chart toolbar when a graph is selected.

In this exercise, you will insert a table into a previously created presentation, and then edit the table contents and table layout.

EXERCISE DIRECTIONS

1. Open **DIAMOND** or **07DIAMOND**.
2. Add a new Data Chart slide.
3. Select Table as the Chart type. Use any desired table layout (see Illustration A on the following page).
4. Enter the following data on the datasheet:

	Region 1	Region 2	Region 3
1st Qtr.	3,557,500	7,537,000	7,003,256
2nd Qtr.	4,875,000	6,755,000	11,412,500
3rd Qtr.	6,226,000	5,896,500	7,987,500
4th Qtr	4,014,500	3,312,000	8,333,000

   a. Use the Range Highlighter tool to shade the legend, label, and data cells on the datasheet.
   b. Change the font size for table text to 30 points.
   c. Change the table layout so that the fill color is solid, the font is white and the range colors are not displayed.
   d. Create the title and subtitle table data shown in Illustration A.

   Hint: Deselect the Display Range Colors option on the Layout tab of the Table Properties dialog box.

5. Switch to Slide Sorter view.
6. Move the new slide to become slide 5.
7. Switch to Slide Editor view.
8. Display slide 5.
   a. View the datasheet.
   b. Edit the data in the cell that contains sales information for Region 3, 1st Qtr to read:
      9,846,500
9. Print one copy as Handouts with 6 slides per page in black and white.
10. Close the file; save the changes.

ILLUSTRATION A

1998 Sales

Congratulations to All Regions on a Successful Year!

	Region 1	Region 2	Region 3
1rst Qtr.	3,557,500	7,537,000	7,003,256
2nd Qtr.	4,875,000	6,755,000	11,412,500
3rd Qtr.	6,226,000	5,896,500	7,987,500
4th Qtr.	4,014,500	3,312,000	8,333,000

KEYSTROKES

CREATE A TABLE

1. **On a new slide:**
   a. Click **Insert a new slide after current** .... slide button on the Application bar.
   b. Click **Insert Data Chart Slide**... or **Insert Combination Slide**.
   c. Double click placeholder.

   OR

   a. Click **Insert** .... Alt+I
   b. Click **New Slide** .... N
   c. Click **Layout** .... Alt+L
   d. Click **Data Chart** or **Combination**.
   e. Click **OK** .... Enter
   f. Double click placeholder.

   OR

   On an existing slide:
   a. Click **Select Layout** button .... on the Property Bar.
   b. Click **Data Chart** or **Combination** ....

   OR
   a. Click **Format** .... Alt+R
   b. Click **Layout Gallery** .... U
   c. Click **Layout** .... Alt+L
      on the Appearance tab.
   d. Click **Data Chart** or **Combination** ....
   e. Click **OK** .... Enter
   f. Double click placeholder.

   OR
   a. Click **Insert** .... Alt+I
   b. Click **Chart** .... A
   c. Drag mouse to desired size and release.

2. Click **Chart type** .... Alt+C
3. Click **Table** ....
4. Click desired table layout.
5. Click **OK** .... Enter
6. Delete the sample data in the datasheet:
   a. Click **Edit** .... Alt+E
   b. Click **Clear All** .... A
   c. Click **Yes** to confirm deletion ...... Y
   d. Click **OK** .... Enter
7. Enter the table data in the datasheet.
8. Press **Tab** to advance to the next datasheet cell.

   OR

   Press **Shift + Tab** .... Shift+Tab
   to move to the previous cell.
9. Click outside the graph to return to Corel Presentations 8 slide.

ADJUST TABLE LAYOUT AND FONT

1. Double-click on table placeholder.
2. Click **Layout** button .... on the Data Chart toolbar.
3. Click **Layout** tab .... Ctrl+Tab
4. Make any desired adjustments.
5. Click **Font** tab .... Ctrl+Tab
6. Make any desired adjustments.
7. Click **OK** .... Enter

COREL PRESENTATIONS 8 Lesson 1: Create, Save, and Print Slides

Exercise 8

■ Insert an Organization Chart on a Slide

Org Chart Toolbar

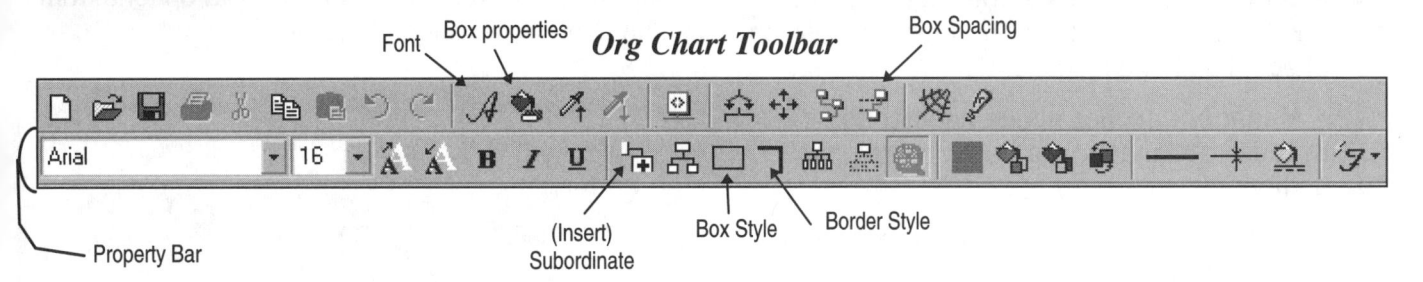

Callouts: Font, Box properties, Box Spacing, Property Bar, (Insert) Subordinate, Box Style, Border Style

NOTES

Insert an Organization Chart on a Slide

- An **Organization Chart** is used to illustrate a company's hierarchy or structure. It may also be used to show the flow of a project or a family tree.

- Corel Presentations 8 contains an organization chart layout that helps to display organizational chart data.

- To create an organization chart in a new slide, click the arrow next to the Insert a New Slide After the Current Slide button on the Application Bar and select Insert Org Chart Slide.

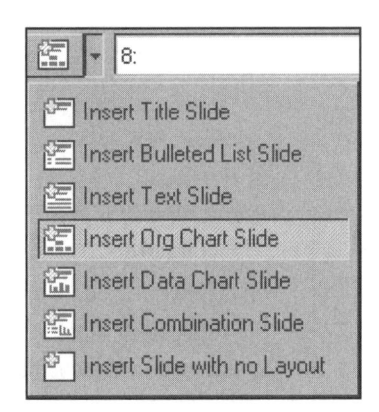

  Menu options: Insert Title Slide, Insert Bulleted List Slide, Insert Text Slide, Insert Org Chart Slide, Insert Data Chart Slide, Insert Combination Slide, Insert Slide with no Layout

- On the organization chart slide that follows, double-click within the placeholder (as directed).

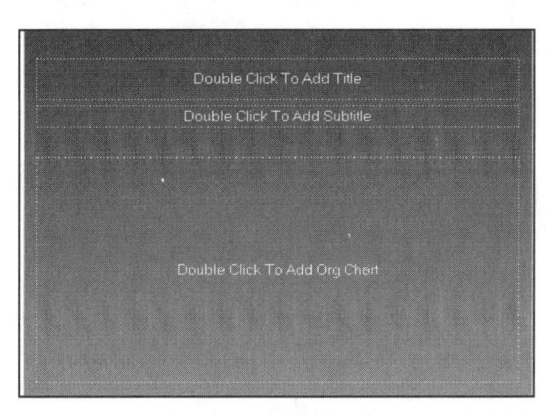

- By default, nine boxes display. (You will note, too, that new menu items appear). You can attach additional boxes to existing boxes, and rearrange boxes. You can format each box with different fonts, font sizes, fill colors, and borders, as well as align text left, center, or right within the box.

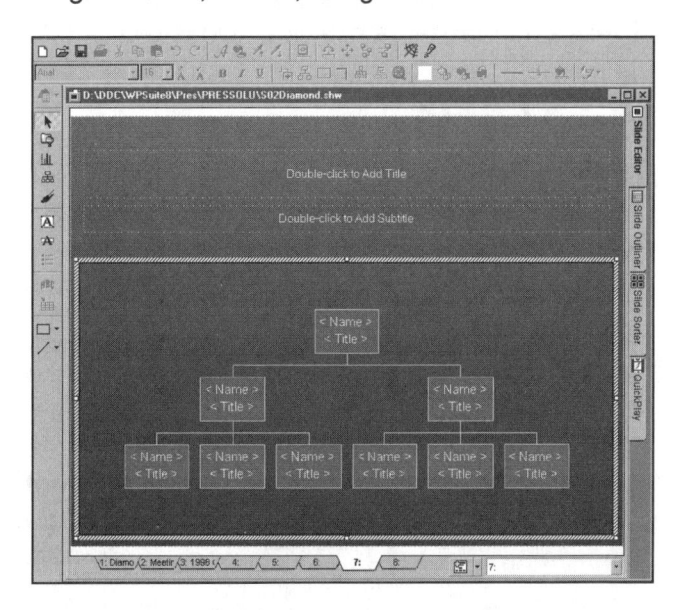

...ert boxes in order to change the ...onal structure. There are four box ...ach one attaches to existing boxes ...ently:

A **S̲ubordinate** attaches below another box because a subordinate is below another position in the chain of command.

- A **Co-w̲orker** attaches to the left or right of another box because a co-worker is a position of equal authority.

- A **M̲anager** attaches above another box because a manager is a position of higher authority.

- **S̲taff** does not attach to another box; it comes off another position.

■ To add a new box, click on an existing box and click the Subordinate button on the Org chart toolbar. Or, select the box type from the I̲nsert menu.

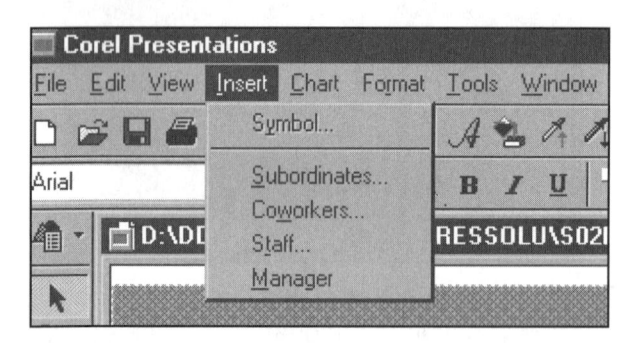

■ The number of lines you can enter in a box is dependent on font size and number of other boxes in the organization chart. You can type text continually; the box expands as you type. Press Enter to start a new line. Double-click the box placeholder and type the desired text to be added.

■ To change the box type, color (fill), or size, click the box to be affected, then click the appropriate formatting button on the Org Chart toolbar or Property Bar. To make several changes at once, click the Box Properties button on the Org Chart toolbar and select the desired options from the Box Properties dialog box.

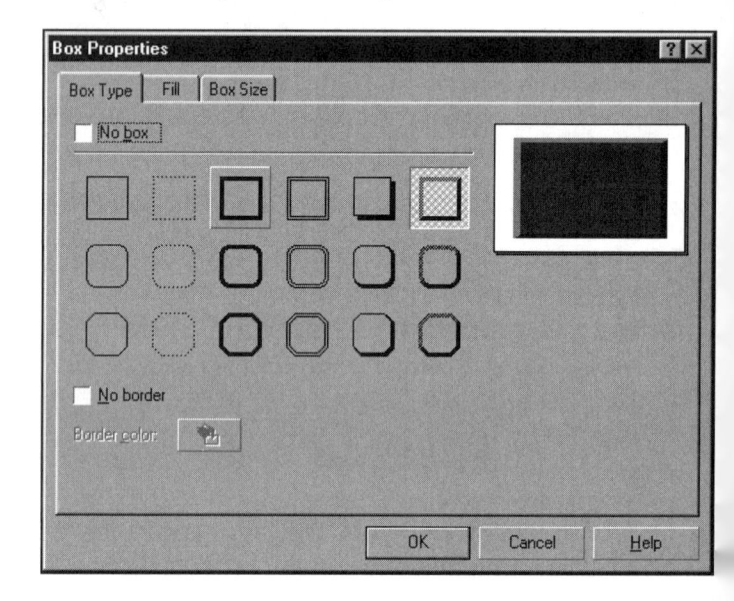

■ To delete a box, click the box, then press the Delete key.

■ To finish the chart, click anywhere outside the organization chart. To re-edit the organization chart (or the style of any of the boxes), double-click on it.

KEYSTROKES

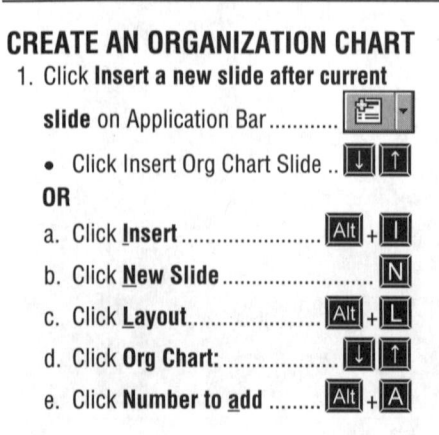

CREATE AN ORGANIZATION CHART

1. Click **Insert a new slide after current slide** on Application Bar............
    - Click Insert Org Chart Slide .. [↓][↑]
    OR
    a. Click **I̲nsert**............................[Alt]+[I]
    b. Click **N̲ew Slide**.......................[N]
    c. Click **L̲ayout**........................[Alt]+[L]
    d. Click **Org Chart:**...................[↓][↑]
    e. Click **Number to a̲dd**.........[Alt]+[A]

    f. Type number of slides to add.[↓][↑]
    g. Click **OK**............................[Enter]
2. Double-click placeholder.
3. Double-click each box to enter text.
4. To add boxes:
    a. Click box to select it.
    b. Click **Subordinate** button on the Property Bar........................
    OR
    - Click **I̲nsert**........................[Alt]+[I]
    - Click desired box type:
        S̲ubordinate............................[S]
        Cow̲orker.............................[W]
        S̲taff....................................[T]
        M̲anager..............................[M]
5. To change box properties (fill, box type and size):
    a. Click **Box Properties** button ...... on Toolbar.
    b. Make desired changes.
    c. Click **OK**............................[Enter]
6. Click outside organization chart to return to slide.

In this exercise, you will add an Org Chart and a Combination slide to a previously created slide show as well as rearrange the slide order.

EXERCISE DIRECTIONS

1. Open ▱SPORTS or ▱08SPORTS.
2. Add a new Org Chart slide as slide 6.
3. Enter the slide title and subtitle as shown in Illustration A below.
   a. Add one additional subordinate box under New Trainers and add the three trainer names (name) and locations (titles) in the boxes as shown.
   b. Delete the extra Subordinate boxes on the third level.
   c. Change the top box to black, the second level of boxes to red, and the third level to blue.
   ✓ Hold the Ctrl key while clicking the mouse to select multiple boxes.
   d. Change text size for each box to 24 points.
4. Add a new Combination slide as slide 7.
   a. Enter the slide title, subtitle and bullet text as shown in Illustration B below.
   b. Select Pie Chart as the Chart type and select the default format.
   c. Delete the data from the datasheet and enter the following new data:

Percentage of Active Membership Plans	
Associate	18%
Associate Plus	30%
Freedom	43%
Freedom Plus	9%

   ✓ Enter the Membership Plans in the Legend column as well as the Labels 1 column. Enter the data in the Pie 1 column.
5. Display all labels.
   Hint: Select the Inside, Percent option from the position tab of the Data Labels dialog box.
6. Switch to Slide Sorter view.
7. Move slide 5 (We're Expanding Every Day) to become slide 4.
8. Move slide 7 (Membership Plans) to become slide 5.
9. Print one copy as Handouts with 6 slides per page in black and white.
10. Close the file; save the changes.

ILLUSTRATION A

World Renowned Trainers Come to FPSC

Recent Guest Trainers Include:

- New Trainers
  - Libby Scala — New York, NY
    - Power Boxing
    - Pilates
  - Tim Sims — Golden, CO
    - Rockclimbing
    - Urban Defense
  - Kaila Douglas — Chicago, IL
    - Power Jazz
    - Yoga

ILLUSTRATION B

Membership Plans

Several Plans Available to Suit Your Personal Needs.

- Associate
  - Full access to one designated facility
- Associate Plus
  - Full access to one designated facility plus access to other facilities during off-peak hours.
- Freedom
  - Full access to ALL facilities.
- Freedom Plus
  - Full access to ALL facilities plus weekly complimentary spa treatments.

Percentage of Active Membership Plans
- Associate Plus 30.0%
- Associate 18.0%
- Freedom Plus 9.0%
- Freedom 43.0%

Legend:
- Associate
- Associate Plus
- Freedom
- Freedom Plus

PRESENTATIONS 8 Lesson 1: Create, Save, and Print Slides

Exercise 9

■ **Summary**

In this exercise, you will create a presentation in Outliner View. You will move the slides, change the background master for the slide show, and then print a handout of the slide show.

EXERCISE DIRECTIONS

1. Create a new slide show.
2. Select a Title layout for the first slide.
3. Use the default Master background.
4. Switch to Slide Outliner view and create the outline shown in Illustration A on the following page.
5. Switch the slide layout to Bulleted List beginning with slide 2.
6. Switch to Slide Editor view.
7. Display slide 1.
8. Change the background to SAND (found in the Nature category of the Master Gallery).
9. Select slide 4 and do the following:
   a. Change Slide layout to Data Chart.
   b. Add a table graph to the slide and insert the information shown in Illustration B on page 486.
   c. Set table font size to 20 points.
10. Select Slide 5 and do the following:
    a. Change Slide layout to Combination.
    b. Return to slide 4.
    c. Copy the top 5 Export countries and their 1998 dollar values (the Legend and "C" columns) from the datasheet.
    d. Paste the data in the slide 5 datasheet and create a Vertical Bar chart.
11. Switch to Slide Sorter view.
12. Move slide 5 to become slide 4.
13. Select slide 3 and change the layout to Title; delete the Subtitle placeholder.
14. Select slide 6 and change the layout to Title.
    ✓ Note that the bulleted items no longer display.
15. Change the layout for slide 6 back to Bulleted List.
16. Delete slide 8 (Stocks to Consider).
17. Display slide 8 (Under Evaluation) and insert a relevant graphic.
18. Insert a new Bulleted List slide after slide 8 (Under Evaluation) that reads:

    > Bonds
    > • Short term
    > • Long term

19. Insert a relevant graphic.
20. Switch to Slide Outliner view.
21. Spell check.
22. Switch to Slide Editor view.
23. Add a new Org Chart slide as slide 11, and enter the text and data as shown in Illustration C on page 486. Delete/Add boxes as necessary.
24. Switch to Slide Sorter view.
25. Move the new Org Chart slide to become slide 10.
26. Display slide 3 (Why Invest in the New Zealand Economy). Insert a relevant graphic.
27. Print one copy as Handouts with six slides per page in black and white.
28. Save the file; name it **INVEST**.
29. Close the slide show window.

ILLUSTRATION A

1. NEW ZEALAND
    Investment Opportunities
2. Brief History of New Zealand Economy
    - Government Deregulation in 1980s
        - Impacts on farming
        - Adjusting to a market-led economy
    - Recent Economic Reform
        - Reserve Bank Act brings inflation below 3%
3. Why Invest in the New Zealand Economy?
4. Tremendous Export Markets
    *Top 5 Performing Markets
    - Australia
    - Japan
    - USA
    - UK
    - Korea
5. Top 10 Export Markets
    Dollars in Millions for Years Ending: March 97 and March 98
6. Rising Export Regions
    Regions Displaying Growth Rates of Over 20%
    - Middle East
    - South East Asia
    - South Asia
    - Africa
7. Additional Economic Contribution
    Not To Be Overlooked When Investing!
    - Tourism
    - Textiles
    - Machinery
    - Manufacturing
    - Transportation equipment
    - Mining
    - Vineyards
8. Stocks to Consider
    - Cattle
    - Electronics
    - Yachting Equipment
9. Under Evaluation
    - Specific Stocks
    - Full Impact of Economic Reform
    - Current Impact of Government Deregulation
10. Conclusion
    - Reasons to Invest with Hartman Investment Inc.
        - Rate of return on investments
        - Global trading
        - Highly trained professionals
    - To Summarize...

ILLUSTRATION B

Top 10 Export Markets

Dollars in Millions for Years Ending: March 97 and March 98

COUNTRY	1997	% of Total	1998	% of Total	% CHANGE
Australia	4,001.7	20	4,099.6	19.8	2.4
Japan	3,119.7	15.6	3,088.4	14.9	-1
USA	1,893.2	9.4	2,294.3	11.1	21.2
UK	1,361.9	6.8	1,300.9	6.3	-4.5
Korea	956.4	4.8	817.6	4	-14.5
China	519.1	2.6	599	2.9	15.4
Hong Kong	609.2	3	579.7	2.8	-4.8
Taiwan	554.6	2.8	565.9	2.7	2
Germany	500.4	2.5	557.2	2.7	11.3
Malaysia	469.6	2.3	480.7	2.3	2.4

ILLUSTRATION C

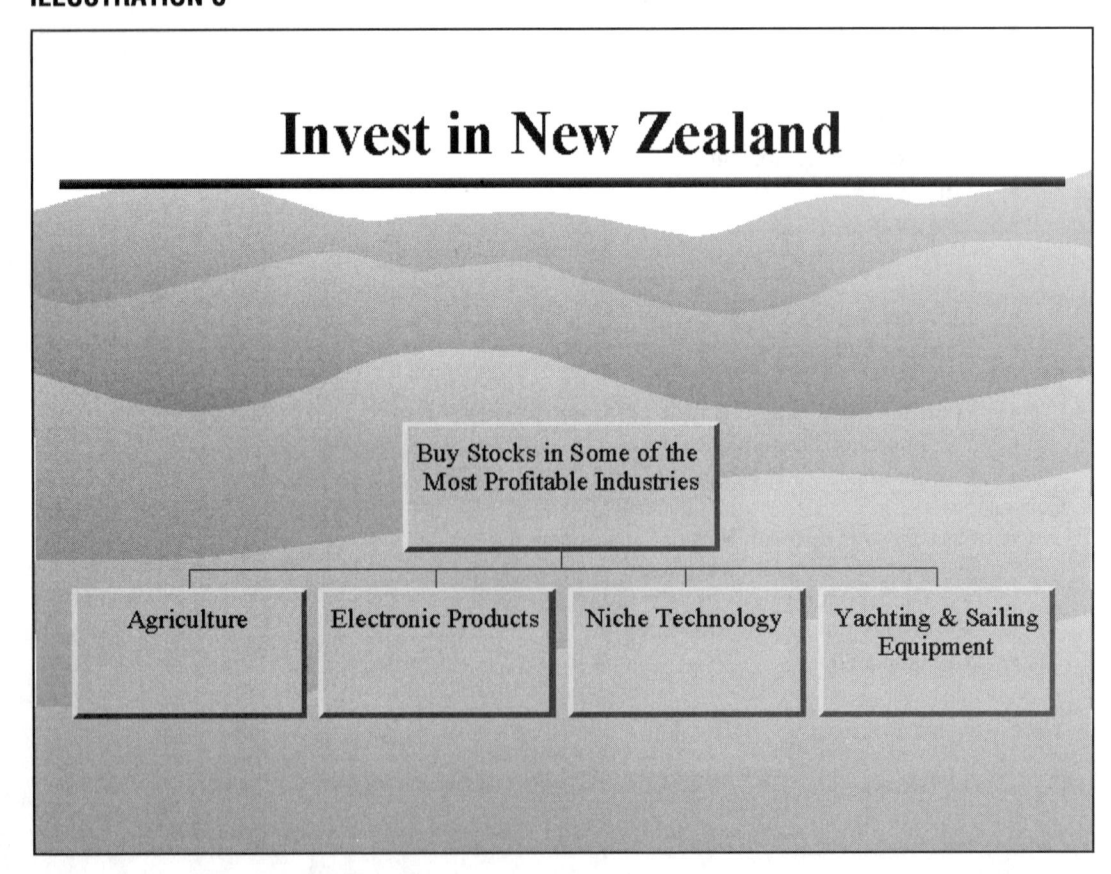

Invest in New Zealand

Buy Stocks in Some of the Most Profitable Industries

- Agriculture
- Electronic Products
- Niche Technology
- Yachting & Sailing Equipment

COREL PRESENTATIONS 8

Lesson 2: Edit and Enhance Slides

Exercise 10

- Select Text
- Align Text
- Change Text Appearance
- Copy and Move Text on a Slide
- Move and Size Placeholders

Property Bar

NOTES

Select Text

- In order to edit text on a slide, you must be in edit mode. To do so, double-click the text you wish to edit. The placeholder will then display with sizing handles, and the insertion point will change to an I-beam, ready for you to select the text you wish to edit. The same techniques for selecting text in WordPerfect 8 apply in Presentations 8:
    - Double-click to select a word.
    - Position the insertion point before the first word to select, hold down the Shift key and click at the end of the text you wish to select in order to highlight several words or a sentence.
    - Click and drag the mouse to highlight text.
- Text may be edited in Slide Editor or Outliner views; text *may not* be edited in Slide Sorter view.
- Some edits affect individual slides, and others affect all slides in a slide show. Changes affecting all slides in a slide show will be covered in Exercise 11.

Align Text

- Corel Presentations 8 lets you left-, right-, or center-justify text in a placeholder on individual slides or for all slides in the slide show. To change alignment, select Justification from the Format menu, then choose Left, Right, or Center. You can also change justification using the following keystrokes:

    - Left: Ctrl+L
    - Right: Ctrl+R
    - Center: Ctrl+E

- Use Slide Editor view to change text alignment because text formatting is displayed in this view.

Change Text Appearance

- Corel Presentations 8 allows you to change the text's font face, style, size, appearance (bold, underline, italic), and color using the same techniques learned in WordPerfect. To do so, select (highlight) the text you want to change and click the appropriate button on the Property Bar.

- To apply more than one change to text, select Font from the Format menu. In the Font Properties dialog box which follows, select the Font tab and make the desired changes.

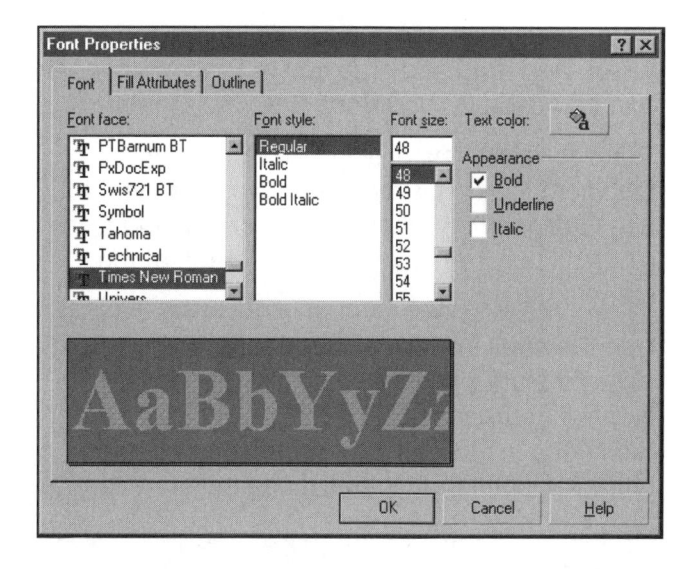

Corel Presentations 8 ■ Lesson 2 ■ Exercise 10

COREL PRESENTATIONS 8 Lesson 2: Edit and Enhance Slides

- To change the text color, click the Text color button and choose a desired font color from the displayed palette.

  ✓ *Note: Clicking the Foreground Fill Color button on the Property Bar will also change the font color.*

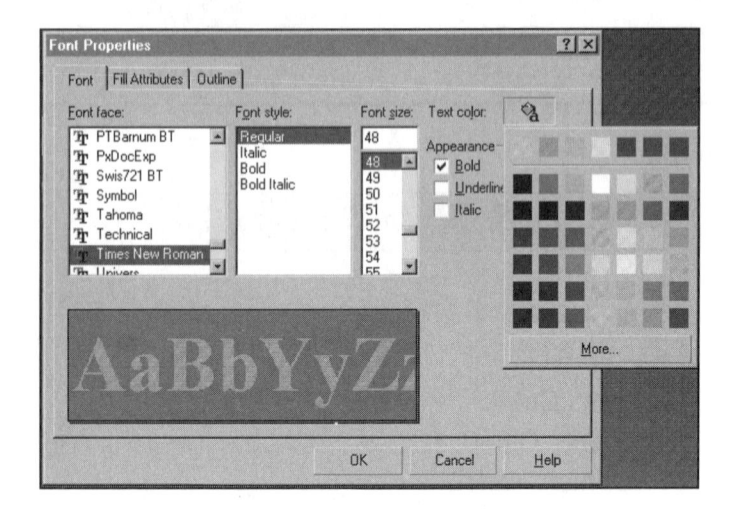

- You can also change the outline color and/or style, as well as the fill pattern of text. For example, you can create a yellow font with a blue outline. Or you can create a white font with a patterned fill. Be careful because some combinations make text difficult to read.

  • To change the text outline color, style, or fill, select the Fill Attributes and/or Outline tab. In the dialog boxes that follow, make the desired selections.

- Remember, text must first be selected in order to receive a format change.

Copy and Move Text on a Slide

- You can use the same methods to cut, copy, paste, and drag and drop text in Presentations 8 that you used in WordPerfect 8.

- You can move text only in Slide Editor or Outliner views. It is more efficient, however, to use Outliner view when moving or copying text since all text can be viewed on screen at the same time.

- Use the copy and paste procedures to copy text to more than one new location or to copy text to a different presentation. Use the drag and drop technique in Outliner view to move or copy text to a new location or to rearrange bulleted items.

- To move or copy an entire slide in Outliner view, point to the slide icon, then click and hold down the mouse button which will highlight all the items on the slide. Drag the highlighted text to the desired point of insertion. (You will see a horizontal red line positioned where you want to insert the text.) Release the mouse button and your text will drop into place.

- To move a bulleted item, point to the bullet you wish to move. When a double-headed arrow appears, click and hold down the mouse button to highlight the text, then drag it to the desired location. Again, you will see a horizontal red line positioned where you want to insert the text. Release the mouse button and your text will drop into place.

Move and Size Placeholders

- Placeholders can be moved, sized, and deleted.

- To move, size, or delete a placeholder, you must first display handles (to put the placeholder into edit mode).

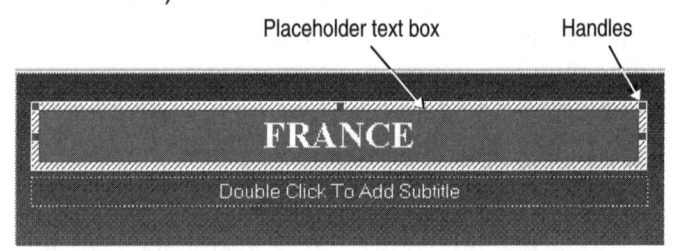

- Double-click the text to display handles and a placeholder box. You can then size the placeholder as you did when working with graphics: Drag a top or bottom middle handle to change the vertical size (height); drag a left or right middle handle to change the horizontal size (width); drag a corner handle to size the placeholder proportionally. When you size a placeholder, the text within it will adjust to the new borders.

  ✓ *If you click the placeholder once, Corel Presentations 8 displays handles without a placeholder box. Sizing the box in this mode will change the size of the text as well as the box. To change only the size of the box, you must double-click the text so that both the placeholder box and handles appears.*

- To move the placeholder box and its contents, double-click the text (to enter edit mode), place the pointer on the border (not on a handle), then click and hold the mouse button while dragging the box to a desired location.

488

In this exercise, you will insert an organization chart and a bubble chart slide to a previously created slide show. In addition, you will manipulate backgrounds and placeholders and change the size and color of text on slides. Check your changes with the Desired Result shown on page 491.

EXERCISE DIRECTIONS

1. Open ⌨**CALIBER** or 💾**10CALIBER**.
2. Add a new Org Chart slide after slide 8 (Weekly CCUG Meetings), as shown in Illustration A on the following page.
   a. Add subordinate boxes to include the information shown.
   b. Color the title red.
   c. Delete/Add boxes as necessary.
   d. Enter text into the boxes using an 18-point font.
   e. Size the Org Chart placeholder to make it as wide as possible (without extending it past the slide borders).
3. Add a new Data Chart slide after slide 9 using a Bubble Chart option as shown in Illustration B on the following page:
   - Delete the data from the datasheet and enter the new data shown below.

POSITION	Jan	Feb	March
Graphic Designers	72	68	92
Web Designers	31	47	62
Office Professionals	110	115	121
Multimedia Designers	12	42	75

   ✓ *Because you will not need all the columns and rows in the datasheet, highlight the row and/or column you do not need and select Exclude Row/Col from the Data menu.*

4. Insert a new Title slide as slide 11.
   a. Add the following text:
      Don't let the learning pass you by!
      Call a CCUG representative today at
      1-800-555-CCUG
   b. Set the font to 44 points and extend the title placeholder so that all title text fits on one line.
   c. Set the subtitle text to 36 points.
   d. Change the color of the telephone number to yellow.
5. Move slide 7 (New Levels of classes) to become slide 5.
6. Change titles in all slides, except the first Title slide, to upper- and lower-case.

7. Display slide 4 (Classes Available).
   a. Left-align the title text as shown in the Desired Result illustrated on page 491.
   b. Change the title to a 48-point decorative font.
   c. Right-align the subtitle text.
   d. Edit the fourth bullet of text to read:
      Desktop Design
   e. Add the following class to the class list:
      Multimedia Production
8. Display slide 5 (New Levels of Classes).
   a. Change the background to Green (found in the Colors category).
   b. Adjust the Bulleted List placeholder and graphic, if necessary.
9. Display slide 9 (Fall Schedule).
   a. Set the subtitle placeholder text to a 32-point decorative font.
   b. Raise the bulleted list placeholder, if necessary.
10. Display slide 10 (Fall Schedule).
    a. Edit the title as follows:
       Spring Schedule
    b. Edit the first line of bulleted text as follows:
       Web Page Design 1
    c. Set the subtitle placeholder text to a 32-point decorative font.
    d. Raise the bulleted list placeholder, if necessary.
11. Move slides 6 (Fall Schedule) and 7 (Spring Schedule) to become slides 9 and 10.
12. Switch to Outliner view.
13. Spell Check.
14. Switch to Slide Sorter view.
15. Check slide order with the Desired Result illustrated on page 491.
16. Switch to Slide Editor view.
17. Print one copy as Handouts with six slides per page in black and white.
18. Close the file; save the changes.

Corel Presentations 8 ■ Lesson 2 ■ Exercise 10

COREL PRESENTATIONS 8 Lesson 2: Edit and Enhance Slides

ILLUSTRATION A

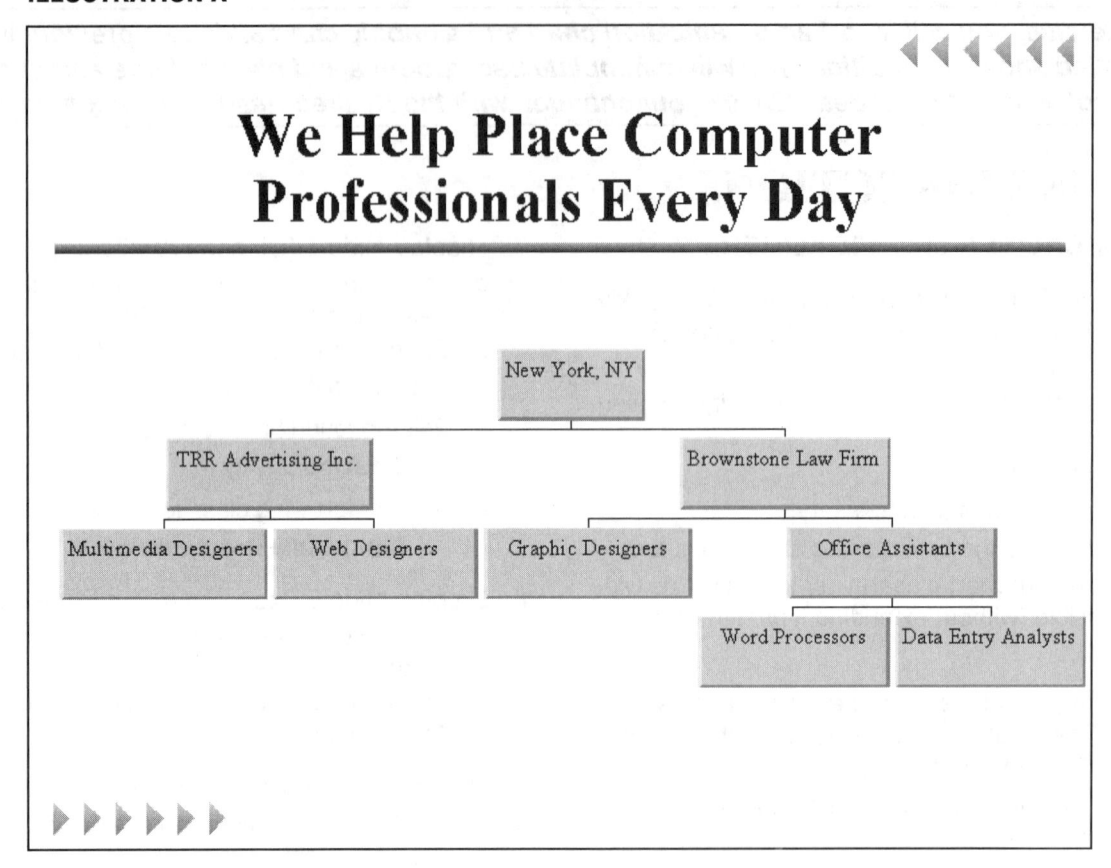

We Help Place Computer Professionals Every Day

- New York, NY
  - TRR Advertising Inc.
    - Multimedia Designers
    - Web Designers
  - Brownstone Law Firm
    - Graphic Designers
    - Office Assistants
      - Word Processors
      - Data Entry Analysts

ILLUSTRATION B

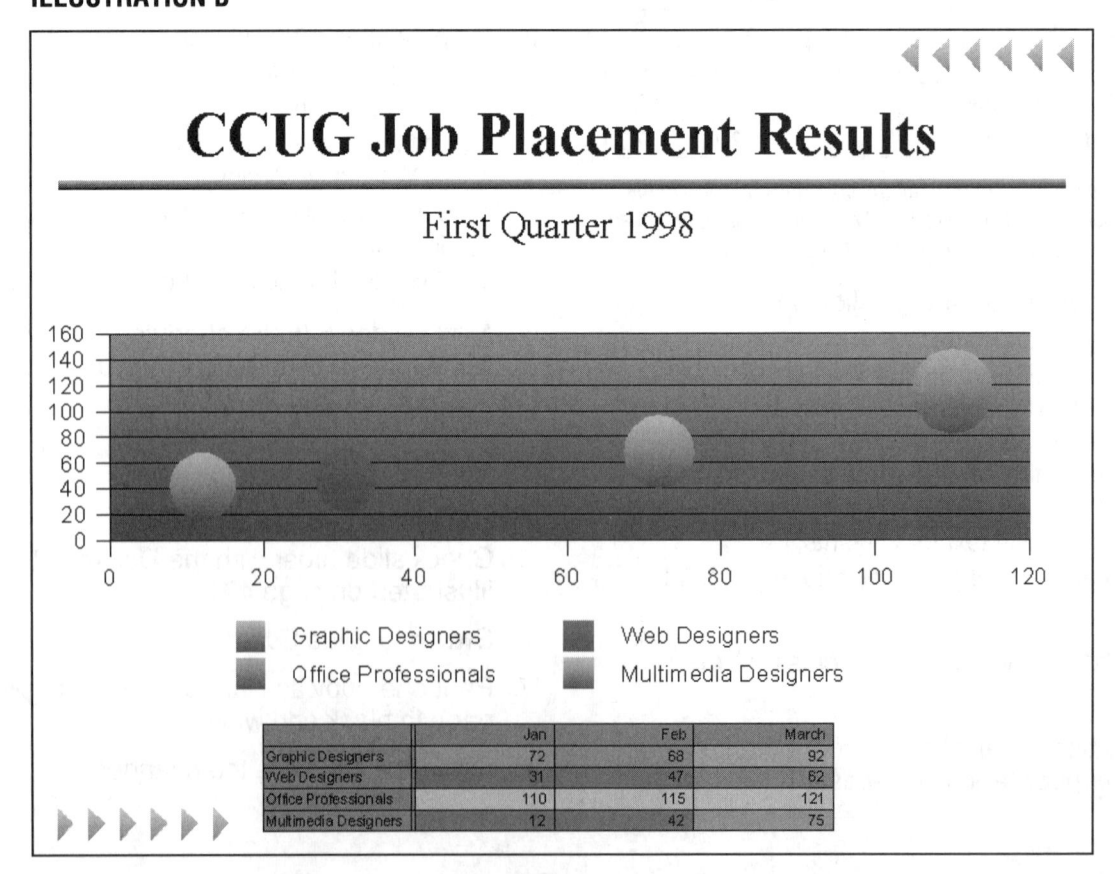

CCUG Job Placement Results

First Quarter 1998

Legend:
- Graphic Designers
- Web Designers
- Office Professionals
- Multimedia Designers

	Jan	Feb	March
Graphic Designers	72	68	92
Web Designers	31	47	62
Office Professionals	110	115	121
Multimedia Designers	12	42	75

DESIRED RESULT

1

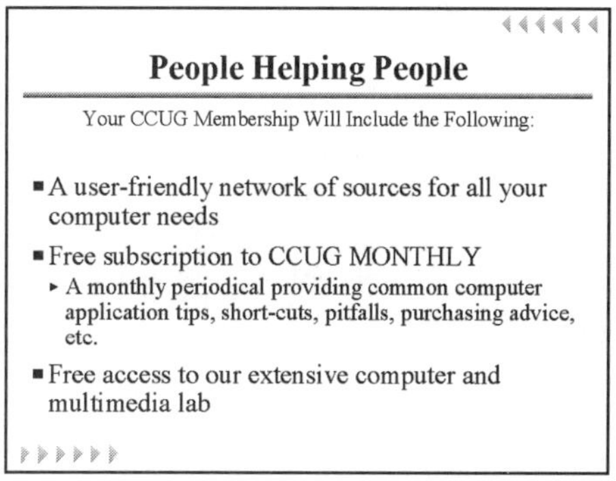

Caliber Computer User Group

Lisa Scully, President

2

People Helping People

Your CCUG Membership Will Include the Following:

- A user-friendly network of sources for all your computer needs
- Free subscription to CCUG MONTHLY
  - A monthly periodical providing common computer application tips, short-cuts, pitfalls, purchasing advice, etc.
- Free access to our extensive computer and multimedia lab

3

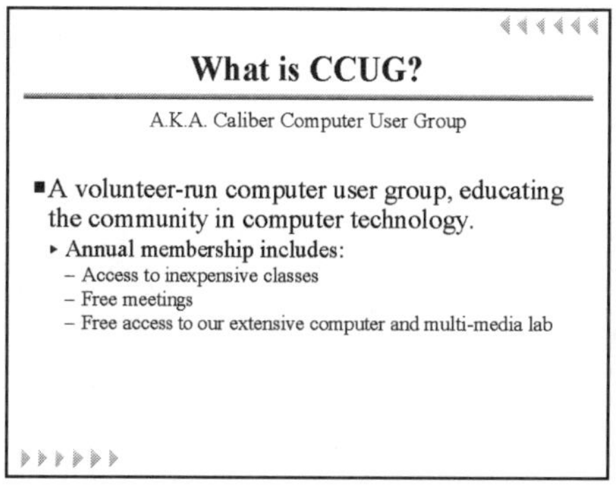

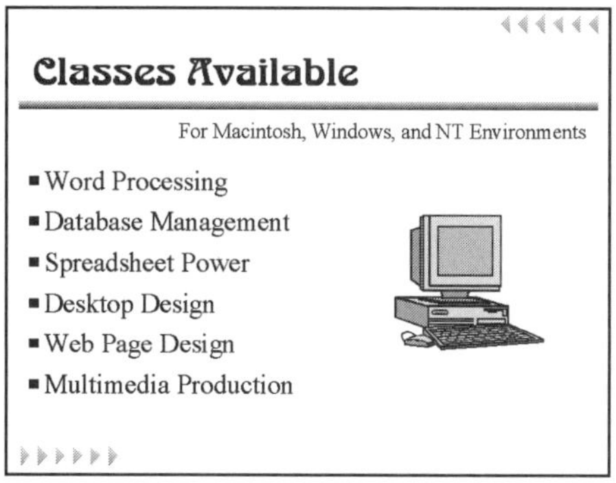

What is CCUG?

A.K.A. Caliber Computer User Group

- A volunteer-run computer user group, educating the community in computer technology.
  - Annual membership includes:
    – Access to inexpensive classes
    – Free meetings
    – Free access to our extensive computer and multi-media lab

---

4

Classes Available

For Macintosh, Windows, and NT Environments

- Word Processing
- Database Management
- Spreadsheet Power
- Desktop Design
- Web Page Design
- Multimedia Production

5

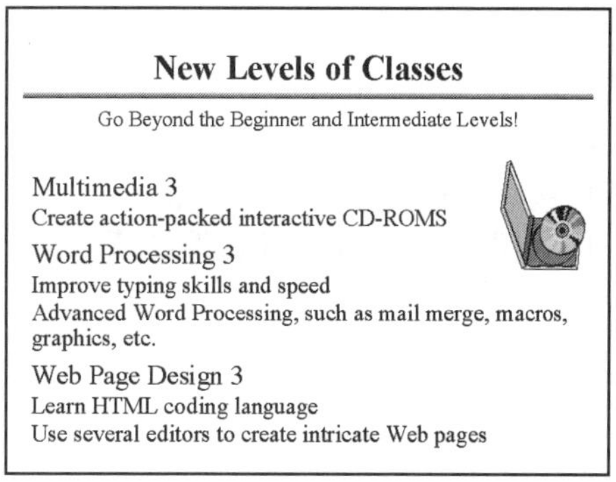

New Levels of Classes

Go Beyond the Beginner and Intermediate Levels!

Multimedia 3
Create action-packed interactive CD-ROMS

Word Processing 3
Improve typing skills and speed
Advanced Word Processing, such as mail merge, macros, graphics, etc.

Web Page Design 3
Learn HTML coding language
Use several editors to create intricate Web pages

6

Weekly SIG Meetings

Valuable Door Prizes Awarded!

- Every Wednesday at 7:00 p.m.
- Topics include:
  - Demos of popular new software and hardware
  - Introduction of new technology
  - Discussion panels regarding popular software
- Meetings hosted by:
  - Popular vendors
  - Computer and multimedia professionals
  - CCUG President, Lisa Scully

7

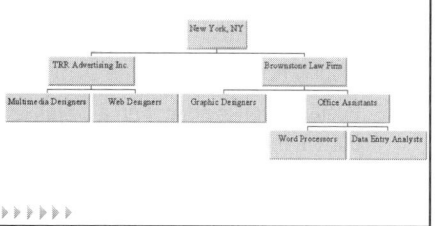

We Help Place Computer Professionals Every Day

(Organizational chart: New York, NY; TRR Advertising Inc.; Brownstone Law Firm; Multimedia Designers; Web Designers; Graphic Designers; Office Assistants; Word Processors; Data Entry Analysts)

8

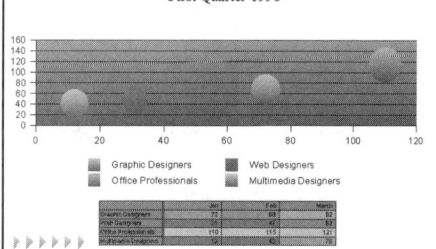

CCUG Job Placement Results

First Quarter 1998

(Bar chart showing Graphic Designers, Web Designers, Office Professionals, Multimedia Designers)

9

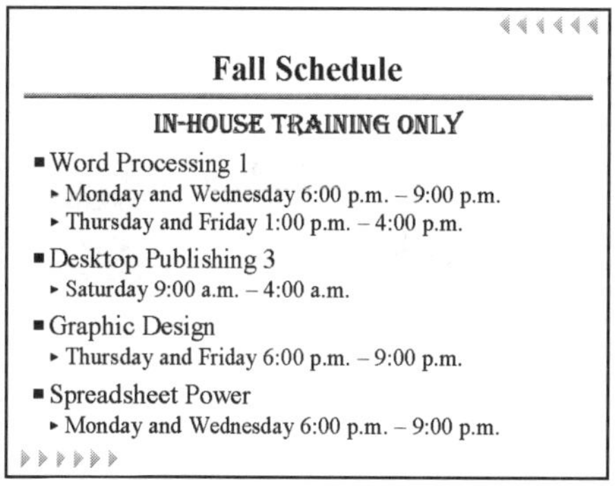

Fall Schedule

IN-HOUSE TRAINING ONLY

- Word Processing 1
  - Monday and Wednesday 6:00 p.m. – 9:00 p.m.
  - Thursday and Friday 1:00 p.m. – 4:00 p.m.
- Desktop Publishing 3
  - Saturday 9:00 a.m. – 4:00 a.m.
- Graphic Design
  - Thursday and Friday 6:00 p.m. – 9:00 p.m.
- Spreadsheet Power
  - Monday and Wednesday 6:00 p.m. – 9:00 p.m.

10

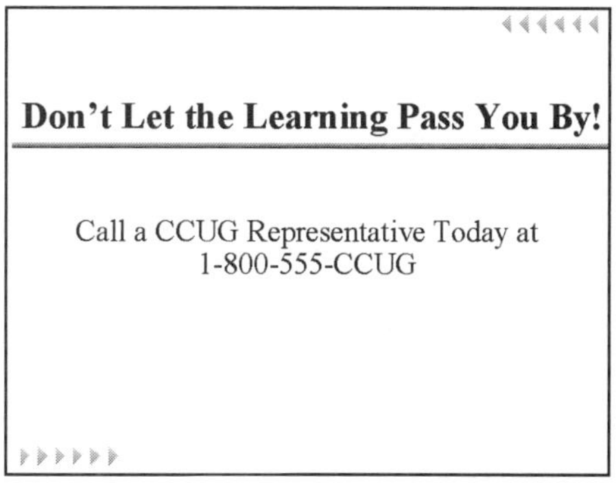

Spring Schedule

IN-HOUSE TRAINING ONLY

- Web Page Design 1
  - Monday and Wednesday 6:00 p.m. – 9:00 p.m.
  - Thursday and Friday 1:00 p.m. – 4:00 p.m.
- Desktop Publishing 3
  - Saturday 9:00 a.m. – 4:00 a.m.
- Graphic Design
  - Thursday and Friday 6:00 p.m. – 9:00 p.m.
- Spreadsheet Power
  - Monday and Wednesday 6:00 p.m. – 9:00 p.m.

11

Don't Let the Learning Pass You By!

Call a CCUG Representative Today at
1-800-555-CCUG

COREL PRESENTATIONS 8 Lesson 2: Edit and Enhance Slides

KEYSTROKES

CHANGE FONT

F9

1. Select text to change.
2. Click **Font** button on Property Bar.... `Arial`
3. Click new font............................. ↓ ↑

OR

1. Click Fo**r**mat....................... `Alt`+`R`
2. Click **F**ont .... `F`
3. Select desired font and options..... ↓ ↑
4. Click **OK**................................. `Enter`

CHANGE FONT SIZE

F9

1. Select text to change.
2. Click **Font Size** drop-down list on Property Bar...................... `48`
   - Select desired font size.

OR

- Click Fo**r**mat....................... `Alt`+`R`
- Click **F**ont .... `F`
3. Select desired font size.............. ↓ ↑
4. Click **OK**................................. `Enter`

CHANGE EMPHASIS (BOLD, ITALIC, SHADOW, UNDERLINE, COLOR)

F9

1. Select text to affect.
2. Click desired attribute.......... **B** *I* U buttons on Property Bar.

OR

- Click Fo**r**mat....................... `Alt`+`R`
- Click **F**ont .... `F`
3. Select desired options .... ↓ ↑
4. Click **OK**................................. `Enter`

EDIT PLACEHOLDERS

To display handles:

- Click once on text to display handles and placeholders box.
- Double-click inside the text placeholder box to display placeholder.

To move:

1. Display handles.
2. Position mouse pointer on border (not on a handle).
3. Hold down left mouse button and drag text to new location.
4. Release mouse button.

To copy:

1. Display handles.
2. Position mouse pointer on border (not on a handle).
3. Press **Ctrl** and position mouse pointer on border (not on a handle).
4. Hold mouse button and drag text to new location.
5. Release mouse button.

To size:

1. Display handles.
2. Position mouse pointer on a top or bottom middle handle to change height, a left or right handle to change width, or a corner handle to change size proportionately.
3. Drag the handle until the placeholder is the desired size.

To delete:

1. Display handles.
2. Press **Delete**.

COREL PRESENTATIONS 8 Lesson 2: Edit and Enhance Slides

Exercise 11

- Customize the Slide Background
- Customize the Layout
- Customize Bulleted List Slides

NOTES

Customize the Slide Background

- In the previous exercise, you learned to make editing changes that affect individual slides. You can, however, edit one slide and have the changes appear on all slides in a slide show.

- To change the background color, add Clipart or a logo and have it affect all slides in a slide show, you must make the changes to the slide show's **Background Layer**. To insert a graphic that will appear on slides, for example, select Background Layer from the Edit menu. Select Graphics, Clipart from Insert menu and position the image on the slide as desired. Then, select Slide Layer from the Edit menu to return to the Slide Layer. The graphic will now appear on all slides in your slide show, regardless of the type of layout being used (Bulleted List, Data Chart, etc.).

Customize the Layout

- To change the font style, font size, color, and/or position of text or placeholders so that they affect all the slides of a particular layout (Title, Bulleted List, Data Chart, etc.), you must make changes to the Layout Layer. For example, if you wish to change the layout of a Bulleted List slide, display a Bulleted List slide, then select Layout Layer from the Edit menu and make any desired changes. If you right-align the title placeholder, all Bulleted List slides in the active slide show will display right-aligned placeholder text. If you change the title text color to red on a Data Chart slide, it will affect the text color on all Data Chart slides. Use the same procedures to edit text as you did in the previous exercise, but remember, any change you make to the template will affect all slides.

- Text formatted on separate slides override changes made on the layout layer.

- After making the desired changes on the Background or Layout Layers, return to Slide Layer and view each slide in the slide show to see its effects. You may need to make adjustments to the Background or Layout Layer after seeing the effects on individual slides.

Customize Bulleted List Slides

- Bulleted List slides contain several parts which can be modified. For example, you can change the appearance and spacing of text and bullets, as well as the box around the bulleted text. (The default option displays no box around the bulleted text.)

  - To make modifications to bulleted lists, click on the bulleted text placeholder, then click the Bulleted List Properties button on the Property Bar or select Bulleted List Properties from the Format menu. In the Bulleted List Properties dialog box which follows, select the Fonts tab to make font changes to bulleted text.

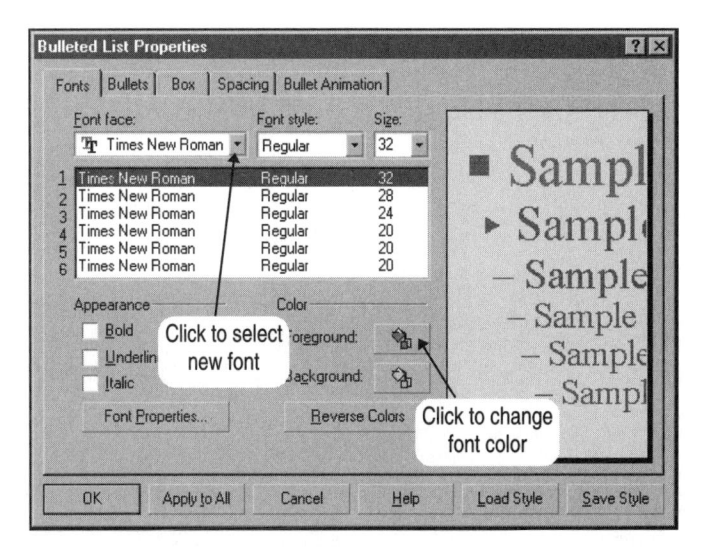

- To change the bullet shape or justification, select the Bullets tab. To select a bullet shape for *all* bullet levels, click the Bullet set drop-down menu and select a set of bullet shapes. To select a bullet style for *individual levels*, select the desired level number you wish to change, then click the Bullet Shapes drop-down list and select a shape. If you select the Other option from the Bullet Shapes, you can create a bullet using the WordPerfect Symbols.

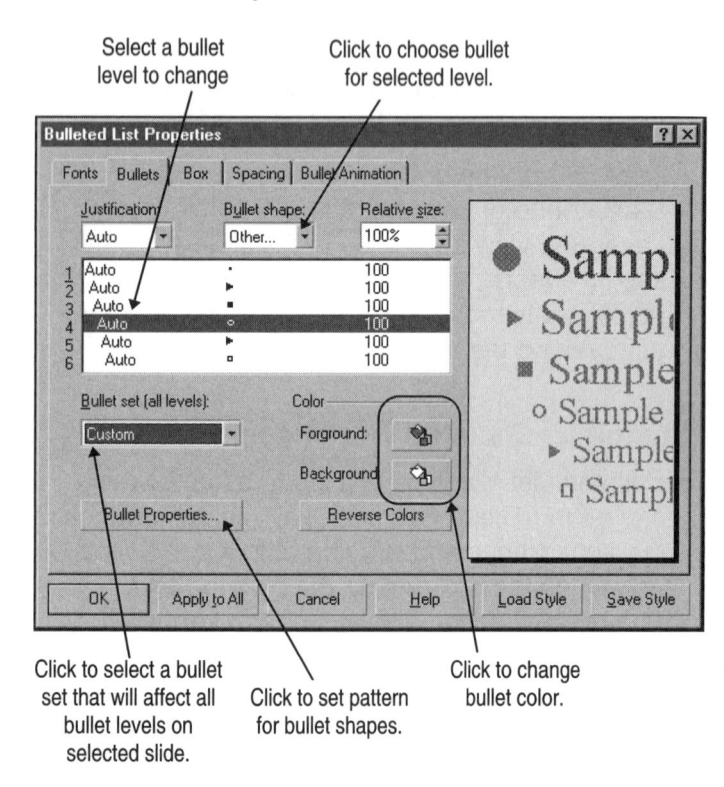

- Click the Box Attributes tab to change the box shape and fill attributes of the box surrounding the bulleted text.

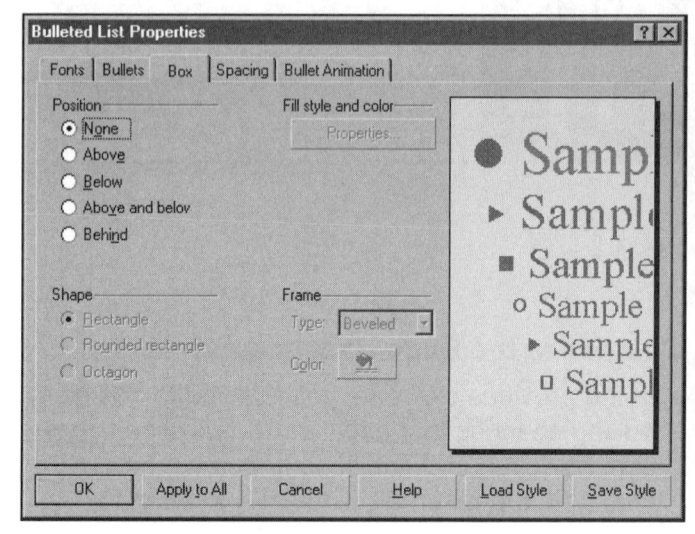

- Click the Bullet Spacing tab to adjust spacing from the bullet to the text and line spacing between bulleted text items.

  ✓Note: The Bullet Animation tab will be discussed in Exercise 15.

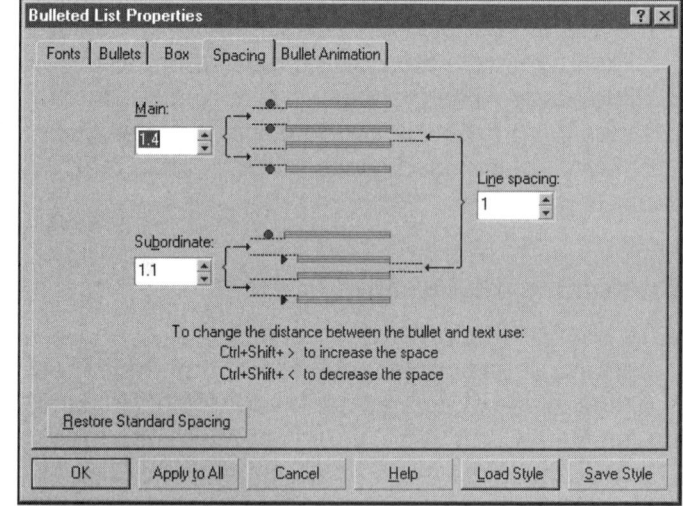

In this exercise, you will edit the Background and Layout Layers by adding a graphic and changing the bulleted list options. Note that all slides in the slide show will be affected.

EXERCISE DIRECTIONS

1. Open **SPORTS** or **11SPORTS**.
2. Change the background master to dark blue (located in the Color category).
3. Edit the background layer by inserting a relevant graphic in the top left corner of the slide. Size it according to Illustration A below.
4. Edit the layout of the Title slide.
   a. Left-align the Title placeholder.
   b. Right-align the Subtitle placeholder.
5. Switch to Slide View.
6. Display slide 1.
   ✓ Note the layout change.
7. Edit the subtitle to read:
   Boston's Number One Fitness Center
8. Switch to Slide Sorter view. Adjust the placeholders as follows:
   ✓ The newly inserted background graphic may be crowding the title and/or subtitle of certain slides.
   a. Click on any Bulleted List slide.
   b. Adjust the Layout Layer so that the Title and Subtitle placeholders are right-aligned.
9. Display slide 5 (Membership Plans).
   • Adjust the Layout Layer so that the Title and Subtitle placeholders are shortened and right-aligned as shown on the Desired Result illustration on pages 496 and 497.
10. Display slide 7 (World Renowned Trainers Come to FPSC).
    • Adjust the placeholders to avoid crowding.
11. Display slide 3 (FPSC's High Success Rate).
    a. Change the first level bullet to a yellow star.
    b. Change the second level bullet to a red star.
12. Insert a new Table Chart slide as slide 8.
    a. Enter the slide title and subtitle information as shown in Illustration B on page 496.
    b. Enter the spa information into the datasheet.
    c. Change the table text to a 24-point font.
    d. Adjust the placeholders as needed so that text does not overlap the background graphic.
13. Print one copy as Handouts with four slides per page in black and white.
14. Close the file; save the changes.

ILLUSTRATION A

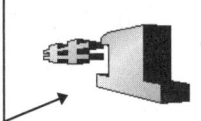

Insert a graphic on background layer.

Fair Play Sports Club

Boston's Number One Fitness Center

COREL PRESENTATIONS 8 Lesson 2: Edit and Enhance Slides

ILLUSTRATION B

Full-Service Salon
Open Seven Days a Week

Pamper Yourself!

	Hair Salon	Massage	Accupressure	Facials
Monday	10 to 8	2 to 10	10 to 10	2 to 10
Tuesday	10 to 6	2 to 10	10 to 10	2 to 10
Wednesday	Noon to 9	2 to 10	10 to 10	2 to 10
Thursday	Noon to 9	2 to 10	10 to 10	2 to 10
Friday	10 to 10	10 to 10	10 to 5	2 to 8
Saturday	Noon to 8	10 to 6	10 to 6	Noon to 8
Sunday	12 to 8	Noon to 5	Noon to 5	Noon to 5

DESIRED RESULT (Slides 1-4)

Slide 1

Fair Play Sports Club

Boston's Number One Fitness Center

Slide 2

FPSC is More Than Just a Gym

We're a Professional Fitness Complex.

★ Professional Fitness Staff and Personal Trainers
★ Classes on the Hour, Every Hour
★ Spa Facility
★ Swimming Pool
★ Rock Climbing Wall
★ Health and Juice Bar

Slide 3

FPSC's High Success Rate

Why More People are Working Out With Us:

★ People want more activity choices.
  ★ Traditional aerobics can be boring.
  ★ Doing the same activity daily can cause repetitive injuries.
★ Our workout equipment is top of the line.
  ★ Updated once a year, or sooner when needed.
  ★ We have more equipment than any fitness center in the New England area.
  ★ Our guarantee: you'll never have to wait in line.

Slide 4

We're Expanding Every Day

Clubs Opening Soon In:

★ Dover
★ Brookline
★ Foxwood
★ Watertown
★ Wellesley
★ Natick

Desired Result continued on next page ➡

DESIRED RESULT (Slides 5-8)

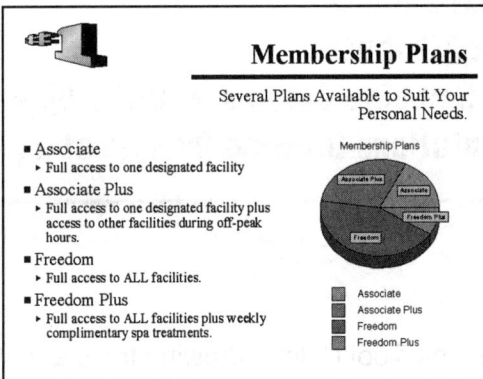

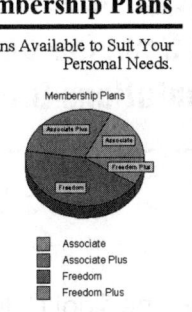

[Slide 5: Membership Plans — Several Plans Available to Suit Your Personal Needs]
- Associate
  - Full access to one designated facility
- Associate Plus
  - Full access to one designated facility plus access to other facilities during off-peak hours.
- Freedom
  - Full access to ALL facilities.
- Freedom Plus
  - Full access to ALL facilities plus weekly complimentary spa treatments.

(Pie chart: Membership Plans — Associate, Associate Plus, Freedom, Freedom Plus)

[Slide 6: Our Professional Staff Means Business — You're Not Alone at FPSC]
- ★ 20 staff members on the floor at all times
- ★ Class limit of 1 instructor per 15 students
- ★ Bi-monthly health readings:
  - ★ Cholesterol readings
  - ★ Body fat and muscle mass analysis.
  - ★ Nutrition advice
- ★ Once a month free private training sessions
  - ★ Additional sessions available at a nominal fee

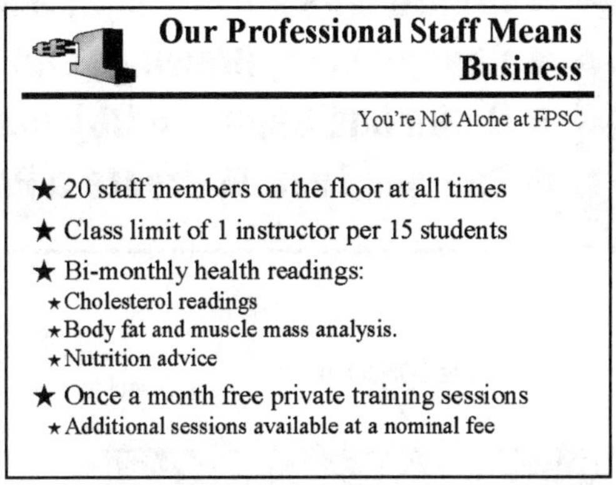

[Slide 7: World Renowned Trainers Come to FPSC — Recent Guest Trainers Include:]

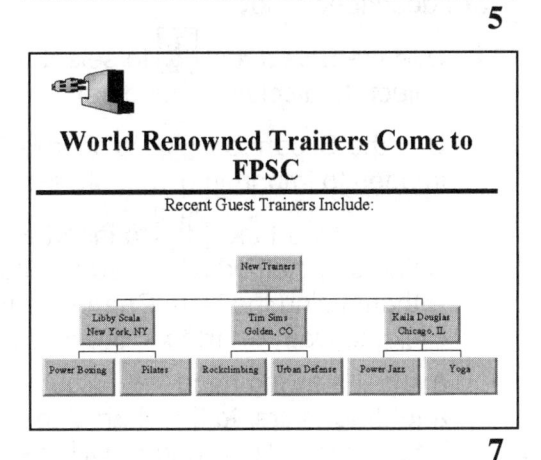

(Org chart: New Trainers → Libby Scala (New York, NY), Tim Sims (Golden, CO), Kaila Douglas (Chicago, IL) → Power Boxing, Pilates, Rockclimbing, Urban Defense, Power Jazz, Yoga)

[Slide 8: Full-Service Salon Open Seven Days a Week — Pamper Yourself!]

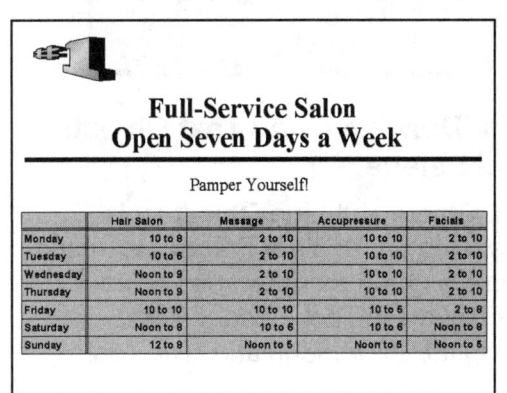

	Hair Salon	Massage	Accupressure	Facials
Monday	10 to 8	2 to 10	10 to 10	2 to 10
Tuesday	10 to 6	2 to 10	10 to 10	2 to 10
Wednesday	Noon to 9	2 to 10	10 to 10	2 to 10
Thursday	Noon to 9	2 to 10	10 to 10	2 to 10
Friday	10 to 10	10 to 10	10 to 5	2 to 8
Saturday	Noon to 8	10 to 6	10 to 6	Noon to 8
Sunday	12 to 8	Noon to 5	Noon to 5	Noon to 5

KEYSTROKES

CUSTOMIZE SLIDE BACKGROUND

1. Click **E**dit .... Alt + E
2. Click **B**ackground Layer .... B
3. Make any additions (add a graphic, if desired).
4. Click **E**dit .... Alt + E
5. Click Slide La**y**er .... Y

CUSTOMIZE LAYOUT

1. Display a slide containing layout you wish to customize (Title, Bulleted List, Data Chart, etc.).
2. Click **E**dit .... Alt + E
3. Click Lay**o**ut Layer .... O
4. Make desired changes.
5. Click **E**dit .... Alt + E
6. Click Slide La**y**er .... Y

✓ To change bullet format on a Bulleted Chart slide, follow steps below.

CHANGE BULLET STYLE

1. Display slide containing a Bulleted List layout.
2. Click once to select the bulleted list placeholder or select individual bulleted items.
3. Click the **Bulleted List Properties** button on the Property Bar.

   OR

   a. Click Fo**r**mat .... Alt + R
   b. Click Bulleted List Prop**e**rties ..... E

4. Click one of the following tabs and make the desired changes:
   - **Fonts** to change font attributes.
   - **Bullets** to change bullet style and/or color.
   - **Box** to add and/or enhance the box around bulleted text.
   - **Spacing** to change line spacing between bulleted items.

5. Click **OK** .... Enter

   OR

   Click Apply **t**o all .... Alt + T
   to apply changes to all
   Bulleted Lists in the current slide show.

Corel Presentations 8 ■ Lesson 2 ■ Exercise 11

COREL PRESENTATIONS 8 Lesson 2: Edit and Enhance Slides

Exercise 12

- Create Lines, Drawings, and Text Objects
- Change Line, Drawing, and Text Attributes
- Group and Separate Objects ■ Combine Objects ■ Order Objects
- Contour Text ■ Create a Presentations Drawing Outside of a Slide Show

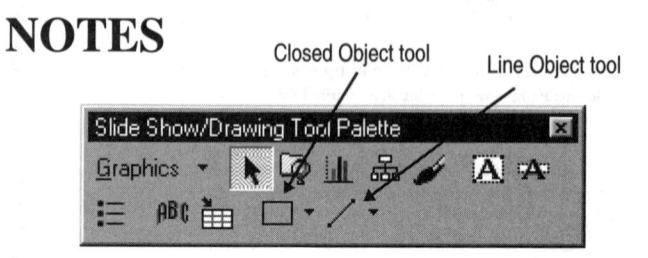

NOTES

Create Lines, Drawings, and Text Objects with the Tool Palette

- The **Closed Object** and **Line Object** tools, which are located on the **Tool Palette**, are used to create simple designs or drawings on your slides. To display the Tool Palette, select Toolbars from the View menu and click Tool Palette.

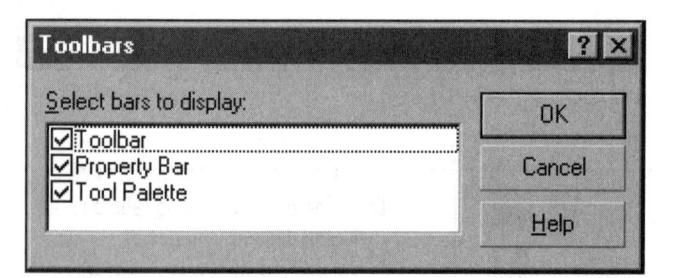

- Drawings created using the Tool Palette are considered graphic objects. Graphic objects include lines, shapes, and freehand designs. Closed shapes may be filled with a color or a pattern.

- Text added to slides thus far has been entered into placeholders. Using the Text Box or Text Line tools on the Tool Palette to add text to a slide creates a separate object that can be moved, sized, deleted, etc. without affecting the layout.

- To draw an object or text box, click the desired object tool on the Tool Palette. The insertion point changes to a crosshair (+). Position the crosshair where you want to create the object; click and drag the crosshair to the point where you want to end the object. To display object handles, click the Select tool and click the object.

- The Tool Palette drawing tools and their uses are described below:

  - Use the Select tool to select a graphic object (to display its handles).

  - Use the Clipart tool to access Clipart images to import into your slides.

  - Use the Chart tool to insert a data chart. Using this method allows you to insert a chart without using the Data Chart layout. After you click the Data Chart tool, the cursor changes to a small drawing hand. You can then click and drag to create the chart size you desire. The Chart Gallery window will open. You can use the same techniques learned in Exercise 6 to complete the chart.

  - Use the Bitmap tool to create or edit a bitmap image. A bitmap image is comprised of small dots or pixels. Working with Bitmap images will not be covered in this book.

  - Use the Text box tool to drag to create a text box object onto a slide.

  - Use the Text Line tool to enter a single line of text anywhere on a slide.

  - Use the Bulleted List tool to create a bulleted list on any slide, without using the Bulleted List layout.

  - Use the TextArt tool to create a TextArt image on any slide. This feature works this same in Presentations as it does within WordPerfect.

- Use Closed Object tools ▭ to create rectangles with square or round corners, circles, arrows, ellipsis, polygons, closed curves, arrow shapes, or polygons with equal sides.

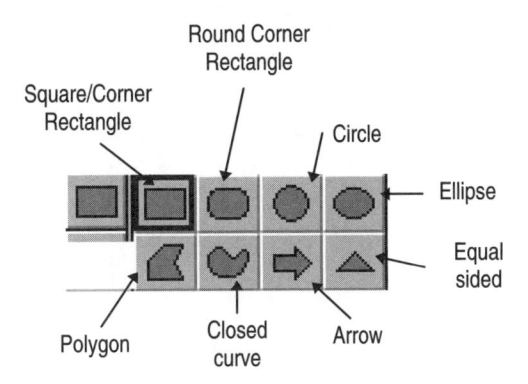

- Use Line Object tools ╱ to draw straight or curved lines, freehand lines or shapes, bezier curves, sections of ellipses or sections of circles.

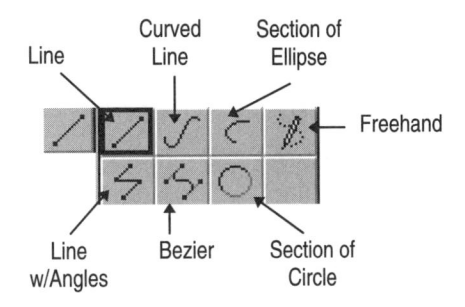

Change Line, Drawing, and Text Attributes

■ Once a line, drawing, or text object is created and selected, the buttons on the Property Bar change to accommodate the attributes of the selected graphics object.

   ✓Note: *Line attributes can change the appearance for lines themselves or for the lines surrounding objects or text.*

- Use the Shadow button to add a shadow effect to a line, a drawing, or text.

- Use the Rotation button to select a rotation amount for a line, drawing, or a text box.

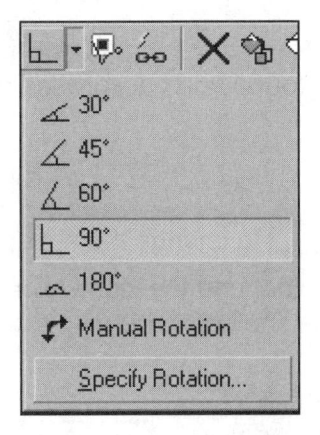

- Use the Fill Patterns button to change the fill pattern of objects and text. (Fill patterns do not apply to lines in Presentations 8)

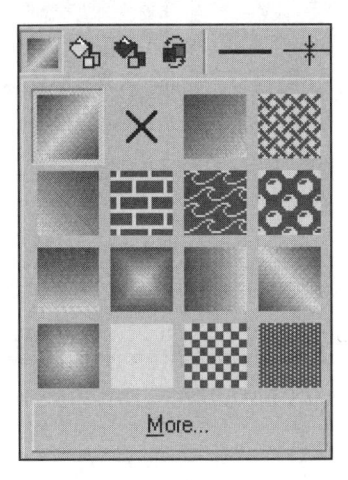

- Use the Foreground Fill Color button to adjust the color and patterns of a drawing or of selected text.

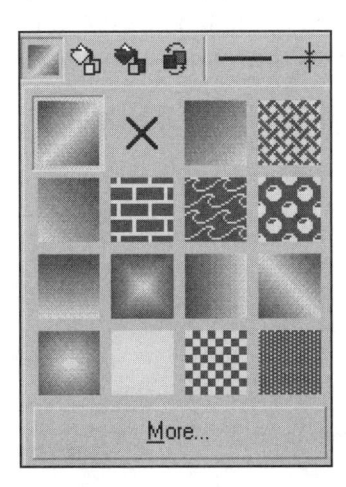

- Use the Background Fill Color button to adjust the background color of a pattern used within a drawing.

COREL PRESENTATIONS 8 Lesson 2: Edit and Enhance Slides

- Use the Reverse Colors button to reverse the foreground and background colors of a drawing.

- Use the Line Width button and Line Style button to change the appearance of a selected line, and the Line Color button to adjust the line color.

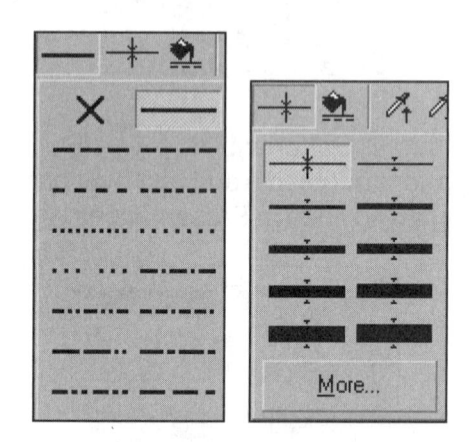

- Use the Get Attributes button to copy all of the attributes of the current selection.

- Use the Apply Attributes button to apply the copied attributes to another object.

- Use the Select Object View button to view the object in a separate window and on the slide simultaneously.

- Use the Fill Attribute button to access the Fill Properties dialog box, which enables you to set several drawing or line attributes at once.

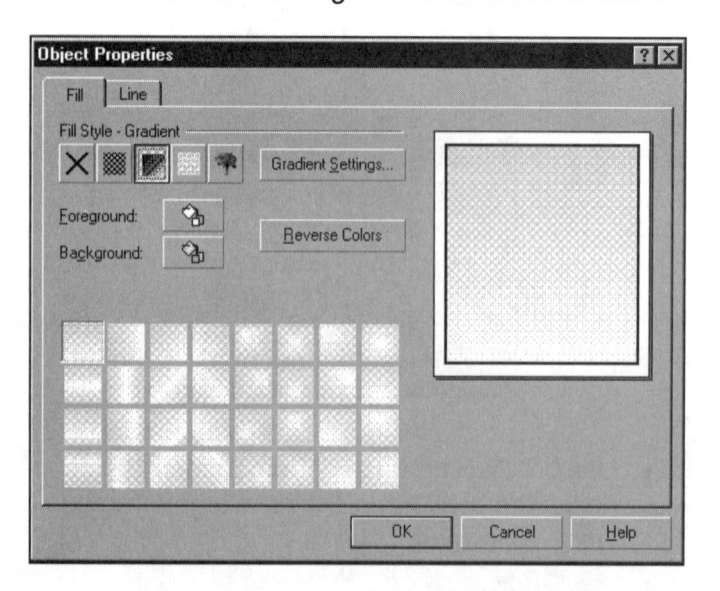

- The Graphics drop-down list on the Property Bar and the Graphics tool on the Tool Palette both contain options to control how objects appear in relation to one another on the slide. These options (Group, Separate, and Combine) are described below and on the next page.

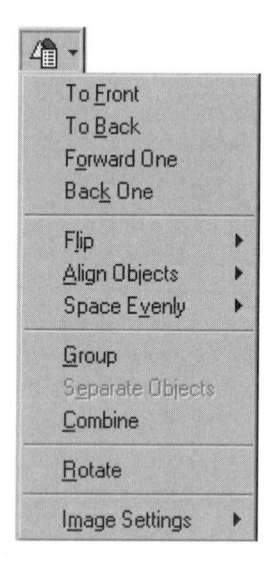

Group and Separate Objects

- When a drawing is composed of several basic shapes, it is difficult to move, copy, or duplicate all the shapes at once. **Grouping** lets you select all the shapes in the group and treat them as a single object so that copying and moving the object becomes easier.

- To group an object composed of individual shapes, select each shape (hold the Shift or Ctrl key down while you click each shape) and select Group from the Graphics button drop-down list. You can undo a grouped object by selecting Separate Objects from the Graphics button drop-down list.

Combine Objects

- The **Combine** option allows you to integrate selected objects into one drawing. For example, suppose you create a blue rectangle and place a yellow arrow within it. Select the two objects, then select Combine from the Graphics button drop-down list. The two objects will integrate. The fill pattern or color of the two objects takes on that of the leftmost object.

Order Objects

- You can **layer** or stack objects on top of each other to create interesting effects. You may adjust the layers by moving them to the back or bringing them to the front. To adjust the layers of shapes or objects, click the shape or object and select one of the following options from the Graphics button drop-down list: To Front, To Back, Forward One, or Back One.

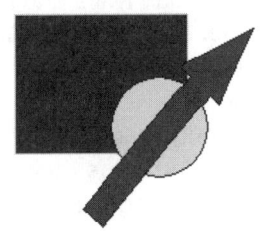

Contour Text

- The **Contour Text** feature allows you to form text around a graphic object. You may display both the graphic object and the text or just the contoured text. Note the samples below.

- To contour text, select the text and the object (hold down the Shift key while you select each object), then select Contour Text from the Tools menu. Deselect the Display text only option if you wish the graphic shape to show.

Create a Presentations Drawing Outside of a Slide Show

- Drawings can be created outside the slide presentation by selecting the **Presentations Drawing** option from the New dialog box when starting Corel Presentations, or after selecting New from the File menu. This enables you to save your drawing using a variety of graphic formats (.PCX, GIF, JPEG). You may then insert the drawing into another document or application.

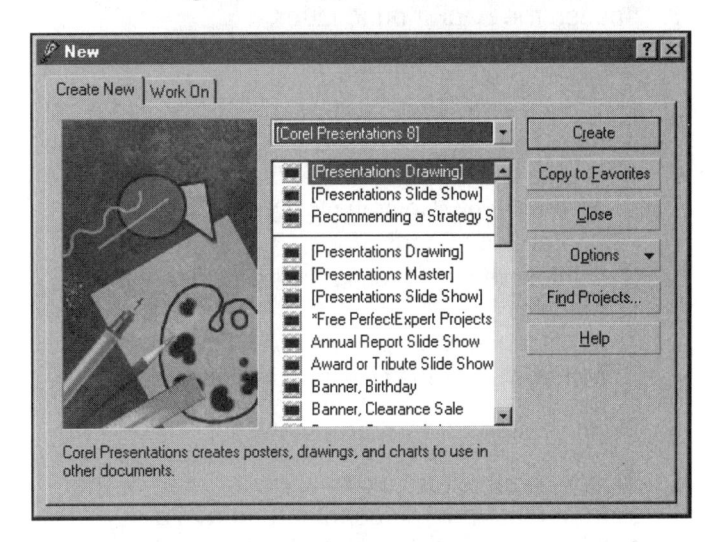

- When you select the Presentations Drawing option from the New dialog box, a blank drawing window appears for you to create your graphic object. After the drawing is complete, save the file.

Corel Presentations 8 ■ Lesson 2 ■ Exercise 12

COREL PRESENTATIONS 8 Lesson 2: Edit and Enhance Slides

> In this exercise, you will open a previously created slide show and create a logo on the background layer by using the Closed Object and Text Object tools. You will then view each slide in your presentation to see the effect.

EXERCISE DIRECTIONS

PART I

1. Open **SPORTS** or **12SPORTS**.
2. Display slide 1.
3. Access the background layer.
4. Create a logo as follows:
   a. Draw a small circle, as shown in Illustration A on page 503 and fill it red.
   b. Create a text line and enter the following text in a 16-point font. Color the text yellow.
      Fair Play Sports Club
   c. Contour the text around the top center of the graphic.
   d. Position the contoured graphic at the bottom-left corner of the slide as shown in Illustration A.
5. Switch to the Slide Sorter view.
6. Display each slide and change the size of the slide objects and placeholders to avoid overlapping of text with the logo.
7. Display slide 3 (FPSC's High Success Rate).
   a. Using the Line and Closed Object tools, create a green dumbbell as shown in Illustration A.
   b. Group the dumbbell and place the grouped object in the lower-right corner, as shown in Illustration A.
   c. Copy the dumbbell and place it as shown in Illustration A.
8. Print one copy as Handouts with eight slides per page.
9. Save the changes; close the file.

PART II

1. Open **CALIBER** or **12CALIBER**.
2. Insert a new Bulleted List slide after slide 10 (Spring Schedule).
   a. Type the bulleted text shown in Illustration B.
   b. Change the arrow style for each of the first three bullet levels.

3. Display slide 12.
   a. Insert any dollar sign Clipart graphic.
   b. Rotate the dollar sign as shown in Illustration B.
   c. Apply a shadow effect and a desired pattern.
   d. Copy the dollar sign twice and align the objects as shown. Set each to a different color.
   e. Insert two relevant pieces of Clipart as shown in Illustration B.
   f. Draw a large purple square.
   g. Add a shadow and a line (border) to the square.
   h. Move the Clipart images over the square, as shown.
   i. Layer the items so that the Clipart is visible.
   j. Group the three items.
   k. Copy the grouped object.
4. Display slide 12 (Don't Let the Learning Pass You By!).
   a. Paste a copy of the grouped object as shown in Illustration C.
   b. Size the object, as shown in Illustration C.
   c. Insert a Text Line near the bottom of the slide using a purple 32-point serif font:
      Ask About Our Free Trial Memberships
   d. Apply a downward shadow to the text.
5. Display any Bulleted List slide and access the layout layer.
   a. Left-align the Title placeholder.
   b. Right-align the Subtitle placeholder.
6. Access the Slide Layer.
   a. Switch to Slide Sorter view. Check for placeholders or graphics overlapping on the slides.
   b. Switch to Slide Editor view and make any necessary adjustments to individual slides.
7. Print one copy as Handouts with eight slides per page.
8. Close the file; save the changes.

ILLUSTRATION A

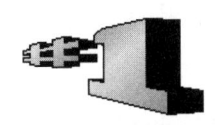

FPSC's High Success Rate

Why More People are Working Out With Us:

★ People want more activity choices.
  ★ Traditional aerobics can be boring.
  ★ Doing the same activity daily can cause repetitive injuries.

★ Our workout equipment is top of the line.
  ★ Updated once a year, or sooner when needed.
  ★ We have more equipment than any fitness center in the New England area.
  ★ Our guarantee: you'll never have to wait in line.

Create logo on background layer.

ILLUSTRATION B

Save Money!

Discounts For all Your Computer Needs

➡ Hardware
  ➡ Mac
  ➡ PC
➡ Software
➡ Peripherals
  ➡ Modems
  ➡ Scanners
    ⇒ Color and Black and White

ILLUSTRATION C

Don't Let the Learning Pass You By!

Call a CCUG Representative Today at
1-800-555-CCUG

Ask about our free trial membership

KEYSTROKES

DRAW SHAPES

1. Select desired tool from **Tools Palette**.
2. Position crosshair (+) at point where shape will start.
3. Click and drag mouse diagonally to shape ending point.
4. Release mouse button.

DRAW POLYGON OR CLOSED CURVE

1. Select **Poloygon** or **Closed Curve** tool from **Closed Object** tools.. [icon] or [icon]
2. Position crosshair (+) at point where shape will start.
3. Move crosshair to draw shape, clicking to change direction or angle, if desired.
4. Double-click to stop drawing.

CREATE TEXT OBJECT

1. Click **Text box tool** on the Tools Palette .... [A]

OR

Click **Text line tool** on the Tools Palette .... [A]

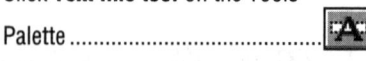

2. Drag to create text box.
3. Type text.

To edit text:

- Highlight text.
- Click **Foreground Fill** button ..... [icon] on the Property Bar to change text color.
- Change font, size, and font attributes by clicking appropriate Property Bar buttons.

4. Click outside text box.
5. Click and drag text box to desired location on slide.

LAYER OBJECTS

F6

1. Select desired object.
2. Click **Graphics tool** .... [Alt]+[G] on Tool Pallet.

OR

Click **Graphics** button .... [Graphics] on Property Bar.

3. Click desired order option:
   - To **F**ront .... [F]
   - To **B**ack .... [B]
   - Forward **O**ne .... [O]
   - Bac**k** One .... [K]

GROUP AND SEPARATE OBJECTS

1. Select first object.
2. Shift-click remaining objects.
3. Click **Graphics tool** .... [Alt]+[G] on Tool Pallet.

OR

Click **Graphics** button .... [Graphics] on Property Bar.

4. Click **Group** .... [G]

To separate:

- Select object.
- Click **Graphics tool** .... [Alt]+[G] on Tool Pallet.

OR

Click **Graphics** button .... [Graphics] on Property Bar.

- Click **S**eparate .... [E]

OR

- Right-click grouped object, choose **S**eparate Objects .... [E]

CONTOUR OBJECTS

1. Draw a shape.
2. Create a text box or text line.
3. Press the Shift key and click the shape and the text box.
4. Click **Tools** .... [Alt]+[T]
5. Click **Contou**r Text .... [U]

To separate:

- Click object.
- Click **Graphics tool** .... [Alt]+[G] on Tool Pallet.

OR

Click **Graphics** button .... [Graphics] on Property Bar.

- Click **S**eparate Objects .... [E]

COREL PRESENTATIONS 8   Lesson 2: Edit and Enhance Slides

Exercise 13

- Use PerfectExpert Projects to Create Presentations
- Insert Date

NOTES

Use PerfectExpert Projects to Create Presentations

- The first step in creating a presentation is to organize your thoughts. To help you plan the content of your presentation, Presentations 8 provides **PerfectExpert Projects,** which serve as templates. Each project consists of an outline for you to follow that indicates what type of information you might include. Some popular PerfectExpert Projects include: Persuasive, Teaching and Training, Sales, Team Meeting, and Year End Report.

- By default, all PerfectExpert Projects are stored on the Corel installation CD-ROM. To access a PerfectExpert Project, you must have the CD-ROM inserted in your CD-ROM drive or have previously installed the projects onto your hard drive or network.

- To launch a PerfectExpert Project, select New from the File menu. Select [Corel Presentations 8] in the top window and then scroll down the second window and select a desired project. Click Create to open it.

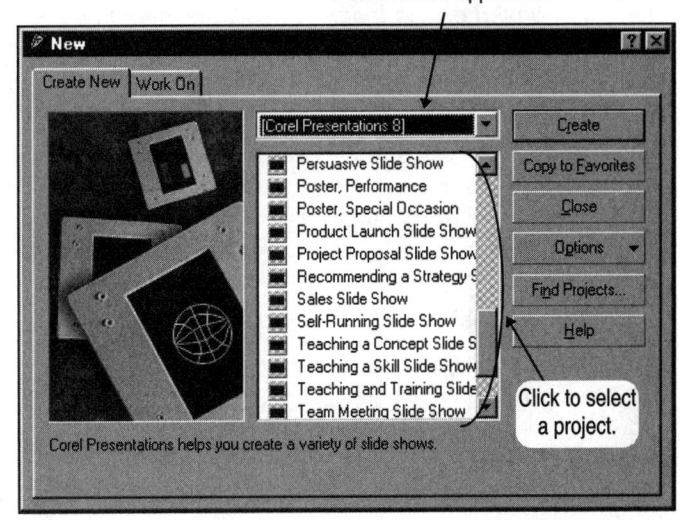

- The project slide show will open with the title slide and the **PerfectExpert panel** automatically displayed. As with the other Corel 8 applications, the PerfectExpert panel provides short cuts for common functions performed when completing a specific task, such as creating a slide show.

COREL PRESENTATIONS 8 Lesson 2: Edit and Enhance Slides

- Each project contains a preset background master and slide layout settings that are consistent with the information being presented. If desired, you may adjust the slide layout and/or background master by using the various options available in the PerfectExpert Panel or by using the methods you learned in earlier exercises.

- To view the full content of the project, switch to Slide Outliner view. You may then review the text, select it, and replace it with your own.

  ✓Note: *The PerfectExpert panel options change based on the features available in each view mode.*

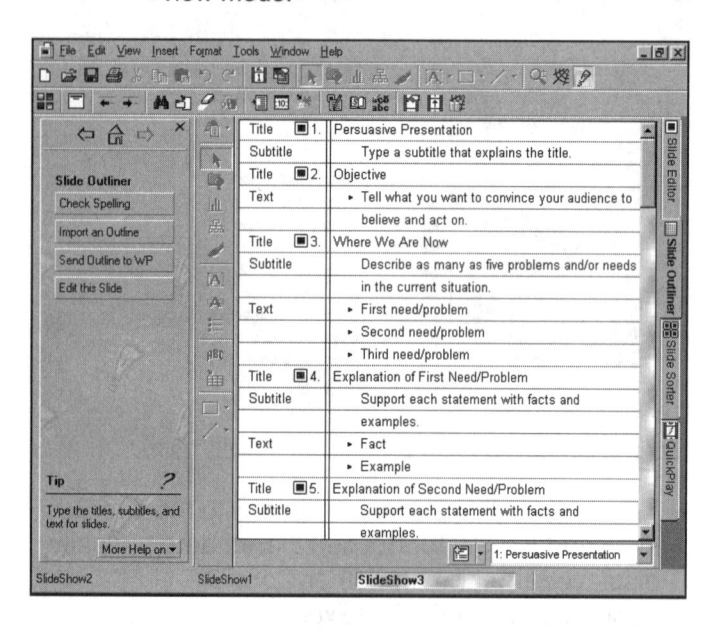

- Proceed to create your slide show using the features and enhancements learned in earlier exercises.

Insert Date

- The **date** may be included on individual slides or on all slides.

- To insert the date, you must first create a text box or text line using the tools on the Tools Palette. Then, select Date/Time from the Insert menu.

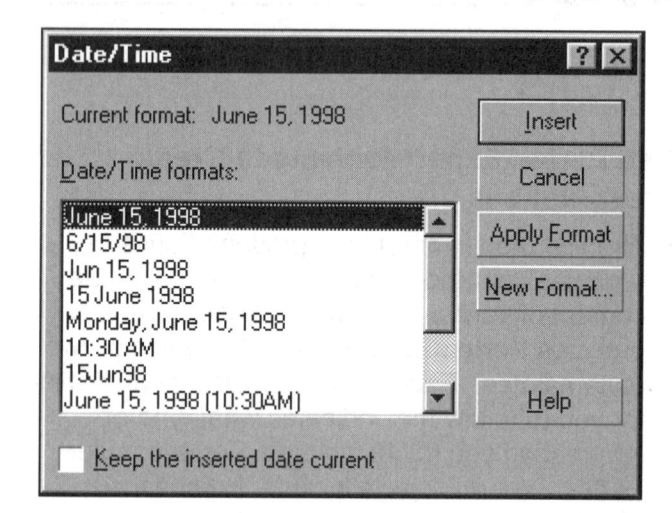

- To automatically update the date whenever you retrieve or print the slide show, click the *Keep the inserted date current* option in the Date/Time dialog box. Otherwise, the original date will remain constant. Remember, to include the date on all slides, insert it on the Background Layer.

- The default date format is month, day, year. To change the format, click to select another option from the Date/Time format list in the Date/Time dialog box or click the New Format button and choose another format.

In this challenge exercise, you will use a PerfectExpert Project to create a sales presentation to persuade the audience to buy a product. You will develop your slide show from information contained in an advertisement.

EXERCISE DIRECTIONS

1. Refer to the advertisement shown in Illustration A on page 508.
2. Use the *Persuasive* PerfectExpert Project template to create a slide presentation based on the information contained in the advertisement. (See Illustration B on page 509 for prompted topics.)
3. Edit the Bulleted List slide Layout Layer:
   a. Left-align all title placeholder text.
   b. Change the first bullet level to blue stars and the second bullet level to red stars.
4. Using the design tools on the Tool Palette, create a logo and include the text, **TIGER**. Place it as desired.
5. Insert today's date on all slides in a sans serif 9 point font. Place it as desired.
6. Add relevant Clipart to desired slides.
7. Spell check.
8. Print one copy as Handouts with eight slides per page in black and white.
9. Save the file; name it **TIGER**.
10. Close the slide show window.

KEYSTROKES

PERFECTEXPERT PROJECT

Open new project.

1. Click **File** .... Alt+F
2. Click **New** .... N
3. Click **Corel Presentations 8** in first window.
4. Click desired project in second window.
5. Click **Create** .... Alt+R
6. Click **Slide Outliner** view tab .... Ctrl+Tab

   OR

   a. Click **View** .... Alt+V
   b. Click **Slide Outliner** .... O
7. Delete project template text and insert your own.

INSERT DATE

1. Click the **Text Box** tool .... A
   on the Tools Palette.

   OR

   Click the **Text Line** tool .... A
   on the Tools Palette
2. Draw the text object.
3. Click **Insert** .... Alt+I
4. Click **Date/Time** .... Alt+D
5. Click **Keep the inserted** .... Alt+K
   date current option if you want date to remain current.
6. Click in **Date/Time** .... Alt+D
   format box.
7. Click desired format .... ↑↓

   OR

   a. Click **New Format** .... Alt+N
   b. Select desired tab .... Ctrl+Tab
   c. Click desired format .... ↑↓
   d. Click **Insert** .... Alt+I
8. Click **OK** .... Enter

ILLUSTRATION A

🖥 TIGER ELECTRONICS
Personal Computers
Creating Technology for a New Millenium

Tiger Electronics is proud to announce its newest desktop series computer, the **Icarus 2000 Home Desktop Package**. At Tiger Electronics, we remain on the cutting edge of technological advancement so that we can bring you the highest performing personal computers available on today's market.

We saw a need for faster, more dependable desktop computers sooner than any of our competitors. That's why we designed the Icarus 2000 Home Desktop Package, which contains a 400 megahertz Pentium processor, 10 gigabytes of hard drive space, 64 megabytes of RAM, a 20X CD-ROM drive, a 56k fax/modem, built-in 100 megabyte zip drive, and built-in speakers as well as a 15" color monitor.

We're aware that space efficiency is a big concern for most home computer users. That's why we designed the Icarus 2000 Home Desktop Package to take up less space. We've enclosed the central processing unit in a small encasement that can easily be stored beneath your desk, as well as a 3" thick 15" monitor that can be mounted to the wall. In addition, we've built our high-fidelity speakers into the monitor unit so that you won't have to worry about excess wires.

The Icarus 2000 Home Desktop Package has been designed for today's home power-users. A minimally stocked computing unit no longer meets the needs of today's strong computer users, who want to create multimedia files, edit video, create Web pages, and more. So, we've created a product that gives you the power, stability, and space efficacy to create dynamic projects—all from the comfort of your very own living room!

The entire Icarus 2000 Home Desktop Package is currently being offered at an unbeatable price of $2,700, which includes a full three-year warranty for all service and parts. And don't forget about our Tiger Electronics guarantee—if you can find an equivalent product for a lower price, we'll beat it.

ILLUSTRATION B

1. Persuasive Presentation
    i. Type a subtitle that explains the title.
2. Objective
    a. Tell what you want to convince your audience to believe and act on.
3. Where We Are Now
    i. Describe as many as five problems and/or needs in the current situation.
    a. First need/problem
    b. Second need/problem
    c. Third need/problem
4. Explanation of First Need/Problem
    i. Support each statement with facts and examples.
    a. Fact
    b. Example
5. Explanation of Second Need/Problem
    i. Support each statement with facts and examples.
    a. Fact
    b. Example
6. Explanation of Third Need/Problem
    i. Support each statement with facts and examples.
    a. Fact
    b. Example
7. What Does It Mean?
    i. Give the implications of the problems/needs you discussed.
    a. First implication
    b. Second implication
    c. Third implication
8. How to Solve the Problems
    a. Give your solution to the problems & needs.
9. Supporting Facts and Examples
    i. Support your solution with concrete facts and examples.
    a. First fact/example
    b. Second fact/example
    c. Third fact/example
10. Benefits of My Solution
    i. List up to 5 benefits of adopting your solution.
    a. First benefit
    b. Second benefit
    c. Third benefit
11. Proof of Benefits
    i. Support each benefit with concrete facts and examples.
    a. First fact/example
    b. Second fact/example
    c. Third fact/example
12. Costs vs. Benefits
    i. Help your audience see the value of adopting your solution vs. the costs.
    a. List areas of savings
    b. Show how savings offset costs
13. Question and Answers
    i. Anticipate objections and answer them, then take further questions.
    a. Prepared questions and answers
    b. Time for audience questions and answers
14. Costs of Rejecting the Solution
    i. Show the costs of not using your solutions with implications in concrete and/or financial values.
    a. Costs
    b. Implications
15. Summary
    i. Summarize your presentation.
    a. Your solution
    b. Benefits of your solution
    c. Savings your solution will yield
    c. Savings your solution will yield
    d. Costs of rejecting your solution
16. What to Do
    i. List the steps to implement your solution.
    a. Step one
    b. Step two
    c. Step three
17. Ask for Any Further Questions
    i. Answer audience questions.
18. Thank You for Coming!
    i. Close with encouragement and thanks to the audience.
19. Blank Slide

COREL PRESENTATIONS 8 Lesson 2: Edit and Enhance Slides

Exercise 14

■ **Summary**

In this exercise, you will create a presentation for New Era Mutual Fund, a company that wants more investors to purchase their securities. This slide show will include a table, organization chart, and data chart slides.

EXERCISE DIRECTIONS

1. Create a new slide show.
2. Select a Title slide for the first slide.
3. Select MARBLE BORDER as the background master (from the Business category).
4. Access the Background Layer.
   a. Insert today's date in the top left corner of the slide in a serif 10 point italic font.
   b. Create the logos on the top and bottom right corners of the slide as shown in Illustration A on page 511.
5. Create the Title slide (1) as shown in Illustration A. Use a sans serif font for the title and subtitle.
6. Select Bulleted List layout for the second slide.
7. Access the Layout Layer.
   a. Change the first two bullet styles to another style and color.
   b. Adjust the placeholders if they interfere with the logo placement.
   c. Set the font for each placeholder to sans serif.
8. Access the Slide Layer.
9. Create slide 2 as shown in Illustration B on page 512.
10. Create the remaining slides using the appropriate slide layouts as shown in Illustration B.
    - Set font to sans serif as indicated in the illustration throughout.
11. Use the names and titles below for the Org Chart slide:
    Kelly Hunter: Head Fund Manager
    Gil Sanchez: Vice President
    Sabine Noir: Vice President
    Katia Reins: Associate
    Shane Taylor: Associate
    Nia Chow: Associate
    David Ovitz: Associate
    - Adjust the organization chart's position so it does not overlap with the logo.
12. Enter the text and data below to create the Data Chart slide:
    New Era Fund Growth
    Continues to Outperform Similar Funds on an Annual Basis

	1996	1997	1998
New Era	212	337	435
Money Now	172	202	190

    - Display the data labels.
    - Adjust the chart's position so it does not overlap the bottom logo.
    - Create a text line that reads: Sales (in $ millions)
13. Display each slide. Adjust the placeholders and/or the font size of the titles so they do not interfere with the logos.
14. Save the file; name it **NEWERA**.
15. Print one copy of each slide in black and white. Compare each slide with those in Illustration B.
16. Close the slide show window.

COREL PRESENTATIONS 8 Lesson 2: Edit and Enhance Slides

ILLUSTRATION A

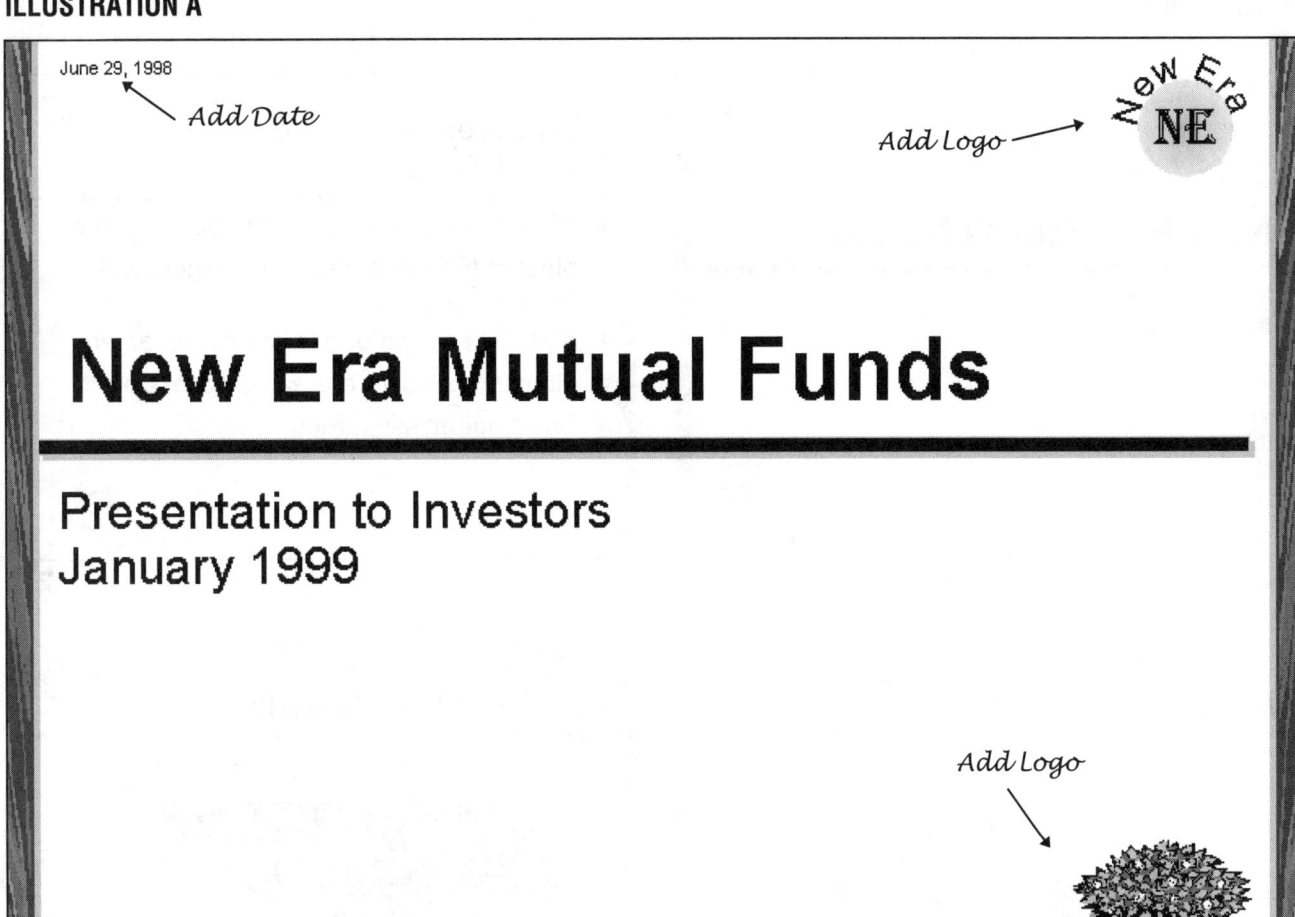

June 29, 1998 ← Add Date

Add Logo → New Era NE

New Era Mutual Funds

Presentation to Investors
January 1999

Add Logo

Watch your money grow!

COREL PRESENTATIONS 8 Lesson 2: Edit and Enhance Slides

ILLUSTRATION B

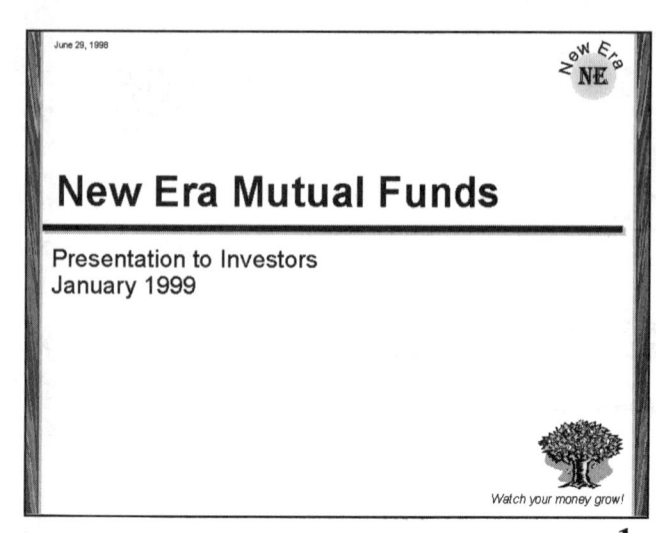

Slide 1

June 29, 1998

New Era Mutual Funds

Presentation to Investors
January 1999

Watch your money grow!

Slide 2

June 15, 1998

Why Invest in New Era Mutual Funds?

- 17 % growth record over the past 3 years
- Most of fund invested in blue-chip stocks and bonds
- Over $22 million under find management
- Money managers are easily accessible
- Small commission fees

Watch your money grow!

Slide 3

June 29, 1998

Management Team

Direct contact with investors is available at any time.

- Kelly Hunter, Head Fund Manager
  - Gil Sanchez, Vice President
    - Katia Reins, Associate
    - Shane Taylor, Associate
  - Sabine Noir, Vice President
    - Nia Chow, Associate
    - David Ovitz, Associate

Watch your money grow!

Slide 4

June 29, 1998

New Era Fund Growth

Continues to Outperform Similar Funds on an Annual Basis

(Bar chart showing 1996, 1997, 1998 data for Money Now and New Era)

Sales (in $ millions)

Watch your money grow!

Slide 5

June 15, 1998

New Era Invests In Many Different Instruments

Instrument	Amount Invested
Treasury Bonds	$12 million
Foreign Currency	$9 million
Foreign Bonds	$7 million
Blue Chip Stocks	$4 million

Watch your money grow!

Slide 6

June 29, 1998

To Invest Your Money with New Era...

- Contact Sabine Noir
  - 800-555-FUND
- Write to:
  - New Era Mutual Funds
  - 575 Fifth Avenue
  - New York, NY 10022
- Inquire with your stockbroker

Watch your money grow!

Exercise 15

- **Show a Presentation**
- **Slide Transitions**
- **Add Animation to Bulleted Lists**
- **Animate Objects**
- **Slide Show Tools**

Play Show

NOTES

Show a Presentation

- Using a projection system or a large monitor, you can show your presentation to an audience. When a slide show is presented, each slide displays on the entire screen without showing Corel Presentations 8 screen elements.

- Slides may be shown one at a time as an oral report is given, or they may run continuously if used at a trade show or at a demonstration counter in a store.

- Changing slides may be activated by clicking the mouse, or by pressing the Spacebar, the Enter key, or the arrow keys on the keyboard.

- Once a group of slides has been created, you may view the presentation as a slide show by doing one of the following:

  - Click the **Play Slide Show** button on the Toolbar. This will automatically start the slide show beginning with the first slide.

    OR

  - Click the **QuickPlay** tab. This will automatically run the slide show beginning with the selected slide.

    OR

  - Click the **Play Slide Show** button on the Property Bar. This will open the Play Slide Show dialog box, enabling you to determine how the slide show will be displayed.

    OR

  - Select **Play Slide Show** from the View menu. This option also opens the Play Show dialog box.

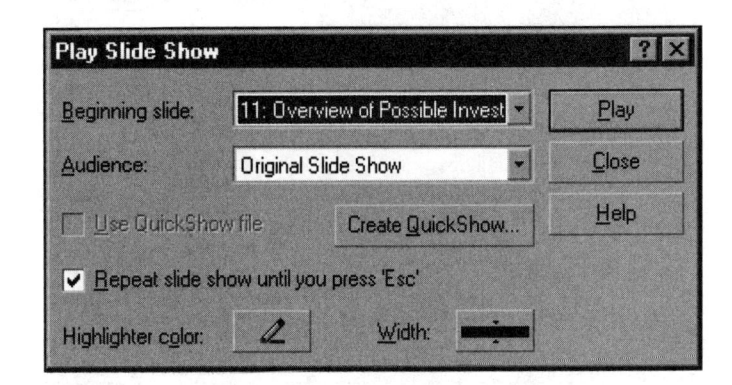

- To run the slide show continuously, click the Repeat slide show until you press 'Esc' option in the dialog box.

- To use an onscreen **Highlighter** tool during your slideshow presentation, select a Highlighter color and highlighter Width. The highlighter tool enables you to temporarily highlight items within a slideshow to call attention to them. The marks that are made with the Highlighter tool are wiped away as you move to the next slide.

- The **Create QuickShow** option allows you to create a QuickShow file. This separate file enables your slide show to run faster by created bitmapped images; however, this option can use a large amount of disk space.

  ✓*Note: Custom audiences may also be accessed from this dialog box. This feature will be discussed in Exercise 16.*

COREL PRESENTATIONS 8 Lesson 3: Work with Slide Shows

Slide Transitions

- **Transitions** add special effects as one slide replaces the other on the screen. Slide transitions can be added to individual slides, all slides in a slide show, or to a selected group of slides. To set slide transition effects:

    - Click the Slide Transition button [Sweep] on the Property Bar (in Slide Editor or Slide Sorter view) and select a transition effect from the drop-down list.

      OR

    - Click the Slide Appearance button on the Toolbar and click the Transitions tab on the Slide Properties dialog box.

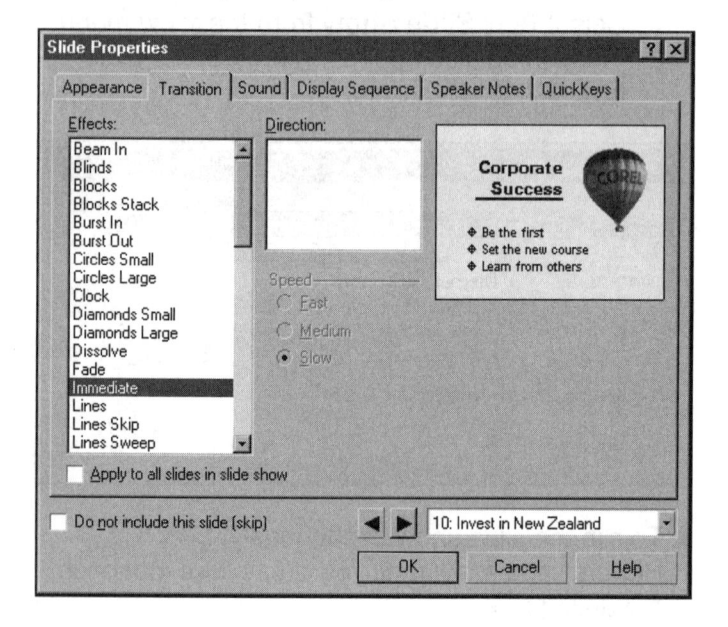

      OR

    - Select Slide Properties, Transition, from the Format menu.

      OR

    - Right-click on the desired slide and select Transitions from the QuickMenu.

- In the Transitions tab of the Slide Properties dialog box which follows, check to see that the desired slide is listed in the bottom right corner. If not, select another slide from the drop-down list. Select the desired transition Effects option. A sample of the effect will display.

- You can also control the speed of the transition by clicking a Speed option. Click Apply to all slides in a slide show if you wish to apply a selected effect to all slides. Click Do not include this slide if you wish to skip the transition effect for the selected slide.

Add Animation to Bulleted Lists

- In addition to adding transition effects to slides, you can also add **bullet animation** to change the way bullets display on Bulleted List slides during a slide show.

- Bullet animation effects are similar to transition effects, except that they only affect the bulleted list placeholders and the bulleted items within those placeholders. Bulleted animation allows you to control the movement of the bulleted text placeholder or of each bulleted item within the placeholder.

- To add animation to a Bulleted List slide, click the bulleted text placeholder, and do the following:

    - Click the Object Animation button on the Property Bar.

      OR

    - Click the Bulleted List Properties button on the Property Bar and click the Bullet Animation tab.

      OR

    - Select Bulleted List Properties from the Format menu and click the Bullet Animation tab.

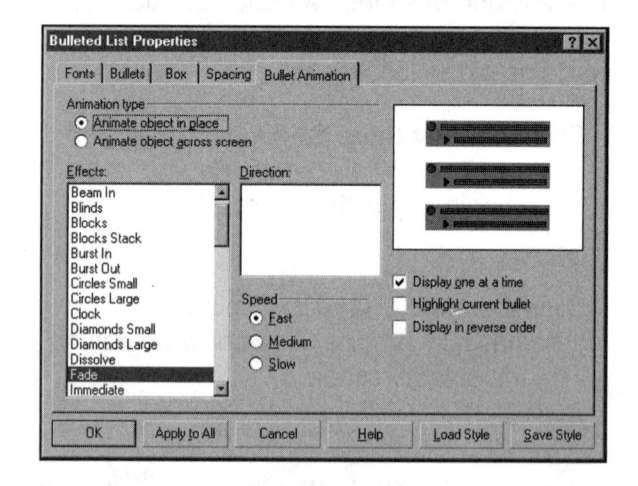

514

- In the Bullet Animation tab of the Bulleted List Properties dialog box, select an Animation Type option. If you select Animate object in place, a list of animation effects will appear in the Effects box that will animate the bulleted items (or placeholders) as they appear—already in place. If you select Animate object across screen, a different list of animation effects will appear that will move the bulleted items (or placeholder) across the screen as the animation effect is taking place.

- If you wish to display one bulleted item at a time and/or highlight it as it displays on screen, or if you wish to display bulleted items in reverse order, click the appropriate check boxes in the Object Animation tab.

- Once all animation effects have been set, click OK to apply the effects to the selected slide(s). Or, Click Apply to all to apply the bullet animation to all Bulleted List slides in the current slide show.

Animate Objects

- In addition to creating transitions and animations to bulleted text, Corel Presentations 8 allows you to animate graphic objects or drawings. For example, you can have a picture bounce into place or crawl into view on the slide.

- To animate a graphic object or drawing, select the object you want to animate and do the following:

  - Click the Object Animation button on the Property Bar.

  OR

  - Select Object Properties, Object Animation from the Format menu.

- In the Object Animation tab of the Object Properties dialog box which follows, note that the animation options and effects are the same as those available for animating bulleted lists.

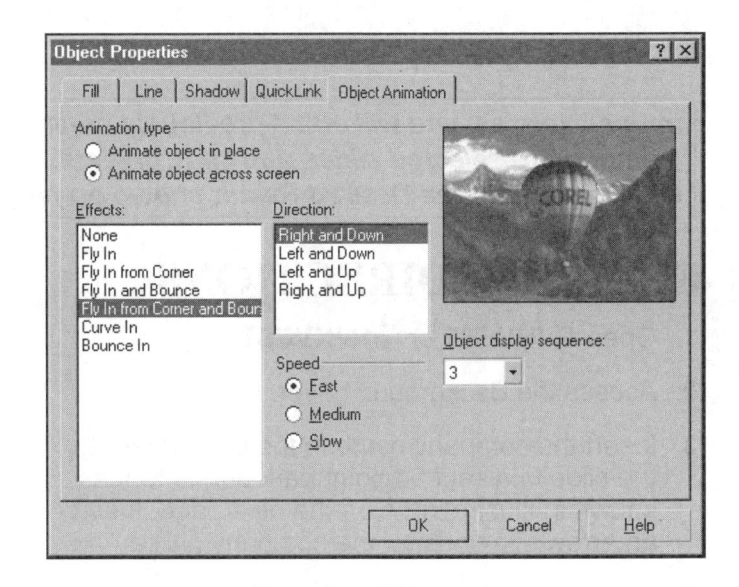

- If the selected slide contains more than one object, you can adjust the display order of those objects by selecting a new order number from the Object display sequence drop-down list.

Slide Show Tools

- **Slide Show Tools** provide short cuts for common activities performed during a slide show presentation. To access the Slide Show Tools dialog box while a slide show is running, right-click anywhere on the presentation. A QuickMenu displays listing all the options that are available to you while you are viewing and/or showing your presentation.

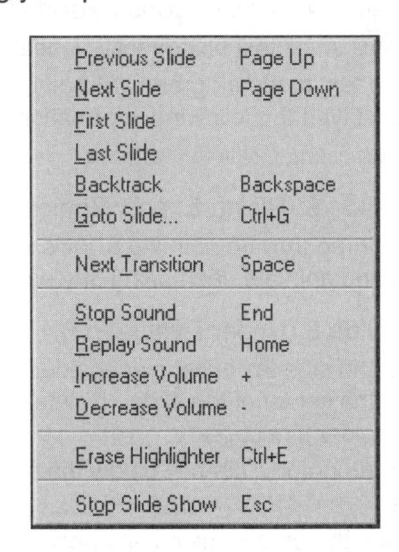

- You can use the Slide Show Tools to move to a particular slide, adjust sound (volume), turn off sound, erase highlighter markings, and close the presentation.

COREL PRESENTATIONS 8 Lesson 3: Work with Slide Shows

In this exercise, you will edit a previously created slide show by adding graphics, transitions and animation to selected slides and slide objects. You will then run your slide show. Check your slide show with the Desired Result shown on page 518.

EXERCISE DIRECTIONS

1. Open ▰INVEST or ▰15INVEST.
2. Access the Background Layer.
3. Insert the company name in the left corner of the slide in a serif 24-point dark purple font as shown in Illustration A on the next page. Insert an arrow symbol after the company name.
4. Insert December 1998 in the right corner of the slide in a serif 10-point italic font. Color the text dark green.
5. Access the Slide Layer.
6. Display slide 2 (Brief History of New Zealand Economy) and insert new text as shown in Illustration A.
7. Switch to Slide Sorter view.
8. Select a transition type for each slide in the show.
9. Create a different animation effect for the text on each Bulleted List slide.
10. Display slide 4 (Tremendous Export Markets)
    a. Create a small text box directly beneath the chart.
    b. Set the text to a dark green, 12-point sans serif font and type the following information:
       * Reflecting Dollars in Millions
11. Display slide 6 (Rising Export Regions).
    - Create three upward pointing arrows in different colors and animate each using any desired effect.
12. Display slide 8 (Under Evaluation).
    a. Move and size the bullet placeholder to place the text in the center of the slide. Delete the subtitle placeholder if necessary.
    b. Move the graphic directly below the bulleted items.
    c. Animate the graphic using any desired effect.
13. Save the changes to the presentation; do not close the file.
14. Display slide 3 (Why Invest in the New Zealand Economy).
    - Animate the graphic using any desired effect.
15. Display slide 9 (Bonds).
    - Click the QuickPlay tab to view the last three slides in the slide show.
16. Play the entire slide show.
17. Display slide 5.
    - Highlight the two top export countries on slide 5 while the slide show is running.
18. Access Slide Show Tools.
    a. Erase the highlighter marks on slide 5.
    b. Display slide 7.
    c. Go to the previous slide.
    d. Play the remainder of the slide show.
20. Print one copy as Handouts with 5 slides per page in black and white.
21. Set the slide show to run continuously and view the slide show again.
22. Save the changes; close the file.

ILLUSTRATION A

New Zealand

Investment Opportunities

Hartman Investment, Inc.

December 1998

Brief History of New Zealand Economy

- Government Deregulation in 1980s
  - Impacts on farming
  - Adjusting to a market-led economy
- Recent Economic Reform
  - Reserve Bank Act brings inflation below 3%
- *Research Department's Report on the History of the Economy* ← *Insert new text*
  - *Positive impact of moving from a regulated economy to a market-driven, deregulated economy*

Hartman Investment, Inc.

December 1998

COREL PRESENTATIONS 8   Lesson 3: Work with Slide Shows

DESIRED RESULT

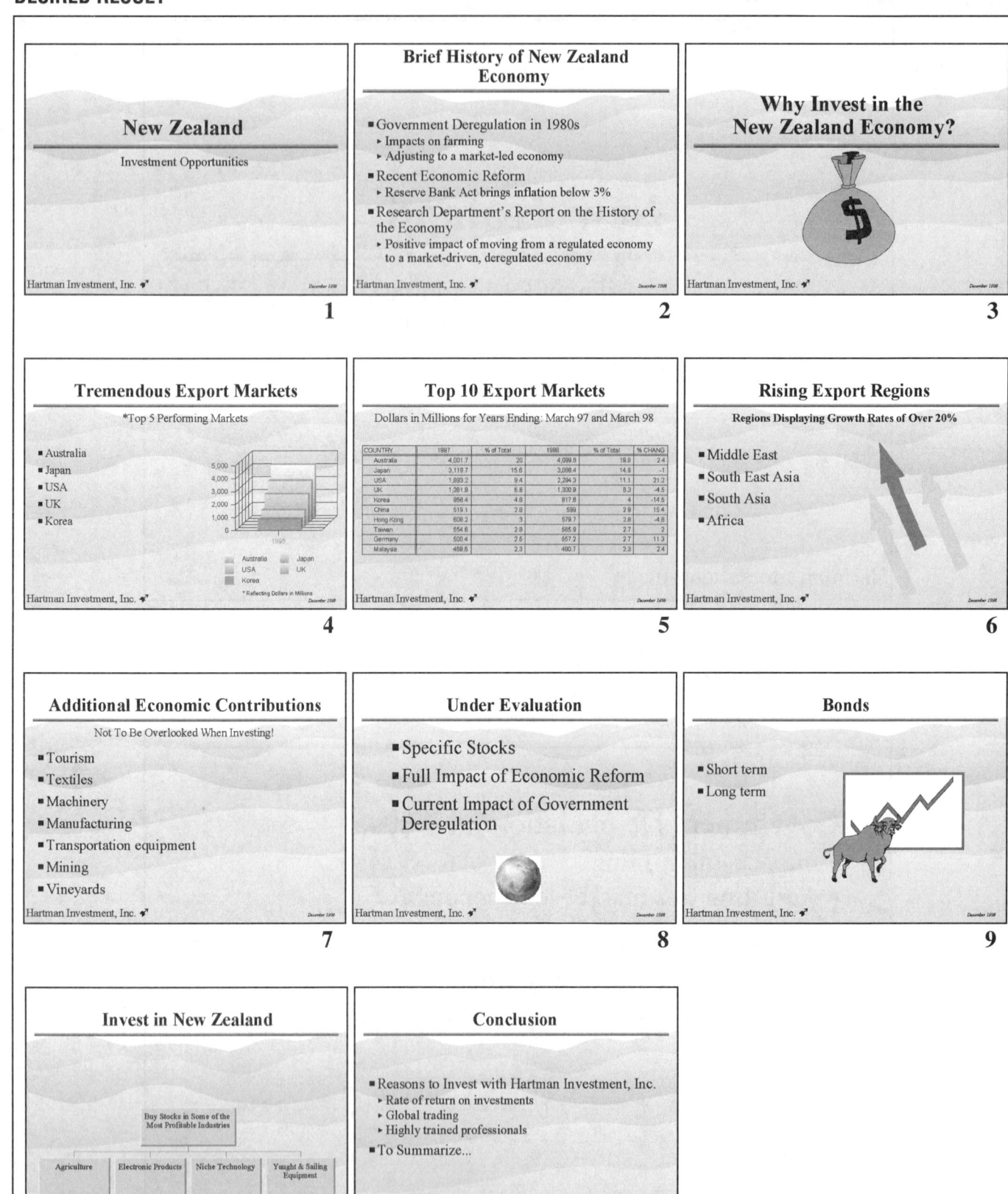

1. New Zealand — Investment Opportunities

2. Brief History of New Zealand Economy
- Government Deregulation in 1980s
  - Impacts on farming
  - Adjusting to a market-led economy
- Recent Economic Reform
  - Reserve Bank Act brings inflation below 3%
- Research Department's Report on the History of the Economy
  - Positive impact of moving from a regulated economy to a market-driven, deregulated economy

3. Why Invest in the New Zealand Economy?

4. Tremendous Export Markets — *Top 5 Performing Markets
- Australia
- Japan
- USA
- UK
- Korea

5. Top 10 Export Markets — Dollars in Millions for Years Ending: March 97 and March 98

COUNTRY	1997	% of Total	1998	% of Total	% CHANG
Australia	4,001.7	20	4,099.8	19.8	2.4
Japan	3,119.7	15.6	3,098.4	14.9	-1
USA	1,893.2	9.4	2,294.3	11.1	21.2
UK	1,361.9	6.8	1,300.9	6.3	-4.5
Korea	958.4	4.8	917.8	4	-14.5
China	519.1	2.6	599	2.9	15.4
Hong Kong	608.2	3	579.7	2.8	-4.8
Taiwan	554.8	2.8	565.9	2.7	2
Germany	500.4	2.5	557.2	2.7	11.3
Malaysia	468.6	2.3	480.7	2.3	2.4

6. Rising Export Regions — Regions Displaying Growth Rates of Over 20%
- Middle East
- South East Asia
- South Asia
- Africa

7. Additional Economic Contributions — Not To Be Overlooked When Investing!
- Tourism
- Textiles
- Machinery
- Manufacturing
- Transportation equipment
- Mining
- Vineyards

8. Under Evaluation
- Specific Stocks
- Full Impact of Economic Reform
- Current Impact of Government Deregulation

9. Bonds
- Short term
- Long term

10. Invest in New Zealand — Buy Stocks in Some of the Most Profitable Industries: Agriculture, Electronic Products, Niche Technology, Yacht & Sailing Equipment

11. Conclusion
- Reasons to Invest with Hartman Investment, Inc.
  - Rate of return on investments
  - Global trading
  - Highly trained professionals
- To Summarize...

KEYSTROKES

SHOW SLIDE SHOW

1. Open desired presentation.
2. Click **Play Slide Show** button .... 🎞️
   on Toolbar.
   OR
   Click **QuickPlay** View tab
   OR
   Double-click slide icon in Outliner view.
3. Click left mouse button press the Enter key, the arrow keys, or press the Spacebar on the keyboard to advance from slide to slide.

To run slide show and set slide show settings:

1. Open desired presentation.
2. Click **Play Slide Show** button .... 🎞️
   on the Property Bar.
   OR
   - Click **View** .... **Alt**+**V**
   - Click **Play Slide Show** .... **W**
3. Set Desired settings in the Play Show dialog box:

To set the starting slide:

- Click **Beginning** slide .... **Alt**+**B**
- Click desired slide .... 🔽

To run show continuously:

- Click **Repeat slide show until you press 'Esc'** .... **Alt**+**R**

To set Highlighter tool options:

- Click **Highlighter color** ...... **Alt**+**O**
- Select a color .... 🔽
- Click **Width** .... **W**
  to set width of highlighter markings.

To create a quick-running slide show:

- Click **Create QuickShow**.... **Alt**+**Q**
  ✓ Note the **Audience** option will be discussed in Exercise 16.

  If prompted, save your document .... **S**
4. Click **Play** .... **Alt**+**P**
5. Click left mouse button press the Enter key, the arrow keys, or press the Spacebar on the keyboard to advance from slide to slide.

ADD SLIDE TRANSITIONS

1. Open desired slide show.
2. Click **Slide Transition** button on the Property Bar..... [Sweep ▼]
   OR
   - Right-click and select **Transition** .... **I**
   OR
   - Click the **Slide Appearance** button on the Toolbar................ 🖼️
   - Click the **Transitions** tab .. **Ctrl**+**Tab**
     on the Slide Properties dialog box.
   OR
   - Click **Format**..................... **Alt**+**R**
   - Click **Slide Properties**................. **S**
   - Click **Transition**........................... **T**
3. Click **Previous** or **Next** button................. **<<** or **>>**
   to go to desired slides.
4. Click **Effects** .... **Alt**+**E**
5. Click desired effect.................... 🔽
6. Select desired transition options.
7. Click **OK** .... **Enter**

ADD ANIMATION TO BULLETED LISTS

1. Open a slide show.
2. Display a Bulleted List slide.
3. Select the bulleted list placeholder.
4. Click **Object Animation** button........ 🖼️
   on the Property Bar.
   OR
   - Click **Format**..................... **Alt**+**R**
   - Click **Bulleted list Properties**...... **E**
   - Click the **Bullet Animation** tab .... **Ctrl**+**Tab**
5. Click **Animate object in place** .... **P**
   OR
   Click **Animate object across the screen**........................... **A**
6. Select an **Effect** .... **Alt**+**E**, ↓ ↑
7. Select a **Direction**, if applicable.............. **Alt**+**D**, ↓ ↑
8. Choose a desired speed:
   - **Fast**................................. **Alt**+**F**
   - **Medium** .... **Alt**+**M**
   - **Slow**................................. **Alt**+**S**
9. If desired click any of the following:
   - Display **one at a time** ...... **Alt**+**O**
   - Highlight current bullet .... **Alt**+**I**
   - Display in **reverse** order... **Alt**+**R**
10. Click **OK** .... **Enter**
    to apply animation to selected slide(s) only.
    OR
    Click **Apply to All** .... **Alt**+**T**

COREL PRESENTATIONS 8   Lesson 3: Work with Slide Shows

ANIMATE OBJECTS

1. Open a slide show.
2. Display slide containing object.
3. Click object to select it.
4. Click **Object Animation** button on the Property Bar.

   OR
   - Click **Format** .... `Alt`+`R`
   - Click **Object Properties** .... `O`
   - Click **Object Animation** .... `N`

5. Click **Animate object in place** .... `P`

   OR

   Click **Animate object across the screen** .... `A`

6. Select an **Effect** .... `Alt`+`E`, `↹`
7. Select a **Direction**, if applicable .... `Alt`+`D`, `↹`
8. Choose a desired speed:
   - **Fast** .... `Alt`+`F`
   - **Medium** .... `Alt`+`M`
   - **Slow** .... `Alt`+`S`
9. Click **Object** .... `Alt`+`O`, `↹` **display sequence** if you want to change display order of objects on the slide.
10. Click **OK** .... `Enter`

USE SLIDE SHOW TOOLS

1. Run a slide show.
2. Right-click on any slide.
3. Select a slide show option .... `↹`

   OR

   Press the short cut keys listed:
   - **Previous Slide** .... `Page Up`
   - **Next Slide** .... `Page Down`
   - **Backtrack** .... `Backspace`
   - **Goto Slide** .... `Ctrl`+`S`
   - **Next Transition** .... `Space`
   - **Stop Sound** .... `End`
   - **Replay Sound** .... `Home`
   - **Increase Volume** .... `+`
   - **Decrease Volume** .... `-`
   - **Erase Highlighter** .... `Ctrl`+`E`
   - **Stop Slide Show** .... `Esc`

4. Click away from dialog box to close.

COREL PRESENTATIONS 8 Lesson 3: Work with Slide Shows

Exercise 16

- Set Slide Timings and Display Sequences
- Add Sound
- Create Custom Audiences

NOTES

Set Slide Timings and Display Sequences

- In the previous exercise, you learned that—by default—a slide stays on screen until you advance it manually by clicking the mouse or by using a keyboard key, such as the Spacebar. You can, however, set a time limit for how long each slide stays on screen. Slide timings are set in second increments.

- Object animation is also activated when you click the mouse or use a keyboard key. You can, however, choose to have objects appear automatically and in various sequences.

- To set **slide timings** and/or **object display sequences**, do the following:

  - Click the Slide Properties button on the Toolbar and click the Display Sequence tab.
    OR
  - Right-click on a slide and select Display Sequence from the QuickMenu.
    OR
  - Select Slide Properties, Display Sequence from the Format menu.

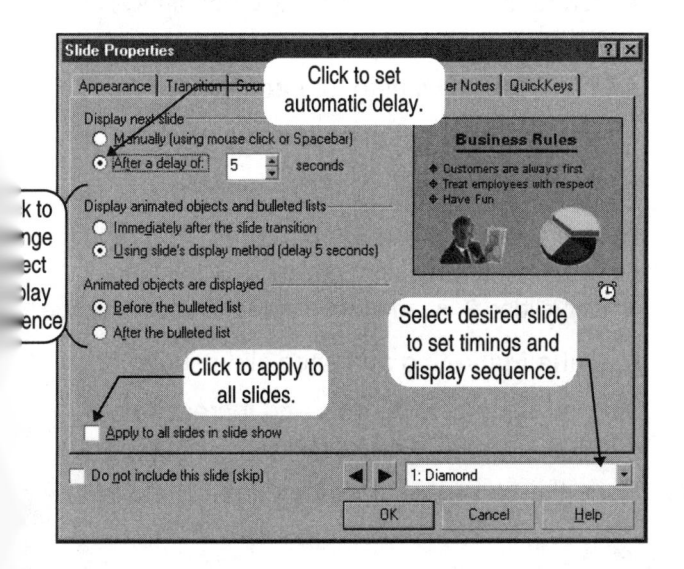

- In the Display Sequence tab of the Slide Properties dialog box that displays, check to see that the desired slide is indicated in the bottom right corner. Then, to set automatic timings between slides, select the After a delay of option and type the desired seconds to be delayed.

- To set objects to display without manual input, select the Immediately after the slide transition option.

- Automated objects display after bulleted list objects by default. Click the Before the bulleted list option to display their animation prior to the animation of a bulleted list.

Add Sound

- In addition to adding visual transitions to slides, you may add **sound** effects so that your slide show can become an entertaining multimedia event. You can add recorded music from a CD, a sound clip, or your own narration to any slide.

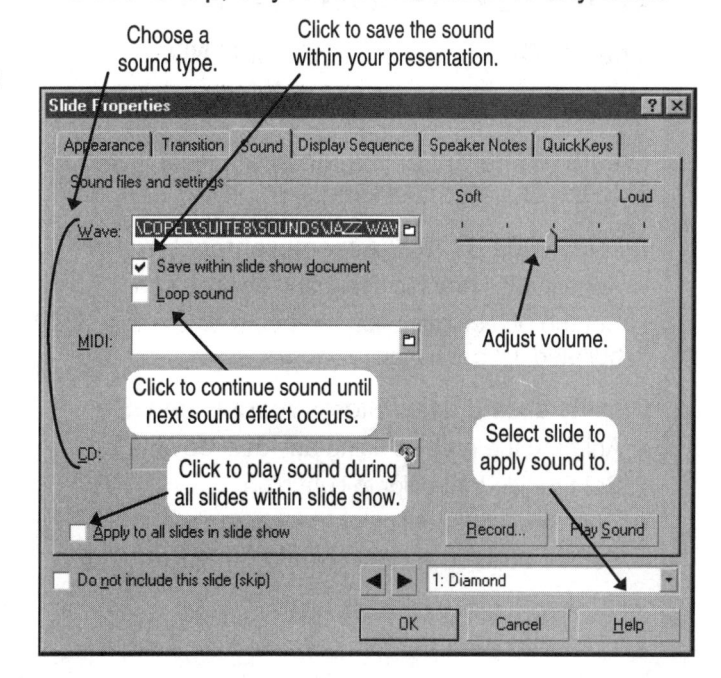

COREL PRESENTATIONS 8 Lesson 3: Work with Slide Shows

- Sounds may be added by selecting Sound from the Insert menu, or by clicking the Sound button on the Property Bar. In the Slide Transition and Sound Properties dialog box that follows, select the slide to which you wish to add a sound. Then click the type of sound you wish to insert: Wave, Midi, or CD. Your Corel Presentations 8 installation CD ROM contains numerous sound clips. Click the Browse button and browse to select a sound to insert.

- If you want a sound to continue until the next sound effect is encountered on a slide, click the Loop sound option.

Create Custom Audiences

- The **Custom Audiences** feature enables you to skip selected slides within a slide show to tailor the presentation for different audiences. By creating different custom audiences within your slide show, you do not need to save several versions of the same presentation.

- To create a custom audience, select Custom Audiences from the Tools menu. Or, select Custom Audience from the Custom Audiences drop-down list on the Property Bar.

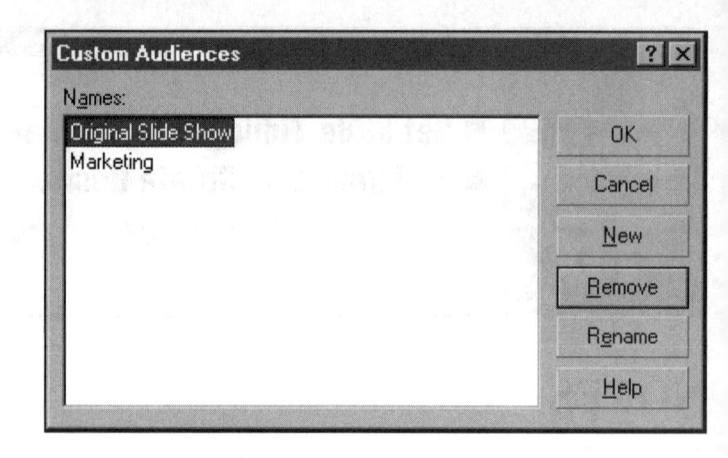

- In the Custom Audiences dialog box, click New and type a name that corresponds with the viewing audience. Click OK and return to the slide show. Select each slide you wish to remove from view (for that particular audience) and click the Skip button on the Property Bar.

- To return to the original view, which contains all slides, click the Custom Audiences drop down list on the Property Bar and select Original Slide Show.

In this exercise, you will edit a previously created presentation by adding sound and timings to selected slides. You will then view your slide show.

EXERCISE DIRECTIONS

1. Open **DIAMOND** or **16DIAMOND**.
2. Create a transition effect for each slide.
3. Create a different animation effect for the text on each Bulleted List slide.
4. Display slide 3 (1998 Accomplishments).
   - Animate the graphic using any desired effect.
   - Set the object animation to appear before the bulleted list animation.
5. Display slide 6 (New Stores Across the US).
   - Animate the graphic using any desired effect.
   - Set the title font color to light blue.
   - Set the subtitle font color to pink.
   - Set the bulleted list font color to light blue.
6. Display slide 7 (Exciting New Product Lines).
   - Animate the graphics using any desired effect.
   - Rearrange the current display order of the graphics.
7. Add a 5-second timing for each slide.
8. Create a sound effect on slides 1 and 3.
9. Set the slide show to run continuously.
10. Create a custom audience.
    - Name the new custom audience: Marketing.
    - Skip slides 2, 4, and 5 for the Marketing audience.
11. Play the Marketing audience slide show.
12. Access Slide Show Tools and increase the volume.
13. Save the changes; close the file.

KEYSTROKES

SET TIMINGS AND DISPLAY SEQUENCE

1. Open slide presentation.
2. Select slide(s) to receive timing.
   OR
   Select the object(s) to receive animation setting.
3. Right-click on a slide and select....... `D` **Display Sequence**.
   OR
   a. Click the **Slide Properties** button on the Toolbar.
   b. Click the **Display Sequence** tab .... `Ctrl`+`Tab`
   OR
   a. Click **Format**............ `Alt`+`R`
   b. Click **Slide Properties**................ `S`
   c. Click **Display Sequence**............. `D`
4. To set slide timings:
   - Click **After a delay** .... `Alt`+`F`
   - Type the number of seconds between slides.
5. To advance animated objects and bulleted lists automatically:
   - Click **Immediately after the slide transition** .... `Alt`+`D`
6. To display animated objects before bulleted lists:
   - Click **Before the bulleted list** .... `Alt`+`B`
7. Click **OK** .... `Enter`
   to apply settings to the current setting.
   OR
   - Click **Apply to all slides in the slide show**............. `Alt`+`A`
   - Click **OK** .... `Enter`

ADD SOUND

1. Open presentation.
2. Display desired slide(s).
3. Right-click on a slide and select **Sound** .... `S`
   OR
   - Click the **Sound** button............... on the Property Bar.
   OR
   a. Click **Insert**.............................. `I`
   b. Click **Sound**............................... `S`
4. Click type of sound file to insert:
   - **Wave**............................. `Alt`+`W`
   - **MIDI**............................. `Alt`+`M`
   - **CD**............................... `Alt`+`C`
   OR
5. Click **Browse** button........................ to find a file type.
6. Choose desired sound.
7. Click **Open** .... `Alt`+`O`
8. If desired, click any of the following:
   - Click **Play Sound**............... `Alt`+`S`
   - Click **Loop Sound** .... `L`
   - Click **Save within slide show document**............. `Alt`+`D`
9. Click **OK** .... `Enter`
   to apply settings to the current setting
   OR
   - Click **Apply to all slides in the slide show**............. `Alt`+`A`
   - Click **OK** .... `Enter`

CREATE CUSTOM AUDIENCES

1. Select **Custom Audiences** from the **Custom Audiences** drop-down list on the Property Bar.
   OR
   a. Click **Tools** .... `Alt`+`T`
   b. Click **Custom Audiences** .... `D`
2. Click **New**............................... `Alt`+`N`
3. Type name of new custom audience.
4. Click **OK** .... `Enter`
5. Select slides to skip for custom audience viewing.
6. Click the **Skip** button....................... on the Property Bar.

To Return to Original Slide Show
   - Select **Original slide show** from the **Custom Audiences** drop-down list on the Property Bar.
   OR
   a. Click **Tools** .... `Alt`+`T`
   b. Click **Custom Audiences** .... `D`
   c. Click in **Names** box .... `Alt`+`N`
   d. Select **Original Slide Show**.......
   e. Click **OK**................................ `Enter`

COREL PRESENTATIONS 8   Lesson 3: Work with Slide Shows

Exercise 17

- **Audience Notes Pages and Handouts**
- **Speaker Notes**

NOTES

Audience Notes Pages and Handouts

- In the previous exercises, you printed your presentation as Handouts with five to eight slides per page. Handouts may be given to the audience so they can follow along with your presentation and/or take them home for reference. Corel Presentations 8 provides other options for printing your presentation as well.

- **Audience Notes** are similar to handouts, but a series of lines are printed below each miniature slide so that the audience can take notes as the presentation is given.

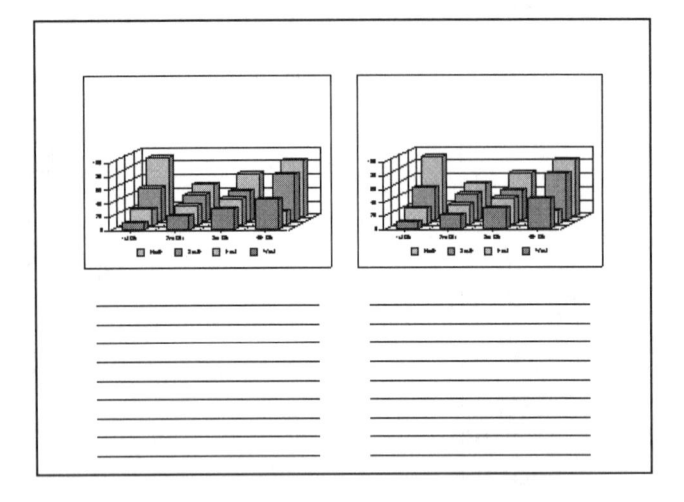

Speaker Notes

- The **Speaker Notes** option allows you type notes and/or your script beneath a thumbnail printout of each slide. Speaker Notes are particularly useful when giving an oral presentation.

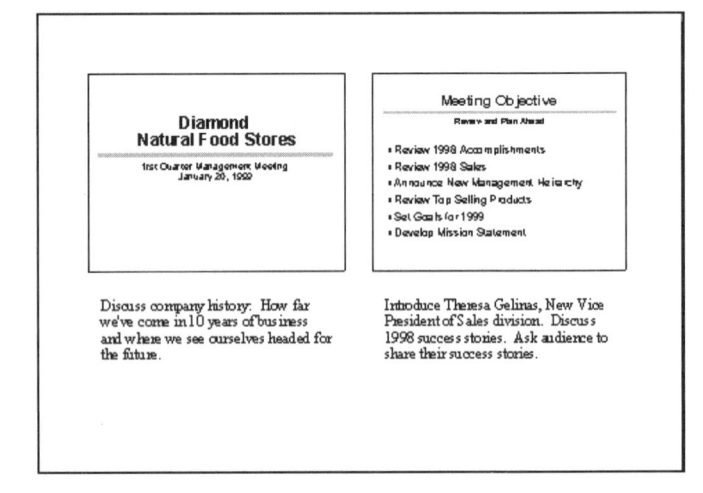

- To create Speaker Notes, click on the slide you wish to add them to (in any view), right-click and select Speaker Notes from the QuickMenu. Or, select Slide Properties, Speaker Notes from the Format menu.

- The Slide Properties dialog box appears with the Notes tab selected. Type the desired information in the text box provided.

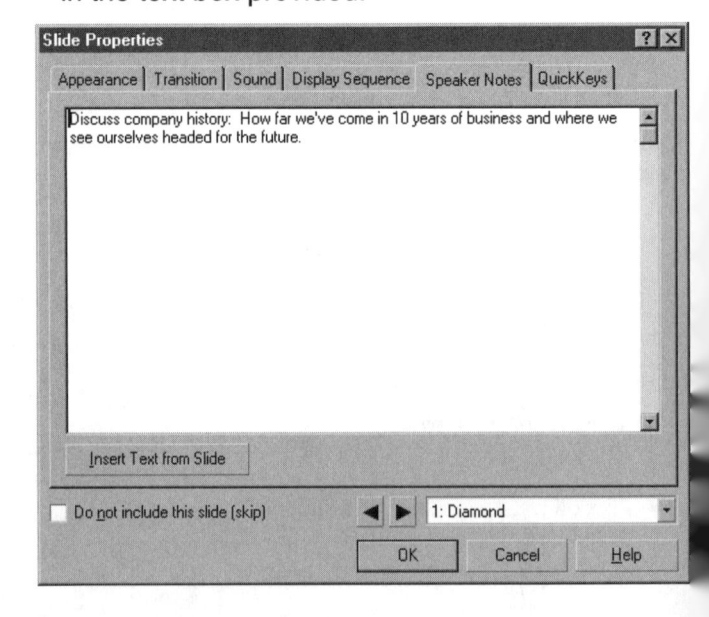

- To add Speaker Notes to additional slides from the Slide Properties dialog box, click the right or left arrow buttons to move to the next or previous slide. Or, select the desired slide from the drop-down list.

- To print Audience Notes Pages or Speaker Notes, select the desired option from the Print dialog box and indicate the desired number of slides to print per page.

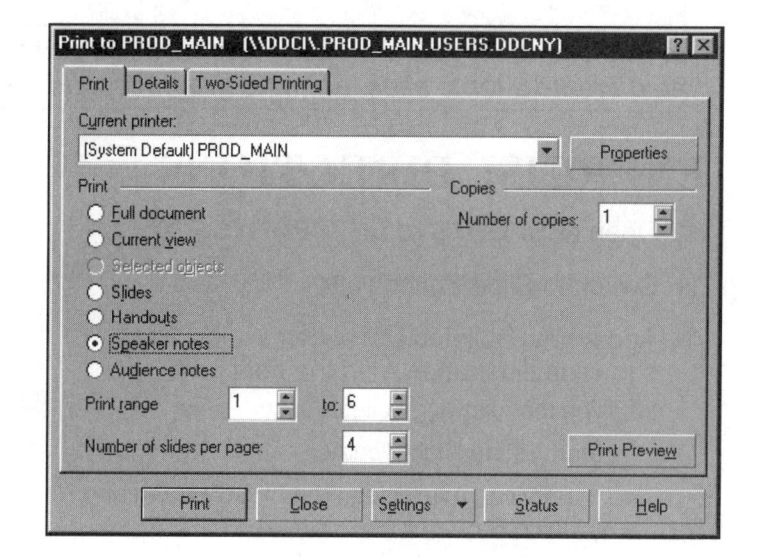

KEYSTROKES

CREATE SPEAKER NOTES

1. Open desired presentation.
2. Click on a slide in any view.
   - Right-click and select **Speaker Notes**.................. N
3. Type notes.
4. Click **Previous** or **Next** button to move to other slides .... ◄ ►
   OR
   Click drop-down list and select desired slide.
5. Click **OK** .... Enter

PRINT SPEAKER NOTES, AUDIENCE NOTES PAGES, AND HANDOUTS

Ctrl + P

1. Click **Print** button on the Toolbar ... 🖨
   OR
   a. Click **File** .... Alt + F
   b. Click **Print** .... P
2. Click **Handouts** .... Alt + T
   OR
   Click **Speaker Notes** .... Alt + P
   OR
   Click **Audience Notes** .... Alt + D

3. Click **Print range**, ... Alt + R
   if desired.
4. Type slide numbers to print .... ↑↓, Tab, ↑↓
5. Click **Number of slides per page** .... Alt + M
6. Type desired number .... ↑↓
7. Click **Print** .... Enter

COREL PRESENTATIONS 8 Lesson 3: Work With Slide Shows

> *In this exercise, you will create a table slide and add reminders on Speaker Note pages. You will also create a table slide, animate graphics, and insert a bulleted list.*

EXERCISE DIRECTIONS

1. Open **SPORTS** or **17SPORTS**.
2. Switch to Slide Editor view.
3. Add a new Bulleted List slide as slide 9 as shown in Illustration A on the next page.
   a. Type the following bulleted text:

      Start Eating Right Today

      Services Available at the FPSC Health and Juice Bar
      - Juice Bar
        - Fresh squeezed fruit and vegetable juices
        - Fruit Smoothies
        - Protein Shakes
      - Vitamins (Our own brand!)
      - Coffee and Cappuccino Bar
      - Lunch and Dinner Service

   b. Insert a text line at the bottom of the slide, using an italic 18-point serif font. Type the following:

      Nutrition Consultants available 9 a.m. to 7 p.m. Monday through Saturday.

   c. Insert a relevant graphic.
   d. Automate the graphic so that it appears after the bulleted list text.
   e. Select a new bullet style.
   f. Select a new automation effect for the bulleted list.
4. Insert a new blank slide (slide with no layout) as slide 10.
   a. Use the Tool Palette to add a bulleted list box in the center of the slide. Type the bulleted text as shown in Illustration B.
   b. Add two text lines and place them as shown in Illustration B.
   c. Set the text line to a 40-point decorative font.
   d. Animate all three items.
5. Insert a new Title slide as slide 11.
   a. Type the title and subtitle as shown in Illustration C.
   b. Insert a relevant graphic, as shown, and animate it so that it displays immediately after the slide transition.
6. Display slide 2 (FPSC is More than Just a Gym).
   - Animate the graphic so that it is displayed before the bulleted text.
7. Display slide 3 (FPSC's High Success Rate).
   - Animate the graphic as desired.
8. Display slide 4 (We're Expanding Every Day).
   - Animate the graphics as desired.
9. Switch to Slide Sorter view.
10. Create a transition effect and set a transition speed for each slide in the presentation.
11. Create a sound effect for slides 1, 2, and 11.
12. Play the slide show. Set each slide to advance automatically.
13. Switch to Slide Sorter view.
14. Add the following Speaker Notes to the slides indicated.

    Slide 1:
    - Introduce the purpose of the presentation.
    - Give a general overview of what will be covered in the presentation.

    Slide 2:
    - Review the numerous facilities available and identify the features of each.

    Slide 4:
    - Identify the location of the new clubs and what specialties each facility will offer.

    Slide 5:
    - Review cost breakdown of each plan.

15. Print one copy of the presentation as Speaker Notes with four slides per page.
16. Print one copy of the presentation as Audience Notes with four slides per page.
17. Save the changes; close the file.

ILLUSTRATION A

Start Eating Right Today

Services Available at the FPSC Health and Juice Bar

★ Juice Bar
  ★ Fresh squeezed fruit and vegetable juices
  ★ Fruit Smoothies
  ★ Protein Shakes
★ Vitamins (Our own brand!)
★ Coffee and Cappuccino Bar
★ Lunch and Dinner Service

Nutrition Consultants Available 9 a.m. to 7 p.m. Monday through Saturday

ILLUSTRATION B

At FPSC we believe in:

- Exercise
- Nutrition
- Stress Management
- Relaxation

And having fun!

ILLUSTRATION C

Join Today

It's the Next Best Thing to Taking a Vacation

Corel Presentations 8 ■ Lesson 3 ■ Exercise 17

Exercise 18

■ QuickKeys ■ QuickLinks ■ Add Movies

NOTES

QuickKeys

- In Exercise 15 you learned how to access the Slide Show Playback Tools to move to specific slides in a slide show. Presentations 8 also allows you to assign QuickKeys to move to slides in your slide show.

- **QuickKeys** are keyboard shortcuts that allow you to automatically jump to a slide or perform an action that you assign. For example, you may have a resource slide in your slide show that you wish to return to, or a specific sound you wish to play during a slide. Assigning a QuickKey to move to a specific slide or to perform a specific action allows you to do so without showing your actions to the audience.

- To assign a QuickKey, select a slide (in any view), right-click and select QuickKeys from the QuickMenu. The QuickKey tab of the Slide Properties dialog box will display.

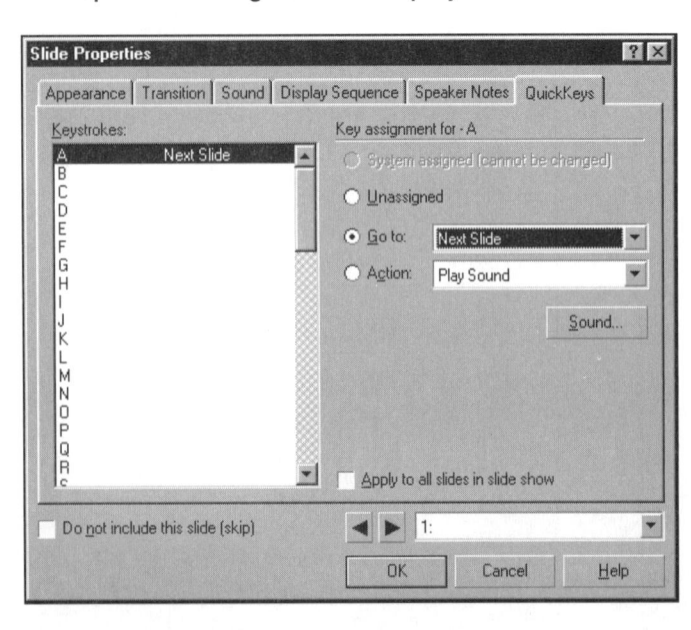

- Select a QuickKey shortcut from the Keystrokes list and click the Go to or Action button. The Go to option provides a list of slides to move to within the presentation. The Action option allows you to assign an action to the keystroke. Actions include Play Sound, Stop Sound, Browse Internet, Launch Program, and Quit Show.

QuickLinks

- **QuickLinks** allow you to assign the same Go to or Actions settings to onscreen objects as you set to keystrokes with QuickKeys. For example, you can create a hyperlink graphic on a slide that, once clicked, will return you to a previous slide.

- To create a QuickLink, select a graphic or text object, right-click, and select QuickLink from the QuickMenu.

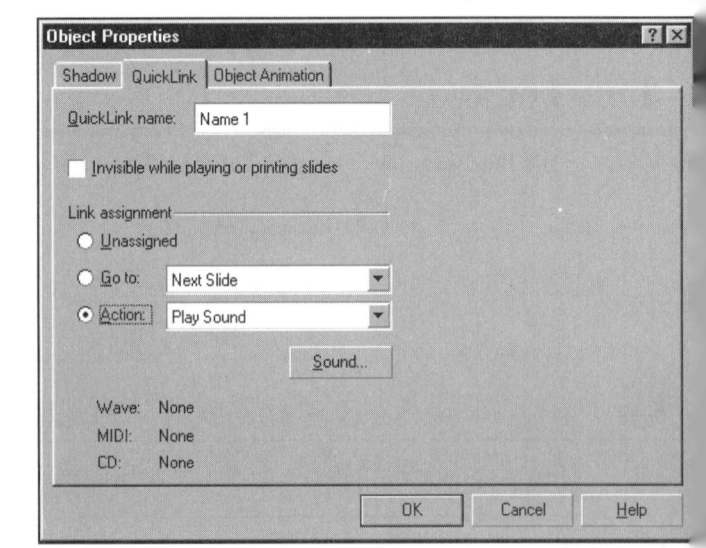

- In the QuickLinks tab of the Object Properties dialog box, you must assign a name for the link in the QuickLink Name box and then click the GoTo or Action button. The shortcut options are the same as with QuickKeys. If you wish to make the link invisible when it is printed or played during a slide show, click to select the Invisible while playing or printing slides option.

- QuickLinks may also be assigned to text to create hyperlinks to specified Internet Web pages. This option—along with all Internet related tasks—will be discussed in the Integration section of this book.

Add Movies

- Moving video images (.AVI, .MOV, .MPEG, or .QT), which Corel refers to as **movies**, can be added to your slide show to create an interesting multimedia effect. Corel provides some movies on the Corel WordPerfect Suite 8 Installation CD-ROM. Additional video images can be imported from the Internet, or from other external sources.

- To insert a video image on a slide, select Movie from the Insert menu, browse to select the desired video image file, and click Insert. To play the movie once it has been inserted, right-click and select Play Movie. Or, double-click the image.

- To control how the movie is displayed on the slide, right-click the image and select Movie Properties. Click to select or deselect any of the desired options.

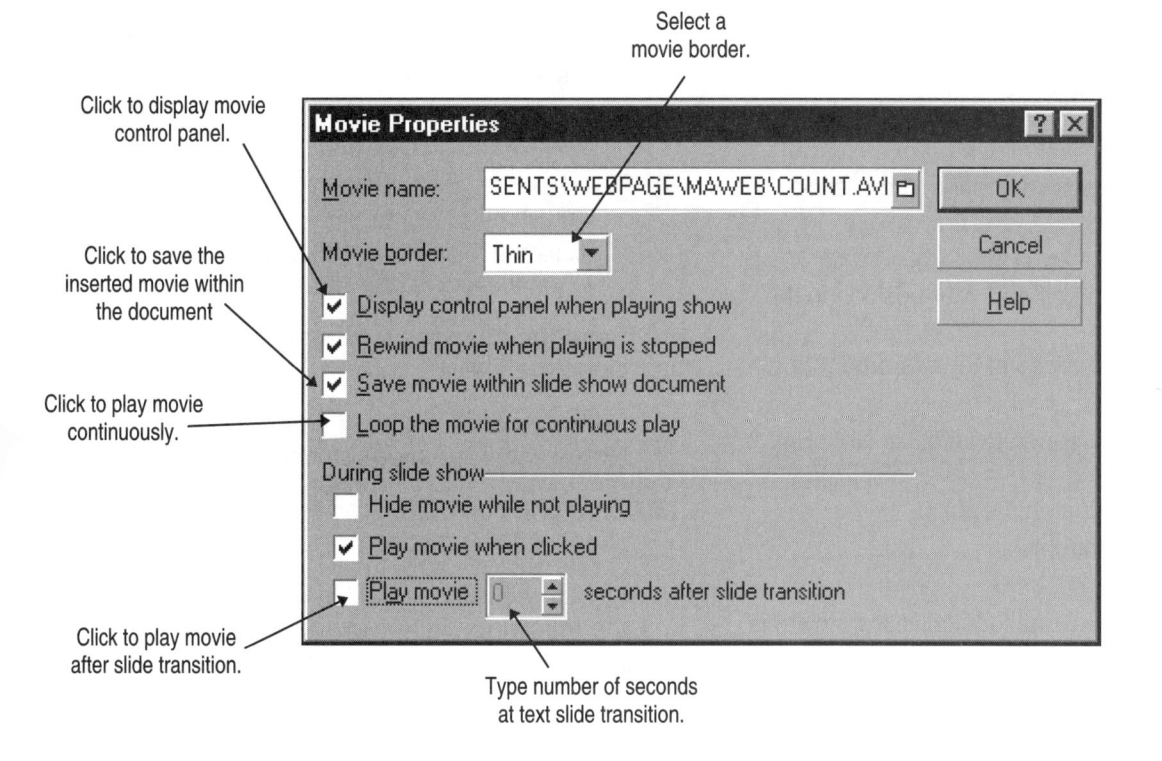

COREL PRESENTATIONS 8 Lesson 3: Work with Slide Shows

In this Exercise, you will assign a QuickKey and a QuickLink to a presentation you created earlier. You will also set transitions and timings for each slide as well as add sound, animation, and a video file to select slides.

EXERCISE DIRECTIONS

1. Open **NEWERA** or **18NEWERA**.
2. Assign a transition effect, a transition speed, and a sound to each slide in the presentation.
3. Set a Timed Advance for each slide.
4. Display Slide 1.
   - Insert a graphic and animate it as desired.
5. Display Slide 2 (Why Invest in New Era Mutual funds).
   - Create an animation effect for the bulleted text.
6. Display Slide 3 (Management Team).
   - Assign a QuickKey to jump to slide 6 (To Invest Your Money With New Era).
7. Add the following speaker notes to the slides indicated:
   Slide 1:
   - Introduce yourself and your position in the company.
   - Explain the purpose of today's presentation.

   Slide 2:
   - Review each reason to invest in New Era Mutual Funds.
   - Emphasize blue-chip stocks.
   - Give three examples.

   Slide 4:
   - Explain the reasons for significant growth in 1998.

   Slide 5:
   - Review each instrument.
8. Insert a new Title slide as slide 7.
   a. Type and center the following text in the Title placeholder. Use a 32-point decorative font.
      You Too Can Be on the Road to Earning More Money
   b. Delete the Subtitle placeholder.
9. Display Slide 7 (To Invest Your Money With New Era).
   a. Create a QuickLink that links to the first slide in the slide show.
   b. Create a text line in a 14-point sans serif font that reads: **Click to return to Slide 1**
   c. Insert a graphic or create a shape below the text line.
   d. Group the text line and the graphic and position it at the bottom-left corner of the slide.
   e. Assign a QuickLink to the image that will link it to the first slide. Name the QuickLink, Slide 1.
   f. Insert a video file.
   g. Loop the movie for continuous play. (Do not display the movie control panels.)
   h. Set the movie to play 1 second after the slide transition.
   i. Assign a QuickKey. Set a sound action to play when the key is pressed.
10. Save the changes to the presentation; do not close the file.
11. Print one copy of the slide show as Speaker Notes with four slides per page.
12. Print one copy of the slide show as Audience Notes with six slides per page.
13. Set the slide show to run continuously and do the following while viewing the slide show:
    a. On Slide 3, access the QuickKey that will advance to slide 6.
    b. Use the Go to option on the Slide Show Play Back Tools to return to slide 3.
    c. Play the remainder of the slide show.
    d. On Slide 7, access the QuickKey to play the sound action.
    e. Click the QuickLink graphic on the last slide to return to the first slide.
14. Save the changes; close the file.

SLIDE 7

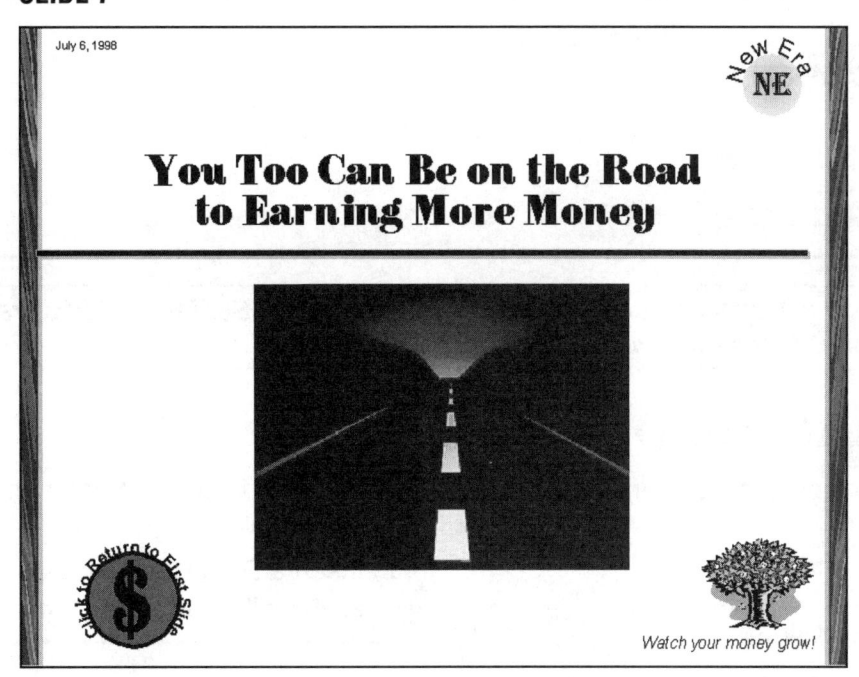

You Too Can Be on the Road to Earning More Money

July 6, 1998

New Era NE

Click to Return to First Slide $

Watch your money grow!

KEYSTROKES

CREATE QUICKKEYS

1. Right-click on desired slide.
2. Click **Q**uickKeys .... Q
3. Click **K**eystrokes .... Alt+K
4. Assign a keystroke .... ↑↓
5. Click **G**o to .... Alt+G
   OR
   Click **A**ction .... Alt+C
6. Assign a slide to go to or an action to perform .... ↑↓
7. Click **OK** .... Enter

CREATE QUICKLINKS

1. Right-click on desired slide.
2. Click **Q**uickLink .... Q
3. Click **Q**uickLink Name .... Alt+Q
4. If desired, click **I**nvisible while playing or printing slide .... Alt+I
5. Click **G**o To .... Alt+G
   OR
   Click **A**ction .... Alt+A

6. Assign a slide to link to or an action to perform .... ↑↓
7. Click **OK** .... Enter

ADD MOVIES

1. Click **I**nsert I
2. Click **M**ovie .... M
3. Browse to select a video file.
4. Click **OK** .... Enter

PLAY MOVIES

   Double-click on movie image.
   OR
   a. Right-click on movie image.
   b. Click P**l**ay Movie L
   OR
   Set Movie Properties setting to Play immediately after slide transition (See Adjust Movie Setting, below).

ADJUST MOVIE SETTINGS

1. Right-click on movie image.
2. Click **M**ovie Properties .... M

3. Click desired options:
   - Movie **b**order .... Alt+B
   - **D**isplay control panel when playing show ...... Alt+D
   - **R**ewind movie when playing is stopped .... Alt+R
   - **S**ave movie within slide show document .... Alt+S
   - **L**oop the movie for continuous play .... Alt+L
   - H**i**de movie while not playing .... Alt+I
   - **P**lay movie when clicked .... Alt+P

To play the slide show after slide transition:

4. Click P**l**ay movie seconds after slide transition. .... Alt+A
5. Type number of seconds to play after transition.
6. Click **OK** .... Enter

COREL PRESENTATIONS 8 Lesson 3: Work with Slide Shows

Exercise 19

■ Summary

In this exercise, you will create a sales presentation for Green Systems. This presentation will be given at the Regional Sales Meeting on February 12, 1999.

EXERCISE DIRECTIONS

1. Create a new presentation. Use any desired background master.
2. Insert a Title slide that reads:
   Green Systems
   Regional Sales Meeting
3. Insert an Org Chart slide as slide 2 and use the following names and titles:

Talia Donovan	VP Sales
Jim Stern	Eastern Region Sales Manager
Joseph Walker	Central Region Sales Manager
Tia Shields	Western Region Sales Manager
Shirley Theison	Eastern Region Assistant Manager

4. Insert a Bulleted List slide as slide 3.
   a. Access the Layout Layer and set the Title placeholder text to a 54-point decorative font.
   b. Set the Subtitle placeholder text to a 32-point decorative font.
   c. Left-align the Title placeholder.
5. Switch to the Background Layer.
   a. Create a company logo (company name or abbreviation and a relevant graphic) and place it where desired on the slide.
   b. Include the date of the meeting in the lower right corner of the slide.
6. Switch to Slide Editor view.
7. Create slide 3-9 as shown in the Desired Result illustration.
   ✓ *The illustration is shown in black and white; the slide background is NOT shown.*
8. Insert graphics where indicated in the illustration and automate each one.
9. Assign a bullet animation effect to each bulleted list.
10. Insert a Data Chart slide as slide 10.
    a. Enter the data below to complete the date chart.

	1996	1997	1998
Green Systems	12	27	42
Smith & Ross Electronics	10	12	14
Arrow Technology	9	8	8
Nevada Systems, Inc.	7.5	20	30

   b. Create a text line as shown in the illustration and type the following in a 20-point sans serif bold font:
      Sales in Millions
   c. Assign a QuickKey on slide 10 that plays a sound when accessed.
11. Insert a blank slide as slide 11.
    a. Create a text box as shown in the Desired Results illustration and type the following text in a 40-point sans serif font that reads:
       Year End Bonuses for All Accounts Whose Sales Are Increased by 5%.
    b. Insert a movie file and place it to the left as shown. Set any desired movie settings.
    c. Create a text line as shown in the illustration and type the following in a 20-point sans serif bold font:
       Click to Review Sales Management Team
    d. Insert a graphic below the text line.
    e. Create a QuickLink that links the graphic to slide 2. Name the Link: Sales Management Team.

COREL PRESENTATIONS 8 Lesson 3: Work with Slide Shows

12. Switch to Slide Outliner view.
13. Spell check.
14. Save the slide show; name it **GREEN**.
15. Switch to Slide Sorter view.
16. Create a transition effect for each slide in the presentation.
17. Create speaker notes where necessary to help you deliver the presentation better.
18. Add a sound effect to the first and last slide.
19. Play the slide show.
    a. At slide 10, click the QuickKey to play the sound you assigned.
    b. At slide 11, play the movie then click the QuickLink to return to slide 2.
    c. Use the Slide Show Play Back Tools to move to the last slide.
    d. Play the movie again.
20. Create a custom slide show and hide slides 2, 10, and 11. Name the custom slide show: District Meeting.
21. Play the custom slide show.
22. Print one copy as Handouts with six slides per page.
23. Print one copy as Speaker Notes with four slides per page.
24. Close the file; save the changes.

DESIRED RESULT (Slides 1-4)

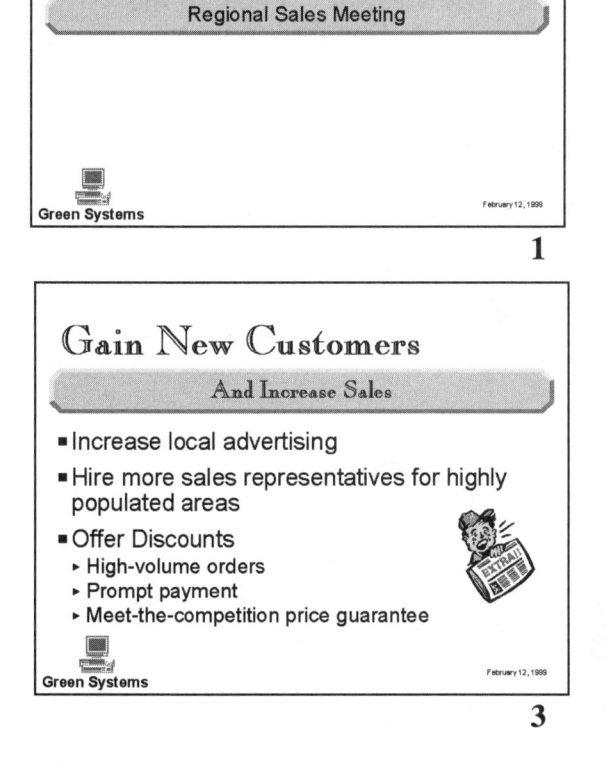

Slide 1:
Green Systems
Regional Sales Meeting
Green Systems — February 12, 1999

Slide 2:
Green Systems
Introducing our Sales Management Team
- Talia Donovan, VP Sales
  - Jim Stern, Eastern Region Sales Manager
    - Shirley Theisen, Eastern Region Assistant Manager
  - Joseph Walker, Central Region Sales Manager
  - Tia Shieds, Western Region Sales Manager
Green Systems — February 12, 1999

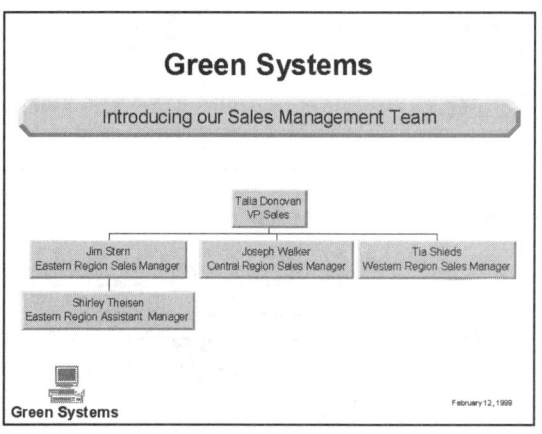

Slide 3:
Gain New Customers
And Increase Sales
- Increase local advertising
- Hire more sales representatives for highly populated areas
- Offer Discounts
  ▸ High-volume orders
  ▸ Prompt payment
  ▸ Meet-the-competition price guarantee
Green Systems — February 12, 1999

Slide 4:
Advertising
Getting Our Name Out There
- Media
  ▸ Television
  ▸ Radio
- Mass mailings
- Internet
  ▸ Search site advertisement
  ▸ Registration with search sites
  ▸ Company Web page
Green Systems — February 12, 1999

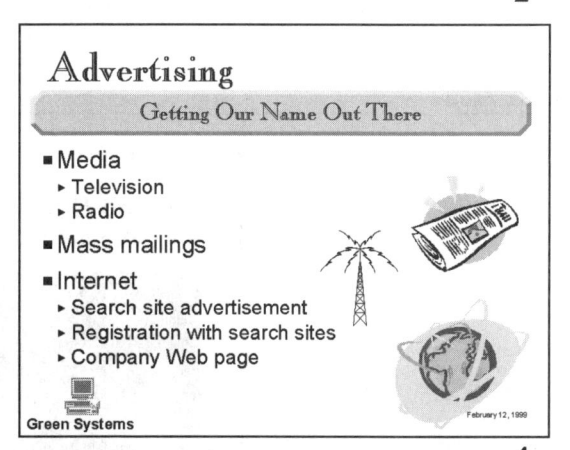

Desired Result continued on next page ➡

COREL PRESENTATIONS 8 Lesson 3: Work with Slide Shows

DESIRED RESULT (Slides 5-11)

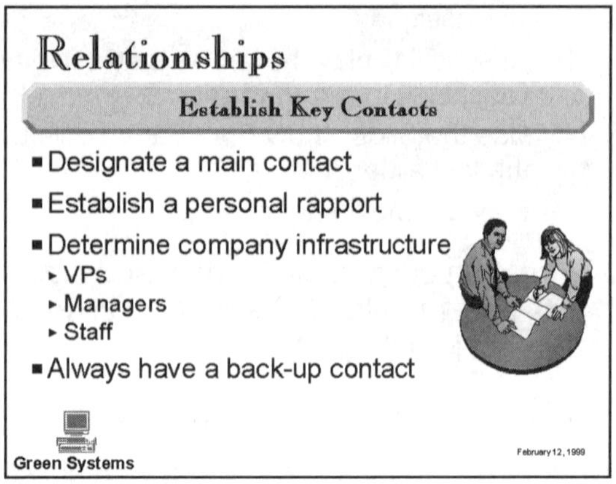

5. Relationships
Establish Key Contacts
- Designate a main contact
- Establish a personal rapport
- Determine company infrastructure
  - VPs
  - Managers
  - Staff
- Always have a back-up contact

Green Systems — February 12, 1999

6. Increase Product Exposure
- Trade conventions
  - Booth layout
  - Product displays
  - Hands-on workshops
- Schools
  - Free workshops
  - Equipment donations
- Computer-user group meetings
  - Product demos
  - Complimentary door prizes

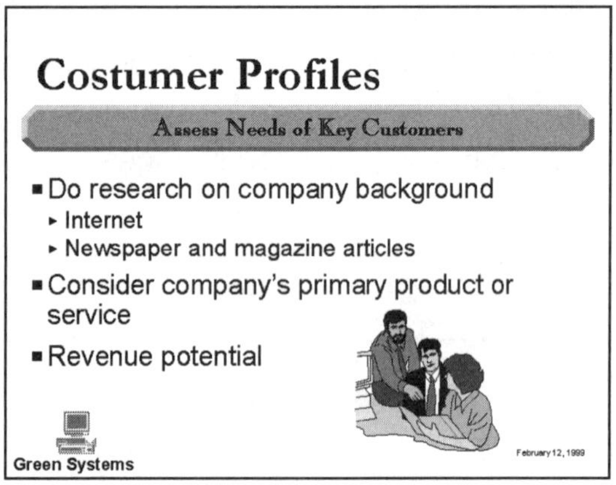

Green Systems — February 12, 1999

7. Costumer Profiles
Assess Needs of Key Customers
- Do research on company background
  - Internet
  - Newspaper and magazine articles
- Consider company's primary product or service
- Revenue potential

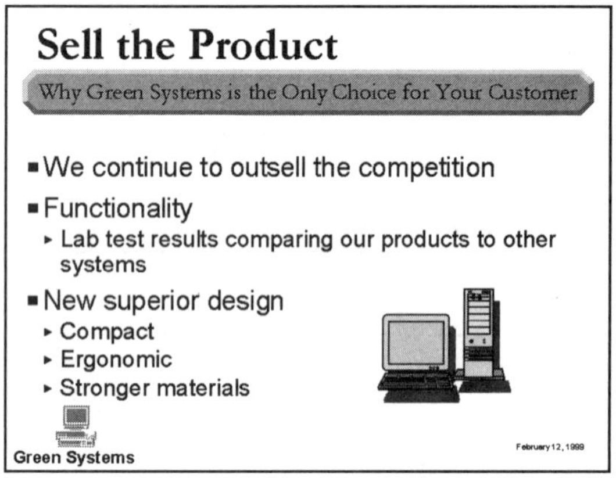

Green Systems — February 12, 1999

8. Sell the Product
Why Green Systems is the Only Choice for Your Customer
- We continue to outsell the competition
- Functionality
  - Lab test results comparing our products to other systems
- New superior design
  - Compact
  - Ergonomic
  - Stronger materials

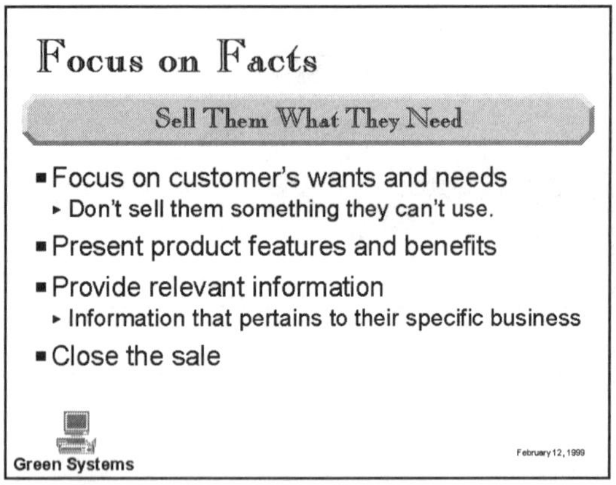

Green Systems — February 12, 1999

9. Focus on Facts
Sell Them What They Need
- Focus on customer's wants and needs
  - Don't sell them something they can't use.
- Present product features and benefits
- Provide relevant information
  - Information that pertains to their specific business
- Close the sale

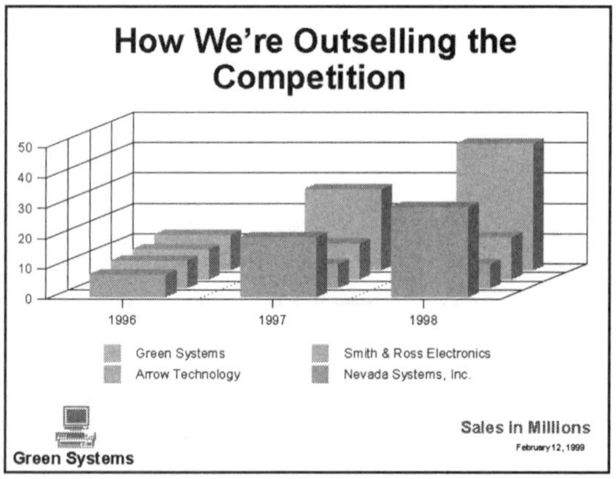

Green Systems — February 12, 1999

10. How We're Outselling the Competition

(Bar chart: 1996, 1997, 1998 — Green Systems, Arrow Technology, Smith & Ross Electronics, Nevada Systems, Inc.)

Sales in Millions

Green Systems — February 12, 1999

11. Year-End Bonuses for All Accounts Whose Sales Are Increased by 5%

Click to Review Sales Management Team

Green Systems — February 12, 1999

534

Corel® WordPerfect® Suite 8 Professional Integration

COREL WORDPERFECT SUITE 8 PROFESSIONAL Integration

Exercise 1

- Use Several Files in One Application
- Work with Files from Different Applications

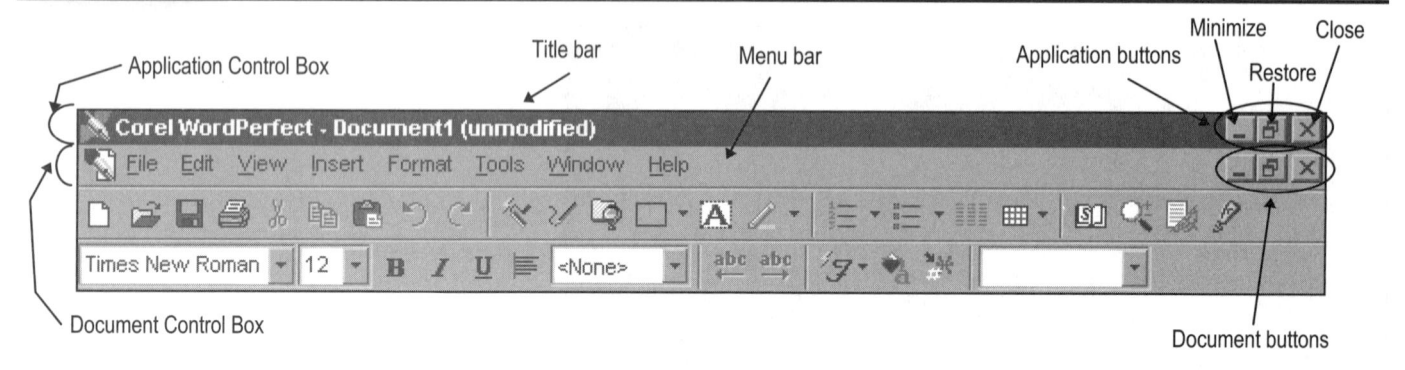

Labels on application window illustration: Application Control Box, Title bar, Menu bar, Application buttons, Minimize, Restore, Close, Document Control Box, Document buttons

Labels on second illustration: Document 1, restored but not maximixed; Document 2 minimized to a title bar and selected; Application Bar showing open documents

NOTES

Use Several Files in One Application

- Corel WordPerfect Suite 8 allows you to work with several files simultaneously by creating a window for each open file. The exact number of files that can be used at once depends on the application and available memory. (Windowing lets you view files as you work with them.)

- When you open an application, Corel WordPerfect Suite 8 displays a full-screen, or maximized window. The control box and buttons on the title bar let you size and arrange files within the Windows screen. (See Chapter 1 - Corel WordPerfect Suite 8 Basics, Exercise 2.) The control box and buttons to the left and right of the menu bar allow you to size and arrange the current application file window.

- Minimizing a window, or reducing its size, allows you to view other open files. To reduce the size of a maximized window, click the restore button on the menu bar. The file will be displayed in a window within the application. The file can be further reduced, or minimized, to a title bar icon by clicking on the minimize button on the file title bar. The file can be restored or maximized by selecting either the restore or maximize button on the title bar. Note the illustration of restored and minimized files.

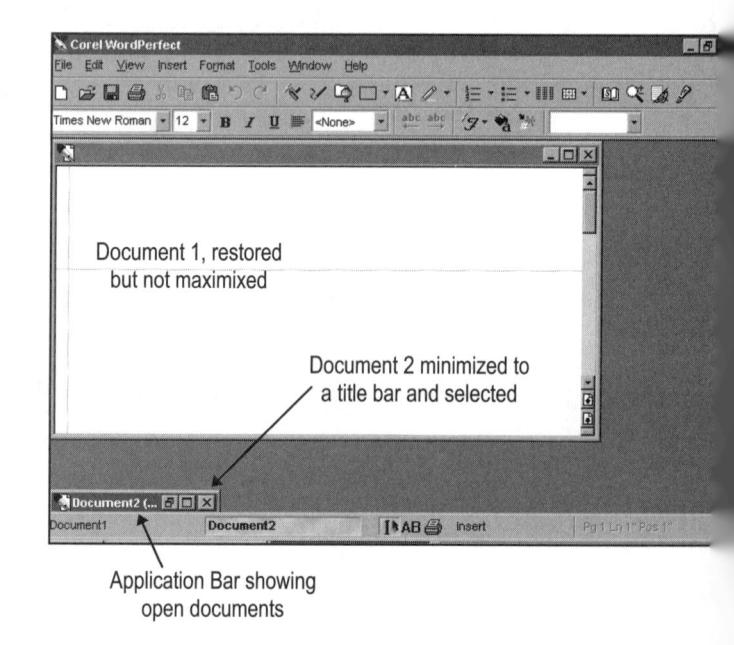

- You can resize a reduced window by dragging the window border. Dragging a corner of the window border allows you to change both the width and length simultaneously.

- If multiple files are open in the same application, you may view them at once by using the Tile Top to Bottom, Tile Side by Side, or Cascade command on the Window menu.

536

- When files are tiled, each file is visible in a window without overlapping. The title bar in the active window will be highlighted and the inactive window title bar will be darkened. Click any window to make it active, and click the maximize button on the title bar to maximize it.

Tiled Files

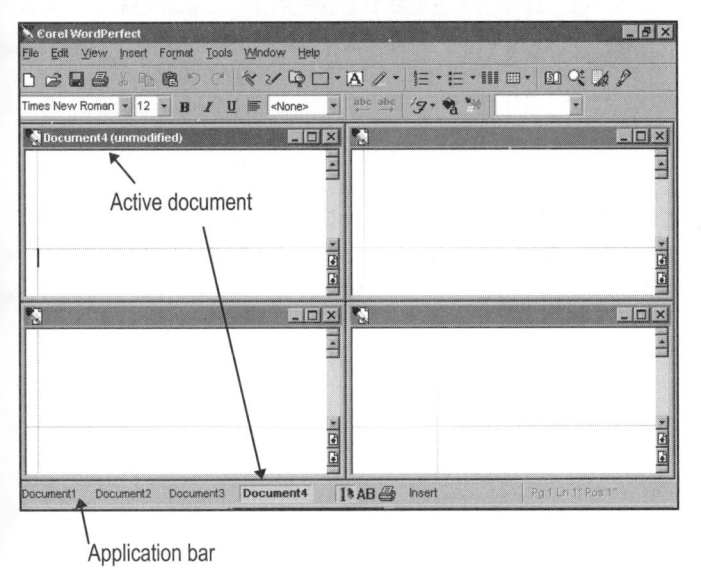

- Cascaded windows allow you to view the title bar of each open file. The windows are overlapped so that the title bar of each file is displayed. Note the illustration of four Quattro Pro files cascaded with the active notebook file on top. To make a window active, click any visible portion of the desired window.

Cascaded Windows

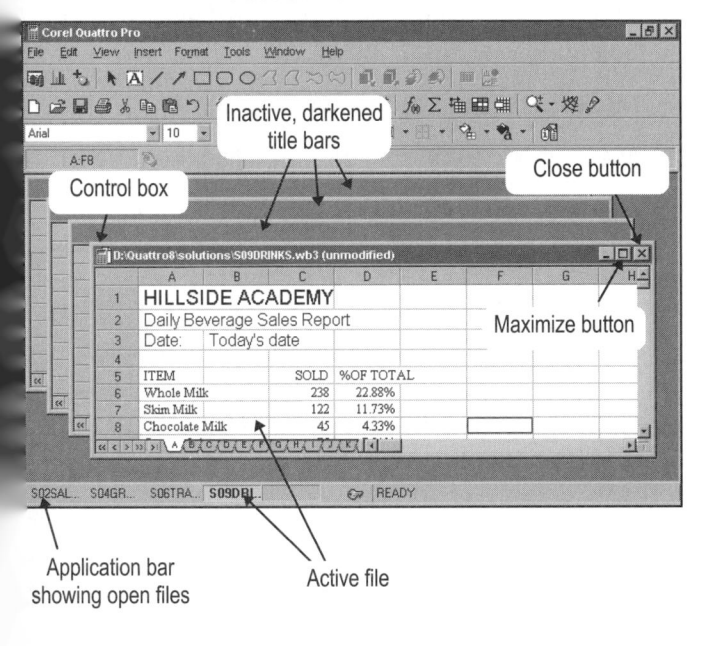

- You can also switch among file windows whether they are currently displayed or not by selecting Window from the menu and choosing the desired file from the open files listed at the bottom.

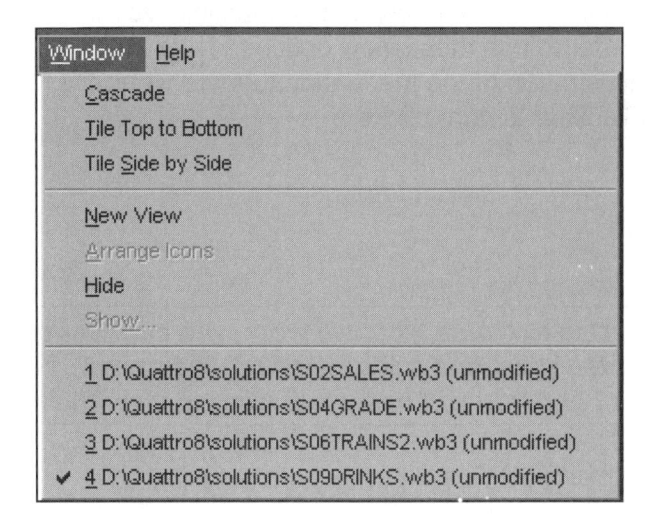

- A window can be closed by double-clicking the control box, which is at the left on the title bar or by clicking the Close button ✕.

  ✓Note: *When you double-click, the control menu is bypassed.*

Use Files from Different Applications

- If you wish to move between a WordPerfect document and a Quattro Pro notebook, or among files open in any Corel WordPerfect Suite 8 application, click the desired DAD icon to open the application. Or, if the application is already open, click an active program icon on the Windows 95 Taskbar as shown below.

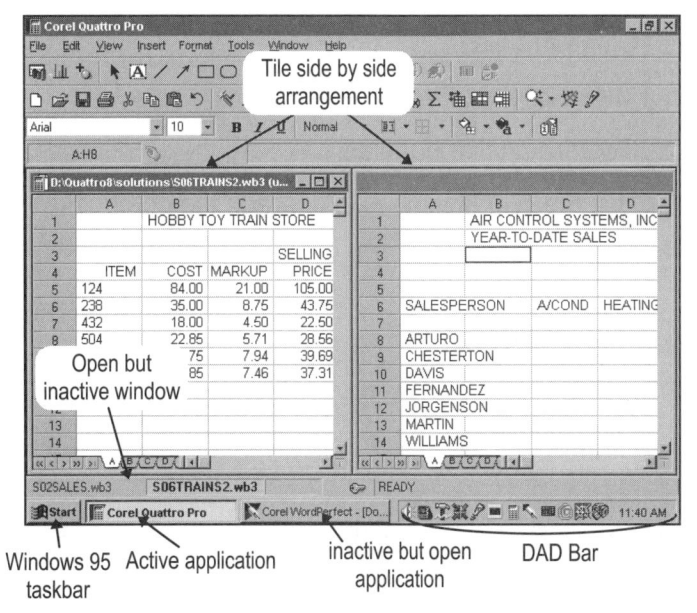

Corel Integration ■ Exercise 1   537

COREL WORDPERFECT SUITE 8 PROFESSIONAL Integration

- However, if you wish to see files from different applications on the screen at the same time, right-click the Windows 95 Taskbar and select the view option you prefer. Each application must be in a window that is not minimized in order to use these view options. Note the illustration of the menu that appears when the Taskbar is right-clicked.

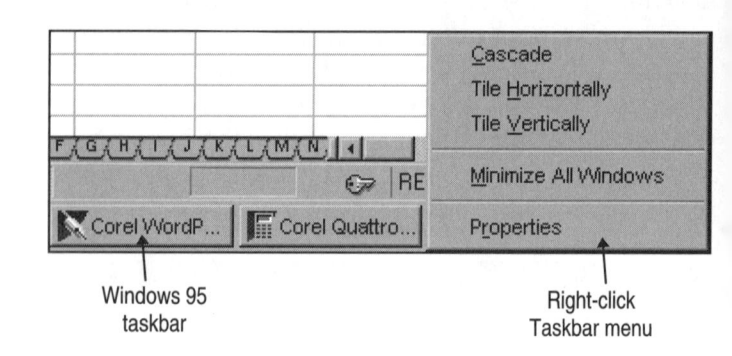

Windows 95 taskbar

Right-click Taskbar menu

In this exercise, you will work with application and document controls, four Quattro Pro notebooks, and a WordPerfect document. You will arrange the notebooks so you can view each file, and you will use windowing to view the notebook pages and the document at the same time.

EXERCISE DIRECTIONS

1. Click the DAD Quattro Pro icon.
2. Open **TRAINS.wb3** or **01TRAINS.wb3**.
3. Open **GRSUM.wb3** or **01GRSUM.wb3**.
4. Open **DRINKS.wb3** or **01DRINKS.wb3**.
5. Open **ACCPAY.wb3** or **01ACCPAY.wb3**.
6. Use the Window menu to tile the notebooks side by side. *Note: Since there are four files, side by side and top to bottom arrangements are the same.*
7. Make GRSUM the active notebook.
8. Minimize it.
9. Make DRINKS the active notebook.
10. Close the file.
11. Minimize ACCPAY to a title bar.
12. Restore all title bar files.
13. Use the Window menu to cascade the notebooks.
14. Use the Window menu to make the last notebook on the list active.
15. Click the WordPerfect icon on the DAD Toolbar to load WordPerfect.
16. Open **SUMMER.wpd** or **01SUMMER.wpd**.
17. Switch back to the Quattro Pro screen by clicking the DAD icon.
    ✓ *Clicking the Taskbar is much quicker.*
18. Switch back to the WordPerfect screen by clicking the Corel WordPerfect icon on the Windows 95 Taskbar.
19. View both applications at once by right-clicking a blank area on the Windows 95 Taskbar and selecting Tile Horizontally.
20. Make SUMMER the active file.
21. Maximize the window so that it fills the screen.
22. Close each window and each application.

KEYSTROKES

WINDOW FILES IN A TILED ARRANGEMENT
Positions file windows next to each other as non-overlapping tiles.

1. Click **Window**.......................... `Alt`+`W`
2. Click **Tile Top to Bottom**.................. `T`
   OR
   Click **Tile Side by Side**.................. `S`

WINDOW FILES IN A CASCADE ARRANGEMENT
Positions file windows in an overlapping format keeping title bars visible.

1. Click **Window**.......................... `Alt`+`W`
2. Click **Cascade**................................ `C`

CLOSE WINDOW

Ctrl + F4

Double-click Control box of active document window.
OR
Click **Close** button.......................... `X`
OR
a. Click Control box.
b. Click **Close**................................ `C`

MAXIMIZE WINDOW
Fills the application window with the active file.

Click **Maximize** button.................... `□`
of active file (not available if window is already maximized).
OR
a. Click Control box.
b. Click **Maximize**.......................... `X`

MINIMIZE WINDOW
Reduces active file window to a title bar icon.

Click **Minimize** button.................... `_`
of active file.
OR
a. Click Control box.
b. Click **Minimize**.......................... `N`

SWITCH AMONG OPEN DOCUMENTS

Click any visible portion of desired document.
OR
a. Click **Window**.................. `Alt`+`W`
b. Click name
   of desired document..................... `↕`
OR
Type document number.

WINDOW FILES FROM DIFFERENT APPLICATIONS

1. Click first DAD icon.
2. Open desired file.
3. Click second DAD icon.
4. Open desired file.
5. Right-click blank area on Windows 95 Taskbar.
6. Select **Tile Horizontally**.................. `H`
   OR
   Select **Tile Vertically**...................... `V`
   OR
   Select **Cascade**.............................. `C`

Corel Integration ■ Exercise 1

Exercise 2

- Copy a Notebook File into a Document File
- Edit a Copied File

NOTES

Copy a Notebook File into a Document File

- Integration is the sharing or combining of data between Corel WordPerfect Suite 8 applications. The source file is used to send data; the destination file is used to receive data. For example, a Quattro Pro graph or notebook page (the source file) can add supporting or visual documentation of material to a WordPerfect document (the destination file).

- There are three methods of integrating data between Corel applications: copying and pasting, linking, and embedding. Linking and embedding will be addressed in the next exercise. The most elementary method is to copy and paste data between applications. This method is most often used when you do not expect to edit or update the data that is copied into the destination document.

- You may use the DAD icons to switch or transfer information between applications, or you may display both files simultaneously as discussed in Exercise 1. To integrate a Quattro Pro table into a WordPerfect document, for example, you can copy and paste the data or use the drag and drop procedure.

- To **copy and paste** between applications: select the data to be copied from the source file, and select Copy from the Edit menu. The copied data is temporarily placed on the system's **clipboard**. To paste the data, switch to the destination file, and select Paste from the Edit menu.

- To **drag and drop** between applications: select the data to be copied from the source file, press Ctrl, and drag the object to the destination file on the screen or to the minimized application button on the Windows 95 Taskbar without releasing the mouse button. This will open the application and you can click or drop the object into place.

  ✓Note: *If you have difficulty placing the notebook data, drag it to any spot on the document, then maximize the document, and adjust the placement.*

Edit a Copied File

- If you are copying a **table**, the copy and paste method pastes the data into the destination file as a table. The drag and drop methods will place the table into the destination document as an object, which can then be edited as table data. However, the integrated table has no connection to the original notebook page and the formulas are not accessible. These methods should only be used when updated or linked data is not necessary and when formulas do not need editing.

In this exercise, you will copy a mortgage payment table prepared in Quattro Pro to a WordPerfect letter for the buyers of a new home. You will save the newly integrated document under a new name.

EXERCISE DIRECTIONS

1. Click the DAD Quattro Pro icon.
2. Open **LOAN.wb3** or **02LOAN.wb3**.
3. Click the DAD WordPerfect icon.
4. Open **02MORTGAGE.wpd** or create the letter shown on the next page.
5. Place your cursor at the beginning of the third paragraph in the letter.
6. Insert the additional text in the document as illustrated, and press Enter to move to the next line.
7. Right-click on a blank area of the Windows 95 Taskbar and tile the Quattro Pro and WordPerfect applications vertically.
8. Select and copy the workbook data in the range A1:G13.
9. Maximize the WordPerfect MORTGAGE document.
10. Paste the notebook table into the document below the new text, as illustrated.
    - ✓ *The notebook will be placed in the document.*
    - ✓ *To practice using drag and drop to copy the data: arrange the files on the screen as in step 7; select the Quattro Pro range A1:G13, and hold down the CTRL key while you drag the data to the WordPerfect document; place below the previous copy and paste table. Note the differences between the two methods. Delete the drag and drop table.*
11. Switch to Quattro Pro using the program button on the Windows 95 Taskbar.
    - ✓ *If the notebook is not there, you moved the notebook instead of copying it when practicing drag and drop in step 10. Click Edit, Undo, and repeat steps 8,9, and 10.*
12. Select the top four rows in the table and delete them. Only table data will be left in the document.
    - ✓ *You can change data, formats, columns, etc., since this data is in table format. However, formulas cannot be changed and data is not linked to the notebook.*
13. Adjust column widths in the table, if necessary.
14. Select the cell with the value 1213 on the top row of the table. Edit the cell to read: YEARS.
15. Move to the top of the document and delete rows before the date so that the letter fits on one page.
16. Print preview to check that the letter fits on one page.
17. Save the file as **LOBUE**.
18. Print one copy.
19. Close all files.

KEYSTROKES

COPY AND PASTE DATA BETWEEN APPLICATIONS

Ctrl+X, Ctrl+V

1. Open both applications and appropriate files.
2. In the source file, highlight the data to be copied.
3. Click **Edit** .... Alt + E
4. Click **Copy** C
5. Switch to the destination file.
6. Place cursor at the point of insertion.
7. Click **Edit** .... Alt + E
8. Click **Paste** .... P

COPY DATA BETWEEN APPLICATIONS WITH DRAG AND DROP

1. Open and display both applications and files.
2. In the source file, highlight the data to be copied.
3. Move mouse button to edge of selected range until the mouse pointer (arrow) changes to a ✥.
4. Hold Ctrl while dragging the data to the desired location in the destination file.
    - ✓ *If you do not hold down the Control key the data will be moved not copied.*

Corel Integration ■ Exercise 2   541

COREL WORDPERFECT SUITE 8 PROFESSIONAL Integration

Action Realty
Farm Boulevard
Mill Neck, New York 11571

Today's date

Mr. and Mrs. Martin Lobue
33 West Street
New York, NY 10024

Dear Mr. and Mrs. Lobue:

We are happy to be working with you to find your dream home. At our last meeting, we discussed your requirements and began to work on the financial arrangements for purchase.

We would like to help you find and select your most comfortable mortgage payment.. The monthly payment depends on your down payment, the number of years for the mortgage loan, and the interest rate in effect at the time. For a small fee, you can lock in the current interest rate after your loan is approved.

Our firm has developed a relationship with several dependable mortgage brokers in the community. We will be glad to assist you with these matters when you are ready. I look forward to our meeting next week and to re-visiting the homes you liked.

Yours truly,

Leonard Caprio
Broker

Insert text

Note the table below, calculated at an 8% interest rate, with examples of mortgage payments for various loan amounts (PRINCIPAL) and loan payment periods (YEARS).

Insert Quattro Pro 8 notebook (LOAN) under inserted text

A	A	B	C	D	E	F	G
1		**ALISHA AND MARTIN LOBUE**					
2		**MONTHLY MORTGAGE TABLE AT 8%**					
3					MARCH		
4					TERM IN YEARS		
5			1213	10	15	20	25	30
6		**PRINCIPAL**	100,000	1,213	956	836	772	734
7			105,000	1,274	1,003	878	810	770
8			110,000	1,335	1,051	920	849	807
9			115,000	1,395	1,099	962	888	844
10			120,000	1,456	1,147	1,004	926	881
11			125,000	1,517	1,195	1,046	965	917
12			130,000	1,577	1,242	1,087	1,003	954
13			135,000	1,638	1,290	1,129	1,042	991
14				0	0	0	0	0
15		Input cells						
16		column:	100000					
17		row:	10					

542

COREL WORDPERFECT SUITE 8 PROFESSIONAL Integration

Exercise 3

- Integrate a Notebook File and a Document File
- Embed a File ■ Edit an Embedded File ■ Link a File
- Edit a Linked File ■ Integrate a Chart File and a Document File

NOTES

Integrate a Notebook File and a Document File

- When integrating data between Corel applications, the copy and paste method discussed in Exercise 2 does not allow the data to be connected to the source document or allow for editing of formulas. The other two methods, **linking** and **embedding**, provide these options and are discussed in this exercise.

- Object Linking and Embedding, or OLE, is the system Corel WordPerfect Suite 8 uses to link or embed objects between applications. You can insert text, charts, graphics, spreadsheets, sound clips, video clips, or any file type using the OLE system, into Corel WordPerfect Suite 8 files.

Embed a File

- Embedding files enables you to edit data in the application but does not change or modify the source file. For example, double-clicking on an embedded Quattro Pro notebook in a WordPerfect document allows you to make edits using Quattro Pro, but will not change the source file. This is preferable if you wish to make changes within Quattro Pro that are not reflected in the source file, or if the source file is not always available. Embedding creates a large destination file since it includes the embedded or integrated object.

- To embed a new object into a file, use the Insert menu, select Object, then the Create New option. As illustrated, you can create a new Quattro Pro notebook object within WordPerfect. When you double-click the new blank object, the menus and Toolbars change to Quattro Pro so that you can develop the notebook within WordPerfect. This will not be practiced in this exercise.

Insert Object Dialog Box with Create New option selected

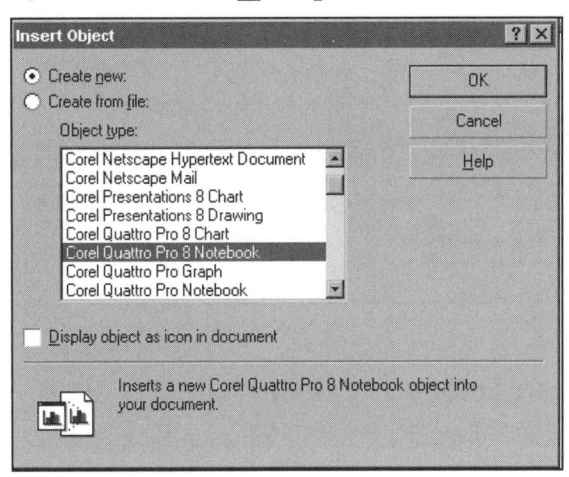

- To create an embedded object from an existing file, use the Create from File option on the Insert, Object dialog box, as illustrated below. The embedded object will be the file you select in the File: box. This procedure will embed the entire file even if it has multiple pages or data that you don't need.

Insert Object Dialog Box with Create from File option selected

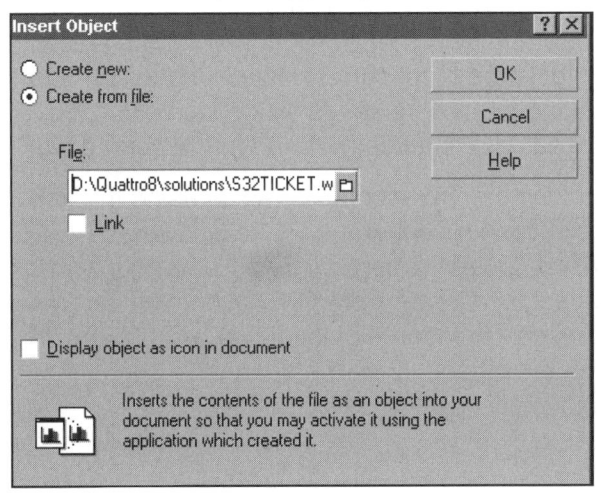

Corel Integration ■ Exercise 3   543

- You can also embed a file by selecting a range to be copied, then using the Edit, Copy, then Edit, Paste Special commands. As illustrated below, the Paste Special dialog box allows you to select the object type to embed the file. This is a good method to use if you want to use a portion of a file because you can select the area to be copied.

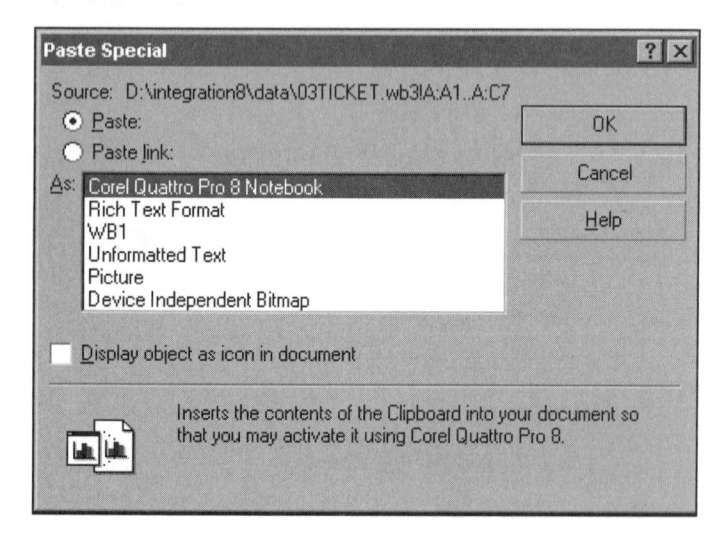

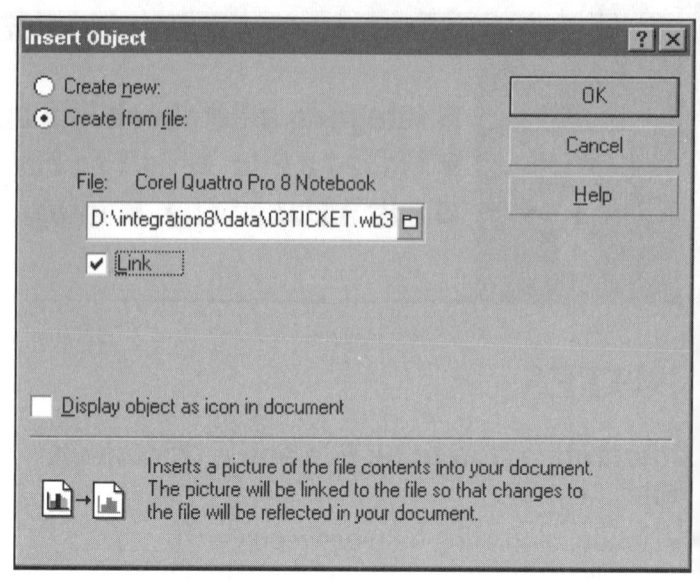

- Or, you can select Paste link on the Paste Special dialog box.

Edit an Embedded File

- Edit an embedded file by double-clicking the file, which will then display the menus for that application. To return to the original file, click outside the object or click the application icon on the Windows 95 Taskbar.

Link a File

- Linking files allows the data in the destination file to change if the source file is updated. For example, if you link a Quattro Pro notebook page (source file) into a WordPerfect document (destination file), and you update the notebook page, the WordPerfect document automatically reflects the most current data. In addition, the linking procedure saves disk space since the linked data is actually stored in the source file.

- Linking can be accomplished by using the link selections on either the Paste Special or the Insert, Object dialog box. As illustrated, if you select the Create from File option, you can select Link on the Insert Object dialog box, which will link the object. Note the change in the explanation at the bottom of the box.

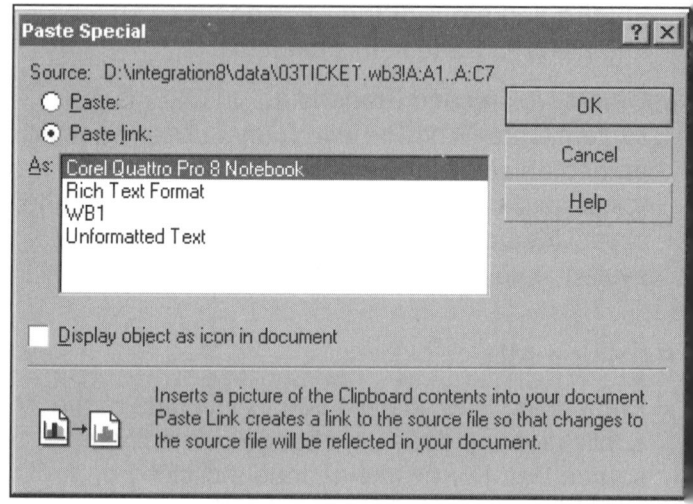

Edit a Linked File

- You can edit a linked file in the source or destination application. When a linked file from one application is double-clicked within another application, the source application and file open. For example, if you double-click a linked Quattro Pro notebook page or chart from within a WordPerfect file, you are brought into the Quattro Pro application. When changes are made to the source file, they will automatically appear in the linked file. Conversely, if you make changes directly into the source file and then open the destination file with the linked data in WordPerfect, the updated notebook page will appear.

Integrate a Chart File and a Document File

- You can insert a Quattro Pro chart into a WordPerfect document using the same linking or embedding commands. The OLE system and the consequences of using linking or embedding for notebook pages apply to charts as well. If the chart is part of a notebook page with data, select the chart and use the Copy, Paste Special procedure since the chart can be selected and isolated. If the chart is on a separate page, the Insert, Object, Create from file procedure may be used if the file is saved with the chart page as the opening window.

- When you double-click on an embedded or linked chart object, you will be in Quattro Pro in chart edit mode. You may make the edits in the chart, or switch back to the notebook by double-clicking the application control button, or by pressing Ctrl+F4. Note the illustration of the application control button in chart edit mode.

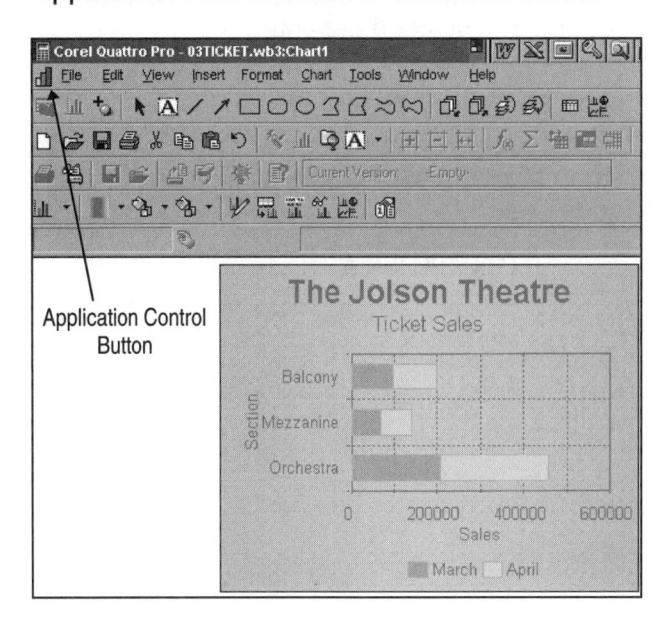

In this exercise, you will provide additional data in a memorandum for The Jolsen Theatre by adding a range from a notebook page and a chart showing sales data for the past two months. You will integrate and edit the data in linked and embedded modes.

EXERCISE DIRECTIONS

1. Click the WordPerfect icon on the DAD Toolbar.
2. Open 📄**03MEMO.wpd** or type the text as shown in Illustration A.
3. Insert the additional text as indicated in the document in Illustration A.
4. Click the DAD Quattro Pro icon.
5. Open 📄**TICKET.wb3** or 📄**03TICKET.wb3**.
6. Switch to the WordPerfect document by clicking the WordPerfect button on the Windows 95 Taskbar.
7. Embed the TICKET file, using Insert, Object, Create from File to embed the Quattro Pro 8 notebook below the memorandum text. (Locate the Quattro Pro file using the Browse button, if necessary.
   - ✓ *Note that the entire file is embedded using this method. This is an embedded object that allows you to work with formulas but changes do not affect the source file.*
8. Double-click on the embedded object in the WordPerfect file. (This brings you into Quattro Pro.)
9. Enter formulas to add the March and April sales.
10. Return to WordPerfect mode by clicking outside the notebook. Switch to Quattro Pro 8 by clicking the Quattro Pro button on the Windows 95 taskbar. Note that the formulas you entered in the destination file do not appear in the source file.
11. Switch to WordPerfect. Select and then delete the embedded object by pressing the delete key.
    - ✓ *When an object is selected, handles appear on the edges of the object box.*
12. Return to Quattro Pro 8. Select and copy only the notebook data shown in Illustration B. Return to WordPerfect to the insertion point under the new text.
13. Link the notebook range, using the Edit, Paste Special, Paste link option, to the Quattro Pro 8 notebook.
    - ✓ *This is a linked object that actually resides in the source file so that the source file will always match the destination file.*
    - ✓ *The text will wrap to the right of the file.*
14. Double click to edit the notebook in Quattro Pro. Bold the two title lines.
15. Use the Taskbar to return to the WordPerfect document and note the update in the linked notebook.

16. Save the file as **TKTMEMO**.
17. Switch to Quattro Pro. Select and copy the rotated 2-D stacked bar chart.
18. Switch to WordPerfect to paste and link the chart so that it is next to the table data.
19. Select and size the objects so that they are the same size and placed side by side under the added text.
20. Select both objects. Right-click, select Wrap, then select Neither Side option.
21. Edit the chart so that the font size for the X-Axis is increased to 30 pt, and the Y-Axis is decreased to 16 pt.
22. Save the file.
23. Print one copy of **TKTMEMO**.
24. Close both files.

ILLUSTRATION A

The Jolson Theatre

MEMORANDUM

To: Nafeesha Jones, Sales Office

From: Your name, Sales Manager

Subject: Ticket sales and prices

Date: May 12, 199-

We are all happy to have a hit on our hands! "Winner's Edge" has garnered good reviews and, despite a slow start in March, we have shown an increase in April ticket sales.

Unfortunately, we will have to raise ticket prices to cover operating costs and to keep up with the market. The March through May prices were at the "Preview" rate. Beginning June 1 we will change to our new rates. Orchestra and Mezzanine seats will now be $50; balcony seats will be increased to $35. We will, however, keep our limited performance schedule of seven performances per week, with no performances on Monday and Tuesday.

We will begin a print media and radio advertising campaign in one week which will continue for four weeks. Please inform your staff about the price changes and the increased exposure that we hope to achieve with our marketing campaign. We hope our sales trends continue to be positive.

For your information, I am including a table and corresponding chart showing the March and April ticket sales. — Insert

Insert — Quattro Pro 8 notebook (TICKET)
Insert — Quattro Pro 8 chart (TICKET) under inserted text

ILLUSTRATION B

	A	B	C
1	THE JOLSON THEATRE		
2	TICKET SALES		
3		March	April
4	Orchestra	208480	250340
5	Mezzanine	68450	73680
6	Balcony	97450	102343

KEYSTROKES

EMBED OBJECTS

This method embeds the entire file.

Create New:

1. Click **I**nsert............................. `Alt` + `I`
2. Click **O**bject .... `J`

    ✓ The **Insert Object** dialog box will appear.

3. Click **C**reate **n**ew option........ `Alt` + `N`
4. Click **O**bject **t**ype list box ...... `Alt` + `T`
5. Select application from which to create object .... `↑/↓`
6. Click **OK** to create....................... `Enter`

    ✓ The selected application will open.

7. Create desired information.
8. Click outside the object to return to the original application.

Create from File:

1. Click **I**nsert............................. `Alt` + `I`
2. Click **O**bject .... `J`

    ✓ The **Insert Object** dialog box will appear.

3. Click **C**reate from **f**ile option. `Alt` + `F`
4. Click the file folder icon.
5. Type or select drive letter of drive containing file you want to insert.
6. Double-click directory containing file you want to insert.
7. Double-click file you want to insert.
8. Select **L**ink, if desired............. `Alt` + `L`
9. Click **OK** .... `Enter`

EMBED DATA USING PASTE SPECIAL

This method allows you select the range to embed.

1. Open both applications and the appropriate files.
2. In the source file, highlight the data to be copied.
3. Click **E**dit............................... `Alt` + `E`
4. Click **C**opy .... `C`
5. Switch to the destination file.
6. Place cursor at the point of insertion.
7. Click **E**dit............................... `Alt` + `E`
8. Click Paste **S**pecial..................... `S`
9. Click **P**aste............................. `Alt` + `P`
10. Click **A**s.............................. `Alt` + `A`
11. Select Application .... `↓/↑`
12. Click **OK** .... `Enter`

LINK DATA BETWEEN APPLICATIONS

1. Open both applications and the appropriate files.
2. In the source file, highlight the data to be copied.
3. Click **E**dit............................... `Alt` + `E`
4. Click **C**opy .... `C`
5. Switch to the destination file.
6. Place cursor at the point of insertion.
7. Click **E**dit............................... `Alt` + `E`
8. Click Paste **S**pecial..................... `S`
9. Select Paste **l**ink.................. `Alt` + `L`
10. Click **A**s list box .... `Alt` + `A`
11. Select Application .... `↓/↑`
12. Click **OK** .... `Enter`

    ✓ You may also link files using the Insert, Object dialog box by following the steps under Embed Objects Create from file: and selecting the **L**ink check box.

EDIT OBJECT

Embedded files:

1. Double-click the object.
2. Edit the file using the source application menus. (The source file will not be changed.)
3. Switch to the destination file using the Taskbar.

Linked file:

1. Double-click the object.
2. Edit the file in the source application. (The source file will be changed.)
3. Switch to the destination file using the Taskbar.

COREL WORDPERFECT SUITE 8 PROFESSIONAL Integration

Exercise 4

- Export a Paradox Database to Quattro Pro
- Insert a Paradox Database into Quattro Pro

NOTES

Export a Paradox Database to Quattro Pro

- You may wish to use a Quattro Pro notebook to summarize and analyze information saved in a Paradox database. One method of accomplishing this is to export, or send, data from Paradox to Quattro Pro. Each record will be a row in Quattro Pro, and each field will be placed in a column. Exporting creates a new notebook file with the database data or with a selected part of a database table.

- To export a table from Paradox, select Export from the File menu. After you select the export format (From Type:, To Type:), the Export Data dialog box allows you to specify the source (From:) and destination files (To:), as illustrated below. Click Export then switch to Quattro Pro and open the new file.

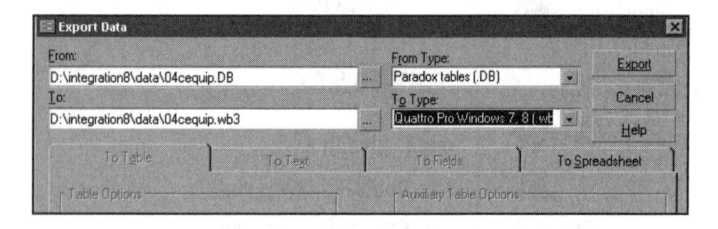

Insert Paradox Database into Quattro Pro

- You can also insert a Paradox file into a Quattro Pro file by selecting File from the Insert menu in Quattro Pro. In the Insert File dialog box, as illustrated below, enter the full file name with its extension or click the folder icon to locate the file.

- If you try to locate a file using the folder icon, the Insert File -data dialog box illustrated below appears. You then have to change the File type to Paradox ("*.db") to find a Paradox file, since the system defaults to inserting a Quattro Pro notebook.

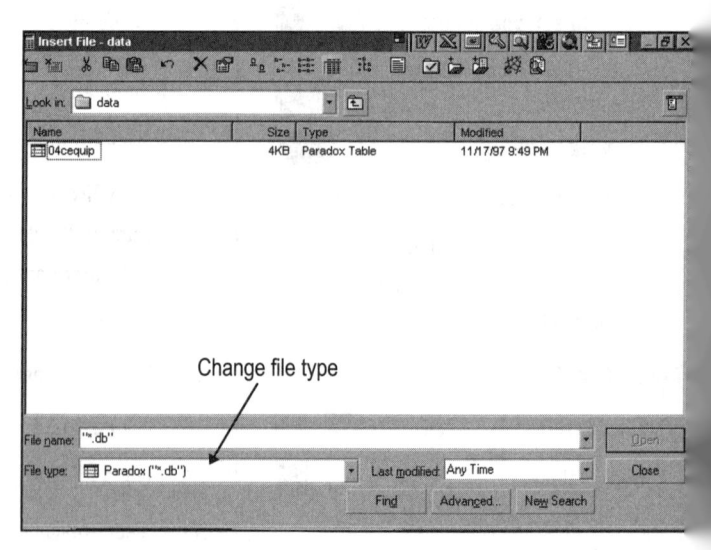

- Quattro Pro translates the format of database data into spreadsheet data and vice versa. You can save a notebook as a database table using the Save As command.

In this exercise, Sports Duds would like to analyze the data in the CEQUIP table to develop depreciation values for the year. You will bring the database into Quattro Pro from Paradox using both methods. The notebook will be formatted for presentation and analysis purposes.

EXERCISE DIRECTIONS

1. To practice exporting a table from Paradox to Quattro Pro:
   - Click the Paradox 8 icon on the DAD bar.
   - Use the File, Export command to export **CEQUIP** or **04CEQUIP** to a Quattro Pro Windows 7,8 (.wb3) file.
   - Click Export in the Export Data dialog box.
   - Click the Quattro Pro icon on the DAD bar.
   - Switch to Quattro Pro and open the new file.
   - ✓ *The file will be in the same directory as the Paradox table. However, you can change the directory and filename if you wish.*

2. Close the file in Quattro Pro without saving the data.

3. To insert a Paradox database table into a Quattro Pro workbook:
   - In Quattro Pro, click the Insert, File commands.
   - Enter **CEQUIP.db** or **04CEQUIP.db** using the full path or location of the file and click OK.
   - ✓ *You can also click the file folder icon at the right of the file name field to locate the file. If this is necessary, change the file type to Paradox to locate the database file.*

4. Make the following changes to the file in Quattro Pro:
   a. Insert three rows above the table to create room for a heading.
   b. Enter a two row heading in column C that reads:
      SPORTS DUDS
      DEPRECIATION SCHEDULE
   c. Delete the Wty and Assigned To: columns.
   d. Move the Cost column to the last position.
   e. Create a new column after the Cost column and enter the title as illustrated: Annual Depreciation.
   f. Change the Purdate column heading to a two-line heading: Date of Purchase.
   g. Select and sort the table in date order.
   ✓ *Use the Tools, Sort commands and select Date of Purchase as the first sort field.*
   h. Bold all titles and column headings.
   i. Find the Annual Depreciation by dividing the Cost by 5.
   ✓ *We are depreciating the hardware over five years.*
   j. Format the Depreciation figures for two place decimals.

5. Save the file as **DEPEQUIP**.

6. Print one copy of the notebook page to fit on one page.

7. Close all files.

COREL WORDPERFECT SUITE 8 PROFESSIONAL Integration

04cequip	A	B	C	D	E	F	G	H	I	J	K
1			SPORTS DUDS								
2			DEPRECIATION SCHEDULE			*Move*		*Delete*			
3											Annual
4	Branch ID	Item	Mfg	Model	Cost	Purdate	Wty	Assigned To	Serial #		Depreciation
5	GA06	Computer	Canton	Notebook	$2,436.00	02/10/98	Y	MIS	98763		
6	CA07	Printer	BP	DeskJet	$429.00	02/06/98	Y	Purchasing	22230		
7	CA05	Printer	BP	Deskjet	$429.00	02/05/98	Y	Accounting	99911		
8	GA06	Printer	NIC	FGE/3V	$539.00	02/03/98	N	Purchasing	87098		
9	NY01	Computer	GBM	PC220	$1,348.50	06/05/97	Y	Accounting	651198		
10	CA07	Computer	GBM	Notepad 500C	$2,199.00	06/10/97	Y	Accounting	AB2059		
11	CA05	Computer	GBM	Notepad 600	$1,399.00	06/15/97	Y	Accounting	671150		
12	CA05	Hard Drive	Barton	LPS80 220MB	$199.00	06/20/97	N	Accounting	54219		
13	CA07	Hard Drive	Wilson	CFS4 330MB	$250.00	06/10/97	N	Purchasing	12345		
14	CA05	Printer	BP	Laserjet	$1,479.00	07/15/97	N	Accounting	8842		
15	PA11	Computer	Debb	Notebook 586	$1,889.00	01/10/98	Y	Accounting	1145A		
16	IL03	Computer	Debb	P200	$2,507.52	01/12/98	Y	Accounting	765498		
17	IL03	Printer	Jokidota	BJ800	$355.00	01/12/98	Y	Accounting	43567		
18	NC09	Computer	Pancard	PE166	$2,095.54	01/25/98	Y	Purchasing	VC2342		
19	NC09	Zip Drive	Howell	Z100	$169.95	01/25/98	N	Purchasing	324222		
20	PA10	Computer	Pancard	PE166	$2,095.54	01/29/98	Y	Accounting	BV3452		
21	PA10	Printer	BP	LaserJet	$1,303.00	01/29/98	Y	Accounting	1213H		
22											

KEYSTROKES

EXPORT A TABLE FROM PARADOX

1. Open Paradox.
2. Click **F**ile .... Alt + F
3. Click Expo**r**t .... T
4. Type the **F**rom file name .... Alt + F
   OR
   a. Click the Select file box to locate the file ....
   b. Select the desired table.
   c. The **Fr**om type is set to Paradox.
5. Type the **T**o file name .... Alt + T
6. Choose the export format in the T**o** type box .... Alt + O
7. Verify **F**rom and **T**o destinations in the Export Data dialog box.
8. Click **E**xport .... Enter
9. Open the destination application.
10. Open the exported file.

INSERT A PARADOX TABLE INTO QUATTRO PRO

1. Open Quattro Pro.
2. Click **I**nsert .... Alt + I
3. Click **F**ile .... F
4. Enter file name and extension.
5. Click OK .... Enter
   OR
6. Click the folder icon to search for the file ....
   a. Click File t**y**pe and change to Paradox ("*.db").
   b. Select the file.
   c. Click **O**pen.

COREL WORDPERFECT SUITE 8 PROFESSIONAL Integration

Exercise 5

■ **Merge a Paradox Table with a WordPerfect Document**

NOTES

Merge a Paradox Table with a WordPerfect Document

- Table data from Paradox can be merged with a document created in WordPerfect. This process is automated with the Merge feature, as was discussed in WordPerfect 8, Exercise 43. Tabular data from a Quattro Pro notebook page or a WordPerfect table may also be used for a merge.

- Merge is a WordPerfect procedure that combines information from a data file with a form file by including merge codes which refer to the data file. You must prepare the **data file** (which in this exercise is a Paradox table) and the **form file** for a merge. For example, a form letter may be merged with a data file of names and addresses. This will produce a form letter for each person in the data file. Note the illustration of the Merge dialog box that appears in WordPerfect 8 when you select the Tools, Merge commands.

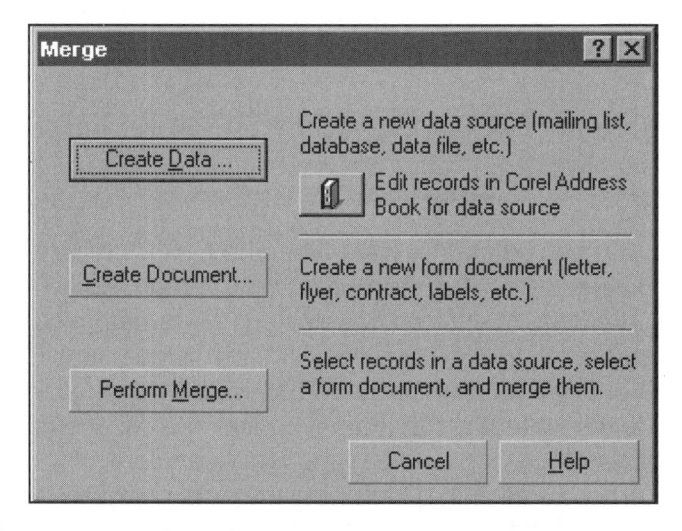

- The **form file** contains the document to be merged. Merge codes, which gather specific information from the data file, are inserted into the form file at the appropriate locations. For example, as shown in the illustration on page 554, the memorandum to members of the staff already includes the merge codes for the name, department and budget amount entered in the appropriate places. The form file must be prepared by inserting the field names from the data file in preparation for the Merge procedure.

- You have two options when using a Paradox table as a **data file**. You can:
  - Merge the data directly into WordPerfect without importing the file.
  - Import or link the data into a WordPerfect table or data file, then merge the files as WordPerfect files.

- To merge the data directly into WordPerfect without importing the file, prepare the form file in the following way:
  - From the Merge dialog box, click Create Document, select Use file in active window.
  - On the Associate Form and Data dialog box, illustrated below, enter the path and name of the Paradox file or locate the file using the folder button.

  ✓Note: You will have to change the file type to All Files to locate the Paradox file.

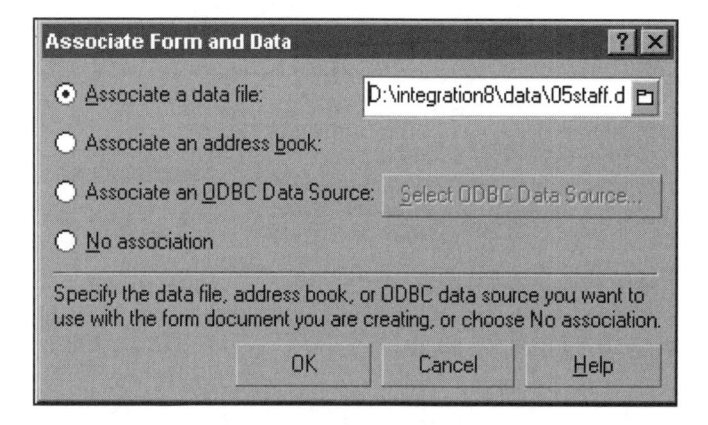

- Use the Insert Field button to insert the fields as shown in the illustration. The Insert Field Name or Number dialog box, illustrated below, appears so that you can select and Insert the fields.

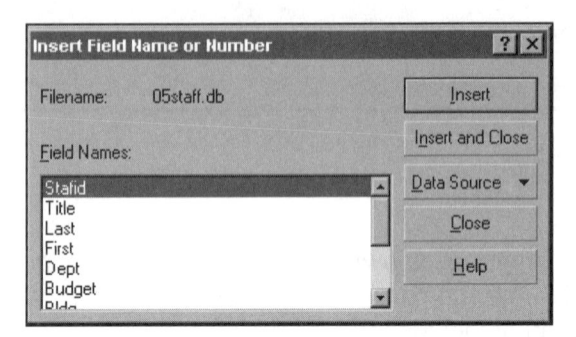

- The merge codes in the form letter refer to the field data in the table so that the merge will take place between the WordPerfect document and the Paradox table. This method ensures that the latest Paradox table information is being merged.

- When you select Merge from the Merge toolbar, the Perform Merge dialog box appears to merge to new documents. Note in the illustration of the Perform Merge dialog box below, you can Select Records to limit the data to be merged.

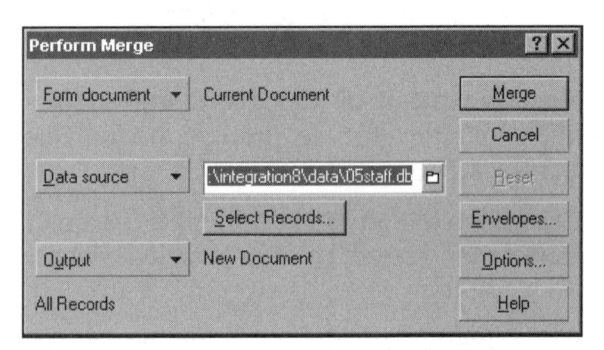

Complete this procedure by pressing Merge on the Merge Feature Bar as illustrated below.

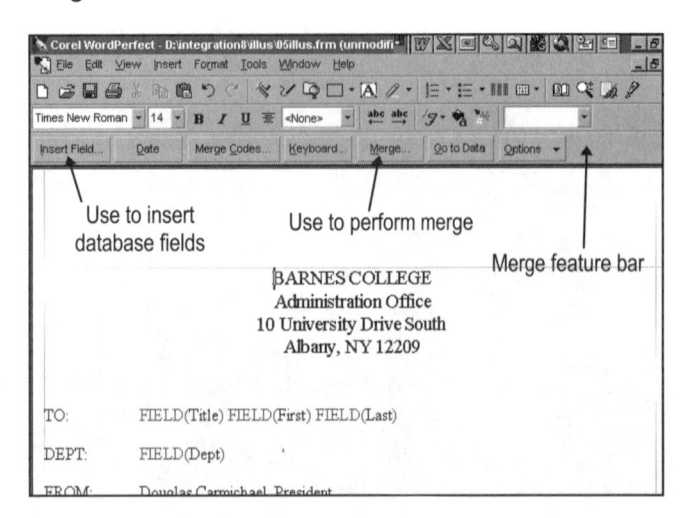

- To create the data file in another way, you can import the data from a Paradox table into a WordPerfect table. To import the data, select Spreadsheet/Database and Import from the Insert menu, or, you can link the Paradox table by selecting Spreadsheet/Database, Create Link from the Insert menu. Note that both commands present similar dialog boxes.

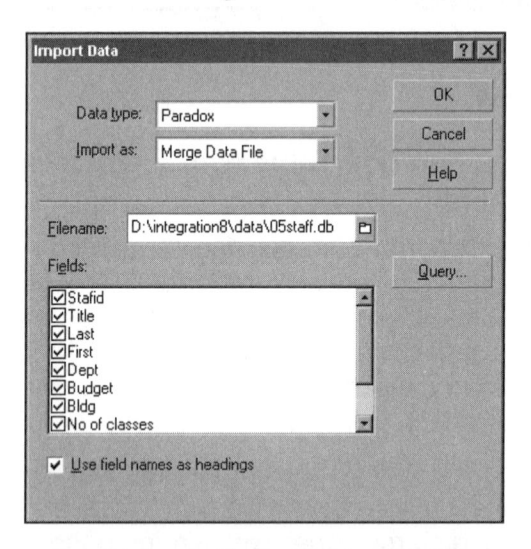

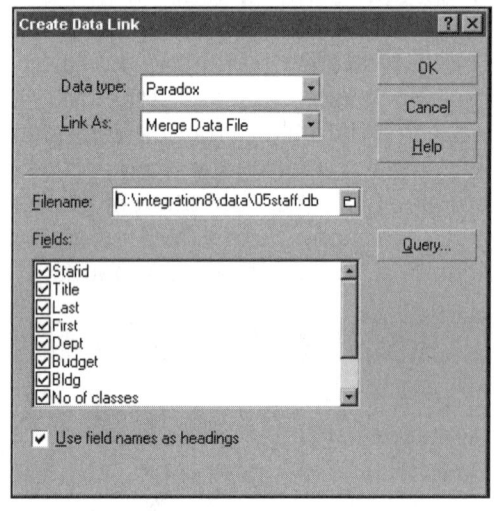

- You can select the Data type and Link or Import settings from the drop-down lists. When the Filename is entered or selected, the table Fields will display. You can deselect any fields you will not need for the merge and/or you can use Query to select records that meet certain specifications. The difference between the import and link procedures is that importing the data brings in the current data, however, linking the data enables updates of the data file when changes are made to the Paradox table. In both cases, by using this method you are importing the Paradox data and creating a WordPerfect data file table.

In Part I of this exercise, the President of Barnes College would like to send a memo to the staff using the information from the colleges STAFF table (created in Paradox) and a memo (created in WordPerfect). You will insert merge codes into the form file and merge the table information to create a memo for each member of the staff. In Part II of this exercise, he would like to send a memo to non-tenured staff. You will edit the form file, and query the STAFF table to create a new memo.

EXERCISE DIRECTIONS

PART I

1. Click the DAD WordPerfect icon.
2. Type the letter on the following page without the field codes or open 🖫**05GRANT.wpd**.
3. To insert the field codes:
   a. Select Merge from the Tools menu.
   b. Click Create Document.
   c. Click Use file in active window.
   d. Click Associate a data file and then Browse to select 📠**STAFF.db** or 🖫**05STAFF.db** as the data file.
       Hint: Select All Files as the file type.
       ✓ *Use the path or drive with the filename either to locate the file that was created earlier or use the data file provided. You will have to change the File type to All files to locate the Paradox file.*
   e. Click Insert Field on the Merge Feature Bar.
   f. Select Title, click Insert, press Spacebar,
   g. Select First, click Insert, press Spacebar,
   h. Select Last, click Insert.
   i. Complete the remaining field entry areas as shown in the illustration.
   j. Close the dialog box.
   k. Save the file as **DEC10**.
   ✓ *The file will be saved as DEC10.frm (a form file).*
4. Click Merge on the Merge Feature Bar.
5. a. Current Document should be set as the form file on the Perform Merge dialog box.
   b. The **05STAFF.db** or **STAFF** table should be set as the Data source.
   c. The Output should be set to a New Document.
6. Click Merge in the Perform Merge dialog box.
   ✓ *A new document will be created with the merged letters, one for each staff member on the list. This merge method provides the data directly from the Paradox table. Scroll down through the merged document and note the merged information and the separation of each memorandum by a page break.*
7. Save the document as **DEC10ALL.wpd**.
8. Print the merged document.
9. Close all open files.

PART II

1. Open a new blank document in WordPerfect.
   a. Click Insert, Spreadsheet/Database, Create Link.
   b. Data type should be set to Paradox.
   c. Link As should be set to Merge Data File.
   d. Filename should be 📠**STAFF.db** or 🖫**05STAFF.db**.
   e. Click OK.
   f. Deselect the Stafid, Bldg, No of classes, Start, Tenure, and Exp fields.
2. Click the Query button.
   a. In the first field box, select Tenure from the drop-down list. (You can query by a field that is not displayed.)
   b. Enter N as Condition 1.
   c. Click OK to close the Define Selection Conditions dialog box.
   d. Click OK to close the Create Data Link dialog box.
3. Scroll through the data file that has been created of non-tenured staff members.
4. Save the file as **NTSTAFF.dat**. Close the file.
5. Open the DEC10 form file and enter the following two-line postscript at the bottom of the memo:
   Please be specific when you list programs, materials and course work.
6. On the form file, click Merge on the Merge Feature Bar.
   a. The Form file should be the current document.
   b. The Data source should be NTSTAFF.dat.
   c. The Output should be New Document.
   d. Click Merge.
   e. Scroll through the memos to check if there are 15 memos for staff such as Anderson, Bergen, Browning, Bryson, etc. Save the file as **NTDEC10.wpd**.
   ✓ *The NTSTAFF.dat data file is linked to Paradox. If any data changes in the Paradox file, it will automatically update in this file when it is reopened. If you have time, you can make a change in Paradox to the STAFF table and note the change in the NTSTAFF .dat file when reopened.*
7. Print the first letter in the file.
8. Save the form file as **NTDEC10.frm**.
9. Save and close all files.

Corel Integration ■ Exercise 5   553

BARNES COLLEGE
Administration Office
10 University Drive South
Albany, NY 12209

TO: FIELD(Title) FIELD(First) FIELD(Last)

DEPT: FIELD(Dept)

FROM: Douglas Carmichael, President

DATE: December 10, 1998

RE: 1999 Budget

Congratulations! Due to your input and assistance with the grant proposal, we are happy to announce that the FIELD(Dept) Department has received a Professional Development Training Grant.

This semester, you received a budget allocation of $FIELD(Budget). To determine your new budget, with the increase in funds due to the grant, we are requesting that you submit an implementation proposal.

Your proposal should include funds for professional development including supplies, and should meet the requirements and limitations of the grant. Copies of the grant proposal with the approximate allocations are located in my office and in each department office.

Your proposals are due before our holiday break. Thank you.

KEYSTROKES

USE PARADOX TABLE FIELDS TO CREATE A FORM FILE

1. Open form document.
2. Click **T**ools .... `Alt`+`T`
3. Click **M**erge .... `E`
4. Click **C**reate Document .... `Alt`+`C`
5. Select **U**se file in active window .... `Alt`+`U`
6. Click OK .... `Enter`
7. Click **A**ssociate a data file ..... `Alt`+`A`
8. Enter a Paradox filename, or click folder to locate.
9. Click OK .... `Enter`
10. Place the cursor at desired location in form document.
11. Click **I**nsert Field on the Merge Feature Bar .... `Alt`+`Shift`+`I`

    ✓ You can re-position the dialog box by placing your mouse pointer on the title bar, then clicking and holding left mouse button while you drag the dialog box to a new location.

12. Select **F**ield Names .... `↓`
13. Click **I**nsert .... `Alt`+`I`

    ✓ The Insert Field Name or Number dialog box will stay open until you either click Insert and close, or Close, but you must re-activate it by clicking in the dialog box after each Insert.

14. Repeat 10-13 until all fields are entered.
15. On the last field to be inserted, Click **I**nsert and Close .... `Alt`+`N`
    OR
16. Click **C**lose .... `Alt`+`C`
17. Save the file.

    ✓ WordPerfect will give the file a .frm extension.

LINK A PARADOX TABLE TO A WORDPERFECT DATA FILE

1. Click **I**nsert .... `Alt`+`I`
2. Click S**p**readsheet/Database .... `R`
3. Click **C**reate Link .... `C`
4. Select Data **t**ype: paradox .... `Alt`+`T`, `↓`
5. Select **L**ink As: Merge Data File .... `Alt`+`L`, `↓`
6. Make sure the **U**se field names as headings option is selected .... `Alt`+`U`
7. Enter **F**ilename.
   OR
   a. Click Folder icon.
   b. Change File type to All Files.
   c. Locate file. Click Select.
8. If desired, deselect unnecessary fields.

To query table:

9. Click **Q**uery .... `Alt`+`Q`
10. Select field for query .... `↓`
11. Enter Condition 1.
12. Repeat 9-10 as required.
13. Click OK to close the Define Selection Conditions dialog box.
14. Make sure the **U**se field names as headings option is selected .... `Alt`+`U`
15. Click OK to close the Create Data Link dialog box.
16. Save the .dat file.

MERGE FILES

1. After the data file and form file are complete, click **M**erge on the Merge Features Toolbar. .... `Alt`+`M`
2. If all settings are correct, click **M**erge on the Perform Merge dialog box. (Use list box arrows to change settings.) .... `Alt`+`M`

COREL WORDPERFECT SUITE 8 PROFESSIONAL Integration

Exercise 6

- Insert A WordPerfect Outline Into A Presentations Slide Show
- Link A Quattro Pro Chart To A Presentations Slide Show

NOTES

Insert a WordPerfect Outline into a Presentations Slide Show

- An outline created in WordPerfect may be used as the text in a Presentations presentation. The outline file is inserted into Presentations in the Slide Outliner view, by selecting File from the Insert menu.

- In a WordPerfect outline, heading levels provide the structure for the data. When the outline is inserted into Presentations, each first level paragraph number becomes the title on a separate slide. The other levels are shown as subtopics or text on the slide. The formatting or styles in the WordPerfect outline will be imported into Presentations. See the illustration below:

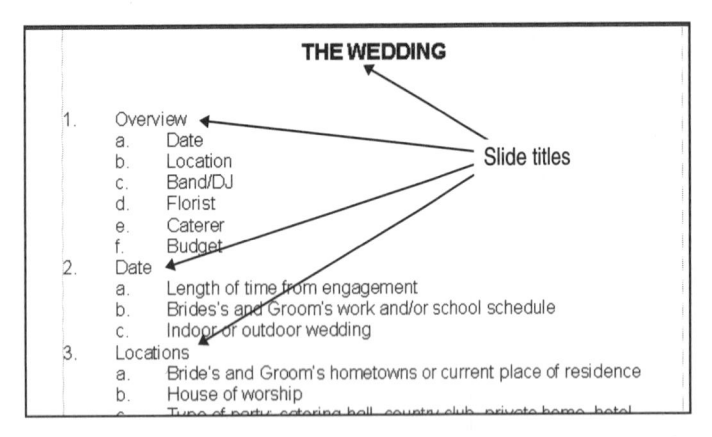

Link a Quattro Pro Chart to a Presentations Slide Show

- Data from WordPerfect or another application can be linked to Presentations so that the Presentations slide will update if the linked file is changed. You can take Quattro Pro data, link it to the slide show and bring it into Presentations as a chart. In preparation for this procedure, you should name the block of data to be charted.

Any charts you have already created in Quattro Pro are automatically named.

- To link Quattro Pro charts or data to a slide:

   a. Add a Data Chart slide template by clicking New Slide from the Insert menu and clicking **Data Chart** on the New Slide dialog box.

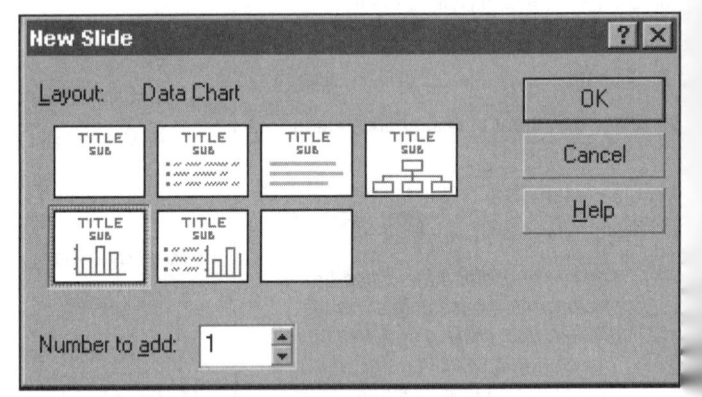

   b. In Slide Editor view, double-click in the area defined to add the data chart. The Data Chart Gallery dialog box will appear, as illustrated below.

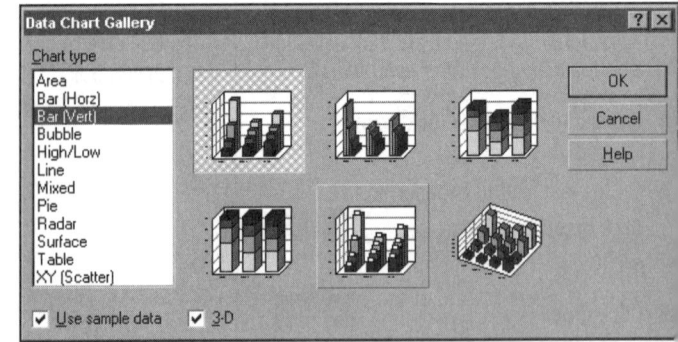

c. After selecting a chart type, Presentations will display a data chart slide with sample data using the format and layout selected.

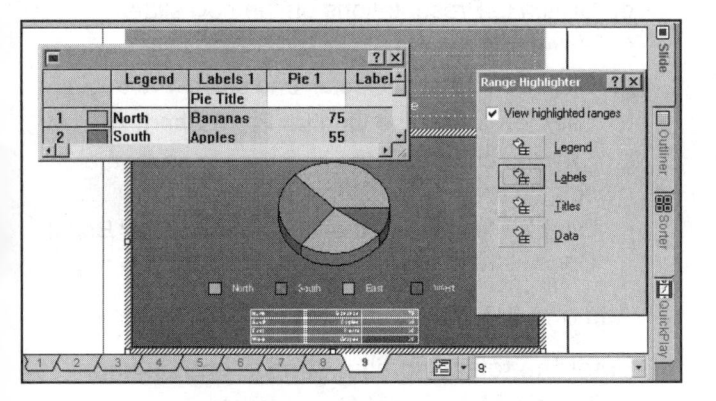

d. Select Import from the Data menu to replace the sample data with imported Quattro Pro data. The Import Data dialog box will display, as illustrated top right. Select Link to Spreadsheet and Clear current data link the Quattro Pro data or chart to the slide. When the filename and block range is selected and entered, the Quattro Pro data and chart will replace the sample data.

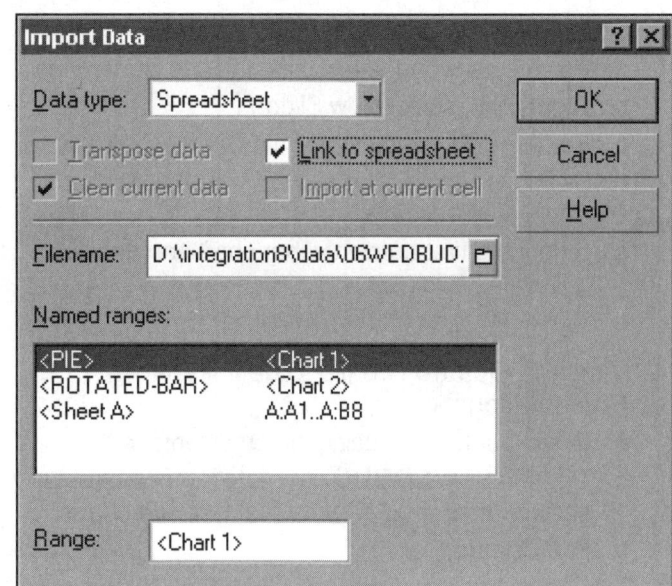

- A Quattro Pro chart or notebook page can also be linked or embedded into a Presentations slide using Copy/Paste Link procedures. To link a chart, the chart should be selected in Quattro Pro, copied, and linked using the Paste Special, Paste Link options on a data chart slide in Presentations. The Copy/Paste Link procedure places the chart on the slide but it does not take on the slide background. The chart created using the first method has a better appearance since Presentations brings the chart into the slide layout.

In this exercise, Patricia May Bridal Consultants will use an outline about weddings, created in WordPerfect, and import it into a presentations slide show. The slides will be edited and a Quattro Pro chart will be linked to the slide show.

EXERCISE DIRECTIONS

1. To insert a WordPerfect outline into Presentations:
   a. Click the Presentations icon on the DAD toolbar.
   b. Click Create on the Create New tab.
   ✓ *Make sure you are creating a new slide show.*
   c. Click OK.
   d. Choose default color.
   e. Change to Slide Outliner View.
   f. Click Insert, File.
   g. Choose the file **WEDDING.wpd** or **06WEDDING.wpd**.
   h. Click Insert.
   ✓ *The outline is inserted into Presentations.*

   i. Click the Slide Sorter to view the outline as slides.

2. Edit the first slide:
   a. Add the following subtitle:
      Patricia May Bridal Consultants
   b. Add the following bullet text:
      ★ *Panel Members:*
         – *Patricia May, President*
         – *Martin Posner, Financial Consultant*
         – *Mary Milner, Design Consultant*
      ★ *Presenter*
         – *Cynthia Wong, Vice President*

3. Add a slide for chart data:
   a. Place cursor on the last slide in Slide Sorter view.
   b. Right-click, select New Slide.
   c. Set the slide template to Data Chart. Click OK.
   d. Switch to Slide Editor and double-click on the Add Data Chart area.
   e. Select the first horizontal bar chart and deselect 3-D style. Click OK.
   ✓ Sample data and a bar chart will appear.

4. View the Quattro Pro file to be linked to Presentations:
   a. Open Quattro Pro using the DAD toolbar.
   b. Open 06WEDBUD or create the notebook as shown on page 559. Note the data and charts.
   c. Exit Quattro Pro.

5. Link Quattro Pro chart to slide show:
   a. Switch back to Presentations in Slide Editor on the last slide.
   b. Click Data, Import.
   c. Click Link to Spreadsheet.
   d. Select 06WEDBUD.wb3 as the spreadsheet data.
   e. Select the named range representing the data. Data and chart will move into slide.
   f. Size chart to fit chart area.
   g. Double-click to add the following title: Patricia May Bridal Consultants.
   h. Double-click to add the following subtitle: Comparison of Low vs. Moderate Costs for 200 Guests.

6. To Link a Quattro Pro chart using the Paste Special, Paste Link commands:
   a. Repeat the procedures in step 3 to add a data chart slide.
   b. Switch to Quattro Pro and open 06WEDBUD.
   c. Select the pie chart by pointing to the edge of the chart. (Handles should appear around the chart.)
   d. Click Edit, Copy.
   e. Switch to Presentations on the new slide.
   f. Select the data chart area.
   g. Click Edit, Paste Special, and select Paste Link.
   h. Click OK to link the Quattro Pro 8 Chart.
   i. Size the chart to fit the slide and to cover the subtitle area.
   j. Double-click to add the title: Patricia May Bridal Consultants.

7. Add a bullet slide to the end of the Presentation.

8. Enter the following title, subtitle and bullets.
   Patricia May Bridal Consultants
   Wedding Services
   - Bookings
   - Invitations/Favors
   - Menu selection
   - Wedding design
   - Flowers
   - Music
   - Financial planning

9. Return to the first slide and play the slide show.

10. Switch to Slide Sorter view and add a Slide Transition and Bullet Chart Animation Property to apply to all slides.

11. Optional: Add graphics to the Florist and Caterer slides.

12. Check the presentation by playing the slide show.

13. Save the file; name it **WEDPLAN**.

14. Close the document window.

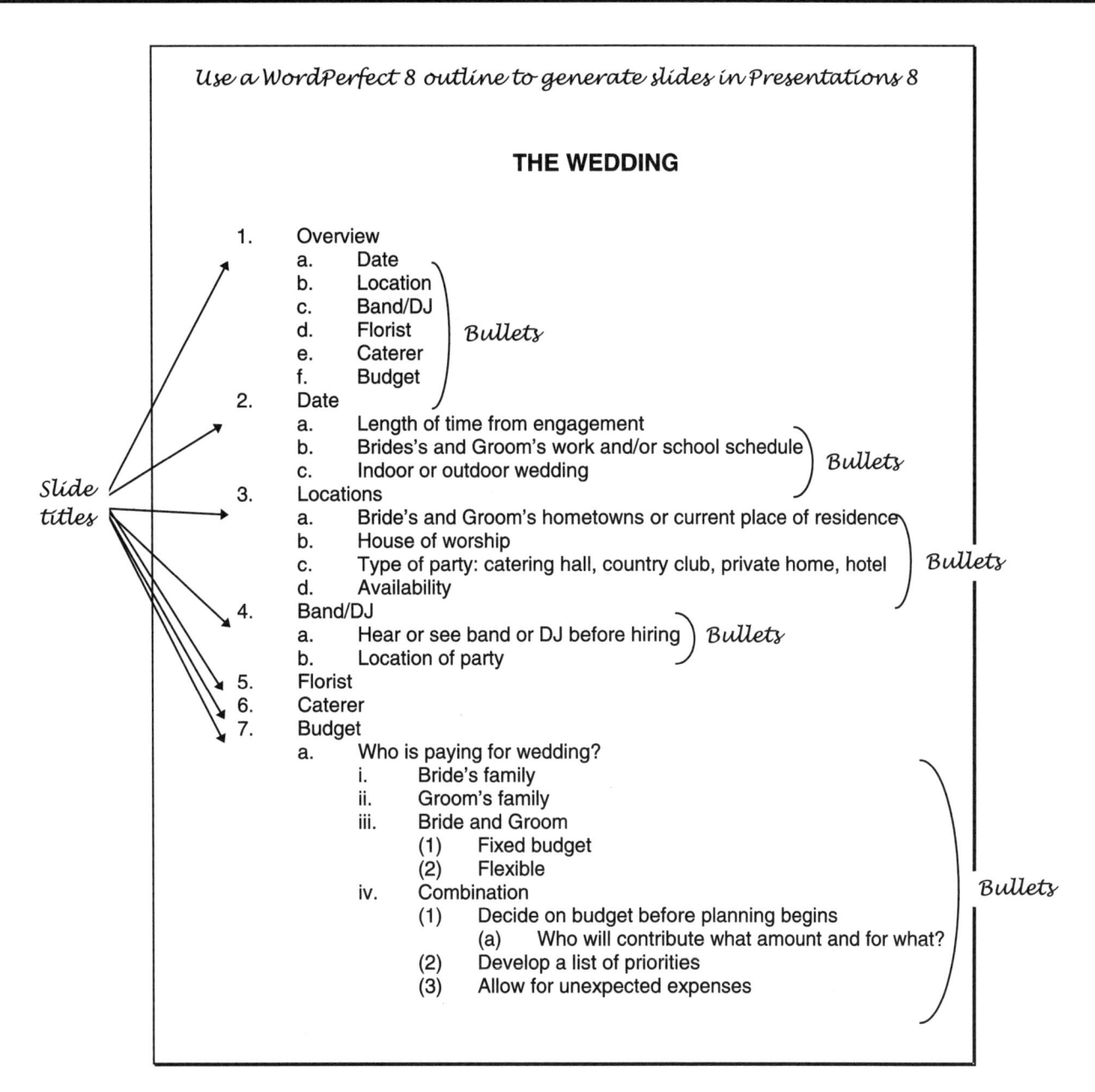

Use a WordPerfect 8 outline to generate slides in Presentations 8

THE WEDDING

1. Overview
   a. Date
   b. Location
   c. Band/DJ
   d. Florist
   e. Caterer
   f. Budget
2. Date
   a. Length of time from engagement
   b. Brides's and Groom's work and/or school schedule
   c. Indoor or outdoor wedding
3. Locations
   a. Bride's and Groom's hometowns or current place of residence
   b. House of worship
   c. Type of party: catering hall, country club, private home, hotel
   d. Availability
4. Band/DJ
   a. Hear or see band or DJ before hiring
   b. Location of party
5. Florist
6. Caterer
7. Budget
   a. Who is paying for wedding?
      i. Bride's family
      ii. Groom's family
      iii. Bride and Groom
          (1) Fixed budget
          (2) Flexible
      iv. Combination
          (1) Decide on budget before planning begins
              (a) Who will contribute what amount and for what?
          (2) Develop a list of priorities
          (3) Allow for unexpected expenses

Slide titles point to items 1–7. *Bullets* group the sub-items.

	A	B	C
1	ESTIMATED WEDDING BUDGET		
2	200 Guests		
3		Low	Moderate
4	Flowers	1000	3500
5	Band/DJ	1200	4500
6	Caterer	12000	20000
7	Other	3000	8000
8		17200	36000
9			
10			
11			
12			
13			
14			
15			
16			
17			
18			
19			
20			
21			
22			

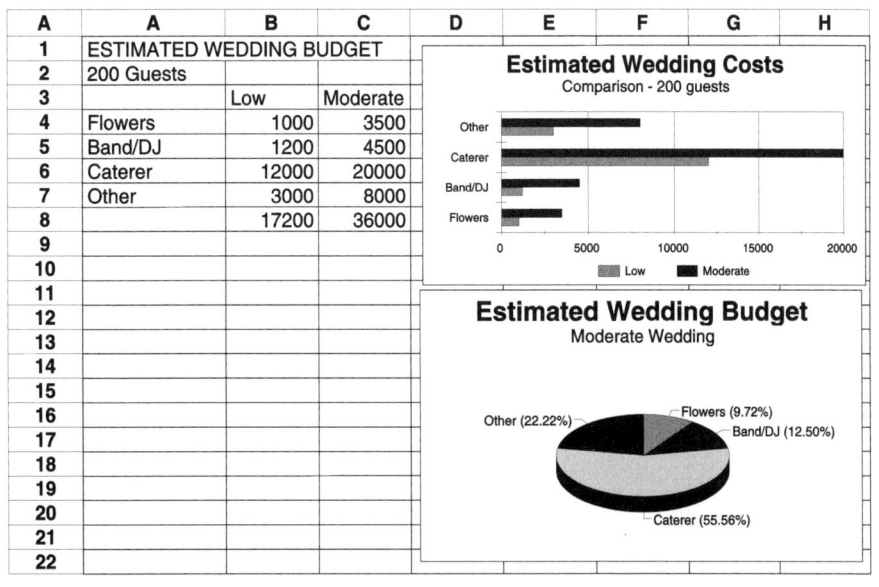

Estimated Wedding Costs
Comparison - 200 guests

Bar chart showing Low and Moderate values for Other, Caterer, Band/DJ, Flowers.

Estimated Wedding Budget
Moderate Wedding

Pie chart: Flowers (9.72%), Band/DJ (12.50%), Caterer (55.56%), Other (22.22%)

KEYSTROKES

INSERT WORD PERFECT OUTLINE INTO PRESENTATIONS

1. Click the Presentations icon on the DAD toolbar.
2. Click Create on the Create New tab .... `Alt`+`C`
3. Click **OK** .... `Enter`
4. Click **V**iew .... `Alt`+`V`
5. Click **Slide Outliner** .... `O`
6. Click **I**nsert .... `Alt`+`I`
7. Click F**i**le .... `I`
8. Select the file.
9. Click **I**nsert .... `Enter`

ADD A SLIDE FOR CHART DATA

(In presentations in slide sorter view)

1. Click **I**nsert .... `Alt`+`I`
2. Click **N**ew Slide .... `N`
3. Select Data Chart.
4. Click **OK** .... `Enter`

LINK QUATTRO PRO CHART TO PRESENTATIONS USING IMPORT METHOD

1. In Slide Editor, double-click Data Chart area.
2. Select chart type.
3. Click **OK** .... `Enter`
4. Click **D**ata .... `Alt`+`D`
5. Click I**m**port .... `M`
6. Click **D**ata type .... `Alt`+`D`
7. Click **S**preadsheet .... `↹`
8. Click **L**ink to Spreadsheet.
9. Select file name to import ...... `Alt`+`F`
10. Select data
    Named ranges .... `Alt`+`N`+`↓`
11. Click **OK** .... `Enter`

LINK QUATTRO PRO CHART TO PRESENTATION SLIDE USING PASTE LINK METHOD

1. Open Quattro Pro notebook.
2. Select chart to be linked.
3. Click **E**dit .... `Alt`+`E`
4. Click **C**opy .... `Alt`+`C`
5. Switch to Presentations and open the slide show.
6. Select the location for the placement of the notebook.
7. Click **E**dit .... `Alt`+`E`
8. Click Paste **S**pecial .... `S`
9. Select Paste **L**ink .... `Alt`+`L`
10. Click **OK** .... `Enter`

COREL WORDPERFECT SUITE 8 PROFESSIONAL Integration

Exercise 7

- **Copy Presentations Text into a WordPerfect Document**
- **Convert Presentations Slide Shows to .wpg Format**
- **Insert a Presentations Slide into a WordPerfect Document**

NOTES

Copy Presentations Text into a WordPerfect Document

- You can bring text developed in Presentations into a WordPerfect document. You can select the desired text in Outliner view, then Copy and Paste the selection into the document. When text is brought into WordPerfect, bulleted text will be organized in outline form and subtitles will be given a level letter or number. You may have to adjust text as desired.

Convert Presentations Slide Shows to .wpg Format

- You may wish to insert a slide into a WordPerfect document. To accomplish this, however, you must first convert the Presentations slide show file to **.wpg** format. Presentations provides a macro that will automatically convert a .shw file to a .wpg file. A macro is a set of instructions that are recorded and played back to complete a task automatically. To convert a Presentations file, click Tools, Macro, Play, or simply press Alt+F10. A Play Macro dialog box will appear with a listing of pre-written macros, ready to automate various tasks. The **Shw2wpg macro** in the Prwin folder, for example, converts each slide in a slide show to separate .wpg files. Note the illustration of the Play Macro dialog box below.

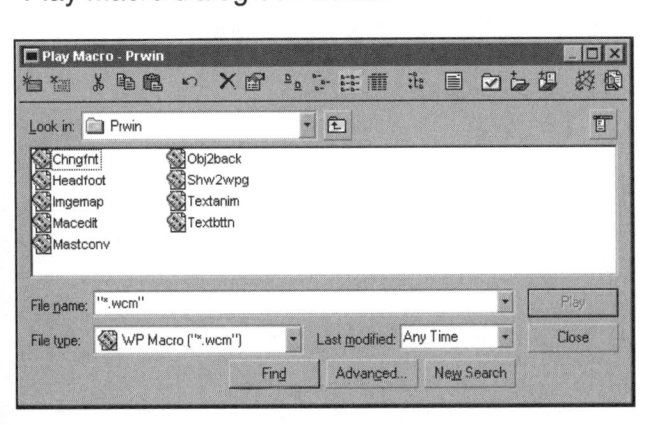

- To convert the presentation file, double-click Shw2wpg in the Play Macro dialog box. The SHW to WPG dialog box will appear. Enter the name of the slide show to convert (including the extension) and enter a directory name for saving the .wpg files. You will have to confirm the creation of the directory if it is a new directory. When you click Convert each slide will be converted to a separate .wpg file in the directory you specified. For example, in the illustration below, the new files will be saved to the A:\WED07 directory. The .wpg files are named using the slide titles.

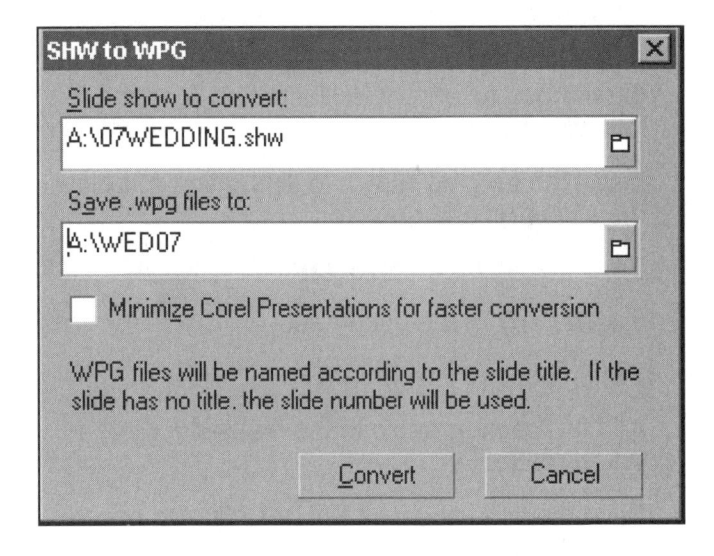

Insert a Presentations Slide into a WordPerfect Document

- Presentations slides that have been converted to .wpg format may be inserted into a WordPerfect document by selecting, File from the Insert menu. Select the file from the Insert File dialog box and click Insert. The slide will be inserted into the document as an image which can then be sized, moved and enhanced.

COREL WORDPERFECT SUITE 8 PROFESSIONAL Integration

In this exercise, Cynthia Wong of Patricia May Bridal Consultants is continuing to prepare for her presentation. Slide text will be used to create a WordPerfect document for prospective clients. In addition, the slide show will be converted to .wpg format so that a slide can be added to a letter about the presentation.

EXERCISE DIRECTIONS

1. Open Presentations using the DAD bar.
2. Open **WEDPLAN** or **07WEDPLAN**.
3. To use slide text in a WordPerfect document:
   a. In Outliner view, move to the last slide containing the Patricia May Bridal Consultants list of Wedding Services.
   b. Select and copy all the text in the last slide.
   c. Open WordPerfect using the DAD icon.
   d. Paste the text into a new document and change font, if necessary.
4. Delete the Wedding Services line.
5. Center the company name and format to 19 points.
6. Enter Patricia May, President, as a centered subtitle.
7. Insert an appropriate clipart or graphic file at the left margin, as shown in Illustration A on the following page.
8. Insert the text, as shown in Illustration A, below the slide text and graphic.
9. Save the file as **LEADS.wpd**.
10. Print a copy of the document.
11. Switch back to Presentations.
12. Add the same graphic to the first slide, WEDDINGS.
13. Save the slide show as **WEDPLAN**. Do not close the file.
14. Switch to WordPerfect.
15. Open **07CONTACT.wpd**, or type the letter shown in Illustration B on page 564.
16. Insert the additional text as illustrated.
17. To insert a slide into a WordPerfect document:
    a. Switch to Presentations. (The .shw file must be converted to a .wpg file.)
    b. Click Tools, Macro, Play, or press Alt+F10.
    c. Select the Prwin folder.
    d. Double-click the Shw2wpg macro.
    e. Enter the name of the slide show to convert, with the extension. (drive:**WEDPLAN**)
    f. Enter a directory name for the .wpg files. (drive:WED07)
    g. Accept the creation of a directory.
    h. Click Convert.
    ✓ *Each slide will be converted to a separate .wpg file in the directory you specified.*
    i. Switch to WordPerfect.
    j. Move the cursor to the insertion point for the slide.
    k. Click Insert, File on the menu.
    l. Select the directory that contains the converted slides and select the WEDDING slide from the Insert File dialog box.
    m. Click Insert.
    ✓ *The slide will be inserted into the document as an image with an edit box.*
    n. Adjust the size and placement so that the slide is centered under the letter text.
18. Print a copy of the letter.
19. Save the file as **CONTACT.wpd**.
20. Close all files.

ILLUSTRATION A

Insert clipart →

Patricia May Bridal Consultants
Patricia May, President

a. Bookings
b. Invitations / Favors
c. Menu selection
d. Wedding design
e. Flowers
f. Music
g. Financial Planning

} *Copy text from presentation slide*

If you are interested in our services, please complete the form below. We will send you our Wedding Planner folder, which includes our rates and services, at no obligation.

Insert text →

BRIDE'S NAME: _____

ADDRESS: _____

CITY: _____ STATE: ____ ZIP: _____

TELEPHONE:
DAY: _____ EVENING: _____

WEDDING DATE: _____

KEYSTROKES

TO CONVERT .SHW FILES TO .WPG FORMAT

In Presentations:

Alt + F10

1. Click **T**ools .... Alt + T
2. Click **M**acro .... M
3. Click **P**lay .... P
4. Select Prwin directory.
5. Click File**n**ame field .... Alt + N, ↓
6. Type **Shw2wpg**.
   OR
   Click the **Shw2wpg** macro .... ↓ ↑

7. Click **P**lay .... Enter
8. In **S**lide show to convert, enter filename of slide show.
   Drive:*filename.shw*
9. In **S**ave files to, enter a directory name for .wpg files.
   drive:*directory name*
10. Accept creation of new directory, if applicable .... Enter
11. Click **C**onvert .... Alt + C

TO INSERT .WPG SLIDES INTO A DOCUMENT

In WordPerfect:

1. Move the cursor to the insertion point for the slide.
2. Click **I**nsert .... Alt + I
3. Click **F**ile I
4. Select directory with converted slides.
5. Select File**n**ame .... Alt + N
   • Enter Slide Name.
   OR
   Click slide name .... ↓
6. Click **I**nsert I

Corel Integration ■ Exercise 7   563

ILLUSTRATION B

Patricia May Bridal Consultants
151 Amsterdam Avenue
New York, NY 10023

December 1, 1998

Ms. Marcie Collingsworth
Professional Women's Club
123 Madison Avenue
New York, NY 10014

Dear Ms. Collingsworth:

Thank you for asking our group to present at your December 15 meeting on Weddings for the Professional Woman. I will present a brief slide show about weddings and will bring the necessary equipment. We will need a power supply and a screen.

After the presentation, our President and members of our staff will be available to field questions from your group.

insert → Thank you.

Sincerely yours,

I am including the first slide below so that you can prepare your agenda and include all participants.

Cynthia Wong
Vice President

Insert Presentations 8 (WEDDING) slide in .WPG format

COREL WORDPERFECT SUITE 8 PROFESSIONAL Integration

Exercise 8

- Internet Basics
- Use Corel WordPerfect to Access the Internet
- Search the Internet

Internet Publisher Toolbar

NOTES

Internet Basics

- The **Internet** is a worldwide network of computers. These computers may be located in businesses, schools, research foundations and/or individuals' homes. Those who are connected to this network can share information with each other, communicate via e-mail and search for information.

- The **World Wide Web** (WWW) is a service of the Internet in which web pages, created by companies, individuals, schools and government agencies around the world, can be accessed.

- In order to access the Internet, you (or your company, or school) must sign up with an Internet Service Provider (ISP). Some popular service providers include America Online, Microsoft Network (MSN), and CompuServe.

- A **Web browser** is a program on your computer that displays the information you retrieve from the Internet in a readable format. The most popular Web browsers are Netscape Navigator and Microsoft Internet Explorer. Some service providers give you a Web browser when you subscribe to them. The Corel Suite 8 package includes Netscape Navigator Web browser.

Use WordPerfect 8 to Access the Internet

- Each Corel WordPerfect Suite 8 tool contains a Browse the Web button on the Toolbar. To discuss the Internet, however, we will use WordPerfect 8 as the basic application. Most of the skills you learn for using the Internet with WordPerfect can be used with the other Corel Suite applications.

- WordPerfect 8 provides easy access to the Internet through menus and toolbar buttons. To access the Internet using WordPerfect 8, click the Netscape Communicator icon on the DAD bar or select Internet Publisher from the File menu. In the Internet Publisher dialog box that follows, click the Browse the Web button. Both methods will launch the Netscape Navigator Web browser.

    ✓Note: *If you are using WordPerfect 8, Netscape Communicator is probably already set up on your computer. The exercises in this lesson assume you are accessing the Internet using Netscape Navigator as your default browser and that the Browse the Web button is displayed on the Internet Publisher Toolbar.*

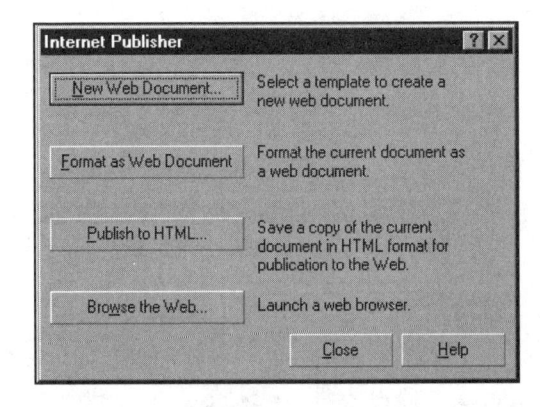

- You can also access the Internet by clicking the Change View button on the WordPerfect 8 Toolbar which displays the Internet

Corel Integration ■ Exercise 8   565

COREL WORDPERFECT SUITE 8 PROFESSIONAL Integration

Publisher Toolbar and changes the view to Web page view. Click the Browse the Web button on the Internet Publisher Toolbar.

Search the Internet

✓ *Note: Because Web sites are constantly changing, those illustrated throughout this lesson may not always match what appears on your screen. When this occurs, you may need to modify some steps to reflect the changes.*

- The Internet provides access to countless Web sites, many of which contain information and documentation that can be used for researching a particular subject or topic.

- After accessing Netscape Navigator using either of the methods described above, either the Netscape Netcenter page or the Corel home page will display in the Navigator window. You can view the contents of this site or you can begin a search on a topic.

Netscape Net Search Page

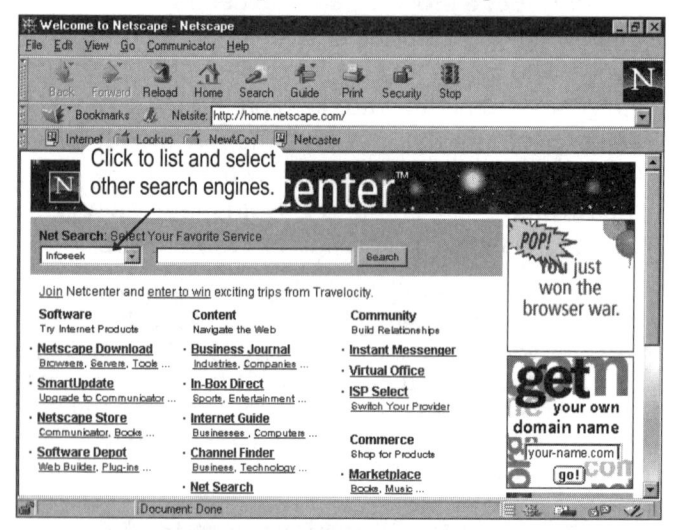

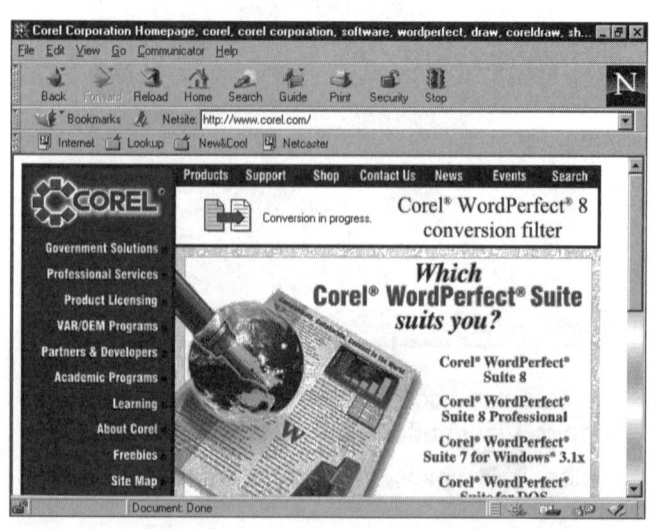

- To locate information on a topic, click the Search on the Internet button and the Netscape Netcenter search page will open. A list of search engines will display with one of the search engine home page displayed (Yahoo, InfoSeek, Magellan, Lycos, Excite). The InfoSeek page is illustrated below.

Netscape Net Search Page

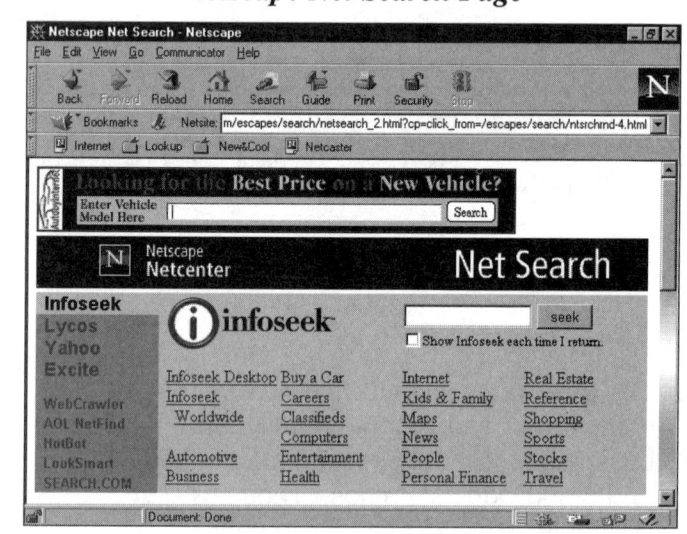

- A **search engine** searches databases around the world for results of your search topic. Some search engines return more results than others. To start a search, select the search engine you want to use. Then, enter the search topic in the search text box and click the appropriate button (e.g., Seek, Submit, Search, Go Get It) to start the search.

- You will go to the search site, and the results of your search will display. For example, if you were searching for information about the Peace Corps, you would enter the words "peace corps" in the search text box. After you click the appropriate search button, the results would display. On the next page is an example of the kind of result you might get.

"Peace Corps" Search Results

Callouts on screenshot:
- Click to move backward and forward through previous links.
- Navigation toolbar
- Location field
- Click to view next page of results.
- Scroll bar
- Hypertext links

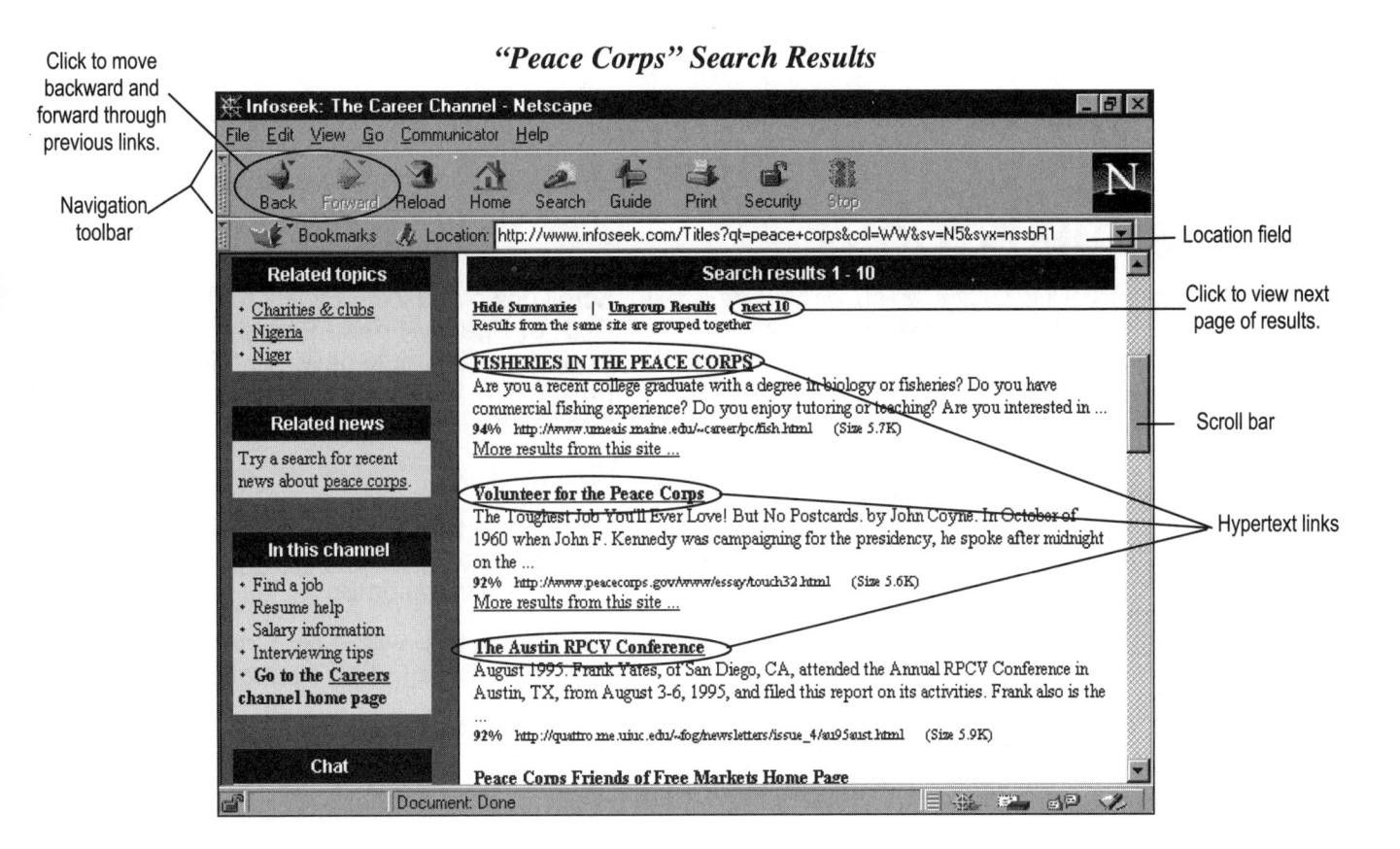

- Once a site is contacted, the Web address displays in the location field text box. (A Web address is also referred to as a URL – Uniform Resource Locator. Opening a Web Site using a URL address will be covered in Exercise 10.)

- You can view the results of your search by dragging the scroll bar.

- You will note that the search result pages display some words in a different color, underlined, or both. Clicking on one of these **hypertext links** takes you to a new page with related information.

- To move among the Web pages that you accessed during the current session, click the Back and Forward buttons on the Navigation toolbar. You can return to the first Search Page by clicking the Search button.

- If a page seems to take too long to load, click the Reload button on the Navigation toolbar. If you decide to take a different action, click the Stop button on the Navigation toolbar.

- Search Sites are updated constantly, so the results you get can vary greatly from day to day as well as from site to site.

    Hints: For the best search results:
    - Always check for misspelled words and typing errors.
    - Use descriptive words and phrases to narrow the search.
    - Use synonyms and variations of words.

- If you do not find what you are looking for, select a different search engine and try the search again.

    ✓*Note:* You will gather information from the Internet for the remaining exercises in this chapter.

    - If you are connected to the Internet, use the suggested sites or select other appropriate Web sites.

COREL WORDPERFECT SUITE 8 PROFESSIONAL Integration

> In this exercise you will launch the Web from inside WordPerfect 8 and search the Web for information.

EXERCISE DIRECTIONS

✓ Since you will be working with an active Web site and Web sites are constantly changing, the following steps may have to be modified to reflect changes.

1. Start WordPerfect 8.
2. Open a new document.
3. Display the Internet Publisher toolbar.
4. Move the mouse pointer over each button on the Internet Publisher toolbar and note the ToolTip that displays for each one.
5. Click the Browse the Web button on the Internet Publisher toolbar.
6. Click the Search button on the Navigation toolbar.
7. Select the Excite Search Engine on the Netscape home page.
8. Type fossil energy international in the text box, and click the Search button.

   ✓ Search words are not case sensitive.
   ✓ The results of your search will appear.

9. Scroll down and locate a link that reads **U.S. Dept of Energy-Fossil Energy International Activities**. It should have the following URL: **http://www.fe.doe.gov/int/international.html**. See Illustration A.
10. Click this link.
11. Scroll down to view the world map. Locate a link that reads **Western Hemisphere**. Click this link. See Illustration B.
12. Scroll down to view the country flags. Click on the flag for **Brazil**. See Illustration C.
13. Scroll down and locate a link that reads **Trade Point USA**. Click this link. See Illustration D.
14. Find information relating to Export Opportunities for Brazil.
15. Close Netscape Communicator.
16. Close WordPerfect.

DESIRED RESULT

✓ Since you are using an active Web site, your results may vary.

ILLUSTRATION A

Select this site.

89% Energy and the Environment: Resources for a Networked World [More Like This]
URL: http://zebu.uoregon.edu/energy.html
Summary: Comprehensive collection of environment and earth science publications. Sustainable Development Dimensions, including sections on Environmental information, Environmental policy, planning and management and Energy for development.

Note the address.

86% U.S. Dept. of Energy - Fossil Energy International Activities [More Like This]
URL: http://www.fe.doe.gov/int/international.html
Summary: Select a Region Africa Russia/Newly Independent States Eastern Europe Western Europe South Asia/Near East Pacific Rim Western Hemisphere Fossil Energy Home Page Options.
Africa | Eastern Europe | Western Europe | Pacific Rim | Western Hemisphere.

ILLUSTRATION B

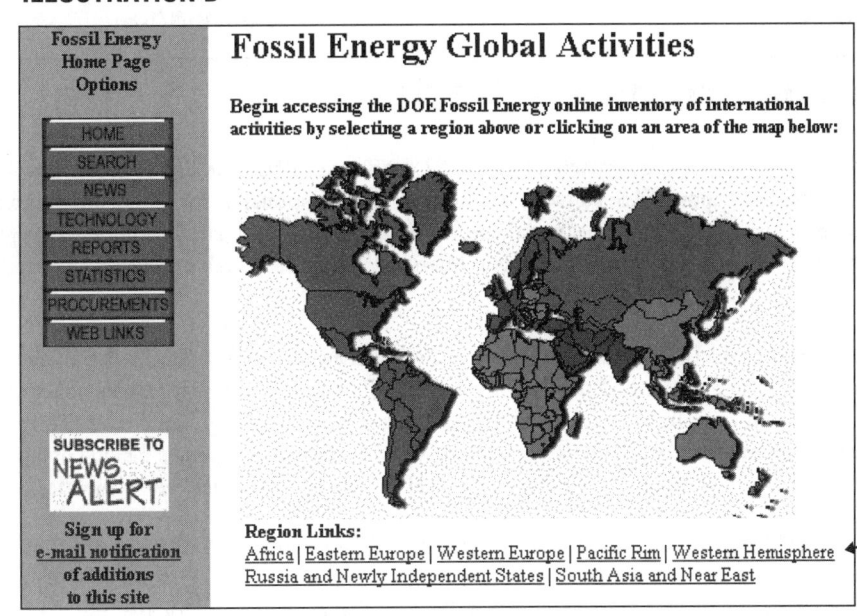

Fossil Energy Global Activities

Fossil Energy Home Page Options
- HOME
- SEARCH
- NEWS
- TECHNOLOGY
- REPORTS
- STATISTICS
- PROCUREMENTS
- WEB LINKS

SUBSCRIBE TO NEWS ALERT
Sign up for e-mail notification of additions to this site

Begin accessing the DOE Fossil Energy online inventory of international activities by selecting a region above or clicking on an area of the map below:

Region Links:
Africa | Eastern Europe | Western Europe | Pacific Rim | Western Hemisphere ← *Click this link.*
Russia and Newly Independent States | South Asia and Near East

---

ILLUSTRATION C

Country Information

The Western Hemispheric region includes the following countries. Please click on a country of interest to learn more about any DOE Fossil Energy activities in that country, or to obtain links to other useful information about that country.

- Argentina
- Bolivia
- Brazil ← *Click this link.*
- Canada
- Chile
- Colombia
- Costa Rica
- Ecuador
- Guatemala
- Honduras
- Mexico
- Nicaragua

ILLUSTRATION C — *Locate and click this link.*

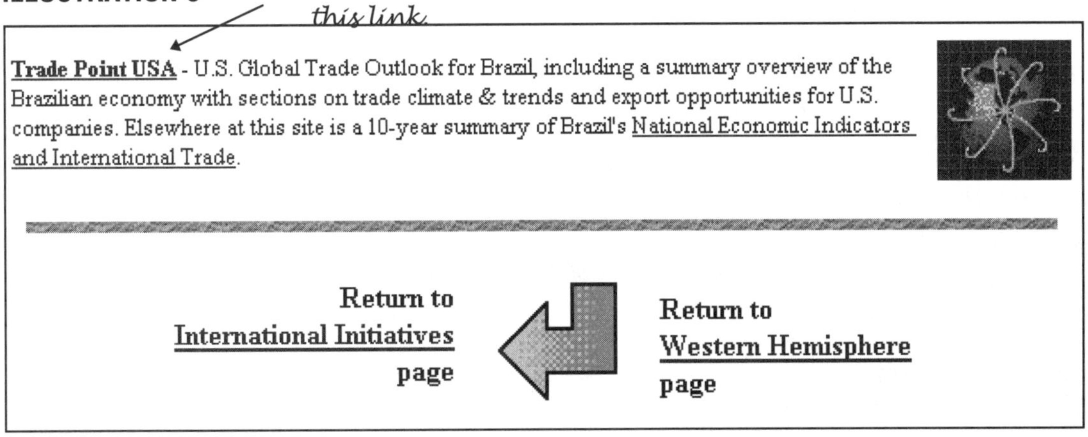

Trade Point USA - U.S. Global Trade Outlook for Brazil, including a summary overview of the Brazilian economy with sections on trade climate & trends and export opportunities for U.S. companies. Elsewhere at this site is a 10-year summary of Brazil's National Economic Indicators and International Trade.

Return to **International Initiatives** page ⬅ Return to **Western Hemisphere** page

COREL WORDPERFECT SUITE 8 PROFESSIONAL Integration

ILLUSTRATION D

Find this information →

Export Opportunities-Brazil

Computer Software. U.S. exports are expected to reach $250 million in 1995. The United States now has a 97 percent share of Brazilian imports. U.S. software manufacturers are responsible for 70 percent of Brazil's software sales; local competitors, principally word processing software producers, account for the rest. Best sales prospects for U.S. exporters include software for personal computers, LANs (local area networks), and graphics.

Computers and Peripherals. U.S. exports were an estimated $892 million in 1994. The United States now has a 60 percent share of total imports, and 15 percent of the market. The Brazilian market reserve policy, restricting foreign participation in the computer industry, ended in October 1992, but the government still offers incentives to the domestic computer industry. The most promising products for U.S. companies include notebooks, subnotebooks, handheld and palmtop computers, high-end microcomputers, disk drives, monitors, and printers.

Plastic Materials and Resins. U.S. exports will be a projected $178 million in 1995. The United States now has a 40 percent share of total imports, but only 4 percent of the overall market. The liberalization of imports since 1990 has had a positive impact on production costs in the Brazilian plastics industry. Imports of plastic materials and resins jumped 74 percent between 1992 and 1993. The packaging industry, the leading national consumer of raw materials, absorbs about 60 percent of the domestic resin supply. Local manufacturers account for more than 90 percent of the production of plastic materials and resins in Brazil.

KEYSTROKES

DISPLAY INTERNET PUBLISHER TOOLBAR

- Click **Change View** button on WordPerfect 8 toolbar.

OR

1. Click **View** .... Alt + V
2. Click We**b** Page .... B

ACCESS NETSCAPE NAVIGATOR

1. Display the Internet Publisher toolbar.
2. Click **Browse the Web** button.
   - ✓ If you are not connected to your Internet Service Provider, a dialog box that lets you sign on to your provider appears. Follow whatever steps are necessary to connect to your ISP.

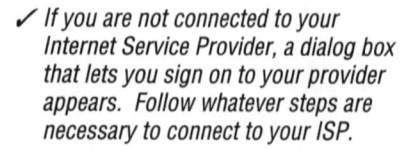

PERFORM A SIMPLE SEARCH
FROM NETSCAPE HOME PAGE

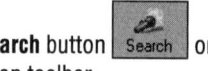

1. Click **Search** button Search on Navigation toolbar.
2. Select a search engine.
3. Enter Search topic in Search text box.
4. Click Seek button.
   - ✓ In some Search Engines, this button may contain different text. Lycos, for example, displays say, "Go Get It."
   - ✓ The results of the search display.

USE A HYPERLINK TO GO TO ANOTHER WEB SITE

1. Point to a link to a site you want to jump to.
2. Click the underlined or graphic link to access the new site.

COREL WORDPERFECT SUITE 8 PROFESSIONAL Integration

Exercise 9

- **Get Help from the Corel Web Site**
- **Print Web Site Information**
- **Save a Web Page**
- **Copy Text from a Web Site into a WordPerfect Document**
- **Copy Images from the Internet**

Netscape Communicator's Navigation Toolbar

NOTES

Get Help from the Corel Web Site

- In addition to the Help features that you have learned about earlier in this book, you can also get help from the Corel Web Site. Corel WordPerfect Suite 8 provides online help and information on the applications including WordPerfect, Quattro Pro, Paradox and Presentations. You must have a modem and Internet software to connect to the online information service

- The Corel home page contains administration and technical information, as well as tips, tricks and task-oriented resources. To get help from the Web site, select Corel Web Site from the Help menu.

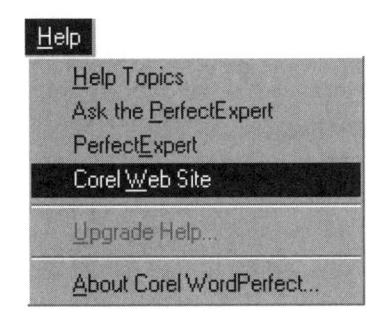

- The Corel Home Products Page displays.

- You can access any other area of the Corel site for additional help from this or any Corel page you open by clicking a topic from those listed on the top of the page.

- If you are unable to select your service or connect using this option, you can sign on to your Internet provider and use your World Wide Web browser to reach http://www.corel.com/ for the home page or http://www.corel.com/products/ for specific tool information. More information on URL's or World Wide Web addresses is in Exercise 10. To get technical assistance, you can click Support on the home page, or, you can select http://www.corel.com/support to connect to the technical support page, shown below.

Print Web Site Information

- You can print Web pages or specified text that you find on the Web.

- To print a Web page, click the Print button on the browser's toolbar or select Print from the File menu.

    ✓Note: *Web pages are constantly changing. You may print a page one day and the page may be different the next day.*

Corel Integration ■ Exercise 9 571

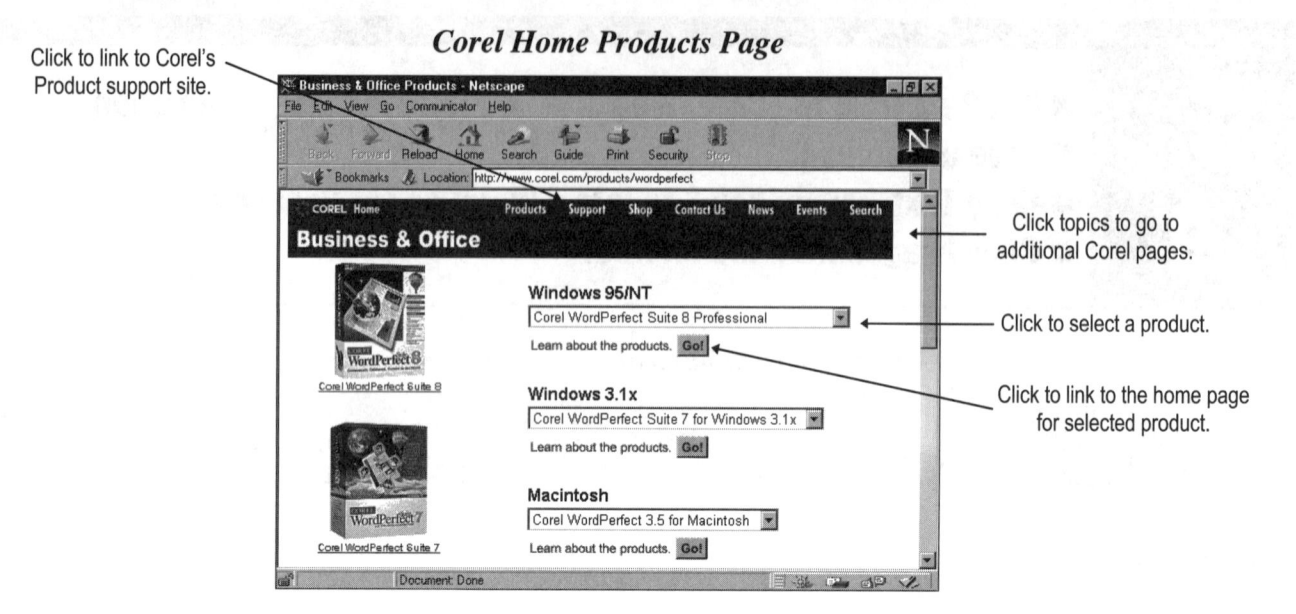

COREL WORDPERFECT SUITE 8 PROFESSIONAL Integration

Corel Home Products Page

Save a Web Page

- You can save a Web page by opening the page and selecting Save As from the File menu. Type the name of the file in the File name box and click Save.

Copy Text from a Web Site into a WordPerfect Document

- It is possible to copy text that you find on the Web into a WordPerfect document. To copy Web text, highlight the text you want copied and select Copy from the Edit menu or right-click and select Copy. Text is copied to the Clipboard. Open or switch to your WordPerfect document and select Paste from the Edit menu or click the Paste button on the WordPerfect 8 toolbar to insert the text into your document.

Copy Images from the Internet

- In addition to clipart images which are available free from Corel, many Web sites offer images such as cartoons, icons, art and photographs that you can copy and save, then insert into your document. Locate the object you want to copy, right-click on it and select Save Image As from the QuickMenu that appears. Enter a filename for this image in the Filename text box in the Save as dialog box and click Save. Then switch to the WordPerfect document and insert the image as you would any other graphics file (Insert, Graphics, From File).

In this exercise, you will access the Corel Help site to find out what's new in CorelDRAW 8. You will also then use a template to create a memo, copy the what's new information from a Web site and insert it into the memo.

EXERCISE DIRECTIONS

1. Create the memo shown in Illustration A or open **09CORHELP** from the data file.
   a. Use the Contemporary Memo Template.
   b. Enter the heading information shown.
   c. Type the paragraphs shown.
   ✓ *Insert the "TM" from the Typographic Symbols set.*
2. Select Corel Web Site from the Help menu.
3. To find out what's new in CorelDRAW 8, click the following links.
   - Products
   - CorelDRAW 8 for Windows 95/Windows NT
   - Go
   - What's Inside the Box
   - CorelDRAW 8 (Core Applications)
4. Copy the What's New heading and bulleted list as shown in Illustration B.
5. Print a copy of this information.
6. Switch to the WordPerfect document.
7. Paste information from the Clipboard into the memo where shown.
8. Format the memo as follows:
   a. If necessary, delete lines before and after inserted text.
   b. If necessary, delete extra spaces preceding each new feature.
   c. Add bullets to the list of new items. Use the check mark bullet style.
   d. Bold "What's New?"
   e. Italicize all the new items.
   f. Insert an appropriate second-page header.
9. Check your printout of What's New Information against your memo text.
10. Return to the browser window and click the Back button to return to "What's Inside the Box" page.
11. Copy a picture of the CorelDRAW 8 software package and save the image as BOX.
12. Insert the image into the WordPerfect document as shown in Illustration C (Desired Result) on page 575.
13. Insert ", Technical Support" after Jim Weston.
14. Double space the heading.
15. Switch the Date with the subject.
16. Preview the document.
17. Print one copy.
18. Save the file; name it **COREL**.
19. Close the document window.
20. Disconnect from your Internet service provider and close your browser.

COREL WORDPERFECT SUITE 8 PROFESSIONAL Integration

ILLUSTRATION A

interoffice MEMORANDUM

To: Rebecca Ishmel, Manager
From: Jim Weston
Date: January 8, 1998
Subject: CorelDRAW 8

In response to your inquiry about what's new in CorelDRAW™ 8, the following information from the Corel Web site should answer your questions.

→ *Insert information from Web site here*

I have included a picture of the box, to make the product identification easier when you purchase the software. If you have any additional questions, please let me know.

ILLUSTRATION B

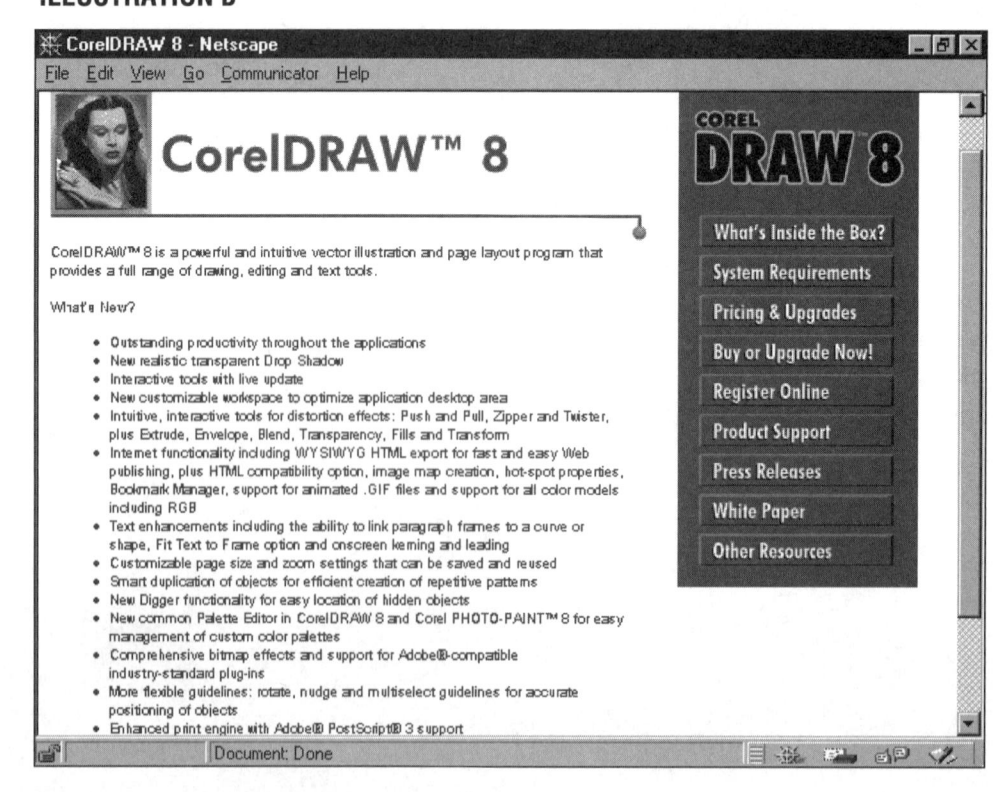

CorelDRAW 8 - Netscape

File Edit View Go Communicator Help

CorelDRAW™ 8

CorelDRAW™ 8 is a powerful and intuitive vector illustration and page layout program that provides a full range of drawing, editing and text tools.

What's New?

- Outstanding productivity throughout the applications
- New realistic transparent Drop Shadow
- Interactive tools with live update
- New customizable workspace to optimize application desktop area
- Intuitive, interactive tools for distortion effects: Push and Pull, Zipper and Twister, plus Extrude, Envelope, Blend, Transparency, Fills and Transform
- Internet functionality including WYSIWYG HTML export for fast and easy Web publishing, plus HTML compatibility option, image map creation, hot-spot properties, Bookmark Manager, support for animated .GIF files and support for all color models including RGB
- Text enhancements including the ability to link paragraph frames to a curve or shape, Fit Text to Frame option and onscreen kerning and leading
- Customizable page size and zoom settings that can be saved and reused
- Smart duplication of objects for efficient creation of repetitive patterns
- New Digger functionality for easy location of hidden objects
- New common Palette Editor in CorelDRAW 8 and Corel PHOTO-PAINT™ 8 for easy management of custom color palettes
- Comprehensive bitmap effects and support for Adobe®-compatible industry-standard plug-ins
- More flexible guidelines: rotate, nudge and multiselect guidelines for accurate positioning of objects
- Enhanced print engine with Adobe® PostScript® 3 support

COREL DRAW 8

- What's Inside the Box?
- System Requirements
- Pricing & Upgrades
- Buy or Upgrade Now!
- Register Online
- Product Support
- Press Releases
- White Paper
- Other Resources

Document: Done

DESIRED RESULT

interoffice
MEMORANDUM

To: Rebecca Ishmel, Manager
From: Jim Weston, Technical Support
Subject: CorelDRAW
Date: January 8, 1998

In response to your inquiry about what's new in CorelDRAW™ 8, the following information from the Corel Web site should answer your questions.

What's New?

- ✓ *Outstanding productivity throughout the applications*
- ✓ *New realistic transparent Drop Shadow*
- ✓ *Interactive tools with live update*
- ✓ *New customizable workspace to optimize application desktop area*
- ✓ *Intuitive, interactive tools for distortion effects: Push and Pull, Zipper and Twister, plus Extrude, Envelope, Blend, Transparency, Fills and Transform*
- ✓ *Internet functionality including WYSIWYG HTML export for fast and easy Web publishing, plus HTML compatibility option, image map creation, hot-spot properties, Bookmark*
- ✓ *Manager, support for animated .GIF files and support for all color models including RGB*
- ✓ *Text enhancements including the ability to link paragraph frames to a curve or shape, Fit Text to Frame option and on-screen kerning and leading*
- ✓ *Customizable page size and zoom settings that can be saved and reused*

Rebecca Ishmel, Manager
Page 2
December 13, 1997

- ✓ *Smart duplication of objects for efficient creation of repetitive patterns*
- ✓ *New Digger functionality for easy location of hidden objects*
- ✓ *New common Palette Editor in CorelDRAW 8 and Corel PHOTO-PAINT™ 8 for easy management of custom color palettes*
- ✓ *Comprehensive bitmap effects and support for Adobe®-compatible industry-standard plug-ins*
- ✓ *More flexible guidelines: rotate, nudge and multiselect guidelines for accurate positioning of objects*
- ✓ *Enhanced print engine with Adobe® PostScript® 3 support*

I have included a picture of the box to make the product identification easier when you purchase the software. If you have any additional questions, please let me know.

COREL WORDPERFECT SUITE 8 PROFESSIONAL Integration

KEYSTROKES

GET HELP ON THE WEB THROUGH COREL

1. Click **H**elp .... `Alt` + `H`
2. Click Corel **W**eb Site .... `W`
3. Click link to desired location:
   - Corel Home
   - Products
   - Support
   - Shop
   - Contact Us
   - News
   - Events
   - Search

   OR

   To go to a product page:
   a. Click the drop-down list arrow for Windows 95/NT.
   b. Select a product .... `↑↓`, `Enter`
   c. Click **Go!** Button `Go`

GET HELP ON THE WEB DIRECTLY

1. Sign on to your Internet provider.
2. Access World Wide Web.
3. Enter:
   http://www.corel.com
   to reach home page.

PRINT WEB SITE INFORMATION

1. Go to a Web site that you want to print.
2. Click **Print** button 🖶 on Navigation toolbar.

   OR

   a. Click **F**ile .... `Alt` + `F`
   b. Click **P**rint .... `P`
3. Click **OK** .... `Enter`

COPY TEXT FROM A WEB SITE TO A WORDPERFECT DOCUMENT

1. Go to a Web site containing text that you want to copy.
2. Highlight text that you want to copy.

   OR

   Select the entire page. .... `Ctrl` + `A`

   ✓ You may need to click in the Navigator window before Ctrl + A will work.

3. Click **Copy** button .... `Ctrl` + `C`
4. Switch to the WordPerfect document where text will be inserted.

   OR

   Open a new WordPerfect document where text will be inserted.

5. Click **Paste** button .... `Ctrl` + `V`

COPY IMAGES FROM A WEB SITE TO A WORDPERFECT DOCUMENT

1. Go to a Web site containing an image that you want to copy.
2. Right-click on the image that you want to copy.
3. Select
   Save **I**mage As .... `I`, `I`, `Enter`
4. Enter filename of image.
5. Click **OK**.

   To insert saved Web image into a WordPerfect document:

   a. Switch to WordPerfect document where image will be inserted.

   OR

   Open a new WordPerfect document where the image will be inserted.

   b. Click **I**nsert .... `Alt` + `I`
   c. Click **G**raphics .... `G`
   d. Click **F**rom File .... `F`
   e. Select Image file to be inserted.
   f. Click **I**nsert .... `Enter`

COREL WORDPERFECT SUITE 8 PROFESSIONAL Integration

Exercise 10

- Hyperlinks
- QuickLinks
- Create Hyperlinks in a WordPerfect Document
- Edit Hyperlinks
- Integrate a Presentations Outline into a WordPerfect Document

NOTES

Hyperlink Toolbar

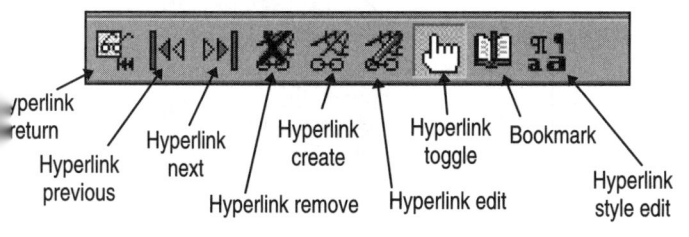

Hyperlink return, Hyperlink previous, Hyperlink next, Hyperlink create, Hyperlink remove, Hyperlink toggle, Hyperlink edit, Bookmark, Hyperlink style edit

Hyperlinks

- As discussed in Exercise 8, **hypertext linked** text on Web pages, underlined and/or displayed in a different color, links you to another Web page.

- You can use **hyperlinks** in all Corel WordPerfect Suite 8 applications to add links to information within the current file, to another file, or to the Internet. This feature allows you to cross-reference data to its source. For example, you can hyperlink a statement in a WordPerfect document with a notebook or chart in Quattro Pro. Or, you can link from a location in a document to a specific site on the Internet to find more information.

- There is a Hyperlink Toolbar, illustrated above, that can be displayed using the View, Toolbars commands, or you can work with Hyperlinks using the Tools menu.

QuickLinks

- QuickLinks is a Corel feature that allows you to automatically create hyperlinks when you type certain kinds of text. For example, when you type text that begins with "WWW," "FTP, "mailto," or "http," QuickLinks automatically converts it to an Internet link. You can specify that QuickLinks convert the link to easier to read text. For example, you might specify that when you type @Corel the visible text would be replaced with "www.corel.com," and linked to the Corel home page at URL http://www.corel.com.

- To create QuickLinks to commonly used Web documents, click Tools, QuickCorrect, and select the QuickLinks tab. In the Link Word: field, type the word you want converted to a QuickLink, then specify the associated URL in the Location to link to: field, as illustrated below.

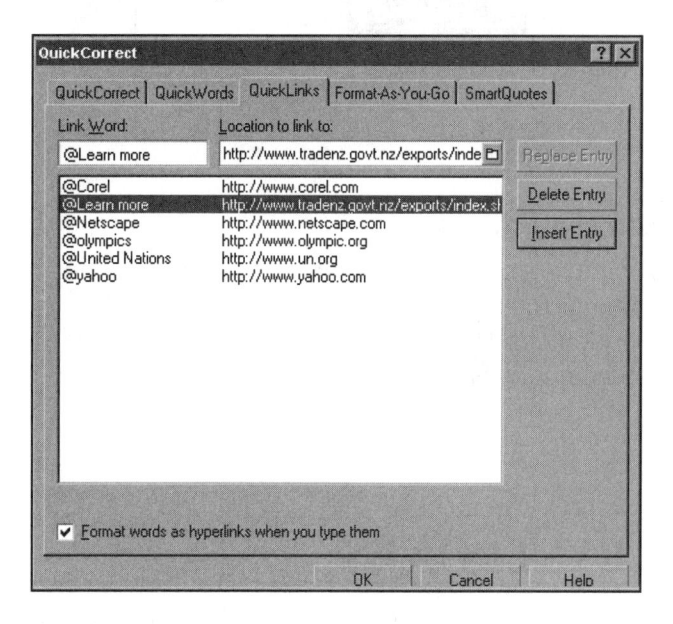

Create Hyperlinks in a WordPerfect Document

- Any text can be used as a hypertext link. You can use the actual path name of the file to be linked or you can use more meaningful text. In either case, you must select the text to be used as the link and click Tools, Hyperlink. The Hyperlink Properties box displays where you can enter the path to the document, filename, macro, or URL, as shown on the following page. You can use the Browse Web button to locate the URL on the web or use the folder button to search for a file.

Corel Integration ■ Exercise 10   577

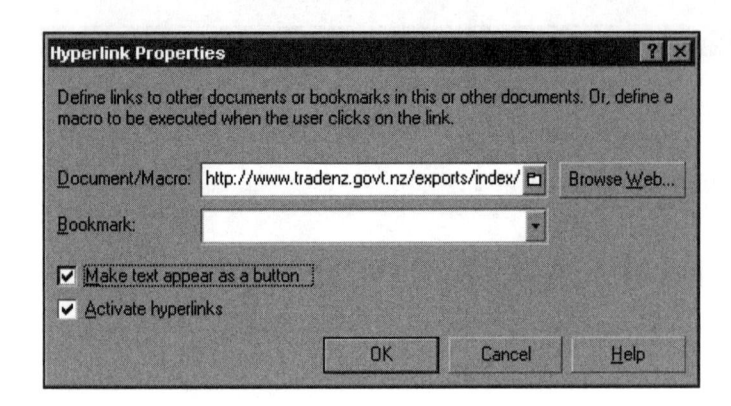

COREL WORDPERFECT SUITE 8 PROFESSIONAL Integration

- You can also choose to make the text you selected appear as a button. If you do not select the button property, the default property is for underlined, blue text. The illustration below shows the two types of hyperlink text, the button and underlined text link. When you place your cursor near a hyperlink, the link displays.

Edit Hyperlinks

- If you wish to edit a hyperlink by changing the text or the link, or changing from a button to underlined text, you must select the hyperlink. Since selecting a hyperlink brings you to the linked page, you must select the hyperlink by using the Hyperlink Toggle button on the toolbar, then use the Edit Hyperlink button. Or, right-click the hyperlink to display the menu illustrated below, and select Edit Hyperlink.

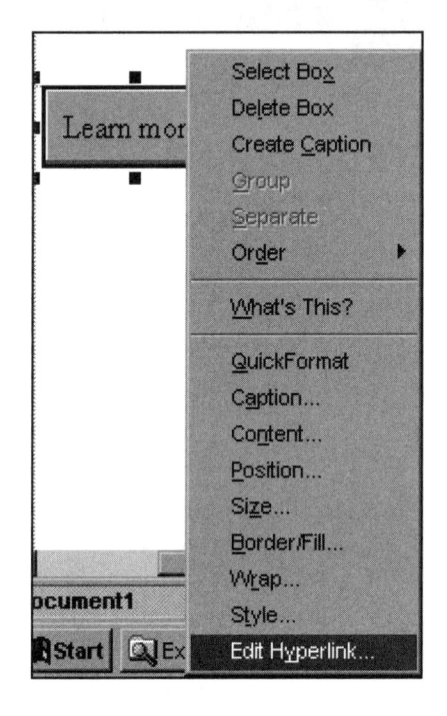

Integrate a Presentations Outline into a WordPerfect document

- You can copy text from a Presentations outline and paste it into a WordPerfect document using Outliner view.

KEYSTROKES

TO CREATE A HYPERLINK IN COREL WORDPERFECT

1. Select the text to be used as the link.
2. Click **Tools** .... Alt + T
3. Click **Hyperlink** .... Y
4. Click **Document/Macro** .... Alt + D
5. Enter path to file or URL
   OR
   Select folder icon to browse for the folder and file.
   OR
   Click **Browse Web**
   to browse for URL .... Alt + W
6. If desired, click **Make text appear as a button** .... Alt + M
7. Make sure that the **Activate hyperlinks** option is selected .... Alt + A
8. Click **OK** .... Enter

CREATE QUICKLINKS

1. Click **Tools** .... Alt + T
2. Click **QuickCorrect** .... Q
3. Select **QuickLinks** tab .... Ctrl + Tab
4. Click **Link Word** .... Alt + W
5. Enter @ sign .... @
6. Enter word .... *link word*
7. Click **Location to link to:** .... Alt + L
8. Enter URL.
   OR
   Select folder icon to browse for the location address.
9. Click **Add Entry** .... Alt + A

578

Hartman Investments, Inc. would like to use the outline from a presentation to create a document on investment opportunities in New Zealand. You will use a Presentations outline to create a WordPerfect document and use hyperlinks to send the user to a Quattro Pro notebook and to a Web site for further information on New Zealand.

EXERCISE DIRECTIONS

1. Click the DAD Presentations icon.
2. Open ⌨**INVEST.shw** or 💾**10INVEST.shw**.
3. Switch to Outliner view and copy the entire outline.
4. Click the DAD WordPerfect icon.
5. Open a new document and paste the outline from the clipboard.
6. Format the outline as shown in Illustration A:
   a. Insert the following two-line heading, as shown in the illustration, at the top of the document: Hartman Investments, Inc., Tucson, AZ 85730.
   b. Format the heading: centered, bold, 16-points, sans serif font (Century Gothic).
   c. Enter a blank line and format the next heading to a 14 point, bold, underlined serif font (Times New Roman).
   d. Move through the outline and reformat the text that was the subtitle on the slides as follows: for items 3i, 4i, 5i, 6i, and 10i:
      i. Place your cursor at the beginning of the bullet.
      ii. Press backspace once.
      iii. Press F7 or on the Indent button.
   e. Enter the following heading for the second page as illustrated: Hartman Investments, Inc. New Zealand Investment Opportunities
   f. Insert a blank line and a horizontal line.
7. Display the Hyperlink Toolbar using the View, Toolbars commands.
8. View and test the QuickLinks that are set in your system:
   a. Click Tools, QuickCorrect, QuickLinks.
   b. Close the dialog box.
   c. Type @Corel anywhere in the document and note that QuickLink has created a Corel hyperlink to the Corel Web page.
   d. Press the Hyperlink Remove button on the Hyperlink toolbar.
9. Create a hyperlink to a Quattro Pro notebook:
   a. Select the subtitle text in item 4, Dollars in Millions for Years Ending: March 97 and March 98.
   b. Select Tools, Hyperlink which displays the Hyperlink Properties dialog box.
   c. Use the folder icon to locate or enter the path to 💾**10EXPORT**. Or, create the notebook as shown in Illustration B on page 581, then close the file and save as **EXPORT**.
   d. Do not select the button property.
   e. Click OK
   ✓ *The selected text will be blue and underlined.*
10. Save the file as **NZ**.
11. Move your mouse over the hyperlink text to view the linked filename.
12. Double click to go to the linked file. Accept the Import Data settings.
    ✓ *The Quattro Pro notebook will be brought into a new WordPerfect document. You will have to reopen the original document.*
13. View the data and close the file without saving it.
14. Reopen ⌨**NZ**.
15. Enter text as illustrated under item 9 in the outline: Learn more!
16. Select the new text and click the Hyperlink Create button.
17. Enter the URL that follows or one you find that provides information on New Zealand exports.
    http://www.tradenz.govt.nz/exports/index.shtml
18. Select the Make text appear as a button property and click OK.
19. If you have an Internet connection, double click the button to link to the New Zealand Web site.
20. View the Web site and then exit from your browser and disconnect from your service provider.
21. Click the Toggle button on the toolbar to deactivate the hyperlinks.
22. Change the button text to: Learn more about it!
23. Click the Toggle button to activate the hyperlinks.
24. Print one copy of the document.
25. Save and close the file.

Corel Integration ■ Exercise 10

ILLUSTRATION A - Page 1 of 2

Hartman Investments, Inc.
Tucson, AZ 85730

Insert: centered, 16 pt bold, sans serif (Century Gothic)

<u>New Zealand Investment Opportunities</u>

Format: centered, 14 pt bold, underlined, serif (Times New Roman)

1. Brief History of New Zealand Economy
    a. Government Deregulation in 1980s
        i. Effects on Farming
        ii. Adjusting to a market-led economy
    b. Recent Economic Reform
        i. Reserve Bank Act brings inflation below 3%
    c. Research Department's report on the history of the economy
        i. Positive impact of moving from a regulated economy to a market-driven, deregulated economy
2. Why Invest in the New Zealand Economy?
3. Tremendous Export Markets
    *Top 5 Performing Markets
    a. Australia
    b. Japan
    c. USA
    d. UK
    e. Korea
4. Top 10 Export Markets
    <u>Dollars in Millions for Years Ending: March 97 and March 98</u>
5. Rising Export Regions
    Regions Displaying Growth Rates of Over 20%
    a. Middle East
    b. South East Asia
    c. South Asia
    d. Africa
6. Additional Economic Contribution
    Not To Be Overlooked When Investing!
    a. Although agriculture remains the key export industry in New Zealand, the following industries are also make significant economic contributions: tourism, textiles, machinery, manufacturing, transportation equipment, financial sector, mining, and wine vineyards.
7. Under Evaluation
    a. Specific stocks
    b. Full Impact of Economic Reform
    c. Current Impact of Government Deregulation

ILLUSTRATION A - PAGE 2 OF 2

Insert heading →

Hartman Investments, Inc.   New Zealand Investment Opportunities

Insert horizontal line →

8. Bonds
   a. Short term
   b. Long term
9. Invest in New Zealand

   [Learn more about it!]

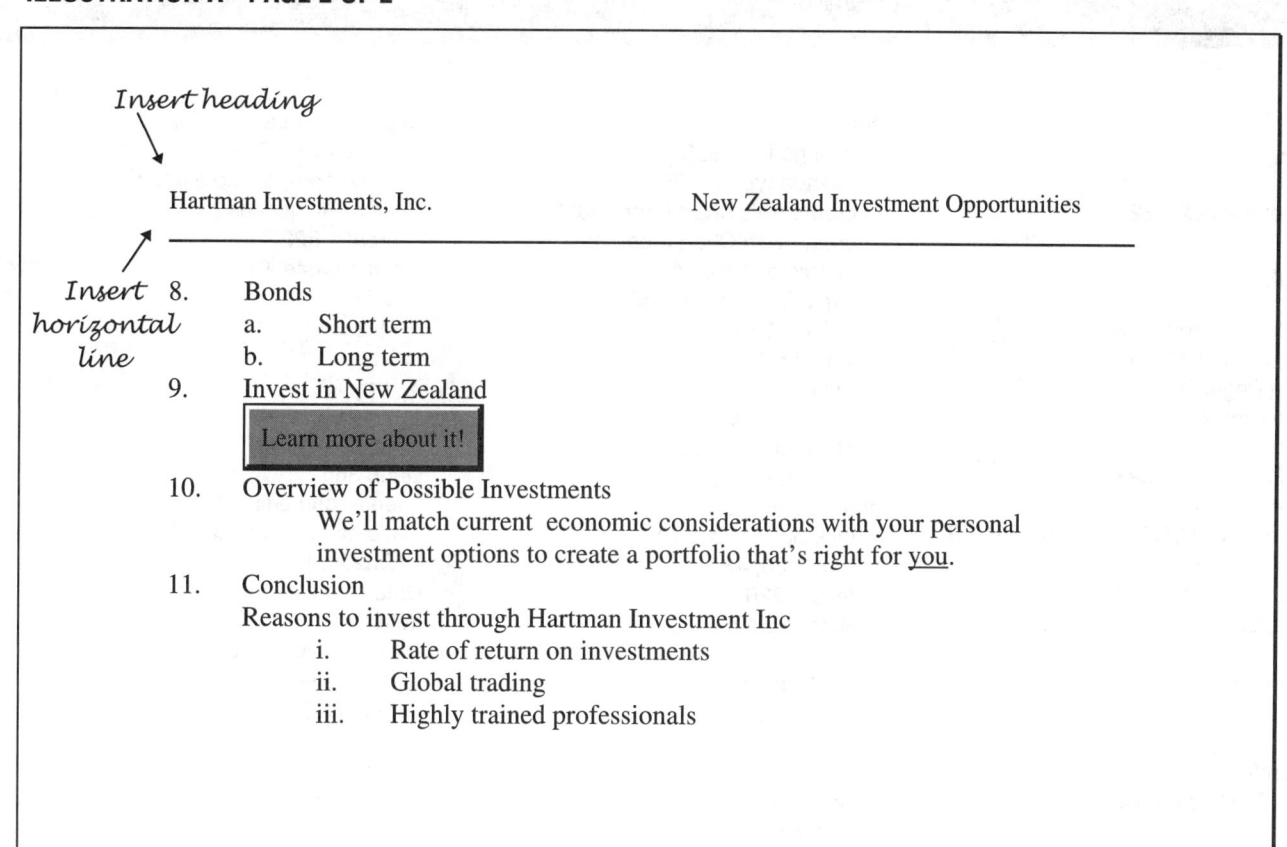

10. Overview of Possible Investments
    We'll match current economic considerations with your personal investment options to create a portfolio that's right for you.
11. Conclusion
    Reasons to invest through Hartman Investment Inc
    i. Rate of return on investments
    ii. Global trading
    iii. Highly trained professionals

ILLUSTRATION B

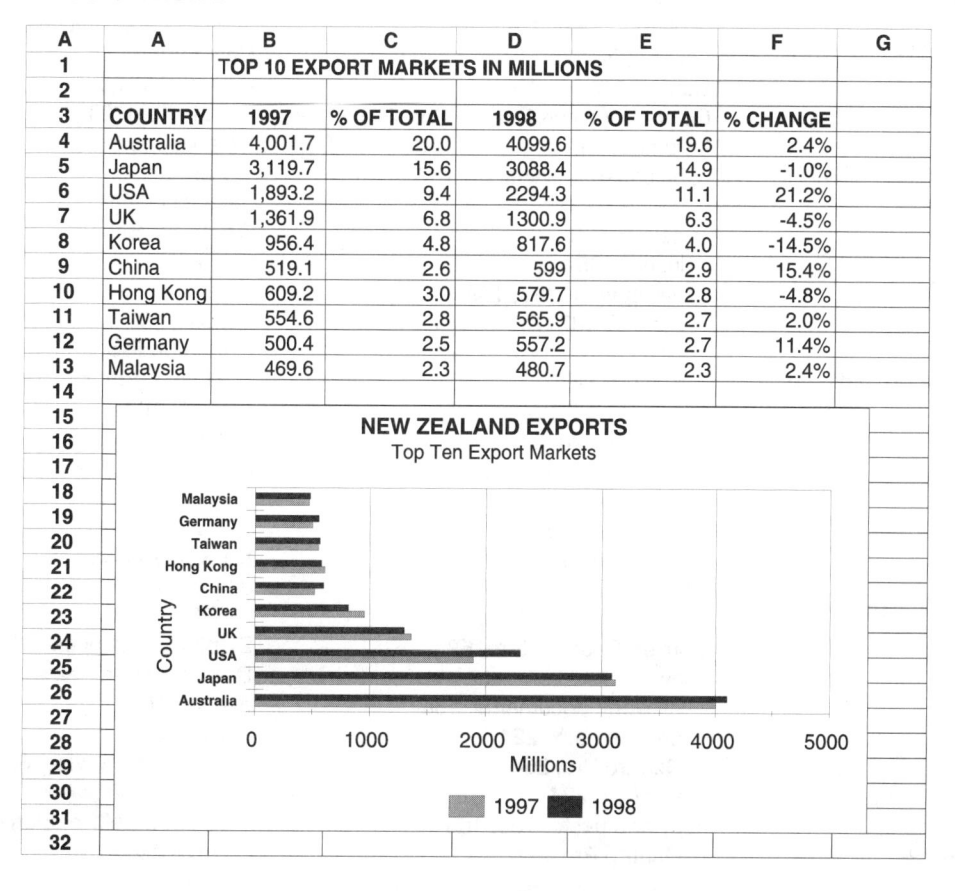

A	A	B	C	D	E	F	G
1		TOP 10 EXPORT MARKETS IN MILLIONS					
2							
3	COUNTRY	1997	% OF TOTAL	1998	% OF TOTAL	% CHANGE	
4	Australia	4,001.7	20.0	4099.6	19.6	2.4%	
5	Japan	3,119.7	15.6	3088.4	14.9	-1.0%	
6	USA	1,893.2	9.4	2294.3	11.1	21.2%	
7	UK	1,361.9	6.8	1300.9	6.3	-4.5%	
8	Korea	956.4	4.8	817.6	4.0	-14.5%	
9	China	519.1	2.6	599	2.9	15.4%	
10	Hong Kong	609.2	3.0	579.7	2.8	-4.8%	
11	Taiwan	554.6	2.8	565.9	2.7	2.0%	
12	Germany	500.4	2.5	557.2	2.7	11.4%	
13	Malaysia	469.6	2.3	480.7	2.3	2.4%	
14							

NEW ZEALAND EXPORTS
Top Ten Export Markets

(Bar chart showing 1997 and 1998 export values in Millions for: Malaysia, Germany, Taiwan, Hong Kong, China, Korea, UK, USA, Japan, Australia)

Index

3
3-D references, 322

A
absolute reference, 267
Access, what it is, 362
Active Page, 309
active window, 164
Add , 285
Add Sound, 521, 523
Address Book, 31
ADJUST NOTEBOOK PAGE PANES, 308
Advanced pattern match, 408
Alpha, 368
appearance attributes, 71
arguments, 272
Arial typeface, 65
arrow keys, 3
Ascending order, 412
Avoid Pasting Blanks, 301

B
Background Layer, 493
Background Master
   change slide show, 462
Blend, 333
   Quattro Pro, 333
Block, 256, 262
Block Properties Active Block, 285
bold font, 71
Bookmark, 133
break
   hard page break, 126
   hard vs. soft page breaks, 126
   soft page break, 126
Break Pages in Quattro Pro, 284, 287
bullet, 80
bullet animation, 514
business letter, create, 27

C
Calc-As-You-Go, 273
Cascade in Quattro Pro, 319
cascade documents, 164, 171
case, convert, 52, 58
Case Sensitive, 408
Cell references, 259
cells in table, 193
center a line, 61
center page vertically, 61
Change Background, 462

chart
   change font, 355
   change types, 345
   create with Chart Expert, 350
   create with Chart Menu, 351
   enable editing, 345
   explode pie slice, 355
   gallery, 356
   line bar, 352
   print, 356
   select and size, 345
   stacked bar, 352
   subtypes, 351
chart legend, 352
Check Box Field, 390
Clipart, 220, 461
   insert, 220
clipboard, 540
close
   application, 4
   document, 19
Closed Object tools, 499
code
   delete, 49
   edit, 49
Color Presentations, 451
Column (Size) to Fit feature, 200
column width
   change, 200, 276
   QuickFit, 276
change, 200
Column Width in Quattro Pro, 276
Columns, 187
   balanced newspaper, 187
   create, 193
   delete, 198
   insert, 198
   newspaper, 187, 189
   parallel, 187, 189
   table, 193
   turn off, 193
Columns and Rows
   delete in QuattroPro, 297
   insert in QuattroPro, 297
Columns dialog box, 187
Comments, 132
Contour text feature, 501
control menu box, 6
Conventions, 12, 21
Convert Case feature, 52
copy
   between documents, 166
   graphics box, 224
   Quattro Pro, 264
   text box, 224
copy and paste, 104, 105
   Quattro Pro, 265

Copy and Paste Special
   QuattroPro, 305
creating an example element, 430
Custom Audiences
   create, 522
cut and paste, 97
Cut/Paste
   QuattroPro, 297

D
DAD, 2, 16
Data, 366
   enter and edit, 376
   locate and replace, 409
   Quattro Pro, 277, 278
Data Chart layout, 473
data file
   create, 208, 216
Data labels, 474
database, 366
   Access, defined, 362
   defined, 362
   plan, 367
database object
   defined, 362
Database objects, 367
Database Table
   create and save, 371
Date feature, 28
   Date Code, 28
   Date Text, 28
Default, 393
   Paradox, 393
default settings, 19
Define Fill Series
   Quattro Pro, 277
Delete, 47
   code, 49
   Quattro Pro, 285
   Reveal Codes mode, 76
   table, 199
Delete feature, 43
Descending order, 412
Design Form, 380
   Paradox, 380
Desktop Application Director , 2
different notebook page In Quattro Pro, 322
Display Sequences, 521
Display Sorted Table, 412
document
   closing, 21
   Open and Revise, 37
   preview, 48
   Preview before opening, 48
   Save As, 40, 42

Index

Save Changes, 38
saving, 20
Document Control button, 19
Document Properties, 24, 26
document window, 164
Documentation Notes, 281
Double Indent text, 90
double underline, 71
drag and drop
   copy, 105
   copy text, 104
   move text, 97
drag margin guidelines, 53
Drag/Drop, 297
draw lines, 242
draw shapes, 504
drop capital, 238, 243

E

Edit in Quattro Pro, 250, 264, 281, 301
edit data in Paradox, 375, 400
endnote, 141, 145
   edit, 141
Enter key, 3
enter records, 373, 379
envelopes, 157
   create while merging, 217
error, keys for recovering from, 19
Escape key, 3
Exact Match, 408
exit
   Quattro Pro, 253
   Corel Presentations 8, 455
   Preview, 35
   Quattro Pro, 254

F

F8 key, 44
field, 366, 408
   defined, 364
field contents, 364, 366
field name, 364, 366
Field roster, 368
file
   close/exit, 454
   insert, 175
   open, 261
   Quattro Pro, 252, 287, 292
File Stamp, 147, 152
filename, 20
Filter fields, 415
Filter Tables, 415
find and replace text, 115
first-line indent, 96
   create, 92
flush right, line, 61
font, 65
   appearance, 71
   facet, 20
   Monotype Sorts, 75

Quattro Pro, 267
remove appearance, 76
sans serif face, 65
script, 65
serif face, 65
size, 20, 67, 268
style, 67
subscript, 76
superscript, 76
Wingdings, 75
ZapfDingbats, 75
footer, 126, 284
footer font
   Quattro Pro, 284
footers
   edit, 127
   insert page numbers, 127
   turn off (suppress), 127
footnote, 139, 145
   edit, 141
form, 379
   add a field, 389
   defined, 363
   delete a field, 389
   move a field, 389
   Paradox, 379
Form Design mode, 380
form file
   create, 209, 216
format numerical dates, 331
Format-As-You-Go, 23, 26
formula, 259
frames, 402
functions, 272, 273

G

Go To, 146, 250
grammar check, 112
Grammar-As-You-Go feature, 111
Grammatik, 111
graphic import, 221
graphics, 220, 461
graphics box, 220, 223
   copy, 224
   delete, 224
   position, 224
   select, 223
   size, 224
Graphics Toolbar, 221
group of pages, 322
grouping, 310, 500

H

hanging indent, 91, 96
   create, 91
hard space, 52, 58
header, 126, 284
header font, 284

headers
   edit, 127
   insert page numbers, 127
   turn off (suppress), 127
Headers/Footers, 287
Help
   Exit, 12
Help
   Microsoft Web site, 571
hidden, 329
   Quattro Pro, 329
highlight, 71, 72
Highlighter, 513
hypertext links, 567
hyphenation, 117
   text, 116

I

IF statement, 327
   Quattro Pro, 327, 329
indent
   hanging, 91
indent
   first-line, 92
   first-line marker, 92
Indent text, 90
   end indent mode, 90
   start, 90
input values, 336
Insert, 272, 287
   date, 506, 507, 531
   file, 172
   graph, 473
   text, 38, 39
insertion point, 27
   express movement keystrokes, 29
   move from column to column, 193
   movements, 27
Internet
   basics, 560
   copy images, 572
   search, 566
Internet service provider, 565

J

Justification, 62
   table examples, 198
   within table, 198

K

Keep Text Together, 142
key, 369
Key Field Data, 376
keyboard, 27
   function keys, 3
   modifier keys, 3

L

Label, 158, 252
Layout
  customize, 493
Legend, 475
  change positions, 352
legends, 352
letters
  attachment notation, 132
  copy notation, 132
  enclosure, 132
  subject line, 132
  with special notations, 132
line
  center, 61, 64
  flush right, 61
  spacing, 87, 89
Line Object tools, 499
Line-Bar chart, 352
link headings, 101
Ln indicator, 20
lock
  Quattro Pro, 337
logical pages, 158

M

macro, 176
  play, 179
  record, 176, 178
Make-It-Fit feature, 107
margins
  default, 19
  set, 53, 58
Margins dialog box, 53
Master Gallery, 462, 451
mathematical operators, 259
Maximize button, 6, 19, 166
Maximum, 393
Menu bar, 6, 7
menu item
  selecting, 7
merge
  feature, 207
  form and data files, 210
  selected records, 210, 216
  with conditions, 211, 217
Minimize button, 6, 19
Minimum, 393
Monotype Sorts, 75
Mouse, 27
  terminology, 3
  using, 3
Move
  between documents, 166
  text, 97, 100

N

name
  Quattro Pro, 314
Navigation tabs, 452, 457
New Set, 285
New Table, 412
notations
  in letters, 132
Notebook Sheets, 309
Notebook Views, 322
Numeric Format, 277
numeric label, 255

O

object animation, 521
objects
  animate, 515
  combine, 500
  order, 501
Objects sheet, 344
open
  Document Not Recently Saved, 37
  Recently Saved File, 37
open a table, 373
Open as Copy, 40, 42
organization chart, 481
Orientation, 284
ornamental fonts, 75
orphan, 142
outlines
  Presentations, 450
  WordPerfect, 119

P

page
  center vertically, 61
Page Break
  Quattro Pro, 287
Page Numbering, 146, 152
Page numbers
  turn off in header/footer, 127
Page Setup, 264, 280, 284
Paper Type, 284
Paragraph Spacing, 87, 89
paste, 97, 104, 264
Paste Formulas as Values, 301
Paste Special
  Quattro Pro, 301
PerfectExpert, 157, 505, 507, 531
  Presentation, 507, 531
  QuattroPro, 318
PerfectExpert Projects, 505
physical page, 158
picture, 393
placeholders, 453
  move and size, 488
Play Slide Show, 513
PMT (payment) function, 337
Pos indicator, 20

presentation, 450
preview
  button, 48
  document, 48
Preview a Document, 32, 35
print, 33, 35, 457
  in landscape, 394
  multiple pages, 133
  Paradox, 394
  Presentation, 457
  Quattro Pro, 264, 280, 284
  Web site information, 571
Print Notebook, 310, 313
Print Preview, 264, 280, 292
project, 318
Project Viewer, 367, 376
Projects
  use, 319
Prompt-As-You-Go, 24, 26
proofreaders' marks, 37, 38
  change case, 53
  close up space, 44
  delete, 44
  indent, 91
  insertion, 38
  move text left, 44
  moving text, 97
  new paragraph, 38
  stet, 49
  stet, 55
Property Bar, 452

Q

query
  defined, 363
Quick Form
  create, 379
Quick Sum, 273
Quick View, 48
QuickCell, 314
QuickCorrect, 23, 26
QuickFill, 314
QuickFit, 276
QuickFonts, 66
QuickFormat, 98, 100, 101, 268
QuickMenus, 7
QuickPlay, 513
QuickPlay view, 457
QuickTip, 2, 7
QuickWords, 28, 29

R

range of notebook pages, 322
Read Only Document, 40
record, 408
  add, 397
  defined, 364
  delete, 397
  merge, 208
records, 366

Index

redline, 71
Redo, 41, 42
Reference text box, 250
relational database, 366
relational database management system, 366
Repeat Next Action, 172
replace text, 115
Replace words as you type, 23
report
    defined, 363
    format in WordPerfect, 90
Reports, 434
Required field, 393
required space, 52
Restore button, 6, 19, 166
Reveal Codes, 49, 50
    delete, 76
Reverse Text, 238, 243
right align a line, 61
Row/Column Borders, 292
rows
    delete, 198
    insert, 198
    table, 193
Ruler, 54

S

Same Table, 412
sans serif, 65
save, 376
    document, 20
    Paradox, 376
    Quattro Pro, 253, 261
Save As, 40, 42, 261, 263
Scrapbook, 461
screen parts of, 17
script font face, 65
scroll, 27, 29, 249
    bars, 6
    box, 6
search engine, 566
Second-Page Headings, 126
select text, 43, 487
Select a slide to go to, 457
selection, 262
serif font face, 65
Set Slide Timings, 521
Shading and Text Colors, 333
Shadow Cursor, 27
Sheet Options, 281, 292
Show a Presentation, 513
Show Symbols, 49, 50
Size Column to Fit feature, 200
sizing handles, 223
Slide Background
    customize, 493
Slide Editor view, 456
    return to, 467

Slide Layers, 452
    Background Master, 452
    Layout, 452
    Slide, 452
Slide Layout
    change, 462
Slide Outliner, 470
Slide Outliner view, 456
Slide Show, 453
    open, 456
    save, 453
Slide Show Tools, 515
Slide Sorter view, 457, 466
Slides
    add new, 453, 470
    copy, 466
    customize bulleted lists, 493
    delete, 466
    move, 466
Smart Color Matching, 451
Sort Just Selected Fields, 412
space
    hard or required, 52, 58
Speaker Notes, 524, 525
SpeedFormats, 333
Spell Check, 24, 26, 460
    Presentation, 457, 460
Spell-As-You-Go, 23, 26
Split Panes, 304
Stacked Bar chart, 352
standard column width, 276
start
    an application, 3
    using Start button, 16
Startup Expert, 367
status of a cell, 252
stet, 49
strikeout, 71
subscript, 76
substitution values, 336
Subtitle placeholder, 453
subtypes, 351
summary operator, 430
superscript, 76
    Paradox, 383
Symbols, 76
    Iconic, 76

T

Tab
    set, 54
    stops default, 19
table, 379
    add a field, 389
    border, 201
    cell lines and fills, 201, 202
    Column Width, 374
    create, 193
    defined, 363, 364
    delete a field, 389
    delete columns and rows, 199

    delete, 199
    enter text, 195, 197
    Expert, 368
    feature, 193
    Guidelines, 376
    horizontal position, 201
    how related other tables, 364
    justification within, 198
    line, 201
    list, 415
    move a field, 389
    move within, 195
    Paradox, 379
    save, 369
    SpeedFormat, 202
    Toolbar, 194
template, 156, 318
text
    copy and paste, 104
    copy to clipboard, 104
    cut and paste, 97
    delete, 43
    Double Indent, 90
    drag and drop copy, 104
    drag and drop move, 97
    find and replace, 115
    highlight, 72
    hyphenation, 116
    Indent, 90
    move, 97
    remove font appearance, 76, 79
    replace, 115
    select, 43
    subscript, 76
    superscript, 76
text alignment
    default, 20
Text Appearance
    change, 487
text box, 221, 223
    copy, 224
    delete, 224
    position, 224
    rotate, 225
    select, 223
Text Object tools, 498
TextArt, 229
Thesaurus, 107, 110
Tile, 319
    document windows, 164
Title placeholder, 453
title bar, 5, 452
Tool Palette, 498
toolbar, 7, 52
top and left headings, 292
Transitions, 514
Transpose, 301
Transpose Rows and Columns, 301
two-variable what-if tables, 336, 340
Type, 284
typeface, 65

U

Undelete, 44, 47
undelete vs. undo, 44
underline, 71
    double, 71
Undo feature, 40
undo vs. undelete, 44
unlock, 338
Update, 285

V

value, 255
variables, 336
vertically center page, 61, 64
View menu
    zoom option, 9
View Modes, 19
    Draft, 19
    Page, 19
    Two page, 19
    Web Page, 19
View tab, 452, 457

W

watermark, 235
    create, 242
    edit, 242
Web browser, 565
Web page
    save, 572
Web Site
    copy text, 572
What-if table, 336
widow, 142
wildcard operator, 409
window
    active, 164
    maximize, 165
    minimize, 166
    parts of, 5
    separate document from app., 165
    switch between open, 165

windowing, 164
Windows Taskbar, 3
Wingdings, 75
word wrap, 20
Work On tab, 456
Working Directories
    create, 371
working directory, 366
World Wide Web, 565
wpd
    file extension, 20
wraparound, 20

Z

ZapfDingbats, 75
Zoom option, 9

NOTES

NOTES

FREE CATALOG AND UPDATED LISTING

We don't just have books that find your answers faster; we also have books that teach you how to use your computer without the fairy tales and the gobbledygook.

We also have books to improve your typing, spelling and punctuation.

Return this card for a free catalog and mailing list update.

DDC Publishing
275 Madison Avenue,
New York, NY 10016

☐ Please send me your catalog and put me on your mailing list.

Name

Firm (if any)

Address

City, State, Zip

Phone (800) 528-3897   Fax (800) 528-3862

SEE OUR COMPLETE CATALOG ON THE INTERNET @: http://www.ddcpub.com

---

FREE CATALOG AND UPDATED LISTING

We don't just have books that find your answers faster; we also have books that teach you how to use your computer without the fairy tales and the gobbledygook.

We also have books to improve your typing, spelling and punctuation.

Return this card for a free catalog and mailing list update.

DDC Publishing
275 Madison Avenue,
New York, NY 10016

☐ Please send me your catalog and put me on your mailing list.

Name

Firm (if any)

Address

City, State, Zip

Phone (800) 528-3897   Fax (800) 528-3862

SEE OUR COMPLETE CATALOG ON THE INTERNET @: http://www.ddcpub.com

---

FREE CATALOG AND UPDATED LISTING

We don't just have books that find your answers faster; we also have books that teach you how to use your computer without the fairy tales and the gobbledygook.

We also have books to improve your typing, spelling and punctuation.

Return this card for a free catalog and mailing list update.

DDC Publishing
275 Madison Avenue,
New York, NY 10016

☐ Please send me your catalog and put me on your mailing list.

Name

Firm (if any)

Address

City, State, Zip

Phone (800) 528-3897   Fax (800) 528-3862

SEE OUR COMPLETE CATALOG ON THE INTERNET @: http://www.ddcpub.com

BUSINESS REPLY MAIL
FIRST CLASS MAIL   PERMIT NO. 7321   NEW YORK, N.Y.

POSTAGE WILL BE PAID BY ADDRESSEE

DDC *Publishing*

275 Madison Avenue
New York, NY 10157-0410

NO POSTAGE
NECESSARY
IF MAILED
IN THE
UNITED STATES

BUSINESS REPLY MAIL
FIRST CLASS MAIL   PERMIT NO. 7321   NEW YORK, N.Y.

POSTAGE WILL BE PAID BY ADDRESSEE

DDC *Publishing*

275 Madison Avenue
New York, NY 10157-0410

NO POSTAGE
NECESSARY
IF MAILED
IN THE
UNITED STATES

BUSINESS REPLY MAIL
FIRST CLASS MAIL   PERMIT NO. 7321   NEW YORK, N.Y.

POSTAGE WILL BE PAID BY ADDRESSEE

DDC *Publishing*

275 Madison Avenue
New York, NY 10157-0410

NO POSTAGE
NECESSARY
IF MAILED
IN THE
UNITED STATES